Collins
French
Dictionary

Collins French Dictionary

HarperCollins Publishers
Westerhill Road
Bishopbriggs
Glasgow
G64 2QT
Great Britain

Fourth Edition 2007

Reprint 10 9 8 7 6 5 4 3

© HarperCollins Publishers 1996, 1998, 2001, 2004, 2007
© Collins Bartholomew 2007

ISBN 978-0-00-725349-4

Collins® and Bank of English® are registered trademarks of HarperCollins Publishers Limited

www.collinslanguage.com

A catalogue record for this book is available from the British Library

HarperCollins Publishers
10 East 53rd Street
New York, NY 10022

COLLINS BEGINNER'S FRENCH DICTIONARY.
Fourth US Edition 2008

ISBN 978-0-06-137492-0

www.harpercollins.com

HarperCollins books may be purchased for educational, business, or sales promotional use. For information, please write to: Special Markets Department, HarperCollins Publishers, 10 East 53rd Street, New York, NY 10022

Art direction by Mark Thomson
Designed by Wolfgang Homola
Typeset by Thomas Callan
Supplements typeset by Davidson Pre-Press, Glasgow

Printed in China through Golden Cup Printing Services

Acknowledgements
We would like to thank those authors and publishers who kindly gave permission for copyright material to be used in the Collins Word Web. We would also like to thank Times Newspapers Ltd for providing valuable data.

MANAGING EDITOR
Maree Airlie

EDITORIAL COORDINATION
Vivian Marr, Nicola Cooke
second edition
Sharon J. Hunter, Caitlin McMahon
third and fourth editions
Gaëlle Amiot-Cadey

EDITORS
Christine Penman, Daphne Day, Chantal Testa, Harry Campbell, Cécile Aubinière-Robb, Gavin Killip, Hélène Bernaërt, Elspeth Anderson, Caroline Lehni, Joane Siksous, Sabine Citron

TECHNICAL SUPPORT
Thomas Callan

SERIES EDITOR
Lorna Knight

Our thanks to the following for their help in researching the project:
Maree Airlie, Teresa Álvarez, Phyllis Gautier, Janet Gough, Sharon Hunter, Mary James, Cordelia Lilly, Carol MacLeod, Jill McNair, Janet Chalmers

William Collins' dream of knowledge for all began with the publication of his first book in 1819. A self-educated mill worker, he not only enriched millions of lives, but also founded a flourishing publishing house. Today, staying true to this spirit, Collins books are packed with inspiration, innovation, and practical expertise. They place you at the centre of a world of possibility and give you exactly what you need to explore it.

Language is the key to this exploration, and at the heart of Collins Dictionaries is language as it is really used. New words, phrases, and meanings spring up every day, and all of them are captured and analysed by the Collins Word Web. Constantly updated, and with over 2.5 billion entries, this living language resource is unique to our dictionaries.

Words are tools for life. And a Collins Dictionary makes them work for you.

Collins. Do more.

Contents

Introduction

Collins Easy Learning French Dictionary is an innovative dictionary designed specifically for anyone starting to learn French. We are grateful to all those teachers who have contributed to its development by advising us on how to tailor it to the needs of their students. We also gratefully acknowledge the help of the examining boards, whom we have consulted throughout this project, and whose word lists and exam papers we carefully studied when compiling this dictionary.

Free downloadable resources are now available for teachers and learners of French at **www.collinsdictionaries.com/easyresources**.

Note on trademarks

Entered words which we have reason to believe constitute trademarks have been designated as such. However, neither the presence nor the absence of such designation should be regarded as affecting the legal status of any trademark.

Dictionary skills

Using a dictionary is a skill you can improve with practice and by following some basic guidelines. This section gives you a detailed explanation of how to use the dictionary to ensure you get the most out of it.

The answers to the questions in this section are on page 18.

Make sure you look in the right side of the dictionary

The French – English side comes first: you look there to find the meaning of a French word. The second part is English – French. That's what you need for translating into French. (To remind yourself which side is which, you could remember the phrase *French first*.) At the side of every page, you will see a tab with either **French – English** or **English – French**. The **French – English** side has a blue tab, the **English – French** side has a black tab, so you can see immediately if you've got the side you want.

1 **Which side of the dictionary would you need to look up to translate 'le vélo'?**

Finding the word you want

When you are looking for a word, for example **nouveau**, look at the first letter – **n** – and find the **N** section in the French – English side. Look at page 182. At the top of the page, you'll find the words **normalement** → **nouvel**. These are the first and last words on that page. Remember that even if a letter has an accent on it, it makes no difference to the alphabetical order.

2 **Which comes first – 'nager' or 'nécessaire'?**
3 **Does 'nouveau' come before or after 'Noël'?**
4 **Does 'chou-fleur' come before or after 'chocolat'?**

To help you expand your vocabulary, we also have suggested possible alternatives in the WORD POWER features at the most common adjectives in English – try looking up **big** on page 318 and learning some of the words you could use.

Make sure you look at the right entry

An entry is made up of a **word**, its translations and, often, example phrases to show you how to use the translations. If there is more than one entry for the same word, then there is a note to tell you so. Look at the following example entries:

flat ADJECTIVE
  ▷ *see also* **flat** NOUN
  1 plat (FEM plate)
    □ a flat roof un toit plat □ flat shoes des chaussures plates
  2 crevé (FEM crevée) *(tyre)*
    □ I've got a flat tyre. J'ai un pneu crevé.

flat NOUN
  ▷ *see also* **flat** ADJECTIVE
  l' appartement *masc*
    □ She lives in a flat. Elle habite un appartement.

5 **Which of the two entries above will help you translate the phrase 'My car has a flat tyre'? Look for the two clues which are there to help you:**
    > **an example similar to what you want to say**
    > **the word ADJECTIVE**

Look out for information notes which have this symbol on the left-hand side. They will give you guidance on grammatical points, and tell you about differences between French and British life.

Choosing the right translation

The main translation of a word is shown on a new line and is underlined to make it stand out from the rest of the entry. If there is more than one main translation for a word, each one is numbered.

Often you will see phrases in light blue, preceded by a white square □. These show how the translation they follow can be used. They also help you choose the translation you want because they give you examples of the context in which it can be used.

6 Use the dictionary to translate *'That's a very hard question'*.

Words often have more than one meaning and more than one translation: if you don't *get* to the station on time, you don't arrive on time, but if you say 'I don't *get* it', you mean you don't understand. When you are translating from English, be careful to choose the French word that has the particular meaning you want. The dictionary offers you a lot of help with this. Look at the following entry:

pool NOUN
1 la flaque *(puddle)*
2 l' étang *masc (pond)*
3 la piscine *(for swimming)*
4 le billard américain *(game)*

A **pool** can be a puddle, a pond or a swimming pool; **pool** can also be a game. Underlining highlights all the main translations, the numbers tell you that there is more than one possible translation and the words in brackets in *italics* after the translations help you choose the translation you want.

7 How would you translate *'I like playing pool'*?

Never take the first translation you see without looking at the others. Always look to see if there is more than one translation underlined.

Phrases in **bold type** preceded by a blue or black square ■ /■ are phrases which are particularly common or important. Sometimes the phrases have a completely different translation from the main translation; sometimes the translation is the same. For example:

le **dommage** NOUN
damage
 □ La tempête a causé d'importants dommages. The storm caused a lot of damage.
 ■ **C'est dommage.** It's a shame. □ C'est dommage que tu ne puisses pas venir. It's shame you can't come.

to **go out** VERB
1 sortir *(person)*
 □ Are you going out tonight? Tu sors ce soir?
 ■ **to go out with somebody** sortir avec quelqu'un □ Are you going out with him? Est-ce que tu sors avec lui?
2 s'éteindre *(light, fire, candle)*
 □ Suddenly the lights went out. Soudain, les lumières se sont éteintes.

When you look up a word, make sure you look beyond the main translations to see if the entry includes any **bold phrases**.

8 **In a job advert you read that applicants 'doivent tous passer une visite médicale'. What must they all do?**

Look up 'visite' and find the answer as quickly as possible by skimming down the *bold phrases*.

Making use of phrases in the dictionary

Sometimes when you look up a word you will find not only the word, but the exact phrase you want. For example, you might want to say *'What's the date today?'*. Look up **date** and you will find:

date NOUN
1 la date
□ my date of birth ma date de naissance
■ **What's the date today?** Quel jour sommes-nous?

Sometimes you have to adapt what you find in the dictionary. If you want to say *'I play darts'* and look up **dart** you will find:

dart NOUN
la fléchette
□ to play darts jouer aux fléchettes

You have to substitute **je joue** for the infinitive form **jouer**. You will often have to adapt the infinitive in this way, adding the correct ending for **je**, **tu**, **il** etc and choosing the present, future or past form. For help with this, look at the verb tables. On the **French – English** side of the dictionary, you will notice that verbs are followed by a number in square brackets, which correspond to verb tables on pages 22-27 in the middle section of this dictionary. **Jouer** is a verb ending in –**er** so it follows the same pattern as verb number [28] **donner**, which is set out on page 35.

9 **How would you say *'We played football'*?**

Phrases containing nouns and adjectives also need to be adapted. You may need to make the noun plural, or the adjective feminine or plural. Remember that some nouns and adjectives have irregular feminine or plural forms and that this is shown in the entry.

10 **How would you say *'The jewels are beautiful'*?**

Don't overuse the dictionary

It takes time to look up words so try to avoid using the dictionary unnecessarily, especially in exams. Think carefully about what you want to say and see if you can put it another way, using words you already know. To rephrase things you can:

> Use a word with a similar meaning. This is particularly easy with adjectives, as there are a lot of words which mean *good*, *bad*, *big* etc and you're sure to know at least one.

> Use negatives: if the cake you made was a total disaster, you could just say it wasn't very good.

> Use particular examples instead of general terms. If you are asked to describe the sports facilities in your area, and time is short, don't look up *facilities* – say something like *'In our town there is a swimming pool and a football ground.'*

11　**You want to ask *'Have you got any pets?'*. How could you avoid using the word *'pet'* if you don't know it?**

12　**How could you say *'The palace of Versailles is huge'* without looking up the word *'huge'*?**

You can also often guess the meaning of a French word by using others to give you a clue. If you see the sentence *'j'écoute de la musique rap'*, you may not know the meaning of the word **écoute**, but you do know it's a verb because it's preceded by **j'**. Therefore it must be something you can do to music: **listen**. So the translation is: *I listen to rap music.*

13　**In a description of a holiday centre you see a picture of bikes and read 'On peut louer des vélos: 10€ la journée'. You may not know the meaning of 'louer', but you can see that you have to pay 10 euros, which gives you a clue to what it could mean. What can you do – ride bikes, borrow bikes or hire bikes?**

Parts of speech

There are two entries for **flat** because this word can be a noun or an adjective. It helps to choose correctly between entries if you know how to recognize these different types of words.

Nouns and pronouns

Nouns often appear with words like *a, the, this, that, my, your* and *his*. They can be singular (abbreviated to SING in the dictionary):

*his **dog***   *her **cat***   *a **street***

or plural (abbreviated to PL in the dictionary):

*the **facts***   *those **people***   *his **shoes***   *our **holidays***

They can be the subject of a verb:

***Vegetables** are good for you*

or the object of a verb:

*I play **tennis***

Words like *I, me, you, he, she, him, her* and *they* are pronouns. They can be used instead of nouns. You can refer to a person as *he* or *she* or to a thing as *it*.

> ***I bought my mother a box of chocolates.***

14   **Which three words are nouns in this sentence?**
15   **Which of the nouns is plural?**
16   **Which word is a pronoun?**

French nouns are either masculine or feminine (abbreviated to MASC and FEM). Masculine nouns are shown by **le**:

***le** bateau*   ***le** chien*   ***le** jardin*

Feminine nouns are shown by **la**:

***la** porte*   ***la** robe*   ***la** souris*

If a noun starts with a vowel or a vowel sound, then **le** or **la** becomes **l'**:

***l'**ami*   ***l'**eau*   ***l'**orage*   ***l'**histoire*

The plural forms of **le**, **la** and **l'** is **les**. As in English, the plural of most French nouns is made by adding **s**:

les chiens   *les* portes   *les* tables

If the singular form already ends in **s**, or if it ends in **x**, then you don't have to add anything:

*l'*ananas   *les* ananas
la voix   *les* voix

Sometimes, however, the plural form is irregular and this is shown in the entry:

le **cheval** (PL les **chevaux**) NOUN
<u>horse</u>

horse NOUN
le <u>cheval</u> (PL les chevaux)

> Je me brosse les dents tous les soirs.

17 **Two words in this sentence are nouns. Which ones?**

18 **Are they singular or plural?**

19 **What is the plural form of 'le choix'?**

20 **Look in the dictionary to find the plural form of 'le travail'.**

Adjectives

Flat can be an adjective as well as a noun. Adjectives describe nouns: your tyre can be **flat**, you can have a pair of **flat** shoes.

21 **'Dark' is an adjective in one of these sentences and a noun in the other. Which is which?**

> *I'm not afraid of the dark.*
> *She's got dark hair.*

French adjectives can be masculine or feminine, singular or plural, depending on the noun they describe:

un **petit** garçon (MASC SING)
une **petite** fille (FEM SING = masculine singular + **e**)
trois **petits** garçons (MASC PL = masculine singular + **s**)
trois **petites** filles (FEM PL = masculine singular + **es**)

The masculine and feminine singular forms of regular adjectives are shown on both sides of the dictionary.

So if you want to find out what sort of shoes **des chaussures plates** are, look under **plat**.

To form the plural of adjectives in French, you generally add **s** to both masculine and feminine forms.

If the masculine form ends in **s** or **x**, then you don't need to add **s** to make the masculine plural.

MASC SING	FEM SING	MASC PL	FEM PL
passé	passée	passés	passées
gris	grise	gris	grises
anxieux	anxieuse	anxieux	anxieuses
agréable	agréable	agréables	agréables

Some adjectives remain the same whether they're masculine, feminine or plural. This is also shown in the dictionary:

arrière (FEM+PL arrière) ADJECTIVE
▷ *see also* **arrière** NOUN
back

back ADJECTIVE, ADVERB
▷ *see also* **back** NOUN, VERB
arrière (FEM+PL arrière)

22 **What is the feminine singular form of 'vert'?**
23 **What is the masculine plural form of 'aimable'?**
24 **What forms can 'heureux' be?**
25 **What is the masculine plural form of 'gras'? And the feminine singular (look in the dictionary for this one)?**

Verbs

She's going to record the programme for me.
His time in the race was a new world record.

Record in the first sentence is a verb. In the second, it is a noun.

One way to recognize a verb is that it frequently comes with a pronoun such as **I**, **you** or **she**, or with somebody's name. Verbs can relate to the present, the past or the future. They have a number of different forms to show this: **I'm going** (present), **he will go** (future), and **Nicola went by herself** (past). Often verbs appear with **to: they promised to go**. This basic form of the verb is called the infinitive.

In this dictionary, verbs are preceded by 'to', so you can identify them at a glance. No matter which of the four previous examples you want to translate, you should look up 'to **go**', not '**going**' or '**went**'. If you want to translate '**I thought**', look up 'to **think**'.

26 **What would you look up to translate the verbs in these phrases?**

| *I* ***went*** | *she****'s crying*** | *he* ***was lying*** |
| *I* ***did*** *it* | *he****'s*** *out* | *they****'ve gone*** |

Verbs have different endings, depending on whether you are talking about **je, tu, nous, ils** etc: **j'aime, tu aimes, nous aimons, ils aiment** etc. They also have different forms for the present, future, past etc. **Nous mangeons** (*we eat* = present), **nous avons mangé** (*we ate* = past). **Manger** is the infinitive and is the form that appears in the dictionary.

Sometimes the verb changes completely between the infinitive form and the **je, tu, ils** etc form. For example, *I go* is **je vais**, but *to go* is **aller**, and **nous faisons** (*we do*) comes from **faire** (*to do*). **J'ai fait** (*I have done* or *I did*) also comes from **faire**.

On pages 28-48 of the middle section of this dictionary, you will find 21 of the most important French verbs shown in full. On the French – English side of the dictionary you will find a number beside all French verbs. When you look up that number in the verb tables on pages 22-27, you will be shown the verb forms for that type of verb. This will help you to work out which is the correct verb form you need, whether that verb is regular or irregular.

27 **Which verb form does the verb plaisanter follow?**

Adverbs

An adverb is a word that describes a verb or an adjective:

Write **soon**.   Check your work **carefully**.
They arrived **late**.   The film was **very** good.

In the sentence '*The swimming pool is open daily*', **daily** is an adverb describing the adjective **open**. In the phrase '*my daily routine*', **daily** is an adjective describing the noun **routine**. We use the same word in English but to get the right French translation, it is important to know if it's being used as an adjective or an adverb. When you look up **daily** you find:

daily ADJECTIVE, ADVERB
1 quotidien (FEM quotidienne)
   □ It's part of my daily routine. Ça fait partie
   de mes occupations quotidiennes.
2 tous les jours
   □ The pool is open daily. La piscine est
   ouverte tous les jours.

The examples show you **daily** being used as an adjective and as an adverb and will help you choose the right French translation.

Take the sentence '*The menu changes daily*'.
28 **Does '*daily*' go with the noun '*menu*' or the verb '*changes*'?**
29 **Is it an adverb or an adjective?**
30 **How would you translate '*daily*' in this sentence?**

Prepositions

Prepositions are words like **for**, **with** and **across**, which are followed by nouns or pronouns:

*I've got a present **for** David.*   *Come **with** me.*   *He ran **across** the road.*

The party's over.
The shop's just over the road.

31 **In one of these sentences 'over' is an adjective describing a noun, in the other it is a preposition followed by a noun. Which is which?**

Answers

1 the French side
2 **nager**
3 **nouveau** comes after **Noël**
4 **chou-fleur** comes after **chocolat**
5 the first entry (the ADJECTIVE entry)
6 **C'est une question très difficile.**
7 **J'aime jouer au billard américain.**
8 they must all have a **medical examination**
9 **Nous avons joué au football.**
10 **Les bijoux sont beaux.**
11 you could ask 'Have you got a cat or a dog?'
12 you could say 'Very big.'
13 you can **hire** bikes
14 **mother**, **box** and **chocolates** are nouns
15 **chocolates** is plural
16 **I** is a pronoun
17 **dents** and **soirs** are nouns
18 they are both plural
19 **les choix**
20 **les travaux**
21 **dark** in the first sentence is a noun and in the second, it's an adjective
22 **verte**
23 **aimables**
24 masculine singular or plural
25 the masculine plural form is **gras** and the feminine singular form is **grasse**
26 to **go**, to **cry**, to **lie**, to **do**, to **be**, to **go**
27 **plaisanter** follows the same verb form as **donner**, number [28]
28 **daily** goes with the verb **changes**
29 it is an adverb
30 **tous les jours**
31 in the first sentence, **over** is an adjective and in the second, it's a preposition

a VERB ▷ *see* **avoir**

> **LANGUAGE TIP** **a** should not be confused with the preposition **à**.

- **Il a beaucoup d'amis.** He has a lot of friends.
- **Il a mangé des frites.** He had some chips.
- **Il a neigé pendant la nuit.** It snowed during the night.
- **il y a** **1** there is □ Il y a un bon film à la télé. There's a good film on TV. **2** there are □ Il y a beaucoup de monde. There are lots of people. **3** ago □ Je l'ai rencontré il y a deux ans. I met him two years ago.
- **Qu'est-ce qu'il y a?** What's the matter?
- **Il n'y a qu'à partir plus tôt.** We'll just have to leave earlier.

à PREPOSITION

> **LANGUAGE TIP** **à** should not be confused with the verb form **a**. See also **au** (=à+le) and **aux** (=à+les).

1 at
  □ être à la maison to be at home □ à trois heures at 3 o'clock
2 in
  □ être à Paris to be in Paris □ habiter au Portugal to live in Portugal □ habiter à la campagne to live in the country □ au printemps in the spring □ au mois de juin in June
3 to
  □ aller à Paris to go to Paris □ aller au Portugal to go to Portugal □ aller à la campagne to go to the country □ donner quelque chose à quelqu'un to give something to somebody □ Cette veste appartient à Marie. This jacket belongs to Marie. □ Je n'ai rien à faire. I've got nothing to do.
- **Ce livre est à Paul.** This book is Paul's.
- **Cette voiture est à nous.** This car is ours.
4 by
  □ à bicyclette by bicycle □ être payé à l'heure to be paid by the hour
- **à pied** on foot

- **C'est à côté de chez moi.** It's near my house.
- **C'est à dix kilomètres d'ici.** It's 10 kilometres from here.
- **C'est à dix minutes d'ici.** It's 10 minutes from here.
- **cent kilomètres à l'heure** 100 kilometres an hour
- **À bientôt!** See you soon! □ À demain! See you tomorrow! □ À samedi! See you on Saturday! □ À tout à l'heure! See you later!

abandonner VERB [28]
1 to abandon
  □ Il a abandonné son chien. He abandonned his dog.
2 to give up
  □ J'ai décidé d'abandonner la natation. I've decided to give up swimming.

l' **abeille** FEM NOUN
  bee

abîmer VERB [28]
  to damage
- **s'abîmer** to get damaged

l' **abonnement** MASC NOUN
1 season ticket
2 subscription *(to magazine)*

s' **abonner** VERB [28]
- **s'abonner à une revue** to take out a subscription to a magazine

l' **abord** MASC NOUN
- **d'abord** first □ Je vais rentrer chez moi d'abord. I'll go home first.

aboyer VERB [53]
  to bark

l' **abri** MASC NOUN
  shelter
- **être à l'abri** to be under cover
- **se mettre à l'abri** to shelter

l' **abricot** MASC NOUN
  apricot

s' **abriter** VERB [28]
  to shelter

l' **absence** FEM NOUN
  absence
- **Il est passé pendant ton absence.** He

came while you were away.

absent (FEM **absente**) ADJECTIVE
absent

absolument ADVERB
absolutely

l' **accélérateur** MASC NOUN
accelerator

accélérer VERB [34]
to accelerate

l' **accent** MASC NOUN
accent
□ Il a l'accent de Marseille. He has a
Marseilles accent.
■ **un accent aigu** an acute accent
■ **un accent grave** a grave accent
■ **un accent circonflexe** a circumflex

accentuer VERB [28]
to stress

accepter VERB [28]
to accept
■ **accepter de faire quelque chose** to
agree to do something

l' **accès** MASC NOUN
access
□ avoir accès à quelque chose to have
access to something
■ **'Accès aux quais'** 'To the trains'

l' **accessoire** MASC NOUN
1   accessory
□ les accessoires de mode fashion
accessories
2   prop

l' **accident** MASC NOUN
accident
□ un accident de la route a road accident
□ Elle a eu un accident de ski. She had a
skiing accident.
■ **par accident** by chance

accompagner VERB [28]
to accompany

accomplir VERB [38]
to carry out
□ Il n'a pas réussi à accomplir cette tâche.
He didn't manage to carry out this task.

l' **accord** MASC NOUN
agreement
■ **être d'accord** to agree □ Tu es d'accord
avec moi? Do you agree with me?
■ **se mettre d'accord** to come to an
agreement
■ **D'accord!** OK!

l' **accordéon** MASC NOUN
accordion
□ Ray joue de l'accordéon. Ray plays the
accordion.

l' **accoudoir** MASC NOUN
armrest

l' **accrochage** MASC NOUN
collision

accrocher VERB [28]
■ **accrocher quelque chose à 1** to hang
something on □ Il a accroché sa veste au
portemanteau. He hung his jacket on the
coat rack. **2** to hitch something up to □ Ils
ont accroché la remorque à leur voiture.
They hitched the trailer up to their car.
■ **s'accrocher à quelque chose** to get
caught on something □ Sa jupe s'est
accrochée aux ronces. Her skirt got caught
on the brambles.

s' **accroupir** VERB [38]
to squat down

l' **accueil** MASC NOUN
welcome
□ Il nous a remerciés de notre accueil. He
thanked us for our welcome.
■ **Elle s'occupe de l'accueil des visiteurs.**
She's in charge of looking after visitors.
■ **'Accueil'** 'Reception'

accueillant (FEM **accueillante**) ADJECTIVE
welcoming
□ Ses parents ont été très accueillants. Her
parents were very welcoming.

accueillir VERB [22]
to welcome

accumuler VERB [28]
to accumulate
■ **s'accumuler** to pile up

l' **accusation** FEM NOUN
accusation

l' **accusé** MASC NOUN
accused
□ L'accusé a déclaré que ... The accused
stated that ...
■ **un accusé de réception** an
acknowledgement of receipt

l' **accusée** FEM NOUN
accused

accuser VERB [28]
to accuse
□ accuser quelqu'un de quelque chose to
accuse somebody of something

l' **achat** MASC NOUN
purchase
■ **faire des achats** to do some shopping

acheter VERB [1]
to buy
□ J'ai acheté des gâteaux à la pâtisserie. I
bought some cakes at the cake shop.
■ **acheter quelque chose à quelqu'un**
1 to buy something for somebody
□ Qu'est-ce que tu lui as acheté pour son
anniversaire? What did you buy him for his
birthday? **2** to buy something from

somebody □ J'ai acheté des œufs au fermier. I bought some eggs from the farmer.

acide (FEM **acide**) ADJECTIVE
▷ *see also* **acide** NOUN
acid
□ Ce pamplemousse est trop acide. This grapefruit is too acid.

l' **acide** MASC NOUN
▷ *see also* **acide** ADJECTIVE
acid

l' **acier** MASC NOUN
steel

l' **acné** FEM NOUN
acne
□ Il a de l'acné. He has acne.

acquérir VERB [2]
to acquire

acquis VERB ▷ *see* **acquérir**

acquitter VERB [28]
to acquit
□ L'accusé a été acquitté. The accused was acquitted.

l' **acte** MASC NOUN
act
■ un acte de naissance a birth certificate

l' **acteur** MASC NOUN
actor
□ Il est acteur. He's an actor. □ un acteur de cinéma a film actor

actif (FEM **active**) ADJECTIVE
active
■ la population active the working population

l' **action** FEM NOUN
action
■ une bonne action a good deed

s' **activer** VERB [28]
1 to bustle about
□ Elle s'activait à préparer le repas. She bustled about preparing the meal.
2 to get moving
□ Allez! Active-toi! Come on! Get moving!

l' **activité** FEM NOUN
activity

l' **actrice** FEM NOUN
actress
□ Elle est actrice. She's an actress. □ une actrice de cinéma a film actress

l' **actualité** FEM NOUN
current events
■ un problème d'actualité a topical issue
■ les actualités the news

actuel (FEM **actuelle**) ADJECTIVE
present
□ le système actuel the present system

■ à l'heure actuelle at the present time
LANGUAGE TIP Be careful! actuel does not mean **actual**.

actuellement ADVERB
at present
LANGUAGE TIP Be careful! actuellement does not mean **actually**.

l' **adaptateur** MASC NOUN
adaptor

l' **addition** FEM NOUN
1 addition
□ l'addition et la soustraction addition and subtraction
2 bill
□ L'addition, s'il vous plaît! Can we have the bill, please?

additionner VERB [28]
to add up

l' **adhérent** MASC NOUN
member

l' **adhérente** FEM NOUN
member

adhésif (FEM **adhésive**) ADJECTIVE
■ le ruban adhésif sticky tape

adieu EXCLAMATION
farewell!

l' **adjectif** MASC NOUN
adjective

admettre VERB [47]
1 to admit
□ Il refuse d'admettre qu'il s'est trompé. He won't admit that he made a mistake.
2 to allow
□ Les chiens ne sont pas admis dans le restaurant. Dogs are not allowed in the restaurant.

l' **administration** FEM NOUN
administration
■ l'Administration the Civil Service

admirable (FEM **admirable**) ADJECTIVE
wonderful

l' **admirateur** MASC NOUN
admirer

l' **admiratrice** FEM NOUN
admirer

admirer VERB [28]
to admire

admis VERB ▷ *see* **admettre**

l' **adolescence** FEM NOUN
adolescence

l' **adolescent** MASC NOUN
teenager

l' **adolescente** FEM NOUN
teenager

adopter VERB [28]
to adopt

adorable – afin de

adorable (FEM **adorable**) ADJECTIVE
lovely

adorer VERB [28]
to love
□ Elle adore le chocolat. She loves chocolate. □ J'adore jouer au tennis. I love playing tennis.

l' **adresse** FEM NOUN
address
□ une adresse web a Web address
■ **mon adresse électronique** my email address

adresser VERB [28]
■ **adresser la parole à quelqu'un** to speak to someone
■ **s'adresser à quelqu'un 1** to speak to somebody □ C'est à toi que je m'adresse. It's you I'm speaking to. **2** to go and see somebody □ Adressez-vous au patron. Go and see the boss. □ Adressez-vous aux renseignements. Ask at the enquiry desk. **3** to be aimed at somebody □ Ce film s'adresse surtout aux enfants. This film is aimed mainly at children.

l' **ADSL** MASC NOUN (= asymmetrical digital subscriber line)
ADSL
■ **On a l'ADSL à la maison.** We have broadband at home.

l' **adulte** MASC/FEM NOUN
adult

l' **adverbe** MASC NOUN
adverb

l' **adversaire** MASC/FEM NOUN
opponent

aérien (FEM **aérienne**) ADJECTIVE
■ **une compagnie aérienne** an airline

l' **aérobic** MASC NOUN
aerobics
□ Teresa fait de l'aérobic. Teresa does aerobics.

l' **aérogare** FEM NOUN
terminal

l' **aéroglisseur** MASC NOUN
hovercraft

l' **aéroport** MASC NOUN
airport

l' **affaire** FEM NOUN
▷ see also **les affaires**
1 case
□ une affaire de drogue a drugs case
2 business
□ Son affaire marche bien. His business is doing well.
■ **une bonne affaire** a real bargain
■ **Ça fera l'affaire.** This will do nicely.
■ **avoir affaire à quelqu'un** to deal with somebody

les **affaires** FEM PL NOUN
▷ see also **l'affaire**
1 things
□ Va chercher tes affaires! Go and get your things!
2 business
□ Les affaires marchent bien en ce moment. Business is good at the moment. □ Mêle-toi de tes affaires. (informal) Mind your own business.
■ **un homme d'affaires** a businessman
■ **le ministre des Affaires étrangères** the Foreign Secretary

l' **affection** FEM NOUN
affection

affectueusement ADVERB
affectionately

affectueux (FEM **affectueuse**) ADJECTIVE
affectionate

l' **affiche** FEM NOUN
poster

afficher VERB [28]
to put up
□ Ils ont affiché les résultats dehors. They've put the results up outside.
■ **'Défense d'afficher'** 'Post no bills'

affilée
■ **d'affilée** ADVERB at a stretch □ Il a travaillé douze heures d'affilée. He worked 12 hours at a stretch.

l' **affirmation** FEM NOUN
assertion

affirmer VERB [28]
to claim
□ Il a affirmé que c'était la vérité. He claimed it was the truth.
■ **s'affirmer** to assert yourself □ Il est trop timide, il faut qu'il s'affirme. He's too shy, he should assert himself.

l' **affluence** FEM NOUN
■ **les heures d'affluence** the rush hour

s' **affoler** VERB [28]
to panic
□ Ne t'affole pas! Don't panic!

affranchir VERB [38]
to stamp

affreux (FEM **affreuse**) ADJECTIVE
awful

affronter VERB [28]
to face
□ L'Allemagne affronte l'Italie en finale. Germany will face Italy in the final.

afin de CONJUNCTION
■ **afin de faire quelque chose** so as to do something □ Je me suis levé très tôt afin d'être prêt à temps. I got up very early so as

to be ready on time.

afin que CONJUNCTION
  so that

> LANGUAGE TIP **afin que** is followed by a verb in the subjunctive.

□ Il m'a téléphoné afin que je sois prêt à temps. He phoned me so that I'd be ready on time.

africain (FEM **africaine**) ADJECTIVE, NOUN
  African

  ■ **un Africain** an African *(man)*
  ■ **une Africaine** an African *(woman)*

l' **Afrique** FEM NOUN
  Africa

  ■ **en Afrique 1** in Africa **2** to Africa
  ■ **l'Afrique du Sud** South Africa

agacer VERB [12]

  ■ **agacer quelqu'un** to get on somebody's nerves □ Tu m'agaces avec tes questions! You're getting on my nerves with all your questions!

l' **âge** MASC NOUN
  age

  ■ **Quel âge as-tu?** How old are you?

âgé (FEM **âgée**) ADJECTIVE
  old

  □ Son père est âgé. His father's old. □ Il est âgé de dix ans. He's 10 years old.

  ■ **les personnes âgées** the elderly

l' **agence** FEM NOUN
1 agency

  □ l'agence pour l'emploi the employment agency

  ■ **une agence de voyages** a travel agency
2 office

  □ l'agence de Londres the London office

  ■ **une agence immobilière** an estate agent's

l' **agenda** MASC NOUN
  diary

  □ J'ai perdu mon agenda. I have lost my diary.

> LANGUAGE TIP Be careful! The French word **agenda** does not mean **agenda**.

s' **agenouiller** VERB [28]
  to kneel down

l' **agent** MASC NOUN

  ■ **un agent de police** a policeman
  ■ **un agent d'entretien** a cleaner

l' **agglomération** FEM NOUN
  town

  ■ **l'agglomération parisienne** Greater Paris

aggraver VERB [28]
  to make worse

  ■ **s'aggraver** to worsen

agir VERB [38]
  to act

  □ Il a agi par vengeance. He acted out of vengeance.

  ■ **Il s'agit de ...** It's about ... □ Il s'agit du club de sport. It's about the sports club.
  □ De quoi s'agit-il? What is it about?

  ■ **Il s'agit de faire attention.** We must be careful.

agité (FEM **agitée**) ADJECTIVE
1 restless

  □ Les élèves sont agités. The pupils are restless.
2 rough

  □ La mer est agitée. The sea is rough.

  ■ **un sommeil agité** broken sleep

agiter VERB [28]
  to shake

  □ Agitez la bouteille. Shake the bottle.

l' **agneau** (PL les **agneaux**) MASC NOUN
  lamb

l' **agrafe** FEM NOUN
  staple *(for papers)*

l' **agrafeuse** FEM NOUN
  stapler

agrandir VERB [38]
1 to enlarge

  □ J'ai fait agrandir mes photos. I've had my photos enlarged.
2 to extend

  □ Ils ont agrandi leur jardin. They've extended their garden.

  ■ **s'agrandir** to expand □ Leur magasin s'est agrandi. Their shop has expanded.

agréable (FEM **agréable**) ADJECTIVE
  nice

agréer VERB [18]

  ■ **Veuillez agréer, Monsieur, l'expression de mes sentiments les meilleurs. Jean Ormal.** Yours sincerely, Jean Ormal.

agressif (FEM **agressive**) ADJECTIVE
  aggressive

l' **agressivité** FEM NOUN
  aggression

  ■ **faire preuve d'agressivité envers de quelqu'un** to be aggressive to somebody
  ■ **l'agressivité au volant** road rage

agricole (FEM **agricole**) ADJECTIVE
  agricultural

  □ le matériel agricole agricultural machinery

  ■ **une exploitation agricole** a farm

l' **agriculteur** MASC NOUN
  farmer

  □ Il est agriculteur. He's a farmer.

l' **agriculture** FEM NOUN

farming

ai VERB ▷*see* **avoir**
- ■ **J'ai deux chats.** I have two cats.
- ■ **J'ai bien dormi.** I slept well.

l' **aide** FEM NOUN
1 help
   - □ J'ai besoin de ton aide. I need your help.
   - □ appeler quelqu'un à l'aide to call to somebody for help
   - ■ **À l'aide!** Help!
2 aid
   - □ une aide financière financial aid
   - ■ **à l'aide de** using □ J'ai réussi à ouvrir la boîte à l'aide d'un couteau. I managed to open the tin using a knife.

aider VERB [28]
   to help

l' **aide-soignant** (PL les **aides-soignants**) MASC NOUN
   auxiliary nurse
   - □ Il est aide-soignant. He's an auxiliary nurse.

l' **aide-soignante** (PL les **aides-soignantes**) FEM NOUN
   auxiliary nurse
   - □ Françoise est aide-soignante. Françoise is an auxiliary nurse.

aie VERB ▷*see* **avoir**

aïe EXCLAMATION
   ouch!

aigre (FEM **aigre**) ADJECTIVE
   sour

aigu (FEM **aiguë**) ADJECTIVE
   sharp (*pain*)
   - □ une douleur aiguë a sharp pain
   - ■ **e accent aigu** e acute

l' **aiguille** FEM NOUN
   needle
   - □ une aiguille à tricoter a knitting needle
   - ■ **les aiguilles d'une montre** the hands of a watch

l' **ail** MASC NOUN
   garlic

l' **aile** FEM NOUN
   wing

aille VERB ▷*see* **aller**

ailleurs ADVERB
   somewhere else
   - ■ **partout ailleurs** everywhere else
   - ■ **nulle part ailleurs** nowhere else
   - ■ **d'ailleurs** besides

aimable (FEM **aimable**) ADJECTIVE
   kind

l' **aimant** MASC NOUN
   magnet

aimer VERB [28]
1 to love

   - □ Elle aime ses enfants. She loves her children.
2 to like
   - □ Tu aimes le chocolat? Do you like chocolate? □ J'aime bien ce garçon. I like this boy. □ J'aime bien jouer au tennis. I like playing tennis. □ J'aimerais aller en Grèce. I'd like to go to Greece.
   - ■ **J'aimerais mieux ne pas y aller.** I'd rather not go.

aîné (FEM **aînée**) ADJECTIVE
   ▷*see also* **aîné** NOUN, **aînée** NOUN
   elder
   - □ mon frère aîné my big brother

l' **aîné** MASC NOUN
   ▷*see also* **aîné** ADJECTIVE
   oldest child
   - □ C'est l'aîné. He's the oldest child.

l' **aînée** FEM NOUN
   ▷*see also* **aînée** ADJECTIVE
   oldest child
   - □ C'est l'aînée. She's the oldest child.

ainsi ADVERB
   in this way
   - □ Il faut faire ainsi. This is the way to do it.
   - ■ **C'est ainsi qu'il a réussi.** That's how he succeeded.
   - ■ **ainsi que** as well as
   - ■ **et ainsi de suite** and so on

l' **air** MASC NOUN
1 air
   - □ l'air chaud warm air
   - ■ **prendre l'air** to get some fresh air
2 tune
   - □ Elle a joué un air au piano. She played a tune on the piano.
   - ■ **Elle a l'air fatiguée.** She looks tired.
   - ■ **Il a l'air d'un clown.** He looks like a clown.

l' **aire de jeux** FEM NOUN
   playground

l' **aire de repos** FEM NOUN
   rest area (*on motorway*)

l' **aise** FEM NOUN
   - ■ **être à l'aise** to be at ease □ Elle est à l'aise avec tout le monde. She's at ease with everybody.
   - ■ **être mal à l'aise** to be ill at ease
   - ■ **se mettre à l'aise** to make oneself comfortable

ait VERB ▷*see* **avoir**

ajouter VERB [28]
   to add

l' **alarme** FEM NOUN
   alarm
   - □ donner l'alarme to raise the alarm

l' **Albanie** FEM NOUN

Albania

l' **album** MASC NOUN
album

l' **alcool** MASC NOUN
alcohol
□ Je ne bois pas d'alcool. I don't drink
alcohol.
■ **les alcools forts** spirits

alcoolisé (FEM **alcoolisée**) ADJECTIVE
alcoholic
■ **une boisson non alcoolisée** a soft drink

les **alentours** MASC PL NOUN
■ **dans les alentours** in the area
■ **aux alentours de Paris** in the Paris area
■ **aux alentours de cinq heures** around 5
o'clock

l' **algèbre** FEM NOUN
algebra

Alger NOUN
Algiers

l' **Algérie** FEM NOUN
Algeria

algérien (FEM **algérienne**) ADJECTIVE, NOUN
Algerian
■ **un Algérien** an Algerian *(man)*
■ **une Algérienne** an Algerian *(woman)*

l' **algue** FEM NOUN
seaweed

l' **aliment** MASC NOUN
food

l' **alimentation** FEM NOUN
1 groceries
□ le rayon alimentation du supermarché
the grocery department in the
supermarket
2 diet
□ Elle a une alimentation saine. She has a
healthy diet.

l' **allée** FEM NOUN
1 path
□ les allées du parc the paths in the park
2 drive *(in street names)*
■ **les allées et venues** comings and
goings

allégé (FEM **allégée**) ADJECTIVE
low-fat
□ un yaourt allégé a low-fat yoghurt

l' **Allemagne** FEM NOUN
Germany
■ **en Allemagne 1** in Germany **2** to
Germany

allemand (FEM **allemande**) ADJECTIVE, NOUN
German
□ Elle parle allemand. She speaks German.
■ **un Allemand** a German *(man)*
■ **une Allemande** a German *(woman)*
■ **les Allemands** the Germans

aller VERB [3]
▷ *see also* **aller** NOUN

PRESENT TENSE	
je vais	nous allons
tu vas	vous allez
il/elle va	ils/elles vont
PAST PARTICIPLE	
allé	

to go
□ Je suis allé à Londres. I went to London.
□ Je dois y aller. I've got to go. □ Elle ira le
voir. She'll go and see him. □ Je vais me
fâcher. I'm going to get angry.
■ **s'en aller** to go away □ Je m'en vais
demain. I'm going tomorrow.
■ **aller bien à quelqu'un** to suit somebody
□ Cette robe te va bien. This dress suits you.
■ **Allez! Dépêche-toi!** Come on! Hurry up!
■ **Comment allez-vous? — Je vais bien.**
How are you? — I'm fine.
■ **Comment ça va? — Ça va bien.** How are
you? — I'm fine.
■ **aller mieux** to be better

l' **aller** MASC NOUN
▷ *see also* **aller** VERB
1 outward journey
□ L'aller nous a pris trois heures. The
journey there took us three hours.
2 single *(ticket)*
□ Je voudrais un aller pour Angers. I'd like a
single to Angers.
■ **un aller simple** a single
■ **un aller retour 1** a return ticket □ Je
voudrais un aller retour pour Londres. I'd
like a return to London. **2** a round trip □ Il a
fait l'aller retour en dix heures. He did the
round trip in ten hours.

allergique (FEM **allergique**) ADJECTIVE
■ **allergique à** allergic to □ Je suis
allergique aux poils de chat. I'm allergic to
cat fur.

allô EXCLAMATION
hello!
□ Allô! Je voudrais parler à Monsieur Simon.
Hello! I'd like to speak to Mr Simon.

l' **allocation** FEM NOUN
allowance
■ **les allocations chômage** unemployment
benefit

s' **allonger** VERB [45]
to lie down
□ Il s'est allongé sur son lit. He lay down on
his bed.

allumer VERB [28]
1 to put on *(light)*
□ Tu peux allumer la lumière? Can you put
the light on?

2 to switch on
□ Allume la radio. Switch on the radio.
3 to light
□ Elle a allumé une cigarette. She lit a cigarette.
■ **s'allumer** (*light*) to come on □ La lumière s'est allumée. The light came on.

l' **allumette** FEM NOUN
match
□ une boîte d'allumettes a box of matches

l' **allure** FEM NOUN
1 speed
□ à toute allure at top speed
2 look
□ avoir une drôle d'allure to look odd

l' **allusion** FEM NOUN
reference

alors ADVERB
1 then
□ Tu as fini? Alors je m'en vais. Have you finished? I'm going then.
2 so
□ Alors je lui ai dit de partir. So I told him to leave.
■ **Et alors?** So what?
3 at that time
□ Il habitait alors à Paris. He was living in Paris at that time.
■ **alors que 1** as □ Il est arrivé alors que je partais. He arrived just as I was leaving.
2 while □ Alors que je travaillais dur, lui se reposait. While I was working hard, he was resting.

les **Alpes** FEM PL NOUN
Alps
□ dans les Alpes in the Alps

l' **alphabet** MASC NOUN
alphabet

alphabétique (FEM **alphabétique**)
ADJECTIVE
alphabetical
□ par ordre alphabétique in alphabetical order

l' **alpinisme** MASC NOUN
mountaineering

l' **alpiniste** MASC/FEM NOUN
mountaineer

l' **Alsace** FEM NOUN
Alsace

l' **amande** FEM NOUN
almond
■ **la pâte d'amandes** marzipan

l' **amant** MASC NOUN
lover

amateur (FEM **amateur**) ADJECTIVE
▷ *see also* **amateur** NOUN
amateur

□ Elle est pianiste amateur. She's an amateur pianist.

l' **amateur** MASC NOUN
▷ *see also* **amateur** ADJECTIVE
amateur
■ **en amateur** as a hobby □ Il fait de la photo en amateur. He takes photos as a hobby.
■ **C'est un amateur de musique.** He's a music lover.

l' **ambassade** FEM NOUN
embassy

l' **ambassadeur** MASC NOUN
ambassador

l' **ambiance** FEM NOUN
atmosphere
□ Je n'aime pas l'ambiance ici. I don't like the atmosphere here. □ Il y a de l'ambiance dans ce café. This café has a lively atmosphere.
■ **la musique d'ambiance** background music

ambitieux (FEM **ambitieuse**) ADJECTIVE
ambitious

l' **ambition** FEM NOUN
ambition
□ Il a l'ambition de devenir Premier ministre. His ambition is to be Prime Minister.
■ **Il a beaucoup d'ambition.** He's very ambitious.

l' **ambulance** FEM NOUN
ambulance

l' **âme** FEM NOUN
soul

l' **amélioration** FEM NOUN
improvement

améliorer VERB [28]
to improve
■ **s'améliorer** to improve □ Le temps s'améliore. The weather's improving.

l' **amende** FEM NOUN
fine
□ une amende de cinquante euros a 50 euro fine

amener VERB [43]
to bring
□ Qu'est-ce qui t'amène? What brings you here? □ Est-ce que je peux amener un ami? Can I bring a friend?

amer (FEM **amère**) ADJECTIVE
bitter

américain (FEM **américaine**) ADJECTIVE, NOUN
American
■ **un Américain** an American (*man*)
■ **une Américaine** an American (*woman*)

l' **Amérique** FEM NOUN

America
- **en Amérique 1** in America **2** to America
- **l'Amérique du Nord** North America
- **l'Amérique du Sud** South America

l' **ami** MASC NOUN
friend
- **C'est son petit ami.** He's her boyfriend.
- **LANGUAGE TIP** Word for word, **petit ami** means 'little friend'.

amical (FEM **amicale**, MASC PL **amicaux**) ADJECTIVE
friendly

amicalement ADVERB
in a friendly way
- **amicalement, Pierre** best wishes, Pierre

l' **amie** FEM NOUN
friend
- **C'est sa petite amie.** She's his girlfriend.
- **LANGUAGE TIP** Word for word, **petite amie** means 'little friend'.

l' **amitié** FEM NOUN
friendship
- **Fais mes amitiés à Paul.** Give my regards to Paul.
- **Amitiés, Christèle.** (in letter) Best wishes, Christèle.

l' **amour** MASC NOUN
love
- **faire l'amour** to make love

amoureux (FEM **amoureuse**) ADJECTIVE
in love
□ **être amoureux de quelqu'un** to be in love with somebody

l' **amour-propre** MASC NOUN
self-esteem

l' **amphithéâtre** MASC NOUN
lecture theatre

amplement ADVERB
- **Nous avons amplement le temps.** We have plenty of time.

l' **ampoule** FEM NOUN
1 light bulb
2 blister
□ **J'ai une ampoule au pied.** I've got a blister on my foot.

amusant (FEM **amusante**) ADJECTIVE
amusing

les **amuse-gueule** MASC PL NOUN
party nibbles

amuser VERB [28]
to amuse
- **s'amuser 1** to play □ **Les enfants s'amusent dehors.** The children are playing outside. **2** to enjoy oneself □ **On s'est bien amusés.** We really enjoyed ourselves.

l' **an** MASC NOUN
year
- **le premier de l'an** New Year's Day
- **le nouvel an** New Year

l' **analyse** FEM NOUN
1 analysis
2 test (medical)
□ **une analyse d'urine** a urine test

l' **ananas** MASC NOUN
pineapple

l' **ancêtre** MASC/FEM NOUN
ancestor

l' **anchois** MASC NOUN
anchovy

ancien (FEM **ancienne**) ADJECTIVE
1 former
□ **C'est une ancienne élève.** She's a former pupil.
2 old
□ **notre ancienne voiture** our old car
3 antique
□ **un fauteuil ancien** an antique chair

l' **ancre** FEM NOUN
anchor

Andorre FEM NOUN
Andorra

l' **âne** MASC NOUN
donkey

l' **ange** MASC NOUN
angel
- **être aux anges** to be over the moon
- **LANGUAGE TIP** Word for word, this means 'to be with the angels'.

l' **angine** FEM NOUN
throat infection

anglais (FEM **anglaise**) ADJECTIVE, NOUN
English
□ **Est-ce que vous parlez anglais?** Do you speak English?
- **un Anglais** an Englishman
- **une Anglaise** an Englishwoman
- **les Anglais** the English

l' **angle** MASC NOUN
1 angle
□ **un angle droit** a right angle
2 corner
□ **à l'angle de la rue** at the corner of the street

l' **Angleterre** FEM NOUN
England
- **en Angleterre 1** in England □ **J'habite en Angleterre.** I live in England. **2** to England □ **Je suis allée en Angleterre le mois dernier.** I went to England last month.

anglo- PREFIX
anglo-
- **les îles Anglo-Normandes** the Channel Islands

anglophone (FEM **anglophone**) ADJECTIVE   9

English-speaking

angoissé (FEM **angoissée**) ADJECTIVE
stressed
▫ Il a l'air angoissé. He looks stressed.

l' **animal** (PL les **animaux**) MASC NOUN
animal

l' **animateur** MASC NOUN
1 host
▫ Il est animateur à la télé. He's a TV host.
2 youth leader
▫ Pierre est animateur au centre sportif.
Pierre is a youth leader at the sports centre.

l' **animatrice** FEM NOUN
1 host
▫ Elle est animatrice à la télé. She's a TV
host.
2 youth leader
▫ Cécile est animatrice au centre sportif.
Cécile is a youth leader at the sports centre.

animé (FEM **animée**) ADJECTIVE
lively
▫ Cette rue est très animée. This is a very
lively street.
■ **un dessin animé** a cartoon

l' **anis** MASC NOUN
aniseed

l' **anneau** (PL les **anneaux**) MASC NOUN
ring

l' **année** FEM NOUN
year
▫ l'année dernière last year ▫ l'année
prochaine next year

l' **anniversaire** MASC NOUN
1 birthday
▫ C'est l'anniversaire de Janet. It's Janet's
birthday.
2 anniversary
▫ un anniversaire de mariage a wedding
anniversary

l' **annonce** FEM NOUN
advert
▫ J'ai lu votre annonce dans le journal. I saw
your advert in the newspaper. ▫ passer une
annonce to place an ad
■ **les petites annonces** the small ads

annoncer VERB [12]
to announce
▫ Ils ont annoncé leurs fiançailles. They've
announced their engagement.

l' **annuaire** MASC NOUN
phone book

annuel (FEM **annuelle**) ADJECTIVE
annual

annuler VERB [28]
to cancel

anonyme (FEM **anonyme**) ADJECTIVE
anonymous

l' **anorak** MASC NOUN
anorak

l' **ANPE** FEM NOUN (= Agence nationale pour
l'emploi)
job centre
▫ Je suis allé à l'ANPE. I went to the job
centre.

l' **Antarctique** MASC NOUN
Antarctic

l' **antenne** FEM NOUN
1 aerial
■ **antenne parabolique** satellite dish
■ **être à l'antenne** to be on the air
2 antenna

l' **antibiotique** MASC NOUN
antibiotic

l' **antidépresseur** MASC NOUN
antidepressant
▫ Elle est sous antidépresseurs depuis un
mois. She's been on antidepressants for a
month.

l' **antigel** MASC NOUN
antifreeze

les **Antilles** FEM PL NOUN
West Indies
■ **aux Antilles 1** in the West Indies **2** to
the West Indies

antipathique (FEM **antipathique**)
ADJECTIVE
unpleasant
▫ Je le trouve plutôt antipathique. I find him
rather unpleasant.

antipelliculaire (FEM **antipelliculaire**)
ADJECTIVE
■ **shampooing antipelliculaire** anti-
dandruff shampoo

l' **antiquaire** MASC/FEM NOUN
antique dealer
▫ Elle est antiquaire. She's an antique
dealer.

l' **antiquité** FEM NOUN
antique
▫ un magasin d'antiquités an antique shop
■ **pendant l'antiquité** in classical times

antiseptique (FEM **antiseptique**) ADJECTIVE
▷ see also **antiseptique** NOUN
antiseptic

l' **antiseptique** MASC NOUN
▷ see also **antiseptique** ADJECTIVE
antiseptic

l' **antivol** MASC NOUN
1 lock (on bike)
2 steering lock (on car)

anxieux (FEM **anxieuse**) ADJECTIVE
anxious
▫ Il est anxieux de nature. He's a born
worrier.

août MASC NOUN
August
- **en août** in August

apercevoir VERB [67]
to see
- □ J'aperçois la côte. I can see the shore.
- **s'apercevoir de quelque chose** to notice something
- **s'apercevoir que ...** to notice that ...

l' **apéritif** MASC NOUN
aperitif
- □ Venez donc prendre l'apéritif ce soir! Come round for drinks this evening!

apparaître VERB [56]
to appear

l' **appareil** MASC NOUN
device
- **un appareil dentaire** a brace *(for teeth)*
- **les appareils ménagers** domestic appliances
- **un appareil photo** a camera
- **Qui est à l'appareil?** *(on phone)* Who's speaking?

apparemment ADVERB
apparently

l' **apparence** FEM NOUN
appearance

l' **apparition** FEM NOUN
appearance
- □ Il n'a fait qu'une brève apparition. He only appeared briefly.

l' **appartement** MASC NOUN
flat

appartenir VERB [83]
- **appartenir à quelqu'un** to belong to somebody

apparu VERB ▷ *see* **apparaître**

l' **appel** MASC NOUN
1 cry
- □ un appel au secours a cry for help
2 phone call
- **faire appel à quelqu'un** to appeal to somebody
- **faire l'appel** *(in school)* to call the register
- **faire un appel de phares** to flash one's headlights

appeler VERB [4]
to call
- □ Elle a appelé le médecin. She called the doctor. □ J'ai appelé Richard à Londres. I called Richard in London.
- **s'appeler** to be called □ Comment ça s'appelle? What is it called? □ Elle s'appelle Muriel. Her name's Muriel. □ Comment tu t'appelles? What's your name?

l' **appendicite** FEM NOUN
appendicitis

appétissant (FEM **appétissante**) ADJECTIVE
appetizing

l' **appétit** MASC NOUN
appetite
- **Bon appétit!** Enjoy your meal!

applaudir VERB [38]
to clap *(applaud)*

les **applaudissements** MASC PL NOUN
applause

appliquer VERB [28]
1 to apply
2 to enforce
- □ appliquer la loi to enforce the law
- **s'appliquer** to apply oneself

apporter VERB [28]
to bring

apprécier VERB [19]
to appreciate

appréhender VERB [28]
to dread
- □ J'appréhende cette réunion. I'm dreading this meeting.

apprendre VERB [65]
1 to learn
- □ apprendre quelque chose par cœur to learn something by heart
- **apprendre à faire quelque chose** to learn to do something □ J'apprends à faire la cuisine. I'm learning to cook.
2 to hear
- □ J'ai appris son départ. I heard that she had left.
- **apprendre quelque chose à quelqu'un** 1 to teach somebody something □ Ma mère m'a appris l'anglais. My mother taught me English. □ Elle lui a appris à conduire. She taught him to drive. 2 to tell somebody something □ Jean-Pierre m'a appris la nouvelle. Jean-Pierre told me the news.

l' **apprentissage** MASC NOUN
learning
- □ On dit que l'apprentissage de l'arabe est très difficile. Learning Arabic is said to be very difficult.

appris VERB ▷ *see* **apprendre**

l' **approbation** FEM NOUN
approval
- □ donner son approbation to give one's approval

approcher VERB [28]
- **approcher de** to approach □ Nous approchons de Paris. We are approaching Paris.
- **s'approcher de** to come closer to □ Ne t'approche pas, j'ai la grippe! Don't get too close to me, I've got flu!

approprié (FEM **appropriée**) ADJECTIVE
suitable
□ une tenue appropriée suitable clothes
approuver VERB [28]
to approve of
□ Je n'approuve pas ses méthodes. I don't approve of his methods.
approximatif (FEM **approximative**) ADJECTIVE
1 approximate
□ un prix approximatif an approximate price
2 rough
□ un calcul approximatif a rough calculation
l' **appui** MASC NOUN
support
□ J'ai besoin de votre appui. I need your support.
appuyer VERB [53]
1 to press
□ appuyer sur un bouton to press a button
2 to lean
□ Elle a appuyé son vélo contre la porte. She leaned her bike against the door.
■ **s'appuyer** to lean □ Elle s'est appuyée contre le mur. She leaned against the wall.
□ Il s'est appuyé sur la table. He leaned on the table.
après PREPOSITION, ADVERB
1 after
□ après le déjeuner after lunch □ après son départ after he had left □ après qu'il est parti after he had left □ Nous viendrons après avoir fait la vaisselle. We'll come after we've done the dishes.
2 afterwards
□ aussitôt après immediately afterwards
■ **après coup** afterwards □ J'y ai repensé après coup. I thought about it again afterwards.
■ **d'après** according to □ D'après lui, c'est une erreur. According to him, that's a mistake.
■ **après tout** after all
après-demain ADVERB
the day after tomorrow
l' **après-midi** MASC OR FEM NOUN
afternoon
l' **après-rasage** MASC NOUN
aftershave
l' **aquarium** MASC NOUN
aquarium
arabe (FEM **arabe**) ADJECTIVE, NOUN
1 Arab
□ les pays arabes the Arab countries
2 Arabic
□ la littérature arabe Arabic literature □ Il parle arabe. He speaks Arabic.

■ **un Arabe** an Arab (man)
■ **une Arabe** an Arab (woman)
l' **Arabie Saoudite** FEM NOUN
Saudi Arabia
l' **araignée** FEM NOUN
spider
l' **arbitre** MASC NOUN
1 referee
2 umpire
l' **arbre** MASC NOUN
tree
■ **un arbre généalogique** a family tree
l' **arbuste** MASC NOUN
shrub
l' **arc** MASC NOUN
bow
□ son arc et ses flèches his bow and arrows
l' **arc-en-ciel** (PL les **arcs-en-ciel**) MASC NOUN
rainbow

LANGUAGE TIP Word for word, arc-en-ciel means 'bow-in-the-sky'.

l' **archéologie** FEM NOUN
archaeology
l' **archéologue** MASC/FEM NOUN
archaeologist
□ Elle est archéologue. She's an archaeologist.
l' **archipel** MASC NOUN
archipelago
l' **architecte** MASC NOUN
architect
□ Il est architecte. He's an architect.
l' **architecture** FEM NOUN
architecture
l' **Arctique** MASC NOUN
Arctic
l' **ardoise** FEM NOUN
slate
l' **arène** FEM NOUN
bullring
■ **des arènes romaines** a Roman amphitheatre
■ **l'arène politique** the political arena
l' **arête** FEM NOUN
fish bone
l' **argent** MASC NOUN
1 silver
□ une bague en argent a silver ring
2 money
□ Je n'ai plus d'argent. I haven't got any more money.
■ **l'argent de poche** pocket money
■ **l'argent liquide** cash
LANGUAGE TIP Word for word, this means 'liquid money'.
argentin (FEM **argentine**) ADJECTIVE, NOUN

Argentinian
- **un Argentin** an Argentinian *(man)*
- **une Argentine** an Argentinian *(woman)*

l' **Argentine** FEM NOUN
Argentina

l' **argile** FEM NOUN
clay

l' **argot** MASC NOUN
slang

l' **arme** FEM NOUN
weapon
- **une arme à feu** a firearm

l' **armée** FEM NOUN
army
- **l'armée de l'air** the Air Force

l' **armistice** MASC NOUN
armistice

l' **armoire** FEM NOUN
wardrobe

l' **armure** FEM NOUN
armour
- un chevalier en armure a knight in armour

arnaquer VERB [28] *(informal)*
to con

l' **arobase** FEM NOUN
@ symbol
- **Mon adresse e-mail, c'est 'lola arobase europost point fr'.** My email address is 'lola@europost.fr'.

aromatisé (FEM **aromatisée**) ADJECTIVE
flavoured

l' **arôme** MASC NOUN
1 aroma
2 flavouring *(added to food)*

arpenter VERB [28]
to pace up and down
- Il arpentait le couloir. He was pacing up and down the corridor.

arrache-pied
- **d'arrache-pied** ADVERB furiously
- travailler d'arrache-pied to work furiously

arracher VERB [28]
1 to take out
- Le dentiste m'a arraché une dent. The dentist took one of my teeth out.
2 to tear out
- Arrachez la page. Tear the page out.
3 to pull up
- Elle a arraché les mauvaises herbes. She pulled up the weeds.
- **arracher quelque chose à quelqu'un** to snatch something from somebody

arranger VERB [45]
1 to arrange
- arranger des fleurs dans un vase to arrange flowers in a vase

2 to suit
- Ça m'arrange de partir plus tôt. It suits me to leave earlier.
- **s'arranger** to come to an agreement
- Arrangez-vous avec le patron. You'll have to come to an agreement with the boss.
- **Je vais m'arranger pour venir.** I'll organize things so that I can come.
- **Ça va s'arranger.** Things will work themselves out.

l' **arrestation** FEM NOUN
arrest
- en état d'arrestation under arrest

l' **arrêt** MASC NOUN
stop
- un arrêt de bus a bus stop
- **sans arrêt 1** non-stop □ Elle travaille sans arrêt. She works non-stop.
- **2** continually □ Ils se disputent sans arrêt. They quarrel continually.

arrêter VERB [28]
1 to stop
- **Arrête!** Stop it!
- **arrêter de faire quelque chose** to stop doing something
2 to switch off
- Il a arrêté le moteur. He switched the engine off.
3 to arrest
- Mon voisin a été arrêté. My neighbour's been arrested
- **s'arrêter** to stop □ Elle s'est arrêtée devant une vitrine. She stopped in front of a shop window.
- **s'arrêter de faire quelque chose** to stop doing something □ s'arrêter de fumer to stop smoking

les **arrhes** FEM PL NOUN
deposit
- verser des arrhes to pay a deposit

l' **arrière** MASC NOUN
▷ *see also* **arrière** ADJECTIVE
back
- l'arrière de la maison the back of the house
- **à l'arrière** at the back
- **en arrière** behind □ Ils sont restés en arrière. They stayed behind.

arrière (FEM+PL **arrière**) ADJECTIVE
▷ *see also* **arrière** NOUN
back
- le siège arrière the back seat □ les roues arrière the rear wheels

l' **arrière-grand-mère** (PL les **arrière-grands-mères**) FEM NOUN
great-grandmother

l' **arrière-grand-père** (PL les **arrière-**

13

grands-pères) MASC NOUN
great-grandfather

l' **arrivée** FEM NOUN
arrival

arriver VERB [5]
1 to arrive
□ J'arrive à l'école à huit heures. I arrive at school at 8 o'clock.
2 to happen
□ Qu'est-ce qui est arrivé à Christian? What happened to Christian?
■ **arriver à faire quelque chose** to manage to do something □ J'espère que je vais y arriver. I hope I'll manage it.
■ **Il m'arrive de dormir jusqu'à midi.** I sometimes sleep till midday.

arrogant (FEM **arrogante**) ADJECTIVE
arrogant

l' **arrondissement** MASC NOUN
district

> DID YOU KNOW...?
> Paris, Lyons and Marseilles are divided into numbered districts called **arrondissements**.

arroser VERB [28]
to water
□ Daphne arrose ses tomates. Daphne is watering her tomatoes.
■ **Ils ont arrosé leur victoire.** They had a drink to celebrate their victory.

l' **arrosoir** MASC NOUN
watering can

l' **art** MASC NOUN
art

l' **artère** FEM NOUN
1 artery
2 thoroughfare
■ **les grandes artères de Paris** the main roads of Paris

l' **artichaut** MASC NOUN
artichoke

l' **article** MASC NOUN
1 article
□ un article de journal a newspaper article
2 item
□ les articles en promotion items on special offer

l' **articulation** FEM NOUN
joint
□ l'articulation du genou the knee joint

articuler VERB [28]
to pronounce clearly

artificiel (FEM **artificielle**) ADJECTIVE
artificial

l' **artisan** MASC NOUN
self-employed craftsman

l' **artiste** MASC/FEM NOUN

1 artist
2 performer

artistique (FEM **artistique**) ADJECTIVE
artistic

as VERB ▷ see **avoir**
▷ see also **as** NOUN
■ **Tu as de beaux cheveux.** You've got nice hair.

l' **as** MASC NOUN
▷ see also **as** VERB
ace
□ l'as de trèfle the ace of clubs

l' **ascenseur** MASC NOUN
lift

l' **Ascension** FEM NOUN
Ascension

asiatique (FEM **asiatique**) ADJECTIVE
Asiatic
□ la cuisine asiatique Oriental cooking □ le Sud-Est asiatique South East Asia

l' **Asie** FEM NOUN
Asia
■ **en Asie 1** in Asia **2** to Asia

l' **aspect** MASC NOUN
appearance

l' **asperge** FEM NOUN
asparagus

l' **aspirateur** MASC NOUN
vacuum cleaner
■ **passer l'aspirateur** to vacuum

l' **aspirine** FEM NOUN
aspirin

assaisonner VERB [28]
to season

l' **assassin** MASC NOUN
murderer

assassiner VERB [28]
to murder

assembler VERB [28]
to assemble
■ **s'assembler** to gather □ Une foule énorme s'était assemblée. A huge crowd had gathered.

s' **asseoir** VERB [6]
to sit down
□ Asseyez-vous! Sit down! □ Assieds-toi! Sit down!

assez ADVERB
1 enough
□ Nous n'avons pas assez de temps. We don't have enough time. □ Est-ce qu'il y a assez de pain? Is there enough bread?
■ **J'en ai assez!** I've had enough!
2 quite
□ Il faisait assez beau. The weather was quite nice.

l' **assiette** FEM NOUN

plate
□ une assiette creuse a soup plate □ une
assiette à dessert a dessert plate
■ une assiette anglaise assorted cold
meats
assis VERB ▷ see asseoir
assis (FEM **assise**) ADJECTIVE
sitting
□ Il est assis par terre. He's sitting on the
floor.
l' **assistance** FEM NOUN
1 audience
□ Y a-t-il un médecin dans l'assistance? Is
there a doctor in the audience?
2 aid
□ l'assistance humanitaire humanitarian
aid
3 assistance
□ avec l'assistance de quelqu'un with the
assistance of somebody
l' **assistant** MASC NOUN
assistant
□ Il était assistant d'anglais à Tourcoing. He
was an English assistant in Tourcoing.
■ un assistant social a social worker
l' **assistante** FEM NOUN
assistant
□ Elle est assistante de français à Oxford.
She's a French assistant in Oxford.
■ une assistante sociale a social worker
assister VERB [28]
■ assister à un accident to witness an
accident
■ assister à un cours to attend a class
■ assister à un concert to be at a concert
l' **association** FEM NOUN
association
l' **associé** MASC NOUN
partner (in business)
l' **associée** FEM NOUN
partner (in business)
s' **associer** VERB [19]
to go into partnership
assommer VERB [28]
to knock out
□ Il l'a assommé avec une bouteille. He
knocked him out with a bottle.
l' **Assomption** FEM NOUN
Assumption
assorti (FEM **assortie**) ADJECTIVE
1 matching
□ des couleurs assorties matching colours
2 assorted
□ des chocolats assortis assorted
chocolates
■ être assorti à quelque chose to match
something □ Son sac est assorti à ses

chaussures. Her bag matches her shoes.
l' **assortiment** MASC NOUN
assortment
l' **assurance** FEM NOUN
1 insurance
□ une assurance maladie medical
insurance
2 confidence
□ parler avec assurance to speak with
confidence
assurer VERB [28]
1 to insure
□ La maison est assurée. The house is
insured. □ être assuré contre quelque chose
to be insured against something
2 to assure
□ Je t'assure que c'est vrai! I assure you it's
true!
■ s'assurer de quelque chose to make
sure of something □ Il s'est assuré que la
porte était fermée. He made sure the door
was shut.
l' **asthme** MASC NOUN
asthma
□ une crise d'asthme an asthma attack
l' **astronaute** MASC/FEM NOUN
astronaut
l' **astronomie** FEM NOUN
astronomy
astucieux (FEM **astucieuse**) ADJECTIVE
clever
l' **atelier** MASC NOUN
1 workshop
2 studio (artist's)
Athènes NOUN
Athens
l' **athlète** MASC/FEM NOUN
athlete
l' **athlétisme** MASC NOUN
athletics
□ un championnat d'athlétisme an athletics
championship
l' **Atlantique** MASC NOUN
Atlantic
l' **atlas** MASC NOUN
atlas
l' **atmosphère** FEM NOUN
atmosphere
atomique (FEM **atomique**) ADJECTIVE
atomic
□ la bombe atomique the atomic bomb
l' **atout** MASC NOUN
1 asset
□ L'atout principal de ce joueur, c'est sa
vitesse. This player's main asset is his
speed.
2 trump card

a

□ J'avais quatre atouts dans mon jeu. I had four trump cards in my hand.

atroce (FEM **atroce**) ADJECTIVE
terrible

attachant (FEM **attachante**) ADJECTIVE
lovable

attacher VERB [28]
to tie up

□ Elle a attaché ses cheveux avec un élastique. She tied her hair up with an elastic band.

■ **s'attacher à quelqu'un** to become attached to somebody

■ **une poêle qui n'attache pas** a non-stick frying pan

attaquer VERB [28]
to attack

atteindre VERB [60]
to reach

attendant

■ **en attendant** ADVERB in the meantime

attendre VERB [7]
to wait

□ attendre quelqu'un to wait for someone
□ J'attends d'avoir un appartement à moi. I'm waiting until I've got a flat of my own.
□ Attends qu'il ne pleuve plus. Wait until it's stopped raining.

■ **attendre un enfant** to be expecting a baby

■ **s'attendre à** to expect □ Je m'attends à une surprise. I'm expecting a surprise.

LANGUAGE TIP Be careful! **attendre** does not mean **to attend**.

l' **attentat** MASC NOUN

■ **un attentat à la bombe** a terrorist bombing

l' **attente** FEM NOUN
wait

□ deux heures d'attente two hours' wait
■ **la salle d'attente** the waiting room

attentif (FEM **attentive**) ADJECTIVE
attentive

l' **attention** FEM NOUN
attention

□ à l'attention de for the attention of
■ **faire attention** to be careful
■ **Attention!** Watch out! □ Attention, tu vas te faire écraser! Watch out, you'll get run over!

attentionné (FEM **attentionnée**) ADJECTIVE
thoughtful

atterrir VERB [38]
to land

l' **atterrissage** MASC NOUN
landing (of plane)

attirant (FEM **attirante**) ADJECTIVE

attractive

attirer VERB [28]
to attract

□ attirer l'attention de quelqu'un to attract somebody's attention

■ **s'attirer des ennuis** to get into trouble
□ Si tu continues, tu vas t'attirer des ennuis. If you keep on like that, you'll get yourself into trouble.

l' **attitude** FEM NOUN
attitude

l' **attraction** FEM NOUN

■ **un parc d'attractions** an amusement park

attraper VERB [28]
to catch

attrayant (FEM **attrayante**) ADJECTIVE
attractive

attrister VERB [28]
to sadden

au PREPOSITION ▷ see à

LANGUAGE TIP **au** is the contracted form of **à** + **le**.

□ au printemps in the spring

l' **aube** FEM NOUN
dawn

□ à l'aube at dawn

l' **auberge** FEM NOUN
inn

■ **une auberge de jeunesse** a youth hostel

l' **aubergine** FEM NOUN
aubergine

aucun (FEM **aucune**) ADJECTIVE, PRONOUN

1 no

□ Il n'a aucun ami. He's got no friends.
□ Aucun enfant ne pourrait le faire. No child could do that.

2 none

□ Aucun d'entre eux n'est venu. None of them came. □ Aucune de mes amies n'aime le football. None of my female friends like football. □ Tu aimes ses films? — Je n'en ai vu aucun. Do you like his films? — I haven't seen any of them.

■ **sans aucun doute** without any doubt

au-delà ADVERB

■ **au-delà de** beyond □ Votre ticket n'est pas valable au-delà de cette limite. Your ticket is not valid beyond this point.

au-dessous ADVERB

1 downstairs

□ Ils habitent au-dessous. They live downstairs.

2 underneath

■ **au-dessous de** under □ au-dessous du pont under the bridge □ dix degrés au-dessous de zéro ten degrees below zero

au-dessus ADVERB
1 upstairs
□ J'habite au-dessus. I live upstairs.
2 above
■ **au-dessus de** above □ au-dessus de la table above the table

audiovisuel (FEM **audiovisuelle**) ADJECTIVE
audiovisual

l' **auditeur** MASC NOUN
listener (to radio)

l' **auditrice** FEM NOUN
listener (to radio)

l' **augmentation** FEM NOUN
rise

augmenter VERB [28]
to increase

aujourd'hui ADVERB
today

auparavant ADVERB
first
□ Vous pouvez utiliser l'ordinateur mais auparavant vous devez taper le mot de passe. You can use the computer but first you have to key in the password.

auquel (MASC PL **auxquels**, FEM PL **auxquelles**) PRONOUN

⊙ LANGUAGE TIP **auquel** is the contracted form of **à** + **lequel**.
□ l'homme auquel j'ai parlé the man I spoke to

aura, aurai, auras, aurez, aurons, auront VERB ▷ see **avoir**

l' **aurore** FEM NOUN
daybreak

ausculter VERB [28]
■ **Le médecin l'a ausculté.** The doctor listened to his chest.

aussi ADVERB
1 too
□ Dors bien. — Toi aussi. Sleep well. — You too. □ Lui aussi parle espagnol. He speaks Spanish too.
2 also
□ J'aimerais aussi que tu achètes le journal. I'd also like you to get the paper. □ Je parle anglais et aussi allemand. I speak English and also German.
■ **aussi ... que** as ... as □ aussi grand que moi as big as me

aussitôt ADVERB
straight away
□ aussitôt après son retour straight after his return
■ **aussitôt que** as soon as □ aussitôt que tu auras fini as soon as you've finished

l' **Australie** FEM NOUN
Australia

■ **en Australie 1** in Australia **2** to Australia

australien (FEM **australienne**) ADJECTIVE, NOUN
Australian
■ **un Australien** an Australian (man)
■ **une Australienne** an Australian (woman)

autant ADVERB
■ **autant de 1** so much □ Je ne veux pas autant de gâteau. I don't want so much cake. **2** so many □ Je n'ai jamais vu autant de monde. I've never seen so many people.
■ **autant ... que 1** as much ... as □ J'ai autant d'argent que toi. I've got as much money as you have. **2** as many ... as □ J'ai autant d'amis que lui. I've got as many friends as he has.
■ **d'autant plus que** all the more since □ Elle est d'autant plus déçue qu'il le lui avait promis. She's all the more disappointed since he had made her a promise.
■ **d'autant moins que** even less since □ C'est d'autant moins pratique pour lui qu'il doit changer deux fois de train. It's even less convenient for him since he has to change trains twice.

l' **auteur** MASC NOUN
author

l' **auto** FEM NOUN
car

l' **autobus** MASC NOUN
bus
□ en autobus by bus

l' **autocar** MASC NOUN
coach
□ en autocar by coach

autocollant (FEM **autocollante**) ADJECTIVE
▷ see also **autocollant** NOUN
self-adhesive
□ une étiquette autocollante a self-adhesive label
■ **une enveloppe autocollante** a self-seal envelope

l' **autocollant** MASC NOUN
▷ see also **autocollant** ADJECTIVE
sticker

l' **auto-école** FEM NOUN
driving school

automatique (FEM **automatique**) ADJECTIVE
automatic

l' **automne** MASC NOUN
autumn
■ **en automne** in autumn

automobile (FEM **automobile**) ADJECTIVE
▷ see also **automobile** NOUN
■ **une course automobile** a motor race

l' **automobile** FEM NOUN

17

▷ *see also* **automobile** ADJECTIVE
car

l' **automobiliste** MASC/FEM NOUN
motorist

l' **autoradio** MASC NOUN
car radio

l' **autorisation** FEM NOUN
1 permission
□ Il m'a donné l'autorisation de sortir ce soir. He's given me permission to go out tonight.
2 permit
□ Il faut une autorisation pour camper ici. You need a permit to camp here.

autoriser VERB [28]
to give permission for
□ Il m'a autorisé à en parler. He's given me permission to talk about it.

autoritaire (FEM **autoritaire**) ADJECTIVE
authoritarian

l' **autorité** FEM NOUN
authority

l' **autoroute** FEM NOUN
motorway

l' **auto-stop** MASC NOUN
■ **faire de l'auto-stop** to hitchhike

l' **auto-stoppeur** MASC NOUN
hitchhiker

l' **auto-stoppeuse** FEM NOUN
hitchhiker

autour ADVERB
around
□ autour de la maison around the house

autre (FEM **autre**) ADJECTIVE, PRONOUN
other
□ Je viendrai un autre jour. I'll come some other day. □ J'ai d'autres projets. I've got other plans.
■ **autre chose** something else
■ **autre part** somewhere else
■ **un autre** another □ Tu veux un autre morceau de gâteau? Would you like another piece of cake?
■ **l'autre** the other □ Non, pas celui-ci, l'autre. No, not that one, the other one.
■ **d'autres** others □ Je t'en apporterai d'autres. I'll bring you some others.
■ **les autres** the others □ Les autres sont arrivés plus tard. The others arrived later.
■ **ni l'un ni l'autre** neither of them
■ **entre autres** among other things
□ Nous avons parlé, entre autres, de nos projets de vacances. We talked about our holiday plans, among other things.

autrefois ADVERB
in the old days

autrement ADVERB

1 differently
□ Il l'a fait autrement. He did it differently.
2 otherwise
□ Je n'ai pas pu faire autrement. I couldn't do otherwise.
■ **autrement dit** in other words

l' **Autriche** FEM NOUN
Austria
■ **en Autriche** 1 in Austria 2 to Austria

autrichien (FEM **autrichienne**) ADJECTIVE, NOUN
Austrian
■ **un Autrichien** an Austrian *(man)*
■ **une Autrichienne** an Austrian *(woman)*

l' **autruche** FEM NOUN
ostrich

aux PREPOSITION ▷ *see* à
LANGUAGE TIP **aux** is the contracted form of à + **les**.
□ J'ai dit aux enfants d'aller jouer. I told the children to go and play.

auxquelles PL PRONOUN
LANGUAGE TIP **auxquelles** is the contracted form of à + **lesquelles**.
□ les revues auxquelles il est abonné the magazines to which he subscribes

auxquels PL PRONOUN
LANGUAGE TIP **auxquels** is the contracted form of à + **lesquels**.
□ les enfants auxquels il a parlé the children he spoke to

avaient, avais, avait VERB ▷ *see* avoir
■ Il y avait beaucoup de monde. There were lots of people.

l' **avalanche** FEM NOUN
avalanche

avaler VERB [28]
to swallow

l' **avance** FEM NOUN
■ **être en avance** to be early
■ **à l'avance** beforehand □ réserver longtemps à l'avance to book well beforehand
■ **d'avance** in advance □ payer d'avance to pay in advance

avancé (FEM **avancée**) ADJECTIVE
advanced
□ à un niveau avancé at an advanced level
■ **bien avancé** well under way □ Les travaux sont déjà bien avancés. The work is already well under way.

avancer VERB [12]
1 to move forward
□ Il avançait prudemment. He was moving forward cautiously.
2 to bring forward
□ La date de l'examen a été avancée. The

date of the exam has been brought forward.
3 to put forward
□ Il a avancé sa montre d'une heure. He put his watch forward an hour.
4 to be fast *(watch)*
□ Ma montre avance d'une heure. My watch is an hour fast.
5 to lend
□ Peux-tu m'avancer dix euros? Can you lend me 10 euros?

avant (FEM+PL **avant**) PREPOSITION, ADJECTIVE
▷ *see also* **avant** NOUN
1 before
□ avant qu'il ne pleuve before it rains
□ avant de partir before leaving
2 front
□ la roue avant the front wheel □ le siège avant the front seat
■ **avant tout** above all

l' **avant** MASC NOUN
▷ *see also* **avant** PREPOSITION
front
□ l'avant de la voiture the front of the car
■ **à l'avant** in front
■ **en avant** forward □ Il a fait un pas en avant. He took a step forward.

l' **avantage** MASC NOUN
advantage

l' **avant-bras** (PL les **avant-bras**) MASC NOUN
forearm

avant-dernier (FEM **avant-dernière**, MASC PL **avant-derniers**) ADJECTIVE
last but one
□ l'avant-dernière page the last page but one □ Ils sont arrivés avant-derniers. They arrived last but one.

avant-hier ADVERB
the day before yesterday
□ Il est arrivé avant-hier. He arrived the day before yesterday.

avare (FEM **avare**) ADJECTIVE
▷ *see also* **avare** NOUN
miserly

l' **avare** MASC/FEM NOUN
▷ *see also* **avare** ADJECTIVE
miser

avec PREPOSITION
with
□ avec mon père with my father
■ **Et avec ça?** Anything else? *(in shop)*

l' **avenir** MASC NOUN
future
■ **à l'avenir** in future □ À l'avenir, essayez d'être à l'heure. Try to be on time in future.
■ **dans un proche avenir** in the near future

l' **aventure** FEM NOUN
adventure

l' **avenue** FEM NOUN
avenue

l' **averse** FEM NOUN
shower *(of rain)*

avertir VERB [38]
to warn
■ **avertir quelqu'un de quelque chose** to warn somebody about something

l' **avertissement** MASC NOUN
warning

aveugle (FEM **aveugle**) ADJECTIVE
blind

l' **avion** MASC NOUN
plane
■ **aller en avion** to fly □ Il est allé en Italie en avion. He flew to Italy.
■ **par avion** by airmail

l' **aviron** MASC NOUN
rowing

l' **avis** MASC NOUN
1 opinion
□ J'aimerais avoir ton avis. I'd like to have your opinion.
■ **à mon avis** in my opinion
2 notice
□ jusqu'à nouvel avis until further notice
■ **changer d'avis** to change one's mind
□ J'ai changé d'avis. I've changed my mind.

l' **avocat** MASC NOUN
1 lawyer
□ Il est avocat. He's a lawyer.
2 avocado

l' **avocate** FEM NOUN
lawyer
□ Elle est avocate. She's a lawyer.

l' **avoine** FEM NOUN
oats
□ les flocons d'avoine porridge oats

avoir VERB [8]

PRESENT TENSE	
j'ai	nous avons
tu as	vous avez
il/elle a	ils/elles ont
PAST PARTICIPLE	
eu	

1 to have
□ Ils ont deux enfants. They have two children. □ Il a les yeux bleus. He's got blue eyes. □ J'ai déjà mangé. I've already eaten. □ Est-ce que tu as vu ce film? Have you seen this film? □ Je lui ai parlé hier. I spoke to him yesterday.
■ **On t'a bien eu!** *(informal)* You've been had!
2 to be
□ Il a trois ans. He's three. □ J'avais dix ans quand je l'ai rencontré. I was ten when I

met him.

■ **il y a 1** there is □ Il y a quelqu'un à la porte. There's somebody at the door.
2 there are □ Il y a des chocolats sur la table. There are some chocolates on the table. **3** ago □ Je l'ai rencontré il y a deux ans. I met him two years ago.

■ **Qu'est-ce qu'il y a?** What's the matter?
■ **Il n'y a qu'à partir plus tôt.** We'll just have to leave earlier.

l' **avortement** MASC NOUN
abortion

avouer VERB [28]
to admit

avril MASC NOUN
April

■ **en avril** in April

ayez, ayons VERB ▷ see **avoir**

a

Bb

le **baby-foot** NOUN
table football

□ jouer au baby-foot to play table football

le **baby-sitting** NOUN
■ faire du baby-sitting to babysit

le **bac** NOUN = baccalauréat

le **baccalauréat** NOUN
A levels

□ Elle a passé son baccalauréat l'année dernière. She did her A levels last year.

> **DID YOU KNOW...?**
> The French **baccalauréat**, or **bac** for short, is taken at the age of 17 or 18. Students have to sit one of a variety of set subject combinations, rather than being able to choose any combination of subjects they want. If you pass you have the right to a place at university.

bâcler VERB [28]
to botch up

□ Je déteste le travail bâclé! I hate botched work!

le **bagage** NOUN
luggage

■ faire ses bagages to pack
■ les bagages à main hand luggage □ un bagage à main a piece of hand luggage

la **bagarre** NOUN
fight

□ Une bagarre a éclaté à la fermeture du pub. A fight broke out when the pub closed.

se **bagarrer** VERB [28]
to fight

□ Il s'est encore bagarré avec son frère. He's been fighting with his brother again.

la **bagnole** NOUN (informal)
car

la **bague** NOUN
ring

la **baguette** NOUN
1 stick of French bread
2 chopstick

□ manger avec des baguettes to eat with chopsticks

■ une baguette magique a magic wand

la **baie** NOUN
bay

la **baignade** NOUN
■ 'baignade interdite' 'no swimming'

se **baigner** VERB [28]
to go swimming

□ Si on allait se baigner? Shall we go swimming?

la **baignoire** NOUN
bath (bathtub)

bâiller VERB [28]
to yawn

le **bain** NOUN
bath

□ prendre un bain to take a bath □ prendre un bain de soleil to sunbathe

le **baiser** NOUN
kiss

la **baisse** NOUN
fall

□ la baisse du taux de chômage the fall in the unemployment rate

■ être en baisse to be falling
■ revoir les chiffres à la baisse to revise figures downwards

baisser VERB [28]
1 to turn down

□ Il fait moins froid, tu peux baisser le chauffage. It's not so cold, you can turn down the heating.

2 to fall

□ Le prix des CD a baissé. The price of CDs has fallen.

■ se baisser to bend down □ Il s'est baissé pour ramasser son mouchoir. He bent down to pick up his handkerchief.

le **bal** NOUN
dance

□ un bal populaire a local dance

la **balade** NOUN (informal)
walk

□ faire une balade to go for a walk

se **balader** VERB [28] (informal)
to wander around

□ J'adore me balader dans les rues de Paris.

French-English

I love to wander around the streets of Paris.

le **baladeur** NOUN
personal stereo

■ **un baladeur numérique** an MP3 player

le **balai** NOUN
broom

■ **Je vais donner un coup de balai dans la cuisine.** I'm going to sweep the kitchen.

la **balance** NOUN
scales *(for weighing)*

■ **la Balance** Libra □ Todd est Balance. Todd is Libra.

se **balancer** VERB [12]
to swing

la **balançoire** NOUN
swing

balayer VERB [59]
1 to sweep
□ Jean-Pierre a balayé la cuisine. Jean-Pierre swept the kitchen.
2 to sweep up
□ Va balayer les feuilles sur la terrasse. Go and sweep up the leaves on the terrace.

le **balayeur** NOUN
roadsweeper

balbutier VERB [19]
to stammer

le **balcon** NOUN
balcony

la **baleine** NOUN
whale

la **balle** NOUN
1 ball
□ une balle de tennis a tennis ball
2 bullet

la **ballerine** NOUN
1 ballet dancer
2 ballet shoe
□ une paire de ballerines rouges a pair of red ballet shoes

le **ballet** NOUN
ballet

le **ballon** NOUN
1 ball
□ lancer le ballon to throw the ball
■ **un ballon de football** a football
2 balloon

balnéaire (FEM **balnéaire**) ADJECTIVE
■ **une station balnéaire** a seaside resort

banal (FEM **banale**, MASC PL **banaux**) ADJECTIVE
1 commonplace
□ La violence est devenue banale à la télévision. Violence has become commonplace on television.
2 hackneyed
□ L'intrigue du film est très banale. The plot of the film is very hackneyed.

la **banane** NOUN
1 banana
□ La banane est un fruit. Banana is a fruit.
2 bumbag
□ Mes clés sont dans ma banane. My keys are in my bumbag.

le **banc** NOUN
bench

bancaire (FEM **bancaire**) ADJECTIVE
■ **une carte bancaire** a bank card

le **bandage** NOUN
bandage

la **bande** NOUN
1 gang
□ une bande de voyous a gang of louts
2 bunch
□ C'est une bande d'idiots! They are a bunch of idiots!
3 bandage
□ une bande Velpeau® a crepe bandage
■ **une bande dessinée** a comic strip

> **DID YOU KNOW...?**
> Comic strips are very popular in France with people of all ages.

■ **une bande magnétique** a tape
■ **la bande sonore** the sound track
■ **Elle fait toujours bande à part.** She always keeps to herself.

le **bandeau** (PL les **bandeaux**) NOUN
headband

bander VERB [28]
to bandage
□ L'infirmière lui a bandé la jambe. The nurse bandaged his leg.

le **bandit** NOUN
bandit

la **banlieue** NOUN
suburbs
□ Christèle habite en banlieue. Christèle lives in the suburbs.
■ **les lignes de banlieue** suburban lines
■ **les trains de banlieue** commuter trains

la **banque** NOUN
bank

le **banquet** NOUN
dinner
□ le banquet annuel de l'association the club's annual dinner

la **banquette** NOUN
seat
□ la banquette arrière de la voiture the back seat of the car

le **banquier** NOUN
banker

le **baptême** NOUN
christening
□ le baptême de notre fille our daughter's

b

christening
■ **C'était mon baptême de l'air.** It was the first time I had flown.
le **baquet** NOUN
tub
le **bar** NOUN
bar
la **baraque** NOUN *(informal)*
house
□ Elle habite dans une belle baraque. She lives in a beautiful house.
barbant (FEM **barbante**) ADJECTIVE *(informal)*
boring
□ Il est vraiment barbant! He's so boring!
barbare (FEM **barbare**) ADJECTIVE
barbaric
la **barbe** NOUN
beard
□ Il porte la barbe. He's got a beard.
■ **Quelle barbe!** *(informal)* What a drag!
■ **la barbe à papa** candyfloss

> **LANGUAGE TIP** Word for word, this means 'dad's beard'.

le **barbecue** NOUN
barbecue
barbouiller VERB [28]
to daub
□ Les murs étaient barbouillés de graffitis. The walls were daubed with graffitis.
■ **J'ai l'estomac barbouillé.** *(informal)* I'm feeling queasy.
barbu (FEM **barbue**) ADJECTIVE
bearded
□ un grand barbu a big, bearded man
barder VERB [28] *(informal)*
■ **Ça va barder!** There's going to be trouble!
le **baromètre** NOUN
barometer
la **barque** NOUN
rowing boat
■ **Ils sont allés faire une promenade en barque.** They've gone for a row.
le **barrage** NOUN
dam
■ **un barrage de police** a police roadblock
la **barre** NOUN
bar *(metal)*
□ une barre de fer an iron bar
le **barreau** (PL les **barreaux**) NOUN
bar *(on window)*
□ Il s'est retrouvé derrière les barreaux. He ended up behind bars.
barrer VERB [28]
to block
□ Il y a un tronc d'arbre qui barre la route. There's a tree trunk blocking the road.
■ **se barrer** *(informal)* to clear off □ Barre-

toi! Clear off!
la **barrette** NOUN
hair slide
la **barrière** NOUN
fence
le **bar-tabac** (PL les **bars-tabacs**) NOUN

> **DID YOU KNOW...?**
> A **bar-tabac** is a bar which also sells cigarettes and stamps; you can tell a **bar-tabac** by the red diamond-shaped sign outside it.

bas (FEM **basse**) ADJECTIVE, ADVERB
▷ *see also* **bas** NOUN
low
□ parler à voix basse to speak in a low voice
■ **en bas 1** down □ Ça me donne le vertige de regarder en bas. I get dizzy if I look down. **2** (down) at the bottom □ Son nom est tout en bas. His name is down at the bottom.
□ Il y a un marchand de journaux en bas de la rue. There's a newsagent's at the bottom of the street. **3** downstairs □ Elle habite en bas. She lives downstairs.
le **bas** NOUN
▷ *see also* **bas** ADJECTIVE
1 bottom
□ en bas de la page at the bottom of the page □ en bas de l'escalier at the bottom of the stairs
2 stocking
□ une paire de bas a pair of stockings
le **bas-côté** NOUN
verge
□ Il s'est garé sur le bas-côté de la route. He stopped his car on the verge.
la **bascule** NOUN
■ **un fauteuil à bascule** a rocking chair
la **base** NOUN
base
□ la base de la pyramide the base of the pyramid
■ **de base** basic □ Le pain et le lait sont des aliments de base. Bread and milk are basic foods.
■ **à base de** made from □ des produits de beauté à base de plantes cosmetics made from plants
■ **une base de données** a database
le **basilic** NOUN
basil
le **basket** NOUN
basketball
□ jouer au basket to play basketball
les **baskets** FEM PL NOUN
trainers
□ une paire de baskets a pair of trainers
le/la **Basque** NOUN

Basque *(person, language)*

basque (FEM **basque**) ADJECTIVE
Basque

basse FEM ADJECTIVE ▷ *see* **bas**

la **basse-cour** (PL les **basses-cours**) NOUN
farmyard

le **bassin** NOUN
1 pond
    □ Il y a un bassin à poissons rouges dans le parc. There's a goldfish pond in the park.
2 pelvis
    □ une fracture du bassin a fractured pelvis

la **bassine** NOUN
bowl *(for washing)*

le **bas-ventre** NOUN
stomach
    □ Elle se plaint de douleurs dans le bas-ventre. She is complaining of pains in her stomach.

la **bataille** NOUN
battle

le **bateau** (PL les **bateaux**) NOUN
boat

le **bateau-mouche** (PL les **bateaux-mouches**) NOUN
pleasure boat

bâti (FEM **bâtie**) ADJECTIVE
■ **bien bâti** well-built

le **bâtiment** NOUN
building

bâtir VERB [38]
to build

le **bâton** NOUN
stick
    □ un coup de bâton a blow with a stick

le **battement** NOUN
■ **J'ai dix minutes de battement.** I've got ten minutes free.

la **batterie** NOUN
1 battery
    □ La batterie est à plat. The battery is flat.
2 drums
    □ jouer de la batterie to play the drums
    ■ **la batterie de cuisine** the pots and pans

le **batteur** NOUN
drummer

battre VERB [9]
to beat
    □ Quand je le vois, mon cœur bat plus vite. When I see him, my heart beats faster.
    ■ **se battre** to fight □ Je me bats souvent avec mon frère. I fight a lot with my brother.
    ■ **battre les cartes** to shuffle the cards
    ■ **Battre les blancs en neige.** Beat the egg whites until stiff.
    ■ **battre son plein** to be in full swing □ A minuit, la fête battait son plein. At

midnight, the party was in full swing.

bavard (FEM **bavarde**) ADJECTIVE
talkative

bavarder VERB [28]
to chat

baver VERB [28]
to dribble

baveux (FEM **baveuse**) ADJECTIVE
runny
    □ une omelette baveuse a runny omelette

la **bavure** NOUN
blunder
    □ une bavure policière a police blunder

le **bazar** NOUN
general store
    ■ **Quel bazar!** *(informal)* What a mess!

BCBG (FEM+PL **BCBG**) ADJECTIVE (= *bon chic bon genre*)
posh

la **BD** (PL les **BD**) NOUN (= *bande dessinée*)
comic strip
    □ Marguerite adore les BD. Marguerite loves comic strips.

béant (FEM **béante**) ADJECTIVE
gaping
    □ un trou béant a gaping hole

beau (MASC SING ALSO **bel**, FEM **belle**, MASC PL **beaux**) ADJECTIVE, ADVERB

> **LANGUAGE TIP** beau changes to **bel** before a vowel and most words beginning with 'h'.

1 lovely
    □ un bel été a lovely summer □ une belle journée a fine day
2 beautiful
    □ C'est une belle femme. She is a beautiful woman.
3 good-looking
    □ C'est un beau garçon. He is a good-looking boy.
4 handsome
    □ un bel homme a handsome man
    ■ **Il fait beau aujourd'hui.** It's a nice day today.
    ■ **J'ai beau essayer, je n'y arrive pas.** However hard I try, I just can't do it.

beaucoup ADVERB
1 a lot
    □ Il boit beaucoup. He drinks a lot.
2 much
    □ Elle n'a pas beaucoup d'argent. She hasn't got much money. □ Janet est beaucoup plus grande que moi. Janet is much taller than me.
    ■ **beaucoup de** a lot of □ Il y avait beaucoup de monde au concert. There were a lot of people at the concert. □ Elle fait

beaucoup de fautes. She makes a lot of mistakes.

■ **J'ai eu beaucoup de chance.** I was very lucky.

le **beau-fils** (PL les **beaux-fils**) NOUN
1 son-in-law
2 stepson

le **beau-frère** (PL les **beaux-frères**) NOUN
brother-in-law

le **beau-père** (PL les **beaux-pères**) NOUN
1 father-in-law
2 stepfather

la **beauté** NOUN
beauty

les **beaux-arts** MASC PL NOUN
fine arts

les **beaux-parents** MASC PL NOUN
in-laws

le **bébé** NOUN
baby

le **bec** NOUN
beak

la **bécane** NOUN (informal)
bike

la **bêche** NOUN
spade

bêcher VERB [28]
to dig
□ Il bêchait son jardin. He was digging the garden.

bégayer VERB [59]
to stammer

beige (FEM **beige**) ADJECTIVE
beige

le **beignet** NOUN
fritter
□ les beignets aux pommes apple fritters

bel MASC ADJECTIVE ▷ see **beau**

le/la **Belge** NOUN
Belgian

belge (FEM **belge**) ADJECTIVE
Belgian

la **Belgique** NOUN
Belgium
■ **en Belgique 1** in Belgium **2** to Belgium

le **bélier** MASC NOUN
ram
■ **le Bélier** Aries □ Christine est Bélier. Christine's Aries.

belle FEM ADJECTIVE ▷ see **beau**

la **belle-famille** (PL les **belles-familles**) NOUN
in-laws

la **belle-fille** (PL les **belles-filles**) NOUN
1 daughter-in-law
2 stepdaughter

la **belle-mère** (PL les **belles-mères**) NOUN

1 mother-in-law
2 stepmother

la **belle-sœur** (PL les **belles-sœurs**) NOUN
sister-in-law

la **bénédiction** NOUN
blessing

le **bénéfice** NOUN
profit
□ La société réalise de gros bénéfices. The company is making big profits.

bénévole (FEM **bénévole**) ADJECTIVE
voluntary
□ du travail bénévole voluntary work

bénir VERB [38]
to bless

bénit (FEM **bénite**) ADJECTIVE
consecrated
■ **l'eau bénite** holy water

la **béquille** NOUN
crutch
□ Il marche avec des béquilles. He walks on crutches.

le **berceau** (PL les **berceaux**) NOUN
cradle

bercer VERB [12]
to rock

la **berceuse** NOUN
lullaby

le **béret** NOUN
beret

la **berge** NOUN
bank (of river)

le **berger** NOUN
shepherd

la **bergère** NOUN
shepherdess

le **besoin** NOUN
need
■ **avoir besoin de quelque chose** to need something □ J'ai besoin d'argent. I need some money. □ J'ai besoin d'y réfléchir. I need to think about it.
■ **une famille dans le besoin** a needy family

le **bétail** NOUN
livestock

bête (FEM **bête**) ADJECTIVE
▷ see also **bête** NOUN
stupid

la **bête** NOUN
▷ see also **bête** ADJECTIVE
animal

la **bêtise** NOUN
■ **faire une bêtise** to do something stupid □ J'ai fait une bêtise. I've done something stupid.
■ **dire des bêtises** to talk nonsense □ Tu

dis des bêtises! You're talking nonsense!

le **béton** NOUN
concrete

- **un alibi en béton** a cast-iron alibi

la **betterave** NOUN
beetroot

□ la salade de betterave beetroot salad

le/la **beur** NOUN (informal)

> **DID YOU KNOW...?**
> A **beur** is a young person of North African origin born in France.

le **beurre** NOUN
butter

□ une sauce au beurre a sauce made with butter

beurrer VERB [28]
to butter

Beyrouth NOUN
Beirut

le **bibelot** NOUN
ornament

le **biberon** NOUN
baby's bottle

la **Bible** NOUN
Bible

le/la **bibliothécaire** NOUN
librarian

la **bibliothèque** NOUN

1 library

□ emprunter un livre à la bibliothèque to borrow a book from the library

2 bookcase

□ une bibliothèque en chêne massif a bookcase made of solid oak

le **bic**® NOUN
Biro®

la **biche** NOUN
doe

la **bicyclette** NOUN
bicycle

le **bidet** NOUN
bidet

le **bidon** NOUN

▷ see also **bidon** ADJECTIVE

can

□ un bidon d'essence a can of petrol

bidon (FEM+PL bidon) ADJECTIVE (informal)

▷ see also **bidon** NOUN

phoney

- **Son histoire est complètement bidon.** His story is a complete load of rubbish.

le **bidonville** NOUN
shanty town

la **Biélorussie** NOUN
Belarus

bien (FEM+PL bien) ADJECTIVE, ADVERB

▷ see also **bien** NOUN

1 well

□ Daphne travaille bien. Daphne works well. □ Je me sens bien. I feel fine. □ Je ne me sens pas bien. I don't feel well.

2 good

□ Ce restaurant est vraiment bien. This restaurant is really good.

3 quite

□ bien assez quite enough

- **Je veux bien le faire.** I'm quite willing to do it.
- **bien mieux** much better
- **J'espère bien y aller.** I very much hope to go.

4 right

□ Ce n'est pas bien de dire du mal des gens. It's not right to say nasty things about people. □ Il croyait bien faire. He thought he was doing the right thing.

- **C'est bien fait pour lui!** It serves him right!

le **bien** NOUN

▷ see also **bien** ADJECTIVE

1 good

□ le bien et le mal good and evil □ Jean m'a dit beaucoup de bien de toi. Jean told me a lot of good things about you. □ C'est pour son bien. It's for his own good.

- **faire du bien à quelqu'un** to do somebody good □ Ses vacances lui ont fait beaucoup de bien. His holiday has done him a lot of good.

2 possession

□ son bien le plus précieux his most treasured possession

le **bien-être** NOUN
well-being

□ une sensation de bien-être a feeling of well-being

la **bienfaisance** NOUN
charity

- **une œuvre de bienfaisance** a charity

bien que CONJUNCTION
although

> **LANGUAGE TIP** bien que is followed by a verb in the subjunctive.

□ Il fait assez chaud bien qu'il n'y ait pas de soleil. It's quite warm although there's no sun.

bien sûr ADVERB
of course

bientôt ADVERB
soon

□ À bientôt! See you soon!

le **bienvenu** NOUN

- **Vous êtes le bienvenu!** You're welcome!

□ Vous êtes tous les bienvenus! You're all

welcome!

la **bienvenue** NOUN
welcome
□ Bienvenue à Paris! Welcome to Paris!
□ Vous êtes la bienvenue! You're welcome!

la **bière** NOUN
beer
■ la bière blonde lager
■ la bière brune brown ale
■ la bière pression draught beer

le **bifteck** NOUN
steak

le **bigoudi** NOUN
roller (in hair)

le **bijou** (PL les **bijoux**) NOUN
jewel

la **bijouterie** NOUN
jeweller's

le **bijoutier** NOUN
jeweller

la **bijoutière** NOUN
jeweller
□ Elle est bijoutière. She's a jeweller.

le **bilan** NOUN
■ faire le bilan de quelque chose to
assess something □ Il faut faire le bilan de la
situation. We need to assess the situation.

bilingue (FEM **bilingue**) ADJECTIVE
bilingual

le **billard** NOUN
billiards
■ le billard américain pool

la **bille** NOUN
marble (toy)
□ jouer aux billes to play marbles

le **billet** NOUN
1 ticket
□ un billet d'avion a plane ticket □ un billet
électronique an e-ticket
2 banknote
□ un billet de dix euros a 10 euro note

le **billion** NOUN
billion

bio (FEM+PL **bio**) ADJECTIVE
organic
□ Je préfère les produits bio. I prefer organic
produce.

la **biographie** NOUN
biography

la **biologie** NOUN
biology

biologique (FEM **biologique**) ADJECTIVE
1 organic
□ des légumes biologiques organic
vegetables
2 biological
□ des armes biologiques biological weapons

la **Birmanie** NOUN
Burma

bis ADVERB
▷ see also **bis** NOUN
□ Il habite au douze bis rue des Fleurs. He
lives at 12A rue des Fleurs.

le **bis** NOUN
▷ see also **bis** ADVERB
encore

la **biscotte** NOUN
toasted bread (sold in packets)

le **biscuit** NOUN
biscuit
■ un biscuit de Savoie a sponge cake

la **bise** NOUN
kiss
□ Grosses bises de Bretagne. Love and
kisses from Brittany.
■ faire la bise à quelqu'un (informal) to
give somebody a peck on the cheek □ Elle
m'a fait la bise. She gave me a peck on the
cheek.

DID YOU KNOW...?
Between girls and boys, and between
girls, the normal French way of saying
hello and goodbye is with kisses,
usually one on each cheek. Boys
shake hands with each other instead.

le **bisou** NOUN (informal)
kiss
□ Viens faire un bisou à maman! Come and
give Mummy a little kiss!

bissextile (FEM **bissextile**) ADJECTIVE
■ une année bissextile a leap year

le **bistrot** NOUN (informal)
café

DID YOU KNOW...?
Cafés in France sell both alcoholic and
non-alcoholic drinks.

bizarre (FEM **bizarre**) ADJECTIVE
strange

la **blague** NOUN (informal)
1 joke
□ raconter une blague to tell a joke
■ Sans blague! No kidding!
2 trick
□ André nous a encore fait une blague!
André has played a trick on us again!

blaguer VERB [28] (informal)
to joke

le **blaireau** (PL les **blaireaux**) NOUN
shaving brush

blâmer VERB [28]
to blame

blanc (FEM **blanche**) ADJECTIVE
▷ see also **blanc** NOUN
1 white

□ un chemisier blanc a white blouse

2 blank

□ une page blanche a blank page

le **blanc** NOUN

▷ *see also* blanc ADJECTIVE

1 white

□ habillé tout en blanc dressed all in white

2 white wine

□ un verre de blanc a glass of white wine

■ **un blanc d'œuf** an egg white

■ **un blanc de poulet** a chicken breast

le **Blanc** NOUN

white man

la **Blanche** NOUN

white woman

blanche FEM ADJECTIVE ▷ *see* blanc

la **blanchisserie** NOUN

laundry

le **blé** NOUN

wheat

blessé (FEM **blessée**) ADJECTIVE

▷ *see also* blessé NOUN, blessée NOUN

injured

le **blessé** NOUN

▷ *see also* blessé ADJECTIVE

injured person

□ L'accident a fait trois blessés. Three people were injured in the accident.

la **blessée** NOUN

▷ *see also* blessée ADJECTIVE

injured person

blesser VERB [28]

1 to injure

□ Il a été blessé dans un accident de voiture. He was injured in a car accident.

2 to hurt

□ Il a fait exprès de le blesser. He hurt him on purpose.

■ **se blesser** to hurt oneself □ Je me suis blessé au pied. I've hurt my foot.

la **blessure** NOUN

injury

bleu (FEM **bleue**) ADJECTIVE

▷ *see also* bleu NOUN

1 blue

□ une veste bleue a blue jacket

■ **bleu marine** navy blue

2 very rare *(steak)*

le **bleu** NOUN

▷ *see also* bleu ADJECTIVE

1 blue

□ J'aime le bleu. I like blue.

2 bruise

□ Il a un bleu au front. He's got a bruise on his forehead.

le **bleuet** NOUN

cornflower

le **bloc** NOUN

pad

□ un bloc de papier à lettres a pad of writing paper

■ **le bloc opératoire** the operating theatre

le **bloc-notes** (PL les **blocs-notes**) NOUN

note pad

le **blog** NOUN

blog *(on the internet)*

bloguer VERB [28]

to blog *(on the internet)*

blond (FEM **blonde**) ADJECTIVE

blond

■ **blond cendré** ash blond □ Andrew a les cheveux blond cendré. Andrew has ash blond hair.

bloquer VERB [28]

to block

□ bloquer le passage to block the way

■ **être bloqué dans un embouteillage** to be stuck in a traffic jam

se **blottir** VERB [38]

to huddle

□ Ils étaient blottis l'un contre l'autre. They were huddled together.

la **blouse** NOUN

overall

le **blouson** NOUN

jacket

□ un blouson en cuir a leather jacket

le **bob** NOUN

cotton sunhat

la **bobine** NOUN

reel

□ une bobine de fil a reel of thread

le **bocal** (PL les **bocaux**) NOUN

jar

le **bœuf** NOUN

1 ox

2 beef

□ un rôti de bœuf a joint of beef

bof EXCLAMATION *(informal)*

■ **Le film t'a plu? — Bof! C'était pas terrible!** Did you like the film? — Well ... it wasn't that great!

■ **Comment ça va? — Bof! Pas terrible.** How is it going? — Oh ... not too well actually.

le **bohémien** NOUN

gipsy

la **bohémienne** NOUN

gipsy

boire VERB [10]

to drink

■ **boire un coup** *(informal)* to have a drink

le **bois** NOUN

wood

■ **en bois** wooden □ une table en bois a wooden table

■ **avoir la gueule de bois** *(informal)* to have a hangover

la **boisson** NOUN
drink
□ une boisson chaude a hot drink □ une boisson non alcoolisée a soft drink

la **boîte** NOUN
1 box
□ une boîte d'allumettes a box of matches
■ **une boîte aux lettres** a letter box
■ **une boîte postale** a PO Box
■ **une boîte vocale** voice mail
2 tin
□ une boîte de sardines a tin of sardines
■ **une boîte de conserve** a tin
■ **en boîte** tinned □ des petits pois en boîte tinned peas
■ **une boîte de nuit** a night club

   LANGUAGE TIP Word for word, this means 'a night box'.

■ **sortir en boîte** to go clubbing

boiter VERB [28]
to limp

le **bol** NOUN
bowl
■ **en avoir ras le bol** *(informal)* to be fed up
□ J'en ai ras le bol de ce boulot. I'm fed up with this job.

bombarder VERB [28]
to bomb

la **bombe** NOUN
1 bomb
2 aerosol
□ du déodorant en bombe aérosol aerosol deodorant

bon (FEM **bonne**) ADJECTIVE, ADVERB
▷ see also **bon** NOUN
1 good
□ un bon restaurant a good restaurant □ Le tabac n'est pas bon pour la santé. Smoking isn't good for you. □ être bon en maths to be good at maths
■ **sentir bon** to smell nice
■ **Bon courage!** Good luck!
■ **Bon voyage!** Have a good trip!
■ **Bon week-end!** Have a nice weekend!
■ **Bonne chance!** Good luck!
■ **Bonne journée!** Have a nice day!
■ **Bonne nuit!** Good night!
■ **Bon anniversaire!** Happy birthday!
■ **Bonne année!** Happy New Year!
2 right
□ Il est arrivé au bon moment. He arrived at the right moment. □ Ce n'est pas la bonne réponse. That's not the right answer.

■ **Il fait bon aujourd'hui.** It's nice today.
■ **de bonne heure** early
■ **bon marché** cheap □ Les fraises ne sont pas bon marché en hiver. Strawberries aren't cheap in winter.
■ **Ah bon?** Really? □ Je pars aux États-Unis la semaine prochaine. — Ah bon? I'm going to the States next week. — Really?
■ **J'aimerais vraiment que tu viennes! — Bon, d'accord.** I'd really like you to come! — OK then, I will.
■ **Est-ce que ce yaourt est encore bon?** Is this yoghurt still OK?

le **bon** NOUN
▷ see also **bon** ADJECTIVE
voucher
□ un bon d'achat a voucher
■ **pour de bon** 1 for good □ Il est parti pour de bon. He's gone for good. 2 for real □ Cette fois, on le fait pour de bon. Let's do it for real this time.
■ **Il est fâché pour de bon.** He's really angry.

le **bonbon** NOUN
sweet

bondé (FEM **bondée**) ADJECTIVE
crowded

bondir VERB [38]
to leap

le **bonheur** NOUN
happiness
■ **porter bonheur** to bring luck

le **bonhomme** (PL les **bonshommes**) NOUN
■ **un bonhomme de neige** a snowman

bonjour EXCLAMATION
1 hello!
□ Donne le bonjour à tes parents de ma part. Say hello to your parents for me.
2 good morning!
3 good afternoon!

   LANGUAGE TIP bonjour is used in the morning and afternoon; in the evening bonsoir is used instead.

■ **C'est simple comme bonjour!** It's easy as pie!

bonne FEM ADJECTIVE ▷ see **bon**

le **bonnet** NOUN
hat
□ un bonnet de laine a woolly hat
■ **un bonnet de bain** a bathing cap

bonsoir EXCLAMATION
good evening!

la **bonté** NOUN
kindness

le **bord** NOUN
1 edge
□ le bord de la table the edge of the table

29

2 side
  □ Jane a garé sa voiture au bord de la route.
  Jane parked her car on the side of the road.
  ■ **au bord de la mer** at the seaside
  ■ **au bord de l'eau** by the water
  ■ **monter à bord** to go on board
  ■ **être au bord des larmes** to be on the
  verge of tears
le **bordeaux** NOUN
  ▷ *see also* **bordeaux** ADJECTIVE
  Bordeaux wine
  ■ **du bordeaux rouge** claret
bordeaux (FEM+PL **bordeaux**) ADJECTIVE
  ▷ *see also* **bordeaux** NOUN
  maroon
  □ une jupe bordeaux a maroon skirt
border VERB [28]
1 to line
  □ une route bordée d'arbres a tree-lined
  street
2 to trim
  □ un col bordé de dentelle a collar trimmed
  with lace
3 to tuck up
  □ Sa mère vient la border tous les soirs. Her
  mother comes and tucks her up every night.
la **bordure** NOUN
  border
  ■ **une villa en bordure de mer** a villa right
  by the sea
la **borne** NOUN
  terminal *(of computer)*
la **Bosnie** NOUN
  Bosnia
  ■ **la Bosnie-Herzégovine** Bosnia-
  Herzegovina
la **bosse** NOUN
  bump
  □ Jacques a une grosse bosse au front.
  Jacques has got a big bump on his forehead.
  □ La route est pleine de bosses. The road is
  very bumpy.
bosser VERB [28]
  to work *(informal)*
  ■ **bosser un examen** to study for an exam
le **bossu** NOUN
  hunchback
la **bossue** NOUN
  hunchback
botanique (FEM **botanique**) ADJECTIVE
  ▷ *see also* **botanique** NOUN
  botanic
  □ les jardins botaniques the botanic
  gardens
la **botanique** NOUN
  ▷ *see also* **botanique** ADJECTIVE
  botany

la **botte** NOUN
1 boot
  □ une paire de bottes a pair of boots
  ■ **les bottes de caoutchouc** Wellington
  boots
2 bunch
  □ une botte de radis a bunch of radishes
le **bottin**® NOUN
  phone book
le **bouc** NOUN
1 goatee beard
2 billy goat
  ■ **un bouc émissaire** a scapegoat
la **bouche** NOUN
  mouth
  ■ **le bouche à bouche** the kiss of life
  ■ **une bouche d'égout** a manhole
  ■ **une bouche de métro** an entrance to the
  underground
la **bouchée** NOUN
  mouthful
  ■ **une bouchée à la reine** a chicken
  vol-au-vent
boucher VERB [28]
  ▷ *see also* **boucher** NOUN
1 to fill
  □ boucher un trou to fill a hole
2 to block
  □ L'évier est bouché. The sink is blocked.
  □ J'ai le nez bouché. My nose is blocked.
le **boucher** NOUN
  ▷ *see also* **boucher** VERB
  butcher
  □ Il est boucher. He's a butcher.
la **bouchère** NOUN
  butcher
  □ Elle est bouchère. She's a butcher.
la **boucherie** NOUN
  butcher's
le **bouchon** NOUN
1 top *(of plastic bottle)*
2 cork *(of wine bottle)*
3 hold-up
  □ Il y avait beaucoup de bouchons sur
  l'autoroute. There were a lot of hold-ups on
  the motorway.
la **boucle** NOUN
  curl *(of hair)*
  ■ **une boucle d'oreille** an earring □ une
  paire de boucles d'oreille a pair of earrings
bouclé (FEM **bouclée**) ADJECTIVE
  curly
le **bouclier** NOUN
  shield
le/la **bouddhiste** NOUN
  Buddhist
bouder VERB [28]

to sulk

le **boudin** NOUN
- **le boudin noir** black pudding
- **le boudin blanc** white pudding

la **boue** NOUN
mud

la **bouée** NOUN
buoy
- **une bouée de sauvetage** a life buoy

boueux (FEM **boueuse**) ADJECTIVE
muddy

la **bouffe** NOUN (informal)
food
□ La bouffe est infecte à la cantine. The food in the canteen is revolting.

la **bouffée** NOUN
- **une bouffée d'air frais** a breath of fresh air

bouffer VERB [28] (informal)
to eat

le **bougeoir** NOUN
candlestick

bouger VERB [45]
to move

la **bougie** NOUN
candle

la **bouillabaisse** NOUN
fish soup

bouillant (FEM **bouillante**) ADJECTIVE
1 boiling
□ Faites cuire les pâtes à l'eau bouillante. Cook the pasta in boiling water.
2 piping hot
□ La soupe est bouillante. The soup is piping hot.

bouillir VERB [11]
to boil
□ L'eau bout. The water's boiling.
- **Je bous d'impatience.** I'm bursting with impatience.

la **bouilloire** NOUN
kettle

le **bouillon** NOUN
stock
□ du bouillon de légumes vegetable stock

la **bouillotte** NOUN
hot-water bottle

le **boulanger** NOUN
baker
□ Il est boulanger. He's a baker.

la **boulangère** NOUN
baker
□ Elle est boulangère. She's a baker.

la **boulangerie** NOUN
baker's

la **boule** NOUN
ball

□ une boule de cristal a crystal ball
- **une boule de neige** a snowball
- **jouer aux boules** to play bowls

> **DID YOU KNOW...?**
> **boules** is played on rough ground, not smooth grass. The balls are smaller than those used in bowls, and are made of metal.

le **boulevard** NOUN
boulevard

bouleverser VERB [28]
1 to move deeply
□ Cette histoire déchirante m'a bouleversée. This heartbreaking story moved me deeply.
2 to shatter
□ La mort de son ami l'a bouleversé. He was shattered by the death of his friend.
3 to turn upside down
□ Cette rencontre a bouleversé sa vie. This meeting turned his life upside down.

le **boulot** NOUN (informal)
1 job
□ Anita a trouvé du boulot. Anita has found a job.
2 work
□ J'ai beaucoup de boulot en ce moment. I've got a lot of work to do at the moment.

la **boum** NOUN (informal)
party

le **bouquet** NOUN
bunch of flowers
□ un bouquet de roses a bunch of roses

le **bouquin** NOUN (informal)
book

bouquiner VERB [28] (informal)
to read

bourdonner VERB [28]
to buzz

le **bourg** NOUN
small market town

bourgeois (FEM **bourgeoise**) ADJECTIVE
middle-class
□ un quartier bourgeois a posh area

le **bourgeon** NOUN
bud

la **Bourgogne** NOUN
Burgundy

bourré (FEM **bourrée**) ADJECTIVE
- **bourré de** stuffed with □ un portefeuille bourré de billets a wallet stuffed with banknotes
- **être bourré** (informal) to be plastered □ Il était complètement bourré. He was completely plastered.

le **bourreau** (PL les **bourreaux**) NOUN
executioner
- **C'est un véritable bourreau de travail.** 31

b

He's a real workaholic.

bourrer VERB [28]
to stuff
□ bourrer une valise de vêtements to stuff clothes into a case

la **bourse** NOUN
grant
■ **la Bourse** the Stock Exchange

bous VERB ▷ *see* **bouillir**

la **bousculade** NOUN
crush
□ la bousculade dans les grands magasins au moment des soldes the crush in the big stores at sale time

bousculer VERB [28]
1 to jostle
□ être bousculé par la foule to be jostled by the crowd
2 to rush
□ Je n'aime pas qu'on me bouscule. I don't like to be rushed.

la **boussole** NOUN
compass

bout VERB ▷ *see* **bouillir**

le **bout** NOUN
1 end
□ Elle habite au bout de la rue. She lives at the end of the street. □ Jane est assise en bout de table. Jane is sitting at the end of the table.
2 tip
□ le bout du nez the tip of the nose
3 bit
□ un petit bout de fromage a bit of cheese
■ **un bout de papier** a scrap of paper
■ **au bout de** after □ Au bout d'un moment, il s'est endormi. After a while he fell asleep.
■ **Elle est à bout.** She's at the end of her tether.

la **bouteille** NOUN
bottle
□ une bouteille de vin rouge a bottle of red wine
■ **une bouteille de gaz** a gas cylinder

la **boutique** NOUN
shop

le **bouton** NOUN
1 button
2 spot *(on skin)*
□ J'ai un bouton sur le nez. I've got a spot on my nose.
3 bud
□ un bouton de rose a rosebud
■ **un bouton d'or** a buttercup
◌ **LANGUAGE TIP** Word for word, this means 'a gold bud'.

le **bowling** NOUN
1 tenpin bowling
2 bowling alley

la **boxe** NOUN
boxing

le **boxeur** NOUN
boxer

le **bracelet** NOUN
bracelet

le **bracelet-montre** (PL les **bracelets-montres**) NOUN
wristwatch

le **brancard** NOUN
stretcher

le **brancardier** NOUN
stretcher-bearer

la **branche** NOUN
branch

branché (FEM **branchée**) ADJECTIVE *(informal)*
trendy
□ avoir un look branché to look trendy

brancher VERB [28]
1 to connect
□ Le téléphone est branché? Is the phone connected?
2 to plug in
□ L'aspirateur n'est pas branché. The hoover isn't plugged in.

le **bras** NOUN
arm

la **brasse** NOUN
breaststroke
□ nager la brasse to do the breaststroke

la **brasserie** NOUN
café-restaurant

brave (FEM **brave**) ADJECTIVE
nice
□ C'est un brave type. He's a nice enough fellow.

bravo EXCLAMATION
bravo!

le **break** NOUN
estate car

la **brebis** NOUN
ewe
■ **le fromage de brebis** sheep's cheese

bref (FEM **brève**) ADJECTIVE, ADVERB
short
□ Sa lettre était brève. His letter was short.
■ **en bref** in brief □ l'actualité en bref the news in brief
■ **... bref, ça s'est bien terminé.** ... to cut a long story short, it turned out all right in the end.

le **Brésil** NOUN
Brazil

la **Bretagne** NOUN

Brittany

la **bretelle** NOUN
strap
▫ La bretelle de son soutien-gorge dépasse. Her bra strap is showing.
■ **les bretelles** braces ▫ Il porte des bretelles. He's wearing braces.

breton (FEM **bretonne**) ADJECTIVE, NOUN
Breton
▫ Ils parlent breton. They speak Breton.
■ **un Breton** a Breton *(man)*
■ **une Bretonne** a Breton *(woman)*
■ **les Bretons** the Bretons

brève FEM ADJECTIVE ▷ *see* **bref**

le **brevet** NOUN
certificate

le **brevet des collèges** NOUN

DID YOU KNOW...?
The **brevet des collèges** is an exam you take at the end of **collège**, at the age of 15.

le **bricolage** NOUN
do-it-yourself
▫ Elle aime le bricolage. She likes doing DIY.
▫ un magasin de bricolage a DIY shop

la **bricole** NOUN *(informal)*
■ **J'ai acheté une bricole pour le bébé de Sabine.** I've bought a little something for Sabine's baby.
■ **J'ai encore quelques bricoles à faire avant de partir.** I've still got a few things to do before I go.

bricoler VERB [28]
to do DIY
▫ Pascal aime bricoler. Pascal loves doing DIY.

le **bricoleur** NOUN
DIY enthusiast

la **bricoleuse** NOUN
DIY enthusiast

le **bridge** NOUN
bridge *(game)*
▫ Horst adore jouer au bridge. Horst loves playing bridge.

brièvement ADVERB
briefly
▫ Expliquez-moi brièvement ce qui s'est passé. Tell me briefly what happened.

la **brigade** NOUN
squad *(of police)*
▫ la brigade des stups *(informal)* the drugs squad

brillamment ADVERB
brilliantly
▫ Il a réussi brillamment à son examen. He did brilliantly in the exam.

brillant (FEM **brillante**) ADJECTIVE

1 brilliant
▫ une brillante carrière a brilliant career
▫ Ses notes ne sont pas brillantes. His marks aren't brilliant.
2 shiny
▫ des cheveux brillants shiny hair

briller VERB [28]
to shine

le **brin** NOUN
■ **un brin d'herbe** a blade of grass
■ **un brin de muguet** a sprig of lily of the valley

la **brindille** NOUN
twig

la **brioche** NOUN
brioche bun

la **brique** NOUN
brick

le **briquet** NOUN
cigarette lighter

la **brise** NOUN
breeze

se **briser** VERB [28]
to break
▫ Le vase s'est brisé en mille morceaux. The vase broke into a thousand pieces.

le/la **Britannique** NOUN
Briton
■ **les Britanniques** the British

britannique (FEM **britannique**) ADJECTIVE
British

la **brocante** NOUN
junk
▫ un magasin de brocante a junk shop

le **brocanteur** NOUN
dealer in second-hand goods

la **brocanteuse** NOUN
dealer in second-hand goods

la **broche** NOUN
brooch
▫ une broche en argent a silver brooch
■ **à la broche** spit-roasted ▫ un poulet à la broche a spit-roasted chicken

la **brochette** NOUN
skewer
■ **les brochettes d'agneau** lamb kebabs

la **brochure** NOUN
brochure

broder VERB [28]
to embroider

la **broderie** NOUN
embroidery

la **bronchite** NOUN
bronchitis
▫ avoir une bronchite to have bronchitis

le **bronze** NOUN
bronze

b

bronzer VERB [28]
to get a tan
□ Il est bien bronzé. He's got a good tan.
■ se bronzer to sunbathe

la **brosse** NOUN
brush
■ une brosse à cheveux a hairbrush
■ une brosse à dents a toothbrush
■ Il est coiffé en brosse. He's got a crew cut.

brosser VERB [28]
to brush
■ se brosser les dents to brush one's teeth
□ Je me brosse les dents tous les soirs. I brush my teeth every night.

la **brouette** NOUN
wheelbarrow

le **brouillard** NOUN
fog
■ Il y a du brouillard. It's foggy.

le **brouillon** NOUN
first draft
□ Ce n'est qu'un brouillon. It's just a first draft.

les **broussailles** FEM PL NOUN
undergrowth

brouter VERB [28]
to graze (animals)

broyer VERB [53]
to crush
■ broyer du noir to be down in the dumps

le **brugnon** NOUN
nectarine

le **bruit** NOUN
1 noise
□ J'ai entendu un bruit. I heard a noise.
□ faire du bruit to make a noise
■ sans bruit without a sound
2 rumour
□ Des bruits circulent à son sujet. There are rumours going round about him.

brûlant (FEM **brûlante**) ADJECTIVE
1 blazing
□ un soleil brûlant a blazing sun
2 boiling hot
□ Marie boit son café brûlant. Marie drinks her coffee boiling hot.

le **brûlé** NOUN
smell of burning
□ Ça sent le brûlé. There's a smell of burning.

brûler VERB [28]
to burn
■ se brûler to burn oneself

la **brûlure** NOUN
burn
■ des brûlures d'estomac heartburn

la **brume** NOUN
mist

brumeux (FEM **brumeuse**) ADJECTIVE
misty

brun (FEM **brune**) ADJECTIVE
brown
■ Elle est brune. She's got dark hair.

le **brushing** NOUN
blow-dry
□ une coupe et un brushing a cut and blow-dry

brusque (FEM **brusque**) ADJECTIVE
abrupt
■ d'un ton brusque brusquely

brusquer VERB [28]
to rush
□ Il ne faut pas la brusquer. You mustn't rush her.

brut (FEM **brute**) ADJECTIVE
■ le champagne brut dry champagne
■ le pétrole brut crude oil
■ son salaire brut his gross salary

brutal (FEM **brutale**, MASC PL **brutaux**) ADJECTIVE
brutal

brutaliser VERB [28]
to knock about
□ Il a été brutalisé par la police. He was treated roughly by the police.

Bruxelles NOUN
Brussels

bruyamment ADVERB
noisily

bruyant (FEM **bruyante**) ADJECTIVE
noisy

la **bruyère** NOUN
heather

bu VERB ▷ see **boire**

la **bûche** NOUN
log
■ la bûche de Noël the Yule log

DID YOU KNOW...?
La bûche de Noël is what is usually eaten in France instead of Christmas pudding.

le **bûcheron** NOUN
woodcutter

le **budget** NOUN
budget

le **buffet** NOUN
1 sideboard
□ un buffet en chêne an oak sideboard
2 buffet
□ un buffet froid a cold buffet □ un buffet de gare a station buffet

le **buisson** NOUN
bush

la **Bulgarie** NOUN
Bulgaria

la **bulle** NOUN
bubble

▫ une bulle de savon a soap bubble

le **bulletin** NOUN

1 bulletin

■ **le bulletin d'informations** the news bulletin

2 report

▫ Ton bulletin n'est pas fameux. Your school report isn't very good.

■ **le bulletin météorologique** the weather report

■ **le bulletin de salaire** pay slip

■ **le bulletin de vote** the ballot paper

le **bureau** (PL les **bureaux**) NOUN

1 desk

▫ Posez le dossier sur mon bureau. Put the file on my desk.

2 office

▫ Il vous attend dans son bureau. He's waiting for you in his office.

■ **un bureau de change** a bureau de change

■ **le bureau de poste** the post office

■ **le bureau de tabac** the tobacconist's

■ **le bureau de vote** the polling station

bus VERB ▷ see **boire**

le **bus** NOUN
bus

le **buste** NOUN
bust

but VERB ▷ see **boire**

le **but** NOUN

1 aim

▫ Ils n'ont pas de but dans la vie. They have no aim in life.

■ **Quel est le but de votre visite?** What's the reason for your visit?

■ **dans le but de** with the intention of ▫ Je suis venue dans le but de vous aider. I came with the intention of helping you.

2 goal

▫ marquer un but to score a goal

le **butane** NOUN
Calor gas®

le **butin** NOUN
loot

▫ Les cambrioleurs se sont partagé le butin. The burglars shared the stolen goods.

buvais, buvait VERB ▷ see **boire**

le **buvard** NOUN
blotter

Cc

c' PRONOUN ▷ see **ce**

ça PRONOUN
1 this
□ Est-ce que vous pouvez me donner un peu de ça? Can you give me a bit of this?
2 that
□ Regarde ça là-bas. Look at that over there.
3 it
□ Ça ne fait rien. It doesn't matter.
■ **Comment ça va?** How are you?
■ **Ça alors!** Well, well!
■ **C'est ça.** That's right.
■ **Ça y est!** That's it!

çà ADVERB
■ **çà et là** here and there

la **cabane** NOUN
hut

le **cabillaud** NOUN
cod

la **cabine** NOUN
cabin (on a ship)
■ **une cabine d'essayage** a fitting room
■ **une cabine téléphonique** a phone box

le **cabinet** NOUN
surgery (of doctor, of dentist)
■ **une chambre avec cabinet de toilette** a room with washing facilities

les **cabinets** MASC PL NOUN
toilet

le **câble** NOUN
cable
■ **la télévision par câble** cable television

cabosser VERB [28]
to dent

la **cacahuète** NOUN
peanut
■ **le beurre de cacahuète** peanut butter

le **cacao** NOUN
cocoa
■ **le beurre de cacao** cocoa butter

cache-cache MASC NOUN
■ **jouer à cache-cache** to play hide-and-seek

le **cachemire** NOUN
cashmere

le **cache-nez** (PL les **cache-nez**) NOUN
long woollen scarf

cacher VERB [28]
to hide
□ J'ai caché les cadeaux sous le lit. I hid the presents under the bed. □ Tu me caches quelque chose! You're hiding something from me!
■ **se cacher** to hide □ Elle s'est cachée sous la table. She's hiding under the table.

le **cachet** NOUN
1 tablet
■ **un cachet d'aspirine** an aspirin
2 fee (for performer)
□ Il a touché un gros cachet pour ce concert. He got a big fee for the concert.
■ **le cachet de la poste** the postmark

la **cachette** NOUN
hiding place
■ **en cachette** on the sly □ Il est sorti en cachette sans réveiller ses parents. He crept out on the sly without waking his parents.

le **cachot** NOUN
dungeon

le **cactus** NOUN
cactus

le **cadavre** NOUN
corpse

le **Caddie**® NOUN
supermarket trolley

le **cadeau** (PL les **cadeaux**) NOUN
present
□ un cadeau d'anniversaire a birthday present □ un cadeau de Noël a Christmas present
■ **faire un cadeau à quelqu'un** to give somebody a present

le **cadenas** NOUN
padlock

cadet (FEM **cadette**) ADJECTIVE
▷ see also **cadet** NOUN, **cadette** NOUN
1 younger (brother, sister)
□ ma sœur cadette my younger sister
2 youngest (son, daughter)
□ son fils cadet his youngest son

le **cadet** NOUN
> ▷ see also **cadet** ADJECTIVE
youngest
□ C'est le cadet de la famille. He's the youngest of the family.

la **cadette** NOUN
> ▷ see also **cadette** ADJECTIVE
youngest
□ C'est la cadette de la famille. She's the youngest of the family.

le **cadre** NOUN
1 frame
□ un cadre en bois a wooden frame
2 surroundings
□ L'hôtel est situé dans un très beau cadre. The hotel is set in beautiful surroundings.
3 executive
□ un cadre supérieur a senior executive

le **cafard** NOUN
cockroach
■ avoir le cafard (informal) to be feeling down □ J'ai le cafard. I'm feeling down.

le **café** NOUN
1 coffee
□ un café au lait a white coffee □ un café crème a strong white coffee
2 café

> **DID YOU KNOW...?**
> Cafés in France sell both alcoholic and non-alcoholic drinks.

le **café-tabac** (PL les **cafés-tabacs**) NOUN

> **DID YOU KNOW...?**
> A **café-tabac** is a bar which also sells cigarettes and stamps; you can tell a **café-tabac** by the red diamond-shaped sign outside it.

la **cafétéria** NOUN
cafeteria

la **cafetière** NOUN
1 coffee maker
2 coffeepot

la **cage** NOUN
cage
■ la cage d'escalier the stairwell

la **cagoule** NOUN
balaclava

le **cahier** NOUN
exercise book
□ mon cahier de brouillon my rough book

la **caille** NOUN
quail

le **caillou** (PL les **cailloux**) NOUN
pebble

la **caisse** NOUN
1 box
□ une caisse à outils a tool box
2 till

□ le ticket de caisse the till receipt
3 checkout
□ J'ai dû faire la queue à la caisse. I had to queue at the checkout.

le **caissier** NOUN
cashier

la **caissière** NOUN
cashier

le **cake** NOUN
fruit cake

le **calcul** NOUN
1 calculation
□ Je me suis trompé dans mes calculs. I made a mistake in my calculations.
2 arithmetic
□ Je ne suis pas très bon en calcul. I'm not very good at arithmetic.

la **calculatrice** NOUN
calculator

calculer VERB [28]
to work out
□ J'ai calculé combien ça allait coûter. I worked out how much it was going to cost.

la **calculette** NOUN
pocket calculator

la **cale** NOUN
wedge

calé (FEM **calée**) ADJECTIVE (informal)
■ Elle est calée en histoire. She's really good at history.

le **caleçon** NOUN
1 boxer shorts
2 leggings

le **calendrier** NOUN
calendar

le **calepin** NOUN
notebook

caler VERB [28]
to stall
□ La voiture a calé dans une côte. The car stalled on a hill.

câlin (FEM **câline**) ADJECTIVE
> ▷ see also **câlin** NOUN
cuddly

le **câlin** NOUN
> ▷ see also **câlin** ADJECTIVE
cuddle
□ faire un câlin à quelqu'un to give somebody a cuddle

le **calmant** NOUN
tranquillizer

calme (FEM **calme**) ADJECTIVE
> ▷ see also **calme** NOUN
1 quiet
□ un endroit calme a quiet place
2 calm
□ Elle est restée très calme. She stayed very

calm.
le **calme** NOUN
 ▷ *see also* **calme** ADJECTIVE
 peace and quiet
 □ J'ai besoin de calme pour travailler. I need peace and quiet to work.
calmer VERB [28]
 to soothe
 □ Cette pommade calme les démangeaisons. This ointment soothes itching.
 ■ **se calmer** to calm down □ Calme-toi! Calm down!
la **calorie** NOUN
 calorie
le/la **camarade** NOUN
 friend
 ■ **un camarade de classe** a school friend
le **cambriolage** NOUN
 burglary
cambrioler VERB [28]
 to burgle
le **cambrioleur** NOUN
 burglar
la **cambrioleuse** NOUN
 burglar
la **camelote** NOUN (*informal*)
 junk
 □ C'est vraiment de la camelote. It's absolute junk.
la **caméra** NOUN
 camera (*cinema, TV*)
 ■ **une caméra numérique** a digital camera
le **caméscope**® NOUN
 camcorder
le **camion** NOUN
 lorry
la **camionnette** NOUN
 van
le **camionneur** NOUN
 lorry driver
la **camomille** NOUN
 camomile tea
le **camp** NOUN
 camp
 □ un camp de prisonniers a prison camp
 □ un camp de vacances a holiday camp
la **campagne** NOUN
 1 country
 ■ **à la campagne** in the country □ Nous passons nos vacances à la campagne. We spend our holidays in the country.
 2 campaign
 □ une campagne de marketing a marketing campaign
camper VERB [28]
 to camp

le **campeur** NOUN
 camper
la **campeuse** NOUN
 camper
le **camping** NOUN
 camping
 □ faire du camping to go camping
 ■ **un terrain de camping** a campsite
le **Canada** NOUN
 Canada
 ■ **au Canada 1** in Canada **2** to Canada
canadien (FEM **canadienne**) ADJECTIVE, NOUN
 Canadian
 ■ **un Canadien** a Canadian (*man*)
 ■ **une Canadienne** a Canadian (*woman*)
le **canal** (PL les **canaux**) NOUN
 canal
le **canapé** NOUN
 1 sofa
 2 open sandwich
le **canard** NOUN
 duck
le **canari** NOUN
 canary
le **cancer** NOUN
 cancer
 □ le cancer du poumon lung cancer
 ■ **le Cancer** Cancer □ Sabine est Cancer. Sabine's Cancer.
le **candidat** NOUN
 1 candidate (*in exam, election*)
 2 applicant (*for job*)
la **candidate** NOUN
 1 candidate (*in exam, election*)
 2 applicant (*for job*)
la **candidature** NOUN
 ■ **poser sa candidature à un poste** to apply for a job □ Il a posé sa candidature à des dizaines de postes. He has applied for dozens of jobs.
le **caneton** NOUN
 duckling
la **canette** NOUN
 ■ **une canette de bière** a small bottle of beer
le **caniche** NOUN
 poodle
la **canicule** NOUN
 scorching heat
le **canif** NOUN
 penknife
le **caniveau** (PL les **caniveaux**) NOUN
 gutter
la **canne** NOUN
 walking stick
 ■ **une canne à pêche** a fishing rod
la **cannelle** NOUN

cinnamon

le **canoë** NOUN
1 canoe
2 canoeing
□ faire du canoë to go canoeing

le **canon** NOUN
1 gun
2 cannon

le **canot** NOUN
dinghy
□ un canot pneumatique a rubber dinghy
■ un canot de sauvetage a lifeboat

la **cantatrice** NOUN
opera singer

la **cantine** NOUN
canteen

le **caoutchouc** NOUN
rubber
■ des bottes en caoutchouc Wellington boots

le **cap** NOUN
cape

capable (FEM **capable**) ADJECTIVE
■ Elle est capable de marcher pendant des heures. She can walk for hours.
■ Il est capable de changer d'avis au dernier moment. He's capable of changing his mind at the last minute.

la **cape** NOUN
cape

le **capitaine** NOUN
captain

la **capitale** NOUN
capital
□ la capitale de la France the capital of France

le **capot** NOUN
bonnet (of car)

la **capote** NOUN (informal)
condom

la **câpre** NOUN
caper (food)

le **caprice** NOUN
■ faire des caprices to make a fuss □ Il n'aime pas les enfants qui font des caprices. He doesn't like children who make a fuss.

capricieux (FEM **capricieuse**) ADJECTIVE
■ un enfant capricieux an awkward child

le **Capricorne** NOUN
Capricorn
□ Helen est Capricorne. Helen's Capricorn.

captivant (FEM **captivante**) ADJECTIVE
fascinating

la **captivité** NOUN
captivity
□ en captivité in captivity

capturer VERB [28]

to capture

la **capuche** NOUN
hood
□ un manteau à capuche a coat with a hood

le **capuchon** NOUN
cap (of pen)

la **capucine** NOUN
nasturtium

le **car** NOUN
▷ see also **car** CONJUNCTION
coach
□ un car scolaire a school bus

car CONJUNCTION
▷ see also **car** NOUN
because
□ Réfléchis bien car c'est important. Think carefully because it's important.

la **carabine** NOUN
rifle

le **caractère** NOUN
personality
□ Il a le même caractère que son père. He's got the same personality as his father.
■ Il a bon caractère. He's good-natured.
■ Elle a mauvais caractère. She's bad-tempered.
■ Il n'a pas un caractère facile. He isn't easy to get on with.

caractéristique (FEM **caractéristique**) ADJECTIVE
▷ see also **caractéristique** NOUN
characteristic

la **caractéristique** NOUN
▷ see also **caractéristique** ADJECTIVE
characteristic

la **carafe** NOUN
jug
□ une carafe d'eau a jug of water

les **Caraïbes** FEM PL NOUN
Caribbean Islands

le **caramel** NOUN
1 caramel
□ la crème caramel crème caramel
2 toffee

la **caravane** NOUN
caravan

carbonique (FEM **carbonique**) ADJECTIVE
■ le gaz carbonique carbon dioxide

le **carburant** NOUN
fuel

cardiaque (FEM **cardiaque**) ADJECTIVE
■ une crise cardiaque a heart attack
■ Ma tante est cardiaque. My aunt has heart trouble.

le **cardigan** NOUN
cardigan

le/la **cardiologue** NOUN

heart specialist

le **carême** NOUN
Lent

la **caresse** NOUN
stroke

□ faire des caresses à un chat to stroke a cat

caresser VERB [28]
to stroke

la **carie** NOUN
tooth decay

■ J'ai une carie. I've got a hole in my tooth.

caritatif (FEM **caritative**) ADJECTIVE

■ une organisation caritative a charity

le **carnaval** NOUN
carnival

le **carnet** NOUN
1 notebook
2 book

□ un carnet d'adresses an address book
□ un carnet de chèques a cheque book
□ un carnet de timbres a book of stamps
□ un carnet de tickets a book of tickets

> DID YOU KNOW...?
In the Paris metro it is cheaper to buy tickets in a book of ten, known as a **carnet**.

■ mon carnet de notes my school report

la **carotte** NOUN
carrot

□ les carottes râpées grated carrots

carré (FEM **carrée**) ADJECTIVE
▷ see also **carré** NOUN
square

■ un mètre carré a square metre

le **carré** NOUN
▷ see also **carré** ADJECTIVE
square

le **carreau** (PL les **carreaux**) NOUN
1 check

□ une chemise à carreaux a checked shirt
2 tile (on floor, wall)

□ des carreaux de terre cuite terracotta tiles
3 pane

□ Il a cassé un carreau. He broke a windowpane.
4 diamonds (cards)

□ l'as de carreau the ace of diamonds

le **carrefour** NOUN
junction

le **carrelage** NOUN
tiled floor

carrément ADVERB
1 completely

□ C'est carrément impossible. It's completely impossible.
2 straight out

□ Dis-lui carrément ce que tu penses. Tell

him straight out what you think.

la **carrière** NOUN
career

■ un militaire de carrière a professional soldier

la **carrure** NOUN
build

□ Il a une carrure d'athlète. He has an athletic build.

le **cartable** NOUN
satchel

la **carte** NOUN
1 card

■ une carte d'anniversaire a birthday card
■ une carte postale a postcard
■ une carte de vœux a Christmas card

> DID YOU KNOW...?
The French send greetings cards (**les cartes de vœux**) in January rather than at Christmas, with best wishes for the New Year.

■ une carte bancaire a cash card
■ une carte bleue

> DID YOU KNOW...?
Carte bleue is a major French debit card.

■ une carte de crédit a credit card
■ une carte de fidélité a loyalty card
■ une carte d'embarquement a boarding card
■ une carte d'identité an identity card
■ une carte de séjour a residence permit
■ une carte téléphonique a phonecard
■ un jeu de cartes 1 a pack of cards 2 a card game

2 map

□ une carte de France a map of France
□ une carte routière a road map

3 menu

□ la carte des vins the wine list
■ manger à la carte to eat à la carte
□ Nous allons manger à la carte. We'll choose from the à la carte menu.

le **carton** NOUN
1 cardboard

□ un morceau de carton a piece of cardboard
2 cardboard box

■ un carton à chaussures a shoe box

la **cartouche** NOUN
cartridge

■ une cartouche de cigarettes a carton of cigarettes

le **cas** (PL les **cas**) NOUN
case

□ plusieurs cas several cases
■ ne faire aucun cas de to take no notice

of
- **en aucun cas** on no account
- **en tout cas** at any rate
- **au cas où** in case □ Prends un sandwich au cas où la cantine serait fermée. Take a sandwich in case the canteen's closed.
- **en cas de** in case of □ En cas d'incendie, appelez ce numéro. In case of fire, call this number.

la **cascade** NOUN
waterfall

le **cascadeur** NOUN
stuntman

la **case** NOUN
1 square (in board game)
2 box (on form)

la **caserne** NOUN
barracks

cash ADVERB
- **payer cash** to pay cash

le **casier** NOUN
locker

le **casque** NOUN
1 helmet
2 headphones

la **casquette** NOUN
cap

cassant (FEM **cassante**) ADJECTIVE
- **Il m'a parlé d'un ton cassant.** He spoke to me curtly.

le **casse-croûte** (PL les **casse-croûte**) NOUN
snack

le **casse-noix** (PL les **casse-noix**) NOUN
nutcrackers

casse-pieds (FEM+PL **casse-pieds**) ADJECTIVE (informal)
- **Il est vraiment casse-pieds!** He's a real pain in the neck!

casser VERB [28]
to break
□ J'ai cassé un verre. I've broken a glass.
- **se casser** to break □ Il s'est cassé la jambe au ski. He broke his leg when he was skiing.
- **se casser la tête** (informal) to go to a lot of trouble □ Ne te casse pas la tête pour le dîner. Don't go to a whole lot of trouble over dinner.

la **casserole** NOUN
saucepan

le **casse-tête** (PL les **casse-tête**) NOUN
- **C'est un vrai casse-tête!** It's a real headache!

la **cassette** NOUN
cassette

le **cassis** NOUN
blackcurrant

le **castor** NOUN
beaver

le **catalogue** NOUN
catalogue

la **catastrophe** NOUN
disaster

le **catch** NOUN
wrestling

le **catéchisme** NOUN
catechism

la **catégorie** NOUN
category

catégorique (FEM **catégorique**) ADJECTIVE
firm
□ un refus catégorique a flat refusal

la **cathédrale** NOUN
cathedral

catholique (FEM **catholique**) ADJECTIVE
▷ see also **catholique** NOUN
Catholic

le/la **catholique** NOUN
▷ see also **catholique** ADJECTIVE
Catholic

le **cauchemar** NOUN
nightmare
□ faire un cauchemar to have a nightmare

la **cause** NOUN
cause
- **à cause de** because of □ Je suis puni à cause de toi. I've been punished because of you.

causer VERB [28]
1 to cause
□ La tempête a causé beaucoup de dégâts. The storm caused a lot of damage.
2 to chat
□ Nous n'avons pas beaucoup eu le temps de causer. We didn't have much time to chat.

la **caution** NOUN
1 bail
2 deposit

le **cavalier** NOUN
1 rider
2 partner (at dance)

la **cavalière** NOUN
rider

la **cave** NOUN
cellar

la **caverne** NOUN
cave

le **CD** (PL les **CD**) NOUN
CD

le **CD-ROM** (PL les **CD-ROM**) NOUN
CD-ROM

ce (MASC SING ALSO **cet**, FEM **cette**, PL **ces**)

ADJECTIVE

▷ *see also* **ce** PRONOUN

> **LANGUAGE TIP** ce changes to **cet** before a vowel and most words beginning with 'h'.

1 this
□ Tu peux prendre ce livre. You can take this book. □ cet après-midi this afternoon □ cet hiver this winter
■ **ce livre-ci** this book
■ **cette voiture-ci** this car
2 that
□ Je n'aime pas du tout ce film. I don't like that film at all.
■ **ce livre-là** that book
■ **cette voiture-là** that car

ce PRONOUN

▷ *see also* **ce** ADJECTIVE

> **LANGUAGE TIP** ce changes to **c'** before the vowel in **est**, **était** and **étaient**.

it
□ Ce n'est pas facile. It's not easy.
■ **c'est 1** it is □ C'est vraiment trop cher. It's really too expensive. □ Ouvre, c'est moi! Open the door, it's me! **2** he is □ C'est un peintre du début du siècle. He's a painter from the turn of the century. **3** she is □ C'est une actrice très célèbre. She's a very famous actress.
■ **ce sont** they are □ Ce sont des amis à mes parents. They're friends of my parents'.
■ **Qui est-ce?** Who is it?
■ **Qu'est-ce que c'est?** What is it?
■ **ce qui** what □ C'est ce qui compte. That's what matters.
■ **tout ce qui** everything that □ J'ai rangé tout ce qui traînait par terre. I've tidied up everything that was on the floor.
■ **ce que** what □ Je vais lui dire ce que je pense. I'm going to tell him what I think.
■ **tout ce que** everything □ Tu peux avoir tout ce que tu veux. You can have everything you want.

ceci PRONOUN
this
□ Prends ceci, tu en auras besoin. Take this, you'll need it.

céder VERB [34]
to give in
□ Elle a tellement insisté qu'il a fini par céder. She went on so much that he eventually gave in.
■ **céder à** to give in to □ Je ne veux pas céder à ses caprices. I'm not going to give in to her whims.

le **cédérom** NOUN
CD-ROM

la **cédille** NOUN
cedilla

la **ceinture** NOUN
belt
□ une ceinture en cuir a leather belt
■ **une ceinture de sauvetage** a lifebelt
■ **votre ceinture de sécurité** your seatbelt

cela PRONOUN
1 it
□ Cela dépend. It depends.
2 that
□ Je n'aime pas cela. I don't like that.
■ **C'est cela.** That's right.
■ **à part cela** apart from that

célèbre (FEM **célèbre**) ADJECTIVE
famous

célébrer VERB [34]
to celebrate

le **céleri** NOUN
■ **le céleri-rave** celeriac
■ **le céleri en branche** celery

célibataire (FEM **célibataire**) ADJECTIVE, NOUN
single
■ **un célibataire** a bachelor
■ **une célibataire** a single woman

celle PRONOUN ▷ *see* **celui**
celles PRONOUN ▷ *see* **ceux**
la **cellule** NOUN
cell

celui (FEM **celle**, MASC PL **ceux**, FEM PL **celles**) PRONOUN
the one
□ Prends celui que tu préfères. Take the one you like best. □ Je n'ai pas d'appareil photo mais je peux emprunter celui de ma sœur. I haven't got a camera but I can borrow my sister's. □ Je n'ai pas de platine laser mais je peux emprunter celle de mon frère. I haven't got a CD player but I can borrow my brother's.
■ **celui-ci** this one
■ **celle-ci** this one
■ **celui-là** that one
■ **celle-là** that one

la **cendre** NOUN
ash

le **cendrier** NOUN
ashtray

censé (FEM **censée**) ADJECTIVE
■ **être censé faire quelque chose** to be supposed to do something □ Vous êtes censé arriver à l'heure. You're supposed to get here on time.

cent NUMBER
a hundred
□ cent euros a hundred euros

> **LANGUAGE TIP** cent is spelt with an -s when there are two or more hundreds, but not when it is followed by another number, as in 'a hundred and two'.

□ trois cents ans three hundred years □ cent deux kilomètres a hundred and two kilometres □ trois cent cinquante kilomètres three hundred and fifty kilometres □ trois cent mille kilomètres three hundred thousand kilometres

le **cent** NOUN
cent *(currency)*

la **centaine** NOUN
about a hundred

□ Il y avait une centaine de personnes. There were about a hundred people.
■ des centaines de hundreds of □ Des centaines de réfugiés se sont présentés à l'ambassade. Hundreds of refugees came to the embassy.

le **centenaire** NOUN
centenary

centième (FEM **centième**) ADJECTIVE
hundredth

le **centilitre** NOUN
centilitre

le **centime** NOUN
1 cent *(one hundredth of a euro)*
□ un centime d'euro a euro cent

> **DID YOU KNOW...?**
> The euro is divided into 100 centimes.

2 centime *(one hundredth of a franc)*
□ une pièce de cinquante centimes a 50-centime coin

le **centimètre** NOUN
centimetre

central (FEM **centrale**, MASC PL **centraux**) ADJECTIVE
central

la **centrale** NOUN
power station
□ une centrale nucléaire a nuclear power station

le **centre** NOUN
centre
■ un centre commercial a shopping centre
■ un centre d'appels a call centre

le **centre-ville** (PL les **centres-villes**) NOUN
town centre

cependant ADVERB
however

le **cercle** NOUN
circle
□ Entourez d'un cercle la bonne réponse.

Put a circle round the right answer.
■ un cercle vicieux a vicious circle

le **cercueil** NOUN
coffin

la **céréale** NOUN
cereal
□ un bol de céréales a bowl of cereal
■ un pain aux cinq céréales a multigrain loaf

la **cérémonie** NOUN
ceremony

le **cerf** NOUN
stag

le **cerf-volant** (PL les **cerfs-volants**) NOUN
kite

> **LANGUAGE TIP** Word for word, cerf-volant means 'flying stag'.

la **cerise** NOUN
cherry

le **cerisier** NOUN
cherry tree

cerné (FEM **cernée**) ADJECTIVE
■ avoir les yeux cernés to have shadows under one's eyes □ Elle avait les yeux cernés. She had shadows under her eyes.

cerner VERB [28]
■ J'ai du mal à le cerner. I can't figure him out.

certain (FEM **certaine**) ADJECTIVE
1 certain
□ Je suis certain que je l'ai remis en place. I'm certain that I put it back. □ Ce n'est pas certain. It's not certain.
2 some
□ Certaines personnes n'aiment pas la crème. Some people don't like cream.
■ un certain temps quite some time □ Ça m'a pris un certain temps. It took me quite some time.

certainement ADVERB
1 definitely
□ C'est certainement le meilleur film que j'ai vu cette année. It's definitely the best film I've seen this year.
2 of course
□ Est-ce que je peux t'emprunter ton stylo? — Mais certainement! Can I borrow your pen? — Of course!

certains (FEM **certaines**) PL PRONOUN
1 some
□ certains d'entre vous some of you
□ certaines de ses amies some of his friends
2 some people
□ Certains pensent que le film est meilleur que le roman. Some people think that the film is better than the novel.

certes ADVERB

43

certainly

□ Nous nous connaissons, certes, mais nous ne sommes pas amis. We know each other, certainly, but we are not friends.

le **certificat** NOUN
certificate

le **cerveau** (PL les **cerveaux**) NOUN
brain

la **cervelle** NOUN
brain

■ **se creuser la cervelle** (informal) to rack one's brains

le **CES** NOUN (= Collège d'enseignement secondaire)
secondary school

DID YOU KNOW...?
In France pupils go to a **CES** between the ages of 11 and 15, and then to a **lycée** until the age of 18.

ces PL ADJECTIVE

1 these

□ Tu peux prendre ces photos si tu veux. You can have these photos if you like.

■ **ces photos-ci** these photos

2 those

□ Ces montagnes sont dangereuses en hiver. Those mountains are dangerous in winter.

■ **ces livres-là** those books

cesse

■ **sans cesse** ADVERB continually □ Elle me dérange sans cesse. She continually interrupts me.

cesser VERB [28]
to stop

□ cesser de faire quelque chose to stop doing something

le **cessez-le-feu** (PL les **cessez-le-feu**) NOUN
ceasefire

c'est-à-dire ADVERB
that is

□ Nous partons lundi prochain, c'est-à-dire le quinze. We're leaving next Monday, that's the 15th.

cet ADJECTIVE ▷ see **ce**

cette ADJECTIVE ▷ see **ce**

ceux (FEM PL **celles**) PL PRONOUN
the ones

□ Prends ceux que tu préfères. Take the ones you like best. □ Je n'ai pas de skis mais je peux emprunter ceux de ma sœur. I haven't got any skis but I can borrow my sister's. □ Je n'ai pas de jumelles mais je peux emprunter celles de mon frère. I haven't got any binoculars but I can borrow my brother's.

■ **ceux-ci** these ones
■ **celles-ci** these ones
■ **ceux-là** those ones
■ **celles-là** those ones

chacun (FEM **chacune**) PRONOUN

1 each

□ Il nous a donné un cadeau à chacun. He gave us each a present. □ Nous avons chacune donné dix euros. We each gave 10 euros.

2 everyone

□ Chacun fait ce qu'il veut. Everyone does what they like.

le **chagrin** NOUN

■ **avoir du chagrin** to be very upset □ Elle a eu beaucoup de chagrin à la mort de sa tante. She was terribly upset by the death of her aunt.

le **chahut** NOUN
bedlam

□ Il y avait du chahut dans la classe. There was bedlam in the classroom.

la **chaîne** NOUN

1 chain

□ une chaîne en or a gold chain

2 channel (on TV)

□ Le film passe sur quelle chaîne? Which channel is the film on?

■ **une chaîne hi-fi** a hi-fi system
■ **une chaîne laser** a CD player
■ **une chaîne stéréo** a music centre
■ **travailler à la chaîne** to work on an assembly line

la **chair** NOUN
flesh

■ **en chair et en os** in the flesh □ J'ai vu Kate Winslet en chair et en os. I saw Kate Winslet in the flesh.

■ **avoir la chair de poule** to have goose pimples

la **chaise** NOUN
chair

■ **une chaise longue** a deckchair

le **châle** NOUN
shawl

la **chaleur** NOUN

1 heat

2 warmth

chaleureux (FEM **chaleureuse**) ADJECTIVE
warm

□ un accueil chaleureux a warm welcome

se **chamailler** VERB [28] (informal)
to squabble

□ Elle se chamaille sans cesse avec son frère. She's always squabbling with her brother.

la **chambre** NOUN

room

□ C'est la chambre de Camille. This is Camille's room.

■ **une chambre à coucher** a bedroom

◯ **LANGUAGE TIP** Word for word, this means 'a room for sleeping'.

■ **une chambre d'amis** a spare room

◯ **LANGUAGE TIP** Word for word, this means 'a friends' room'.

■ **une chambre à un lit** a single room

■ **une chambre pour une personne** a single room

■ **une chambre pour deux personnes** a double room

■ **'Chambres d'hôte'** 'Bed and Breakfast'

le **chameau** (PL les **chameaux**) NOUN
camel

le **champ** NOUN
field

le **champagne** NOUN
champagne

le **champignon** NOUN
mushroom

□ une omelette aux champignons a mushroom omelette

■ **un champignon de Paris** a button mushroom

le **champion** NOUN
champion

le **championnat** NOUN
championship

□ le championnat du monde the world championship

la **championne** NOUN
champion

la **chance** NOUN
1 luck

■ **Bonne chance!** Good luck!

■ **par chance** luckily

■ **avoir de la chance** to be lucky □ Tu as de la chance de partir au soleil! You're lucky, going off to the sun!

2 chance

□ Il n'a aucune chance. He's got no chance. □ Il a des chances de réussir. He's got a good chance of passing.

le **change** NOUN
exchange

□ le taux de change the exchange rate

le **changement** NOUN
change

□ Il n'aime pas le changement. He doesn't like change.

changer VERB [45]
to change

□ Il n'a pas beaucoup changé. He hasn't changed much. □ J'ai changé les draps ce

matin. I changed the sheets this morning. □ J'ai changé trois cents euros. I changed 300 euros.

■ **se changer** to get changed □ Je vais me changer avant de sortir. I'm going to get changed before I go out.

■ **changer de** to change □ Je change de chaussures et j'arrive! I'll change my shoes and then I'll be ready!

■ **changer d'avis** to change one's mind

□ Appelle-moi si tu changes d'avis. Give me a ring if you change your mind.

■ **changer de chaîne** to change the channel

la **chanson** NOUN
song

le **chant** NOUN
singing

□ des cours de chant singing lessons

■ **un chant de Noël** a Christmas carol

le **chantage** NOUN
blackmail

□ faire du chantage à quelqu'un to blackmail somebody

chanter VERB [28]
to sing

le **chanteur** NOUN
singer

la **chanteuse** NOUN
singer

le **chantier** NOUN
building site

la **Chantilly** NOUN
whipped cream

chantonner VERB [28]
to hum

le **chapeau** (PL les **chapeaux**) NOUN
hat

la **chapelle** NOUN
chapel

le **chapitre** NOUN
chapter

chaque (FEM **chaque**) ADJECTIVE
1 every

□ chaque année every year

2 each

□ Ces verres coûtent cinq euros chaque. These glasses cost 5 euros each.

le **char** NOUN
tank (military)

le **charabia** NOUN (informal)
gibberish

□ Je n'y comprends rien: c'est du charabia. I don't understand any of it: it's gibberish.

la **charade** NOUN
1 riddle

2 charade

□ jouer aux charades to play charades

le **charbon** NOUN
coal

■ **le charbon de bois** charcoal

la **charcuterie** NOUN
1 pork butcher's

> **DID YOU KNOW...?**
> A **charcuterie** sells cuts of pork and
> pork products such as sausages,
> salami and pâté, as well as various
> cooked dishes and salads.

2 cold meats

le **charcutier** NOUN
pork butcher

la **charcutière** NOUN
pork butcher

le **chardon** NOUN
thistle

charger VERB [45]
to load

■ **charger quelqu'un de faire quelque
chose** to tell somebody to do something
□ Paul m'a chargé de vous dire que la clé est
sous le paillasson. Paul told me to tell you
that the key's under the mat.

le **chariot** NOUN
trolley (at supermarket)

charmant (FEM **charmante**) ADJECTIVE
charming

le **charme** NOUN
charm

charmer VERB [28]
to charm

la **charrue** NOUN
plough

la **chasse** NOUN
1 hunting
□ un chien de chasse a hunting dog
2 shooting
□ la chasse au canard duck shooting
■ **tirer la chasse d'eau** to flush the toilet

le **chasse-neige** (PL les **chasse-neige**)
NOUN
snowplough

chasser VERB [28]
1 to hunt
□ Mon père chasse le lapin. My father hunts
rabbits.
2 to chase away
□ Ils ont chassé les cambrioleurs. They
chased away the robbers.
3 to get rid of
□ Ouvre donc la fenêtre pour chasser les
odeurs de cuisine. Open the window to get
rid of the cooking smells.

le **chasseur** NOUN
hunter

le **chat** NOUN
1 cat

■ **appeler un chat un chat** to call a spade a
spade

> **LANGUAGE TIP** Word for word, this
> means 'to call a cat a cat'.

2 chat

> **LANGUAGE TIP** This word has two
> pronunciations. **chat** meaning **cat** is
> pronounced 'shah', and the internet
> one is pronounced the same as the
> word 'chat' in English.

la **châtaigne** NOUN
chestnut

le **châtaignier** NOUN
chestnut tree

châtain (FEM+PL **châtain**) ADJECTIVE
brown
□ J'ai les cheveux châtain. I've got brown
hair.

le **château** (PL les **châteaux**) NOUN
1 castle
■ **un château fort** a castle
2 palace
□ le château de Versailles the palace of
Versailles

le **chaton** NOUN
kitten

chatouiller VERB [28]
to tickle

chatouilleux (FEM **chatouilleuse**) ADJECTIVE
ticklish

la **chatte** NOUN
cat (female)

chatter VERB [28]
to chat (on the internet)

chaud (FEM **chaude**) ADJECTIVE
1 warm
□ des vêtements chauds warm clothes
■ **avoir chaud** to be warm □ J'ai assez
chaud. I'm warm enough.
2 hot
□ Il fait chaud aujourd'hui. It's hot today.
□ un plat chaud a hot dish □ Attention,
c'est chaud! Mind, it's hot! □ J'ai trop
chaud! I'm too hot!

le **chauffage** NOUN
heating
□ Le chauffage est en panne. The heating
isn't working.
■ **le chauffage central** central heating

le **chauffe-eau** (PL les **chauffe-eau**) NOUN
water heater

chauffer VERB [28]
to heat
□ Je vais mettre de l'eau à chauffer pour
faire du thé. I'm going to heat some water

to make tea.

le **chauffeur** NOUN
driver

☐ un chauffeur de taxi a taxi driver

le **chaume** NOUN

■ un toit de chaume a thatched roof

la **chaussée** NOUN
road surface

☐ 'Attention! Chaussée déformée' 'Uneven road surface'

chausser VERB [28]

■ Vous chaussez du combien? What size shoe do you take?

la **chaussette** NOUN
sock

le **chausson** NOUN
slipper

■ un chausson aux pommes an apple turnover

la **chaussure** NOUN
shoe

■ les chaussures de ski ski boots

chauve (FEM **chauve**) ADJECTIVE
bald

la **chauve-souris** (PL les **chauves-souris**) NOUN
bat (animal)

LANGUAGE TIP Word for word, this means 'bald mouse'.

le **chef** NOUN
1 head

☐ le chef de famille the head of the family

■ le chef de l'État the Head of State

2 boss

☐ Je dois demander la permission à mon chef. I have to get permission from my boss.

■ un chef d'entreprise a company director

3 chef

☐ la spécialité du chef the chef's speciality

■ un chef d'orchestre a conductor

le **chef-d'œuvre** (PL les **chefs-d'œuvre**) NOUN
masterpiece

le **chemin** NOUN
1 path

☐ un chemin de montagne a mountain path

2 way

☐ Quel est le chemin le plus court pour aller à l'aéroport? What's the quickest way to the airport?

■ en chemin on the way ☐ Je mangerai mon sandwich en chemin. I'll eat my sandwich on the way.

■ le chemin de fer the railway

la **cheminée** NOUN
1 chimney
2 fireplace

la **chemise** NOUN
1 shirt

☐ une chemise à carreaux a checked shirt

■ une chemise de nuit a nightdress

2 folder

☐ une chemise en plastique a plastic folder

le **chemisier** NOUN
blouse

le **chêne** NOUN
oak

☐ une armoire en chêne an oak wardrobe

le **chenil** NOUN
kennels

la **chenille** NOUN
caterpillar

le **chèque** NOUN
cheque

■ les chèques de voyage traveller's cheques

le **chéquier** NOUN
cheque book

cher (FEM **chère**) ADJECTIVE, ADVERB
1 dear

☐ Chère Mélusine ... Dear Mélusine ...

2 expensive

☐ C'est trop cher. It's too expensive.

☐ coûter cher to be expensive

chercher VERB [28]
1 to look for

☐ Je cherche mes clés. I'm looking for my keys.

2 to look up

☐ chercher un mot dans le dictionnaire to look up a word in the dictionary

■ aller chercher 1 to go to get ☐ Elle est allée chercher du pain. She's gone to get some bread. 2 to pick up ☐ J'irai te chercher à la gare. I'll pick you up at the station.

le **chercheur** NOUN
scientist

la **chercheuse** NOUN
scientist

chère FEM ADJECTIVE ▷ see **cher**

chéri (FEM **chérie**) ADJECTIVE

▷ see also **chéri** NOUN, **chérie** NOUN
darling

☐ ma petite fille chérie my darling daughter

le **chéri** NOUN

▷ see also **chéri** ADJECTIVE
darling

■ mon chéri darling

la **chérie** NOUN

▷ see also **chérie** ADJECTIVE
darling

■ ma chérie darling

le **cheval** (PL les **chevaux**) NOUN

French-English

horse
- ■ **un cheval de course** a racehorse
- ■ **à cheval** on horseback
- ■ **faire du cheval** to go riding

le **chevalier** NOUN
knight

la **chevalière** NOUN
signet ring

chevalin (FEM **chevaline**) ADJECTIVE
- ■ **une boucherie chevaline** a horsemeat butcher's

les **chevaux** MASC PL NOUN ▷ *see* **cheval**

le **chevet** NOUN
- ■ **une table de chevet** a bedside table
- ■ **une lampe de chevet** a bedside lamp

les **cheveux** MASC PL NOUN
hair
- □ Elle a les cheveux courts. She's got short hair.

la **cheville** NOUN
ankle
- □ Il s'est foulé la cheville. He sprained his ankle.

la **chèvre** NOUN
goat
- ■ **le fromage de chèvre** goat's cheese

le **chevreau** (PL les **chevreaux**) NOUN
kid (*animal, leather*)

le **chèvrefeuille** NOUN
honeysuckle

le **chevreuil** NOUN
1 roe deer
2 venison
- □ un rôti de chevreuil roast venison

le **chewing-gum** NOUN
chewing gum

chez PREPOSITION
- ■ **chez Pierre** 1 at Pierre's house 2 to Pierre's house
- ■ **chez moi** 1 at my house □ Mes amis sont restés chez moi. My friends stayed at my house. 2 to my house □ Allons chez moi. Let's go to my house.
- ■ **chez le dentiste** 1 at the dentist's □ J'ai rendez-vous chez le dentiste demain matin. I've got an appointment at the dentist's tomorrow morning. 2 to the dentist's □ Je vais chez le dentiste. I'm going to the dentist's.
- ■ **Je rentre chez moi.** I'm going home.

chic (FEM+PL **chic**) ADJECTIVE
1 smart
- □ une tenue chic a smart outfit
2 nice
- □ C'est chic de ta part de m'avoir invité. (*informal*) It was nice of you to invite me.

la **chicorée** NOUN

endive

le **chien** NOUN
dog
- ■ **'Attention, chien méchant'** 'Beware of the dog'

la **chienne** NOUN
bitch (*dog*)

le **chiffon** NOUN
cloth

chiffonner VERB [28]
to crease
- □ Ma robe est toute chiffonnée. My dress is all creased.

le **chiffre** NOUN
figure
- □ en chiffres ronds in round figures
- ■ **les chiffres romains** Roman numerals

le **chignon** NOUN
bun (*in hair*)
- □ Elle s'est fait un chignon. She put her hair in a bun.

le **Chili** NOUN
Chile

la **chimie** NOUN
chemistry
- □ un cours de chimie a chemistry lesson

chimique (FEM **chimique**) ADJECTIVE
chemical
- □ une réaction chimique a chemical reaction
- ■ **les produits chimiques** chemicals

la **Chine** NOUN
China

chinois (FEM **chinoise**) ADJECTIVE, NOUN
Chinese
- □ Il apprend le chinois. He's learning Chinese.
- ■ **un Chinois** a Chinese (*man*)
- ■ **une Chinoise** a Chinese (*woman*)
- ■ **les Chinois** the Chinese

le **chiot** NOUN
puppy

les **chips** FEM PL NOUN
crisps
- □ un paquet de chips a packet of crisps

chirurgical (FEM **chirurgicale**, MASC PL **chirurgicaux**) ADJECTIVE
- ■ **une intervention chirurgicale** an operation

la **chirurgie** NOUN
surgery
- ■ **la chirurgie esthétique** plastic surgery

le **chirurgien** NOUN
surgeon

le **choc** NOUN
shock
- □ Ça m'a fait un sacré choc de le voir comme

ça. It gave me a hell of a shock to see him in that state.

■ **Elle est encore sous le choc.** She's still in shock.

le **chocolat** NOUN
chocolate

■ **un chocolat chaud** a hot chocolate

■ **le chocolat à croquer** dark chocolate

le **chœur** NOUN
choir

choisir VERB [38]
to choose

le **choix** NOUN

1 choice

■ **avoir le choix** to have the choice

2 selection

□ Il n'y a pas beaucoup de choix dans ce magasin. There's not a very wide selection of things in this shop.

le **chômage** NOUN
unemployment

■ **être au chômage** to be unemployed

le **chômeur** NOUN
unemployed person

□ Il est chômeur. He's unemployed.

la **chômeuse** NOUN
unemployed woman

□ Elle est chômeuse. She's unemployed.

choquer VERB [28]
to shock

□ Cette remarque m'a choqué. I was shocked by that remark.

la **chorale** NOUN
choir

la **chose** NOUN
thing

□ J'ai des tas de choses à te raconter. I've got loads of things to tell you.

■ **C'est peu de chose.** It's nothing really.

le **chou** (PL les **choux**) NOUN
cabbage

■ **les choux de Bruxelles** Brussels sprouts

■ **un chou à la crème** a choux bun

le **chouchou** NOUN (informal)
teacher's pet

la **chouchoute** NOUN (informal)
teacher's pet

la **choucroute** NOUN
sauerkraut (with sausages and ham)

la **chouette** NOUN
▷ see also **chouette** ADJECTIVE
owl

chouette (FEM **chouette**) ADJECTIVE
(informal)
▷ see also **chouette** NOUN
brilliant

□ Chouette alors! Brilliant!

le **chou-fleur** (PL les **choux-fleurs**) NOUN
cauliflower

chrétien (FEM **chrétienne**) ADJECTIVE
Christian

□ Il est chrétien. He's a Christian.

le **Christ** NOUN
Christ

chronologique (FEM **chronologique**)
ADJECTIVE
chronological

le **chronomètre** NOUN
stopwatch

chronométrer VERB [34]
to time

le **chrysanthème** NOUN
chrysanthemum

DID YOU KNOW...?
Chrysanthemums are strongly associated with funerals in France.

chuchoter VERB [28]
to whisper

chut EXCLAMATION
shh!

la **chute** NOUN
fall

■ **faire une chute** to fall

■ **une chute d'eau** a waterfall

■ **la chute des cheveux** hair loss

■ **les chutes de neige** snowfalls

Chypre NOUN
Cyprus

-ci ADVERB

■ **ce livre-ci** this book

■ **ces bottes-ci** these boots

la **cible** NOUN
target

la **ciboulette** NOUN
chives

la **cicatrice** NOUN
scar

se **cicatriser** VERB [28]
to heal up

□ Cette plaie s'est vite cicatrisée. This wound has healed up quickly.

ci-contre ADVERB
opposite

□ la page ci-contre the opposite page

ci-dessous ADVERB
below

□ la photo ci-dessous the picture below

ci-dessus ADVERB
above

le **cidre** NOUN
cider

le **ciel** NOUN

1 sky

□ un ciel nuageux a cloudy sky

C

49

French-English

C

2 heaven
□ être au ciel to be in heaven

le **cierge** NOUN
candle *(in church)*

la **cigale** NOUN
cicada

le **cigare** NOUN
cigar
□ Il fume le cigare. He smokes cigars.

la **cigarette** NOUN
cigarette

la **cigogne** NOUN
stork

ci-joint ADVERB
enclosed
□ Veuillez trouver ci-joint mon curriculum
vitae. Please find enclosed my CV.

le **cil** NOUN
eyelash

le **ciment** NOUN
cement

le **cimetière** NOUN
cemetery

le/la **cinéaste** NOUN
film-maker

le **cinéma** NOUN
cinema

cinq NUMBER
five
□ Il est cinq heures du matin. It's five in the
morning. □ Il a cinq ans. He's five.
■ **le cinq février** the fifth of February

la **cinquantaine** NOUN
about fifty
□ Il y avait une cinquantaine de personnes.
There were about fifty people there.
■ **Il a la cinquantaine.** He's in his fifties.

cinquante NUMBER
fifty
□ Il a cinquante ans. He's fifty.
■ **cinquante et un** fifty-one
■ **cinquante-deux** fifty-two

cinquième (FEM **cinquième**) ADJECTIVE
▷ *see also* **cinquième** NOUN
fifth
□ au cinquième étage on the fifth floor

la **cinquième** NOUN
▷ *see also* **cinquième** ADJECTIVE
year 8
□ Mon frère est en cinquième. My brother's
in year 8.

┌─ **DID YOU KNOW...?**
│ In French secondary schools, years
│ are counted from the **sixième**
│ (youngest) to **première** and
└─ **terminale** (oldest).

50 le **cintre** NOUN

coat hanger

le **cirage** NOUN
shoe polish

circonflexe (FEM **circonflexe**) ADJECTIVE
■ **un accent circonflexe** a circumflex

la **circonstance** NOUN
circumstance
□ dans les circonstances actuelles in the
present circumstances

la **circulation** NOUN
1 traffic
□ Il y avait beaucoup de circulation. There
was a lot of traffic.
2 circulation
□ Elle a des problèmes de circulation. She
has bad circulation.

circuler VERB [28]
to run
□ Il n'y a qu'un bus sur trois qui circule.
Only one bus in three is running.

la **cire** NOUN
wax

le **ciré** NOUN
oilskin jacket

cirer VERB [28]
to polish *(shoes, floor)*

le **cirque** NOUN
circus

les **ciseaux** MASC PL NOUN
■ **une paire de ciseaux** a pair of scissors

le **citadin** NOUN
city dweller

la **citation** NOUN
quotation

la **cité** NOUN
estate
□ J'habite dans une cité. I live on an estate.
■ **une cité universitaire** halls of residence
■ **une cité-dortoir** a dormitory town

citer VERB [28]
to quote

le **citoyen** NOUN
citizen

la **citoyenne** NOUN
citizen

la **citoyenneté** NOUN
citizenship

le **citron** NOUN
lemon
■ **un citron vert** a lime
  LANGUAGE TIP Word for word, this
  means 'a green lemon'.
■ **un citron pressé** a fresh lemon juice

la **citronnade** NOUN
still lemonade

la **citrouille** NOUN
pumpkin

le **civet** NOUN
stew
□ du civet de lapin rabbit stew

civil (FEM **civile**) ADJECTIVE
civilian
■ en civil in civilian clothes

la **civilisation** NOUN
civilization

civique (FEM **civique**) ADJECTIVE
■ l'instruction civique PSHE

clair (FEM **claire**) ADJECTIVE, ADVERB
1 light
□ vert clair light green □ C'est une pièce très claire. It's a very light room.
2 clear *(water)*
■ voir clair to see clearly
■ le clair de lune moonlight

clairement ADVERB
clearly

la **clairière** NOUN
clearing

clandestin (FEM **clandestine**) ADJECTIVE
■ un passager clandestin a stowaway

la **claque** NOUN
slap
□ Elle m'a donné une claque. She gave me a slap.

claquer VERB [28]
1 to bang
□ On entend des volets qui claquent. You can hear shutters banging.
2 to slam
□ Elle est partie en claquant la porte. She left, slamming the door behind her.

les **claquettes** FEM PL NOUN
■ faire des claquettes to tap-dance

la **clarinette** NOUN
clarinet

la **classe** NOUN
1 class
□ C'est la meilleure élève de la classe. She's the best pupil in the class. □ voyager en première classe to travel first class
2 classroom

classer VERB [28]
to arrange
□ Les livres sont classés par ordre alphabétique. The books are arranged in alphabetical order.

le **classeur** NOUN
ring binder

classique (FEM **classique**) ADJECTIVE
1 classical
□ de la musique classique classical music
2 classic
□ un style classique a classic style

le **clavier** NOUN
keyboard *(of computer, typewriter)*

la **clé** NOUN
1 key
2 clef
□ la clé de sol the treble clef □ la clé de fa the bass clef □ une clé de voiture a car key

la **clef** NOUN = clé

le **client** NOUN
customer

la **cliente** NOUN
customer

la **clientèle** NOUN
customers

cligner VERB [28]
■ cligner des yeux to blink

le **clignotant** NOUN
indicator
□ Il a mis son clignotant à gauche. He's indicating left.

le **climat** NOUN
climate

la **climatisation** NOUN
air conditioning

climatisé (FEM **climatisée**) ADJECTIVE
air-conditioned
□ L'hôtel est climatisé. The hotel is air-conditioned.

le **clin d'œil** (PL les **clins d'œil**) NOUN
wink
■ en un clin d'œil in a flash

la **clinique** NOUN
private hospital

cliquer VERB [28]
to click
□ cliquer sur une icône to click on an icon

le **clochard** NOUN
tramp

la **cloche** NOUN
bell

le **clocher** NOUN
1 church tower
2 steeple

le **clone** NOUN
clone

cloner VERB [28]
to clone

le **clou** NOUN
nail
■ un clou de girofle a clove

le **clown** NOUN
clown

le **club** NOUN
club

le **cobaye** NOUN
guinea pig

le **coca** NOUN
Coke®

la **cocaïne** NOUN
cocaine

la **coccinelle** NOUN
ladybird

cocher VERB [28]
to tick
□ Cochez la bonne réponse. Tick the right
answer.

le **cochon** NOUN
▷ *see also* **cochon** ADJECTIVE
pig
■ **un cochon d'Inde** a guinea pig
LANGUAGE TIP Word for word, this
means 'a pig from India'.

cochon (FEM **cochonne**) ADJECTIVE (*informal*)
▷ *see also* **cochon** NOUN
dirty
□ une histoire cochonne a dirty story

le **cocktail** NOUN
1 cocktail
2 cocktail party

le **coco** NOUN
■ **une noix de coco** a coconut

cocorico EXCLAMATION
1 cock-a-doodle-doo!
2 three cheers for France!

DID YOU KNOW...?
The symbol of France is the cockerel
and so **cocorico!** is sometimes used
as an expression of French national
pride.

la **cocotte** NOUN
casserole (*pan*)
■ **une cocotte-minute®** a pressure cooker

le **code** NOUN
code
■ **le code de la route** the highway code
■ **le code postal** the postcode

le **cœur** NOUN
heart
■ **avoir bon cœur** to be kind-hearted
■ **la dame de cœur** the queen of hearts
■ **avoir mal au cœur** to feel sick
■ **par cœur** by heart □ apprendre quelque
chose par cœur to learn something by heart

le **coffre** NOUN
1 boot (*of car*)
2 chest (*furniture*)

le **coffre-fort** (PL les **coffres-forts**) NOUN
safe

le **coffret** NOUN
■ **un coffret à bijoux** a jewellery box

le **cognac** NOUN
brandy

se **cogner** VERB [28]
■ **se cogner à quelque chose** to bang into
something □ Je me suis cogné à la table. I

banged into the table. □ Je me suis cogné la
tête contre la porte du placard. I banged my
head on the cupboard door.

coiffé (FEM **coiffée**) ADJECTIVE
■ **Tu es bien coiffée.** Your hair looks nice.

coiffer VERB [28]
■ **se coiffer** to do one's hair

le **coiffeur** NOUN
hairdresser

la **coiffeuse** NOUN
hairdresser

la **coiffure** NOUN
hairstyle
□ Cette coiffure te va bien. That hairstyle
suits you.
■ **un salon de coiffure** a hairdresser's

le **coin** NOUN
corner
□ au coin de la rue on the corner of the
street
■ **Tu habites dans le coin?** Do you live near
here?
■ **Je ne suis pas du coin.** I'm not from here.
■ **le bistrot du coin** the local pub

coincé (FEM **coincée**) ADJECTIVE
1 stuck
□ La clé est coincée dans la serrure. The key
is stuck in the keyhole.
2 stuffy
□ Il est un peu coincé. (*informal*) He's a bit
stuffy.

coincer VERB [12]
to jam
□ La porte est coincée. The door's jammed.

la **coïncidence** NOUN
coincidence

le **col** NOUN
1 collar
2 pass (*of mountain*)

la **colère** NOUN
anger
■ **Je suis en colère.** I'm angry.
■ **se mettre en colère** to get angry

le **colin** NOUN
hake

la **colique** NOUN
diarrhoea

le **colis** NOUN
parcel

collaborer VERB [28]
to collaborate

le **collant** NOUN
▷ *see also* **collant** ADJECTIVE
tights
□ un collant en laine woollen tights

collant (FEM **collante**) ADJECTIVE
▷ *see also* **collant** NOUN

1 sticky
2 clingy
  □ Je le trouve un peu collant. *(informal)* I
  find him a bit clingy.
la **colle** NOUN
1 glue
  □ un tube de colle a tube of glue
2 detention
  □ J'ai une heure de colle samedi prochain.
  (informal) I've got an hour's detention next
  Saturday.
  ■ **Je n'en sais rien: tu me poses une colle.**
  (informal) I really don't know: you've got me
  there.
la **collecte** NOUN
  collection *(of money)*
  □ On a fait une collecte au profit des
  victimes. There was a collection for the
  victims.
la **collection** NOUN
  collection
  □ une collection de timbres a stamp
  collection
collectionner VERB [28]
  to collect
le **collège** NOUN
  secondary school

> **DID YOU KNOW...?**
> In France pupils go to a **collège**
> between the ages of 11 and 15, and
> then to a **lycée** until the age of 18.

le **collégien** NOUN
  schoolboy
la **collégienne** NOUN
  schoolgirl
le/la **collègue** NOUN
  colleague
coller VERB [28]
1 to stick
  □ Il y a un chewing-gum collé sous la chaise.
  There's a bit of chewing gum stuck under
  the chair. □ Ce timbre ne colle plus. This
  stamp won't stick on.
2 to press
  □ J'ai collé mon oreille au mur. I pressed my
  ear against the wall.
le **collier** NOUN
1 necklace
  □ un collier de perles a pearl necklace
2 collar *(of dog, cat)*
la **colline** NOUN
  hill
la **collision** NOUN
  crash
la **colombe** NOUN
  dove
la **colonie** NOUN
  ■ **aller en colonie de vacances** to go to
  summer camp
la **colonne** NOUN
  column
  ■ **la colonne vertébrale** the spine
le **colorant** NOUN
  colouring
le **coloris** NOUN
  colour
le **coma** NOUN
  coma
  ■ **être dans le coma** to be in a coma
le **combat** NOUN
  fighting
  □ Les combats ont repris ce matin. Fighting
  started again this morning.
  ■ **un combat de boxe** a boxing match
le **combattant** NOUN
  ■ **un ancien combattant** a war veteran
combattre VERB [9]
  to fight
combien ADVERB
1 how much
  □ Vous en voulez combien? Un kilo? How
  much do you want? One kilo?
  ■ **C'est combien?** How much is that?
  □ Combien est-ce que ça coûte? How much
  does it cost? □ Combien ça fait? How much
  does it come to?
2 how many
  □ Tu en veux combien? Deux? How many
  do you want? Two?
  ■ **combien de 1** how much □ Combien de
  purée est-ce que je vous sers? How much
  mashed potato shall I give you? **2** how
  many □ Combien de personnes as-tu
  invitées? How many people have you
  invited?
  ■ **combien de temps** how long □ Combien
  de temps est-ce que tu seras absente? How
  long will you be away?
  ■ **Il y a combien de temps?** How long ago?
  □ Il est parti il y a combien de temps? How
  long ago did he leave?
  ■ **On est le combien aujourd'hui? — On
  est le vingt.** What's the date today? — It's
  the 20th.
la **combinaison** NOUN
1 combination
  □ J'ai changé la combinaison de mon
  antivol. I've changed the combination on
  my bike lock.
2 slip *(petticoat)*
  ■ **une combinaison de plongée** a wetsuit
  ■ **une combinaison de ski** a ski suit
le **comble** NOUN
  ■ **Alors ça, c'est le comble!** That's the last

straw!

la **comédie** NOUN
comedy
■ **une comédie musicale** a musical

le **comédien** NOUN
actor

la **comédienne** NOUN
actress

comestible (FEM **comestible**) ADJECTIVE
edible

comique (FEM **comique**) ADJECTIVE
▷ *see also* **comique** NOUN
comical

le **comique** NOUN
▷ *see also* **comique** ADJECTIVE
comedian

le **comité** NOUN
committee

le **commandant** NOUN
captain (of ship, plane)

la **commande** NOUN
order
□ un bon de commande an order form
■ **être aux commandes** to be at the
controls

commander VERB [28]
1 to order
□ J'ai commandé une robe par catalogue.
I've ordered a dress from a catalogue.
2 to give orders
□ C'est moi qui commande ici, pas vous! I
give the orders here, not you!

comme CONJUNCTION, ADVERB
1 like
□ Il est comme son père. He's like his
father. □ Je voudrais un manteau comme
celui de la photo. I'd like a coat like the one
in the picture.
2 for
□ Qu'est-ce que tu veux comme dessert?
What would you like for pudding?
3 as
□ J'ai travaillé comme serveuse cet été. I
worked as a waitress this summer. □ Faites
comme vous voulez. Do as you like.
■ **comme ça** like this □ Ça se plie comme
ça. You fold it like this. □ C'était un poisson
grand comme ça. The fish was this big.
■ **comme il faut** properly □ Mets le couvert
comme il faut! Set the table properly!
■ **Comme tu as grandi!** How you've grown!
■ **Regarde comme c'est beau!** Look, isn't
it lovely!
■ **comme ci comme ça** so-so □ Comment
est-ce que tu as trouvé le film? — Comme ci
comme ça. What did you think of the film?
— So-so.

le **commencement** NOUN
beginning

commencer VERB [12]
to start
□ Les cours commencent à huit heures.
Lessons start at 8 o'clock. □ Il a commencé
à pleuvoir. It started raining. □ J'ai
commencé de réviser pour les examens.
I've started revising for the exams.

comment ADVERB
how
□ Comment arrives-tu à travailler dans ce
bruit? How can you possibly work with this
noise?
■ **Comment allez-vous?** How are you?
■ **Comment dit-on 'pomme' en anglais?**
How do you say 'pomme' in English?
■ **Comment s'appelle-t-il?** What's his
name?
■ **Comment?** What did you say?

le **commentaire** NOUN
comment

les **commérages** MASC PL NOUN
gossip

le **commerçant** NOUN
shopkeeper

le **commerce** NOUN
1 trade
□ le commerce extérieur foreign trade
■ **le commerce électronique** e-commerce
2 business
□ Il fait des études de commerce. He's
studying business.
3 shop
□ tenir un commerce to have a shop
■ **On trouve ça dans le commerce.** You
can find it in the shops.

commercial (FEM **commerciale**, MASC PL
commerciaux) ADJECTIVE
■ **un centre commercial** a shopping
centre

commettre VERB [47]
to commit
□ Il a commis un crime grave. He has
committed a serious crime.

le **commissaire** NOUN
police superintendent

le **commissariat** NOUN
police station

les **commissions** FEM PL NOUN
shopping
□ J'ai quelques commissions à faire. I've got
some shopping to do.

la **commode** NOUN
▷ *see also* **commode** ADJECTIVE
chest of drawers

commode (FEM **commode**) ADJECTIVE

▷ *see also* **commode** NOUN
handy

□ Ce sac est très commode pour les voyages. This bag is very handy for travelling.

■ **Son père n'est pas commode.** His father is a difficult character.

commun (FEM **commune**) ADJECTIVE
shared

□ une salle de bain commune a shared bathroom □ Nous avons des intérêts communs. We have interests in common.

■ **en commun** in common □ Ils n'ont rien en commun. They've got nothing in common.

■ **les transports en commun** public transport

■ **mettre quelque chose en commun** to share something □ Nous mettons tous nos livres en commun. We share all our books.

la **communauté** NOUN
community

la **communication** NOUN
communication

■ **une communication téléphonique** a telephone call

la **communion** NOUN
communion

□ faire sa première communion to make one's first communion

communiquer VERB [28]
to communicate

communiste (FEM **communiste**) ADJECTIVE
communist

□ le Parti communiste the Communist Party

compact (FEM **compacte**) ADJECTIVE
compact

■ **un disque compact** a compact disc

la **compagne** NOUN
1 companion
2 partner *(living together)*

la **compagnie** NOUN
company

□ J'aime avoir de la compagnie. I like to have company. □ Je viendrai te tenir compagnie. I'll come to keep you company.

■ **une compagnie d'assurances** an insurance company

■ **une compagnie aérienne** an airline

le **compagnon** NOUN
1 companion
2 partner *(living together)*

la **comparaison** NOUN
comparison

□ en comparaison de in comparison with

comparer VERB [28]

to compare

le **compartiment** NOUN
compartment *(on train)*

le **compas** NOUN
compass *(for drawing circles)*

compatible (FEM **compatible**) ADJECTIVE
compatible

la **compétence** NOUN
competence

compétent (FEM **compétente**) ADJECTIVE
competent

compétitif (FEM **compétitive**) ADJECTIVE
competitive

la **compétition** NOUN
competition

■ **avoir l'esprit de compétition** to be competitive

complet (FEM **complète**) ADJECTIVE
▷ *see also* **complet** NOUN
1 complete

□ les œuvres complètes de Shakespeare the complete works of Shakespeare

2 full

□ L'hôtel est complet. The hotel is full.

■ **'complet'** 'no vacancies'

■ **le pain complet** wholemeal bread

le **complet** NOUN
▷ *see also* **complet** ADJECTIVE
suit *(for man)*

complètement ADVERB
completely

□ J'avais complètement oublié que tu venais. I'd completely forgotten that you were coming.

compléter VERB [34]
to complete

□ Complétez les phrases suivantes. Complete the following phrases.

complexe (FEM **complexe**) ADJECTIVE
complex

complexé (FEM **complexée**) ADJECTIVE
screwed-up

la **complication** NOUN
complication

le/la **complice** NOUN
accomplice

les **compliments** MASC PL NOUN
compliment

■ **faire des compliments** to compliment □ Il m'a fait des compliments sur ma robe. He complimented me on my dress.

compliqué (FEM **compliquée**) ADJECTIVE
complicated

□ C'est une histoire compliquée. It's a complicated story.

le **complot** NOUN
plot

le **comportement** NOUN
behaviour

comporter VERB [28]

1 to consist of
□ Le château comporte trois parties. The castle consists of three parts.

2 to have
□ Ce modèle comporte un écran couleur. This model has a colour screen.
■ **se comporter** to behave □ Il s'est comporté de façon odieuse. He behaved atrociously.

composer VERB [28]
to compose (*music, text*)
■ **composer un numéro** to dial a number
■ **se composer de** to consist of □ L'uniforme se compose d'une veste, d'un pantalon et d'une cravate. The uniform consists of a jacket, trousers and a tie.

le **compositeur** NOUN
composer

la **composition** NOUN
test
□ Nous avons une composition de français cet après-midi. We've got a French test this afternoon.

la **compositrice** NOUN
composer

le **compostage** NOUN
date stamping

composter VERB [28]
to punch
□ N'oublie pas de composter ton billet avant de monter dans le train. Remember to punch your ticket before you get on the train.

> **DID YOU KNOW...?**
> In France you have to punch your ticket on the platform to validate it before getting onto the train.

la **compote** NOUN
stewed fruit
■ **la compote de prunes** stewed plums

compréhensible (FEM **compréhensible**) ADJECTIVE
understandable

compréhensif (FEM **compréhensive**) ADJECTIVE
understanding

> **LANGUAGE TIP** Be careful!
> **compréhensif** does not mean **comprehensive**.

la **compréhension** NOUN

1 comprehension
□ la compréhension orale listening comprehension

2 sympathy

□ Elle a fait preuve de beaucoup de compréhension à mon égard. She showed a lot of sympathy for me.

comprendre VERB [65]

1 to understand
□ Je ne comprends pas ce que vous dites. I don't understand what you're saying.

2 to include
□ Le forfait ne comprend pas la location des skis. The price doesn't include ski hire.

le **comprimé** NOUN
tablet
□ un comprimé d'aspirine an aspirin

compris (FEM **comprise**) ADJECTIVE
included
□ Le service n'est pas compris. Service is not included.
■ **y compris** including □ Ils ont tout vendu, y compris leur voiture. They sold everything, including their car.
■ **non compris** excluding □ un menu à vingt euros, vin non compris a set menu for 20 euros, excluding wine
■ **cent euros tout compris** 100 euros all-inclusive

compromettre VERB [47]
to compromise

le **compromis** NOUN
compromise
□ Ils sont parvenus à un compromis. They came to a compromise.

la **comptabilité** NOUN
accounting
□ un cours de comptabilité a course in accounting

le/la **comptable** NOUN
accountant
□ Il est comptable. He's an accountant.

comptant ADVERB
■ **payer comptant** to pay cash

le **compte** NOUN
account
□ J'ai déposé le chèque sur mon compte. I've paid the cheque into my account.
■ **Le compte est bon.** That's the right amount.
■ **tenir compte de 1** to take into account □ Ils ont tenu compte de mon expérience. They took my experience into account. **2** to take notice of □ Il n'a pas tenu compte de mes conseils. He took no notice of my advice.
■ **travailler à son compte** to be self-employed
■ **en fin de compte** all things considered □ Le voyage ne s'est pas mal passé, en fin de compte. The journey wasn't bad, all things

considered.
compter VERB [28]
to count
le **compte rendu** (PL les **comptes rendus**)
NOUN
report
le **compteur** NOUN
meter
le **comptoir** NOUN
bar
□ au comptoir at the bar
se **concentrer** VERB [28]
to concentrate
□ J'ai du mal à me concentrer. I find it hard
to concentrate.
la **conception** NOUN
design
concernant PREPOSITION
regarding
□ Concernant notre nouveau projet, je
voudrais ajouter que … Regarding our new
project, I would like to add that …
concerner VERB [28]
to concern
□ en ce qui me concerne as far as I'm
concerned
■ **Je ne me sens pas concerné.** I don't feel
it's anything to do with me.
le **concert** NOUN
concert
le/la **concierge** NOUN
caretaker
conclure VERB [13]
to conclude
la **conclusion** NOUN
conclusion
le **concombre** NOUN
cucumber
concorder VERB [28]
to tally
□ Les dates concordent. The dates tally.
le **concours** NOUN
1 competition
□ un concours de chant a singing
competition
2 competitive exam (for a job or a place in a
school)
concret (FEM **concrète**) ADJECTIVE
concrete
conçu VERB
designed
□ Ces appartements sont très mal conçus.
These flats are very badly designed.
la **concurrence** NOUN
competition
□ La concurrence est vive sur ce marché.
There's a lot of competition in this market.

le **concurrent** NOUN
competitor
la **concurrente** NOUN
competitor
condamner VERB [28]
1 to sentence
□ Il a été condamné à deux ans de prison.
He was sentenced to two years in prison.
□ condamner à mort to sentence to death
2 to condemn
□ Le gouvernement a condamné cette
décision. The government condemned this
decision.
la **condition** NOUN
condition
□ Je le ferai à une condition … I'll do it, on
one condition …
■ **à condition que** provided that □ Je
viendrai à condition qu'il me le demande.
I'll come provided he asks me to.
■ **les conditions de travail** working
conditions
le **conditionnel** NOUN
conditional tense
le **conducteur** NOUN
driver
la **conductrice** NOUN
driver
conduire VERB [23]
to drive
□ Est-ce que tu sais conduire? Can you
drive? □ Je te conduirai chez le docteur. I'll
drive you to the doctor's.
■ **se conduire** to behave □ Il s'est mal
conduit. He behaved badly.
la **conduite** NOUN
behaviour
la **conférence** NOUN
1 lecture
□ donner une conférence to give a lecture
2 conference
□ une conférence internationale an
international conference
se **confesser** VERB [28]
to go to confession
les **confettis** MASC PL NOUN
confetti
la **confiance** NOUN
1 trust
■ **avoir confiance en quelqu'un** to trust
somebody □ Je n'ai pas confiance en lui. I
don't trust him.
2 confidence
■ **Tu peux avoir confiance. Il sera à
l'heure.** You don't need to worry. He'll be
on time.
■ **confiance en soi** self-confidence □ Elle

manque de confiance en elle. She lacks self-confidence.

confiant (FEM **confiante**) ADJECTIVE
confident

les **confidences** FEM PL NOUN
■ **faire des confidences à quelqu'un** to confide in someone □ Elle me fait quelquefois des confidences. She sometimes confides in me.

confidentiel (FEM **confidentielle**) ADJECTIVE
confidential

confier VERB [19]
■ **se confier à quelqu'un** to confide in somebody □ Elle s'est confiée à sa meilleure amie. She confided in her best friend.

confirmer VERB [28]
to confirm

la **confiserie** NOUN
sweet shop

confisquer VERB [28]
to confiscate

confit (FEM **confite**) ADJECTIVE
■ **des fruits confits** crystallized fruits

la **confiture** NOUN
jam
□ la confiture de fraises strawberry jam
■ **la confiture d'oranges** marmalade

le **conflit** NOUN
conflict

confondre VERB [69]
to mix up
□ On le confond souvent avec son frère. People often mix him up with his brother.

le **confort** NOUN
comfort
■ **tout confort** with all mod cons □ un appartement tout confort a flat with all mod cons

confortable (FEM **confortable**) ADJECTIVE
comfortable
□ des chaussures confortables comfortable shoes

confus (FEM **confuse**) ADJECTIVE
1 unclear
□ J'ai trouvé ses explications confuses. I thought his explanation was unclear.
2 embarrassed
□ Il avait l'air confus. He looked embarrassed.

la **confusion** NOUN
1 confusion
2 embarrassment
□ rougir de confusion to go red with embarrassment

le **congé** NOUN
holiday
□ une semaine de congé a week's holiday

■ **en congé** on holiday □ Je serai en congé la semaine prochaine. I'll be on holiday next week.
■ **un congé de maladie** sick leave □ Il est en congé de maladie. He's on sick leave.

le **congélateur** NOUN
freezer

congeler VERB [1]
to freeze

la **conjonction** NOUN
conjunction

la **conjonctivite** NOUN
conjunctivitis

la **conjugaison** NOUN
conjugation

la **connaissance** NOUN
1 knowledge
□ ... pour approfondir vos connaissances ... to increase your knowledge
2 acquaintance
□ Ce n'est pas vraiment une amie, juste une connaissance. She's not really a friend, just an acquaintance.
■ **perdre connaissance** to lose consciousness
■ **faire la connaissance de quelqu'un** to meet somebody □ J'ai fait la connaissance de son frère. I met her brother.

connaître VERB [14]
to know
□ Je ne connais pas du tout cette région. I don't know this area at all. □ Je le connais de vue. I know him by sight.
■ **Ils se sont connus à Nantes.** They first met in Nantes.
■ **s'y connaître en quelque chose** to know about something □ Je ne m'y connais pas beaucoup en musique classique. I don't know much about classical music.

se **connecter** VERB [28]
to log on
□ Je me suis connecté sur Internet il y a dix minutes. I logged onto the internet ten minutes ago.

connu (FEM **connue**) ADJECTIVE
well-known
□ C'est un acteur connu. He's a well-known actor.

conquérir VERB [2]
to conquer

consacrer VERB [28]
to devote
□ Il consacre beaucoup de temps à ses enfants. He devotes a lot of time to his children. □ Je suis désolé, je n'ai pas beaucoup de temps à vous consacrer. I'm afraid I can't spare much time for you.

la **conscience** NOUN
conscience
□ avoir mauvaise conscience to have a
guilty conscience
■ **prendre conscience de** to become
aware of □ Ils ont fini par prendre
conscience de la gravité de la situation.
They eventually became aware of the
seriousness of the situation.

consciencieux (FEM **consciencieuse**)
ADJECTIVE
conscientious

conscient (FEM **consciente**) ADJECTIVE
conscious

consécutif (FEM **consécutive**) ADJECTIVE
consecutive

le **conseil** NOUN
advice
□ Est-ce que je peux te demander conseil?
Can I ask you for some advice?
■ **un conseil** a piece of advice

conseiller VERB [28]
▷ see also **conseiller** NOUN
1 to advise
□ Il a été mal conseillé. He has been badly
advised.
2 to recommend
□ Il m'a conseillé ce livre. He recommended
this book to me.

le **conseiller** NOUN
▷ see also **conseiller** VERB
1 councillor (political)
□ un conseiller municipal a town councillor
2 adviser
□ le conseiller d'orientation the careers
adviser

le **consentement** NOUN
consent
□ le consentement des parents the parents'
consent

consentir VERB [77]
to agree
□ consentir à quelque chose to agree to
something

la **conséquence** NOUN
consequence
■ **en conséquence** consequently

conséquent (FEM **conséquente**) ADJECTIVE
■ **par conséquent** consequently

le **conservatoire** NOUN
school of music
□ Elle fait du piano au conservatoire. She's
learning the piano at the school of music.

la **conserve** NOUN
tin
□ Je vais ouvrir une conserve. I'll open a tin.
■ **une boîte de conserve** a tin

■ **les conserves** tinned food □ Il n'est pas
bon de manger tous les jours des conserves.
It's not healthy to eat tinned food every day.
■ **en conserve** tinned □ des petits pois en
conserve tinned peas

conserver VERB [28]
to keep
□ J'ai conservé toutes ses lettres. I've kept
all her letters.
■ **se conserver** to keep □ Ce pain se
conserve plus d'une semaine. This bread
will keep for more than a week.

considérable (FEM **considérable**) ADJECTIVE
considerable
□ Il a fait des progrès considérables. He's
made considerable progress.

la **considération** NOUN
■ **prendre quelque chose en
considération** to take something into
consideration

considérer VERB [34]
■ **considérer que** to believe that □ Je
considère que le gouvernement devrait
investir davantage dans l'éducation. I
believe that the government should invest
more money in education.

la **consigne** NOUN
left-luggage office
■ **une consigne automatique** a left-
luggage locker

consistant (FEM **consistante**) ADJECTIVE
substantial
□ un petit déjeuner consistant a substantial
breakfast

consister VERB [28]
■ **consister à** to consist of □ Mon travail
consiste à répondre au téléphone et à
recevoir les clients. My job consists of
answering the phone and welcoming the
customers.
■ **En quoi consiste votre travail?** What
does your job involve?

la **console de jeu** NOUN
games console

consoler VERB [28]
to console

le **consommateur** NOUN
1 consumer
2 customer (in café)

la **consommation** NOUN
1 consumption
□ la consommation d'électricité electricity
consumption
2 drink
□ Le billet d'entrée donne droit à une
consommation gratuite. The ticket entitles
you to one free drink.

la **consommatrice** NOUN
1 consumer
2 customer (in café)

consommer VERB [28]
1 to use
 □ Ces grosses voitures consomment beaucoup d'essence. These big cars use a lot of petrol.
2 to have a drink
 □ Est-ce qu'on peut consommer à la terrasse? Can we have drinks outside?

la **consonne** NOUN
 consonant

constamment ADVERB
 constantly
 □ Elle se plaint constamment. She's constantly complaining.

constant (FEM **constante**) ADJECTIVE
 constant

constater VERB [28]
 to notice

constipé (FEM **constipée**) ADJECTIVE
 constipated

constitué (FEM **constituée**) ADJECTIVE
 ■ être constitué de to consist of

constituer VERB [28]
 to make up
 □ les États qui constituent la Fédération russe the states which make up the Russian Federation

la **construction** NOUN
 building
 □ des matériaux de construction building materials
 ■ une maison en construction a house being built

construire VERB [23]
 to build
 □ Ils font construire une maison neuve. They're having a new house built.

le **consulat** NOUN
 consulate
 □ le consulat de France the French consulate

la **consultation** NOUN
 ■ les heures de consultation surgery hours

consulter VERB [28]
1 to consult
 □ Il vaut toujours mieux consulter un médecin. It's always best to consult a doctor.
2 to see patients
 □ Le docteur ne consulte pas le samedi. The doctor doesn't see patients on Saturdays.

le **contact** NOUN
 contact

 □ les contacts humains human contact
 ■ Il a le contact facile. He's very approachable.
 ■ garder le contact avec quelqu'un to keep in touch with somebody

contacter VERB [28]
 to get in touch with
 □ Je te contacterai dès que j'aurai des nouvelles. I'll get in touch with you as soon as I have some news.

contagieux (FEM **contagieuse**) ADJECTIVE
 infectious
 □ une maladie contagieuse an infectious disease □ Je suis peut-être contagieux. I might have something infectious.

contaminer VERB [28]
 to contaminate

le **conte de fées** (PL les **contes de fées**) NOUN
 fairy tale

contempler VERB [28]
 to gaze at

contemporain (FEM **contemporaine**) ADJECTIVE
 contemporary
 ■ un auteur contemporain a modern writer

contenir VERB [83]
 to contain
 □ un portefeuille contenant de l'argent a wallet containing money

content (FEM **contente**) ADJECTIVE
 glad
 □ Je suis content que tu sois venu. I'm glad you've come.
 ■ content de pleased with □ Elle est contente de mon travail. She is pleased with my work.

contenter VERB [28]
 to please
 □ Il est difficile à contenter. He's hard to please.
 ■ Je me contente de peu. I can make do with very little.

contesté (FEM **contestée**) ADJECTIVE
 controversial
 □ Cette décision est très contestée. This is a very controversial decision.

le **continent** NOUN
 continent

continu (FEM **continue**) ADJECTIVE
 continuous
 ■ faire la journée continue to work without taking a full lunch break

continuellement ADVERB
 constantly

continuer VERB [28]

to carry on

□ Continuez sans moi! Carry on without me!

□ Il ne veut pas continuer ses études. He doesn't want to carry on studying.

■ **continuer à faire quelque chose** to go on doing something □ Ils ont continué à regarder la télé sans me dire bonjour. They went on watching TV without saying hello to me.

■ **continuer de faire quelque chose** to keep on doing something □ Il continue de fumer malgré son asthme. He keeps on smoking, despite his asthma.

contourner VERB [28]

to go round

□ La route contourne la ville. The road goes round the town.

le **contraceptif** NOUN
contraceptive

la **contraception** NOUN
contraception

le **contractuel** NOUN
traffic warden

la **contractuelle** NOUN
traffic warden

la **contradiction** NOUN
contradiction

■ **par esprit de contradiction** just to be awkward □ Il a refusé de venir par esprit de contradiction. He refused to come, just to be awkward.

le **contraire** NOUN
opposite

□ Il a fait le contraire de ce que je lui avais demandé. He did the opposite of what I asked him.

■ **au contraire** on the contrary

contrarier VERB [19]

1 to annoy

□ Il avait l'air contrarié. He looked annoyed.

2 to upset

□ Est-ce que tu serais contrariée si je ne venais pas? Would you be upset if I didn't come?

le **contraste** NOUN
contrast

le **contrat** NOUN
contract

□ un contrat de travail an employment contract

la **contravention** NOUN
parking ticket

contre PREPOSITION

1 against

□ Ne mets pas ton vélo contre le mur. Don't put your bike against the wall. □ Tu es pour ou contre ce projet? Are you for or against

this plan?

2 for

□ échanger quelque chose contre quelque chose to swap something for something

■ **par contre** on the other hand

la **contrebande** NOUN
smuggling

■ **des produits de contrebande** smuggled goods

la **contrebasse** NOUN
double bass

contrecœur

■ **à contrecœur** ADVERB reluctantly □ Il est venu à contrecœur. He came reluctantly.

contredire VERB [27]

to contradict

□ Il ne supporte pas d'être contredit. He can't stand being contradicted.

la **contre-indication** NOUN

■ 'Contre-indication en cas d'eczéma' 'Not to be used by people with eczema'

le **contresens** NOUN
mistranslation

le **contretemps** NOUN

■ **Désolé d'être en retard: j'ai eu un contretemps.** Sorry I'm late: I was held up.

contribuer VERB [28]

■ **contribuer à** to contribute to □ Est-ce que tu veux contribuer au cadeau pour Marie? Do you want to contribute to Marie's present?

le **contrôle** NOUN

1 control

□ le contrôle des passeports passport control

2 check

■ **un contrôle d'identité** an identity check

■ **le contrôle des billets** ticket inspection

3 test

□ un contrôle antidopage a drugs test

■ **le contrôle continu** continuous assessment

contrôler VERB [28]

to check

□ Personne n'a contrôlé mon billet. Nobody checked my ticket.

le **contrôleur** NOUN
ticket inspector

la **contrôleuse** NOUN
ticket inspector

controversé (FEM **controversée**) ADJECTIVE
controversial

convaincre VERB [86]

1 to persuade

□ Il a essayé de me convaincre de rester. He tried to persuade me to stay.

2 to convince

61

□ Tu n'as pas l'air convaincu. You don't look convinced.

la **convalescence** NOUN
convalescence

convenable (FEM **convenable**) ADJECTIVE
decent

□ un hôtel convenable a decent hotel

■ **Ce n'est pas convenable.** It's bad manners.

convenir VERB [89]

■ **convenir à** to suit □ Est-ce que cette date te convient? Does this date suit you?

□ J'espère que cela vous conviendra. I hope this will suit you.

■ **convenir de** to agree on □ Nous avons convenu d'une date. We've agreed on a date.

conventionné (FEM **conventionnée**) ADJECTIVE

■ **un médecin conventionné** a Health Service doctor

> **DID YOU KNOW…?**
> All doctors in France charge for treatment, but patients of Health Service doctors get their money refunded by the government.

convenu (FEM **convenue**) ADJECTIVE
agreed

□ au moment convenu at the agreed time

la **conversation** NOUN
conversation

la **convocation** NOUN
notification

convoquer VERB [28]

■ **convoquer quelqu'un à une réunion** to invite somebody to a meeting

■ **Le directeur m'a convoqué dans son bureau.** The headteacher asked me into his office.

cool (FEM+PL **cool**) ADJECTIVE (informal)
cool

la **coopération** NOUN
co-operation

coopérer VERB [34]
to co-operate

les **coordonnées** FEM PL NOUN
contact details

□ As-tu ses coordonnées? Do you have his contact details?

le **copain** NOUN (informal)
1 friend

□ C'est un bon copain. He's a good friend.

2 boyfriend

□ Elle a un copain. She's got a boyfriend.

la **copie** NOUN
1 copy

□ Ce tableau n'est qu'une copie. This

picture is only a copy.

2 paper

□ Il a des copies à corriger ce week-end. He's got some papers to mark this weekend.

copier VERB [19]
to copy

■ **copier-coller** to copy and paste

copieux (FEM **copieuse**) ADJECTIVE
hearty

□ un repas copieux a hearty meal

la **copine** NOUN (informal)
1 friend

□ Je sors avec une copine ce soir. I'm going out with a friend tonight.

2 girlfriend

□ Il a une copine. He's got a girlfriend.

le **coq** NOUN
cockerel

la **coque** NOUN
hull (of boat)

■ **un œuf à la coque** a soft-boiled egg

> **LANGUAGE TIP** Word for word, this means 'an egg in its shell'.

le **coquelicot** NOUN
poppy

la **coqueluche** NOUN
whooping cough

le **coquillage** NOUN
1 shellfish
2 shell

□ Nous avons ramassé des coquillages sur la plage. We picked up some shells on the beach.

la **coquille** NOUN
shell

■ **une coquille d'œuf** an eggshell

■ **une coquille Saint-Jacques** a scallop

coquin (FEM **coquine**) ADJECTIVE
cheeky

□ Il m'a regardé d'un air coquin. He gave me a cheeky look.

le **cor** NOUN
horn

□ Je joue du cor. I play the horn.

le **corbeau** (PL les **corbeaux**) NOUN
crow

la **corbeille** NOUN
1 basket

□ une corbeille de fruits a basket of fruit

2 recycle bin (of a computer)

■ **une corbeille à papier** a wastepaper basket

la **corde** NOUN
1 rope
2 string (of violin, tennis racket)

■ **une corde à linge** a clothes line

■ **pleuvoir des cordes** to be bucketing down

◯ **LANGUAGE TIP** Word for word, this means 'to be raining ropes'.

la **cordonnerie** NOUN
shoe repair shop

le **cordonnier** NOUN
cobbler

coriace (FEM **coriace**) ADJECTIVE
tough

la **corne** NOUN
horn

la **cornemuse** NOUN
bagpipes
□ jouer de la cornemuse to play the bagpipes

le **cornet** NOUN
■ **un cornet de frites** a bag of chips
■ **un cornet de glace** an ice cream cone

le **cornichon** NOUN
gherkin

la **Cornouailles** NOUN
Cornwall

le **corps** NOUN
body

correct (FEM **correcte**) ADJECTIVE
1 correct
□ Ce n'est pas tout à fait correct. That's not quite correct.
2 reasonable
□ un salaire correct a reasonable salary
□ Le repas était tout à fait correct. The meal was quite reasonable.

la **correction** NOUN
correction

la **correspondance** NOUN
1 correspondence
■ **un cours par correspondance** a correspondence course
2 connection (train, plane)
□ Il y a une correspondance pour Toulouse à dix heures. There's a connection for Toulouse at ten o'clock.

le **correspondant** NOUN
penfriend

la **correspondante** NOUN
penfriend

correspondre VERB [69]
to correspond
■ **Faites correspondre les phrases.** Match the sentences together.

le **corridor** NOUN
corridor

corriger VERB [45]
to mark
□ Vous pouvez corriger mon test? Can you mark my test?

le **corsage** NOUN

blouse

corse (FEM **corse**) ADJECTIVE, NOUN
Corsican
■ **un Corse** a Corsican (man)
■ **une Corse** a Corsican (woman)

la **Corse** NOUN
Corsica

la **corvée** NOUN
chore
□ Quelle corvée! What a chore!

costaud (FEM **costaude**) ADJECTIVE
brawny

le **costume** NOUN
1 suit (man's)
□ Il porte toujours un costume. He always wears a suit.
2 costume (theatre)
□ de superbes costumes superb costumes

la **côte** NOUN
1 coastline
□ La route longe la côte. The road follows the coastline.
■ **la Côte d'Azur** the French Riviera
2 hill
□ J'ai grimpé la côte. I went up the hill.
3 rib
□ Il s'est cassé une côte en tombant. He broke a rib when he fell.
4 chop
□ une côte de porc a pork chop
□ **une côte de bœuf** a rib of beef
■ **côte à côte** side by side

le **côté** NOUN
side
■ **à côté de 1** next to □ Le café est à côté du sucre. The coffee's next to the sugar.
2 next door to □ Il habite à côté de chez moi. He lives next door to me.
■ **de l'autre côté** on the other side □ La pharmacie est de l'autre côté de la rue. The chemist's is on the other side of the street.
■ **De quel côté est-il parti?** Which way did he go?
■ **mettre quelque chose de côté** to save something □ J'ai mis de l'argent de côté. I've saved some money.

la **côtelette** NOUN
chop
□ une côtelette d'agneau a lamb chop

la **cotisation** NOUN
1 subscription (to club, union)
2 contributions (to pension, national insurance)
■ **cotisations sociales** social security contributions

le **coton** NOUN
cotton
□ une chemise en coton a cotton shirt

■ **le coton hydrophile** cotton wool
le **Coton-tige®** (PL les **Cotons-tiges**) NOUN
cotton bud
le **cou** NOUN
neck
couchant (FEM **couchante**) ADJECTIVE
■ **le soleil couchant** the setting sun
la **couche** NOUN
1 layer
□ **la couche d'ozone** the ozone layer
2 coat (of paint, varnish)
3 nappy
couché (FEM **couchée**) ADJECTIVE
1 lying down
□ **Il était couché sur le tapis.** He was lying on the carpet.
2 in bed
□ **Il est déjà couché.** He's already in bed.
se **coucher** VERB [28]
▷ see also **coucher** NOUN
1 to go to bed
□ **Je me suis couché tard hier soir.** I went to bed late last night.
2 to set (sun)
le **coucher** NOUN
▷ see also **se coucher** VERB
■ **un coucher de soleil** a sunset
la **couchette** NOUN
1 couchette (on train)
2 bunk (on boat)
le **coude** NOUN
elbow
coudre VERB [15]
1 to sew
□ **J'aime coudre.** I like sewing.
2 to sew on
□ **Il ne sait même pas coudre un bouton.** He can't even sew a button on.
la **couette** NOUN
duvet
les **couettes** FEM PL NOUN
bunches
□ **la petite fille avec les couettes** the little girl with her hair in bunches
couler VERB [28]
1 to run
□ **Ne laissez pas couler les robinets.** Don't leave the taps running. □ **J'ai le nez qui coule.** My nose is running.
2 to flow
□ **La rivière coulait lentement.** The river was flowing slowly.
3 to leak
□ **Mon stylo coule.** My pen's leaking.
4 to sink
□ **Le bateau a coulé.** The boat sank.
la **couleur** NOUN

colour
□ **De quelle couleur est leur voiture?** What colour is their car? □ **une pellicule couleur** a colour film
■ **Tu as pris des couleurs.** You've got a tan.
la **couleuvre** NOUN
grass snake
les **coulisses** FEM PL NOUN
wings (in theatre)
■ **dans les coulisses** behind the scenes
le **couloir** NOUN
corridor
le **coup** NOUN
1 knock
□ **donner un coup à quelque chose** to give something a knock
2 blow
■ **Il m'a donné un coup!** He hit me!
■ **un coup de pied** a kick
■ **un coup de poing** a punch
3 shock
□ **Ça m'a fait un coup de le voir comme ça!** (informal) It gave me a shock to see him like that!
■ **un coup de feu** a shot
■ **un coup de fil** (informal) a ring □ **Je te donnerai un coup de fil demain.** I'll give you a ring tomorrow.
■ **donner un coup de main à quelqu'un** to give somebody a hand □ **Je viendrai te donner un coup de main.** I'll come and give you a hand.
■ **un coup d'œil** a quick look □ **jeter un coup d'œil** to have a quick look
■ **attraper un coup de soleil** to get sunburnt
■ **un coup de téléphone** a phone call
■ **un coup de tonnerre** a clap of thunder
■ **boire un coup** (informal) to have a drink
■ **après coup** afterwards □ **Après coup j'ai regretté de m'être mis en colère.** Afterwards I was sorry I'd got angry.
■ **à tous les coups** (informal) every time □ **Je me trompe de rue à tous les coups.** I get the street wrong every time.
■ **du premier coup** first time □ **Il a été reçu au permis du premier coup.** He passed his driving test first time.
■ **sur le coup** at first □ **Sur le coup je ne l'ai pas reconnu.** I didn't recognize him at first.
coupable (FEM **coupable**) ADJECTIVE
▷ see also **coupable** NOUN
guilty
le/la **coupable** NOUN
▷ see also **coupable** ADJECTIVE
culprit
la **coupe** NOUN

cup (sport)
□ la coupe du monde the World Cup
■ une coupe de cheveux a haircut
■ une coupe de champagne a glass of
champagne

le **coupe-ongle** NOUN
nail clippers

couper VERB [28]
1 to cut
2 to turn off
□ couper le courant to turn off the
electricity
3 to take a short-cut
□ On peut couper par la forêt. We could take
a short-cut through the woods.
■ couper l'appétit to spoil one's appetite
■ se couper to cut oneself □ Je me suis
coupé le doigt avec une boîte de conserve. I
cut my finger on a tin.
■ couper la parole à quelqu'un to
interrupt somebody

le **couple** NOUN
couple

le **couplet** NOUN
verse
□ le premier couplet the first verse

la **coupure** NOUN
cut
■ une coupure de courant a power cut

la **cour** NOUN
1 yard
□ la cour de l'école the school yard
2 court
□ la cour de Louis XIV the court of Louis XIV
□ la cour d'assises the criminal court

le **courage** NOUN
courage

courageux (FEM **courageuse**) ADJECTIVE
brave

couramment ADVERB
1 fluently
□ Elle parle couramment japonais. She
speaks Japanese fluently.
2 commonly
□ C'est une expression que l'on emploie
couramment. It's a commonly used phrase.

courant (FEM **courante**) ADJECTIVE
▷ see also **courant** NOUN
1 common
□ C'est une erreur courante. It's a common
mistake.
2 standard
□ C'est un modèle courant. It's a standard
model.

le **courant** NOUN
▷ see also **courant** ADJECTIVE
1 current (of river)

■ un courant d'air a draught
2 power
□ une panne de courant a power cut
■ Je le ferai dans le courant de la
semaine. I'll do it some time during the
week.
■ être au courant de quelque chose to
know about something □ Je n'étais pas au
courant de l'accident. I didn't know about
the accident.
■ mettre quelqu'un au courant de
quelque chose to tell somebody about
something
■ Tu es au courant? Have you heard about
it?
■ se tenir au courant de quelque chose
to keep up with something □ J'essaie de me
tenir au courant de l'actualité. I try to keep
up with the news.

le **coureur** NOUN
runner
■ un coureur à pied a runner
■ un coureur cycliste a racing cyclist
■ un coureur automobile a racing driver

la **coureuse** NOUN
runner

la **courgette** NOUN
courgette

courir VERB [16]
to run
□ Elle a traversé la rue en courant. She ran
across the street.
■ courir un risque to run a risk

la **couronne** NOUN
crown

courons, courez VERB ▷ see **courir**

le **courriel** NOUN
email

le **courrier** NOUN
mail
□ Est-ce qu'il y avait du courrier ce matin?
Was there any mail this morning?
■ N'oublie pas de poster le courrier.
Don't forget to post the letters.
■ le courrier électronique email
LANGUAGE TIP Be careful! The French
word **courrier** does not mean
courier.

la **courroie** NOUN
■ la courroie du ventilateur fan belt

le **cours** NOUN
1 lesson
□ un cours d'espagnol a Spanish lesson
□ des cours particuliers private lessons
2 course
□ un cours intensif a crash course
3 rate

□ le cours du change the exchange rate

■ **au cours de** during □ Il a été réveillé trois fois au cours de la nuit. He was woken up three times during the night.

la **course** NOUN

1 running

□ la course de fond long-distance running

2 race

□ une course hippique a horse race

3 shopping

□ J'ai juste une course à faire. I've just got a bit of shopping to do.

■ **faire les courses** to go shopping □ Elle est partie faire les courses de la semaine. She's gone to do her weekly shopping.

court (FEM **courte**) ADJECTIVE

▷ *see also* **court** NOUN

short

le **court** NOUN

▷ *see also* **court** ADJECTIVE

■ **un court de tennis** a tennis court

couru VERB ▷ *see* **courir**

le **couscous** NOUN

couscous

> **DID YOU KNOW...?**
> **couscous** is a spicy North African dish made with meat, vegetables and steamed semolina.

le **cousin** NOUN

cousin

la **cousine** NOUN

cousin

le **coussin** NOUN

cushion

le **coût** NOUN

cost

□ le coût de la vie the cost of living

le **couteau** (PL les **couteaux**) NOUN

knife

coûter VERB [28]

to cost

□ Est-ce que ça coûte cher? Does it cost a lot?

■ **Combien ça coûte?** How much is it?

coûteux (FEM **coûteuse**) ADJECTIVE

expensive

la **coutume** NOUN

custom

la **couture** NOUN

1 sewing

□ Je n'aime pas la couture. I don't like sewing.

■ **faire de la couture** to sew

2 seam

□ La couture de mon pantalon s'est défaite. The seam of my trousers has come undone.

le **couturier** NOUN

fashion designer

□ un grand couturier a top designer

la **couturière** NOUN

dressmaker

le **couvercle** NOUN

1 lid *(of pan)*

2 top *(of tube, jar, spray can)*

couvert VERB ▷ *see* **couvrir**

couvert (FEM **couverte**) ADJECTIVE

▷ *see also* **couvert** NOUN

1 covered

■ **couvert de** covered with □ Cet arbre est couvert de fleurs au printemps. This tree is covered with blossom in spring.

2 overcast *(sky)*

le **couvert** NOUN

▷ *see also* **couvert** ADJECTIVE

■ **mettre le couvert** to lay the table

les **couverts** MASC PL NOUN

cutlery

□ Les couverts sont dans le tiroir de gauche. The cutlery is in the left-hand drawer.

la **couverture** NOUN

blanket

le **couvre-lit** NOUN

bedspread

couvrir VERB [55]

to cover

□ Le chien est revenu couvert de boue. The dog came back covered with mud.

■ **se couvrir 1** to wrap up □ Couvre-toi bien: il fait très froid dehors. Wrap up well: it's very cold outside. **2** to cloud over □ Le ciel se couvre. The sky's clouding over.

le **crabe** NOUN

crab

cracher VERB [28]

to spit

le **crachin** NOUN

drizzle

la **craie** NOUN

chalk

craindre VERB [17]

to fear

□ Tu n'as rien à craindre. You've got nothing to fear.

la **crainte** NOUN

fear

■ **de crainte de** for fear of □ Il n'ose rien dire de crainte de la vexer. He daren't say anything for fear of upsetting her.

craintif (FEM **craintive**) ADJECTIVE

timid

la **crampe** NOUN

cramp

□ J'ai une crampe au mollet. I've got a cramp in my calf.

le **cran** NOUN
hole *(in belt)*
- **avoir du cran** *(informal)* to have guts

le **crâne** NOUN
skull

crâner VERB [28] *(informal)*
to show off

le **crapaud** NOUN
toad

craquer VERB [28]
1 to creak
□ Le plancher craque. The floor creaks.
2 to burst
□ Ma fermeture éclair a craqué. My zip's burst.
3 to crack up
□ Je vais finir par craquer! *(informal)* I'm going to crack up at this rate!
- **Quand j'ai vu cette robe, j'ai craqué!** *(informal)* When I saw that dress, I couldn't resist it!

la **crasse** NOUN
filth

la **cravate** NOUN
tie

le **crawl** NOUN
crawl
□ nager le crawl to do the crawl

le **crayon** NOUN
pencil
□ un crayon de couleur a coloured pencil
- **un crayon feutre** a felt-tip pen

la **création** NOUN
creation

la **crèche** NOUN
1 nursery
□ Elle dépose son fils à la crèche à huit heures. She leaves her son at the nursery at 8 o'clock.
2 nativity scene

le **crédit** NOUN
credit

créer VERB [18]
to create

la **crémaillère** NOUN
- **pendre la crémaillère** to have a house warming party

la **crème** NOUN
▷ *see also* **le crème**
cream
- **la crème anglaise** custard
- **la crème Chantilly** whipped cream
- **la crème fouettée** whipped cream
- **une crème caramel** a crème caramel
- **une crème au chocolat** a chocolate dessert

le **crème** NOUN

▷ *see also* **la crème**
white coffee
□ un grand crème a large white coffee

la **crémerie** NOUN
cheese shop

crémeux (FEM **crémeuse**) ADJECTIVE
creamy

la **crêpe** NOUN
pancake

la **crêperie** NOUN
pancake restaurant

le **crépuscule** NOUN
dusk

le **cresson** NOUN
watercress

la **Crète** NOUN
Crete

creuser VERB [28]
to dig *(a hole)*
- **Ça creuse!** That gives you a real appetite!
- **se creuser la cervelle** *(informal)* to rack one's brains

creux (FEM **creuse**) ADJECTIVE
hollow

la **crevaison** NOUN
puncture

crevé (FEM **crevée**) ADJECTIVE
1 punctured
□ un pneu crevé a puncture
2 knackered
□ Je suis complètement crevé! *(informal)* I'm completely knackered!

crever VERB [43]
1 to burst *(balloon)*
2 to have a puncture *(motorist)*
□ J'ai crevé sur l'autoroute. I had a puncture on the motorway.
- **Je crève de faim!** *(informal)* I'm starving!
- **Je crève de froid!** *(informal)* I'm freezing!

la **crevette** NOUN
prawn
- **une crevette rose** a prawn
- **une crevette grise** a shrimp

le **cri** NOUN
1 scream
□ J'ai entendu un cri. I heard a scream.
□ pousser des cris de douleur to scream with pain
2 call
□ Il sait reconnaître les cris des oiseaux. He can identify the calls of birds.
- **C'est le dernier cri.** It's the latest fashion. □ Ce haut est du dernier cri. This top is the latest fashion.

criard (FEM **criarde**) ADJECTIVE
garish *(colours)*

le **cric** NOUN

jack (for car)

crier VERB [19]
to shout
■ **crier de douleur** to scream with pain

le **crime** NOUN
1 crime
□ un crime de guerre a war crime
2 murder
□ Un crime a été commis ici. There was a murder here.

le **criminel** NOUN
1 criminal
□ un criminel de guerre a war criminal
2 murderer

la **criminelle** NOUN
1 criminal
2 murderer

le **crin** NOUN
horsehair

la **crinière** NOUN
mane

le **criquet** NOUN
grasshopper

la **crise** NOUN
1 crisis
■ **la crise économique** the recession
2 attack
□ une crise d'asthme an asthma attack
□ une crise cardiaque a heart attack
■ **une crise de foie** an upset stomach
■ **piquer une crise de nerfs** to go hysterical
■ **avoir une crise de fou rire** to have a fit of the giggles

le **cristal** (PL les **cristaux**) NOUN
crystal
□ un verre en cristal a crystal glass

le **critère** NOUN
criterion

critique (FEM **critique**) ADJECTIVE
▷ see also **critique** NOUN
critical

le **critique** NOUN
▷ see also **la critique** NOUN, **critique** ADJECTIVE
critic
□ un critique de cinéma a film critic

la **critique** NOUN
▷ see also **le critique** NOUN, **critique** ADJECTIVE
1 criticism
□ Elle ne supporte pas les critiques. She can't stand being criticized.
2 review
□ Le film a reçu de bonnes critiques. The film's had good reviews.

critiquer VERB [28]
to criticize

la **Croatie** NOUN

Croatia

le **crochet** NOUN
1 hook
2 detour
□ faire un crochet to make a detour
3 crochet
□ un pull au crochet a crocheted sweater

le **crocodile** NOUN
crocodile

croire VERB [20]
to believe
□ Il croit tout ce qu'on lui raconte. He believes everything he's told.
■ **croire que** to think that □ Tu crois qu'il fera meilleur demain? Do you think the weather will be better tomorrow?
■ **croire à quelque chose** to believe in something
■ **croire en Dieu** to believe in God

crois VERB ▷ see **croire**

croîs VERB ▷ see **croître**

le **croisement** NOUN
crossroads
□ Tournez à gauche au croisement. Turn left at the crossroads.

croiser VERB [28]
■ **J'ai croisé Anne-Laure dans la rue.** I bumped into Anne-Laure in the street.
■ **croiser les bras** to fold one's arms
■ **croiser les jambes** to cross one's legs
■ **se croiser** to pass each other □ Nous nous croisons dans l'escalier tous les matins. We pass each other on the stairs every morning.

la **croisière** NOUN
cruise

la **croissance** NOUN
growth

le **croissant** NOUN
croissant
□ un croissant au beurre a butter croissant

croit VERB ▷ see **croire**

croître VERB [21]
to grow

la **croix** NOUN
cross
■ **la Croix-Rouge** the Red Cross

le **croque-madame** (PL les **croque-madame**) NOUN
toasted ham and cheese sandwich with fried egg on top

le **croque-monsieur** (PL les **croque-monsieur**) NOUN
toasted ham and cheese sandwich

croquer VERB [28]
to munch
□ croquer une pomme to munch an apple

■ **le chocolat à croquer** plain chocolate

le **croquis** NOUN
sketch

la **crotte** NOUN
■ **une crotte de chien** dog dirt

le **crottin** NOUN
1 manure
□ **du crottin de cheval** horse manure
2 small goat's cheese

croustillant (FEM **croustillante**) ADJECTIVE
crusty

la **croûte** NOUN
1 crust (of bread)
■ **en croûte** in pastry
2 rind (of cheese)
3 scab (on skin)

le **croûton** NOUN
1 crust (end of loaf)
2 crouton
□ **des croûtons frottés d'ail** garlic croutons

croyons, croyez VERB ▷ see **croire**

les **CRS** MASC PL NOUN
French riot police

cru VERB ▷ see **croire**

cru (FEM **crue**) ADJECTIVE
raw
□ **la viande crue** raw meat
■ **le jambon cru** Parma ham

crû VERB ▷ see **croître**

la **cruauté** NOUN
cruelty

la **cruche** NOUN
jug

les **crudités** FEM PL NOUN
assorted raw vegetables

cruel (FEM **cruelle**) ADJECTIVE
cruel

les **crustacés** MASC PL NOUN
shellfish

le **cube** NOUN
cube
■ **un mètre cube** a cubic metre

la **cueillette** NOUN
picking
□ **la cueillette des champignons** mushroom picking

cueillir VERB [22]
to pick (flowers, fruit)

la **cuiller** NOUN
spoon
■ **une cuiller à café** a teaspoon
■ **une cuiller à soupe** a soup spoon

la **cuillère** NOUN
spoon
■ **une cuillère à café** a teaspoon
■ **une cuillère à soupe** a soup spoon

la **cuillerée** NOUN
spoonful

le **cuir** NOUN
leather
□ **un sac en cuir** a leather bag
■ **le cuir chevelu** the scalp

cuire VERB [23]
to cook
□ **cuire quelque chose à feu vif** to cook something on a high heat
■ **cuire quelque chose au four** to bake something
■ **cuire quelque chose à la vapeur** to steam something
■ **faire cuire** to cook □ 'Faire cuire pendant une heure' 'Cook for one hour'
■ **bien cuit** well done
■ **trop cuit** overdone

la **cuisine** NOUN
1 kitchen
2 cooking
□ **la cuisine française** French cooking
■ **faire la cuisine** to cook

cuisiné (FEM **cuisinée**) ADJECTIVE
■ **un plat cuisiné** a ready-made meal

cuisiner VERB [28]
to cook
□ **J'aime beaucoup cuisiner.** I love cooking.

le **cuisinier** NOUN
cook

la **cuisinière** NOUN
1 cook
2 cooker
□ **une cuisinière à gaz** a gas cooker

la **cuisse** NOUN
thigh
■ **une cuisse de poulet** a chicken leg

la **cuisson** NOUN
cooking
□ 'une heure de cuisson' 'cooking time: one hour'

cuit VERB ▷ see **cuire**

le **cuivre** NOUN
copper

le **culot** NOUN (informal)
cheek
□ **Quel culot!** What a cheek! □ **Il a un sacré culot!** He's got a damn cheek!

la **culotte** NOUN
knickers

la **culpabilité** NOUN
guilt

le **cultivateur** NOUN
farmer

la **cultivatrice** NOUN
farmer

cultivé (FEM **cultivée**) ADJECTIVE
cultured

C

□ Il est très cultivé. He's very cultured.

cultiver VERB [28]
to grow
□ Il cultive la vigne. He grows grapes.
■ **cultiver la terre** to farm the land

la **culture** NOUN
1 farming
□ les cultures intensives intensive farming
2 education
□ une bonne culture générale a good general education
■ **la culture physique** physical education

le **culturisme** NOUN
body-building

le **curé** NOUN
parish priest

le **cure-dent** NOUN
toothpick

curieux (FEM **curieuse**) ADJECTIVE
curious

la **curiosité** NOUN
curiosity

le **curriculum vitae** NOUN
CV

le **curseur** NOUN
cursor

la **cuvette** NOUN
bowl
□ une cuvette en plastique a plastic bowl

le **CV** NOUN (= curriculum vitae)
CV

le **cybercafé** NOUN
internet café

cyclable (FEM **cyclable**) ADJECTIVE
■ **une piste cyclable** a cycle track

le **cycle** NOUN
cycle

le **cyclisme** NOUN
cycling

le/la **cycliste** NOUN
cyclist

le **cyclomoteur** NOUN
moped

le **cyclone** NOUN
hurricane

le **cygne** NOUN
swan

Dd

d' PREPOSITION, ARTICLE ▷ *see* **de**

la **dactylo** NOUN
1 typist
   □ Elle est dactylo. She's a typist.
2 typing
   □ Je prends des cours de dactylo. I'm taking typing lessons.

le **daim** NOUN
   suede
   □ une veste en daim a suede jacket

la **dame** NOUN
1 lady
2 queen *(in cards, chess)*

les **dames** FEM PL NOUN
   draughts

le **Danemark** NOUN
   Denmark

le **danger** NOUN
   danger
   ■ **être en danger** to be in danger
   ■ **'Danger de mort'** 'Extremely dangerous'

dangereux (FEM **dangereuse**) ADJECTIVE
   dangerous

danois (FEM **danoise**) ADJECTIVE, NOUN
   Danish
   □ Il parle danois. He speaks Danish.
   ■ **un Danois** a Dane *(man)*
   ■ **une Danoise** a Dane *(woman)*
   ■ **les Danois** the Danish

dans PREPOSITION
1 in
   □ Il est dans sa chambre. He's in his bedroom. □ dans deux mois in two months' time
2 into
   □ Il est entré dans mon bureau. He came into my office.
3 out of
   □ On a bu dans des verres en plastique. We drank out of plastic glasses.

la **danse** NOUN
1 dance
   □ la danse moderne modern dance □ des danses folkloriques folk dances
   ■ **la danse classique** ballet
2 dancing
   □ des cours de danse dancing lessons

danser VERB [28]
   to dance

le **danseur** NOUN
   dancer

la **danseuse** NOUN
   dancer

la **date** NOUN
   date
   □ votre date de naissance your date of birth
   □ la date limite de vente the sell-by date
   ■ **un ami de longue date** an old friend

dater VERB [28]
   ■ **dater de** to date from □ Cette coutume date du moyen âge. This custom dates from the Middle Ages.

la **datte** NOUN
   date *(fruit)*

le **dauphin** NOUN
   dolphin

davantage ADVERB
   ■ **davantage de** more □ Il faudrait davantage de stages de formation. There should be more training courses.

de PREPOSITION, ARTICLE

> **LANGUAGE TIP** See also **du** (=de+le) and **des** (=de+les). **de** changes to **d'** before a vowel and most words beginning with 'h'.

1 of
   □ le toit de la maison the roof of the house □ la voiture de Paul Paul's car □ la voiture de mes parents my parents' car □ la voiture d'Hélène Hélène's car □ deux bouteilles de vin two bottles of wine □ un litre d'essence a litre of petrol
   ■ **un bébé d'un an** a one-year-old baby
   ■ **un billet de cinquante euros** a 50-euro note
2 from
   □ de Londres à Paris from London to Paris □ Il vient de Londres. He comes from London. □ une lettre de Victor a letter from Victor

3 by

□ augmenter de dix euros to increase by ten euros

> **LANGUAGE TIP** You use **de** to form expressions with the meaning of 'some' and 'any'.

■ **Je voudrais de l'eau.** I'd like some water.

■ **du pain et de la confiture** bread and jam

■ **Il n'a pas de famille.** He hasn't got any family.

■ **Il n'y a plus de biscuits.** There aren't any more biscuits.

le **dé** NOUN

1 dice

2 thimble

le **dealer** NOUN (informal)
drug-pusher

déballer VERB [28]
to unpack

le **débardeur** NOUN
tank top

débarquer VERB [28]
to disembark

□ Nous avons dû débarquer à Marseille. We had to disembark at Marseilles.

■ **débarquer chez quelqu'un** (informal) to descend on somebody □ Ils ont débarqué chez nous à dix heures du soir. They descended on us at ten o'clock at night.

le **débarras** NOUN
junk room

■ **Bon débarras!** Good riddance!

débarrasser VERB [28]
to clear

□ Tu peux débarrasser la table, s'il te plaît? Can you clear the table please?

■ **se débarrasser de quelque chose** to get rid of something □ Je me suis débarrassé de mon vieux frigo. I got rid of my old fridge.

le **débat** NOUN
debate

se **débattre** VERB [9]
to struggle

débile (FEM **débile**) ADJECTIVE
crazy

□ C'est complètement débile! (informal) That's totally crazy!

débordé (FEM **débordée**) ADJECTIVE

■ **être débordé** to be snowed under

déborder VERB [28]
to overflow (river)

■ **déborder d'énergie** to be full of energy

le **débouché** NOUN
job prospect

□ Quels débouchés y a-t-il après ces études? What are the job prospects after this course?

déboucher VERB [28]

1 to unblock (sink, pipe)

2 to open (bottle)

■ **déboucher sur** to lead into □ La rue débouche sur une place. The street leads into a square.

debout ADVERB

1 standing up

□ Il a mangé ses céréales debout. He ate his cereal standing up.

2 upright

□ Mets les livres debout sur l'étagère. Put the books upright on the shelf.

3 up

□ Tu es déjà debout? Are you up already?

■ **Debout!** Get up!

déboutonner VERB [28]
to unbutton

débraillé (FEM **débraillée**) ADJECTIVE
sloppily dressed

débrancher VERB [28]
to unplug

le **débris** NOUN

■ **des débris de verre** bits of glass

débrouillard (FEM **débrouillarde**) ADJECTIVE
streetwise

se **débrouiller** VERB [28]
to manage

□ C'était difficile, mais je ne me suis pas trop mal débrouillé. It was difficult, but I managed OK.

■ **Débrouille-toi tout seul.** Sort things out for yourself.

le **début** NOUN
beginning

□ au début at the beginning

■ **début mai** in early May

le **débutant** NOUN
beginner

la **débutante** NOUN
beginner

débuter VERB [28]
to start

décaféiné (FEM **décaféinée**) ADJECTIVE
decaffeinated

le **décalage horaire** NOUN
time difference (between time zones)

□ Il y a une heure de décalage horaire entre la France et la Grande-Bretagne. There's an hour's time difference between France and Britain.

décalquer VERB [28]
to trace

décapiter VERB [28]
to behead

décapotable (FEM **décapotable**) ADJECTIVE
convertible

décapsuler VERB [28]
- **décapsuler une bouteille** to take the top off a bottle

le **décapsuleur** NOUN
bottle-opener

décéder VERB [34]
to die
□ Son père est décédé il y a trois ans. His father died three years ago.

décembre MASC NOUN
December
- **en décembre** in December

décemment ADVERB
decently

décent (FEM **décente**) ADJECTIVE
decent

la **déception** NOUN
disappointment

décerner VERB [28]
to award

le **décès** NOUN
death

décevant (FEM **décevante**) ADJECTIVE
disappointing
□ Ses résultats sont plutôt décevants. His results are rather disappointing.

décevoir VERB [67]
to disappoint

décharger VERB [45]
to unload

se **déchausser** VERB [28]
to take off one's shoes

les **déchets** MASC PL NOUN
waste
□ les déchets nucléaires nuclear waste
□ les déchets toxiques toxic waste

déchiffrer VERB [28]
to decipher

déchirant (FEM **déchirante**) ADJECTIVE
heart-rending

déchirer VERB [28]
1 to tear (clothes)
2 to tear up
□ déchirer une lettre to tear up a letter
3 to tear out
□ déchirer une page d'un livre to tear a page out of a book
- **se déchirer** to tear □ se déchirer un muscle to tear a muscle

la **déchirure** NOUN
tear (rip)
- **une déchirure musculaire** a torn muscle

décidé (FEM **décidée**) ADJECTIVE
determined
- **C'est décidé.** It's decided.

décidément ADVERB
certainly

□ Décidément, je n'ai pas de chance aujourd'hui. I'm certainly not having much luck today.

décider VERB [28]
to decide
- **décider de faire quelque chose** to decide to do something □ Ils ont décidé de rester. They decided to stay.
- **se décider** to make up one's mind □ Elle n'arrive pas à se décider. She can't make up her mind.

décisif (FEM **décisive**) ADJECTIVE
decisive

la **décision** NOUN
decision

la **déclaration** NOUN
statement
□ Je n'ai aucune déclaration à faire. I have no statement to make.
- **faire une déclaration de vol** to report something as stolen

déclarer VERB [28]
to declare
□ déclarer la guerre à un pays to declare war on a country
- **se déclarer** to break out □ Le feu s'est déclaré dans la cantine. The fire broke out in the canteen.

déclencher VERB [28]
to set off (alarm, explosion)
- **se déclencher** to go off

le **déclic** NOUN
click

décoiffé (FEM **décoiffée**) ADJECTIVE
- **Elle était toute décoiffée.** Her hair was in a real mess.

le **décollage** NOUN
takeoff (of plane)

décollé (FEM **décollée**) ADJECTIVE
- **avoir les oreilles décollées** to have sticking-out ears

décoller VERB [28]
1 to unstick
□ décoller une étiquette to unstick a label
- **se décoller** to come unstuck
2 to take off
□ L'avion a décollé avec dix minutes de retard. The plane took off ten minutes late.

décolleté (FEM **décolletée**) ADJECTIVE
▷ see also **décolleté** NOUN
low-cut

le **décolleté** NOUN
▷ see also **décolleté** ADJECTIVE
- **un décolleté plongeant** a plunging neckline

se **décolorer** VERB [28]
to fade

□ Ce T-shirt s'est décoloré au lavage. This T-shirt has faded in the wash.

■ **se faire décolorer les cheveux** to have one's hair bleached

les **décombres** MASC PL NOUN
rubble

se **décommander** VERB [28]
to cry off

□ Elle devait venir mais elle s'est décommandée à la dernière minute. She was supposed to be coming, but she cried off at the last minute.

déconcerté (FEM **déconcertée**) ADJECTIVE
disconcerted

décongeler VERB [1]
to thaw

se **déconnecter** VERB [28]
to log out

déconseiller VERB [28]

■ **déconseiller à quelqu'un de faire quelque chose** to advise somebody not to do something □ Je lui ai déconseillé d'y aller. I advised him not to go.

■ **C'est déconseillé.** It's not recommended.

décontenancé (FEM **décontenancée**) ADJECTIVE
disconcerted

décontracté (FEM **décontractée**) ADJECTIVE
relaxed

■ **s'habiller décontracté** to dress casually

se **décontracter** VERB [28]
to relax

□ Il est allé faire du footing pour se décontracter. He went jogging to relax.

le **décor** NOUN
décor

le **décorateur** NOUN
interior decorator

la **décoration** NOUN
decoration

la **décoratrice** NOUN
interior decorator

décorer VERB [28]
to decorate

les **décors** MASC PL NOUN
1 scenery (in play)
2 set (in film)

décortiquer VERB [28]
to shell

■ **des crevettes décortiquées** peeled shrimps

découdre VERB [15]
to unpick

■ **se découdre** to come unstitched

découper VERB [28]
1 to cut out

□ J'ai découpé cet article dans le journal. I cut this article out of the paper.
2 to carve (meat)

décourageant (FEM **décourageante**) ADJECTIVE
discouraging

décourager VERB [45]
to discourage

■ **se décourager** to get discouraged
■ **Ne te décourage pas!** Don't give up!

décousu (FEM **décousue**) ADJECTIVE
unstitched

□ L'ourlet est décousu. The hem's come unstitched.

le **découvert** NOUN
overdraft

la **découverte** NOUN
discovery

découvrir VERB [55]
to discover

décrire VERB [30]
to describe

le **décrochage** NOUN

■ **le décrochage scolaire** truancy

décrocher VERB [28]
1 to take down

□ Tu peux m'aider à décrocher les rideaux? Can you help me take down the curtains?
2 to pick up the phone

□ Il a décroché et a composé le numéro. He picked up the phone and dialled the number.

■ **décrocher le téléphone** to take the phone off the hook

déçu VERB
disappointed

dédaigneux (FEM **dédaigneuse**) ADJECTIVE
disdainful

□ d'un air dédaigneux disdainfully

le **dédain** NOUN
disdain

□ avec dédain with disdain

dedans ADVERB
inside

□ C'est une jolie boîte: qu'est-ce qu'il y a dedans? That's a nice box: what's in it?

■ **là-dedans 1** in there □ J'ai trouvé les clés là-dedans. I found the keys in there. **2** in that □ Il y a du vrai là-dedans. There's some truth in that.

dédicacé (FEM **dédicacée**) ADJECTIVE

■ **un exemplaire dédicacé** a signed copy

dédier VERB [19]
to dedicate

déduire VERB [23]
to take off

□ Tu as déduit les vingt euros que je te

devais? Did you take off the twenty euros I owed you?

■ **J'en déduis qu'il m'a menti.** That means he must have been lying.

défaire VERB [36]
to undo

■ **défaire sa valise** to unpack
■ **se défaire** to come undone

la **défaite** NOUN
defeat

le **défaut** NOUN
fault

défavorable (FEM **défavorable**) ADJECTIVE
unfavourable

défavorisé (FEM **défavorisée**) ADJECTIVE
underprivileged

défectueux (FEM **défectueuse**) ADJECTIVE
faulty

défendre VERB [88]
1 to forbid

■ **défendre à quelqu'un de faire quelque chose** to forbid somebody to do something □ Sa mère lui a défendu de le revoir. Her mother forbade her to see him again.
2 to defend

□ défendre ses idées to defend your ideas
□ défendre quelqu'un to defend somebody

défendu (FEM **défendue**) ADJECTIVE
forbidden

□ C'est défendu. It's forbidden.

la **défense** NOUN
1 defence

■ **prendre la défense de quelqu'un** to back somebody up
■ **'défense de fumer'** 'no smoking'
2 tusk *(of elephant)*

le **défi** NOUN
challenge

■ **d'un air de défi** defiantly
■ **sur un ton de défi** defiantly

défier VERB [19]
1 to challenge

□ Je te défie de trouver un meilleur exemple. I challenge you to find a better example.
2 to dare

□ Il m'a défié d'aller à l'école en pyjama. He dared me to go to school in my pyjamas.

défigurer VERB [28]
to disfigure

le **défilé** NOUN
1 parade

■ **un défilé de mode** a fashion show
2 march

défiler VERB [28]
to march

définir VERB [38]
to define

définitif (FEM **définitive**) ADJECTIVE
final

■ **en définitive** in the end □ En définitive, ils ont décidé de rester. In the end, they decided to stay.

définitivement ADVERB
for good

□ Elle s'est définitivement installée en Écosse en 2004. She settled in Scotland for good in 2004.

déformer VERB [28]
to stretch

□ Ne tire pas sur ton pull, tu vas le déformer. Don't pull at your sweater, you'll stretch it.

■ **se déformer** to stretch □ Ce T-shirt s'est déformé au lavage. This T-shirt has stretched in the wash.

se **défouler** VERB [28]
to unwind

□ Je fais de l'aérobic pour me défouler. I do aerobics to unwind.

dégagé (FEM **dégagée**) ADJECTIVE
■ **d'un air dégagé** casually
■ **sur un ton dégagé** casually

dégager VERB [45]
1 to free

□ Ils ont mis une heure à dégager les victimes. They took an hour to free the victims.
2 to clear

□ des gouttes qui dégagent le nez drops to clear your nose

■ **Ça se dégage.** *(weather)* It's clearing up.

se **dégarnir** VERB [38]
to go bald

les **dégâts** MASC PL NOUN
damage

le **dégel** NOUN
thaw

dégeler VERB [1]
to thaw

□ faire dégeler un poulet congelé to thaw out a frozen chicken

dégivrer VERB [28]
1 to defrost
2 to de-ice

dégonfler VERB [28]
to let down

□ Quelqu'un a dégonflé mes pneus. Somebody let down my tyres.

■ **se dégonfler** *(informal)* to chicken out

dégouliner VERB [28]
to trickle

dégourdi (FEM **dégourdie**) ADJECTIVE
smart

□ Il n'est pas très dégourdi. He's pretty clueless.

dégourdir – délice

dégourdir VERB [38]
- **se dégourdir les jambes** to stretch one's legs

le **dégoût** NOUN
disgust
- □ une expression de dégoût a disgusted expression
- **avec dégoût** disgustedly

dégoûtant (FEM **dégoûtante**) ADJECTIVE
disgusting

dégoûté (FEM **dégoûtée**) ADJECTIVE
disgusted
- **être dégoûté de tout** to be sick of everything

dégoûter VERB [28]
to disgust
- □ Ce genre de comportement me dégoûte. That kind of behaviour disgusts me.
- **dégoûter quelqu'un de quelque chose** to put somebody off something □ Ça m'a dégoûté de la viande. That put me off meat.

se **dégrader** VERB [28]
to deteriorate

le **degré** NOUN
degree
- **de l'alcool à 90 degrés** surgical spirit

dégringoler VERB [28]
1 to rush down
- □ Il a dégringolé l'escalier. He rushed down the stairs.
2 to collapse
- □ Elle a fait dégringoler la pile de livres. She knocked over the stack of books.

le **déguisement** NOUN
disguise

déguiser VERB [28]
- **se déguiser en quelque chose** to dress up as something □ Elle s'était déguisée en vampire. She was dressed up as a vampire.

la **dégustation** NOUN
tasting

déguster VERB [28]
1 to taste (food, wine)
2 to enjoy

dehors ADVERB
outside
- □ Je t'attends dehors. I'll wait for you outside.
- **jeter quelqu'un dehors** to throw somebody out
- **en dehors de** apart from □ En dehors de lui, tout le monde était content. Apart from him, everybody was happy.

déjà ADVERB
1 already
- □ J'ai déjà fini. I've already finished.
2 before

- □ Tu es déjà venu en France? Have you been to France before?

déjeuner VERB [28]
- ▷ see also **déjeuner** NOUN
to have lunch

le **déjeuner** NOUN
- ▷ see also **déjeuner** VERB
lunch

le **délai** NOUN
1 extension
- □ J'ai demandé un délai d'une semaine. I've asked for a week's extension.
2 time limit
- □ être dans les délais to be within the time limit

> **LANGUAGE TIP** Be careful! **délai** does not mean **delay**.

délasser VERB [28]
to relax
- □ La lecture délasse. Reading's relaxing.
- **se délasser** to relax □ J'ai pris un bain pour me délasser. I had a bath to relax.

délavé (FEM **délavée**) ADJECTIVE
faded
- □ un jean délavé a pair of faded jeans

le **délégué** NOUN
representative
- □ les délégués de classe the class representatives

> **DID YOU KNOW...?**
> In French schools, each class elects two representatives or **délégués de classe**, one boy and one girl.

la **déléguée** NOUN
representative

déléguer VERB [34]
to delegate

délibéré (FEM **délibérée**) ADJECTIVE
deliberate

délicat (FEM **délicate**) ADJECTIVE
1 delicate
- □ avoir la peau délicate to have delicate skin
2 tricky
- □ une situation délicate a tricky situation
3 tactful
- □ Il est toujours très délicat. He's always very tactful.
4 thoughtful
- □ C'est une attention délicate de sa part. That was thoughtful on his part.

délicatement ADVERB
1 gently
2 tactfully

le **délice** NOUN
delight
- □ Vivre ici est un vrai délice. Living here is a real delight.

■ **Ce gâteau est un vrai délice.** This cake's a real treat.

délicieux (FEM **délicieuse**) ADJECTIVE
delicious

la **délinquance** NOUN
crime

□ de nouvelles mesures pour combattre la petite délinquance new measures to fight petty crime

■ **la délinquance juvénile** juvenile delinquency

le **délinquant** NOUN
criminal

la **délinquante** NOUN
criminal

délirer VERB [28]
■ **Mais tu délires!** (informal) You're crazy!

le **délit** NOUN
criminal offence

délivrer VERB [28]
to set free (prisoner)

le **deltaplane** NOUN
hang-glider

■ **faire du deltaplane** to go hang-gliding

demain ADVERB
tomorrow

■ **À demain!** See you tomorrow!

la **demande** NOUN
request

■ **une demande en mariage** an offer of marriage

■ **'demandes d'emploi'** 'situations wanted'

demandé (FEM **demandée**) ADJECTIVE
■ **très demandé** very much in demand

demander VERB [28]
1 to ask for
□ J'ai demandé la permission. I've asked for permission. □ On a demandé notre chemin à un chauffeur de taxi. We asked a taxi driver the way. □ Je lui ai demandé de m'aider. I asked him to help me.

2 to require
□ un travail qui demande beaucoup de temps a job that requires a lot of time

■ **se demander** to wonder □ Je me demande à quelle heure il va venir. I wonder what time he'll come.

⌁ **LANGUAGE TIP** Be careful! demander does not mean **to demand**.

le **demandeur d'asile** NOUN
asylum seeker

le **demandeur d'emploi** NOUN
job-seeker

la **demandeuse d'asile** NOUN
asylum seeker

la **demandeuse d'emploi** NOUN
job-seeker

la **démangeaison** NOUN
itching

démanger VERB [45]
to itch
□ Ça me démange. It itches.

le **démaquillant** NOUN
make-up remover

démaquiller VERB [28]
■ **se démaquiller** to remove one's make-up

la **démarche** NOUN
1 walk
□ Il a une drôle de démarche. He's got a funny walk.

2 step
□ faire les démarches nécessaires pour obtenir quelque chose to take the necessary steps to obtain something

démarrer VERB [28]
to start (car)

démêler VERB [28]
to untangle

le **déménagement** NOUN
move
□ C'était le jour de notre déménagement. It was the day we moved house.

■ **un camion de déménagement** a removal van

déménager VERB [45]
to move house

le **déménageur** NOUN
removal man

dément (FEM **démente**) ADJECTIVE
crazy

démentiel (FEM **démentielle**) ADJECTIVE
insane

demeurer VERB [28]
to live

demi (FEM **demie**) ADJECTIVE, ADVERB
▷ see also **demi** NOUN
half
□ Il a trois ans et demi. He's three and a half.

■ **Il est trois heures et demie.** It's half past three.

■ **Il est midi et demi.** It's half past twelve.

■ **à demi endormi** half-asleep

le **demi** NOUN
▷ see also **demi** ADJECTIVE
half pint of beer

■ **Un demi, s'il vous plaît!** A beer please!

la **demi-baguette** NOUN
half a baguette

le **demi-cercle** NOUN
semicircle

la **demi-douzaine** NOUN

half-dozen

□ une demi-douzaine d'œufs half a dozen eggs

la **demie** NOUN
half-hour
□ Le bus passe à la demie. The bus comes by on the half-hour.

demi-écrémé (FEM **demi-écrémée**) ADJECTIVE
semi-skimmed

la **demi-finale** NOUN
semi-final

le **demi-frère** NOUN
half-brother

la **demi-heure** NOUN
half an hour
□ dans une demi-heure in half an hour
□ toutes les demi-heures every half an hour

la **demi-journée** NOUN
half-day
□ On peut louer un parasol à la demi-journée. You can hire a sun umbrella for a half-day.

le **demi-litre** NOUN
half litre
□ un demi-litre de lait half a litre of milk

la **demi-livre** NOUN
half-pound
□ une demi-livre de tomates half a pound of tomatoes

la **demi-pension** NOUN
half board
□ Cet hôtel propose des tarifs raisonnables en demi-pension. This hotel has reasonable rates for half board.

le/la **demi-pensionnaire** NOUN
■ être demi-pensionnaire to have school lunches

demi-sel (FEM+PL **demi-sel**) ADJECTIVE
■ du beurre demi-sel slightly salted butter

la **demi-sœur** NOUN
half-sister

la **démission** NOUN
resignation
■ donner sa démission to resign

démissionner VERB [28]
to resign

le **demi-tarif** NOUN
1 half-price
□ un billet à demi-tarif a half-price season ticket
2 half-fare
□ voyager à demi-tarif to travel half-fare

le **demi-tour** NOUN
■ faire demi-tour to turn back □ La nuit commence à tomber; il est temps de faire demi-tour. It's getting dark; it's time we turned back.

la **démocratie** NOUN
democracy

démocratique (FEM **démocratique**) ADJECTIVE
democratic

démodé (FEM **démodée**) ADJECTIVE
old-fashioned

la **demoiselle** NOUN
young lady
■ une demoiselle d'honneur a bridesmaid

démolir VERB [38]
to demolish

le **démon** NOUN
devil

démonter VERB [28]
1 to take down (tent)
2 to take apart (machine)

démontrer VERB [28]
to show

dénoncer VERB [12]
to denounce
■ se dénoncer to give oneself up □ Il s'est dénoncé à la police. He gave himself up to the police.

le **dénouement** NOUN
outcome

la **densité** NOUN
density

la **dent** NOUN
tooth
□ une dent de lait a milk tooth □ une dent de sagesse a wisdom tooth

dentaire (FEM **dentaire**) ADJECTIVE
dental

la **dentelle** NOUN
lace
□ un chemisier en dentelle a lacy blouse

le **dentier** NOUN
denture

le **dentifrice** NOUN
toothpaste

le/la **dentiste** NOUN
dentist

le **déodorant** NOUN
deodorant

le **dépannage** NOUN
■ un service de dépannage a breakdown service

dépanner VERB [28]
1 to fix
□ Il a dépanné la voiture en cinq minutes. He fixed the car in five minutes.
2 to help out
□ Il m'a prêté dix euros pour me dépanner. (informal) He lent me 10 euros to help me out.

la **dépanneuse** NOUN
breakdown lorry

le **départ** NOUN
departure
□ Le départ est à onze heures. The departure is at 11.
■ **Je lui téléphonerai la veille de son départ.** I'll phone him the day before he leaves.

le **département** NOUN
1 department
□ le département d'anglais à l'université the English department at the university
2 administrative area
□ le département du Vaucluse the Vaucluse region

> **DID YOU KNOW...?**
> France is divided into 96 **départements**, administrative areas rather like counties.

dépasser VERB [58]
1 to overtake
□ Il y a une voiture qui essaie de nous dépasser. There's a car trying to overtake us.
2 to pass
□ Nous avons dépassé Dijon. We've passed Dijon.
3 to exceed (sum, limit)

dépaysé (FEM **dépaysée**) ADJECTIVE
■ **se sentir un peu dépaysé** to feel a bit lost

se **dépêcher** VERB [28]
to hurry
□ Dépêche-toi! Hurry up!

dépendre VERB [88]
■ **dépendre de** to depend on □ Ça dépend du temps. It depends on the weather.
■ **dépendre de quelqu'un** to be dependent on somebody
■ **Ça dépend.** It depends.

dépenser VERB [28]
to spend (money)

dépensier (FEM **dépensière**) ADJECTIVE
■ **Il est dépensier.** He's a big spender.
■ **Elle n'est pas dépensière.** She's not exactly extravagant.

dépilatoire (FEM **dépilatoire**) ADJECTIVE
■ **une crème dépilatoire** a hair-removing cream

le **dépit** NOUN
■ **en dépit de** in spite of □ Il y est allé en dépit de mes conseils. He went in spite of my advice.

déplacé (FEM **déplacée**) ADJECTIVE
uncalled-for
□ C'était une remarque déplacée. That remark was uncalled-for.

le **déplacement** NOUN
trip
□ Ça vaut le déplacement. It's worth the trip.

déplacer VERB [12]
1 to move
□ Tu peux m'aider à déplacer la table? Can you help me move the table?
2 to put off
□ déplacer un rendez-vous to put off an appointment
■ **se déplacer 1** to travel around □ Il se déplace beaucoup pour son travail. He travels around a lot for his work. **2** to get around □ Il a du mal à se déplacer. He has difficulty getting around.
■ **se déplacer une vertèbre** to slip a disc

déplaire VERB [62]
■ **Cela me déplaît.** I dislike this.

déplaisant (FEM **déplaisante**) ADJECTIVE
unpleasant

le **dépliant** NOUN
leaflet

déplier VERB [19]
to unfold

déposer VERB [28]
1 to leave
□ J'ai déposé mon sac à la consigne. I left my bag at the left-luggage office.
2 to put down
□ Déposez le paquet sur la table. Put the parcel down on the table.
■ **déposer quelqu'un** to drop somebody off

dépourvu (FEM **dépourvue**) ADJECTIVE
■ **prendre quelqu'un au dépourvu** to take somebody by surprise □ Sa question m'a pris au dépourvu. His question took me by surprise.

la **dépression** NOUN
depression
■ **faire de la dépression** to be suffering from depression
■ **faire une dépression** to have a breakdown

déprimant (FEM **déprimante**) ADJECTIVE
depressing

déprimer VERB [28]
to get depressed
□ Il déprime tout le temps. He gets depressed all the time. □ Ce genre de temps me déprime. This kind of weather makes me depressed.

depuis PREPOSITION, ADVERB
1 since
□ Il habite Paris depuis 1983. He's been

living in Paris since 1983. □ Je ne lui ai pas parlé depuis. I haven't spoken to him since.
■ **depuis que** since □ Il a plu tous les jours depuis qu'elle est arrivée. It's rained every day since she arrived.

2 for
□ Il habite Paris depuis cinq ans. He's been living in Paris for five years.
■ **Depuis combien de temps?** How long?
□ Depuis combien de temps est-ce que vous le connaissez? How long have you known him?
■ **Depuis quand?** How long? □ Depuis quand est-ce que vous le connaissez? How long have you known him?

le **député** NOUN
Member of Parliament

la **députée** NOUN
Member of Parliament

déraciner VERB [28]
to uproot

le **dérangement** NOUN
■ **en dérangement** out of order □ Le téléphone est en dérangement. The phone's out of order.

déranger VERB [45]
1 to bother
□ Excusez-moi de vous déranger. I'm sorry to bother you.
■ **Ne vous dérangez pas, je vais répondre au téléphone.** You stay there, I'll answer the phone.
2 to mess up
□ Ne dérange pas mes livres, s'il te plaît. Don't mess up my books, please.

déraper VERB [28]
to skid

le/la **dermatologue** NOUN
dermatologist
□ Elle est dermatologue. She's a dermatologist.

dernier (FEM **dernière**) ADJECTIVE
1 last
□ Il est arrivé dernier. He arrived last. □ la dernière fois the last time
2 latest
□ le dernier film de Spielberg Spielberg's latest film
■ **en dernier** last □ Ajoutez le lait en dernier. Put the milk in last.

dernièrement ADVERB
recently

dérouler VERB [28]
1 to unroll
2 to unwind
■ **se dérouler** to take place □ L'action se déroule dans les années vingt. The action

takes place in the 1920s.
■ **Tout s'est déroulé comme prévu.** Everything went as planned.

derrière ADVERB, PREPOSITION
▷ see also **derrière** NOUN
behind

le **derrière** NOUN
▷ see also **derrière** ADVERB
1 back
□ la porte de derrière the back door
2 backside
□ un coup de pied dans le derrière a kick up the backside

des ARTICLE
LANGUAGE TIP **des** is the contracted form of **de + les**.
1 some
□ Tu veux des chips? Would you like some crisps?
LANGUAGE TIP **des** is sometimes not translated.
□ J'ai des cousins en France. I have cousins in France. □ pendant des mois for months
2 any
□ Tu as des frères? Have you got any brothers? □ la fin des vacances the end of the holidays □ la voiture des Durand the Durands' car □ Il arrive des États-Unis. He's arriving from the United States.

dès PREPOSITION
as early as
□ dès le mois de novembre from November
■ **dès le début** right from the start
■ **Il vous appellera dès son retour.** He'll call you as soon as he gets back.
■ **dès que** as soon as □ Il m'a reconnu dès qu'il m'a vu. He recognized me as soon as he saw me.

désabusé (FEM **désabusée**) ADJECTIVE
disillusioned

le **désaccord** NOUN
disagreement

désagréable (FEM **désagréable**) ADJECTIVE
unpleasant

désaltérer VERB [34]
■ **L'eau gazeuse désaltère bien.** Sparkling water is very thirst-quenching.
■ **se désaltérer** to quench one's thirst
□ Nous sommes allés dans un café pour nous désaltérer. We went into a café to have a drink.

désapprobateur (FEM **désapprobatrice**) ADJECTIVE
disapproving
□ un regard désapprobateur a disapproving look

le **désastre** NOUN

disaster

le **désavantage** NOUN
disadvantage

désavantager VERB [45]

■ **désavantager quelqu'un** to put somebody at a disadvantage □ Cette nouvelle loi va désavantager les femmes. The new law will put women at a disadvantage.

descendre VERB [24]

1 to go down
□ Je suis tombé en descendant l'escalier. I fell as I was going down the stairs.

2 to come down
□ Attends en bas; je descends! Wait downstairs; I'm coming down!

3 to get down
□ Vous pouvez descendre ma valise, s'il vous plaît? Can you get my suitcase down, please?

4 to get off
□ Nous descendons à la prochaine station. We're getting off at the next station.

la **descente** NOUN
way down
□ Je t'attendrai au bas de la descente. I'll wait for you at the bottom of the hill.

■ **une descente de police** a police raid

la **description** NOUN
description

déséquilibré (FEM **déséquilibrée**) ADJECTIVE
unbalanced

déséquilibrer VERB [28]

■ **déséquilibrer quelqu'un** to throw somebody off balance □ Le coup de poing l'a déséquilibré. The punch threw him off balance.

désert (FEM **déserte**) ADJECTIVE
▷ see also **désert** NOUN
deserted
□ Le dimanche, le centre commercial est désert. On Sundays, the shopping centre is deserted.

■ **une île déserte** a desert island

le **désert** NOUN
▷ see also **désert** ADJECTIVE
desert

déserter VERB [28]
to desert

désertique (FEM **désertique**) ADJECTIVE
desert
□ une région désertique a desert region

désespéré (FEM **désespérée**) ADJECTIVE
desperate

désespérer VERB [34]
to despair
□ Il ne faut pas désespérer. Don't despair.

le **désespoir** NOUN
despair

déshabiller VERB [28]
to undress

■ **se déshabiller** to get undressed

déshériter VERB [28]
to disinherit

■ **les déshérités** the underprivileged

déshydraté (FEM **déshydratée**) ADJECTIVE
dehydrated

désigner VERB [28]
to choose
□ On l'a désignée pour remettre le prix. She was chosen to present the prize.

■ **désigner quelque chose du doigt** to point at something

le **désinfectant** NOUN
disinfectant

désinfecter VERB [28]
to disinfect

désintéressé (FEM **désintéressée**) ADJECTIVE

1 unselfish
□ un acte désintéressé an unselfish action

2 impartial
□ un conseil désintéressé impartial advice

désintéresser VERB [28]

■ **se désintéresser de quelque chose** to lose interest in something

le **désir** NOUN

1 wish
□ Vos désirs sont des ordres. Your wish is my command.

2 will
□ le désir de réussir the will to succeed

3 desire
□ Ses yeux brillaient de désir. Her eyes were shining with desire.

désirer VERB [28]
to want
□ Vous désirez? (in shop) What would you like?

désobéir VERB [38]

■ **désobéir à quelqu'un** to disobey somebody

désobéissant (FEM **désobéissante**) ADJECTIVE
disobedient

désobligeant (FEM **désobligeante**) ADJECTIVE
unpleasant
□ faire une remarque désobligeante to make an unpleasant remark

le **désodorisant** NOUN
air freshener

désolé (FEM **désolée**) ADJECTIVE
sorry

□ Je suis vraiment désolé. I'm very sorry.
■ **Désolé!** Sorry!

désopilant (FEM **désopilante**) ADJECTIVE
underline: hilarious

désordonné (FEM **désordonnée**) ADJECTIVE
untidy

le **désordre** NOUN
untidiness
■ **Quel désordre!** What a mess!
■ **en désordre** untidy □ Sa chambre est
toujours en désordre. His bedroom is
always untidy.

désormais ADVERB
from now on
□ Désormais, je boirai de l'eau. From now
on I'll drink water.

desquelles PL PRONOUN
LANGUAGE TIP **desquelles** is the
contracted form of **de** + **lesquelles**.
□ des négociations au cours desquelles les
patrons ont fait des concessions
negotiations during which the employers
made concessions

desquels PL PRONOUN
LANGUAGE TIP **desquels** is the
contracted form of **de** + **lesquels**.
□ les lacs au bord desquels nous avons
campé the lakes on the banks of which we
camped

dessécher VERB [34]
to dry out
□ Le soleil dessèche la peau. The sun dries
your skin out.

desserrer VERB [28]
to loosen

le **dessert** NOUN
pudding
□ Qu'est-ce que vous désirez comme
dessert? What would you like for pudding?

le **dessin** NOUN
drawing
□ C'est un dessin de ma petite sœur. It's a
drawing my little sister did.
■ **un dessin animé** (film) a cartoon
■ **un dessin humoristique** (drawing) a
cartoon

le **dessinateur** NOUN
■ **un dessinateur industriel** a
draughtsman

dessiner VERB [28]
to draw

dessous ADVERB
▷ see also **dessous** NOUN
underneath
■ **en dessous** underneath □ Soulève le pot
de fleurs, la clé est en dessous. Lift the
flowerpot, the key's underneath.

■ **par-dessous** underneath □ Le grillage ne
sert à rien, les lapins passent par-dessous.
The fence is useless, the rabbits get in
underneath.
■ **là-dessous** under there □ Il s'est caché
là-dessous. He hid under there.
■ **ci-dessous** below □ Complétez les
phrases ci-dessous. Complete the
sentences below.
■ **au-dessous de** below □ vingt degrés
au-dessous de zéro 20 degrees below zero

le **dessous** NOUN
▷ see also **dessous** ADVERB
underneath
■ **les voisins du dessous** the downstairs
neighbours
■ **avoir le dessus** to have the upper hand
■ **les dessous** underwear □ des dessous en
soie silk underwear

le **dessous-de-plat** (PL les **dessous-de-
plat**) NOUN
tablemat

dessus ADVERB
▷ see also **dessus** NOUN
on top
□ un gâteau avec des bougies dessus a cake
with candles on top
■ **par-dessus** over □ Nous avons sauté
par-dessus la barrière. We jumped over the
gate.
■ **au-dessus** above □ la taille au-dessus
the size above □ au-dessus du lit above the
bed
■ **là-dessus 1** on there □ Tu peux écrire
là-dessus. You can write on there. **2** with
that □ 'Je démissionne!' Là-dessus, il est
parti. 'I resign!' With that, he left.
■ **ci-dessus** above □ l'exemple ci-dessus
the example above

le **dessus** NOUN
▷ see also **dessus** ADVERB
top
■ **les voisins du dessus** the upstairs
neighbours

le/la **destinataire** NOUN
addressee

la **destination** NOUN
destination
■ **les passagers à destination de Paris**
passengers travelling to Paris

destiné (FEM **destinée**) ADJECTIVE
intended for
□ Ce livre est destiné aux enfants. This book
is intended for children.
■ **Elle était destinée à faire ce métier.**
She was destined to go into that job.

la **destruction** NOUN

destruction

le **détachant** NOUN
stain remover

détacher VERB [28]
to undo

■ **se détacher de quelque chose** 1 to come off something □ La poignée de la porte s'est détachée. The door handle came off. 2 to break away from something □ Un wagon s'est détaché du reste du train. A carriage broke away from the rest of the train.

le **détail** NOUN
detail

■ **en détail** in detail

le **détective** NOUN
detective

□ un détective privé a private detective

déteindre VERB [60]
to fade (in wash)

détendre VERB [88]
to relax

□ La lecture, ça me détend. I find reading relaxing.

■ **se détendre** to relax □ Il est allé prendre un bain pour se détendre. He's gone to have a bath to relax.

la **détente** NOUN
relaxation

le **détenu** NOUN
prisoner

la **détenue** NOUN
prisoner

se **détériorer** VERB [28]
to deteriorate

déterminé (FEM **déterminée**) ADJECTIVE
1 determined

□ C'est un homme déterminé. He's a determined man.

2 specific

□ un but déterminé a specific aim

détestable (FEM **détestable**) ADJECTIVE
horrible

détester VERB [28]
to hate

la **détonation** NOUN
bang

□ J'ai entendu une détonation. I heard a bang.

le **détour** NOUN
detour

■ **Ça vaut le détour.** It's worth the trip.

le **détournement** NOUN

■ **un détournement d'avion** a hijacking

détrempé (FEM **détrempée**) ADJECTIVE
waterlogged

les **détritus** MASC PL NOUN

litter

détruire VERB [23]
to destroy

la **dette** NOUN
debt

le **deuil** NOUN

■ **être en deuil** to be in mourning

deux NUMBER
two

□ Il était deux heures. It was two o'clock.
□ Elle a deux ans. She's two.

■ **deux fois** twice

■ **deux points** colon

■ **tous les deux** both □ Nous y sommes allées toutes les deux. We both went.

■ **le deux février** the second of February

deuxième (FEM **deuxième**) ADJECTIVE
second

□ au deuxième étage on the second floor

deuxièmement ADVERB
secondly

devais, devait, devaient VERB ▷ see
devoir

dévaliser VERB [28]
to rob

devant ADVERB, PREPOSITION
▷ see also **devant** NOUN

1 in front

□ Il marchait devant. He was walking in front.

2 in front of

□ Il était assis devant moi. He was sitting in front of me.

■ **passer devant** to go past □ Nous sommes passés devant chez toi. We went past your house.

le **devant** NOUN
▷ see also **devant** ADVERB
front

□ le devant de la maison the front of the house

■ **les pattes de devant** the front legs

le **développement** NOUN
development

■ **les pays en voie de développement** developing countries

développer VERB [28]
to develop

□ donner une pellicule à développer to take a film to be developed

■ **se développer** to develop

devenir VERB [25]
to become

devez VERB ▷ see devoir

la **déviation** NOUN
diversion

deviez VERB ▷ see devoir

deviner VERB [28]
to guess

la **devinette** NOUN
riddle
□ poser une devinette à quelqu'un to ask somebody a riddle

devions VERB ▷see devoir

dévisager VERB [45]
■ dévisager quelqu'un to stare at somebody

la **devise** NOUN
currency
□ les devises étrangères foreign currency

dévisser VERB [28]
to unscrew

dévoiler VERB [28]
to unveil

devoir VERB [26]
▷see also devoir NOUN

PRESENT TENSE	
je dois	nous devons
tu dois	vous devez
il/elle doit	ils/elles doivent
PAST PARTICIPLE	
dû	

1 to have to
□ Je dois partir. I've got to go.
2 must
□ Tu dois être fatigué. You must be tired.
3 to be due to
□ Le nouveau centre commercial doit ouvrir en mai. The new shopping centre is due to open in May.
■ devoir quelque chose à quelqu'un to owe somebody something □ Combien est-ce que je vous dois? How much do I owe you?

le **devoir** NOUN
▷see also devoir VERB
1 exercise
■ les devoirs homework
■ un devoir sur table a written test
2 duty
□ Aller voter fait partie des devoirs du citoyen. Voting is part of one's duty as a citizen.

devons VERB ▷see devoir

dévorer VERB [28]
to devour

dévoué (FEM dévouée) ADJECTIVE
devoted

devra, devrai, devras, devrez, devrons, devront VERB ▷see devoir

le **diabète** NOUN
diabetes

diabétique (FEM diabétique) ADJECTIVE
diabetic

□ Je suis diabétique. I'm diabetic.

le **diable** NOUN
devil

le **diabolo** NOUN
fruit cordial and lemonade
■ un diabolo menthe a mint cordial and lemonade

diagonal (FEM diagonale, MASC PL diagonaux) ADJECTIVE
diagonal

la **diagonale** NOUN
diagonal
■ en diagonale diagonally

le **diagramme** NOUN
diagram

le **dialecte** NOUN
dialect

le **dialogue** NOUN
dialogue

le **diamant** NOUN
diamond

le **diamètre** NOUN
diameter

la **diapo** NOUN (informal)
slide
■ une pellicule diapo a slide film

la **diapositive** NOUN
slide
□ projeter des diapositives to show some slides

la **diarrhée** NOUN
diarrhoea
□ avoir la diarrhée to have diarrhoea

le **dictateur** NOUN
dictator

la **dictature** NOUN
dictatorship

la **dictée** NOUN
dictation

dicter VERB [28]
to dictate

le **dictionnaire** NOUN
dictionary

diététique (FEM diététique) ADJECTIVE
■ un magasin diététique a health food shop

le **dieu** (PL les dieux) NOUN
god
■ Dieu God □ Mon Dieu! Oh my God!

le **différé** NOUN
■ une émission en différé a recording

la **différence** NOUN
difference
■ la différence d'âge the age difference
■ à la différence de unlike

différent (FEM différente) ADJECTIVE
1 different

□ pour des raisons différentes for different reasons

2 various

□ pour différentes raisons for various reasons

■ **différent de** different to □ Son point de vue est différent du mien. His point of view is different to mine.

difficile (FEM **difficile**) ADJECTIVE
difficult

□ C'est difficile à comprendre. It's difficult to understand.

difficilement ADVERB

■ **faire quelque chose difficilement** to have trouble doing something □ Ma grand-mère se déplace difficilement. My grandmother has trouble getting around.

■ **Je pouvais difficilement refuser.** It was difficult for me to refuse.

la **difficulté** NOUN
difficulty

□ avec difficulté with difficulty

■ **être en difficulté** to be in difficulties

digérer VERB [34]
to digest

le **digestif** NOUN
after-dinner liqueur

digne (FEM **digne**) ADJECTIVE

■ **digne de** worthy of □ digne de confiance trustworthy

la **dignité** NOUN
dignity

le **dilemme** NOUN
dilemma

□ être devant un dilemme to be faced with a dilemma

diluer VERB [28]
to dilute

le **dimanche** NOUN

1 Sunday

□ Aujourd'hui, on est dimanche. It's Sunday today.

2 on Sunday

□ Dimanche, nous allons déjeuner chez mes grands-parents. On Sunday we're having lunch at my grandparents'.

■ **le dimanche** on Sundays □ Le dimanche, je fais la grasse matinée. I have a lie-in on Sundays.

■ **tous les dimanches** every Sunday

■ **dimanche dernier** last Sunday

■ **dimanche prochain** next Sunday

diminuer VERB [28]
to decrease

□ Est-ce que tu peux diminuer le son? Could you turn down the sound?

le **diminutif** NOUN

pet name

la **diminution** NOUN

1 reduction

2 decrease

la **dinde** NOUN
turkey (meat)

□ la dinde de Noël the Christmas turkey

le **dindon** NOUN
turkey (bird)

le **dîner** NOUN

▷ see also **dîner** VERB
dinner (evening meal)

dîner VERB [28]

▷ see also **dîner** NOUN
to have dinner (evening meal)

dingue (FEM **dingue**) ADJECTIVE (informal)
crazy

diplomate (FEM **diplomate**) ADJECTIVE

▷ see also **diplomate** NOUN
diplomatic

le **diplomate** NOUN

▷ see also **diplomate** ADJECTIVE
diplomat

la **diplomatie** NOUN
diplomacy

le **diplôme** NOUN
qualification

diplômé (FEM **diplômée**) ADJECTIVE
qualified

dire VERB [27]

1 to say

□ Il a dit qu'il ne viendrait pas. He said he wouldn't come.

■ **on dit que ...** they say that ... □ On dit que la nourriture est excellente là-bas. They say that the food is excellent there.

2 to tell

■ **dire quelque chose à quelqu'un** to tell somebody something □ Elle m'a dit la vérité. She told me the truth. □ Il nous a dit de regarder cette émission. He told us to watch this programme.

■ **On dirait qu'il va pleuvoir.** It looks as if it's going to rain.

■ **se dire quelque chose** to think something □ Quand je l'ai vu, je me suis dit qu'il avait vieilli. When I saw him, I thought to myself that he'd aged.

■ **Est-ce que ça se dit?** Can you say that?

■ **Ça ne me dit rien.** That doesn't appeal to me.

direct (FEM **directe**) ADJECTIVE
direct

■ **en direct** live □ une émission en direct a live broadcast

directement ADVERB
straight

□ Il est rentré directement chez lui. He went straight home.

le **directeur** NOUN
1 headteacher
□ Il est directeur. He's a headteacher.
2 manager
□ Il est directeur du personnel. He's a personnel manager.

la **direction** NOUN
1 management
□ la direction et les ouvriers the management and the workers
2 direction
□ 'toutes directions' 'all directions'

la **directrice** NOUN
1 headteacher
□ Elle est directrice. She's a headteacher.
2 manager
□ Elle est directrice commerciale. She's a sales manager.

dirent VERB ▷ see dire

le **dirigeant** NOUN
leader

la **dirigeante** NOUN
leader

diriger VERB [45]
to manage
□ Il dirige une petite entreprise. He manages a small company.
■ **se diriger vers** to head for □ Il se dirigeait vers la gare. He was heading for the station.

dis VERB ▷ see dire
■ **Dis-moi la vérité!** Tell me the truth!
■ **dis donc** hey □ Il a drôlement changé, dis donc! Hey, he's really changed! □ Dis donc, tu te souviens de Sam? Hey, do you remember Sam?

disaient, disais, disait VERB ▷ see dire

la **discothèque** NOUN
disco (club)

le **discours** NOUN
speech

discret (FEM **discrète**) ADJECTIVE
discreet

la **discrimination** NOUN
discrimination
□ la discrimination raciale racial discrimination □ la discrimination sexuelle sex discrimination

la **discussion** NOUN
discussion

discutable (FEM **discutable**) ADJECTIVE
debatable

discuter VERB [28]
1 to talk
□ Nous avons discuté pendant des heures. We talked for hours.

2 to argue
□ C'est ce que j'ai décidé, alors ne discutez pas! That's what I've decided, so don't argue!

disent, disiez, disions VERB ▷ see dire

disons VERB ▷ see dire
let's say
□ C'est à, disons, une demi-heure à pied. It's half an hour's walk, say.

disparaître VERB [56]
to disappear
■ **faire disparaître quelque chose 1** to make something disappear □ Il a fait disparaître le lapin dans son chapeau. He made the rabbit disappear in his hat. **2** to get rid of something □ Ils ont fait disparaître tous les documents compromettants. They got rid of all the incriminating documents.

la **disparition** NOUN
disappearance
■ **une espèce en voie de disparition** an endangered species

disparu (FEM **disparue**) ADJECTIVE
■ **être porté disparu** to be reported missing

le **dispensaire** NOUN
community clinic

dispensé (FEM **dispensée**) ADJECTIVE
■ **être dispensé de quelque chose** to be excused something □ Elle est dispensée de gymnastique. She's excused gym.

disperser VERB [28]
to break up
□ La police a dispersé les manifestants. The police broke up the demonstrators.
■ **se disperser** to break up □ Une fois l'ambulance partie, la foule s'est dispersée. Once the ambulance had left, the crowd broke up.

disponible (FEM **disponible**) ADJECTIVE
available

disposé (FEM **disposée**) ADJECTIVE
■ **être disposé à faire quelque chose** to be willing to do something □ Il était disposé à m'aider. He was willing to help me.

disposer VERB [28]
■ **disposer de quelque chose** to have access to something □ Je dispose d'un ordinateur. I have access to a computer.

la **disposition** NOUN
■ **prendre ses dispositions** to make arrangements □ Est-ce que vous avez pris vos dispositions pour partir en France? Have you made arrangements to go to France?
■ **avoir quelque chose à sa disposition** to have something at one's disposal □ J'ai une voiture à ma disposition pour la semaine. I

d

have a car at my disposal for the week.
- **Je suis à votre disposition.** I am at your service.
- **Je tiens ces livres à votre disposition.** The books are at your disposal.

la **dispute** NOUN
argument

se **disputer** VERB [28]
to argue

le **disquaire** NOUN
record dealer

le **disque** NOUN
record
- **un disque compact** a compact disc
- **le disque dur** hard disk

la **disquette** NOUN
floppy disk

disséminé (FEM **disséminée**) ADJECTIVE
scattered

disséquer VERB [34]
to dissect

la **dissertation** NOUN
essay

dissimuler VERB [28]
to conceal

se **dissiper** VERB [28]
to clear
□ Le brouillard va se dissiper dans l'après-midi. The fog will clear during the afternoon.

le **dissolvant** NOUN
nail polish remover

dissoudre VERB [70]
to dissolve
- **se dissoudre** to dissolve

dissuader VERB [28]
- **dissuader quelqu'un de faire quelque chose** to dissuade somebody from doing something □ Elle m'a dissuadé d'aller voir ce film. She dissuaded me from going to see the film.

la **distance** NOUN
distance

la **distillerie** NOUN
distillery

distingué (FEM **distinguée**) ADJECTIVE
distinguished

distinguer VERB [28]
to distinguish

la **distraction** NOUN
entertainment
□ Il lit beaucoup: c'est sa seule distraction. He reads a lot: it's his only form of entertainment.

distraire VERB [85]
- **Va voir un film, ça te distraira.** Go and see a film, it'll take your mind off things.

distrait (FEM **distraite**) ADJECTIVE
absent-minded

distribuer VERB [28]
1 to give out
□ Distribue les livres, s'il te plaît. Give out the books, please.
2 to deal (cards)

le **distributeur** NOUN
- **un distributeur automatique** a vending machine
- **un distributeur de billets** a cash dispenser

dit VERB ▷ see **dire**

dit (FEM **dite**) ADJECTIVE
known as
□ Pierre, dit Pierrot Pierre, known as Pierrot

dites VERB ▷ see **dire**
- **Dites-moi ce que vous pensez.** Tell me what you think.
- **dites donc** hey □ Dites donc, vous, là-bas! Hey, you there!

divers (FEM **diverse**) ADJECTIVE
diverse
- **pour diverses raisons** for various reasons

se **divertir** VERB [38]
to enjoy oneself

divin (FEM **divine**) ADJECTIVE
divine

diviser VERB [28]
to divide
□ Quatre divisé par deux égalent deux. 4 divided by 2 equals 2.

le **divorcé** NOUN
divorcee

la **divorcée** NOUN
divorcee

divorcer VERB [12]
to get divorced

dix NUMBER
ten
□ Elle a dix ans. She's ten. □ à dix heures at ten o'clock
- **le dix février** the tenth of February

dix-huit NUMBER
□ Elle a dix huit ans. She's eighteen.
□ à dix-huit heures at 6 p.m.

dixième (FEM **dixième**) ADJECTIVE
tenth
□ au dixième étage on the tenth floor

dix-neuf NUMBER
□ Elle a dix-neuf ans. She's nineteen.
□ à dix-neuf heures at 7 p.m.

dix-sept NUMBER
□ Elle a dix-sept ans. She's seventeen.
□ à dix-sept heures at 5 p.m.

la **dizaine** NOUN

about ten
□ une dizaine de jours about ten days
le **do** NOUN
1 C
□ en do majeur in C major
2 do
□ do, ré, mi ... do, re, mi ...
le **docteur** NOUN
doctor
□ Elle est docteur. She's a doctor.
le **document** NOUN
document
le **documentaire** NOUN
documentary
le/la **documentaliste** NOUN
librarian
la **documentation** NOUN
documentation
documenter VERB [28]
■ se documenter sur quelque chose to gather information on something
dodu (FEM **dodue**) ADJECTIVE
plump
le **doigt** NOUN
finger
■ les doigts de pied the toes

　　LANGUAGE TIP Word for word, **doigts de pied** means 'foot fingers'.

dois, doit, doivent VERB ▷ see **devoir**
le **domaine** NOUN
1 estate
□ Il possède un immense domaine en Normandie. He owns a huge estate in Normandy.
2 field
□ La chimie n'est pas mon domaine. Chemistry's not my field.
domestique (FEM **domestique**) ADJECTIVE
▷ see also **domestique** NOUN
domestic
■ les animaux domestiques pets
le/la **domestique** NOUN
▷ see also **domestique** ADJECTIVE
servant
le **domicile** NOUN
place of residence
■ à domicile at home □ Il travaille à domicile. He works at home.
domicilié (FEM **domiciliée**) ADJECTIVE
■ 'domicilié à: ...' 'address: ...'
dominer VERB [28]
to dominate
■ se dominer to control oneself
les **dominos** MASC PL NOUN
dominoes
□ jouer aux dominos to play dominoes
le **dommage** NOUN

damage
□ La tempête a causé d'importants dommages. The storm caused a lot of damage.
■ C'est dommage. It's a shame. □ C'est dommage que tu ne puisses pas venir. It's a shame you can't come.
dompter VERB [28]
to tame
le **dompteur** NOUN
animal tamer
la **dompteuse** NOUN
animal tamer
le **don** NOUN
1 donation
2 gift
□ avoir un don pour quelque chose to have a gift for something
■ Elle a le don de m'énerver. She's got a knack of getting on my nerves.
donc CONJUNCTION
so
le **donjon** NOUN
keep (of castle)
les **données** FEM PL NOUN
data
donner VERB [28]
1 to give
■ donner quelque chose à quelqu'un to give somebody something □ Elle m'a donné son adresse. She gave me her address.
■ Ça m'a donné faim. That made me feel hungry.
2 to give away
□ Tu as toujours ta veste en daim? — Non, je l'ai donnée. Have you still got your suede jacket? — No, I gave it away.
■ donner sur quelque chose to overlook something □ une fenêtre qui donne sur la mer a window overlooking the sea
dont PRONOUN
1 of which
□ deux livres, dont l'un est en anglais two books, one of which is in English □ le prix dont il est si fier the prize he's so proud of
2 of whom
□ dix blessés, dont deux grièvement ten people injured, two of whom are seriously injured □ la fille dont je t'ai parlé the girl I told you about
doré (FEM **dorée**) ADJECTIVE
golden
□ une étoile dorée a golden star
dorénavant ADVERB
from now on
□ Dorénavant, tu feras attention. From now on, you'll be careful.

dorloter VERB [28]
to pamper

dormir VERB [29]
1 to sleep
□ Tu as bien dormi? Did you sleep well?
2 to be asleep
□ Tu dors? Are you asleep?

le **dortoir** NOUN
dormitory

le **dos** NOUN
back
□ dos à dos back to back
■ **faire quelque chose dans le dos de quelqu'un** to do something behind somebody's back □ Elle me critique dans mon dos. She criticizes me behind my back.
■ **de dos** from behind
■ **nager le dos crawlé** to swim backstroke
■ **'voir au dos'** 'see over'

la **dose** NOUN
dose
□ Ne pas dépasser la dose prescrite. Do not exceed the stated dose.

le **dossier** NOUN
1 file
□ une pile de dossiers a stack of files
2 report
□ un bon dossier scolaire a good school report
3 feature (in magazine)
4 back (of chair)

la **douane** NOUN
customs

le **douanier** NOUN
customs officer

le **double** NOUN
■ **le double** twice as much □ Il gagne le double. He earns twice as much. □ le double du prix normal twice the normal price
■ **en double** in duplicate □ Garde cette photo, je l'ai en double. Keep this photo, I've got a copy of it.
■ **le double messieurs** (tennis) the men's doubles

double-cliquer VERB [28]
to double-click
□ double-cliquer sur une icône to double-click on an icon

doubler VERB [28]
1 to double
□ Le prix a doublé en dix ans. The price has doubled in 10 years.
2 to overtake
□ Il est dangereux de doubler sur cette route. It's dangerous to overtake on this road.

■ **un film doublé** a dubbed film

douce FEM ADJECTIVE ▷ see **doux**

doucement ADVERB
1 gently
□ Il a frappé doucement à la porte. He knocked gently at the door.
2 slowly
□ Roulez doucement! Drive slowly! □ Je ne comprends pas, parle plus doucement. I don't understand, speak more slowly.

la **douceur** NOUN
1 softness
□ Cette crème maintient la douceur de votre peau. This cream keeps your skin soft.
2 gentleness
□ parler avec douceur to speak gently
■ **L'avion a atterri en douceur.** The plane made a smooth landing.

la **douche** NOUN
shower
■ **les douches** the shower room
■ **prendre une douche** to have a shower

se **doucher** VERB [28]
to have a shower

doué (FEM **douée**) ADJECTIVE
talented
■ **être doué en quelque chose** to be good at something □ Il est doué en maths. He's good at maths.

douillet (FEM **douillette**) ADJECTIVE
1 cosy
□ un anorak douillet a cosy anorak
2 soft
□ Je ne supporte pas la douleur: je suis très douillette. I can't stand pain: I'm a real softie.

la **douleur** NOUN
pain

douloureux (FEM **douloureuse**) ADJECTIVE
painful

le **doute** NOUN
doubt
■ **sans doute** probably

douter VERB [28]
to doubt
■ **douter de quelque chose** to have doubts about something □ Je doute de sa sincérité. I have my doubts about his sincerity.
■ **se douter de quelque chose** to suspect something □ Je ne me doutais de rien. I didn't suspect anything.
■ **Je m'en doutais.** I suspected as much.

douteux (FEM **douteuse**) ADJECTIVE
1 dubious
□ une plaisanterie d'un goût douteux a joke in dubious taste
2 suspicious-looking

□ un individu douteux a suspicious-looking person

Douvres NOUN
Dover

doux (FEM **douce**, MASC PL **doux**) ADJECTIVE
1 soft
□ un tissu doux soft material □ les drogues douces soft drugs
2 sweet
□ du cidre doux sweet cider
3 mild
□ Il fait doux aujourd'hui. It's mild today.
4 gentle
□ C'est quelqu'un de très doux. He's a very gentle person.
■ **en douce** on the quiet □ Il m'a donné cinq euros en douce. He slipped me 5 euros on the quiet.

la **douzaine** NOUN
dozen
□ une douzaine d'œufs a dozen eggs
■ **une douzaine de personnes** about twelve people

douze NUMBER
twelve
□ Il a douze ans. He's twelve.
■ **le douze février** the twelfth of February

douzième (FEM **douzième**) ADJECTIVE
twelfth
□ au douzième étage on the twelfth floor

la **dragée** NOUN
sugared almond

draguer VERB [28] (informal)
■ **draguer quelqu'un** to chat somebody up
□ Il est en train de la draguer. He's chatting her up.
■ **se faire draguer** to get chatted up □ Elle aime se faire draguer. She likes getting chatted up.

le **dragueur** NOUN (informal)
flirt (person)

la **dragueuse** NOUN (informal)
flirt (person)

dramatique (FEM **dramatique**) ADJECTIVE
tragic
□ une situation dramatique a tragic situation
■ **l'art dramatique** drama

le **drame** NOUN
drama (incident)
■ **Ça n'est pas un drame si tu ne viens pas.** It's not the end of the world if you don't come.

le **drap** NOUN
sheet (for bed)

le **drapeau** (PL les **drapeaux**) NOUN
flag

□ le drapeau français the French flag □ le drapeau tricolore the French flag

⌐ **DID YOU KNOW…?**
le drapeau tricolore is the French flag: its three colours are blue, white and red.

dressé (FEM **dressée**) ADJECTIVE
trained
□ un chien bien dressé a well-trained dog

dresser VERB [28]
1 to draw up
□ dresser une liste to draw up a list
2 to train
□ dresser un chien to train a dog
■ **dresser l'oreille** to prick up one's ears
□ Quand elle a dit ça, il a dressé l'oreille. When she said that, he pricked up his ears.

la **drogue** NOUN
drug
□ le problème de la drogue the drugs problem □ la lutte contre la drogue the war against drugs
■ **les drogues douces** soft drugs
■ **les drogues dures** hard drugs

le **drogué** NOUN
drug addict

la **droguée** NOUN
drug addict

droguer VERB [28]
■ **droguer quelqu'un** to drug somebody
■ **se droguer** to take drugs

la **droguerie** NOUN
hardware shop

droit (FEM **droite**) ADJECTIVE, ADVERB
▷ see also **droit** NOUN, **droite** NOUN
1 right
□ le bras droit the right arm □ le côté droit the right-hand side
2 straight
□ une ligne droite a straight line □ Tiens-toi droite! Stand up straight!
■ **tout droit** straight on

le **droit** NOUN
▷ see also **droit** ADJECTIVE
1 right
□ les droits de l'homme human rights
■ **avoir le droit de faire quelque chose** to be allowed to do something □ On n'a pas le droit de fumer à l'école. We're not allowed to smoke at school.
2 law
□ faire son droit to study law □ un étudiant en droit a law student

la **droite** NOUN
▷ see also **droite** ADJECTIVE, **droite** NOUN
right
□ sur votre droite on your right

■ **à droite 1** on the right □ **la troisième rue à droite** the third street on the right **2** to the right □ **à droite de la fenêtre** to the right of the window

■ **Tournez à droite.** Turn right.

■ **la voie de droite** the right-hand lane

■ **la droite** *(in politics)* the right

■ **Elle est très à droite.** She's very right-wing.

droitier (FEM **droitière**) ADJECTIVE
right-handed

□ **Elle est droitière.** She's right-handed.

drôle (FEM **drôle**) ADJECTIVE
funny

□ **Ça n'est pas drôle.** It's not funny.

■ **un drôle de temps** funny weather

drôlement ADVERB *(informal)*
really

□ **C'est drôlement bon.** It's really good.

du ARTICLE

◌ **LANGUAGE TIP** du is the contracted form of **de** + **le**.

1 some

□ **Tu veux du fromage?** Would you like some cheese?

2 any

□ **Tu as du chocolat?** Have you got any chocolate?

3 of the

□ **la porte du garage** the door of the garage □ **la femme du directeur** the headmaster's wife

dû VERB ▷*see* **devoir**

▷*see also* **dû** ADJECTIVE

■ **Nous avons dû nous arrêter.** We had to stop.

dû (FEM **due**, MASC PL **dus**) ADJECTIVE

▷*see also* **dû** VERB

■ **dû à** due to □ **un retard dû au mauvais temps** a delay due to bad weather

le duc NOUN
duke

la duchesse NOUN
duchess

dupe (FEM **dupe**) ADJECTIVE

■ **Elle me ment mais je ne suis pas dupe.** She lies to me but I'm not taken in by that.

duquel (MASC PL **desquels**, FEM PL **desquelles**)
PRONOUN

◌ **LANGUAGE TIP** duquel is the contracted form of **de** + **lequel**.

□ **l'homme duquel il parle** the man he is talking about

dur (FEM **dure**) ADJECTIVE, ADVERB
hard

□ **travailler dur** to work hard □ **être dur avec quelqu'un** to be hard on somebody

durant PREPOSITION

1 during

□ **durant la nuit** during the night

2 for

□ **durant des années** for years □ **des mois durant** for months

la durée NOUN
length

□ **Quelle est la durée des études d'ingénieur?** How long does it take to train as an engineer?

■ **pour une durée de quinze jours** for a period of two weeks

■ **de courte durée** short □ **un séjour de courte durée** a short stay

■ **de longue durée** long □ **une absence de longue durée** a long absence

durement ADVERB
harshly

durer VERB [28]
to last

la dureté NOUN
harshness

□ **traiter quelqu'un avec dureté** to treat somebody harshly

le DVD NOUN
DVD

dynamique (FEM **dynamique**) ADJECTIVE
dynamic

dyslexique (FEM **dyslexique**) ADJECTIVE
dyslexic

e

l' **eau** (PL les **eaux**) FEM NOUN
water

■ **l'eau minérale** mineral water
■ **l'eau plate** still water
■ **tomber à l'eau** to fall through □ Nos projets sont tombés à l'eau. Our plans have fallen through.

ébahi (FEM **ébahie**) ADJECTIVE
amazed

éblouir VERB [38]
to dazzle

l' **éboueur** MASC NOUN
dustman

ébouillanter VERB [28]
to scald

l' **écaille** FEM NOUN
scale (of fish)

s' **écailler** VERB [28]
to flake

l' **écart** MASC NOUN
gap

■ **à l'écart de** away from □ Ils se sont assis à l'écart des autres. They sat down away from the others.

écarté (FEM **écartée**) ADJECTIVE
remote

■ **les bras écartés** arms outstretched
■ **les jambes écartées** legs apart

écarter VERB [28]
to open wide (arms, legs)

■ **s'écarter** to move □ Ils se sont écartés pour le laisser passer. They moved to let him pass.

l' **échafaudage** MASC NOUN
scaffolding

l' **échalote** FEM NOUN
shallot

l' **échange** MASC NOUN
exchange

□ en échange de in exchange for

échanger VERB [45]
to swap

□ Je t'échange ce timbre contre celui-là. I'll swap you this stamp for that one.

l' **échantillon** MASC NOUN
sample

échapper VERB [28]

■ **échapper à** to escape from □ Le prisonnier a réussi à échapper à la police. The prisoner managed to escape from the police.

■ **s'échapper** to escape □ Il s'est échappé de prison. He escaped from prison.

■ **l'échapper belle** to have a narrow escape □ Nous l'avons échappé belle. We had a narrow escape.

l' **écharde** FEM NOUN
splinter of wood

l' **écharpe** FEM NOUN
scarf

s' **échauffer** VERB [28]
to warm up (before exercise)

l' **échec** MASC NOUN
failure

les **échecs** MASC PL NOUN
chess

□ jouer aux échecs to play chess

l' **échelle** FEM NOUN
1 ladder
2 scale (of map)

échevelé (FEM **échevelée**) ADJECTIVE
dishevelled

l' **écho** MASC NOUN
echo

échouer VERB [28]

■ **échouer à un examen** to fail an exam

éclabousser VERB [28]
to splash

l' **éclair** MASC NOUN
flash of lightning

■ **un éclair au chocolat** a chocolate éclair

l' **éclairage** MASC NOUN
lighting

l' **éclaircie** FEM NOUN
bright interval

éclairer VERB [28]

■ **Cette lampe éclaire bien.** This lamp gives a good light.

l' **éclat** MASC NOUN
1 piece (of glass)

□ La vase a volé en éclats. The vase smashed into pieces.

2 brightness (of sun, colour)

■ des éclats de rire roars of laughter

éclatant (FEM **éclatante**) ADJECTIVE
brilliant

□ des dents d'une blancheur éclatante brilliant white teeth

éclater VERB [28]

1 to burst (tyre, balloon)

■ éclater de rire to burst out laughing

■ éclater en sanglots to burst into tears

2 to break out

□ La Seconde Guerre mondiale a éclaté en 1939. The Second World War broke out in 1939.

écœurant (FEM **écœurante**) ADJECTIVE
sickly

écœurer VERB [28]

■ Tous ces mensonges m'écœurent. All these lies make me sick.

l' **école** FEM NOUN
school

□ aller à l'école to go to school □ une école privée a private school □ une école publique a state school □ une école maternelle a nursery school

> **DID YOU KNOW...?**
> The **école maternelle** is a state school for 2–6 year-olds.

l' **écolier** MASC NOUN
schoolboy

l' **écolière** FEM NOUN
schoolgirl

l' **écologie** FEM NOUN
ecology

écologique (FEM **écologique**) ADJECTIVE
ecological

□ une lessive écologique an ecological washing powder

l' **économie** FEM NOUN

1 economy

□ l'économie de la France the French economy

2 economics

□ un cours d'économie an economics class

les **économies** FEM PL NOUN
savings

■ faire des économies to save up □ Je fais des économies pour partir en vacances. I'm saving up for my holidays.

économique (FEM **économique**) ADJECTIVE

1 economic

□ une crise économique an economic crisis

2 economical

□ Il est plus économique d'acheter une grande boîte de lessive. It's more economical to buy a big box of washing powder. □ Cette petite voiture est économique. This little car is economical.

économiser VERB [28]
to save

l' **économiseur d'écran** MASC NOUN
screen saver

l' **écorce** FEM NOUN

1 bark (of tree)

2 peel (of orange, lemon)

s' **écorcher** VERB [28]

■ Je me suis écorché le genou. I've grazed my knee.

écossais (FEM **écossaise**) ADJECTIVE, NOUN

1 Scottish

□ Elle est écossaise. She's Scottish.

■ un Écossais a Scot (man)

■ une Écossaise a Scot (woman)

■ les Écossais the Scots

2 tartan

□ une jupe écossaise a tartan skirt

l' **Écosse** FEM NOUN
Scotland

■ en Écosse 1 in Scotland □ Il a passé une semaine en Écosse. He spent a week in Scotland. 2 to Scotland □ Nous allons en Écosse l'été prochain. We're going to Scotland next summer.

s' **écouler** VERB [28]

1 to flow out (water)

2 to pass

□ Le temps s'écoule trop vite. Time passes too quickly.

écouter VERB [28]
to listen to

□ J'aime écouter de la musique. I like listening to music.

■ Écoute-moi! Listen!

l' **écouteur** MASC NOUN
earpiece (of phone)

l' **écran** MASC NOUN
screen

■ le petit écran television

■ l'écran total sunblock

écraser VERB [28]

1 to crush

□ Écrasez une gousse d'ail. Crush a clove of garlic.

2 to run over

□ Mon chien s'est fait écraser par une voiture. My dog got run over by a car.

■ s'écraser to crash □ L'avion s'est écrasé dans le désert. The plane crashed in the desert.

écrémé (FEM **écrémée**) ADJECTIVE
skimmed

□ le lait écrémé skimmed milk

l' **écrevisse** FEM NOUN
crayfish

écrire VERB [30]
to write
□ Nous nous écrivons régulièrement. We write to each other regularly.
■ **Ça s'écrit comment?** How do you spell that?

l' **écrit** MASC NOUN
written paper
□ L'écrit d'anglais a lieu la semaine prochaine. The written paper in English is next week.
■ **par écrit** in writing

l' **écriteau** (PL les **écriteaux**) MASC NOUN
notice

l' **écriture** FEM NOUN
writing
□ J'ai du mal à lire son écriture. I can't read his writing.

l' **écrivain** MASC NOUN
writer
□ Elle est écrivain. She's a writer.

l' **écrou** MASC NOUN
nut *(metal)*

s' **écrouler** VERB [28]
to collapse

écru (FEM **écrue**) ADJECTIVE
off-white

l' **écureuil** MASC NOUN
squirrel

l' **écurie** FEM NOUN
stable

EDF FEM NOUN (= *Électricité de France*)
French electricity company

Édimbourg NOUN
Edinburgh

éditer VERB [28]
to publish
□ On vient d'éditer un nouveau dictionnaire. A new dictionary has just been published.

l' **éditeur** MASC NOUN
publisher

l' **édition** FEM NOUN
1 edition
□ une édition de poche a paperback edition
2 publishing
□ Il travaille dans l'édition. He works in publishing.

l' **édredon** MASC NOUN
eiderdown

l' **éducateur** MASC NOUN
teacher *(of people with special needs)*

éducatif (FEM **éducative**) ADJECTIVE
educational
□ un jeu éducatif an educational game

l' **éducation** FEM NOUN

1 education
□ l'éducation physique physical education
■ **Il n'a pas beaucoup d'éducation.** He's not very well educated.
2 upbringing
□ Il a reçu une éducation très stricte. He had a very strict upbringing.

l' **éducatrice** FEM NOUN
teacher *(of people with special needs)*

éduquer VERB [28]
to educate

effacer VERB [12]
to rub out

effarant (FEM **effarante**) ADJECTIVE
amazing
□ Il a mangé une quantité effarante de pain. He ate an amazing amount of bread.

effectivement ADVERB
indeed
□ Il est effectivement plus rapide de passer par là. It is indeed quicker to go this way.
□ Oui, effectivement. Yes, indeed.
LANGUAGE TIP Be careful!
effectivement does not mean **effectively**.

effectuer VERB [28]
1 to make
□ Ils ont effectué de nombreux changements. They have made a lot of changes.
2 to do
□ On vient d'effectuer des travaux dans le bâtiment. They have just done some work in the building.

effervescent (FEM **effervescente**) ADJECTIVE
effervescent
□ un comprimé effervescent an effervescent tablet

l' **effet** MASC NOUN
effect
■ **faire de l'effet** to take effect □ Ce médicament fait rapidement de l'effet. This medicine takes effect quickly.
■ **Ça m'a fait un drôle d'effet de le revoir.** It gave me a strange feeling to see him again.
■ **en effet** yes indeed □ Je ne me sens pas très bien. — En effet, tu as l'air pâle. I don't feel very well. — Yes, you do look pale.

efficace (FEM **efficace**) ADJECTIVE
1 efficient
□ C'est une femme efficace. She's an efficient woman.
2 effective
□ un médicament efficace an effective medicine

s' **effondrer** VERB [28]
to collapse

s' **efforcer** VERB [12]
- s'efforcer de faire quelque chose to try hard to do something □ Il s'efforce d'être aimable avec la clientèle. He tries hard to be polite to the customers.

l' **effort** MASC NOUN
effort
□ faire un effort to make an effort

effrayant (FEM **effrayante**) ADJECTIVE
frightening

effrayer VERB [59]
to frighten

effronté (FEM **effrontée**) ADJECTIVE
cheeky
□ Ce gamin est vraiment effronté. This kid's really cheeky.

effroyable (FEM **effroyable**) ADJECTIVE
horrifying

égal (FEM **égale**, MASC PL **égaux**) ADJECTIVE
equal
□ une quantité égale de farine et de sucre an equal quantity of flour and sugar
- Ça m'est égal. 1 I don't mind. □ Tu préfères du riz ou des pâtes? — Ça m'est égal. Would you rather have rice or pasta? — I don't mind. 2 I don't care. □ Fais ce que tu veux, ça m'est égal. Do what you like, I don't care.

également ADVERB
also

égaler VERB [28]
to equal

l' **égalité** FEM NOUN
equality
- être à égalité to be level □ Maintenant les deux joueurs sont à égalité. The two players are now level.

l' **égard** MASC NOUN
- à cet égard in this respect

égarer VERB [28]
to mislay
□ J'ai égaré mes clés. I've mislaid my keys.
- s'égarer to get lost □ Ils se sont égarés dans la forêt. They got lost in the forest.

l' **église** FEM NOUN
church
□ aller à l'église to go to church

l' **égoïsme** MASC NOUN
selfishness

égoïste (FEM **égoïste**) ADJECTIVE
selfish

l' **égout** MASC NOUN
sewer

l' **égratignure** FEM NOUN
scratch

l' **Égypte** FEM NOUN
Egypt

égyptien (FEM **égyptienne**) ADJECTIVE
Egyptian

eh EXCLAMATION
hey!
- eh bien well

l' **élan** MASC NOUN
- prendre de l'élan to gather speed

s' **élancer** VERB [12]
to hurl oneself

élargir VERB [38]
to widen

l' **élastique** MASC NOUN
rubber band

l' **électeur** MASC NOUN
voter (man)

l' **élection** FEM NOUN
election
□ les élections présidentielles the presidential election

l' **électrice** FEM NOUN
voter (woman)

l' **électricien** MASC NOUN
electrician

l' **électricité** FEM NOUN
electricity
□ une facture d'électricité an electricity bill
- allumer l'électricité to turn on the light
- éteindre l'électricité to turn off the light

électrique (FEM **électrique**) ADJECTIVE
electric
□ le courant électrique the electric current

l' **électronique** FEM NOUN
electronics

élégant (FEM **élégante**) ADJECTIVE
smart

élémentaire (FEM **élémentaire**) ADJECTIVE
elementary

l' **éléphant** MASC NOUN
elephant

l' **élevage** MASC NOUN
cattle rearing
□ faire de l'élevage to rear cattle
- un élevage de porcs a pig farm
- un élevage de poulets a chicken farm
- les truites d'élevage farmed trout

élevé (FEM **élevée**) ADJECTIVE
high
□ Le prix est trop élevé. The price is too high.
- être bien élevé to have good manners
- être mal élevé to have bad manners

l' **élève** MASC/FEM NOUN
pupil

élever VERB [43]
1 to bring up

□ Il a été élevé par sa grand-mère. He was brought up by his grandmother.

2 to breed

□ Son oncle élève des chevaux. His uncle breeds horses.

■ **élever la voix** to raise one's voice
■ **s'élever à** to come to □ À combien s'élèvent les dégâts? How much does the damage come to?

l' **éleveur** MASC NOUN
breeder

éliminatoire (FEM **éliminatoire**) ADJECTIVE

■ **une note éliminatoire** a fail mark
■ **une épreuve éliminatoire** (sport) a qualifying round

éliminer VERB [28]
to eliminate

élire VERB [44]
to elect

elle PRONOUN

1 she

□ Elle est institutrice. She is a primary school teacher.

2 her

□ Vous pouvez avoir confiance en elle. You can trust her.

3 it

□ Prends cette chaise: elle est plus confortable. Take this chair: it's more comfortable.

LANGUAGE TIP **elle** is also used for emphasis.

□ Elle, elle est toujours en retard! Oh, SHE's always late!

■ **elle-même** herself □ Elle l'a choisi elle-même. She chose it herself.

elles PL PRONOUN
they

□ Où sont Anne et Rachel? — Elles sont allées au cinéma. Where are Anne and Rachel? — They've gone to the cinema.

■ **elles-mêmes** themselves

élogieux (FEM **élogieuse**) ADJECTIVE
complimentary

□ Ton professeur a été très élogieux à propos de ton travail. Your teacher was very complimentary about your work.

éloigné (FEM **éloignée**) ADJECTIVE
distant

s' **éloigner** VERB [28]
to go far away

□ Ne vous éloignez pas: le dîner est bientôt prêt! Don't go far away: dinner will soon be ready!

■ **Vous vous éloignez du sujet.** You are getting off the point.

l' **Élysée** MASC NOUN

Élysée Palace

DID YOU KNOW...?
The **Élysée** is the residence of the French president.

l' **e-mail** MASC NOUN
email

l' **emballage** MASC NOUN

■ **le papier d'emballage** wrapping paper

emballer VERB [28]
to wrap

■ **s'emballer** (informal) to get excited □ Il s'est emballé pour ce projet. He got really excited about this plan.

l' **embarquement** MASC NOUN
boarding

□ 'embarquement immédiat' 'now boarding' □ L'embarquement des passagers n'a pas encore été annoncé. Passenger boarding has not been announced yet.

l' **embarras** MASC NOUN
embarrassment

□ Votre question me met dans l'embarras. It's difficult for me to answer your question.

■ **Vous n'avez que l'embarras du choix.** The only problem is choosing.

embarrassant (FEM **embarrassante**) ADJECTIVE
embarrassing

embarrasser VERB [28]
to embarrass

□ Cela m'embarrasse de vous demander encore un service. I feel embarrassed to ask you to do something more for me.

embaucher VERB [28]
to take on

□ L'entreprise vient d'embaucher cinquante ouvriers. The firm has just taken on fifty workers.

embêtant (FEM **embêtante**) ADJECTIVE
annoying

les **embêtements** MASC PL NOUN
trouble

embêter VERB [28]
to bother

■ **s'embêter** to be bored □ Qu'est-ce qu'on s'embête ici! Isn't it boring here!

l' **embouteillage** MASC NOUN
traffic jam

embrasser VERB [28]
to kiss

□ Ils se sont embrassés. They kissed each other.

s' **embrouiller** VERB [28]
to get confused

□ Il s'embrouille dans ses explications. He gets confused when he explains things.

émerveiller VERB [28]

to dazzle

l' **émeute** FEM NOUN
riot

émigrer VERB [28]
to emigrate

l' **émission** FEM NOUN
programme
□ une émission de télévision a TV
programme

s' **emmêler** VERB [28]
to get tangled
□ Ma laine s'est emmêlée. My wool has got tangled.

emménager VERB [45]
to move in
□ Nous venons d'emménager dans une nouvelle maison. We've just moved into a new house.

emmener VERB [43]
to take
□ Ils m'ont emmené au cinéma pour mon anniversaire. They took me to the cinema for my birthday.

l' **émoticon** MASC NOUN
smiley (computing)

émotif (FEM **émotive**) ADJECTIVE
emotional
□ Il est très émotif. He's very emotional.

l' **émotion** FEM NOUN
emotion

émouvoir VERB [31]
to move
□ Sa lettre l'a beaucoup émue. She was deeply moved by his letter.

emparer VERB [28]
■ s'emparer de to grab □ Il s'est emparé de ma valise. He grabbed my case.

l' **empêchement** MASC NOUN
■ Nous avons eu un empêchement de dernière minute. We were held up at the last minute.

empêcher VERB [28]
to prevent
□ Le café le soir m'empêche de dormir. Coffee at night keeps me awake.
■ Il n'a pas pu s'empêcher de rire. He couldn't help laughing.

l' **empereur** MASC NOUN
emperor

s' **empiffrer** VERB [28] (informal)
to stuff one's face
□ Arrête de t'empiffrer! Stop stuffing your face!

empiler VERB [28]
to pile up

empirer VERB [28]
to worsen

□ La situation a encore empiré. The situation got even worse.

l' **emplacement** MASC NOUN
site
□ Un panneau indique l'emplacement du château. A sign shows the site of the castle.

l' **emploi** MASC NOUN
1 use
□ prêt à l'emploi ready for use
■ le mode d'emploi directions for use
2 job
□ la création d'emplois job creation
■ un emploi du temps a timetable

l' **employé** MASC NOUN
employee
■ un employé de bureau an office worker

l' **employée** FEM NOUN
employee
■ une employée de banque a bank clerk

employer VERB [53]
1 to use
□ Quelle méthode employez-vous? What method do you use?
2 to employ
□ L'entreprise emploie dix ingénieurs. The firm employs ten engineers.

l' **employeur** MASC NOUN
employer

empoisonner VERB [28]
to poison

emporter VERB [28]
to take
□ N'emportez que le strict nécessaire. Only take the bare minimum.
■ plats à emporter take-away meals
■ s'emporter to lose one's temper □ Je m'emporte facilement. I'm quick to lose my temper.

l' **empreinte** FEM NOUN
■ une empreinte digitale a fingerprint

s' **empresser** VERB [28]
■ s'empresser de faire quelque chose to be quick to do something □ Ils se sont empressés de nous annoncer la nouvelle. They were quick to tell us the news.

emprisonner VERB [28]
to imprison

l' **emprunt** MASC NOUN
loan

emprunter VERB [28]
to borrow
■ emprunter quelque chose à quelqu'un to borrow something from somebody □ Je peux t'emprunter dix euros? Can I borrow ten euros from you?

l' **EMT** FEM NOUN (= éducation manuelle et technique)

97

design and technology

ému (FEM **émue**) ADJECTIVE
touched
□ J'ai été très ému par sa gentillesse. I was very touched by her kindness.

en PREPOSITION, PRONOUN
1 in
□ Il habite en France. He lives in France. □ La mariée est en blanc. The bride is in white. □ Je le verrai en mai. I'll see him in May.
2 to
□ Je vais en France cet été. I'm going to France this summer.
3 by
□ C'est plus rapide en voiture. It's quicker by car.
4 made of
□ C'est en verre. It's made of glass. □ un collier en argent a silver necklace
5 while
□ Il s'est coupé le doigt en ouvrant une boîte de conserve. He cut his finger while opening a tin.
■ Elle est sortie en courant. She ran out.

> **LANGUAGE TIP** When en is used with **avoir** and **il y a**, it is not translated in English.

□ Est-ce que tu as un dictionnaire? — Oui, j'en ai un. Have you got a dictionary? — Yes, I've got one. □ Combien d'élèves y a-t-il dans ta classe? — Il y en a trente. How many pupils are there in your class? — There are 30.

> **LANGUAGE TIP** en is also used with verbs and expressions normally followed by **de** to avoid repeating the same word.

□ Si tu as un problème, tu peux m'en parler. If you've got a problem, you can talk to me about it. □ Est-ce que tu peux me rendre ce livre? J'en ai besoin. Can you give me back that book? I need it. □ Il a un beau jardin et il en est très fier. He's got a beautiful garden and is very proud of it.
■ J'en ai assez. I've had enough.

encaisser VERB [28]
to cash (money)

enceinte FEM ADJECTIVE
pregnant
□ Elle est enceinte de six mois. She's 6 months pregnant.

enchanté (FEM **enchantée**) ADJECTIVE
delighted
□ Ma mère est enchantée de sa nouvelle voiture. My mother's delighted with her new car.

■ Enchanté! Pleased to meet you!

encombrant (FEM **encombrante**) ADJECTIVE
bulky

encombrer VERB [28]
to clutter

encore ADVERB
1 still
□ Il est encore au travail. He's still at work. □ Il reste encore deux morceaux de gâteau. There are two bits of cake left.
2 even
□ C'est encore mieux. That's even better.
3 again
□ Il m'a encore demandé de l'argent. He asked me for money again.
■ encore une fois once again
■ pas encore not yet □ Je n'ai pas encore fini. I haven't finished yet.

encourager VERB [45]
to encourage

l' **encre** FEM NOUN
ink

l' **encyclopédie** FEM NOUN
encyclopaedia

l' **endive** FEM NOUN
chicory

endommager VERB [45]
to damage

endormi (FEM **endormie**) ADJECTIVE
asleep

endormir VERB [29]
to deaden
□ Cette piqûre sert à endormir le nerf. This injection is to deaden the nerve.
■ s'endormir to go to sleep

l' **endroit** MASC NOUN
place
□ C'est un endroit très tranquille. It's a very quiet place.
■ à l'endroit 1 the right way out 2 the right way up

endurant (FEM **endurante**) ADJECTIVE
tough (person)

endurcir VERB [38]
to toughen up
□ Ces exercices servent à endurcir les soldats. These exercises are to toughen up the soldiers.
■ s'endurcir to become hardened

endurer VERB [28]
to endure

l' **énergie** FEM NOUN
1 energy
□ Je n'ai pas beaucoup d'énergie ce matin. I haven't got much energy this morning.
2 power
□ l'énergie nucléaire nuclear power

■ **avec énergie** vigorously □ Il a protesté avec énergie. He protested vigorously.

énergique (FEM **énergique**) ADJECTIVE
energetic

■ **des mesures énergiques** strong measures

énerver VERB [28]

■ **Il m'énerve!** He gets on my nerves!
■ **Ce bruit m'énerve.** This noise gets on my nerves.
■ **s'énerver** to get worked up
■ **Ne t'énerve pas!** Take it easy!

l' **enfance** FEM NOUN
childhood

□ Je le connais depuis l'enfance. I've known him since I was a child.

l' **enfant** MASC/FEM NOUN
child

l' **enfer** MASC NOUN
hell

s' **enfermer** VERB [28]

■ **Il s'est enfermé dans sa chambre.** He shut himself up in his bedroom.

enfiler VERB [28]

1 to put on
□ J'ai rapidement enfilé un pull avant de sortir. I quickly put on a sweater before going out.

2 to thread
□ J'ai du mal à enfiler cette aiguille. I am having difficulty threading this needle.

enfin ADVERB
at last

□ J'ai enfin réussi à le joindre. I have at last managed to contact him.

enflé (FEM **enflée**) ADJECTIVE
swollen

enfler VERB [28]
to swell

enfoncer VERB [12]

■ **Il marchait, les mains enfoncées dans les poches.** He was walking with his hands thrust into his pockets.
■ **s'enfoncer** to sink □ Les roues de la voiture s'enfonçaient dans la boue. The wheels of the car were sinking into the mud.

s' **enfuir** VERB [39]
to run off

l' **engagement** MASC NOUN
commitment

engager VERB [45]
to take on (person)

□ engager quelqu'un to take somebody on

s' **engager** VERB [45]
to commit oneself

□ Le Premier ministre s'est engagé à combattre le chômage. The Prime Minister

has committed himself to fighting unemployment.

■ **Il s'est engagé dans l'armée à dix-huit ans.** He joined the army when he was 18.

les **engelures** FEM PL NOUN
chilblains

l' **engin** MASC NOUN
device

LANGUAGE TIP Be careful! The French word **engin** does not mean **engine**.

s' **engourdir** VERB [38]
to go numb

□ Mes doigts se sont engourdis avec le froid. My fingers have gone numb with the cold.

engueuler VERB [28] (informal)

■ **engueuler quelqu'un** to tell somebody off □ Tu vas te faire engueuler! You're going to get a telling-off!

l' **énigme** FEM NOUN
riddle

s' **enivrer** VERB [28]
to get drunk

enjamber VERB [28]
to stride over

□ enjamber une barrière to stride over a fence

l' **enlèvement** MASC NOUN
kidnapping

enlever VERB [43]

1 to take off
□ Enlève donc ton manteau! Take off your coat!

2 to kidnap
□ Un groupe terroriste a enlevé la femme de l'ambassadeur. A terrorist group has kidnapped the ambassador's wife.

enneigé (FEM **enneigée**) ADJECTIVE
snowed up

□ Les routes sont encore enneigées. The roads are still snowed up.

l' **ennemi** MASC NOUN
enemy

l' **ennemie** FEM NOUN
enemy

l' **ennui** MASC NOUN

1 boredom
□ C'est à mourir d'ennui. It would make you die of boredom.

2 problem
□ avoir des ennuis to have problems

ennuyer VERB [53]
to bother

□ J'espère que cela ne vous ennuie pas trop. I hope it doesn't bother you too much.

■ **s'ennuyer** to be bored

ennuyeux (FEM **ennuyeuse**) ADJECTIVE

1 boring

2 awkward
□ Tu ne peux pas venir plus tôt? C'est bien ennuyeux. You can't come any earlier? That's rather awkward.

énorme (FEM **énorme**) ADJECTIVE
huge

énormément ADVERB
■ **Il a énormément grossi.** He's got terribly fat.
■ **Il y a énormément de neige.** There's an enormous amount of snow.

l' **enquête** FEM NOUN
1 investigation
□ La police a ouvert une enquête. The police have begun an investigation.
2 survey
□ une enquête parmi les étudiants a montré que ... a survey of students has shown that ...

enquêter VERB [28]
to investigate
□ La police enquête actuellement sur le crime. The police are currently investigating the crime.

enrageant (FEM **enrageante**) ADJECTIVE
infuriating

enrager VERB [45]
to be furious
□ J'enrage de n'avoir pas pu profiter de cette occasion. I'm furious I wasn't able to take advantage of this opportunity.

l' **enregistrement** MASC NOUN
recording
■ **l'enregistrement des bagages** baggage check-in

enregistrer VERB [28]
1 to record
□ Ils viennent d'enregistrer un nouvel album. They've just recorded a new album.
2 to check in
□ Vous pouvez enregistrer plusieurs valises. You can check in several cases.

s' **enrhumer** VERB [28]
to catch a cold
□ Je suis enrhumé. I've got a cold.

s' **enrichir** VERB [38]
to get rich

enrouler VERB [28]
to wind
□ Enroulez le fil autour de la bobine. Wind the thread round the bobbin.

l' **enseignant** MASC NOUN
teacher

l' **enseignante** FEM NOUN
teacher

l' **enseignement** MASC NOUN
1 education

□ les réformes de l'enseignement education reforms
2 teaching
□ l'enseignement des langues étrangères the teaching of foreign languages

enseigner VERB [28]
to teach
□ Mon père enseigne les maths dans un lycée. My father teaches maths in a secondary school.

ensemble ADVERB
▷ see also **ensemble** NOUN
together
□ tous ensemble all together

l' **ensemble** MASC NOUN
▷ see also **ensemble** ADVERB
outfit
□ Elle portait un ensemble vert. She was wearing a green outfit.
■ **l'ensemble de** the whole of
□ L'ensemble du personnel est en grève. The whole workforce is on strike.
■ **dans l'ensemble** on the whole

ensoleillé (FEM **ensoleillée**) ADJECTIVE
sunny

ensuite ADVERB
then
□ Nous sommes allés au cinéma et ensuite au restaurant. We went to the cinema and then to a restaurant.

entamer VERB [28]
to start
□ Qui a entamé le gâteau? Who's started the cake?

s' **entasser** VERB [28]
to cram
□ Ils se sont tous entassés dans ma voiture. They all crammed into my car.

entendre VERB [88]
1 to hear
□ Je ne t'entends pas. I can't hear you.
■ **J'ai entendu dire qu'il est dangereux de nager ici.** I've heard that it's dangerous to swim here.
2 to mean
□ Qu'est-ce que tu entends par là? What do you mean by that?
■ **s'entendre** to get on □ Il s'entend bien avec sa sœur. He gets on well with his sister.

entendu (FEM **entendue**) ADJECTIVE
■ **C'est entendu!** Agreed! □ Je passerai te prendre à sept heures, c'est entendu. That's agreed then, I'll pick you up at 7 o'clock.
■ **bien entendu** of course □ Il est bien entendu que je n'en parlerai à personne. I won't tell anybody about it of course.

l' **enterrement** MASC NOUN
funeral *(burial)*

enterrer VERB [28]
to bury

entêté (FEM **entêtée**) ADJECTIVE
stubborn

s' **entêter** VERB [28]
to persist
  □ Il s'entête à refuser de voir le médecin. He persists in refusing to go to the doctor.

l' **enthousiasme** MASC NOUN
enthusiasm

s' **enthousiasmer** VERB [28]
to get enthusiastic
  □ Il s'enthousiasme facilement. He gets very enthusiastic about things.

entier (FEM **entière**) ADJECTIVE
whole
  □ Il a mangé une quiche entière. He ate a whole quiche. □ Je n'ai pas lu le livre en entier. I haven't read the whole book.
  ■ **le lait entier** full fat milk

entièrement ADVERB
completely

l' **entorse** FEM NOUN
sprain
  □ Il s'est fait une entorse à la cheville. He's sprained his ankle.

entourer VERB [28]
to surround
  □ Le jardin est entouré d'un mur de pierres. The garden is surrounded by a stone wall.

l' **entracte** MASC NOUN
interval

l' **entraînement** MASC NOUN
training

entraîner VERB [28]
1 to lead
  □ Il se laisse facilement entraîner par les autres. He's easily led.
2 to train
  □ Il entraîne l'équipe de France depuis cinq ans. He's been training the French team for five years.
3 to involve
  □ Un mariage entraîne beaucoup de dépenses. A wedding involves a lot of expense.
  ■ **s'entraîner** to train □ Il s'entraîne au foot tous les samedis matins. He does football training every Saturday morning.

l' **entraîneur** MASC NOUN
trainer

entre PREPOSITION
between
  □ Il est assis entre son père et son oncle. He's sitting between his father and his uncle.
  ■ **entre eux** among themselves
  ■ **l'un d'entre eux** one of them

l' **entrecôte** FEM NOUN
rib steak

l' **entrée** FEM NOUN
1 entrance
2 starter *(of meal)*
  □ Qu'est ce que vous prenez comme entrée? What would you like for the starter?

entreprendre VERB [65]
to start on
  □ Elle a entrepris des démarches pour adopter un enfant. She's started on the procedures for adopting a child.

l' **entrepreneur** MASC NOUN
contractor

l' **entreprise** FEM NOUN
firm

entrer VERB [32]
1 to come in
  □ Entrez donc! Come on in!
2 to go in
  □ Ils sont tous entrés dans la maison. They all went into the house.
  ■ **entrer à l'hôpital** to go into hospital
  ■ **entrer des données** to enter data □ J'ai entré toutes les adresses de mon agenda sur mon ordinateur. I've entered all the addresses in my diary onto my computer.

entre-temps ADVERB
meanwhile

l' **entretien** MASC NOUN
1 maintenance
  □ un contrat d'entretien a maintenance contract
2 interview
  □ On m'a convoqué à un entretien pour un travail. I've been called for a job interview.

l' **entrevue** FEM NOUN
interview
  □ une entrevue avec le ministre an interview with the minister

entrouvert (FEM **entrouverte**) ADJECTIVE
half open
  □ La porte était entrouverte. The door was half open.

envahir VERB [38]
to invade

l' **enveloppe** FEM NOUN
envelope

envelopper VERB [28]
to wrap

envers PREPOSITION
▷ *see also* **envers** NOUN
towards
  □ Il est bien disposé envers elle. He's well

101

disposed towards her. □ son attitude envers moi his attitude to me

l' **envers** MASC NOUN

▷ see also **envers** PREPOSITION

■ **à l'envers** inside out □ Je dois repasser ce chemisier à l'envers. I have to iron this blouse inside out.

l' **envie** FEM NOUN

■ **avoir envie de faire quelque chose** to feel like doing something □ J'avais envie de pleurer. I felt like crying. □ J'ai envie d'aller aux toilettes. I want to go to the toilet.

■ **Cette glace me fait envie.** I fancy some of that ice cream.

envier VERB [19]

to envy

environ ADVERB

about

□ C'est à soixante kilomètres environ. It's about 60 kilometres.

l' **environnement** MASC NOUN

environment

les **environs** MASC PL NOUN

area

□ les environs de Nantes the Nantes area □ Il y a beaucoup de choses intéressantes à voir dans les environs. There are a lot of interesting things to see in the area.

■ **aux environs de dix-neuf heures** around 7 p.m.

envisager VERB [45]

to consider

□ Est-ce que vous envisagez de travailler à l'étranger? Are you considering working abroad?

s' **envoler** VERB [28]

1 to fly away

□ Le papillon s'est envolé. The butterfly flew away.

2 to blow away

□ Toutes mes feuilles de cours se sont envolées. All my lecture notes blew away.

envoyer VERB [33]

to send

□ Ma tante m'a envoyé une carte pour mon anniversaire. My aunt sent me a card for my birthday.

■ **envoyer quelqu'un chercher quelque chose** to send somebody to get something □ Sa mère l'a envoyé chercher du pain. His mother sent him to get some bread.

■ **envoyer un e-mail à quelqu'un** to send sb an email

épais (FEM **épaisse**) ADJECTIVE

thick

l' **épaisseur** FEM NOUN

thickness

épatant (FEM **épatante**) ADJECTIVE (informal)

great

□ C'est un type épatant. He's a great guy.

l' **épaule** FEM NOUN

shoulder

l' **épée** FEM NOUN

sword

épeler VERB [4]

to spell

□ Est-ce que vous pouvez épeler votre nom, s'il vous plaît? Can you spell your name, please?

l' **épice** FEM NOUN

spice

épicé (FEM **épicée**) ADJECTIVE

spicy

□ un plat épicé a spicy dish

l' **épicerie** FEM NOUN

grocer's shop

l' **épicier** MASC NOUN

grocer

l' **épicière** FEM NOUN

grocer

l' **épidémie** FEM NOUN

epidemic

épiler VERB [28]

■ **s'épiler les jambes** to wax one's legs

■ **s'épiler les sourcils** to pluck one's eyebrows

les **épinards** MASC PL NOUN

spinach

l' **épine** FEM NOUN

thorn

l' **épingle** FEM NOUN

pin

■ **une épingle de sûreté** a safety pin

l' **épisode** MASC NOUN

episode

éplucher VERB [28]

to peel

l' **éponge** FEM NOUN

sponge

l' **époque** FEM NOUN

time

□ à cette époque de l'année at this time of year

■ **à l'époque** at that time □ À l'époque, beaucoup de gens n'avaient pas l'eau courante. At that time a lot of people didn't have running water.

l' **épouse** FEM NOUN

wife

épouser VERB [28]

to marry

épouvantable (FEM **épouvantable**) ADJECTIVE

awful

e

l' **épouvante** FEM NOUN
terror

■ un film d'épouvante a horror film

épouvanter VERB [28]
to terrify

l' **époux** MASC NOUN
husband

■ les nouveaux époux the newly-weds

l' **épreuve** FEM NOUN
1 test

□ une épreuve orale an oral test □ une épreuve écrite a written test
2 event (sport)

éprouver VERB [28]
to feel

□ Qu'est-ce que vous avez éprouvé à ce moment-là? What did you feel at that moment?

l' **EPS** FEM NOUN (= éducation physique et sportive)
PE (= physical education)

épuisé (FEM **épuisée**) ADJECTIVE
exhausted

épuiser VERB [28]
to wear out

□ Ce travail m'a complètement épuisé. This job has completely worn me out.

■ s'épuiser to wear oneself out □ Il s'épuise à garder un jardin impeccable. He wears himself out keeping his garden immaculate.

l' **Équateur** MASC NOUN
Ecuador

l' **équateur** MASC NOUN
equator

l' **équation** FEM NOUN
equation

l' **équerre** FEM NOUN
set square

l' **équilibre** MASC NOUN
balance

□ J'ai failli perdre l'équilibre. I nearly lost my balance.

équilibré (FEM **équilibrée**) ADJECTIVE
well-balanced

l' **équipage** MASC NOUN
crew

l' **équipe** FEM NOUN
team

équipé (FEM **équipée**) ADJECTIVE
■ bien équipé well-equipped

l' **équipement** MASC NOUN
equipment

les **équipements** MASC PL NOUN
facilities

□ les équipements sportifs sports facilities

l' **équitation** FEM NOUN
riding

□ faire de l'équitation to go riding

l' **équivalent** MASC NOUN
equivalent

l' **erreur** FEM NOUN
mistake

■ faire erreur to be mistaken

es VERB ▷ see être

■ Tu es très gentille. You're very kind.

l' **ESB** FEM NOUN (= encéphalite spongiforme bovine)
BSE

l' **escabeau** (PL les **escabeaux**) MASC NOUN
stepladder

l' **escalade** FEM NOUN
climbing

□ faire de l'escalade to go climbing

escalader VERB [28]
to climb

l' **escale** FEM NOUN
■ faire escale to stop off

l' **escalier** MASC NOUN
stairs

□ un escalier roulant an escalator

l' **escargot** MASC NOUN
snail

l' **esclavage** MASC NOUN
slavery

l' **esclave** MASC/FEM NOUN
slave

l' **escrime** FEM NOUN
fencing

l' **escroc** MASC NOUN
crook

l' **espace** MASC NOUN
space

■ espace de travail workspace

s' **espacer** VERB [12]
to become less frequent

□ Ses visites se sont peu à peu espacées. His visits became less and less frequent.

l' **espadrille** FEM NOUN
rope-soled sandal

l' **Espagne** FEM NOUN
Spain

■ en Espagne 1 in Spain 2 to Spain

espagnol (FEM **espagnole**) ADJECTIVE, NOUN
Spanish

□ J'apprends l'espagnol. I'm learning Spanish.

■ un Espagnol a Spaniard (man)
■ une Espagnole a Spaniard (woman)

l' **espèce** FEM NOUN
1 sort

□ Elle portait une espèce de cape en velours. She was wearing a sort of velvet cloak.
2 species

French-English

□ **une espèce en voie de disparition** an endangered species

■ **Espèce d'idiot!** You idiot!

les **espèces** FEM PL NOUN
cash

□ **payer en espèces** to pay cash

espérer VERB [34]
to hope

■ **J'espère bien.** I hope so. □ **Tu penses avoir réussi? — Oui, j'espère bien.** Do you think you've passed? — Yes, I hope so.

espiègle (FEM **espiègle**) ADJECTIVE
mischievous

l' **espion** MASC NOUN
spy

l' **espionnage** MASC NOUN
spying

■ **un roman d'espionnage** a spy novel

l' **espionne** FEM NOUN
spy

l' **espoir** MASC NOUN
hope

l' **esprit** MASC NOUN
mind

□ **Ça ne m'est pas venu à l'esprit.** It didn't cross my mind.

■ **avoir de l'esprit** to be witty □ **Il a beaucoup d'esprit.** He's very witty.

l' **esquimau®** (PL les **esquimaux**) MASC NOUN
ice lolly

l' **Esquimau** (PL les **Esquimaux**) MASC NOUN
Eskimo

l' **Esquimaude** FEM NOUN
Eskimo

l' **essai** MASC NOUN
attempt

□ **Ce n'est pas mal pour un coup d'essai.** It's not bad for a first attempt.

■ **prendre quelqu'un à l'essai** to take somebody on for a trial period

essayer VERB [59]

1 to try

□ **Essaie de rentrer de bonne heure.** Try to come home early.

2 to try on

□ **Essaie ce pull: il devrait bien t'aller.** Try this sweater on: it ought to look good on you.

l' **essence** FEM NOUN
petrol

essentiel (FEM **essentielle**) ADJECTIVE
essential

■ **Tu es là: c'est l'essentiel.** You're here: that's the main thing.

s' **essouffler** VERB [28]
to get out of breath

l' **essuie-glace** MASC NOUN
windscreen wiper

essuyer VERB [53]
to wipe

■ **essuyer la vaisselle** to dry the dishes

■ **s'essuyer** to dry oneself □ **Vous pouvez vous essuyer les mains avec cette serviette.** You can dry your hands on this towel.

est VERB ▷ see **être**

▷ see also **est** ADJECTIVE, NOUN

■ **Elle est merveilleuse.** She's marvellous.

⋯ **LANGUAGE TIP** **est** is pronounced 'ay' when it comes from the verb **être**.

est (FEM+PL **est**) ADJECTIVE

▷ see also **est** VERB, NOUN

1 east

□ **la côte est des États-Unis** the east coast of the United States

2 eastern

□ **dans la partie est du pays** in the eastern part of the country

⋯ **LANGUAGE TIP** **est** is pronounced 'ayst' when it means **east** or **eastern**.

l' **est** MASC NOUN

▷ see also **est** VERB, ADJECTIVE

east

□ **Je vis dans l'est de la France.** I live in the East of France.

■ **vers l'est** eastwards

■ **à l'est de Paris** east of Paris

■ **l'Europe de l'Est** Eastern Europe

■ **le vent d'est** the east wind

⋯ **LANGUAGE TIP** **est** is pronounced 'ayst' when it means **east** or **eastern**.

est-ce que ADVERB

■ **Est-ce que c'est cher?** Is it expensive?

■ **Quand est-ce qu'il part?** When is he leaving?

l' **esthéticienne** FEM NOUN
beautician

l' **estime** FEM NOUN

■ **J'ai beaucoup d'estime pour elle.** I think a lot of her.

estimer VERB [28]

■ **estimer quelqu'un** to have great respect for somebody □ **Mon père l'estime beaucoup.** My father has a lot of respect for him.

■ **estimer que** to consider that □ **J'estime que c'est de sa faute.** I consider that it's his fault.

l' **estivant** MASC NOUN
holiday-maker

l' **estivante** FEM NOUN
holiday-maker

l' **estomac** MASC NOUN
stomach

l' **Estonie** FEM NOUN
Estonia

l' **estrade** FEM NOUN
platform

et CONJUNCTION
and

établir VERB [30]
to establish
  ■ **s'établir à son compte** to set up in business

l' **établissement** MASC NOUN
establishment
  ■ **un établissement scolaire** a school

l' **étage** MASC NOUN
floor
  □ **au premier étage** on the first floor
  ■ **à l'étage** upstairs

l' **étagère** FEM NOUN
shelf

étaient VERB ▷ see **être**

l' **étain** MASC NOUN
tin

étais, était VERB ▷ see **être**
  ■ **Il était très jeune.** He was very young.

l' **étalage** MASC NOUN
display

étaler VERB [28]
to spread
  □ **Il a étalé la carte sur la table.** He spread the map on the table.

étanche (FEM **étanche**) ADJECTIVE
1 watertight
  □ **Le toit n'est pas étanche.** The roof isn't watertight.
2 waterproof (watch)

l' **étang** MASC NOUN
pond

étant VERB ▷ see **être**
  ■ **Mes revenus étant limités ...** My income being limited ...

l' **étape** FEM NOUN
stage
  □ **une étape importante de la vie** an important stage in life
  ■ **faire étape** to stop off

l' **État** MASC NOUN
state (nation)
  □ **un chef d'État** a head of state

l' **état** MASC NOUN
1 state (country)
2 condition
  □ **en bon état** in good condition □ **en mauvais état** in poor condition
  ■ **remettre quelque chose en état** to repair something
  ■ **le bureau d'état civil** the registry office

les **États-Unis** MASC PL NOUN
United States
  ■ **aux États-Unis 1** in the United States
  2 to the United States

été VERB ▷ see **être**
  ▷ see also **été** NOUN
  ■ **Il a été licencié.** He's been made redundant.

l' **été** MASC NOUN
  ▷ see also **été** VERB
summer
  ■ **en été** in the summer

éteindre VERB [60]
1 to switch off
  □ **Éteins la lumière.** Switch the light off.
2 to put out (cigarette)

étendre VERB [88]
to spread
  □ **Elle a étendu une nappe propre sur la table.** She spread a clean cloth on the table.
  ■ **étendre le linge** to hang out the washing
  ■ **s'étendre** to lie down □ **Je vais m'étendre cinq minutes.** I'm going to lie down for five minutes.

l' **éternité** FEM NOUN
  ■ **J'ai attendu une éternité chez le médecin.** I waited for ages at the doctor's.

éternuer VERB [28]
to sneeze

êtes VERB ▷ see **être**
  ■ **Vous êtes en retard.** You're late.

étiez VERB ▷ see **être**

étinceler VERB [4]
to sparkle

étions VERB ▷ see **être**

l' **étiquette** FEM NOUN
label
  □ **L'étiquette du pot de confiture s'est décollée.** The label has come off the jam pot.

s' **étirer** VERB [28]
to stretch
  □ **Elle s'est étirée paresseusement.** She stretched lazily.

l' **étoile** FEM NOUN
star
  ■ **une étoile de mer** a starfish
  ◌ **LANGUAGE TIP** Word for word, **étoile de mer** means 'sea star'.
  ■ **une étoile filante** a shooting star
  ■ **dormir à la belle étoile** to sleep under the stars

étonnant (FEM **étonnante**) ADJECTIVE
amazing

étonner VERB [28]
to surprise
  □ **Cela m'étonnerait que le colis soit déjà arrivé.** I'd be surprised if the parcel had

arrived yet.

étouffer VERB [28]
■ **On étouffe ici: ouvre donc les fenêtres.** It's stifling in here: open the windows.
■ **s'étouffer** to choke □ Ne mange pas si vite: tu vas t'étouffer! Don't eat so fast: you'll choke!

l' **étourderie** FEM NOUN
absent-mindedness
■ **une erreur d'étourderie** a slip

étourdi (FEM **étourdie**) ADJECTIVE
scatterbrained

l' **étourdissement** MASC NOUN
■ **avoir des étourdissements** to feel dizzy

étrange (FEM **étrange**) ADJECTIVE
strange

étranger (FEM **étrangère**) ADJECTIVE
▷ see also **étranger** NOUN
foreign
□ un pays étranger a foreign country
■ **une personne étrangère** a stranger

l' **étranger** MASC NOUN
▷ see also **étranger** ADJECTIVE
1 foreigner
2 stranger
■ **à l'étranger** abroad

l' **étrangère** FEM NOUN
1 foreigner
2 stranger

étrangler VERB [28]
to strangle
■ **s'étrangler** to choke □ s'étrangler avec quelque chose to choke on something

l' **être** MASC NOUN
▷ see also **être** VERB
■ **un être humain** a human being

être VERB [35]
▷ see also **être** NOUN

PRESENT TENSE

je suis	nous sommes
tu es	vous êtes
il/elle est	ils/elles sont

PAST PARTICIPLE
été

1 to be
□ Je suis heureux. I'm happy. □ Mon père est instituteur. My father's a primary school teacher. □ Il est dix heures. It's 10 o'clock.
2 to have
□ Il n'est pas encore arrivé. He hasn't arrived yet.

les **étrennes** FEM PL NOUN
■ **Nous avons donné des étrennes à la gardienne.** We gave the caretaker a New Year gift.

étroit (FEM **étroite**) ADJECTIVE
narrow

■ **être à l'étroit** to be cramped □ Nous sommes un peu à l'étroit dans cet appartement. We're a bit cramped in this flat.

l' **étude** FEM NOUN
study
□ une étude de cas a case study
■ **faire des études** to be studying □ Il fait des études de droit. He's studying law.

l' **étudiant** MASC NOUN
student

l' **étudiante** FEM NOUN
student

étudier VERB [19]
to study

l' **étui** MASC NOUN
case
□ un étui à lunettes a glasses case

eu VERB ▷ see **avoir**
■ **J'ai eu une bonne note.** I got a good mark.

euh EXCLAMATION
er
□ Euh … je ne m'en souviens pas. Er … I can't remember.

l' **euro** MASC NOUN
euro

l' **Europe** FEM NOUN
Europe
■ **en Europe 1** in Europe **2** to Europe

européen (FEM **européenne**) ADJECTIVE
European

eux PL PRONOUN
them
□ Je pense souvent à eux. I often think of them.

○ **LANGUAGE TIP** eux is also used for emphasis.

□ Elle a accepté l'invitation, mais eux ont refusé. She accepted the invitation, but THEY refused.

évacuer VERB [28]
to evacuate

s' **évader** VERB [28]
to escape

l' **évangile** MASC NOUN
gospel

s' **évanouir** VERB [38]
to faint

s' **évaporer** VERB [28]
to evaporate

évasif (FEM **évasive**) ADJECTIVE
evasive

l' **évasion** FEM NOUN
escape
□ Ils ont préparé leur évasion pendant des mois. They spent months planning their

escape.

éveillé (FEM **éveillée**) ADJECTIVE
1 awake
  □ Il est resté éveillé toute la nuit. He stayed awake all night.
2 bright
  □ C'est un enfant très éveillé pour son âge. He's very bright for his age.

s' **éveiller** VERB [28]
  to awaken

l' **événement** MASC NOUN
  event

l' **éventail** MASC NOUN
  fan (hand-held)
  ■ un large éventail de prix a wide range of prices

l' **éventualité** FEM NOUN
  ■ dans l'éventualité d'un retard in the event of a delay

éventuel (FEM **éventuelle**) ADJECTIVE
  possible
  □ une solution éventuelle a possible solution □ les conséquences éventuelles the possible consequences

  LANGUAGE TIP Be careful! éventuel does not mean **eventual**.

éventuellement ADVERB
  possibly
  □ Nous pourrions éventuellement avoir besoin de vous. We may possibly need you. □ les difficultés que vous pourriez éventuellement rencontrer the difficulties that you may have

  LANGUAGE TIP Be careful! éventuellement does not mean **eventually**.

l' **évêque** MASC NOUN
  bishop

évidemment ADVERB
1 obviously
  □ Les tomates sont évidemment chères en cette saison. Tomatoes are obviously dear at this time of year.
2 of course
  □ Est-ce que je peux utiliser ton téléphone? — Évidemment, tu n'as pas besoin de demander. Can I use your phone? — Of course, you don't need to ask.

l' **évidence** FEM NOUN
  ■ C'est une évidence. It's quite obvious.
  ■ de toute évidence obviously □ De toute évidence, il ne veut pas nous voir. Obviously he doesn't want to see us.
  ■ être en évidence to be clearly visible □ La lettre était en évidence sur la table. The letter was clearly visible on the table.
  ■ mettre en évidence to reveal

évident (FEM **évidente**) ADJECTIVE
  obvious

l' **évier** MASC NOUN
  sink

éviter VERB [28]
  to avoid

évolué (FEM **évoluée**) ADJECTIVE
  advanced

évoluer VERB [28]
  to progress
  □ La chirurgie esthétique a beaucoup évolué. Plastic surgery has progressed a great deal.
  ■ Il a beaucoup évolué. He has come on a great deal.

l' **évolution** FEM NOUN
1 development
  □ une évolution rapide rapid development
2 evolution
  □ la théorie de l'évolution the theory of evolution

évoquer VERB [28]
  to mention
  □ Il a évoqué divers problèmes dans son discours. He mentioned various problems in his speech.

exact (FEM **exacte**) ADJECTIVE
1 right
  □ Avez-vous l'heure exacte? Have you got the right time? □ Votre voiture est garée dehors, n'est-ce pas? — C'est exact. Your car's parked outside, isn't it? — That's right.
2 exact
  □ Est-ce que vous pouvez m'indiquer le prix exact du billet? Can you tell me the exact price of the ticket?

exactement ADVERB
  exactly
  □ C'est exactement ce que je cherchais. That's exactly what I was looking for.

ex aequo (FEM+PL **ex aequo**) ADJECTIVE
  ■ Ils sont arrivés ex aequo. They finished neck and neck.

exagérer VERB [34]
1 to exaggerate
  □ Vous exagérez! You're exaggerating!
2 to go too far
  □ Ça fait trois fois que tu arrives en retard: tu exagères! That's three times you've been late: you really go too far sometimes!

l' **examen** MASC NOUN
  exam
  □ Nous allons passer l'examen d'anglais vendredi matin. We're doing our English exam on Friday morning. □ un examen de français a French exam
  ■ un examen médical a medical

examiner VERB [28]
to examine

exaspérant (FEM **exaspérante**) ADJECTIVE
infuriating

exaspérer VERB [34]
to infuriate

l' **excédent** MASC NOUN
■ l' excédent de bagages excess baggage

excéder VERB [34]
to exceed
□ un contrat dont la durée n'excède pas deux ans a contract for a period not exceeding two years
■ **excéder quelqu'un** to drive somebody mad □ Les cris des enfants l'excédaient. The noise of the children was driving her mad.

excellent (FEM **excellente**) ADJECTIVE
excellent

excentrique (FEM **excentrique**) ADJECTIVE
eccentric

excepté PREPOSITION
except
□ Toutes les chaussures excepté les sandales sont en solde. All the shoes except sandals are reduced.

l' **exception** FEM NOUN
exception
■ **à l'exception de** except

exceptionnel (FEM **exceptionnelle**) ADJECTIVE
exceptional

l' **excès** MASC NOUN
■ **faire des excès** to overindulge □ On fait souvent des excès aux environs de Noël. People often overindulge around Christmas.
■ **les excès de vitesse** speeding

excessif (FEM **excessive**) ADJECTIVE
excessive

excitant (FEM **excitante**) ADJECTIVE
▷ see also **excitant** NOUN
exciting

l' **excitant** MASC NOUN
▷ see also **excitant** ADJECTIVE
stimulant
□ Le thé et le café sont des excitants. Tea and coffee are stimulants.

l' **excitation** FEM NOUN
excitement

exciter VERB [28]
to excite
□ Il était tout excité à l'idée de revoir ses cousins. He was all excited about seeing his cousins again.
■ **s'exciter** (informal) to get excited □ Ne t'excite pas trop vite: ça ne va peut-être pas

marcher! Don't get excited too soon: it may not work!

l' **exclamation** FEM NOUN
exclamation

exclu (FEM **exclue**) ADJECTIVE
■ **Il n'est pas exclu que ...** It's not impossible that ...

exclusif (FEM **exclusive**) ADJECTIVE
exclusive

l' **excursion** FEM NOUN
1 trip
□ faire une excursion to go on a trip
2 walk
□ une excursion dans la montagne a walk in the hills

l' **excuse** FEM NOUN
1 excuse
□ une bonne excuse a good excuse
2 apology
□ présenter ses excuses to offer one's apologies
■ **un mot d'excuse** a note □ Vous devez apporter un mot d'excuse signé par vos parents. You have to bring a note signed by your parents.

excuser VERB [28]
to excuse
■ **Excusez-moi. 1** Sorry! □ Excusez-moi, je ne vous avais pas vu. Sorry, I didn't see you.
2 Excuse me. □ Excusez-moi, est-ce que vous avez l'heure? Excuse me, have you got the time?
■ **s'excuser** to apologize □ Il s'est excusé de son retard. He apologized for being late.

exécuter VERB [28]
1 to execute
□ Le prisonnier a été exécuté à l'aube. The prisoner was executed at dawn.
2 to perform
□ Le pianiste va maintenant exécuter une valse de Chopin. The pianist is now going to perform a waltz by Chopin.

l' **exemplaire** MASC NOUN
copy

l' **exemple** MASC NOUN
example
□ donner l'exemple to set an example
■ **par exemple** for example

s' **exercer** VERB [12]
to practise

l' **exercice** MASC NOUN
exercise

exhiber VERB [28]
to show off
□ Il aime bien exhiber ses décorations. He likes showing off his medals.
■ **s'exhiber** to expose oneself

l' **exhibitionniste** MASC NOUN
flasher

exigeant (FEM **exigeante**) ADJECTIVE
hard to please
□ Elle est vraiment exigeante. She's really
hard to please.

exiger VERB [45]
1 to demand
□ Le propriétaire exige d'être payé
immédiatement. The landlord is
demanding to be paid immediately.
2 to require
□ Ce travail exige beaucoup de patience.
This job requires a lot of patience.

l' **exil** MASC NOUN
exile

exister VERB [28]
to exist
□ Ça n'existe pas. It doesn't exist. □ Ce
manteau existe également en rose. This
coat is also available in pink.

exotique (FEM **exotique**) ADJECTIVE
exotic
□ une plante exotique an exotic plant
■ un yaourt aux fruits exotiques a tropical
fruit yoghurt

expédier VERB [19]
to send
□ expédier un colis to send a parcel

l' **expéditeur** MASC NOUN
sender

l' **expédition** FEM NOUN
expedition
■ l'expédition du courrier the dispatch of
the mail

l' **expéditrice** FEM NOUN
sender

l' **expérience** FEM NOUN
1 experience
□ Elle a plusieurs années d'expérience.
She's got several years' experience.
2 experiment
□ une expérience de chimie a chemistry
experiment

expérimenter VERB [28]
to test
□ Ces produits de beauté n'ont pas été
expérimentés sur des animaux. These
cosmetics have not been tested on animals.

l' **expert** MASC NOUN
expert

expirer VERB [28]
1 to expire (document, passport)
2 to run out (time allowed)
3 to breathe out (person)

l' **explication** FEM NOUN
explanation

■ une explication de texte a critical
analysis (of a text)

expliquer VERB [28]
to explain
□ Il m'a expliqué comment faire. He
explained to me how to do it.
■ ça s'explique it's understandable

l' **exploit** MASC NOUN
achievement

l' **exploitation** FEM NOUN
exploitation
□ C'est de l'exploitation. It's exploitation.
■ une exploitation agricole a farm

exploiter VERB [28]
to exploit
□ Il se fait exploiter par son patron. He gets
exploited by his boss.

explorer VERB [28]
to explore

exploser VERB [28]
to explode
□ La bombe a explosé en pleine rue. The
bomb exploded in the middle of the street.

l' **explosif** MASC NOUN
explosive

l' **explosion** FEM NOUN
explosion

l' **exportateur** MASC NOUN
exporter

l' **exportation** FEM NOUN
export

l' **exportatrice** FEM NOUN
exporter

exporter VERB [28]
to export

l' **exposé** MASC NOUN
talk
□ un exposé sur l'environnement a talk on
the environment

exposer VERB [28]
1 to show
□ Il expose ses peintures dans une galerie
d'art. He shows his paintings in a private art
gallery.
2 to expose
□ N'exposez pas la pellicule à la lumière. Do
not expose the film to light.
3 to set out
□ Il nous a exposé les raisons de son départ.
He set out the reasons for his departure.
■ s'exposer au soleil to stay out in the sun
□ Ne vous exposez pas trop longtemps au
soleil. Don't stay out too long in the sun.

l' **exposition** FEM NOUN
exhibition
□ une exposition de peinture an exhibition
of paintings

exprès – extrémité

exprès ADVERB
1 on purpose
  □ Il l'a fait exprès. He did it on purpose.
2 specially
  □ J'ai fait ce gâteau exprès pour toi. I made this cake specially for you.

l' **express** MASC NOUN
1 espresso (coffee)
2 fast train
  □ Il a décidé de prendre l'express de dix heures. He decided to catch the fast train at 10 o'clock.

l' **expression** FEM NOUN
1 expression
2 phrase

exprimer VERB [28]
  to express
  ■ **s'exprimer** to express oneself □ Il s'exprime très bien pour un enfant de huit ans. For a child of 8, he expresses himself very well.

exquis (FEM **exquise**) ADJECTIVE
  exquisite

extérieur (FEM **extérieure**) ADJECTIVE
  ▷ see also **extérieur** NOUN
  outside

l' **extérieur** MASC NOUN
  ▷ see also **extérieur** ADJECTIVE
  outside
  ■ **à l'extérieur** outside □ Les toilettes sont à l'extérieur. The toilet is outside.

l' **externat** MASC NOUN
  day school

l' **externe** MASC/FEM NOUN
  day pupil

l' **extincteur** MASC NOUN
  fire extinguisher

extra (FEM+PL **extra**) ADJECTIVE
  excellent
  □ Ce fromage est extra! This cheese is excellent!

extraire VERB [85]
  to extract

l' **extrait** MASC NOUN
  extract

extraordinaire (FEM **extraordinaire**) ADJECTIVE
  extraordinary

extravagant (FEM **extravagante**) ADJECTIVE
  extravagant

extrême (FEM **extrême**) ADJECTIVE
  ▷ see also **extrême** NOUN
  extreme
  □ l'extrême droite et l'extrême gauche the far right and the far left

l' **extrême** MASC NOUN
  ▷ see also **extrême** ADJECTIVE
  extreme

extrêmement ADVERB
  extremely

l' **Extrême-Orient** MASC NOUN
  the Far East

l' **extrémité** FEM NOUN
  end
  □ La gare est à l'autre extrémité de la ville. The station is at the other end of the town.

Ff

F ABBREVIATION
franc (currency in Switzerland and many former French colonies)

le **fa** NOUN
F

la **fabrication** NOUN
manufacture

fabriquer VERB [28]
to make
□ fabriqué en France made in France
■ **Qu'est-ce qu'il fabrique?** (informal) What's he up to?

la **fac** NOUN (informal)
university
■ **à la fac** at university

la **face** NOUN
■ **face à face** face to face
■ **en face de** opposite □ Le bus s'arrête en face de chez moi. The bus stops opposite my house.
■ **faire face à quelque chose** to face something
■ **Pile ou face? — Face.** Heads or tails? — Heads.

fâché (FEM **fâchée**) ADJECTIVE
angry
■ **être fâché contre quelqu'un** to be angry with somebody □ Elle est fâchée contre moi. She's angry with me.
■ **être fâché avec quelqu'un** to be on bad terms with somebody □ Elle est fâchée avec sa sœur. She's on bad terms with her sister.

se **fâcher** VERB [28]
■ **se fâcher contre quelqu'un** to lose one's temper with somebody
■ **se fâcher avec quelqu'un** to fall out with somebody □ Il s'est fâché avec son frère. He's fallen out with his brother.

facile (FEM **facile**) ADJECTIVE
easy
■ **facile à faire** easy to do

facilement ADVERB
easily

la **facilité** NOUN
■ **un logiciel d'une grande facilité d'utilisation** a very user-friendly piece of software
■ **Il a des facilités en langues.** He has a gift for languages.

   ○ **LANGUAGE TIP** Be careful! facilité does not mean **facility**.

la **façon** NOUN
way
□ De quelle façon? In what way?
■ **de toute façon** anyway

le **facteur** NOUN
postman
□ Il est facteur. He's a postman.

la **facture** NOUN
bill
□ une facture de gaz a gas bill

facultatif (FEM **facultative**) ADJECTIVE
optional

la **faculté** NOUN
faculty
■ **avoir une grande faculté de concentration** to have great powers of concentration

fade (FEM **fade**) ADJECTIVE
tasteless
□ La soupe est un peu fade. The soup is a bit tasteless.

faible (FEM **faible**) ADJECTIVE
weak
□ Je me sens encore faible. I still feel a bit weak.
■ **Il est faible en maths.** He's not very good at maths.

la **faiblesse** NOUN
weakness

la **faïence** NOUN
pottery

faillir VERB [12]
■ **J'ai failli tomber.** I nearly fell down.

la **faillite** NOUN
bankruptcy
■ **une entreprise en faillite** a bankrupt business
■ **faire faillite** to go bankrupt

la **faim** NOUN

hunger
- **avoir faim** to be hungry

fainéant (FEM **fainéante**) ADJECTIVE
lazy

faire VERB [36]

PRESENT TENSE	
je fais	nous faisons
tu fais	vous faites
il/elle fait	ils/elles font

PAST PARTICIPLE
fait

1 to make
  □ Je vais faire un gâteau pour ce soir. I'm going to make a cake for tonight. □ Ils font trop de bruit. They're making too much noise. □ Je voudrais me faire de nouveaux amis. I'd like to make new friends.

2 to do
  □ Qu'est-ce que tu fais? What are you doing? □ Il fait de l'italien. He's doing Italian. □ Qui veut faire la vaisselle? Who'll do the dishes?

3 to play
  □ Il fait du piano. He plays the piano.

4 to be
  □ Qu'est-ce qu'il fait chaud! Isn't it hot! □ Espérons qu'il fera beau demain. Let's hope it'll be nice weather tomorrow.
  - **Ça ne fait rien.** It doesn't matter.
  - **Ça fait cinquante-trois euros en tout.** That makes fifty-three euros in all.
  - **Ça fait trois ans qu'il habite à Paris.** He's lived in Paris for three years.
  - **faire tomber** to knock over □ Le chat a fait tomber le vase. The cat knocked over the vase.
  - **faire faire quelque chose** to get something done □ Je dois faire réparer ma voiture. I've got to get my car repaired.
  - **Je vais me faire couper les cheveux.** I'm going to get my hair cut.
  - **Ne t'en fais pas!** Don't worry!

fais, faisaient, faisais, faisait VERB
  ▷ see faire

le **faisan** NOUN
pheasant

faisiez, faisions, faisons, fait VERB
  ▷ see faire

le **fait** NOUN
fact
  □ Le fait que ... The fact that ...
  - **un fait divers** a news item
  - **au fait** by the way □ Au fait, tu as aimé le film d'hier? By the way, did you enjoy the film yesterday?
  - **en fait** actually □ En fait je n'ai pas beaucoup de temps. I haven't got much time actually.

faites VERB ▷ see faire

la **falaise** NOUN
cliff

falloir VERB [37] ▷ see faut, faudra, faudrait

famé (FEM **famée**) ADJECTIVE
  - **un quartier mal famé** a rough area

fameux (FEM **fameuse**) ADJECTIVE
  - **Ce n'est pas fameux.** It's not great.

familial (FEM **familiale**, MASC PL **familiaux**) ADJECTIVE
family
  □ une atmosphère familiale a family atmosphere
  - **les allocations familiales** child benefit

familier (FEM **familière**) ADJECTIVE
familiar

la **famille** NOUN

1 family
  □ une famille nombreuse a big family
  □ Nous passons Noël en famille. We have a family Christmas.

2 relatives
  □ Il a de la famille à Paris. He's got relatives in Paris.

la **famine** NOUN
famine

fanatique (FEM **fanatique**) ADJECTIVE
  ▷ see also **fanatique** NOUN
fanatical

le/la **fanatique** NOUN
  ▷ see also **fanatique** ADJECTIVE
fanatic

la **fanfare** NOUN
brass band

fantaisie (FEM+PL **fantaisie**) ADJECTIVE
  - **des bijoux fantaisie** costume jewellery

fantastique (FEM **fantastique**) ADJECTIVE
fantastic

le **fantôme** NOUN
ghost

la **farce** NOUN

1 stuffing (for chicken, turkey)

2 practical joke
  □ Il aime faire des farces. He likes to play practical jokes.

farci (FEM **farcie**) ADJECTIVE
stuffed
  □ des tomates farcies stuffed tomatoes

la **farine** NOUN
flour

fascinant (FEM **fascinante**) ADJECTIVE
fascinating

fasciner VERB [28]
to fascinate

le **fascisme** NOUN
fascism

fasse, fassent, fasses, fassiez, fassions VERB ▷ see **faire**
- **Pourvu qu'il fasse beau demain!** Let's hope it'll be fine tomorrow!

fatal (FEM **fatale**) ADJECTIVE
fatal
- **C'était fatal.** It was bound to happen.

la **fatalité** NOUN
fate

fatigant (FEM **fatigante**) ADJECTIVE
tiring

la **fatigue** NOUN
tiredness

fatigué (FEM **fatiguée**) ADJECTIVE
tired

se **fatiguer** VERB [28]
to get tired

fauché (FEM **fauchée**) ADJECTIVE (informal)
hard up

faudra VERB
> LANGUAGE TIP **faudra** is the future tense of **falloir**.
- **Il faudra qu'on soit plus rapide.** We'll have to be quicker.

faudrait VERB
> LANGUAGE TIP **faudrait** is the conditional tense of **falloir**.
- **Il faudrait qu'on fasse attention.** We ought to be careful.

se **faufiler** VERB [28]
- **Il s'est faufilé à travers la foule.** He made his way through the crowd.

la **faune** NOUN
wildlife

fausse (FEM **fausse**) ADJECTIVE ▷ see **faux**

faut VERB
> LANGUAGE TIP **faut** is the present tense of **falloir**.
- **Il faut faire attention.** You've got to be careful.
- **Nous n'avons pas le choix, il faut y aller.** We've no choice, we've got to go.
- **Il faut que je parte.** I've got to go.
- **Il faut du courage pour faire ce métier.** It takes courage to do that job.
- **Il me faut de l'argent.** I need money.

la **faute** NOUN
1 mistake
□ **faire une faute** to make a mistake
2 fault
□ **Ce n'est pas de ma faute.** It's not my fault.
- **sans faute** without fail □ **Je t'appellerai sans faute.** I'll phone you without fail.

le **fauteuil** NOUN
armchair
- **un fauteuil roulant** a wheelchair

faux (FEM **fausse**) ADJECTIVE, ADVERB

▷ see also **faux** NOUN
untrue
□ **C'est entièrement faux.** It's totally untrue.
- **faire un faux pas** to trip
- **Il chante faux.** He sings out of tune.

le **faux** NOUN
▷ see also **faux** ADJECTIVE
fake
□ **Ce tableau est un faux.** This painting is a fake.

la **faveur** NOUN
favour

favori (FEM **favorite**) ADJECTIVE
favourite

favoriser VERB [28]
to favour
□ **Ce système d'examen favorise ceux qui ont de la mémoire.** This exam system favours people with good memories.

le **fax** NOUN
fax

faxer VERB [28]
to fax
- **faxer un document à quelqu'un** to fax somebody a document

la **fée** NOUN
fairy

feignant (FEM **feignante**) ADJECTIVE
(informal)
lazy

les **félicitations** FEM PL NOUN
congratulations

féliciter VERB [28]
to congratulate

la **femelle** NOUN
female (animal)

féminin (FEM **féminine**) ADJECTIVE
1 female
□ **les personnages féminins du roman** the female characters in the novel
2 feminine
□ **Elle est très féminine.** She's very feminine.
3 women's
□ **Elle joue dans l'équipe féminine de France.** She plays in the French women's team.

féministe (FEM **féministe**) ADJECTIVE
feminist

la **femme** NOUN
1 woman
2 wife
□ **la femme du directeur** the headmaster's wife
- **une femme au foyer** a housewife
- **une femme de ménage** a cleaning woman

113

f

■ **une femme de chambre** a chambermaid

se **fendre** VERB [88]
to crack

la **fenêtre** NOUN
window

le **fenouil** NOUN
fennel

la **fente** NOUN
slot

le **fer** NOUN
iron
■ **un fer à cheval** a horseshoe
■ **un fer à repasser** an iron

fera, ferai, feras, ferez VERB ▷ see **faire**

férié (FEM **fériée**) ADJECTIVE
■ **un jour férié** a public holiday

feriez, ferions VERB ▷ see **faire**

ferme (FEM **ferme**) ADJECTIVE
▷ see also **ferme** NOUN
firm
□ Elle s'est montrée très ferme à mon égard.
She was very firm with me.

la **ferme** NOUN
▷ see also **ferme** ADJECTIVE
farm

fermé (FEM **fermée**) ADJECTIVE
1 closed
□ La pharmacie est fermée. The chemist's is
closed.
2 off
□ Est-ce que le gaz est fermé? Is the gas off?

fermer VERB [28]
1 to close
□ Ferme la fenêtre. Close the window.
2 to turn off
□ As-tu bien fermé le robinet? Have you
turned the tap off?
■ **fermer à clef** to lock □ N'oublie pas de
fermer la porte à clef! Don't forget to lock
the door!

la **fermeture** NOUN
■ **les heures de fermeture** closing times
■ **une fermeture éclair®** a zip

le **fermier** NOUN
farmer

la **fermière** NOUN
1 farmer (woman)
2 farmer's wife

féroce (FEM **féroce**) ADJECTIVE
fierce

ferons, feront VERB ▷ see **faire**

les **fesses** FEM PL NOUN
buttocks

le **festival** NOUN
festival

les **festivités** FEM PL NOUN
festivities

la **fête** NOUN
1 party
□ On organise une petite fête pour son
anniversaire. We're having a little party for
his birthday.
■ **faire la fête** to party
2 name day
□ C'est sa fête aujourd'hui. It's his name
day today.
■ **Bonne fête!** Happy Saint's Day!

> DID YOU KNOW...?
> As part of the weather forecast on
> most TV channels, the presenter will
> remind the viewers which Saint is
> being celebrated the following day.

■ **une fête foraine** a funfair
■ **la Fête Nationale** Bastille Day
■ **les fêtes de fin d'année** the festive
season

fêter VERB [28]
to celebrate

le **feu** (PL les **feux**) NOUN
1 fire
□ prendre feu to catch fire □ faire du feu to
make a fire
■ **Au feu!** Fire!
■ **un feu de joie** a bonfire
2 traffic light
□ un feu rouge a red light □ le feu vert the
green light □ Tournez à gauche aux feux.
Turn left at the lights.
■ **Avez-vous du feu?** Have you got a light?
3 heat
□ ... mijoter à feu doux ... simmer over a
gentle heat
■ **un feu d'artifice** a firework display

le **feuillage** NOUN
leaves

la **feuille** NOUN
1 leaf
□ des feuilles mortes fallen leaves
2 sheet
□ une feuille de papier a sheet of paper
■ **une feuille de maladie** a claim form for
medical expenses

feuilleté (FEM **feuilletée**) ADJECTIVE
■ **de la pâte feuilletée** flaky pastry

feuilleter VERB [41]
to leaf through

le **feuilleton** NOUN
serial

le **feutre** NOUN
felt
■ **un stylo-feutre** a felt-tip pen

la **fève** NOUN
broad bean

février MASC NOUN

February
- **en février** in February

fiable (FEM fiable) ADJECTIVE
reliable

les **fiançailles** FEM PL NOUN
engagement

fiancé (FEM fiancée) ADJECTIVE
- **être fiancé à quelqu'un** to be engaged to somebody

se **fiancer** VERB [12]
to get engaged

la **ficelle** NOUN
1 string
□ Passe-moi un bout de ficelle. Give me a piece of string.
2 thin baguette (bread)

la **fiche** NOUN
form
□ Remplissez cette fiche s'il vous plaît. Fill in this form please.

se **ficher** VERB [28] (informal)
- **Je m'en fiche!** I don't care!
- **Fiche-moi la paix!** Leave me alone!
- **Quoi, tu n'as fait que ça? Tu te fiches de moi?** You've only done that much? You can't be serious!

le **fichier** NOUN
file

fichu (FEM fichue) ADJECTIVE (informal)
- **Ce parapluie est fichu.** This umbrella's knackered.

fidèle (FEM fidèle) ADJECTIVE
faithful

fier (FEM fière) ADJECTIVE
proud

la **fierté** NOUN
pride

la **fièvre** NOUN
fever
- **avoir de la fièvre** to have a temperature
□ J'ai de la fièvre. I've got a temperature.
□ Il a trente neuf de fièvre. He's got a temperature of 39°C.

fiévreux (FEM fiévreuse) ADJECTIVE
feverish

la **figue** NOUN
fig

la **figure** NOUN
1 face
□ Il a reçu le ballon en pleine figure. The ball hit him smack in the face.
2 figure (illustration)
□ Voir figure 2.1, page 32. See figure 2.1, page 32.

le **fil** NOUN
thread
□ le fil à coudre sewing thread

- **le fil de fer** wire
- **un coup de fil** a phone call

la **file** NOUN
line (of people, objects)
- **une file d'attente** a queue □ se mettre à la file to join the queue
- **à la file** one after the other
- **en file indienne** in single file

filer VERB [28]
to speed along
□ Les voitures filent sur l'autoroute. The cars are speeding along the motorway.
- **File dans ta chambre!** Off to your room with you!

le **filet** NOUN
net

la **fille** NOUN
1 girl
□ C'est une école de filles. It's a girls' school.
2 daughter
□ C'est leur fille aînée. She's their oldest daughter.

la **fillette** NOUN
little girl

le **filleul** NOUN
godson

la **filleule** NOUN
goddaughter

le **film** NOUN
film
- **un film policier** a thriller
- **un film d'aventures** an adventure film
- **un film d'épouvante** a horror film
- **le film alimentaire** Clingfilm®

le **fils** NOUN
son

la **fin** NOUN
▷ see also **fin** ADJECTIVE
end
□ à la fin du film at the end of the film □ À la fin, il a réussi à se décider. In the end he managed to make up his mind.
- **'Fin'** 'The End'
- **Il sera en vacances fin juin.** He'll be on holiday at the end of June.
- **en fin de journée** at the end of the day
- **en fin de compte** when all's said and done
- **sans fin** endless

fin (FEM fine) ADJECTIVE
▷ see also **fin** NOUN
fine
- **des fines herbes** mixed herbs

la **finale** NOUN
final
□ les quarts de finale the quarter finals

115

finalement ADVERB
1 at last
  □ Nous sommes finalement arrivés. At last we arrived.
2 after all
  □ Finalement, tu avais raison. You were right after all.

fini (FEM **finie**) ADJECTIVE
  finished

finir VERB [38]
  to finish
  □ Le cours finit à onze heures. The lesson finishes at 11 o'clock. □ Je viens de finir ce livre. I've just finished this book.
  ■ **Il a fini par se décider.** He made up his mind in the end.

finlandais (FEM **finlandaise**) ADJECTIVE, NOUN
  Finnish
  □ Ils parlent finlandais. They speak Finnish.
  ■ **un Finlandais** a Finn (man)
  ■ **une Finlandaise** a Finn (woman)
  ■ **les Finlandais** the Finns

la **Finlande** NOUN
  Finland

la **firme** NOUN
  firm

fis VERB ▷ see **faire**

la **fissure** NOUN
  crack

fit VERB ▷ see **faire**

fixe (FEM **fixe**) ADJECTIVE
1 steady
  □ Il n'a pas d'emploi fixe. He hasn't got a steady job.
2 set
  □ Il mange toujours à heures fixes. He always eats at set times.
  ■ **un menu à prix fixe** a set menu

fixer VERB [28]
1 to fix
  □ Les volets sont fixés avec des crochets. The shutters are fixed with hooks. □ Nous avons fixé une heure pour nous retrouver. We fixed a time to meet.
2 to stare at
  □ Ne fixe pas les gens comme ça! Don't stare at people like that!

le **flacon** NOUN
  bottle
  □ un flacon de parfum a bottle of perfume

le **flageolet** NOUN
  small haricot bean

flamand (FEM **flamande**) ADJECTIVE, NOUN
  Flemish
  □ Il parle flamand chez lui. He speaks Flemish at home.
  ■ **les Flamands** the Dutch-speaking Belgians

flambé (FEM **flambée**) ADJECTIVE
  ■ **des bananes flambées** flambéed bananas

la **flamme** NOUN
  flame
  ■ **en flammes** on fire

le **flan** NOUN
  baked custard

flâner VERB [28]
  to stroll

la **flaque** NOUN
  puddle (of water)

le **flash** (PL les **flashes**) NOUN
  flash (of camera)
  ■ **un flash d'information** a newsflash

flatter VERB [28]
  to flatter

la **flèche** NOUN
  arrow

les **fléchettes** FEM PL NOUN
  darts
  □ jouer aux fléchettes to play darts

la **fleur** NOUN
  flower

fleuri (FEM **fleurie**) ADJECTIVE
1 full of flowers
  □ Son jardin était très fleuri. Her garden was full of flowers.
2 flowery
  □ un papier peint fleuri flowery wallpaper

fleurir VERB [38]
  to flower
  □ Cette plante fleurit en automne. This plant flowers in autumn.

le/la **fleuriste** NOUN
  florist

le **fleuve** NOUN
  river

le **flic** NOUN (informal)
  cop

le **flipper** NOUN
  pinball machine

flirter VERB [28]
  to flirt

le **flocon** NOUN
  flake

flotter VERB [28]
  to float

flou (FEM **floue**) ADJECTIVE
  blurred

le **fluor** NOUN
  ■ **le dentifrice au fluor** fluoride toothpaste

la **flûte** NOUN
  flute
  □ Je joue de la flûte. I play the flute.
  ■ **une flûte à bec** a recorder

■ **Flûte!** *(informal)* Heck!

la **foi** NOUN
faith

le **foie** NOUN
liver

■ **une crise de foie** a stomach upset

le **foin** NOUN
hay

■ **un rhume des foins** hay fever

la **foire** NOUN
fair

la **fois** NOUN
time

□ **la première fois** the first time □ **à chaque fois** each time □ **À chaque fois que je vais à la bibliothèque, j'oublie ma carte.** Every time I go to the library, I forget my card.
□ **Deux fois deux font quatre.** 2 times 2 is 4.
■ **une fois** once
■ **deux fois** twice □ **deux fois plus de gens** twice as many people
■ **une fois que** once □ **Tu te sentiras mieux une fois que tu auras mangé.** You'll feel better once you've had something to eat.
■ **à la fois** at once □ **Je ne peux pas faire deux choses à la fois.** I can't do two things at once.

fol MASC ADJECTIVE ▷ *see* **fou**

la **folie** NOUN
madness

□ **C'est de la folie pure!** It's absolute madness!
■ **faire une folie** to be extravagant

folklorique (FEM **folklorique**) ADJECTIVE
folk

□ **de la musique folklorique** folk music

folle FEM ADJECTIVE ▷ *see* **fou**

foncé (FEM **foncée**) ADJECTIVE
dark

□ **bleu foncé** dark blue

foncer VERB [12] *(informal)*

■ **Je vais foncer à la boulangerie.** I'm just going to dash to the baker's.

la **fonction** NOUN
function

■ **une voiture de fonction** a company car

le/la **fonctionnaire** NOUN
civil servant

fonctionner VERB [28]
to work

le **fond** NOUN
1 bottom

□ **Mon porte-monnaie est au fond de mon sac.** My purse is at the bottom of my bag.
2 end

□ **Les toilettes sont au fond du couloir.** The toilets are at the end of the corridor.

■ **dans le fond** all things considered

□ **Dans le fond, ce n'est pas si grave.** All things considered, it's not that bad.

fonder VERB [28]
to found

fondre VERB [69]
to melt

□ **La tablette de chocolat a fondu dans ma poche.** The bar of chocolate melted in my pocket.

■ **fondre en larmes** to burst into tears

fondu (FEM **fondue**) ADJECTIVE

■ **du beurre fondu** melted butter

font VERB ▷ *see* **faire**

la **fontaine** NOUN
fountain

le **foot** NOUN *(informal)*
footie

le **football** NOUN
football

□ **jouer au football** to play football

le **footballeur** NOUN
footballer

le **footing** NOUN
jogging

□ **faire du footing** to go jogging

forain (FEM **foraine**) ADJECTIVE
▷ *see also* **forain** NOUN

■ **une fête foraine** a funfair

le **forain** NOUN
▷ *see also* **forain** ADJECTIVE
fairground worker

la **force** NOUN
strength

□ **Je n'ai pas beaucoup de force dans les bras.** I haven't got much strength in my arms.

■ **à force de** by □ **Il a grossi à force de manger autant.** He got fat by eating so much.

■ **de force** by force □ **Ils lui ont enlevé son pistolet de force.** They took the gun from him by force.

forcé (FEM **forcée**) ADJECTIVE
forced

□ **un sourire forcé** a forced smile

■ **C'est forcé.** *(informal)* It's inevitable.

forcément ADVERB

■ **Ça devait forcément arriver.** That was bound to happen.

■ **pas forcément** not necessarily

la **forêt** NOUN
forest

le **forfait** NOUN
all-in price

■ **C'est compris dans le forfait.** It's included in the price.

le forgeron NOUN
blacksmith

la formalité NOUN
formality
□ Ce n'est qu'une simple formalité. It's just a formality.

le format NOUN
size

la formation NOUN
training
□ la formation professionnelle vocational training
■ **la formation continue** in-house training
■ **Il a une formation d'ingénieur.** He is a trained engineer.

la forme NOUN
shape
■ **être en forme** to be in good shape
■ **Je ne suis pas en forme aujourd'hui.** I'm not feeling too good today.
■ **Tu as l'air en forme.** You're looking well.

formellement ADVERB
strictly
□ Il est formellement interdit de fumer dans les couloirs. It is strictly forbidden to smoke in the corridors.

former VERB [28]
to form

formidable (FEM **formidable**) ADJECTIVE
great

le formulaire NOUN
form

fort (FEM **forte**) ADJECTIVE, ADVERB
1 strong
□ Le café est trop fort. The coffee's too strong.
2 good
□ Il est très fort en espagnol. He's very good at Spanish.
3 loud
□ Est-ce vous pouvez parler plus fort? Can you speak louder?
■ **frapper fort** to hit hard

le fortifiant NOUN
tonic (medicine)

la fortune NOUN
fortune
■ **de fortune** makeshift □ un radeau de fortune a makeshift raft

le forum de discussion NOUN
chatroom

le fossé NOUN
ditch

fou (MASC SING ALSO **fol**, FEM **folle**) ADJECTIVE

LANGUAGE TIP **fou** changes to **fol** before a vowel or most words beginning with 'h'.

118

mad
■ **Il y a un monde fou sur la plage!** (informal) There are loads of people on the beach!
■ **attraper le fou rire** to get the giggles

la foudre NOUN
lightning
□ Il a été frappé par la foudre. He was struck by lightning.

foudroyant (FEM **foudroyante**) ADJECTIVE
instant
□ un succès foudroyant an instant hit

le fouet NOUN
whisk

la fougère NOUN
fern

fouiller VERB [28]
to rummage

le fouillis NOUN
mess
□ Il y a du fouillis dans sa chambre. His bedroom is a mess.

le foulard NOUN
scarf
□ un foulard en soie a silk scarf

la foule NOUN
crowd
■ **une foule de** masses of □ J'ai une foule de choses à faire ce week-end. I've got masses of things to do this weekend.

se fouler VERB [28]
■ **se fouler la cheville** to sprain one's ankle

le four NOUN
oven
□ un four à micro-ondes a microwave oven

la fourchette NOUN
fork

la fourmi NOUN
ant
■ **avoir des fourmis dans les jambes** to have pins and needles

LANGUAGE TIP Word for word, this means 'to have ants in one's legs'.

le fourneau (PL les **fourneaux**) NOUN
stove

fourni (FEM **fournie**) ADJECTIVE
thick (beard, hair)

fournir VERB [38]
to supply

le fournisseur NOUN
supplier
■ **un fournisseur d'accès à Internet** an internet service provider

les fournitures FEM PL NOUN
■ **les fournitures scolaires** school stationery

fourré (FEM **fourrée**) ADJECTIVE

filled

□ un gâteau fourré à la confiture d'abricot a cake filled with apricot jam

fourrer VERB [28] (informal)
to put

□ Où as-tu fourré mon sac? Where have you put my bag?

le **fourre-tout** (PL les **fourre-tout**) NOUN
holdall

la **fourrure** NOUN
fur

□ un manteau de fourrure a fur coat

le **foyer** NOUN
home

□ dans la plupart des foyers français in most French homes

■ **un foyer de jeunes** a youth club

la **fracture** NOUN
fracture

fragile (FEM **fragile**) ADJECTIVE
fragile

□ Attention, c'est fragile! Be careful, it's fragile!

la **fragilité** NOUN
fragility

fraîche FEM ADJECTIVE ▷ see **frais**

la **fraîcheur** NOUN
1 cool

□ la fraîcheur du soir the cool of the evening
2 freshness

□ Je ne suis pas sûre de la fraîcheur du poisson. I'm not sure about the freshness of the fish.

frais (FEM **fraîche**) ADJECTIVE
▷ see also **frais** NOUN
1 fresh

□ des œufs frais fresh eggs □ Cette salade n'est pas très fraîche. This lettuce isn't very fresh.

2 chilly

□ Il fait un peu frais ce soir. It's a bit chilly this evening.

3 cool

□ des boissons fraîches cool drinks

■ **'servir frais'** 'serve chilled'

■ **mettre au frais** to put in a cool place

les **frais** MASC PL NOUN
▷ see also **frais** ADJECTIVE
expenses

la **fraise** NOUN
strawberry

□ une fraise des bois a wild strawberry

la **framboise** NOUN
raspberry

franc (FEM **franche**) ADJECTIVE
▷ see also **franc** NOUN
frank

le **franc** NOUN
▷ see also **franc** ADJECTIVE
franc

┌──────────────────────
DID YOU KNOW...?
The **franc** is the unit of currency in Switzerland and many former French colonies.
└──────────────────────

français (FEM **française**) ADJECTIVE, NOUN
French

□ Il parle français couramment. He speaks French fluently.

■ **un Français** a Frenchman

■ **une Française** a Frenchwoman

■ **les Français** the French

la **France** NOUN
France

■ **en France 1** in France □ Je suis né en France. I was born in France. **2** to France □ Je pars en France pour Noël. I'm going to France for Christmas.

franche FEM ADJECTIVE ▷ see **franc**

franchement ADVERB
1 frankly

□ Il m'a parlé franchement. He spoke to me frankly.

2 really

□ C'est franchement mauvais. It's really bad.

franchir VERB [38]
to get over

la **franchise** NOUN
frankness

francophone (FEM **francophone**) ADJECTIVE
French-speaking

la **frange** NOUN
fringe

la **frangipane** NOUN
almond cream

frapper VERB [28]
to strike

□ Il l'a frappée au visage. He struck her in the face. □ Son air fatigué m'a frappé. I was struck by how tired she looked.

fredonner VERB [28]
to hum

le **freezer** NOUN
freezing compartment

le **frein** NOUN
brake

■ **le frein à main** handbrake

freiner VERB [28]
to brake

frêle (FEM **frêle**) ADJECTIVE
frail

le **frelon** NOUN
hornet

frémir VERB [38]

shudder
□ Cette idée me fait frémir. The idea makes me shudder.

fréquemment ADVERB
frequently

fréquent (FEM **fréquente**) ADJECTIVE
frequent

fréquenté (FEM **fréquentée**) ADJECTIVE
busy
□ une rue très fréquentée a very busy street
■ un bar mal fréquenté a rough pub

fréquenter VERB [28]
to see (person)
□ Je ne le fréquente pas beaucoup. I don't see him often.

le **frère** NOUN
brother

le **friand** NOUN
■ un friand au fromage a cheese puff

la **friandise** NOUN
sweet

le **fric** NOUN (informal)
cash

le **frigidaire**® NOUN
refrigerator

le **frigo** NOUN (informal)
fridge

frileux (FEM **frileuse**) ADJECTIVE
■ être frileux to feel the cold □ Je suis très frileuse. I really feel the cold.

frimer VERB [28] (informal)
to show off

les **fringues** FEM PL NOUN (informal)
clothes

fripé (FEM **fripée**) ADJECTIVE
crumpled

frire VERB [80]
■ faire frire to fry □ Faites frire les boulettes dans de l'huile très chaude. Fry the meatballs in very hot oil.

frisé (FEM **frisée**) ADJECTIVE
curly
□ Elle est très frisée. She's got very curly hair.

le **frisson** NOUN
shiver

frissonner VERB [28]
to shiver

frit (FEM **frite**) ADJECTIVE
fried
□ du poisson frit fried fish

les **frites** FEM PL NOUN
chips

la **friture** NOUN
1 fried food
□ On lui a conseillé d'éviter les fritures. He's been advised to avoid fried food.

2 fried fish
□ Nous allons faire une friture ce soir. We are going to have fried fish tonight.

froid (FEM **froide**) ADJECTIVE
▷ see also froid NOUN
cold
□ Ça me laisse froid. It leaves me cold. □ de la viande froide cold meat

le **froid** NOUN
▷ see also froid ADJECTIVE
cold
■ Il fait froid. It's cold.
■ avoir froid to be cold □ Est-ce que tu as froid? Are you cold?

se **froisser** VERB [28]
1 to crease
□ Ce tissu se froisse très facilement. This material creases very easily.

2 to take offence
□ Paul se froisse très facilement. Paul's very quick to take offence.
■ se froisser un muscle to strain a muscle

frôler VERB [28]
1 to brush against
□ Le chat m'a frôlé au passage. The cat brushed against me as it went past.

2 to narrowly avoid
□ Nous avons frôlé la catastrophe. We narrowly avoided disaster.

le **fromage** NOUN
cheese
■ du fromage blanc soft white cheese

le **froment** NOUN
wheat
■ une crêpe de froment a pancake (made with wheat flour)

froncer VERB [12]
■ froncer les sourcils to frown

le **front** NOUN
forehead

la **frontière** NOUN
border

frotter VERB [28]
to rub
□ se frotter les yeux to rub one's eyes
■ frotter une allumette to strike a match

le **fruit** NOUN
fruit
■ un fruit a piece of fruit □ Est-ce que vous voulez manger un fruit? Would you like some fruit?
■ les fruits de mer seafood
　　LANGUAGE TIP Word for word, this means 'sea fruit'.

fruité (FEM **fruitée**) ADJECTIVE
fruity

frustrer VERB [28]

to frustrate

la **fugue** NOUN
- ■ **faire une fugue** to run away

fuir VERB [39]
1 to flee
  - □ fuir devant un danger to flee from danger
2 to drip
  - □ Le robinet fuit. The tap's dripping.

la **fuite** NOUN
1 leak
  - □ Il y a une fuite de gaz. There is a gas leak.
2 flight (escape)
  - ■ **être en fuite** to be on the run

fumé (FEM **fumée**) ADJECTIVE
  - ▷ see also **fumée** NOUN
  smoked
  - □ du saumon fumé smoked salmon

la **fumée** NOUN
  - ▷ see also **fumée** ADJECTIVE
  smoke

fumer VERB [28]
  to smoke

le **fumeur** NOUN
  smoker

la **fumeuse** NOUN
  smoker

le **fur** NOUN
  - ■ **au fur et à mesure** as you go along □ Je

vérifie mon travail au fur et à mesure. I check my work as I go along.
  - ■ **au fur et à mesure que** as □ Je réponds à mon courrier au fur et à mesure que je le reçois. I answer my mail as I receive it.

le **furet** NOUN
  ferret

la **fureur** NOUN
  fury
  - ■ **faire fureur** to be all the rage □ Ce genre de sac fait fureur actuellement. This sort of bag is all the rage at the moment.

furieux (FEM **furieuse**) ADJECTIVE
  furious

le **furoncle** NOUN
  boil (on skin)

fus VERB ▷ see être

le **fuseau** (PL les **fuseaux**) NOUN
  ski pants

la **fusée** NOUN
  rocket

le **fusil** NOUN
  gun

fut VERB ▷ see être

futé (FEM **futée**) ADJECTIVE
  crafty

le **futur** NOUN
  future

f

Gg

gâcher VERB [28]
to waste
□ Je n'aime pas gâcher la nourriture. I don't like to waste food.

le **gâchis** NOUN
waste

la **gaffe** NOUN
■ **faire une gaffe** to do something stupid
■ **Fais gaffe!** *(informal)* Watch out! □ Fais gaffe: la peinture est encore humide! Watch out: the paint's still wet!

le **gage** NOUN
forfeit *(in a game)*
□ recevoir un gage to pay a forfeit

le **gagnant** NOUN
winner

la **gagnante** NOUN
winner

gagner VERB [28]
to win
□ Qui a gagné? Who won?
■ **gagner du temps** to gain time
■ **Il gagne bien sa vie.** He makes a good living.

gai (FEM **gaie**) ADJECTIVE
cheerful
□ Elle est très gaie. She's very cheerful.

la **gaieté** NOUN
cheerfulness

la **galerie** NOUN
gallery
□ une galerie de peinture an art gallery
■ **une galerie marchande** a shopping arcade
■ **une galerie de jeux d'arcade** an amusement arcade

le **galet** NOUN
pebble

la **galette** NOUN
1 round flat cake
■ **une galette de blé noir** a buckwheat pancake
2 biscuit
□ des galettes pur beurre shortbread biscuits

■ **la galette des Rois**

> **DID YOU KNOW...?**
> A **galette des Rois** is a cake eaten on Twelfth Night containing a figurine. The person who finds it is the king (or queen) and gets a paper crown. They then choose someone else to be their queen (or king).

Galles FEM NOUN
■ **le pays de Galles** Wales
■ **le prince de Galles** the Prince of Wales

gallois (FEM **galloise**) ADJECTIVE, NOUN
Welsh
□ un peintre gallois a Welsh painter
■ **un Gallois** a Welshman
■ **une Galloise** a Welshwoman
■ **les Gallois** the Welsh

le **galop** NOUN
gallop

galoper VERB [28]
to gallop

le **gamin** NOUN *(informal)*
kid

la **gamine** NOUN *(informal)*
kid

la **gamme** NOUN
scale *(in music)*
□ faire des gammes to do scales
■ **une gamme de produits** a range of products

gammée (FEM **gammée**) ADJECTIVE
■ **la croix gammée** the swastika

le **gant** NOUN
glove
□ des gants en laine woollen gloves
■ **un gant de toilette** a face cloth

le **garage** NOUN
garage

le/la **garagiste** NOUN
1 garage owner
2 mechanic

la **garantie** NOUN
guarantee

garantir VERB [38]
to guarantee

le **garçon** NOUN
boy
- **un vieux garçon** a bachelor
  - 🔅 **LANGUAGE TIP** Word for word, **vieux garçon** means 'old boy'.

le **garde** NOUN
▷ see also **la garde**
1 warder (in prison)
2 security man
- **un garde du corps** a bodyguard

la **garde** NOUN
▷ see also **le garde**
1 guarding
  □ Il est chargé de la garde des prisonniers. He's responsible for guarding the prisoners.
2 guard
  □ la relève de la garde the changing of the guard
- **un chien de garde** a guard dog
- **être de garde** to be on duty □ Mon père est de garde ce soir. My father is on duty tonight. □ La pharmacie de garde ce week-end est ... The duty chemist this weekend is ...
- **mettre en garde** to warn □ Elle m'a mis en garde contre les pickpockets. She warned me about pickpockets.

le **garde-côte** (PL les **garde-côtes**) NOUN
coastguard

garder VERB [28]
1 to keep
  □ Tu as gardé toutes ses lettres? Have you kept all his letters?
2 to look after
  □ Je garde ma nièce samedi après-midi. I'm looking after my niece on Saturday afternoon.
3 to guard
  □ Ils ont pris un gros chien pour garder la maison. They got a big dog to guard the house.
- **garder le lit** to stay in bed
- **se garder** to keep □ Ces crêpes se gardent bien. These pancakes keep well.

la **garderie** NOUN
nursery

la **garde-robe** NOUN
wardrobe (clothes)
  □ Elle a une garde-robe bien fournie. She's got an extensive wardrobe.

le **gardien** NOUN
1 caretaker
2 attendant (in a museum)
- **un gardien de but** a goalkeeper
- **un gardien de la paix** a police officer

la **gardienne** NOUN
1 caretaker

2 attendant (in a museum)

la **gare** NOUN
▷ see also **gare** EXCLAMATION
station
  □ la gare routière the bus station

gare EXCLAMATION
▷ see also **gare** NOUN
- **Gare aux serpents!** Watch out for snakes!

garer VERB [28]
to park
- **se garer** to park □ Où t'es-tu garé? Where are you parked?

garni (FEM **garnie**) ADJECTIVE
- **un plat garni** a dish served with accompaniments (vegetables, chips, rice etc)

le **gars** NOUN (informal)
guy

gaspiller VERB [28]
to waste

le **gâteau** (PL les **gâteaux**) NOUN
cake
- **les gâteaux secs** biscuits

gâter VERB [28]
to spoil
  □ Il aime gâter ses petits enfants. He likes to spoil his grandchildren.
- **se gâter** to go bad □ Les pommes vont se gâter si on ne les mange pas ce soir. The apples will go bad if we don't eat them tonight.
- **Le temps va se gâter.** The weather's going to break.

gauche (FEM **gauche**) ADJECTIVE
▷ see also **gauche** NOUN
left
  □ le bras gauche the left arm □ le côté gauche the left-hand side

la **gauche** NOUN
▷ see also **gauche** ADJECTIVE
left
  □ sur votre gauche on your left
- **à gauche 1** on the left □ la deuxième rue à gauche the second street on the left **2** to the left □ à gauche de l'armoire to the left of the cupboard
- **Tournez à gauche.** Turn left.
- **la voie de gauche** the left-hand lane
- **la gauche** (in politics) the left
- **Il est de gauche.** He's left-wing.

gaucher (FEM **gauchère**) ADJECTIVE
left-handed

la **gaufre** NOUN
waffle

la **gaufrette** NOUN
wafer

le **Gaulois** NOUN

Gaul

□ Astérix le Gaulois Asterix the Gaul

gaulois (FEM **gauloise**) ADJECTIVE
Gallic

le **gaz** NOUN
gas

gazeux (FEM **gazeuse**) ADJECTIVE

■ une boisson gazeuse a fizzy drink

■ de l'eau gazeuse sparkling water

le **gazole** NOUN
diesel (fuel)

le **gazon** NOUN
lawn

le **GDF** NOUN (= Gaz de France)
French gas company

le **géant** NOUN
giant

le **gel** NOUN
frost

la **gelée** NOUN
jelly

geler VERB [43]
to freeze

■ Il a gelé cette nuit. There was a frost last
night.

la **gélule** NOUN
capsule (containing medicine)

les **Gémeaux** MASC PL NOUN
Gemini

□ Henry est Gémeaux. Henry's Gemini.

gémir VERB [38]
to moan

gênant (FEM **gênante**) ADJECTIVE
awkward

□ un silence gênant an awkward silence

la **gencive** NOUN
gum (in mouth)

le **gendarme** NOUN
policeman

la **gendarmerie** NOUN
1 police force
2 police station

□ Vous devriez porter plainte à la
gendarmerie. You should go to the police
station and report it.

le **gendre** NOUN
son-in-law

gêné (FEM **gênée**) ADJECTIVE
embarrassed

gêner VERB [28]
1 to bother

□ Je ne voudrais pas vous gêner. I don't
want to bother you.

2 to feel awkward

□ Son regard la gênait. The way he was
looking at her made her feel awkward.

général (FEM **générale**, MASC PL **généraux**)

ADJECTIVE

▷ see also **général** NOUN
general

■ en général usually

le **général** (PL les **généraux**) NOUN

▷ see also **général** ADJECTIVE
general

généralement ADVERB
generally

le/la **généraliste** NOUN
family doctor

la **génération** NOUN
generation

généreux (FEM **généreuse**) ADJECTIVE
generous

la **générosité** NOUN
generosity

le **genêt** NOUN
broom (bush)

la **génétique** NOUN
genetics

génétiquement ADVERB
genetically

□ génétiquement modifié genetically-
modified □ les aliments génétiquement
modifiés GM foods □ un organisme
génétiquement modifié a genetically-
modified organism

Genève NOUN
Geneva

génial (FEM **géniale**, MASC PL **géniaux**)
ADJECTIVE (informal)
great

□ Le film d'hier soir était génial. The film
last night was great.

le **genou** (PL les **genoux**) NOUN
knee

□ Elle est à genoux. She's on her knees.
□ se mettre à genoux to kneel down

le **genre** NOUN
kind

□ C'est un genre de gâteau à la crème. It's a
kind of cream cake.

les **gens** MASC PL NOUN
people

gentil (FEM **gentille**) ADJECTIVE
1 nice

□ Nos voisins sont très gentils. Our
neighbours are very nice.

2 kind

□ C'était très gentil de votre part. It was very
kind of you.

la **gentillesse** NOUN
kindness

□ Je l'ai remerciée de sa gentillesse. I
thanked her for her kindness.

■ C'est un homme d'une grande

gentillesse. He is a very nice man.

gentiment ADVERB

1 <u>nicely</u>
□ Demande-le lui gentiment. Ask him nicely.

2 <u>kindly</u>
□ Ils nous ont gentiment proposé de rester dîner. They kindly invited us to stay for dinner.

la **géographie** NOUN
<u>geography</u>

la **géométrie** NOUN
<u>geometry</u>

le **gérant** NOUN
<u>manager</u>

la **gérante** NOUN
<u>manager</u>

gérer VERB [34]
<u>to manage</u>

germain (FEM **germaine**) ADJECTIVE
■ **un cousin germain** a first cousin

le **geste** NOUN
<u>gesture</u>
□ Il a voulu faire un geste. He wanted to make a gesture.
■ **Ne faites pas un geste!** Don't move!

la **gestion** NOUN
<u>management</u>

le/la **gestionnaire de site** NOUN
<u>webmaster</u>

la **gifle** NOUN
<u>slap across the face</u>

gifler VERB [28]
<u>to slap across the face</u>

gigantesque (FEM **gigantesque**) ADJECTIVE
<u>gigantic</u>

le **gigot** NOUN
<u>leg of lamb</u>

le **gilet** NOUN

1 <u>waistcoat</u>
□ un gilet en cuir a leather waistcoat

2 <u>cardigan</u>
□ un gilet tricoté main a hand-knitted cardigan
■ **un gilet de sauvetage** a life jacket

le **gingembre** NOUN
<u>ginger</u>

la **girafe** NOUN
<u>giraffe</u>

le **gitan** NOUN
<u>gipsy</u>

la **gitane** NOUN
<u>gipsy</u>

le **gîte** NOUN
■ **un gîte rural** a holiday house

la **glace** NOUN

1 <u>ice</u>
□ L'étang est recouvert de glace. The pond is covered with ice.

2 <u>ice cream</u>
□ une glace à la fraise a strawberry ice cream

3 <u>mirror</u>
□ Il se regarde souvent dans la glace. He often looks at himself in the mirror.

glacé (FEM **glacée**) ADJECTIVE

1 <u>icy</u>
□ un vent glacé an icy wind

2 <u>iced</u>
□ un thé glacé an iced tea

glacial (FEM **glaciale**, MASC PL **glaciaux**) ADJECTIVE
<u>icy</u>

le **glaçon** NOUN
<u>ice cube</u>

glissant (FEM **glissante**) ADJECTIVE
<u>slippery</u>

glisser VERB [28]

1 <u>to slip</u>
□ Il a glissé sur une peau de banane. He slipped on a banana skin.

2 <u>to be slippery</u>
□ Attention, ça glisse! Watch out, it's slippery!

global (FEM **globale**, MASC PL **globaux**) ADJECTIVE
<u>total</u>
□ la somme globale the total amount

la **gloire** NOUN
<u>glory</u>

la **godasse** NOUN (informal)
<u>shoe</u>

le **goéland** NOUN
<u>seagull</u>

le **golf** NOUN

1 <u>golf</u>
□ Il joue au golf. He plays golf.

2 <u>golf course</u>
□ un golf dix-huit trous an 18-hole golf course

le **golfe** NOUN
<u>gulf</u>
■ **le golfe de Gascogne** the Bay of Biscay

la **gomme** NOUN
<u>rubber</u>

gommer VERB [28]
<u>to rub out</u>

gonflé (FEM **gonflée**) ADJECTIVE

1 <u>swollen</u> (arm, finger, stomach)
□ Elle a les pieds gonflés. Her feet are swollen.

2 <u>inflated</u> (ball, tyre)
□ Le ballon de foot était mal gonflé. The football wasn't properly inflated.

■ **Il est gonflé!** He's got a nerve!

gonfler VERB [28]

1 to blow up

□ gonfler un ballon to blow up a balloon

2 to pump up

□ gonfler un pneu to pump up a tyre

la **gorge** NOUN

1 throat

□ J'ai mal à la gorge. I've got a sore throat.

2 gorge

□ les gorges du Tarn the Tarn gorges

la **gorgée** NOUN

sip

□ une gorgée d'eau a sip of water

le **gorille** NOUN

gorilla

le/la **gosse** NOUN (informal)

kid

le **goudron** NOUN

tar

le **gouffre** NOUN

chasm

■ **Cette voiture est un vrai gouffre!** This car eats up money!

la **gourde** NOUN

water bottle

gourmand (FEM **gourmande**) ADJECTIVE

greedy

la **gourmandise** NOUN

greed

la **gousse** NOUN

■ **une gousse d'ail** a clove of garlic

le **goût** NOUN

taste

□ Ça n'a pas de goût. It's got no taste. □ Elle a très bon goût. She's got very good taste.

goûter VERB [28]

▷ see also **goûter** NOUN

1 to taste

□ Goûte ce fromage. Taste this cheese.

2 to have a snack (in the afternoon)

□ Les enfants goûtent généralement vers quatre heures. The children usually have a snack around 4 o'clock.

le **goûter** NOUN

▷ see also **goûter** VERB

afternoon snack

la **goutte** NOUN

drop

le **gouvernement** NOUN

government

gouverner VERB [28]

to govern

la **grâce** NOUN

■ **grâce à** thanks to □ Je suis arrivé à l'heure grâce à toi. I arrived on time thanks to you.

gracieux (FEM **gracieuse**) ADJECTIVE

graceful

les **gradins** MASC PL NOUN

terraces (in stadium)

graduel (FEM **graduelle**) ADJECTIVE

gradual

les **graffiti** MASC PL NOUN

graffiti

le **grain** NOUN

grain

□ un grain de sable a grain of sand

■ **un grain de beauté** a beauty spot

■ **un grain de café** a coffee bean

■ **un grain de raisin** a grape

la **graine** NOUN

seed

la **graisse** NOUN

fat

la **grammaire** NOUN

grammar

le **gramme** NOUN

gramme

grand (FEM **grande**) ADJECTIVE, ADVERB

1 tall

□ Il est grand pour son âge. He's tall for his age.

2 big

□ une grande valise a big suitcase □ C'est sa grande sœur. She's his big sister.

■ **une grande personne** a grown-up

3 long

□ un grand voyage a long journey

■ **les grandes vacances** the summer holidays

4 great

□ C'est un grand ami à moi. He's a great friend of mine.

■ **un grand magasin** a department store

■ **une grande surface** a hypermarket

■ **les grandes écoles** top ranking colleges (at university level)

■ **au grand air** out in the open air □ Ça te fera beaucoup de bien d'être au grand air. It'll be very good for you to be out in the open air.

■ **grand ouvert** wide open

grand-chose NOUN

■ **pas grand-chose** not much □ Je n'ai pas acheté grand-chose au marché. I didn't buy much at the market. □ Voici un petit cadeau: ce n'est pas grand-chose. Here's a little present: it's nothing much.

la **Grande-Bretagne** NOUN

Britain

la **grandeur** NOUN

size

grandir VERB [38]

to grow
□ Il a beaucoup grandi. He's grown a lot.

la **grand-mère** (PL les **grands-mères**) NOUN
grandmother

grand-peine
■ a grand-peine ADVERB with great difficulty

le **grand-père** (PL les **grands-pères**) NOUN
grandfather

les **grands-parents** MASC PL NOUN
grandparents

la **grange** NOUN
barn

la **grappe** NOUN
■ une grappe de raisin a bunch of grapes

gras (FEM **grasse**) ADJECTIVE
1 fatty (food)
□ Évitez les aliments gras. Avoid fatty foods.
2 greasy
□ des cheveux gras greasy hair
3 oily
□ une peau grasse oily skin
■ faire la grasse matinée to have a lie-in

gratis (FEM+PL **gratis**) ADJECTIVE, ADVERB
free
□ J'ai eu ce stylo gratis. I got this pen free.

le **gratte-ciel** (PL les **gratte-ciel**) NOUN
skyscraper

gratter VERB [28]
1 to scratch
□ Ne gratte pas tes piqûres de moustiques! Don't scratch your mosquito bites!
2 to be itchy
□ C'est épouvantable comme ça gratte! It's terribly itchy!

gratuit (FEM **gratuite**) ADJECTIVE
free
□ entrée gratuite entrance free □ J'ai deux places gratuites pour le film. I've got two free tickets for the film.

grave (FEM **grave**) ADJECTIVE
1 serious
□ une maladie grave a serious illness □ Il avait l'air grave. He was looking serious.
2 deep
□ Il a une voix grave. He's got a deep voice.
■ Ce n'est pas grave. It doesn't matter.
□ J'ai oublié ma clé. — Ce n'est pas grave, j'ai la mienne. I've forgotten my key. — It doesn't matter, I've got mine.

gravement ADVERB
seriously
□ Il a été gravement blessé. He was seriously injured.

le **graveur** NOUN

■ un graveur de CD a CD burner

grec (FEM **grecque**) ADJECTIVE, NOUN
Greek
■ J'apprends le grec. I'm learning Greek.
■ un Grec a Greek (man)
■ une Grecque a Greek (woman)
■ les Grecs the Greeks

la **Grèce** NOUN
Greece
■ en Grèce 1 in Greece 2 to Greece

la **grêle** NOUN
hail

grêler VERB [28]
■ Il grêle. It's hailing.

grelotter VERB [28]
to shiver

la **grenade** NOUN
1 pomegranate
2 grenade

la **grenadine** NOUN
grenadine

> **DID YOU KNOW...?**
> Grenadine is a bright pink drink which is very popular with children in France.

le **grenier** NOUN
attic

la **grenouille** NOUN
frog

la **grève** NOUN
1 strike
■ en grève on strike □ Ils sont en grève depuis dix jours. They have been on strike for ten days.
■ faire grève to be on strike
2 shore
□ Nous nous sommes promenés le long de la grève. We went for a walk along the shore.

le/la **gréviste** NOUN
striker

grièvement ADVERB
■ grièvement blessé seriously injured

la **griffe** NOUN
1 claw
■ donner un coup de griffe to scratch
□ Le chat m'a donné un coup de griffe. The cat scratched me.
2 label
□ la griffe d'un grand couturier the label of a top designer

griffer VERB [28]
to scratch
□ Le chat m'a griffé. The cat scratched me.

grignoter VERB [28]
to nibble

la **grillade** NOUN

g

127

grilled food

□ une grillade d'agneau grilled lamb

la **grille** NOUN

1 wire fence

□ L'usine est entourée d'une haute grille. The factory is surrounded by a high wire fence.

2 metal gate

□ Le facteur a sonné à la grille du jardin. The postman rang at the garden gate.

le **grille-pain** (PL les **grille-pain**) NOUN

toaster

griller VERB [28]

1 to toast

■ **du pain grillé** toast

2 to grill

□ des saucisses grillées grilled sausages

la **grimace** NOUN

■ **faire des grimaces** to make faces

grimper VERB [28]

to climb

grincer VERB [12]

to creak

grincheux (FEM **grincheuse**) ADJECTIVE

grumpy

la **grippe** NOUN

flu

■ **avoir la grippe** to have flu □ J'ai eu une mauvaise grippe l'hiver dernier. I had a bad bout of flu last winter.

grippé (FEM **grippée**) ADJECTIVE

■ **être grippé** to have flu

gris (FEM **grise**) ADJECTIVE

grey

le **Groenland** NOUN

Greenland

grogner VERB [28]

1 to growl

□ Le chien a grogné quand je me suis approché de lui. The dog growled when I went near it.

2 to complain

□ Arrête donc de grogner! Stop complaining!

gronder VERB [28]

■ **se faire gronder** to get a telling-off

□ Tu vas te faire gronder par ton père! You're going to get a telling-off from your father!

gros (FEM **grosse**) ADJECTIVE

1 big

□ une grosse pomme a big apple

2 fat

□ Je suis trop grosse pour porter ça! I'm too fat to wear that!

la **groseille** NOUN

■ **la groseille rouge** redcurrant

■ **la groseille à maquereau** gooseberry

LANGUAGE TIP Word for word, groseille à maquereau means 'currant for mackerel'.

la **grossesse** NOUN

pregnancy

grossier (FEM **grossière**) ADJECTIVE

rude

□ Ne sois pas si grossier! Don't be so rude!

■ **une erreur grossière** a bad mistake

grossir VERB [38]

to put on weight

□ Il a beaucoup grossi. He's put on a lot of weight.

grosso modo ADVERB

roughly

□ Dis-moi grosso modo ce que tu en penses. Tell me roughly what you think of it.

la **grotte** NOUN

cave

le **groupe** NOUN

group

□ votre groupe sanguin your blood group

grouper VERB [28]

to group

□ On nous a groupés dans différentes classes selon notre niveau. We were grouped in different classes according to our level.

■ **se grouper** to gather □ Nous nous sommes groupés autour du feu. We gathered round the fire.

le **guépard** NOUN

cheetah

la **guêpe** NOUN

wasp

guérir VERB [38]

to recover

□ Il est maintenant complètement guéri. He's now completely recovered.

la **guérison** NOUN

recovery

la **guerre** NOUN

war

□ en guerre at war □ une guerre civile a civil war □ la Deuxième Guerre mondiale the Second World War

guetter VERB [28]

to look out for

□ Elle guette l'arrivée du facteur tous les matins. She looks out for the postman every morning.

la **gueule** NOUN

mouth

□ Le chat a ramené une souris dans sa gueule. The cat brought in a mouse in its mouth.

■ **Ta gueule!** *(rude)* Shut your face!
■ **avoir la gueule de bois** *(informal)* to have a hangover

> **LANGUAGE TIP** **gueule** is an impolite way of talking about a person's mouth but it is the correct term for an animal's.

gueuler VERB [28] *(informal)*
to bawl

le **guichet** NOUN
counter *(in bank, booking office)*

le **guide** NOUN
guide

guider VERB [28]
to guide

le **guidon** NOUN
handlebars

les **guillemets** MASC PL NOUN
inverted commas
□ entre guillemets in inverted commas

la **guirlande** NOUN
tinsel
□ Nous avons décoré le sapin de Noël avec des guirlandes. We decorated the Christmas tree with tinsel.
■ **des guirlandes en papier** paper chains

la **guitare** NOUN
guitar
□ Sais-tu jouer de la guitare? Can you play the guitar?

la **gym** NOUN *(informal)*
PE

le **gymnase** NOUN
gym
□ Le lycée a un nouveau gymnase. The school's got a new gym.

la **gymnastique** NOUN
gymnastics
■ **faire de la gymnastique** to do one's exercises

g

Hh

h

habile (FEM **habile**) ADJECTIVE
skilful
□ Il est très habile de ses mains. He is very clever with his hands.

habillé (FEM **habillée**) ADJECTIVE
1 dressed
□ Il n'est pas encore habillé. He's not dressed yet.
2 smart
□ Cette robe fait très habillé. This dress looks very smart.

s' **habiller** VERB [28]
1 to get dressed
□ Je me suis rapidement habillé. I got dressed quickly.
2 to dress up
□ Est-ce qu'il faut s'habiller pour la réception? Do you have to dress up to go to the party?

l' **habitant** MASC NOUN
inhabitant
■ **les habitants du quartier** the local people

l' **habitante** FEM NOUN
inhabitant

habiter VERB [28]
to live
□ Il habite à Montpellier. He lives in Montpellier.

les **habits** MASC PL NOUN
clothes

l' **habitude** FEM NOUN
habit
□ une mauvaise habitude a bad habit
■ **avoir l'habitude de quelque chose** to be used to something □ Elle a l'habitude des enfants. She's used to children. □ Je n'ai pas l'habitude de parler en public. I'm not used to speaking in public.
■ **d'habitude** usually
■ **comme d'habitude** as usual

habituel (FEM **habituelle**) ADJECTIVE
usual

s' **habituer** VERB [28]
■ **s'habituer à quelque chose** to get used

to something □ Il faudra que tu t'habitues à te lever tôt. You'll have to get used to getting up early.

le **hachis** NOUN
mince
■ **le hachis Parmentier** shepherd's pie

la **haie** NOUN
hedge

la **haine** NOUN
hatred

haïr VERB [40]
to hate

l' **haleine** FEM NOUN
breath
□ avoir mauvaise haleine to have bad breath □ être hors d'haleine to be out of breath

les **halles** FEM PL NOUN
covered market

la **halte** NOUN
stop
□ faire halte to make a stop
■ **Halte!** Stop!

l' **haltérophilie** FEM NOUN
weightlifting

le **hamburger** NOUN
hamburger

l' **hameçon** MASC NOUN
fish hook

le **hamster** NOUN
hamster

la **hanche** NOUN
hip

le **handball** NOUN
handball
□ jouer au handball to play handball

le **handicapé** NOUN
disabled man

la **handicapée** NOUN
disabled woman

le **harcèlement** NOUN
harassment
□ le harcèlement sexuel sexual harassment

le **hareng** NOUN
herring

■ **un hareng saur** a kipper

le **haricot** NOUN
bean

■ **les haricots verts** runner beans
■ **les haricots blancs** haricot beans
■ **C'est la fin des haricots.** *(informal)* It's the last straw.

◯ **LANGUAGE TIP** Word for word, this means 'it's the end of the beans'.

l' **harmonica** MASC NOUN
mouth organ

la **harpe** NOUN
harp

le **hasard** NOUN
coincidence
□ C'était un pur hasard. It was pure coincidence.
■ **au hasard** at random □ Choisis un numéro au hasard. Choose a number at random.
■ **par hasard** by chance □ rencontrer quelqu'un par hasard to meet somebody by chance
■ **à tout hasard 1** just in case □ Prends un parapluie à tout hasard. Take an umbrella just in case. **2** on the off chance □ Je ne sais pas s'il est chez lui, mais je vais l'appeler à tout hasard. I don't know if he's at home, but I'll phone on the off chance.

la **hâte** NOUN
■ **à la hâte** hurriedly □ Elle s'est habillée à la hâte. She got dressed hurriedly.
■ **J'ai hâte de te voir.** I can't wait to see you.

la **hausse** NOUN
1 increase
□ la hausse des prix price increase
2 rise
□ On annonce une légère hausse de température. The forecast is for a slight rise in temperature.

hausser VERB [28]
■ **hausser les épaules** to shrug one's shoulders

haut (FEM **haute**) ADJECTIVE, ADVERB
▷ *see also* **haut** NOUN
1 high
□ une haute montagne a high mountain
2 aloud
□ penser tout haut to think aloud

le **haut** NOUN
▷ *see also* **haut** ADJECTIVE
top
■ **un mur de trois mètres de haut** a wall 3 metres high
■ **en haut 1** upstairs □ La salle de bain est en haut. The bathroom is upstairs. **2** at the top □ Le nid est tout en haut de l'arbre. The nest is right at the top of the tree.

la **hauteur** NOUN
height

le **haut-parleur** NOUN
loudspeaker

l' **hebdomadaire** MASC NOUN
weekly *(magazine)*

l' **hébergement** MASC NOUN
accommodation

héberger VERB [45]
to put up
□ Mon cousin a dit qu'il nous hébergerait. My cousin said he would put us up.

hein? EXCLAMATION
eh?
□ Hein? Qu'est-ce que tu dis? Eh? What did you say?

hélas ADVERB
unfortunately
□ Hélas, il ne restait plus de billets. Unfortunately there were no tickets left.

l' **hélicoptère** MASC NOUN
helicopter

l' **hémorragie** FEM NOUN
haemorrhage

l' **herbe** FEM NOUN
grass
■ **les herbes de Provence** mixed herbs

le **hérisson** NOUN
hedgehog

hériter VERB [28]
to inherit

l' **héritier** MASC NOUN
heir

l' **héritière** FEM NOUN
heiress

hermétique (FEM **hermétique**) ADJECTIVE
airtight

l' **héroïne** FEM NOUN
1 heroine
□ l'héroïne du roman the heroine of the novel
2 heroin *(drug)*

le **héros** NOUN
hero

l' **hésitation** FEM NOUN
hesitation

hésiter VERB [28]
to hesitate
□ Il n'a pas hésité à nous aider. He didn't hesitate to help us.
■ **J'ai hésité entre le pull vert et le cardigan jaune.** I couldn't decide between the green pullover and the yellow cardigan.
■ **Est-ce que tu viens ce soir? — J'hésite ...** Are you coming this evening? — I'm not

sure ...
- **sans hésiter** without hesitating

l' **heure** FEM NOUN
1 hour
   □ Le trajet dure six heures. The journey lasts six hours.
2 time
   □ Vous avez l'heure? Have you got the time?
   - **Quelle heure est-il?** What time is it?
   - **À quelle heure?** What time? □ À quelle heure arrivons-nous? What time do we arrive?
   - **deux heures du matin** 2 o'clock in the morning
   - **être à l'heure** to be on time
   - **une heure de français** a period of French

heureusement ADVERB
luckily
   □ Heureusement qu'il n'a pas été blessé. Luckily he wasn't hurt.

heureux (FEM **heureuse**) ADJECTIVE
happy

heurter VERB [28]
to hit

l' **hexagone** MASC NOUN
hexagon
   - **l'Hexagone** France

> **DID YOU KNOW...?**
> France is often referred to as **l'Hexagone** because of its six-sided shape.

le **hibou** (PL les **hiboux**) NOUN
owl

hier ADVERB
yesterday
   - **avant-hier** the day before yesterday

la **hi-fi** NOUN
stereo
   - **une chaîne hi-fi** a stereo system

hippique (FEM **hippique**) ADJECTIVE
   - **un club hippique** a riding centre
   - **un concours hippique** a horse show

l' **hippopotame** MASC NOUN
hippopotamus

l' **hirondelle** FEM NOUN
swallow (bird)

l' **histoire** FEM NOUN
1 history
   □ un cours d'histoire a history lesson
2 story
   □ C'est l'histoire de deux enfants. It's the story of two children.
   - **Ne fais pas d'histoires!** Don't make a fuss!

historique (FEM **historique**) ADJECTIVE

historic
   □ un monument historique a historic monument

l' **hiver** MASC NOUN
winter
   - **en hiver** in winter

la **HLM** NOUN (= *habitation à loyer modéré*)
council flat
   - **des HLM** council housing

le **hockey** NOUN
hockey
   - **le hockey sur glace** ice hockey

hollandais (FEM **hollandaise**) ADJECTIVE, NOUN
Dutch
   - **J'apprends le hollandais.** I'm learning Dutch.
   - **un Hollandais** a Dutch man
   - **une Hollandaise** a Dutch woman
   - **les Hollandais** the Dutch

la **Hollande** NOUN
Holland
   - **en Hollande 1** in Holland **2** to Holland

le **homard** NOUN
lobster

homéopathique (FEM **homéopathique**) ADJECTIVE
homeopathic

l' **hommage** MASC NOUN
tribute

l' **homme** MASC NOUN
man
   - **un homme d'affaires** a businessman

homosexuel (FEM **homosexuelle**) ADJECTIVE
homosexual

la **Hongrie** NOUN
Hungary

hongrois (FEM **hongroise**) ADJECTIVE, NOUN
Hungarian
   - **Il parle le hongrois.** He speaks Hungarian.
   - **un Hongrois** a Hungarian (*man*)
   - **une Hongroise** a Hungarian (*woman*)
   - **les Hollandais** the Dutch

honnête (FEM **honnête**) ADJECTIVE
honest

l' **honnêteté** FEM NOUN
honesty

l' **honneur** MASC NOUN
honour

la **honte** NOUN
shame
   - **avoir honte de quelque chose** to be ashamed of something

l' **hôpital** (PL les **hôpitaux**) MASC NOUN
hospital

le **hoquet** NOUN

■ **avoir le hoquet** to have hiccups

l' **horaire** MASC NOUN
timetable

■ **les horaires de train** the train timetable

l' **horizon** MASC NOUN
horizon

horizontal (FEM **horizontale**, MASC PL
horizontaux) ADJECTIVE
horizontal

l' **horloge** FEM NOUN
clock

l' **horreur** FEM NOUN
horror

□ un film d'horreur a horror film

■ **avoir horreur de** to hate □ J'ai horreur
du chou. I hate cabbage.

horrible (FEM **horrible**) ADJECTIVE
horrible

hors PREPOSITION

■ **hors de** out of □ Elle est hors de danger
maintenant. She's out of danger now.

■ **hors taxes** duty-free

le **hors-d'œuvre** (PL les **hors-d'œuvre**)
NOUN
starter (food)

hospitalier (FEM **hospitalière**) ADJECTIVE
hospitable

□ Ils sont très hospitaliers. They're very
hospitable.

■ **les services hospitaliers** hospital
services

l' **hospitalité** FEM NOUN
hospitality

hostile (FEM **hostile**) ADJECTIVE
hostile

l' **hôte** MASC/FEM NOUN

1 host
□ N'oubliez pas de remercier vos hôtes.
Don't forget to thank your hosts.

2 guest
□ Cette ferme accueille des hôtes payants.
This farm takes paying guests.

l' **hôtel** MASC NOUN
hotel

■ **l'hôtel de ville** the town hall

l' **hôtesse** FEM NOUN
hostess

■ **une hôtesse de l'air** a stewardess

la **housse** NOUN
cover
□ une housse de couette a quilt cover
□ une housse de téléphone a phone cover

le **houx** NOUN
holly

l' **huile** FEM NOUN
oil

■ **l'huile solaire** suntan oil

huit NUMBER
eight
□ Il est huit heures du matin. It's eight in
the morning. □ Il a huit ans. He's eight.

■ **le huit février** the eighth of February

■ **dans huit jours** in a week's time

la **huitaine** NOUN

■ **une huitaine de jours** about a week
□ Nous serons de retour dans une
huitaine de jours. We'll be back in about a
week.

huitième (FEM **huitième**) ADJECTIVE
eighth
□ au huitième étage on the eighth floor

l' **huître** FEM NOUN
oyster

humain (FEM **humaine**) ADJECTIVE
▷ see also **humain** NOUN
human

l' **humain** MASC NOUN
▷ see also **humain** ADJECTIVE
human being

l' **humeur** FEM NOUN
mood
□ Il est de bonne humeur. He's in a good
mood. □ Elle était de mauvaise humeur.
She was in a bad mood.

humide (FEM **humide**) ADJECTIVE
damp
□ L'herbe est humide. The grass is damp.
□ un climat humide a damp climate

humilier VERB [19]
to humiliate

humoristique (FEM **humoristique**)
ADJECTIVE
humorous

■ **des dessins humoristiques** cartoons

l' **humour** MASC NOUN
humour
□ Il n'a pas beaucoup d'humour. He hasn't
got much of a sense of humour.

hurler VERB [28]
to howl

la **hutte** NOUN
hut

hydratant (FEM **hydratante**) ADJECTIVE

■ **une crème hydratante** a moisturizing
cream

l' **hygiène** FEM NOUN
hygiene

hygiénique (FEM **hygiénique**) ADJECTIVE
hygienic

■ **une serviette hygiénique** a sanitary
towel

■ **le papier hygiénique** toilet paper

l' **hymne** MASC NOUN

■ **l'hymne national** the national anthem

l' **hyperlien** MASC NOUN
   hyperlink
l' **hypermarché** MASC NOUN
   hypermarket
hypermétrope (FEM **hypermétrope**)
   ADJECTIVE

   long-sighted
hypocrite (FEM **hypocrite**) ADJECTIVE
   hypocritical
   □ Il est hypocrite. He's a hypocrite.
l' **hypothèse** FEM NOUN
   hypothesis

Ii

l' **iceberg** MASC NOUN
iceberg

ici ADVERB
here

□ Les assiettes sont ici. The plates are here.
■ **La mer monte parfois jusqu'ici.** The sea sometimes comes in as far as this.
■ **Jusqu'ici nous n'avons eu aucun problème avec la voiture.** So far we haven't had any problems with the car.

l' **icône** FEM NOUN
icon

idéal (FEM **idéale**, MASC PL **idéaux**) ADJECTIVE
ideal

□ C'est l'endroit idéal pour faire un pique-nique. It's an ideal place to have a picnic.

l' **idée** FEM NOUN
idea

□ C'est une bonne idée. It's a good idea.

l' **identifiant** MASC NOUN
login (on a computer)

identifier VERB [19]
to identify

□ La police a identifié le meurtrier. The police have identified the murderer.

identique (FEM **identique**) ADJECTIVE
identical

□ Ils ont obtenu des résultats identiques. They obtained identical results.

l' **identité** FEM NOUN
identity

■ **une pièce d'identité** a form of identification □ Avez-vous une pièce d'identité? Have you got any form of identification?

idiot (FEM **idiote**) ADJECTIVE
▷ see also **idiot** NOUN, **idiote** NOUN
1 stupid

□ une plaisanterie idiote a stupid joke
2 silly

□ Ne sois pas idiot! Don't be silly!

l' **idiot** MASC NOUN
▷ see also **idiot** ADJECTIVE
idiot

l' **idiote** FEM NOUN

▷ see also **idiote** ADJECTIVE
idiot

ignoble (FEM **ignoble**) ADJECTIVE
horrible

□ Il a été ignoble avec elle. He was horrible to her.

ignorant (FEM **ignorante**) ADJECTIVE
ignorant

ignorer VERB [28]
1 not to know

□ J'ignore son nom. I don't know his name.
2 to ignore

□ Il m'a complètement ignoré. He completely ignored me.

il PRONOUN
1 he

□ Il est parti ce matin de bonne heure. He left early this morning.
2 it

□ Méfie-toi de ce chien: il mord. Be careful of that dog: it bites. □ Il pleut. It's raining.

l' **île** FEM NOUN
island

■ **les îles Anglo-Normandes** the Channel Islands
■ **les îles Britanniques** the British Isles
■ **les îles Féroé** the Faroe Islands

illégal (FEM **illégale**, MASC PL **illégaux**)
ADJECTIVE
illegal

illimité (FEM **illimitée**) ADJECTIVE
unlimited

illisible (FEM **illisible**) ADJECTIVE
illegible

□ une écriture illisible illegible handwriting

illuminer VERB [28]
to floodlight

□ Le château est illuminé tous les soirs pendant l'été. The castle is floodlit every night in the summer.

l' **illusion** FEM NOUN
illusion

■ **Tu te fais des illusions!** You're deluding yourself!

l' **illustration** FEM NOUN

illustration

illustré (FEM **illustrée**) ADJECTIVE
▷ see also **illustré** NOUN
illustrated

l' **illustré** MASC NOUN
▷ see also **illustré** ADJECTIVE
comic

illustrer VERB [28]
to illustrate

□ Vous pouvez illustrer votre rédaction avec des exemples. You may illustrate your essay with examples.

ils PL PRONOUN
they

□ Ils nous ont appelés hier soir. They phoned us last night.

l' **image** FEM NOUN
picture

□ Les films donnent une fausse image de l'Amérique. Films give a false picture of America.

l' **imagination** FEM NOUN
imagination

□ Elle a beaucoup d'imagination. She's got a vivid imagination.

imaginer VERB [28]
to imagine

l' **imbécile** MASC/FEM NOUN
idiot

l' **imitation** FEM NOUN
imitation

imiter VERB [28]
to imitate

l' **immatriculation** FEM NOUN
■ une plaque d'immatriculation a numberplate (of car)

l' **immédiat** MASC NOUN
■ dans l'immédiat for the moment □ Je n'ai pas besoin de ce livre dans l'immédiat. I don't need this book for the moment.

immédiatement ADVERB
immediately

immense (FEM **immense**) ADJECTIVE
1 huge
□ une immense fortune a huge fortune
2 tremendous
□ un immense soulagement a tremendous relief

l' **immeuble** MASC NOUN
block of flats

l' **immigration** FEM NOUN
immigration

l' **immigré** MASC NOUN
immigrant

l' **immigrée** FEM NOUN
immigrant

immobile (FEM **immobile**) ADJECTIVE

motionless

immobilier (FEM **immobilière**) ADJECTIVE
■ une agence immobilière an estate agent's

immobiliser VERB [28]
to immobilize

immunisé (FEM **immunisée**) ADJECTIVE
immunized

l' **impact** MASC NOUN
impact

impair (FEM **impaire**) ADJECTIVE
odd

□ un nombre impair an odd number

impardonnable (FEM **impardonnable**) ADJECTIVE
unforgivable

l' **impasse** FEM NOUN
cul-de-sac

l' **impatience** FEM NOUN
impatience

impatient (FEM **impatiente**) ADJECTIVE
impatient

impeccable (FEM **impeccable**) ADJECTIVE
1 immaculate
□ Elle est toujours impeccable. She's always immaculate.
2 perfect
□ Il a fait un travail impeccable. He's done a perfect job. □ C'est impeccable! That's perfect!

l' **imper** MASC NOUN (informal)
mac

l' **impératif** MASC NOUN
imperative

l' **impératrice** FEM NOUN
empress

l' **imperméable** MASC NOUN
raincoat

impertinent (FEM **impertinente**) ADJECTIVE
cheeky
□ Ne sois pas impertinent! Don't be cheeky!

impitoyable (FEM **impitoyable**) ADJECTIVE
merciless

impliquer VERB [28]
to mean
□ Son silence implique qu'il est d'accord. His silence means he agrees.
■ être impliqué dans to be involved in □ Il est impliqué dans un scandale financier. He's involved in a financial scandal.

impoli (FEM **impolie**) ADJECTIVE
rude

l' **importance** FEM NOUN
importance
■ C'est sans importance. It doesn't matter.

important (FEM **importante**) ADJECTIVE

1 important
  □ un rôle important an important role
2 considerable
  □ une somme importante a considerable sum

l' **importation** FEM NOUN
import
  □ Les importations de pétrole ont baissé. Oil imports have fallen.

importer VERB [28]
  ▷ see also n'importe
1 to import (goods)
2 to matter
  □ Peu importe. It doesn't matter.

imposant (FEM imposante) ADJECTIVE
imposing

imposer VERB [28]
to impose
  ■ imposer quelque chose à quelqu'un to make somebody do something

impossible (FEM impossible) ADJECTIVE
  ▷ see also impossible NOUN
impossible

l' **impossible** MASC NOUN
  ▷ see also impossible ADJECTIVE
  ■ Nous ferons l'impossible pour finir à temps. We'll do our utmost to finish on time.

l' **impôt** MASC NOUN
tax

imprécis (FEM imprécise) ADJECTIVE
imprecise

l' **impression** FEM NOUN
impression
  □ Il a fait bonne impression à ma mère. He made a good impression on my mother.

impressionnant (FEM impressionnante) ADJECTIVE
impressive

impressionner VERB [28]
to impress

imprévisible (FEM imprévisible) ADJECTIVE
unpredictable

imprévu (FEM imprévue) ADJECTIVE
unexpected

l' **imprimante** FEM NOUN
printer (for computer)

imprimé (FEM imprimée) ADJECTIVE
printed
  □ un tissu imprimé a printed fabric □ C'est imprimé en grandes lettres. It's printed in large letters.

imprimer VERB [28]
to print

impropre (FEM impropre) ADJECTIVE
  ■ impropre à la consommation unfit for human consumption

improviser VERB [28]
to improvise

improviste ADVERB
  ■ arriver à l'improviste to arrive unexpectedly

l' **imprudence** FEM NOUN
carelessness
  ■ Ne fais pas d'imprudences! Don't do anything silly!

imprudent (FEM imprudente) ADJECTIVE
1 unwise
  □ Il serait imprudent de prendre la voiture aujourd'hui. It would be unwise to take the car today.
2 careless
  □ un conducteur imprudent a careless driver

impuissant (FEM impuissante) ADJECTIVE
helpless
  □ Elle se sentait complètement impuissante. She felt completely helpless.

impulsif (FEM impulsive) ADJECTIVE
impulsive

inabordable (FEM inabordable) ADJECTIVE
prohibitive
  □ des prix inabordables prohibitive prices

inaccessible (FEM inaccessible) ADJECTIVE
inaccessible
  □ Cette plage est inaccessible par la route. This beach is inaccessible by road.

inachevé (FEM inachevée) ADJECTIVE
unfinished

inadmissible (FEM inadmissible) ADJECTIVE
intolerable
  □ Ce type de comportement est inadmissible! This sort of behaviour is intolerable!

inanimé (FEM inanimée) ADJECTIVE
unconscious
  □ On l'a retrouvé inanimé sur la route. He was found unconscious on the road.

inaperçu (FEM inaperçue) ADJECTIVE
  ■ passer inaperçu to go unnoticed

inattendu (FEM inattendue) ADJECTIVE
unexpected

l' **inattention** FEM NOUN
  ■ une faute d'inattention a careless mistake

inaugurer VERB [28]
to open (an exhibition)

incapable (FEM incapable) ADJECTIVE
incapable
  □ être incapable de faire quelque chose to be incapable of doing something

incassable (FEM incassable) ADJECTIVE
unbreakable

l' **incendie** MASC NOUN

fire
□ un incendie de forêt a forest fire
incertain (FEM **incertaine**) ADJECTIVE
1 uncertain
□ Son avenir est encore incertain. His future is still uncertain.
2 unsettled
□ Le temps est incertain. The weather is unsettled.
l' **incident** MASC NOUN
incident
inciter VERB [28]
■ **inciter quelqu'un à faire quelque chose** to encourage somebody to do something
□ J'ai incité mes parents à partir en voyage. I encouraged my parents to go on a trip.
inclure VERB [13]
to enclose
□ Veuillez inclure une enveloppe timbrée libellée à votre adresse. Please enclose a stamped addressed envelope.
■ **jusqu'au dix mars inclus** until 10th March inclusive
incohérent (FEM **incohérente**) ADJECTIVE
incoherent
incollable (FEM **incollable**) ADJECTIVE
■ **être incollable sur quelque chose** *(informal)* to know everything there is to know about something
■ **le riz incollable** non-stick rice
incolore (FEM **incolore**) ADJECTIVE
colourless
incompétent (FEM **incompétente**) ADJECTIVE
incompetent
incompris (FEM **incomprise**) ADJECTIVE
misunderstood
l' **inconnu** MASC NOUN
stranger
□ Ne parle pas à des inconnus. Don't speak to strangers.
■ **l'inconnu** the unknown □ la peur de l'inconnu the fear of the unknown
l' **inconnue** FEM NOUN
stranger
inconsciemment ADVERB
unconsciously
inconscient (FEM **inconsciente**) ADJECTIVE
unconscious
□ Il est resté inconscient quelques minutes. He was unconscious for several minutes.
incontestable (FEM **incontestable**) ADJECTIVE
indisputable
incontournable (FEM **incontournable**) ADJECTIVE
inevitable

□ l'incontournable petite robe noire the inevitable little black dress
l' **inconvénient** MASC NOUN
disadvantage
■ **si vous n'y voyez pas d'inconvénient** if you have no objection
incorrect (FEM **incorrecte**) ADJECTIVE
1 incorrect
□ une réponse incorrecte an incorrect answer
2 rude
□ Il a été incorrect avec la voisine. He was rude to the woman next door.
incroyable (FEM **incroyable**) ADJECTIVE
incredible
inculper VERB [28]
■ **inculper de** to charge with □ Il a été inculpé de meurtre. He was charged with murder.
l' **Inde** FEM NOUN
India
indécis (FEM **indécise**) ADJECTIVE
1 indecisive
□ Il est constamment indécis. He's always indecisive.
2 undecided
□ Je suis encore indécis. I'm still undecided.
indéfiniment ADVERB
indefinitely
indélicat (FEM **indélicate**) ADJECTIVE
tactless
indemne (FEM **indemne**) ADJECTIVE
unharmed
□ Il s'en est sorti indemne. He escaped unharmed.
indemniser VERB [28]
to compensate
□ Les victimes demandent maintenant à être indemnisées. The victims are now demanding compensation.
indépendamment ADVERB
independently
■ **indépendamment de** irrespective of
□ Les allocations familiales sont versées indépendamment des revenus. Child benefit is given irrespective of income.
l' **indépendance** FEM NOUN
independence
indépendant (FEM **indépendante**) ADJECTIVE
independent
l' **index** MASC NOUN
1 index finger
2 index *(in book)*
l' **indicatif** MASC NOUN
▷ *see also* **indicatif** ADJECTIVE
1 dialling code

2 indicative *(of verb)*

3 theme tune *(of TV programme)*

indicatif (FEM **indicative**) ADJECTIVE
▷ *see also* **indicatif** NOUN
■ **à titre indicatif** for your information

les **indications** FEM PL NOUN
instructions
□ Il suffit de suivre les indications. You just have to follow the instructions.

l' **indice** MASC NOUN
clue
□ La police cherche des indices. The police are looking for clues.

indien (FEM **indienne**) ADJECTIVE, NOUN
Indian
■ **un Indien** an Indian *(man)*
■ **une Indienne** an Indian *(woman)*

l' **indifférence** FEM NOUN
indifference

indifférent (FEM **indifférente**) ADJECTIVE
indifferent

l' **indigène** MASC/FEM NOUN
native

indigeste (FEM **indigeste**) ADJECTIVE
indigestible

l' **indigestion** FEM NOUN
indigestion

indigne (FEM **indigne**) ADJECTIVE
unworthy

indigner VERB [28]
■ **s'indigner de quelque chose** to get indignant about something

indiqué (FEM **indiquée**) ADJECTIVE
advisable
□ Ce n'est pas très indiqué. It's not really advisable.

indiquer VERB [28]
to point out
□ Il m'a indiqué la mairie. He pointed out the town hall.

indirect (FEM **indirecte**) ADJECTIVE
indirect

indiscipliné (FEM **indisciplinée**) ADJECTIVE
unruly

indiscret (FEM **indiscrète**) ADJECTIVE
indiscreet

indispensable (FEM **indispensable**) ADJECTIVE
indispensable

indisposé (FEM **indisposée**) ADJECTIVE
indisposed
■ **être indisposée** to be having one's period

l' **individu** MASC NOUN
individual

individuel (FEM **individuelle**) ADJECTIVE
individual

□ une portion individuelle an individual portion
■ **Vous aurez une chambre individuelle.** You'll have a room of your own.

indolore (FEM **indolore**) ADJECTIVE
painless

l' **Indonésie** FEM NOUN
Indonesia

indulgent (FEM **indulgente**) ADJECTIVE
indulgent
■ **Elle est trop indulgente avec son fils.** She's not firm enough with her son.

l' **industrie** FEM NOUN
industry

industriel (FEM **industrielle**) ADJECTIVE
▷ *see also* **industriel** NOUN
industrial

l' **industriel** MASC NOUN
▷ *see also* **industriel** ADJECTIVE
industrialist

inédit (FEM **inédite**) ADJECTIVE
unpublished

inefficace (FEM **inefficace**) ADJECTIVE
1 ineffective *(treatment)*
2 inefficient
□ un service de transports publics inefficace an inefficient public transport system

inégal (FEM **inégale**, MASC PL **inégaux**) ADJECTIVE
1 unequal
□ un combat inégal an unequal struggle
2 uneven
■ **La qualité est inégale.** The quality varies.

inévitable (FEM **inévitable**) ADJECTIVE
unavoidable
■ **C'était inévitable!** That was bound to happen!

inexact (FEM **inexacte**) ADJECTIVE
inaccurate

in extremis ADVERB
■ **Il a réussi à attraper son train in extremis.** He just managed to catch his train.
■ **Ils ont évité un accident in extremis.** They avoided an accident by the skin of their teeth.

l' **infarctus** MASC NOUN
coronary

infatigable (FEM **infatigable**) ADJECTIVE
indefatigable
□ Il est infatigable. He's indefatigable.

infect (FEM **infecte**) ADJECTIVE
revolting *(meal)*

s' **infecter** VERB [28]
to go septic
□ La plaie s'est infectée. The wound has

139

gone septic.

l' **infection** FEM NOUN
infection

inférieur (FEM **inférieure**) ADJECTIVE
lower
□ les membres inférieurs the lower limbs
□ C'est moins cher, mais de qualité
inférieure. It's cheaper but of lower quality.

infernal (FEM **infernale**, MASC PL **infernaux**)
ADJECTIVE
terrible
□ Ils faisaient un bruit infernal. They were
making a terrible noise.

l' **infini** MASC NOUN
■ à l'infini indefinitely □ On pourrait en
parler à l'infini. We could discuss this
indefinitely.

l' **infinitif** MASC NOUN
infinitive

l' **infirme** MASC/FEM NOUN
disabled person

l' **infirmerie** FEM NOUN
medical room
□ Elle est à l'infirmerie. She's in the medical
room.

l' **infirmier** MASC NOUN
nurse

l' **infirmière** FEM NOUN
nurse

inflammable (FEM **inflammable**) ADJECTIVE
inflammable

l' **influence** FEM NOUN
influence

influencer VERB [12]
to influence

l' **informaticien** MASC NOUN
computer scientist

l' **informaticienne** FEM NOUN
computer scientist

les **informations** FEM PL NOUN
1 news (on TV)
□ les informations de vingt heures the 8
o'clock news
2 information
□ Je voudrais quelques informations, s'il
vous plaît. I'd like some information, please.
■ une information a piece of information

l' **informatique** FEM NOUN
computing

informer VERB [28]
to inform
■ s'informer to find out □ Je vais
m'informer des heures de fermeture. I'm
going to find out when they close.

infuser VERB [28]
1 to brew (tea)
2 to infuse (herbal tea)

l' **infusion** FEM NOUN
herbal tea

l' **ingénieur** MASC NOUN
engineer

ingrat (FEM **ingrate**) ADJECTIVE
ungrateful

l' **ingrédient** MASC NOUN
ingredient

inhabituel (FEM **inhabituelle**) ADJECTIVE
unusual

l' **inhalateur** MASC NOUN
inhaler

inhumain (FEM **inhumaine**) ADJECTIVE
inhuman

initial (FEM **initiale**, MASC PL **initiaux**) ADJECTIVE
▷ see also **initiale** NOUN
initial

l' **initiale** FEM NOUN
▷ see also **initiale** ADJECTIVE
initial

l' **initiation** FEM NOUN
introduction
□ un stage d'initiation à la planche à voile
an introductory course in windsurfing

l' **initiative** FEM NOUN
initiative
□ avoir de l'initiative to have initiative

injecter VERB [28]
to inject

l' **injection** FEM NOUN
injection

l' **injure** FEM NOUN
1 insult
□ Il a pris ça comme une injure. He took this
as an insult.
2 abuse
□ lancer des injures à quelqu'un to hurl
abuse at somebody

injurier VERB [19]
to insult

injurieux (FEM **injurieuse**) ADJECTIVE
abusive (language)

injuste (FEM **injuste**) ADJECTIVE
unfair

innocent (FEM **innocente**) ADJECTIVE
innocent

innombrable (FEM **innombrable**) ADJECTIVE
innumerable

innover VERB [28]
to break new ground

inoccupé (FEM **inoccupée**) ADJECTIVE
empty
□ un appartement inoccupé an empty flat

inoffensif (FEM **inoffensive**) ADJECTIVE
harmless

l' **inondation** FEM NOUN
flood

inoubliable (FEM **inoubliable**) ADJECTIVE
unforgettable

inoxydable (FEM **inoxydable**) ADJECTIVE
■ l'acier inoxydable stainless steel

inquiet (FEM **inquiète**) ADJECTIVE
worried

inquiétant (FEM **inquiétante**) ADJECTIVE
worrying

s' **inquiéter** VERB [34]
to worry
□ Ne t'inquiète pas! Don't worry!

l' **inquiétude** FEM NOUN
anxiety

insatisfait (FEM **insatisfaite**) ADJECTIVE
dissatisfied

l' **inscription** FEM NOUN
registration (for school, course)

s' **inscrire** VERB [30]
■ s'inscrire à 1 to join □ Je me suis inscrit
au club de tennis. I've joined the tennis
club. 2 to register □ N'attends pas trop
pour t'inscrire à la fac. Don't leave it too
long to register at the university.

l' **insecte** MASC NOUN
insect

insensible (FEM **insensible**) ADJECTIVE
insensitive
□ Il la trouve insensible. He thinks she's
insensitive.

l' **insigne** MASC NOUN
badge

insignifiant (FEM **insignifiante**) ADJECTIVE
insignificant

insister VERB [28]
to insist
■ N'insiste pas! Don't keep on!

l' **insolation** FEM NOUN
sunstroke

insolent (FEM **insolente**) ADJECTIVE
cheeky

insouciant (FEM **insouciante**) ADJECTIVE
carefree

insoutenable (FEM **insoutenable**)
ADJECTIVE
unbearable
□ une douleur insoutenable an unbearable
pain

inspecter VERB [28]
to inspect

l' **inspecteur** MASC NOUN
inspector

l' **inspection** FEM NOUN
inspection

l' **inspectrice** FEM NOUN
inspector

inspirer VERB [28]
1 to inspire

■ s'inspirer de to take one's inspiration
from □ Le peintre s'est inspiré d'un poème.
The painter took his inspiration from a
poem.

2 to breathe in
□ Inspirez! Expirez! Breathe in! Breathe out!

instable (FEM **instable**) ADJECTIVE
1 unsteady (piece of furniture)
2 unstable (person)

les **installations** FEM PL NOUN
facilities
□ Cet appartement est pourvu de toutes les
installations modernes. This flat has all
modern facilities.

installer VERB [28]
1 to put up (shelves)
2 to install (gas, telephone)
■ s'installer to settle in □ Nous nous
sommes installés dans notre nouvel
appartement. We've settled into our new
flat.
■ Installez-vous, je vous en prie. Have a
seat, please.

l' **instant** MASC NOUN
moment
□ pour l'instant for the moment
■ dans un instant in a moment □ Le dîner
sera prêt dans un instant. Dinner will be
ready in a moment.

instantané (FEM **instantanée**) ADJECTIVE
instant
□ du café instantané instant coffee

l' **instinct** MASC NOUN
instinct

l' **institut** MASC NOUN
institute

l' **instituteur** MASC NOUN
primary school teacher

l' **institution** FEM NOUN
institution

l' **institutrice** FEM NOUN
primary school teacher

l' **instruction** FEM NOUN
1 instruction
□ J'ai suivi ses instructions. I followed his
instructions.
2 education
□ Il n'a pas beaucoup d'instruction. He's
not very well-educated.

s' **instruire** VERB [23]
to educate oneself

instruit (FEM **instruite**) ADJECTIVE
educated

l' **instrument** MASC NOUN
instrument
□ un instrument de musique a musical
instrument

insuffisant (FEM **insuffisante**) ADJECTIVE
insufficient
■ 'travail insuffisant' (on school report)
'must try harder'

l' **insuline** FEM NOUN
insulin

insultant (FEM **insultante**) ADJECTIVE
insulting
□ Il s'est montré insultant avec elle. He was insulting to her.

l' **insulte** FEM NOUN
insult

insulter VERB [28]
to insult

insupportable (FEM **insupportable**) ADJECTIVE
unbearable

intact (FEM **intacte**) ADJECTIVE
intact

intégral (FEM **intégrale**, MASC PL **intégraux**) ADJECTIVE
■ le texte intégral unabridged version
■ un remboursement intégral a full refund

l' **intégrisme** MASC NOUN
fundamentalism

l' **intelligence** FEM NOUN
intelligence

intelligent (FEM **intelligente**) ADJECTIVE
intelligent

intense (FEM **intense**) ADJECTIVE
intense

intensif (FEM **intensive**) ADJECTIVE
intensive
■ un cours intensif a crash course

l' **intention** FEM NOUN
intention
■ avoir l'intention de faire quelque chose to intend to do something □ J'ai l'intention de lui en parler. I intend to speak to him about it.

l' **interdiction** FEM NOUN
■ 'interdiction de stationner' 'no parking'
■ 'interdiction de fumer' 'no smoking'

interdire VERB [27]
to forbid
□ Ses parents lui ont interdit de sortir. His parents have forbidden him to go out.

interdit (FEM **interdite**) ADJECTIVE
forbidden
□ Il est interdit de fumer dans les couloirs. Smoking in the corridors is forbidden.

intéressant (FEM **intéressante**) ADJECTIVE
interesting
□ un livre intéressant an interesting book
■ On lui a fait une offre intéressante. They made him an attractive offer.

■ On trouve des CD à des prix très intéressants dans ce magasin. You can get very cheap CDs in this shop.

intéresser VERB [28]
to interest
■ s'intéresser à to be interested in
□ Est-ce que vous vous intéressez à la politique? Are you interested in politics?

l' **intérêt** MASC NOUN
interest
■ avoir intérêt à faire quelque chose to do well to do something □ Tu as intérêt à accepter. You'd do well to accept.

l' **intérieur** MASC NOUN
inside
□ à l'intérieur de la maison inside the house

l' **interlocuteur** MASC NOUN
■ son interlocuteur the man he's speaking to

l' **interlocutrice** FEM NOUN
■ son interlocutrice the woman he's speaking to

l' **intermédiaire** MASC NOUN
intermediary
■ par l'intermédiaire de through □ Je l'ai rencontré par l'intermédiaire de sa sœur. I met him through his sister.

l' **internat** MASC NOUN
boarding school

international (FEM **internationale**, MASC PL **internationaux**) ADJECTIVE
international

l' **internaute** MASC/FEM NOUN
internet user

l' **interne** MASC/FEM NOUN
boarder

l' **Internet** MASC NOUN
internet
□ sur Internet on the internet

l' **interphone** MASC NOUN
intercom

l' **interprète** MASC/FEM NOUN
interpreter

interpréter VERB [34]
to interpret

interrogatif (FEM **interrogative**) ADJECTIVE
interrogative

l' **interrogation** FEM NOUN
1 question
2 test
□ une interrogation écrite a written test
□ une interrogation orale an oral test

l' **interrogatoire** MASC NOUN
questioning
■ C'est un interrogatoire ou quoi? Am I being cross-examined?

interroger VERB [45]

to question

interrompre VERB [75]
to interrupt

l' **interrupteur** MASC NOUN
switch

l' **interruption** FEM NOUN
interruption

■ **sans interruption** without stopping
□ Il a parlé pendant deux heures sans
interruption. He spoke for two hours
without stopping.

l' **intervalle** MASC NOUN
interval

■ **dans l'intervalle** in the meantime

intervenir VERB [89]
1 to intervene
2 to take action
□ La police est intervenue. The police took
action.

l' **intervention** FEM NOUN
intervention
□ une intervention militaire a military
intervention
■ **une intervention chirurgicale** a surgical
operation

l' **interview** FEM NOUN
interview *(on radio, TV)*

l' **intestin** MASC NOUN
intestine

intime (FEM **intime**) ADJECTIVE
intimate
■ **un journal intime** a diary

intimider VERB [28]
to intimidate

l' **intimité** FEM NOUN
■ **dans l'intimité** in private □ Ce que vous
faites dans l'intimité ne m'intéresse pas.
What you do in private doesn't interest me.
■ **Le mariage a eu lieu dans l'intimité.**
The wedding ceremony was private.

intitulé (FEM **intitulée**) ADJECTIVE
entitled

intolérable (FEM **intolérable**) ADJECTIVE
intolerable

l' **intoxication** FEM NOUN
■ **une intoxication alimentaire** food
poisoning

l' **Intranet** MASC NOUN
Intranet

intransigeant (FEM **intransigeante**)
ADJECTIVE
uncompromising

l' **intrigue** FEM NOUN
plot *(of book, film)*

l' **introduction** FEM NOUN
introduction

introduire VERB [23]

to introduce

l' **intuition** FEM NOUN
intuition

inusable (FEM **inusable**) ADJECTIVE
hard-wearing

inutile (FEM **inutile**) ADJECTIVE
useless

l' **invalide** MASC/FEM NOUN
disabled person

l' **invasion** FEM NOUN
invasion

inventer VERB [28]
1 to invent
2 to make up
□ inventer une excuse to make up an
excuse

l' **inventeur** MASC NOUN
inventor

l' **invention** FEM NOUN
invention

inverse (FEM **inverse**) ADJECTIVE
▷ *see also* **inverse** NOUN
■ **dans l'ordre inverse** in reverse order
■ **en sens inverse** in the opposite direction

l' **inverse** MASC NOUN
▷ *see also* **inverse** ADJECTIVE
reverse
■ **Tu t'es trompé, c'est l'inverse.** You've
got it wrong, it's the other way round.

l' **investissement** MASC NOUN
investment

invisible (FEM **invisible**) ADJECTIVE
invisible

l' **invitation** FEM NOUN
invitation

l' **invité** MASC NOUN
guest

l' **invitée** FEM NOUN
guest

inviter VERB [28]
to invite

involontaire (FEM **involontaire**) ADJECTIVE
unintentional
□ C'était tout à fait involontaire. It was quite
unintentional.

invraisemblable (FEM **invraisemblable**)
ADJECTIVE
unlikely
□ une histoire invraisemblable an unlikely
story

l' **iPod**® MASC NOUN
iPod®

ira, irai, iraient, irais VERB ▷ *see* aller
■ **J'irai demain au supermarché.** I'll go to
the supermarket tomorrow.

l' **Irak** MASC NOUN
Iraq

l' **Iran** MASC NOUN
Iran

iras, irez VERB ▷ *see* aller

irlandais (FEM **irlandaise**) ADJECTIVE, NOUN
Irish
- **un Irlandais** an Irishman
- **une Irlandaise** an Irishwoman
- **les Irlandais** the Irish

l' **Irlande** FEM NOUN
Ireland
- **en Irlande 1** in Ireland **2** to Ireland
- **la République d'Irlande** the Irish
Republic
- **l'Irlande du Nord** Northern Ireland

l' **ironie** FEM NOUN
irony

ironique (FEM **ironique**) ADJECTIVE
ironical

irons, iront VERB ▷ *see* aller
- **Nous irons à la plage cet après-midi.**
We'll go to the beach this afternoon.

irrationnel (FEM **irrationnelle**) ADJECTIVE
irrational

irréel (FEM **irréelle**) ADJECTIVE
unreal

irrégulier (FEM **irrégulière**) ADJECTIVE
irregular

irrésistible (FEM **irrésistible**) ADJECTIVE
irresistible

irritable (FEM **irritable**) ADJECTIVE
irritable

irriter VERB [28]
to irritate

islamique (FEM **islamique**) ADJECTIVE
Islamic

l' **Islande** FEM NOUN
Iceland

isolé (FEM **isolée**) ADJECTIVE
isolated
- □ une ferme isolée an isolated farm

Israël MASC NOUN
Israel

israélien (FEM **israélienne**) ADJECTIVE, NOUN
Israeli
- **un Israélien** an Israeli *(man)*
- **une Israélienne** an Israeli *(woman)*
- **les Israéliens** the Israelis

israélite (FEM **israélite**) ADJECTIVE
Jewish

l' **issue** FEM NOUN
- **une voie sans issue** a dead end
- **l'issue de secours** emergency exit

l' **Italie** FEM NOUN
Italy
- **en Italie 1** in Italy **2** to Italy

italien (FEM **italienne**) ADJECTIVE, NOUN
Italian
- □ J'apprends l'italien. I'm learning Italian.
- **un Italien** an Italian *(man)*
- **une Italienne** an Italian *(woman)*
- **les Italiens** the Italians

l' **itinéraire** MASC NOUN
route

l' **IUT** MASC NOUN (= *Institut universitaire de technologie*)
institute of technology *(at university level)*

ivre (FEM **ivre**) ADJECTIVE
drunk

l' **ivrogne** MASC/FEM NOUN
drunkard

J j

j' PRONOUN ▷ see **je**

la **jalousie** NOUN
jealousy

jaloux (FEM **jalouse**) ADJECTIVE
jealous

jamais ADVERB
1 never
□ Tu vas souvent au cinéma? — Non, jamais. Do you go to the cinema often? — No, never. □ Il ne boit jamais d'alcool. He never drinks alcohol.
2 ever

> LANGUAGE TIP Phrases with **jamais** meaning 'ever' are followed by a verb in the subjunctive.

□ C'est la plus belle chose que j'aie jamais vue. It's the most beautiful thing I've ever seen.

la **jambe** NOUN
leg

le **jambon** NOUN
ham
■ **le jambon cru** Parma ham

le **jambonneau** (PL les **jambonneaux**) NOUN
knuckle of ham

janvier MASC NOUN
January
■ **en janvier** in January

le **Japon** NOUN
Japan
■ **au Japon 1** in Japan **2** to Japan

japonais (FEM **japonaise**) ADJECTIVE, NOUN
Japanese
□ Elle parle japonais. She speaks Japanese.
■ **un Japonais** a Japanese *(man)*
■ **une Japonaise** a Japanese *(woman)*
■ **les Japonais** the Japanese

le **jardin** NOUN
garden
□ un jardin potager a vegetable garden

le **jardinage** NOUN
gardening

le **jardinier** NOUN
gardener

la **jardinière** NOUN
gardener

jaune (FEM **jaune**) ADJECTIVE
▷ see also **jaune** NOUN
yellow

le **jaune** NOUN
▷ see also **jaune** ADJECTIVE
yellow
■ **un jaune d'œuf** an egg yolk

> LANGUAGE TIP Word for word, **un jaune d'œuf** means 'an egg yellow'.

jaunir VERB [38]
to turn yellow

la **jaunisse** NOUN
jaundice

Javel NOUN
■ **l'eau de Javel** bleach

le **jazz** NOUN
jazz

J.-C. ABBREVIATION (= *Jésus-Christ*)
■ **44 avant J.-C.** 44 BC
■ **115 après J.-C.** 115 AD

je PRONOUN

> LANGUAGE TIP **je** changes to **j'** before a vowel and most words beginning with 'h'.

I
□ Je t'appellerai ce soir. I'll phone you this evening. □ J'arrive! I'm coming! □ J'hésite. I'm not sure.

le **jean** NOUN
jeans

la **jeannette** NOUN
Brownie
□ Elle est jeannette. She's a Brownie.

Jésus-Christ MASC NOUN
Jesus Christ

le **jet** NOUN
1 jet *(of water)*
■ **un jet d'eau** a fountain
2 jet plane

jetable (FEM **jetable**) ADJECTIVE
disposable

la **jetée** NOUN
jetty

jeter VERB [41]
1 to throw
  □ Il a jeté son sac sur le lit. He threw his bag onto the bed.
2 to throw away
  □ Ils ne jettent jamais rien. They never throw anything away.
  ■ **jeter un coup d'œil** to have a look

le **jeton** NOUN
counter (in board game)

le **jeu** (PL les **jeux**) NOUN
game
  □ Les enfants jouaient à un jeu. The children were playing a game.
  ■ **un jeu d'arcade** an arcade video game
  ■ **un jeu de cartes** 1 a pack of cards 2 a card game
  ■ **un jeu de mots** a pun
  ■ **un jeu de société** a board game
  ■ **un jeu électronique** an electronic game
  ■ **les jeux vidéo** video games
  ■ **en jeu** at stake □ Des vies humaines sont en jeu. Human lives are at stake.

le **jeudi** NOUN
1 Thursday
  □ Aujourd'hui, nous sommes jeudi. It's Thursday today.
2 on Thursday
  □ Il arrivera jeudi matin. He's arriving on Thursday morning.
  ■ **le jeudi** on Thursdays □ Le musée est fermé le jeudi. The museum is closed on Thursdays.
  ■ **tous les jeudis** every Thursday
  ■ **jeudi dernier** last Thursday
  ■ **jeudi prochain** next Thursday

jeun
  ■ **à jeun** ADVERB on an empty stomach □ à prendre à jeun to be taken on an empty stomach □ Il faut être à jeun pour la prise de sang. You mustn't have eaten anything before giving a blood sample.

jeune (FEM **jeune**) ADJECTIVE
  ▷ see also **jeune** NOUN
young
  □ un jeune homme a young man □ une jeune femme a young woman
  ■ **une jeune fille** a girl

jeune NOUN
  ▷ see also **jeune** ADJECTIVE
young person
  □ les jeunes young people

la **jeunesse** NOUN
youth

le **job** NOUN (informal)
job

le **jogging** NOUN

1 jogging
  □ Il fait du jogging. He goes jogging.
2 tracksuit
  □ un jogging rose a pink tracksuit

la **joie** NOUN
joy

joindre VERB [42]
1 to put together
  □ On va joindre les deux tables. We're going to put the two tables together.
2 to contact
  □ Vous pouvez le joindre chez lui. You can contact him at home.

joint (FEM **jointe**) ADJECTIVE
  ■ **une pièce jointe** (in email) an attachment

joli (FEM **jolie**) ADJECTIVE
pretty

le **jonc** NOUN
rush

la **jonquille** NOUN
daffodil

la **joue** NOUN
cheek

jouer VERB [28]
1 to play
  □ Viens jouer avec nous. Come and play with us.
  ■ **jouer de** to play (instrument)
  □ Il joue de la guitare et du piano. He plays the guitar and the piano.
  ■ **jouer à** to play (sport, game)
  □ Elle joue au tennis. She plays tennis.
  □ jouer aux cartes to play cards
2 to act
  □ Je trouve qu'il joue très bien dans ce film. I think he acts very well in this film.
  ■ **On joue Hamlet au Théâtre de la Ville.** Hamlet is on at the Théâtre de la Ville.

le **jouet** NOUN
toy

le **joueur** NOUN
player
  ■ **être mauvais joueur** to be a bad loser

la **joueuse** NOUN
player

le **jour** NOUN
day
  □ J'ai passé trois jours chez mes cousins. I stayed with my cousins for three days.
  ■ **Il fait jour.** It's daylight.
  ■ **mettre quelque chose à jour** to update something
  ■ **le jour de l'An** New Year's Day
  ■ **un jour de congé** a day off
  ■ **un jour férié** a public holiday
  ■ **dans huit jours** in a week

■ **dans quinze jours** in a fortnight

le **journal** (PL les **journaux**) NOUN
1 newspaper
■ **le journal télévisé** the television news
2 diary
□ Elle tient un journal depuis l'âge de douze ans. She has been keeping a diary since she was 12.

journalier (FEM **journalière**) ADJECTIVE
daily

le **journalisme** NOUN
journalism

le/la **journaliste** NOUN
journalist
□ Elle est journaliste. She's a journalist.

la **journée** NOUN
day

joyeux (FEM **joyeuse**) ADJECTIVE
happy
■ **Joyeux anniversaire!** Happy birthday!
■ **Joyeux Noël!** Merry Christmas!

le **judo** NOUN
judo

le **juge** NOUN
judge

juger VERB [45]
to judge

juif (FEM **juive**) ADJECTIVE
Jewish
□ la cuisine juive Jewish cooking
■ **un juif** a Jew (man)
■ **une juive** a Jew (woman)

juillet MASC NOUN
July
■ **en juillet** in July

juin MASC NOUN
June
■ **en juin** in June

le **jumeau** (PL les **jumeaux**) NOUN
twin

jumeler VERB [4]
to twin
□ Saint-Brieuc est jumelée avec Aberystwyth. Saint-Brieuc is twinned with Aberystwyth.

la **jumelle** NOUN
twin

les **jumelles** FEM PL NOUN
binoculars

la **jument** NOUN
mare

la **jungle** NOUN
jungle

la **jupe** NOUN
skirt

jurer VERB [28]
to swear
□ Je jure que c'est vrai! I swear it's true!

juridique (FEM **juridique**) ADJECTIVE
legal

le **jury** NOUN
jury

le **jus** NOUN
juice
■ **un jus de fruit** a fruit juice

jusqu'à PREPOSITION
1 as far as
□ Nous avons marché jusqu'au village. We walked as far as the village.
2 until
□ Il fait généralement chaud jusqu'à la mi-août. It's usually hot until mid-August.
■ **jusqu'à ce que** until □ Tu peux rester ici jusqu'à ce qu'il cesse de pleuvoir. You can stay here until it stops raining.
■ **jusqu'à présent** so far

jusque PREPOSITION
as far as
□ Je l'ai raccompagnée jusque chez elle. I went with her as far as her house.
□ Jusqu'ici nous n'avons pas eu de problèmes. So far we've had no problems.
□ Jusqu'où es-tu allé? How far did you go?

juste (FEM **juste**) ADJECTIVE, ADVERB
1 fair
□ Il est sévère, mais juste. He's strict but fair.
2 tight
□ Cette veste est un peu juste. This jacket is a bit tight.
■ **juste assez** just enough
■ **chanter juste** to sing in tune

justement ADVERB
just
□ C'est justement pour cela qu'il est parti! That's just the reason he left!

la **justesse** NOUN
■ **de justesse** only just □ Il a eu son permis de justesse. He only just passed his driving test.

la **justice** NOUN
justice

justifier VERB [19]
to justify

juteux (FEM **juteuse**) ADJECTIVE
juicy

juvénile (FEM **juvénile**) ADJECTIVE
youthful

Kk

kaki (FEM+PL **kaki**) ADJECTIVE
  khaki

le **kangourou** NOUN
  kangaroo

le **karaté** NOUN
  karate

la **kermesse** NOUN
  fair

kidnapper VERB [28]
  to kidnap

le **kilo** NOUN
  kilo

le **kilogramme** NOUN
  kilogramme

le **kilomètre** NOUN
  kilometre

le/la **kinésithérapeute** NOUN
  physiotherapist

le **kiosque** NOUN
  ■ un kiosque à journaux a news stand

le **kit** NOUN
  kit

▢ en kit in kit form ▢ un kit mains libres a hands-free kit ▢ un kit piéton a hands-free kit

le **klaxon** NOUN
  horn *(of car)*

klaxonner VERB [28]
  to sound the horn

km ABBREVIATION *(= kilomètre)*
  km *(= kilometre)*

km/h ABBREVIATION *(= kilomètres/heure)*
  kph *(= kilometres per hour)*

KO (FEM+PL **KO**) ADJECTIVE
  knocked out
  ■ mettre quelqu'un KO to knock somebody out ▢ Il l'a mis KO au troisième round. He knocked him out in the third round.
  ■ Je suis complètement KO. *(informal)* I'm completely knackered.

le **K-way**® NOUN
  cagoule

Ll

l' ARTICLE, PRONOUN ▷ see **la**, **le**

la ARTICLE, PRONOUN
> ▷ see also **la** NOUN

> **LANGUAGE TIP** **la** changes to **l'** before a vowel and most words beginning with 'h'.

1 the
   □ la maison the house □ l'actrice the actress □ l'herbe the grass
2 her
   □ Je la connais depuis longtemps. I've known her for a long time. □ C'est une femme intelligente: je l'admire beaucoup. She's an intelligent woman: I admire her very much.
3 it
   □ C'est une bonne émission: je la regarde tous les jours. It's a good programme: I watch it every day.
4 one's
   ■ **se mordre la langue** to bite one's tongue □ Je me suis mordu la langue. I've bitten my tongue.
   ■ **six euros la douzaine** six euros a dozen

le la NOUN
> ▷ see also **la** ARTICLE

1 A
   □ en la bémol in A flat
2 la
   □ sol, la, si, do so, la, ti, do

là ADVERB
1 there
   □ Ton livre est là, sur la table. Your book's there, on the table.
2 here
   □ Elle n'est pas là. She isn't here.
   ■ **C'est là que ...** 1 That's where ... □ C'est là que je suis né. That's where I was born.
   2 That's when ... □ C'est là que j'ai réalisé que je m'étais trompé. That's when I realized that I had made a mistake.

là-bas ADVERB
over there

le labo NOUN (informal)
lab

le laboratoire NOUN
laboratory

labourer VERB [28]
to plough

le labyrinthe NOUN
maze

le lac NOUN
lake

lacer VERB [12]
to do up (shoes)

le lacet NOUN
lace
   ■ **des chaussures à lacets** lace-up shoes

lâche (FEM **lâche**) ADJECTIVE
> ▷ see also **lâche** NOUN

1 loose
   □ Le nœud est trop lâche. The knot's too loose.
2 cowardly
   ■ **Il est lâche.** He's a coward.

le lâche NOUN
> ▷ see also **lâche** ADJECTIVE
coward

lâcher VERB [28]
1 to let go of
   □ Il n'a pas lâché ma main de tout le film. He didn't let go of my hand until the end of the film.
2 to drop
   □ Il a été tellement surpris qu'il a lâché son verre. He was so surprised that he dropped his glass.
3 to fail
   □ Les freins ont lâché. The brakes failed.

la lâcheté NOUN
cowardice

lacrymogène (FEM **lacrymogène**) ADJECTIVE
   ■ **le gaz lacrymogène** tear gas

la lacune NOUN
gap

là-dedans ADVERB
in there
   □ Qu'est-ce qu'il y a là-dedans? What's in there?

là-dessous ADVERB

1 under there

□ Mon carnet d'adresses est quelque part là-dessous. My address book is under there somewhere.

2 behind it

□ Il y a quelque chose de louche là-dessous. There's something fishy behind it.

là-dessus ADVERB
on there

là-haut ADVERB
up there

laid (FEM **laide**) ADJECTIVE
ugly

la **laideur** NOUN
ugliness

le **lainage** NOUN
woollen garment

la **laine** NOUN
wool

□ un pull en laine a wool jumper

■ une laine polaire a fleece (jacket)

laïque (FEM **laïque**) ADJECTIVE

■ une école laïque a state school

la **laisse** NOUN
lead

□ Tenez votre chien en laisse. Keep your dog on a lead.

laisser VERB [28]

1 to leave

□ J'ai laissé mon parapluie à la maison. I've left my umbrella at home.

2 to let

□ Laisse-le parler. Let him speak.

■ Il se laisse aller. He's letting himself go.

le **laisser-aller** NOUN
carelessness

le **lait** NOUN
milk

■ un café au lait a white coffee

la **laitue** NOUN
lettuce

les **lambeaux** MASC PL NOUN

■ en lambeaux tattered

la **lame** NOUN
blade

□ une lame de rasoir a razor blade

la **lamelle** NOUN
thin strip

lamentable (FEM **lamentable**) ADJECTIVE
appalling

se **lamenter** VERB [28]
to moan

le **lampadaire** NOUN
standard lamp

la **lampe** NOUN
lamp

■ une lampe de poche a torch

LANGUAGE TIP Word for word, **lampe de poche** means 'pocket lamp'.

la **lance** NOUN
spear

le **lancement** NOUN
launch

lancer VERB [12]
▷ see also **lancer** NOUN

1 to throw

□ Lance-moi le ballon! Throw me the ball!

2 to launch

□ Ils viennent de lancer un nouveau modèle. They've just launched a new model.

■ se lancer dans to embark on □ Il s'est lancé là-dedans sans bien réfléchir. He embarked on it without thinking properly.

le **lancer** NOUN
▷ see also **lancer** VERB

■ le lancer de poids putting the shot

lancinant (FEM **lancinante**) ADJECTIVE

■ une douleur lancinante a shooting pain

le **landau** NOUN
pram

la **lande** NOUN
moor

le **langage** NOUN
language

la **langouste** NOUN
crayfish

la **langue** NOUN

1 tongue

□ Il m'a tiré la langue. He stuck out his tongue at me.

■ sa langue maternelle his mother tongue

2 language

□ une langue étrangère a foreign language

■ les langues vivantes modern languages

la **lanière** NOUN
strap

le **lapin** NOUN
rabbit

le **laps** NOUN

■ un laps de temps a space of time

la **laque** NOUN
hair spray

laquelle (PL **lesquelles**) FEM PRONOUN

1 which

□ Laquelle de ces photos préfères-tu? Which of these photos do you prefer?

□ À laquelle de tes sœurs ressembles-tu? Which of your sisters do you look like?

2 whom

□ la personne à laquelle vous faites référence the person to whom you are referring

LANGUAGE TIP **laquelle** is often not translated in English.

□ la personne à laquelle je pense the person I'm thinking of

le **lard** NOUN
streaky bacon

les **lardons** MASC PL NOUN
chunks of bacon

large (FEM **large**) ADJECTIVE, ADVERB
▷ see also **large** NOUN
wide

■ **voir large** to allow a bit extra □ Achète un autre pain: il vaut mieux voir large. Buy another loaf of bread: it's better to have a bit extra.

le **large** NOUN
▷ see also **large** ADJECTIVE
■ **cinq mètres de large** 5 m wide
■ **le large** the open sea
■ **au large de** off the coast of □ Le bateau est actuellement au large du Portugal. The boat is off the coast of Portugal at the moment.

largement ADVERB
■ **Vous avez largement le temps.** You have plenty of time.
■ **C'est largement suffisant.** That's ample.

la **largeur** NOUN
width

la **larme** NOUN
tear
□ être en larmes to be in tears

la **laryngite** NOUN
laryngitis

le **laser** NOUN
laser
■ **une chaîne laser** a compact disc player
■ **un disque laser** a compact disc

lasser VERB [28]
■ **se lasser de** to get tired of □ Tu vas te lasser de cette couleur. You're going to get tired of this colour.

le **latin** NOUN
Latin

le **laurier** NOUN
laurel tree
□ une feuille de laurier a bay leaf

lavable (FEM **lavable**) ADJECTIVE
washable

le **lavabo** NOUN
washbasin

le **lavage** NOUN
wash
□ Ce pull a rétréci au lavage. This jumper has shrunk in the wash.

la **lavande** NOUN
lavender

le **lave-linge** (PL les **lave-linge**) NOUN
washing machine

laver VERB [28]
to wash
■ **se laver** to wash □ se laver les mains to wash one's hands

la **laverie** NOUN
■ **une laverie automatique** a launderette

le **lave-vaisselle** (PL les **lave-vaisselle**) NOUN
dishwasher

le ARTICLE, PRONOUN

> **LANGUAGE TIP** le changes to l' before a vowel and most words beginning with 'h'.

1 the
□ le livre the book □ l'arbre the tree
□ l'hélicoptère the helicopter

2 him
□ Daniel est un vieil ami: je le connais depuis plus de vingt ans. Daniel is an old friend: I've known him for over 20 years.

3 it
□ Où est mon stylo? Je ne le trouve plus. Where's my pen? I can't find it. □ Où est le fromage? — Je l'ai mis au frigo. Where's the cheese? — I've put it in the fridge.

4 one's
■ **se laver le visage** to wash one's face
□ Évitez de vous laver le visage avec du savon. Avoid washing your face with soap.
■ **dix euros le kilo** 10 euros a kilo
■ **Il est arrivé le douze mai.** He arrived on 12 May.

lécher VERB [34]
to lick

le **lèche-vitrine** NOUN
■ **faire du lèche-vitrine** to go window-shopping

> **LANGUAGE TIP** Word for word, this means 'to dome some window-licking'.

la **leçon** NOUN
lesson

le **lecteur** NOUN
1 reader
2 foreign language assistant (at a university)
■ **un lecteur de CD** a CD player
■ **un lecteur de DVD** a DVD player
■ **un lecteur MP3** an MP3 player

la **lectrice** NOUN
1 reader
2 foreign language assistant (at a university)

la **lecture** NOUN
reading

> **LANGUAGE TIP** Be careful! The French word **lecture** does not mean **lecture**.

légal (FEM **légale**, MASC PL **légaux**) ADJECTIVE
legal

la **légende** NOUN
1 legend
2 key *(of map)*
3 caption *(of picture)*

léger (FEM **légère**) ADJECTIVE
1 light
2 slight
□ un léger retard a slight delay
■ **à la légère** thoughtlessly □ Il a agi à la légère. He acted thoughtlessly.

légèrement ADVERB
1 lightly
□ Habille-toi légèrement: il va faire chaud. Wear light clothes: it's going to be hot.
2 slightly
□ Il est légèrement plus grand que son frère. He's slightly taller than his brother.

les **législatives** FEM PL NOUN
general election

le **légume** NOUN
vegetable

le **lendemain** NOUN
next day
□ le lendemain de son arrivée the day after he arrived
■ **le lendemain matin** the next morning

lent (FEM **lente**) ADJECTIVE
slow

lentement ADVERB
slowly

la **lenteur** NOUN
slowness

la **lentille** NOUN
1 contact lens
□ Est-ce que tu portes des lentilles? Do you wear contact lenses?
2 lentil
□ un rôti de porc aux lentilles roast pork with lentils

le **léopard** NOUN
leopard

lequel (FEM **laquelle**, MASC PL **lesquels**, FEM PL **lesquelles**) PRONOUN
1 which
□ Lequel de ces films as-tu préféré? Which of the films did you prefer?
2 whom
□ l'homme avec lequel elle a été vue pour la dernière fois the man with whom she was last seen
○ **LANGUAGE TIP** lequel is often not translated in English.
□ le garçon avec lequel elle est sortie the boy she went out with

les ARTICLE, PRONOUN
1 the
□ les arbres the trees

2 them
□ Elle les a invités à dîner. She invited them to dinner.
3 one's
■ **se brosser les dents** to brush one's teeth
□ Elle s'est brossé les dents. She brushed her teeth.
■ **dix euros les cinq** 10 euros for 5

la **lesbienne** NOUN
lesbian

lesquels (FEM **lesquelles**) PL PRONOUN
1 which
□ Lesquelles de ces photos préfères-tu? Which of the photos do you prefer?
2 whom
□ les personnes avec lesquelles il est associé the people with whom he is in partnership
○ **LANGUAGE TIP** lesquels is often not translated in English.
□ les gens chez lesquels nous avons dîné the people we had dinner with

la **lessive** NOUN
1 washing powder
□ une marque de lessive a brand of washing powder
2 washing
□ Il y a beaucoup de lessive à faire/étendre. There's a lot of washing to do/hang out.
■ **faire la lessive** to do the washing

leste (FEM **leste**) ADJECTIVE
nimble

la **Lettonie** NOUN
Latvia

la **lettre** NOUN
letter
□ écrire une lettre to write a letter

les **lettres** FEM PL NOUN
arts
□ la faculté de lettres the Faculty of Arts

leur (FEM **leur**) ADJECTIVE, PRONOUN
1 their
□ leur ami their friend
2 them
□ Je leur ai dit la vérité. I told them the truth.
■ **le leur** theirs □ mon camion et le leur my truck and theirs □ Ma voiture est rouge, la leur est bleue. My car's red, theirs is blue.

leurs (FEM **leurs**) PL ADJECTIVE, PL PRONOUN
their
□ leurs amis their friends
■ **les leurs** theirs □ tes livres et les leurs your books and theirs

levé (FEM **levée**) ADJECTIVE
▷ *see also* **levée** NOUN
■ **être levé** to be up □ Est-ce qu'il est levé? Is he up?

la **levée** NOUN
▷ *see also* **levée** ADJECTIVE
collection *(of mail)*
   □ Prochaine levée: 17 heures Next
   collection: 5 p.m.
lever VERB [43]
   ▷ *see also* **lever** NOUN
   to raise
   □ Levez vos verres! Raise your glasses!
   ■ **Levez la main!** Put your hand up!
   ■ **lever les yeux** to look up
   ■ **se lever 1** to get up □ Il se lève tous les
   jours à six heures. He gets up at 6 o'clock
   every day. □ Lève-toi! Get up! **2** to rise
   □ Le soleil se lève actuellement à cinq heures.
   At the moment the sun rises at 5 o'clock.
   3 to stand up □ Levez-vous! Stand up!
le **lever** NOUN
   ▷ *see also* **lever** VERB
   ■ **le lever du soleil** sunrise
le **levier** NOUN
   lever
la **lèvre** NOUN
   lip
le **lévrier** NOUN
   greyhound
la **levure** NOUN
   yeast
   ■ **la levure chimique** baking powder
le **lexique** NOUN
   word list
le **lézard** NOUN
   lizard
la **liaison** NOUN
   affair
   □ Ils ont eu une liaison dans leur jeunesse.
   They had an affair when they were younger.
la **libellule** NOUN
   dragonfly
libérer VERB [34]
   to free
   □ Les otages ont été libérés hier soir. The
   hostages were freed last night.
   ■ **se libérer** to find time □ J'essaierai de me
   libérer cet après-midi. I'll try to find time
   this afternoon.
la **liberté** NOUN
   freedom
   ■ **mettre en liberté** to release □ Il a été
   mis en liberté au bout d'un an de prison. He
   was released after a year in prison.
le/la **libraire** NOUN
   bookseller
la **librairie** NOUN
   bookshop
   ⬤ **LANGUAGE TIP** Be careful! **librairie**
   does not mean **library**.

libre (FEM **libre**) ADJECTIVE
1 free
   □ Tu es libre de faire ce que tu veux. You are
   free to do as you wish. □ Est-ce que cette
   place est libre? Is this seat free?
   ■ **Avez-vous une chambre de libre?** Have
   you got a free room?
2 clear
   □ La route est libre: vous pouvez traverser.
   The road is clear: you can cross.
   ■ **une école libre** a private school
le **libre-service** (PL les **libres-services**)
   NOUN
   self-service store
la **Libye** NOUN
   Libya
la **licence** NOUN
1 degree
   □ une licence de droit a law degree
2 licence
   □ une licence d'exportation an export licence
le **licencié** NOUN
   graduate
la **licenciée** NOUN
   graduate
le **licenciement** NOUN
   redundancy
licencier VERB [19]
   to make redundant
   □ Ils viennent de licencier sept employés.
   They've just made 7 employees redundant
le **liège** NOUN
   cork
   □ des sets en liège cork mats
   ■ **un bouchon en liège** a cork *(for bottle)*
le **lien** NOUN
1 connection
   □ Il n'y a aucun lien entre ces deux
   événements. There's no connection
   between these two events.
   ■ **un lien de parenté** a family tie
2 link *(in computing)*
lier VERB [19]
   ■ **lier conversation avec quelqu'un** to get
   into conversation with somebody
   ■ **se lier avec quelqu'un** to make friends
   with somebody □ Je ne me lie pas
   facilement. I don't make friends easily.
le **lierre** NOUN
   ivy
le **lieu** (PL les **lieux**) NOUN
   place
   □ votre lieu de travail your place of work
   ■ **avoir lieu** to take place □ La cérémonie a
   eu lieu dans la salle des fêtes. The
   ceremony took place in the village hall.
   ■ **au lieu de** instead of □ J'aimerais une

pomme au lieu de la glace. I'd like an apple instead of ice cream.

le **lièvre** NOUN
hare

la **ligne** NOUN
1 line (phone, train)
   □ La ligne est mauvaise. It's a bad line. □ la ligne de bus numéro six the number 6 bus
   ■ **en ligne** (computing) on-line
2 figure
   □ C'est mauvais pour la ligne. It's bad for your figure.

ligoter VERB [28]
   to tie up

la **ligue** NOUN
   league

le **lilas** NOUN
   lilac

la **limace** NOUN
   slug

la **lime** NOUN
   ■ **une lime à ongles** a nail file

la **limitation** NOUN
   ■ **la limitation de vitesse** the speed limit

la **limite** NOUN
1 boundary (of property, football pitch)
2 limit
   □ Est-ce qu'il y a une limite d'âge? Is there an age limit?
   ■ **À la limite, on pourrait prendre le bus.** At a pinch we could go by bus.
   ■ **la date limite** the deadline
   ■ **la date limite de vente** the sell-by-date

limiter VERB [28]
   to limit
   □ Le nombre de billets est limité à deux par personne. The number of tickets is limited to two per person.

la **limonade** NOUN
   lemonade

le **lin** NOUN
   linen
   □ une veste en lin a linen jacket

le **linge** NOUN
1 linen
   □ le linge sale dirty linen
2 washing
   □ laver le linge to do the washing
   ■ **du linge de corps** underwear

la **lingerie** NOUN
   underwear (women's)

le **lion** NOUN
   lion
   ■ **le Lion** Leo □ Louise est Lion. Louise is Leo.

la **lionne** NOUN
   lioness

la **liqueur** NOUN
   liqueur

liquide (FEM **liquide**) ADJECTIVE
   ▷ see also **liquide** NOUN
   liquid

le **liquide** NOUN
   ▷ see also **liquide** ADJECTIVE
   liquid
   ■ **payer quelque chose en liquide** to pay cash for something

lire VERB [44]
   to read
   □ Tu as lu 'Madame Bovary'? Have you read 'Madame Bovary'?

lis, lisent, lisez VERB ▷ see **lire**
   ■ **Je lis beaucoup.** I read a lot.

lisible (FEM **lisible**) ADJECTIVE
   legible

lisse (FEM **lisse**) ADJECTIVE
   smooth

la **liste** NOUN
   list
   ■ **faire la liste de** to make a list of □ J'ai fait la liste de tout ce dont j'ai besoin. I've made a list of all the things I need.

le **lit** NOUN
   bed
   □ un grand lit a double bed □ aller au lit to go to bed
   ■ **faire son lit** to make one's bed □ Il ne fait jamais son lit. He never makes his bed.
   ■ **un lit de camp** a campbed

lit VERB ▷ see **lire**

la **literie** NOUN
   bedding

la **litière** NOUN
1 litter (for cat)
2 bedding (of caged pet)

le **litre** NOUN
   litre

littéraire (FEM **littéraire**) ADJECTIVE
   ■ **une œuvre littéraire** a work of literature

la **littérature** NOUN
   literature

le **littoral** (PL les **littoraux**) NOUN
   coast

la **Lituanie** NOUN
   Lithuania

la **livraison** NOUN
   delivery
   ■ **la livraison des bagages** baggage reclaim

le **livre** NOUN
   ▷ see also **la livre**
   book
   ■ **un livre de poche** a paperback

LANGUAGE TIP Word for word, **livre de poche** means 'pocket book'.

la **livre** NOUN
▷ see also **le livre**
pound

DID YOU KNOW...?
The French **livre** is 500 grams.

□ une livre de beurre a pound of butter
■ **la livre sterling** the pound sterling □ Ce jouet coûte trois livres. This toy costs £3.

livrer VERB [28]
to deliver

le **livret** NOUN
booklet

■ **le livret scolaire** the school report book

le **livreur** NOUN
delivery man

local (FEM **locale**, MASC PL **locaux**) ADJECTIVE
▷ see also **local** NOUN
local

le **local** (PL les **locaux**) NOUN
▷ see also **local** ADJECTIVE
premises

□ Nous cherchons un local pour les répétitions. We are looking for premises to rehearse in.

le/la **locataire** NOUN
1 tenant
2 lodger

□ Ils ont décidé de prendre un locataire. They have decided to take a lodger.

la **location** NOUN
■ **location de voitures** car rental
■ **location de skis** ski hire

LANGUAGE TIP Be careful! The French word **location** does not mean **location**.

locaux ADJECTIVE, NOUN ▷ see **local**

la **locomotive** NOUN
locomotive

la **loge** NOUN
dressing room

le **logement** NOUN
1 housing
2 accommodation

loger VERB [45]
to stay

□ Elle loge chez sa cousine quand elle revient dans la région. She stays with her cousin when she comes back to the area.

■ **trouver à se loger** to find somewhere to live □ J'ai eu du mal à trouver à me loger. I had difficulty finding somewhere to live.

le **logiciel** NOUN
software

logique (FEM **logique**) ADJECTIVE
▷ see also **logique** NOUN
logical

la **logique** NOUN
▷ see also **logique** ADJECTIVE
logic

la **loi** NOUN
law

loin ADVERB
1 far

□ La gare n'est pas très loin d'ici. The station is not very far from here.
2 far off

□ Noël n'est plus tellement loin. Christmas isn't far off now.
3 a long time ago

□ Les vacances paraissent déjà tellement loin! The holidays already seem such a long time ago!

■ **au loin** in the distance □ On aperçoit la mer au loin. You can see the sea in the distance.

■ **de loin 1** from a long way away □ On voit l'église de loin. You can see the church from a long way away. **2** by far □ C'est de loin l'élève la plus brillante. She is by far the brightest pupil.

■ **C'est plus loin que la gare.** It's further on than the station.

lointain (FEM **lointaine**) ADJECTIVE
▷ see also **lointain** NOUN
distant

□ un pays lointain a distant country □ C'est un parent lointain de ma mère. He's a distant relation of my mother.

le **lointain** NOUN
▷ see also **lointain** ADJECTIVE
■ **dans le lointain** in the distance

le **loir** NOUN
dormouse

■ **dormir comme un loir** to sleep like a log

LANGUAGE TIP Word for word, this means 'to sleep like a doormouse'.

les **loisirs** MASC PL NOUN
1 free time

□ Qu'est-ce que vous faites pendant vos loisirs? What do you do in your free time?
2 hobby

□ Le ski et l'équitation sont des loisirs coûteux. Skiing and riding are expensive hobbies.

le **Londonien** NOUN
Londoner

la **Londonienne** NOUN
Londoner

Londres NOUN
London

□ le métro de Londres the London underground

■ **à Londres 1** in London **2** to London

long (FEM **longue**) ADJECTIVE

▷ *see also* **long** NOUN, **longue** NOUN

long

le **long** NOUN

▷ *see also* **long** ADJECTIVE

■ **un bateau de trois mètres de long** a boat 3 m long

■ **tout le long de** all along □ Il y a des chemins de randonnée tout le long de la côte. There are footpaths all along the coast.

■ **marcher de long en large** to walk up and down

longer VERB [45]

■ **La route longe la forêt.** The road runs along the edge of the forest.

■ **Nous avons longé la Seine à pied.** We walked along the Seine.

longtemps ADVERB

a long time

□ J'ai attendu longtemps chez le dentiste. I waited a long time at the dentist's.

■ **pendant longtemps** for a long time □ On a cru pendant longtemps que la Terre était plate. For a long time people thought the Earth was flat.

■ **mettre longtemps à faire quelque chose** to take a long time to do something □ Il a mis longtemps à répondre à ma lettre. He took a long time to answer my letter.

la **longue** NOUN

▷ *see also* **longue** ADJECTIVE

■ **à la longue** in the end □ Elle a fini par agacer tout le monde à la longue. In the end she got on everybody's nerves.

longuement ADVERB

at length

□ Elle m'a longuement parlé de ses projets d'avenir. She talked to me at length about her plans for the future.

la **longueur** NOUN

length

■ **à longueur de journée** all day long □ Elle mâche du chewing-gum à longueur de journée. She chews gum all day long.

le **look** NOUN

look

□ Il a un look d'enfer. He looks so cool.

les **loques** FEM PL NOUN

■ **être en loques** to be torn to bits □ Sa chemise était en loques. His shirt was torn to bits.

lors de PREPOSITION

during

□ Je l'ai rencontré lors de mon stage en entreprise. I met him during my work placement.

lorsque CONJUNCTION

when

□ J'allais composer ton numéro lorsque tu as appelé. I was about to dial your number when you called.

le **lot** NOUN

prize

■ **le gros lot** the jackpot

la **loterie** NOUN

1 lottery

□ la loterie nationale the National Lottery

2 raffle

□ J'ai gagné cet ours en peluche dans une loterie. I won this teddy in a raffle.

la **lotion** NOUN

lotion

□ une bouteille de lotion solaire a bottle of suntan lotion

■ **une lotion après-rasage** an aftershave

■ **une lotion démaquillante** cleansing milk

le **lotissement** NOUN

housing estate

le **loto** NOUN

lottery

■ **le loto sportif** the pools

le **loubard** NOUN (*informal*)

lout

louche (FEM **louche**) ADJECTIVE

▷ *see also* **louche** NOUN

fishy

□ une histoire louche a fishy story

la **louche** NOUN

▷ *see also* **louche** ADJECTIVE

ladle

loucher VERB [28]

to squint

louer VERB [28]

1 to let

□ Ils louent des chambres à des étudiants. They let rooms to students.

■ **'à louer'** 'to let'

2 to rent

□ Je loue un petit appartement au centre-ville. I rent a little flat in the centre of town.

3 to hire

□ Est-ce que vous louez des vélos? Do you hire bikes? □ Nous allons louer une voiture. We're going to hire a car.

4 to praise

□ Les journaux ont loué le courage des pompiers. The newspapers praised the courage of the firefighters.

le **loup** NOUN

wolf

■ **J'ai une faim de loup!** I'm ravenous!

LANGUAGE TIP Word for word, this means 'I'm as hungry as a wolf'.

la **loupe** NOUN
magnifying glass

louper VERB [28] (informal)
to miss
□ J'ai loupé mon bus. I've missed my bus.

lourd (FEM **lourde**) ADJECTIVE
▷ see also **lourd** ADVERB
heavy
□ Mon sac est très lourd. My bag's very heavy.

lourd ADVERB
▷ see also **lourd** ADJECTIVE
close (weather)
□ Il fait très lourd aujourd'hui. It's very close today.

la **loutre** NOUN
otter

la **loyauté** NOUN
loyalty

le **loyer** NOUN
rent

lu VERB ▷ see **lire**

la **lucarne** NOUN
skylight

la **luge** NOUN
sledge

lugubre (FEM **lugubre**) ADJECTIVE
gloomy

lui PRONOUN
1 him
□ Il a été très content du cadeau que je lui ai offert. He was very pleased with the present I gave him. □ C'est bien lui! It's definitely him! □ J'ai pensé à lui toute la journée. I thought about him all day long.
2 to him
□ Mon père est d'accord: je lui ai parlé ce matin. My father said yes: I spoke to him this morning.
3 her
□ Elle a été très contente du cadeau que je lui ai offert. She was very pleased with the present I gave her.
4 to her
□ Ma mère est d'accord: je lui ai parlé ce matin. My mother said yes: I spoke to her this morning.
5 it
□ Qu'est-ce que tu donnes à ton chat? — Je lui donne de la viande crue. What do you give your cat? — I give it raw meat.

LANGUAGE TIP lui is also used for emphasis.

□ Lui, il est toujours en retard! Oh him, he's always late!

■ **lui-même** himself □ Il a construit son bateau lui-même. He built his boat himself.

la **lumière** NOUN
light
■ **la lumière du jour** daylight

lumineux (FEM **lumineuse**) ADJECTIVE
■ **une enseigne lumineuse** a neon sign

lunatique (FEM **lunatique**) ADJECTIVE
temperamental
□ Il est plutôt lunatique. He's rather temperamental.

le **lundi** NOUN
1 Monday
□ Aujourd'hui, nous sommes lundi. It's Monday today.
2 on Monday
□ Ils sont arrivés lundi. They arrived on Monday.
■ **le lundi** on Mondays □ Le lundi, je vais à la piscine. I go swimming on Mondays.
■ **tous les lundis** every Monday
■ **lundi dernier** last Monday
■ **lundi prochain** next Monday
■ **le lundi de Pâques** Easter Monday

la **lune** NOUN
moon
■ **la lune de miel** honeymoon

les **lunettes** FEM PL NOUN
glasses
■ **des lunettes de soleil** sunglasses
■ **des lunettes de plongée** swimming goggles

la **lutte** NOUN
1 fight
□ la lutte contre le racisme the fight against racism
2 wrestling
□ une épreuve de lutte a wrestling bout

lutter VERB [28]
to fight

le **luxe** NOUN
luxury
■ **de luxe** luxury □ un hôtel de luxe a luxury hotel

luxueux (FEM **luxueuse**) ADJECTIVE
luxurious

le **lycée** NOUN
secondary school
■ **lycée technique** technical college

DID YOU KNOW...?
In France pupils go to a **collège** between the ages of 11 and 15, and then to a **lycée** until the age of 18.

le **lycéen** NOUN
secondary school pupil

la **lycéenne** NOUN
secondary school pupil

Mm

M. ABBREVIATION (= *Monsieur*)
Mr
□ M. Bernard Mr Bernard
m' PRONOUN ▷ *see* me
ma FEM ADJECTIVE
my
□ ma mère my mother □ ma montre my
watch
les **macaronis** MASC PL NOUN
macaroni
la **Macédoine** NOUN
Macedonia
la **macédoine** NOUN
■ la macédoine de fruits fruit salad
■ la macédoine de légumes mixed
vegetables
mâcher VERB [28]
to chew
le **machin** NOUN (*informal*)
thingy
□ Passe-moi le machin pour râper les
carottes. Pass me the thingy for grating
carrots. □ Qu'est-ce que c'est que ce vieux
machin? What's this old thing?
machinalement ADVERB
■ Elle a regardé sa montre
machinalement. She looked at her watch
without thinking.
la **machine** NOUN
machine
■ une machine à laver a washing machine
■ une machine à écrire a typewriter
■ une machine à coudre a sewing
machine
■ une machine à sous a fruit machine
le **machiste** NOUN
male chauvinist
le **macho** NOUN (*informal*)
male chauvinist pig
la **mâchoire** NOUN
jaw
mâchonner VERB [28]
to chew
le **maçon** NOUN
bricklayer

Madame (PL **Mesdames**) FEM NOUN
1 Mrs
□ Madame Legall Mrs Legall
2 lady
□ Occupez-vous de Madame. Could you
look after this lady?
3 Madam
□ Madame, ... Dear Madam, ... (*in letter*)
□ Madame! Vous avez oublié votre
parapluie! Excuse me! You've forgotten your
umbrella!
Mademoiselle (PL **Mesdemoiselles**) FEM
NOUN
1 Miss
□ Mademoiselle Martin Miss Martin
2 Madam
□ Mademoiselle, ... Dear Madam, ... (*in
letter*)
le **magasin** NOUN
shop
□ Les magasins ouvrent à huit heures. The
shops open at 8 o'clock.
■ faire les magasins to go shopping
le **magazine** NOUN
magazine
le **magicien** NOUN
magician
la **magicienne** NOUN
magician
la **magie** NOUN
magic
□ un tour de magie a magic trick
magique (FEM **magique**) ADJECTIVE
magic
□ une baguette magique a magic wand
magistral (FEM **magistrale**, MASC PL
magistraux) ADJECTIVE
■ un cours magistral a lecture (*at
university*)
magnétique (FEM **magnétique**) ADJECTIVE
magnetic
le **magnétophone** NOUN
tape recorder
■ un magnétophone à cassettes a
cassette recorder

le **magnétoscope** NOUN
video recorder

magnifique (FEM **magnifique**) ADJECTIVE
superb

mai MASC NOUN
May
■ **en mai** in May

maigre (FEM **maigre**) ADJECTIVE
1 skinny
□ Ma mère me trouve trop maigre. My
mother says I'm too skinny.
2 lean *(meat)*
3 low-fat *(cheese, yoghurt)*

maigrir VERB [38]
to lose weight
□ Il fait un régime pour essayer de maigrir.
He's on a diet, to try to lose weight. □ Elle a
maigri de deux kilos en un mois. She's lost
two kilos in a month.

le **mail** NOUN
email

le **maillot de bain** NOUN
1 swimsuit
2 swimming trunks

la **main** NOUN
hand
□ Donne-moi la main! Give me your hand!
■ **serrer la main à quelqu'un** to shake
hands with somebody
■ **se serrer la main** to shake hands □ Les
deux présidents se sont serré la main. The
two presidents shook hands.
■ **sous la main** to hand □ Est-ce que tu as
son adresse sous la main? Have you got his
address to hand?

la **main-d'œuvre** NOUN
workforce
□ la main-d'œuvre de l'usine the workforce
of the factory
■ **la main-d'œuvre immigrée** immigrant
labour

maintenant ADVERB
1 now
□ Qu'est-ce que tu veux faire maintenant?
What do you want to do now? □ C'est
maintenant ou jamais. It's now or never.
2 nowadays
□ Maintenant la plupart des gens font leurs
courses au supermarché. Nowadays most
people do their shopping at the
supermarket.

maintenir VERB [83]
to maintain
□ Il maintient qu'il est innocent. He
maintains he is innocent.
■ **se maintenir** to hold □ Espérons que le
beau temps va se maintenir pour le week-

end! Let's hope the good weather will hold
over the weekend!

le **maire** NOUN
mayor

la **mairie** NOUN
town hall

mais CONJUNCTION
but
□ C'est cher mais de très bonne qualité. It's
expensive, but very good quality.

le **maïs** NOUN
1 maize
2 sweetcorn

la **maison** NOUN
▷ *see also* **maison** ADJECTIVE
house
□ C'est la maison de Colette. It's Colette's
house.
■ **une maison des jeunes** a youth club
■ **des maisons mitoyennes** 1 semi-
detached houses 2 terraced houses
■ **à la maison** 1 at home □ Je serai à la
maison cet après-midi. I'll be at home this
afternoon. 2 home □ Elle est rentrée à la
maison. She's gone home.

maison (FEM+PL **maison**) ADJECTIVE
▷ *see also* **maison** NOUN
home-made
□ Je préfère les tartes maison à celles qu'on
achète. I prefer home-made pies to bought
ones.

le **maître** NOUN
1 teacher *(in primary school)*
2 master *(of dog)*
■ **un maître d'hôtel** a head waiter *(in
restaurant)*
■ **un maître nageur** a lifeguard

la **maîtresse** NOUN
1 teacher *(in primary school)*
2 mistress
□ Il paraît qu'il a une maîtresse. They say
he's got a mistress.

la **maîtrise** NOUN
master's degree
□ Elle a une maîtrise d'anglais. She's got a
master's degree in English.
■ **la maîtrise de soi** self-control

maîtriser VERB [28]
■ **se maîtriser** to control oneself □ Il se
met facilement en colère et a du mal à se
maîtriser. He loses his temper easily and
finds it hard to control himself.

majestueux (FEM **majestueuse**) ADJECTIVE
majestic

majeur (FEM **majeure**) ADJECTIVE
■ **être majeur** to be 18 □ Tu feras ce que tu
voudras quand tu seras majeure. You can

159

m

do what you like once you're 18. □ Elle sera majeure en août. She will be 18 in August.

■ **la majeure partie** most □ la majeure partie de mon salaire most of my salary

la **majorité** NOUN
majority

□ dans la majorité des cas in the majority of cases

■ **la majorité et l'opposition** the government and the opposition

Majorque FEM NOUN
Majorca

la **majuscule** NOUN
capital letter

□ un M majuscule a capital M

mal (FEM+PL **mal**) ADVERB, ADJECTIVE
▷ *see also* **mal** NOUN

1 badly

□ Ce travail a été mal fait. The work was badly done.

■ **Il a mal compris.** He misunderstood.

2 wrong

□ C'est mal de mentir. It's wrong to tell lies.

■ **aller mal** to be ill □ Son grand-père va très mal. His grandfather is very ill.

■ **pas mal** quite good □ Je te trouve pas mal sur cette photo. I think you look quite good in this photo.

le **mal** (PL les **maux**) NOUN
▷ *see also* **mal** ADVERB

1 ache

□ J'ai mal à la tête. I've got a headache.
□ J'ai mal aux dents. I've got toothache.
□ J'ai mal au dos. My back hurts. □ Est-ce que vous avez mal à la gorge? Have you got a sore throat?

■ **Ça fait mal.** It hurts.

■ **Où est-ce que tu as mal?** Where does it hurt?

■ **faire mal à quelqu'un** to hurt somebody □ Attention, tu me fais mal! Be careful, you're hurting me!

■ **se faire mal** to hurt oneself □ Je me suis fait mal au bras. I hurt my arm.

■ **se donner du mal pour faire quelque chose** to go to a lot of trouble to do something □ Il s'est donné beaucoup de mal pour que cette soirée soit réussie. He went to a lot of trouble to make the party a success.

■ **avoir le mal de mer** to be seasick

■ **avoir le mal du pays** to be homesick

2 evil

□ le bien et le mal good and evil

■ **dire du mal de quelqu'un** to speak ill of somebody

malade (FEM **malade**) ADJECTIVE

▷ *see also* **malade** NOUN
ill

■ **tomber malade** to fall ill

le/la **malade** NOUN
▷ *see also* **malade** ADJECTIVE
patient

la **maladie** NOUN
illness

maladif (FEM **maladive**) ADJECTIVE
sickly

□ C'est un enfant maladif. He's a sickly child.

la **maladresse** NOUN
clumsiness

maladroit (FEM **maladroite**) ADJECTIVE
clumsy

le **malaise** NOUN

■ **avoir un malaise** to feel faint □ Elle a eu un malaise après le déjeuner. She felt faint after lunch.

■ **Son arrivée a créé un malaise parmi les invités.** Her arrival made the guests feel uncomfortable.

la **malchance** NOUN
bad luck

mâle (FEM **mâle**) ADJECTIVE
male

la **malédiction** NOUN
curse

mal en point (FEM+PL **mal en point**) ADJECTIVE

■ **Il avait l'air mal en point quand je l'ai vu hier soir.** He didn't look too good when I saw him last night.

le **malentendu** NOUN
misunderstanding

le **malfaiteur** NOUN
criminal

mal famé (FEM **mal famée**, MASC PL **mal famés**) ADJECTIVE

■ **un quartier mal famé** a seedy area

malgache (FEM **malgache**) ADJECTIVE
from Madagascar

□ Sa mère est malgache. His mother's from Madagascar.

malgré PREPOSITION
in spite of

□ Il est toujours généreux malgré ses problèmes d'argent. He's always generous in spite of his financial problems.

■ **malgré tout** all the same □ Il faisait mauvais mais nous sommes sortis malgré tout. The weather was bad but we went out all the same.

le **malheur** NOUN
tragedy

□ Elle a eu beaucoup de malheurs dans sa

vie. She's had a lot of tragedy in her life.
- **faire un malheur** *(informal)* to be a smash hit □ Leur dernier album a fait un malheur. Their latest album was a smash hit.

malheureusement ADVERB
unfortunately

malheureux (FEM **malheureuse**) ADJECTIVE
miserable
□ Il a l'air malheureux. He looks miserable.

malhonnête (FEM **malhonnête**) ADJECTIVE
dishonest

la **malice** NOUN
mischief
□ Son regard était plein de malice. His eyes were full of mischief.

malicieux (FEM **malicieuse**) ADJECTIVE
mischievous

○ **LANGUAGE TIP** Be careful! malicieux does not mean **malicious**.

malin (FEM **maligne**) ADJECTIVE
crafty
- **C'est malin!** *(informal)* That's clever! □ Ah c'est malin! Nous voilà enfermés à cause de toi! That's clever! You've got us locked in!

la **malle** NOUN
trunk

malodorant (FEM **malodorante**) ADJECTIVE
foul-smelling

malpropre (FEM **malpropre**) ADJECTIVE
dirty

malsain (FEM **malsaine**) ADJECTIVE
unhealthy

Malte MASC NOUN
Malta

maltraiter VERB [28]
to ill-treat
□ Il maltraite son chien. He ill-treats his dog.
- **des enfants maltraités** battered children

malveillant (FEM **malveillante**) ADJECTIVE
malicious
□ des rumeurs malveillantes malicious rumours

la **maman** NOUN
mum

la **mamie** NOUN
granny

le **mammifère** NOUN
mammal

la **manche** NOUN
▷ *see also* **le manche**
1 sleeve *(of clothes)*
2 leg *(of game)*
□ Ils ont gagné la première manche du match. They won the first leg of the match.

- **la Manche** the Channel

le **manche** NOUN
▷ *see also* **la manche**
handle *(of pan)*

la **mandarine** NOUN
mandarin orange

le **manège** NOUN
merry-go-round

la **manette** NOUN
lever

mangeable (FEM **mangeable**) ADJECTIVE
edible
□ C'est à peine mangeable! It's practically inedible!

manger VERB [45]
to eat

la **mangue** NOUN
mango

maniaque (FEM **maniaque**) ADJECTIVE
fussy

la **manie** NOUN
1 obsession
- **avoir la manie de** to be obsessive about □ Il a la manie du rangement. He's obsessive about tidying up.
2 habit
□ J'essaie de respecter ses petites manies. I try to go along with her little ways.

manier VERB [19]
to handle

la **manière** NOUN
▷ *see also* **les manières** PL NOUN
way
- **de manière à** so as to □ Nous sommes partis tôt de manière à éviter la circulation. We left early so as to avoid the traffic.
- **de toute manière** in any case □ Je n'aurais pas pu venir de toute manière. I couldn't have come in any case.

maniéré (FEM **maniérée**) ADJECTIVE
affected

les **manières** FEM PL NOUN
▷ *see also* **la manière** SING NOUN
1 manners
□ apprendre les bonnes manières to learn good manners
2 fuss
□ Ne fais pas de manières: mange ta soupe! Don't make a fuss: eat your soup!

le **manifestant** NOUN
demonstrator

la **manifestante** NOUN
demonstrator

la **manifestation** NOUN
demonstration
□ une manifestation pour la paix a peace demonstration

161

manifester VERB [28]
to demonstrate

manipuler VERB [28]
1 to handle
□ Ce vase doit être manipulé avec soin. This vase must be handled with care.
2 to manipulate
□ Tous les partis essaient de manipuler l'opinion publique. All the parties are trying to manipulate public opinion.

le **mannequin** NOUN
model
□ Elle est mannequin. She's a model.

manœuvrer VERB [28]
to manœuvre

le **manque** NOUN
■ **le manque de** lack of □ Le manque de sommeil peut provoquer toutes sortes de troubles. Lack of sleep can cause all sorts of problems.
withdrawal
□ un drogué en état de manque a drug addict suffering withdrawal symptoms

manqué (FEM **manquée**) ADJECTIVE
■ **un garçon manqué** a tomboy

manquer VERB [28]
to miss
□ Tu n'as rien manqué: c'était nul. You didn't miss anything: it was rubbish. □ Il manque des pages à ce livre. There are some pages missing from this book.
■ **Mes parents me manquent.** I miss my parents.
■ **Ma sœur me manque.** I miss my sister.
■ **Il manque encore dix euros.** We are still 10 euros short.
■ **manquer de** to lack □ La quiche manque de sel. The quiche hasn't got enough salt in it. □ Je trouve qu'il a manqué de tact. I don't think he was very tactful.
■ **Il a manqué se tuer.** He nearly got killed.

le **manteau** (PL les **manteaux**) NOUN
coat

manuel (FEM **manuelle**) ADJECTIVE
▷ see also **manuel** NOUN
manual

le **manuel** NOUN
▷ see also **manuel** ADJECTIVE
1 textbook
2 handbook

le **maquereau** (PL les **maquereaux**) NOUN
mackerel

la **maquette** NOUN
model
□ une maquette de bateau a model boat

le **maquillage** NOUN
make-up

se **maquiller** VERB [28]
to put on one's make-up
□ Je vais me maquiller en vitesse. I'll just quickly put on my make-up.

le **marais** NOUN
marsh

le **marbre** NOUN
marble
□ une statue en marbre a marble statue

le **marchand** NOUN
1 shopkeeper
■ **un marchand de journaux** a newsagent
2 stallholder (in market)

la **marchande** NOUN
1 shopkeeper
■ **une marchande de fruits et de légumes** a greengrocer
2 stallholder (in market)

marchander VERB [28]
to haggle

la **marchandise** NOUN
goods

la **marche** NOUN
1 step
□ Fais attention à la marche! Mind the step!
2 walking
□ La marche me fait du bien. Walking does me good.
■ **être en état de marche** to be in working order □ Cette voiture est en parfait état de marche. This car is in perfect running order.
■ **Ne montez jamais dans un train en marche.** Never try to get into a moving train.
■ **mettre en marche** to start □ Comment est-ce qu'on met la machine à laver en marche? How do you start the washing machine?
■ **la marche arrière** reverse gear
■ **faire marche arrière** to reverse
3 march
□ une marche militaire a military march

le **marché** NOUN
market
■ **un marché aux puces** a flea market
■ **le marché noir** the black market

marcher VERB [28]
1 to walk
□ Elle marche cinq kilomètres par jour. She walks 5 kilometres every day.
2 to run
□ Le métro marche normalement aujourd'hui. The underground is running normally today.
3 to work
□ Est-ce que l'ascenseur marche? Is the lift working?

m

4 to go well

□ Est-ce que les affaires marchent actuellement? Is business going well at the moment?

■ **Alors les études, ça marche?** *(informal)* How are you getting on at school?

■ **faire marcher quelqu'un** to pull somebody's leg □ Il essaie de te faire marcher. He's pulling your leg.

le **marcheur** NOUN
walker

la **marcheuse** NOUN
walker

le **mardi** NOUN

1 Tuesday

□ Aujourd'hui, nous sommes mardi. It's Tuesday today.

2 on Tuesday

□ Ils reviennent mardi. They're coming back on Tuesday.

■ **le mardi** on Tuesdays □ Le mardi, je vais à la gym. I go to the gym on Tuesdays.

■ **tous les mardis** every Tuesday

■ **mardi dernier** last Tuesday

■ **mardi prochain** next Tuesday

■ **Mardi gras** Shrove Tuesday

LANGUAGE TIP Word for word, **Mardi gras** means 'fat Tuesday'.

la **mare** NOUN
pond

le **marécage** NOUN
marsh

la **marée** NOUN
tide

□ la marée haute high tide □ la marée basse low tide □ la marée montante the rising tide □ la marée descendante the ebb tide

■ **une marée noire** an oil slick

la **margarine** NOUN
margarine

la **marge** NOUN
margin

le **mari** NOUN
husband

□ son mari her husband

le **mariage** NOUN

1 marriage

2 wedding

□ un mariage civil a registry office wedding
□ un mariage religieux a church wedding

marié (FEM **mariée**) ADJECTIVE

▷ *see also* **marié** NOUN, **mariée** NOUN
married

le **marié** NOUN

▷ *see also* **marié** ADJECTIVE
bridegroom

■ **les mariés** the bride and groom

la **mariée** NOUN

▷ *see also* **marié** ADJECTIVE
bride

se **marier** VERB [19]
to marry

□ Elle s'est mariée avec un ami d'enfance. She married a childhood friend.

marin (FEM **marine**) ADJECTIVE

▷ *see also* **marin** NOUN, **marine** NOUN, ADJECTIVE
sea

□ l'air marin the sea air

■ **un pull marin** a sailor's jersey

le **marin** NOUN

▷ *see also* **marin** ADJECTIVE
sailor

marine (FEM+PL **marine**) ADJECTIVE

▷ *see also* **marine** NOUN, **marin** ADJECTIVE

■ **bleu marine** navy-blue □ un pull bleu marine a navy-blue sweater

la **marine** NOUN

▷ *see also* **marine** ADJECTIVE
navy

■ **la marine nationale** the French navy

la **marionnette** NOUN
puppet

le **marketing** NOUN
marketing

la **marmelade** NOUN
stewed fruit

■ **la marmelade de pommes** stewed apple

■ **la marmelade d'oranges** marmalade

la **marmite** NOUN
cooking pot

marmonner VERB [28]
to mumble

le **Maroc** NOUN
Morocco

marocain (FEM **marocaine**) ADJECTIVE
Moroccan

la **maroquinerie** NOUN
leather goods shop

marquant (FEM **marquante**) ADJECTIVE
significant

□ un événement marquant a significant event

la **marque** NOUN

1 mark

□ des marques de doigts fingermarks

2 make

□ De quelle marque est ton jean? What make are your jeans?

3 brand

□ une grande marque de cognac a well-known brand of cognac

■ **l'image de marque** the public image □ Le ministre tient à son image de marque.

The minister cares about his public image.
- **une marque déposée** a registered trademark
- **A vos marques! prêts! partez!** Ready, steady, go!

marquer VERB [28]
1 to mark
  □ Peux-tu marquer sur la carte où se trouve le village? Can you mark where the village is on the map?
2 to score
  □ L'équipe irlandaise a marqué dix points. The Irish team scored ten points.
3 to celebrate
  □ On va sortir au restaurant pour marquer ton anniversaire. We'll eat out to celebrate your birthday.

la **marraine** NOUN
godmother

marrant (FEM **marrante**) ADJECTIVE (informal)
funny

marre ADVERB (informal)
- **en avoir marre de quelque chose** to be fed up with something □ J'en ai marre de faire la vaisselle. I'm fed up with doing the dishes.

se **marrer** VERB [28] (informal)
to have a good laugh
  □ On s'est bien marrés. We had a good laugh.

le **marron** NOUN
▷ see also **marron** ADJECTIVE
chestnut
  □ la crème de marrons chestnut purée

marron (FEM+PL **marron**) ADJECTIVE
▷ see also **marron** NOUN
brown
  □ des chaussures marron brown shoes

le **marronnier** NOUN
chestnut tree

mars MASC NOUN
March
- **en mars** in March

le **marteau** (PL les **marteaux**) NOUN
hammer

martyriser VERB [28]
to batter
  □ des enfants martyrisés battered children

masculin (FEM **masculine**) ADJECTIVE
1 men's
  □ la mode masculine men's fashion
2 masculine
  □ 'chat' est un nom masculin. 'chat' is a masculine noun. □ Elle a une allure assez masculine. She looks rather masculine.

le **masque** NOUN
mask

le **massacre** NOUN
massacre

massacrer VERB [28]
to massacre

le **massage** NOUN
massage

la **masse** NOUN
- **une masse de** (informal) masses of □ J'ai une masse de choses à faire. I've got masses of things to do.
- **produire en masse** to mass-produce □ des meubles produits en masse mass-produced furniture
- **venir en masse** to come en masse □ Les gens sont venus en masse pour accueillir Nelson Mandela. People came en masse to welcome Nelson Mandela.

masser VERB [28]
to massage
- **se masser** to gather □ Les manifestants se sont massés devant l'ambassade. The demonstrators gathered in front of the embassy.

massif (FEM **massive**) ADJECTIVE
1 solid (gold, silver, wood)
  □ un bracelet en or massif a solid gold bracelet
2 massive
  □ une dose massive d'antibiotiques a massive dose of antibiotics
3 mass
  □ des départs massifs a mass exodus

mat (FEM **mate**) ADJECTIVE
matt
  □ blanc mat matt white □ Je voudrais mes photos en mat. I would like my photos matt.
- **être mat** to be checkmate (chess)

le **match** NOUN
match
  □ un match de football a football match
- **le match aller** the first leg
- **le match retour** the second leg
- **faire match nul** to draw

le **matelas** NOUN
mattress
- **un matelas pneumatique** an air bed

matelassé (FEM **matelassée**) ADJECTIVE
quilted
  □ une veste matelassée a quilted jacket

le **matelot** NOUN
sailor

les **matériaux** MASC PL NOUN
materials

le **matériel** NOUN
1 equipment
  □ du matériel de laboratoire laboratory

equipment
2 gear

□ Il a pris tout son matériel de pêche avec lui. He took all his fishing gear with him.

maternel (FEM **maternelle**) ADJECTIVE
▷ see also **maternelle** NOUN
motherly

□ Elle est très maternelle. She's very motherly.

■ **ma grand-mère maternelle** my mother's mother

■ **mon oncle maternel** my mother's brother

la **maternelle** NOUN
▷ see also **maternelle** ADJECTIVE
nursery school

> **DID YOU KNOW...?**
> The **maternelle** is a state school for 2–6 year-olds.

la **maternité** NOUN

■ **le congé de maternité** maternity leave

□ Notre professeur de musique est en congé de maternité. Our music teacher is on maternity leave.

les **mathématiques** FEM PL NOUN
mathematics

les **maths** FEM PL NOUN (informal)
maths

la **matière** NOUN
subject

□ Le latin est une matière facultative. Latin is an optional subject.

■ **sans matières grasses** fat-free

■ **les matières premières** raw materials

le **matin** NOUN
morning

□ à trois heures du matin at 3 o'clock in the morning □ du matin au soir from morning till night

■ **Je suis du matin.** I'm at my best in the morning.

■ **de bon matin** early in the morning

matinal (FEM **matinale**, MASC PL **matinaux**) ADJECTIVE
morning

□ Je fais ma gymnastique matinale avant de déjeuner. I do my morning exercises before breakfast.

■ **être matinal** to be up early □ Tu es bien matinal aujourd'hui! You're up early today!

la **matinée** NOUN
morning

□ Je t'appellerai demain dans la matinée. I'll call you sometime tomorrow morning. □ en début de matinée early in the morning

le **matou** NOUN
tomcat

matrimonial (FEM **matrimoniale**, MASC PL **matrimoniaux**) ADJECTIVE

■ **une agence matrimoniale** a marriage bureau

maudire VERB [46]
to curse

maudit (FEM **maudite**) ADJECTIVE (informal)
blasted

□ Où est passé ce maudit parapluie? Where's that blasted umbrella got to?

maussade (FEM **maussade**) ADJECTIVE
sullen

mauvais (FEM **mauvaise**) ADJECTIVE, ADVERB
1 bad

□ une mauvaise note a bad mark □ Tu arrives au mauvais moment. You've come at a bad time.

■ **Il fait mauvais.** The weather's bad.

■ **être mauvais en** to be bad at □ Je suis mauvais en allemand. I'm bad at German.

2 poor

□ J'ai trouvé que le film était mauvais. I thought the film was poor. □ Il est en mauvaise santé. His health is poor.

■ **Tu as mauvaise mine.** You don't look well.

3 wrong

□ Vous avez fait le mauvais numéro. You've dialled the wrong number.

■ **des mauvaises herbes** weeds

■ **sentir mauvais** to smell

les **maux** MASC PL NOUN ▷ see **mal**

■ **des maux de ventre** stomachache

■ **des maux de tête** headache

maximal (FEM **maximale**, MASC PL **maximaux**) ADJECTIVE
maximum

le **maximum** NOUN
maximum

■ **au maximum 1** as much as one can □ Remplis le seau au maximum. Fill the bucket as full as you can. **2** at the very most □ Ça va vous coûter deux cents euros au maximum. It'll cost you 200 euros at the very most.

la **mayonnaise** NOUN
mayonnaise

le **mazout** NOUN
fuel oil

me PRONOUN

> **LANGUAGE TIP** me changes to m' before a vowel and most words beginning with 'h'.

1 me

□ Elle me téléphone tous les jours. She phones me every day. □ Il m'attend depuis une heure. He's been waiting for me for an

m

hour.

2 to me

□ Il me parle en allemand. He talks to me in German. □ Elle m'a expliqué la situation. She explained the situation to me.

3 myself

□ Je vais me préparer quelque chose à manger. I'm going to make myself something to eat.

LANGUAGE TIP With reflexive verbs, me is often not translated.

□ Je me lève à sept heures tous les matins. I get up at 7 every morning.

le **mec** NOUN (informal)
guy

le **mécanicien** NOUN
mechanic

la **mécanique** NOUN
1 mechanics
2 mechanism (of watch, clock)

le **mécanisme** NOUN
mechanism

méchamment ADVERB
nastily
□ Il lui a répondu méchamment. He answered him nastily.

la **méchanceté** NOUN
nastiness

méchant (FEM **méchante**) ADJECTIVE
nasty
□ C'est un homme méchant. He's a nasty man. □ Ne sois pas méchant avec ton petit frère. Don't be nasty to your little brother.
■ 'Attention, chien méchant' 'Beware of the dog'

la **mèche** NOUN
lock (of hair)

mécontent (FEM **mécontente**) ADJECTIVE
■ mécontent de unhappy with □ Elle est mécontente de sa coupe de cheveux. She's unhappy with her haircut.

le **mécontentement** NOUN
displeasure
□ Il a exprimé son mécontentement. He expressed his displeasure.

la **médaille** NOUN
medal

le **médecin** NOUN
doctor
□ aller chez le médecin to go to the doctor

la **médecine** NOUN
medicine (subject)
□ Il fait médecine. He's studying medicine.

les **médias** MASC PL NOUN
media

médical (FEM **médicale**, MASC PL **médicaux**)
ADJECTIVE

medical
□ la recherche médicale medical research
■ passer une visite médicale to have a medical

le **médicament** NOUN
medicine (drug)

médiéval (FEM **médiévale**, MASC PL **médiévaux**) ADJECTIVE
medieval

médiocre (FEM **médiocre**) ADJECTIVE
poor
□ des notes médiocres poor marks

la **Méditerranée** NOUN
Mediterranean

méditerranéen (FEM **méditerranéenne**)
ADJECTIVE
Mediterranean

la **méduse** NOUN
jellyfish

la **méfiance** NOUN
mistrust

méfiant (FEM **méfiante**) ADJECTIVE
mistrustful

se **méfier** VERB [19]
■ se méfier de quelqu'un to distrust somebody □ Si j'étais toi, je me méfierais de lui. If I were you, I wouldn't trust him.

la **mégarde** NOUN
■ par mégarde by mistake □ J'ai emporté son livre par mégarde. I took his book by mistake.

le **mégot** NOUN
cigarette end

meilleur (FEM **meilleure**) ADJECTIVE, ADVERB, NOUN
better
□ Ce serait meilleur avec du fromage râpé. It would be better with grated cheese. □ Il paraît que le film est meilleur que le livre. They say that the film is better than the book.
■ le meilleur the best □ Je préfère garder le meilleur pour la fin. I like to keep the best for last. □ C'est elle qui est la meilleure en sport. She's the best at sport.
■ le meilleur des deux the better of the two
■ meilleur marché cheaper □ La bière est meilleur marché en France. Beer's cheaper in France.

le **mél** NOUN
email

mélancolique (FEM **mélancolique**)
ADJECTIVE
melancholy

le **mélange** NOUN
mixture

mélanger VERB [45]
1 to mix
  □ Mélangez le tout. Mix everything together.
2 to muddle up
  □ Tu mélanges tout! You're muddling everything up!
la **mêlée** NOUN
  scrum
mêler VERB [28]
  ■ **se mêler** to mix □ Il ne cherche pas à se mêler aux autres. He doesn't try to mix with the others.
  ■ **Mêle-toi de ce qui te regarde!** (informal) Mind your own business!
la **mélodie** NOUN
  melody
le **melon** NOUN
  melon
le **membre** NOUN
1 limb
2 member
  □ un membre de la famille a member of the family □ les pays membres de l'Union européenne the member countries of the European Union
la **mémé** NOUN (informal)
  granny
même (FEM **même**) ADJECTIVE, ADVERB, PRONOUN
1 same
  □ J'ai le même manteau. I've got the same coat. □ Tiens, c'est curieux j'ai le même! That's strange, I've got the same one!
  ■ **en même temps** at the same time
  ■ **moi-même** myself □ Je l'ai fait moi-même. I did it myself.
  ■ **toi-même** yourself □ Est-ce que tu vas faire les travaux toi-même? Are you going to do the work yourself?
  ■ **eux-mêmes** themselves
2 even
  □ Il n'a même pas pleuré. He didn't even cry.
la **mémoire** NOUN
  memory
la **menace** NOUN
  threat
menacer VERB [12]
  to threaten
le **ménage** NOUN
  housework
  □ faire le ménage to do the housework
  ■ **une femme de ménage** a cleaning woman
ménager (FEM **ménagère**) ADJECTIVE
  ■ **les travaux ménagers** housework
la **ménagère** NOUN

housewife
le **mendiant** NOUN
  beggar
la **mendiante** NOUN
  beggar
mendier VERB [19]
  to beg
mener VERB [43]
  to lead
  □ Cette rue mène directement à la gare. This street leads straight to the station.
  ■ **Cela ne vous mènera à rien!** That will get you nowhere!
la **méningite** NOUN
  meningitis
les **menottes** FEM PL NOUN
  handcuffs
le **mensonge** NOUN
  lie
la **mensualité** NOUN
  monthly payment
  □ en dix mensualités in ten monthly payments
mensuel (FEM **mensuelle**) ADJECTIVE
  monthly
les **mensurations** FEM PL NOUN
  measurements
la **mentalité** NOUN
  mentality
le **menteur** NOUN
  liar
la **menteuse** NOUN
  liar
la **menthe** NOUN
  mint
la **mention** NOUN
  grade
  □ Il a été reçu avec mention bien. He got a grade B pass.
mentionner VERB [28]
  to mention
mentir VERB [77]
  to lie
  □ Tu mens! You're lying!
le **menton** NOUN
  chin
le **menu** NOUN
  ▷ see also **menu** ADJECTIVE
  menu
  □ le menu du jour today's menu □ le menu touristique the tourist menu □ le menu d'aide (on a computer) the help menu
menu (FEM **menue**) ADJECTIVE, ADVERB
  ▷ see also **menu** NOUN
1 slim
  □ Elle est menue. She's slim. □ Elle est petite et menue. She's petite.

m

2 very fine

□ Les oignons doivent être coupés menu.
The onions have to be cut up very fine.

la **menuiserie** NOUN
woodwork

le **menuisier** NOUN
joiner

le **mépris** NOUN
contempt

□ Il nous a traités avec mépris. He treated
us with contempt.

méprisant (FEM **méprisante**) ADJECTIVE
contemptuous

mépriser VERB [28]
to despise

la **mer** NOUN

1 sea

□ en mer at sea
■ **au bord de la mer** at the seaside
■ **la mer du Nord** the North Sea

2 tide

□ La mer est basse. The tide is out. □ La
mer sera haute à sept heures. It'll be high
tide at 7 o'clock.

la **mercerie** NOUN

1 haberdashery

2 haberdasher's shop

merci EXCLAMATION
thank you

□ Merci de m'avoir raccompagné. Thank
you for taking me home.
■ **merci beaucoup** thank you very much

le **mercredi** NOUN

1 Wednesday

□ Aujourd'hui, nous sommes mercredi. It's
Wednesday today.

2 on Wednesday

□ Nous comptons partir mercredi. We plan
to leave on Wednesday.
■ **le mercredi** on Wednesdays □ Le musée
est fermé le mercredi. The museum is shut
on Wednesdays.
■ **tous les mercredis** every Wednesday
■ **mercredi dernier** last Wednesday
■ **mercredi prochain** next Wednesday

la **mère** NOUN
mother

la **merguez** NOUN
spicy sausage

méridional (FEM **méridionale**, MASC PL
méridionaux) ADJECTIVE
southern

□ Il a un accent méridional. He's got a
southern accent.

la **meringue** NOUN
meringue

mériter VERB [28]

to deserve

le **merlan** NOUN
whiting

le **merle** NOUN
blackbird

la **merveille** NOUN

■ Cet ordinateur est une vraie merveille!
This computer's really wonderful!
■ **à merveille** wonderfully □ Elle se porte à
merveille depuis son opération. She's been
wonderfully well since the operation.

merveilleux (FEM **merveilleuse**) ADJECTIVE
marvellous

mes PL ADJECTIVE
my

□ mes parents my parents

Mesdames FEM NOUN
ladies

□ Bonjour, Mesdames. Good morning,
ladies.

Mesdemoiselles FEM NOUN
ladies

□ Bonjour, Mesdemoiselles. Good morning,
ladies.

mesquin (FEM **mesquine**) ADJECTIVE
mean

le **message** NOUN
message

■ **un message SMS** a text message

la **messagerie** NOUN

■ **une messagerie vocale** voice mail
■ **la messagerie électronique** email

la **messe** NOUN
mass

□ aller à la messe to go to mass □ la messe
de minuit midnight mass

messieurs MASC NOUN
gentlemen

□ Que puis-je faire pour vous, Messieurs?
What can I do for you, gentlemen?
■ **Messieurs, ...** *(in letter)* Dear Sirs, ...

la **mesure** NOUN

1 measurement

□ J'ai pris les mesures de la fenêtre. I took
the measurements of the window.
■ **sur mesure** tailor-made □ un costume
sur mesure a tailor-made suit

2 measure

□ L'établissement a pris des mesures pour
lutter contre le vandalisme. The school has
taken measures to combat vandalism.
■ **au fur et à mesure** as one goes along
□ Quand je cuisine, je préfère faire la
vaisselle au fur et à mesure. When I'm
cooking, I prefer to wash up as I go along.
■ **être en mesure de faire quelque chose**
to be in a position to do something □ Nous

m

ne sommes pas en mesure de vous renseigner. We are not in a position to give you any information.

mesurer VERB [28]
to measure
□ Mesurez la longueur et la largeur. Measure the length and the width.
■ Il mesure un mètre quatre-vingts. He's 1 m 80 tall.

met VERB ▷ see **mettre**

le **métal** (PL les **métaux**) NOUN
metal

métallique (FEM **métallique**) ADJECTIVE
metallic

la **météo** NOUN
weather forecast
□ Qu'est-ce que dit la météo pour cet après-midi? What's the weather forecast for this afternoon?

la **méthode** NOUN
1 method
□ des méthodes d'enseignement modernes modern teaching methods
2 tutor
□ une méthode de guitare a guitar tutor

le **métier** NOUN
job
□ Tu aimerais faire quel métier plus tard? What job would you like to do when you're older?

le **mètre** NOUN
metre
■ un mètre ruban a tape measure

le **métro** NOUN
underground
□ prendre le métro to go by underground

mets VERB ▷ see **mettre**

le **metteur en scène** (PL les **metteurs en scène**) NOUN
1 producer (of play)
2 director (of film)

mettre VERB [47]

PRESENT TENSE	
je mets	nous mettons
tu mets	vous mettez
il/elle met	ils/elles mettent

PAST PARTICIPLE	
mis	

1 to put
□ Où est-ce que tu as mis les clés? Where have you put the keys?
2 to put on
□ Je mets mon manteau et j'arrive. I'll put on my coat and then I'll be ready. □ Il fait froid, je vais mettre le chauffage. It's cold, I'm going to put the heating on.
3 to wear

□ Elle ne met pas souvent de jupe. She doesn't often wear a skirt. □ Je n'ai rien à me mettre! I've got nothing to wear!
4 to take
□ Combien de temps as-tu mis pour aller à Lille? How long did it take you to get to Lille? □ Elle met des heures à se préparer. She takes hours getting ready.
■ mettre en marche to start □ Comment met-on la machine à laver en marche? How do you start the washing machine?
■ Vous pouvez vous mettre là. You can sit there.
■ se mettre au lit to get into bed
■ se mettre en maillot de bain to put on one's swimsuit
■ se mettre à to start □ Il s'est mis à la peinture à cinquante ans. He started painting when he was 50. □ Il est temps de se mettre au travail. It's time to start work. □ Elle s'est mise à pleurer. She started crying.

le **meuble** NOUN
piece of furniture
□ Je me suis cogné contre un meuble. I bumped into a piece of furniture. □ de beaux meubles nice furniture

le **meublé** NOUN
1 furnished flat
2 furnished room

meubler VERB [28]
to furnish

le **meurtre** NOUN
murder

le **meurtrier** NOUN
murderer

la **meurtrière** NOUN
murderess

Mexico NOUN
Mexico City

le **Mexique** NOUN
Mexico

le **mi** NOUN
1 E
□ mi bémol E flat
2 mi
□ do, ré, mi ... do, re, mi ...

mi- PREFIX
1 half-
□ mi-clos half-shut
2 mid-
□ à la mi-janvier in mid-January

miauler VERB [28]
to mew

la **miche** NOUN
loaf

mi-chemin

■ **à mi-chemin** ADVERB halfway

le **micro** NOUN
microphone

le **microbe** NOUN
germ

le **micro-ondes** NOUN
microwave oven

le **micro-ordinateur** NOUN
microcomputer

le **microscope** NOUN
microscope

le **midi** NOUN
1 midday
□ à midi at midday
■ **midi et demi** half past twelve
2 lunchtime
□ On a bien mangé à midi. We had a good meal at lunchtime.
■ **le Midi** the South of France

la **mie** NOUN
breadcrumbs

le **miel** NOUN
honey

mien MASC PRONOUN
■ **le mien** mine □ Ce vélo-là, c'est le mien. That bike's mine.

mienne FEM PRONOUN
■ **la mienne** mine □ Cette valise-là, c'est la mienne. That case is mine.

miennes FEM PL PRONOUN
■ **les miennes** mine □ Tu as tes clés? J'ai oublié les miennes. Have you got your keys? I forgot mine.

miens MASC PL PRONOUN
■ **les miens** mine □ Ces CD-là, ce sont les miens. Those CDs are mine.

la **miette** NOUN
crumb (of bread, cake)

mieux (FEM+PL **mieux**) ADVERB, ADJECTIVE, NOUN
better
□ Je la connais mieux que son frère. I know her better than her brother. □ Elle va mieux. She's better. □ Les cheveux courts lui vont mieux. She looks better with short hair.
■ **Il vaut mieux que tu appelles ta mère.** You'd better phone your mother.
■ **le mieux** the best □ C'est la région que je connais le mieux. It's the region I know best.
■ **faire de son mieux** to do one's best □ Essaie de faire de ton mieux. Try to do your best.
■ **de mieux en mieux** better and better
■ **au mieux** at best

mignon (FEM **mignonne**) ADJECTIVE
sweet
□ Qu'est-ce qu'il est mignon! Isn't he

sweet!

la **migraine** NOUN
migraine
□ J'ai la migraine. I've got a migraine.

mijoter VERB [28]
to simmer

le **milieu** (PL les **milieux**) NOUN
1 middle
■ **au milieu de** in the middle of □ Place le vase au milieu de la table. Put the vase in the middle of the table.
■ **au beau milieu de** in the middle of □ Il est arrivé au beau milieu de la nuit. He arrived in the middle of the night.
2 background
□ le milieu familial the family background
□ Il vient d'un milieu modeste. He comes from a modest background.
3 environment
□ le milieu marin the marine environment

militaire (FEM **militaire**) ADJECTIVE
▷ see also **militaire** NOUN
military
□ faire son service militaire to do one's military service

le **militaire** NOUN
▷ see also **militaire** ADJECTIVE
serviceman
□ Son père est militaire. His father is in the services.
■ **un militaire de carrière** a professional soldier

mille NUMBER
a thousand
□ mille euros a thousand euros □ deux mille personnes two thousand people

le **millénaire** NOUN
millennium
□ le troisième millénaire the third millennium

le **millefeuille** NOUN
vanilla slice

le **millénium** NOUN
millennium

le **milliard** NOUN
thousand million
□ cinq milliards d'euros five thousand million euros

le/la **milliardaire** NOUN
multimillionaire

le **millier** NOUN
thousand
□ des milliers de personnes thousands of people
■ **par milliers** by the thousand

le **milligramme** NOUN
milligramme

le millimètre NOUN
millimetre

le million NOUN
million
□ deux millions de personnes two million
people

le/la millionnaire NOUN
millionaire

le/la mime NOUN
mime artist

mimer VERB [28]
to mimic

minable (FEM **minable**) ADJECTIVE
1 shabby
□ un imperméable minable a shabby
raincoat
2 pathetic

mince (FEM **mince**) ADJECTIVE
1 thin
□ une mince tranche de jambon a thin slice
of ham
2 slim
□ Il est grand et mince. He's tall and slim.
■ Mince alors! *(informal)* Oh bother!

la minceur NOUN
1 thinness
□ la minceur des murs the thinness of the
walls
2 slimness
□ Elle enviait la minceur de sa sœur. She
envied her sister's slimness.

la mine NOUN
1 expression
2 look
□ Tu as bonne mine. You look well. □ Il a
mauvaise mine. He doesn't look well. □ Elle
avait une mine fatiguée. She was looking
tired.
3 appearance
□ Il ne faut pas juger les gens d'après leur
mine. You shouldn't judge people by their
appearance.
4 lead *(of pencil)*
5 mine
□ une mine de charbon a coal mine
■ faire mine de faire quelque chose to
pretend to do something □ Elle a fait mine
de le croire. She pretended to believe him.
■ mine de rien somehow or other □ Mine
de rien elle est arrivée à l'heure. Somehow
or other she got here on time.

minéral (FEM **minérale**, MASC PL **minéraux**)
ADJECTIVE
mineral
□ l'eau minérale mineral water

minéralogique (FEM **minéralogique**)
ADJECTIVE

■ une plaque minéralogique a number
plate

le minet NOUN
pussycat

la minette NOUN
pussycat *(female)*

mineur (FEM **mineure**) ADJECTIVE
▷ see also **mineur** NOUN, **mineure** NOUN
minor

le mineur NOUN
▷ see also **mineur** ADJECTIVE
1 boy under 18
■ les mineurs the under-18s
2 miner
□ Mon grand-père était mineur. My
grandfather was a miner.

la mineure NOUN
▷ see also **mineure** ADJECTIVE
girl under 18

le minidisque NOUN
Minidisc®

la minijupe NOUN
miniskirt

minimal (FEM **minimale**, MASC PL **minimaux**)
ADJECTIVE
minimum

le minimessage NOUN
text message

le minimum NOUN
minimum
□ Il en fait le minimum. He does the
absolute minimum.
■ au minimum at the very least

le ministère NOUN
ministry
□ le ministère des Affaires étrangères the
Foreign Office

le ministre NOUN
minister
□ le ministre des Affaires étrangères the
Foreign Secretary

le Minitel® NOUN
DID YOU KNOW...?
Minitel is a system for getting
information online which pre-dates
the Internet. People still use it to get
phone numbers and train times, but
they increasingly rely on the Internet
for other things.

la minorité NOUN
minority

Minorque FEM NOUN
Minorca

le minuit NOUN
midnight
□ à minuit et quart at a quarter past
midnight

minuscule (FEM **minuscule**) ADJECTIVE
▷ *see also* **minuscule** NOUN
tiny

la **minuscule** NOUN
▷ *see also* **minuscule** ADJECTIVE
small letter

la **minute** NOUN
minute
■ **à la minute** just this minute □ Je viens de l'appeler à la minute. I've just this minute called him.

minutieux (FEM **minutieuse**) ADJECTIVE
meticulous
■ **C'est un travail minutieux.** It's a fiddly job.

la **mirabelle** NOUN
small yellow plum

le **miracle** NOUN
miracle

le **miroir** NOUN
mirror

mis VERB ▷ *see* **mettre**

mis (FEM **mise**) ADJECTIVE
■ **bien mis** well turned out □ Elle est toujours bien mise. She's always well turned out.

miser VERB [28] (*informal*)
to bank on
□ On ne peut pas miser là-dessus. We can't bank on it.

misérable (FEM **misérable**) ADJECTIVE
shabby-looking
□ une femme d'aspect misérable a shabby-looking woman

la **misère** NOUN
extreme poverty
■ **un salaire de misère** starvation wages

le/la **missionnaire** NOUN
missionary

mit VERB ▷ *see* **mettre**

la **mi-temps** NOUN
1 half (*of match*)
□ la première mi-temps the first half □ la deuxième mi-temps the second half
2 half-time
□ Je lui parlerai à la mi-temps. I'll speak to him at half-time.
■ **travailler à mi-temps** to work part-time

la **mitraillette** NOUN
submachine gun

mixte (FEM **mixte**) ADJECTIVE
■ **une école mixte** a mixed school

Mlle (PL **Mlles**) ABBREVIATION (= *Mademoiselle*)
Miss
□ Mlle Renoir Miss Renoir

Mme (PL **Mmes**) ABBREVIATION (= *Madame*)
Mrs

□ Mme Leroy Mrs Leroy

le **mobile** NOUN
1 motive
□ Quel était le mobile du crime? What was the motive for the crime?
2 mobile phone
□ Tu me donnes ton numéro de mobile? Can you give me your mobile number?

le **mobilier** NOUN
furniture

la **mobylette**® NOUN
moped

moche (FEM **moche**) ADJECTIVE (*informal*)
1 awful
□ Cette couleur est vraiment moche. That colour's really awful. □ Je me trouve moche! I think I look awful!
2 rotten
□ Il a la grippe, c'est moche pour lui. He's got flu, that's rotten for him.

la **mode** NOUN
▷ *see also* **le mode**
fashion
□ être à la mode to be fashionable

le **mode** NOUN
▷ *see also* **la mode**
■ **le mode d'emploi** directions for use
■ **le mode de vie** the way of life

le **modèle** NOUN
1 model
□ Le nouveau modèle sort en septembre. The new model is coming out in September.
2 style (*of clothes*)
□ Est-ce que vous avez le même modèle en plus grand? Have you got the same style in a bigger size?

modéré (FEM **modérée**) ADJECTIVE
moderate

moderne (FEM **moderne**) ADJECTIVE
modern

moderniser VERB [28]
to modernize

modeste (FEM **modeste**) ADJECTIVE
modest
□ Ne sois pas si modeste! Don't be so modest!

la **modestie** NOUN
modesty

moelleux (FEM **moelleuse**) ADJECTIVE
soft
□ un coussin moelleux a soft cushion

les **mœurs** FEM PL NOUN
social attitudes
■ **l'évolution des mœurs** changing attitudes

moi PRONOUN
me

□ Coucou, c'est moi! Hello, it's me!
■ **Moi, je pense que tu as tort.** I personally think you're wrong.
■ **à moi** mine □ Ce livre n'est pas à moi. This book isn't mine. □ un ami à moi a friend of mine

moi-même PRONOUN
myself
□ J'ai tricoté ce pull moi-même. I knitted this jumper myself.

moindre (FEM **moindre**) ADJECTIVE
■ **le moindre** the slightest □ Il ne fait pas le moindre effort. He doesn't make the slightest effort. □ Je n'en ai pas la moindre idée. I haven't the slightest idea.

le **moine** NOUN
monk

le **moineau** (PL les **moineaux**) NOUN
sparrow

moins ADVERB, PREPOSITION
1 less
□ Ça coûte moins de deux cents euros. It costs less than 200 euros.
2 fewer
□ Il y a moins de gens aujourd'hui. There are fewer people today.
■ **Il est cinq heures moins dix.** It's 10 to 5.
3 minus
□ quatre moins trois 4 minus 3 □ Il a fait moins cinq la nuit dernière. It was minus five last night.
■ **le moins** the least □ C'est le modèle le moins cher. It's the least expensive model. □ Ce sont les plages qui sont les moins polluées. These are the least polluted beaches. □ C'est l'album que j'aime le moins. This is the album I like the least.
■ **de moins en moins** less and less □ Il vient nous voir de moins en moins. He comes to see us less and less often.
■ **Il a trois ans de moins que moi.** He's three years younger than me.
■ **au moins** at least □ Ne te plains pas: au moins il ne pleut pas! Don't complain: at least it's not raining!
■ **à moins que** unless

○ **LANGUAGE TIP** **à moins que** is followed by a verb in the subjunctive.
□ Je te retrouverai à dix heures à moins que le train n'ait du retard. I'll meet you at 10 o'clock unless the train's late.

le **mois** NOUN
month

le **moisi** NOUN
■ **Ça sent le moisi.** It smells musty.

moisir VERB [38]
to go mouldy

□ Le pain a moisi. The bread's gone mouldy.

la **moisson** NOUN
harvest

moite (FEM **moite**) ADJECTIVE
sweaty
□ J'ai toujours les mains moites. My hands are always sweaty.

la **moitié** NOUN
half
□ Il a mangé la moitié du gâteau. He ate half the cake.
■ **la moitié du temps** half the time
■ **à la moitié de** halfway through □ Elle est partie à la moitié du film. She left halfway through the film.
■ **à moitié** half □ Ton verre est encore à moitié plein. Your glass is still half-full. □ Ce sac était à moitié prix. This bag was half-price.
■ **partager moitié moitié** to go halves □ On partage moitié moitié, d'accord? We'll go halves, OK?

la **molaire** NOUN
back tooth

la **Moldavie** NOUN
Moldova

molle FEM ADJECTIVE ▷ see **mou**

le **mollet** NOUN
▷ see also **mollet** ADJECTIVE
calf (of leg)

mollet (FEM **mollette**) ADJECTIVE
▷ see also **mollet** NOUN
■ **un œuf mollet** a soft-boiled egg

le/la **môme** NOUN (informal)
kid

le **moment** NOUN
moment
■ **en ce moment** at the moment □ Nous avons beaucoup de travail en ce moment. We have a lot of work at the moment.
■ **pour le moment** for the moment □ Nous ne pensons pas déménager pour le moment. We're not thinking of moving for the moment.
■ **au moment où** just as □ Il est arrivé au moment où j'allais partir. He turned up just as I was leaving.
■ **à ce moment-là 1** at that point □ À ce moment-là, on a vu arriver la police. At that point, we saw the police coming. **2** in that case □ À ce moment-là, je devrai partir plus tôt. In that case I'll have to leave earlier.
■ **à tout moment 1** at any moment □ Elle peut arriver à tout moment. She could arrive at any moment. **2** constantly □ Il nous dérange à tout moment pour des riens. He's constantly bothering us about

m

173

silly little things.

■ **sur le moment** at the time □ Sur le moment je n'ai rien dit. At the time I didn't say anything.

■ **par moments** at times □ Elle se sent seule par moments. She feels lonely at times.

momentané (FEM **momentanée**) ADJECTIVE
momentary

la **momie** NOUN
mummy *(Egyptian)*

mon (FEM **ma**, PL **mes**) ADJECTIVE
my
□ mon frère my brother □ mon ami my friend

la **monarchie** NOUN
monarchy

le **monastère** NOUN
monastery

le **monde** NOUN
world
□ faire le tour du monde to go round the world

■ **Il y a du monde.** There are a lot of people.

■ **beaucoup de monde** a lot of people □ Il y avait beaucoup de monde au concert. There were a lot of people at the concert.

■ **peu de monde** not many people

mondial (FEM **mondiale**, MASC PL **mondiaux**) ADJECTIVE
1 world
□ la population mondiale the world population
2 world-wide
□ une crise mondiale a world-wide crisis

le **moniteur** NOUN
1 instructor
□ un moniteur de voile a sailing instructor
2 monitor
□ le moniteur de mon ordinateur my computer monitor

la **monitrice** NOUN
instructor
□ une monitrice de ski a ski instructor

la **monnaie** NOUN
■ **une pièce de monnaie** a coin
■ **avoir de la monnaie** to have change
□ Est-ce que tu as de la monnaie? Have you got any change? □ Est-ce que vous avez la monnaie de dix euros? Do you have change for 10 euros?
■ **rendre la monnaie à quelqu'un** to give somebody their change

monotone (FEM **monotone**) ADJECTIVE
monotonous

Monsieur (PL **Messieurs**) MASC NOUN
1 Mr

□ Monsieur Dupont Mr Dupont
2 man
□ Il y a un monsieur qui veut te voir. There's a man to see you.
3 Sir
□ Monsieur, … Dear Sir, … *(in letter)*
□ Monsieur! Vous avez oublié votre parapluie! Excuse me! You've forgotten your umbrella!

le **monstre** NOUN
▷ *see also* **monstre** ADJECTIVE
monster

monstre (FEM **monstre**) ADJECTIVE
▷ *see also* **monstre** NOUN
■ **Nous avons un travail monstre.** We've got a terrific amount of work.

le **mont** NOUN
mount
■ **le mont Everest** Mount Everest
■ **le mont Blanc** Mont Blanc

la **montagne** NOUN
mountain
□ de hautes montagnes high mountains
□ des vacances à la montagne holidays in the mountains
■ **les montagnes russes** roller coaster

> **LANGUAGE TIP** Word for word, montagnes russes means 'Russian mountains'.

montagneux (FEM **montagneuse**) ADJECTIVE
mountainous
□ une région montagneuse a mountainous area

montant (FEM **montante**) ADJECTIVE
1 rising
□ la marée montante the rising tide
2 high
□ un pull à col montant a high-necked jumper

monter VERB [48]
1 to go up
□ Elle a du mal à monter les escaliers. She has difficulty going upstairs. □ Les prix ont encore monté. Prices have gone up again.
2 to assemble
□ Est-ce que ces étagères sont difficiles à monter? Are these shelves difficult to assemble?
■ **monter dans** to get on □ Il est temps de monter dans l'avion. It's time to get on the plane.
■ **monter sur** to stand on □ Monte sur la chaise: tu verras mieux. Stand on the chair: you'll see better.
■ **monter à cheval** to ride

la **montre** NOUN

watch

montrer VERB [28]
to show
□ Montre-moi ton nouveau manteau. Show me your new coat.

la **monture** NOUN
frames (of glasses)

le **monument** NOUN
monument

se **moquer** VERB [28]
■ **se moquer de 1** to make fun of □ Ils se sont moqués de mes chaussures jaunes. They made fun of my yellow shoes.
2 (informal) not to care about □ Il se moque complètement de la mode. He couldn't care less about fashion.

la **moquette** NOUN
fitted carpet

moqueur (FEM **moqueuse**) ADJECTIVE
mocking

le **moral** NOUN
■ Elle a le moral. She's in good spirits.
■ J'ai le moral à zéro. I'm feeling really down.

la **morale** NOUN
moral
□ La morale de cette histoire est ... The moral of the story is ...
■ faire la morale à quelqu'un to lecture somebody

le **morceau** (PL les **morceaux**) NOUN
piece
□ un morceau de pain a piece of bread

mordre VERB [49]
to bite

mordu (FEM **mordue**) ADJECTIVE
■ Il est mordu de jazz. (informal) He's crazy about jazz.

la **morgue** NOUN
mortuary

le **morse** NOUN
walrus

la **morsure** NOUN
bite

la **mort** NOUN
▷ see also **mort** ADJECTIVE
death

mort (FEM **morte**) ADJECTIVE
▷ see also **mort** NOUN
dead
□ Nous avons trouvé un oiseau mort. We found a dead bird. □ Napoléon est mort en 1821. Napoleon died in 1821.
■ Il était mort de peur. He was scared to death.
■ Je suis morte de fatigue. I'm dead tired.

mortel (FEM **mortelle**) ADJECTIVE

1 deadly
□ un poison mortel a deadly poison □ Ces réunions de famille sont mortelles! (informal) These family gatherings are deadly!

2 fatal
□ une chute mortelle a fatal fall

la **morue** NOUN
cod

Moscou NOUN
Moscow

la **mosquée** NOUN
mosque

le **mot** NOUN

1 word
□ mot à mot word for word
■ des mots croisés a crossword
■ le mot de passe the password

2 note
□ Je vais lui écrire un mot pour lui dire qu'on arrive. I'll write her a note to say we're coming.

le **motard** NOUN

1 biker

2 motorcycle cop (informal)
□ Il s'est fait arrêter par un motard. He was stopped by a motorcycle cop.

le **moteur** NOUN
engine
■ un bateau à moteur a motor boat
■ un moteur de recherche a search engine

le **motif** NOUN
pattern
□ des rideaux avec un motif d'oiseaux curtains with a bird pattern
■ sans motif for no reason □ Il s'est fâché sans motif. He got angry for no reason.

motivé (FEM **motivée**) ADJECTIVE
motivated

la **moto** NOUN
motorbike

le/la **motocycliste** NOUN
motorcyclist

mou (FEM **molle**) ADJECTIVE

1 soft
□ Mon matelas est trop mou. My mattress is too soft.

2 lethargic
□ Je le trouve un peu mou. I find him a bit lethargic.

la **mouche** NOUN
fly
■ prendre la mouche to get into a huff

se **moucher** VERB [28]
to blow one's nose

le **moucheron** NOUN

midge

le **mouchoir** NOUN
handkerchief
■ un mouchoir en papier a tissue

moudre VERB [50]
to grind

la **moue** NOUN
pout
■ faire la moue to pout

la **mouette** NOUN
seagull

la **moufle** NOUN
mitt

mouillé (FEM **mouillée**) ADJECTIVE
wet

mouiller VERB [28]
to get wet
□ J'ai mouillé les manches de mon pull. I got the sleeves of my jumper wet.
■ se mouiller to get wet □ Attention, tu vas te mouiller! Careful, you'll get wet!

moulant (FEM **moulante**) ADJECTIVE
figure-hugging
□ une robe moulante a figure-hugging dress

la **moule** NOUN
▷ see also le moule
mussel

le **moule** NOUN
▷ see also la moule
■ un moule à gâteaux a cake tin

le **moulin** NOUN
mill

moulu VERB ▷ see moudre

mourir VERB [51]
to die
■ mourir de faim to starve to death □ Des centaines de personnes sont mortes de faim. Hundreds of people starved to death.
■ Je meurs de faim! I'm starving!
■ mourir de froid to die of exposure
■ Je meurs de froid! I'm freezing!
■ mourir d'envie de faire quelque chose to be dying to do something □ Je meurs d'envie d'aller me baigner. I'm dying to go for a swim.

la **mousse** NOUN
1 moss
□ un rocher recouvert de mousse a rock covered with moss
2 froth (on beer)
3 lather (of soap, shampoo)
4 mousse
□ une mousse au chocolat a chocolate mousse □ une mousse de poisson a fish mousse
■ la mousse à raser shaving foam

mousseux (FEM **mousseuse**) ADJECTIVE
■ un vin mousseux a sparkling wine

la **moustache** NOUN
moustache
■ les moustaches (of a cat) whiskers

le **moustique** NOUN
mosquito

la **moutarde** NOUN
mustard

le **mouton** NOUN
1 sheep
□ une peau de mouton a sheepskin
2 mutton
□ un gigot de mouton a leg of mutton

le **mouvement** NOUN
movement

mouvementé (FEM **mouvementée**) ADJECTIVE
eventful
□ des vacances mouvementées eventful holidays

moyen (FEM **moyenne**) ADJECTIVE
▷ see also moyen NOUN, moyenne NOUN
1 average
□ Je suis plutôt moyenne en langues. I'm just average at languages.
2 medium
□ Elle est de taille moyenne. She's of medium height.
■ le moyen âge the Middle Ages

le **moyen** NOUN
▷ see also moyen ADJECTIVE
way
□ Quel est le meilleur moyen de le convaincre? What's the best way of convincing him?
■ Je n'en ai pas les moyens. I can't afford it.
■ Ils n'ont pas les moyens de s'acheter une voiture. They can't afford to buy a car.
■ un moyen de transport a means of transport
■ par tous les moyens by every possible means

la **moyenne** NOUN
▷ see also moyenne ADJECTIVE
■ avoir la moyenne to get a pass mark
□ J'espère avoir la moyenne en maths. I hope to get a pass mark in maths.
■ en moyenne on average
■ la moyenne d'âge the average age

le **Moyen-Orient** NOUN
Middle East

muet (FEM **muette**) ADJECTIVE
dumb
■ un film muet a silent film

le **muguet** NOUN

m

lily of the valley

multiple (FEM **multiple**) ADJECTIVE
numerous
□ en de multiples occasions on numerous occasions

multiplier VERB [19]
to multiply

municipal (FEM **municipale**, MASC PL **municipaux**) ADJECTIVE
■ la bibliothèque municipale the public library

la **municipalité** NOUN
town council

munir VERB [38]
■ munir quelqu'un de to equip someone with
■ se munir de to equip oneself with

les **munitions** FEM PL NOUN
ammunition

le **mur** NOUN
wall

mûr (FEM **mûre**) ADJECTIVE
▷ see also **mûre** NOUN
1 ripe (fruit)
2 mature (person)

la **mûre** NOUN
▷ see also **mûr** ADJECTIVE
bramble

mûrir VERB [38]
1 to ripen
□ Les fraises ont mis du temps à mûrir. The strawberries took a while to ripen.
2 to make mature
□ Cette expérience l'a beaucoup mûrie. That experience has made her much more mature.

murmurer VERB [28]
to whisper
□ Il m'a murmuré à l'oreille qu'il allait partir. He whispered in my ear that he was going to go.

la **muscade** NOUN
nutmeg

le **muscat** NOUN
1 muscat grape
2 muscatel (wine)
□ un verre de muscat a glass of muscatel

le **muscle** NOUN
muscle

musclé (FEM **musclée**) ADJECTIVE
muscular

le **museau** (PL les **museaux**) NOUN
muzzle

le **musée** NOUN
museum

musical (FEM **musicale**, MASC PL **musicaux**) ADJECTIVE
musical
■ avoir l'oreille musicale to be musical

le **music-hall** NOUN
variety
□ une chanteuse de music-hall a variety singer

le **musicien** NOUN
musician

la **musicienne** NOUN
musician

la **musique** NOUN
music

musulman (FEM **musulmane**) ADJECTIVE, NOUN
Muslim
■ un musulman a Muslim (man)
■ une musulmane a Muslim (woman)

la **mutation** NOUN
transfer
□ Il a demandé sa mutation à Paris. He asked for a transfer to Paris.

myope (FEM **myope**) ADJECTIVE
short-sighted

le **mystère** NOUN
mystery

mystérieux (FEM **mystérieuse**) ADJECTIVE
mysterious

le **mythe** NOUN
myth

m

Nn

n' PRONOUN ▷ *see* **ne**

la **nage** NOUN
- **traverser une rivière à la nage** to swim across a river
- **être en nage** to be sweating profusely

la **nageoire** NOUN
fin

nager VERB [45]
to swim

le **nageur** NOUN
swimmer

la **nageuse** NOUN
swimmer

naïf (FEM **naïve**) ADJECTIVE
naïve

le **nain** NOUN
dwarf

la **naissance** NOUN
birth
- **votre date de naissance** your date of birth

naître VERB [52]
to be born
- **Il est né en 1992.** He was born in 1992.

naïve FEM ADJECTIVE ▷ *see* **naïf**

la **nana** NOUN (informal)
girl

la **nappe** NOUN
tablecloth

la **narine** NOUN
nostril

natal (FEM **natale**) ADJECTIVE
native
- □ mon pays natal my native country

la **natation** NOUN
swimming
- □ La natation est mon sport favori. Swimming's my favourite sport.
- **faire de la natation** to go swimming

la **nation** NOUN
nation
- □ les Nations unies the United Nations

national (FEM **nationale**, MASC PL **nationaux**) ADJECTIVE
▷ *see also* **nationale** NOUN

national
- **la fête nationale espagnole** the national day of Spain

la **nationale** NOUN
▷ *see also* **nationale** ADJECTIVE
main road
- □ En vélo, il vaut mieux éviter les nationales. When on a bike it's better to avoid main roads.

la **nationalité** NOUN
nationality

la **natte** NOUN
plait
- □ Cécile avait des nattes. Cécile had plaits.

la **nature** NOUN
▷ *see also* **nature** ADJECTIVE
nature

nature (FEM **nature**) ADJECTIVE
▷ *see also* **nature** NOUN
plain
- □ un yaourt nature a plain yoghurt

naturel (FEM **naturelle**) ADJECTIVE
natural

naturellement ADVERB
of course
- □ Vous viendrez à notre fête? — Naturellement! Are you coming to our party? — Of course! □ Naturellement, il est encore en retard. Of course, he's late again.

le **naufrage** NOUN
shipwreck

nautique (FEM **nautique**) ADJECTIVE
water
- **les sports nautiques** water sports
- **le ski nautique** water-skiing

le **navet** NOUN
turnip

la **navette** NOUN
shuttle
- □ la navette entre la gare et l'aéroport the shuttle between the station and the airport
- **faire la navette** to commute □ Je fais la navette entre Paris et Ivry. I commute between Paris and Ivry.

le **navigateur** NOUN
browser (on computer)

la **navigation** NOUN
■ **La navigation est interdite ici.** Boats are not allowed here.
naviguer VERB [28]
to sail
le **navire** NOUN
ship
ne ADVERB

> LANGUAGE TIP **ne** is combined with words such as **pas, personne, plus** and **jamais** to form negative phrases.

□ Je ne peux pas venir. I can't come. □ Ils ne vont jamais en boîte. They never go to discos. □ Je ne connais personne ici. I don't know anyone here.

> LANGUAGE TIP **ne** changes to **n'** before a vowel and most words beginning with 'h'.

□ Je n'ai pas d'argent. I haven't got any money. □ Il n'habite plus à Paris. He doesn't live in Paris any more.

> LANGUAGE TIP **ne** is sometimes not translated.

□ C'est plus loin que je ne le croyais. It's further than I thought.

né VERB ▷see **naître**
born
□ Elle est née en 1980. She was born in 1980.
néanmoins ADVERB
nevertheless
nécessaire (FEM **nécessaire**) ADJECTIVE
necessary
□ Il est nécessaire de réserver. It's necessary to book.
le **nectar** NOUN
■ **le nectar d'abricot** apricot drink
néerlandais (FEM **néerlandaise**) ADJECTIVE, NOUN
Dutch
□ Manon parle néerlandais. Manon speaks Dutch.
■ **un Néerlandais** a Dutchman
■ **une Néerlandaise** a Dutchwoman
■ **les Néerlandais** the Dutch
négatif (FEM **négative**) ADJECTIVE
▷see also **négatif** NOUN
negative
le **négatif** NOUN
▷see also **négatif** ADJECTIVE
negative (of photo)
négligé (FEM **négligée**) ADJECTIVE
scruffy
□ une tenue négligée scruffy clothes
négliger VERB [45]
to neglect
□ Ces derniers temps il a négligé son travail.

He's been neglecting his work recently.
négocier VERB [19]
to negotiate
la **neige** NOUN
snow
■ **un bonhomme de neige** a snowman
neiger VERB [45]
to snow
le **nénuphar** NOUN
water lily
le **néon** NOUN
neon
□ une lampe au néon a neon light □ La cuisine est éclairée au néon. The kitchen has a neon light.
néo-zélandais (FEM **néo-zélandaise**) ADJECTIVE, NOUN
New Zealand
□ Le champion néo-zélandais a gagné la course. The New Zealand champion won the race.
■ **un Néo-Zélandais** a New Zealander (man)
■ **une Néo-Zélandaise** a New Zealander (woman)
le **nerf** NOUN
nerve
■ **taper sur les nerfs de quelqu'un** to get on somebody's nerves □ Il me tape sur les nerfs. He's getting on my nerves.

> LANGUAGE TIP Word for word, this means 'he's banging on my nerves'.

nerveux (FEM **nerveuse**) ADJECTIVE
nervous
la **nervosité** NOUN
nervousness
n'est-ce pas ADVERB

> LANGUAGE TIP **n'est-ce pas** is used to check that something is true.

□ Nous sommes le douze aujourd'hui, n'est-ce pas? It's the 12th today, isn't it? □ Ils sont venus l'an dernier, n'est-ce pas? They came last year, didn't they? □ Elle aura dix-huit ans en octobre, n'est-ce pas? She'll be 18 in October, won't she?
le **Net** NOUN
the Net
net (FEM **nette**) ADJECTIVE, ADVERB
1 clear
□ L'image n'est pas nette. The picture isn't very clear.
2 net
□ Poids net: 500 g. Net weight: 500 g.
3 flatly
□ Il a refusé net de nous aider. He flatly refused to help us.
■ **s'arrêter net** to stop dead

nettement ADVERB
much
□ Ce magasin est nettement plus cher. This shop is much more expensive.

le **nettoyage** NOUN
cleaning
■ le nettoyage à sec dry cleaning

nettoyer VERB [53]
to clean

neuf NUMBER
▷ *see also* **neuf** ADJECTIVE
nine
□ Claire a neuf ans. Claire's nine. □ Il est neuf heures du matin. It's nine in the morning.
■ le neuf février the ninth of February

neuf (FEM **neuve**) ADJECTIVE
▷ *see also* **neuf** NUMBER
new
□ des chaussures neuves new shoes

neutre (FEM **neutre**) ADJECTIVE
neutral

neuve FEM ADJECTIVE ▷ *see* **neuf**

neuvième (FEM **neuvième**) ADJECTIVE
ninth
□ au neuvième étage on the ninth floor

le **neveu** (PL les **neveux**) NOUN
nephew

le **nez** NOUN
nose
■ se trouver nez à nez avec quelqu'un to come face to face with somebody

ni CONJUNCTION
■ ni ... ni ... neither ... nor ... □ Je n'aime ni les lentilles ni les épinards. I like neither lentils nor spinach. □ Elles ne sont venues ni l'une ni l'autre. Neither of them came.

la **niche** NOUN
kennel

le **nid** NOUN
nest

la **nièce** NOUN
niece

nier VERB [19]
to deny

n'importe ADVERB
■ n'importe quel any old □ N'importe quel stylo fera l'affaire. Any old pen will do.
■ n'importe qui anybody □ N'ouvre pas la porte à n'importe qui. Don't open the door to just anybody.
■ n'importe quoi anything □ Je ferais n'importe quoi pour elle. I'd do anything for her.
■ Tu dis n'importe quoi. You're talking rubbish.
■ n'importe où anywhere □ On trouve ces fleurs n'importe où. You can find these flowers anywhere.
■ Ne laisse pas tes affaires n'importe où. Don't leave your things lying everywhere.
■ n'importe quand any time □ Tu peux venir n'importe quand. You can come any time.
■ n'importe comment any old how □ Ces livres sont rangés n'importe comment. These books have been put away any old how.

le **niveau** (PL les **niveaux**) NOUN
1 level
□ le niveau de l'eau the water level
2 standard
□ Ces deux enfants n'ont pas le même niveau. These two children aren't at the same level.
■ le niveau de vie the standard of living

noble (FEM **noble**) ADJECTIVE
noble

la **noblesse** NOUN
nobility

la **noce** NOUN
wedding
■ un repas de noce a wedding reception
■ Leurs noces d'or. Their golden wedding anniversary.

nocif (FEM **nocive**) ADJECTIVE
harmful
□ une substance nocive a harmful substance

nocturne (FEM **nocturne**) ADJECTIVE
▷ *see also* **nocturne** NOUN
1 nocturnal
□ un oiseau nocturne a nocturnal bird
2 by night
□ Découvrez le Paris nocturne! Discover Paris by night!

la **nocturne** NOUN
▷ *see also* **nocturne** ADJECTIVE
late-night opening
□ Nocturne le vendredi jusqu'à vingt-trois heures. Late-night opening until 11 p.m. on Fridays.

le **Noël** NOUN
Christmas
□ Qu'est-ce que tu as eu pour Noël? What did you get for Christmas?
■ Joyeux Noël! Merry Christmas!

le **nœud** NOUN
1 knot
□ Il a fait un nœud à la corde. He tied a knot in the rope.
2 bow
□ Janet avait un nœud dans les cheveux. Janet had a bow in her hair.

- **un nœud papillon** a bow tie

  🗨 **LANGUAGE TIP** Word for word, this means 'a butterfly bow'.

noir (FEM **noire**) ADJECTIVE
▷ see also **noir** NOUN
1 black
  □ Elle porte une robe noire. She's wearing a black dress. □ Elle est noire. She's black.
2 dark
  □ Il fait noir dehors. It's dark outside.

le **noir** NOUN
▷ see also **noir** ADJECTIVE
dark
  □ J'ai peur du noir. I'm afraid of the dark.
- **le travail au noir** moonlighting

  🗨 **LANGUAGE TIP** Word for word, **travail au noir** means 'work in the dark'.

le **Noir** NOUN
black man
- **les Noirs** black people

la **Noire** NOUN
black woman

la **noisette** NOUN
hazelnut

la **noix** (PL les **noix**) NOUN
walnut
- **une noix de coco** a coconut
- **les noix de cajou** cashew nuts
- **une noix de beurre** a knob of butter

le **nom** NOUN
1 name
  □ votre nom your name
- **mon nom de famille** my surname
- **son nom de jeune fille** her maiden name
2 noun (in grammar)
  □ un nom commun a common noun □ un nom propre a proper noun

le **nombre** NOUN
number
  □ Treize est un nombre impair. Thirteen is an odd number. □ un grand nombre d'amis a large number of friends

nombreux (FEM **nombreuse**) ADJECTIVE
1 many
  □ Il a gagné de nombreux matchs. He's won many matches.
2 large
  □ une famille nombreuse a large family
- **peu nombreux** few □ Nous étions peu nombreux à la réunion. There were few of us at the meeting.

le **nombril** NOUN
navel

nommer VERB [28]
1 to name
  □ Il n'a voulu nommer personne. He didn't want to name anybody.
2 to appoint
  □ Il a été nommé directeur. He was appointed director.

non ADVERB
no
  □ Tu as vu Jean-Pierre? — Non. Have you seen Jean-Pierre? — No.
- **non seulement** not only □ Il est non seulement intelligent, mais aussi très gentil. Not only is he intelligent, he's also very nice.
- **moi non plus** Neither do I. □ Je n'aime pas les hamburgers. — Moi non plus. I don't like hamburgers. — Neither do I. □ Il n'y est pas allé et moi non plus. He didn't go and neither did I.

non alcoolisé (FEM **non alcoolisée**) ADJECTIVE
non-alcoholic
  □ les boissons non alcoolisées non-alcoholic drinks

le **non-fumeur** NOUN
non-smoker
  □ Gavin est un non-fumeur. Gavin's a non-smoker.
- **une voiture non-fumeurs** a no-smoking carriage

le **nord** NOUN
▷ see also **nord** ADJECTIVE
north
  □ Ils vivent dans le nord de l'île. They live in the north of the island.
- **vers le nord** northwards
- **au nord de Paris** north of Paris
- **l'Afrique du Nord** North Africa
- **le vent du nord** the north wind

nord (FEM+PL **nord**) ADJECTIVE
▷ see also **nord** NOUN
1 north
  □ la face nord du Mont-Blanc the north face of Mont-Blanc
- **le pôle Nord** the North Pole
2 northern
  □ Nous avons visité la partie nord de l'île. We visited the northern part of the island.

le **nord-est** NOUN
north-east
  □ les régions du nord-est north-eastern regions

le **nord-ouest** NOUN
north-west
- **l'Europe du nord-ouest** north-west Europe

normal (FEM **normale**, MASC PL **normaux**) ADJECTIVE
1 normal
  □ un bébé normal a normal baby
2 natural

n

□ C'est tout à fait normal. It's perfectly natural.

■ Vous trouvez que c'est normal? Does that seem right to you?

normalement ADVERB
normally

□ Les aéroports fonctionnent tous normalement. The airports are all working normally.

■ Normalement, elle doit arriver à huit heures. She's supposed to arrive at 8 o'clock.

■ Tu es libre ce week-end? — Oui, normalement. Are you free this weekend? — Yes, I should be.

normand (FEM **normande**) ADJECTIVE

■ un village normand a village in Normandy

■ la côte normande the coast of Normandy

la **Normandie** NOUN
Normandy

la **Norvège** NOUN
Norway

norvégien (FEM **norvégienne**) ADJECTIVE, NOUN
Norwegian

■ Elle parle norvégien. She speaks Norwegian.

■ un Norvégien a Norwegian (man)

■ une Norvégienne a Norwegian (woman)

nos PL ADJECTIVE
our

□ Où sont nos affaires? Where are our things?

le **notaire** NOUN
solicitor

□ Son père est notaire. His father's a solicitor.

la **note** NOUN
1 note

□ J'ai pris des notes pendant la conférence. I took notes at the lecture. □ Il a joué quelques notes au piano. He played a few notes on the piano.

2 mark

□ Vincent a de bonnes notes en maths. Vincent's got good marks in maths.

3 bill

□ Il n'a pas payé sa note. He didn't pay his bill.

noter VERB [28]
to make a note of

□ Tu as noté leur adresse? Did you make a note of their address?

les **notions** FEM PL NOUN
basics

□ Il faut avoir des notions d'anglais. You have to have some basic English. □ Elle a des notions de comptabilité. She knows the basics of accounting.

notre (FEM **notre**, PL **nos**) ADJECTIVE
our

□ Voici notre maison. Here's our house.

nôtre PRONOUN

■ le nôtre ours □ À qui est ce chien? — C'est le nôtre. Whose dog is it? — It's ours. □ Leur voiture est rouge, la nôtre est bleue. Their car is red, ours is blue.

nôtres PL PRONOUN

■ les nôtres ours □ Ces places-là sont les nôtres. Those seats are ours.

nouer VERB [28]
to tie

les **nouilles** FEM PL NOUN
noodles

le **nounours** NOUN
teddy bear

nourrir VERB [38]
to feed

la **nourriture** NOUN
food

nous PL PRONOUN
1 we

□ Nous avons deux enfants. We have two children.

2 us

□ Viens avec nous. Come with us.

■ nous-mêmes ourselves

nouveau (MASC SING ALSO **nouvel**, FEM **nouvelle**, MASC PL **nouveaux**) ADJECTIVE
▷ see also **nouveau** NOUN
new

□ Il me faut un nouveau pantalon. I need some new trousers. □ Elle a une nouvelle voiture. She's got a new car.

> LANGUAGE TIP nouveau changes to nouvel before a vowel and most words beginning with 'h'.

□ le nouvel élève dans ma classe The new boy in my class

■ le nouvel an New Year

le **nouveau** (PL les **nouveaux**) NOUN
▷ see also **nouveau** ADJECTIVE
new pupil

□ Il y a plusieurs nouveaux dans la classe. There are several new pupils in the class.

■ de nouveau again □ Il pleut de nouveau. It's raining again.

le **nouveau-né** NOUN
newborn child

la **nouveauté** NOUN
novelty

nouvel, nouvelle ADJECTIVE ▷ see **nouveau**

n

la **nouvelle** NOUN
1 news
  □ Tu connais la nouvelle? Teresa a gagné au loto. Have you heard the news? Teresa won the lottery. □ C'est une bonne nouvelle. That's good news.
2 short story
  □ une nouvelle de Balsac a short story by Balsac
  ■ **les nouvelles** the news □ J'ai écouté les nouvelles à la radio. I listened to the news on the radio.
  ■ **avoir des nouvelles de quelqu'un** to hear from somebody □ Je n'ai pas eu de nouvelles de lui. I haven't heard from him.

la **Nouvelle-Zélande** NOUN
New Zealand

novembre MASC NOUN
November
  ■ **en novembre** in November

le **noyau** (PL les **noyaux**) NOUN
stone (of fruit)
  □ un noyau d'abricot an apricot stone

le **noyer** NOUN
  ▷ see also **noyer** VERB
walnut tree

se **noyer** VERB [53]
  ▷ see also **noyer** NOUN
to drown
  □ Il s'est noyé dans la rivière. He drowned in the river.

nu (FEM **nue**) ADJECTIVE
1 naked
  □ Ils se sont baignés nus. They went for a swim naked. □ tout nus stark naked
2 bare
  □ Elle avait les bras nus. Her arms were bare. □ Les murs étaient nus. The walls were bare.

le **nuage** NOUN
cloud
  ■ **un nuage de lait** a drop of milk

nuageux (FEM **nuageuse**) ADJECTIVE
cloudy

nucléaire (FEM **nucléaire**) ADJECTIVE
nuclear
  □ l'énergie nucléaire nuclear power

le/la **nudiste** NOUN
nudist

la **nuit** NOUN
night
  □ Ils ont fait du bruit toute la nuit. They were noisy all night.
  ■ **Il fait nuit.** It's dark.
  ■ **cette nuit** tonight □ Il va rentrer cette nuit. He'll be back tonight.
  ■ **Bonne nuit!** Good night!
  ■ **de nuit** by night

nul (FEM **nulle**) ADJECTIVE
rubbish
  □ Ce film est nul. (informal) This film's rubbish.
  ■ **être nul** to be no good □ Je suis nul en maths. I'm no good at maths.
  ■ **un match nul** a draw (in sport)
  □ Ils ont fait match nul. It was a draw.
  ■ **nulle part** nowhere □ Je ne le vois nulle part. I can't see it anywhere.

numérique (FEM **numérique**) ADJECTIVE
digital
  □ un appareil photo numérique a digital camera

le **numéro** NOUN
number
  □ J'habite au numéro trois. I live at number 3.
  ■ **mon numéro de téléphone** my phone number
  ■ **le numéro de compte** the account number

nu-pieds (FEM+PL **nu-pieds**) ADJECTIVE, ADVERB
barefoot
  □ Il se promenait nu-pieds. He was walking barefoot.

la **nuque** NOUN
nape of the neck

le **nylon** NOUN
nylon

n

Oo

obéir VERB [38]
to obey
- **obéir à quelqu'un** to obey somebody
□ Elle refuse d'obéir à ses parents. She refuses to obey her parents.

obéissant (FEM **obéissante**) ADJECTIVE
obedient

l' **objet** MASC NOUN
object
- **les objets de valeur** valuables
- **les objets trouvés** the lost property office

obligatoire (FEM **obligatoire**) ADJECTIVE
compulsory

obliger VERB [45]
- **obliger quelqu'un à faire quelque chose** to force somebody to do something
- **Je suis bien obligé d'accepter.** I can't really refuse.

obscur (FEM **obscure**) ADJECTIVE
dark

l' **obscurité** FEM NOUN
darkness
□ dans l'obscurité in the dark

l' **obsédé** MASC NOUN
sex maniac
- **un obsédé sexuel** a sex maniac

obséder VERB [34]
to obsess
□ Il est obsédé par le travail. He's obsessed by work.

l' **observation** FEM NOUN
comment
□ J'ai une ou deux observations à faire. I've got one or two comments to make.

observer VERB [28]
1 to watch
□ Il observait les canards sur le lac. He watched the ducks on the lake.
2 to observe
□ Ils observent le règlement. They observe the rules.

l' **obstacle** MASC NOUN
1 obstacle
□ surmonter un obstacle to overcome an obstacle

2 fence (in show jumping)
- **une course d'obstacles** an obstacle race

obstiné (FEM **obstinée**) ADJECTIVE
stubborn

obtenir VERB [83]
1 to get
□ Ils ont obtenu cinquante pour cent des voix. They got 50% of the votes.
2 to achieve
□ Nous avons obtenu de bons résultats. We achieved good results.

l' **occasion** FEM NOUN
1 opportunity
□ C'est une occasion à ne pas manquer. It's an opportunity not to be missed.
2 occasion
□ à l'occasion de son anniversaire on the occasion of his birthday □ à plusieurs occasions on several occasions
3 bargain
□ Cet ordinateur est une bonne occasion. This computer's a real bargain.
- **d'occasion** second-hand □ une voiture d'occasion a second-hand car

l' **Occident** MASC NOUN
West
□ en Occident in the West

occidental (FEM **occidentale**, MASC PL **occidentaux**) ADJECTIVE
western
- **les pays occidentaux** the West

l' **occupation** FEM NOUN
occupation
□ la France sous l'Occupation France during the Occupation

occupé (FEM **occupée**) ADJECTIVE
1 busy
□ Le directeur est très occupé. The director's very busy.
2 taken
□ Est-ce que cette place est occupée? Is this seat taken?
3 engaged
□ Les toilettes sont occupées. The toilet's engaged. □ La ligne est occupée. The line's

engaged.

occuper VERB [28]
to occupy
□ Les enfants ne sont pas faciles à occuper quand il pleut. Children aren't easy to keep occupied when it rains.
■ **s'occuper de quelque chose 1** to be in charge of something □ Elle s'occupe d'un club de sport. She's in charge of a sports club. **2** to deal with something □ Je vais m'occuper de ce dossier. I'm going to deal with this file.
■ **On s'occupe de vous?** *(in a shop)* Are you being attended to?

l' **océan** MASC NOUN
ocean
□ l'océan Indien the Indian Ocean

octobre MASC NOUN
October
■ **en octobre** in October

l' **odeur** FEM NOUN
smell
□ Il y a une drôle d'odeur ici. There's a funny smell round here.

odieux (FEM **odieuse**) ADJECTIVE
horrible
□ Elle a été odieuse avec nous. She was horrible to us.

l' **œil** (PL les **yeux**) MASC NOUN
eye
□ J'ai quelque chose dans l'œil. I've got something in my eye.
■ **à l'œil** *(informal)* for free □ Il est entré à l'œil. He got in for free.

l' **œillet** MASC NOUN
carnation

l' **œuf** MASC NOUN
egg
■ **un œuf à la coque** a soft-boiled egg
■ **un œuf dur** a hard-boiled egg
■ **un œuf au plat** a fried egg
■ **les œufs brouillés** scrambled eggs
■ **un œuf de Pâques** an Easter egg

l' **œuvre** FEM NOUN
work
□ J'étudie une œuvre de Molière. I'm studying one of Molière's works.
■ **une œuvre d'art** a work of art

offert VERB ▷ *see* **offrir**

l' **office** MASC NOUN
■ **un office du tourisme** a tourist office

officiel (FEM **officielle**) ADJECTIVE
official

l' **officier** MASC NOUN
officer
□ Il est officier de marine. He's a naval officer.

l' **offre** FEM NOUN
offer
□ une offre spéciale a special offer
■ **'offres d'emploi'** 'situations vacant'

offrir VERB [54]
■ **offrir quelque chose 1** to offer something □ On lui a offert un poste de secrétaire. They offered her a secretarial post. □ Elle lui a offert à boire. She offered him a drink. **2** to give something □ Il lui a offert des roses. He gave her roses.
■ **s'offrir quelque chose** to treat oneself to something □ Je me suis offert un nouveau sac. I treated myself to a new bag.

l' **oie** FEM NOUN
goose

l' **oignon** MASC NOUN
onion
■ **Ce ne sont pas mes oignons!** *(informal)* It's none of my business!

　LANGUAGE TIP Word for word, this means 'these aren't my onions'.

l' **oiseau** (PL les **oiseaux**) MASC NOUN
bird

l' **olive** FEM NOUN
olive
□ l'huile d'olive olive oil

olympique (FEM **olympique**) ADJECTIVE
■ **les Jeux olympiques** the Olympic Games

l' **ombre** FEM NOUN
1 shade
□ Je vais me mettre à l'ombre. I'm going to sit in the shade.
2 shadow
■ **l'ombre à paupières** eye shadow

l' **omelette** FEM NOUN
omelette

l' **omnibus** MASC NOUN
local train

on PRONOUN
1 we
□ On va à la plage demain. We're going to the beach tomorrow. □ On a pensé que ça te ferait plaisir. We thought you'd be pleased.
2 someone
□ On m'a volé mon sac. Someone has stolen my bag.
■ **On m'a dit d'attendre.** I was told to wait.
■ **On vous demande au téléphone.** There's a phone call for you.
3 you
□ On peut visiter le château en été. You can visit the castle in the summer. □ D'ici on peut voir la côte française. From here you can see the French coast.

l' **oncle** MASC NOUN

o

uncle

l' **onde** FEM NOUN
wave *(on radio)*
□ sur les grandes ondes on long wave

l' **ongle** MASC NOUN
nail
■ **se couper les ongles** to cut one's nails
□ Elle s'est coupé les ongles. She cut her nails.

ont VERB ▷ *see* **avoir**
■ **Ils ont beaucoup d'argent.** They've got lots of money.
■ **Elles ont passé de bonnes vacances.** They had a good holiday.

l' **ONU** FEM NOUN *(= Organisation des Nations unies)*
UN *(= United Nations)*

onze NUMBER
eleven
□ Elle a onze ans. She's eleven. □ à onze heures at eleven o'clock
■ **le onze février** the eleventh of February

onzième (FEM **onzième**) ADJECTIVE
eleventh
□ au onzième étage on the eleventh floor

l' **opéra** MASC NOUN
opera

l' **opération** FEM NOUN
operation

opérer VERB [34]
to operate on
□ Elle a été opérée de l'appendicite. She was operated on for appendicitis.
■ **se faire opérer** to have an operation
□ Elle s'est fait opérer. She's had an operation.

l' **opinion** FEM NOUN
opinion

opposé (FEM **opposée**) ADJECTIVE
▷ *see also* **opposé** NOUN
opposite
□ Elle est partie dans la direction opposée. She went off in the opposite direction.
■ **être opposé à quelque chose** to be opposed to something

l' **opposé** MASC NOUN
▷ *see also* **opposé** ADJECTIVE
the opposite

opposer VERB [28]
■ **opposer quelqu'un à quelqu'un** to pit somebody against somebody □ Ce match oppose les Français aux Allemands. This match pits the French against the Germans.
■ **s'opposer** to conflict □ Ces deux points de vue s'opposent. These two points of view conflict.
■ **s'opposer à quelque chose** to oppose

something □ Son père s'oppose à son mariage. Her father's against her marriage.

l' **opposition** FEM NOUN
opposition
■ **par opposition à** as opposed to □ la littérature contemporaine par opposition à la littérature classique modern literature, as opposed to classics
■ **faire opposition à un chèque** to stop a cheque

l' **opticien** MASC NOUN
optician
□ Il est opticien. He's an optician.

l' **opticienne** FEM NOUN
optician
□ Elle est opticienne. She's an optician.

optimiste (FEM **optimiste**) ADJECTIVE
optimistic

l' **option** FEM NOUN
option
■ **une matière à option** an optional subject

l' **or** MASC NOUN
▷ *see also* **or** CONJUNCTION
gold
□ un bracelet en or a gold bracelet

or CONJUNCTION
▷ *see also* **or** NOUN
and yet
□ Il était sûr de gagner, or il a perdu. He was sure he would win, and yet he lost.

l' **orage** MASC NOUN
thunderstorm

orageux (FEM **orageuse**) ADJECTIVE
stormy

oral (FEM **orale**, MASC PL **oraux**) ADJECTIVE
▷ *see also* **oral** NOUN
■ **une épreuve orale** an oral exam
■ **à prendre par voie orale** to be taken orally

l' **oral** (PL les **oraux**) MASC NOUN
▷ *see also* **oral** ADJECTIVE
oral *(exam)*
□ un oral de français a French oral

l' **orange** FEM NOUN
▷ *see also* **orange** ADJECTIVE
orange *(fruit)*

orange (FEM+PL **orange**) ADJECTIVE
▷ *see also* **orange** NOUN
orange *(in colour)*
□ des fleurs orange orange flowers

l' **orchestre** MASC NOUN
1 orchestra
□ un orchestre symphonique a symphony orchestra
2 band
□ un orchestre de jazz a jazz band

o

l' **ordi** MASC NOUN *(informal)*
computer

ordinaire (FEM **ordinaire**) ADJECTIVE
▷ *see also* **ordinaire** NOUN
1 ordinary
  □ des gens ordinaires ordinary people
2 standard
  □ un format ordinaire a standard size

l' **ordinaire** MASC NOUN
▷ *see also* **ordinaire** ADJECTIVE
two-star (petrol)
  ■ **sortir de l'ordinaire** to be out of the ordinary

l' **ordinateur** MASC NOUN
computer
  ■ **un ordinateur portable** a laptop computer

l' **ordonnance** FEM NOUN
prescription

ordonné (FEM **ordonnée**) ADJECTIVE
tidy

ordonner VERB [28]
  ■ **ordonner à quelqu'un de faire quelque chose** to order somebody to do something

l' **ordre** MASC NOUN
order
  □ par ordre alphabétique in alphabetical order
  ■ **dans l'ordre** in order □ dans le bon ordre in the right order
  ■ **mettre en ordre** to tidy up
  ■ **jusqu'à nouvel ordre** until further notice

les **ordures** FEM PL NOUN
rubbish
  ■ **jeter quelque chose aux ordures** to throw something in the bin

l' **oreille** FEM NOUN
ear

l' **oreiller** MASC NOUN
pillow

les **oreillons** MASC PL NOUN
mumps

l' **organe** MASC NOUN
organ *(in body)*

l' **organisateur** MASC NOUN
organizer

l' **organisation** FEM NOUN
organization

l' **organisatrice** FEM NOUN
organizer

organiser VERB [28]
to organize
  ■ **s'organiser** to get organized □ Il ne sait pas s'organiser. He can't get himself organized.

l' **organisme** MASC NOUN
body *(organization)*

l' **orgue** MASC NOUN
organ
  □ Carl joue de l'orgue. Carl plays the organ.

orgueilleux (FEM **orgueilleuse**) ADJECTIVE
proud

l' **Orient** MASC NOUN
East
  □ en Orient in the East

oriental (FEM **orientale**, MASC PL **orientaux**)
ADJECTIVE
1 oriental
  □ un palais oriental an oriental palace
2 eastern
  □ la frontière orientale de la Pologne Poland's eastern border

l' **orientation** FEM NOUN
orientation
  ■ **avoir le sens de l'orientation** to have a good sense of direction
  ■ **l'orientation professionnelle** careers advice

originaire (FEM **originaire**) ADJECTIVE
  ■ **Elle est originaire de Paris.** She's from Paris.

original (FEM **originale**, MASC PL **originaux**)
ADJECTIVE
▷ *see also* **original** NOUN
original
  □ un film en version originale a film in the original language

l' **original** (PL les **originaux**) MASC NOUN
▷ *see also* **original** ADJECTIVE
original
  □ L'original est au Louvre. The original is in the Louvre.
  ■ **un vieil original** an old eccentric

l' **origine** FEM NOUN
origin
  ■ **à l'origine** originally

l' **orphelin** MASC NOUN
orphan

l' **orpheline** FEM NOUN
orphan

l' **orteil** MASC NOUN
toe

l' **orthographe** FEM NOUN
spelling

l' **os** MASC NOUN
bone
  ■ **tomber sur un os** *(informal)* to hit a snag
  ○ **LANGUAGE TIP** Word for word, this means 'to come across a bone'.

oser VERB [28]
to dare
  ■ **oser faire quelque chose** to dare to do something

l' **otage** MASC NOUN

hostage

ôter VERB [28]

1 to take off

□ Elle a ôté son manteau. She took off her coat.

2 to take away

ou CONJUNCTION

or

■ ou ... ou ... either ... or ...

■ ou bien or else □ On pourrait aller au cinéma ou bien rentrer directement. We could go to the cinema or else go straight home.

où PRONOUN, ADVERB

1 where

□ Où est Nick? Where's Nick? □ Où allez-vous? Where are you going? □ Je sais où il est. I know where he is. □ C'est la maison où je suis né. That's the house where I was born. □ la ville d'où je viens the town I come from

2 that

□ Le jour où il est parti, tout le monde a pleuré. The day that he left, everyone cried.

■ Par où allons-nous passer? Which way are we going to go?

l' **ouate** FEM NOUN

cotton wool

oublier VERB [19]

1 to forget

□ N'oublie pas de fermer la porte. Don't forget to shut the door.

2 to leave

□ J'ai oublié mon sac chez Sabine. I left my bag at Sabine's.

l' **ouest** MASC NOUN

▷ see also **ouest** ADJECTIVE

west

□ Elle vit dans l'ouest de l'Angleterre. She lives in the West of England.

■ à l'ouest de Paris west of Paris

■ vers l'ouest westwards

■ l'Europe de l'Ouest Western Europe

■ le vent d'ouest the west wind

ouest (FEM+PL **ouest**) ADJECTIVE

▷ see also **ouest** NOUN

1 west

□ la côte ouest de l'Écosse the west coast of Scotland

2 western

□ la partie ouest du pays the western part of the country

ouf EXCLAMATION

phew!

oui ADVERB

yes

l' **ouragan** MASC NOUN

hurricane

l' **ourlet** MASC NOUN

seam

l' **ours** MASC NOUN

bear

■ un ours en peluche a teddy bear

l' **outil** MASC NOUN

tool

outré (FEM **outrée**) ADJECTIVE

outraged

□ Il a été outré de son insolence. He was outraged at her cheek.

ouvert VERB ▷ see ouvrir

ouvert (FEM **ouverte**) ADJECTIVE

1 open

□ Le magasin est ouvert. The shop's open.

2 on

□ Il a laissé le robinet ouvert. He left the tap on.

■ avoir l'esprit ouvert to be open-minded

l' **ouverture** FEM NOUN

opening

□ les heures d'ouverture opening hours

l' **ouvre-boîte** MASC NOUN

tin opener

l' **ouvre-bouteille** MASC NOUN

bottle-opener

l' **ouvreuse** FEM NOUN

usherette

l' **ouvrier** MASC NOUN

worker

□ Son père est ouvrier dans une usine. His father's a factory worker.

l' **ouvrière** FEM NOUN

worker

ouvrir VERB [55]

to open

□ Ouvrez! Open up! □ Elle a ouvert la porte. She opened the door.

■ s'ouvrir to open □ La porte s'est ouverte. The door opened.

ovale (FEM **ovale**) ADJECTIVE

oval

l' **ovni** MASC NOUN (= objet volant non identifié)

UFO

l' **oxygène** MASC NOUN

oxygen

l' **ozone** MASC NOUN

ozone

Pp

le **Pacifique** NOUN
Pacific
□ l'océan Pacifique the Pacific Ocean

le **pacifiste** NOUN
pacifist

la **pagaille** NOUN
mess
□ Quelle pagaille! What a mess!

la **page** NOUN
page
□ Tournez la page. Turn the page.
■ **la page d'accueil** (on internet) the home page

la **paie** NOUN
wages

le **paiement** NOUN
payment

le **paillasson** NOUN
doormat

la **paille** NOUN
straw

le **pain** NOUN
1 bread
□ un morceau de pain a piece of bread
□ une tranche de pain a slice of bread
2 loaf
□ J'ai acheté un pain. I bought a loaf of bread.
■ **le pain complet** wholemeal bread
■ **le pain d'épice** gingerbread
■ **le pain de mie** sandwich loaf
■ **le pain grillé** toast

> **DID YOU KNOW...?**
> Bread is always served with a meal in French restaurants, at no extra cost.

pair (FEM **paire**) ADJECTIVE
▷ see also **paire** NOUN
even
□ un nombre pair an even number
■ **une jeune fille au pair** an au pair

la **paire** NOUN
▷ see also **paire** ADJECTIVE
pair
□ une paire de chaussures a pair of shoes

paisible (FEM **paisible**) ADJECTIVE

peaceful
□ un village paisible a peaceful village

la **paix** NOUN
peace
■ **faire la paix** 1 to make peace □ Les deux pays ont fait la paix. The two countries have made peace with each other. 2 to make it up □ Laure a fait la paix avec son frère. Laure made it up with her brother.
■ **avoir la paix** to have peace and quiet
□ J'aimerais bien avoir la paix. I'd like to have a bit of peace and quiet.
■ **Fiche-moi la paix!** (informal) Leave me alone!

le **palais** NOUN
1 palace
□ le palais de Buckingham Buckingham Palace
2 palate (in mouth)

pâle (FEM **pâle**) ADJECTIVE
pale
□ bleu pâle pale blue

la **Palestine** NOUN
Palestine

la **pâleur** NOUN
paleness

le **palier** NOUN
landing
□ Il m'attendait sur le palier. He was waiting for me on the landing.

pâlir VERB [38]
to go pale

la **palme** NOUN
flipper (for swimming)

palmé (FEM **palmée**) ADJECTIVE
webbed
□ Les canards ont les pieds palmés. Ducks have webbed feet.

le **palmier** NOUN
palm tree

palpitant (FEM **palpitante**) ADJECTIVE
thrilling
□ un roman palpitant a thrilling novel

le **pamplemousse** NOUN
grapefruit

P

le **panaché** NOUN
shandy

la **pancarte** NOUN
sign
□ Il y a une pancarte dans la vitrine. There's a sign in the window.

pané (FEM **panée**) ADJECTIVE
fried in breadcrumbs
□ du poisson pané fish in breadcrumbs

le **panier** NOUN
basket

la **panique** NOUN
panic

paniquer VERB [28]
to panic

la **panne** NOUN
breakdown
■ **être en panne** to have broken down
□ L'ascenseur est en panne. The lift's not working.
■ **tomber en panne** to break down □ Nous sommes tombés en panne sur l'autoroute. We broke down on the motorway.
■ **Nous sommes tombés en panne d'essence.** We've run out of petrol.
■ **une panne de courant** a power cut

le **panneau** (PL les **panneaux**) NOUN
sign
□ Ce panneau dit que la maison est à vendre. This sign says that the house is for sale.
■ **panneau d'affichage 1** advertising hoarding **2** (in station) arrivals and departures board **3** (on internet) a bulletin board

le **panorama** NOUN
panorama

le **pansement** NOUN
1 dressing (bandage)
2 sticking plaster

le **pantalon** NOUN
trousers
□ Son pantalon est trop court. His trousers are too short.
■ **un pantalon de ski** a pair of ski pants

la **panthère** NOUN
panther

la **pantoufle** NOUN
slipper

la **PAO** ABBREVIATION (= publication assistée par ordinateur)
DTP (= desktop publishing)

le **paon** NOUN
peacock

le **papa** NOUN
dad

le **pape** NOUN

pope

la **papeterie** NOUN
stationer's

le **papi** NOUN (informal)
granddad

le **papier** NOUN
paper
□ une feuille de papier a sheet of paper
■ **Vos papiers, s'il vous plaît.** Your identity papers, please.
■ **les papiers d'identité** identity papers
■ **le papier à lettres** writing paper
■ **le papier hygiénique** toilet paper
■ **le papier peint** wallpaper

le **papillon** NOUN
butterfly

le **paquebot** NOUN
liner

la **pâquerette** NOUN
daisy

Pâques MASC NOUN
Easter
□ Je viendrai te voir à Pâques. I'll come and see you at Easter.
■ **les œufs de Pâques** Easter eggs

DID YOU KNOW...?
In France, Easter eggs are said to be brought by the Easter bells or **cloches de Pâques** which fly from Rome and drop them in people's gardens.

le **paquet** NOUN
1 packet
□ Je voudrais un paquet de chewing-gums. I'd like a packet of chewing-gum.
2 parcel
□ Sa mère lui a envoyé un paquet. His mother sent him a parcel.

le **paquet-cadeau** (PL les **paquets-cadeaux**) NOUN
gift-wrapped parcel
□ La vendeuse m'a fait un paquet-cadeau. The shop assistant gift-wrapped it for me.

par PREPOSITION
1 by
□ L'Amérique a été découverte par Christophe Colomb. America was discovered by Christopher Columbus.
■ **deux par deux** two by two □ Les élèves sont entrés deux par deux. The pupils went in two by two.
2 with
□ Son nom commence par un H. His name begins with H.
3 out of
□ Elle regardait par la fenêtre. She was looking out of the window. □ par habitude out of habit

4 via

□ Nous sommes passés par Lyon pour aller à Grenoble. We went via Lyons to Grenoble.

5 through

□ Il faut passer par la douane avant de prendre l'avion. You have to go through customs before boarding the plane.

6 per

□ Prenez trois cachets par jour. Take three tablets per day. □ Le voyage coûte deux mille euros par personne. The trip costs two thousand euros per person.

■ **par ici 1** this way □ Il faut passer par ici pour y arriver. You have to go this way to get there. **2** round here □ Il y a beaucoup de touristes par ici. There are lots of tourists round here.

■ **par-ci, par-là** here and there

le **parachute** NOUN
parachute

le/la **parachutiste** NOUN
parachutist

le **paradis** NOUN
heaven

les **parages** MASC PL NOUN

■ **dans les parages** in the area □ Il n'y a pas d'hôtel dans les parages. There are no hotels in the area.

le **paragraphe** NOUN
paragraph

paraître VERB [56]

1 to seem

□ Ça paraît incroyable. It seems unbelievable.

2 to look

□ Elle paraît plus jeune que son frère. She looks younger than her brother.

■ **il paraît que** it seems that □ Il paraît que c'est la faute de la direction. It seems that it's the management's fault.

le **parallèle** NOUN
▷ see also **la parallèle**
parallel

□ Il a fait un parallèle entre ces deux événements. He drew a parallel between the two events.

la **parallèle** NOUN
▷ see also **le parallèle**
parallel line

paralysé (FEM **paralysée**) ADJECTIVE
paralysed

le **parapluie** NOUN
umbrella

le **parasol** NOUN
parasol

le **parc** NOUN

1 park

□ Le dimanche, Chantal va se promener au parc. On Sundays Chantal goes for a walk in the park.

■ **un parc d'attractions** an amusement park

2 grounds

□ Le château est situé au milieu d'un grand parc. The castle is surrounded by extensive grounds.

parce que CONJUNCTION
because

□ Il n'est pas venu parce qu'il n'avait pas de voiture. He didn't come because he didn't have a car.

le **parcmètre** NOUN
parking meter

parcourir VERB [16]

1 to cover

□ Gavin a parcouru cinquante kilomètres à vélo. Gavin covered 50 kilometres on his bike.

2 to glance through

□ J'ai parcouru le journal d'aujourd'hui. I glanced through today's newspaper.

le **parcours** NOUN
journey

par-dessous ADVERB
underneath

□ Il portait un pull et une chemise par-dessous. He was wearing a jumper with a shirt underneath.

par-dessus ADVERB, PREPOSITION

1 on top

□ Elle porte un chemisier et un pull rouge par-dessus. She's wearing a blouse with a red jumper on top.

2 over

□ Elle a sauté par-dessus le mur. She jumped over the wall.

■ **en avoir par-dessus la tête** to have had enough □ J'en ai par-dessus la tête de tous ces problèmes. I've had enough of all these problems.

le **pardessus** NOUN
overcoat

le **pardon** NOUN
▷ see also **pardon** EXCLAMATION
forgiveness

pardon EXCLAMATION
▷ see also **pardon** NOUN

1 sorry!

□ Oh, pardon! J'espère que je ne vous ai pas fait mal. Oh, sorry! I hope I didn't hurt you.

■ **demander pardon à quelqu'un** to apologize to somebody □ Il leur a demandé pardon. He apologized to them.

■ **Je vous demande pardon.** I'm sorry.

2 excuse me!

□ Pardon, madame! Pouvez-vous me dire

P

où se trouve la poste? Excuse me! Could you tell me where the post office is?

3 pardon?

□ Pardon? Je n'ai pas compris ce que vous avez dit. Pardon? I didn't understand what you said.

pardonner VERB [28]
to forgive

□ Nous lui avons pardonné de nous avoir menti. We forgave him for lying to us.

le **pare-brise** (PL les **pare-brise**) NOUN
windscreen

le **pare-chocs** NOUN
bumper

pareil (FEM **pareille**) ADJECTIVE

1 the same

□ Ces deux maisons ne sont pas pareilles. These two houses aren't the same.

2 like that

□ J'aime bien sa voiture. J'en voudrais une pareille. I like his car. I'd like one like that.

3 such

□ Je refuse d'écouter des bêtises pareilles. I won't listen to such nonsense.

■ **sans pareil** unequalled □ un talent sans pareil. an unequalled talent.

la **parenthèse** NOUN
bracket

□ entre parenthèses in brackets

les **parents** MASC PL NOUN

1 parents (mother and father)

2 relatives

□ parents et amis friends and relatives

la **paresse** NOUN
laziness

paresseux (FEM **paresseuse**) ADJECTIVE
lazy

parfait (FEM **parfaite**) ADJECTIVE
perfect

parfaitement ADVERB
perfectly

□ Il parle parfaitement l'arabe. He speaks perfect Arabic.

parfois ADVERB
sometimes

le **parfum** NOUN

1 perfume

2 flavour

□ Je voudrais une glace. — Quel parfum veux-tu? I'd like an ice cream. — What flavour would you like?

parfumé (FEM **parfumée**) ADJECTIVE

1 fragrant

□ une rose très parfumée a very fragrant rose

2 flavoured

□ des biscuits parfumés au café coffee-

flavoured biscuits

la **parfumerie** NOUN
perfume shop

le **pari** NOUN
bet

parier VERB [19]
to bet

Paris NOUN
Paris

■ **à Paris 1** in Paris **2** to Paris

parisien (FEM **parisienne**) ADJECTIVE, NOUN

1 Parisian

□ un célèbre couturier parisien a famous Parisian designer

2 Paris

□ le métro parisien the Paris metro

■ **un Parisien** a Parisian (man)

■ **une Parisienne** a Parisian (woman)

le **parking** NOUN
car park

> **LANGUAGE TIP** Be careful! The French word **parking** does not mean **parking**.

le **parlement** NOUN
parliament

parler VERB [28]

1 to speak

□ Vous parlez français? Do you speak French?

2 to talk

□ Nous étions en train de parler quand le directeur est entré. We were talking when the headmaster came in.

■ **parler de quelque chose à quelqu'un** to tell somebody about something □ Il m'a parlé de sa nouvelle voiture. He told me about his new car.

parmi PREPOSITION
among

□ Ils étaient parmi les meilleurs de la classe. They were among the best pupils in the class.

la **paroi** NOUN
wall

la **paroisse** NOUN
parish

la **parole** NOUN

1 speech

□ l'usage de la parole the power of speech

2 word

□ Il m'a donné sa parole. He gave me his word. □ Elle a tenu parole. She kept her word.

■ **les paroles** lyrics □ J'aime les paroles de cette chanson. I like the lyrics of this song.

le **parquet** NOUN
floor (wooden)

le **parrain** NOUN
godfather

parrainer VERB [28]
to sponsor
□ Cette entreprise parraine notre équipe de rugby. This firm is sponsoring our rugby team

pars VERB ▷ see partir

la **part** NOUN
1 share
□ Vous n'avez pas eu votre part. You haven't had your share.
2 piece
□ une part de gâteau a piece of cake
■ **prendre part à quelque chose** to take part in something □ Il va prendre part à la réunion. He's going to take part in the meeting.
■ **de la part de 1** on behalf of □ Je dois vous remercier de la part de mon frère. I must thank you on behalf of my brother. **2** from □ C'est un cadeau pour toi, de la part de Françoise. It's a present for you, from Françoise.
■ **à part** except □ Ils sont tous venus, à part Christian. They all came, except Christian.

partager VERB [45]
1 to share
□ Ils partagent un appartement. They share a flat.
2 to divide
□ Janet a partagé le gâteau en quatre. Janet divided the cake into four.

le/la **partenaire** NOUN
partner

le **parti** NOUN
party
□ le Parti socialiste the Socialist Party

le **participant** NOUN
participant

la **participante** NOUN
participant

la **participation** NOUN
participation

le **participe** NOUN
participle
■ **le participe passé** the past participle
■ **le participe présent** the present participle

participer VERB [28]
■ **participer à quelque chose 1** to take part in something □ André va participer à la course. André is going to take part in the race. **2** to contribute to something □ Je voudrais participer aux frais. I would like to contribute to the cost.

la **particularité** NOUN
characteristic

particulier (FEM **particulière**) ADJECTIVE
1 private
□ une maison particulière a private house
2 distinctive
□ Ce vin a un arôme particulier. This wine has a distinctive flavour.
3 particular
□ Dans ce cas particulier, je ne peux rien faire. In this particular case, I can't do anything.
■ **en particulier 1** particularly □ J'aime les fruits, en particulier les fraises. I like fruit, particularly strawberries. **2** in private □ Est-ce que je peux vous parler en particulier? Can I speak to you in private?

particulièrement ADVERB
particularly

la **partie** NOUN
1 part
□ Une partie du groupe partira en Italie. Part of the group will go to Italy.
2 game
□ Nous avons fait une partie de tennis. We played a game of tennis. □ une partie de cartes a game of cards
■ **en partie** partly □ Cela explique en partie le problème. That partly explains the problem.
■ **en grande partie** largely □ Son histoire est en grande partie vraie. His story is largely true.
■ **faire partie de** to be part of □ Ce tableau fait partie d'une très belle collection. This picture is part of a very beautiful collection.

partiel (FEM **partielle**) ADJECTIVE
partial

partir VERB [57]
to go
□ Je lui ai téléphoné mais il était déjà parti. I phoned him but he'd already gone.
■ **partir en vacances** to go on holiday
■ **partir de** to leave □ Il est parti de Nice à sept heures. He left Nice at 7.
■ **à partir de** from □ Je serai chez moi à partir de huit heures. I'll be at home from eight o'clock onwards.

la **partition** NOUN
score (in music)
□ une partition de piano a piano score

partout ADVERB
everywhere

paru VERB ▷ see paraître

la **parution** NOUN
publication
□ Ce roman a eu beaucoup de succès dès sa parution. This novel was very successful

from the moment it came out.

parvenir VERB [89]

■ **parvenir à faire quelque chose** to manage to do something □ Elle est finalement parvenue à ouvrir la porte. She finally managed to open the door.

■ **faire parvenir quelque chose à quelqu'un** to send something to somebody □ Je vous ferai parvenir le colis avant lundi. I'll send you the parcel before Monday.

pas ADVERB

▷ *see also* **pas** NOUN

■ **ne ... pas** not □ Il ne pleut pas. It's not raining. □ Elle n'est pas venue. She didn't come. □ Ils n'ont pas de voiture. They haven't got a car.

■ **Vous viendrez à notre soirée, n'est-ce pas?** You're coming to our party, aren't you?

■ **C'est Harry qui a gagné, n'est-ce pas?** Harry won, didn't he?

■ **pas moi** not me □ Elle veut aller au cinéma, pas moi. She wants to go to the cinema, but I don't.

■ **pas du tout** not at all □ Je n'aime pas du tout ça. I don't like that at all.

■ **pas mal** not bad □ Ce n'est pas mal pour un début. That's not bad for a first attempt. □ Comment allez-vous? — Pas mal. How are you? — Not bad.

■ **pas mal de** quite a lot of □ Il y avait pas mal de monde au concert. There were quite a lot of people at the concert.

le pas NOUN

▷ *see also* **pas** ADVERB

1 pace
□ Il marchait d'un pas rapide. He walked at a fast pace.

2 step
□ Faites trois pas en avant. Take three steps forward. □ un pas en arrière a step backwards

3 footstep
□ J'entends des pas dans l'escalier. I can hear footsteps on the stairs.

■ **au pas** at walking pace □ Le cheval est parti au pas. The horse set off at walking pace.

■ **faire les cent pas** to pace up and down □ Il faisait les cent pas dans le couloir. He was pacing up and down the corridor.

le passage NOUN
passage
□ J'ai traduit un passage de ce livre. I translated a passage from this book.

■ **Il a été éclaboussé au passage de la voiture.** He was soaked by a passing car.

■ **de passage** passing through □ Nous

sommes de passage à Toulouse. We're just passing through Toulouse.

■ **un passage à niveau** a level crossing

■ **un passage clouté** a pedestrian crossing

■ **un passage protégé** a pedestrian crossing

■ **un passage souterrain** a subway

passager (FEM **passagère**) ADJECTIVE
▷ *see also* **passager** NOUN, **passagère** NOUN
temporary

le passager NOUN
▷ *see also* **passager** ADJECTIVE
passenger

■ **un passager clandestin** a stowaway

la passagère NOUN
▷ *see also* **passagère** ADJECTIVE
passenger

le passant NOUN
passer-by

la passante NOUN
passer-by

passé (FEM **passée**) ADJECTIVE
▷ *see also* **passé** NOUN

1 last
□ Je l'ai vu la semaine passée. I saw him last week.

2 past
□ Il est minuit passé. It's past midnight.

le passé NOUN
▷ *see also* **passé** ADJECTIVE

1 past
□ dans le passé in the past

2 past tense
□ Mettez ce verbe au passé. Put this verb into the past tense.

■ **le passé composé** the perfect tense

■ **le passé simple** the past historic

le passeport NOUN
passport

passer VERB [58]

1 to cross
□ Nous avons passé la frontière belge. We crossed the Belgian border.

2 to go through
□ Il faut passer la douane en sortant. You have to go through customs on the way out.

3 to spend
□ Elle a passé la journée à ne rien faire. She spent the day doing nothing. □ Ils passent toujours leurs vacances au Danemark. They always spend their holidays in Denmark.

4 to take
□ Gordon a passé ses examens la semaine dernière. Gordon took his exams last week.

LANGUAGE TIP Be careful! passer un examen does not mean **to pass an exam**.

5 to pass
□ Passe-moi le sel, s'il te plaît. Pass me the salt, please.

6 to show
□ On passe 'Le Kid' au cinéma cette semaine. They're showing 'The Kid' at the cinema this week.

7 to call in
□ Je passerai chez vous ce soir. I'll call in this evening.

■ **passer à la radio** to be on the radio
□ Mon père passe à la radio demain soir. My father's on the radio tomorrow night.

■ **passer à la télévision** to be on the television □ 'Titanic' passe à la télé ce soir. Titanic is on TV tonight.

■ **Ne quittez pas, je vous passe Madame Chevalier.** Hold on please, I'm putting you through to Mrs Chevalier.

■ **passer par** to go through □ Ils sont passés par Paris pour aller à Tours. They went through Paris to get to Tours.

■ **en passant** in passing □ Je lui ai dit en passant que j'allais me marier. I told him in passing that I was getting married.

■ **laisser passer** to let through □ Il m'a laissé passer. He let me through.

■ **se passer 1** to take place □ Cette histoire se passe au moyen âge. This story takes place in the Middle Ages. **2** to go □ Comment se sont passés tes examens? How did your exams go? **3** to happen □ Que s'est-il passé? Un accident? What happened? Was there an accident?

■ **Qu'est-ce qui se passe? Pourquoi est-ce qu'elle pleure?** What's the matter? Why is she crying?

■ **se passer de** to do without □ Je me passerai de café ce matin. I'll do without coffee this morning.

la **passerelle** NOUN
1 footbridge (over river)
2 gangway (onto plane, boat)

le **passe-temps** NOUN
pastime

passif (FEM **passive**) ADJECTIVE
▷ see also **passif** NOUN
passive

le **passif** NOUN
▷ see also **passif** ADJECTIVE
passive
□ Mettez ce verbe au passif. Put this verb into the passive.

la **passion** NOUN
passion

passionnant (FEM **passionnante**) ADJECTIVE
fascinating

passionné (FEM **passionnée**) ADJECTIVE
keen
□ Donald est un lecteur passionné. Donald is a keen reader.

■ **Il est passionné de voile.** He's a sailing fanatic.

passionner VERB [28]
■ **Son travail le passionne.** He's passionate about his work.

■ **se passionner pour quelque chose** to have a passion for something □ Jack se passionne pour les perroquets. Jack has a passion for parrots.

la **passoire** NOUN
sieve

la **pastèque** NOUN
watermelon

le **pasteur** NOUN
minister (priest)

la **pastille** NOUN
cough sweet

la **patate** NOUN (informal)
potato

■ **une patate douce** a sweet potato

la **pâte** NOUN
1 pastry
2 dough
3 cake mixture

■ **la pâte à crêpes** pancake batter

■ **la pâte à modeler** Plasticine®

■ **la pâte d'amandes** marzipan

le **pâté** NOUN
pâté
□ Nous avons mangé du pâté en entrée. We had pâté as a starter.

■ **un pâté de maisons** a block (of houses)

paternel (FEM **paternelle**) ADJECTIVE
■ **ma grand-mère paternelle** my father's mother

■ **mon oncle paternel** my father's brother

les **pâtes** FEM PL NOUN
pasta

la **patience** NOUN
patience

patient (FEM **patiente**) ADJECTIVE
▷ see also **patient** NOUN, **patiente** NOUN
patient

le **patient** NOUN
▷ see also **patient** ADJECTIVE
patient

la **patiente** NOUN
▷ see also **patiente** ADJECTIVE
patient

patienter VERB [28]
to wait
□ Veuillez patienter un instant, s'il vous plaît. Please wait a moment.

le **patin** NOUN
1 skate
 □ Nic a enfilé ses patins. Nic put her skates on.
2 skating
 □ Ils font du patin tous les mercredis. They go skating every Wednesday.
 ■ **les patins à glace** ice skates
 ■ **les patins en ligne** Rollerblades®
 ■ **les patins à roulettes** roller skates

le **patinage** NOUN
 skating
 ■ **le patinage artistique** figure skating

patiner VERB [28]
 to skate

le **patineur** NOUN
 skater

la **patineuse** NOUN
 skater

la **patinoire** NOUN
 ice rink

la **pâtisserie** NOUN
 cake shop
 ■ **faire de la pâtisserie** to bake □ J'adore faire de la pâtisserie. I love baking.
 ■ **les pâtisseries** cakes

le **pâtissier** NOUN
 confectioner

la **pâtissière** NOUN
 confectioner

la **patrie** NOUN
 homeland

le **patron** NOUN
1 boss
2 pattern (for dressmaking)

la **patronne** NOUN
 boss
 ■ **Elle est patronne de café.** She runs a café.

patronner VERB [28]
 to sponsor
 □ Le festival est patronné par des entreprises locales. The festival is sponsored by local businesses.

la **patrouille** NOUN
 patrol

la **patte** NOUN
1 paw (of dog, cat)
2 leg (of bird, animal)

paumer VERB [28] (informal)
 to lose
 □ J'ai paumé mes clefs. I've lost my keys.

la **paupière** NOUN
 eyelid

la **pause** NOUN
1 break
 □ Ils font une pause. They're having a break.
 □ une pause de midi a lunch break
2 pause
 □ Il y a eu une pause dans la conversation. There was a pause in the conversation.

pauvre (FEM **pauvre**) ADJECTIVE
 poor
 □ Sa famille est pauvre. His family is poor.
 □ Pauvre Jean-Pierre! Il n'a pas eu de chance! Poor Jean-Pierre! He was unlucky!

la **pauvreté** NOUN
 poverty

pavé (FEM **pavée**) ADJECTIVE
 cobbled
 □ Les rues étaient pavées. The streets were cobbled.

le **pavillon** NOUN
 house
 □ Ils habitent un pavillon de banlieue. They've got a house in the suburbs.

payant (FEM **payante**) ADJECTIVE
 paying
 □ Ce sont des hôtes payants. They're paying guests.
 ■ **C'est payant.** You have to pay. □ L'entrée de la boîte est payante. You have to pay to get into the nightclub.

la **paye** NOUN
 wages

payer VERB [59]
1 to pay for
 □ Combien as-tu payé ta voiture? How much did you pay for your car?
 ■ **J'ai payé ce T-shirt vingt euros.** I paid 20 euros for this T-shirt.
2 to pay
 □ Elle a été payée aujourd'hui. She got paid today. □ Son métier paye bien. His job pays good money. □ Elle est mal payée. She is badly paid.
 ■ **faire payer quelque chose à quelqu'un** to charge somebody for something □ Il me l'a fait payer dix euros. He charged me 10 euros for it.
 ■ **payer quelque chose à quelqu'un** to buy somebody something □ Allez, je vous paye un verre. Come on, I'll buy you a drink.

le **pays** NOUN
 country
 ■ **du pays** local □ le vin du pays the local wine

le **paysage** NOUN
 landscape

le **paysan** NOUN
 farmer

la **paysanne** NOUN
 farmer

les **Pays-Bas** MASC PL NOUN

Netherlands
■ **aux Pays-Bas 1** in the Netherlands **2** to the Netherlands

le **pays de Galles** NOUN
Wales

■ **au pays de Galles 1** in Wales □ Daphne habite au pays de Galles. Daphne lives in Wales. **2** to Wales □ Elle part au pays de Galles la semaine prochaine. She is going to Wales next week.

le **PC** NOUN
▷ *see also* **PC** ABBREVIATION
PC (= *personal computer*)
□ Il a tapé le rapport sur son PC. He typed the report on his PC.

PC ABBREVIATION (= *Parti communiste*)
▷ *see also* **PC** NOUN
Communist Party

le **PDG** NOUN (= *président-directeur général*)
MD (= *managing director*)

le **péage** NOUN
1 toll
□ Nous avons payé vingt euros de péage. We paid a toll of 20 euros.
2 tollbooth
□ Sabine s'est arrêtée au péage de l'autoroute. Sabine stopped at the motorway tollbooth.

⊙ **DID YOU KNOW...?**
French motorways charge a toll.

la **peau** (PL les **peaux**) NOUN
skin
□ Elle a la peau douce. She's got soft skin.

le/la **Peau-Rouge** (PL les **Peaux-Rouges**) NOUN
Red Indian

la **pêche** NOUN
1 peach
2 fishing
■ **aller à la pêche** to go fishing
■ **la pêche à la ligne** angling

le **péché** NOUN
sin

pêcher VERB [28]
1 to fish for
□ Ils sont partis pêcher la truite. They've gone fishing for trout.
2 to catch
□ Jacques a pêché deux saumons. Jacques caught two salmon.

le **pêcheur** NOUN
fisherman
□ Son père est pêcheur. His father's a fisherman.
■ **un pêcheur à la ligne** an angler

pédagogique (FEM **pédagogique**) ADJECTIVE
educational

la **pédale** NOUN
pedal

le **pédalo** NOUN
pedalo

pédestre (FEM **pédestre**) ADJECTIVE
■ **une randonnée pédestre** a ramble

le **peigne** NOUN
comb

peigner VERB [28]
to comb
□ Elle peigne sa poupée. She's combing her doll's hair.
■ **se peigner** to comb one's hair □ Il faut que je me peigne. I must comb my hair.

le **peignoir** NOUN
dressing gown
■ **un peignoir de bain** a bathrobe

peindre VERB [60]
to paint

la **peine** NOUN
trouble
■ **avoir de la peine à faire quelque chose** to have trouble doing something □ J'ai eu beaucoup de peine à la convaincre. I had a lot of trouble convincing her.
■ **se donner de la peine** to make a real effort □ Il s'est donné beaucoup de peine pour obtenir ces renseignements. He made a real effort to get this information.
■ **prendre la peine de faire quelque chose** to go to the trouble of doing something □ Il a pris la peine de me rapporter ma valise. He went to the trouble of returning my case to me.
■ **faire de la peine à quelqu'un** to upset somebody □ Ça me fait de la peine de la voir pleurer. It upsets me to see her crying.
■ **ce n'est pas la peine** there's no point □ Ce n'est pas la peine de téléphoner. There's no point in phoning.
■ **à peine 1** hardly □ J'ai à peine eu le temps de me changer. I hardly had time to get changed. **2** only just □ Elle vient à peine de se lever. She's only just got up.

le **peintre** NOUN
painter

la **peinture** NOUN
1 painting
□ On expose des peintures d'Aurélie au musée. There's an exhibition of Aurélie's paintings at the museum.
2 paint
□ J'ai acheté de la peinture verte. I bought some green paint.
■ **'peinture fraîche'** 'wet paint'

pêle-mêle ADVERB
higgledy-piggledy

197

peler VERB [43]
to peel

la **pelle** NOUN
1 shovel
2 spade

la **pellicule** NOUN
film
□ une pellicule couleur a colour film

les **pellicules** FEM PL NOUN
dandruff

la **pelote** NOUN
ball
□ une pelote de laine a ball of wool

la **pelouse** NOUN
lawn

la **peluche** NOUN
■ un animal en peluche a soft toy

le **penchant** NOUN
■ avoir un penchant pour quelque chose
to have a liking for something

pencher VERB [28]
to tilt
□ Ce tableau penche vers la droite. The
picture's tilting to the right.
■ se pencher 1 to lean over □ Françoise
s'est penchée sur son cahier. Françoise
leant over her exercise book. 2 to bend
down □ Il s'est penché pour ramasser sa
casquette. He bent down to pick his cap up.
3 to lean out □ Annick s'est penchée par la
fenêtre. Annick leant out of the window.

pendant PREPOSITION
during
□ Ça s'est passé pendant l'été. It happened
during the summer.
■ pendant que while □ Christian a
téléphoné pendant que Chantal prenait son
bain. Christian phoned while Chantal was
having a bath.

le **pendentif** NOUN
pendant

la **penderie** NOUN
wardrobe (for hanging clothes)

pendre VERB [88]
to hang
□ Il a pendu sa veste dans l'armoire. He
hung his jacket in the wardrobe.
■ pendre quelqu'un to hang somebody
□ L'assassin a été pendu. The murderer was
hanged.

la **pendule** NOUN
clock

pénétrer VERB [34]
1 to enter
□ Ils ont pénétré dans la maison en passant
par le jardin. They entered the house
through the garden.

2 to penetrate
□ L'armée a pénétré sur le territoire ennemi.
The army penetrated enemy territory.

pénible (FEM **pénible**) ADJECTIVE
hard
□ Travailler sur un chantier est pénible.
Working on a building site is hard.
■ Il est vraiment pénible. He's a real
nuisance.

péniblement ADVERB
with difficulty

la **péniche** NOUN
barge

le **pénis** NOUN
penis

la **pénombre** NOUN
half-light

la **pensée** NOUN
thought
□ Il était perdu dans ses pensées. He was
lost in thought.

penser VERB [28]
to think
□ Je pense que Yann a eu raison de partir. I
think Yann was right to leave.
■ penser à quelque chose to think about
something □ Je pense à mes vacances. I'm
thinking about my holidays. □ Pensez-y.
Think about it.
■ faire penser quelqu'un à quelque chose
to remind someone of something □ Cette
photo me fait penser à la Grèce. This photo
reminds me of Greece.
■ faire penser quelqu'un à faire quelque
chose to remind someone to do something
□ Fais-moi penser à téléphoner à Claire.
Remind me to phone Claire.
■ penser faire quelque chose to be
planning to do something □ Ils pensent
partir en Espagne en juillet. They're
planning to go to Spain in July.

la **pension** NOUN
1 boarding school
□ Leur fille est en pension. Their daughter is
at boarding school.
2 pension
□ Ma grand-mère reçoit sa pension tous les
mois. My grandma gets her pension every
month.
3 boarding house
■ la pension complète full board

le/la **pensionnaire** NOUN
boarder

le **pensionnat** NOUN
boarding school

la **pente** NOUN
slope

□ une pente raide a steep slope

■ **en pente** sloping □ Le toit de cette maison est en pente. This house has a sloping roof.

la **Pentecôte** NOUN
Whitsun

le **pépin** NOUN

1 pip

□ Cette orange est pleine de pépins. This orange is full of pips.

2 problem

□ avoir un pépin (informal) to have a slight problem

perçant (FEM **perçante**) ADJECTIVE

1 sharp

□ Il a une vue perçante. He has very sharp eyes.

2 piercing

□ un cri perçant a piercing cry

percer VERB [12]
to pierce

□ Elle s'est fait percer les oreilles. She's had her ears pierced.

percuter VERB [28]
to smash into

le **perdant** NOUN
loser

la **perdante** NOUN
loser

perdre VERB [61]
to lose

□ Cécile a perdu ses clés. Cécile's lost her keys.

■ **J'ai perdu mon chemin.** I've lost my way.

■ **perdre un match** to lose a match

■ **perdre du temps** to waste time □ J'ai perdu beaucoup de temps ce matin. I've wasted a lot of time this morning. □ Nous avons perdu notre temps à cette réunion. That meeting was a waste of time.

■ **se perdre** to get lost □ Je me suis perdu en route. I got lost on the way here.

perdu VERB ▷ see perdre

le **père** NOUN
father

■ **le père Noël** Father Christmas

perfectionné (FEM **perfectionnée**) ADJECTIVE
sophisticated

perfectionner VERB [28]
to improve

□ Elle a besoin de perfectionner son anglais. She needs to improve her English.

périmé (FEM **périmée**) ADJECTIVE
out-of-date

□ Mon passeport est périmé. My passport's out of date.

■ Ces yaourts sont périmés. These yoghurts are past their use-by date.

la **période** NOUN
period

périodique (FEM **périodique**) ADJECTIVE
periodic

périphérique (FEM **périphérique**) ADJECTIVE
▷ see also **périphérique** NOUN
outlying

□ un quartier périphérique an outlying district

le **périphérique** NOUN
▷ see also **périphérique** ADJECTIVE
ring road

la **perle** NOUN
pearl

la **permanence** NOUN

■ **assurer une permanence** to operate a basic service □ Ma banque assure une permanence le samedi matin. My bank operates a basic service on Saturday mornings.

■ **être de permanence** to be on duty □ Sophie ne peut pas venir, elle est de permanence ce soir. Sophie can't come, she's on duty tonight.

■ **en permanence** permanently □ Elle se plaint en permanence. She's always complaining.

permanent (FEM **permanente**) ADJECTIVE
▷ see also **permanente** NOUN

1 permanent

□ Il a un poste permanent. He has a permanent job.

2 continuous

□ J'en ai assez de tes critiques permanentes. I've had enough of your constant criticism.

la **permanente** NOUN
▷ see also **permanente** ADJECTIVE
perm

permettre VERB [47]
to allow

■ **permettre à quelqu'un de faire quelque chose** to allow somebody to do something □ Sa mère lui permet de sortir le soir. His mother allows him to go out at night.

le **permis** NOUN
permit

□ Il vous faut un permis pour camper ici. You need a permit to camp here.

■ **le permis de conduire** driving licence

■ **un permis de séjour** a residence permit

■ **un permis de travail** a work permit

la **permission** NOUN
permission

□ Qui t'a donné la permission d'entrer?

Who gave you permission to come in?

■ **avoir la permission de faire quelque chose** to have permission to do something □ J'ai la permission d'utiliser sa chaîne hi-fi. I've got his permission to use his hi-fi.

■ **être en permission** to be on leave (from the army)

le **Pérou** NOUN
Peru

perpétuel (FEM **perpétuelle**) ADJECTIVE
perpetual

perplexe (FEM **perplexe**) ADJECTIVE
puzzled
□ Ma question l'a laissé perplexe. She was puzzled by my question.

le **perroquet** NOUN
parrot

la **perruche** NOUN
budgie

la **perruque** NOUN
wig

le **persil** NOUN
parsley
□ un bouquet de persil a bunch of parsley

> DID YOU KNOW...?
> Most sellers at vegetable stalls on French markets will give you un bouquet de persil with any fruit or vegetables you buy.

le **personnage** NOUN
1 figure
□ les grands personnages de l'histoire de France the important figures in French history
2 character
□ le personnage principal du film the main character in the film

la **personnalité** NOUN
1 personality
□ Ray a une personnalité forte. Ray has a strong personality.
2 prominent figure
□ Il y avait beaucoup de personnalités politiques à ce dîner. There were lots of prominent political figures at the dinner.

la **personne** NOUN
▷ see also **personne** PRONOUN
person
□ Il y avait une trentaine de personnes dans la pièce. There were about 30 people in the room. □ une personne âgée an elderly person
■ **en personne** in person

personne PRONOUN
▷ see also **personne** NOUN
1 nobody
□ Il n'y a personne à la maison. There's

nobody at home. □ Personne n'est venu le chercher. Nobody came to fetch him.
2 anybody
□ Elle ne veut voir personne. She doesn't want to see anybody.

personnel (FEM **personnelle**) ADJECTIVE
▷ see also **personnel** NOUN
personal

le **personnel** NOUN
▷ see also **personnel** ADJECTIVE
staff
□ Il nous faut plus de personnel. We need more staff.
■ **le service du personnel** the personnel department

personnellement ADVERB
personally
□ Personnellement, je ne suis pas d'accord. Personally, I don't agree.

la **perspective** NOUN
prospect
□ Les perspectives sont bonnes. The prospects are good.
■ **perspectives d'avenir** prospects □ Il y a des perspectives d'avenir dans ce métier. This job has good prospects.
■ **en perspective 1** in prospect □ Il y a des changements en perspective. Changes are in prospect. **2** in perspective □ Il a dessiné la maison en perspective. He drew the house in perspective.

persuader VERB [28]
to persuade
■ **persuader quelqu'un de faire quelque chose** to persuade somebody to do something □ Elle m'a persuadé de l'accompagner au cinéma. She persuaded me to go to the cinema with her.

la **perte** NOUN
1 loss
□ des pertes d'emploi job losses
2 waste
□ Cette réunion a été une perte de temps. The meeting was a waste of time.

perturber VERB [28]
to disrupt
□ Les manifestations perturbaient la circulation. The demonstrations disrupted the traffic.

le **pèse-personne** NOUN
bathroom scales
> LANGUAGE TIP Word for word, this means 'a person-weigher'.

peser VERB [43]
to weigh
□ Elle pèse cent kilos. She weighs 100 kilos.

pessimiste (FEM **pessimiste**) ADJECTIVE

pessimistic

le **pétale** NOUN
petal

la **pétanque** NOUN

> **DID YOU KNOW...?**
> **pétanque** is a type of bowls played in France, especially in the south.

le **pétard** NOUN
firecracker

péter VERB [34] *(rude)*
to fart

pétillant (FEM **pétillante**) ADJECTIVE
sparkling

petit (FEM **petite**) ADJECTIVE
1 small
□ Sonia habite une petite ville. Sonia lives in a small town.
2 little
□ Elle a une jolie petite maison. She has a nice little house.
■ **petit à petit** bit by bit
■ **un petit ami** a boyfriend
■ **une petite amie** a girlfriend
■ **le petit déjeuner** breakfast □ prendre le petit déjeuner to have breakfast

> **LANGUAGE TIP** Word for word, **petit déjeuner** means 'little lunch'.

■ **un petit pain** a bread roll
■ **les petites annonces** the small ads
■ **des petits pois** garden peas
■ **les petits** young *(of animal)*
□ la lionne et ses petits the lioness and her young

la **petite-fille** (PL les **petites-filles**) NOUN
granddaughter

le **petit-fils** (PL les **petits-fils**) NOUN
grandson

les **petits-enfants** MASC PL NOUN
grandchildren

le **pétrole** NOUN
oil
□ une lampe à pétrole an oil lamp

> **LANGUAGE TIP** Be careful! **pétrole** does not mean **petrol**.

peu ADVERB, NOUN
not much
□ J'ai peu mangé à midi. I didn't eat much for lunch. □ Il voyage peu. He doesn't travel much.
■ **un peu** a bit □ Elle est un peu timide. She's a bit shy. □ un peu de gâteau a bit of cake
■ **un petit peu** a little bit □ un petit peu de crème a little bit of cream
■ **peu de 1** not many □ Il y a peu de bons films au cinéma. There aren't very many good films on at the cinema. □ Elle a peu

d'amis. She hasn't got many friends. **2** not much □ Il a peu d'espoir de réussir. He doesn't have much hope of succeeding. □ Il lui reste peu d'argent. He hasn't got much money left.
■ **à peu près 1** more or less □ J'ai à peu près fini. I've more or less finished. **2** about □ Le voyage prend à peu près deux heures. The journey takes about two hours.
■ **peu à peu** little by little
■ **peu avant** shortly before
■ **peu après** shortly afterwards
■ **de peu** only just □ Il a manqué son train de peu. He only just missed his train.

le **peuple** NOUN
people
□ le peuple français the French people

la **peur** NOUN
fear
■ **avoir peur de** to be afraid of □ Il a peur du noir. He's afraid of the dark.
■ **avoir peur de faire quelque chose** to be frightened of doing something □ Elle a peur d'y aller toute seule. She's frightened of going on her own.
■ **faire peur à quelqu'un** to frighten somebody □ Cet homme-là me fait peur. That man frightens me.

peureux (FEM **peureuse**) ADJECTIVE
fearful

peut VERB ▷ *see* **pouvoir**
■ **Il ne peut pas venir.** He can't come.

peut-être ADVERB
perhaps
□ Je l'ai peut-être oublié à la maison. Perhaps I've left it at home.
■ **peut-être que** perhaps □ Peut-être qu'elles n'ont pas pu téléphoner. Perhaps they weren't able to phone.

peuvent, peux VERB ▷ *see* **pouvoir**
■ **Je ne peux pas le faire.** I can't do it.

p. ex. ABBREVIATION (= *par exemple*)
e.g.

le **phare** NOUN
1 lighthouse
□ On voit le phare depuis le pont du bateau. You can see the lighthouse from the ship's deck.
2 headlight
□ Elle a laissé ses phares allumés. She left her headlights on.

la **pharmacie** NOUN
chemist's

> **DID YOU KNOW...?**
> Chemist's shops in France are identified by a special green cross outside the shop.

le **pharmacien** NOUN
pharmacist

la **pharmacienne** NOUN
pharmacist

le **phasme** NOUN
stick insect

le **phénomène** NOUN
phenomenon

la **philosophie** NOUN
philosophy

le **phoque** NOUN
seal (animal)

la **photo** NOUN
photograph
□ Elle a fait développé ses photos. She's
had her photographs developed.
■ **en photo** in photographs □ Je n'ai vu
Venise qu'en photo. I've only seen Venice in
photographs.
■ **prendre quelqu'un en photo** to take a
photo of somebody □ Claire nous a pris en
photo. Claire took a photo of us.
■ **une photo d'identité** a passport
photograph

la **photocopie** NOUN
photocopy

photocopier VERB [19]
to photocopy

la **photocopieuse** NOUN
photocopier

le/la **photographe** NOUN
photographer

la **photographie** NOUN
1 photography
2 photograph

photographier VERB [19]
to photograph

le **photophone** NOUN
camera phone

la **phrase** NOUN
sentence

physique (FEM **physique**) ADJECTIVE
▷ see also **physique** NOUN
physical

le **physique** NOUN
▷ see also **la physique** NOUN, **physique**
ADJECTIVE
■ **Il a un physique agréable.** He's quite
good-looking.

la **physique** NOUN
▷ see also **le physique** NOUN, **physique**
ADJECTIVE
physics
□ Il est professeur de physique. He's a
physics teacher.

le/la **pianiste** NOUN
pianist

□ Elle est pianiste. She's a pianist.

le **piano** NOUN
piano

le **pic** NOUN
peak
□ les pics enneigés des Alpes the snowy
peaks of the Alps
■ **à pic 1** vertically □ La falaise tombe à pic
dans la mer. The cliff drops vertically into
the sea.
■ **à pic 1** just at the right time □ Tu es
arrivé à pic. You arrived just at the right
time.

la **pièce** NOUN
1 room
□ Mon lit est au centre de la pièce. My bed is
in the middle of the room.
■ **un cinq-pièces** a five-roomed flat
2 play
□ On joue une pièce de Shakespeare au
théâtre. There's a play by Shakespeare on at
the theatre.
3 part
□ Il faut changer une pièce du moteur.
There's an engine part which needs
changing.
4 coin
□ des pièces d'un euro some one-euro
coins
■ **cinquante euros pièce** 50 euros each
□ J'ai acheté ces T-shirts dix euros pièce. I
bought these T-shirts for ten euros each.
■ **un maillot une pièce** a one-piece
swimsuit
■ **un maillot deux-pièces** a bikini
■ **Avez-vous une pièce d'identité?** Have
you got any identification?
■ **une pièce jointe** an email attachment

le **pied** NOUN
foot
□ J'ai mal aux pieds. My feet are hurting.
■ **à pied** on foot
■ **avoir pied** to be able to touch the bottom
□ Justine n'aime pas nager là où elle n'a pas
pied. Justine doesn't like swimming where
she can't touch the bottom.

le **pied-noir** (PL les **pieds-noirs**) NOUN
> DID YOU KNOW...?
> A **pied-noir** is a French person born in
> Algeria; most of them moved to
> France during the Algerian war in the
> 1950s.

□ Sa grand-mère est pied-noir. His
grandmother was born in Algeria.

le **piège** NOUN
trap
■ **prendre quelqu'un au piège** to trap

somebody

piéger VERB [66]
to trap
■ **un colis piégé** a parcel bomb
■ **une voiture piégée** a car bomb

la **pierre** NOUN
stone
■ **une pierre précieuse** a precious stone

le **piéton** NOUN
pedestrian

la **piétonne** NOUN
pedestrian

piétonnier (FEM **piétonnière**) ADJECTIVE
■ **une rue piétonnière** a pedestrianized
street
■ **un quartier piétonnier** a pedestrianized
area

la **pieuvre** NOUN
octopus

le **pigeon** NOUN
pigeon

piger VERB [45] (informal)
to understand

la **pile** NOUN
▷ see also **pile** ADVERB
1 pile
□ Il y a une pile de disques sur la table.
There's a pile of records on the table.
2 battery
□ La pile de ma montre est usée. The
battery in my watch has run out.

pile ADVERB
▷ see also **pile** NOUN
■ **à deux heures pile** at two on the dot
■ **jouer à pile ou face** to toss up
■ **Pile ou face?** Heads or tails?

le **pilote** NOUN
pilot
■ **un pilote de course** a racing driver
■ **un pilote de ligne** an airline pilot

piloter VERB [28]
to fly (a plane)

la **pilule** NOUN
pill
■ **prendre la pilule** to be on the pill

le **piment** NOUN
chilli

le **pin** NOUN
pine

le **pinard** NOUN (informal)
wine

la **pince** NOUN
1 pliers (tool)
2 pincer (of crab)
■ **une pince à épiler** tweezers
■ **une pince à linge** a clothes peg

le **pinceau** (PL les **pinceaux**) NOUN

paintbrush

la **pincée** NOUN
■ **une pincée de sel** a pinch of salt

pincer VERB [12]
to pinch
□ Elle m'a pincé le bras. She pinched my
arm.

le **pingouin** NOUN
penguin

le **ping-pong** NOUN
table tennis
□ jouer au ping-pong to play table tennis

la **pintade** NOUN
guinea fowl

le **pion** NOUN
1 pawn (in chess)
2 piece (in draughts)
3 supervisor (man)

> **DID YOU KNOW...?**
> In French secondary schools, the
> teachers are not responsible for
> supervising the pupils outside class.
> This job is done by people called
> **pions** or **surveillants**.

la **pionne** NOUN
supervisor (woman)

la **pipe** NOUN
pipe
□ Mon grand-père fume la pipe. My
granddad smokes a pipe.

piquant (FFM **piquante**) ADJECTIVE
1 prickly
2 spicy

le **pique** NOUN
▷ see also **la pique**
spades
□ l'as de pique the ace of spades

la **pique** NOUN
▷ see also **le pique**
cutting remark
□ envoyer des piques à quelqu'un to make
cutting remarks to somebody

le **pique-nique** NOUN
picnic

piquer VERB [28]
1 to bite
□ Nous avons été piqués par les
moustiques. We were bitten by mosquitoes.
2 to burn
□ Cette sauce me pique la langue. This
sauce is burning my tongue.
3 to steal
□ On m'a piqué mon porte-monnaie.
(informal) I've had my purse stolen.
■ **se piquer** to prick oneself □ Il s'est piqué
avec une aiguille. He pricked himself with a
needle.

le **piquet** NOUN
1 post
  □ Le chien est attaché à un piquet. The dog is tied to a post.
2 peg
  □ Il nous manque un des piquets de la tente. One of our tent pegs is missing.

la **piqûre** NOUN
1 injection
  □ Le médecin lui a fait une piqûre. The doctor gave him an injection.
2 bite
  □ une piqûre de moustique a mosquito bite
3 sting
  □ une piqûre d'abeille a bee sting

le **pirate** NOUN
  pirate
  ■ **un pirate informatique** a hacker

pire (FEM **pire**) ADJECTIVE, NOUN
  worse
  □ C'est encore pire qu'avant. It's even worse than before.
  ■ **le pire** the worst □ C'est la pire journée que j'aie jamais passée. That's the worst day I've ever had. □ Ce gamin est le pire de la bande. That boy is the worst in the group.
  ■ **le pire de** the worst of □ Le pire de tout, c'est qu'on s'ennuie tout le temps. The worst of it is that we're always bored.

la **piscine** NOUN
  swimming pool

pisser VERB [28] (informal)
  to have a pee

la **pistache** NOUN
  pistachio
  □ une glace à la pistache a pistachio ice cream

la **piste** NOUN
1 lead
  □ La police est sur une piste. The police are following a lead.
2 runway
  □ L'avion s'est posé sur la piste. The plane landed on the runway.
3 ski run
  □ Le skieur a descendu la piste. The skier came down the ski run.
  ■ **une piste artificielle** a dry ski slope
  ■ **la piste de danse** the dance floor
  ■ **une piste cyclable** a cycle lane

le **pistolet** NOUN
  pistol

pistonner VERB [28]
  ■ Il a été pistonné pour avoir ce travail. They pulled some strings to get him this job.

la **pitié** NOUN
  pity

■ Il me fait pitié. I feel sorry for him.
■ **avoir pitié de quelqu'un** to feel sorry for somebody

pittoresque (FEM **pittoresque**) ADJECTIVE
  picturesque

la **pizza** NOUN
  pizza

le **placard** NOUN
  cupboard

la **place** NOUN
1 place
  □ Vincent a eu la troisième place au concours. Vincent got third place in the competition.
2 square
  □ la place du village the village square
3 space
  □ Il ne reste plus de place pour se garer. There's no more space to park. □ Ça prend de la place. It takes up a lot of room.
4 seat
  □ Toutes les places ont été vendues. All the seats have been sold. □ Il y a vingt places assises. There are 20 seats.
  ■ **remettre quelque chose en place** to put something back in its place
  ■ **sur place** on the spot
  ■ **à la place** instead □ Il ne reste plus de tarte; désirez-vous quelque chose d'autre à la place? There's no pie left; would you like something else instead?
  ■ **à la place de** instead of

placer VERB [12]
1 to seat
  □ Nous étions placés à côté du directeur. We were seated next to the manager.
2 to invest
  □ Il a placé ses économies en Bourse. He invested his money on the Stock Exchange.

le **plafond** NOUN
  ceiling

la **plage** NOUN
  beach

la **plaie** NOUN
  wound

plaindre VERB [17]
  ■ **plaindre quelqu'un** to feel sorry for somebody □ Je te plains. I feel sorry for you.
  ■ **se plaindre** to complain □ Il n'arrête pas de se plaindre. He never stops complaining.
  ■ **se plaindre à quelqu'un** to complain to somebody □ Ils se sont plaints au directeur. They complained to the manager.
  ■ **se plaindre de quelque chose** to complain about something □ Elle s'est plainte du bruit. She complained about the noise.

la **plaine** NOUN
plain *(level area)*

la **plainte** NOUN
complaint

■ **porter plainte** to lodge a complaint

plaire VERB [62]

■ **Ce cadeau me plaît beaucoup.** I like this present a lot.

■ **Ce film plaît beaucoup aux jeunes.** The film is very popular with young people.

■ **Ça t'a plu d'aller en Italie?** Did you enjoy going to Italy?

■ **Elle lui plaît.** He fancies her.

■ **s'il te plaît** please

■ **s'il vous plaît** please

plaisanter VERB [28]
to joke

la **plaisanterie** NOUN
joke

le **plaisir** NOUN
pleasure

■ **faire plaisir à quelqu'un** to please somebody □ J'y suis allé pour lui faire plaisir. I went there to please him. □ Ce cadeau me fait très plaisir. I'm very pleased with this present.

plaît VERB ▷ *see* **plaire**

le **plan** NOUN
plan

■ **un plan de la ville** a street map

■ **au premier plan** in the foreground

la **planche** NOUN
plank

■ **une planche à repasser** an ironing board

■ **une planche à roulettes** a skateboard

■ **une planche à voile** a sailboard

le **plancher** NOUN
floor

planer VERB [28]

1 to glide

□ L'avion planait dans le ciel. The plane was gliding in the sky.

2 to have one's head in the clouds

□ Ce garçon plane complètement. *(informal)* He's not with us at all.

la **planète** NOUN
planet

la **plante** NOUN
plant

planter VERB [28]

1 to plant

□ Daphné a planté des tomates. Daphne planted some tomatoes.

2 to hammer in

□ Jean-Pierre a planté un clou dans le mur. Jean-Pierre hammered a nail into the wall.

3 to pitch

□ André a planté sa tente au bord du lac. André pitched his tent next to the lake.

■ **Ne reste pas planté là!** Don't just stand there!

■ **se planter** *(informal)* to fail □ Je me suis planté en maths. I failed maths.

la **plaque** NOUN
(metal) plate

■ **une plaque de verglas** a patch of ice

■ **une plaque de chocolat** a bar of chocolate

plaqué (FEM **plaquée** ADJECTIVE

■ **plaqué or** gold-plated

■ **plaqué argent** silver-plated

plaquer VERB [28] *(informal)*

1 to ditch

□ Elle a plaqué son copain. She ditched her boyfriend.

2 to pack in

□ Il a plaqué son boulot. He packed in his job.

la **plaquette** NOUN

■ **une plaquette de chocolat** a bar of chocolate

■ **une plaquette de beurre** a pack of butter

le **plastique** NOUN
plastic

plat (FEM **plate** ADJECTIVE
▷ *see also* **plat** NOUN
flat

■ **être à plat ventre** to be lying face down

■ **l'eau plate** still water

le **plat** NOUN
▷ *see also* **plat** ADJECTIVE

1 dish

2 course

□ le plat principal the main course

■ **un plat cuisiné** a pre-cooked meal

■ **le plat de résistance** the main course

■ **le plat du jour** the dish of the day

le **platane** NOUN
plane tree

le **plateau** (PL les **plateaux** NOUN

1 tray

■ **un plateau de fromages** a selection of cheeses

2 plateau

le **platine** NOUN
▷ *see also* **la platine**
platinum

la **platine** NOUN
▷ *see also* **le platine**
turntable *(of record player)*

■ **une platine laser** a CD player

le **plâtre** NOUN
plaster

plein – plus

□ une statue en plâtre a statue made of plaster □ avoir un bras dans le plâtre to have an arm in plaster

plein (FEM **pleine**) ADJECTIVE
▷ see also **plein** NOUN
full
■ **à plein temps** full-time □ Elle travaille à plein temps. She works full-time.
■ **plein de** (informal) lots of □ un gâteau avec plein de crème a cake with lots of cream
■ **Il y a plein de gens dans la rue.** The street is full of people.
■ **en plein air** in the open air
■ **en pleine nuit** in the middle of the night
■ **en plein jour** in broad daylight

le **plein** NOUN
▷ see also **plein** ADJECTIVE
■ **faire le plein** to fill up (petrol tank) □ Faites le plein, s'il vous plaît. Fill it up, please.

pleurer VERB [28]
to cry

pleut VERB ▷ see **pleuvoir**

pleuvoir VERB [63]
to rain
□ Il pleut. It's raining.

le **pli** NOUN
1 fold
2 pleat
□ Elle a repassé les plis de sa jupe. She ironed the pleats of her skirt.
3 crease
□ Il y a un pli sur la manche de ta chemise. There's a crease in the sleeve of your shirt.

pliant (FEM **pliante**) ADJECTIVE
folding
□ un lit pliant a folding bed

plier VERB [19]
1 to fold
□ Elle a plié sa serviette. She folded her towel.
2 to bend
□ Elle a plié le bras. She bent her arm.

le **plomb** NOUN
1 lead
□ Ces jouets sont en plomb. These toys are made of lead.
2 fuse
□ Les plombs ont sauté. The fuses have blown.
■ **l'essence sans plomb** unleaded petrol

le **plombier** NOUN
plumber
■ **Il est plombier.** He's a plumber.

la **plongée** NOUN
diving

□ faire de la plongée to go diving

le **plongeoir** NOUN
diving board

le **plongeon** NOUN
dive

plonger VERB [45]
to dive
□ Jean a plongé dans la piscine. Jean dived into the swimming pool.
■ **J'ai plongé ma main dans l'eau.** I plunged my hand into the water.
■ **être plongé dans son travail** to be absorbed in your work
■ **se plonger dans un livre** to get absorbed in a book

plu VERB ▷ see **plaire**, **pleuvoir**

la **pluie** NOUN
rain
□ sous la pluie in the rain

la **plume** NOUN
feather
□ une plume d'oiseau a bird's feather
■ **un stylo à plume** a fountain pen
LANGUAGE TIP Word for word, **stylo à plume** means 'feather pen'.

plupart
■ **la plupart** PRONOUN most (of them) □ La plupart ont moins de quinze ans. Most of them are under 15.
■ **la plupart des** most □ La plupart des gens ont vu ce film. Most people have seen this film.
■ **la plupart du temps** most of the time

le **pluriel** NOUN
plural
■ **au pluriel** in the plural

plus ADVERB, PREPOSITION
■ **ne ... plus 1** not ... any more □ Je ne veux plus le voir. I don't want to see him any more. **2** no longer □ Il ne travaille plus ici. He's no longer working here.
■ **Je n'ai plus de pain.** I've got no bread left.
■ **plus ... que** more ... than □ Il est plus intelligent que son frère. He's more intelligent than his brother. □ Il travaille plus que moi. He works more than me. □ Elle est plus grande que moi. She's bigger than me.
■ **C'est le plus grand de la famille.** He's the tallest in his family.
■ **plus ... plus ...** the more ... the more ... □ Plus il gagne d'argent, plus il en veut. The more money he earns, the more he wants.
■ **plus de 1** more □ Il nous faut plus de pain. We need more bread. **2** more than □ Il y avait plus de dix personnes. There were more than 10 people.

■ **de plus** more □ Il nous faut un joueur de plus. We need one more player. □ Le voyage a pris trois heures de plus que prévu. The journey took 3 hours more than planned.

■ **en plus** more □ J'ai apporté quelques gâteaux en plus. I brought a few more cakes.

■ **de plus en plus** more and more □ Il y a de plus en plus de touristes par ici. There are more and more tourists round here. □ Il fait de plus en plus chaud. It's getting hotter and hotter.

■ **un peu plus difficile** a bit more difficult □ Il fait un peu plus froid qu'hier. It's a bit colder than yesterday.

■ **plus ou moins** more or less

■ **Quatre plus deux égalent six.** 4 plus 2 is 6.

plusieurs PL PRONOUN

several

□ Elle a acheté plusieurs chemises. She bought several shirts. □ Il y en a plusieurs. There are several of them.

le **plus-que-parfait** NOUN

pluperfect

plutôt ADVERB

1 quite

□ Elle est plutôt jolie. She's quite pretty.

2 rather

□ L'eau est plutôt froide. The water's rather cold.

3 instead

□ Demande-leur plutôt de venir avec toi. Ask them to come with you instead.

■ **plutôt que** rather than □ Invite Marie plutôt que Nathalie. Invite Marie rather than Nathalie.

pluvieux (FEM **pluvieuse**) ADJECTIVE

rainy

le **pneu** NOUN

tyre

la **pneumonie** NOUN

pneumonia

la **poche** NOUN

pocket

■ **l'argent de poche** pocket money

■ **un livre de poche** a paperback

○ **LANGUAGE TIP** Word for word, **livre de poche** means 'pocket book'.

le **podcast** NOUN

podcast

podcaster VERB [28]

to podcast

la **poêle** NOUN

frying pan

■ **une poêle à frire** a frying pan

le **poème** NOUN

poem

la **poésie** NOUN

1 poetry

2 poem

le **poète** NOUN

poet

le **poids** NOUN

weight

□ vendre quelque chose au poids to sell something by weight

■ **prendre du poids** to put on weight □ Il a pris du poids. He's put on weight.

■ **perdre du poids** to lose weight □ Elle a perdu du poids. She's lost weight.

■ **un poids lourd** a lorry

la **poignée** NOUN

1 handful

□ une poignée de sel a handful of salt

2 handle

□ la poignée de la porte the door handle

■ **une poignée de main** a handshake

le **poignet** NOUN

1 wrist

□ Je me suis fait mal au poignet. I've hurt my wrist.

2 cuff (of shirt)

le **poil** NOUN

1 hair

□ Il y a des poils de chat partout sur la moquette. There are cat hairs all over the carpet.

2 fur

□ Ton chien a un beau poil. Your dog's got lovely fur.

■ **à poil** (informal) stark naked

poilu (FEM **poilue**) ADJECTIVE

hairy

poinçonner VERB [28]

to punch

□ Le contrôleur a poinçonné les billets. The conductor punched the tickets.

le **poing** NOUN

fist

■ **un coup de poing** a punch

le **point** NOUN

1 point

□ Je ne suis pas d'accord sur ce point. I don't agree with this point. □ Son point faible, c'est qu'elle est trop gentille. Her weak point is she's too nice.

■ **point de vue** point of view

2 full stop

■ **être sur le point de faire quelque chose** to be just about to do something □ J'étais sur le point de te téléphoner. I was just about to phone you.

■ **mettre au point** to finalize

P

■ **Ce n'est pas encore au point.** It's not finalized yet.

■ **à point** medium □ Comment voulez-vous votre steak? — À point. How would you like your steak? — Medium.

■ **un point d'exclamation** an exclamation mark

■ **un point d'interrogation** a question mark

■ **un point noir** a blackhead

la **pointe** NOUN
point
□ la pointe d'un couteau the point of a knife
■ **être à la pointe du progrès** to be in the forefront of progress
■ **sur la pointe des pieds** on tiptoe
■ **les heures de pointe** peak hours

le **pointillé** NOUN
dotted line

pointu (FEM **pointue**) ADJECTIVE
pointed
□ un chapeau pointu a pointed hat

la **pointure** NOUN
size (of shoes)
□ Quelle est votre pointure? What size shoes do you take?

le **point-virgule** (PL **points-virgules**) NOUN
semicolon

la **poire** NOUN
pear

le **poireau** (PL les **poireaux**) NOUN
leek
□ la soupe aux poireaux leek soup

le **pois** NOUN
pea
■ **les petits pois** peas
■ **les pois chiches** chickpeas
■ **à pois** spotted □ une robe à pois a spotted dress

le **poison** NOUN
poison

le **poisson** NOUN
fish
□ Je n'aime pas le poisson. I don't like fish.
□ André a pêché deux poissons. André caught two fish.
■ **les Poissons** Pisces □ Monique est Poissons. Monique is Pisces.
■ **Poisson d'avril!** April fool!

> **DID YOU KNOW...?**
> Pinning a paper fish to somebody's back is a traditional April fool joke in France.

■ **un poisson rouge** a goldfish

la **poissonnerie** NOUN
fish shop

le **poissonnier** NOUN
fishmonger

la **poitrine** NOUN
1 chest
□ J'ai mal à la poitrine. My chest hurts.
2 bust
□ Quel est votre tour de poitrine? What's your bust size?

le **poivre** NOUN
pepper (spice)

le **poivron** NOUN
pepper (vegetable)

le **pôle** NOUN
pole
■ **le pôle Nord** the North Pole
■ **le pôle Sud** the South Pole

poli (FEM **polie**) ADJECTIVE
polite

la **police** NOUN
police
□ La police recherche le voleur. The police are looking for the thief.
■ **police secours** emergency services □ Ils ont appelé police secours. They phoned the emergency services.
■ **une police d'assurance** an insurance policy

policier (FEM **policière**) ADJECTIVE
▷ see also **policier** NOUN
■ **un roman policier** a detective novel

le **policier** NOUN
▷ see also **policier** ADJECTIVE
policeman
□ Il est policier. He's a policeman.

la **politesse** NOUN
politeness

la **politique** NOUN
politics
□ La politique ne l'intéresse pas du tout. He's not at all interested in politics.
■ **un homme politique** a politician

pollué (FEM **polluée**) ADJECTIVE
polluted

polluer VERB [28]
to pollute

la **pollution** NOUN
pollution

le **polo** NOUN
polo shirt

la **Pologne** NOUN
Poland

polonais (FEM **polonaise**) ADJECTIVE, NOUN
Polish
□ Elle parle polonais. She speaks Polish.
■ **un Polonais** a Pole (man)
■ **une Polonaise** a Pole (woman)
■ **les Polonais** the Poles

la **Polynésie** NOUN
Polynesia

la **pommade** NOUN
ointment

la **pomme** NOUN
apple

- **les pommes de terre** potatoes
- **les pommes frites** chips
- **les pommes vapeur** boiled potatoes
- **tomber dans les pommes** (*informal*) to faint

LANGUAGE TIP Word for word, this means 'to fall into the apples'.

la **pompe** NOUN
pump

- **une pompe à essence** a petrol pump
- **les pompes funèbres** undertakers

le **pompier** NOUN
fireman

le **pompiste** NOUN
petrol pump attendant

ponctuel (FEM **ponctuelle**) ADJECTIVE
1 punctual
  □ Elle est toujours très ponctuelle. She's always very punctual.
2 occasional
  - **On a rencontré quelques problèmes ponctuels.** We've had the occasional problem.

pondre VERB [69]
to lay (*eggs*)

le **poney** NOUN
pony

le **pont** NOUN
1 bridge
2 deck (*of ship*)
  - **faire le pont** to take a long weekend
  □ Nous faisons le pont pour la Pentecôte. We're taking a long weekend for Whitsun.

populaire (FEM **populaire**) ADJECTIVE
1 popular
  □ Ce chanteur est très populaire en France. This singer's very popular in France.
2 working-class
  □ un quartier populaire de la ville a working-class area of town

la **population** NOUN
population

le **porc** NOUN
1 pig
  □ Ils élèvent des porcs. They breed pigs.
2 pork
  □ du rôti de porc roast pork

la **porcelaine** NOUN
china
  □ une tasse en porcelaine a china cup

le **port** NOUN

1 harbour
2 port

portable (FEM **portable**) ADJECTIVE
  ▷ *see also* **portable** NOUN
  mobile (*telephone*)
  - **un ordinateur portable** a laptop

le **portable** NOUN
  ▷ *see also* **portable** ADJECTIVE
1 mobile phone
  □ Je vais appeler Marie sur mon portable. I'll phone Marie on my mobile.
2 laptop
  □ Je vais te montrer sur mon portable. I'll show you on my laptop.

le **portail** NOUN
gate

portatif (FEM **portative**) ADJECTIVE
portable

la **porte** NOUN
1 door
  □ Ferme la porte, s'il te plaît. Close the door, please.
  - **la porte d'entrée** the front door
2 gate
  □ Vol 432 à destination de Paris: porte numéro trois. Flight 432 to Paris: gate 3.
  - **mettre quelqu'un à la porte** to sack somebody

le **porte-bagages** NOUN
luggage rack

le **porte-clés** NOUN
key ring

la **portée** NOUN
  - **à portée de main** within arm's reach
  - **hors de portée** out of reach

le **portefeuille** NOUN
wallet

le **portemanteau** (PL les **portemanteaux**) NOUN
1 coat hanger
2 coat rack

le **porte-monnaie** (PL les **porte-monnaie**) NOUN
purse

LANGUAGE TIP Word for word, **porte-monnaie** means 'a change carrier'.

porter VERB [28]
1 to carry
  □ Il portait une valise. He was carrying a suitcase.
2 to wear
  □ Elle porte une robe bleue. She's wearing a blue dress.
  - **se porter bien** to be well
  - **se porter mal** to be unwell

le **porteur** NOUN
porter

209

la **portière** NOUN
door *(of car)*

la **portion** NOUN
portion

le **porto** NOUN
port *(wine)*

le **portrait** NOUN
portrait

portugais (FEM **portugaise**) ADJECTIVE, NOUN
Portuguese
□ Il parle portugais. He speaks Portuguese.
■ **un Portugais** a Portuguese *(man)*
■ **une Portugaise** a Portuguese *(woman)*
■ **les Portugais** the Portuguese

le **Portugal** NOUN
Portugal
■ **au Portugal 1** in Portugal **2** to Portugal

poser VERB [28]
1 to put down
□ J'ai posé la cafetière sur la table. I put the
coffee pot down on the table.
2 to pose
□ Cela pose un problème. That poses a
problem.
■ **poser une question à quelqu'un** to ask
somebody a question
■ **se poser** to land □ L'avion s'est posé à
huit heures. The plane landed at 8 o'clock.

positif (FEM **positive**) ADJECTIVE
positive

la **position** NOUN
position

posséder VERB [34]
to own
□ Ils possèdent une jolie maison. They own
a lovely house.

la **possibilité** NOUN
possibility

possible (FEM **possible**) ADJECTIVE
possible
□ Alain leur a dit que ce n'était pas possible.
Alain told them it wasn't possible.
■ **le plus de gens possible** as many people
as possible
■ **le plus tôt possible** as early as possible
■ **le moins d'argent possible** as little
money as possible
■ **Il travaille le moins possible.** He works
as little as possible.
■ **dès que possible** as soon as possible
■ **faire son possible** to do all one can □ Je
ferai tout mon possible. I'll do all I can.

la **poste** NOUN
▷ *see also* **le poste**
1 post
□ Je vais l'envoyer par la poste. I'm going to
send it by post.

2 post office
□ Je vais à la poste pour acheter des timbres.
I'm going to the post office to buy some
stamps.
■ **mettre une lettre à la poste** to post a
letter

le **poste** NOUN
▷ *see also* **la poste**
1 post
□ Jean-Pierre a trouvé un poste de
professeur. Jean-Pierre has found a
teaching post.
2 extension *(phone)*
□ Pouvez-vous me passer le poste de M.
Salzedo? Can you put me through to Mr
Salzedo's extension?
3 set
□ un poste de radio a radio set
■ **un poste de police** a police station

poster VERB [28]
▷ *see also* **poster** NOUN
to post
□ Je vais poster ce colis. I'm going to post
this parcel.
LANGUAGE TIP **poster** is pronounced
'postay' when it means **to post**.

le **poster** NOUN
▷ *see also* **poster** VERB
poster
□ un poster de la Grèce a poster of Greece
LANGUAGE TIP **poster** is pronounced
'post-air' when it means **a poster**.

postérieur (FEM **postérieure**) ADJECTIVE
1 later
□ Ce document est postérieur à 1314. This
document is from later than 1314.
2 back
□ la partie postérieure de ma jambe the
back of my leg

le **pot** NOUN
jar
□ J'ai fait trois pots de confiture. I've made
three jars of jam.
■ **prendre un pot** *(informal)* to have a drink
□ On va prendre un pot ce soir. We're going
for a drink tonight.
■ **un pot de fleurs** a plant pot

potable (FEM **potable**) ADJECTIVE
■ **eau potable** drinking water
■ **'eau non potable'** 'not drinking water'

le **potage** NOUN
soup

le **potager** NOUN
vegetable garden

le **pot-au-feu** (PL les **pot-au-feu**) NOUN
beef stew

le **pot-de-vin** (PL les **pots-de-vin**) NOUN

bribe

le **pote** NOUN (informal)
mate
□ Je sors avec mes potes ce soir. I'm going out with my mates tonight.

le **poteau** (PL les **poteaux**) NOUN
post
□ Il s'est appuyé contre un poteau. He leant against a post.
■ **un poteau indicateur** a signpost

potentiel (FEM **potentielle**) ADJECTIVE
potential

la **poterie** NOUN
1 pottery
□ Elle fait de la poterie à l'école. She does pottery at school.
2 piece of pottery
□ J'ai acheté deux poteries. I bought two pieces of pottery.

le **potier** NOUN
potter

le **pou** (PL les **poux**) NOUN
louse

la **poubelle** NOUN
dustbin

le **pouce** NOUN
1 thumb
□ Je me suis coincé le pouce dans la porte. I trapped my thumb in the door.
2 inch
□ Un pouce fait à peu près deux virgule cinq centimètres. 1 inch equals roughly 2.5 centimetres.
■ **manger sur le pouce** to have a quick snack

la **poudre** NOUN
1 powder
2 face powder
■ **la poudre à laver** washing powder
■ **le lait en poudre** powdered milk
■ **le café en poudre** instant coffee

le **poulain** NOUN
foal

la **poule** NOUN
hen
■ **quand les poules auront des dents** (informal) pigs might fly
○ **LANGUAGE TIP** Word for word, this means 'when hens have teeth'.

le **poulet** NOUN
1 chicken
□ J'adore le poulet. I love chicken. □ un poulet rôti a roast chicken
2 cop
□ Il s'est fait attraper par les poulets. (informal) He got caught by the cops.

le **pouls** NOUN

pulse
□ Il m'a pris le pouls. He took my pulse.

le **poumon** NOUN
lung

la **poupée** NOUN
doll

pour PREPOSITION
for
□ C'est un cadeau pour toi. It's a present for you. □ Qu'est-ce que tu veux pour ton petit déjeuner? What would you like for breakfast?
■ **pour faire quelque chose** to do something □ Je lui ai téléphoné pour l'inviter. I phoned him to invite him.
■ **Pour aller à Strasbourg, s'il vous plaît?** Which way is it to Strasbourg, please?
■ **pour que** so that
○ **LANGUAGE TIP** pour que is followed by a verb in the subjunctive.
□ Je lui ai prêté mon pull pour qu'elle n'ait pas froid. I lent her my jumper so that she wouldn't be cold.
■ **pour cent** per cent

le **pourboire** NOUN
tip
□ Il a donné un pourboire au garçon. He gave the waiter a tip.

le **pourcentage** NOUN
percentage

pourquoi ADVERB, CONJUNCTION
why
□ Pourquoi est-ce qu'il ne vient pas avec nous? Why isn't he coming with us? □ Elle ne m'a pas dit pourquoi. She didn't tell me why.

pourra, pourrai, pourras, pourrez
VERB ▷ see **pouvoir**

pourri (FEM **pourrie**) ADJECTIVE
rotten

le **pourriel** NOUN
spam (email)

pourrir VERB [38]
to go bad
□ Ces poires ont pourri. These pears have gone bad.

pourrons, pourront VERB ▷ see **pouvoir**

la **poursuite** NOUN
chase
■ **se lancer à la poursuite de quelqu'un** to chase after somebody

poursuivre VERB [81]
to carry on with
□ Ils ont poursuivi leur travail. They carried on with their work.
■ **se poursuivre** to go on □ Le concert s'est poursuivi très tard. The concert went on

P

211

very late.

pourtant ADVERB

yet

□ Il a raté son examen. Pourtant, il n'est pas bête. He failed his exam, yet he's not stupid.

■ **C'est pourtant facile!** But it's easy!

pourvu (FEM **pourvue**) ADJECTIVE

■ **pourvu que ...** let's hope that ...

◌ LANGUAGE TIP **pourvu que** is followed by a verb in the subjunctive.

□ Pourvu qu'il ne pleuve pas! Let's hope it doesn't rain!

pousser VERB [28]

1 to push

□ Ils ont dû pousser la voiture. They had to push the car.

2 to grow

□ Mes cheveux poussent vite. My hair grows quickly.

■ **pousser un cri** to give a cry

■ **se pousser** to move over □ Pousse-toi, je ne vois rien. Move over, I can't see a thing.

la **poussette** NOUN

pushchair

la **poussière** NOUN

1 dust

□ La table est couverte de poussière. The table's covered in dust.

2 speck of dust

□ J'ai une poussière dans l'œil. I've got a speck of dust in my eye.

poussiéreux (FEM **poussiéreuse**) ADJECTIVE

dusty

le **poussin** NOUN

chick

pouvoir VERB [64]

▷ see also **pouvoir** NOUN

PRESENT TENSE

je peux	nous pouvons
tu peux	vous pouvez
il/elle peut	ils/elles peuvent

PAST PARTICIPLE

pu

can

□ Je peux lui téléphoner si tu veux. I can phone her if you want. □ Puis-je venir vous voir samedi? May I come and see you on Saturday? □ Je ne pourrai pas venir samedi. I can't come on Saturday. □ J'ai fait tout ce que j'ai pu. I did all I could.

■ **Je n'en peux plus.** I'm exhausted.

■ **Il se peut que ...** It's possible that ...

◌ LANGUAGE TIP **il se peut que** is followed by a verb in the subjunctive.

□ Il se peut qu'elle ait déménagé. It's possible that she's moved house. □ Il se peut que j'y aille. I might go.

le **pouvoir** NOUN

▷ see also **pouvoir** VERB

power

□ Le Premier ministre a beaucoup de pouvoir. The prime minister has a lot of power.

la **prairie** NOUN

meadow

la **pratique** NOUN

▷ see also **pratique** ADJECTIVE

practice

□ Je manque de pratique. I'm out of practice.

pratique (FEM **pratique**) ADJECTIVE

▷ see also **pratique** NOUN

practical

□ Ce sac est très pratique. This bag's very practical.

pratiquement ADVERB

virtually

□ J'ai pratiquement fini. I've virtually finished.

pratiquer VERB [28]

to practise

□ Je dois pratiquer mon espagnol. I need to practise my Spanish.

■ **Pratiquez-vous un sport?** Do you do any sport?

le **pré** NOUN

meadow

la **précaution** NOUN

precaution

□ prendre ses précautions to take precautions

■ **par précaution** as a precaution □ Il a pris une assurance par précaution. He took out insurance as a precaution.

■ **avec précaution** cautiously

■ **'à manipuler avec précaution'** 'handle with care'

précédemment ADVERB

previously

précédent (FEM **précédente**) ADJECTIVE

previous

précieux (FEM **précieuse**) ADJECTIVE

precious

■ **une pierre précieuse** a precious stone

■ **de précieux conseils** invaluable advice

le **précipice** NOUN

ravine

□ Leur voiture est tombée dans un précipice. Their car fell into a ravine.

précipitamment ADVERB

hurriedly

□ Chantal est partie précipitamment. Chantal left hurriedly.

la **précipitation** NOUN

P

haste

□ Il a agi avec précipitation. He acted hastily.

se **précipiter** VERB [28]
to rush

précis (FEM **précise**) ADJECTIVE
precise

■ **à huit heures précises** at exactly eight o'clock

précisément ADVERB
precisely

préciser VERB [28]
1 to be more specific about

□ Pouvez-vous préciser ce que vous voulez dire? Can you be more specific about what you want to say?
2 to specify

□ Pouvez-vous préciser les raisons de ce changement? Can you specify the reasons for this change?

la **précision** NOUN
1 precision
2 detail

□ Je vais vous donner quelques précisions. I'm going to give you some details.

la **préfecture** NOUN

> **DID YOU KNOW…?**
> A **préfecture** is the headquarters of a **département**, one of the 96 administrative areas of France.

■ **la préfecture de police** the police headquarters

préférable (FEM **préférable**) ADJECTIVE
preferable

préféré (FEM **préférée**) ADJECTIVE
favourite

la **préférence** NOUN
preference

□ Je n'ai pas de préférence. I've no preference.

■ **de préférence** preferably

préférer VERB [34]
to prefer

□ Je préfère la cuisine de Teresa. I prefer Teresa's cooking. □ Je préfère manger à la cantine. I prefer to eat in the canteen.

■ **Je préférerais du thé.** I'd rather have tea.

■ **préférer quelqu'un à quelqu'un** to prefer somebody to somebody □ Je le préfère à son frère. I prefer him to his brother.

préhistorique (FEM **préhistorique**) ADJECTIVE
prehistoric

le **préjugé** NOUN
prejudice

□ avoir des préjugés contre quelqu'un to be

prejudiced against somebody

premier (FEM **première**) ADJECTIVE
▷ see also **première** NOUN
first

□ au premier étage on the first floor □ C'est notre premier jour de vacances. It's the first day of our holiday. □ C'est la première fois que je viens ici. It's the first time I've been here. □ le premier mai the first of May □ Il est arrivé premier. He came first.

■ **le Premier ministre** the Prime Minister

la **première** NOUN
▷ see also **premier** ADJECTIVE
1 first class

□ Nous avons voyagé en première. We travelled first class.
2 first gear

□ Passe en première pour prendre ce virage. Change into first to go round this bend.
3 lower sixth form

□ Ma sœur est en première. My sister's in the lower sixth.

> **DID YOU KNOW…?**
> In French secondary schools, years are counted from the **sixième** (youngest) to **première** and **terminale** (oldest).

premièrement ADVERB
firstly

prendre VERB [65]
to take

□ Prends tes affaires et viens avec moi. Take your things and come with me.

■ **prendre quelque chose à quelqu'un** to take something from somebody □ Il m'a pris mon stylo! He's taken my pen!

■ **Nous avons pris le train de huit heures.** We took the eight o'clock train.

■ **Je prends toujours le train pour aller à Paris.** I always go to Paris by train.

■ **passer prendre** to pick up □ Je dois passer prendre Richard. I have to pick up Richard.

■ **prendre à gauche** to turn left □ Prenez à gauche en arrivant au rond-point. Turn left at the roundabout.

■ **Il se prend pour Napoléon.** He thinks he's Napoleon.

■ **s'en prendre à quelqu'un** to lay into somebody *(verbally)*

□ Il s'en est pris à moi. He laid into me.

■ **s'y prendre** to set about it □ Tu t'y prends mal! You're setting about it the wrong way!

le **prénom** NOUN
first name

□ Quel est votre prénom? What's your first

name?

préoccupé (FEM **préoccupée**) ADJECTIVE
worried

la **préparation** NOUN
preparation

préparer VERB [28]
1 to prepare
□ Elle prépare le dîner. She's preparing dinner.
2 to make
□ Je vais préparer le café. I'm going to make the coffee.
3 to prepare for
□ Laure prépare son examen d'économie. Laure's preparing for her economics exam.
■ **se préparer** to get ready □ Ils se préparent à partir. They're getting ready to go.

la **préposition** NOUN
preposition

près ADVERB
■ **tout près** nearby □ J'habite tout près. I live nearby.
■ **près de 1** near (to) □ Est-ce que c'est près d'ici? Is it near here? **2** next to □ Assieds-toi près de moi. Sit down next to me. **3** nearly □ Il y avait près de cinq cents spectateurs. There were nearly 500 spectators.
■ **de près** closely □ Il a regardé la photo de près. He looked closely at the photo.
■ **à peu de chose près** more or less

la **présence** NOUN
1 presence
□ Sa présence est rassurante. His presence is reassuring.
2 attendance
□ La présence aux cours est obligatoire. Attendance at lessons is compulsory.

présent (FEM **présente**) ADJECTIVE
▷ see also **présent** NOUN
present

le **présent** NOUN
▷ see also **présent** ADJECTIVE
present tense
■ **à présent** now

la **présentation** NOUN
presentation
■ **faire les présentations** to do the introductions

présenter VERB [28]
to present
□ Il présentait le spectacle. He presented the show.
■ **présenter quelqu'un à quelqu'un** to introduce somebody to somebody □ Il m'a présenté à sa sœur. He introduced me to

his sister.
■ **Marc, je te présente Anaïs.** Marc, this is Anaïs.
■ **se présenter 1** to introduce oneself □ Elle s'est présentée à ses collègues. She introduced herself to her colleagues. **2** to arise □ Si l'occasion se présente, nous irons en Écosse. If the chance arises, we'll go to Scotland. **3** to stand □ Monsieur Legros se présente encore aux élections. Mr Legros is standing for election again.

le **préservatif** NOUN
condom

préserver VERB [28]
to protect
□ préserver du froid to protect from the cold

le **président** NOUN
1 president
□ le président des États-Unis the president of the United States
2 chairman
□ le président du conseil d'administration the chairman of the board of directors
■ **le président directeur général** the chairman and managing director

présider VERB [28]
1 to chair
□ Duncan a présidé la réunion. Duncan chaired the meeting.
2 to be the guest of honour
□ Il présidait à table. He was the guest of honour at the table.

presque ADVERB
nearly
□ Il est presque six heures. It's nearly 6 o'clock. □ Nous sommes presque arrivés. We're nearly there.
■ **presque rien** hardly anything □ Elle n'a presque rien mangé. She's hardly eaten anything.
■ **presque pas** hardly at all □ Il ne dort presque pas. He hardly sleeps at all.
■ **presque pas de** hardly any □ Il n'y a presque pas de place. There's hardly any space.

la **presqu'île** NOUN
peninsula

la **presse** NOUN
press
□ les représentants de la presse representatives of the press

pressé (FEM **pressée**) ADJECTIVE
1 in a hurry
□ Je ne peux pas rester, je suis pressé. I can't stay, I'm in a hurry.
2 urgent
□ Ce n'est pas très pressé. It's not very

urgent.

■ **une orange pressée** a fresh orange juice

presser VERB [28]

1 to squeeze

□ Tu peux me presser un citron? Can you squeeze me a lemon?

2 to be urgent

□ Est-ce que ça presse? Is it urgent?

■ **se presser** to hurry up □ Allez, presse-toi, on va être en retard! Come on, hurry up, we're going to be late!

■ **Rien ne presse.** There's no hurry.

le pressing NOUN

dry-cleaner's

la pression NOUN

1 pressure

■ **faire pression sur quelqu'un** to put pressure on somebody

2 draught beer (informal)

prêt (FEM **prête**) ADJECTIVE

▷ see also **prêt** NOUN

ready

□ Le déjeuner est prêt. Lunch is ready. □ Tu es prête? Are you ready?

le prêt NOUN

▷ see also **prêt** ADJECTIVE

loan

le prêt-à-porter NOUN

ready-to-wear clothes

prétendre VERB [88]

■ **prétendre que** to claim that □ Il prétend qu'il ne la connaît pas. He claims he doesn't know her.

⚬ **LANGUAGE TIP** Be careful! **prétendre** does not mean **to pretend**.

prétendu (FEM **prétendue**) ADJECTIVE

so-called

□ un prétendu expert a so-called expert

prétentieux (FEM **prétentieuse**) ADJECTIVE

pretentious

prêter VERB [28]

■ **prêter quelque chose à quelqu'un** to lend something to someone □ Il m'a prêté sa voiture. He lent me his car.

■ **prêter attention à quelque chose** to pay attention to something

le prétexte NOUN

excuse

□ Il avait un prétexte pour ne pas venir. He had an excuse for not coming.

■ **sous aucun prétexte** on no account

□ Ne le dérangez sous aucun prétexte. On no account must you disturb him.

prétexter VERB [28]

to give as an excuse

□ Elle a prétexté une réunion. She gave a meeting as her excuse. □ Il a prétexté qu'il

avait un rendez-vous. He gave the excuse that he had an appointment.

le prêtre NOUN

priest

la preuve NOUN

1 evidence

□ Il y a des preuves contre lui. There's evidence against him.

2 proof

□ Vous n'avez aucune preuve. You haven't got any proof.

■ **faire preuve de courage** to show courage

■ **faire ses preuves** to prove oneself

□ Pour être embauché ici, il faut faire ses preuves. To be employed here, you need to prove yourself.

prévenir VERB [89]

■ **prévenir quelqu'un** to warn somebody

□ Je te préviens, il est de mauvaise humeur. I'm warning you, he's in a bad mood.

la prévention NOUN

prevention

■ **des mesures de prévention** preventative measures

■ **la prévention routière** road safety

la prévision NOUN

■ **les prévisions météorologiques** the weather forecast

■ **en prévision de quelque chose** in anticipation of something

prévoir VERB [92]

1 to plan

□ Nous prévoyons un pique-nique pour dimanche. We're planning to have a picnic on Sunday.

■ **Le départ est prévu pour dix heures.** The departure's scheduled for 10 o'clock.

2 to allow

□ J'ai prévu assez à manger pour quatre. I allowed enough food for four.

3 to foresee

□ J'avais prévu qu'il serait en retard. I'd foreseen that he'd be late.

■ **Je prévois qu'il me faudra une heure de plus.** I reckon on it taking me another hour.

prier VERB [19]

to pray to

□ Les Grecs priaient Dionysos. The Greeks prayed to Dionysos.

■ **prier quelqu'un de faire quelque chose** to ask somebody to do something □ Elle l'a prié de sortir. She asked him to leave.

■ **je vous en prie 1** please do □ Je peux m'asseoir? — Je vous en prie. May I sit down? — Please do. **2** please □ Je vous en prie, ne me laissez pas seule. Please, don't

leave me alone. **3** don't mention it □ Merci pour votre aide. — Je vous en prie. Thanks for your help. — Don't mention it.

la prière NOUN
prayer
□ faire ses prières to say one's prayers
■ **'prière de ne pas fumer'** 'no smoking please'

le primaire NOUN
primary education
□ Ses enfants sont encore en primaire. His children are still in primary education.
■ **l'école primaire** primary school

la prime NOUN
1 bonus
□ Il a eu une prime en récompense de son travail. He received a bonus for his work.
2 free gift
□ J'ai eu ce stylo en prime avec l'agenda. I got this pen as a free gift with the diary.
3 premium
□ une prime d'assurance an insurance premium

la primevère NOUN
primrose

le prince NOUN
prince
□ le prince Charles Prince Charles

la princesse NOUN
princess
□ la princesse Diana Princess Diana

principal (FEM **principale**, MASC PL **principaux**) ADJECTIVE
▷ see also **principal** NOUN
main
□ le rôle principal the main role

le principal (PL les **principaux**) NOUN
▷ see also **principal** ADJECTIVE
1 headmaster
□ le principal du collège the headmaster of the school
2 main thing
□ Personne n'a été blessé; c'est le principal. Nobody was injured; that's the main thing.

le principe NOUN
principle
■ **pour le principe** on principle
■ **en principe 1** as a rule □ Il déjeune en principe à midi et demi. As a rule he has lunch at 12.30. **2** in theory □ En principe Anne doit arriver lundi. In theory, Anne should arrive on Monday.

le printemps NOUN
spring
■ **au printemps** in spring

la priorité NOUN

1 priority
□ C'est à faire en priorité. It needs to be done as a priority.
2 right of way
□ Tu n'as pas la priorité. You haven't got right of way.

pris VERB ▷ see **prendre**

pris (FEM **prise**) ADJECTIVE
▷ see also **prise** NOUN
1 taken
□ Est-ce que cette place est prise? Is this seat taken?
2 busy
□ Je serai très pris la semaine prochaine. I'll be very busy next week.
■ **avoir le nez pris** to have a stuffy nose
■ **être pris de panique** to be panic-stricken

la prise NOUN
▷ see also **prise** ADJECTIVE
1 plug
2 socket
■ **une prise de courant** a power point
■ **une prise multiple** an adaptor
■ **une prise de sang** a blood test

la prison NOUN
prison
□ aller en prison to go to prison □ être en prison to be in prison

prisonnier (FEM **prisonnière**) ADJECTIVE
▷ see also **prisonnier** NOUN, **prisonnière** NOUN
captive

le prisonnier NOUN
▷ see also **prisonnier** ADJECTIVE
prisoner

la prisonnière NOUN
▷ see also **prisonnière** ADJECTIVE
prisoner

prit VERB ▷ see **prendre**

privé (FEM **privée**) ADJECTIVE
private
□ la propriété privée private property □ ma vie privée my private life
■ **en privé** in private

priver VERB [28]
■ **priver quelqu'un de quelque chose** to deprive somebody of something □ Le prisonnier a été privé de nourriture. The prisoner was deprived of food.
■ **Tu seras privé de dessert!** You won't get any pudding!

le prix NOUN
1 price
□ Je n'arrive pas à lire le prix de ce livre. I can't see the price of this book.
2 prize
□ Cécile a eu le prix de la meilleure actrice. Cécile got the prize for best actress.

■ **hors de prix** exorbitantly priced □ Les repas sont hors de prix ici! The price of meals here is exorbitant!

■ **à aucun prix** not at any price □ Je n'irai là-bas à aucun prix. I'm not going there, not at any price.

■ **à tout prix** at all costs □ Je veux à tout prix voir ce film. I want to see this film at all costs.

probable (FEM **probable**) ADJECTIVE
likely

□ Il est probable qu'elle viendra. It's likely she'll come.

■ **C'est peu probable.** That's unlikely.

probablement ADVERB
probably

le **problème** NOUN
problem

le **procédé** NOUN
process

le **procès** NOUN
trial

□ Le procès du meurtrier commence mardi. The murder trial starts on Tuesday.

■ **Il est en procès avec son employeur.** He's involved in a lawsuit with his employer.

prochain (FEM **prochaine**) ADJECTIVE
next

□ Nous descendons au prochain arrêt. We're getting off at the next stop.

■ **la prochaine fois** next time

■ **la semaine prochaine** next week

■ **À la prochaine!** See you!

prochainement ADVERB
soon

proche (FEM **proche**) ADJECTIVE
1 near

□ Les magasins les plus proches étaient à trois kilomètres. The nearest shops were 3 kilometres away. □ dans un proche avenir in the near future

2 close

□ un ami proche a close friend

■ **proche de** near to □ La cathédrale est proche du château. The cathedral is near the castle.

■ **le Proche-Orient** the Middle East

les **proches** MASC PL NOUN
close relatives

proclamer VERB [28]
to proclaim

procurer VERB [28]

■ **procurer quelque chose à quelqu'un** to get something for somebody □ C'est lui qui m'a procuré ce travail. He got me this job.

■ **se procurer quelque chose** to get something □ Je me suis procuré leur dernier

catalogue. I got their latest catalogue.

le **producteur** NOUN
producer

la **production** NOUN
production

la **productrice** NOUN
producer

produire VERB [23]
to produce

■ **se produire** to take place □ Ces changements se sont produits l'an dernier. The changes took place last year.

le **produit** NOUN
product

□ les produits de beauté beauty products

le/la **prof** NOUN (informal)
teacher

□ Elle est prof de maths. She's a maths teacher.

le **professeur** NOUN
1 teacher

□ Philippe est professeur d'histoire. Philippe's a history teacher.

2 professor

□ le professeur Dupont Professor Dupont

■ **un professeur de faculté** a university lecturer

la **profession** NOUN
profession

□ Quelle est votre profession? What's your profession?

■ **'sans profession'** 'unemployed'

professionnel (FEM **professionnelle**)
ADJECTIVE
professional

le **profil** NOUN
1 profile (of person)

□ de profil in profile

2 contours (of object)

le **profit** NOUN
profit

□ La société a fait des profits importants. The company made significant profits.

■ **tirer profit de quelque chose** to profit from something

■ **au profit de** in aid of □ un spectacle au profit de l'UNICEF a show in aid of UNICEF

profiter VERB [28]

■ **profiter de quelque chose** to take advantage of something □ Profitez du beau temps pour aller faire du vélo. Take advantage of the good weather and go cycling.

■ **Profitez-en bien!** Make the most of it!

profond (FEM **profonde**) ADJECTIVE
deep

■ **peu profond** shallow

la **profondeur** NOUN
depth

le **programme** NOUN
1 programme
  □ le programme du festival the festival programme
2 syllabus
  □ le programme de maths the maths syllabus
3 program
  □ un programme informatique a computer program

programmer VERB [28]
1 to show
  □ Ce film est programmé dimanche soir. The film is scheduled for Sunday evening.
2 to program
  □ Mon ordinateur n'est pas programmé pour ça. My computer isn't programmed to do that.

le **programmeur** NOUN
programmer
  □ Marc est programmeur. Marc is a programmer.

la **programmeuse** NOUN
programmer
  □ Elle est programmeuse. She's a programmer.

le **progrès** NOUN
progress
  □ faire des progrès to make progress

progresser VERB [28]
to progress

progressif (FEM **progressive**) ADJECTIVE
progressive

le **projecteur** NOUN
1 projector
  □ Le projecteur de diapositives est en panne. The slide projector is broken.
2 spotlight
  □ sous les projecteurs under the spotlight

le **projet** NOUN
1 plan
  □ des projets de vacances holiday plans
2 draft
  □ le projet de construction d'un musée the draft for the construction of a museum
  ■ **un projet de loi** a bill (in parliament)

projeter VERB [41]
1 to plan
  □ Ils projettent d'acheter une maison. They're planning to buy a house.
2 to cast
  □ une ombre projetée sur le mur a shadow cast onto the wall
  ■ **Elle a été projetée hors de la voiture.** She was thrown out of the car.

prolonger VERB [45]
1 to prolong
  □ Je vais prolonger mes vacances en Espagne. I'm going to prolong my holidays in Spain.
2 to extend
  □ Je vais prolonger mon abonnement. I'm going to extend my subscription.
  ■ **se prolonger** to go on □ La réunion s'est prolongée tard. The meeting went on late.

la **promenade** NOUN
walk
  □ Il y a de belles promenades par ici. There are some nice walks round here.
  ■ **faire une promenade** to go for a walk
  ■ **faire une promenade en voiture** to go for a drive
  ■ **faire une promenade à vélo** to go for a bike ride

promener VERB [43]
to take for a walk
  □ Cordelia promène son chien tous les jours. Cordelia takes her dog for a walk every day.
  ■ **se promener** to go for a walk □ Chantal est partie se promener. Chantal has gone for a walk.

la **promesse** NOUN
promise
  □ faire une promesse to make a promise
  □ tenir sa promesse to keep one's promise

promettre VERB [47]
to promise
  □ On m'a promis une augmentation. They promised me a pay rise. □ Elle m'a promis de me téléphoner. She promised to phone me.

la **promotion** NOUN
promotion
  □ Il espère avoir bientôt une promotion. He's hoping to get promotion soon.
  ■ **être en promotion** to be on special offer
  □ Les côtes de porc sont en promotion. Pork chops are on special offer.

le **pronom** NOUN
pronoun

prononcer VERB [12]
1 to pronounce
  □ Le russe est difficile à prononcer. Russian is difficult to pronounce.
2 to deliver
  □ prononcer un discours to deliver a speech
  ■ **se prononcer** to be pronounced □ Le 'e' final ne se prononce pas. The final 'e' isn't pronounced.

la **prononciation** NOUN
pronunciation

la **propagande** NOUN

propaganda

se **propager** VERB [45]
to spread
□ Le feu s'est propagé rapidement. The fire spread quickly.

la **proportion** NOUN
proportion

le **propos** NOUN
■ **à propos** by the way □ À propos, quand est-ce que tu viens? By the way, when are you coming?
■ **à propos de quelque chose** about something □ C'est à propos de la soirée de vendredi. It's about the party on Friday.

proposer VERB [28]
■ **proposer quelque chose à quelqu'un**
1 to suggest something to somebody □ Nous lui avons proposé une promenade en bateau. We suggested going on a boat ride to him. 2 to offer somebody something □ Ils m'ont proposé des chocolats. They offered me some chocolates.

la **proposition** NOUN
offer
□ J'accepte ta proposition avec plaisir. I'll be pleased to accept your offer.

propre (FEM **propre**) ADJECTIVE
▷ see also **propre** NOUN
1 clean
□ Ce mouchoir n'est pas propre. This handkerchief isn't clean.
2 own
□ Gordon l'a fabriqué de ses propres mains. Gordon made it with his own hands.
■ **propre à** characteristic of □ C'est une coutume propre au Berry. It's a custom you find in the Berry region.

le **propre** NOUN
▷ see also **propre** ADJECTIVE
■ **recopier quelque chose au propre** to make a fair copy of something

proprement ADVERB
properly
□ Mange proprement! Eat properly!
■ **le village proprement dit** the village itself
■ **à proprement parler** strictly speaking

la **propreté** NOUN
cleanliness

le **propriétaire** NOUN
▷ see also **la propriétaire**
1 owner
2 landlord

la **propriétaire** NOUN
▷ see also **le propriétaire**
1 owner
2 landlady

la **propriété** NOUN
property
□ la propriété privée private property

le **prospectus** NOUN
leaflet

prospère (FEM **prospère**) ADJECTIVE
prosperous

la **prostituée** NOUN
prostitute

protecteur (FEM **protectrice**) ADJECTIVE
1 protective
□ un vernis protecteur a protective varnish
2 patronizing
□ un ton protecteur a patronizing tone

la **protection** NOUN
protection

protéger VERB [66]
to protect

la **protéine** NOUN
protein

protestant (FEM **protestante**) ADJECTIVE
Protestant
□ une église protestante a Protestant church
■ **Il est protestant.** He's a Protestant.

la **protestation** NOUN
protest

protester VERB [28]
to protest
□ Ils protestent contre leurs conditions de travail. They're protesting about their working conditions.

prouver VERB [28]
to prove

la **provenance** NOUN
origin
■ **un avion en provenance de Berlin** a plane arriving from Berlin

provenir VERB [89]
■ **provenir de** 1 to come from □ Ces tomates proviennent d'Espagne. These tomatoes come from Spain. 2 to be the result of □ Cela provient d'un manque d'organisation. This is the result of a lack of organization.

le **proverbe** NOUN
proverb

la **province** NOUN
province
■ **en province** in the provinces □ Ils habitent en province. They live in the provinces.

le **proviseur** NOUN
headteacher (of state secondary school)
□ Elle est proviseur. She's a headteacher.

la **provision** NOUN
supply

□ une provision de pommes de terre a supply of potatoes

les **provisions** FEM PL NOUN
food
□ Nous n'avons plus beaucoup de provisions. We haven't got much food left.

provisoire (FEM **provisoire**) ADJECTIVE
temporary
□ un emploi provisoire a temporary job

provoquer VERB [28]
1 to provoke
□ Il l'a provoquée en la traitant d'imbécile. He provoked her by calling her stupid.
2 to cause
□ Cet accident a provoqué la mort de quarante personnes. The accident caused the death of 40 people.

la **proximité** NOUN
proximity
■ **à proximité** nearby □ Sabine habite à proximité. Sabine lives nearby.

prudemment ADVERB
1 carefully
□ Conduisez prudemment! Drive carefully!
2 wisely
□ Prudemment, il a fait des économies. Wisely, he saved some money.
3 cautiously
□ Le gouvernement a réagi prudemment. The government reacted cautiously.

la **prudence** NOUN
caution
■ **avec prudence** carefully □ Ils ont conduit avec prudence. They drove carefully.

prudent (FEM **prudente**) ADJECTIVE
1 careful
□ Soyez prudents! Be careful!
2 wise
□ Laisse ton passeport à la maison, c'est plus prudent. It would be wiser to leave your passport at home.

la **prune** NOUN
plum

le **pruneau** (PL les **pruneaux**) NOUN
prune

le/la **psychiatre** NOUN
psychiatrist

la **psychologie** NOUN
psychology

psychologique (FEM **psychologique**) ADJECTIVE
psychological

le/la **psychologue** NOUN
psychologist

pu VERB ▷ see **pouvoir**
■ **Je n'ai pas pu venir.** I couldn't come.

la **pub** NOUN (informal)
1 advertising
□ Il y a trop de pub à la télé. There's too much advertising on TV.
2 adverts
□ Le film a été coupé par la pub. The film was interrupted by adverts.

public (FEM **publique**) ADJECTIVE
▷ see also **public** NOUN
public
□ un jardin public a public park
■ **une école publique** a state school

le **public** NOUN
▷ see also **public** ADJECTIVE
1 public
□ Ce parc est ouvert au public. The park's open to the public.
2 audience
□ Le public a applaudi le chanteur. The audience applauded the singer.
■ **en public** in public □ Je déteste parler en public. I hate speaking in public.

publicitaire (FEM **publicitaire**) ADJECTIVE
■ **une agence publicitaire** an advertising agency
■ **un film publicitaire** a publicity film

la **publicité** NOUN
1 advertising
□ Muriel travaille dans la publicité. Muriel works in advertising.
2 advert
□ Il y a trop de publicités dans ce journal. There are too many adverts in this newspaper.
■ **faire de la publicité pour quelque chose** to publicize something

publier VERB [19]
to publish
□ Bob vient de publier son nouveau roman. Bob has just published his new novel.

publique FEM ADJECTIVE ▷ see **public**

la **puce** NOUN
1 flea
□ Ce chien a des puces. This dog has fleas.
2 chip
□ une puce électronique a microchip
■ **une carte à puce** a smart card

les **puces** FEM PL NOUN
flea market

puer VERB [28]
to stink
□ Ça pue le tabac ici! It stinks of tobacco round here!

puéril (FEM **puérile**) ADJECTIVE
childish

puis VERB
▷ see also **puis** ADVERB ▷ see **pouvoir**

P

■ **Puis-je venir vous voir samedi?** May I come and see you on Saturday?

puis ADVERB
▷ *see also* **puis** VERB
then
□ Faites dorer le poulet, puis ajoutez le vin blanc. Fry the chicken till golden, then add white wine.

puisque CONJUNCTION
since
□ Puisque c'est si cher, nous irons manger ailleurs. Since it's so expensive, we'll eat elsewhere.

la **puissance** NOUN
power

puissant (FEM **puissante**) ADJECTIVE
powerful

le **puits** NOUN
well
□ Il a un puits dans son jardin. He's got a well in his garden.

le **pull** NOUN
jumper

le **pull-over** NOUN
jumper

le **pulvérisateur** NOUN
spray
□ un pulvérisateur de parfum a perfume spray

pulvériser VERB [28]
1 to pulverize
□ L'explosion a pulvérisé le bâtiment. The explosion pulverized the building.
2 to spray
□ Il a pulvérisé de l'insecticide sur ses plantes. He sprayed insecticide on his plants.

la **punaise** NOUN
drawing pin

punir VERB [38]
to punish
□ Il a été puni pour avoir menti. He was punished for lying.

la **punition** NOUN
punishment

le **pupitre** NOUN
desk *(for pupil)*

pur (FEM **pure**) ADJECTIVE
1 pure
□ L'eau de cette source est très pure. The water from this spring is very pure.
2 neat *(undiluted)*
□ du whisky pur neat whisky □ de l'eau de Javel pure concentrated bleach
■ **c'est de la folie pure** it's sheer madness

la **purée** NOUN
mashed potatoes
■ **la purée de marrons** chestnut purée

le **puzzle** NOUN
jigsaw puzzle

le **PV** NOUN *(= procès-verbal)*
parking ticket

le **pyjama** NOUN
pyjamas

la **pyramide** NOUN
pyramid

les **Pyrénées** FEM PL NOUN
Pyrenees
■ **dans les Pyrénées** in the Pyrenees

P

Qq

le **QI** NOUN (= *quotient intellectuel*)
IQ

le **quai** NOUN
1 quay
□ être à quai to be alongside the quay
2 platform
□ Le train partira du quai numéro quatre.
The train will leave from platform 4.

qualifié (FEM **qualifiée**) ADJECTIVE
qualified

qualifier VERB [19]
■ **se qualifier** to qualify □ Bob s'est qualifié
pour la demi-finale. Bob has qualified for
the semifinal.

la **qualité** NOUN
quality
□ Ces outils sont de très bonne qualité.
These are very good quality tools.

quand CONJUNCTION, ADVERB
when
□ Quand est-ce que tu pars en vacances?
When are you going on holiday? □ Quand je
serai riche, j'achèterai une belle maison.
When I'm rich, I'll buy a nice house.
■ **quand même** all the same □ Je ne
voulais pas de dessert, mais j'en ai mangé
quand même. I didn't want any dessert, but
I had some all the same.

quant à PREPOSITION
regarding
□ Quant au problème de chauffage …
Regarding the problem with the heating …
□ Quant à moi, je n'arriverai qu'à dix heures.
As for me, I won't be arriving till 10 o'clock.

la **quantité** NOUN
amount
■ **des quantités de** a great deal of

la **quarantaine** NOUN
about forty
□ une quarantaine de personnes about
forty people
■ **Elle a la quarantaine.** She's in her
forties.

quarante NUMBER
forty

□ Elle a quarante ans. She's forty.
■ **quarante et un** forty-one
■ **quarante-deux** forty-two

le **quart** NOUN
quarter
■ **le quart de** a quarter of □ Elle a mangé le
quart du gâteau. She ate a quarter of the
cake.
■ **trois quarts** three quarters
■ **un quart d'heure** a quarter of an hour
■ **deux heures et quart** a quarter past two
■ **dix heures moins le quart** a quarter to
ten
■ **Un quart d'eau minérale, s'il vous plaît.**
A small bottle of mineral water, please.

le **quartier** NOUN
1 area (*of town*)
□ un quartier tranquille a quiet area
□ un cinéma de quartier a local cinema
2 piece
□ un quartier d'orange a piece of orange

le **quartz** NOUN
■ **une montre à quartz** a quartz watch

quasi ADVERB
nearly
□ La quasi-totalité des récoltes a été
détruite. Nearly all of the crop was
destroyed.

quasiment ADVERB
nearly
□ Le film est quasiment fini. The film's
nearly finished.
■ **quasiment jamais** hardly ever □ Ils ne
vont quasiment jamais en boîte. They
hardly ever go clubbing.

quatorze NUMBER
fourteen
□ Mon frère a quatorze ans. My brother's
fourteen. □ à quatorze heures at 2 p.m.
■ **le quatorze février** the fourteenth of
February

quatre NUMBER
four
□ Il est quatre heures du matin. It's four in
the morning. □ Il a quatre ans. He's four.

■ **le quatre février** the fourth of February
■ **faire les quatre cents coups** to be a bit wild □ Todd a fait les quatre cents coups dans sa jeunesse. Todd was a bit wild in his youth.

quatre-vingts NUMBER
eighty

> LANGUAGE TIP **quatre-vingts** is spelt with an **-s** when it is followed by a noun, but not when it is followed by another number.

□ quatre-vingts euros eighty euros □ Elle a quatre-vingt-deux ans. She's eighty-two.
■ **quatre-vingt-dix** ninety
■ **quatre-vingt-onze** ninety-one
■ **quatre-vingt-quinze** ninety-five
■ **quatre-vingt-dix-huit** ninety-eight

> LANGUAGE TIP Word for word, **quatre-vingts** means 'four twenties'.

quatrième (FEM **quatrième**) ADJECTIVE
▷ see also **quatrième** NOUN
fourth
□ au quatrième étage on the fourth floor

la **quatrième** NOUN
▷ see also **quatrième** ADJECTIVE
year 9
□ Mon frère est en quatrième. My brother's in year 9.

> DID YOU KNOW...?
> In French secondary schools, years are counted from the **sixième** (youngest) to **première** and **terminale** (oldest).

que CONJUNCTION, PRONOUN, ADVERB
1 that
□ Il sait que tu es là. He knows that you're here. □ la dame que j'ai rencontrée hier the lady that I met yesterday □ Le gâteau qu'elle a fait est délicieux. The cake she's made is delicious.
■ **Je veux que tu viennes.** I want you to come.
2 what
□ Que fais-tu? What are you doing? □ Que vas-tu lui dire? What are you going to tell him?
■ **Qu'est-ce que ...?** What ...? □ Qu'est-ce que tu fais? What are you doing? □ Qu'est-ce que c'est? What's that?
■ **plus ... que** more ... than □ C'est plus difficile que je ne le pensais. It's more difficult than I thought. □ Il est plus grand que moi. He's bigger than me.
■ **aussi ... que** as ... as □ Elle est aussi jolie que sa sœur. She's as pretty as her sister. □ Le train est aussi cher que l'avion. The train is as expensive as the plane.

■ **ne ... que** only □ Il ne boit que de l'eau. He only drinks water. □ Je ne l'ai vu qu'une fois. I've only seen him once.
■ **Qu'il est bête!** He's so silly!

quel (FEM **quelle**) ADJECTIVE
1 who
□ Quel est ton chanteur préféré? Who's your favourite singer?
2 what
□ Quelle est ta couleur préférée? What's your favourite colour? □ Quelle heure est-il? What time is it? □ Quelle bonne surprise! What a surprise!
3 which
□ Quel groupe préfères-tu? Which band do you like best?
■ **quel que soit 1** whoever □ quel que soit le coupable whoever is guilty **2** whatever □ quel que soit votre avis whatever your opinion

quelle FEM ADJECTIVE ▷ see **quel**

quelque (FEM **quelque**) ADJECTIVE, ADVERB
1 some
□ Il a quelques amis à Paris. He has some friends in Paris. □ J'ai acheté quelques disques. I bought some records.
2 a few
□ Il reste quelques bouteilles. There are a few bottles left.
3 few
□ Ils ont fini les quelques bouteilles qui restaient. They finished the few bottles that were left.
■ **quelque chose 1** something □ J'ai quelque chose pour toi. I've got something for you. □ Je voudrais quelque chose de moins cher. I'd like something cheaper. **2** anything □ Avez-vous quelque chose à déclarer? Have you got anything to declare? □ Tu as pensé à quelque chose d'autre? Did you think of anything else?
■ **quelque part 1** somewhere □ J'ai oublié mon sac quelque part. I've left my bag somewhere. **2** anywhere □ Vous allez quelque part ce week-end? Are you going anywhere this weekend?

quelquefois ADVERB
sometimes

quelques-uns (FEM **quelques-unes**) PL PRONOUN
some
□ As-tu vu ses films? J'en ai vu quelques-uns. Have you seen his films? I've seen some of them.

quelqu'un PRONOUN
1 somebody
□ Quelqu'un t'a appelé. Somebody phoned

q

223

you. □ Il y a quelqu'un à la porte. There's somebody at the door.

2 anybody

□ Est-ce que quelqu'un a vu mon parapluie? Has anybody seen my umbrella? □ Il y a quelqu'un? Is there anybody there?

la **querelle** NOUN
quarrel

qu'est-ce que ▷ see que
qu'est-ce qui ▷ see qui
la **question** NOUN

1 question

□ Je t'ai posé une question. I asked you a question.

2 matter

□ Ils se sont disputés pour des questions d'argent. They argued over money matters.
■ **Il n'en est pas question.** There's no question of it. □ Il n'est pas question que je paye. There's no question of me paying.
■ **De quoi est-il question?** What's it about? □ Il est question de l'organisation du concert. It's about the organization of the concert.
■ **hors de question** out of the question □ Il est hors de question que nous restions ici. It's out of the question that we stay here.

le **questionnaire** NOUN
questionnaire

questionner VERB [28]
to question

la **queue** NOUN

1 tail

□ Le chien a agité la queue. The dog wagged its tail.
■ **faire la queue** to queue
■ **une queue de cheval** a ponytail

2 rear

□ en queue du train at the rear of the train

3 bottom

□ en queue de liste at the bottom of the list

4 stalk (of fruit, leaf)

□ la queue d'une cerise a cherry stalk

qui PRONOUN

1 who

□ Qui a téléphoné? Who phoned?
□ Einstein, qui était un génie ... Einstein, who was a genius ...

2 whom

□ C'est la personne à qui j'ai parlé hier. It's the person whom I spoke to yesterday.

3 that

□ Donne-moi la veste qui est sur la chaise. Give me the jacket that's on the chair.
■ **Qui est-ce qui ...?** Who ...? □ Qui est-ce qui t'emmène au spectacle? Who's taking you to the show?

■ **Qui est-ce que ...?** Who ...? □ Qui est-ce que tu as vu à cette soirée? Who did you see at the party?
■ **Qu'est-ce qui ...?** What ...? □ Qu'est-ce qui est sur la table? What's on the table? □ Qu'est-ce qui te prend? What's the matter with you?
■ **À qui est ce sac?** Whose bag is this?
■ **À qui parlais-tu?** Who were you talking to?

la **quille** NOUN
■ **un jeu de quilles** skittles

la **quincaillerie** NOUN
ironmonger's (shop)

le **quinquennat** NOUN

⟨ DID YOU KNOW...?
le quinquennat is the five-year term of office of the French President. ⟩

la **quinzaine** NOUN
about fifteen

□ Il y avait une quinzaine de personnes. There were about fifteen people there.
■ **une quinzaine de jours** a fortnight

quinze NUMBER
fifteen

□ Anaïs a quinze ans. Anaïs is fifteen. □ à quinze heures at 3 p.m.
■ **le quinze février** the fifteenth of February
■ **dans quinze jours** in a fortnight's time

la **quittance** NOUN

1 receipt

2 bill

quitter VERB [28]
to leave

□ J'ai quitté la maison à huit heures. I left the house at 8 o'clock.
■ **se quitter** to part □ Les deux amis se sont quittés devant le café. The two friends parted in front of the café.
■ **Ne quittez pas.** (on telephone) Hold the line. □ Ne quittez pas, je vous passe Monsieur Divan. Hold the line, I'll put you through to Monsieur Divan.

quoi PRONOUN
what?

□ À quoi penses-tu? What are you thinking about? □ C'est quoi, ce truc? What's this thing?
■ **Quoi de neuf?** What's new?
■ **As-tu de quoi écrire?** Have you got anything to write with?
■ **Je n'ai pas de quoi acheter une voiture.** I can't afford to buy a car.
■ **Quoi qu'il arrive.** Whatever happens.
■ **Il n'y a pas de quoi.** Don't mention it.
■ **Il n'y a pas de quoi s'énerver.** There's no

reason for getting worked up.

■ **En quoi puis-je vous aider?** How may I help you?

quoique CONJUNCTION

even though

> 🔅 **LANGUAGE TIP** **quoique** is followed by a verb in the subjunctive.

□ Il va l'acheter quoique ce soit cher. He's going to buy it even though it's expensive.

quotidien (FEM **quotidienne**) ADJECTIVE

▷ *see also* **quotidien** NOUN

daily

□ Il est parti faire sa promenade quotidienne. He's gone for his daily walk.

■ **la vie quotidienne** everyday life

le **quotidien** NOUN

▷ *see also* **quotidien** ADJECTIVE

daily paper

□ Le Monde est un quotidien. Le Monde is a daily paper.

Rr

le **rab** NOUN (informal)
seconds (of meal)
□ Il y a du rab? Are there any seconds?

le **rabais** NOUN
reduction (in price)
■ **au rabais** at a discount

la **racaille** NOUN
riff-raff

raccompagner VERB [28]
to take home
□ Tu peux me raccompagner? Can you take
me home?

le **raccourci** NOUN
shortcut

raccrocher VERB [28]
to hang up (telephone)

la **race** NOUN
1 race
□ la race humaine the human race
2 breed
□ De quelle race est ton chat? What breed is
your cat?
■ **de race** pedigree □ un chien de race a
pedigree dog

racheter VERB [1]
1 to buy another
□ J'ai racheté un portefeuille. I've bought
another wallet. □ racheter du lait to buy
more milk
2 to buy
□ Il m'a racheté ma moto. He bought my
bike from me.

la **racine** NOUN
root

le **racisme** NOUN
racism

raciste (FEM **raciste**) ADJECTIVE
racist

raconter VERB [28]
■ **raconter quelque chose à quelqu'un** to
tell somebody about something □ Raconte-
moi ce qui s'est passé. Tell me what
happened. □ Raconte-moi une histoire. Tell
me a story.
■ **Qu'est-ce que tu racontes?** What are

you talking about?

le **radar** NOUN
radar

le **radiateur** NOUN
radiator
■ **un radiateur électrique** an electric
heater

radin (FEM **radine**) ADJECTIVE (informal)
stingy

la **radio** NOUN
1 radio
□ à la radio on the radio
■ **une radio numérique** a digital radio
2 X-ray
■ **passer une radio** to have an X-ray □ Elle
a passé une radio des poumons. She had a
chest X-ray.

le **radio-réveil** (PL les **radios-réveils**) NOUN
clock radio

le **radis** NOUN
radish

raffoler VERB [28]
■ **raffoler de** to be crazy about □ Elle
raffole de la tarte aux pommes. She really
loves apple tart.

rafraîchir VERB [38]
to cool down
■ **se rafraîchir 1** to get cooler □ Le temps
se rafraîchit. The weather's getting cooler.
2 to freshen up □ Il a pris une douche pour
se rafraîchir. He had a shower to freshen up.

rafraîchissant (FEM **rafraîchissante**)
ADJECTIVE
refreshing

la **rage** NOUN
rabies
■ **une rage de dents** raging toothache

le **ragoût** NOUN
stew

raide (FEM **raide**) ADJECTIVE
1 steep
□ Cette pente est raide. This is a steep
slope.
2 straight
□ Laure a les cheveux raides. Laure has

straight hair.

3 stiff

□ Son bras est encore raide. His arm's still stiff.

4 flat broke

□ Je suis raide ce mois-ci. *(informal)* I'm flat broke this month.

la **raie** NOUN

1 skate *(fish)*

2 parting *(in hair)*

le **rail** NOUN

rail

□ par rail by rail

le **raisin** NOUN

grapes

□ le raisin blanc green grapes

■ **des raisins secs** raisins

la **raison** NOUN

reason

□ sans raison for no reason □ Raison de plus pour y aller. All the more reason for going.

■ **Ce n'est pas une raison.** That's no excuse.

■ **avoir raison** to be right □ Tu as raison. You're right.

■ **en raison de** because of □ en raison d'une grève because of a strike

raisonnable (FEM **raisonnable**) ADJECTIVE

sensible

□ Elle est très raisonnable pour son âge. She's very sensible for her age.

le **raisonnement** NOUN

reasoning

□ J'ai du mal à suivre son raisonnement. I have difficulty following his reasoning.

rajouter VERB [28]

to add

ralentir VERB [38]

to slow down

râler VERB [28] *(informal)*

to moan

le **ramassage** NOUN

■ **le ramassage scolaire** the school bus service

ramasser VERB [28]

1 to pick up

□ Il a ramassé son crayon. He picked up his pencil.

2 to take in

□ Il a ramassé les copies. He took in the exam papers.

la **rame** NOUN

1 oar *(of boat)*

2 train *(on the underground)*

le **rameau** (PL les **rameaux**) NOUN

branch

■ **le dimanche des Rameaux** Palm Sunday

ramener VERB [43]

1 to bring back

□ Je t'ai ramené un souvenir de Grèce. I've brought you back a present from Greece.

2 to take home

□ Tu me ramènes? Will you take me home?

ramer VERB [28]

to row

□ C'est Jean-Pierre qui ramait. Jean-Pierre was rowing.

la **rampe** NOUN

banister

la **rancune** NOUN

■ **garder rancune à quelqu'un** to bear somebody a grudge

■ **Sans rancune!** No hard feelings!

rancunier (FEM **rancunière**) ADJECTIVE

vindictive

la **randonnée** NOUN

■ **une randonnée à vélo** a bike ride

■ **une randonnée pédestre** a ramble

■ **faire de la randonnée** to go hiking

le **randonneur** NOUN

hiker

la **randonneuse** NOUN

hiker

le **rang** NOUN

row *(line)*

□ au premier rang in the front row □ se mettre en rangs to get into rows

la **rangée** NOUN

row *(line)*

□ une rangée de chaises a row of chairs

ranger VERB [45]

1 to put away

□ J'ai rangé tes affaires. I've put your things away.

2 to tidy up

□ Va ranger ta chambre. Go and tidy up your room.

le **rap** NOUN

rap

□ C'est un chanteur de rap très connu. He's a well-known rap singer.

râper VERB [28]

to grate

□ le fromage râpé grated cheese

rapide (FEM **rapide**) ADJECTIVE

1 fast

□ Cette voiture est très rapide. This is a very fast car.

2 quick

□ J'ai jeté un coup d'œil rapide sur ton travail. I had a quick glance at your work.

rapidement ADVERB

quickly

le **rappel** NOUN
1 booster *(vaccination)*
2 curtain call
rappeler VERB [4]
to call back
□ Je te rappelle dans cinq minutes. I'll call you back in 5 minutes.
■ **rappeler quelque chose à quelqu'un** to remind somebody of something □ Cette odeur me rappelle mon enfance. This smell reminds me of my childhood.
■ **rappeler à quelqu'un de faire quelque chose** to remind somebody to do something □ Rappelle-moi d'acheter des billets. Remind me to get tickets.
■ **se rappeler** to remember □ Il s'est rappelé qu'il avait une course à faire. He remembered he had some shopping to do.
le **rapport** NOUN
▷ *see also* **les rapports**
1 report
□ Il a écrit un rapport. He wrote a report.
2 connection
□ Je ne vois pas le rapport. I can't see the connection.
■ **par rapport à** in comparison with
rapporter VERB [28]
to bring back
□ Je leur ai rapporté un cadeau. I brought them back a present.
le **rapporteur** NOUN
telltale
la **rapporteuse** NOUN
telltale
les **rapports** MASC PL NOUN
▷ *see also* **le rapport**
relations
□ Leurs rapports avec leurs voisins se sont améliorés. Their relations with their neighbours have improved.
■ **les rapports sexuels** sexual intercourse
rapprocher VERB [28]
1 to bring together
□ Cet accident a rapproché les deux frères. The accident brought the two brothers together.
2 to bring closer
□ Il a rapproché le fauteuil de la télé. He brought the armchair closer to the TV.
■ **se rapprocher** to come closer
□ Rapproche-toi, tu verras mieux. Come closer, you'll see better.
la **raquette** NOUN
1 racket *(tennis)*
2 bat *(table tennis)*
rare (FEM **rare**) ADJECTIVE
rare

□ une plante rare a rare plant
rarement ADVERB
rarely
ras (FEM **rase**) ADJECTIVE, ADVERB
short
□ un chien à poil ras a short-haired dog
■ **à ras bords** to the brim □ Il a rempli son verre à ras bords. He filled his glass to the brim.
■ **en avoir ras le bol de quelque chose** *(informal)* to be fed up with something
■ **un pull ras du cou** a crew-neck jumper
raser VERB [28]
to shave off
□ Ray a rasé sa barbe. Ray has shaved off his beard.
■ **se raser** to shave
le **rasoir** NOUN
▷ *see also* **rasoir** ADJECTIVE
razor
rasoir (FEM+PL **rasoir**) ADJECTIVE *(informal)*
▷ *see also* **rasoir** NOUN
dead boring
rassembler VERB [28]
to assemble
□ Il a rassemblé les enfants dans la cour. He assembled the children in the playground.
■ **se rassembler** to gather together □ Les passagers se sont rassemblés près du car. The passengers gathered near the coach.
rassurer VERB [28]
to reassure
■ **Je suis rassuré.** I don't need to worry any more.
■ **se rassurer** to be reassured
■ **Rassure-toi!** Don't worry!
le **rat** NOUN
rat
raté (FEM **ratée**) ADJECTIVE
failed
□ une tentative ratée a failed attempt □ Il a raté sa pizza. His pizza was a failure.
le **râteau** (PL les **râteaux**) NOUN
rake
rater VERB [28]
1 to miss
□ Chantal a raté son train. Chantal missed her train.
2 to fail
□ J'ai raté mon examen de maths. I failed my maths exam. □ Elle a raté sa pizza. Her pizza didn't turn out right.
la **RATP** NOUN
Paris transport authority
rattacher VERB [28]
to tie up again
□ rattacher ses lacets to retie one's laces

rattraper VERB [28]
1 to recapture
□ La police a rattrapé le voleur. The police recaptured the thief.
2 to catch up with
□ Je vais rattraper Cécile. I'll catch up with Cécile.
3 to make up for
□ Il faut rattraper le temps perdu. We must make up for lost time.
■ **se rattraper** to make up for it □ Quand il ne mange pas à midi il se rattrape au dîner. When he doesn't have lunch he makes up for it at dinnertime.

la **rature** NOUN
correction
□ un texte sans ratures a text with no corrections

ravi (FEM **ravie**) ADJECTIVE
■ **être ravi** to be delighted □ Ils étaient ravis de nous voir. They were delighted to see us. □ Je suis ravi que vous puissiez venir. I'm delighted that you can come.

se **raviser** VERB [28]
to change your mind
□ Il allait accepter, mais il s'est ravisé. He was going to accept, but he changed his mind.

ravissant (FEM **ravissante**) ADJECTIVE
lovely

rayé (FEM **rayée**) ADJECTIVE
striped
□ une chemise rayée a striped shirt

rayer VERB [59]
1 to scratch
□ Il a rayé la peinture de sa voiture. He scratched the paintwork of his car.
2 to cross off
□ Son nom a été rayé de la liste. His name has been crossed off the list.

le **rayon** NOUN
1 ray
□ un rayon de soleil a ray of sunshine
2 radius
□ le rayon d'un cercle the radius of a circle
3 shelf
□ les rayons d'une bibliothèque the shelves of a bookcase
4 department
□ le rayon hi-fi vidéo the hi-fi and video department
■ **les rayons X** X-rays

la **rayure** NOUN
stripe

le **ré** NOUN
1 D
□ en ré majeur in D major

2 re
□ do, ré, mi … do, re, mi …

la **réaction** NOUN
reaction

réagir VERB [38]
to react

le **réalisateur** NOUN
director (of film)
□ Spielberg est réalisateur. Spielberg is a film director.

la **réalisatrice** NOUN
director (of film)
□ Elle est réalisatrice. She's a film director.

réaliser VERB [28]
1 to carry out
□ Ils ont réalisé leur projet. They carried out their plan.
2 to fulfil
□ Il a réalisé son rêve. He has fulfilled his dream.
3 to realize
□ Tu réalises ce que tu dis? Do you realize what you're saying?
4 to make
□ réaliser un film to make a film
■ **se réaliser** to come true □ Mon rêve s'est réalisé. My dream has come true.

réaliste (FEM **réaliste**) ADJECTIVE
realistic

la **réalité** NOUN
reality
■ **en réalité** in fact

le **rebelle** NOUN
rebel

rebondir VERB [38]
to bounce

le **rebord** NOUN
edge
□ le rebord du lavabo the edge of the washbasin
■ **le rebord de la fenêtre** the window ledge

recaler VERB [28] (informal)
■ **J'ai été recalé en maths.** I failed maths.

récemment ADVERB
recently

récent (FEM **récente**) ADJECTIVE
recent

le **récepteur** NOUN
receiver

la **réception** NOUN
reception desk

le/la **réceptionniste** NOUN
receptionist
□ Elle est réceptionniste. She's a receptionist.

la **recette** NOUN

recipe

recevoir VERB [67]
1 to receive
□ J'ai reçu une lettre. I received a letter.
2 to see
□ Il a déjà reçu trois clients. He has already seen three clients.
3 to have round
□ Je reçois des amis à dîner. I'm having friends round for dinner.
■ **être reçu à un examen** to pass an exam

le **rechange** NOUN
■ **de rechange** spare (battery, bulb)
■ **des vêtements de rechange** a change of clothes

la **recharge** NOUN
refill

le **réchaud** NOUN
stove

réchauffer VERB [28]
1 to reheat
□ Je vais réchauffer les légumes. I'll reheat the vegetables.
2 to warm up
□ Un bon café va te réchauffer. A nice cup of coffee will warm you up.
■ **se réchauffer** to warm oneself □ Je vais me réchauffer près du feu. I'll go and warm myself by the fire.

la **recherche** NOUN
research
□ Je voudrais faire de la recherche. I'd like to do some research.
■ **être à la recherche de quelque chose** to be looking for something □ Je suis à la recherche d'un emploi. I'm looking for a job.
■ **les recherches** search □ La police a interrompu les recherches. The police called off the search.

recherché (FEM **recherchée**) ADJECTIVE
much sought-after

rechercher VERB [28]
to look for
□ La police recherche l'assassin. The police are looking for the killer.

la **rechute** NOUN
relapse

le **récipient** NOUN
container

le **récit** NOUN
story

réciter VERB [28]
to recite

la **réclamation** NOUN
complaint
□ J'ai une réclamation à faire. I want to

make a complaint.
■ **les réclamations** the complaints department

la **réclame** NOUN
advert
□ une réclame de lessive an advert for washing powder
■ **en réclame** on special offer □ Le saumon était en réclame au supermarché. Salmon was on special offer at the supermarket.

réclamer VERB [28]
1 to demand
□ Nous réclamons la semaine de trente heures. We demand a 30-hour week.
2 to complain
□ Elles sont toujours en train de réclamer. They're always complaining about something.

reçois VERB ▷ see recevoir

la **récolte** NOUN
harvest

récolter VERB [28]
1 to harvest
□ Ils ont récolté le blé. They harvested the wheat.
2 to collect
□ Ils ont récolté deux cents euros. They collected 200 euros.
3 to get
□ Il a récolté une amende. (informal) He got a fine.

le **recommandé** NOUN
■ **en recommandé** by registered mail □ Je voudrais envoyer ce paquet en recommandé. I'd like to send this parcel registered.

recommander VERB [28]
to recommend
□ Je vous recommande ce restaurant. I recommend this restaurant.

recommencer VERB [12]
1 to start again
□ Il a recommencé à pleuvoir. It's started raining again.
2 to do again
□ S'il n'est pas puni, il va recommencer. If he's not punished he'll do it again.

la **récompense** NOUN
reward

récompenser VERB [28]
to reward
□ Il m'a récompensée de mes efforts. He rewarded me for my efforts.

réconcilier VERB [19]
■ **se réconcilier avec quelqu'un** to make it up with somebody □ Il s'est réconcilié avec sa sœur. He has made it up with his sister.

reconnaissant (FEM **reconnaissante**)
ADJECTIVE
grateful

reconnaître VERB [14]
1 to recognize
□ Je ne l'ai pas reconnu. I didn't recognize him.
2 to admit
□ Je reconnais que j'ai eu tort. I admit I was wrong.

reconstruire VERB [23]
to rebuild

le **record** NOUN
record
□ battre un record to break a record

recouvrir VERB [55]
to cover
□ La neige recouvre le sol. The ground is covered in snow.

la **récréation** NOUN
break
□ Les élèves sont en récréation. The pupils are having their break.
■ **la cour de récréation** the playground (of school)

le **rectangle** NOUN
rectangle

rectangulaire (FEM **rectangulaire**)
ADJECTIVE
rectangular

rectifier VERB [19]
to correct

le **reçu** NOUN
▷ see also **reçu** VERB
receipt

reçu VERB ▷ see **recevoir**
▷ see also **reçu** NOUN
■ **J'ai reçu un colis ce matin.** I received a parcel this morning.
■ **être reçu à un examen** to pass an exam

reculer VERB [28]
1 to step back
□ Il a reculé pour la laisser entrer. He stepped back to let her in.
2 to reverse
□ J'ai reculé pour laisser passer le camion. I reversed to let the lorry past.
3 to postpone
□ Ils ont reculé la date du spectacle. They postponed the show.

reculons
■ **à reculons** ADVERB backwards □ Elle est entrée à reculons. She came in backwards.

récupérer VERB [34]
1 to get back
□ Je vais récupérer ma voiture au garage. I'm going to get my car back from the garage.
2 to make up
□ J'ai des heures à récupérer. I've got time to make up.
3 to recover
□ J'ai besoin de récupérer. I need to recover.

recycler VERB [28]
to recycle
■ **se recycler** to retrain □ Il a décidé de se recycler en informatique. He decided to retrain as a computer programmer.

la **rédaction** NOUN
essay

redemander VERB [28]
1 to ask again for
□ Je vais lui redemander son adresse. I'll ask him for his address again.
2 to ask for more
□ Je vais redemander des carottes. I'm going to ask for more carrots.

redescendre VERB [24]
to go back down
□ Il est redescendu au premier étage. He went back down to the first floor. □ Elle a redescendu l'escalier. She went back down the stairs.

rédiger VERB [45]
to write (an essay)

redoubler VERB [28]
to repeat a year
□ Il a raté son examen et doit redoubler. He's failed his exam and will have to repeat the year.

la **réduction** NOUN
1 reduction
□ une réduction du nombre des touristes a reduction in the number of tourists
2 discount
□ une réduction de vingt euros a 20 euro discount

réduire VERB [23]
to cut
□ Ils ont réduit leurs prix. They've cut their prices. □ Il a réduit de moitié ses dépenses. He has cut his spending by half.

réel (FEM **réelle**) ADJECTIVE
real

réellement ADVERB
really

refaire VERB [36]
1 to do again
□ Je dois refaire ce rapport. I've got to do this report again.
2 to take up again
□ Je voudrais refaire de la gym. I'd like to take up gymnastics again.

le **réfectoire** NOUN

r

231

refectory

la référence NOUN
reference

■ **faire référence à quelque chose** to refer to something

■ **Ce n'est pas une référence!** That's no recommendation!

réfléchi (FEM **réfléchie**) ADJECTIVE
reflexive *(verb)*

■ **C'est tout réfléchi.** My mind's made up.

réfléchir VERB [38]
to think

□ Il est en train de réfléchir. He's thinking.

■ **réfléchir à quelque chose** to think about something □ Je vais réfléchir à ta proposition. I'll think about your suggestion.

le reflet NOUN
reflection

□ les reflets du soleil sur la mer the reflection of the sun on the sea

refléter VERB [34]
to reflect

le réflexe NOUN
reflex

□ avoir de bons réflexes to have good reflexes

la réflexion NOUN

1 thought

□ Elle est en pleine réflexion. She's deep in thought.

2 remark

□ faire des réflexions désagréables to make nasty remarks

■ **réflexion faite** on reflection

le refrain NOUN
chorus *(of song)*

le réfrigérateur NOUN
refrigerator

refroidir VERB [38]
to cool

□ Laissez le gâteau refroidir. Leave the cake to cool.

■ **se refroidir** to get colder □ Le temps se refroidit. It's getting colder.

se réfugier VERB [19]
to take shelter

□ Je me suis réfugié sous un arbre. I took shelter under a tree.

le refus NOUN
refusal

■ **Ce n'est pas de refus.** I wouldn't say no. □ Voulez-vous une bière? — Ce n'est pas de refus. Would you like a beer? — I wouldn't say no.

refuser VERB [28]
to refuse

□ Il a refusé de payer sa part. He refused to pay his share. □ On lui a refusé une augmentation. He was refused a pay rise.

■ **Je refuse qu'on me parle ainsi!** I won't let anybody talk to me like that!

se régaler VERB [28]

■ **Merci beaucoup: je me suis régalé!** Thank you very much: it was absolutely delicious!

le regard NOUN
look

□ Il lui a jeté un regard méfiant. He gave him a mistrustful look. □ On voyait à son regard qu'elle était contrariée. You could tell from the look in her eyes that she was upset.

■ **Tous les regards se sont tournés vers lui.** All eyes turned towards him.

regarder VERB [28]

1 to look at

□ Il regardait ses photos de vacances. He was looking at his holiday photos. □ Regarde! J'ai presque fini. Look! I've nearly finished.

2 to watch

□ Je regarde la télévision. I'm watching television. □ Regarde où tu mets les pieds! Watch where you put your feet!

3 to concern

□ Ça ne nous regarde pas. It doesn't concern us.

■ **ne pas regarder à la dépense** to spare no expense

le régime NOUN

1 régime *(of a country)*

2 diet

□ un régime sans sel a salt-free diet □ se mettre au régime to go on a diet □ suivre un régime to be on a diet

■ **un régime de bananes** a bunch of bananas

la région NOUN
region

régional (FEM **régionale**, MASC PL **régionaux**) ADJECTIVE
regional

le registre NOUN
register

la règle NOUN

1 ruler

□ Il a souligné son nom avec une règle. He underlined his name with a ruler.

2 rule

□ C'est la règle. That's the rule. □ en règle générale as a general rule

■ **être en règle** to be in order □ Mes papiers sont en règle. My papers are in

order.
- **les règles** period (menstruation)

le **règlement** NOUN
rules
□ Le règlement est affiché à l'entrée. The rules are up on the wall by the entrance.

régler VERB [34]
1 to adjust
□ Il faut que je règle mon rétroviseur. I'll have to adjust my rear-view mirror.
2 to tune
□ J'ai réglé ma radio sur 476 FM. I tuned my radio to 476 FM.
3 to set
□ J'ai réglé le thermostat à vingt degrés. I've set the thermostat to 20 degrees.
4 to solve
□ Le problème est réglé. The problem's solved.
5 to settle
□ Elle a réglé sa facture. She's settled her bill. □ J'ai réglé Jean-Pierre pour l'essence. I've settled up with Jean-Pierre for the petrol.

la **réglisse** NOUN
liquorice

le **règne** NOUN
reign
□ sous le règne de Henri IV in the reign of Henry IV

régner VERB [34]
to reign

le **regret** NOUN
regret
- **à regret** reluctantly

regretter VERB [28]
1 to regret
□ Elle regrette ce qu'elle a dit. She regrets saying what she did.
- **Je regrette.** I'm sorry. □ Je regrette, je ne peux pas vous aider. I'm sorry, I can't help you.
2 to miss
□ Je regrette mon ancien travail. I miss my old job.

regrouper VERB [28]
to group together
□ Nous avons regroupé les enfants suivant leur âge. We grouped the children together according to age.
- **se regrouper** to gather together □ Les agriculteurs se sont regroupés pour constituer un syndicat. The farmers joined together to form a union.

régulier (FEM **régulière**) ADJECTIVE
1 regular
□ des livraisons régulières regular deliveries

□ des bus réguliers a regular bus service
2 steady
□ à un rythme régulier at a steady rate
3 scheduled
□ des vols réguliers pour Marseille scheduled flights to Marseilles

régulièrement ADVERB
regularly

le **rein** NOUN
kidney
- **les reins** back (of body)
□ J'ai mal aux reins. My back hurts.

la **reine** NOUN
queen

rejoindre VERB [42]
to go back to
□ J'ai rejoint mes amis. I went back to my friends.
- **Je te rejoins au café.** I'll see you at the café.
- **se rejoindre** to meet up □ Elles se sont rejointes une heure après. They met up an hour later.

relâcher VERB [28]
to release (prisoner, animal)
- **se relâcher** to get slack □ Il se relâche dans son travail. He is slacking in his work.

le **relais** NOUN
relay race
□ le relais quatre fois cent mètres the 4 x 100 metre relay
- **prendre le relais** to take over

la **relation** NOUN
relationship
- **les relations franco-britanniques** Anglo-French relations

se **relaxer** VERB [28]
to relax

se **relayer** VERB [59]
- **se relayer pour faire quelque chose** to take it in turns to do something

le **relevé** NOUN
- **un relevé de compte** a bank statement

relever VERB [43]
1 to collect
□ Je relève les copies dans cinq minutes. I'll collect the papers in five minutes.
2 to react to
□ Je n'ai pas relevé sa réflexion. I didn't react to his remark.
- **relever la tête** to look up
- **se relever** to get up □ Il est tombé mais s'est relevé aussitôt. He fell, but got up immediately.

la **religieuse** NOUN
1 nun
2 choux cream bun

□ des religieuses au chocolat choux buns with chocolate cream and icing

religieux (FEM **religieuse**) ADJECTIVE
religious

la **religion** NOUN
religion

relire VERB [44]
1 to read over
□ Il a relu sa copie avant de la rendre. He read his exam paper over before handing it in.
2 to read again
□ Je voudrais relire ce roman. I'd like to read this novel again.

remarquable (FEM **remarquable**) ADJECTIVE
remarkable

la **remarque** NOUN
1 remark
□ Il a fait une remarque désagréable. He made a nasty remark.
2 comment
□ Avez-vous des remarques à faire? Have you any comments to make?

remarquer VERB [28]
to notice
□ J'ai remarqué qu'elle avait l'air triste. I noticed she was looking sad.
■ **faire remarquer quelque chose à quelqu'un** to point something out to somebody □ Je lui ai fait remarquer que c'était un peu cher. I pointed out to him that it was rather expensive.
■ **Remarquez, il n'est pas si bête que ça.** Mind you, he's not as stupid as all that.
■ **se remarquer** to be noticeable □ David ne s'est pas rasé ce matin. Ça se remarque. It's obvious David didn't shave this morning.
■ **se faire remarquer** to call attention to oneself

le **remboursement** NOUN
refund

rembourser VERB [28]
to pay back
□ Il m'a remboursé l'argent qu'il me devait. He paid me back the money he owed me.
■ **'satisfait ou remboursé'** 'satisfaction or your money back'

le **remède** NOUN
1 medicine
2 cure

remercier VERB [19]
to thank
□ Je te remercie pour ton cadeau. Thank you for your present.
■ **remercier quelqu'un d'avoir fait quelque chose** to thank somebody for doing something □ Je vous remercie de

m'avoir invité. Thank you for inviting me.

remettre VERB [47]
1 to put back on
□ Il a remis son pull. He put his sweater back on.
2 to put back
□ Il a remis sa veste dans l'armoire. He put his jacket back in the wardrobe.
3 to put off
□ J'ai dû remettre mon rendez-vous. I've had to put my appointment off.
■ **se remettre** to recover (from illness)
□ Mélusine s'est bien remise de son opération. Mélusine has fully recovered from her operation.

le **remonte-pente** NOUN
ski-lift

remonter VERB [48]
1 to go back up
□ Il est remonté au premier étage. He has gone back up to the first floor.
2 to go up
□ Ils ont remonté la pente. They went up the hill.
3 to buck up
□ Cette nouvelle m'a un peu remontée. The news bucked me up a bit.
■ **remonter le moral à quelqu'un** to cheer somebody up

le **remords** NOUN
■ **avoir des remords** to feel remorse

la **remorque** NOUN
trailer (of car)

les **remparts** MASC PL NOUN
city walls

le **remplaçant** NOUN
supply teacher

la **remplaçante** NOUN
supply teacher

remplacer VERB [12]
to replace
□ Il faut remplacer cette ampoule. We need to replace this bulb. □ Il remplace le prof de maths. He's replacing the maths teacher.
■ **remplacer par** to replace with

rempli (FEM **remplie**) ADJECTIVE
busy
□ une journée bien remplie a very busy day
■ **rempli de** full of □ La salle était remplie de monde. The room was full of people.

remplir VERB [38]
1 to fill up
□ Elle a rempli son verre de vin. She filled her glass with wine.
2 to fill in
□ Tu as rempli ton formulaire? Have you filled in your form?

■ **se remplir** to fill up □ La salle s'est remplie de monde. The room filled up with people.

remuer VERB [28]

1 to move

□ Elle a remué le bras. She moved her arm.

2 to stir

□ Remuez la sauce pendant deux minutes. Stir the sauce for two minutes.

■ **se remuer** (informal) to go to a lot of trouble □ Ils se sont beaucoup remués pour organiser cette soirée. They went to a lot of trouble organizing this party.

le **renard** NOUN
fox

la **rencontre** NOUN

■ **faire la rencontre de quelqu'un** to meet somebody □ J'ai fait la rencontre de personnes intéressantes ce soir. I met some interesting people this evening.

■ **aller à la rencontre de quelqu'un** to go and meet somebody □ Je viendrai à ta rencontre. I'll come and meet you.

rencontrer VERB [28]
to meet

■ **se rencontrer** to meet □ Ils se sont rencontrés il y a deux ans. They met two years ago.

le **rendez-vous** NOUN

1 appointment

□ J'ai rendez-vous chez le coiffeur. I've got an appointment at the hairdresser's.

□ prendre rendez-vous avec quelqu'un to make an appointment with somebody

2 date

□ Tu sors ce soir? — Oui, j'ai un rendez-vous. Are you going out tonight? — Yes, I've got a date.

■ **donner rendez-vous à quelqu'un** to arrange to meet somebody

rendre VERB [7]

1 to give back

□ J'ai rendu ses CD à Christine. I've given Christine her CDs back.

2 to take back

□ J'ai rendu mes livres à la bibliothèque. I've taken my books back to the library.

■ **rendre quelqu'un célèbre** to make somebody famous

■ **se rendre** to give oneself up □ Le meurtrier s'est rendu à la police. The murderer gave himself up to the police.

■ **se rendre compte de quelque chose** to realize something

le **renfermé** NOUN

■ **sentir le renfermé** to smell stuffy

renifler VERB [28]

to sniff

le **renne** NOUN
reindeer

renommé (FEM **renommée**) ADJECTIVE
renowned

□ La Bretagne est renommée pour ses plages. Brittany is renowned for its beaches.

renoncer VERB [12]

■ **renoncer à** to give up □ Ils ont renoncé à leur projet. They've given up their plan.

■ **renoncer à faire quelque chose** to give up the idea of doing something

renouvelable (FEM **renouvelable**) ADJECTIVE
renewable

□ une énergie renouvelable a renewable energy source

renouveler VERB [4]
to renew (passport, contract)

■ **se renouveler** to happen again □ J'espère que ça ne se renouvellera pas. I hope that won't happen again.

le **renseignement** NOUN
piece of information

□ Il me manque un renseignement. There's one piece of information I still need.

■ **les renseignements 1** information □ Il m'a donné des renseignements. He gave me some information. **2** information desk **3** directory inquiries

renseigner VERB [28]

■ **renseigner quelqu'un sur quelque chose** to give somebody information about something

■ **Est-ce que je peux vous renseigner?** Can I help you?

■ **se renseigner** to find out □ Je vais me renseigner pour voir s'il n'y a pas un vol direct. I'm going to find out if there's a direct flight.

rentable (FEM **rentable**) ADJECTIVE
profitable

la **rentrée** NOUN

■ **la rentrée (des classes)** the start of the new school year

rentrer VERB [68]

1 to come in

□ Rentre, tu vas prendre froid. Come in, you'll catch cold.

2 to go in

□ Elle est rentrée dans le magasin. She went into the shop.

3 to get home

□ Je suis rentré à sept heures hier soir. I got home at 7 o'clock last night.

4 to put away

□ Tu as rentré la voiture? Have you put the

car away?
- ■ **rentrer dans** to crash into □ Sa voiture est rentrée dans un arbre. He crashed into a tree.
- ■ **rentrer dans l'ordre** to get back to normal

la **renverse** NOUN
- ■ **tomber à la renverse** to fall backwards

renverser VERB [28]
1 to knock over
   □ J'ai renversé mon verre. I knocked my glass over.
2 to knock down
   □ Elle a été renversée par une voiture. She was knocked down by a car.
3 to spill
   □ Il a renversé de l'eau partout. He has spilt water everywhere.
- ■ **se renverser** (glass, vase) to fall over

renvoyer VERB [33]
1 to send back
   □ Je t'ai renvoyé ton courrier. I've sent your mail back to you.
2 to dismiss
   □ On a renvoyé deux employés. Two employees have been dismissed.

répandu (FEM **répandue**) ADJECTIVE
common
   □ C'est un préjugé très répandu. It's a very common prejudice.
- ■ **du vin répandu sur la table** wine spilt on the table
- ■ **des papiers répandus sur le sol** papers scattered over the floor

le **réparateur** NOUN
repairman

la **réparation** NOUN
repair

réparer VERB [28]
to repair

repartir VERB [57]
to set off again
   □ Il s'est arrêté pour déjeuner avant de repartir. He stopped for lunch before setting off again. □ Il était là tout à l'heure, mais il est reparti. He was here a moment ago, but he's gone again.
- ■ **repartir à zéro** to start again from scratch

le **repas** NOUN
meal
- ■ **le repas de midi** lunch
- ■ **le repas du soir** dinner

le **repassage** NOUN
ironing
   □ Je déteste le repassage. I hate ironing.

repasser VERB [28]

1 to come back
   □ Je repasserai demain. I'll come back tomorrow.
2 to go back
   □ Je dois repasser au magasin. I've got to go back to the shop.
3 to iron
   □ J'ai repassé ma chemise. I've ironed my shirt.
4 to resit
   □ Elle doit repasser son examen. She's got to resit her exam.

repérer VERB [34]
to spot
   □ J'ai repéré deux fautes. I spotted two mistakes.
- ■ **se repérer** to find one's way around
   □ J'ai du mal à me repérer de nuit. I have difficulty finding my way around when it's dark.

le **répertoire** NOUN
directory

répéter VERB [34]
1 to repeat
   □ Elle répète toujours la même chose. She keeps repeating the same thing.
2 to rehearse
   □ Les acteurs répètent une scène. The actors are rehearsing a scene.
- ■ **se répéter** to happen again □ J'espère que cela ne se répétera pas! I hope this won't happen again!

la **répétition** NOUN
1 repetition
   □ Il y a beaucoup de répétitions dans ce texte. There's a lot of repetition in this text.
- ■ **des grèves à répétition** repeated strikes
2 rehearsal
   □ Ils ont une répétition cet après-midi. They've got a rehearsal this afternoon.
- ■ **la répétition générale** the dress rehearsal

le **répondeur** NOUN
answering machine

répondre VERB [69]
to answer
   □ répondre à quelqu'un to answer somebody

la **réponse** NOUN
answer
   □ C'est la bonne réponse. That's the right answer.

le **reportage** NOUN
1 report
   □ J'ai vu ce reportage aux informations. I saw that report on the news.
2 story

□ J'ai lu ce reportage dans 'La Gazette'. I read that story in 'La Gazette'.

le **reporter** NOUN
reporter
□ Christian est reporter. Christian is a reporter.

le **repos** NOUN
rest

reposer VERB [28]
to put back down
□ Elle a reposé son verre sur la table. She put her glass back down on the table.
■ **se reposer** to have a rest □ Tu pourras te reposer demain. You'll be able to have a rest tomorrow.
■ **se reposer sur quelqu'un** to rely on somebody

repousser VERB [28]
1 to grow again
□ Ses cheveux ont repoussé. Her hair has grown again.
2 to postpone
□ Le voyage est repoussé. The trip's been postponed.

reprendre VERB [65]
1 to take back
□ Il a repris son livre. He's taken his book back.
2 to go back to
□ Elle a repris le travail. She went back to work.
3 to start again
□ La réunion reprendra à deux heures. The meeting will start again at 2 o'clock.
■ **reprendre du pain** to take more bread
■ **reprendre la route** to set off again
■ **reprendre son souffle** to get one's breath back

le **représentant** NOUN
rep
□ Il est représentant chez Harper Collins. He's a rep for Harper Collins.

la **représentante** NOUN
rep
□ Elle est représentante. She's a sales rep.

la **représentation** NOUN
performance
□ la dernière représentation d'une pièce the final performance of a play

représenter VERB [28]
to show
□ Le tableau représente un enfant et un chat. The picture shows a child with a cat.
■ **se représenter** to arise again □ Cette occasion ne se représentera pas. This opportunity won't arise again.

le **reproche** NOUN

■ **faire des reproches à quelqu'un** to reproach somebody

reprocher VERB [28]
■ **reprocher quelque chose à quelqu'un** to reproach somebody for something □ Il m'a reproché mon retard. He reproached me for being late
■ **Qu'est-ce que tu lui reproches?** What have you got against him?

la **reproduction** NOUN
reproduction

reproduire VERB [23]
to reproduce
■ **se reproduire** to happen again □ Je te promets que ça ne se reproduira pas! I promise it won't happen again!

républicain (FEM **républicaine**) ADJECTIVE
republican

la **république** NOUN
republic
□ la République française the French Republic

répugnant (FEM **répugnante**) ADJECTIVE
repulsive

la **réputation** NOUN
reputation

le **requin** NOUN
shark

le **RER** NOUN
Greater Paris high-speed train service

le **réseau** (PL les **réseaux**) NOUN
network

la **réservation** NOUN
reservation

la **réserve** NOUN
stock
□ avoir quelque chose en réserve to have a stock of something
■ **mettre quelque chose en réserve** to put something aside

réservé (FEM **réservée**) ADJECTIVE
reserved
□ Cette table est réservée. This table's reserved.

réserver VERB [28]
1 to reserve
□ Je voudrais réserver une table. I'd like to reserve a table.
2 to book
□ Nous avons réservé une chambre. We've booked a room.
3 to save
□ Je t'ai réservé une part de gâteau. I've saved you a piece of cake.

le **réservoir** NOUN
petrol tank

la **résidence** NOUN

block of flats
■ **une résidence secondaire** a second home

résistant (FEM **résistante**) ADJECTIVE
1 hard-wearing
  □ Ce tissu est résistant. This fabric is hard-wearing.
2 robust
  □ Il est très résistant. He's very robust.

résister VERB [28]
  to resist

résolu (FEM **résolue**) ADJECTIVE
  ■ **Le problème est résolu.** The problem's solved.

résoudre VERB [70]
  to solve

le **respect** NOUN
  respect

respecter VERB [28]
  to respect

la **respiration** NOUN
  breathing

respirer VERB [28]
  to breathe

la **responsabilité** NOUN
  responsibility

responsable (FEM **responsable**) ADJECTIVE
  ▷ see also **responsable** NOUN
  responsible
  □ être responsable de quelque chose to be responsible for something

le/la **responsable** NOUN
  ▷ see also **responsable** ADJECTIVE
1 person in charge
  □ Je voudrais parler au responsable. I'd like to speak to the person in charge.
2 person responsible
  □ Il faut punir les responsables. The people responsible must be punished.

ressembler VERB [28]
  ■ **ressembler à 1** to look like □ Elle ne ressemble pas à sa sœur. She doesn't look like her sister. **2** to be like □ Ça ressemble à un conte de fées. It's like a fairy tale.
  ■ **se ressembler 1** to look alike □ Les deux frères ne se ressemblent pas. The two brothers don't look alike. **2** to be alike □ Ces deux pays ne se ressemblent pas. These two countries aren't alike.

le **ressort** NOUN
  spring (metal)
  □ Le ressort est cassé. The spring is broken.

ressortir VERB [79]
  to go out again

le **restaurant** NOUN
  restaurant

le **reste** NOUN

rest
■ **un reste de poulet** some left-over chicken
■ **les restes** the left-overs

rester VERB [71]
1 to stay
  □ Je reste à la maison ce week-end. I'm staying at home this weekend.
2 to be left
  □ Il reste du pain. There's some bread left.
  □ Il me reste assez de temps. I still have enough time.
  ■ **Il ne me reste plus qu'à ...** I've just got to ... □ Il ne me reste plus qu'à ranger mes affaires. I've just got to put my things away.
  ■ **Restons-en là.** Let's leave it at that.

le **résultat** NOUN
  result
  □ le résultat des examens the exam results

le **résumé** NOUN
  summary

résumer VERB [28]
  to summarize

  ⌣ **LANGUAGE TIP** Be careful! **résumer** does not mean **to resume**.

se **rétablir** VERB [38]
  to get well

le **retard** NOUN
  delay
  □ un retard de livraison a delay in delivery
  ■ **avoir du retard** to be late
  ■ **être en retard de deux heures** to be two hours late
  ■ **prendre du retard** to be delayed

retarder VERB [28]
1 to be slow
  □ Ma montre retarde. My watch is slow.
2 to put back
  □ Je dois retarder la pendule d'une heure. I've got to put the clock back an hour.
  ■ **être retardé** to be delayed □ J'ai été retardé par un coup de téléphone. I was held up by a phone call.

retenir VERB [83]
1 to remember
  □ Tu as retenu leur adresse? Do you remember their address?
2 to book
  □ J'ai retenu une chambre à l'hôtel. I've booked a room at the hotel.
  ■ **retenir son souffle** to hold one's breath

retenu (FEM **retenue**) ADJECTIVE
  ▷ see also **retenue** NOUN
1 reserved
  □ Cette place est retenue. This seat is reserved.
2 held up

□ J'ai été retenu par un coup de téléphone. I was held up by a phone call.

la **retenue** NOUN

▷ *see also* **retenue** ADJECTIVE

detention

□ Gerry est en retenue. Gerry's in detention.

retirer VERB [28]

1 to withdraw

□ Elle a retiré de l'argent. She withdrew some money.

2 to take off

□ Il a retiré son pull. He took off his sweater.

le **retour** NOUN

return

■ **être de retour** to be back □ Je serai de retour la semaine prochaine. I'll be back next week.

retourner VERB [72]

1 to go back

□ Est-ce que tu es retourné à Londres? Have you been back to London?

2 to turn over

□ Elle a retourné la crêpe. She turned the pancake over. □ Il a retourné la poubelle. He turned the bin upside down.

■ **se retourner 1** to turn round □ Janet s'est retournée. Janet turned round. **2** to turn over □ La voiture s'est retournée. The car turned over.

la **retraite** NOUN

■ **être à la retraite** to be retired

■ **prendre sa retraite** to retire

retraité (FEM **retraitée**) ADJECTIVE

▷ *see also* **retraité** NOUN, **retraitée** NOUN

retired

□ Mon oncle est maintenant retraité. My uncle's now retired.

le **retraité** NOUN

▷ *see also* **retraité** ADJECTIVE

pensioner

la **retraitée** NOUN

▷ *see also* **retraité** ADJECTIVE

pensioner

rétrécir VERB [38]

to shrink

□ Son pull a rétréci au lavage. Her sweater shrank in the wash.

■ **se rétrécir** to get narrower □ La rue se rétrécit. The street gets narrower.

retrouver VERB [28]

1 to find

□ J'ai retrouvé mon portefeuille. I've found my wallet.

2 to meet up with

□ Je te retrouve au café à trois heures. I'll meet you at the café at 3 o'clock.

■ **se retrouver 1** to meet up □ Ils se sont retrouvés devant le cinéma. They met up in front of the cinema. **2** to find one's way around □ Je n'arrive pas à me retrouver. I can't find my way around.

le **rétroviseur** NOUN

rear-view mirror

la **réunion** NOUN

meeting

se **réunir** VERB [38]

to meet

□ Ils se sont réunis à cinq heures. They met at 5 o'clock.

réussi (FEM **réussie**) ADJECTIVE

successful

□ une soirée très réussie a very successful party

■ **être réussi** to be a success □ Le repas était très réussi. The meal was a success.

réussir VERB [38]

to be successful

□ Tous ses enfants ont très bien réussi. All her children are very successful.

■ **réussir à faire quelque chose** to succeed in doing something

■ **réussir à un examen** to pass an exam

la **réussite** NOUN

success

la **revanche** NOUN

return match

■ **prendre sa revanche** to get one's own back □ Il a pris sa revanche en refusant de lui prêter son vélo. He got his own back by refusing to lend him his bike.

■ **en revanche** on the other hand □ C'est cher mais en revanche c'est de la bonne qualité. It is dear but on the other hand it's good quality.

le **rêve** NOUN

dream

■ **de rêve** fantastic □ des vacances de rêve fantastic holidays

le **réveil** NOUN

alarm clock

■ **mettre le réveil à huit heures** to set the alarm for eight o'clock

le **réveille-matin** (PL les **réveille-matin**) NOUN

alarm clock

réveiller VERB [28]

to wake up

□ réveiller quelqu'un to wake somebody up

■ **se réveiller** to wake up

le **réveillon** NOUN

■ **le réveillon du premier de l'an** New Year's Eve celebrations

■ **le réveillon de Noël** Christmas Eve celebrations

r

réveillonner VERB [28]
1 to celebrate New Year's Eve
2 to celebrate Christmas Eve
revenir VERB [73]
to come back
□ Reviens vite! Come back soon! □ Son nom m'est revenu cinq minutes après. His name came back to me five minutes later.
■ **Ça revient au même.** It comes to the same thing.
■ **Ça revient cher.** It costs a lot.
■ **Je n'en reviens pas!** I can't get over it!
■ **revenir sur ses pas** to retrace one's steps
le **revenu** NOUN
income
rêver VERB [28]
to dream
■ **rêver de quelque chose** to dream of something □ J'ai rêvé de mes vacances cette nuit. I dreamt about my holidays last night.
le **réverbère** NOUN
street lamp
le **revers** NOUN
1 backhand
□ Henman a un excellent revers. Henman has an excellent backhand.
2 lapel (of jacket)
■ **le revers de la médaille** the other side of the coin
revient VERB ▷ see revenir
réviser VERB [28]
1 to revise
□ Je dois réviser mon anglais. I've got to revise my English.
2 to service
□ Je dois faire réviser ma voiture. I must get my car serviced.
la **révision** NOUN
revision
revoir VERB [92]
1 to see again
□ J'ai revu Sophie hier soir. I saw Sophie again last night.
2 to revise
□ Il est en train de revoir sa géographie. He's revising his geography.
■ **au revoir** goodbye
la **révolution** NOUN
revolution
□ la Révolution française the French Revolution
le **revolver** NOUN
revolver
la **revue** NOUN
magazine
le **rez-de-chaussée** NOUN

ground floor
□ au rez-de-chaussée on the ground floor
le **Rhin** NOUN
Rhine
le **rhinocéros** NOUN
rhinoceros
le **Rhône** NOUN
Rhone
la **rhubarbe** NOUN
rhubarb
le **rhum** NOUN
rum
le **rhume** NOUN
cold
□ J'ai attrapé un rhume. I've caught a cold.
■ **un rhume de cerveau** a head cold
■ **le rhume des foins** hay fever
ri VERB ▷ see rire
■ **Nous avons bien ri.** We had a good laugh.
riche (FEM **riche**) ADJECTIVE
1 well-off
□ Sa famille est très riche. His family's very well-off.
2 rich
□ riche en vitamines rich in vitamins
le **rideau** (PL les **rideaux**) NOUN
curtain
■ **tirer les rideaux** to draw the curtains
ridicule (FEM **ridicule**) ADJECTIVE
ridiculous
□ Je trouve ça complètement ridicule. I think that's absolutely ridiculous.
rien PRONOUN
▷ see also **rien** NOUN
1 nothing
□ Qu'est-ce que tu as acheté? — Rien. What have you bought? — Nothing. □ Ça n'a rien à voir. It has nothing to do with it.
■ **rien d'intéressant** nothing interesting
■ **rien d'autre** nothing else
■ **rien du tout** nothing at all
2 anything
□ Il n'a rien dit. He didn't say anything.
■ **rien que 1** just □ rien que pour lui faire plaisir just to please him □ Rien que la voiture coûte un million. The car alone costs a million. **2** nothing but □ rien que la vérité nothing but the truth
■ **De rien!** Not at all! □ Merci beaucoup! — De rien! Thank you very much! — Not at all!
le **rien** NOUN
▷ see also **rien** PRONOUN
■ **pour un rien** at the slightest thing □ Il se met en colère pour un rien. He loses his temper over the slightest thing.
■ **en un rien de temps** in no time at all

rigoler VERB [28] *(informal)*
1 to laugh
□ Elle a rigolé en le voyant tomber. She laughed when she saw him fall.
2 to have fun
□ On a bien rigolé hier soir. We had good fun last night.
3 to be joking
□ Ne te fâche pas, je rigolais. Don't get upset, I was only joking.
■ **pour rigoler** for a laugh

rigolo (FEM **rigolote**) ADJECTIVE *(informal)*
funny

rincer VERB [12]
to rinse

rire VERB [74]
▷ *see also* **rire** NOUN
to laugh
□ Ce film m'a vraiment fait rire. That film really made me laugh. □ Nous avons bien ri. We had a good laugh.
■ **pour rire** for a laugh

le rire NOUN
▷ *see also* **rire** VERB
laughter
□ Il a un rire bruyant. He has a loud laugh.

le risque NOUN
1 risk
□ prendre des risques. to take risks □ à tes risques et périls at your own risk
2 danger
□ Il n'y a pas de risque qu'il l'apprenne. There's no danger of him finding out.

risqué (FEM **risquée**) ADJECTIVE
risky

risquer VERB [28]
to risk
■ **Ça ne risque rien.** It's quite safe.
■ **Il risque de se tuer.** He could get himself killed.
■ **C'est ce qui risque de se passer.** That's what might well happen.

le rivage NOUN
shore

la rivière NOUN
river

le riz NOUN
rice

le RMI NOUN
Income Support
□ Il touche le RMI. He's on Income Support.

la RN NOUN (= *route nationale*)
A road

la robe NOUN
dress
■ **une robe de soirée** an evening dress

■ **une robe de mariée** a wedding dress
■ **une robe de chambre** a dressing gown
LANGUAGE TIP Word for word, une robe de chambre means 'a bedroom dress'.

le robinet NOUN
tap

le robot NOUN
robot

la roche NOUN
rock *(stone)*

le rocher NOUN
rock

le rock NOUN
rock *(music)*
□ un chanteur de rock a rock singer

rôder VERB [28]
to loiter
□ Il y a un homme louche qui rôde autour de l'école. There's a suspicious man loitering around the school.

les rognons MASC PL NOUN
kidneys *(in cooking)*

le roi NOUN
king
■ **le jour des Rois** Twelfth Night

le rôle NOUN
role

les rollers MASC PL NOUN
Rollerblades®

romain (FEM **romaine**) ADJECTIVE
Roman
□ des ruines romaines Roman remains

le roman NOUN
novel
■ **un roman policier** a detective story
■ **un roman d'espionnage** a spy story

le romancier NOUN
novelist

romantique (FEM **romantique**) ADJECTIVE
romantic

rompre VERB [75]
1 to split up
□ Paul et Justine ont rompu. Paul and Justine have split up.
2 to break off
□ Ils ont rompu leurs fiançailles. They've broken off their engagement.

les ronces FEM PL NOUN
brambles

ronchonner VERB [28] *(informal)*
to grouse

rond (FEM **ronde**) ADJECTIVE
▷ *see also* **rond** NOUN
1 round
□ La Terre est ronde. The earth is round.
■ **ouvrir des yeux ronds** to stare in

241

amazement

2 chubby

□ Il a les joues rondes. He has chubby cheeks.

3 drunk

□ Il est complètement rond. (*informal*) He's completely drunk.

le **rond** NOUN

▷ *see also* **rond** ADJECTIVE

circle

□ Elle a dessiné un rond sur le sable. She drew a circle in the sand.

■ **en rond** in a circle □ Ils se sont assis en rond. They sat down in a circle.

■ **tourner en rond** to go round in circles

■ **Je n'ai plus un rond.** (*informal*) I haven't a penny left.

la **rondelle** NOUN

slice

□ une rondelle de citron a slice of lemon

le **rond-point** (PL les **ronds-points**) NOUN

roundabout

□ La voiture s'est arrêtée au rond-point. The car stopped at the roundabout.

ronfler VERB [28]

to snore

le **rosbif** NOUN

roast beef

la **rose** NOUN

▷ *see also* **rose** ADJECTIVE

rose

rose (FEM **rose**) ADJECTIVE

▷ *see also* **rose** NOUN

pink

le **rosé** NOUN

rosé (wine)

□ Je prendrai un verre de rosé. I'll have a glass of rosé.

le **rosier** NOUN

rosebush

le **rôti** NOUN

roast meat

■ **un rôti de bœuf** a joint of beef

rôtir VERB [38]

to roast

□ faire rôtir quelque chose to roast something

la **roue** NOUN

wheel

□ une roue de secours a spare wheel

rouge (FEM **rouge**) ADJECTIVE

▷ *see also* **rouge** NOUN

red

le **rouge** NOUN

▷ *see also* **rouge** ADJECTIVE

1 red

□ Le rouge est ma couleur préférée. Red is

my favourite colour.

2 red wine

□ un verre de rouge a glass of red wine

■ **passer au rouge 1** to change to red □ Le feu est passé au rouge. The light changed to red. **2** to go through a red light □ Jean-Pierre est passé au rouge. Jean-Pierre went through a red light.

■ **un rouge à lèvres** a lipstick

◯ **LANGUAGE TIP** Word for word, this means 'red for lips'.

la **rougeole** NOUN

measles

rougir VERB [38]

1 to blush

□ Il a rougi en me voyant. He blushed when he saw me.

2 to flush

□ Il a rougi de colère. He flushed with anger.

la **rouille** NOUN

rust

rouillé (FEM **rouillée**) ADJECTIVE

rusty

rouiller VERB [28]

to go rusty

roulant (FEM **roulante**) ADJECTIVE

■ **un fauteuil roulant** a wheelchair

■ **une table roulante** a trolley

le **rouleau** (PL les **rouleaux**) NOUN

roll

□ un rouleau de papier peint a roll of wallpaper

■ **un rouleau à pâtisserie** a rolling pin

rouler VERB [28]

1 to go

□ Le train roulait à 250 km/h. The train was going at 250 km an hour.

2 to drive

□ Il a roulé sans s'arrêter. He drove without stopping.

3 to roll

□ Gilles a roulé une cigarette. Gilles rolled a cigarette.

4 to roll up

□ Il a roulé le tapis. He rolled the carpet up.

5 to con

□ Ils se sont fait rouler. (*informal*) They were conned.

■ **Alors, ça roule?** (*informal*) How's it going?

la **Roumanie** NOUN

Romania

le **rouquin** NOUN (*informal*)

redhead

la **rouquine** NOUN (*informal*)

redhead

r

rousse FEM ADJECTIVE ▷*see* **roux**

la **rousse** NOUN
>▷*see also* **rousse** ADJECTIVE
redhead

la **route** NOUN
1 road
□ au bord de la route at the roadside
■ une route nationale an A road
2 way
□ Je ne connais pas la route. I don't know the way.
■ Il y a trois heures de route. It's a 3-hour journey.
■ en route on the way □ Ils se sont arrêtés en route. They stopped on the way.
■ mettre en route to start up □ Il a mis le moteur en route. He started the engine up.
■ se mettre en route to set off □ Il s'est mis en route à cinq heures. He set off at 5 o'clock.

le **routier** NOUN
1 lorry driver
□ Son père est routier. His father's a lorry driver.
2 transport café
□ Nous avons mangé dans un routier. We ate in a transport café.

la **routine** NOUN
routine

roux (FEM **rousse**) ADJECTIVE
>▷*see also* **roux** NOUN
1 red
□ Harry a les cheveux roux. Harry has red hair.
2 red-haired
□ Isobel est rousse. Isobel's red-haired.

le **roux** NOUN
>▷*see also* **roux** ADJECTIVE
redhead

royal (FEM **royale**, MASC PL **royaux**) ADJECTIVE
royal

le **royaume** NOUN
kingdom
■ le Royaume-Uni the United Kingdom

le **ruban** NOUN
ribbon
■ le ruban adhésif adhesive tape

la **rubéole** NOUN
German measles

la **ruche** NOUN
hive

rudement ADVERB (*informal*)
terribly
□ C'était rudement bon. It was terribly good.

la **rue** NOUN
street

la **ruelle** NOUN
alley

le **rugby** NOUN
rugby
□ Yann joue au rugby. Yann plays rugby.

rugueux (FEM **rugueuse**) ADJECTIVE
rough

la **ruine** NOUN
ruin
□ les ruines de la cathédrale the ruins of the cathedral

ruiner VERB [28]
to ruin

le **ruisseau** (PL les **ruisseaux**) NOUN
stream

la **rumeur** NOUN
rumour

la **rupture** NOUN
break-up

la **ruse** NOUN
trickery
□ une ruse a trick

rusé (FEM **rusée**) ADJECTIVE
cunning

russe (FEM **russe**) ADJECTIVE, NOUN
Russian
□ Il parle russe. He speaks Russian.
■ un Russe a Russian (*man*)
■ une Russe a Russian (*woman*)
■ les Russes the Russians

la **Russie** NOUN
Russia

le **rythme** NOUN
1 rhythm
□ J'aime le rythme de cette musique. I like the beat of this music.
2 pace
□ Il marche à un bon rythme. He walks at a good pace.

r

Ss

s' PRONOUN ▷ see **se**

sa FEM ADJECTIVE
1 his
  □ Paul est allé voir sa grand-mère. Paul's gone to see his grandmother.
2 her
  □ Elle a embrassé sa mère. She kissed her mother.

le **sable** NOUN
  sand
  ■ des sables mouvants quicksand

le **sablé** NOUN
  shortbread biscuit

le **sabot** NOUN
1 clog
2 hoof (of horse)

le **sac** NOUN
  bag
  ■ un sac de voyage a travel bag
  ■ un sac de couchage a sleeping bag
  ■ un sac à main a handbag
  ■ un sac à dos a rucksack
  ■ voyager sac au dos to go backpacking

le **sachet** NOUN
  sachet (of sugar, coffee)
  ■ du potage en sachet packet soup
  ■ un sachet de thé a tea bag

la **sacoche** NOUN
  bag
  ■ une sacoche de bicyclette a saddlebag

sacré (FEM **sacrée**) ADJECTIVE
  sacred

sage (FEM **sage**) ADJECTIVE
1 good (well-behaved)
  □ Sois sage. Be good.
2 wise (sensible)
  □ Il serait plus sage d'attendre. It would be wiser to wait.

la **sagesse** NOUN
  wisdom
  □ Il a eu la sagesse de ne pas y aller. He wisely didn't go.
  ■ une dent de sagesse a wisdom tooth

le **Sagittaire** NOUN
  Sagittarius

  □ Il est Sagittaire. He is Sagittarius.

saignant (FEM **saignante**) ADJECTIVE
  rare (meat)

saigner VERB [28]
  to bleed
  ■ saigner du nez to have a nosebleed

sain (FEM **saine**) ADJECTIVE
  healthy
  ■ sain et sauf safe and sound

saint (FEM **sainte**) ADJECTIVE
  ▷ see also **saint** NOUN, **sainte** NOUN
  holy
  □ la semaine sainte Holy Week □ le Saint-Esprit the Holy Spirit
  ■ la Sainte Vierge the Blessed Virgin
  ■ le vendredi saint Good Friday
  ■ la Saint-Sylvestre New Year's Eve

le **saint** NOUN
  ▷ see also **saint** ADJECTIVE
  saint

la **sainte** NOUN
  ▷ see also **sainte** ADJECTIVE
  saint

sais VERB ▷ see **savoir**
  ■ Je ne sais pas. I don't know.

saisir VERB [38]
  to take hold of
  ■ saisir l'occasion de faire quelque chose to seize the opportunity to do something

la **saison** NOUN
  season
  □ Ce n'est pas la saison des fraises. Strawberries are out of season. □ un temps de saison seasonable weather
  ■ la saison des vendanges harvest time

sait VERB ▷ see **savoir**
  ■ Il sait que ... He knows that ...
  ■ On ne sait jamais! You never know!

la **salade** NOUN
1 lettuce
2 salad
  □ une salade composée a mixed salad
  □ une salade de fruits a fruit salad

le **saladier** NOUN
  salad bowl

le **salaire** NOUN
salary

le **salami** NOUN
salami

le **salarié** NOUN
salaried employee

la **salariée** NOUN
salaried employee

sale (FEM **sale**) ADJECTIVE
dirty

salé (FEM **salée**) ADJECTIVE
1 salty
  □ La soupe est trop salée. The soup's too salty.
2 salted
  □ du beurre salé salted butter
3 savoury
  □ des biscuits salés savoury biscuits

saler VERB [28]
to put salt in
  □ J'ai oublié de saler la soupe. I forgot to put salt in the soup.

la **saleté** NOUN
dirt
  □ J'ai horreur de la saleté. I hate dirt. □ Il y a une saleté sur ta chemise. There's some dirt on your shirt.
  ■ **faire des saletés** to make a mess

salir VERB [38]
  ■ **salir quelque chose** to get something dirty
  ■ **se salir** to get oneself dirty □ Mets un tablier, sinon tu vas te salir. Put on an apron or you'll get yourself dirty.

la **salle** NOUN
1 room
2 audience
  □ Toute la salle l'a applaudi. The whole audience applauded him.
3 ward (in hospital)
  □ Il est à la salle douze. He's in Ward 12.
  ■ **la salle à manger** the dining room
  ■ **la salle de séjour** the living room
  ■ **la salle de bains** the bathroom
  ■ **la salle d'attente** the waiting room
  ■ **une salle de classe** a classroom
  ■ **la salle des professeurs** the staffroom
  ■ **une salle de concert** a concert hall
  ■ **la salle d'embarquement** the departure lounge

le **salon** NOUN
lounge
  ■ **un salon de thé** a tearoom
  ■ **un salon de coiffure** a hair salon
  ■ **un salon de beauté** a beauty salon
  ■ **un salon de discussion** a chatroom

la **salopette** NOUN

1 dungarees
2 overalls

saluer VERB [28]
  ■ **saluer quelqu'un 1** to say hello to somebody □ Je l'ai croisé dans la rue et il m'a salué. I met him in the street and he said hello. **2** to say goodbye to somebody □ Il nous a salués et il est parti. He said goodbye and left.

salut EXCLAMATION (informal)
hi!

la **salutation** NOUN
greeting

le **samedi** NOUN
1 Saturday
  □ Aujourd'hui, nous sommes samedi. It's Saturday today.
2 on Saturday
  □ Nous sommes allés au cinéma samedi. We went to the cinema on Saturday.
  ■ **le samedi** on Saturdays □ Le magasin ferme à dix-huit heures le samedi. The shop closes at 6 p.m. on Saturdays.
  ■ **tous les samedis** every Saturday
  ■ **samedi dernier** last Saturday
  ■ **samedi prochain** next Saturday

le **SAMU** NOUN
ambulance service

la **sandale** NOUN
sandal

le **sandwich** NOUN
sandwich

le **sang** NOUN
blood
  ■ **en sang** covered in blood

le **sang-froid** NOUN
  ■ **garder son sang-froid** to keep calm
  ■ **perdre son sang-froid** to lose one's cool
  ■ **faire quelque chose de sang-froid** to do something in cold blood

le **sanglier** NOUN
wild boar

le **sanglot** NOUN
  ■ **éclater en sanglots** to burst into tears

sans PREPOSITION
without
  □ Elle est venue sans son frère. She came without her brother.
  ■ **un pull sans manches** a sleeveless sweater

le/la **sans-abri** (PL les **sans-abri**) NOUN
homeless person
  □ les sans-abri the homeless

sans-gêne (FEM **sans-gêne**) ADJECTIVE
inconsiderate

la **santé** NOUN
health

□ en bonne santé in good health

■ **Santé!** Cheers!

saoudien (FEM **saoudienne**) ADJECTIVE, NOUN
Saudi Arabian

■ un **Saoudien** a Saudi Arabian *(man)*

■ une **Saoudienne** a Saudi Arabian *(woman)*

le **sapeur-pompier** (PL les **sapeurs-pompiers**) NOUN
fireman

■ **les sapeurs-pompiers** the fire brigade

le **sapin** NOUN
fir tree

■ un **sapin de Noël** a Christmas tree

la **Sardaigne** NOUN
Sardinia

la **sardine** NOUN
sardine

le **satellite** NOUN
satellite

□ la télévision par satellite satellite TV

satisfaire VERB [36]
to satisfy

satisfaisant (FEM **satisfaisante**) ADJECTIVE
satisfactory

satisfait (FEM **satisfaite**) ADJECTIVE
satisfied

□ être satisfait de quelque chose to be satisfied with something

la **sauce** NOUN

1 sauce

2 gravy

la **saucisse** NOUN
sausage

le **saucisson** NOUN
salami

sauf PREPOSITION
except

□ Tout le monde est venu sauf lui. Everyone came except him.

■ **sauf si** unless □ On ira se promener, sauf s'il fait mauvais. We'll go for a walk, unless the weather's bad.

■ **sauf que** except that □ Tout s'est bien passé, sauf que nous sommes arrivés en retard. Everything went OK, except that we arrived late.

le **saumon** NOUN
salmon

saur MASC ADJECTIVE

■ un **hareng saur** a kipper

le **saut** NOUN
jump

■ **le saut en longueur** the long jump

■ **le saut en hauteur** the high jump

■ **le saut à la perche** the pole vault

■ **le saut à l'élastique** bungee jumping

■ **un saut périlleux** a somersault

sauter VERB [28]
to jump

□ Nous avons sauté par-dessus la barrière. We jumped over the gate.

■ **sauter à la corde** to skip *(with a rope)*

■ **faire sauter quelque chose** to blow something up □ Ils ont fait sauter le pont. They blew up the bridge.

la **sauterelle** NOUN
grasshopper

sauvage (FEM **sauvage**) ADJECTIVE

1 wild

□ les animaux sauvages wild animals

□ faire du camping sauvage to camp in the wild

■ **une région sauvage** an unspoiled area

2 shy

□ Il est sauvage. He's shy.

sauvegarder VERB [28]
to save *(file on computer)*

sauver VERB [28]
to save

■ **se sauver 1** to run away □ Il s'est sauvé à toutes jambes. He ran away as fast as he could. **2** *(informal)* to be off □ Allez, je me sauve! Right, I'm off.

le **sauvetage** NOUN
rescue

le **sauveur** NOUN
saviour

savais, savait VERB ▷ *see* savoir

■ **Je ne savais pas qu'il devait venir.** I didn't know he was going to come.

le **savant** NOUN
scientist

savent VERB ▷ *see* savoir

■ **Ils ne savent pas ce qu'ils veulent.** They don't know what they want.

la **saveur** NOUN
flavour

savez VERB ▷ *see* savoir

■ **Est-ce que vous savez où elle habite?** Do you know where she lives?

savoir VERB [76]
to know

□ Je ne sais pas où il est allé. I don't know where he's gone. □ Nous ne savons pas s'il est bien arrivé. We don't know if he's arrived safely. □ Tu savais que Canberra était la capitale de l'Australie? Did you know that Canberra was the capital of Australia? □ Il ne sait pas ce qu'il va faire ce week-end. He doesn't know what he's going to do this weekend.

■ **Tu sais nager?** Can you swim?

le **savon** NOUN
soap

la **savonnette** NOUN
bar of soap

savons VERB ▷ see savoir

savoureux (FEM **savoureuse**) ADJECTIVE
tasty

le **saxo** NOUN (informal)
▷ see also la saxo
1 sax
2 sax player

la **saxo** NOUN (informal)
▷ see also le saxo
sax player

le **scandale** NOUN
scandal
■ **faire scandale** to cause a scandal □ Ce
film a fait scandale. The film caused a scandal.

scandaleux (FEM **scandaleuse**) ADJECTIVE
outrageous

le/la **Scandinave** NOUN
Scandinavian

scandinave (FEM **scandinave**) ADJECTIVE
Scandinavian

la **Scandinavie** NOUN
Scandinavia

le **scarabée** NOUN
beetle

la **scène** NOUN
scene
□ une scène d'amour a love scene □ la
scène du crime the scene of the crime □ Il
m'a fait une scène. He made a scene.
■ **une scène de ménage** a domestic row

sceptique (FEM **sceptique**) ADJECTIVE
sceptical

le **schéma** NOUN
diagram

schématique (FEM **schématique**) ADJECTIVE
■ **l'explication schématique d'une
théorie** the broad outline of a theory
■ **Cette interprétation est un peu trop
schématique.** This interpretation is a bit
oversimplified.

la **scie** NOUN
saw
■ **une scie à métaux** a hacksaw

la **science** NOUN
science
■ **Elle est forte en sciences.** She is good at
science.
■ **les sciences physiques** physics
■ **les sciences naturelles** biology
■ **les sciences économiques** economics
■ **sciences po** (informal) politics □ Mon
frère fait sciences po à Paris. My brother is
studying politics in Paris.

la **science-fiction** NOUN
science fiction

scientifique (FEM **scientifique**) ADJECTIVE
▷ see also **scientifique** NOUN
scientific

le/la **scientifique** NOUN
▷ see also **scientifique** ADJECTIVE
1 scientist
2 science student

scier VERB [19]
to saw

scolaire (FEM **scolaire**) ADJECTIVE
school
□ l'année scolaire the school year □ les
vacances scolaires the school holidays
□ mon livret scolaire my school report

le **Scorpion** NOUN
Scorpio
□ Catherine est Scorpion. Catherine is
Scorpio.

le **Scotch**® NOUN
adhesive tape

le **scrupule** NOUN
scruple

sculpter VERB [28]
to sculpt

le **sculpteur** NOUN
sculptor

la **sculpture** NOUN
sculpture

le/la **SDF** NOUN (= sans domicile fixe)
homeless person
■ **les SDF** the homeless

se PRONOUN

LANGUAGE TIP se forms part of
reflexive constructions.

1 himself
□ Il se regarde dans la glace. He's looking at
himself in the mirror.

2 herself
□ Elle se regarde dans la glace. She's
looking at herself in the mirror.

3 itself
□ Le chien s'est fait mal. The dog hurt itself.

4 oneself
□ se regarder dans une glace to look at
oneself in a mirror

5 themselves
□ Ils se sont regardés dans la glace. They
looked at themselves in the mirror.

LANGUAGE TIP se changes to s' before
a vowel and most words beginning
with 'h'.

□ Elle s'admire dans sa nouvelle robe. She's
admiring herself in her new dress.

6 each other
□ Ils s'aiment. They love each other.

la **séance** NOUN
1 session

□ une séance de rééducation a physiotherapy session

2 showing *(at the cinema)*

□ La prochaine séance est à dix-neuf heures. The next showing is at 7 p.m.

le **seau** (PL les **seaux**) NOUN
bucket

sec (FEM **sèche**) ADJECTIVE

1 dry

□ Mon jean n'est pas encore sec. My jeans aren't dry yet.

2 dried

□ des figues sèches dried figs

le **sèche-cheveux** (PL les **sèche-cheveux**) NOUN
hair dryer

le **sèche-linge** (PL les **sèche-linge**) NOUN
tumble dryer

sécher VERB [34]

1 to dry

2 to be stumped

□ J'ai complètement séché à l'interrogation de maths. *(informal)* I was completely stumped in the maths test.

■ **se sécher** to dry oneself □ Sèche-toi avec cette serviette. Dry yourself with this towel.

la **sécheresse** NOUN
drought

□ une terrible sécheresse a terrible drought

le **séchoir** NOUN
dryer

second (FEM **seconde**) ADJECTIVE
▷ *see also* **second** NOUN, **seconde** NOUN
second

□ Il est arrivé second. He came second.

le **second** NOUN
▷ *see also* **second** ADJECTIVE
second floor

□ Elle habite au second. She lives on the second floor.

secondaire (FEM **secondaire**) ADJECTIVE
secondary

□ l'enseignement secondaire secondary education

■ **des effets secondaires** side effects

la **seconde** NOUN
▷ *see also* **seconde** ADJECTIVE

1 second

□ Attends une seconde! Wait a second!

2 year 11

□ Ma sœur est en seconde. My sister's in year 11.

DID YOU KNOW…?

In French secondary schools, years are counted from the **sixième** (youngest) to **première** and **terminale** (oldest).

3 second class

□ voyager en seconde to travel second-class

secouer VERB [28]
to shake

□ secouer la tête to shake one's head

secourir VERB [16]
to rescue

le **secourisme** NOUN
first aid

□ J'ai un brevet de secourisme. I've got a first aid qualification.

le **secours** NOUN
help

□ Il est allé chercher du secours. He went to get help. □ Au secours! Help!

■ **les premiers secours** first aid

■ **une sortie de secours** an emergency exit

■ **la roue de secours** the spare wheel

le **secret** NOUN
▷ *see also* **secret** ADJECTIVE
secret

secret (FEM **secrète**) ADJECTIVE
▷ *see also* **secret** NOUN
secret

le **secrétaire** NOUN
▷ *see also* **la secrétaire**

1 secretary

2 writing desk

la **secrétaire** NOUN
▷ *see also* **le secrétaire**
secretary

le **secrétariat** NOUN
secretary's office

le **secteur** NOUN
sector

□ le secteur public the public sector □ le secteur privé the private sector

la **section** NOUN
department *(of school)*

la **sécu** NOUN *(informal)*
Social Security

la **sécurité** NOUN

1 safety

■ **être en sécurité** to be safe □ On ne se sent pas en sécurité dans ce quartier. You don't feel safe in this neighbourhood.

■ **la sécurité routière** road safety

■ **une ceinture de sécurité** a seatbelt

2 security

□ par mesure de sécurité as a security measure

■ **la sécurité sociale** Social Security

■ **la sécurité de l'emploi** job security

séduisant (FEM **séduisante**) ADJECTIVE
attractive

le **seigle** NOUN
rye

▫ un pain de seigle a loaf of rye bread

le **seigneur** NOUN
lord

▪ **le Seigneur** the Lord

le **sein** NOUN
breast

▪ **au sein de** within ▫ Chaque pays est autonome au sein de l'Europe. Each country is independent within Europe.

seize NUMBER
sixteen

▫ Elle a seize ans. She's sixteen. ▫ à seize heures at 4 p.m.

▪ **le seize février** the sixteenth of February

seizième (FEM **seizième**) ADJECTIVE
sixteenth

le **séjour** NOUN
stay

▫ J'ai fait un séjour d'une semaine en Italie. I stayed in Italy for a week.

le **sel** NOUN
salt

sélectionner VERB [28]
to select

le **self** NOUN (informal)
self-service restaurant

le **self-service** NOUN
self-service restaurant

la **selle** NOUN
saddle

selon PREPOSITION
according to

▫ selon lui according to him ▫ selon mon humeur according to what mood I'm in ▫ Ils sont répartis selon leur âge. They're divided up according to age.

la **semaine** NOUN
week

▪ **en semaine** on weekdays

semblable (FEM **semblable**) ADJECTIVE
similar

le **semblant** NOUN

▪ **faire semblant de faire quelque chose** to pretend to do something ▫ Il fait semblant de dormir. He's pretending to be asleep.

sembler VERB [28]
to seem

▫ Le temps semble s'améliorer. The weather seems to be improving. ▫ Il me semble inutile de s'en inquiéter. It seems pointless to me to worry about it.

la **semelle** NOUN
1 sole
2 insole

la **semoule** NOUN
semolina

le **sens** NOUN
1 sense

▫ avoir le sens de l'humour to have a sense of humour ▫ Je n'ai pas le sens de l'orientation. I've got no sense of direction. ▫ avoir le sens du rythme to have a sense of rhythm ▫ Ça n'a pas de sens. It doesn't make sense.

▪ **le bon sens** common sense
2 direction

▫ Tu tournes la poignée dans le mauvais sens. You're turning the handle in the wrong direction.

▪ **sens dessus dessous** upside down
▪ **un sens interdit** a one-way street ▫ J'ai failli prendre un sens interdit. I nearly went the wrong way down a one-way street.

▪ **un sens unique** a one-way street

la **sensation** NOUN
feeling

sensationnel (FEM **sensationnelle**)
ADJECTIVE
sensational

sensé (FEM **sensée**) ADJECTIVE
sensible

sensible (FEM **sensible**) ADJECTIVE
1 sensitive

▫ Elle est très sensible. She's very sensitive.

▪ **Ce film est déconseillé aux personnes sensibles.** This film contains scenes which some viewers may find disturbing.
2 visible

▫ une amélioration sensible a visible improvement

> **LANGUAGE TIP** Be careful! The French word **sensible** does not mean **sensible**.

sensiblement ADVERB
1 visibly

▫ Elle a sensiblement progressé. She's made visible progress.
2 approximately

▫ Elles sont sensiblement de la même taille. They are approximately the same height.

la **sentence** NOUN
sentence (judgement)

le **sentier** NOUN
path

le **sentiment** NOUN
feeling

sentimental (FEM **sentimentale**, MASC PL **sentimentaux**) ADJECTIVE
sentimental

sentir VERB [77]
1 to smell

▫ Ça sent bon. That smells good. ▫ Ça sent mauvais. It smells bad.

2 to smell of

□ Ça sent les frites ici. It smells of chips in here.

3 to taste

□ Tu sens l'ail dans le rôti? Can you taste the garlic in the roast?

4 to feel

□ Ça t'a fait mal? — Non, je n'ai rien senti. Did it hurt? — No, I didn't feel a thing. □ Je ne me sens pas bien. I don't feel well.

■ Il ne peut pas la sentir. *(informal)* He can't stand her.

séparé (FEM **séparée**) ADJECTIVE
separated

□ Mes parents sont séparés. My parents are separated.

séparément ADVERB
separately

séparer VERB [28]
to separate

□ Séparez le blanc du jaune. Separate the yolk from the white.

■ **se séparer** to separate □ Mes parents se sont séparés l'année dernière. My parents separated last year.

sept NUMBER
seven

□ Il est arrivé à sept heures. He arrived at seven o'clock. □ Elle a sept ans. She's seven.

■ **le sept février** the seventh of February

septembre MASC NOUN
September

■ **en septembre** in September

septième (FEM **septième**) ADJECTIVE
seventh

□ au septième étage on the seventh floor

sera, serai, seras, serez VERB ▷ see être

■ **Je serai de retour à dix heures.** I'll be back at 10 o'clock.

la série NOUN
series

sérieusement ADVERB
seriously

sérieux (FEM **sérieuse**) ADJECTIVE
▷ see also **sérieux** NOUN

1 serious

□ Il plaisantait? — Non, il était sérieux. Was he joking? — No, he was serious.

2 responsible

□ C'est un employé très sérieux. He's a very responsible employee.

le sérieux NOUN
▷ see also **sérieux** ADJECTIVE

■ **garder son sérieux** to keep a straight face □ J'ai eu du mal à garder mon sérieux. I had trouble keeping a straight face.

■ **prendre quelque chose au sérieux** to take something seriously

■ **prendre quelqu'un au sérieux** to take somebody seriously

■ **Il manque un peu de sérieux.** He's not very responsible.

la seringue NOUN
syringe

séronégatif (FEM **séronégative**) ADJECTIVE
HIV-negative

serons, seront VERB ▷ see être

séropositif (FEM **séropositive**) ADJECTIVE
HIV-positive

le serpent NOUN
snake

la serre NOUN
greenhouse

■ **l'effet de serre** the greenhouse effect

serré (FEM **serrée**) ADJECTIVE

1 tight

□ Mon pantalon est trop serré. My trousers are too tight.

2 close-fought

□ Ça a été un match serré. It was a close-fought game.

serrer VERB [28]

■ **Ce pantalon me serre trop.** These trousers are too tight for me.

■ **serrer la main à quelqu'un** to shake hands with somebody

■ **se serrer** to squeeze up □ Serrez-vous un peu pour que je puisse m'asseoir. Squeeze up a bit so I can sit down.

■ **serrer quelqu'un dans ses bras** to hug somebody

■ **'Serrer à droite'** 'Keep right'

la serrure NOUN
lock

sers, sert VERB ▷ see servir

le serveur NOUN

1 waiter *(in café)*

2 server *(computer)*

la serveuse NOUN
waitress

serviable (FEM **serviable**) ADJECTIVE
helpful

le service NOUN

1 service *(in restaurant)*

□ Le service est compris. Service is included.

■ **être de service** to be on duty

■ **hors service** out of order

■ **faire le service** to serve *(at table)*

□ Tu peux faire le service s'il te plaît? Could you serve please?

2 favour

□ rendre service à quelqu'un to do somebody a favour □ Est-ce que je peux te

demander un service? Can I ask you a favour?

3 serve *(sport)*
- □ Il a un bon service. He's got a good serve.
- ■ **le service militaire** military service
- ■ **les services sociaux** the social services
- ■ **les services secrets** the secret service

la **serviette** NOUN
1 towel
- □ une serviette de bain a bath towel
- ■ **une serviette hygiénique** a sanitary towel
2 serviette *(napkin)*
3 briefcase

servir VERB [78]
to serve
- □ On vous sert? Are you being served?
- ■ **À toi de servir.** *(tennis)* It's your serve.
- ■ **se servir** to help oneself □ Servez-vous. Help yourself.
- ■ **se servir de** to use □ Tu te sers souvent de ton vélo? Do you use your bike a lot?
- ■ **servir à quelqu'un** to be of use to somebody □ Ça m'a beaucoup servi. I found it very useful.
- ■ **À quoi ça sert?** What's it for?
- ■ **Ça ne sert à rien.** It's no use. □ Ça ne sert à rien d'insister. It's no use insisting.

ses PL ADJECTIVE
1 his
- □ Il est parti voir ses grands-parents. He's gone to see his grandparents.
2 her
- □ Delphine a oublié ses baskets. Delphine's forgotten her trainers.
3 its
- □ la ville et ses alentours the town and its surroundings

le **set** NOUN
1 tablemat *(on table)*
2 set *(in tennis)*

le **seuil** NOUN
doorstep

seul (FEM **seule**) ADJECTIVE, ADVERB
1 alone
- □ vivre seul to live alone
2 by oneself
- □ Elle est venue seule. She came by herself.
- ■ **faire quelque chose tout seul** to do something by oneself □ Elle a fait ça toute seule? Did she do it by herself?
- ■ **se sentir seul** to feel lonely
- ■ **un seul livre** one book only □ Vous avez droit à un seul livre. You're entitled to one book only.
- ■ **Il reste une seule nectarine.** There's only one nectarine left.

- ■ **le seul livre que ...** the only book that ...
- □ C'est le seul Agatha Christie que je n'aie pas lu. That's the only Agatha Christie I haven't read.
- ■ **le seul** the only one □ C'est la seule que je ne connaisse pas. She's the only one I don't know.

seulement ADVERB
only
- ■ **non seulement ... mais** not only ... but
- □ Non seulement il a plu, mais en plus il a fait froid. Not only did it rain, but it was cold as well.

sévère (FEM **sévère**) ADJECTIVE
strict
- □ Mon prof de maths est très sévère. My maths teacher is very strict.

le **sexe** NOUN
sex

sexuel (FEM **sexuelle**) ADJECTIVE
sexual
- □ l'éducation sexuelle sex education

le **shampooing** NOUN
shampoo
- ■ **se faire un shampooing** to wash one's hair

le **short** NOUN
shorts
- □ Il était en short. He was wearing shorts.

si CONJUNCTION, ADVERB
▷ *see also* **si** NOUN
1 if
- □ si tu veux if you like □ Je me demande si elle va venir. I wonder if she'll come. □ si seulement if only
2 so
- □ Elle est si gentille. She's so kind. □ Tout s'est passé si vite. Everything happened so fast.
3 yes
- □ Tu n'es pas allé à l'école habillé comme ça? — Si. You didn't go to school dressed like that? — Yes I did.

le **si** NOUN
▷ *see also* **si** CONJUNCTION
1 B
- □ en si bémol in B flat
2 ti
- □ la, si, do la, ti, do

la **Sicile** NOUN
Sicily

le **sida** NOUN
AIDS
- □ Il a le sida. He's got AIDS.

le **siècle** NOUN
century
- □ le vingtième siècle the twentieth century

251

le **siège** NOUN
1 seat (in vehicle)
2 head office

sien MASC PRONOUN
■ **le sien 1** his □ C'est le vélo de Paul? —
Oui, c'est le sien. Is this Paul's bike? — Yes,
it's his. **2** hers □ C'est le vélo d'Isabelle? —
Oui, c'est le sien. Is this Isabelle's bike? —
Yes, it's hers.

sienne FEM PRONOUN
■ **la sienne 1** his □ C'est la montre de
Paul? — Oui, c'est la sienne. Is this Paul's
watch? — Yes, it's his. **2** hers □ C'est la
montre d'Isabelle? — Oui, c'est la sienne. Is
this Isabelle's watch? — Yes, it's hers.

siennes FEM PL PRONOUN
■ **les siennes 1** his □ Ce sont les
chaussures de Christian? — Oui, ce sont les
siennes. Are these Christian's shoes? —
Yes, they're his. **2** hers □ Ce sont les
lunettes de Daphne? — Oui, ce sont les
siennes. Are these Daphne's glasses? —
Yes, they're hers.

siens MASC PL PRONOUN
■ **les siens 1** his □ Ce sont les sandwichs
de Pierre? — Oui, ce sont les siens. Are
these Pierre's sandwiches? — Yes, they're
his. **2** hers □ Ce sont les sandwichs de
Justine? — Oui, ce sont les siens. Are these
Justine's sandwiches? — Yes, they're hers.

la **sieste** NOUN
nap
□ faire la sieste to have a nap

siffler VERB [28]
to whistle

le **sifflet** NOUN
whistle

le **sigle** NOUN
acronym

le **signal** (PL les **signaux**) NOUN
signal

la **signature** NOUN
signature

le **signe** NOUN
sign
■ **faire un signe de la main** to wave
■ **faire signe à quelqu'un d'entrer** to
beckon to somebody to come in
■ **les signes du zodiaque** the signs of the
zodiac

signer VERB [28]
to sign

le **signet** NOUN
bookmark

la **signification** NOUN
meaning

signifier VERB [19]

to mean
□ Que signifie ce mot? What does this word
mean?

le **silence** NOUN
silence
■ **Silence!** Be quiet!

silencieux (FEM **silencieuse**) ADJECTIVE
1 silent
□ Elle est restée silencieuse. She remained
silent.
2 quiet
□ C'est très silencieux ici. It's very quiet
here.

la **silhouette** NOUN
figure
□ J'ai vu une silhouette dans le brouillard. I
saw a figure in the mist.

similaire (FEM **similaire**) ADJECTIVE
similar

le **simple** NOUN
▷ see also **simple** ADJECTIVE
singles (tennis)
□ le simple messieurs the men's singles
□ le simple dames the ladies' singles

simple (FEM **simple**) ADJECTIVE
▷ see also **simple** NOUN
simple

simplement ADVERB
simply
□ C'est tout simplement inadmissible. It's
quite simply unacceptable.

simuler VERB [28]
to simulate

simultané (FEM **simultanée**) ADJECTIVE
simultaneous

sincère (FEM **sincère**) ADJECTIVE
sincere

sincèrement ADVERB
sincerely

la **sincérité** NOUN
sincerity

le **singe** NOUN
monkey

le **singulier** NOUN
singular
□ au féminin singulier in the feminine
singular

sinistre (FEM **sinistre**) ADJECTIVE
sinister

sinon CONJUNCTION
otherwise
□ Dépêche-toi, sinon je pars sans toi. Hurry
up, otherwise I'll leave without you.

la **sinusite** NOUN
sinusitis
□ avoir de la sinusite to have sinusitis

la **sirène** NOUN

mermaid
- **la sirène d'alarme** the fire alarm

le **sirop** NOUN
syrup
- **le sirop contre la toux** cough mixture

le **site** NOUN
setting
□ un site très sauvage a totally unspoiled setting
- **un site pittoresque** a beauty spot
- **un site touristique** a tourist attraction
- **un site archéologique** an archaeological site
- **un site Web** a website

sitôt ADVERB
- **sitôt dit, sitôt fait** no sooner said than done
- **pas de sitôt** not for a long time □ On ne le reverra pas de sitôt. We won't see him again for a long time.

la **situation** NOUN
1 situation
- **la situation de famille** marital status
2 job
□ Il a une belle situation. He's got a good job.

se **situer** VERB [28]
to be situated
□ Versailles se situe à l'ouest de Paris. Versailles is situated to the west of Paris.
- **bien situé** well situated

six NUMBER
six
□ Il est rentré à six heures. He got back at six o'clock. □ Il a six ans. He's six.
- **le six février** the sixth of February

sixième (FEM **sixième**) ADJECTIVE
▷ see also **sixième** NOUN
sixth
□ au sixième étage on the sixth floor

la **sixième** NOUN
▷ see also **sixième** ADJECTIVE
year 7
□ Mon frère est en sixième. My brother's in year 7.

> DID YOU KNOW…?
> In French secondary schools, years are counted from the **sixième** (youngest) to **première** and **terminale** (oldest).

le **ski** NOUN
1 ski
□ J'ai loué des skis. I hired skis.
2 skiing
□ J'adore le ski. I love skiing. □ faire du ski to go skiing
- **le ski de fond** cross-country skiing

- **le ski nautique** water-skiing
- **le ski de piste** downhill skiing
- **le ski de randonnée** cross-country skiing

skier VERB [19]
to ski

le **skieur** NOUN
skier

la **skieuse** NOUN
skier

le **slip** NOUN
pants
- **un slip de bain** swimming trunks

la **Slovaquie** NOUN
Slovakia

la **Slovénie** NOUN
Slovenia

le **SMIC** NOUN
guaranteed minimum wage
□ Il touche le SMIC. He's on the legal minimum wage.

le **smoking** NOUN
dinner suit

le **SMS** NOUN
text message

la **SNCF** NOUN (= Société nationale des chemins de fer français)
French railways

snob (FEM **snob**) ADJECTIVE
snobbish

sobre (FEM **sobre**) ADJECTIVE
1 sober
2 plain
□ C'est une veste très sobre. It's a very plain jacket.

social (FEM **sociale**, MASC PL **sociaux**) ADJECTIVE
social

le/la **socialiste** NOUN
socialist

la **société** NOUN
1 society
2 company
□ une société financière a finance company

la **sociologie** NOUN
sociology

la **socquette** NOUN
ankle sock

la **sœur** NOUN
sister
- **une bonne sœur** (informal) a nun

soi PRONOUN
oneself
□ avoir confiance en soi to have confidence in oneself
- **rester chez soi** to stay at home
- **Ça va de soi.** It goes without saying.

soi-disant (FEM **soi-disante**) ADVERB, ADJECTIVE

supposedly

□ Il était soi-disant parti à Paris. He had supposedly left for Paris.

■ **un soi-disant poète** a so-called poet

la **soie** NOUN
silk

la **soif** NOUN
thirst

■ **avoir soif** to be thirsty

soigner VERB [28]
to look after (ill person, animal)

□ Soigne-toi bien ce week-end! Take good care of yourself this weekend!

soigneux (FEM **soigneuse**) ADJECTIVE
careful

□ Tu devrais être plus soigneux avec tes livres. You should be more careful with your books.

soi-même PRONOUN
oneself

□ Il vaut mieux le faire soi-même. It's better to do it oneself.

le **soin** NOUN
care

■ **prendre soin de quelque chose** to take care of something □ Prends bien soin de ce livre. Take good care of this book.

les **soins** MASC PL NOUN
treatment

■ **les premiers soins** first aid

■ **'aux bons soins de Madame Martin'** (on letter) 'c/o Mrs Martin'

le **soir** NOUN
evening

□ ce soir this evening

■ **à sept heures du soir** at 7 p.m.

■ **demain soir** tomorrow night

■ **hier soir** last night

la **soirée** NOUN
evening

□ en tenue de soirée in evening dress

sois VERB ▷ see être

■ **Sois tranquille!** Be quiet!

soit CONJUNCTION

■ **soit ..., soit ...** either ... or ... □ soit lundi, soit mardi either Monday or Tuesday

la **soixantaine** NOUN
about sixty

□ une soixantaine de personnes about sixty people

■ **Elle a la soixantaine.** She's in her sixties.

soixante NUMBER
sixty

□ Il a soixante ans. He's sixty. □ soixante et un sixty-one □ soixante-deux sixty-two

■ **soixante et onze** seventy-one

■ **soixante-quinze** seventy-five

soixante-dix NUMBER
seventy

□ Il a soixante-dix ans. He's seventy.

le **soja** NOUN
soya

■ **des germes de soja** beansprouts

le **sol** NOUN

1 floor

□ un sol carrelé a tiled floor

■ **à même le sol** on the floor

2 soil

□ sur le sol français on French soil

3 G

□ sol dièse G sharp

4 so

□ do, ré, mi, fa, sol ... do, re, mi, fa, so ...

solaire (FEM **solaire**) ADJECTIVE
solar

□ le système solaire the solar system

■ **la crème solaire** sun cream

le **soldat** NOUN
soldier

le **solde** NOUN

■ **être en solde** to be reduced □ Les chemisiers sont en solde. The blouses are reduced.

■ **les soldes** the sales □ faire les soldes to go round the sales □ les soldes de janvier the January sales

soldé (FEM **soldée**) ADJECTIVE

■ **être soldé** to be reduced □ un article soldé à dix euros an item reduced to 10 euros

la **sole** NOUN
sole (fish)

le **soleil** NOUN
sun

□ au soleil in the sun

■ **Il y a du soleil.** It's sunny.

le **solfège** NOUN
musical theory

□ un cours de solfège a music theory lesson

■ **Il joue du violon sans connaître le solfège.** He plays the violin but he can't read music.

solidaire (FEM **solidaire**) ADJECTIVE

■ **être solidaire de quelqu'un** to back somebody up

solide (FEM **solide**) ADJECTIVE

1 strong (person)

2 solid (object)

solitaire (FEM **solitaire**) ADJECTIVE
▷ see also **solitaire** NOUN
solitary

le/la **solitaire** NOUN
▷ see also **solitaire** ADJECTIVE
loner

la solitude NOUN
loneliness

la solution NOUN
solution
- **une solution de facilité** an easy way out

sombre (FEM **sombre**) ADJECTIVE
dark

le sommaire NOUN
summary

la somme NOUN
▷ *see also* **le somme**
sum

le somme NOUN
▷ *see also* **la somme**
nap
□ faire un somme to take a nap

le sommeil NOUN
sleep
- **avoir sommeil** to be sleepy

sommes VERB ▷ *see* être
- **Nous sommes en vacances.** We're on holiday.

le sommet NOUN
summit

le somnifère NOUN
sleeping pill

somptueux (FEM **somptueuse**) ADJECTIVE
sumptuous

son (FEM **sa**, PL **ses**) ADJECTIVE
▷ *see also* **son** NOUN
1 his
□ son père his father □ Il a perdu son portefeuille. He's lost his wallet.
2 her
□ son père her father □ Elle a perdu son sac. She's lost her bag.

le son NOUN
▷ *see also* **son** ADJECTIVE
1 sound
□ Le son n'est pas très bon. The sound's not very good. □ baisser le son to turn the sound down
2 bran
- **le pain de son** brown bread

le sondage NOUN
survey
- **un sondage d'opinion** an opinion poll

sonner VERB [28]
to ring
□ On a sonné. Somebody rang the doorbell.
□ Le téléphone a sonné. The phone rang.

la sonnerie NOUN
1 bell (electric)
□ La sonnerie du téléphone l'a réveillé. He was woken by the phone ringing.
2 ringtone (on mobile phone)
□ J'ai téléchargé une nouvelle sonnerie sur

mon portable. I've downoaded a new ringtone onto my mobile.

la sonnette NOUN
bell
□ la sonnette d'alarme the alarm bell

la sono NOUN (informal)
sound system

sont VERB ▷ *see* être
- **Ils sont en vacances.** They're on holiday.

sophistiqué (FEM **sophistiquée**) ADJECTIVE
sophisticated

la sorcière NOUN
witch

le sort NOUN
1 spell
□ jeter un sort à quelqu'un to cast a spell on somebody
- **un mauvais sort** a curse
2 fate
□ abandonner quelqu'un à son triste sort to leave somebody to their fate
- **tirer au sort** to draw lots

la sorte NOUN
sort
□ C'est une sorte de gâteau. It's a sort of cake. □ toutes sortes de choses all sorts of things

la sortie NOUN
way out
□ Où est la sortie? Where's the way out?
- **la sortie de secours** the emergency exit
- **Attends-moi à la sortie de l'école.** Meet me after school.

sortir VERB [79]
1 to go out
□ Il est sorti sans rien dire. He went out without saying a word. □ Il est sorti acheter un journal. He's gone out to buy a newspaper. □ J'aime sortir. I like going out.
2 to come out
□ Elle sort de l'hôpital demain. She's coming out of hospital tomorrow. □ Je l'ai rencontré en sortant de la pharmacie. I met him coming out of the chemist's. □ Ce modèle vient juste de sortir. This model has just come out.
3 to take out
□ Elle a sorti son porte-monnaie de son sac. She took her purse out of her handbag. □ Je vais sortir la voiture du garage. I'll get the car out of the garage.
- **sortir avec quelqu'un** to be going out with somebody □ Tu sors avec lui? Are you going out with him?
- **s'en sortir** to manage □ Ne t'en fais pas, tu t'en sortiras. Don't worry, you'll manage OK.

la **sottise** NOUN
- **Ne fais pas de sottises.** Don't do anything silly.
- **Ne dis pas de sottises.** Don't talk nonsense.

le **sou** NOUN
- **une machine à sous** a fruit machine
- **Je n'ai pas un sou sur moi.** I haven't got a penny on me.
- **être près de ses sous** (informal) to be tight-fisted

le **souci** NOUN
worry
- **se faire du souci** to worry

soucieux (FEM **soucieuse**) ADJECTIVE
worried
- □ Tu as l'air soucieux. You look worried.

la **soucoupe** NOUN
saucer
- **une soucoupe volante** a flying saucer

soudain (FEM **soudaine**) ADJECTIVE, ADVERB
1 sudden
- □ une douleur soudaine a sudden pain
2 suddenly
- □ Soudain, il s'est fâché. Suddenly, he got angry.

le **souffle** NOUN
breath
- **à bout de souffle** out of breath

le **soufflé** NOUN
soufflé
- □ un soufflé au fromage a cheese soufflé

souffler VERB [28]
1 to blow
- □ Le vent soufflait fort. The wind was blowing hard.
2 to blow out
- □ Souffle les bougies! Blow out the candles!

la **souffrance** NOUN
suffering

souffrant (FEM **souffrante**) ADJECTIVE
unwell

souffrir VERB [54]
to be in pain
- □ Il souffre beaucoup. He's in a lot of pain.

le **souhait** NOUN
wish
- □ faire un souhait to make a wish □ Tous nos souhaits de réussite. All our best wishes for your success. □ les souhaits de bonne année New Year's wishes
- **Atchoum! — À tes souhaits!** Atchoo! — Bless you!

souhaiter VERB [28]
to wish
- □ Il souhaite aller à l'université. He wishes to go to university. □ Nous vous souhaitons une bonne année. We wish you a happy New Year.

soûl (FEM **soûle**) ADJECTIVE (informal)
drunk

soulager VERB [45]
to relieve

soulever VERB [43]
1 to lift
- □ Je n'arrive pas à soulever cette valise. I can't lift this suitcase.
2 to raise
- □ Il faudra soulever la question lors de la réunion. We'll have to raise the matter at the meeting.

le **soulier** NOUN
shoe

souligner VERB [28]
to underline

le **soupçon** NOUN
suspicion
- **un soupçon de** a dash of □ Ajoutez un soupçon de rhum. Add a dash of rum.

soupçonner VERB [28]
to suspect

la **soupe** NOUN
soup

souper VERB [28]
to have supper

le **soupir** NOUN
sigh

soupirer VERB [28]
to sigh

souple (FEM **souple**) ADJECTIVE
1 supple (person)
2 flexible (system)

la **source** NOUN
spring
- □ l'eau de source spring water

le **sourcil** NOUN
eyebrow

sourd (FEM **sourde**) ADJECTIVE
deaf

souriant (FEM **souriante**) ADJECTIVE
cheerful

le **sourire** NOUN
▷ see also **sourire** VERB
smile

sourire VERB [74]
▷ see also **sourire** NOUN
to smile
- □ sourire à quelqu'un to smile at somebody

la **souris** NOUN
mouse

sournois (FEM **sournoise**) ADJECTIVE
sly

sous PREPOSITION
under

■ **sous terre** underground
■ **sous la pluie** in the rain

sous-entendu (FEM **sous-entendue**)
ADJECTIVE
▷ *see also* **sous-entendu** NOUN
implied

le **sous-entendu** NOUN
▷ *see also* **sous-entendu** ADJECTIVE
insinuation

sous-marin (FEM **sous-marine**) ADJECTIVE
▷ *see also* **sous-marin** NOUN
underwater

le **sous-marin** NOUN
▷ *see also* **sous-marin** ADJECTIVE
submarine

le **sous-sol** NOUN
basement

le **sous-titre** NOUN
subtitle

sous-titré (FEM **sous-titrée**) ADJECTIVE
with subtitles

la **soustraction** NOUN
subtraction

les **sous-vêtements** MASC PL NOUN
underwear

soutenir VERB [83]
to support
□ Il m'a toujours soutenu contre elle. He's
always supported me against her.
■ **soutenir que** to maintain that □ Elle
soutenait que c'était impossible. She
maintained that it was impossible.
■ **soutenir l'allure** to keep up □ Il marchait
trop vite et je n'arrivais pas à soutenir
l'allure. He was walking too fast and I
couldn't keep up.

souterrain (FEM **souterraine**) ADJECTIVE
▷ *see also* **souterrain** NOUN
underground

le **souterrain** NOUN
▷ *see also* **souterrain** ADJECTIVE
underground passage

le **soutien** NOUN
support

le **soutien-gorge** (PL les **soutiens-gorge**)
NOUN
bra

le **souvenir** NOUN
▷ *see also* **se souvenir** VERB
1 memory
□ garder un bon souvenir de quelque chose
to have happy memories of something
2 souvenir
■ **Garde ce livre en souvenir de moi.** Keep
the book: it'll remind you of me.

se **souvenir** VERB [83]
▷ *see also* **souvenir** NOUN

■ **se souvenir de quelque chose** to
remember something □ Je ne me souviens
pas de son adresse. I can't remember his
address.
■ **se souvenir que** to remember that □ Je
me souviens qu'il neigeait. I remember it
was snowing.

souvent ADVERB
often

soyez, soyons VERB ▷ *see* **être**
■ **Soyons clairs!** Let's be clear about this!

la **SPA** NOUN (= *Société protectrice des
animaux*)
RSPCA

spacieux (FEM **spacieuse**) ADJECTIVE
spacious

les **spaghettis** MASC PL NOUN
spaghetti

le **sparadrap** NOUN
sticking plaster

le **speaker** NOUN
announcer

la **speakerine** NOUN
announcer

spécial (FEM **spéciale**, MASC PL **spéciaux**)
ADJECTIVE
1 special
□ Qu'est-ce que tu fais ce week-end? —
Rien de spécial. What are you doing this
weekend? — Nothing special.
■ **les effets spéciaux** special effects
2 peculiar
□ Elle a des goûts un peu spéciaux. She has
rather peculiar tastes.

spécialement ADVERB
1 specially
□ Il est venu spécialement pour te parler.
He came specially to speak to you.
2 particularly
□ Ce n'est pas spécialement difficile. It's not
particularly difficult.

se **spécialiser** VERB [28]
■ **se spécialiser dans quelque chose** to
specialize in something □ Je me suis
spécialisé en histoire contemporaine. I
specialized in modern history.

le/la **spécialiste** NOUN
specialist

la **spécialité** NOUN
speciality

spécifier VERB [19]
to specify

le **spectacle** NOUN
show

spectaculaire (FEM **spectaculaire**)
ADJECTIVE
spectacular

S

le **spectateur** NOUN
1 member of the audience
2 spectator
la **spectatrice** NOUN
1 member of the audience
2 spectator
la **spéléologie** NOUN
potholing
spirituel (FEM **spirituelle**) ADJECTIVE
1 spiritual
2 witty
splendide (FEM **splendide**) ADJECTIVE
magnificent
spontané (FEM **spontanée**) ADJECTIVE
spontaneous
le **sport** NOUN
▷ see also **sport** ADJECTIVE
sport
□ faire du sport to do sport
■ les sports d'hiver winter sports
sport (FEM+PL **sport**) ADJECTIVE
▷ see also **sport** NOUN
casual
□ une veste sport a casual jacket
sportif (FEM **sportive**) ADJECTIVE
▷ see also **sportif** NOUN
1 sporty
□ Elle est très sportive. She's very sporty.
2 sports
□ un club sportif a sports club
le **sportif** NOUN
▷ see also **sportif** ADJECTIVE
sportsman
la **sportive** NOUN
sportswoman
le **spot** NOUN
spotlight
■ un spot publicitaire a commercial break
le **square** NOUN
public gardens
le **squelette** NOUN
skeleton
stable (FEM **stable**) ADJECTIVE
stable
■ un emploi stable a steady job
le **stade** NOUN
stadium
le **stage** NOUN
1 training course
□ faire un stage de formation
professionnelle to go on a vocational
training course
2 work experience
□ Caroline a fait un stage chez Collins.
Caroline did work experience at Collins.
■ faire un stage en entreprise to do a
work placement

LANGUAGE TIP Be careful! The French
word stage does not mean **stage**.
le/la **stagiaire** NOUN
▷ see also **stagiaire** ADJECTIVE
trainee
stagiaire (FEM **stagiaire**) ADJECTIVE
▷ see also **stagiaire** NOUN
trainee
□ un professeur stagiaire a trainee teacher
le **stand** NOUN
1 stand (at exhibition)
2 stall (at fair)
le/la **standardiste** NOUN
operator
la **station** NOUN
■ une station de métro an underground
station
■ une station de taxis a taxi rank
■ une station de ski a ski resort
le **stationnement** NOUN
parking
■ 'stationnement interdit' 'no parking'
stationner VERB [28]
to park
la **station-service** (PL les **stations-
service**) NOUN
service station
la **statistique** NOUN
statistic
le **steak** NOUN
steak
■ un steak frites steak and chips
■ un steak haché a hamburger
la **sténo** NOUN
shorthand
□ un cours de sténo a shorthand course
la **sténodactylo** NOUN
shorthand typist
stérile (FEM **stérile**) ADJECTIVE
sterile
stimulant (FEM **stimulante**) ADJECTIVE
stimulating
stimuler VERB [28]
to stimulate
le **stop** NOUN
stop sign
■ faire du stop to hitchhike
stopper VERB [28]
to stop
le **store** NOUN
1 blind (on window)
2 awning
le **strapontin** NOUN
foldaway seat
la **stratégie** NOUN
strategy
stratégique (FEM **stratégique**) ADJECTIVE

strategic

stressant (FEM **stressante**) ADJECTIVE
stressful

stressé (FEM **stressée**) ADJECTIVE
stressed out

strict (FEM **stricte**) ADJECTIVE
1 strict *(person)*
   □ Ma prof de français est très stricte. My French teacher's very strict.
2 severe *(clothes)*
   □ une tenue très stricte a very severe outfit
   ■ **le strict minimum** the bare minimum

la **strophe** NOUN
stanza

studieux (FEM **studieuse**) ADJECTIVE
studious

le **studio** NOUN
1 studio flat
2 studio
   □ un studio de télévision a television studio

stupéfait (FEM **stupéfaite**) ADJECTIVE
astonished

les **stupéfiants** MASC PL NOUN
narcotics

stupéfier VERB [19]
to astonish
   □ Sa réponse m'a stupéfié. I was astonished by his answer.

stupide (FEM **stupide**) ADJECTIVE
stupid

le **style** NOUN
style

le/la **styliste** NOUN
designer

le **stylo** NOUN
pen
   ■ **un stylo plume** a fountain pen
   ■ **un stylo bille** a ballpoint pen
   ■ **un stylo-feutre** a felt-tip pen

su VERB ▷ see **savoir**
   ■ **Si j'avais su ...** If I'd known ...

subir VERB [38]
to suffer *(defeat)*
   ■ **subir une opération** to have an operation

subit (FEM **subite**) ADJECTIVE
sudden

subitement ADVERB
suddenly

subjectif (FEM **subjective**) ADJECTIVE
subjective

le **subjonctif** NOUN
subjunctive

substituer VERB [28]
to substitute
   □ substituer un mot à un autre to substitute one word for another

subtil (FEM **subtile**) ADJECTIVE
subtle

la **subvention** NOUN
subsidy

subventionner VERB [28]
to subsidize

le **succès** NOUN
success
   ■ **avoir du succès** to be successful

le **successeur** NOUN
successor

la **succursale** NOUN
branch *(of company)*

sucer VERB [12]
to suck

la **sucette** NOUN
lollipop

le **sucre** NOUN
sugar
   ■ **un sucre** a sugar lump □ Je prends deux sucres dans mon café. I take two lumps of sugar in my coffee.
   ■ **du sucre en morceaux** lump sugar
   ■ **un sucre d'orge** a barley sugar
   ■ **du sucre en poudre** caster sugar
   ■ **du sucre glace** icing sugar

sucré (FEM **sucrée**) ADJECTIVE
1 sweet
   □ Ce gâteau est un peu trop sucré. This cake is a bit too sweet.
2 sweetened
   □ du lait concentré sucré sweetened condensed milk

les **sucreries** FEM PL NOUN
sweet things

le **sucrier** NOUN
sugar bowl

le **sud** NOUN
   ▷ see also **sud** ADJECTIVE
south
   □ Ils vivent dans le sud de la France. They live in the South of France.
   ■ **vers le sud** southwards
   ■ **au sud de Paris** south of Paris
   ■ **l'Amérique du Sud** South America
   ■ **le vent du sud** the south wind

sud (FEM+PL **sud**) ADJECTIVE
   ▷ see also **sud** NOUN
1 south
   □ la côte sud de l'Espagne the south coast of Spain
   ■ **le pôle sud** the South Pole
2 southern
   □ Nous avons visité la partie sud du pays. We visited the southern part of the country.

sud-africain (FEM **sud-africaine**) ADJECTIVE
South African

sud-américain (FEM **sud-américaine**)
ADJECTIVE
South American

le **sud-est** NOUN
south-east
□ au sud-est in the south-east

le **sud-ouest** NOUN
south-west
□ au sud-ouest in the south-west

la **Suède** NOUN
Sweden

suédois (FEM **suédoise**) ADJECTIVE, NOUN
Swedish
□ Ils parlent suédois. They speak Swedish.
■ **un Suédois** a Swede (man)
■ **une Suédoise** a Swede (woman)
■ **les Suédois** the Swedes

suer VERB [28]
to sweat

la **sueur** NOUN
sweat
■ **en sueur** sweating

suffire VERB [80]
to be enough
□ Tiens, voilà dix euros. Ça te suffit? Here's
10 euros. Is that enough for you?
■ **Ça suffit!** That's enough!

suffisamment ADVERB
enough
□ Ça n'est pas suffisamment grand. It's not
big enough. □ Il n'y a pas suffisamment de
chaises. There aren't enough chairs.

suffisant (FEM **suffisante**) ADJECTIVE
1 sufficient
□ Ça n'est pas une raison suffisante. That's
not sufficient reason.
2 smug
□ Il est un peu trop suffisant. He's rather
smug.

suffoquer VERB [28]
to suffocate

suggérer VERB [34]
to suggest

se **suicider** VERB [28]
to commit suicide

suis VERB ▷ see **être** ▷ see **suivre**
■ **Je suis écossais.** I'm Scottish.
■ **Suis-moi.** Follow me.

suisse (FEM **suisse**) ADJECTIVE, NOUN
▷ see also **la Suisse**
Swiss
□ le franc suisse the Swiss franc
■ **un Suisse** a Swiss man
■ **une Suisse** a Swiss woman
■ **les Suisses** the Swiss

la **Suisse** NOUN
▷ see also **suisse** ADJECTIVE

Switzerland
□ la Suisse allemande German-speaking
Switzerland □ la Suisse romande French-
speaking Switzerland

la **suite** NOUN
1 rest
□ Je vous raconterai la suite de l'histoire
demain. I'll tell you the rest of the story
tomorrow.
2 sequel (to book, film)
■ **tout de suite** straightaway □ J'y vais tout
de suite. I'll go straightaway.
■ **de suite** in succession □ Il a commis la
même erreur trois fois de suite. He made
the same mistake three times in succession.
■ **par la suite** subsequently □ Il s'est avéré
par la suite qu'il était coupable. He
subsequently turned out to be guilty.

suivant (FEM **suivante**) ADJECTIVE
following
□ le jour suivant the following day
□ l'exercice suivant the following exercise
■ **Au suivant!** Next!

suivre VERB [81]
1 to follow
□ Il m'a suivie jusque chez moi. He followed
me home. □ Vous me suivez ou est-ce que
je parle trop vite? Are you following me or
am I speaking too fast?
2 to do
□ Je suis un cours d'anglais à la fac. I'm
doing an English course at college.
3 to keep up
□ Il n'arrive pas à suivre en maths. He can't
keep up in maths. □ J'aime suivre
l'actualité. I like to keep up with the news.
■ **'à suivre'** 'to be continued'
■ **suivre un régime** to be on a diet

le **sujet** NOUN
▷ see also **sujet** ADJECTIVE
subject
■ **au sujet de** about □ C'est à quel sujet? —
C'est au sujet de l'annonce parue dans 'Le
Monde' d'aujourd'hui. What's it about? —
It's about the advertisement in today's 'Le
Monde'.
■ **un sujet de conversation** a topic of
conversation
■ **un sujet d'examen** an examination
question
■ **un sujet de plaisanterie** something to
joke about

sujet (FEM **sujette**) ADJECTIVE
▷ see also **sujet** NOUN
■ **être sujet à** to be prone to □ Il est sujet à
des crises de panique. He is prone to panic
attacks.

super (FEM+PL **super**) ADJECTIVE
▷ *see also* **super** NOUN
great

le **super** NOUN
▷ *see also* **super** ADJECTIVE
super *(petrol)*

superficiel (FEM **superficielle**) ADJECTIVE
superficial

superflu (FEM **superflue**) ADJECTIVE
superfluous

supérieur (FEM **supérieure**) ADJECTIVE
▷ *see also* **supérieur** NOUN
1 upper
□ la lèvre supérieure the upper lip
2 superior
□ qualité supérieure superior quality □ Il a
toujours l'air tellement supérieur! He
always looks so superior!
■ **supérieur à** greater than □ Choisissez un
nombre supérieur à cent. Choose a number
greater than 100.

le **supérieur** NOUN
▷ *see also* **supérieur** ADJECTIVE
superior
□ mon supérieur hiérarchique my
immediate superior

le **supermarché** NOUN
supermarket

superposé (FEM **superposée**) ADJECTIVE
■ **des lits superposés** bunk beds

superstitieux (FEM **superstitieuse**)
ADJECTIVE
superstitious

le **suppléant** NOUN
supply teacher

la **suppléante** NOUN
supply teacher

le **supplément** NOUN
■ **payer un supplément** to pay an
additional charge
■ **Le vin est en supplément.** Wine is extra.
■ **un supplément de travail** extra work

supplémentaire (FEM **supplémentaire**)
ADJECTIVE
additional
□ Voici quelques exercices supplémentaires.
Here are some additional exercises.
■ **faire des heures supplémentaires** to do
overtime

le **supplice** NOUN
torture
□ C'était un supplice. It was torture.

supplier VERB [19]
■ **supplier quelqu'un de faire quelque
chose** to beg somebody to do something
□ Je t'en supplie! I'm begging you!

supportable (FEM **supportable**) ADJECTIVE
bearable

supporter VERB [28]
to stand *(tolerate)*
□ Je ne supporte pas l'hypocrisie. I can't
stand hypocrisy. □ Elle ne supporte pas
qu'on la critique. She can't stand being
criticized. □ Je ne peux pas la supporter. I
can't stand her. □ Je supporte mal la
chaleur. I can't stand hot weather.
LANGUAGE TIP Be careful! **supporter**
does not mean **to support**.

supposer VERB [28]
to suppose

supprimer VERB [28]
1 to cut
□ Deux mille emplois ont été supprimés.
Two thousand jobs have been cut.
2 to cancel
□ Le train de Londres a été supprimé. The
train to London has been cancelled.
3 to get rid of
□ Ils ont supprimé les témoins gênants.
They got rid of the awkward witnesses.

sur PREPOSITION
1 on
□ Pose-le sur la table. Put it down on the
table. □ Vous verrez l'hôpital sur votre
droite. You'll see the hospital on your right.
□ une conférence sur Balzac a lecture on
Balzac
2 in
□ une personne sur dix 1 person in 10
3 out of
□ J'ai eu onze sur vingt en maths. I got 11
out of 20 in maths.
4 by
□ quatre mètres sur deux 4 metres by 2

sûr (FEM **sûre**) ADJECTIVE
1 sure
□ Tu es sûr? Are you sure?
■ **sûr et certain** absolutely certain
2 reliable
□ C'est quelqu'un de très sûr. He's a very
reliable person.
3 safe
□ Ce quartier n'est pas très sûr la nuit. This
neighbourhood isn't very safe at night.
■ **sûr de soi** self-confident □ Elle est très
sûre d'elle. She's very self-confident.

sûrement ADVERB
certainly
□ Sûrement pas! Certainly not! □ Il est
sûrement déjà parti. He'll certainly already
have left.

la **sûreté** NOUN
■ **mettre quelque chose en sûreté** to put
something in a safe place

le **surf** NOUN
surfing

la **surface** NOUN
surface
- **les grandes surfaces** the supermarkets

surfer VERB [28]
to go surfing
- **surfer sur le Net** to surf the Net

surgelé (FEM **surgelée**) ADJECTIVE
frozen
□ des frites surgelées frozen chips

les **surgelés** MASC PL NOUN
frozen food

surhumain (FEM **surhumaine**) ADJECTIVE
superhuman

sur-le-champ ADVERB
immediately

le **surlendemain** NOUN
- **le surlendemain de son arrivée** two days after he arrived
- **le surlendemain dans la matinée** two days later, in the morning

se **surmener** VERB [43]
to work too hard
□ Ne te surmène pas trop pendant le week-end. Don't work too hard over the weekend.

surmonter VERB [48]
to overcome
□ Il nous reste de nombreux obstacles à surmonter. We still have many obstacles to overcome.

surnaturel (FEM **surnaturelle**) ADJECTIVE
supernatural

le **surnom** NOUN
nickname

surnommer NOUN
to nickname
□ On l'a surnommé 'Kiki'. We nicknamed him 'Kiki'.

surpeuplé (FEM **surpeuplée**) ADJECTIVE
overpopulated

surprenant (FEM **surprenante**) ADJECTIVE
surprising

surprendre VERB [65]
to surprise
□ Ça me surprendrait beaucoup qu'il arrive à l'heure. I'd be very surprised if he arrived on time.
- **surprendre quelqu'un en train de faire quelque chose** to catch somebody doing something □ Je l'ai surpris en train de fouiller dans mon placard. I caught him rummaging in my cupboard.

surpris (FEM **surprise**) ADJECTIVE
▷ see also **surprise** NOUN
surprised
□ Il était surpris de me voir. He was

surprised to see me.

la **surprise** NOUN
▷ see also **surprise** ADJECTIVE
surprise
□ faire une surprise à quelqu'un to give somebody a surprise

sursauter VERB [28]
to jump
□ J'ai sursauté en entendant mon nom. I jumped when I heard my name.

surtout ADVERB
1 especially
□ Il est assez timide, surtout avec les filles. He's rather shy, especially with girls.
2 crucially
□ Ce canapé est joli et surtout, il n'est pas salissant. This sofa is pretty and, crucially, it doesn't show the dirt.
- **Surtout, ne répète pas ce que je t'ai dit!** Whatever you do, don't repeat what I told you!

le **surveillant** NOUN
supervisor (man)

> **DID YOU KNOW...?**
> In French secondary schools, the teachers are not responsible for supervising the pupils outside class. This job is done by people called **surveillants** or **pions**.

la **surveillante** NOUN
supervisor (woman)

surveiller VERB [28]
1 to keep an eye on
□ Tu peux surveiller mes bagages? Can you keep an eye on my luggage?
2 to keep a watch on
□ La police a surveillé la maison pendant une semaine. The police kept the house under surveillance for a week.
3 to supervise
□ Nous sommes toujours surveillés pendant la récréation. We're always supervised during break.
- **surveiller un examen** to invigilate an exam
- **surveiller sa ligne** to watch one's figure

le **survêtement** NOUN
tracksuit
□ un haut de survêtement a tracksuit top
□ un pantalon de survêtement tracksuit bottoms

la **survie** NOUN
survival

le **survivant** NOUN
survivor

la **survivante** NOUN
survivor

survivre VERB [91]
to survive
□ survivre à un accident to survive an accident
survoler VERB [28]
to fly over
sus ADVERB
■ en sus in addition
susceptible (FEM **susceptible**) ADJECTIVE
touchy
suspect (FEM **suspecte**) ADJECTIVE
suspicious
□ dans des circonstances suspectes under suspicious circumstances
suspecter VERB [28]
to suspect
le **suspense** NOUN
suspense
■ un film à suspense a thriller
la **suture** NOUN
■ un point de suture a stitch
svelte (FEM **svelte**) ADJECTIVE
slender
SVP ABBREVIATION (= s'il vous plaît)
please
le **sweat** NOUN
sweatshirt
la **syllabe** NOUN
syllable
le **symbole** NOUN
symbol
symbolique (FEM **symbolique**) ADJECTIVE
symbolic
symboliser VERB [28]
to symbolize
symétrique (FEM **symétrique**) ADJECTIVE
symmetrical
sympa (FEM+PL **sympa**) ADJECTIVE (informal)
nice
□ Elle est très sympa. She's a really nice person.
la **sympathie** NOUN

■ J'ai beaucoup de sympathie pour lui. I like him a lot.
sympathique (FEM **sympathique**)
ADJECTIVE
nice
□ Ce sont des gens très sympathiques. They're very nice people.

> LANGUAGE TIP Be careful!
> sympathique does not mean
> sympathetic.

sympathiser VERB [28]
to get on well
□ Nous avons immédiatement sympathisé avec nos voisins. We got on well with our neighbours straight away.
le **symptôme** NOUN
symptom
la **synagogue** NOUN
synagogue
le **syndicat** NOUN
trade union
■ le syndicat d'initiative the tourist information office
synonyme (FEM **synonyme**) ADJECTIVE
▷ see also synonyme NOUN
synonymous
□ être synonyme de to be synonymous with
le **synonyme** NOUN
▷ see also synonyme ADJECTIVE
synonym
synthétique (FEM **synthétique**) ADJECTIVE
synthetic
la **Syrie** NOUN
Syria
syrien (FEM **syrienne**) ADJECTIVE
Syrian
systématique (FEM **systématique**)
ADJECTIVE
systematic
le **système** NOUN
system

S

Tt

t' PRONOUN ▷ *see* **te**

ta FEM ADJECTIVE
your
□ J'ai vu ta sœur hier. I saw your sister yesterday.

le **tabac** NOUN
1 tobacco
□ le tabac blond light tobacco □ le tabac brun dark tobacco
2 smoking
□ Le tabac est mauvais pour la santé. Smoking is bad for you.

la **table** NOUN
table
■ **mettre la table** to lay the table
■ **se mettre à table** to sit down to eat
■ **À table!** Dinner's ready!
■ **une table de nuit** a bedside table
■ **'table des matières'** 'contents'

le **tableau** (PL les **tableaux**) NOUN
painting
□ un tableau de Monet a painting by Monet
■ **le tableau d'affichage** the notice board
■ **le tableau noir** the blackboard

la **tablette** NOUN
■ **une tablette de chocolat** a bar of chocolate

le **tableur** NOUN
spreadsheet

le **tablier** NOUN
apron

le **tabouret** NOUN
stool

la **tache** NOUN
mark *(stain)*
■ **des taches de rousseur** freckles

la **tâche** NOUN
task

tacher VERB [28]
to leave a stain

tâcher VERB [28]
■ **tâcher de faire quelque chose** to try to do something □ Tâche d'être à l'heure! Try to be on time!

le **tact** NOUN

tact
■ **avoir du tact** to be tactful

la **tactique** NOUN
tactics
■ **changer de tactique** to try something different

la **taie** NOUN
■ **une taie d'oreiller** a pillowcase

la **taille** NOUN
1 waist
□ Elle a la taille fine. She has a slim waist.
2 height
□ un homme de taille moyenne a man of average height
3 size
□ Avez-vous ma taille? Have you got my size?

le **taille-crayon** NOUN
pencil sharpener

le **tailleur** NOUN
1 tailor
2 suit *(lady's)*
■ **Il est assis en tailleur.** He's sitting cross-legged.

se **taire** VERB [82]
to stop talking
■ **Taisez-vous!** Be quiet!

le **talon** NOUN
heel

le **tambour** NOUN
drum

la **Tamise** NOUN
Thames

le **tampon** NOUN
pad
□ un tampon à récurer a scouring pad
■ **un tampon hygiénique** a tampon

tamponneuse FEM ADJECTIVE
■ **les autos tamponneuses** dodgems

tandis que CONJUNCTION
while
□ Il a toujours de bonnes notes, tandis que les miennes sont mauvaises. He always gets good marks, while mine are poor.

tant ADVERB

so much
□ Je l'aime tant! I love him so much!
■ **tant de 1** so much □ tant de nourriture
so much food **2** so many □ tant de livres
so many books
■ **tant que 1** until □ Tu ne sortiras pas tant
que tu n'auras pas fini tes devoirs. You're
not going out until you've finished your
homework. **2** while □ Profites-en tant que
tu peux. Make the most of it while you can.
■ **tant mieux** so much the better
■ **tant pis** never mind

la **tante** NOUN
aunt

tantôt ADVERB
sometimes
□ Nous venons tantôt à pied, tantôt en bus.
Sometimes we walk, sometimes we come
by bus.

le **tapage** NOUN
1 racket
□ Ils ont fait du tapage toute la nuit. They
made a racket all night long.
2 fuss
□ On a fait beaucoup de tapage autour de
cette affaire. There was a lot of fuss about
that business.

taper VERB [28]
to beat down
□ Le soleil tape. The sun's really beating
down
■ **taper quelqu'un** to hit somebody
□ Maman, il m'a tapé! Mum, he hit me!
■ **taper sur quelque chose** to bang on
something
■ **taper des pieds** to stamp one's feet
■ **taper des mains** to clap one's hands
■ **taper à la machine** to type □ Tu sais
taper à la machine? Can you type? □ Je vais
taper cette lettre. I'm going to type this
letter.

le **tapis** NOUN
carpet
■ **le tapis roulant 1** (for people) the
Travelator® **2** (in factory) the conveyer belt
3 (at baggage reclaim) the carousel
■ **un tapis de souris** a mouse mat

tapisser VERB [28]
to paper

la **tapisserie** NOUN
1 wallpaper
□ Tu aimes la tapisserie de ma chambre? Do
you like the wallpaper in my bedroom?
2 tapestry

taquiner VERB [28]
to tease

tard ADVERB

late
□ Il est tard. It's late.
■ **plus tard** later on
■ **au plus tard** at the latest

tardif (FEM **tardive**) ADJECTIVE
late
□ un petit déjeuner tardif a late breakfast

le **tarif** NOUN
■ **le tarif des consommations** (in café) the
price list
■ **une communication à tarif réduit** an
off-peak phone call
■ **un billet de train à tarif réduit** a
concessionary train ticket
■ **un billet de train à plein tarif** a full-price
train ticket
■ **Est-ce que vous faites un tarif de
groupe?** Is there a reduction for groups?

la **tarte** NOUN
tart

la **tartine** NOUN
slice of bread
□ une tartine de confiture a slice of bread
and jam

tartiner VERB [28]
to spread
■ **le fromage à tartiner** cheese spread

le **tas** NOUN
heap
□ un tas de charbon a heap of coal
■ **un tas de** (informal) loads of □ J'ai lu un
tas de livres pendant les vacances. I read
loads of books in the holidays.

la **tasse** NOUN
cup

le **taureau** (PL les **taureaux**) NOUN
bull
■ **le Taureau** Taurus □ Ils sont tous les
deux Taureau. They're both Taurus.

le **taux** NOUN
rate
□ le taux de change the exchange rate

la **taxe** NOUN
tax
■ **la boutique hors taxes** the duty-free
shop

le **taxi** NOUN
taxi

tchèque (FEM **tchèque**) ADJECTIVE
Czech
■ **la République tchèque** the Czech
Republic

te PRONOUN
LANGUAGE TIP te changes to t' before
a vowel and most words beginning
with 'h'.
1 you

□ Je te vois. I can see you. □ Il t'a vu? Did he see you?

2 to you

□ Est-ce qu'il te parle en français? Does he talk to you in French? □ Elle t'a parlé? Did she speak to you?

3 yourself

□ Tu vas te rendre malade. You'll make yourself sick.

> **LANGUAGE TIP** With reflexive verbs, **te** is often not translated.

□ Comment tu t'appelles? What's your name?

le **technicien** NOUN
technician

la **technicienne** NOUN
technician

technique (FEM **technique**) ADJECTIVE
▷ see also **technique** NOUN
technical

la **technique** NOUN
▷ see also **technique** ADJECTIVE
technique

la **techno** NOUN
techno music

la **technologie** NOUN
technology

le **teint** NOUN
complexion

□ Elle a le teint clair. She's got a fair complexion.

la **teinte** NOUN
shade (colour)

le **teinturier** NOUN
dry cleaner's

□ Je vais porter ce manteau chez le teinturier. I'm going to take this coat to the dry cleaner's.

tel (FEM **telle**) ADJECTIVE

■ **Il a un tel enthousiasme!** He's got such enthusiasm!

■ **rien de tel** nothing like □ Il n'y a rien de tel qu'une bonne nuit de sommeil. There's nothing like a good night's sleep.

■ **J'ai tout laissé tel quel.** I left everything as it was.

■ **tel que** such as

la **télé** NOUN
telly

□ à la télé on telly

la **télécarte** NOUN
phonecard

le **téléchargement** NOUN
download

télécharger VERB [45]
to download

la **télécommande** NOUN
remote control

la **téléconférence** NOUN
video conference

la **télécopie** NOUN
fax

le **télégramme** NOUN
telegram

télépéage NOUN
motorway toll payment system

> **DID YOU KNOW...?**
> Certain lanes at motorway tolls are reserved for drivers who have a sensor inside their car which allows them to pay monthly rather than on the spot. These lanes are marked with a yellow T and should be avoided by tourists.

le **téléphérique** NOUN
cable car

le **téléphone** NOUN
telephone

□ Elle est au téléphone. She's on the phone.

■ **un téléphone portable** a mobile phone

■ **un téléphone appareil photo** a camera phone

téléphoner VERB [28]
to phone

□ Je vais téléphoner à Claire. I'll phone Claire. □ Je peux téléphoner? Can I make a phone call?

la **téléréalité** NOUN
reality TV

le **télésiège** NOUN
chairlift

le **téléski** NOUN
ski-tow

le **téléspectateur** NOUN
viewer (TV)

la **téléspectatrice** NOUN
viewer (TV)

le **téléviseur** NOUN
television set

la **télévision** NOUN
television

□ à la télévision on television

■ **la télévision en circuit fermé** CCTV

■ **la télévision numérique** digital TV

telle FEM ADJECTIVE

■ **Je n'ai jamais eu une telle peur.** I've never had such a fright.

■ **telle que** such as

tellement ADVERB

1 so

□ Andrew est tellement gentil. Andrew's so nice. □ Il travaille tellement. He works so hard.

2 so much

□ Il a tellement mangé que ... He ate so

much that …
3 so many

□ Il y avait tellement de monde. There were so many people.

telles FEM PL ADJECTIVE
such

□ Je n'ai jamais entendu de telles bêtises! I've never heard such nonsense!

tels MASC PL ADJECTIVE
such

□ Nous n'avons pas de tels orages chez nous. We don't have such storms back home.

le **témoignage** NOUN
testimony

témoigner VERB [28]
to testify

le **témoin** NOUN
witness

la **température** NOUN
temperature

□ avoir de la température to have a temperature

la **tempête** NOUN
storm

le **temple** NOUN
1 church (Protestant)
2 temple (Hindu, Sikh, Buddhist)

temporaire (FEM **temporaire**) ADJECTIVE
temporary

le **temps** NOUN
1 weather

□ Quel temps fait-il? What's the weather like?
2 time

□ Je n'ai pas le temps. I haven't got time. □ Prends ton temps. Take your time. □ Il est temps de partir. It's time to go.

■ **juste à temps** just in time
■ **de temps en temps** from time to time
■ **en même temps** at the same time
■ **à temps** in time □ Il est arrivé à temps pour le match. He arrived in time for the match.
■ **à plein temps** full time □ Elle travaille à plein temps. She works full time.
■ **à temps complet** full time
■ **à temps partiel** part time □ le travail à temps partiel part-time work
■ **dans le temps** at one time □ Dans le temps, on pouvait circuler en vélo sans danger. At one time, it was safe to go around by bike.
3 tense (of verb)

tenais, tenait VERB ▷ see tenir

la **tendance** NOUN
■ **avoir tendance à faire quelque chose**

to tend to do something □ Il a tendance à exagérer. He tends to exaggerate.

tendre (FEM **tendre**) ADJECTIVE
▷ see also **tendre** VERB
tender

tendre VERB [88]
▷ see also **tendre** ADJECTIVE
to stretch out

□ Ils ont tendu une corde entre deux arbres. They stretched out a rope between two trees.

■ **tendre quelque chose à quelqu'un** to hold something out to somebody □ Il lui a tendu les clés. He held out the keys to her.
■ **tendre la main** to hold out one's hand
■ **tendre le bras** to reach out
■ **tendre un piège à quelqu'un** to set a trap for someone

tendrement ADVERB
tenderly

la **tendresse** NOUN
tenderness

tendu (FEM **tendue**) ADJECTIVE
tense

□ Il était très tendu aujourd'hui. He was very tense today.

tenir VERB [83]
to hold

□ Tu peux tenir la lampe, s'il te plaît? Can you hold the torch, please? □ Il tenait un enfant par la main. He was holding a child by the hand.

■ **Tenez votre chien en laisse.** Keep your dog on the lead.
■ **tenir à quelqu'un** to be attached to somebody □ Il tient beaucoup à elle. He's very attached to her.
■ **tenir à faire quelque chose** to be determined to do something □ Elle tient à y aller. She's determined to go.
■ **tenir de quelqu'un** to take after somebody □ Il tient de son père. He takes after his father.
■ **Tiens, voilà un stylo.** Here's a pen.
■ **Tiens, c'est Alain là-bas!** Look, that's Alain over there!
■ **Tiens? Really?**
■ **se tenir 1** to stand □ Il se tenait près de la porte. He was standing by the door. **2** to be held □ La foire va se tenir place du marché. The fair will be held in the market place.
■ **se tenir droit 1** to stand up straight □ Tiens-toi droit! Stand up straight! **2** to sit up straight □ Arrête de manger le nez dans ton assiette, tiens-toi droit. Don't slouch while you're eating, sit up straight.

t

■ **Tiens-toi bien!** Behave yourself!

le **tennis** NOUN

1 tennis
□ Elle joue au tennis. She plays tennis.
■ **le tennis de table** table tennis

2 tennis court
□ Il est au tennis. He's at the tennis court.
■ **les tennis** trainers

tentant (FEM **tentante**) ADJECTIVE
tempting

la **tentation** NOUN
temptation

la **tentative** NOUN
attempt

la **tente** NOUN
tent

tenter VERB [28]
to tempt
□ J'ai été tenté de tout abandonner. I was tempted to give up. □ Ça ne me tente vraiment pas d'aller à la piscine. I don't really fancy going to the swimming pool.
■ **tenter de faire quelque chose** to try to do something □ Il a tenté plusieurs fois de s'évader. He tried several times to escape.

tenu VERB ▷ see tenir

la **tenue** NOUN
clothes
■ **en tenue de soirée** in evening dress

le **terme** NOUN
■ **à court terme** short-term
■ **à long terme** long-term

la **terminale** NOUN
upper sixth
□ Je suis en terminale. I'm in the upper sixth.

> **DID YOU KNOW…?**
> In French secondary schools, years are counted from the **sixième** (youngest) to **première** and **terminale** (oldest).

terminer VERB [28]
to finish
■ **se terminer** to end □ Les vacances se terminent demain. The holidays end tomorrow.

le **terminus** NOUN
terminus

le **terrain** NOUN
land
□ Il veut acheter un terrain en Normandie. He wants to buy some land in Normandy.
■ **un terrain de camping** a campsite
■ **un terrain de football** a football pitch
■ **un terrain de golf** a golf course
■ **un terrain de jeu** a playground
■ **un terrain de sport** a sports ground

■ **un terrain vague** a piece of waste ground

la **terrasse** NOUN
terrace
■ **Si on s'asseyait en terrasse?** (at café) Shall we sit outside?

la **terre** NOUN
earth
■ **la Terre** the Earth
■ **Elle s'est assise par terre.** She sat on the floor.
■ **Il est tombé par terre.** He fell down.
■ **la terre cuite** terracotta □ un pot en terre cuite a terracotta pot
■ **la terre glaise** clay

terrible (FEM **terrible**) ADJECTIVE
terrible
□ Quelque chose de terrible est arrivé. Something terrible has happened.
■ **pas terrible** (informal) nothing special
□ Ce film n'est pas terrible. The film's nothing special.

la **terrine** NOUN
pâté

le **territoire** NOUN
territory

terrorisé (FEM **terrorisée**) ADJECTIVE
terrified

le **terrorisme** NOUN
terrorism

le/la **terroriste** NOUN
terrorist

tes PL ADJECTIVE
your
□ J'aime bien tes baskets. I like your trainers.

le **test** NOUN
test

le **testament** NOUN
will
□ Il est mort sans testament. He died without leaving a will.

tester VERB [28]
to test

le **tétanos** NOUN
tetanus

le **têtard** NOUN
tadpole

la **tête** NOUN
head
□ de la tête aux pieds from head to foot
■ **se laver la tête** to wash one's hair
■ **la tête la première** headfirst
■ **tenir tête à quelqu'un** to stand up to somebody
■ **faire la tête** to sulk
■ **en avoir par-dessus la tête** to be fed up

têtu (FEM **têtue**) ADJECTIVE

stubborn

le **texte** NOUN
text *(written work)*

le **Texto**® NOUN
text message

le **TGV** NOUN (= *train à grande vitesse*)
high-speed train

le **thé** NOUN
tea
□ Je vous offre un thé? Would you like a cup of tea? □ un thé au lait a white tea

le **théâtre** NOUN
theatre
■ **faire du théâtre** to act □ Est-ce que tu as déjà fait du théâtre? Have you ever acted?

la **théière** NOUN
teapot

le **thème** NOUN
1 subject
□ Quel est le thème de l'émission? What's the programme about?
2 prose *(translation into the foreign language)*

la **théorie** NOUN
theory

le **thermomètre** NOUN
thermometer

le **thon** NOUN
tuna

la **thune** NOUN *(informal)*
dosh

le **tibia** NOUN
1 shinbone
□ une fracture du tibia a broken shinbone
2 shin
□ Il m'a donné un coup de pied dans le tibia. He kicked me in the shin.

les **TIC** FEM PL NOUN (= *technologies de l'information et de la communication*)
ICT

le **tic** NOUN
nervous twitch

le **ticket** NOUN
ticket
□ un ticket de métro an underground ticket
■ **le ticket de caisse** the till receipt

tiède (FEM **tiède**) ADJECTIVE
1 warm *(water, air)*
2 lukewarm *(food, drink)*

tien MASC PRONOUN
■ **le tien** yours □ J'ai oublié mon stylo. Tu peux me prêter le tien? I've forgotten my pen. Can you lend me yours?

tienne FEM PRONOUN
■ **la tienne** yours □ Ce n'est pas ma raquette, c'est la tienne. It's not my racket, it's yours.

■ **À la tienne!** Cheers!

tiennes FEM PL PRONOUN
■ **les tiennes** yours □ J'ai pris mes baskets, mais j'ai oublié les tiennes. I've brought my trainers, but I've forgotten yours.

tiens MASC PL PRONOUN
■ **les tiens** yours □ Je ne trouve pas mes feutres. Je peux utiliser les tiens? I can't find my felt pens. Can I use yours?

tiens, tient VERB ▷ *see* **tenir**

le **tiers** NOUN
third
□ Un tiers de la classe était pour. A third of the class were in favour.
■ **le tiers monde** the Third World

la **tige** NOUN
stem

le **tigre** NOUN
tiger

le **tilleul** NOUN
lime tea

le **timbre** NOUN
stamp

le **timbre-poste** NOUN
postage stamp

timide (FEM **timide**) ADJECTIVE
shy

timidement ADVERB
shyly

la **timidité** NOUN
shyness

le **tir** NOUN
shooting
■ **le tir à l'arc** archery

le **tirage** NOUN
■ **par tirage au sort** by drawing lots □ Les prix seront attribués par tirage au sort. The prizes will be awarded by drawing lots.

le **tire-bouchon** NOUN
corkscrew
○ **LANGUAGE TIP** Word for word, **tire-bouchon** means 'cork-puller'.

la **tirelire** NOUN
money box

tirer VERB [28]
1 to pull
□ Elle a tiré un mouchoir de son sac. She pulled a handkerchief out of her bag. □ Il m'a tiré les cheveux. He pulled my hair. □ 'Tirer' 'Pull'
2 to draw
□ tirer les rideaux to draw the curtains □ tirer un trait to draw a line □ tirer des conclusions to draw conclusions
■ **tirer au sort** to draw lots
3 to fire
□ Il a tiré plusieurs coups de feu. He fired

several shots. □ Il a tiré sur les policiers. He fired at the police.
■ **Tu t'en tires bien.** You're doing well.

le **tiret** NOUN
dash (hyphen)

le **tiroir** NOUN
drawer

la **tisane** NOUN
herbal tea

tisser VERB [28]
to weave

le **tissu** NOUN
material
■ **un sac en tissu** a cloth bag

le **titre** NOUN
title
■ **les gros titres** the headlines
■ **un titre de transport** a travel ticket

tituber VERB [28]
to stagger

la **TNT** NOUN (= télévision numérique terrestre)
digital television

le **toast** NOUN
1 piece of toast
2 toast
□ porter un toast à quelqu'un to drink a toast to somebody

le **toboggan** NOUN
slide

toi PRONOUN
you
□ Ça va? — Oui, et toi? How are you? — Fine, and you? □ J'ai faim, pas toi? I'm hungry, aren't you?
■ **Assieds-toi.** Sit down.
■ **C'est à toi de jouer.** It's your turn to play.
■ **Est-ce que ce stylo est à toi?** Is this pen yours?

la **toile** NOUN
■ **un pantalon de toile** cotton trousers
■ **un sac de toile** a canvas bag
■ **une toile cirée** an oilcloth
■ **une toile d'araignée** a cobweb

la **toilette** NOUN
1 wash
□ faire sa toilette to have a wash
2 outfit
□ une toilette élégante an elegant outfit

les **toilettes** FEM PL NOUN
toilet

toi-même PRONOUN
yourself
□ Tu as fait ça toi-même? Did you do it yourself?

le **toit** NOUN
roof
■ **un toit ouvrant** a sunroof

tolérant (FEM **tolérante**) ADJECTIVE
tolerant

tolérer VERB [34]
to tolerate

la **tomate** NOUN
tomato

la **tombe** NOUN
grave

le **tombeau** (PL les **tombeaux**) NOUN
tomb

la **tombée** NOUN
■ **à la tombée de la nuit** at nightfall

tomber VERB [84]
to fall
□ Attention, tu vas tomber! Be careful, you'll fall!
■ **laisser tomber 1** to drop □ Elle a laissé tomber son stylo. She dropped her pen.
2 to give up □ Il a laissé tomber le piano. He gave up the piano. **3** to let down □ Il ne laisse jamais tomber ses amis. He never lets his friends down.
■ **tomber sur quelqu'un** to bump into someone □ Je suis tombé sur lui en sortant de chez Pierre. I bumped into him coming out of Pierre's place.
■ **Ça tombe bien.** That's lucky.
■ **Il tombe de sommeil.** He's asleep on his feet.

ton (FEM **ta**, PL **tes**) ADJECTIVE
▷ see also **ton** NOUN
your
□ C'est ton stylo? Is this your pen?

le **ton** NOUN
▷ see also **ton** ADJECTIVE
1 tone of voice
□ Ne me parle pas sur ce ton. Don't speak to me in that tone of voice.
2 colour
□ J'adore les tons pastel. I love pastel colours.

la **tonalité** NOUN
dialling tone

la **tondeuse** NOUN
lawnmower

tondre VERB [69]
to mow

tonique (FEM **tonique**) ADJECTIVE
fortifying

la **tonne** NOUN
tonne

le **tonneau** (PL les **tonneaux**) NOUN
barrel

le **tonnerre** NOUN
thunder

le **tonus** NOUN
■ **avoir du tonus** to be energetic

le **torchon** NOUN
tea towel

tordre VERB [49]
- **se tordre la cheville** to twist one's ankle

tordu (FEM **tordue**) ADJECTIVE
1 bent
  □ Ce clou est un peu tordu. This nail's a bit bent.
2 crazy
  □ une histoire complètement tordue a crazy story

le **torrent** NOUN
mountain stream

le **torse** NOUN
chest
  □ Il était torse nu. He was bare-chested.

le **tort** NOUN
- **avoir tort** to be wrong
- **donner tort à quelqu'un** to lay the blame on somebody

le **torticolis** NOUN
stiff neck
  □ J'ai le torticolis. I've got a stiff neck.

la **tortue** NOUN
tortoise

la **torture** NOUN
torture

torturer VERB [28]
to torture

tôt ADVERB
early
- **au plus tôt** at the earliest
- **tôt ou tard** sooner or later

total (FEM **totale**, MASC PL **totaux**) ADJECTIVE
▷ see also **total** NOUN
total

le **total** (PL les **totaux**) NOUN
▷ see also **total** ADJECTIVE
total
  □ faire le total to work out the total
- **au total** in total

totalement ADVERB
totally

la **totalité** NOUN
- **la totalité des profs** all the teachers
- **la totalité du personnel** the entire staff

touchant (FEM **touchante**) ADJECTIVE
touching

toucher VERB [28]
1 to touch
  □ Ne touche pas à mes livres! Don't touch my books!
- **Nos deux jardins se touchent.** Our gardens are next to each other.
2 to feel
  □ Ce pull a l'air doux. Je peux toucher? That sweater looks soft. Can I feel it?

3 to hit
  □ La balle l'a touché en pleine poitrine. The bullet hit him right in the chest.
4 to affect
  □ Ces nouvelles réformes ne nous touchent pas. The new reforms don't affect us.
5 to receive
  □ Il a touché une grosse somme d'argent. He received a large sum of money.

toujours ADVERB
1 always
  □ Il est toujours très gentil. He's always very nice.
- **pour toujours** forever
2 still
  □ Quand on est revenus, Pierre était toujours là. When we got back Pierre was still there.

le **toupet** NOUN (informal)
- **avoir du toupet** to have a nerve

la **tour** NOUN
▷ see also **le tour**
1 tower
  □ la Tour Eiffel the Eiffel Tower
2 tower block
  □ Il y a beaucoup de tours dans ce quartier. There are a lot of tower blocks in this area.

le **tour** NOUN
▷ see also **la tour**
turn
  □ C'est ton tour de jouer. It's your turn to play.
- **faire un tour** to go for a walk □ Allons faire un tour dans le parc. Let's go for a walk in the park.
- **faire un tour en voiture** to go for a drive
- **faire un tour à vélo** to go for a ride □ Tu veux aller faire un tour à vélo? Do you want to go for a bike ride?
- **faire le tour du monde** to travel round the world
- **à tour de rôle** alternately

le **tourbillon** NOUN
whirlpool

le **tourisme** NOUN
tourism

le/la **touriste** NOUN
tourist

touristique (FEM **touristique**) ADJECTIVE
tourist

se **tourmenter** VERB [28]
to fret
  □ Ne te tourmente pas, ça s'arrangera. Don't fret about it, it'll be all right.

le **tournant** NOUN
1 bend
  □ Il y a beaucoup de tournants dangereux

sur cette route. There are a lot of dangerous bends on this road.

2 turning point

□ Ça a été un tournant dans sa vie. It was a turning point in his life.

la **tournée** NOUN

1 round

□ Le facteur commence sa tournée à sept heures du matin. The postman starts his round at 7 o'clock in the morning. □ Allez, qu'est-ce que vous voulez boire? C'est ma tournée. Right, what are you drinking? It's my round.

2 tour

□ Il est en tournée aux États-Unis. He's on tour in the United States.

tourner VERB [28]

1 to turn

□ Tournez à droite au prochain feu. Turn right at the lights. □ Tourne-toi un peu plus vers moi, et souris! Turn towards me a bit more, and smile!

2 to go sour

□ Le lait a tourné. The milk's gone sour.

■ **mal tourner** to go wrong □ Ça a mal tourné. It all went wrong.

■ **tourner le dos à quelqu'un** to have one's back to somebody

■ **tourner un film** to make a film

le **tournesol** NOUN
sunflower

le **tournevis** NOUN
screwdriver

le **tournoi** NOUN
tournament

la **tourte** NOUN
pie

□ une tourte aux poireaux a leek pie

tous PL ADJECTIVE, PL PRONOUN ▷see tout

la **Toussaint** NOUN
All Saints' Day

tousser VERB [28]
to cough

tout (FEM **toute**, MASC PL **tous**) ADJECTIVE, ADVERB, PRONOUN

1 all

□ tout le lait all the milk □ toute la nuit all night □ tous les livres all the books □ toutes les filles all the girls □ toute la journée all day □ tout le temps all the time □ C'est tout. That's all. □ Je les connais tous. I know them all. □ Nous y sommes toutes allées. We all went. □ Ça fait combien en tout? How much is that all together?

■ **Il est tout seul.** He's all alone.

■ **pas du tout** not at all

■ **tout de même** all the same

2 every

□ tous les jours every day □ tous les deux jours every two days

■ **tout le monde** everybody

■ **tous les deux** both □ Nous y sommes allés tous les deux. We both went.

■ **tous les trois** all three □ Je les ai invités tous les trois. I invited all three of them.

3 everything

□ Il a tout organisé. He organized everything.

4 very

□ Elle habite tout près. She lives very close.

■ **tout en haut** right at the top

■ **tout droit** straight ahead

■ **tout d'abord** first of all

■ **tout à coup** suddenly

■ **tout à fait** absolutely

■ **tout à l'heure 1** just now □ Je l'ai vu tout à l'heure. I saw him just now. **2** in a moment □ Je finirai ça tout à l'heure. I'll finish it in a moment.

■ **À tout à l'heure!** See you later!

■ **tout de suite** straight away

■ **Il a fait son travail tout en chantant.** He sang as he worked.

toutefois ADVERB
however

toutes FEM PL ADJECTIVE, FEM PL PRONOUN
▷see tout

la **toux** NOUN
cough

le/la **toxicomane** NOUN
drug addict

la **toxicomanie** NOUN
drug addiction

le **TP** NOUN (= travaux pratiques)
practical class

□ J'ai un TP de biologie à deux heures. I've got a biology practical at two o'clock.

le **trac** NOUN

■ **avoir le trac** to be feeling nervous

tracasser VERB [28]
to worry

□ La santé de mon père me tracasse. My dad's health worries me.

■ **se tracasser** to worry □ Arrête de te tracasser pour rien! Stop worrying about nothing!

la **trace** NOUN

1 trace

□ Le voleur n'a pas laissé de traces. The thief left no traces.

2 mark

□ des traces de doigts finger marks

■ **des traces de pas** footprints

tracer VERB [12]
  to draw
  □ tracer un trait to draw a line

le tracteur NOUN
  tractor

la tradition NOUN
  tradition

traditionnel (FEM **traditionnelle**) ADJECTIVE
  traditional

le traducteur NOUN
  translator

la traduction NOUN
  translation

la traductrice NOUN
  translator

traduire VERB [23]
  to translate

le trafic NOUN
  traffic
  ■ **le trafic de drogue** drug trafficking

le trafiquant NOUN
  ■ **un trafiquant de drogue** a drug trafficker

tragique (FEM **tragique**) ADJECTIVE
  tragic

trahir VERB [38]
  to betray

la trahison NOUN
  betrayal

le train NOUN
  train
  ■ **un train électrique** a train set
  ■ **Il est en train de manger.** He's eating.

le traîneau (PL les **traîneaux**) NOUN
  sledge

traîner VERB [28]
1 to wander around
  □ J'ai vu des jeunes qui traînaient en ville. I saw some young people wandering around town.
2 to hang about
  □ Dépêche-toi, ne traîne pas! Hurry up, don't hang about!
3 to drag on
  □ La réunion a traîné jusqu'à midi. The meeting dragged on till 12 o'clock.
  ■ **traîner des pieds** to drag one's feet
  ■ **laisser traîner qch** to leave sth lying around □ Ne laisse pas traîner tes affaires. Don't leave your things lying around.

le train-train NOUN
  humdrum routine

traire VERB [85]
  to milk

le trait NOUN
1 line
  □ Tracez un trait. Draw a line.
2 feature

  □ Elle a les traits fins. She has delicate features.
  ■ **boire quelque chose d'un trait** to drink something down in one gulp
  ■ **un trait d'union** a hyphen

le traitement NOUN
  treatment
  ■ **le traitement de texte** word processing

traiter VERB [28]
  to treat
  □ Elle le traite comme un chien. She treats him like a dog.
  ■ **Il m'a traité d'imbécile.** He called me an idiot.
  ■ **traiter de** to be about □ Cet article traite des sans-abri. This article is about the homeless.

le traiteur NOUN
  caterer

le trajet NOUN
1 journey
  □ Il n'a pas arrêté de parler pendant tout le trajet. He talked for the whole journey.
  □ J'ai une heure de trajet pour aller au travail. My journey to work takes an hour.
2 route
  □ C'est le trajet le plus court. It's the shortest route.

le tramway NOUN
  tram

tranchant (FEM **tranchante**) ADJECTIVE
  sharp *(knife)*

la tranche NOUN
  slice

tranquille (FEM **tranquille**) ADJECTIVE
  quiet
  □ Cette rue est très tranquille. This is a very quiet street.
  ■ **Sois tranquille, il ne va rien lui arriver.** Don't worry, nothing will happen to him.
  ■ **Tiens-toi tranquille!** Be quiet!
  ■ **Laisse-moi tranquille.** Leave me alone.
  ■ **Laisse ça tranquille.** Leave it alone.

tranquillement ADVERB
  quietly
  □ Nous étions tranquillement installés dans le salon. We were just sitting quietly in the living room.
  ■ **Je peux travailler tranquillement cinq minutes?** Can I have five minutes to myself to work in peace?

la tranquillité NOUN
  peace and quiet

transférer VERB [34]
  to transfer

transformer VERB [28]
1 to transform

□ Son séjour en France l'a transformé. His stay in France has transformed him.

2 to convert

□ Ils ont transformé la grange en garage. They've converted the barn into a garage.

■ **se transformer en** to turn into □ La chenille se transforme en papillon. The caterpillar turns into a butterfly.

la **transfusion** NOUN

■ **une transfusion sanguine** a blood transfusion

transiger VERB [45]
to compromise

transmettre VERB [47]

■ **transmettre quelque chose à quelqu'un** to pass something on to somebody

transpercer VERB [12]
to go through

□ La pluie a transpercé mes vêtements. The rain went through my clothes.

la **transpiration** NOUN
perspiration

transpirer VERB [28]
to perspire

le **transport** NOUN
transport

■ **les transports en commun** public transport

transporter VERB [28]

1 to carry

□ Le train transportait des marchandises. The train was carrying freight.

2 to move

□ Je ne sais pas comment je vais transporter mes affaires. I don't know how I'm going to move my stuff.

traumatiser VERB [28]
to traumatize

le **travail** (PL les **travaux**) NOUN

1 work

□ J'ai beaucoup de travail. I've got a lot of work.

2 job

□ Il a un travail intéressant. He's got an interesting job.

■ **Il est sans travail depuis un an.** He has been out of work for a year.

■ **le travail au noir** moonlighting

travailler VERB [28]
to work

travailleur (FEM **travailleuse**) ADJECTIVE
▷ see also **travailleur** NOUN, **travailleuse** NOUN
hard-working

le **travailleur** NOUN
▷ see also **travailleur** ADJECTIVE

worker

la **travailleuse** NOUN
▷ see also **travailleuse** ADJECTIVE
worker

les **travaillistes** MASC PL NOUN
the Labour Party

les **travaux** MASC PL NOUN

1 work

□ des travaux de construction building work

2 roadworks

□ Il y a beaucoup de bruit à cause des travaux dans la rue. There's a lot of noise from the roadworks.

■ **être en travaux** to be undergoing alterations

■ **les travaux dirigés** supervised practical work

■ **les travaux manuels** handicrafts

■ **les travaux ménagers** housework

■ **les travaux pratiques** practical work

le **travers** NOUN

■ **en travers de** across □ Il y avait un arbre en travers de la route. There was a tree lying across the road.

■ **de travers** crooked □ Son chapeau était de travers. His hat was crooked.

■ **comprendre de travers** to misunderstand □ Elle comprend toujours tout de travers. She always gets the wrong idea.

■ **J'ai avalé de travers.** Something went down the wrong way.

■ **à travers** through □ Cette vitre est tellement sale qu'on ne voit rien à travers. This window is so dirty you can't see anything through it.

la **traversée** NOUN
crossing

traverser VERB [28]

1 to cross

□ Traversez la rue. Cross the street.

2 to go through

□ Nous avons traversé la France pour aller en Espagne. We went through France on the way to Spain. □ La pluie a traversé mon manteau. The rain went through my coat.

le **traversin** NOUN
bolster

trébucher VERB [28]
to trip up

le **trèfle** NOUN

1 clover

2 clubs (at cards)

□ le roi de trèfle the king of clubs

treize NUMBER
thirteen

□ Il a treize ans. He's thirteen. □ à treize

t

heures at 1 p.m.

■ **le treize février** the thirteenth of February

treizième (FEM **treizième**) ADJECTIVE
thirteenth

le **tréma** NOUN
diaeresis

le **tremblement de terre** NOUN
earthquake

trembler VERB [28]
to shake
□ trembler de peur to shake with fear
■ **trembler de froid** to shiver

trempé (FEM **trempée**) ADJECTIVE
soaking wet
■ **trempé jusqu'aux os** soaked to the skin

tremper VERB [28]
to soak
■ **tremper sa main dans l'eau** to dip one's hand in the water

le **tremplin** NOUN
springboard

la **trentaine** NOUN
about thirty
□ une trentaine de personnes about thirty people
■ **Il a la trentaine.** He's in his thirties.

trente NUMBER
thirty
□ Elle a trente ans. She's thirty.
■ **le trente janvier** the thirtieth of January
■ **trente et un** thirty-one
■ **trente-deux** thirty-two

trentième (FEM **trentième**) ADJECTIVE
thirtieth

très ADVERB
very

le **trésor** NOUN
treasure

la **tresse** NOUN
plait

le **triangle** NOUN
triangle

la **tribu** NOUN
tribe

le **tribunal** (PL les **tribunaux**) NOUN
court

tricher VERB [28]
to cheat

tricolore (FEM **tricolore**) ADJECTIVE
three-coloured
■ **le drapeau tricolore** the French flag

> **DID YOU KNOW...?**
> **le drapeau tricolore** is the French flag which is blue, white and red.

le **tricot** NOUN
1 knitting
□ On fait du tricot à l'école. We do knitting

at school.
2 sweater
□ Mets un tricot, il fait froid. Put a sweater on, it's cold.

tricoter VERB [28]
to knit

trier VERB [19]
to sort out
□ Je vais trier mes papiers avant les vacances. I'm going to sort out my papers before the holidays.

le **trimestre** NOUN
term

trinquer VERB [28]
to clink glasses

le **triomphe** NOUN
triumph

triompher VERB [28]
to triumph

les **tripes** FEM PL NOUN
tripe

le **triple** NOUN
■ **Ça m'a coûté le triple.** It cost me three times as much.
■ **Il gagne le triple de mon salaire.** He earns three times my salary.

tripler VERB [28]
to treble

les **triplés** MASC PL NOUN
triplets

triste (FEM **triste**) ADJECTIVE
sad

la **tristesse** NOUN
sadness

le **trognon** NOUN
core
□ un trognon de pomme an apple core

trois NUMBER
three
□ à trois heures du matin at three in the morning □ Elle a trois ans. She's three.
□ trois fois three times
■ **le trois février** the third of February

troisième (FEM **troisième**) ADJECTIVE
▷ see also **troisième** NOUN
third
□ au troisième étage on the third floor

la **troisième** NOUN
▷ see also **troisième** ADJECTIVE
year 10
□ Mon frère est en troisième. My brother's in year 10.

> **DID YOU KNOW...?**
> In French secondary schools, years are counted from the **sixième** (youngest) to **première** and **terminale** (oldest).

t

275

les **trois-quarts** MASC PL NOUN
three-quarters
▫ les trois-quarts de la classe three-quarters of the class

le **trombone** NOUN
1 trombone
▫ Il joue du trombone. He plays the trombone.
2 paper clip

la **trompe** NOUN
trunk
▫ la trompe d'un éléphant an elephant's trunk

tromper VERB [28]
to deceive
■ **se tromper** to make a mistake ▫ Tout le monde peut se tromper. Anyone can make a mistake.
■ **se tromper de jour** to get the wrong day
■ **Vous vous êtes trompé de numéro.** You've got the wrong number.

la **trompette** NOUN
trumpet
▫ Il joue de la trompette. He plays the trumpet.
■ **Il a le nez en trompette.** He's got a turned-up nose.

le **tronc** NOUN
trunk
▫ un tronc d'arbre a tree trunk

trop ADVERB
1 too
▫ Il conduit trop vite. He drives too fast.
2 too much
▫ J'ai trop mangé. I've eaten too much.
■ **trop de 1** too much ▫ J'ai acheté trop de pain. I bought too much bread. ▫ trois euros de trop 3 euros too much **2** too many ▫ J'ai apporté trop de vêtements. I've brought too many clothes.
■ **trois personnes de trop** 3 people too many

le **tropique** NOUN
tropic

le **trottoir** NOUN
pavement

le **trou** NOUN
hole
■ **J'ai eu un trou de mémoire.** My mind went blank.

  LANGUAGE TIP Word for word, avoir un trou de mémoire means 'to have a hole in one's memory'.

trouble (FEM **trouble**) ADJECTIVE, ADVERB
cloudy
▫ L'eau est trouble. The water's cloudy.
■ **Sans mes lunettes je vois trouble.**

Without my glasses I can't see properly.

les **troubles** MASC PL NOUN
■ **une période de troubles politiques** a period of political instability

trouer VERB [28]
to make a hole in
▫ Il a troué la moquette avec sa cigarette. He made a hole in the carpet with his cigarette.

la **trouille** NOUN
■ **avoir la trouille** (informal) to be scared to death

la **troupe** NOUN
troop
■ **une troupe de théâtre** a theatre company

le **troupeau** (PL les **troupeaux**) NOUN
■ **un troupeau de moutons** a flock of sheep
■ **un troupeau de vaches** a herd of cows

la **trousse** NOUN
pencil case
■ **une trousse de secours** a first-aid kit
■ **une trousse de toilette** a toilet bag

trouver VERB [28]
1 to find
▫ Je ne trouve pas mes lunettes. I can't find my glasses.
2 to think
▫ Je trouve que c'est bête. I think it's stupid.
■ **se trouver** to be ▫ Où se trouve la poste? Where is the post office? ▫ Nice se trouve dans le sud de la France. Nice is in the South of France.
■ **se trouver mal** to pass out

le **truc** NOUN (informal)
1 thing
▫ un truc en plastique a plastic thing ▫ J'ai plein de trucs à faire ce week-end. I've got loads of things to do this weekend.
2 trick
▫ Je vais te montrer un truc qui réussit à tous les coups. I'll show you a trick that never fails.

la **truite** NOUN
trout

le **T-shirt** NOUN
T-shirt

TSVP ABBREVIATION (= tournez s'il vous plaît)
PTO (= please turn over)

tu PRONOUN

  LANGUAGE TIP tu is used when speaking to one person your own age or younger.

you
▫ Est-ce que tu as un animal familier? Have you got a pet?

le **tuba** NOUN
1 tuba
  □ Je joue du tuba. I play the tuba.
2 snorkel

le **tube** NOUN
1 tube
  □ un tube de dentifrice a tube of toothpaste
  ■ **un tube de rouge à lèvres** a lipstick
2 hit
  □ Ça va être le tube de l'été. It's going to be this summer's hit.

tuer VERB [28]
to kill
  ■ **se tuer** to get killed □ Il s'est tué dans un accident de voiture. He got killed in a car accident.

tue-tête
  ■ **à tue-tête** ADVERB at the top of one's voice □ crier à tue-tête to shout at the top of one's voice □ Il chantait à tue-tête. He was singing at the top of his voice.

la **tuile** NOUN
tile
  □ un toit en tuiles a tiled roof

la **tunique** NOUN
tunic

la **Tunisie** NOUN
Tunisia

tunisien (FEM **tunisienne**) ADJECTIVE
Tunisian

le **tunnel** NOUN
tunnel
  ■ **le tunnel sous la Manche** the Channel Tunnel

turbulent (FEM **turbulente**) ADJECTIVE
boisterous

turc (FEM **turque**) ADJECTIVE, NOUN
Turkish

  □ Il parle turc. He speaks Turkish.
  ■ **un Turc** a Turk (man)
  ■ **une Turque** a Turk (woman)

la **Turquie** NOUN
Turkey

tutoyer VERB [53]
  ■ **tutoyer quelqu'un** to address somebody as 'tu' □ On se tutoie? Shall we use 'tu' to each other?

> **DID YOU KNOW...?**
> tutoyer quelqu'un means to use **tu** when speaking to someone, rather than **vous**. Use **tu** only when talking to one person and when that person is someone of your own age or whom you know well; use **vous** to everyone else. If in doubt use **vous**.

le **tuyau** (PL les **tuyaux**) NOUN
1 pipe
  ■ **un tuyau d'arrosage** a hosepipe
2 tip
  □ Il m'a donné un bon tuyau. (informal) He gave me a handy tip.

la **TVA** NOUN (= taxe sur la valeur ajoutée)
VAT

le **tympan** NOUN
eardrum

le **type** NOUN (informal)
guy
  □ C'est un type formidable. He's a great guy.

typique (FEM **typique**) ADJECTIVE
typical

le **tyran** NOUN
tyrant
  □ C'est un vrai tyran. He's a real tyrant.

le/la **tzigane** NOUN
gipsy

Uu

l' **UE** FEM NOUN (= *Union européenne*)
the EU (= *European Union*)

un (FEM **une**) ARTICLE, MASC PRONOUN, MASC ADJECTIVE

1 a
□ un garçon a boy
an
□ un œuf an egg

2 one
□ l'un des meilleurs one of the best □ un citron et deux oranges one lemon and two oranges □ Combien de timbres? — Un. How many stamps? — One. □ Elle a un an. She's one year old.
■ **l'un ..., l'autre ...** one ..., the other ...
□ L'un est grand, l'autre est petit. One is tall, the other is short.
■ **les uns ..., les autres ...** some ..., others ... □ Les uns marchaient, les autres couraient. Some were walking, others were running.
■ **l'un ou l'autre** either of them □ Prends l'un ou l'autre, ça m'est égal. Take either of them, I don't mind.
■ **un par un** one by one □ Ils entraient un par un. They went in one by one.

unanime (FEM **unanime**) ADJECTIVE
unanimous

l' **unanimité** FEM NOUN
■ **à l'unanimité** unanimously

une ARTICLE, FEM PRONOUN, FEM ADJECTIVE

1 a
□ une fille a girl
an
□ une pomme an apple

2 one
□ une pomme et deux bananes one apple and two bananas □ Combien de cartes postales? — Une. How many postcards? — One. □ à une heure du matin at one in the morning □ l'une des meilleures one of the best
■ **l'une ..., l'autre ...** one ..., the other ...
□ L'une est grande, l'autre est petite. One is tall, the other is short.
■ **les unes..., les autres...** some ..., others ... □ Les unes marchaient, les autres couraient. Some were walking, others were running.
■ **l'une ou l'autre** either of them □ Prends l'une ou l'autre, ça m'est égal. Take either of them, I don't mind.
■ **une par une** one by one □ Elles entraient une par une. They went in one by one.

uni (FEM **unie**) ADJECTIVE

1 plain
□ un tissu uni a plain fabric

2 close-knit
□ une famille unie a close-knit family

l' **uniforme** MASC NOUN
uniform

l' **union** FEM NOUN
union
■ **l'Union européenne** the European Union

unique (FEM **unique**) ADJECTIVE
unique
□ Tout individu a des empreintes uniques. Everyone's fingerprints are unique. □ C'est une occasion unique. It's a unique opportunity.
■ **Il est fils unique.** He's an only child.
■ **Elle est fille unique.** She's an only child.

uniquement ADVERB
only

l' **unité** FEM NOUN

1 unity
□ l'unité européenne European unity

2 unit
□ une unité de mesure a unit of measurement

l' **univers** MASC NOUN
universe

universitaire (FEM **universitaire**) ADJECTIVE
university
□ un diplôme universitaire a university degree
■ **faire des études universitaires** to study at university

l' **université** FEM NOUN

university

□ aller à l'université to go to university

l' **urgence** FEM NOUN

■ **C'est une urgence.** It's urgent.

■ **Il n'y a pas urgence.** It's not urgent.

■ **le service des urgences** the accident and emergency department

■ **Il a été transporté d'urgence à l'hôpital.** He was rushed to hospital.

■ **Téléphonez d'urgence.** Phone as soon as possible.

urgent (FEM **urgente**) ADJECTIVE

urgent

l' **urine** FEM NOUN

urine

les **USA** MASC PL NOUN

USA

■ **aux USA 1** in the USA **2** to the USA

l' **usage** MASC NOUN

use

□ à usage interne for internal use □ à usage externe for external use only

■ **hors d'usage** out of action □ Cet appareil est hors d'usage. That machine's out of action.

usagé (FEM **usagée**) ADJECTIVE

1 old

□ un manteau usagé an old coat

2 used

□ une seringue usagée a used syringe

l' **usager** MASC NOUN

user

□ les usagers de la route road users

usé (FEM **usée**) ADJECTIVE

worn

□ Mon jean est un peu usé. My jeans are a bit worn.

s' **user** VERB [28]

to wear out

□ Mes baskets se sont usées en quinze jours. My trainers wore out in two weeks.

l' **usine** FEM NOUN

factory

□ une usine de sardines a sardine factory

l' **ustensile** MASC NOUN

■ **un ustensile de cuisine** a kitchen utensil

usuel (FEM **usuelle**) ADJECTIVE

everyday

□ la langue usuelle everyday language

utile (FEM **utile**) ADJECTIVE

useful

l' **utilisation** FEM NOUN

use

□ L'utilisation des calculatrices est interdite. It is forbidden to use calculators.

utiliser VERB [28]

to use

l' **utilité** FEM NOUN

use

□ Cet objet n'est pas d'une grande utilité. This object isn't much use.

Vv

va VERB ▷ see **aller**

les **vacances** FEM PL NOUN
holidays
  □ aller en vacances to go on holiday □ être
  en vacances to be on holiday
  ■ **les vacances de Noël** the Christmas
  holidays
  ■ **les vacances de Pâques** the Easter
  holidays
  ■ **les grandes vacances** the summer
  holidays

le **vacancier** NOUN
holiday-maker

la **vacancière** NOUN
holiday-maker

le **vacarme** NOUN
racket
  □ Qu'est-ce que c'est que ce vacarme?
  What's all this racket?

le **vaccin** NOUN
vaccination

la **vaccination** NOUN
vaccination
  □ La vaccination est obligatoire. Vaccination
  is compulsory.

vacciner VERB [28]
to vaccinate
  □ se faire vacciner contre la rubéole to be
  vaccinated against German measles

la **vache** NOUN
  ▷ see also **vache** ADJECTIVE
cow

vache (FEM **vache**) ADJECTIVE (informal)
  ▷ see also **vache** NOUN
mean
  □ C'est vraiment vache, ce qu'il a dit. What
  he said was really mean. □ Il est vache. He's
  a mean sod.

vachement ADVERB (informal)
really
  □ Viens te baigner, l'eau est vachement
  chaude. Come in the water, it's really warm.

le **vagabond** NOUN
tramp

le **vagin** NOUN

vagina

la **vague** NOUN
  ▷ see also **vague** ADJECTIVE
wave (in sea)
  ■ **une vague de chaleur** a heat wave

vague (FEM **vague**) ADJECTIVE
  ▷ see also **vague** NOUN
vague
  □ J'ai un vague souvenir de lui. I vaguely
  remember him.

vain (FEM **vaine**) ADJECTIVE
  ■ **en vain** in vain

vaincre VERB [86]
1 to defeat
  □ L'armée a été vaincue. The army was
  defeated.
2 to overcome
  □ Il a réussi à vaincre sa timidité. He
  managed to overcome his shyness.

le **vainqueur** NOUN
winner

vais VERB ▷ see **aller**
  ■ **Je vais écrire à mes cousins.** I'm going
  to write to my cousins.

le **vaisseau** (PL les **vaisseaux**) NOUN
  ■ **un vaisseau spatial** a spaceship
  ■ **un vaisseau sanguin** a blood vessel

la **vaisselle** NOUN
1 washing-up
  □ Je vais faire la vaisselle. I'll do the
  washing-up.
2 dishes
  □ Tu peux ranger la vaisselle s'il te plaît?
  Can you put the dishes away please?

valable (FEM **valable**) ADJECTIVE
valid
  □ Ce billet d'avion est valable un an. This
  plane ticket is valid for one year.

le **valet** NOUN
jack (in card games)
  □ le valet de carreau the jack of diamonds

la **valeur** NOUN
value
  □ sans valeur of no value
  ■ **des objets de valeur** valuables □ Ne

laissez pas d'objets de valeur dans votre chambre. Don't leave any valuables in your room.

valider VERB [28]
to stamp
□ Vous devez faire valider votre billet avant votre départ. You must get your ticket stamped before you leave.

la **valise** NOUN
suitcase
■ **faire sa valise** to pack

la **vallée** NOUN
valley

valoir VERB [87]
to be worth
□ Ça vaut combien? How much is it worth?
□ Cette voiture vaut très cher. This car's worth a lot of money.
■ **Ça vaut mieux.** That would be better. □ Il vaut mieux ne rien dire. It would be better to say nothing.
■ **valoir la peine** to be worth it □ Ça vaudrait la peine d'essayer. It would be worth a try.

le **vampire** NOUN
vampire

le **vandalisme** NOUN
vandalism

la **vanille** NOUN
vanilla
□ une glace à la vanille a vanilla ice cream

la **vanité** NOUN
vanity

vaniteux (FEM **vaniteuse**) ADJECTIVE
conceited

se **vanter** VERB [28]
to boast

la **vapeur** NOUN
steam
□ des légumes cuits à la vapeur steamed vegetables

la **varappe** NOUN
rock climbing
□ faire de la varappe to go rock climbing

variable (FEM **variable**) ADJECTIVE
changeable (weather)

la **varicelle** NOUN
chickenpox
□ Elle a la varicelle. She's got chickenpox.

varié (FEM **variée**) ADJECTIVE
varied
□ Son travail est très varié. His job is very varied.

varier VERB [19]
to vary
■ **Le menu varie tous les jours.** The menu changes every day.

la **variété** NOUN
variety
□ Il n'y a pas beaucoup de variété. There isn't much variety.
■ **une émission de variétés** a television variety show

vas VERB ▷ see **aller**

le **vase** NOUN
▷ see also la **vase**
vase

la **vase** NOUN
▷ see also le **vase**
mud

vaste (FEM **vaste**) ADJECTIVE
vast

vaudrait, vaut VERB ▷ see **valoir**

le **vautour** NOUN
vulture

le **veau** (PL les **veaux**) NOUN
1 calf (animal)
2 veal (meat)

vécu VERB ▷ see **vivre**
■ **Il a vécu à Paris pendant dix ans.** He lived in Paris for ten years.

la **vedette** NOUN
1 star
□ une vedette de cinéma a film star
2 motor boat
■ **une vedette de police** a police launch

végétal (FEM **végétale**, MASC PL **végétaux**) ADJECTIVE
vegetable
□ l'huile végétale vegetable oil

végétarien (FEM **végétarienne**) ADJECTIVE
vegetarian
□ Je suis végétarien. I'm a vegetarian.

la **végétation** NOUN
vegetation

le **véhicule** NOUN
vehicle

la **veille** NOUN
the day before
□ la veille de son départ the day before he left □ la veille au soir the previous evening
■ **la veille de Noël** Christmas Eve
■ **la veille du jour de l'An** New Year's Eve

veiller VERB [28]
to stay up
■ **veiller sur quelqu'un** to watch over somebody

veinard (FEM **veinarde**) ADJECTIVE (informal)
■ **Qu'est-ce qu'il est veinard!** He's such a lucky devil!

la **veine** NOUN
vein
■ **avoir de la veine** (informal) to be lucky

le/la **véliplanchiste** NOUN

windsurfer

le **vélo** NOUN
bike
□ faire du vélo to go cycling
■ un vélo tout-terrain a mountain bike

le **vélomoteur** NOUN
moped

le **velours** NOUN
velvet
□ une robe en velours a velvet dress
■ le velours côtelé corduroy □ un pantalon en velours côtelé corduroy trousers

les **vendanges** FEM PL NOUN
grape harvest
□ On fait les vendanges en septembre. The grape harvest is in September.

le **vendeur** NOUN
shop assistant

la **vendeuse** NOUN
shop assistant

vendre VERB [88]
to sell
■ vendre quelque chose à quelqu'un to sell somebody something □ Il m'a vendu son vélo. He sold me his bike.
■ 'à vendre' 'for sale'

le **vendredi** NOUN
1 Friday
□ Aujourd'hui, nous sommes vendredi. It's Friday today.
2 on Friday
□ Il est venu vendredi. He came on Friday.
■ le vendredi on Fridays □ Je joue au foot le vendredi. I play football on Fridays.
■ tous les vendredis every Friday
■ vendredi dernier last Friday
■ vendredi prochain next Friday
■ le Vendredi saint Good Friday

vénéneux (FEM **vénéneuse**) ADJECTIVE
poisonous *(plant)*
□ un champignon vénéneux a poisonous mushroom

la **vengeance** NOUN
revenge

se **venger** VERB [45]
to get revenge

venimeux (FEM **venimeuse**) ADJECTIVE
poisonous *(animal)*
□ un serpent venimeux a poisonous snake

le **venin** NOUN
poison

venir VERB [89]
to come
□ Il viendra demain. He'll come tomorrow.
□ Il est venu nous voir. He came to see us.
■ venir de to have just □ Je viens de le voir.

I've just seen him. □ Je viens de lui téléphoner. I've just phoned him.
■ faire venir quelqu'un to call somebody out □ faire venir le médecin to call the doctor out

le **vent** NOUN
wind
□ Il y a du vent. It's windy.

la **vente** NOUN
sale
■ en vente on sale □ Ce modèle est en vente dans les grands magasins. This model is on sale in the department stores.
■ la vente par téléphone telesales
■ une vente aux enchères an auction

le **ventilateur** NOUN
fan *(for cooling)*

le **ventre** NOUN
stomach
□ avoir mal au ventre to have stomachache

venu VERB ▷ see venir

le **ver** NOUN
worm
■ un ver de terre an earthworm

le **verbe** NOUN
verb

le **verdict** NOUN
verdict

le **verger** NOUN
orchard

verglacé (FEM **verglacée**) ADJECTIVE
icy
□ La route était verglacée. The road was icy.

le **verglas** NOUN
black ice

véridique (FEM **véridique**) ADJECTIVE
truthful

la **vérification** NOUN
check
□ une vérification d'identité an identity check

vérifier VERB [19]
to check

véritable (FEM **véritable**) ADJECTIVE
real
□ C'était un véritable cauchemar. It was a real nightmare.
■ en cuir véritable made of real leather

la **vérité** NOUN
truth
□ dire la vérité to tell the truth

verni (FEM **vernie**) ADJECTIVE
varnished
■ des chaussures vernies patent leather shoes

vernir VERB [38]
to varnish

le **vernis** NOUN
varnish
□ le vernis à ongles nail varnish
verra, verrai, verras VERB ▷ *see* **voir**
■ on verra ... we'll see ...
le **verre** NOUN
1 glass
□ une table en verre a glass table □ un verre d'eau a glass of water
■ boire un verre to have a drink
2 lens *(of spectacles)*
□ des verres de contact contact lenses
verrez, verrons, verront VERB ▷ *see* **voir**
le **verrou** NOUN
bolt *(on door)*
verrouiller VERB [28]
to bolt
□ N'oublie pas de verrouiller la porte du garage. Don't forget to bolt the garage door.
la **verrue** NOUN
wart
le **vers** NOUN
▷ *see also* **vers** PREPOSITION
line *(of poetry)*
□ au troisième vers in the third line
vers PREPOSITION
▷ *see also* **vers** NOUN
1 towards
□ Il allait vers la gare. He was going towards the station.
2 at about
□ Il est rentré chez lui vers cinq heures. He went home at about 5 o'clock.
verse
■ à verse ADVERB
□ Il pleut à verse. It's pouring with rain.
le **Verseau** NOUN
Aquarius
□ Georges est Verseau. Georges is Aquarius.
le **versement** NOUN
instalment
□ en cinq versements in 5 instalments
verser VERB [28]
to pour
□ Est-ce que tu peux me verser un verre d'eau? Could you pour me a glass of water?
la **version** NOUN
1 version
2 translation *(from the foreign language)*
■ un film en version originale a film in the original language
le **verso** NOUN
back *(of sheet of paper)*
■ voir au verso see overleaf
vert (FEM **verte**) ADJECTIVE
green
la **vertèbre** NOUN

vertebra
vertical (FEM **verticale**, MASC PL **verticaux**) ADJECTIVE
vertical
le **vertige** NOUN
vertigo
□ avoir le vertige to have vertigo
la **verveine** NOUN
verbena tea
la **vessie** NOUN
bladder
la **veste** NOUN
jacket
le **vestiaire** NOUN
1 cloakroom *(in theatre, museum)*
2 changing room *(at sports ground)*
le **vestibule** NOUN
hall
le **vêtement** NOUN
garment
■ les vêtements clothes
le/la **vétérinaire** NOUN
vet
□ Elle est vétérinaire. She's a vet.
le **veuf** NOUN
widower
□ Il est veuf. He's a widower.
veuille, veuillez, veuillons, veulent, veut VERB ▷ *see* **vouloir**
■ Veuillez fermer la porte en sortant. Please shut the door when you go out.
la **veuve** NOUN
widow
□ Elle est veuve. She's a widow.
veux VERB ▷ *see* **vouloir**
vexer VERB [28]
■ vexer quelqu'un to hurt somebody's feelings
■ se vexer to be offended
la **viande** NOUN
meat
■ la viande hachée mince
vibrer VERB [28]
to vibrate
le **vice** NOUN
vice
vicieux (FEM **vicieuse**) ADJECTIVE
lecherous
□ Il est un peu vicieux. He's a bit of a lecher.
la **victime** NOUN
victim
la **victoire** NOUN
victory
vide (FEM **vide**) ADJECTIVE
▷ *see also* **vide** NOUN
empty
le **vide** NOUN

V

▷ *see also* vide ADJECTIVE
vacuum

□ emballé sous vide vacuum-packed

■ **avoir peur du vide** to be afraid of heights

la **vidéo** NOUN
▷ *see also* vidéo ADJECTIVE
video

vidéo (FEM+PL vidéo) ADJECTIVE
▷ *see also* vidéo NOUN
video

□ une cassette vidéo a video cassette □ un jeu vidéo a video game □ une caméra vidéo a video camera

le **vidéoclip** NOUN
music video

le **vidéoclub** NOUN
video shop

vider VERB [28]
to empty

la **vie** NOUN
life

■ **être en vie** to be alive

vieil MASC ADJECTIVE

⚬ **LANGUAGE TIP** vieil is used in place of vieux when the noun begins with a vowel sound.

old

□ un vieil arbre an old tree □ un vieil homme an old man

le **vieillard** NOUN
old man

vieille FEM ADJECTIVE ▷ *see* vieux

la **vieille** NOUN
▷ *see also* vieille ADJECTIVE
old woman

■ **Eh bien, ma vieille ...** *(informal)* Well, my dear ...

la **vieillesse** NOUN
old age

vieillir VERB [38]
to age

□ Il a beaucoup vieilli. He's aged a lot.

viendrai, vienne, viens VERB ▷ *see* venir

■ **Je viendrai dès que possible.** I'll come as soon as possible.

■ **Je voudrais que tu viennes.** I'd like you to come.

■ **Viens ici!** Come here!

la **Vierge** NOUN
▷ *see also* vierge ADJECTIVE
Virgo

□ Pascal est Vierge. Pascal is Virgo.

■ **la Vierge** the Virgin Mary

vierge (FEM vierge) ADJECTIVE
▷ *see also* Vierge NOUN

1 virgin

□ Il est vierge. He's a virgin.

2 blank

□ un CD vierge a blank CD

le **Viêt-Nam** NOUN
Vietnam

vietnamien (FEM vietnamienne) ADJECTIVE, NOUN
Vietnamese

■ **un Vietnamien** a Vietnamese *(man)*

■ **une Vietnamienne** a Vietnamese *(woman)*

■ **les Vietnamiens** the Vietnamese

vieux (MASC SING ALSO vieil, FEM vieille) ADJECTIVE
▷ *see also* vieux NOUN, vieille NOUN
old

□ Il fait plus vieux que son âge. He looks older than he is. □ une vieille dame an old lady

■ **un vieux garçon** a bachelor

⚬ **LANGUAGE TIP** Word for word, un vieux garçon means 'an old boy'.

■ **une vieille fille** an old maid

⚬ **LANGUAGE TIP** Word for word, une vieille fille means 'an old girl'.

le **vieux** NOUN
▷ *see also* vieux ADJECTIVE
old man

□ Eh bien, mon vieux ... *(informal)* Well, my old mate ...

■ **les vieux** old people

vieux jeu (FEM+PL vieux jeu) ADJECTIVE
old-fashioned

□ Il est un peu vieux jeu. He's a bit old-fashioned.

vif (FEM vive) ADJECTIVE

1 sharp *(mentally)*

□ Il est très vif. He's very sharp.

■ **avoir l'esprit vif** to be quick-witted

2 crisp

□ L'air est plus vif à la campagne qu'en ville. The air is crisper in the country than in the town.

3 bright *(colour)*

□ un bleu vif a bright blue

■ **à vive allure** at a brisk pace

■ **de vive voix** in person □ Je te le dirai de vive voix. I'll tell you about it when I see you.

la **vigne** NOUN
vine

■ **des champs de vigne** vineyards

le **vigneron** NOUN
wine grower

la **vignette** NOUN
tax disc

le **vignoble** NOUN
vineyard

vilain (FEM vilaine) ADJECTIVE

1 naughty

□ C'est très vilain de dire des mensonges.
It's very naughty to tell lies.

2 ugly

□ Il n'est pas vilain. He's not bad-looking.

la **villa** NOUN
villa

□ une villa en multipropriété a time-share villa

le **village** NOUN
village

le **villageois** NOUN
villager

la **villageoise** NOUN
villager

la **ville** NOUN
town

□ Je vais en ville. I'm going into town.

■ **une grande ville** a city

le **vin** NOUN
wine

□ le vin blanc white wine □ le vin rouge red wine □ le vin de pays the local wine □ le vin ordinaire table wine

le **vinaigre** NOUN
vinegar

la **vinaigrette** NOUN
French dressing

vingt NUMBER
twenty

□ Elle a vingt ans. She's twenty. □ à vingt heures at 8 p.m.

■ **le vingt février** the twentieth of February

■ **vingt et un** twenty-one

■ **vingt-deux** twenty-two

la **vingtaine** NOUN
about twenty

□ une vingtaine de personnes about twenty people

■ **Il a une vingtaine d'années.** He's about twenty.

vingtième (FEM **vingtième**) ADJECTIVE
twentieth

le **viol** NOUN
rape

violemment ADVERB
violently

la **violence** NOUN
violence

violent (FEM **violente**) ADJECTIVE
violent

violer VERB [28]
to rape

violet (FEM **violette**) ADJECTIVE
purple

la **violette** NOUN
violet *(flower)*

le **violon** NOUN
violin

□ Je joue du violon. I play the violin.

le **violoncelle** NOUN
cello

□ Elle joue du violoncelle. She plays the cello.

le/la **violoniste** NOUN
violinist

la **vipère** NOUN
viper

le **virage** NOUN
bend

□ une route pleine de virages dangereux a road full of dangerous bends

la **virgule** NOUN

1 comma

2 decimal point

□ trois virgule cinq three point five

le **virus** NOUN
virus

vis VERB ▷ see vivre
▷ see also **vis** NOUN

■ **Je vis en Écosse.** I live in Scotland.

la **vis** NOUN
▷ see also **vis** VERB
screw

le **visa** NOUN
visa

le **visage** NOUN
face

□ Elle a le visage rond. She's got a round face.

vis-à-vis de PREPOSITION
with regard to

□ Ce n'est pas très juste vis-à-vis de lui. It's not very fair to him.

viser VERB [28]
to aim at

□ Il faut viser la cible. You have to aim at the target.

la **visibilité** NOUN
visibility

visible (FEM **visible**) ADJECTIVE
visible

la **visière** NOUN
peak *(of cap)*

la **visite** NOUN
visit

■ **rendre visite à quelqu'un** to visit somebody □ Je vais rendre visite à mon grand-père. I'm going to visit my grandfather.

■ **avoir de la visite** to have visitors □ Nous avons de la visite aujourd'hui. We've got visitors today.

■ **une visite guidée** a guided tour

■ **une visite médicale** a medical

V

examination

visiter VERB [28]
to visit

le **visiteur** NOUN
visitor

la **visiteuse** NOUN
visitor

le **vison** NOUN
mink (fur)
□ un manteau en vison a mink coat

vit VERB ▷see **vivre**

vital (FEM **vitale**, MASC PL **vitaux**) ADJECTIVE
vital
□ C'est une question vitale. It's of vital importance.

la **vitamine** NOUN
vitamin

vite ADVERB
1 quick
□ Vite, ils arrivent! Quick, they're coming! □ Je peux aller dire au revoir à Claire? — Oui, mais fais vite! Can I go and say goodbye to Claire? — Yes, but be quick! □ Prenons la voiture, ça ira plus vite. Let's take the car, it'll be quicker.
■ **Le temps passe vite.** Time flies.
2 fast
□ Il roule trop vite. He drives too fast.
3 soon
□ Il va vite oublier. He'll soon forget.
■ **Il a vite compris.** He understood immediately.

la **vitesse** NOUN
1 speed
□ à toute vitesse at top speed □ Nous sommes rentrés à toute vitesse. We rushed back home.
2 gear
□ en première vitesse in first gear

le **viticulteur** NOUN
wine grower
□ Mon oncle est viticulteur. My uncle is a wine grower.

le **vitrail** (PL les **vitraux**) NOUN
stained-glass window

la **vitre** NOUN
window
□ Il a cassé une vitre. He broke a window.

la **vitrine** NOUN
shop window

vivant (FEM **vivante**) ADJECTIVE
1 living
□ les êtres vivants living creatures □ les expériences sur les animaux vivants experiments on live animals
2 lively
□ Elle est très vivante. She's very lively.

vive FEM ADJECTIVE ▷see **vif**

vive EXCLAMATION
▷see also **vive** ADJECTIVE
■ **Vive le roi!** Long live the king!

vivement EXCLAMATION
■ **Vivement les vacances!** Roll on the holidays!

vivre VERB [91]
to live
□ J'aimerais vivre à l'étranger. I'd like to live abroad. □ Et ton grand-père? Il vit encore? What about your grandfather? Is he still alive?

vlan EXCLAMATION
wham!

la **VO** NOUN
■ **un film en VO** a film in the original language

le **vocabulaire** NOUN
vocabulary

la **vocation** NOUN
vocation

le **vœu** (PL les **vœux**) NOUN
wish
□ faire un vœu to make a wish □ Meilleurs vœux de bonne année! Best wishes for the New Year!

la **vogue** NOUN
fashion
□ C'est très en vogue en ce moment. It's very fashionable at the moment.

voici PREPOSITION
1 this is
□ Voici mon frère et voilà ma sœur. This is my brother and that's my sister.
2 here is
□ Tu as perdu ton stylo? Tiens, en voici un autre. Have you lost your pen? Here's another one.
■ **Le voici!** Here he is! □ Tu veux tes clés? Tiens, les voici! You want your keys? Here you are!

la **voie** NOUN
lane
□ une route à trois voies a 3-lane road
■ **par voie orale** orally □ à prendre par voie orale to be taken orally
■ **la voie ferrée** the railway track

voilà PREPOSITION
1 there is
□ Tiens! Voilà Paul. Look! There's Paul. □ Tu as perdu ton stylo? Tiens, en voilà un autre. Have you lost your pen? There's another one.
■ **Les voilà!** There they are!
2 that is
□ Voilà ma sœur. That's my sister.

la **voile** NOUN
▷ *see also* le voile
1 sail
2 sailing
□ faire de la voile to go sailing
■ un bateau à voiles a sailing boat

le **voile** NOUN
▷ *see also* la voile
veil
□ un voile de mariée a wedding veil

le **voilier** NOUN
sailing boat

voir VERB [92]

PRESENT TENSE	
je vois	nous voyons
tu vois	vous voyez
il/elle voit	ils/elles voient

PAST PARTICIPLE
vu

to see
□ Venez me voir quand vous serez à Paris.
Come and see me when you're in Paris. □ Je
ne vois pas pourquoi il a fait ça. I can't see
why he did that.
■ faire voir quelque chose à quelqu'un to
show somebody something □ Il m'a fait voir
sa maison. He showed me his house.
■ se voir to be obvious □ Ça fait des années
qu'elle n'a pas joué au tennis — Oui, ça se
voit! She hasn't played tennis for years —
Yes, that's obvious! □ Est-ce que cette tache
se voit? Does that stain show?
■ avoir quelque chose à voir avec to have
something to do with □ Ça n'a rien à voir
avec lui, c'est entre toi et moi. It's nothing
to do with him, it's between you and me.
■ Je ne peux vraiment pas la voir.
(informal) I really can't stand her.

le **voisin** NOUN
neighbour

le **voisinage** NOUN
■ dans le voisinage in the vicinity

la **voisine** NOUN
neighbour

la **voiture** NOUN
car
□ une voiture de sport a sports car

la **voix** (PL les voix) NOUN
1 voice
□ à voix basse in a low voice
■ à haute voix aloud
2 vote
□ Il a obtenu cinquante pour cent des voix.
He got 50% of the votes.

le **vol** NOUN
1 flight
■ à vol d'oiseau as the crow flies
■ le vol à voile gliding
2 theft
□ un vol à main armée an armed robbery

la **volaille** NOUN
poultry

le **volant** NOUN
1 steering wheel
2 shuttlecock

le **volcan** NOUN
volcano

la **volée** NOUN
volley *(in tennis)*
■ rattraper une balle à la volée to catch a
ball in mid-air

voler VERB [28]
1 to fly
□ J'aimerais savoir voler. I'd like to be able to
fly.
2 to steal
□ On a volé mon appareil photo. My
camera's been stolen.
■ voler quelque chose à quelqu'un to
steal something from somebody □ Ça n'est
pas son stylo, il me l'a volé. That's not his
pen, he stole it from me.
■ voler quelqu'un to rob somebody

le **volet** NOUN
shutter

le **voleur** NOUN
thief
■ Au voleur! Stop thief!

la **voleuse** NOUN
thief

le **volley** NOUN
volleyball
□ jouer au volley to play volleyball

le/la **volontaire** NOUN
volunteer

la **volonté** NOUN
willpower
□ Il a beaucoup de volonté. He's got a lot of
willpower.
■ la bonne volonté goodwill
■ la mauvaise volonté lack of goodwill

volontiers ADVERB
1 gladly
□ Je l'aiderais volontiers s'il me le
demandait. I'd gladly help him if he asked
me.
2 please
□ Voulez-vous boire quelque chose? —
Volontiers! Would you like something to
drink? — Yes, please!

le **volume** NOUN
volume
□ un dictionnaire en deux volumes a two-
volume dictionary

V

volumineux (FEM **volumineuse**) ADJECTIVE
bulky

vomir VERB [38]
to vomit
□ Il a vomi toute la nuit. He was vomiting all night.

vont VERB ▷see aller

vos PL ADJECTIVE
your
□ Rangez vos jouets, les enfants! Children, put your toys away! □ Merci pour vos fleurs, M. Durand. Thanks for your flowers, Mr Durand.

le **vote** NOUN
vote

voter VERB [28]
to vote

votre (FEM **votre**, PL **vos**) ADJECTIVE
your
□ C'est votre manteau? Is this your coat?

vôtre PRONOUN
■ **le vôtre** yours □ J'aime bien notre prof de maths, mais le vôtre est plus patient. I like our maths teacher, but yours is more patient. □ À qui est cette écharpe? C'est la vôtre? Whose is this scarf? Is it yours?
■ **À la vôtre!** Cheers!

vôtres PL PRONOUN
■ **les vôtres** yours □ J'ai oublié mes lunettes de soleil. Vous avez les vôtres? I've forgotten my sunglasses. Have you got yours?

voudra, voudrai, voudrais, voudras, voudrez, voudrons, voudront VERB ▷see vouloir
■ **Je voudrais …** I'd like … □ Je voudrais deux litres de lait, s'il vous plaît. I'd like two litres of milk, please.

vouloir VERB [93]

PRESENT TENSE	
je veux	nous voulons
tu veux	vous voulez
il/elle veut	ils/elles veulent
PAST PARTICIPLE	
voulu	

to want
□ Elle veut un vélo pour Noël. She wants a bike for Christmas. □ Je ne veux pas de dessert. I don't want any pudding. □ Il ne veut pas venir. He doesn't want to come. □ On va au cinéma? — Si tu veux. Shall we go to the cinema? — If you like.
■ **Je veux bien.** I'll be happy to. □ Je veux bien le faire à ta place si ça t'arrange. I'd be happy to do it for you if you prefer.
■ **Voulez-vous une tasse de thé?** — **Je veux bien.** Would you like a cup of tea? —

Yes, please.
■ **sans le vouloir** without meaning to □ Je l'ai vexé sans le vouloir. I upset him without meaning to.
■ **en vouloir à quelqu'un** to be angry with somebody □ Il m'en veut de ne pas l'avoir invité. He's angry with me for not inviting him.
■ **vouloir dire** to mean □ Qu'est-ce que ça veut dire? What does that mean?

voulu VERB ▷see vouloir

vous SING, PL PRONOUN
💬 LANGUAGE TIP vous is used when speaking to several people, or to one person you don't know well.
1 you
□ Vous aimez la pizza? Do you like pizza?
2 to you
□ Je vous écrirai bientôt. I'll write to you soon.
3 yourself
□ Vous vous êtes fait mal? Have you hurt yourself?
■ **vous-même** yourself □ Vous l'avez fait vous-même? Did you do it yourself?

vouvoyer VERB [53]
■ **vouvoyer quelqu'un** to address somebody as 'vous' □ Est-ce que je dois vouvoyer ta sœur? Should I use 'vous' to your sister?
💡 DID YOU KNOW…?
vouvoyer quelqu'un means to use vous when speaking to someone, rather than tu. Use tu only when talking to one person and when that person is someone of your own age or whom you know well; use vous to everyone else. If in doubt use vous.

le **voyage** NOUN
journey
□ Avez-vous fait bon voyage? Did you have a good journey?
■ **Bon voyage!** Have a good trip!

voyager VERB [45]
to travel

le **voyageur** NOUN
passenger

la **voyageuse** NOUN
passenger

voyaient, voyais, voyait VERB ▷see voir

la **voyelle** NOUN
vowel

voyez, voyiez, voyions VERB ▷see voir
voyons VERB ▷see voir
1 let's see
□ Voyons ce qu'on peut faire. Let's see what we can do.

2 come on
 □ Voyons, sois raisonnable! **Come on, be
 reasonable!**
le **voyou** NOUN
 hooligan
vrac
 ■ **en vrac** ADVERB loose □ du thé en vrac
 loose tea
vrai (FEM **vraie**) ADJECTIVE
 true
 □ une histoire vraie a true story □ C'est
 vrai? Is that true?
 ■ **à vrai dire** to tell the truth
vraiment ADVERB
 really
vraisemblable (FEM **vraisemblable**)
 ADJECTIVE
 likely
 □ C'est peu vraisemblable. That's not very
 likely.
 ■ **une excuse vraisemblable** a convincing
 excuse
le **VTT** NOUN (= *vélo tout-terrain*)

mountain bike
vu VERB ▷ *see* **voir**
 □ J'ai vu ce film au cinéma. I saw this film at
 the cinema.
 ■ **être bien vu** *(person)* to be popular
 □ Est-ce qu'il est bien vu à l'école? Is he
 popular at school?
 ■ **C'est mal vu de fumer ici.** They don't like
 people smoking here.
la **vue** NOUN
1 eyesight
 □ J'ai une mauvaise vue. I've got bad
 eyesight.
2 view
 □ Il y a une belle vue d'ici. There's a lovely
 view from here.
 ■ **à vue d'œil** visibly □ Elle grandit à vue
 d'œil. Every time you see her, she's got
 taller.
vulgaire (FEM **vulgaire**) ADJECTIVE
 vulgar
 □ Ne dit pas ça, c'est très vulgaire. Don't say
 that, it's very vulgar.

v

Ww

le **wagon** NOUN
railway carriage

le **wagon-lit** (PL les **wagons-lits**) NOUN
sleeper *(on train)*

> **LANGUAGE TIP** Word for word, wagon-
> lit means **bed carriage**.

le **wagon-restaurant** (PL les **wagons-
restaurants**) NOUN
restaurant car

le **walkman**® NOUN
Walkman®

wallon (FEM **wallonne**) ADJECTIVE, NOUN
Walloon *(French-speaking Belgian)*

■ **les Wallons** the French-speaking Belgians

la **Wallonie** NOUN
French-speaking Belgium

les **W.-C.** MASC PL NOUN
toilet

le **Web** NOUN
Web

la **webcam** NOUN
webcam

le **webmaster** NOUN
webmaster

le **webzine** NOUN
webzine

le **week-end** NOUN
weekend

le **western** NOUN
western *(film)*

le **wifi** NOUN
wifi

le **whisky** (PL les **whiskies**) NOUN
whisky

xénophobe (FEM **xénophobe**) ADJECTIVE
prejudiced against foreigners

la **xénophobie** NOUN
prejudice against foreigners

le **xylophone** NOUN
xylophone
□ Elle joue du xylophone. She plays the xylophone.

Yy

y PRONOUN
there
□ Nous y sommes allés l'été dernier. We went there last summer. □ Regarde dans le tiroir: je pense que les clés y sont. Look in the drawer: I think the keys are in there.

○ **LANGUAGE TIP** y replaces phrases with à in constructions like the ones below:

■ **Je pensais à l'examen. — Mais arrête d'y penser!** I was thinking about the exam. — Well, stop thinking about it!

■ **Je ne m'attendais pas à ça. — Moi, je m'y attendais.** I wasn't expecting that. — I was expecting it.

le **yaourt** NOUN
yoghurt

□ un yaourt nature a plain yoghurt □ un yaourt aux fruits a fruit yoghurt

les **yeux** (SING œil) MASC PL NOUN
eyes
□ Elle a les yeux bleus. She's got blue eyes.

le **yoga** NOUN
yoga

le **yoghourt** NOUN
yoghurt

la **Yougoslavie** NOUN
Yugoslavia

■ l'ex-Yougoslavie the former Yugoslavia

youpi EXCLAMATION
yippee!

le **yoyo** NOUN
yo-yo

Zz

zapper VERB [28]
  to channel hop
le **zèbre** NOUN
  zebra
le **zéro** NOUN
  zero
  ■ **Ils ont gagné trois à zéro.** They won three-nil.
zézayer VERB [59]
  to lisp
  □ Il zézaie. He's got a lisp.
le **zigzag** NOUN
  ■ **faire des zigzags** to zigzag

la **zone** NOUN
  zone
  ■ **une zone industrielle** an industrial estate
  ■ **une zone piétonne** a pedestrian precinct
le **zoo** NOUN
  zoo
zoologique (FEM **zoologique**) ADJECTIVE
  zoological
  □ un jardin zoologique zoological gardens
zut EXCLAMATION
  oh heck!

French in Action

©Collins Bartholomew Ltd 2007

- France is the biggest country by area in Western Europe, covering 549 000 km² (well over twice the size of the UK).

- The Loire is the longest river in France, and is around 1010 km long. It rises in the Cévennes mountains and flows into the Atlantic Ocean at Saint-Nazaire.

- The highest mountain in the Alps, Mont Blanc (4807 m), lies just within France's border with Italy.

- 59.3 million people live in metropolitan France, and there are another 1.7 million in the overseas *départements*.

Relationships and feelings

Some useful phrases

Voici ma sœur Sandrine.	This is my sister, Sandrine.
Elle va se marier l'été prochain.	She's getting married next summer.
J'ai un frère jumeau.	I have a twin brother.
J'ai une sœur jumelle.	I have a twin sister.
J'ai un demi-frère.	I have a half-brother.
Je suis fils unique.	I'm an only child. (boy)
Je suis fille unique.	I'm an only child. (girl)
Mes parents sont séparés/divorcés.	My parents are separated/divorced.
Mon grand-père est mort l'année dernière.	My grandfather died last year.
Ma mère s'est remariée.	My mother has got married again.

Les relations / Relationships

Je m'entends bien avec ma sœur.	I get on well with my sister.
Je ne m'entends pas du tout avec mon frère.	I don't get on at all with my brother.
Mon meilleur copain s'appelle Tamir.	My best friend is called Tamir.
J'ai trois meilleures copines.	I've got three best friends.
Nous sommes inséparables.	We're always together.
Je me suis disputée avec Rachida.	I've had a quarrel with Rachida.
On ne se parle plus avec Bertrand.	I'm not talking to Bertrand any more.

Les membres de la famille / Members of the family

mon père	my father, my dad
ma mère	my mother, my mum
mon frère	my brother
ma sœur	my sister
mon oncle	my uncle
ma tante	my aunt
mon cousin	my cousin (male)
ma cousine	my cousin (female)
mon grand-père	my grandfather, my granddad
ma grand-mère	my grandmother, my gran
mes grands-parents	my grandparents
mon grand frère	my big brother
ma petite sœur	my little sister
le copain de ma sœur	my sister's boyfriend
la copine de mon frère	my brother's girlfriend
le fiancé de ma sœur	my sister's fiancé
la fiancée de mon frère	my brother's fiancée

Les émotions / Emotions

être ...	to be ...
triste	sad
content/contente	pleased
heureux/heureuse	happy
fâché/fâchée	angry
amoureux/amoureuse	in love
vexé/vexée	hurt

Je suis amoureuse de Fabien.	I'm in love with Fabien.
Bruno et moi, on s'est séparés.	Bruno and I have split up.
Je suis contente que tu viennes.	I'm pleased you're coming.
Je suis triste de partir.	I'm sad to be leaving.
J'espère que tu n'es pas trop fâché.	I hope you're not too angry.
Elle était vexée de ne pas avoir été invitée.	She was hurt that she wasn't invited.

3

At home

Où habites-tu? Where do you live?

J'habite ...	I live ...
dans un village	in a village
dans une petite ville	in a small town
dans le centre-ville	in the town centre
dans la banlieue de Londres	in the suburbs of London
à la campagne	in the countryside
au bord de la mer	at the seaside
à 100 km de Manchester	100 km from Manchester
au nord de Birmingham	north of Birmingham
dans une maison individuelle	in a detached house
dans une maison jumelée	in a semi-detached house
dans une maison à deux étages	in a two-storey house
dans un immeuble	in a block of flats
dans un appartement	in a flat
dans un lotissement	on a housing estate

J'habite dans un appartement ...	I live in a flat ...
au rez-de-chaussée	on the ground floor
au premier étage	on the first floor
au deuxième étage	on the second floor
au dernier étage	on the top floor

J'habite ...	I live ...
dans une maison moderne	in a modern house
dans une maison neuve	in a new house
dans une vieille maison edwardienne	in an old Edwardian house

De la maison au collège / From home to school

Le collège est assez loin de chez moi.	School is quite a long way from my house.
J'habite à cinq minutes à pied du collège.	I live five minutes' walk from school.
Mon père m'emmène au collège en voiture.	My father takes me to school in the car.
Je vais au collège en bus.	I go to school by bus.

À la maison / At home

Au rez-de-chaussée, il y a ...	On the ground floor there is ...
la cuisine	the kitchen
la salle de séjour	the living room
la salle à manger	the dining room
le salon	the lounge
À l'étage, il y a ...	Upstairs there is ...
ma chambre	my bedroom
la chambre de mon frère	my brother's bedroom
la chambre de mes parents	my parents' room
la chambre d'amis	the spare bedroom
la salle de bains	the bathroom
un bureau	a study
un jardin	a garden
un terrain de football	a football pitch
un court de tennis	a tennis court
un voisin	a neighbour
les voisins d'en face	the people opposite
les voisins d'à côté	the next-door neighbours

Some useful phrases

Chez moi, c'est tout petit.	My house is very small.
Ma chambre est bien rangée.	My room is tidy.
Je partage ma chambre avec mon frère.	I share my bedroom with my brother.
Mon meilleur copain habite dans la même rue que moi.	My best friend lives in the same street as me.
Il y a un court de tennis à côté de chez moi.	There's a tennis court next to my house.
Nous déménageons le mois prochain.	We're moving next month.

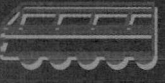  

Quelques endroits importants	A few landmarks
un cinéma	a cinema
un théâtre	a theatre
un musée	a museum
un square	public gardens
un distributeur de billets	a cash dispenser
l'office de tourisme	the tourist office
une cathédrale	a cathedral
une église	a church
une mosquée	a mosque
une rue piétonne	a pedestrian street
une banque	a bank
la piscine	the swimming pool
la patinoire	the ice rink
la bibliothèque	the library
la mairie	the town hall
la place du marché	the market square

Les moyens de transport	Means of transport
un bus	a bus
un car	a coach
le métro	the underground
le tramway	the tram
le train	the train
la gare	the station
la gare routière	the bus station
une station de métro	an underground station
À quelle heure est le prochain train pour Marseille?	What time is the next train to Marseilles?
Je voudrais un aller simple pour Lille.	I'd like a single to Lille.
Un aller-retour pour Paris, s'il vous plaît.	A return to Paris, please.
Où est le quai numéro 10?	Where is platform 10?
Où est la station de métro la plus proche?	Where is the nearest underground station?

Les directions	Directions
en face de	opposite
à côté de	next to
près de	near
entre ... et ...	between ... and ...
Où se trouve la gare routière?	Where's the bus station?
Je cherche l'office de tourisme.	I'm looking for the tourist office.
Allez jusqu'au bout de la rue.	Go right to the end of the street.
Tournez à droite.	Turn right.
Traversez le pont.	Cross the bridge.
Prenez la première rue à gauche.	Take the first street on the left.
C'est sur votre droite.	It's on your right.
C'est en face du cinéma.	It's opposite the cinema.
C'est à côté de la poste.	It's next to the post office.

My plans for the future

Le travail	Work
Je voudrais faire des études ...	**I'd like to study ...**
de médecine	medicine
d'ingénieur	engineering
de droit	law
de sociologie	sociology
de psychologie	psychology
de langues	languages
d'architecture	architecture
Je voudrais ...	**I'd like to ...**
gagner beaucoup d'argent	earn lots of money
travailler dans un magasin	work in a shop
travailler dans une banque	work in a bank
travailler dans le tourisme	work in tourism
faire un apprentissage	do an apprenticeship
faire un diplôme	do a qualification
Je voudrais être ...	**I'd like to be ...**
avocat(e)	a solicitor
prof	a teacher
dentiste	a dentist
actrice	an actress
chanteur/chanteuse	a singer
coiffeur/coiffeuse	a hairdresser
journaliste	a journalist
acteur	an actor
footballeur professionel	a professional footballer
musicien(ne)	a musician
politicien(ne)	a politician
Je pense que c'est ...	**I think it's ...**
intéressant	interesting
fatigant	tiring
gratifiant	rewarding
stressant	stressful
bien payé	well paid
mal payé	badly paid

Les ambitions	Ambitions
J'ai l'intention d'aller à l'université.	I'm planning to go to university.
Après, j'aimerais bien aller à l'étranger.	Afterwards I'd like to go abroad.
Je voudrais me marier et avoir beaucoup d'enfants.	I'd like to get married and have lots of children.
Je ne sais pas encore ce que je veux faire.	I don't know yet what I want to do.

Les examens	Exams
un examen	an exam
un examen blanc	a mock exam
les résultats	the results
Cette année, je prépare le GCSE.	I'm doing my GCSEs this year.
Je vais passer mon premier examen blanc lundi prochain.	I'm going to do my first mock exam next Monday.
J'espère réussir à mes examens.	I hope I'll pass my exams.
Je crois que j'ai raté mon examen de maths.	I think I've failed my maths exam.
J'aurai les résultats au mois d'août.	I'll get the results in August.
J'ai bien réussi à mes examens.	I've done well in my exams.
L'année prochaine, je vais préparer huit examens.	I'm going to do eight exams next year.

Les sports	Sports
Je joue ...	**I play ...**
au foot	football
au basket	basketball
au netball	netball
au rugby	rugby
au tennis	tennis
au ping-pong	table tennis
Je fais ...	**I ...**
du ski	ski
du kayak	canoe
de la gymnastique	do gymnastics
de la natation	swim
de l'équitation	go horse riding
de la voile	go sailing
Cet été, je vais faire un stage de voile.	I'm going to do a sailing course this summer.
Je n'ai jamais fait de ski.	I've never been skiing.
Je vais apprendre à faire du kayak.	I'm going to learn how to canoe.

Les petits boulots	Jobs
un CV	a CV
un entretien	an interview
Je travaille ...	**I work ...**
à la pharmacie le samedi	at the chemist's on Saturdays
au supermarché pendant les vacances	at the supermarket in the holidays
dans un magasin de vêtements le week-end	in a clothes shop at the weekend
Je fais du baby-sitting.	I do baby-sitting.
Je fais les courses pour une vieille dame.	I do an old lady's shopping for her.
Je distribue les journaux.	I deliver papers.
Je gagne 7,50 euros de l'heure.	I earn 7.50 euros an hour.
Je n'ai jamais travaillé.	I've never had a job.
Je vais chercher un boulot pour cet été.	I'm going to look for a job for this summer.

Les instruments de musique	Musical instruments
Je joue ...	**I play the ...**
du violon	violin
du piano	piano
de la guitare	guitar
de la flûte	flute
Je joue du violon depuis l'âge de huit ans.	I've been playing the violin since I was eight.
Je joue dans l'orchestre du collège.	I play in the school orchestra.
Je voudrais apprendre à jouer de la guitare.	I'd like to learn to play the guitar.

Cuisiner chez soi	Cooking at home
J'aime faire la cuisine.	I like cooking.
Je ne sais pas cuisiner.	I can't cook.
Je fais très bien les gâteaux.	I'm very good at making cakes.

Mes passe-temps préférés	My favourite hobbies
J'aime lire des romans.	I like reading novels.
J'adore écouter de la musique dans ma chambre.	I love listening to music in my room.
J'aime bien aller en ville avec mes copines.	I love going into town with my friends.
Mon passe-temps préféré, c'est l'équitation.	My favourite hobby is riding.
Je préfère sortir avec mes copains.	I'd rather go out with my friends.
Je déteste les jeux vidéo.	I hate video games.

Describing someone

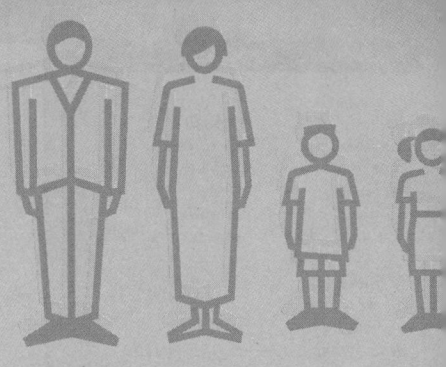

La personnalité / Personality

La personnalité	Personality
Il / Elle est ...	**He/She is ...**
drôle	funny
sympa	nice
timide	shy
réservé/réservée	quiet
énervant/énervante	annoying
généreux/généreuse	generous
bavarde/bavarde	talkative
intelligent/intelligente	intelligent
bête	stupid
radin	stingy
bizarre	strange

Les couleurs / Colours

Les couleurs	Colours
jaune	yellow
orange (masc, fem, pl)	orange
rouge	red
rose	pink
violet, violette	purple
bleu, bleue	blue
vert, verte	green
marron (masc, fem, pl)	brown
gris, grise	grey
noir, noire	black
blanc, blanche	white
bordeaux (masc, fem, pl)	maroon
bleu marine (masc, fem, pl)	navy (blue)
turquoise (masc, fem, pl)	turquoise
beige	beige
crème (masc, fem, pl)	cream

aussi pour les yeux:	**For eyes:**
noisette (masc, fem, pl)	hazel

aussi pour les cheveux:	**For hair:**
auburn	auburn
blond, blonde	blonde
châtain	brown
châtain clair (masc, fem, pl)	light brown
brun, brune	dark brown
roux, rousse	red

J'ai les yeux noisette.	I've got hazel eyes.
Il a les cheveux châtains.	He's got brown hair.
Elle a les cheveux gris et courts.	She's got short grey hair.
Elle est rousse.	She's got red hair.
Il est chauve.	He's bald.
Elle a les cheveux blonds, longs et frisés.	She's got long curly blonde hair.

Describing someone

Les caractéristiques	Characteristics
Il/Elle est ...	He/She is ...
grand/grande	tall
petit/petite	small
mince	slim
gros/grosse	fat
beau/belle	good-looking
jeune	young
vieux/vieille	old
Il a une trentaine d'années.	He's about thirty.
Elle est grande, mince et assez jolie.	She's tall, slim and quite nice-looking.
Elle ressemble à Cameron Diaz.	She looks like Cameron Diaz.

Les vêtements	Clothes
un pull	a jumper
un pantalon	trousers
un chemisier	a blouse
un T-shirt	a T-shirt
un manteau	a coat
un blouson	a jacket
un gilet	a cardigan
une robe	a dress
une jupe	a skirt
une cravate	a tie
une veste	a jacket
une chemise	a shirt
des chaussures	shoes
des baskets	trainers
des bottes	boots
Elle porte un T-shirt bleu clair.	She's wearing a light blue T-shirt.
Il porte un costume gris foncé.	He's wearing a dark grey suit.
Mon uniforme comprend une jupe bleu marine, un chemisier blanc, une cravate rayée bordeaux et gris, des chaussettes grises, un blazer bordeaux et des chaussures noires.	My uniform consists of a navy blue skirt, a white blouse, a tie with maroon and grey stripes, grey socks, a maroon blazer and black shoes.

Keeping fit and healthy

Les repas	Meals
le petit déjeuner	breakfast
le déjeuner	lunch
le goûter	afternoon snack
le dîner	dinner
J'adore ...	**I love ...**
le chocolat	chocolate
la salade	salad
les fraises	strawberries
J'aime ...	**I like ...**
le poisson	fish
la limonade	lemonade
les légumes	vegetables
Je n'aime pas ...	**I don't like ...**
le jus d'orange	orange juice
l'eau pétillante	sparkling water
les bananes	bananas
Je ne mange pas de porc.	I don't eat pork.
Je mange beaucoup de fruits.	I eat a lot of fruit.
Je ne mange pas de cochonneries entre les repas.	I don't eat junk food between meals.
J'évite les boissons gazeuses.	I avoid fizzy drinks.
Je suis végétarien/ végétarienne.	I'm a vegetarian.
Je suis allergique aux arachides.	I'm allergic to peanuts.

Les maladies	Ailments
J'ai mal au ...	**I have a sore ...**
ventre	stomach
dos	back
genou	knee
pied	foot
cou	neck
J'ai mal à la ...	**I have a sore ...**
tête	head
gorge	throat
jambe	leg
J'ai mal aux dents.	I've got toothache.
J'ai mal aux oreilles.	I've got earache.
J'ai mal aux yeux.	My eyes are hurting.
J'ai le rhume.	I've got a cold.
J'ai la grippe.	I've got flu.
J'ai envie de vomir.	I feel sick.
Je suis fatigué.	I'm tired.
Je suis malade.	I'm ill.
avoir ...	**to be ...**
froid	cold
chaud	hot
peur	scared
soif	thirsty
faim	hungry

J'ai peur d'échouer à mon examen.
I'm afraid that I'm going to fail the exam.

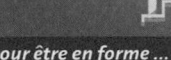

Pour être en forme ...	To be fit ...
Je fais beaucoup de sport.	I do a lot of sport.
Je ne fume pas.	I don't smoke.
Je me couche de bonne heure.	I go to bed early.
Je vais au collège à pied.	I walk to school.
C'est bon pour la santé.	It's good for your health.
L'alcool est mauvais pour la santé.	Alcohol is bad for your health.

When your number answers

Bonjour! J'aimerais parler à Valérie.	Hello! Could I speak to Valérie, please?
Pourriez-vous lui demander de me rappeler, s'il vous plaît?	Would you ask him/her to call me back, please?
Je rappellerai dans une demi-heure.	I'll call back in half an hour.

Answering the telephone

Bonjour! C'est Marc à l'appareil.	Hello! It's Marc speaking.
C'est moi.	Speaking.
Qui est à l'appareil?	Who's speaking?

When the switchboard answers

C'est de la part de qui?	Who shall I say is calling?
Je vous le/la passe.	I'm putting you through.
Ne quittez pas.	Please hold.
Voulez-vous laisser un message?	Would you like to leave a message?

Difficulties

Je n'arrive pas à avoir le numéro.	I can't get through.
Je suis désolé, j'ai dû faire un faux numéro.	I'm sorry, I dialled the wrong number.
La ligne est très mauvaise.	This is a very bad line.
Leur téléphone est en dérangement.	Their phone is out of order.
Je ne te capte plus!	You're breaking up!
Je n'ai plus de crédit sur mon portable.	I've no credit left on my phone.

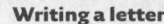

Writing a letter

Nathalie Leduc
18 rue des Tulipes
65004 Gervais
Gervais, le 14 février 2007

Chers papi et mamie,

Merci beaucoup pour les CD que vous m'avez envoyés. Vous avez vraiment bien choisi puisqu'il s'agit de mes deux chanteurs préférés: je n'arrête pas de les écouter!

Sinon, rien de nouveau ici. Je passe presque tout mon temps à préparer mes examens, qui commencent dans quinze jours. J'espère que je les réussirai tous, mais j'ai le trac pour mon examen de maths: c'est la matière que j'aime le moins.

Maman m'a dit que vous partiez en Crète la semaine prochaine. Je vous souhaite de très bonnes vacances, et je suis sûre que vous reviendrez tout bronzés.

Grosses bises,

Nathalie

Alternatively
Affectueusement
Amicalement

Writing a personal letter
Your own name and address
Town/city you are writing from, and the date

Starting a personal letter

Merci pour ta lettre.	Thank you for your letter.
Ça m'a fait plaisir d'avoir de tes nouvelles.	It was lovely to hear from you.
Je suis désolé de ne pas t'avoir écrit plus tôt.	I'm sorry I didn't write sooner.

Ending a personal letter

Écris-moi bientôt!	Write soon!
Embrasse Sophie pour moi.	Give my love to Sophie.
Paul te fait ses amitiés.	Paul sends his best wishes.

Writing an email

Fichier	Edition	Affichage	Composer	Aide	Envoyer
			Nouveau message		
A:	alice@ntnet.co.fr		Répondre à tous		
Cc:	antoine@blt.com		Faire suivre		
Objet:	show		Fichier joint		
Copie cachée:					

Salut!

Je viens d'acheter le nouvel album de Rockstar. Il est génial!

J'ai trois billets gratuits pour leur show à Orléans samedi prochain, et j'espère que vous pourrez venir avec moi tous les deux!

À bientôt!

Saying your email address
To give your email address to someone in French, say:
"Alice at n t net point co point f r"

French	English
nouveau message (m)	new message
à	to
de	from
objet (m)	subject
cc	cc (carbon copy)
copie cachée	bcc
fichier joint (m)	attachment
Envoyer	send
fichier (m)	file
édition (f)	edit
affichage (m)	view
outils (mpl)	tools
composer	compose
aide (f)	help
répondre	reply to sender
répondre à tous	reply to all
faire suivre	forward
date (f)	sent

Texto	French	English
@+	à plus (tard)	see you later
@2m1	à demain	see you tomorrow
bi1to	bientôt	soon
cpg	c'est pas grave	it's no big deal
dsl	désolé	I'm sorry
entouK	en tout cas	in any case
G la N	J'ai la haine	I'm gutted
je t'M	je t'aime	I love you
mdr	mort de rire	rolling on the floor laughing
mr6	merci	thanks
msg	message	message
p2k	pas de quoi	you're welcome
parske	parce que	because
qqn	quelqu'un	someone
ri1	rien	nothing
svp	s'il vous plaît	please
TOK?	t'es OK?	are you OK?
TOQP?	t'es occupé?	are you busy?
we	week-end	weekend
Xlnt	excellent	excellent

You will notice that just as the numbers 2, 4 and 8 are used in English in text messages (C U 2moro; R U coming 4 Xmas?; Gr8!), French texts also use 1 for all "in/un/ain/" sounds, 2 for "de/deu" sounds and 6 for "si/sis" sounds.

Dates, festivals and holidays

Les jours de la semaine	Days of the week
lundi	Monday
mardi	Tuesday
mercredi	Wednesday
jeudi	Thursday
vendredi	Friday
samedi	Saturday
dimanche	Sunday
lundi	on Monday
lundi dernier	last Monday
lundi prochain	next Monday
hier	yesterday
aujourd'hui	today
demain	tomorrow

Les fêtes	Festivals
Noël (masc)	Christmas
le jour de Noël	Christmas Day
la veille de Noël	Christmas Eve
le réveillon de Noël	Christmas Eve celebrations
le lendemain de Noël	Boxing Day
la Saint-Sylvestre	New Year's Eve
le Nouvel An	New Year's Day
la Saint-Valentin	Valentine's Day
mardi gras	Pancake Day
le premier avril	April Fool's Day
Pâques (fem pl)	Easter
la fête des Mères	Mother's Day
la fête des Pères	Father's Day
la Toussaint	All Saints' Day
le 11 novembre	Remembrance Day
le ramadan	Ramadan
Joyeux Noël!	Happy Christmas!
Poisson d'avril!	April fool!
à Pâques	at Easter
fêter le Nouvel An	to celebrate New Year
Qu'est-ce que tu fais le jour de Noël?	What do you do on Christmas Day?
Nous passons le lendemain de Noël à la maison.	We spend Boxing Day at home.
Nous allons chez mes cousins pour le jour de l'An.	We go to my cousins' for New Year.

Les mois de l'année	Months of the year
janvier	January
février	February
mars	March
avril	April
mai	May
juin	June
juillet	July
août	August
septembre	September
octobre	October
novembre	November
décembre	December

Quelle est la date aujourd'hui?	What date is it today?
Nous sommes le 16 juin.	It's 16 June.
Quelle est la date de ton anniversaire?	What date is your birthday?
C'est le 22 mai.	It's 22 May.

Les vacances	Holidays
les grandes vacances	the summer holidays
les vacances de la Toussaint	the autumn half-term
les vacances de Noël	the Christmas holidays
les vacances de février	the spring half-term
les vacances de Pâques	the Easter holidays
le bord de la mer	the seaside
la montagne	the mountains

Qu'est-ce que tu vas faire pendant les vacances?	What are you going to do in the holidays?
Cet été, nous partons une semaine en Italie.	We're going to Italy for a week this summer.
Nous ne partons pas en vacances cette année.	We're not going on holiday this year.
Nous allons toujours aux sports d'hiver en février.	We always go skiing in February.
L'été prochain, je vais passer une semaine chez ma tante.	I'm going to stay with my aunt for a week next year.
L'été dernier je suis allé aux États-Unis.	Last summer I went to the United States.

Time

Quelle heure est-il? Il est...	What time is it? It's...

une heure

une heure dix

une heure et quart

une heure et demie

deux heures moins vingt

deux heures moins le quart

A quelle heure?	At what time?

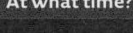

à minuit

à midi

à une heure (de l'après-midi)

à huit heures (du soir)

à 11h15 or *onze heures quinze*

à 20h45 or *vingt heures quarante-cinq*

In French times are often given in the twenty-four hour clock.

Numbers

Numbers

1	*un(e)*
2	*deux*
3	*trois*
4	*quatre*
5	*cinq*
6	*six*
7	*sept*
8	*huit*
9	*neuf*
10	*dix*
11	*onze*
12	*douze*
13	*treize*
14	*quatorze*
15	*quinze*
16	*seize*
17	*dix-sept*
18	*dix-huit*
19	*dix-neuf*
20	*vingt*
21	*vingt et un(e)*
22	*vingt-deux*
30	*trente*
40	*quarante*
50	*cinquante*
60	*soixante*
70	*soixante-dix*
71	*soixante et onze*
72	*soixante-douze*
80	*quatre-vingts*
81	*quatre-vingt-un(e)*
90	*quatre-vingt-dix*
91	*quatre-vingt-onze*
100	*cent*
101	*cent un(e)*
300	*trois cents*
301	*trois cent un(e)*
1,000	*mille*
2,000	*deux mille*
1,000,000	*un million*

Examples
il habite au dix - he lives at number ten
à la page dix-neuf - on page nineteen
au chapitre sept - in chapter seven

I
II
III
IV
V
VI
VII
VIII
IX
X

Fractions etc

1/2	*un demi*
1/3	*un tiers*
2/3	*deux tiers*
1/4	*un quart*
1/5	*un cinquième*
0.5	*zéro virgule cinq (0,5)*
3.4	*trois virgule quatre (3,4)*
10%	*dix pour cent*
100%	*cent pour cent*

1st	*premier (1er), première (1re)*
2nd	*deuxième (2e)*
3rd	*troisième (3e)*
4th	*quatrième (4e)*
5th	*cinquième (5e)*
6th	*sixième (6e)*
7th	*septième (7e)*
8th	*huitième (8e)*
9th	*neuvième (9e)*
10th	*dixième (10e)*
11th	*onzième (11e)*
12th	*douzième (12e)*
13th	*treizième (13e)*
14th	*quatorzième (14e)*
15th	*quinzième (15e)*
16th	*seizième (16e)*
17th	*dix-septième (17e)*
18th	*dix-huitième (18e)*
19th	*dix-neuvième (19e)*
20th	*vingtième (20e)*
21st	*vingt et unième (21e)*
22nd	*vingt-deuxième (22e)*
30th	*trentième (30e)*
100th	*centième (100e)*
101st	*cent unième (101e)*
1000th	*millième (1000e)*

Examples
il habite au cinquième (étage) - he lives on the fifth floor
il est arrivé troisième - he came in third
échelle au vingt-cinq millième - scale one to twenty-five thousand

Contents

French verb tables

This section is designed to help you find all the verb forms you need in French. From pages 22–27 you will find a list of 93 regular and irregular verbs with a summary of their main forms, followed on pages 28-48 by some very common regular and irregular verbs shown in full, with example phrases.

How to find the verb you need

All the verbs on the **French – English** side of the dictionary are followed by a number in square brackets. Each of these numbers corresponds to a verb in this section.

> **regarder** VERB [28]
> **1** to look at

In this example, the number [28] after the verb **regarder** means that **regarder** follows the same pattern as verb number 28 in the list, which is **donner**. In this instance, **donner** is given in full on page 35.

> **avancer** VERB [12]
> **1** to move forward

For other verbs, a summary of the main forms is given. In the example above, **avancer** follows the same pattern as verb number [12] in the list, which is **commencer**. On page 22 of this section, you can see that the main forms of **commencer** are given to show you how this verb (and others like it) works.

In the full verb tables, you will find examples of regular verbs: a regular -er verb (**donner**), a regular -ir verb (**finir**) and a regular -re verb (**vendre**). Regular verbs follow one of three set patterns. When you have learnt these patterns, you will be able to form any regular verb.

You will also find **avoir** (to have) and **être** (to be) in the full verb tables. These are very important verbs which must be learnt. You use them when you want to say 'I have' *etc* or 'I am' *etc*. The present tense of **avoir** or **être** is also used to form the **perfect tense**. In most cases, **avoir** is used to form the perfect, but reflexive verbs like **se taire** (to stop talking) and verbs of movement like **aller** (to go) and **venir** (to come) use **être** – e.g. the French for both 'he's gone' and 'he went' is **il** *est* **allé**, not **il** *a* **allé**.

Finally, there are some other very common irregular verbs shown in full in the verb tables on pages 28-48. And remember to visit **www.collinsdictionaries.com/easyresources** for further help with verb tables.

Verb tenses

The present tense

The present tense is used to talk about what is true at the moment, what happens regularly and what is happening now, for example, 'I'm a student'; 'he works as a consultant'; 'I'm studying French'.

There is more than one way to express the present tense in English. For example, you can either say 'I give', 'I am giving' or occasionally 'I do give'. In French, you use the same form **je donne** for all these.

In English you can also use the present to talk about something that is going to happen in the near future. You can do the same in French.

J'emménage à la fin du mois.	**I'm moving in** at the end of the month.
On sort avec Aurélie ce soir.	**We're going out** with Aurélie tonight.

The future tense

The future tense is used to talk about something that will happen or will be true. There are several ways to express the future tense in English: you can use the future tense ('I'll ask him on Tuesday'), the present tense ('I'm not working tomorrow'), or going to followed by an infinitive ('she's going to study in France for a year'). In French you can also use the future tense, the present tense, or the verb **aller** (to go) followed by an infinitive.

Elle ne rentrera pas avant minuit.	**She won't be back** before midnight.
Il arrive dans dix minutes.	**He's coming** in ten minutes.
Je vais me faire couper les cheveux.	**I'm going to** have my hair cut.

The imperfect tense

The imperfect tense is one of the tenses used to talk about the past, especially in descriptions, and to say what used to happen, for example 'I used to work in Manchester'; 'it was sunny yesterday'.

Je ne faisais rien de spécial.	**I wasn't doing anything** special.
C'était une super fête.	**It was** a great party.
Avant, **il était** professeur.	**He used to be** a teacher.

The perfect tense

The perfect tense is made up of two parts: the present tense of **avoir** or **être**, and the French past participle (like 'given', 'finished' and 'done' in English).

Most verbs form the perfect tense with **avoir**. There are two main groups of verbs which form their perfect tense with **être** instead of **avoir**: all reflexive verbs (see **s'asseoir** page 30 and **se taire** page 44) and a group of verbs that are mainly used to talk about movement or a change of some kind, including:

aller	to go
venir	to come
arriver	to arrive, to happen
partir	to leave, to go
descendre	to go down, to come down, to get off
monter	to go up, to come up
entrer	to go in, to come in
sortir	to go out, to come out
mourir	to die
naître	to be born
devenir	to become
rester	to stay
tomber	to fall

Richard **est parti** de bonne heure.   Richard **left** early.
Tu es sortie hier soir?   **Did you go out** last night?
On est resté trois jours à Toulouse.   **We stayed** in Toulouse for three days.

The imperative

An imperative is a form of the verb used when giving orders and instructions, for example, 'Be quiet!', 'Don't forget your passport!', 'Please fill in this form'.

In French, there are several forms of the imperative that are used to give instructions or orders to someone. These correspond to **tu**, **vous** and **nous**. The **nous** form means the same as 'let's' in English. For regular verbs, the imperative is the same as the **tu**, **nous** and **vous** forms of the present tense, except that you do not say the pronouns **tu**, **nous** and **vous**. Also, in the **tu** form of –er verbs like **donner**, the final –s is dropped.

Arrête de me faire rire!   **Stop** making me laugh!
Venez déjeuner chez nous.   **Come** round to ours for lunch.
Allons voir ce qu'ils font.   **Let's go** and see what they're up to.

The subjunctive

The subjunctive is a verb form that is used in certain circumstances to express some sort of feeling, or to show there is doubt about whether something will happen or something is true. It is used after certain structures in French, for example, **il faut que** and **il faudrait que**.

Il faut que je rentre.	**I have to** get back.
Il faudrait qu'on loue une voiture.	**We should** hire a car.
Je veux que tu viennes avec moi.	**I want** you to come with me.

The conditional

The conditional is a verb form used to talk about things that would happen or that would be true under certain conditions, for instance, 'I would help you if I could'. It is also used to say what you would like or need, for example, 'Could you give me the bill?'.

Je voudrais deux billets.	**I'd like** two tickets.
Si j'étais toi, **je téléphonerais**.	**I'd call** if I were you.

French verb forms

INFINITIVE	PRESENT	PERFECT	IMPERFECT	FUTURE	PRESENT SUBJUNCTIVE
1 acheter -er verb with a spelling change	j'achète tu achètes il achète nous achetons vous achetez ils achètent	j'ai acheté	j'achetais	j'achèterai	j'achète
2 acquérir	see full verb table page 28				
3 aller	see full verb table page 29				
4 appeler -er verb with a spelling change	j'appelle tu appelles il appelle nous appelons vous appelez ils appellent	j'ai appelé	j'appelais	j'appellerai	j'appelle
5 arriver similar to donner [28], apart from the perfect tense	j'arrive	je suis arrivé(e)	j'arrivais	j'arriverai	j'arrive
6 s'asseoir	see full verb table page 30				
7 attendre similar to vendre [88]	j'attends	j'ai attendu	j'attendais	j'attendrai	j'attende
8 avoir	see full verb table page 31				
9 battre	je bats	j'ai battu	je battais	je battrai	je batte
10 boire	je bois nous buvons ils boivent	j'ai bu	je buvais	je boirai	je boive
11 bouillir	je bous nous bouillons	j'ai bouilli	je bouillais	je bouillirai	je bouille
12 commencer -er verb with a spelling change	je commence nous commençons vous commencez ils commencent	j'ai commencé	je commençais nous commencions ils commençaient	je commencerai	je commence
13 conclure	je conclus nous concluons	j'ai conclu	je concluais	je concluerai	je conclue
14 connaître	je connais il connaît nous connaissons	j'ai connu	je connaissais	je connaîtrai tu connaîtras	je connaisse
15 coudre	je couds nous cousons ils cousent	j'ai cousu	je cousais	je coudrai	je couse
16 courir	je cours nous courons	j'ai couru	je courais	je courrai	je coure
17 craindre	je crains nous craignons	j'ai craint	je craignais	je craindrai	je craigne

INFINITIVE	PRESENT	PERFECT	IMPERFECT	FUTURE	PRESENT SUBJUNCTIVE
18 créer similar to donner [28]	je crée	j'ai créé	je créais	je créerai	je crée
19 crier similar to donner [28]	je crie	j'ai crié	je criais nous criions vous criiez	je crierai	je crie
20 croire	see full verb table page 32				
21 croître	je croîs nous croissons	j'ai crû	je croissais	je croîtrai	je croisse
22 cueillir	je cueille nous cueillons	j'ai cueilli	je cueillais	je cueillerai	je cueille
23 cuire	je cuis nous cuisons ils cuisent	j'ai cuit	je cuisais	je cuirai	je cuise
24 descendre similar to vendre [88], apart from the perfect tense	je descends	je suis descendu(e)	je descendais	je descendrai	je descende
25 devenir similar to venir [89]	je deviens	je suis devenu(e)	je devenais	je deviendrai	je devienne
26 devoir	see full verb table page 33				
27 dire	see full verb table page 34				
28 donner	see full verb table page 35				
29 dormir	je dors nous dormons	j'ai dormi	je dormais	je dormirai	je dorme
30 écrire	j'écris nous écrivons	j'ai écrit	j'écrivais	j'écrirai	j'écrive
31 émouvoir	j'émeus nous émouvons ils émeuvent	j'ai ému	j'émouvais	j'émouvrai	j'émeuve
32 entrer similar to donner [28], apart from the perfect tense	j'entre	je suis entré(e)	j'entrais	j'entrerai	j'entre
33 envoyer -er verb with a spelling change	j'envoie nous envoyons ils envoient	j'ai envoyé	j'envoyais	j'enverrai	j'envoie
34 espérer -er verb with a spelling change	j'espère tu espères il espère nous espérons vous espérez ils espèrent	j'ai espéré	j'espérais	j'espérerai	j'espère

INFINITIVE	PRESENT	PERFECT	IMPERFECT	FUTURE	PRESENT SUBJUNCTIVE
35 être	see full verb table page 36				
36 faire	see full verb table page 37				
37 falloir	il faut	il a fallu	il fallait	il faudra	il faille
38 finir	see full verb table page 38				
39 fuir	je fuis nous fuyons vous fuyez ils fuient	j'ai fui	je fuyais nous fuyions vous fuyiez	je fuirai	je fuie
40 haïr	je hais tu hais il hait nous haïssons vous haïssez ils haïssent	j'ai haï	je haïssais	je haïrai	je haïsse
41 jeter -er verb with a spelling change	je jette tu jettes il jette nous jetons vous jetez ils jettent	j'ai jeté	je jetais	je jetterai	je jette
42 joindre	je joins nous joignons	j'ai joint	je joignais	je joindrai	je joigne
43 lever -er verb with a spelling change	je lève tu lèves il lève nous levons vous levez ils lèvent	j'ai levé	je levais	je lèverai	je lève
44 lire	je lis nous lisons	j'ai lu	je lisais	je lirai	je lise
45 manger -er verb with a spelling change	je mange nous mangeons vous mangez ils mangent	j'ai mangé	je mangeais nous mangions vous mangiez ils mangeaient	je mangerai	je mange
46 maudire	je maudis nous maudissons	j'ai maudit	je maudissais	je maudirai	je maudisse
47 mettre	see full verb table page 39				
48 monter similar to **donner** [28], apart from the perfect tense	je monte	je suis monté(e)	je montais	je monterai	je monte
49 mordre similar to **vendre** [88]	je mords	j'ai mordu	je mordais	je mordrai	je morde
50 moudre	je mouds nous moulons ils moulent	j'ai moulu	je moulais	je moudrai	je moule

INFINITIVE	PRESENT	PERFECT	IMPERFECT	FUTURE	PRESENT SUBJUNCTIVE
51 mourir	je meurs nous mourons ils meurent	je suis mort(e)	je mourais	je mourrai	je meure
52 naître	je nais il naît nous naissons	je suis né(e)	je naissais	je naîtrai	je naisse
53 nettoyer -er verb with a spelling change	je nettoie nous nettoyons ils nettoient	j'ai nettoyé	je nettoyais	je nettoierai	je nettoie nous nettoyions ils nettoient
54 offrir similar to **ouvrir [55]**	j'offre	j'ai offert	j'offrais	j'offrirai	j'offre
55 ouvrir	see full verb table page 40				
56 paraître	je parais il paraît nous paraissons	j'ai paru	je paraissais	je paraîtrai tu paraîtras	je paraisse
57 partir similar to **sentir [77]**, apart from the perfect tense	je pars nous partons ils partent	je suis parti(e)	je partais	je partirai	je parte
58 passer similar to **donner [28]**, apart from the perfect tense	je passe	je suis passé(e)	je passais	je passerai	je passe
59 payer -er verb with a spelling change	je paie *or* paye nous payons ils paient *or* payent	j'ai payé	je payais	je paierai *or* payerai	je paie *or* paye
60 peindre	je peins nous peignons ils peignent	j'ai peint	je peignais	je peindrai	je peigne
61 perdre	je perds	j'ai perdu	je perdais	je perdrai	je perde
62 plaire	je plais nous plaisons	j'ai plu	je plaisais	je plairai	je plaise
63 pleuvoir	il pleut	il a plu	il pleuvait	il pleuvra	il pleuve
64 pouvoir	see full verb table page 41				
65 prendre	je prends nous prenons ils prennent	j'ai pris	je prenais	je prendrai	je prenne
66 protéger -er verb with a spelling change	je protège tu protèges il protège nous protégeons vous protégez ils protègent	j'ai protégé	je protégeais nous protégions ils protégeaient	je protégerai	je protège

INFINITIVE	PRESENT	PERFECT	IMPERFECT	FUTURE	PRESENT SUBJUNCTIVE
67 **recevoir**	je reçois nous recevons ils reçoivent	j'ai reçu	je recevais	je recevrai	je reçoive
68 **rentrer** similar to **donner** [28], apart from the perfect tense	je rentre	je suis rentrée	je rentrais	je rentrerai	je rentre
69 **répondre**	je réponds	j'ai répondu	je répondais	je répondrai	je réponde
70 **résoudre**	je résous tu résous il résout nous résolvons vous résolvez ils résolvent	j'ai résolu	je résolvais	je résoudrai	je résolve
71 **rester** similar to **donner** [28], apart from the perfect tense	je reste	je suis resté(e)	je restais	je resterai	je reste
72 **retourner** similar to **donner** [28], apart from the perfect tense	je retourne	je suis retourné(e)	je retournais	je retournerai	je retourne
73 **revenir** similar to **venir** [89]	je reviens	je suis revenu(e)	je revenais	je reviendrai	je revienne
74 **rire**	je ris il rit nous rions ils rient	j'ai ri	je riais nous riions ils riaient	je rirai	je rie nous riions
75 **rompre**	je romps	j'ai rompu	je rompais	je romprai	je rompe
76 **savoir**	see full verb table page 42				
77 **sentir**	see full verb table page 43				
78 **servir**	je sers nous servons ils servent	j'ai servi	je servais	je servirai	je serve
79 **sortir** similar to **sentir** [77], apart from the perfect tense	je sors	je suis sorti(e)	je sortais	je sortirai	je sorte

INFINITIVE	PRESENT	PERFECT	IMPERFECT	FUTURE	PRESENT SUBJUNCTIVE
80 **suffire**	je suffis nous suffisons	j'ai suffi	je suffisais	je suffirai	je suffise
81 **suivre**	je suis nous suivons ils suivent	j'ai suivi	je suivais	je suivrai	je suive
82 **se taire**	see full verb table page 44				
83 **tenir** similar to **venir [89]**, apart from the perfect tense	je tiens	j'ai tenu	je tenais	je tiendrai	je tienne
84 **tomber** similar to **donner [28]**, apart from the perfect tense	je tombe	je suis tombé(e)	je tombais	je tomberai	je tombe
85 **traire**	je trais nous trayons ils traient	j'ai trait	je trayais	je trairai	je traie nous trayions ils traient
86 **vaincre**	je vaincs tu vaincs il vainc nous vain**qu**ons vous vain**qu**ez ils vain**qu**ent	j'ai vaincu	je vain**qu**ais	je vaincrai	je vain**qu**e
87 **valoir**	je v**aux** il v**aut** nous valons ils valent	j'ai valu	je valais	je v**aud**rai	je vai**ll**e nous valions vous valiez ils vai**ll**ent
88 **vendre**	see full verb table page 45				
89 **venir**	see full verb table page 46				
90 **vêtir**	je vêts	j'ai vêtu	je vêtais	je vêtirai	je vête
91 **vivre**	je vis nous vivons ils vivent	j'ai vécu	je vivais	je vivrai	je vive
92 **voir**	see full verb table page 47				
93 **vouloir**	see full verb table page 48				

acquérir (to acquire)

	PRESENT		PRESENT SUBJUNCTIVE
j'	acquiers	j'	acquière
tu	acquiers	tu	acquières
il/elle/on	acquiert	il/elle/on	acquière
nous	acquérons	nous	acquérions
vous	acquérez	vous	acquériez
ils/elles	acquièrent	ils/elles	acquièrent

	PERFECT		IMPERFECT
j'	ai acquis	j'	acquérais
tu	as acquis	tu	acquérais
il/elle/on	a acquis	il/elle/on	acquérait
nous	avons acquis	nous	acquérions
vous	avez acquis	vous	acquériez
ils/elles	ont acquis	ils/elles	acquéraient

	FUTURE		CONDITIONAL
j'	acquerrai	j'	acquerrais
tu	acquerras	tu	acquerrais
il/elle/on	acquerra	il/elle/on	acquerrait
nous	acquerrons	nous	acquerrions
vous	acquerrez	vous	acquerriez
ils/elles	acquerront	ils/elles	acquerraient

PRESENT PARTICIPLE	PAST PARTICIPLE
acquérant	acquis

IMPERATIVE

acquiers / acquérons / acquérez

EXAMPLE PHRASES

Elle **a acquis** la nationalité française en 2003.   She acquired French nationality in 2003.

je/j' = I tu = you il = he/it elle = she/it on = we/one nous = we vous = you ils/elles = they

aller (to go)

	PRESENT		PRESENT SUBJUNCTIVE
je	vais	j'	aille
tu	vas	tu	ailles
il/elle/on	va	il/elle/on	aille
nous	allons	nous	allions
vous	allez	vous	alliez
ils/elles	vont	ils/elles	aillent

	PERFECT		IMPERFECT
je	suis allé(e)	j'	allais
tu	es allé(e)	tu	allais
il/elle/on	est allé(e)	il/elle/on	allait
nous	sommes allé(e)s	nous	allions
vous	êtes allé(e)(s)	vous	alliez
ils/elles	sont allé(e)s	ils/elles	allaient

	FUTURE		CONDITIONAL
j'	irai	j'	irais
tu	iras	tu	irais
il/elle/on	ira	il/elle/on	irait
nous	irons	nous	irions
vous	irez	vous	iriez
ils/elles	iront	ils/elles	iraient

PRESENT PARTICIPLE	PAST PARTICIPLE
allant	allé

IMPERATIVE

va / allons / allez

EXAMPLE PHRASES

Vous **allez** au cinéma? Are you going to the cinema?
Je **suis allé** à Londres. I went to London.
Est-ce que tu **es** déjà **allé** en Allemagne? Have you ever been to Germany?

je/j' = I tu = you il = he/it elle = she/it on = we/one nous = we vous = you ils/elles = they

s'asseoir (to sit down)

	PRESENT		**PRESENT SUBJUNCTIVE**
je	m'assieds/m'assois	je	m'asseye
tu	t'assieds/t'assois	tu	t'asseyes
il/elle/on	s'assied/s'assoit	il/elle/on	s'asseye
nous	nous asseyons/	nous	nous asseyions
	nous assoyons	vous	vous asseyiez
vous	vous asseyez/	ils/elles	s'asseyent
	vous assoyez		
ils/elles	s'asseyent/s'assoient		

	PERFECT		**IMPERFECT**
je	me suis assis(e)	je	m'asseyais
tu	t'es assis(e)	tu	t'asseyais
il/elle/on	s'est assis(e)	il/elle/on	s'asseyait
nous	nous sommes assis(es)	nous	nous asseyions
vous	vous êtes assis(e(s))	vous	vous asseyiez
ils/elles	se sont assis(es)	ils/elles	s'asseyaient

	FUTURE		**CONDITIONAL**
je	m'assiérai	je	m'assiérais
tu	t'assiéras	tu	t'assiérais
il/elle/on	s'assiéra	il/elle/on	s'assiérait
nous	nous assiérons	nous	nous assiérions
vous	vous assiérez	vous	vous assiériez
ils/elles	s'assiéront	ils/elles	s'assiéraient

PRESENT PARTICIPLE	**PAST PARTICIPLE**
s'asseyant	assis

IMPERATIVE

assieds-toi / asseyons-nous / asseyez-vous

EXAMPLE PHRASES

Assieds-toi, Nicole.   Sit down Nicole.
Asseyez-vous, les enfants.   Sit down children.
Je peux **m'assoir**?   May I sit down?
Je **me suis assise** sur un chewing-gum!   I've sat on some chewing gum!

je/j' = I **tu** = you **il** = he/it **elle** = she/it **on** = we/one **nous** = we **vous** = you **ils/elles** = they

avoir (to have)

	PRESENT			PRESENT SUBJUNCTIVE
j'	ai		j'	aie
tu	as		tu	aies
il/elle/on	a		il/elle/on	ait
nous	avons		nous	ayons
vous	avez		vous	ayez
ils/elles	ont		ils/elles	aient

	PERFECT			IMPERFECT
j'	ai eu		j'	avais
tu	as eu		tu	avais
il/elle/on	a eu		il/elle/on	avait
nous	avons eu		nous	avions
vous	avez eu		vous	aviez
ils/elles	ont eu		ils/elles	avaient

	FUTURE			CONDITIONAL
j'	aurai		j'	aurais
tu	auras		tu	aurais
il/elle/on	aura		il/elle/on	aurait
nous	aurons		nous	aurions
vous	aurez		vous	auriez
ils/elles	auront		ils/elles	auraient

PRESENT PARTICIPLE

ayant

PAST PARTICIPLE

eu

IMPERATIVE

aie / ayons / ayez

EXAMPLE PHRASES

Il **a** les yeux bleus.   He's got blue eyes.
Quel âge **as**-tu?   How old are you?
Il **a eu** un accident.   He's had an accident.
J'**avais** faim.   I was hungry.
Il y **a** beaucoup de monde.   There are lots of people.

je/j' = I tu = you il = he/it elle = she/it on = we/one nous = we vous = you ils/elles = they

croire (to believe)

	PRESENT		PRESENT SUBJUNCTIVE
je	crois	je	croie
tu	crois	tu	croies
il/elle/on	croit	il/elle/on	croie
nous	croyons	nous	croyions
vous	croyez	vous	croyiez
ils/elles	croient	ils/elles	croient

	PERFECT		IMPERFECT
j'	ai cru	je	croyais
tu	as cru	tu	croyais
il/elle/on	a cru	il/elle/on	croyait
nous	avons cru	nous	croyions
vous	avez cru	vous	croyiez
ils/elles	ont cru	ils/elles	croyaient

	FUTURE		CONDITIONAL
je	croirai	je	croirais
tu	croiras	tu	croirais
il/elle/on	croira	il/elle/on	croirait
nous	croirons	nous	croirions
vous	croirez	vous	croiriez
ils/elles	croiront	ils/elles	croiraient

PRESENT PARTICIPLE

croyant

PAST PARTICIPLE

cru

IMPERATIVE

crois / croyons / croyez

EXAMPLE PHRASES

Je ne te **crois** pas.   I don't believe you.
J'**ai cru** que tu n'allais pas venir.   I thought you weren't going to come.
Elle **croyait** encore au père Noël.   She still believed in Santa.

je/j' = I **tu** = you **il** = he/it **elle** = she/it **on** = we/one **nous** = we **vous** = you **ils/elles** = they

32

devoir (to have to; to owe)

PRESENT

je	**dois**
tu	**dois**
il/elle/on	**doit**
nous	**devons**
vous	**devez**
ils/elles	**doivent**

PRESENT SUBJUNCTIVE

je	**doive**
tu	**doives**
il/elle/on	**doive**
nous	**devions**
vous	**deviez**
ils/elles	**doivent**

PERFECT

j'	**ai dû**
tu	**as dû**
il/elle/on	**a dû**
nous	**avons dû**
vous	**avez dû**
ils/elles	**ont dû**

IMPERFECT

je	**devais**
tu	**devais**
il/elle/on	**devait**
nous	**devions**
vous	**deviez**
ils/elles	**devaient**

FUTURE

je	**devrai**
tu	**devras**
il/elle/on	**devra**
nous	**devrons**
vous	**devrez**
ils/elles	**devront**

CONDITIONAL

je	**devrais**
tu	**devrais**
il/elle/on	**devrait**
nous	**devrions**
vous	**devriez**
ils/elles	**devraient**

PRESENT PARTICIPLE

devant

PAST PARTICIPLE

dû (*NB*: **due, dus, dues**)

IMPERATIVE

dois / devons / devez

EXAMPLE PHRASES

Je **dois** aller faire les courses ce matin.   I have to do the shopping this morning.
À quelle heure est-ce que tu **dois** partir?   What time do you have to leave?
Il **a dû** faire ses devoirs hier soir.   He had to do his homework last night.
Il **devait** prendre le train pour aller travailler.   He had to go to work by train.

je/j' = I **tu** = you **il** = he/it **elle** = she/it **on** = we/one **nous** = we **vous** = you **ils/elles** = they

dire (to say)

	PRESENT		PRESENT SUBJUNCTIVE
je	dis	je	dise
tu	dis	tu	dises
il/elle/on	dit	il/elle/on	dise
nous	disons	nous	disions
vous	dites	vous	disiez
ils/elles	disent	ils/elles	disent

	PERFECT		IMPERFECT
j'	ai dit	je	disais
tu	as dit	tu	disais
il/elle/on	a dit	il/elle/on	disait
nous	avons dit	nous	disions
vous	avez dit	vous	disiez
ils/elles	ont dit	ils/elles	disaient

	FUTURE		CONDITIONAL
je	dirai	je	dirais
tu	diras	tu	dirais
il/elle/on	dira	il/elle/on	dirait
nous	dirons	nous	dirions
vous	direz	vous	diriez
ils/elles	diront	ils/elles	diraient

PRESENT PARTICIPLE
disant

PAST PARTICIPLE
dit

IMPERATIVE
dis / disons / dites

EXAMPLE PHRASES

Qu'est-ce qu'elle **dit**? What is she saying?
"Bonjour!", **a**-t-il **dit**. "Hello!" he said.
Ils m'**ont dit** que le film était nul. They told me that the film was rubbish.
Comment ça **se dit** en anglais? How do you say that in English?

je/j' = I tu = you il = he/it elle = she/it on = we/one nous = we vous = you ils/elles = they

donner (to give)

	PRESENT		PRESENT SUBJUNCTIVE
je	donne	je	donne
tu	donnes	tu	donnes
il/elle/on	donne	il/elle/on	donne
nous	donnons	nous	donnions
vous	donnez	vous	donniez
ils/elles	donnent	ils/elles	donnent

	PERFECT		IMPERFECT
j'	ai donné	je	donnais
tu	as donné	tu	donnais
il/elle/on	a donné	il/elle/on	donnait
nous	avons donné	nous	donnions
vous	avez donné	vous	donniez
ils/elles	ont donné	ils/elles	donnaient

	FUTURE		CONDITIONAL
je	donnerai	je	donnerais
tu	donneras	tu	donnerais
il/elle/on	donnera	il/elle/on	donnerait
nous	donnerons	nous	donnerions
vous	donnerez	vous	donneriez
ils/elles	donneront	ils/elles	donneraient

PRESENT PARTICIPLE

donnant

PAST PARTICIPLE

donné

IMPERATIVE

donne / donnons / donnez

EXAMPLE PHRASES

Donne-moi la main. Give me your hand.
Est-ce que je t'**ai donné** mon adresse? Did I give you my address?
L'appartement **donne** sur la place. The flat overlooks the square.

je/j' = I tu = you il = he/it elle = she/it on = we/one nous = we vous = you ils/elles = they

être (to be)

	PRESENT			PRESENT SUBJUNCTIVE
je	**suis**		je	**sois**
tu	**es**		tu	**sois**
il/elle/on	**est**		il/elle/on	**soit**
nous	**sommes**		nous	**soyons**
vous	**êtes**		vous	**soyez**
ils/elles	**sont**		ils/elles	**soient**

	PERFECT			IMPERFECT
j'	**ai été**		j'	**étais**
tu	**as été**		tu	**étais**
il/elle/on	**a été**		il/elle/on	**était**
nous	**avons été**		nous	**étions**
vous	**avez été**		vous	**étiez**
ils/elles	**ont été**		ils/elles	**étaient**

	FUTURE			CONDITIONAL
je	**serai**		je	**serais**
tu	**seras**		tu	**serais**
il/elle/on	**sera**		il/elle/on	**serait**
nous	**serons**		nous	**serions**
vous	**serez**		vous	**seriez**
ils/elles	**seront**		ils/elles	**seraient**

PRESENT PARTICIPLE
étant

PAST PARTICIPLE
été

IMPERATIVE
sois / soyons / soyez

EXAMPLE PHRASES

Mon père **est** professeur.   My father's a teacher.
Quelle heure **est**-il? – Il **est** dix heures.   What time is it? – It's 10 o'clock.
Ils ne **sont** pas encore arrivés.   They haven't arrived yet.

je/j' = I **tu** = you **il** = he/it **elle** = she/it **on** = we/one **nous** = we **vous** = you **ils/elles** = they

faire (to do; to make)

	PRESENT		PRESENT SUBJUNCTIVE
je	fais	je	fasse
tu	fais	tu	fasses
il/elle/on	fait	il/elle/on	fasse
nous	faisons	nous	fassions
vous	faites	vous	fassiez
ils/elles	font	ils/elles	fassent

	PERFECT		IMPERFECT
j'	ai fait	je	faisais
tu	as fait	tu	faisais
il/elle/on	a fait	il/elle/on	faisait
nous	avons fait	nous	faisions
vous	avez fait	vous	faisiez
ils/elles	ont fait	ils/elles	faisaient

	FUTURE		CONDITIONAL
je	ferai	je	ferais
tu	feras	tu	ferais
il/elle/on	fera	il/elle/on	ferait
nous	ferons	nous	ferions
vous	ferez	vous	feriez
ils/elles	feront	ils/elles	feraient

PRESENT PARTICIPLE

faisant

PAST PARTICIPLE

fait

IMPERATIVE

fais / faisons / faites

EXAMPLE PHRASES

Qu'est-ce que tu **fais**?   What are you doing?
Qu'est-ce qu'il **a fait**?   What has he done? *or* What did he do?
J'**ai fait** un gâteau.   I've made a cake *or* I made a cake.
Il **s'est fait** couper les cheveux.   He's had his hair cut.

je/j' = I   tu = you   il = he/it   elle = she/it   on = we/one   nous = we   vous = you   ils/elles = they

finir (to finish)

PRESENT		PRESENT SUBJUNCTIVE	
je	finis	je	finisse
tu	finis	tu	finisses
il/elle/on	finit	il/elle/on	finisse
nous	finissons	nous	finissions
vous	finissez	vous	finissiez
ils/elles	finissent	ils/elles	finissent

PERFECT		IMPERFECT	
j'	ai fini	je	finissais
tu	as fini	tu	finissais
il/elle/on	a fini	il/elle/on	finissait
nous	avons fini	nous	finissions
vous	avez fini	vous	finissiez
ils/elles	ont fini	ils/elles	finissaient

FUTURE		CONDITIONAL	
je	finirai	je	finirais
tu	finiras	tu	finirais
il/elle/on	finira	il/elle/on	finirait
nous	finirons	nous	finirions
vous	finirez	vous	finiriez
ils/elles	finiront	ils/elles	finiraient

PRESENT PARTICIPLE

finissant

PAST PARTICIPLE

fini

IMPERATIVE

finis / finissons / finissez

EXAMPLE PHRASES

Finis ta soupe! Finish your soup!
J'ai **fini**! I've finished!
Je **finirai** mes devoirs demain. I'll finish my homework tomorrow.

je/j' = I **tu** = you **il** = he/it **elle** = she/it **on** = we/one **nous** = we **vous** = you **ils/elles** = they

mettre (to put)

PRESENT		PRESENT SUBJUNCTIVE	
je	mets	je	mette
tu	mets	tu	mettes
il/elle/on	met	il/elle/on	mette
nous	mettons	nous	mettions
vous	mettez	vous	mettiez
ils/elles	mettent	ils/elles	mettent

PERFECT		IMPERFECT	
j'	ai mis	je	mettais
tu	as mis	tu	mettais
il/elle/on	a mis	il/elle/on	mettait
nous	avons mis	nous	mettions
vous	avez mis	vous	mettiez
ils/elles	ont mis	ils/elles	mettaient

FUTURE		CONDITIONAL	
je	mettrai	je	mettrais
tu	mettras	tu	mettrais
il/elle/on	mettra	il/elle/on	mettrait
nous	mettrons	nous	mettrions
vous	mettrez	vous	mettriez
ils/elles	mettront	ils/elles	mettraient

PRESENT PARTICIPLE

mettant

PAST PARTICIPLE

mis

IMPERATIVE

mets / mettons / mettez

EXAMPLE PHRASES

Mets ton manteau!   Put your coat on!
Où est-ce que tu **as mis** les clés?   Where have you put the keys?
J'**ai mis** le livre sur la table.   I put the book on the table.
Elle **s'est mise** à pleurer.   She started crying.

je/j' = I   tu = you   il = he/it   elle = she/it   on = we/one   nous = we   vous = you   ils/elles = they

ouvrir (to open)

	PRESENT		PRESENT SUBJUNCTIVE
j'	ouvre	j'	ouvre
tu	ouvres	tu	ouvres
il/elle/on	ouvre	il/elle/on	ouvre
nous	ouvrons	nous	ouvrions
vous	ouvrez	vous	ouvriez
ils/elles	ouvrent	ils/elles	ouvrent

	PERFECT		IMPERFECT
j'	ai ouvert	j'	ouvrais
tu	as ouvert	tu	ouvrais
il/elle/on	a ouvert	il/elle/on	ouvrait
nous	avons ouvert	nous	ouvrions
vous	avez ouvert	vous	ouvriez
ils/elles	ont ouvert	ils/elles	ouvraient

	FUTURE		CONDITIONAL
j'	ouvrirai	j'	ouvrirais
tu	ouvriras	tu	ouvrirais
il/elle/on	ouvrira	il/elle/on	ouvrirait
nous	ouvrirons	nous	ouvririons
vous	ouvrirez	vous	ouvririez
ils/elles	ouvriront	ils/elles	ouvriraient

PRESENT PARTICIPLE

ouvrant

PAST PARTICIPLE

ouvert

IMPERATIVE

ouvre / ouvrons / ouvrez

EXAMPLE PHRASES

Elle **a ouvert** la porte.   She opened the door.
Est-ce que tu pourrais **ouvrir** la fenêtre?   Could you open the window?
Je me suis coupé en **ouvrant** une boîte de conserve.   I cut myself opening a tin.
La porte **s'est ouverte**.   The door opened.

je/j' = I **tu** = you **il** = he/it **elle** = she/it **on** = we/one **nous** = we **vous** = you **ils/elles** = they

pouvoir (to be able)

PRESENT		PRESENT SUBJUNCTIVE	
je	**peux**	je	**puisse**
tu	**peux**	tu	**puisses**
il/elle/on	**peut**	il/elle/on	**puisse**
nous	**pouvons**	nous	**puissions**
vous	**pouvez**	vous	**puissiez**
ils/elles	**peuvent**	ils/elles	**puissent**

PERFECT		IMPERFECT	
j'	**ai pu**	je	**pouvais**
tu	**as pu**	tu	**pouvais**
il/elle/on	**a pu**	il/elle/on	**pouvait**
nous	**avons pu**	nous	**pouvions**
vous	**avez pu**	vous	**pouviez**
ils/elles	**ont pu**	ils/elles	**pouvaient**

FUTURE		CONDITIONAL	
je	**pourrai**	je	**pourrais**
tu	**pourras**	tu	**pourrais**
il/elle/on	**pourra**	il/elle/on	**pourrait**
nous	**pourrons**	nous	**pourrions**
vous	**pourrez**	vous	**pourriez**
ils/elles	**pourront**	ils/elles	**pourraient**

PRESENT PARTICIPLE	PAST PARTICIPLE
pouvant	pu

IMPERATIVE

not used

EXAMPLE PHRASES

Je **peux** t'aider, si tu veux.   I can help you if you like.
J'ai fait tout ce que j'**ai pu**.   I did all I could.
Je ne **pourrai** pas venir samedi.   I won't be able to come on Saturday.

je/j' = I tu = you il = he/it elle = she/it on = we/one nous = we vous = you ils/elles = they

savoir (to know)

	PRESENT		PRESENT SUBJUNCTIVE
je	sais	je	sache
tu	sais	tu	saches
il/elle/on	sait	il/elle/on	sache
nous	savons	nous	sachions
vous	savez	vous	sachiez
ils/elles	savent	ils/elles	sachent

	PERFECT		IMPERFECT
j'	ai su	je	savais
tu	as su	tu	savais
il/elle/on	a su	il/elle/on	savait
nous	avons su	nous	savions
vous	avez su	vous	saviez
ils/elles	ont su	ils/elles	savaient

	FUTURE		CONDITIONAL
je	saurai	je	saurais
tu	sauras	tu	saurais
il/elle/on	saura	il/elle/on	saurait
nous	saurons	nous	saurions
vous	saurez	vous	sauriez
ils/elles	sauront	ils/elles	sauraient

PRESENT PARTICIPLE
sachant

PAST PARTICIPLE
su

IMPERATIVE
sache / sachons / sachez

EXAMPLE PHRASES

Tu **sais** ce que tu vas faire l'année prochaine?   Do you know what you're doing next year?
Je ne **sais** pas.   I don't know.
Elle ne **sait** pas nager.   She can't swim.
Tu **savais** que son père était pakistanais?   Did you know her father was Pakistani?

je/j' = I **tu** = you **il** = he/it **elle** = she/it **on** = we/one **nous** = we **vous** = you **ils/elles** = they

sentir (to smell; to feel)

	PRESENT		PRESENT SUBJUNCTIVE
je	sens	je	sente
tu	sens	tu	sentes
il/elle/on	sent	il/elle/on	sente
nous	sentons	nous	sentions
vous	sentez	vous	sentiez
ils/elles	sentent	ils/elles	sentent

	PERFECT		IMPERFECT
j'	ai senti	je	sentais
tu	as senti	tu	sentais
il/elle/on	a senti	il/elle/on	sentait
nous	avons senti	nous	sentions
vous	avez senti	vous	sentiez
ils/elles	ont senti	ils/elles	sentaient

	FUTURE		CONDITIONAL
je	sentirai	je	sentirais
tu	sentiras	tu	sentirais
il/elle/on	sentira	il/elle/on	sentirait
nous	sentirons	nous	sentirions
vous	sentirez	vous	sentiriez
ils/elles	sentiront	ils/elles	sentiraient

PRESENT PARTICIPLE	PAST PARTICIPLE
sentant	senti

IMPERATIVE

sens / sentons / sentez

EXAMPLE PHRASES

Ça **sentait** mauvais.   It smelt bad.
Je n'**ai** rien **senti**.   I didn't feel a thing.
Elle ne **se sent** pas bien.   She's not feeling well.

se taire (to stop talking)

	PRESENT		PRESENT SUBJUNCTIVE
je	me tais	je	me taise
tu	te tais	tu	te taises
il/elle/on	se tait	il/elle/on	se taise
nous	nous taisons	nous	nous taisions
vous	vous taisez	vous	vous taisiez
ils/elles	se taisent	ils/elles	se taisent

	PERFECT		IMPERFECT
je	me suis tu(e)	je	me taisais
tu	t'es tu(e)	tu	te taisais
il/elle/on	s'est tu(e)	il/elle/on	se taisait
nous	nous sommes tu(e)s	nous	nous taisions
vous	vous êtes tu(e)(s)	vous	vous taisiez
ils/elles	se sont tu(e)s	ils/elles	se taisaient

	FUTURE		CONDITIONAL
je	me tairai	je	me tairais
tu	te tairas	tu	te tairais
il/elle/on	se taira	il/elle/on	se tairait
nous	nous tairons	nous	nous tairions
vous	vous tairez	vous	vous tairiez
ils/elles	se tairont	ils/elles	se tairaient

PRESENT PARTICIPLE	PAST PARTICIPLE
se taisant	tu

IMPERATIVE

tais-toi / taisons-nous / taisez-vous

EXAMPLE PHRASES

Il **s'est tu**. He stopped talking.
Taisez-vous! Be quiet!
Sophie, **tais-toi**! Be quiet Sophie!

je/j' = I tu = you il = he/it elle = she/it on = we/one nous = we vous = you ils/elles = they

vendre (to sell)

PRESENT		PRESENT SUBJUNCTIVE	
je	**vends**	je	**vende**
tu	**vends**	tu	**vendes**
il/elle/on	**vend**	il/elle/on	**vende**
nous	**vendons**	nous	**vendions**
vous	**vendez**	vous	**vendiez**
ils/elles	**vendent**	ils/elles	**vendent**

PERFECT		IMPERFECT	
j'	**ai vendu**	je	**vendais**
tu	**as vendu**	tu	**vendais**
il/elle/on	**a vendu**	il/elle/on	**vendait**
nous	**avons vendu**	nous	**vendions**
vous	**avez vendu**	vous	**vendiez**
ils/elles	**ont vendu**	ils/elles	**vendaient**

FUTURE		CONDITIONAL	
je	**vendrai**	je	**vendrais**
tu	**vendras**	tu	**vendrais**
il/elle/on	**vendra**	il/elle/on	**vendrait**
nous	**vendrons**	nous	**vendrions**
vous	**vendrez**	vous	**vendriez**
ils/elles	**vendront**	ils/elles	**vendraient**

PRESENT PARTICIPLE	PAST PARTICIPLE
vendant	vendu

IMPERATIVE

vends / vendons / vendez

EXAMPLE PHRASES

Il m'**a vendu** son vélo pour 50 euros.   He sold me his bike for 50 euros.
Est-ce que vous **vendez** des piles?   Do you sell batteries?
Elle voudrait **vendre** sa voiture.   She would like to sell her car.

je/j' = I **tu** = you **il** = he/it **elle** = she/it **on** = we/one **nous** = we **vous** = you **ils/elles** = they

venir (to come)

	PRESENT		PRESENT SUBJUNCTIVE
je	viens	je	vienne
tu	viens	tu	viennes
il/elle/on	vient	il/elle/on	vienne
nous	venons	nous	venions
vous	venez	vous	veniez
ils/elles	viennent	ils/elles	viennent

	PERFECT		IMPERFECT
je	suis venu(e)	je	venais
tu	es venu(e)	tu	venais
il/elle/on	est venu(e)	il/elle/on	venait
nous	sommes venu(e)s	nous	venions
vous	êtes venu(e)(s)	vous	veniez
ils/elles	sont venu(e)s	ils/elles	venaient

	FUTURE		CONDITIONAL
je	viendrai	je	viendrais
tu	viendras	tu	viendrais
il/elle/on	viendra	il/elle/on	viendrait
nous	viendrons	nous	viendrions
vous	viendrez	vous	viendriez
ils/elles	viendront	ils/elles	viendraient

PRESENT PARTICIPLE	PAST PARTICIPLE
venant	venu

IMPERATIVE

viens / venons / venez

EXAMPLE PHRASES

Elle ne **viendra** pas cette année.   She won't be coming this year.
Fatou et Malik **viennent** du Sénégal.   Fatou and Malik come from Senegal.
Je **viens** de manger.   I've just eaten.

je/j' = I tu = you il = he/it elle = she/it on = we/one nous = we vous = you ils/elles = they

voir (to see)

	PRESENT		PRESENT SUBJUNCTIVE
je	**vois**	je	**voie**
tu	**vois**	tu	**voies**
il/elle/on	**voit**	il/elle/on	**voie**
nous	**voyons**	nous	**voyions**
vous	**voyez**	vous	**voyiez**
ils/elles	**voient**	ils/elles	**voient**

	PERFECT		IMPERFECT
j'	**ai vu**	je	**voyais**
tu	**as vu**	tu	**voyais**
il/elle/on	**a vu**	il/elle/on	**voyait**
nous	**avons vu**	nous	**voyions**
vous	**avez vu**	vous	**voyiez**
ils/elles	**ont vu**	ils/elles	**voyaient**

	FUTURE		CONDITIONAL
je	**verrai**	je	**verrais**
tu	**verras**	tu	**verrais**
il/elle/on	**verra**	il/elle/on	**verrait**
nous	**verrons**	nous	**verrions**
vous	**verrez**	vous	**verriez**
ils/elles	**verront**	ils/elles	**verraient**

PRESENT PARTICIPLE	PAST PARTICIPLE
voyant	vu

IMPERATIVE

vois / voyons / voyez

EXAMPLE PHRASES

Venez me **voir** quand vous serez à Paris.   Come and see me when you're in Paris.
Je ne **vois** rien sans mes lunettes.   I can't see anything without my glasses.
Est-ce que tu l'**as vu**?   Did you see him? *or* Have you seen him?
Est-ce que cette tache **se voit**?   Does that stain show?

je/j' = I tu = you il = he/it elle = she/it on = we/one nous = we vous = you ils/elles = they

vouloir (to want)

	PRESENT		PRESENT SUBJUNCTIVE
je	veux	je	veuille
tu	veux	tu	veuilles
il/elle/on	veut	il/elle/on	veuille
nous	voulons	nous	voulions
vous	voulez	vous	vouliez
ils/elles	veulent	ils/elles	veuillent

	PERFECT		IMPERFECT
j'	ai voulu	je	voulais
tu	as voulu	tu	voulais
il/elle/on	a voulu	il/elle/on	voulait
nous	avons voulu	nous	voulions
vous	avez voulu	vous	vouliez
ils/elles	ont voulu	ils/elles	voulaient

	FUTURE		CONDITIONAL
je	voudrai	je	voudrais
tu	voudras	tu	voudrais
il/elle/on	voudra	il/elle/on	voudrait
nous	voudrons	nous	voudrions
vous	voudrez	vous	voudriez
ils/elles	voudront	ils/elles	voudraient

PRESENT PARTICIPLE	PAST PARTICIPLE
voulant	voulu

IMPERATIVE

veuille / veuillons / veuillez

....

EXAMPLE PHRASES

Elle **veut** un vélo pour Noël.   She wants a bike for Christmas.
Ils **voulaient** aller au cinéma.   They wanted to go to the cinema.
Tu **voudrais** une tasse de thé?   Would you like a cup of tea?

je/j' = I tu = you il = he/it elle = she/it on = we/one nous = we vous = you ils/elles = they

Aa

a ARTICLE

> **LANGUAGE TIP** Use **un** for masculine nouns, **une** for feminine nouns.

un *masc*

□ a book un livre □ a year ago il y a un an

une *fem*

□ an apple une pomme

> **LANGUAGE TIP** You do not translate 'a' when you want to describe somebody's job in French.

□ He's a butcher. Il est boucher. □ She's a doctor. Elle est médecin.

■ **once a week** une fois par semaine
■ **10 km an hour** dix kilomètres à l'heure
■ **30 pence a kilo** trente pence le kilo
■ **a hundred pounds** cent livres

AA NOUN (= *Automobile Association*)
la société de dépannage

aback ADVERB

■ **I was taken aback by his reaction.** Sa réaction m'a déconcentré.

to **abandon** VERB
abandonner

abbey NOUN
l' abbaye *fem*

abbreviation NOUN
l' abréviation *fem*

ability NOUN

■ **to have the ability to do something** être capable de faire quelque chose

able ADJECTIVE

■ **to be able to do something** être capable de faire quelque chose

to **abolish** VERB
abolir

abortion NOUN
l' avortement *masc*

■ **She had an abortion.** Elle s'est fait avorter.

about PREPOSITION, ADVERB

1 à propos de (*concerning*)

□ I'm phoning you about tomorrow's meeting. Je vous appelle à propos de la réunion de demain.

2 environ (*approximately*)

□ It takes about 10 hours. Ça prend dix heures environ.

■ **about a hundred pounds** une centaine de livres

■ **at about 11 o'clock** vers onze heures

3 dans (*around*)

□ to walk about the town se promener dans la ville

4 sur

□ a book about London un livre sur Londres

■ **to be about to do something** être sur le point de faire quelque chose □ I was about to go out. J'étais sur le point de sortir.

■ **to talk about something** parler de quelque chose

■ **What's it about?** De quoi s'agit-il?

■ **How about going to the cinema?** Et si nous allions au cinéma?

above PREPOSITION, ADVERB

1 au-dessus de (*higher than*)

□ He put his hands above his head. Il a mis ses mains au-dessus de sa tête.

■ **the flat above** l'appartement du dessus
■ **mentioned above** mentionné ci-dessus
■ **above all** par-dessus tout

2 plus de (*more than*)

□ above 40 degrees plus de quarante degrés

abroad ADVERB
à l'étranger

□ to go abroad partir à l'étranger

abrupt ADJECTIVE
brusque (FEM brusque)

□ He was a bit abrupt with me. Il s'est montré un peu brusque avec moi.

abruptly ADVERB
brusquement

□ He got up abruptly. Il s'est levé brusquement.

absence NOUN
l' absence *fem*

absent ADJECTIVE
absent (FEM absente)

absent-minded ADJECTIVE
distrait (FEM distraite)

□ She's a bit absent-minded. Elle est un peu

distraite.

absolutely ADVERB

1 tout à fait (completely)

□ Chantal's absolutely right. Chantal a tout à fait raison.

2 absolument

□ Do you think it's a good idea? — Absolutely! Tu trouves que c'est une bonne idée? — Absolument!

absorbed ADJECTIVE

■ **to be absorbed in something** être absorbé par quelque chose

■ **to be absorbed in a book** être plongé dans un livre

absurd ADJECTIVE

absurde (FEM absurde)

□ That's absurd! C'est absurde!

abuse NOUN

▷ see also **abuse** VERB

l' abus masc (misuse)

■ **to shout abuse at somebody** insulter quelqu'un

■ **the issue of child abuse** la question des enfants maltraités

■ **the problem of drug abuse** le problème de la drogue

to **abuse** VERB

▷ see also **abuse** NOUN

1 maltraiter

□ abused children les enfants maltraités masc pl

■ **to be abused** être maltraité (child, woman)

2 injurier (insult)

■ **to abuse drugs** se droguer

abusive ADJECTIVE

insultant (FEM insultante) (insulting)

□ abusive behaviour un comportement insultant

■ **When I refused, he became abusive.** Quand j'ai refusé, il s'est mis à m'injurier.

■ **children with abusive parents** les enfants maltraités par leurs parents

academic ADJECTIVE

universitaire (FEM universitaire)

□ the academic year l'année universitaire fem

academy NOUN

le collège

□ a military academy un collège militaire

to **accelerate** VERB

accélérer

accelerator NOUN

l' accélérateur masc

accent NOUN

l' accent masc

□ He's got a French accent. Il a l'accent

français.

to **accept** VERB

accepter

acceptable ADJECTIVE

acceptable (FEM acceptable)

access NOUN

1 l' accès masc

□ He has access to confidential information. Il a accès à des renseignements confidentiels.

2 le droit de visite

□ Her ex-husband has access to the children. Son ex-mari a le droit de visite.

accessible ADJECTIVE

accessible (FEM accessible)

accessory NOUN

l' accessoire masc

□ fashion accessories les accessoires de mode

accident NOUN

l' accident masc

□ to have an accident avoir un accident

■ **by accident 1** (by mistake) accidentellement □ The burglar killed him by accident. Le cambrioleur l'a tué accidentellement. **2** (by chance) par hasard □ She met him by accident. Elle l'a rencontré par hasard.

accidental ADJECTIVE

accidentel (FEM accidentelle)

to **accommodate** VERB

recevoir

□ The hotel can accommodate 50 people. L'hôtel peut recevoir cinquante personnes.

accommodation NOUN

le logement

to **accompany** VERB

accompagner

accord NOUN

■ **of his own accord** de son plein gré □ He left of his own accord. Il est parti de son plein gré.

accordingly ADVERB

en conséquence

according to PREPOSITION

selon

□ According to him, everyone had gone. Selon lui, tout le monde était parti.

accordion NOUN

l' accordéon masc

account NOUN

1 le compte

□ a bank account un compte en banque

■ **to do the accounts** tenir la comptabilité

2 le compte rendu (PL les comptes rendus) (report)

□ He gave a detailed account of what

happened. Il a donné un compte rendu
détaillé des événements.

■ **to take something into account** tenir
compte de quelque chose

■ **on account of** à cause de □ We couldn't
go out on account of the bad weather. Nous
n'avons pas pu sortir à cause du mauvais
temps.

to **account for** VERB
expliquer

□ She had to account for her absence. Elle a
dû expliquer son absence.

accountable ADJECTIVE

■ **to be accountable to someone for
something** être responsable de quelque
chose devant quelqu'un

accountancy NOUN
la comptabilité

accountant NOUN
le/la comptable

□ She's an accountant. Elle est comptable.

accuracy NOUN
l' exactitude *fem*

accurate ADJECTIVE
précis (FEM précise)

□ accurate information les renseignements
précis *masc pl*

accurately ADVERB
avec précision

accusation NOUN
l' accusation *fem*

to **accuse** VERB

■ **to accuse somebody of something**
accuser quelqu'un de quelque chose □ The
police are accusing her of murder. La police
l'accuse de meurtre.

ace NOUN
l' as *masc*

□ the ace of hearts l'as de cœur

ache NOUN
▷ *see also* **ache** VERB
la douleur

to **ache** VERB
▷ *see also* **ache** NOUN

■ **My leg's aching.** J'ai mal à la jambe.

to **achieve** VERB
1 atteindre *(an aim)*
2 remporter *(victory)*

achievement NOUN
l' exploit *masc*

□ That was quite an achievement. C'était
un véritable exploit.

acid NOUN
l' acide *masc*

acid rain NOUN
les pluies acides *fem pl*

acne NOUN

l' acné *fem*

acre NOUN
le demi-hectare

> **DID YOU KNOW...?**
> In France, land is measured in
> hectares. One acre is about 0.4
> hectares.

acrobat NOUN
l' acrobate *masc/fem*

□ He's an acrobat. Il est acrobate.

across PREPOSITION, ADVERB
de l'autre côté de

□ the shop across the road la boutique de
l'autre côté de la rue

■ **to walk across the road** traverser la rue

■ **to run across the road** traverser la rue en
courant

■ **across from** *(opposite)* en face de □ He
sat down across from her. Il s'est assis en
face d'elle.

to **act** VERB
▷ *see also* **act** NOUN
1 jouer *(in play, film)*

□ He acts really well. Il joue vraiment bien.
□ She's acting the part of Juliet. Elle joue le
rôle de Juliette.
2 agir *(take action)*

□ The police acted quickly. La police a agi
rapidement.

■ **She acts as his interpreter.** Elle lui sert
d'interprète.

act NOUN
▷ *see also* **act** VERB
l' acte *masc (in play)*

□ in the first act au premier acte

action NOUN
l' action *fem*

□ The film was full of action. Il y avait
beaucoup d'action dans le film.

■ **to take firm action against** prendre des
mesures énergiques contre

active ADJECTIVE
actif (FEM active)

□ He's a very active person. Il est très actif.

■ **an active volcano** un volcan en activité

activity NOUN
l' activité *fem*

□ outdoor activities les activités de plein air

actor NOUN
l' acteur *masc*

□ Brad Pitt is a well-known actor. Brad Pitt
est un acteur connu.

actress NOUN
l' actrice *fem*

□ Julia Roberts is a well-known actress. Julia
Roberts est une actrice connue.

actual ADJECTIVE

réel (FEM réelle)

□ The film is based on actual events. Le film repose sur des faits réels.

■ **What's the actual amount?** Quel est le montant exact?

◯ **LANGUAGE TIP** Be careful not to translate **actual** by **actuel**.

actually ADVERB

1 vraiment (really)

□ Did it actually happen? Est-ce que c'est vraiment arrivé?

2 en fait (in fact)

□ Actually, I don't know him at all. En fait, je ne le connais pas du tout.

◯ **LANGUAGE TIP** Be careful not to translate **actually** by **actuellement**.

acupuncture NOUN

l' acuponcture fem

ad NOUN

1 l' annonce fem (in paper)

2 la pub (on TV, radio)

AD ABBREVIATION

ap. J.-C. (= après Jésus-Christ)

□ in 800 AD en huit cents après Jésus-Christ

to **adapt** VERB

adapter

□ His novel was adapted for television. Son roman a été adapté pour la télévision.

■ **to adapt to something** (get used to) s'adapter à quelque chose □ He adapted to his new school very quickly. Il s'est adapté très vite à sa nouvelle école.

adaptor NOUN

l' adaptateur masc

to **add** VERB

ajouter

□ Add two eggs to the mixture. Ajoutez deux œufs au mélange.

to **add up** VERB

additionner

□ Add the figures up. Additionnez les chiffres.

addict NOUN

le drogué

la droguée (drug addict)

■ **Jean-Pierre's a football addict.** Jean-Pierre est un mordu de football.

addicted ADJECTIVE

■ **to be addicted to** (drug) s'adonner à □ She's addicted to heroin. Elle s'adonne à l'héroïne.

■ **She's addicted to soap operas.** C'est une mordue des soaps.

addition NOUN

■ **in addition** en plus □ He's broken his leg and, in addition, he's caught a cold. Il s'est cassé la jambe et en plus, il a attrapé un

rhume.

■ **in addition to** en plus de □ There's a postage fee in addition to the repair charge. Il y a des frais de port en plus du prix de la réparation.

address NOUN

l' adresse fem

□ What's your address? Quelle est votre adresse?

adjective NOUN

l' adjectif masc

to **adjust** VERB

régler

□ You can adjust the height of the chair. Tu peux régler la hauteur de la chaise.

■ **to adjust to something** (get used to) s'adapter à quelque chose □ He adjusted to his new school very quickly. Il s'est adapté très vite à sa nouvelle école.

adjustable ADJECTIVE

réglable (FEM réglable)

administration NOUN

l' administration fem

admiral NOUN

l' amiral masc

to **admire** VERB

admirer

admission NOUN

l' entrée fem

■ **'admission free'** 'entrée gratuite'

to **admit** VERB

1 admettre (agree)

□ I must admit that ... Je dois admettre que ...

2 reconnaître (confess)

□ He admitted that he'd done it. Il a reconnu qu'il l'avait fait.

admittance NOUN

■ **'no admittance'** 'accès interdit'

adolescence NOUN

l' adolescence fem

adolescent NOUN

l' adolescent masc

l' adolescente fem

to **adopt** VERB

adopter

□ Phil was adopted. Phil a été adopté.

adopted ADJECTIVE

adoptif (FEM adoptive)

□ an adopted son un fils adoptif

adoption NOUN

l' adoption fem

to **adore** VERB

adorer

Adriatic Sea NOUN

la mer Adriatique

adult NOUN

l' adulte *masc/fem*
- **adult education** l'enseignement pour adultes *masc*

to **advance** VERB
▷ *see also* **advance** NOUN
1 avancer *(move forward)*
□ The troops are advancing. Les troupes avancent.
2 progresser *(progress)*
□ Technology has advanced a lot. La technologie a beaucoup progressé.

advance NOUN
▷ *see also* **advance** VERB
- **in advance** à l'avance □ They bought the tickets in advance. Ils ont acheté les billets à l'avance.

advance booking NOUN
- **Advance booking is essential.** Il est indispensable de réserver.

advanced ADJECTIVE
avancé (FEM avancée)

advantage NOUN
l' avantage *masc*
□ Going to university has many advantages. Aller à l'université présente de nombreux avantages.
- **to take advantage of something** profiter de quelque chose □ He took advantage of the good weather to go for a walk. Il a profité du beau temps pour faire une promenade.
- **to take advantage of somebody** exploiter quelqu'un □ The company was taking advantage of its employees. La société exploitait ses employés.

adventure NOUN
l' aventure *fem*

adverb NOUN
l' adverbe *masc*

advert, advertisement NOUN
1 la publicité *(on TV)*
2 l' annonce *fem (in newspaper)*

to **advertise** VERB
faire de la publicité pour
□ They're advertising the new model. Ils font de la publicité pour leur nouveau modèle.
- **Jobs are advertised in the paper.** Le journal publie des annonces d'emplois.

advertising NOUN
la publicité

advice NOUN
les conseils *masc pl*
□ to give somebody advice donner des conseils à quelqu'un
- **a piece of advice** un conseil □ He gave me a good piece of advice. Il m'a donné un

bon conseil.

to **advise** VERB
conseiller
□ He advised me to wait. Il m'a conseillé d'attendre. □ He advised me not to go there. Il m'a conseillé de ne pas y aller.

aerial NOUN
l' antenne *fem*

aerobics NOUN
l' aérobic *fem*
□ I'm going to aerobics tonight. Je vais au cours d'aérobic ce soir.

aeroplane NOUN
l' avion *masc*

aerosol NOUN
la bombe

affair NOUN
1 l' aventure *fem (romantic)*
□ to have an affair with somebody avoir une aventure avec quelqu'un
2 l' affaire *fem (event)*

to **affect** VERB
affecter

affectionate ADJECTIVE
affectueux (FEM affectueuse)

to **afford** VERB
avoir les moyens d'acheter
□ I can't afford a new pair of jeans. Je n'ai pas les moyens d'acheter un nouveau jean.
- **We can't afford to go on holiday.** Nous n'avons pas les moyens de partir en vacances.

afraid ADJECTIVE
- **to be afraid of something** avoir peur de quelque chose □ I'm afraid of spiders. J'ai peur des araignées.
- **I'm afraid I can't come.** Je crains de ne pouvoir venir.
- **I'm afraid so.** Hélas oui.
- **I'm afraid not.** Hélas non.

Africa NOUN
l' Afrique *fem*
- **in Africa** en Afrique

African NOUN
▷ *see also* **African** ADJECTIVE
l' Africain *masc*
l' Africaine *fem*

African ADJECTIVE
▷ *see also* **African** NOUN
africain (FEM africaine)

after PREPOSITION, ADVERB, CONJUNCTION
après
□ after dinner après le dîner □ He ran after me. Il a couru après moi. □ soon after peu après
- **after I'd had a rest** après m'être reposé
- **after having asked** après avoir demandé

299

■ **after all** après tout □ After all, nobody can make us go. Après tout, personne ne peut nous obliger à y aller.

afternoon NOUN
l' après-midi *masc/fem*
□ 3 o'clock in the afternoon trois heures de l'après-midi □ this afternoon cet après-midi □ on Saturday afternoon samedi après-midi

afters NOUN
le dessert

aftershave NOUN
l' après-rasage *masc*

afterwards ADVERB
après
□ She left not long afterwards. Elle est partie peu de temps après.

again ADVERB
1 de nouveau *(once more)*
□ They're friends again. Ils sont de nouveau amis.
2 encore une fois *(one more time)*
□ Can you tell me again? Tu peux me le dire encore une fois?
■ **not ... again** ne ... plus □ I won't go there again. Je n'y retournerai plus.
■ **Do it again!** Refais-le!
■ **again and again** à plusieurs reprises

against PREPOSITION
contre
□ He leant against the wall. Il s'est appuyé contre le mur. □ I'm against nuclear testing. Je suis contre les essais nucléaires.

age NOUN
l' âge *masc*
□ at the age of 16 à l'âge de seize ans □ an age limit une limite d'âge
■ **I haven't been to the cinema for ages.** Ça fait une éternité que je ne suis pas allé au cinéma.

aged ADJECTIVE
■ **aged 10** âgé de dix ans

agenda NOUN
l' ordre du jour *masc*
□ on the agenda à l'ordre du jour □ the agenda for today's meeting l'ordre du jour de la réunion d'aujourd'hui

> LANGUAGE TIP Be careful not to translate **agenda** by the French word **agenda**.

agent NOUN
l' agent *masc*
□ an estate agent un agent immobilier □ a travel agent un agent de voyage

aggressive ADJECTIVE
agressif (FEM agressive)

ago ADVERB

■ **two days ago** il y a deux jours
■ **two years ago** il y a deux ans
■ **not long ago** il n'y a pas longtemps
■ **How long ago did it happen?** Il y a combien de temps que c'est arrivé?

agony NOUN
■ **to be in agony** souffrir le martyre □ He was in agony. Il souffrait le martyre.

to **agree** VERB
■ **to agree with** être d'accord avec □ I agree with Carol. Je suis d'accord avec Carol.
■ **to agree to do something** accepter de faire quelque chose □ He agreed to go and pick her up. Il a accepté d'aller la chercher.
■ **to agree that ...** admettre que ... □ I agree that it's difficult. J'admets que c'est difficile.
■ **Garlic doesn't agree with me.** Je ne supporte pas l'ail.

agreed ADJECTIVE
convenu (FEM convenue)
□ at the agreed time au moment convenu

agreement NOUN
l' accord *masc*
■ **to be in agreement** être d'accord □ Everybody was in agreement with Ray. Tout le monde était d'accord avec Ray.

agricultural ADJECTIVE
agricole (FEM agricole)

agriculture NOUN
l' agriculture *fem*

ahead ADVERB
devant
□ She looked straight ahead. Elle regardait droit devant elle.
■ **ahead of time** en avance
■ **to plan ahead** organiser à l'avance
■ **The French are 5 points ahead.** Les Français ont cinq points d'avance.
■ **Go ahead!** Allez-y!

aid NOUN
■ **in aid of charity** au profit d'associations caritatives

AIDS NOUN
le sida

to **aim** VERB
▷ *see also* **aim** NOUN
■ **to aim at** braquer sur □ He aimed a gun at me. Il a braqué un revolver sur moi.
■ **The film is aimed at children.** Le film est destiné aux enfants.
■ **to aim to do something** avoir l'intention de faire quelque chose □ Janice aimed to leave at 5 o'clock. Janice avait l'intention de partir à cinq heures.

aim NOUN
▷ *see also* **aim** VERB

l' objectif *masc*
□ The aim of the festival is to raise money. L'objectif du festival est de collecter des fonds.

air NOUN
l' air *masc*
□ to get some fresh air prendre l'air
■ **by air** en avion □ I prefer to travel by air. Je préfère voyager en avion.

air-conditioned ADJECTIVE
climatisé (FEM climatisée)

air conditioning NOUN
la climatisation

Air Force NOUN
l' armée de l'air *fem*

air hostess NOUN
l' hôtesse de l'air *fem*
□ She's an air hostess. Elle est hôtesse de l'air.

airline NOUN
la compagnie aérienne

airmail NOUN
■ **by airmail** par avion

airplane NOUN (US)
l' avion *masc*

airport NOUN
l' aéroport *masc*

aisle NOUN
l' allée centrale *fem*

alarm NOUN
l' alarme *fem (warning)*
■ **a fire alarm** un avertisseur d'incendie

alarm clock NOUN
le réveil

album NOUN
l' album *masc*

alcohol NOUN
l' alcool *masc*

alcoholic NOUN
▷ *see also* **alcoholic** ADJECTIVE
l' alcoolique *masc/fem*
□ He's an alcoholic. C'est un alcoolique.

alcoholic ADJECTIVE
▷ *see also* **alcoholic** NOUN
alcoolisé (FEM alcoolisée)
□ alcoholic drinks des boissons alcoolisées

alert ADJECTIVE
1 vif (FEM vive) *(bright)*
□ a very alert baby un bébé très vif
2 vigilant (FEM vigilante) *(paying attention)*
□ We must stay alert. Nous devons rester vigilants.

A levels PL NOUN
le baccalauréat *sing*

> **DID YOU KNOW...?**
> The **baccalauréat** (or **bac** for short) is taken at the age of 17 or 18. Students

have to sit one of a variety of set subject combinations, rather than being able to choose any combination of subjects they want. If you pass you have the right to a place at university.

Algeria NOUN
l' Algérie *fem*
■ **in Algeria** en Algérie

alien NOUN
l' extra-terrestre *masc/fem (from outer space)*

alike ADVERB
■ **to look alike** se ressembler □ The two sisters look alike. Les deux sœurs se ressemblent.

alive ADJECTIVE
vivant (FEM vivante)

all ADJECTIVE, PRONOUN, ADVERB
tout (FEM toute, MASC PL tous)
□ all the time tout le temps □ I ate all of it. J'ai tout mangé. □ all day toute la journée □ all the books tous les livres □ all the girls toutes les filles
■ **All of us went.** Nous y sommes tous allés.
■ **after all** après tout □ After all, nobody can make us go. Après tout, personne ne peut nous obliger à y aller.
■ **all alone** tout seul □ She's all alone. Elle est toute seule.
■ **not at all** pas du tout □ I'm not tired at all. Je ne suis pas du tout fatigué.
■ **The score is 5 all.** Le score est de cinq partout.

allergic ADJECTIVE
allergique (FEM allergique)
■ **to be allergic to something** être allergique à quelque chose □ I'm allergic to cats' hair. Je suis allergique aux poils de chat.

alley NOUN
la ruelle

to **allow** VERB
■ **to be allowed to do something** être autorisé à faire quelque chose □ He's not allowed to go out at night. Il n'est pas autorisé à sortir le soir.
■ **to allow somebody to do something** permettre à quelqu'un de faire quelque chose □ His mum allowed him to go out. Sa mère lui a permis de sortir.

all right ADVERB
1 bien *(okay)*
□ Everything turned out all right. Tout s'est bien terminé.
■ **Are you all right?** Ça va?
2 pas mal *(not bad)*
□ The film was all right. Le film n'était pas

mal.
3 d'accord *(when agreeing)*
  □ We'll talk about it later. — All right. On en reparlera plus tard. — D'accord.
  ■ **Is that all right with you?** Tu es d'accord?
almond NOUN
  l' amande *fem*
almost ADVERB
  presque
  □ I've almost finished. J'ai presque fini.
alone ADJECTIVE, ADVERB
  seul (FEM seule)
  □ She lives alone. Elle habite seule.
  ■ **to leave somebody alone** laisser quelqu'un tranquille □ Leave her alone! Laisse-la tranquille!
  ■ **to leave something alone** ne pas toucher à quelque chose □ Leave my things alone! Ne touche pas à mes affaires!
along PREPOSITION, ADVERB
  le long de
  □ Chris was walking along the beach. Chris se promenait le long de la plage.
  ■ **all along** depuis le début □ He was lying to me all along. Il m'a menti depuis le début.
aloud ADVERB
  à haute voix
  □ He read the poem aloud. Il a lu le poème à haute voix.
alphabet NOUN
  l' alphabet *masc*
Alps PL NOUN
  les Alpes *fem pl*
already ADVERB
  déjà
  □ Liz had already gone. Liz était déjà partie.
also ADVERB
  aussi
altar NOUN
  l' autel *masc*
to **alter** VERB
  changer
alternate ADJECTIVE
  ■ **on alternate days** tous les deux jours
alternative NOUN
  ▷ *see also* **alternative** ADJECTIVE
  le choix
  □ You have no alternative. Tu n'a pas le choix.
  ■ **Fruit is a healthy alternative to chocolate.** Les fruits sont plus sains que le chocolat.
  ■ **There are several alternatives.** Il y a plusieurs possibilités.
alternative ADJECTIVE

▷ *see also* **alternative** NOUN
  autre (FEM autre)
  □ They made alternative plans. Ils ont pris d'autres dispositions.
  ■ **an alternative solution** une solution de rechange
  ■ **alternative medicine** la médecine douce
alternatively ADVERB
  ■ **Alternatively, we could just stay at home.** On pourrait aussi rester à la maison.
although CONJUNCTION
  bien que

  🗨 **LANGUAGE TIP** bien que has to be followed by a verb in the subjunctive.

  □ Although she was tired, she stayed up late. Bien qu'elle soit fatiguée, elle s'est couchée tard.
altogether ADVERB
1 en tout *(in total)*
  □ You owe me £20 altogether. Tu me dois vingt livres en tout.
2 tout à fait *(completely)*
  □ I'm not altogether happy with your work. Je ne suis pas tout à fait satisfait de votre travail.
aluminium (US **aluminum**) NOUN
  l' aluminium *masc*
always ADVERB
  toujours
  □ He's always moaning. Il est toujours en train de ronchonner.
am VERB ▷ *see* be
a.m. ABBREVIATION
  du matin
  □ at 4 a.m. à quatre heures du matin
amateur NOUN
  l' amateur *masc*
to **amaze** VERB
  ■ **to be amazed** être stupéfait □ I was amazed that I managed to do it. J'étais stupéfait d'avoir réussi.
amazed ADJECTIVE
  stupéfait (FEM stupéfaite)
amazing ADJECTIVE
1 stupéfiant (FEM stupéfiante) *(surprising)*
  □ That's amazing news! C'est une nouvelle stupéfiante!
2 exceptionnel (FEM exceptionnelle) *(excellent)*
  □ Vivian's an amazing cook. Vivian est une cuisinière exceptionnelle.
ambassador NOUN
  l' ambassadeur *masc*
  l' ambassadrice *fem*
amber ADJECTIVE
  ■ **an amber light** un feu orange
ambition NOUN
  l' ambition *fem*

ambitious ADJECTIVE
ambitieux (FEM ambitieuse)
□ She's very ambitious. Elle est très ambitieuse.

ambulance NOUN
l' ambulance fem

amenities PL NOUN
les aménagements masc pl
■ **The hotel has very good amenities.** L'hôtel est très bien aménagé.

America NOUN
l' Amérique fem
■ **in America** en Amérique
■ **to America** en Amérique

American NOUN
▷ see also **American** ADJECTIVE
l' Américain masc
l' Américaine fem
■ **the Americans** les Américains

American ADJECTIVE
▷ see also **American** NOUN
américain (FEM américaine)
□ He's American. Il est américain. □ She's American. Elle est américaine.

among PREPOSITION
parmi
□ There were six children among them. Il y avait six enfants parmi eux.
■ **We were among friends.** Nous étions entre amis.
■ **among other things** entre autres

amount NOUN
1 la somme
□ a large amount of money une grosse somme d'argent
2 la quantité
□ a huge amount of rice une énorme quantité de riz

amp NOUN
1 l' ampère masc (of electricity)
2 l' ampli masc (for hi-fi)

amplifier NOUN
l' amplificateur masc (for hi-fi)

to **amuse** VERB
amuser
□ He was most amused by the story. L'histoire l'a beaucoup amusé.

amusement arcade NOUN
la salle de jeux électroniques

an ARTICLE ▷ see **a**

to **analyse** VERB
analyser

analysis NOUN
l' analyse fem

to **analyze** VERB (US)
analyser

ancestor NOUN

l' ancêtre masc/fem

anchor NOUN
l' ancre fem

ancient ADJECTIVE
1 antique (FEM antique) (civilization)
□ ancient Greece la Grèce antique
2 ancien (FEM ancienne) (custom, building)
□ an ancient monument un monument ancien

and CONJUNCTION
et
□ you and me toi et moi □ 2 and 2 are 4 deux et deux font quatre
■ **Please try and come!** Essaie de venir!
■ **He talked and talked.** Il n'a pas arrêté de parler.
■ **better and better** de mieux en mieux

angel NOUN
l' ange masc

anger NOUN
la colère

angle NOUN
l' angle masc

angler NOUN
le pêcheur à la ligne
la pêcheuse à la ligne

angling NOUN
la pêche à la ligne

angry ADJECTIVE
en colère
□ Dad looks very angry. Papa a l'air très en colère.
■ **to be angry with somebody** être furieux contre quelqu'un □ Mum's really angry with you. Maman est vraiment furieuse contre toi.
■ **to get angry** se fâcher

animal NOUN
l' animal masc (PL les animaux)

ankle NOUN
la cheville

anniversary NOUN
l' anniversaire masc
□ a wedding anniversary un anniversaire de mariage

to **announce** VERB
annoncer

announcement NOUN
l' annonce fem

to **annoy** VERB
agacer
□ He's really annoying me. Il m'agace vraiment.
■ **to get annoyed** se fâcher □ Don't get so annoyed! Ne vous fâchez pas!

annoying ADJECTIVE
agaçant (FEM agaçante)

a

□ It's really annoying. C'est vraiment agaçant.

annual ADJECTIVE
annuel (FEM annuelle)
□ an annual meeting une réunion annuelle

anorak NOUN
l' anorak *masc*

anorexic ADJECTIVE
anorexique (FEM anorexique)

another ADJECTIVE
un autre (FEM une autre)
□ Would you like another piece of cake? Tu veux un autre morceau de gâteau? □ Have you got another skirt? Tu as une autre jupe?

to **answer** VERB
▷ *see also* **answer** NOUN
répondre à
□ Can you answer my question? Peux-tu répondre à ma question? □ to answer the phone répondre au téléphone
■ **to answer the door** aller ouvrir □ Can you answer the door please? Tu peux aller ouvrir s'il te plaît?

answer NOUN
▷ *see also* **answer** VERB
1 la réponse *(to question)*
2 la solution *(to problem)*

answering machine NOUN
le répondeur

ant NOUN
la fourmi

to **antagonize** VERB
contrarier
□ He didn't want to antagonize her. Il ne voulait pas la contrarier.

Antarctic NOUN
l' Antarctique *fem*

anthem NOUN
■ **the national anthem** l'hymne national *masc*

antibiotic NOUN
l' antibiotique *masc*

antidepressant NOUN
l' antidépresseur *masc*

antique NOUN
le meuble ancien *(furniture)*

antique shop NOUN
le magasin d'antiquités

antiseptic NOUN
l' antiseptique *masc*

any ADJECTIVE, PRONOUN, ADVERB
> LANGUAGE TIP Use **du**, **de la** or **des** to translate 'any' according to the gender of the French noun that follows it. **du** and **de la** become **de l'** when they're followed by a noun starting with a vowel.

1 du
□ Would you like any bread? Voulez-vous du pain?
de la
□ Would you like any beer? Voulez-vous de la bière?
de l'
□ Have you got any mineral water? Avez-vous de l'eau minérale?
des
□ Have you got any Madonna CDs? Avez-vous des CD de Madonna?
> LANGUAGE TIP If you want to say you haven't got any of something, use **de** whatever the gender of the following noun is. **de** becomes **d'** when it comes before a noun starting with a vowel.

2 de
□ I haven't got any books. Je n'ai pas de livres.
d'
□ I haven't got any money. Je n'ai pas d'argent.

3 en
> LANGUAGE TIP Use **en** where there is no noun after 'any'.
□ Sorry, I haven't got any. Désolé, je n'en ai pas.
■ **any more 1** *(additional)* encore de
□ Would you like any more coffee? Est-ce que tu veux encore du café? **2** *(no longer)* ne ... plus □ I don't love him any more. Je ne l'aime plus.

anybody PRONOUN
1 quelqu'un *(in question)*
□ Has anybody got a pen? Est-ce que quelqu'un a un stylo?
2 n'importe qui *(no matter who)*
□ Anybody can learn to swim. N'importe qui peut apprendre à nager.
3 ne ... personne
> LANGUAGE TIP Use **ne ... personne** in a negative sentence. **ne** comes before the verb, **personne** after it.
□ I can't see anybody. Je ne vois personne.

anyhow ADVERB
de toute façon
□ He doesn't want to go out and anyhow he's not allowed. Il ne veut pas sortir et de toute façon il n'y est pas autorisé.

anyone PRONOUN
1 quelqu'un *(in question)*
□ Has anyone got a pen? Est-ce que quelqu'un a un stylo?
2 n'importe qui *(no matter who)*
□ Anyone can learn to swim. N'importe qui

peut apprendre à nager.

3 ne ... personne

> **LANGUAGE TIP** Use **ne ... personne** in a negative sentence. **ne** comes before the verb, **personne** after it.

□ I can't see anyone. Je ne vois personne.

anything PRONOUN

1 quelque chose *(in question)*

□ Would you like anything to eat? Tu veux manger quelque chose?

2 n'importe quoi *(no matter what)*

□ Anything could happen. Il pourrait arriver n'importe quoi.

3 ne ... rien

> **LANGUAGE TIP** Use **ne ... rien** in a negative sentence. **ne** comes before the verb, **rien** after it.

□ I can't hear anything. Je n'entends rien.

anyway ADVERB

de toute façon

□ He doesn't want to go out and anyway he's not allowed. Il ne veut pas sortir et de toute façon il n'y est pas autorisé.

anywhere ADVERB

1 quelque part *(in question)*

□ Have you seen my coat anywhere? Est-ce que tu as vu mon manteau quelque part?

2 n'importe où

□ You can buy stamps almost anywhere. On peut acheter des timbres presque n'importe où.

3 ne ... nulle part

> **LANGUAGE TIP** Use **ne ... nulle part** in a negative sentence. **ne** comes before the verb, **nulle part** after it.

□ I can't find it anywhere. Je ne le trouve nulle part.

apart ADVERB

■ **The two towns are 10 kilometres apart.** Les deux villes sont à dix kilomètres l'une de l'autre.

■ **apart from** à part □ Apart from that, everything's fine. À part ça, tout va bien.

apartment NOUN

l' appartement *masc*

to **apologize** VERB

s'excuser

□ He apologized for being late. Il s'est excusé de son retard.

■ **I apologize!** Je vous prie de m'excuser.

apology NOUN

les excuses *fem pl*

apostrophe NOUN

l' apostrophe *fem*

apparatus NOUN

1 le matériel *(in lab)*

2 les agrès *masc pl (in gym)*

apparent ADJECTIVE

apparent (FEM apparente)

apparently ADVERB

apparemment

to **appeal** VERB

▷ *see also* **appeal** NOUN

lancer un appel

□ They appealed for help. Ils ont lancé un appel au secours.

■ **Greece doesn't appeal to me.** Ça ne me tente pas d'aller en Grèce.

■ **Does that appeal to you?** Ça te tente?

appeal NOUN

▷ *see also* **appeal** VERB

l' appel *masc*

□ They have launched an appeal. Ils ont lancé un appel.

to **appear** VERB

1 apparaître *(come into view)*

□ The bus appeared around the corner. Le bus est apparu au coin de la rue.

■ **to appear on TV** passer à la télé

2 paraître *(seem)*

□ She appeared to be asleep. Elle paraissait dormir.

appearance NOUN

l' apparence *fem (looks)*

□ She takes great care over her appearance. Elle prend grand soin de son apparence.

appendicitis NOUN

l' appendicite *fem*

appetite NOUN

l' appétit *masc*

to **applaud** VERB

applaudir

applause NOUN

les applaudissements *masc pl*

apple NOUN

la pomme

■ **an apple tree** un pommier

applicant NOUN

le candidat

la candidate

□ There were a hundred applicants for the job. Il y avait cent candidats pour ce poste.

application NOUN

■ **a job application** une candidature

application form NOUN

1 le dossier de candidature *(for job)*

2 le dossier d'inscription *(for university)*

to **apply** VERB

■ **to apply for a job** poser sa candidature à un poste

■ **to apply to** *(be relevant)* s'appliquer à

□ This rule doesn't apply to us. Ce règlement ne s'applique pas à nous.

appointment NOUN

le rendez-vous

□ I've got a dental appointment. J'ai rendez-vous chez le dentiste.

to **appreciate** VERB
être reconnaissant de

□ I really appreciate your help. Je vous suis extrêmement reconnaissant de votre aide.

apprentice NOUN
l' apprenti *masc*
l' apprentie *fem*

to **approach** VERB
1 s'approcher de *(get nearer to)*
□ He approached the house. Il s'est approché de la maison.
2 aborder *(tackle)*
□ to approach a problem aborder un problème

appropriate ADJECTIVE
approprié (FEM appropriée)

□ That dress isn't very appropriate for an interview. Cette robe n'est pas très appropriée pour un entretien.

approval NOUN
l' approbation *fem*

to **approve** VERB
■ **to approve of** approuver □ I don't approve of his choice. Je n'approuve pas son choix.

■ **They didn't approve of his girlfriend.** Sa copine ne leur a pas plu.

approximate ADJECTIVE
approximatif (FEM approximative)

apricot NOUN
l' abricot *masc*

April NOUN
avril *masc*

■ **in April** en avril

■ **April Fool's Day** le premier avril

DID YOU KNOW...?
Pinning a paper fish to somebody's back is a traditional April Fool joke in France.

apron NOUN
le tablier

Aquarius NOUN
le Verseau

□ I'm Aquarius. Je suis Verseau.

Arab NOUN
▷ see also **Arab** ADJECTIVE
l' Arabe *masc/fem*

Arab ADJECTIVE
▷ see also **Arab** NOUN
arabe (FEM arabe)
□ the Arab countries les pays arabes

Arabic NOUN
l' arabe *masc*

arch NOUN

l' arc *masc*

archaeologist NOUN
l' archéologue *masc/fem*
□ He's an archaeologist. Il est archéologue.

archaeology NOUN
l' archéologie *fem*

archbishop NOUN
l' archevêque *masc*

archeologist NOUN (US)
l' archéologue *masc/fem*
□ He's an archeologist. Il est archéologue.

archeology NOUN (US)
l' archéologie *fem*

architect NOUN
l' architecte *masc/fem*
□ She's an architect. Elle est architecte.

architecture NOUN
l' architecture *fem*

Arctic NOUN
l' Arctique *masc*

are VERB ▷ see **be**

area NOUN
1 la région
□ She lives in the Paris area. Elle habite dans la région parisienne.
2 le quartier
□ My favourite area of Paris is Montmartre. Montmartre est le quartier de Paris que je préfère.
3 la superficie
□ The field has an area of 1500m². Le champ a une superficie de mille cinq cent mètres carrés.

Argentina NOUN
l' Argentine *fem*
■ **in Argentina** en Argentine

Argentinian ADJECTIVE
argentin (FEM argentine)

to **argue** VERB
se disputer
□ They never stop arguing. Ils n'arrêtent pas de se disputer.

argument NOUN
■ **to have an argument** se disputer □ They had an argument. Ils se sont disputés.

Aries NOUN
le Bélier
□ I'm Aries. Je suis Bélier.

arm NOUN
le bras

armchair NOUN
le fauteuil

armour (US **armor**) NOUN
l' armure *fem*

army NOUN
l' armée *fem*

around PREPOSITION, ADVERB

1 autour de
□ She wore a scarf around her neck. Elle portait une écharpe autour du cou.
2 environ *(approximately)*
□ It costs around £100. Cela coûte environ cent livres.
3 vers *(date, time)*
□ Let's meet at around 8 p.m. Retrouvons-nous vers vingt heures.

■ **around here 1** *(nearby)* près d'ici □ Is there a chemist's around here? Est-ce qu'il y a une pharmacie près d'ici? **2** *(in this area)* dans les parages □ He lives around here. Il habite dans les parages.

to **arrange** VERB

■ **to arrange to do something** prévoir de faire quelque chose □ They arranged to go out together on Friday. Ils ont prévu de sortir ensemble vendredi.
■ **to arrange a meeting** convenir d'un rendez-vous □ Can we arrange a meeting? Pouvons-nous convenir d'un rendez-vous?
■ **to arrange a party** organiser une fête

arrangement NOUN
l' arrangement *masc (plan)*
■ **They made arrangements to go out on Friday night.** Ils ont organisé une sortie vendredi soir.

to **arrest** VERB
▷ *see also* **arrest** NOUN
arrêter
□ The police have arrested 5 people. La police a arrêté cinq personnes.

arrest NOUN
▷ *see also* **arrest** VERB
l' arrestation *fem*
■ **to be under arrest** être en état d'arrestation □ You're under arrest! Vous êtes en état d'arrestation!

arrival NOUN
l' arrivée *fem*

to **arrive** VERB
arriver
□ I arrived at 5 o'clock. Je suis arrivé à cinq heures.

arrow NOUN
la flèche

art NOUN
l' art *masc*

artery NOUN
l' artère *fem*

art gallery NOUN
le musée

article NOUN
l' article *masc*
□ a newspaper article un article de journal

artificial ADJECTIVE

artificiel (FEM artificielle)

artist NOUN
l' artiste *masc/fem*
□ She's an artist. C'est une artiste.

artistic ADJECTIVE
artistique (FEM artistique)

as CONJUNCTION, ADVERB
1 au moment où *(while)*
□ He came in as I was leaving. Il est arrivé au moment où je partais.
2 puisque *(since)*
□ As it's Sunday, you can have a lie-in. Tu peux faire la grasse matinée, puisque c'est dimanche.

■ **as ... as** aussi ... que □ Pierre's as tall as Michel. Pierre est aussi grand que Michel.
■ **twice as ... as** deux fois plus ... que □ Her coat cost twice as much as mine. Son manteau a coûté deux fois plus cher que le mien.
■ **as much ... as** autant ... que □ I haven't got as much money as you. Je n'ai pas autant d'argent que toi.
■ **as soon as possible** dès que possible □ I'll do it as soon as possible. Je le ferai dès que possible.
■ **as from tomorrow** à partir de demain □ As from tomorrow, the shop will be closed on Sundays. À partir de demain, le magasin sera fermé le dimanche .
■ **as though** comme si □ She acted as though she hadn't seen me. Elle a fait comme si elle ne m'avait pas vu.
■ **as if** comme si
■ **He works as a waiter in the holidays.** Il travaille comme serveur pendant les vacances.

asap ABBREVIATION *(= as soon as possible)*
dès que possible

ashamed ADJECTIVE
■ **to be ashamed** avoir honte □ You should be ashamed of yourself! Tu devrais avoir honte!

ashtray NOUN
le cendrier

Asia NOUN
l' Asie *fem*
■ **in Asia** en Asie

Asian NOUN
▷ *see also* **Asian** ADJECTIVE
l' Asiatique *masc/fem*

Asian ADJECTIVE
▷ *see also* **Asian** NOUN
asiatique (FEM asiatique)
■ **He's Asian.** C'est un Asiatique.
■ **She's Asian.** C'est une Asiatique.

to **ask** VERB

1 demander *(inquire, request)*
□ 'Have you finished?' she asked. 'Tu as fini?' a-t-elle demandé.

■ **to ask somebody something** demander quelque chose à quelqu'un □ He asked her how old she was. Il lui a demandé quel âge elle avait.

■ **to ask for something** demander quelque chose □ He asked for a cup of tea. Il a demandé une tasse de thé.

■ **to ask somebody to do something** demander à quelqu'un de faire quelque chose □ She asked him to do the shopping. Elle lui a demandé de faire les courses.

■ **to ask about something** se renseigner sur quelque chose □ I asked about train times to Leeds. Je me suis renseigné sur les horaires des trains pour Leeds.

■ **to ask somebody a question** poser une question à quelqu'un

2 inviter
□ Have you asked Matthew to the party? Est-ce que tu as invité Matthew à la fête?

■ **He asked her out.** *(on a date)* Il lui a demandé de sortir avec lui.

asleep ADJECTIVE
■ **to be asleep** dormir □ He's asleep. Il dort.

■ **to fall asleep** s'endormir □ I fell asleep in front of the TV. Je me suis endormi devant la télé.

asparagus NOUN
les asperges *fem pl*

aspect NOUN
l' aspect *masc*

aspirin NOUN
l' aspirine *fem*

assembly NOUN

> **DID YOU KNOW...?**
> There is no assembly in French schools.

asset NOUN
l' atout *masc*
□ Her experience will be an asset to the firm. Son expérience sera un atout pour l'entreprise.

assignment NOUN
le devoir *(in school)*

assistance NOUN
l' aide *fem*

assistant NOUN
1 le vendeur
la vendeuse *(in shop)*
2 l' assistant *masc*
l' assistante *fem (helper)*

association NOUN
l' association *fem*

assortment NOUN
l' assortiment *masc*

to **assume** VERB
supposer
□ I assume she won't be coming. Je suppose qu'elle ne viendra pas.

to **assure** VERB
assurer
□ He assured me he was coming. Il m'a assuré qu'il viendrait.

asthma NOUN
l' asthme *masc*
□ I've got asthma. J'ai de l'asthme.

to **astonish** VERB
étonner

astonished ADJECTIVE
étonné (FEM étonnée)

astonishing ADJECTIVE
étonnant (FEM étonnante)

astrology NOUN
l' astrologie *fem*

astronaut NOUN
l' astronaute *masc/fem*

astronomy NOUN
l' astronomie *fem*

asylum seeker NOUN
le demandeur d'asile
la demandeuse d'asile

at PREPOSITION
▷ *see also* **at** NOUN

> **LANGUAGE TIP** à + **le** becomes **au**, à + **les** becomes **aux**.

à
□ at 4 o'clock à quatre heures □ at Christmas à Noël □ at 50 km/h à cinquante km/h □ at home à la maison □ two at a time deux à la fois □ at school à l'école
au
□ at the office au bureau
aux
□ at the races aux courses
■ **at night** la nuit
■ **What are you doing at the weekend?** Qu'est-ce que tu fais ce week-end?

at NOUN
l' arobase *fem (@ symbol)*

ate VERB ▷ *see* eat

Athens NOUN
Athènes
■ **in Athens** à Athènes

athlete NOUN
l' athlète *masc/fem*

athletic ADJECTIVE
athlétique (FEM athlétique)

athletics NOUN
l' athlétisme *masc*

□ I love athletics. J'aime l'athlétisme.

Atlantic NOUN
l' océan Atlantique *masc*

atlas NOUN
l' atlas *masc*

atmosphere NOUN
l' atmosphère *fem*

atom NOUN
l' atome *masc*

atomic ADJECTIVE
atomique (FEM atomique)

to **attach** VERB
fixer

□ He attached a rope to the car. Il a fixé une corde à la voiture.

■ **Please find attached ...** Veuillez trouver ci-joint ...

attached ADJECTIVE
■ **to be attached to** être attaché à □ He's very attached to his family. Il est très attaché à sa famille.

attachment NOUN
la pièce jointe *(email)*

to **attack** VERB
▷ *see also* **attack** NOUN
attaquer

□ The dog attacked her. Le chien l'a attaquée.

attack NOUN
▷ *see also* **attack** VERB
l' attaque *fem*

attempt NOUN
▷ *see also* **attempt** VERB
la tentative

□ She gave up after several attempts. Elle y a renoncé après plusieurs tentatives.

to **attempt** VERB
▷ *see also* **attempt** NOUN
■ **to attempt to do something** essayer de faire quelque chose □ I attempted to write a song. J'ai essayé d'écrire une chanson.

to **attend** VERB
assister à

□ to attend a meeting assister à une réunion

⚬ **LANGUAGE TIP** Be careful not to translate **to attend** by **attendre**.

attention NOUN
■ **to pay attention to** faire attention à □ He didn't pay attention to what I was saying. Il ne faisait pas attention à ce que je disais.

attic NOUN
le grenier

attitude NOUN
l' attitude *fem (way of thinking)*
□ I really don't like your attitude! Je n'aime

pas du tout ton attitude!

attorney NOUN (US)
l' avocat *masc*
l' avocate *fem*

to **attract** VERB
attirer

□ The Lake District attracts lots of tourists. La région des lacs attire de nombreux touristes.

attraction NOUN
l' attraction *fem*
□ a tourist attraction une attraction touristique

attractive ADJECTIVE
séduisant (FEM séduisante)
□ She's very attractive. Elle est très séduisante.

aubergine NOUN
l' aubergine *fem*

auction NOUN
la vente aux enchères

audience NOUN
les spectateurs *masc pl (in theatre)*

audition NOUN
l' audition *fem*

August NOUN
août *masc*
■ **in August** en août

aunt, aunty NOUN
la tante
□ my aunt ma tante

au pair NOUN
la jeune fille au pair
□ She's an au pair. Elle est jeune fille au pair.

Australia NOUN
l' Australie *fem*
■ **in Australia** en Australie
■ **to Australia** en Australie

Australian NOUN
▷ *see also* **Australian** ADJECTIVE
l' Australien *masc*
l' Australienne *fem*
■ **the Australians** les Australiens

Australian ADJECTIVE
▷ *see also* **Australian** NOUN
australien (FEM australienne)
□ He's Australian. Il est australien.

Austria NOUN
l' Autriche *fem*
■ **in Austria** en Autriche

Austrian NOUN
▷ *see also* **Austrian** ADJECTIVE
l' Autrichien *masc*
l' Autrichienne *fem*
■ **the Austrians** les Autrichiens

Austrian ADJECTIVE
▷ *see also* **Austrian** NOUN

autrichien (FEM autrichienne)
□ She's Austrian. Elle est autrichienne.

author NOUN
l' auteur *masc*
□ She's a famous author. C'est un auteur connu.

autobiography NOUN
l' autobiographie *fem*

autograph NOUN
l' autographe *masc*

automatic ADJECTIVE
automatique (FEM automatique)
□ an automatic door une porte automatique

automatically ADVERB
automatiquement

autumn NOUN
l' automne *masc*
■ **in autumn** en automne

availability NOUN
la disponibilité

available ADJECTIVE
disponible (FEM disponible)
□ Free brochures are available on request. Des brochures gratuites sont disponibles sur demande. □ Is Mr Cooke available today? Est-ce que Monsieur Cooke est disponible aujourd'hui?

avalanche NOUN
l' avalanche *fem*

avenue NOUN
l' avenue *fem*

average NOUN
▷ *see also* **average** ADJECTIVE
la moyenne
□ on average en moyenne

average ADJECTIVE
▷ *see also* **average** NOUN
moyen (FEM moyenne)
□ the average price le prix moyen

avocado NOUN
l' avocat *masc*

to **avoid** VERB
éviter
□ He avoids her when she's in a bad mood. Il l'évite lorsqu'elle est de mauvaise humeur.
■ **to avoid doing something** éviter de faire

quelque chose □ Avoid going out on your own at night. Évite de sortir seul le soir.

awake ADJECTIVE
■ **to be awake** être réveillé □ Is she awake? Elle est réveillée?
■ **He was still awake.** Il ne dormait pas encore.

award NOUN
le prix
□ He's won an award. Il a remporté un prix.
□ the award for the best actor le prix du meilleur acteur

away ADJECTIVE, ADVERB
absent (FEM absente) *(not here)*
□ André's away today. André est absent aujourd'hui.
■ **He's away for a week.** Il est parti pour une semaine.
■ **The town's 2 kilometres away.** La ville est à deux kilomètres d'ici.
■ **The coast is 2 hours away by car.** La côte est à deux heures de route.
■ **Go away!** Va-t'en!
■ **to put something away** ranger quelque chose □ He put the books away in the cupboard. Il a rangé les livres dans le placard.

away match NOUN
le match à l'extérieur

awful ADJECTIVE
affreux (FEM affreuse)
□ That's awful! C'est affreux!
■ **an awful lot of ...** énormément de ...

awfully ADVERB
■ **I'm awfully sorry.** Je suis vraiment désolé.

awkward ADJECTIVE
1 délicat (FEM délicate) *(difficult to deal with)*
□ an awkward situation une situation délicate
2 gênant (FEM gênante) *(embarrassing)*
□ an awkward question une question gênante
■ **It's a bit awkward for me to come and see you.** Ce n'est pas très pratique pour moi de venir vous voir.

axe NOUN
la hache

Bb

BA NOUN
la licence

■ **a BA in French** une licence de français

baby NOUN
le bébé

baby carriage NOUN (US)
le landau

to **babysit** VERB
faire du baby-sitting

babysitter NOUN
le/la baby-sitter

babysitting NOUN
le baby-sitting

bachelor NOUN
le célibataire

□ He's a bachelor. Il est célibataire.

back NOUN
▷ *see also* **back** ADJECTIVE, VERB
1 le dos *(of person, horse, book)*
2 l' arrière *masc (of car, house)*
□ in the back à l'arrière
3 le verso *(of page)*
□ on the back au verso
4 le fond *(of room, garden)*
□ at the back au fond

back ADJECTIVE, ADVERB
▷ *see also* **back** NOUN, VERB
arrière (FEM+PL arrière)
□ the back seat le siège arrière □ the back
wheel of my bike la roue arrière de mon vélo

■ **the back door** la porte de derrière

■ **to get back** rentrer □ What time did you
get back? À quelle heure est-ce que tu es
rentré?

■ **We went there by bus and walked
back.** Nous y sommes allés en bus et nous
sommes rentrés à pied.

■ **He's not back yet.** Il n'est pas encore
rentré.

■ **to call somebody back** rappeler
quelqu'un □ I'll call back later. Je rappellerai
plus tard.

to **back** VERB
▷ *see also* **back** NOUN, ADJECTIVE
soutenir *(support)*

□ I'm backing Tony Blair. Je soutiens Tony
Blair.

■ **to back a horse** parier sur un cheval

to **back out** VERB
se désister

□ They backed out at the last minute. Ils se
sont désistés au dernier moment.

to **back up** VERB

■ **to back somebody up** soutenir
quelqu'un

backache NOUN
le mal au dos

□ to have backache avoir mal au dos

backbone NOUN
la colonne vertébrale

to **backfire** VERB
échouer *(go wrong)*

background NOUN
1 l' arrière-plan *masc (of picture)*
□ a house in the background une maison à
l'arrière-plan

■ **background noise** les bruits de fond
masc pl
2 le milieu (PL les milieux)
□ his family background son milieu familial

backhand NOUN
le revers

backing NOUN
le soutien *(support)*

backpack NOUN
le sac à dos

backpacker NOUN
1 le routard
la routarde *(globe-trotter)*
2 le randonneur
la randonneuse *(hill-walker)*

backpacking NOUN

■ **to go backpacking** voyager sac au dos

back pain NOUN
le mal au dos

□ to have back pain avoir mal au dos

backside NOUN
le derrière

backstroke NOUN
le dos crawlé

backup NOUN
le soutien *(support)*
- **a backup file** une sauvegarde

backwards ADVERB
en arrière
□ to take a step backwards faire un pas en arrière
- **to fall backwards** tomber à la renverse

back yard NOUN
la cour

bacon NOUN
1 le lard *(French type)*
2 le bacon *(British type)*
□ bacon and eggs des œufs au bacon

bad ADJECTIVE
1 mauvais *(FEM mauvaise)*
□ a bad film un mauvais film □ the bad weather le mauvais temps □ to be in a bad mood être de mauvaise humeur

---

WORD POWER

You can use a number of other words instead of **bad** to mean 'terrible':
awful affreux
□ an awful day une journée affreuse
dreadful terrible
□ a dreadful mistake une terrible erreur
rubbish nul
□ a rubbish team une équipe nulle
terrible épouvantable
□ a terrible book un livre épouvantable

- **to be bad at something** être mauvais en quelque chose □ I'm really bad at maths. Je suis vraiment mauvais en maths.
2 grave *(FEM grave) (serious)*
□ a bad accident un accident grave
3 vilain *(FEM vilaine) (naughty)*
□ You bad boy! Vilain!
- **to go bad** *(food)* se gâter
- **I feel bad about it.** Ça m'ennuie.
- **not bad** pas mal □ That's not bad at all. Ce n'est pas mal du tout.

badge NOUN
le badge

badly ADVERB
mal
□ badly paid mal payé
- **badly wounded** grièvement blessé
- **He badly needs a rest.** Il a sérieusement besoin de se reposer.

badminton NOUN
le badminton
□ to play badminton jouer au badminton

bad-tempered ADJECTIVE
- **to be bad-tempered 1** *(by nature)* avoir mauvais caractère □ He's a really bad-tempered person. Il a vraiment mauvais caractère. **2** *(temporarily)* être de mauvaise humeur □ He was really bad-tempered yesterday. Il était vraiment de mauvaise humeur hier.

baffled ADJECTIVE
déconcerté *(FEM déconcertée)*

bag NOUN
le sac
- **an old bag** *(person)* une vieille peau

baggage NOUN
les bagages *masc pl*

baggage reclaim NOUN
la livraison des bagages

baggy ADJECTIVE
ample *(FEM ample)*

bagpipes PL NOUN
la cornemuse *sing*
□ Ed plays the bagpipes. Ed joue de la cornemuse.

to **bake** VERB
- **to bake a cake** faire un gâteau

baked ADJECTIVE
cuit au four *(FEM cuite au four)*
□ baked potatoes les pommes de terre cuites au four *fem pl*
- **baked beans** les haricots blancs à la sauce tomate *masc pl*

baker NOUN
le boulanger
la boulangère
□ He's a baker. Il est boulanger.

bakery NOUN
la boulangerie

baking ADJECTIVE
- **It's baking in here!** Il fait une chaleur torride ici!

balance NOUN
l' équilibre *masc*
□ to lose one's balance perdre l'équilibre

balanced ADJECTIVE
équilibré *(FEM équilibrée)*

balcony NOUN
le balcon

bald ADJECTIVE
chauve *(FEM chauve)*

ball NOUN
1 la balle *(tennis, golf, cricket)*
2 le ballon *(football, rugby)*

ballet NOUN
le ballet
□ We went to a ballet. Nous sommes allés voir un ballet.
- **ballet lessons** les cours de danse *masc pl*

ballet dancer NOUN
le danseur classique
la danseuse classique

ballet shoes PL NOUN
les chaussons de danse *masc pl*

balloon NOUN
le ballon *(for parties)*
■ **a hot-air balloon** une montgolfière

ballpoint pen NOUN
le stylo à bille

ballroom dancing NOUN
la danse de salon

ban NOUN
▷ *see also* **ban** VERB
l' interdiction *fem*

to **ban** VERB
▷ *see also* **ban** NOUN
interdire

banana NOUN
la banane
□ a banana skin une peau de banane

band NOUN
1 le groupe *(rock band)*
2 la fanfare *(brass band)*

bandage NOUN
▷ *see also* **bandage** VERB
le bandage

to **bandage** VERB
▷ *see also* **bandage** NOUN
mettre un bandage à
□ The nurse bandaged his arm. L'infirmière lui a mis un bandage au bras.

Band-Aid® NOUN (US)
le pansement adhésif

bandit NOUN
le bandit

bang NOUN
▷ *see also* **bang** VERB
1 la détonation
□ I heard a loud bang. J'ai entendu une forte détonation.
2 le coup
□ a bang on the head un coup sur la tête
■ **Bang!** Pan!

to **bang** VERB
▷ *see also* **bang** NOUN
se cogner *(part of body)*
□ I banged my head. Je me suis cogné la tête.
■ **to bang the door** claquer la porte
■ **to bang on the door** cogner à la porte

banger NOUN
1 le tacot *(old car)*
□ His car's an old banger. Sa voiture est un vieux tacot.
2 la saucisse *(sausage)*
□ bangers and mash les saucisses à la purée

Bangladesh NOUN
le Bangladesh
■ **from Bangladesh** du Bangladesh

bank NOUN
1 la banque *(financial)*
2 le bord *(of river, lake)*

bank account NOUN
le compte en banque

banker NOUN
le banquier

bank holiday NOUN
le jour férié

banknote NOUN
le billet de banque

banned ADJECTIVE
interdit (FEM interdite)

bar NOUN
1 le bar *(pub)*
2 le comptoir *(counter)*
■ **a bar of chocolate** une tablette de chocolat
■ **a bar of soap** une savonnette

barbaric ADJECTIVE
barbare (FEM barbare)

barbecue NOUN
le barbecue

barber NOUN
le coiffeur pour hommes

bare ADJECTIVE
nu (FEM nue)

barefoot ADJECTIVE, ADVERB
nu-pieds (FEM+PL nu-pieds)
□ The children go around barefoot. Les enfants se promènent nu-pieds.
■ **to be barefoot** avoir les pieds nus □ She was barefoot. Elle avait les pieds nus.

barely ADVERB
à peine
□ I could barely hear what she was saying. J'entendais à peine ce qu'elle disait.

bargain NOUN
l' affaire *fem*
□ It was a bargain! C'était une affaire!

barge NOUN
la péniche

to **bark** VERB
aboyer

barmaid NOUN
la barmaid
□ She's a barmaid. Elle est barmaid.

barman NOUN
le barman
□ He's a barman. Il est barman.

barn NOUN
la grange

barrel NOUN
le tonneau (PL les tonneaux)

barrier NOUN
la barrière

bartender NOUN (US)

base – be

le barman

□ He's a bartender. Il est barman.

base NOUN
la base

baseball NOUN
le base-ball

■ **a baseball cap** une casquette de base-ball

based ADJECTIVE
■ **based on** fondé sur

basement NOUN
le sous-sol

to **bash** VERB
▷ see also **bash** NOUN
■ **to bash something** taper sur quelque chose

bash NOUN
▷ see also **bash** VERB
■ **I'll have a bash.** Je vais essayer.

basic ADJECTIVE
1 de base
□ It's a basic model. C'est un modèle de base.
2 rudimentaire (FEM rudimentaire)
□ The accommodation is pretty basic. Le logement est plutôt rudimentaire.

basically ADVERB
tout simplement
□ Basically, I just don't like him. Tout simplement, je ne l'aime pas.

basics PL NOUN
les rudiments masc pl

basil NOUN
le basilic

basin NOUN
le lavabo (washbasin)

basis NOUN
■ **on a daily basis** quotidiennement
■ **on a regular basis** régulièrement

basket NOUN
le panier

basketball NOUN
le basket

bass NOUN
1 la basse (guitar, singer)
□ He plays the bass. Il joue de la basse.
□ He's a bass. Il est basse.
■ **a bass guitar** une guitare basse
■ **a double bass** une contrebasse
2 les graves masc pl (on hi-fi)

bass drum NOUN
la grosse caisse

bassoon NOUN
le basson
□ I play the bassoon. Je joue du basson.

bat NOUN
1 la batte (for cricket, rounders)

2 la raquette (for table tennis)
3 la chauve-souris (PL les chauves-souris) (animal)

bath NOUN
1 le bain
□ to have a bath prendre un bain
■ **a hot bath** un bain chaud
2 la baignoire (bathtub)
□ There's a spider in the bath. Il y a une araignée dans la baignoire.

to **bathe** VERB
se baigner

bathing suit NOUN (US)
le maillot de bain

bathroom NOUN
la salle de bains

baths PL NOUN
la piscine sing

bath towel NOUN
la serviette de bain

batter NOUN
la pâte à frire

battery NOUN
1 la pile (for torch, toy)
2 la batterie (of car)

battle NOUN
la bataille
□ the Battle of Hastings la bataille de Hastings
■ **It was a battle, but we managed in the end.** Il a fallu se battre, mais on a fini par y arriver.

battleship NOUN
le cuirassé

bay NOUN
la baie

BC ABBREVIATION (= before Christ)
av. J.-C. (= avant Jésus-Christ)
□ in 200 BC en deux cents avant Jésus-Christ

to **be** VERB
être
□ I'm tired. Je suis fatigué. □ You're late. Tu es en retard. □ She's English. Elle est anglaise. □ Edinburgh is in Scotland. Édimbourg est en Écosse. □ It's 4 o'clock. Il est quatre heures. □ We are all happy. Nous sommes tous heureux. □ They are in Paris at the moment. Ils sont à Paris en ce moment. □ I've been ill. J'ai été malade.
■ **It's the 28th of October today.** Nous sommes le vingt-huit octobre.
■ **Have you been to Greece before?** Est-ce que tu es déjà allé en Grèce?
■ **I've never been to Paris.** Je ne suis jamais allé à Paris.
■ **to be killed** être tué

LANGUAGE TIP When you are saying what somebody's occupation is, you leave out the 'a' in French.

□ She's a doctor. Elle est médecin. □ He's a student. Il est étudiant.

LANGUAGE TIP With certain adjectives, such as 'cold', 'hot', 'hungry' and 'thirsty', use **avoir** instead of **être**.

■ I'm cold. J'ai froid.
■ I'm hungry. J'ai faim.

LANGUAGE TIP When saying how old somebody is, use **avoir** not **être**.

■ I'm fourteen. J'ai quatorze ans.
■ How old are you? Quel âge as-tu?

LANGUAGE TIP When referring to the weather, use **faire**.

■ It's cold. Il fait froid.
■ It's too hot. Il fait trop chaud.
■ It's a nice day. Il fait beau.

beach NOUN
la plage

bead NOUN
la perle

beak NOUN
le bec

beam NOUN
le rayon

beans PL NOUN
1 les haricots *masc pl*
2 les haricots blancs à la sauce tomate *masc pl* (baked beans)
■ broad beans les fèves *fem pl*
■ green beans les haricots verts *masc pl*
■ kidney beans les haricots rouges *masc pl*

bear NOUN
▷ see also **bear** VERB
l' ours *masc*

to **bear** VERB
▷ see also **bear** NOUN
■ I can't bear it! C'est insupportable!

to **bear up** VERB
tenir le coup
■ Bear up! Tiens bon!

beard NOUN
la barbe
■ He's got a beard. Il est barbu.
■ a man with a beard un barbu

bearded ADJECTIVE
barbu (FEM barbue)

beat NOUN
▷ see also **beat** VERB
le rythme

to **beat** VERB
▷ see also **beat** NOUN
battre
□ We beat them 3-0. On les a battus trois à zéro.

■ Beat it! Fiche le camp! *(informal)*
■ to beat somebody up *(informal)* tabasser quelqu'un

beautiful ADJECTIVE
beau (FEM belle, MASC PL beaux)

beautifully ADVERB
admirablement

beauty NOUN
la beauté

beauty spot NOUN
le site pittoresque

became VERB ▷ see **become**

because CONJUNCTION
parce que
□ I did it because ... Je l'ai fait parce que ...
■ because of à cause de □ because of the weather à cause du temps

to **become** VERB
devenir
□ He became a famous writer. Il est devenu un grand écrivain.

bed NOUN
le lit
□ in bed au lit
■ to go to bed aller se coucher
■ to go to bed with somebody coucher avec quelqu'un

bed and breakfast NOUN
la chambre d'hôte
□ We stayed in a bed and breakfast. Nous avons logé dans une chambre d'hôte.
■ How much is it for bed and breakfast? C'est combien pour la chambre et le petit déjeuner?

bedclothes PL NOUN
les draps et les couvertures *masc pl*

bedding NOUN
la literie

bedroom NOUN
la chambre

bedsit NOUN
la chambre meublée

bedspread NOUN
le dessus-de-lit (PL les dessus-de-lit)

bedtime NOUN
■ Ten o'clock is my usual bedtime. Je me couche généralement à dix heures.
■ Bedtime! Au lit!

bee NOUN
l' abeille *fem*

beef NOUN
le bœuf
■ roast beef le rosbif

beefburger NOUN
le hamburger

been VERB ▷ see **be**

beer NOUN

la bière
beetle NOUN
le scarabée
beetroot NOUN
la betterave rouge
before PREPOSITION, CONJUNCTION, ADVERB
1 avant
  □ before Tuesday avant mardi
2 avant de
  □ before going avant de partir □ Before opening the packet, read the instructions. Avant d'ouvrir le paquet, lisez le mode d'emploi. □ I'll phone before I leave. J'appellerai avant de partir.
3 déjà (already)
  □ I've seen this film before. J'ai déjà vu ce film. □ Have you been to Scotland before? Vous êtes déjà venu en Écosse?
  ■ the day before la veille
  ■ the week before la semaine précédente
beforehand ADVERB
à l'avance
to **beg** VERB
1 mendier (for money)
2 supplier
  □ He begged me to stop. Il m'a supplié d'arrêter.
began VERB ▷ see begin
beggar NOUN
le mendiant
la mendiante
to **begin** VERB
commencer
  ■ to begin doing something commencer à faire quelque chose
beginner NOUN
le débutant
la débutante
  □ I'm just a beginner. Je ne suis qu'un débutant.
beginning NOUN
le début
  □ in the beginning au début
begun VERB ▷ see begin
behalf NOUN
  ■ on behalf of somebody pour quelqu'un
to **behave** VERB
se comporter
  □ He behaved like an idiot. Il s'est comporté comme un idiot. □ She behaved very badly. Elle s'est très mal comportée.
  ■ to behave oneself être sage □ Did the children behave themselves? Est-ce que les enfants ont été sages?
  ■ Behave! Sois sage!
behaviour (US **behavior**) NOUN
le comportement

behind PREPOSITION, ADVERB
  ▷ see also **behind** NOUN
derrière
  □ behind the television derrière la télévision
  ■ to be behind (late) avoir du retard □ I'm behind with my revision. J'ai du retard dans mes révisions.
behind NOUN
  ▷ see also **behind** PREPOSITION, ADVERB
le derrière
beige ADJECTIVE
beige (FEM beige)
Belgian NOUN
  ▷ see also **Belgian** ADJECTIVE
le/la Belge
  ■ the Belgians les Belges
Belgian ADJECTIVE
  ▷ see also **Belgian** NOUN
belge (FEM belge)
  □ Belgian chocolate le chocolat belge
  □ She's Belgian. Elle est belge.
Belgium NOUN
la Belgique
  ■ in Belgium en Belgique
to **believe** VERB
croire
  □ I don't believe you. Je ne te crois pas.
  ■ to believe in something croire à quelque chose □ Do you believe in ghosts? Tu crois aux fantômes?
  ■ to believe in God croire en Dieu
bell NOUN
1 la sonnette (doorbell)
  ■ to ring the bell sonner à la porte
2 la cloche (in church)
3 la sonnerie (in school)
4 la clochette
  □ Our cat has a bell on its collar. Notre chat a une clochette sur son collier.
belly NOUN
le ventre
to **belong** VERB
  ■ to belong to somebody être à quelqu'un
  □ Who does it belong to? C'est à qui?
  □ That belongs to me. C'est à moi.
  ■ Do you belong to any clubs? Est-ce que tu es membre d'un club?
  ■ Where does this belong? Où est-ce que ça va?
belongings PL NOUN
les affaires fem pl
below PREPOSITION, ADVERB
1 au-dessous de
  □ below the castle au-dessous du château
2 en dessous
  □ on the floor below à l'étage en dessous
  ■ 10 degrees below freezing moins dix

belt NOUN
la ceinture

beltway NOUN (US)
le périphérique

bench NOUN
1 le banc *(seat)*
2 l' établi *masc (for woodwork)*

bend NOUN
▷ *see also* **bend** VERB
1 le virage *(in road)*
2 le coude *(in river)*

to **bend** VERB
▷ *see also* **bend** NOUN
1 courber *(back)*
2 plier *(leg, arm)*
□ I can't bend my arm. Je n'arrive pas à plier le bras.
■ **'do not bend'** 'ne pas plier'
3 tordre *(object)*
□ You've bent it. Tu l'as tordu.
4 se tordre
□ It bends easily. Ça se tord facilement.

to **bend down** VERB
se baisser

to **bend over** VERB
se pencher

beneath PREPOSITION
sous

benefit NOUN
▷ *see also* **benefit** VERB
l' avantage *masc (advantage)*
■ **unemployment benefit** les allocations de chômage

to **benefit** VERB
▷ *see also* **benefit** NOUN
■ **He'll benefit from the change.** Le changement lui fera du bien.

bent VERB ▷ *see* **bend**

bent ADJECTIVE
tordu *(FEM tordue)*
□ a bent fork une fourchette tordue

beret NOUN
le béret

berserk ADJECTIVE
■ **to go berserk** devenir fou furieux □ She went berserk. Elle est devenue folle furieuse.

berth NOUN
la couchette

beside PREPOSITION
à côté de
□ beside the television à côté de la télévision
■ **He was beside himself.** Il était hors de lui.
■ **That's beside the point.** Cela n'a rien à voir.

besides ADVERB

en plus
□ Besides, it's too expensive. En plus, c'est trop cher.

best ADJECTIVE, ADVERB
1 meilleur *(FEM meilleure)*
□ He's the best player in the team. Il est le meilleur joueur de l'équipe. □ Janet's the best at maths. Janet est la meilleure en maths.
2 le mieux
□ Emma sings best. C'est Emma qui chante le mieux. □ That's the best I can do. Je ne peux pas faire mieux.
■ **to do one's best** faire de son mieux □ It's not perfect, but I did my best. Ça n'est pas parfait, mais j'ai fait de mon mieux.
■ **to make the best of it** s'en contenter
□ We'll have to make the best of it. Il va falloir nous en contenter.

best man NOUN
le garçon d'honneur

bet NOUN
▷ *see also* **bet** VERB
le pari
□ to make a bet faire un pari

to **bet** VERB
▷ *see also* **bet** NOUN
parier
□ I bet you he won't come. Je te parie qu'il ne viendra pas. □ I bet he forgot. Je parie qu'il a oublié.

to **betray** VERB
trahir

better ADJECTIVE, ADVERB
1 meilleur *(FEM meilleure)*
□ This one's better than that one. Celui-ci est meilleur que celui-là. □ a better way to do it une meilleure façon de le faire
2 mieux
□ That's better! C'est mieux comme ça.
■ **better still** encore mieux □ Go and see her tomorrow, or better still, go today. Va la voir demain, ou encore mieux, vas-y aujourd'hui.
■ **the sooner the better** le plus tôt sera le mieux □ Phone her, the sooner the better. Appelle-la, le plus tôt sera le mieux.
■ **to get better 1** *(improve)* s'améliorer □ I hope the weather gets better soon. J'espère que le temps va s'améliorer bientôt. □ My French is getting better. Mon français s'améliore. **2** *(from illness)* se remettre □ I hope you get better soon. J'espère que tu vas vite te remettre.
■ **to feel better** se sentir mieux □ Are you feeling better now? Tu te sens mieux maintenant?

■ **You'd better do it straight away.** Vous feriez mieux de le faire immédiatement.
■ **I'd better go home.** Je ferais mieux de rentrer.
betting shop NOUN
le bureau de paris
between PREPOSITION
entre
□ Stroud is between Oxford and Bristol. Stroud est entre Oxford et Bristol.
□ between 15 and 20 minutes entre quinze et vingt minutes
bewildered ADJECTIVE
■ **He looked bewildered.** Il avait l'air perplexe.
beyond PREPOSITION
au-delà de
□ There was a lake beyond the mountain. Il y avait un lac au-delà de la montagne.
■ **beyond belief** incroyable
■ **beyond repair** irréparable
biased ADJECTIVE
partial (FEM partiale)
Bible NOUN
la Bible
bicycle NOUN
le vélo
bifocals PL NOUN
les verres à double foyer masc pl
big ADJECTIVE
1 grand (FEM grande)
□ a big house une grande maison □ my big brother mon grand frère □ her big sister sa grande sœur

---

WORD POWER
You can use a number of other words instead of **big** to mean 'large':
enormous énorme
□ an enormous cake un gâteau énorme
gigantic gigantesque
□ a gigantic house une maison gigantesque
huge immense
□ a huge garden un jardin immense
massive énorme
□ a massive TV une télé énorme

■ **He's a big guy.** C'est un grand gaillard.
2 gros (FEM grosse) (car, animal, book, parcel)
□ a big car une grosse voiture
bigheaded ADJECTIVE
■ **to be bigheaded** avoir la grosse tête
bike NOUN
le vélo
□ by bike en vélo
bikini NOUN

le bikini
bilingual ADJECTIVE
bilingue (FEM bilingue)
bill NOUN
1 l' addition fem (in restaurant)
□ Can we have the bill, please? L'addition, s'il vous plaît.
2 la facture (for gas, electricity)
3 le billet (US)
□ a five-dollar bill un billet de cinq dólars
billiards NOUN
le billard
□ to play billiards jouer au billard
billion NOUN
le milliard
bin NOUN
la poubelle
bingo NOUN
le bingo
binoculars PL NOUN
les jumelles fem pl
■ **a pair of binoculars** des jumelles
biochemistry NOUN
la biochimie
biography NOUN
la biographie
biology NOUN
la biologie
bird NOUN
l' oiseau masc (PL les oiseaux)
birdwatching NOUN
■ **My hobby's birdwatching.** Mon passe-temps favori est d'observer les oiseaux.
■ **to go birdwatching** aller observer les oiseaux
Biro® NOUN
le bic®
birth NOUN
la naissance
□ date of birth la date de naissance
birth certificate NOUN
l' acte de naissance masc
birth control NOUN
la contraception
birthday NOUN
l' anniversaire masc
□ When's your birthday? Quelle est la date de ton anniversaire?
■ **a birthday cake** un gâteau d'anniversaire
■ **a birthday card** une carte d'anniversaire
■ **I'm going to have a birthday party.** Je vais faire une fête pour mon anniversaire.
biscuit NOUN
le gâteau sec (PL les gâteaux secs)
bishop NOUN
l' évêque masc
bit VERB ▷ see bite

bit NOUN
le morceau (PL les morceaux)
□ Would you like another bit? Est-ce que tu en veux un autre morceau?
■ **a bit of 1** (piece of) un morceau de □ a bit of cake un morceau de gâteau **2** (a little) un peu de □ a bit of music un peu de musique
■ **It's a bit of a nuisance.** C'est ennuyeux.
■ **a bit** un peu □ He's a bit mad. Il est un peu fou. □ a bit too hot un peu trop chaud □ Wait a bit! Attends un peu! □ Do you play football? — A bit. Tu joues au football? — Un peu.
■ **to fall to bits** se désintégrer
■ **to take something to bits** démonter quelque chose
■ **bit by bit** petit à petit

bitch NOUN
la chienne (female dog)

to **bite** VERB
▷ see also **bite** NOUN
1 mordre (person, dog)
2 piquer (insect)
□ I got bitten by mosquitoes. Je me suis fait piquer par des moustiques.
■ **to bite one's nails** se ronger les ongles

bite NOUN
▷ see also **bite** VERB
1 la piqûre (insect bite)
2 la morsure (animal bite)
■ **to have a bite to eat** manger un morceau

bitten VERB ▷ see **bite**

bitter ADJECTIVE
▷ see also **bitter** NOUN
1 amer (FEM amère)
2 glacial (FEM glaciale, MASC PL glaciaux) (weather, wind)
□ It's bitter today. Il fait un froid glacial aujourd'hui.

bitter NOUN
▷ see also **bitter** ADJECTIVE
la bière brune

black ADJECTIVE
noir (FEM noire)
□ a black jacket une veste noire □ She's black. Elle est noire.

blackberry NOUN
la mûre

blackbird NOUN
le merle

blackboard NOUN
le tableau noir (PL les tableaux noirs)

black coffee NOUN
le café

blackcurrant NOUN
le cassis

blackmail NOUN
▷ see also **blackmail** VERB
le chantage
□ That's blackmail! C'est du chantage!

to **blackmail** VERB
▷ see also **blackmail** NOUN
■ **to blackmail somebody** faire chanter quelqu'un □ He blackmailed her. Il l'a fait chanter.

blackout NOUN
la panne d'électricité (power cut)
■ **to have a blackout** (faint) s'évanouir

black pudding NOUN
le boudin

blade NOUN
la lame

to **blame** VERB
■ **Don't blame me!** Ça n'est pas ma faute!
■ **I blame the police.** À mon avis, c'est la faute de la police.
■ **He blamed it on my sister.** Il a dit que c'était la faute de ma sœur.

blank ADJECTIVE
▷ see also **blank** NOUN
1 blanc (FEM blanche) (paper)
2 vierge (FEM vierge) (video, page)
■ **My mind went blank.** J'ai eu un trou.

blank NOUN
▷ see also **blank** ADJECTIVE
le blanc
□ Fill in the blanks. Remplissez les blancs.

blank cheque NOUN
le chèque en blanc

blanket NOUN
la couverture

blast NOUN
■ **a bomb blast** une explosion

blatant ADJECTIVE
flagrant (FEM flagrante)

blaze NOUN
l' incendie masc

blazer NOUN
le blazer

bleach NOUN
l' eau de Javel fem

bleached ADJECTIVE
décoloré (FEM décolorée)
□ bleached hair les cheveux décolorés

bleak ADJECTIVE
désolé (FEM désolée) (place)
■ **The future looks bleak.** L'avenir semble peu prometteur.

to **bleed** VERB
saigner
□ My nose is bleeding. Je saigne du nez.

bleeper NOUN

319

le bip
blender NOUN
le mixer
to **bless** VERB
bénir *(religiously)*
■ **Bless you!** *(after sneezing)* À tes souhaits!
blew VERB ▷*see* **blow**
blind ADJECTIVE
▷*see also* **blind** NOUN
aveugle (FEM aveugle)
blind NOUN
▷*see also* **blind** ADJECTIVE
le store *(for window)*
blindfold NOUN
▷*see also* **blindfold** VERB
le bandeau (PL les bandeaux)
to **blindfold** VERB
▷*see also* **blindfold** NOUN
■ **to blindfold somebody** bander les yeux à
quelqu'un
to **blink** VERB
cligner des yeux
bliss NOUN
■ **It was bliss!** C'était merveilleux!
blister NOUN
l' ampoule *fem*
blizzard NOUN
la tempête de neige
blob NOUN
la goutte
□ a blob of glue une goutte de colle
block NOUN
▷*see also* **block** VERB
l' immeuble *masc*
□ He lives in our block. Il habite dans notre
immeuble.
■ **a block of flats** un immeuble
to **block** VERB
▷*see also* **block** NOUN
bloquer
blockage NOUN
l' obstruction *fem*
bloke NOUN
le mec *(informal)*
blonde ADJECTIVE
blond (FEM blonde)
□ She's got blonde hair. Elle a les cheveux
blonds.
blood NOUN
le sang
blood pressure NOUN
■ **to have high blood pressure** faire de la
tension
blood sports NOUN
les sports sanguinaires *masc pl*
blood test NOUN
la prise de sang

bloody ADJECTIVE
■ **bloody difficult** sacrément difficile
■ **that bloody television** cette putain de
télévision
■ **Bloody hell!** Merde!
blouse NOUN
le chemisier
blow NOUN
▷*see also* **blow** VERB
le coup
to **blow** VERB
▷*see also* **blow** NOUN
souffler *(wind, person)*
■ **to blow one's nose** se moucher
■ **to blow a whistle** siffler
■ **to blow out a candle** éteindre une
bougie
to **blow up** VERB
1 faire sauter
□ The terrorists blew up a police station. Les
terroristes ont fait sauter un commissariat
de police.
2 gonfler
□ to blow up a balloon gonfler un ballon
■ **The house blew up.** La maison a sauté.
blow-dry NOUN
le brushing
■ **A cut and blow-dry, please.** Une coupe
brushing, s'il vous plaît.
blown VERB ▷*see* **blow**
blue ADJECTIVE
bleu (FEM bleue)
□ a blue dress une robe bleue
■ **a blue film** un film pornographique
■ **It came out of the blue.** C'était
complètement inattendu.
blues PL NOUN
le blues *sing*
to **bluff** VERB
▷*see also* **bluff** NOUN
bluffer
bluff NOUN
▷*see also* **bluff** VERB
le bluff
□ It's just a bluff. C'est du bluff.
blunder NOUN
la gaffe
blunt ADJECTIVE
1 brusque (FEM brusque) *(person)*
2 émoussé (FEM émoussée) *(knife)*
to **blush** VERB
rougir
board NOUN
1 la planche *(wooden)*
2 le tableau (PL les tableaux) *(blackboard)*
□ on the board au tableau
3 le panneau (PL les panneaux) *(noticeboard)*

4 le jeu (PL les jeux) *(for board games)*
5 l' échiquier *masc (for chess)*
■ **on board** à bord
■ **'full board'** 'pension complète'
boarder NOUN
l' interne *masc/fem*
board game NOUN
le jeu de société (PL les jeux de société)
boarding card NOUN
la carte d'embarquement
boarding school NOUN
le pensionnat
■ **I go to boarding school.** Je suis interne.
to **boast** VERB
se vanter
□ Stop boasting! Arrête de te vanter!
■ **to boast about something** se vanter de
quelque chose
boat NOUN
le bateau (PL les bateaux)
body NOUN
le corps
bodybuilding NOUN
le culturisme
bodyguard NOUN
le garde du corps
bog NOUN
la tourbière *(marsh)*
boil NOUN
▷ *see also* **boil** VERB
le furoncle
to **boil** VERB
▷ *see also* **boil** NOUN
1 faire bouillir
□ to boil some water faire bouillir de l'eau
■ **to boil an egg** faire cuire un œuf
2 bouillir
□ The water's boiling. L'eau bout. □ The
water's boiled. L'eau a bouilli.
to **boil over** VERB
déborder
boiled ADJECTIVE
à l'eau
□ boiled potatoes des pommes de terre à
l'eau
■ **a boiled egg** un œuf à la coque
boiling ADJECTIVE
■ **It's boiling in here!** Il fait une chaleur
torride ici!
■ **boiling hot** torride □ a boiling hot day
une journée torride
bolt NOUN
1 le verrou *(on door)*
2 le boulon *(with nut)*
bomb NOUN
▷ *see also* **bomb** VERB
la bombe

to **bomb** VERB
▷ *see also* **bomb** NOUN
bombarder
bomber NOUN
le bombardier
bombing NOUN
l' attentat à la bombe *masc*
bond NOUN
le lien
bone NOUN
1 l' os *masc (of human, animal)*
2 l' arête *fem (of fish)*
bone dry ADJECTIVE
complètement sec (FEM complètement
sèche)
bonfire NOUN
le feu (PL les feux)

> **DID YOU KNOW…?**
> The French do not celebrate Bonfire
> Night, though they have fireworks on
> the 14th July, which is Bastille Day.

bonnet NOUN
le capot *(of car)*
bonus NOUN
1 la prime *(extra payment)*
2 le plus *(added advantage)*
book NOUN
▷ *see also* **book** VERB
le livre
to **book** VERB
▷ *see also* **book** NOUN
réserver
□ We haven't booked. Nous n'avons pas
réservé.
bookcase NOUN
la bibliothèque
booklet NOUN
la brochure
bookmark NOUN
le signet *(computing)*
bookshelf NOUN
l' étagère à livres *fem*
bookshop NOUN
la librairie
to **boost** VERB
stimuler
□ to boost the economy stimuler
l'économie
■ **The win boosted the team's morale.** La
victoire a remonté le moral de l'équipe.
boot NOUN
1 le coffre *(of car)*
2 la botte *(fashion boot)*
3 la chaussure de marche *(for hiking)*
■ **football boots** des chaussures de foot
booze NOUN
l' alcool *masc*

321

border NOUN
la frontière

bore VERB ▷ see **bear**

bored ADJECTIVE
- **to be bored** s'ennuyer □ I was bored. Je m'ennuyais.
- **to get bored** s'ennuyer

boredom NOUN
l' ennui *masc*

boring ADJECTIVE
ennuyeux (FEM ennuyeuse)

born ADJECTIVE
- **to be born** naître □ I was born in 1990. Je suis né en mille neuf cent quatre-vingt-dix.

to **borrow** VERB
emprunter
□ Can I borrow your pen? Je peux emprunter ton stylo?
- **to borrow something from somebody** emprunter quelque chose à quelqu'un □ I borrowed some money from a friend. J'ai emprunté de l'argent à un ami.

Bosnia NOUN
la Bosnie

Bosnian ADJECTIVE
bosniaque (FEM bosniaque)

boss NOUN
le patron
la patronne

to **boss around** VERB
- **to boss somebody around** donner des ordres à quelqu'un

bossy ADJECTIVE
autoritaire (FEM autoritaire)

both ADJECTIVE, PRONOUN
tous les deux *masc pl*
toutes les deux *fem pl*
□ We both went. Nous y sommes allés tous les deux. □ Emma and Jane both went. Emma et Jane y sont allées toutes les deux. □ Both of your answers are wrong. Vos réponses sont toutes les deux mauvaises. □ Both of them have left. Ils sont partis tous les deux. □ Both of us went. Nous y sommes allés tous les deux. □ Both Maggie and John are against it. Maggie et John sont tous les deux contre.
- **He speaks both German and Italian.** Il parle allemand et italien.

to **bother** VERB
1 tracasser *(worry)*
□ What's bothering you? Qu'est-ce qui te tracasse?
2 déranger *(disturb)*
□ I'm sorry to bother you. Je suis désolé de vous déranger.
- **no bother** aucun problème

- **Don't bother!** Ça n'est pas la peine!
- **to bother to do something** prendre la peine de faire quelque chose □ He didn't bother to tell me about it. Il n'a pas pris la peine de m'en parler.

bottle NOUN
la bouteille

bottle bank NOUN
le conteneur à verre

bottle-opener NOUN
l' ouvre-bouteille *masc*

bottom NOUN
▷ see also **bottom** ADJECTIVE
1 le fond *(of container, bag, sea)*
2 le derrière *(buttocks)*
3 le bas *(of page, list)*

bottom ADJECTIVE
▷ see also **bottom** NOUN
inférieur (FEM inférieure)
□ the bottom shelf l'étagère inférieure
- **the bottom sheet** le drap de dessous

bought VERB ▷ see **buy**

to **bounce** VERB
rebondir

bouncer NOUN
le videur

bound ADJECTIVE
- **He's bound to fail.** Il va sûrement échouer.

boundary NOUN
la frontière

bow NOUN
▷ see also **bow** VERB
1 le nœud *(knot)*
□ to tie a bow faire un nœud
2 l' arc *masc*
□ a bow and arrows un arc et des flèches

to **bow** VERB
▷ see also **bow** NOUN
faire une révérence

bowels PL NOUN
les intestins *masc pl*

bowl NOUN
▷ see also **bowl** VERB
le bol *(for soup, cereal)*

to **bowl** VERB
▷ see also **bowl** NOUN
lancer la balle *(in cricket)*

bowler NOUN
le lanceur *(in cricket)*

bowling NOUN
le bowling
- **to go bowling** jouer au bowling
- **a bowling alley** un bowling

bowls NOUN
les boules *fem pl*
□ to play bowls jouer aux boules

bow tie NOUN
le nœud papillon

box NOUN
la boîte
  □ a box of matches une boîte d'allumettes
  ■ a cardboard box un carton

boxer NOUN
le boxeur

boxer shorts PL NOUN
le caleçon *sing*

boxing NOUN
la boxe

Boxing Day NOUN
le lendemain de Noël
  □ on Boxing Day le lendemain de Noël
  ○ **LANGUAGE TIP** Word for word, this
  means 'the day after Christmas'.

boy NOUN
le garçon

boyfriend NOUN
le copain
  □ Have you got a boyfriend? Est-ce que tu
as un copain?

bra NOUN
le soutien-gorge (PL les soutiens-gorge)

brace NOUN
l' appareil *masc (on teeth)*
  □ She wears a brace. Elle a un appareil.

bracelet NOUN
le bracelet

braces PL NOUN
l' appareil *masc sing (on teeth)*
  □ She wears braces. Elle a un appareil.

brackets PL NOUN
  ■ in brackets entre parenthèses

brain NOUN
le cerveau (PL les cerveaux)

brainy ADJECTIVE
intelligent (FEM intelligente)

brake NOUN
  ▷ *see also* **brake** VERB
le frein

to **brake** VERB
  ▷ *see also* **brake** NOUN
freiner

branch NOUN
1 la branche *(of tree)*
2 l' agence *fem (of bank)*

brand NOUN
la marque
  □ a well-known brand of coffee une marque
de café bien connue

brand name NOUN
la marque

brand-new ADJECTIVE
tout neuf (FEM toute neuve)

brandy NOUN

le cognac

brass NOUN
le cuivre
  ■ the brass section les cuivres

brass band NOUN
la fanfare

brat NOUN
  ■ He's a spoiled brat. C'est un enfant gâté.

brave ADJECTIVE
courageux (FEM courageuse)

Brazil NOUN
le Brésil
  ■ in Brazil au Brésil

bread NOUN
le pain
  □ brown bread le pain complet □ white
bread le pain blanc
  ■ bread and butter les tartines de pain
beurrées *fem pl*

break NOUN
  ▷ *see also* **break** VERB
1 la pause *(rest)*
  □ to take a break faire une pause
2 la récréation *(at school)*
  □ during morning break pendant la
récréation du matin
  ■ the Christmas break les vacances de
Noël
  ■ Give me a break! Laisse-moi tranquille!

to **break** VERB
  ▷ *see also* **break** NOUN
1 casser
  □ Careful, you'll break something!
Attention, tu vas casser quelque chose!
2 se casser *(get broken)*
  □ Careful, it'll break! Attention, ça va se
casser!
  ■ to break one's leg se casser la jambe □ I
broke my leg. Je me suis cassé la jambe.
  ■ He broke his arm. Il s'est cassé le bras.
  ■ to break a promise rompre une
promesse
  ■ to break a record battre un record
  ■ to break the law violer la loi

to **break down** VERB
tomber en panne
  □ The car broke down. La voiture est
tombée en panne.

to **break in** VERB
entrer par effraction

to **break off** VERB
1 casser
  □ He broke off a piece of chocolate. Il a
cassé un bout de chocolat.
2 se casser
  □ The branch broke off in the storm. La
branche s'est cassée pendant l'orage.

to **break open** VERB
forcer *(door, cupboard)*

to **break out** VERB
1 se déclarer *(fire)*
2 éclater *(war)*
3 s'évader *(prisoner)*
■ **to break out in a rash** être couvert de boutons

to **break up** VERB
1 se disperser *(crowd)*
2 se terminer *(meeting, party)*
3 se séparer *(couple)*
■ **to break up a fight** mettre fin à une bagarre
■ **We break up next Wednesday.** Nos vacances commencent mercredi.
■ **You're breaking up!** Je ne te capte plus!

breakdown NOUN
1 la panne *(in vehicle)*
□ **to have a breakdown** tomber en panne
2 la dépression *(mental)*
□ **to have a breakdown** faire une dépression

breakdown van NOUN
la dépanneuse

breakfast NOUN
le petit déjeuner
□ **What would you like for breakfast?** Qu'est-ce vous voulez pour le petit déjeuner?

break-in NOUN
le cambriolage

breast NOUN
le sein *(of woman)*
■ **chicken breast** le blanc de poulet

to **breast-feed** VERB
allaiter

breaststroke NOUN
la brasse

breath NOUN
l' haleine *fem*
□ **to have bad breath** avoir mauvaise haleine
■ **to be out of breath** être essoufflé
■ **to get one's breath back** reprendre son souffle

to **breathe** VERB
respirer

to **breathe in** VERB
inspirer

to **breathe out** VERB
expirer

to **breed** VERB
▷ *see also* **breed** NOUN
se reproduire *(reproduce)*
■ **to breed dogs** faire de l'élevage de chiens

breed NOUN
▷ *see also* **breed** VERB

la race

breeze NOUN
la brise

brewery NOUN
la brasserie

to **bribe** VERB
soudoyer

brick NOUN
la brique
□ **a brick wall** un mur en brique

bricklayer NOUN
le maçon

bride NOUN
la mariée

bridegroom NOUN
le marié

bridesmaid NOUN
la demoiselle d'honneur

bridge NOUN
1 le pont
□ **a suspension bridge** un pont suspendu
2 le bridge
□ **to play bridge** jouer au bridge

brief ADJECTIVE
bref (FEM brève)

briefcase NOUN
la serviette

briefly ADVERB
brièvement

briefs PL NOUN
le slip *sing*
■ **a pair of briefs** un slip

bright ADJECTIVE
1 vif (FEM vive) *(colour, light)*
□ **a bright colour** une couleur vive
■ **bright blue** bleu vif □ **a bright blue car** une voiture bleu vif
2 intelligent (FEM intelligente)
□ **He's not very bright.** Il n'est pas très intelligent.

brilliant ADJECTIVE
1 génial (FEM géniale, MASC PL géniaux) *(wonderful)*
□ **Brilliant!** Génial!
2 brillant (FEM brillante) *(clever)*
□ **a brilliant scientist** un savant brillant

to **bring** VERB
1 apporter
□ **Bring warm clothes.** Apportez des vêtements chauds. □ **Could you bring me my trainers?** Tu peux m'apporter mes baskets?
2 amener *(person)*
□ **Can I bring a friend?** Est-ce que je peux amener un ami?

to **bring back** VERB
rapporter

to **bring forward** VERB
avancer
□ The meeting was brought forward. On a avancé la réunion.

to **bring up** VERB
élever
□ She brought up 5 children on her own. Elle a élevé cinq enfants toute seule.

Britain NOUN
la Grande-Bretagne
■ **in Britain** en Grande-Bretagne
■ **to Britain** en Grande-Bretagne
■ **I'm from Britain.** Je suis britannique.
■ **Great Britain** la Grande-Bretagne

British ADJECTIVE
britannique (FEM britannique)
■ **the British** les Britanniques *masc pl*
■ **the British Isles** les îles Britanniques *fem pl*

Brittany NOUN
la Bretagne
■ **in Brittany** en Bretagne
■ **to Brittany** en Bretagne
■ **She's from Brittany.** Elle est bretonne.

broad ADJECTIVE
large (FEM large) *(wide)*
■ **in broad daylight** en plein jour
■ **broad beans** les fèves *fem pl*

broadband NOUN
l' ADSL *masc*
□ Do you have broadband? Tu as l'ADSL?

broadcast NOUN
▷ *see also* **broadcast** VERB
l' émission *fem*

to **broadcast** VERB
▷ *see also* **broadcast** NOUN
diffuser
□ The interview was broadcast yesterday. L'interview a été diffusée hier.
■ **to broadcast live** retransmettre en direct

broad-minded ADJECTIVE
large d'esprit (FEM large d'esprit)

broccoli NOUN
les brocolis *masc pl*

brochure NOUN
la brochure

to **broil** VERB (US)
■ **to broil something** faire griller quelque chose

broke VERB ▷ *see* **break**

broke ADJECTIVE
■ **to be broke** *(without money)* être fauché

broken ADJECTIVE
cassé (FEM cassée)
□ It's broken. C'est cassé. □ a broken leg une jambe cassée □ He's got a broken arm. Il a le bras cassé.

bronchitis NOUN
la bronchite

bronze NOUN
le bronze
□ the bronze medal la médaille de bronze

brooch NOUN
la broche

broom NOUN
le balai

brother NOUN
le frère
□ my brother mon frère □ my big brother mon grand frère

brother-in-law NOUN
le beau-frère (PL les beaux-frères)

brought VERB ▷ *see* **bring**

brown ADJECTIVE
1 marron (FEM+PL marron) *(clothes)*
2 brun (FEM brune) *(hair)*
3 bronzé (FEM bronzée) *(tanned)*
■ **brown bread** le pain complet

Brownie NOUN
la jeannette

to **browse** VERB
parcourir le Net *(on internet)*

browser NOUN
le navigateur *(for internet)*

bruise NOUN
le bleu

brush NOUN
▷ *see also* **brush** VERB
1 la brosse
2 le pinceau (PL les pinceaux) *(paintbrush)*

to **brush** VERB
▷ *see also* **brush** NOUN
brosser
■ **to brush one's hair** se brosser les cheveux □ I brushed my hair. Je me suis brossé les cheveux.
■ **to brush one's teeth** se brosser les dents □ I brush my teeth every night. Je me brosse les dents tous les soirs.

Brussels NOUN
Bruxelles
■ **in Brussels** à Bruxelles
■ **to Brussels** à Bruxelles

Brussels sprouts PL NOUN
les choux de Bruxelles *masc pl*

brutal ADJECTIVE
brutal (FEM brutale, MASC PL brutaux)

BSc NOUN (= *Bachelor of Science*)
la licence
■ **a BSc in Mathematics** une licence de mathématiques

BSE NOUN (= *bovine spongiform encephalopathy*)
l' ESB *fem* (= *l'encéphalite spongiforme*

bovine)

bubble NOUN
la bulle

bubble bath NOUN
le bain moussant

bubble gum NOUN
le chewing-gum

bucket NOUN
le seau (PL les seaux)

buckle NOUN
la boucle *(on belt, watch, shoe)*

Buddhism NOUN
le bouddhisme

Buddhist ADJECTIVE
bouddhiste (FEM bouddhiste)

buddy NOUN (US)
le copain
la copine

budget NOUN
le budget

budgie NOUN
la perruche

buffet NOUN
le buffet

buffet car NOUN
la voiture-bar

bug NOUN
1 l' insecte *masc (insect)*
2 le microbe *(infection)*
  □ There's a bug going round. Il y a un
  microbe qui traîne.
  ■ **a stomach bug** une gastroentérite
3 le bug *(in computer)*

bugged ADJECTIVE
sur écoute
  □ The room was bugged. La pièce était sur
  écoute.

to **build** VERB
construire
  □ He's building a garage. Il construit un
  garage.

to **build up** VERB
s'accumuler *(increase)*

builder NOUN
1 l' entrepreneur *masc (owner of firm)*
2 le maçon *(worker)*

building NOUN
le bâtiment
  ■ **a building site** un chantier

built VERB ▷ *see* **build**

bulb NOUN
l' ampoule *fem (electric)*

Bulgaria NOUN
la Bulgarie

bull NOUN
le taureau (PL les taureaux)

bullet NOUN

la balle

bulletin board NOUN
le panneau d'affichage électronique
(computer)

bullfighting NOUN
la tauromachie

bully NOUN
  ▷ *see also* **bully** VERB
la brute
  □ He's a big bully. C'est une brute.

to **bully** VERB
  ▷ *see also* **bully** NOUN
tyranniser

bum NOUN
le derrière *(bottom)*

bum bag NOUN
la banane

bump NOUN
  ▷ *see also* **bump** VERB
1 la bosse *(lump)*
2 l' accrochage *masc (minor accident)*
  □ We had a bump. Nous avons eu un
  accrochage.

to **bump** VERB
  ▷ *see also* **bump** NOUN
  ■ **to bump into something** rentrer dans
  quelque chose □ I bumped into the table in
  the dark. Je suis rentrée dans la table dans
  le noir.
  ■ **to bump into somebody** 1 *(literally)*
  rentrer dans quelqu'un □ He stopped
  suddenly and I bumped into him. Il s'est
  arrêté subitement et je lui suis rentré
  dedans. **2** *(meet by chance)* rencontrer par
  hasard □ I bumped into Jane in the
  supermarket. J'ai rencontré Jane par hasard
  au supermarché.

bumper NOUN
le pare-chocs (PL les pare-chocs)

bumpy ADJECTIVE
cahoteux (FEM cahoteuse)

bun NOUN
le petit pain au lait

bunch NOUN
  ■ **a bunch of flowers** un bouquet de fleurs
  ■ **a bunch of grapes** une grappe de raisin
  ■ **a bunch of keys** un trousseau de clés

bunches PL NOUN
les couettes *fem pl*
  □ She has her hair in bunches. Elle a des
  couettes.

bungalow NOUN
le bungalow

bunk NOUN
la couchette
  ■ **bunk beds** les lits superposés *masc pl*

burger NOUN

le hamburger

burglar NOUN
le cambrioleur
la cambrioleuse

to **burglarize** VERB (US)
cambrioler

burglary NOUN
le cambriolage

to **burgle** VERB
cambrioler
□ Her house was burgled. Sa maison a été cambriolée.

burn NOUN
▷ see also **burn** VERB
la brûlure

to **burn** VERB
▷ see also **burn** NOUN
1 brûler (rubbish, documents)
2 faire brûler (food)
□ I burned the cake. J'ai fait brûler le gâteau.
3 graver (CD, DVD)
■ **to burn oneself** se brûler □ I burned myself on the oven door. Je me suis brûlé sur la porte du four.
■ **I've burned my hand.** Je me suis brûlé la main.

to **burn down** VERB
brûler
□ The factory burned down. L'usine a brûlé.

to **burst** VERB
éclater
□ The balloon burst. Le ballon a éclaté.
■ **to burst a balloon** faire éclater un ballon
■ **to burst out laughing** éclater de rire
■ **to burst into flames** prendre feu
■ **to burst into tears** fondre en larmes

to **bury** VERB
enterrer

bus NOUN
l' autobus masc
□ the bus driver le conducteur d'autobus
□ a bus stop un arrêt d'autobus
■ **the school bus** le car scolaire
■ **a bus pass** une carte d'abonnement pour le bus
■ **a bus station** une gare routière
■ **a bus ticket** un ticket de bus

bush NOUN
le buisson

business NOUN
1 l' entreprise fem (firm)
□ He's got his own business. Il a sa propre entreprise.
2 les affaires fem pl (commerce)
□ He's away on business. Il est en voyage d'affaires.
■ **a business trip** un voyage d'affaires

■ **It's none of my business.** Ça ne me regarde pas.

businessman NOUN
l' homme d'affaires masc

businesswoman NOUN
la femme d'affaires

busker NOUN
le musicien de rue
la musicienne de rue

bust NOUN
la poitrine (chest)

busy ADJECTIVE
1 occupé (FEM occupée) (person, phone line)
2 chargé (FEM chargée) (day, schedule)
3 très fréquenté (FEM très fréquentée) (shop, street)

busy signal NOUN (US)
la tonalité 'occupé'

but CONJUNCTION
mais
□ I'd like to come, but I'm busy. J'aimerais venir mais je suis occupé.

butcher NOUN
le boucher
□ He's a butcher. Il est boucher.

butcher's NOUN
la boucherie

butter NOUN
le beurre

butterfly NOUN
le papillon

buttocks PL NOUN
les fesses fem pl

button NOUN
le bouton

to **buy** VERB
▷ see also **buy** NOUN
acheter
□ I bought him an ice cream. Je lui ai acheté une glace.
■ **to buy something from somebody**
acheter quelque chose à quelqu'un □ I bought a watch from him. Je lui ai acheté une montre.

buy NOUN
▷ see also **buy** VERB
■ **It was a good buy.** C'était une bonne affaire.

by PREPOSITION
1 par
□ The thieves were caught by the police. Les voleurs ont été arrêtés par la police.
2 de
□ a painting by Picasso un tableau de Picasso □ a book by Balzac un livre de Balzac
3 en

327

□ by car en voiture □ by train en train □ by bus en autobus

4 à côté de *(close to)*

□ Where's the bank? — It's by the post office. Où est la banque? — Elle est à côté de la poste.

5 avant *(not later than)*

□ We have to be there by 4 o'clock. Nous devons y être avant quatre heures.

■ **by the time ...** quand ... □ By the time I got there it was too late. Quand je suis arrivé il était déjà trop tard. □ It'll be ready by the time you get back. Ça sera prêt quand vous reviendrez.

■ **That's fine by me.** Ça me va.

■ **all by himself** tout seul

■ **all by herself** toute seule

■ **I did it all by myself.** Je l'ai fait tout seul.

■ **by the way** au fait

bye EXCLAMATION
salut!

bypass NOUN
la route de contournement

Cc

cab NOUN
le taxi

cabbage NOUN
le chou (PL les choux)

cabin NOUN
la cabine (on ship)

cabinet NOUN
■ **a bathroom cabinet** une armoire de salle
de bain
■ **a drinks cabinet** un bar

cable NOUN
le câble

cable car NOUN
le téléphérique

cable television NOUN
la télévision par câble

cactus NOUN
le cactus

cadet NOUN
■ **a police cadet** un élève policier
■ **a cadet officer** un élève officier

café NOUN
le café

> **DID YOU KNOW...?**
> Cafés in France sell both alcoholic and
> non-alcoholic drinks.

cafeteria NOUN
la cafétéria

cage NOUN
la cage

cagoule NOUN
le K-way®

cake NOUN
le gâteau (PL les gâteaux)

to **calculate** VERB
calculer

calculation NOUN
le calcul

calculator NOUN
la machine à calculer

calendar NOUN
le calendrier

calf NOUN
1 le veau (PL les veaux) (of cow)
2 le mollet (of leg)

call NOUN
▷ see also **call** VERB
l' appel masc (by phone)
□ Thanks for your call. Merci de votre appel.
■ **a phone call** un coup de téléphone
■ **to be on call** (doctor) être de permanence
□ He's on call this evening. Il est de
permanence ce soir.

to **call** VERB
▷ see also **call** NOUN
appeler
□ I'll tell him you called. Je lui dirai que vous
avez appelé. □ This is the number to call.
C'est le numéro à appeler. □ We called the
police. Nous avons appelé la police.
□ Everyone calls him Jimmy. Tout le monde
l'appelle Jimmy.
■ **to be called** s'appeler □ He's called
Fluffy. Il s'appelle Fluffy. □ What's she
called? Elle s'appelle comment?
■ **to call somebody names** insulter
quelqu'un
■ **He called me an idiot.** Il m'a traité
d'idiot.

to **call back** VERB
rappeler (phone again)
□ I'll call back at 6 o'clock. Je rappellerai à
six heures.

to **call for** VERB
passer prendre
□ I'll call for you at 2.30. Je passerai te
prendre à deux heures et demie.

to **call off** VERB
annuler
□ The match was called off. Le match a été
annulé.

call box NOUN
la cabine téléphonique

call centre NOUN
le centre d'appels

calm ADJECTIVE
calme (FEM calme)

to **calm down** VERB
se calmer
□ Calm down! Calme-toi!

C

Calor gas® NOUN
le butane

calorie NOUN
la calorie

calves PL NOUN ▷ see **calf**

Cambodia NOUN
le Cambodge

■ **in Cambodia** au Cambodge

camcorder NOUN
le caméscope

came VERB ▷ see **come**

camel NOUN
le chameau (PL les chameaux)

camera NOUN
1 l' appareil photo *masc* (PL les appareils photo) *(for photos)*
2 la caméra *(for filming, TV)*

cameraman NOUN
le caméraman

camera phone NOUN
le téléphone appareil photo

to **camp** VERB
▷ see also **camp** NOUN
camper

camp NOUN
▷ see also **camp** VERB
le camp

■ **a camp bed** un lit de camp

campaign NOUN
la campagne

camper NOUN
1 le campeur
la campeuse *(person)*
2 le camping-car *(van)*

camping NOUN
le camping

■ **to go camping** faire du camping □ We went camping in Cornwall. Nous avons fait du camping en Cornouailles.

camping gas® NOUN
le butane

campsite NOUN
le terrain de camping

campus NOUN
le campus

can NOUN
▷ see also **can** VERB
1 la boîte *(tin)*
□ a can of sweetcorn une boîte de maïs □ a can of beer une boîte de bière
2 le bidon *(container)*
□ a can of petrol un bidon d'essence

can VERB
▷ see also **can** NOUN
1 pouvoir *(be able to, be allowed to)*
□ I can't come. Je ne peux pas venir. □ Can I help you? Est-ce que je peux vous aider?

□ Can I use your phone? Est-ce que je peux me servir de votre téléphone? □ You could hire a bike. Tu pourrais louer un vélo. □ I couldn't sleep because of the noise. Je ne pouvais pas dormir à cause du bruit.

○ **LANGUAGE TIP** 'can' is sometimes not translated.

□ I can't hear you. Je ne t'entends pas. □ I can't remember. Je ne m'en souviens pas. □ Can you speak French? Parlez-vous français?
2 savoir *(have learnt how to)*
□ I can swim. Je sais nager. □ He can't drive. Il ne sait pas conduire.

■ **That can't be true!** Ce n'est pas possible!
■ **You could be right.** Vous avez peut-être raison.

Canada NOUN
le Canada

■ **in Canada** au Canada
■ **to Canada** au Canada

Canadian NOUN
▷ see also **Canadian** ADJECTIVE
le Canadien
la Canadienne

Canadian ADJECTIVE
▷ see also **Canadian** NOUN
canadien (FEM canadienne)

canal NOUN
le canal (PL les canaux)

Canaries PL NOUN
■ **the Canaries** les îles Canaries *fem pl*

canary NOUN
le canari

to **cancel** VERB
annuler
□ The match was cancelled. Le match a été annulé.

cancellation NOUN
l' annulation *fem*

cancer NOUN
1 le cancer
□ He's got cancer. Il a le cancer.
2 le Cancer
□ I'm Cancer. Je suis Cancer.

candidate NOUN
le candidat
la candidate

candle NOUN
la bougie

candy NOUN (US)
les bonbons *masc pl*

■ **a candy** un bonbon

candyfloss NOUN
la barbe à papa

cannabis NOUN
le cannabis

canned ADJECTIVE
en conserve *(food)*

cannot VERB ▷ *see* **can**

canoe NOUN
le canoë

canoeing NOUN
■ **to go canoeing** faire du canoë □ We went canoeing. Nous avons fait du canoë.

can-opener NOUN
l' ouvre-boîte *masc*

can't VERB ▷ *see* **can**

canteen NOUN
la cantine

to **canter** VERB
aller au petit galop

canvas NOUN
la toile

cap NOUN
1 la casquette *(hat)*
2 le bouchon *(of bottle, tube)*

capable ADJECTIVE
capable (FEM capable)

capacity NOUN
la capacité

capital NOUN
1 la capitale
□ Cardiff is the capital of Wales. Cardiff est la capitale du pays de Galles.
2 la majuscule *(letter)*
□ Write your address in capitals. Écris ton adresse en majuscules.

capitalism NOUN
le capitalisme

capital punishment NOUN
la peine capitale

Capricorn NOUN
le Capricorne
□ I'm Capricorn. Je suis Capricorne.

to **capsize** VERB
chavirer

captain NOUN
le capitaine
□ She's captain of the hockey team. Elle est capitaine de l'équipe de hockey.

caption NOUN
la légende

to **capture** VERB
capturer

car NOUN
la voiture
■ **to go by car** aller en voiture □ We went by car. Nous y sommes allés en voiture.
■ **a car crash** un accident de voiture

caramel NOUN
le caramel

caravan NOUN
la caravane

□ a caravan site un camping pour caravanes

card NOUN
la carte
■ **a card game** un jeu de cartes

cardboard NOUN
le carton
■ **a cardboard box** un carton

cardigan NOUN
le cardigan

cardphone NOUN
le téléphone à carte

care NOUN
▷ *see also* **care** VERB
le soin
□ with care avec soin
■ **to take care of** s'occuper de □ I take care of the children on Saturdays. Le samedi, je m'occupe des enfants.
■ **Take care! 1** *(Be careful!)* Fais attention!
2 *(Look after yourself!)* Prends bien soin de toi!

to **care** VERB
▷ *see also* **care** NOUN
■ **to care about** se soucier de □ They don't really care about their image. Ils se soucient pas trop de leur image.
■ **I don't care!** Ça m'est égal! □ She doesn't care. Ça lui est égal.
■ **to care for somebody** *(patients, old people)* s'occuper de quelqu'un

career NOUN
la carrière
■ **a careers adviser** un conseiller d'orientation

careful ADJECTIVE
■ **Be careful!** Fais attention!

carefully ADVERB
1 soigneusement
□ She carefully avoided talking about it. Elle évitait soigneusement d'en parler.
2 prudemment *(safely)*
□ Drive carefully! Conduisez prudemment!
■ **Think carefully!** Réfléchis bien!

careless ADJECTIVE
1 peu soigné (FEM peu soignée) *(work)*
■ **a careless mistake** une faute d'inattention
2 peu soigneux (FEM peu soigneuse) *(person)*
□ She's very careless. Elle est bien peu soigneuse.
3 imprudent (FEM imprudente)
□ a careless driver un conducteur imprudent

caretaker NOUN
le gardien
la gardienne

car-ferry NOUN

le ferry
cargo NOUN
la cargaison
car hire NOUN
la location de voitures
Caribbean NOUN
▷ see also **Caribbean** ADJECTIVE
1 les Caraïbes *fem pl (islands)*
□ We're going to the Caribbean. Nous allons aux Caraïbes.
■ **He's from the Caribbean.** Il est antillais.
2 la mer des Caraïbes *(sea)*
Caribbean ADJECTIVE
▷ see also **Caribbean** NOUN
antillais (FEM antillaise)
□ Caribbean food la cuisine antillaise
caring ADJECTIVE
■ **She's a very caring teacher.** C'est un professeur qui se préoccupe du bien-être de ses élèves.
■ **She has very caring parents.** Ses parents sont très affectueux.
carnation NOUN
l' œillet *masc*
carnival NOUN
le carnaval
carol NOUN
■ **a Christmas carol** un chant de Noël
car park NOUN
le parking
carpenter NOUN
le charpentier
□ He's a carpenter. Il est charpentier.
carpentry NOUN
la menuiserie
carpet NOUN
1 le tapis
□ a Persian carpet un tapis persan
2 la moquette *(fitted)*
car phone NOUN
le téléphone de voiture
car rental NOUN (US)
la location de voitures
carriage NOUN
la voiture
carrier bag NOUN
le sac en plastique
carrot NOUN
la carotte
to **carry** VERB
1 porter
□ I'll carry your bag. Je vais porter ton sac.
2 transporter
□ a plane carrying 100 passengers un avion transportant cent passagers
to **carry on** VERB
continuer

□ Carry on! Continue! □ She carried on talking. Elle a continué à parler.
to **carry out** VERB
exécuter *(orders)*
carrycot NOUN
le porte-bébé
cart NOUN
la charrette
carton NOUN
la brique *(of milk, juice)*
cartoon NOUN
1 le dessin animé *(film)*
2 le dessin humoristique *(in newspaper)*
■ **a strip cartoon** une bande dessinée
cartridge NOUN
la cartouche
to **carve** VERB
découper *(meat)*
case NOUN
1 la valise
□ I've packed my case. J'ai fait ma valise.
2 le cas (PL les cas)
□ in some cases dans certains cas
■ **in that case** dans ce cas □ I don't want it. — In that case, I'll take it. Je n'en veux pas. — Dans ce cas, je le prends.
■ **in case** au cas où □ in case it rains au cas où il pleuvrait
■ **just in case** à tout hasard □ Take some money, just in case. Prends de l'argent à tout hasard.
cash NOUN
l' argent *masc*
□ I'm a bit short of cash. Je suis un peu à court d'argent.
■ **in cash** en liquide □ £2000 in cash deux mille livres en liquide
■ **to pay cash** payer comptant
■ **a cash card** une carte de retrait
■ **the cash desk** la caisse
■ **a cash dispenser** un distributeur automatique de billets
■ **a cash register** une caisse
cashew NOUN
la noix de cajou (PL les noix de cajou)
cashier NOUN
le caissier
la caissière
cashmere NOUN
le cachemire
□ a cashmere sweater un pull en cachemire
casino NOUN
le casino
casserole NOUN
le ragoût
□ I'm going to make a casserole. Je vais faire un ragoût.

c

■ **a casserole dish** une cocotte

cassette NOUN
la cassette

■ **a cassette player** un lecteur de cassettes
■ **a cassette recorder** un magnétophone

cast NOUN
les acteurs *masc pl*
□ the cast of Eastenders les acteurs de la série Eastenders

castle NOUN
le château (PL les châteaux)

casual ADJECTIVE
1 décontracté (FEM décontractée)
□ casual clothes les vêtements décontractés
2 désinvolte (FEM désinvolte)
□ a casual attitude une attitude désinvolte
3 en passant
□ It was just a casual remark. C'était juste une remarque en passant.

casually ADVERB
■ **to dress casually** s'habiller de façon décontractée

casualty NOUN
les urgences *fem pl (in hospital)*

cat NOUN
le chat
la chatte *(female)*
□ Have you got a cat? Est-ce que tu as un chat?

catalogue NOUN
le catalogue

catalytic converter NOUN
le catalyseur

catarrh NOUN
le rhume chronique

catastrophe NOUN
la catastrophe

to **catch** VERB
1 attraper
□ to catch a thief attraper un voleur □ My cat catches birds. Mon chat attrape des oiseaux.
■ **to catch somebody doing something** attraper quelqu'un en train de faire quelque chose □ If they catch you smoking ... S'ils t'attrapent en train de fumer ...
■ **to catch a cold** attraper un rhume
2 prendre *(bus, train)*
□ We caught the last bus. On a pris le dernier bus.
3 saisir *(hear)*
□ I didn't catch his name. Je n'ai pas saisi son nom.

to **catch up** VERB
rattraper son retard
□ I've got to catch up: I was off yesterday. Je

dois rattraper mon retard: j'étais absent hier.

catching ADJECTIVE
contagieux (FEM contagieuse)
□ It's not catching. Ce n'est pas contagieux.

catering NOUN
la restauration

cathedral NOUN
la cathédrale

Catholic ADJECTIVE
▷ see also **Catholic** NOUN
catholique (FEM catholique)

Catholic NOUN
▷ see also **Catholic** ADJECTIVE
le/la catholique
□ I'm a Catholic. Je suis catholique.

cattle PL NOUN
le bétail *sing*

caught VERB ▷ see **catch**

cauliflower NOUN
le chou-fleur (PL les choux-fleurs)

cause NOUN
▷ see also **cause** VERB
la cause

to **cause** VERB
▷ see also **cause** NOUN
provoquer
□ to cause an accident provoquer un accident

cautious ADJECTIVE
prudent (FEM prudente)

cautiously ADVERB
avec précaution
□ She cautiously opened the door. Elle a ouvert la porte avec précaution.
■ **The government reacted cautiously.** Le gouvernement a réagi prudemment.

cave NOUN
la grotte

CCTV NOUN (= closed-circuit television)
la télévision en circuit fermé

CD NOUN
le CD (PL les CD)

CD burner NOUN
le graveur de CD

CD player NOUN
la platine laser

CD-ROM NOUN
le CD-ROM (PL les CD-ROM)

ceasefire NOUN
le cessez-le-feu (PL les cessez-le-feu)

ceiling NOUN
le plafond

to **celebrate** VERB
fêter *(birthday)*

celebrity NOUN
la célébrité

celery NOUN
le céleri

cell NOUN
la cellule

cell phone NOUN (US)
le téléphone portable

cellar NOUN
la cave
□ a wine cellar une cave à vins

cello NOUN
le violoncelle
□ I play the cello. Je joue du violoncelle.

cement NOUN
le ciment

cemetery NOUN
le cimetière

cent NOUN
le cent
□ twenty cents vingt cents

centenary NOUN
le centenaire

center NOUN (US)
le centre

centigrade ADJECTIVE
centigrade (FEM centigrade)
□ 20 degrees centigrade vingt degrés
centigrade

centimetre (US **centimeter**) NOUN
le centimètre

central ADJECTIVE
central (FEM centrale, MASC PL centraux)

central heating NOUN
le chauffage central

centre NOUN
le centre
□ a sports centre un centre sportif

century NOUN
le siècle
□ the 20th century le vingtième siècle
□ the 21st century le vingt et unième
siècle

cereal NOUN
les céréales *fem pl*
□ I have cereal for breakfast. Je prends des
céréales au petit déjeuner.

ceremony NOUN
la cérémonie

certain ADJECTIVE
certain (FEM certaine)
□ a certain person une certaine personne
□ I'm absolutely certain it was him. Je suis
absolument certain que c'était lui.
■ I don't know for certain. Je n'en suis pas
certain.
■ to make certain s'assurer □ I made
certain the door was locked. Je me suis
assuré que la porte était fermée à clé.

certainly ADVERB
vraiment
□ I certainly expected something better. Je
m'attendais vraiment à quelque chose de
mieux.
■ Certainly not! Certainement pas!
■ So it was a surprise? — It certainly was!
C'était donc une surprise? — Ça oui alors!

certificate NOUN
le certificat

CFCs PL NOUN
les CFC *masc pl*

chain NOUN
la chaîne

chair NOUN
1 la chaise
□ a table and 4 chairs une table et quatre
chaises
2 le fauteuil *(armchair)*

chairlift NOUN
le télésiège

chairman NOUN
le président

chalet NOUN
le chalet

chalk NOUN
la craie

challenge NOUN
▷ *see also* **challenge** VERB
le défi

to **challenge** VERB
▷ *see also* **challenge** NOUN
■ She challenged me to a race. Elle m'a
proposé de faire la course avec elle.

challenging ADJECTIVE
stimulant (FEM stimulante)
□ a challenging job un travail stimulant

chambermaid NOUN
la femme de chambre

champagne NOUN
le champagne

champion NOUN
le champion
la championne

championship NOUN
le championnat

chance NOUN
1 la chance
□ Do you think I've got any chance? Tu crois
que j'ai une chance? □ Their chances of
winning are very good. Ils ont de fortes
chances de gagner.
■ No chance! Pas question!
2 l' occasion *fem*
□ I'd like to have a chance to travel.
J'aimerais avoir l'occasion de voyager.
■ I'll write when I get the chance. J'écrirai

quand j'aurai un moment.

■ **by chance** par hasard □ We met by chance. Nous nous sommes rencontrés par hasard.

■ **to take a chance** prendre un risque □ I'm taking no chances! Je ne veux prendre aucun risque!

Chancellor of the Exchequer NOUN
le chancelier de l'Échiquier

to **change** VERB
▷ *see also* **change** NOUN
1 changer
□ The town has changed a lot. La ville a beaucoup changé. □ I'd like to change £50. Je voudrais changer cinquante livres.
2 changer de

> **LANGUAGE TIP** Use **changer de** when you change one thing for another.

□ You have to change trains in Paris. Il faut changer de train à Paris. □ I'm going to change my shoes. Je vais changer de chaussures. □ He wants to change his job. Il veut changer d'emploi.

■ **to change one's mind** changer d'avis □ I've changed my mind. J'ai changé d'avis.

■ **to change gear** changer de vitesse
3 se changer
□ She changed to go to the party. Elle s'est changée pour aller à la fête.

■ **to get changed** se changer □ I'm going to get changed. Je vais me changer.
4 échanger *(swap)*
□ Can I change this sweater? It's too small. Est-ce que je peux échanger ce pull? Il est trop petit.

change NOUN
▷ *see also* **change** VERB
1 le changement
□ There's been a change of plan. Il y a eu un changement de programme.
2 la monnaie *(money)*
□ I haven't got any change. Je n'ai pas de monnaie.

■ **a change of clothes** des vêtements de rechange

■ **for a change** pour changer □ Let's play tennis for a change. Si on jouait au tennis pour changer?

changeable ADJECTIVE
variable (FEM variable)

changing room NOUN
1 le salon d'essayage *(in shop)*
2 le vestiaire *(for sport)*

channel NOUN
la chaîne *(TV)*
□ There's football on the other channel. Il y a du football sur l'autre chaîne.

■ **the Channel** la Manche

■ **the Channel Islands** les îles Anglo-Normandes *fem pl*

■ **the Channel Tunnel** le tunnel sous la Manche

chaos NOUN
le chaos

chap NOUN
le type
□ He's a nice chap. C'est un type sympa.

chapel NOUN
la chapelle *(part of church)*

chapter NOUN
le chapitre

character NOUN
1 le caractère
■ She's quite a character. C'est un drôle de numéro.
2 le personnage *(in play, film)*
□ The character played by Depardieu ... Le personnage joué par Depardieu ...

characteristic NOUN
la caractéristique

charcoal NOUN
le charbon de bois

charge NOUN
▷ *see also* **charge** VERB
les frais *masc pl*
□ Is there a charge for delivery? Est-ce qu'il y a des frais de livraison?

■ **an extra charge** un supplément

■ **free of charge** gratuit

■ **to reverse the charges** appeler en P.C.V. □ I'd like to reverse the charges. Je voudrais appeler en P.C.V.

■ **to be in charge** être responsable □ Mrs Munday was in charge of the group. Madame Munday était responsable du groupe.

to **charge** VERB
▷ *see also* **charge** NOUN
1 prendre *(money)*
□ How much did he charge you? Combien est-ce qu'il vous a pris? □ They charge £10 an hour. Ils prennent dix livres de l'heure.
2 inculper *(with crime)*
□ The police have charged him with murder. La police l'a inculpé de meurtre.

charity NOUN
l' association caritative *fem*
□ He gave the money to charity. Il a donné l'argent à une association caritative.

charm NOUN
le charme
□ He's got a lot of charm. Il a beaucoup de charme.

charming ADJECTIVE

charmant (FEM charmante)

chart NOUN
le tableau (PL les tableaux)
□ The chart shows the rise of
unemployment. Le tableau indique la
progression du chômage.
■ **the charts** le hit-parade □ This album is
number one in the charts. Cet album est
numéro un au hit-parade.

charter flight NOUN
le charter

to **chase** VERB
▷ see also **chase** NOUN
pourchasser

chase NOUN
▷ see also **chase** VERB
la poursuite
□ a car chase une poursuite en voiture

chat NOUN
▷ see also **chat** VERB
■ **to have a chat** bavarder

to **chat** VERB
▷ see also **chat** NOUN
bavarder
■ **to chat somebody up** draguer quelqu'un
(informal) □ He likes to chat up the girls. Il
aime bien draguer les filles.
■ **She likes chatting online.** Elle aime
chatter sur internet.

chatroom NOUN
le forum de discussion

chat show NOUN
le talk-show

chauvinist NOUN
■ **a male chauvinist** un machiste

cheap ADJECTIVE
bon marché (FEM+PL bon marché)
□ a cheap T-shirt un T-shirt bon marché

cheaper ADJECTIVE
moins cher (FEM moins chère)
□ It's cheaper by bus. C'est moins cher en
bus.

to **cheat** VERB
▷ see also **cheat** NOUN
tricher
□ You're cheating! Tu triches!

cheat NOUN
▷ see also **cheat** VERB
le tricheur
la tricheuse

check NOUN
▷ see also **check** VERB
1 le contrôle
□ a security check un contrôle de sécurité
2 le chèque (US)
□ to write a check faire un chèque
3 l' addition fem (US)

□ Can we have the check, please?
L'addition, s'il vous plaît.

to **check** VERB
▷ see also **check** NOUN
vérifier
□ I'll check the time of the train. Je vais
vérifier l'heure du train. □ Could you check
the oil, please? Pourriez-vous vérifier le
niveau d'huile, s'il vous plaît?

to **check in** VERB
1 se présenter à l'enregistrement (at airport)
□ Where do we check in? Où est-ce qu'on
doit se présenter à l'enregistrement?
2 se présenter à la réception (in hotel)
■ **I'd like to check in.** Je voudrais prendre
ma chambre.

to **check out** VERB
régler la note (from hotel)
□ Can I check out, please? Je peux régler la
note, s'il vous plaît?

checked ADJECTIVE
à carreaux (fabric)

checkers NOUN (US)
les dames fem pl
□ to play checkers jouer aux dames

check-in NOUN
l' enregistrement masc

checking account NOUN (US)
le compte courant (PL les comptes
courants)

checkout NOUN
la caisse

check-up NOUN
l' examen de routine masc

cheek NOUN
1 la joue
□ He kissed her on the cheek. Il l'a
embrassée sur la joue.
2 le culot
□ What a cheek! Quel culot!

cheeky ADJECTIVE
effronté (FEM effrontée)
□ Don't be cheeky! Ne sois pas effronté!
■ **a cheeky smile** un sourire malicieux

cheer NOUN
▷ see also **cheer** VERB
les hourras masc pl
■ **to give a cheer** pousser des hourras
■ **Cheers! 1** (good health) À la vôtre!
2 (thanks) Merci!

to **cheer** VERB
▷ see also **cheer** NOUN
applaudir
■ **to cheer somebody up** remonter le
moral à quelqu'un □ I was trying to cheer
him up. J'essayais de lui remonter le moral.
■ **Cheer up!** Ne te laisse pas abattre!

cheerful ADJECTIVE
gai (FEM gaie)

cheerio EXCLAMATION
salut!

cheese NOUN
le fromage

chef NOUN
le chef

chemical NOUN
le produit chimique

chemist NOUN
1 le pharmacien
la pharmacienne *(dispenser)*
2 la pharmacie *(shop)*
□ You get it from the chemist. C'est vendu
en pharmacie.

> **DID YOU KNOW...?**
> Chemists' shops in France are
> identified by a special green cross
> outside the shop.

3 le/la chimiste *(scientist)*

chemistry NOUN
la chimie
□ the chemistry lab le laboratoire de
chimie

cheque NOUN
le chèque
□ to write a cheque faire un chèque □ to
pay by cheque payer par chèque

chequebook NOUN
le carnet de chèques

cherry NOUN
la cerise

chess NOUN
les échecs *masc pl*
□ to play chess jouer aux échecs

chessboard NOUN
l' échiquier *masc*

chest NOUN
la poitrine *(of person)*
□ his chest measurement son tour de
poitrine
■ **a chest of drawers** une commode

chestnut NOUN
le marron
□ We have turkey with chestnuts. Nous
mangeons de la dinde aux marrons.

to **chew** VERB
mâcher

chewing gum NOUN
le chewing-gum

chick NOUN
le poussin
□ a hen and her chicks une poule et ses
poussins

chicken NOUN
le poulet

chickenpox NOUN
la varicelle

chickpeas PL NOUN
les pois chiches *masc pl*

chief NOUN
▷ *see also* **chief** ADJECTIVE
le chef
□ the chief of security le chef de la sécurité

chief ADJECTIVE
▷ *see also* **chief** NOUN
principal (FEM principale)
□ His chief reason for resigning was stress.
La principale raison de sa démission était le
stress.

child NOUN
l' enfant *masc/fem*
□ all the children tous les enfants

childish ADJECTIVE
puéril (FEM puérile)

child minder NOUN
la nourrice

children PL NOUN ▷ *see* **child**

Chile NOUN
le Chili
■ **in Chile** au Chili

to **chill** VERB
mettre au frais
□ Put the wine in the fridge to chill. Mets le
vin au frais dans le réfrigérateur.

chilli NOUN
le piment

chilly ADJECTIVE
froid (FEM froide)

chimney NOUN
la cheminée

chin NOUN
le menton

China NOUN
la Chine
■ **in China** en Chine

china NOUN
la porcelaine
□ a china plate une assiette en porcelaine

Chinese NOUN
▷ *see also* **Chinese** ADJECTIVE
le chinois *(language)*
■ **the Chinese** *(people)* les Chinois

Chinese ADJECTIVE
▷ *see also* **Chinese** NOUN
chinois (FEM chinoise)
□ a Chinese restaurant un restaurant
chinois
■ **a Chinese man** un Chinois
■ **a Chinese woman** une Chinoise

chip NOUN
1 la frite *(food)*
□ We bought some chips. Nous avons

C

acheté des frites.

2 la puce *(in computer)*

chiropodist NOUN
le/la pédicure
□ He's a chiropodist. Il est pédicure.

chives PL NOUN
la ciboulette *sing*

chocolate NOUN
le chocolat
□ a chocolate cake un gâteau au chocolat
■ **hot chocolate** le chocolat chaud

choice NOUN
le choix
□ I had no choice. Je n'avais pas le choix.

choir NOUN
la chorale
□ I sing in the school choir. Je chante dans
la chorale de l'école.

to **choke** VERB
s'étrangler
■ **He choked on a fishbone.** Il s'est
étranglé avec une arête de poisson.

to **choose** VERB
choisir
□ It's difficult to choose. C'est difficile de
choisir.

to **chop** VERB
▷ *see also* **chop** NOUN
émincer
□ Chop the onions. Émincez les oignons.

chop NOUN
▷ *see also* **chop** VERB
la côte
□ a pork chop une côte de porc

chopsticks PL NOUN
les baguettes *fem pl*

chose, chosen VERB ▷ *see* **choose**

Christ NOUN
le Christ
□ the birth of Christ la naissance du Christ

christening NOUN
le baptême

Christian NOUN
▷ *see also* **Christian** ADJECTIVE
le chrétien
la chrétienne

Christian ADJECTIVE
▷ *see also* **Christian** NOUN
chrétien (FEM chrétienne)

Christian name NOUN
le prénom

Christmas NOUN
Noël *masc*
□ Happy Christmas! Joyeux Noël!
■ **Christmas Day** le jour de Noël
■ **Christmas Eve** la veille de Noël
■ **a Christmas tree** un arbre de Noël

■ **a Christmas card** une carte de Noël

DID YOU KNOW...?
The French more often send greetings
cards (**une carte de vœux**) in January
rather than at Christmas, with best
wishes for the New Year.

■ **Christmas dinner** le repas de Noël

DID YOU KNOW...?
Most French people have their
Christmas meal (**réveillon de Noël**)
on the evening of Christmas Eve,
though some have a **repas de Noël**
on Christmas Day. The French usually
have a Yule log (**une bûche de Noël**)
for pudding at the Christmas meal.

chubby ADJECTIVE
potelé (FEM potelée)
□ a chubby baby un bébé potelé

chunk NOUN
le gros morceau (PL les gros morceaux)
□ Cut the meat into chunks. Coupez la
viande en gros morceaux.

church NOUN
l'église *fem*
□ I don't go to church every Sunday. Je ne
vais pas à l'église tous les dimanches.
■ **the Church of England** l'Église anglicane

cider NOUN
le cidre

cigar NOUN
le cigare

cigarette NOUN
la cigarette

cigarette lighter NOUN
le briquet

cinema NOUN
le cinéma
□ I'm going to the cinema this evening. Je
vais au cinéma ce soir.

cinnamon NOUN
la cannelle

circle NOUN
le cercle

circular ADJECTIVE
circulaire (FEM circulaire)

circulation NOUN
1 la circulation *(of blood)*
2 le tirage *(of newspaper)*

circumflex NOUN
l'accent circonflexe *masc*

circumstances PL NOUN
les circonstances *fem pl*

circus NOUN
le cirque

citizen NOUN
le citoyen
la citoyenne

□ a French citizen un citoyen français

citizenship NOUN
la citoyenneté

City NOUN
■ **the City** la City de Londres

city NOUN
la ville
■ **the city centre** le centre-ville □ It's in the city centre. C'est au centre-ville.

city technology college NOUN
le collège technique

civilization NOUN
la civilisation

civil servant NOUN
le/la fonctionnaire

civil war NOUN
la guerre civile

to **claim** VERB
▷ see also **claim** NOUN
1 prétendre
□ He claims to have found the money. Il prétend avoir trouvé l'argent.
2 percevoir (receive)
□ She's claiming unemployment benefit. Elle perçoit des allocations chômage.
■ **She can't claim unemployment benefit.** Elle n'a pas droit aux allocations chômage.
■ **to claim on one's insurance** se faire rembourser par son assurance □ We claimed on our insurance. On s'est fait rembourser par notre assurance.

claim NOUN
▷ see also **claim** VERB
la demande d'indemnité (on insurance policy)
□ to make a claim faire une demande d'indemnité

to **clap** VERB
applaudir (applaud)
■ **to clap one's hands** frapper dans ses mains □ My dog sits when I clap my hands. Mon chien s'asseoit quand je frappe dans mes mains.

clarinet NOUN
la clarinette
□ I play the clarinet. Je joue de la clarinette.

to **clash** VERB
1 jurer (colours)
□ These two colours clash. Ces deux couleurs jurent.
2 tomber en même temps (events)
□ The concert clashes with Ann's party. Le concert tombe en même temps que la soirée d'Ann.

clasp NOUN
le fermoir (of necklace)

class NOUN

1 la classe (group)
□ We're in the same class. Nous sommes dans la même classe.
2 le cours (lesson)
□ I go to dancing classes. Je vais à des cours de danse.

classic ADJECTIVE
▷ see also **classic** NOUN
classique (FEM classique)
□ a classic example un cas classique

classic NOUN
▷ see also **classic** ADJECTIVE
le classique (book, film)

classical ADJECTIVE
classique (FEM classique)
□ I like classical music. J'aime la musique classique.

classmate NOUN
le camarade de classe
la camarade de classe

classroom NOUN
la classe

classroom assistant NOUN
l' aide-éducateur masc
l' aide-éducatrice fem

claw NOUN
1 la griffe (of cat, dog)
2 la serre (of bird)
3 la pince (of crab, lobster)

clean ADJECTIVE
▷ see also **clean** VERB
propre (FEM propre)
□ a clean shirt une chemise propre

to **clean** VERB
▷ see also **clean** ADJECTIVE
nettoyer

cleaner NOUN
la femme de ménage (woman)
l' agent d'entretien masc (man)

cleaner's NOUN
la teinturerie

cleaning lady NOUN
la femme de ménage

cleansing lotion NOUN
la lotion démaquillante

clear ADJECTIVE
▷ see also **clear** VERB
1 clair (FEM claire)
□ a clear explanation une explication claire
□ It's clear you don't believe me. Il est clair que tu ne me crois pas.
2 libre (FEM libre) (road, way)
□ The road's clear now. La route est libre maintenant.

to **clear** VERB
▷ see also **clear** ADJECTIVE
1 dégager

□ The police are clearing the road after the accident. La police dégage la route après l'accident.

2 se dissiper *(fog, mist)*

□ The mist cleared. La brume s'est dissipée.

■ **to be cleared of a crime** être reconnu non coupable d'un crime □ She was cleared of murder. Elle a été reconnu non coupable du meurtre.

■ **to clear the table** débarrasser la table

□ I'll clear the table. Je vais débarrasser la table.

to **clear off** VERB

filer

□ Clear off and leave me alone! File et laisse-moi tranquille!

to **clear up** VERB

ranger

□ Who's going to clear all this up? Qui va ranger tout ça?

■ **I think it's going to clear up.** *(weather)* Je pense que le temps va se lever.

clearly ADVERB

1 clairement

□ She explained it very clearly. Elle l'a expliqué très clairement.

2 nettement

□ You could clearly make out the French coast. On distinguait nettement la côte française.

3 distinctement

□ to speak clearly parler distinctement

clementine NOUN

la clémentine

clever ADJECTIVE

1 intelligent (FEM intelligente)

□ She's very clever. Elle est très intelligente.

2 astucieux (FEM astucieuse) *(ingenious)*

□ a clever system un système astucieux

■ **What a clever idea!** Quelle bonne idée!

click NOUN

▷ *see also* **click** VERB

le petit bruit *(of door, camera)*

to **click** VERB

▷ *see also* **click** NOUN

cliquer *(with mouse)*

□ to click on an icon cliquer sur une icône

client NOUN

le client

la cliente

cliff NOUN

la falaise

climate NOUN

le climat

to **climb** VERB

1 escalader

□ We're going to climb Snowdon. Nous allons escalader le Snowdon.

2 monter *(stairs)*

climber NOUN

le grimpeur

la grimpeuse

climbing NOUN

l' escalade *fem*

■ **to go climbing** faire de l'escalade

□ We're going climbing in Scotland. Nous allons faire de l'escalade en Écosse.

Clingfilm® NOUN

le film alimentaire

clinic NOUN

le centre médical (PL les centres médicaux)

clip NOUN

1 la barrette *(for hair)*

2 le court extrait *(film)*

□ some clips from Disney's latest film quelques courts extraits du dernier film Disney

clippers PL NOUN

■ **nail clippers** le coupe-ongle *sing*

cloakroom NOUN

1 le vestiaire *(for coats)*

2 les toilettes *fem pl (toilet)*

clock NOUN

1 l' horloge *fem*

□ the church clock l'horloge de l'église

2 la pendule *(smaller)*

■ **an alarm clock** un réveil

■ **a clock-radio** un radio-réveil

clockwork NOUN

■ **Everything went like clockwork.** Tout a marché comme sur des roulettes.

clog NOUN

le sabot

clone NOUN

▷ *see also* **clone** VERB

le clone *(animal, plant)*

to **clone** VERB

▷ *see also* **clone** NOUN

cloner

□ a cloned sheep un mouton cloné

close ADJECTIVE, ADVERB

▷ *see also* **close** VERB

1 près (FEM+PL près) *(near)*

□ The shops are very close. Les magasins sont tout près.

■ **close to** près de □ The youth hostel is close to the station. L'auberge de jeunesse est près de la gare.

■ **Come closer.** Rapproche-toi.

2 proche (FEM proche) *(in relationship)*

□ We're just inviting close relations. Nous n'invitons que les parents proches. □ She's a close friend of mine. C'est une proche amie. □ I'm very close to my sister. Je suis

très proche de ma sœur.

3 très serré (FEM très serrée) *(contest)*

□ It's going to be very close. Ça va être très très serré.

4 lourd (FEM lourde) *(weather)*

□ It's close this afternoon. Il fait lourd cet après-midi.

to **close** VERB

▷ *see also* **close** ADJECTIVE

1 fermer

□ What time does the pool close? La piscine ferme à quelle heure? □ The shops close at 5.30. Les magasins ferment à cinq heures et demie. □ Please close the door. Fermez la porte, s'il vous plaît.

2 se fermer

□ The doors close automatically. Les portes se ferment automatiquement.

closed ADJECTIVE

fermé (FEM fermée)

□ The bank's closed. La banque est fermée.

closely ADVERB

de près *(look, examine)*

cloth NOUN

le tissu *(material)*

■ **a cloth** un chiffon □ Wipe it with a damp cloth. Nettoyez-le avec un chiffon humide.

clothes PL NOUN

les vêtements *masc pl*

□ new clothes des vêtements neufs

■ **a clothes line** un fil à linge

■ **a clothes peg** une pince à linge

cloud NOUN

le nuage

cloudy ADJECTIVE

nuageux (FEM nuageuse)

clove NOUN

■ **a clove of garlic** une gousse d'ail

clown NOUN

le clown

club NOUN

le club

□ a golf club un club de golf

■ **the youth club** la maison des jeunes

■ **clubs** *(in cards)* le trèfle □ the ace of clubs l'as de trèfle

to **club together** VERB

se cotiser

□ We clubbed together to buy her a present. Nous nous sommes cotisés pour lui acheter un cadeau.

clubbing NOUN

■ **to go clubbing** sortir en boîte

clue NOUN

l' indice *masc*

□ an important clue un indice important

■ **I haven't a clue.** Je n'en ai pas la moindre

idée.

clumsy ADJECTIVE

maladroit (FEM maladroite)

clutch NOUN

la pédale d'embrayage *(of car)*

clutter NOUN

le désordre

□ There's too much clutter in here. Il y a trop de désordre ici.

coach NOUN

1 le car *masc*

□ We went there by coach. Nous y sommes allés en car.

■ **the coach station** la gare routière

■ **a coach trip** une excursion en car

2 l' entraîneur *masc (trainer)*

□ the French coach l'entraîneur de l'équipe de France

coal NOUN

le charbon

■ **a coal mine** une mine de charbon

■ **a coal miner** un mineur

coarse ADJECTIVE

1 rugueux (FEM rugueuse) *(surface, fabric)*

□ The bag was made of coarse cloth. Le sac était fait d'un tissu rugueux.

2 grossier (FEM grossière) *(vulgar)*

□ coarse language un langage grossier

coast NOUN

la côte

□ It's on the west coast of Scotland. C'est sur la côte ouest de l'Écosse.

coastguard NOUN

le garde-côte (PL les garde-côtes)

coat NOUN

le manteau (PL les manteaux)

□ a warm coat un manteau chaud

■ **a coat of paint** une couche de peinture

coat hanger NOUN

le cintre

cobweb NOUN

la toile d'araignée

cocaine NOUN

la cocaïne

cock NOUN

le coq *(cockerel)*

cockerel NOUN

le coq

cockney NOUN

le cockney

□ I'm a cockney. Je suis cockney.

cocoa NOUN

le cacao

□ a cup of cocoa une tasse de cacao

coconut NOUN

la noix de coco

cod NOUN

le cabillaud

code NOUN
le code

coffee NOUN
le café
■ **a white coffee** un café au lait
■ **A cup of coffee, please.** Un café, s'il vous plaît.

coffeepot NOUN
la cafetière

coffee table NOUN
la table basse

coffin NOUN
le cercueil

coin NOUN
la pièce de monnaie
■ **a 2 euro coin** une pièce de deux euros

coincidence NOUN
la coïncidence

coinphone NOUN
le téléphone à pièces

Coke® NOUN
le coca
□ **a can of Coke®** une boîte de coca

colander NOUN
la passoire

cold ADJECTIVE
▷ see also **cold** NOUN
froid (FEM froide)
□ The water's cold. L'eau est froide.
■ **It's cold today.** Il fait froid aujourd'hui.
■ **to be cold** (person) avoir froid □ I'm cold. J'ai froid. □ Are you cold? Est-ce que tu as froid?

cold NOUN
▷ see also **cold** ADJECTIVE
1 le froid
□ I can't stand the cold. Je ne supporte pas le froid.
2 le rhume
□ to catch a cold attraper un rhume
■ **to have a cold** avoir un rhume □ I've got a bad cold. J'ai un gros rhume.
■ **a cold sore** un bouton de fièvre

coleslaw NOUN
la salade de chou cru à la mayonnaise

to **collapse** VERB
s'effondrer
□ He collapsed. Il s'est effondré.

collar NOUN
1 le col (of coat, shirt)
2 le collier (for animal)

collarbone NOUN
la clavicule
□ I broke my collarbone. Je me suis cassé la clavicule.

colleague NOUN

le/la collègue

to **collect** VERB
1 ramasser
□ The teacher collected the exercise books. Le professeur a ramassé les cahiers. □ They collect the rubbish on Fridays. Ils ramassent les ordures le vendredi.
2 faire collection de
□ I collect stamps. Je fais collection de timbres.
3 aller chercher
□ Their mother collects them from school. Leur mère va les chercher à l'école.
4 faire une collecte
□ They're collecting for charity. Ils font une collecte pour une association caritative.

collect call NOUN (US)
la communication en PCV

collection NOUN
1 la collection
□ my DVD collection ma collection de DVD
2 la collecte
□ a collection for charity une collecte pour une association caritative
3 la levée (of mail)
□ Next collection: 5pm Prochaine levée: 17 heures

collector NOUN
le collectionneur
la collectionneuse

college NOUN
le collège
□ a technical college un collège d'enseignement technique

to **collide** VERB
entrer en collision

collie NOUN
le colley

colliery NOUN
la houillère

collision NOUN
la collision

colon NOUN
les deux points masc pl (punctuation mark)

colonel NOUN
le colonel

colour (US **color**) NOUN
la couleur
□ What colour is it? C'est de quelle couleur?
■ **a colour film** (for camera) une pellicule en couleur

colourful (US **colorful**) ADJECTIVE
coloré (FEM colorée)

colouring (US **coloring**) NOUN
le colorant (for food)

comb NOUN
▷ see also **comb** VERB

le peigne
to **comb** VERB
  ▷ *see also* **comb** NOUN
  ■ **to comb one's hair** se peigner □ You
  haven't combed your hair. Tu ne t'es pas
  peigné.
combination NOUN
  la combinaison
to **combine** VERB
1 allier
  □ The film combines humour with
  suspense. Le film allie l'humour au
  suspense.
2 concilier
  □ It's difficult to combine a career with a
  family. Il est difficile de concilier carrière et
  vie de famille.
to **come** VERB
1 venir
  □ Can I come too? Est-ce que je peux venir
  aussi? □ Some friends came to see us.
  Quelques amis sont venus nous voir. □ I'll
  come with you. Je viens avec toi.
2 arriver *(arrive)*
  □ I'm coming! J'arrive! □ They came late. Ils
  sont arrivés en retard. □ The letter came
  this morning. La lettre est arrivée ce matin.
  ■ **Where do you come from?** Tu viens
  d'où?
  ■ **Come on!** Allez!
to **come back** VERB
  revenir
  □ Come back! Reviens!
to **come down** VERB
1 descendre *(person, lift)*
2 baisser *(prices)*
to **come in** VERB
  entrer
  □ Come in! Entrez!
to **come out** VERB
  sortir
  □ I tripped as we came out of the cinema.
  J'ai trébuché quand nous sommes sortis du
  cinéma. □ It's just come out on DVD. Ça
  vient de sortir en DVD.
  ■ **None of my photos came out.** Mes
  photos n'ont rien donné.
to **come round** VERB
  reprendre connaissance *(after faint,
  operation)*
to **come up** VERB
  monter
  □ Come up here! Monte!
  ■ **to come up to somebody 1** s'approcher
  de quelqu'un □ She came up to me and
  kissed me. Elle s'est approchée de moi et
  m'a embrassé. **2** *(to speak to them)* aborder

quelqu'un □ A man came up to me and
said … Un homme m'a abordé et m'a dit …
comedian NOUN
  le comique
comedy NOUN
  la comédie
comfortable ADJECTIVE
1 confortable (FEM confortable) *(bed, chair)*
2 à l'aise *(person)*
  □ I'm very comfortable, thanks. Je suis
  parfaitement à l'aise, merci.
comic NOUN
  l' illustré *masc (magazine)*
comic strip NOUN
  la bande dessinée
coming ADJECTIVE
  prochain (FEM prochaine)
  □ in the coming months au cours des
  prochains mois
comma NOUN
  la virgule
command NOUN
  l' ordre *masc*
comment NOUN
  ▷ *see also* **comment** VERB
  le commentaire
  □ He made no comment. Il n'a fait aucun
  commentaire.
  ■ **No comment!** Je n'ai rien à dire!
to **comment** VERB
  ▷ *see also* **comment** NOUN
  ■ **to comment on something** faire des
  commentaires sur quelque chose
commentary NOUN
  le reportage en direct *(on TV, radio)*
commentator NOUN
  le commentateur sportif
  la commentatrice sportive
commercial NOUN
  le spot publicitaire
commission NOUN
  la commission
  □ Salesmen work on commission. Les
  représentants travaillent à la commission.
to **commit** VERB
  ■ **to commit a crime** commettre un crime
  ■ **to commit oneself** s'engager □ I don't
  want to commit myself. Je ne veux pas
  m'engager.
  ■ **to commit suicide** se suicider □ He
  committed suicide. Il s'est suicidé.
committee NOUN
  le comité
common ADJECTIVE
  ▷ *see also* **common** NOUN
  courant (FEM courante)
  □ 'Smith' is a very common surname.

343

'Smith' est un nom de famille très courant.
■ **in common** en commun □ We've got a lot in common. Nous avons beaucoup de choses en commun.

common NOUN
▷ *see also* **common** ADJECTIVE
le terrain communal
□ The boys play football on the common. Les garçons jouent au football sur le terrain communal.

Commons PL NOUN
■ **the House of Commons** la Chambre des communes

common sense NOUN
le bon sens
□ Use your common sense! Sers-toi de ton bon sens!

to communicate VERB
communiquer

communication NOUN
la communication

communion NOUN
la communion
□ my First Communion ma première communion

communism NOUN
le communisme

communist NOUN
▷ *see also* **communist** ADJECTIVE
le/la communiste

communist ADJECTIVE
▷ *see also* **communist** NOUN
communiste (FEM communiste)
■ **the Communist Party** le Parti communiste

community NOUN
la communauté

to commute VERB
faire la navette
□ She commutes between Liss and London. Elle fait la navette entre Liss et Londres.

compact disc NOUN
le disque compact
■ **a compact disc player** une platine laser

companion NOUN
le compagnon
la compagne

company NOUN
1 la société
□ He works for a big company. Il travaille pour une grosse société.
2 la compagnie
□ an insurance company une compagnie d'assurance □ a theatre company une compagnie théâtrale
■ **to keep somebody company** tenir compagnie à quelqu'un □ I'll keep you

company. Je vais te tenir compagnie.

comparatively ADVERB
relativement

to compare VERB
comparer
□ People always compare him with his brother. On le compare toujours à son frère.
■ **compared with** en comparaison de
□ Oxford is small compared with London. Oxford est une petite ville en comparaison de Londres.

comparison NOUN
la comparaison

compartment NOUN
le compartiment

compass NOUN
la boussole

compensation NOUN
l' indemnité *fem*
□ They got £2000 compensation. Ils ont reçu une indemnité de deux mille livres.

compere NOUN
l' animateur *masc*
l' animatrice *fem*

to compete VERB
participer
□ I'm competing in the marathon. Je participe au marathon.
■ **to compete for something** se disputer quelque chose □ There are 50 students competing for 6 places. Ils sont cinquante étudiants à se disputer six places.

competent ADJECTIVE
compétent (FEM compétente)

competition NOUN
le concours
□ a singing competition un concours de chant

competitive ADJECTIVE
compétitif (FEM compétitive)
□ a very competitive price un prix très compétitif
■ **to be competitive** *(person)* avoir l'esprit de compétition
□ He's a very competitive person. Il a vraiment l'esprit de compétition.

competitor NOUN
le concurrent
la concurrente

to complain VERB
se plaindre
□ I'm going to complain to the manager. Je vais me plaindre au directeur. □ We complained about the noise. Nous nous sommes plaints du bruit.

complaint NOUN
la plainte

□ There were lots of complaints about the food. Il y a eu beaucoup de plaintes à propos de la nourriture.

■ **to make a complaint** faire une réclamation □ I'd like to make a complaint. J'ai une réclamation à faire.

complete ADJECTIVE
complet (FEM complète)

completely ADVERB
complètement

complexion NOUN
le teint

complicated ADJECTIVE
compliqué (FEM compliquée)

compliment NOUN
▷ see also **compliment** VERB
le compliment

to **compliment** VERB
▷ see also **compliment** NOUN
complimenter

□ They complimented me on my French. Ils m'ont complimenté sur mon français.

complimentary ADJECTIVE
1 élogieux (FEM élogieuse) (flattering)
□ He was very complimentary about my garden. Il a été très élogieux à propos de mon jardin.
2 gratuit (FEM gratuite) (free)
□ I've got two complimentary tickets for tonight. J'ai deux places gratuites pour ce soir.

composer NOUN
le compositeur
la compositrice

comprehension NOUN
1 la compréhension (understanding)
2 l' exercice de compréhension masc (school exercise)

comprehensive ADJECTIVE
complet (FEM complète)

□ a comprehensive guide un guide complet

> **LANGUAGE TIP** Be careful not to translate **comprehensive** by compréhensif.

comprehensive school NOUN
1 le collège
2 le lycée

> **DID YOU KNOW...?**
> In France pupils go to a **collège** between the ages of 11 and 15, and then to a **lycée** until the age of 18.

compromise NOUN
▷ see also **compromise** VERB
le compromis

□ We reached a compromise. Nous sommes parvenus à un compromis.

to **compromise** VERB

▷ see also **compromise** NOUN
■ Let's compromise. Essayons de trouver un compromis.

compulsory ADJECTIVE
obligatoire (FEM obligatoire)

computer NOUN
l' ordinateur masc

computer game NOUN
le jeu électronique (PL les jeux électroniques)

computer programmer NOUN
le programmeur
la programmeuse
□ She's a computer programmer. Elle est programmeuse.

computer room NOUN
la salle d'informatique

computer science NOUN
l' informatique fem

computing NOUN
l' informatique fem

to **concentrate** VERB
se concentrer
□ I couldn't concentrate. Je n'arrivais pas à me concentrer.

concentration NOUN
la concentration

concern NOUN
l' inquiétude fem (preoccupation)
□ They expressed concern about her health. Ils ont exprimé leur inquiétude concernant sa santé.

concerned ADJECTIVE
■ **to be concerned** s'inquiéter □ His mother is concerned about him. Sa mère s'inquiète à son sujet.
■ **as far as I'm concerned** en ce qui me concerne

concerning PREPOSITION
concernant
□ For further information concerning the job, contact ... Pour plus d'informations concernant cet emploi, contacter ...

concert NOUN
le concert

concrete NOUN
le béton

to **condemn** VERB
condamner
□ The government has condemned the decision. Le gouvernement a condamné cette décision.

condition NOUN
1 la condition
□ I'll do it, on one condition ... Je veux bien le faire, à une condition ...
2 l' état masc

□ **in bad condition** en mauvais état □ **in good condition** en bon état

conditional NOUN
le conditionnel

conditioner NOUN
le baume démêlant *(for hair)*

condom NOUN
le préservatif

to **conduct** VERB
diriger *(orchestra)*

conductor NOUN
le chef d'orchestre

cone NOUN
le cornet
□ **an ice-cream cone** un cornet de glace

conference NOUN
la conférence

to **confess** VERB
avouer
□ **He finally confessed.** Il a fini par avouer.
□ **He confessed to the murder.** Il a avoué avoir commis le meurtre.

confession NOUN
la confession

confetti NOUN
les confettis *masc pl*

confidence NOUN
1 la confiance
□ **I've got confidence in you.** J'ai confiance en toi.
2 l' assurance *fem*
□ **She lacks confidence.** Elle manque d'assurance.

confident ADJECTIVE
sûr (FEM sûre)
□ **I'm confident everything will be okay.** Je suis sûr que tout ira bien.
■ **She's seems quite confident.** Elle a l'air sûre d'elle.

confidential ADJECTIVE
confidentiel (FEM confidentielle)

to **confirm** VERB
confirmer *(booking)*

confirmation NOUN
la confirmation

conflict NOUN
le conflit

to **confuse** VERB
■ **to confuse somebody** embrouiller les idées de quelqu'un □ **Don't confuse me!** Ne m'embrouille pas les idées!

confused ADJECTIVE
désorienté (FEM désorientée)

confusing ADJECTIVE
■ **The traffic signs are confusing.** Les panneaux de signalisation ne sont pas clairs.

confusion NOUN

la confusion

to **congratulate** VERB
féliciter
□ **My aunt congratulated me on my results.** Ma tante m'a félicité pour mes résultats.

congratulations PL NOUN
les félicitations *fem pl*
□ **Congratulations on your new job!** Félicitations pour votre nouveau poste!

conjunction NOUN
la conjonction

conjurer NOUN
le prestidigitateur

connection NOUN
1 le rapport
□ **There's no connection between the two events.** Il n'y a aucun rapport entre les deux événements.
2 le contact *(electrical)*
□ **There's a loose connection.** Il y a un mauvais contact.
3 la correspondance *(of trains, planes)*
□ **We missed our connection.** Nous avons raté la correspondance.

to **conquer** VERB
conquérir

conscience NOUN
la conscience

conscious ADJECTIVE
conscient (FEM consciente)

consciousness NOUN
la connaissance
■ **to lose consciousness** perdre connaissance □ **I lost consciousness.** J'ai perdu connaissance.

consequence NOUN
la conséquence
□ **What are the consequences for the environment?** Quelles sont les conséquences pour l'environnement?
■ **as a consequence** en conséquence

consequently ADVERB
par conséquent

conservation NOUN
la protection

conservative ADJECTIVE
▷ *see also* **conservative** NOUN
conservateur (FEM conservatrice)
■ **the Conservative Party** le Parti conservateur

Conservative NOUN
▷ *see also* **conservative** ADJECTIVE
le conservateur
la conservatrice
■ **to vote Conservative** voter conservateur
■ **the Conservatives** les conservateurs

conservatory NOUN

le jardin d'hiver

to **consider** VERB
1 considérer
□ He considers it a waste of time. Il considère que c'est une perte de temps.
2 envisager
□ We considered cancelling our holiday. Nous avons envisagé d'annuler nos vacances.
■ **I'm considering the idea.** J'y songe.

considerate ADJECTIVE
délicat (FEM délicate)

considering PREPOSITION
1 étant donné
□ Considering we were there for a month … Étant donné que nous étions là pour un mois …
2 tout compte fait
□ I got a good mark, considering. J'ai eu une bonne note, tout compte fait.

to **consist** VERB
■ **to consist of** être composé de □ The band consists of a singer and a guitarist. Le groupe est composé d'un chanteur et d'un guitariste.

consonant NOUN
la consonne

constant ADJECTIVE
constant (FEM constante)

constantly ADVERB
constamment

constipated ADJECTIVE
constipé (FEM constipée)

to **construct** VERB
construire

construction NOUN
la construction

to **consult** VERB
consulter

consumer NOUN
le consommateur
la consommatrice

contact NOUN
▷ see also **contact** VERB
le contact
□ I'm in contact with her. Je suis en contact avec elle.

to **contact** VERB
▷ see also **contact** NOUN
joindre
□ Where can we contact you? Où pouvons-nous vous joindre?

contact lenses PL NOUN
les verres de contact masc pl

to **contain** VERB
contenir

container NOUN

le récipient

contempt NOUN
le mépris

contents PL NOUN
1 le contenu sing (of container)
2 la table des matières sing (of book)

contest NOUN
le concours

contestant NOUN
le concurrent
la concurrente

context NOUN
le contexte

continent NOUN
le continent
□ How many continents are there? Combien y a-t-il de continents?
■ **the Continent** l'Europe fem □ I've never been to the Continent. Je ne suis jamais allé en Europe.

continental breakfast NOUN
le petit déjeuner à la française

to **continue** VERB
1 continuer
□ She continued talking to her friend. Elle a continué à parler à son amie.
2 reprendre (after interruption)
□ We continued working after lunch. Nous avons repris le travail après le déjeuner.

continuous ADJECTIVE
continu (FEM continue)
■ **continuous assessment** le contrôle continu

contraceptive NOUN
le contraceptif

contract NOUN
le contrat

to **contradict** VERB
contredire

contrary NOUN
le contraire
■ **on the contrary** au contraire

contrast NOUN
le contraste

to **contribute** VERB
1 contribuer (to success, achievement)
□ The treaty will contribute to world peace. Le traité va contribuer à la paix dans le monde.
2 participer (share in)
□ He didn't contribute to the discussion. Il n'a pas participé à la discussion.
3 donner (give)
□ She contributed £10. Elle a donné dix livres.

contribution NOUN
1 la contribution

347

2 la cotisation (to pension, national insurance)

control NOUN
  ▷ see also **control** VERB
  le contrôle
  ■ **to lose control** (of vehicle) perdre le contrôle □ He lost control of the car. Il a perdu le contrôle de son véhicule.
  ■ **the controls** les commandes fem pl (of machine)
  ■ **to be in control** être maître de la situation
  ■ **to keep control** (of people) se faire obéir □ He can't keep control of the class. Il ne se fait pas obéir de sa classe.
  ■ **out of control** (child, class) déchaîné

to control VERB
  ▷ see also **control** NOUN
1 diriger (country, organization)
2 se faire obéir de
  □ He can't control the class. Il ne se fait pas obéir de sa classe.
3 maîtriser
  □ I couldn't control the horse. Je ne suis pas arrivé à maîtriser le cheval.
  ■ **to control oneself** se contrôler

controversial ADJECTIVE
  controversé (FEM controversée)
  □ a controversial book un livre controversé

convenient ADJECTIVE
  bien situé (FEM bien située) (place)
  □ The hotel's convenient for the airport. L'hôtel est bien situé par rapport à l'aéroport.
  ■ **It's not a convenient time for me.** C'est une heure qui ne m'arrange pas.
  ■ **Would Monday be convenient for you?** Est-ce que lundi vous conviendrait?

conventional ADJECTIVE
  conventionnel (FEM conventionnelle)

convent school NOUN
  le couvent
  □ She goes to convent school. Elle va au couvent.

conversation NOUN
  la conversation
  □ a French conversation class un cours de conversation française

to convert VERB
  transformer
  □ We've converted the loft into a spare room. Nous avons transformé le grenier en chambre d'amis.

to convict VERB
  reconnaître coupable
  □ He was convicted of the murder. Il a été reconnu coupable du meurtre.

to convince VERB

persuader
  □ I'm not convinced. Je n'en suis pas persuadé.

to cook VERB
  ▷ see also **cook** NOUN
1 faire la cuisine
  □ I can't cook. Je ne sais pas faire la cuisine.
2 préparer
  □ She's cooking lunch. Elle est en train de préparer le déjeuner.
3 faire cuire
  □ Cook the pasta for 10 minutes. Faites cuire les pâtes pendant dix minutes.
  ■ **to be cooked** être cuit □ When the potatoes are cooked … Lorsque les pommes de terre sont cuites …

cook NOUN
  ▷ see also **cook** VERB
  le cuisinier
  la cuisinière
  □ Matthew's an excellent cook. Matthew est un excellent cuisinier.

cookbook NOUN
  le livre de cuisine

cooker NOUN
  la cuisinière
  □ a gas cooker une cuisinière à gaz

cookery NOUN
  la cuisine

cookie NOUN (US)
  le gâteau sec (PL les gâteaux secs)

cooking NOUN
  la cuisine
  □ I like cooking. J'aime bien faire la cuisine.

cool ADJECTIVE
1 frais (FEM fraîche)
  □ a cool place un endroit frais
2 cool (FEM+PL cool) (great)
  □ That's really cool! C'est vraiment cool!

cooperation NOUN
  la coopération

cop NOUN
  le flic (informal)

to cope VERB
  se débrouiller
  □ It was hard, but we coped. C'était dur, mais nous nous sommes débrouillés.
  ■ **to cope with** faire face à □ She's got a lot of problems to cope with. Elle doit faire face à de nombreux problèmes.

copper NOUN
1 le cuivre
  □ a copper bracelet un bracelet en cuivre
2 le flic (informal: policeman)

copy NOUN
  ▷ see also **copy** VERB
1 la copie (of letter, document)

2 l' exemplaire *masc (of book)*

to **copy** VERB
▷ *see also* **copy** NOUN
copier
□ The teacher accused him of copying. Le professeur l'a accusé d'avoir copié.
■ **to copy and paste** copier-coller

core NOUN
le trognon *(of fruit)*
□ an apple core un trognon de pomme

cork NOUN
1 le bouchon *(of bottle)*
2 le liège *(material)*
□ a cork table mat un set de table en liège

corkscrew NOUN
le tire-bouchon

corn NOUN
1 le blé *(wheat)*
2 le maïs *(sweetcorn)*
■ **corn on the cob** l'épi de maïs *masc*

corner NOUN
1 le coin
□ in a corner of the room dans un coin de la pièce
■ **the shop on the corner** la boutique au coin de la rue
■ **He lives just round the corner.** Il habite tout près d'ici.
2 le corner *(in football)*

cornet NOUN
1 le cornet à pistons
□ He plays the cornet. Il joue du cornet à pistons.
2 le cornet *(ice cream)*

cornflakes PL NOUN
les corn-flakes *masc pl*

cornstarch NOUN (US)
la farine de maïs

Cornwall NOUN
la Cornouailles
■ **in Cornwall** en Cornouailles

corporal NOUN
le caporal

corporal punishment NOUN
le châtiment corporel

corpse NOUN
le cadavre

correct ADJECTIVE
▷ *see also* **correct** VERB
exact (FEM exacte)
□ That's correct. C'est exact.
■ **the correct choice** le bon choix
■ **the correct answer** la bonne réponse

to **correct** VERB
▷ *see also* **correct** ADJECTIVE
corriger

correction NOUN

la correction

correctly ADVERB
correctement

correspondent NOUN
le correspondant
la correspondante
□ our foreign correspondent notre correspondant à l'étranger

corridor NOUN
le couloir

corruption NOUN
la corruption

Corsica NOUN
la Corse
■ **in Corsica** en Corse

cosmetics PL NOUN
les produits de beauté *masc pl*

cosmetic surgery NOUN
la chirurgie esthétique

to **cost** VERB
▷ *see also* **cost** NOUN
coûter
□ The meal costs a hundred euros. Le repas coûte cent euros. □ How much does it cost? Combien est-ce que ça coûte? □ It costs too much. Ça coûte trop cher.

cost NOUN
▷ *see also* **cost** VERB
le coût
■ **the cost of living** le coût de la vie
■ **at all costs** à tout prix

costume NOUN
le costume

cosy ADJECTIVE
douillet (FEM douillette)

cot NOUN
le lit d'enfant

cottage NOUN
le cottage
■ **a thatched cottage** une chaumière

cottage cheese NOUN
le cottage cheese

cotton NOUN
le coton
□ a cotton shirt une chemise en coton
■ **cotton wool** le coton hydrophile

couch NOUN
le canapé

couchette NOUN
la couchette

to **cough** VERB
▷ *see also* **cough** NOUN
tousser

cough NOUN
▷ *see also* **cough** VERB
la toux
□ a bad cough une mauvaise toux

■ **I've got a cough.** Je tousse.
■ **a cough sweet** une pastille
could VERB ▷ *see* **can**
council NOUN
le conseil

> **DID YOU KNOW...?**
> The nearest French equivalent of a local council would be a **conseil municipal**, which administers a **commune**.

■ **He's on the council.** Il fait partie du conseil municipal.
■ **a council estate** une cité HLM
■ **a council house** une HLM

> **DID YOU KNOW...?**
> HLM stands for **habitation à loyer modéré** which means 'low-rent home'.

councillor NOUN
■ **She's a local councillor.** Elle fait partie du conseil municipal.
to **count** VERB
compter
to **count on** VERB
compter sur
□ **You can count on me.** Tu peux compter sur moi.
counter NOUN
1 le comptoir *(in shop)*
2 le guichet *(in post office, bank)*
3 le jeton *(in game)*
country NOUN
1 le pays
□ **the border between the two countries** la frontière entre les deux pays
2 la campagne
□ **I live in the country.** J'habite à la campagne.
■ **country dancing** la danse folklorique
countryside NOUN
la campagne
county NOUN
le comté

> **DID YOU KNOW...?**
> The nearest French equivalent of a county would be a **département**.

■ **the county council**

> **DID YOU KNOW...?**
> The nearest French equivalent of a county council would be a **conseil général**, which administers a **département**.

couple NOUN
le couple
□ **the couple who live next door** le couple qui habite à côté
■ **a couple** deux □ **a couple of hours** deux

heures
■ **Could you wait a couple of minutes?** Pourriez-vous attendre quelques minutes?
courage NOUN
le courage
courgette NOUN
la courgette
courier NOUN
1 l' accompagnateur *masc*
l' accompagnatrice *fem (for tourists)*
2 le coursier *(delivery service)*
□ **They sent it by courier.** Ils l'ont envoyé par coursier.

> **LANGUAGE TIP** Be careful not to translate **courier** by **courrier**.

course NOUN
1 le cours
□ **a French course** un cours de français □ **to go on a course** suivre un cours
2 le plat
□ **the main course** le plat principal
■ **the first course** l'entrée *fem*
3 le terrain
□ **a golf course** un terrain de golf
■ **of course** bien sûr □ **Do you love me?** — **Of course I do!** Tu m'aimes? — Bien sûr que oui!
court NOUN
1 le tribunal (PL les tribunaux) *(of law)*
□ **He was in court yesterday.** Il est passé devant le tribunal hier.
2 le court *(tennis)*
□ **There are tennis and squash courts.** Il y a des courts de tennis et de squash.
courtyard NOUN
la cour
cousin NOUN
le cousin
la cousine
cover NOUN
▷ *see also* **cover** VERB
1 la couverture *(of book)*
2 la housse *(of duvet)*
to **cover** VERB
▷ *see also* **cover** NOUN
1 couvrir
□ **My face was covered with mosquito bites.** J'avais le visage couvert de piqûres de moustique.
2 prendre en charge
□ **Our insurance didn't cover it.** Notre assurance ne l'a pas pris en charge.
■ **to cover up a scandal** étouffer un scandale
cow NOUN
la vache
coward NOUN

le lâche
□ She's a coward. Elle est lâche.

cowardly ADJECTIVE
lâche (FEM lâche)

cowboy NOUN
le cow-boy

crab NOUN
le crabe

crack NOUN
▷ *see also* **crack** VERB
1 la fissure *(in wall)*
2 la fêlure *(in cup, window)*
3 le crack *(drug)*
■ **I'll have a crack at it.** Je vais tenter le coup.

to **crack** VERB
▷ *see also* **crack** NOUN
casser *(nut, egg)*
■ **to crack a joke** sortir une blague

to **crack down on** VERB
être ferme avec
□ The police are cracking down on drink-drivers. La police va être ferme avec les automobilistes en état d'ébriété.

cracked ADJECTIVE
fêlé (FEM fêlée) *(cup, window)*

cracker NOUN
1 la papillote *(biscuit)*
2 le diablotin *(Christmas cracker)*

DID YOU KNOW...?
Papillotes are different from crackers in Britain. They consist of a sweet with a joke and a banger wrapped around it, covered in foil. You unwrap the **papillote** and then pull the banger.

cradle NOUN
le berceau (PL les berceaux)

craft NOUN
les travaux manuels *masc pl*
□ We do craft at school. Nous avons des cours de travaux manuels à l'école.
■ **a craft centre** un centre artisanal

craftsman NOUN
l' artisan *masc*

to **cram** VERB
1 entasser
□ We crammed our stuff into the boot. Nous avons entassé nos affaires dans le coffre.
2 bachoter *(for exams)*

crammed ADJECTIVE
■ **crammed with** bourré de □ Her bag was crammed with books. Son sac était bourré de livres.

crane NOUN
la grue *(machine)*

to **crash** VERB
▷ *see also* **crash** NOUN
avoir un accident
□ He's crashed his car. Il a eu un accident de voiture.
■ **The plane crashed.** L'avion s'est écrasé.

crash NOUN
▷ *see also* **crash** VERB
1 la collision *(of car)*
2 l' accident *masc (of plane)*
■ **a crash helmet** un casque
■ **a crash course** un cours intensif

to **crawl** VERB
▷ *see also* **crawl** NOUN
marcher à quatre pattes *(baby)*

crawl NOUN
▷ *see also* **crawl** VERB
le crawl
□ to do the crawl nager le crawl

crazy ADJECTIVE
fou (FEM folle)

LANGUAGE TIP fou changes to fol before a vowel and most words beginning with 'h'.

cream ADJECTIVE
▷ *see also* **cream** NOUN
crème (FEM+PL crème) *(colour)*

cream NOUN
▷ *see also* **cream** ADJECTIVE
la crème
□ strawberries and cream les fraises à la crème
■ **a cream cake** un gâteau à la crème
■ **cream cheese** le fromage à la crème
■ **sun cream** la crème solaire

crease NOUN
le pli

creased ADJECTIVE
froissé (FEM froissée)

to **create** VERB
créer

creation NOUN
la création

creative ADJECTIVE
créatif (FEM créative)

creature NOUN
la créature

crèche NOUN
la crèche

credit NOUN
le crédit
□ on credit à crédit
■ **I've no credit left on my phone.** Je n'ai plus de crédit sur mon portable.

credit card NOUN
la carte de crédit

creeps PL NOUN

■ **It gives me the creeps.** Ça me donne la chair de poule.

to **creep up** VERB

■ **to creep up on somebody** s'approcher de quelqu'un à pas de loup

crept VERB ▷ see **creep up**

cress NOUN
le cresson

crew NOUN
1 l'équipage masc (of ship, plane)
2 l'équipe fem
□ a film crew une équipe de tournage

crew cut NOUN
les cheveux en brosse masc pl

cricket NOUN
1 le cricket
□ I play cricket. Je joue au cricket.
■ **a cricket bat** une batte de cricket
2 le grillon (insect)

crime NOUN
1 le délit
□ Murder is a crime. Le meurtre est un délit.
2 la criminalité (lawlessness)
■ **Crime is rising.** La criminalité augmente.

criminal NOUN
▷ see also **criminal** ADJECTIVE
le criminel
la criminelle

criminal ADJECTIVE
▷ see also **criminal** NOUN
criminel (FEM criminelle)
□ It's criminal! C'est criminel!
■ **It's a criminal offence.** C'est un crime puni par la loi.
■ **to have a criminal record** avoir un casier judiciaire

crisis NOUN
la crise

crisp ADJECTIVE
croquant (FEM croquante) (food)

crisps PL NOUN
les chips fem pl
□ a bag of crisps un paquet de chips

criterion NOUN
le critère

critic NOUN
le critique

critical ADJECTIVE
critique (FEM critique)
■ **a critical remark** une critique

criticism NOUN
la critique

to **criticize** VERB
critiquer

Croatia NOUN
la Croatie
■ **in Croatia** en Croatie

to **crochet** VERB
crocheter

crocodile NOUN
le crocodile

crook NOUN
l'escroc masc (criminal)

crop NOUN
la récolte
□ a good crop of apples une bonne récolte de pommes

cross NOUN
▷ see also **cross** ADJECTIVE, VERB
la croix

cross ADJECTIVE
▷ see also **cross** NOUN, VERB
fâché (FEM fâchée)
□ to be cross about something être fâché à propos de quelque chose

to **cross** VERB
▷ see also **cross** ADJECTIVE, NOUN
traverser (street, bridge)

to **cross out** VERB
barrer

to **cross over** VERB
traverser

cross-country NOUN
le cross (race)
■ **cross-country skiing** le ski de fond

crossing NOUN
1 la traversée (by boat)
□ the crossing from Dover to Calais la traversée de Douvres à Calais
2 le passage clouté (for pedestrians)

crossroads NOUN
le carrefour

crossword NOUN
les mots croisés masc pl
□ I like doing crosswords. J'aime faire les mots croisés.

to **crouch down** VERB
s'accroupir

crow NOUN
le corbeau (PL les corbeaux)

crowd NOUN
la foule
■ **the crowd** (at sports match) les spectateurs

crowded ADJECTIVE
bondé (FEM bondée)

crown NOUN
la couronne

crucifix NOUN
le crucifix

crude ADJECTIVE
grossier (FEM grossière) (vulgar)

cruel ADJECTIVE
cruel (FEM cruelle)

cruise NOUN
la croisière
□ to go on a cruise faire une croisière

crumb NOUN
la miette

to **crush** VERB
écraser

crutch NOUN
la béquille

cry NOUN
▷ see also **cry** VERB
le cri
□ He gave a cry of surprise. Il a poussé un cri de surprise.
■ Go on, have a good cry! Vas-y, pleure un bon coup!

to **cry** VERB
▷ see also **cry** NOUN
pleurer
□ The baby's crying. Le bébé pleure.

crystal NOUN
le cristal (PL les cristaux)

CTC NOUN (= city technology college)
le collège technique

cub NOUN
1 le petit (animal)
2 le louveteau (PL les louveteaux) (scout)

cube NOUN
le cube

cubic ADJECTIVE
■ a cubic metre un mètre cube

cucumber NOUN
le concombre

cuddle NOUN
▷ see also **cuddle** VERB
le câlin
□ Come and give me a cuddle. Viens me faire un câlin.

cuddle VERB
▷ see also **cuddle** NOUN
■ to cuddle something faire un câlin à quelque chose □ Emma cuddled her teddy bear. Emma a fait un câlin à son nounours.

cue NOUN
la queue de billard (for snooker, pool)

culottes PL NOUN
la jupe-culotte sing

culture NOUN
la culture

cunning ADJECTIVE
1 rusé (FEM rusée) (person)
2 astucieux (FEM astucieuse) (plan, idea)

cup NOUN
1 la tasse
□ a china cup une tasse en porcelaine
■ a cup of coffee un café
2 la coupe (trophy)

cupboard NOUN
le placard

to **cure** VERB
▷ see also **cure** NOUN
guérir

cure NOUN
▷ see also **cure** VERB
le remède

curious ADJECTIVE
curieux (FEM curieuse)

curl NOUN
la boucle (in hair)

curly ADJECTIVE
1 bouclé (FEM bouclée) (loosely curled)
2 frisé (FEM frisée) (tightly curled)

currant NOUN
le raisin de Corinthe (dried fruit)

currency NOUN
la devise
□ foreign currency les devises étrangères

current NOUN
▷ see also **current** ADJECTIVE
le courant
□ The current is very strong. Le courant est très fort.

current ADJECTIVE
▷ see also **current** NOUN
actuel (FEM actuelle)
□ the current situation la situation actuelle

current account NOUN
le compte courant

current affairs PL NOUN
l' actualité fem

curriculum NOUN
le programme

curriculum vitae NOUN
le curriculum vitae

curry NOUN
le curry

curse NOUN
la malédiction (spell)

curtain NOUN
le rideau (PL les rideaux)
□ to draw the curtains tirer les rideaux

cushion NOUN
le coussin

custard NOUN
la crème anglaise (for pouring)

custody NOUN
la garde (of child)

custom NOUN
la coutume masc
□ It's an old custom. C'est une ancienne coutume.

customer NOUN
le client
la cliente

353

customs PL NOUN
la douane *sing*

customs officer NOUN
le douanier
la douanière

cut NOUN
▷ *see also* **cut** VERB
1 la coupure
  □ He's got a cut on his forehead. Il a une coupure au front.
2 la coupe
  □ a cut and blow-dry une coupe brushing
3 la réduction *(in price, spending)*

to **cut** VERB
▷ *see also* **cut** NOUN
1 couper
  □ I'll cut some bread. Je vais couper du pain.
  ■ **to cut oneself** se couper □ I cut my foot on a piece of glass. Je me suis coupé au pied avec un morceau de verre.
2 réduire *(price, spending)*

to **cut down** VERB
abattre *(tree)*

to **cut off** VERB
couper
  □ The electricity was cut off. L'électricité a été coupée.

to **cut up** VERB
hacher *(vegetables, meat)*

cutback NOUN
la réduction
  □ staff cutbacks des réductions de personnel

cute ADJECTIVE
mignon (FEM mignonne)

cutlery NOUN
les couverts *masc pl*

cutting NOUN
la coupure de presse *(from newspaper)*

CV NOUN
le C.V.

cybercafé NOUN
le cybercafé

to **cycle** VERB
▷ *see also* **cycle** NOUN
faire de la bicyclette
  □ I like cycling. J'aime faire de la bicyclette.
  ■ **I cycle to school.** Je vais à l'école à bicyclette.

cycle NOUN
▷ *see also* **cycle** VERB
la bicyclette
  ■ **a cycle ride** une promenade à bicyclette
  ■ **a cycle lane** une piste cyclable

cycling NOUN
le cyclisme

cyclist NOUN
le/la cycliste

cylinder NOUN
le cylindre

Cyprus NOUN
Chypre
  ■ **in Cyprus** à Chypre
  ■ **We went to Cyprus.** Nous sommes allés à Chypre.

Czech NOUN
▷ *see also* **Czech** ADJECTIVE
1 le/la Tchèque *(person)*
2 le tchèque *(language)*

Czech ADJECTIVE
▷ *see also* **Czech** NOUN
tchèque (FEM tchèque)
  ■ **the Czech Republic** la République tchèque

Dd

dad NOUN
1 le père
   □ my dad mon père □ his dad son père
2 le papa

> **LANGUAGE TIP** Use **papa** only when you are talking to your father or using it as his name; otherwise use **père**.

   ■ **Dad!** Papa! □ I'll ask Dad. Je vais demander à papa.

daddy NOUN
le papa
   □ Say hello to your daddy! Dis bonjour à ton papa! □ Hello Daddy! Bonjour Papa!

daffodil NOUN
la jonquille

daft ADJECTIVE
idiot (FEM idiote)

daily ADJECTIVE, ADVERB
1 quotidien (FEM quotidienne)
   □ It's part of my daily routine. Ça fait partie de mes occupations quotidiennes.
2 tous les jours
   □ The pool is open daily. La piscine est ouverte tous les jours.

dairy NOUN
la crémerie *(shop)*

dairy products PL NOUN
les produits laitiers *masc pl*

daisy NOUN
la pâquerette

dam NOUN
le barrage

damage NOUN
   ▷ *see also* **damage** VERB
   les dégâts *masc pl*
   □ The storm did a lot of damage. La tempête a fait beaucoup de dégâts.

to **damage** VERB
   ▷ *see also* **damage** NOUN
   endommager

damn NOUN
   ▷ *see also* **damn** ADJECTIVE
   ■ I don't give a damn! *(informal)* Je m'en fiche!
   ■ **Damn!** *(informal)* Zut!

damn ADJECTIVE, ADVERB
   ▷ *see also* **damn** NOUN
   ■ It's a damn nuisance! Quelle barbe!

damp ADJECTIVE
humide (FEM humide)

dance NOUN
   ▷ *see also* **dance** VERB
1 la danse
   □ The last dance was a waltz. La dernière danse était une valse.
2 le bal
   □ Are you going to the dance tonight? Tu vas au bal ce soir?

to **dance** VERB
   ▷ *see also* **dance** NOUN
   danser
   ■ **to go dancing** aller danser □ Let's go dancing! Si on allait danser?

dancer NOUN
le danseur
la danseuse

dandruff NOUN
les pellicules *fem pl*

Dane NOUN
1 le Danois
2 la Danoise

danger NOUN
le danger
   ■ **in danger** en danger □ His life is in danger. Sa vie est en danger.
   ■ **to be in danger of** risquer de □ We were in danger of missing the plane. Nous risquions de rater l'avion.

dangerous ADJECTIVE
dangereux (FEM dangereuse)

Danish ADJECTIVE
   ▷ *see also* **Danish** NOUN
   danois (FEM danoise)

Danish NOUN
   ▷ *see also* **Danish** ADJECTIVE
   le danois *(language)*

to **dare** VERB
oser
   ■ **to dare to do something** oser faire quelque chose □ I didn't dare to tell my

parents. Je n'ai pas osé le dire à mes parents.
■ **I dare say it'll be okay.** Je suppose que ça va aller.

daring ADJECTIVE
audacieux (FEM audacieuse)

dark ADJECTIVE
▷ *see also* **dark** NOUN
1 sombre (FEM sombre) *(room)*
□ It's dark. *(inside)* Il fait sombre.
■ **It's dark outside.** Il fait nuit dehors.
■ **It's getting dark.** La nuit tombe.
2 foncé (FEM foncée) *(colour)*
□ She's got dark hair. Elle a les cheveux foncés. □ a dark green sweater un pull vert foncé

dark NOUN
▷ *see also* **dark** ADJECTIVE
le noir
□ I'm afraid of the dark. J'ai peur du noir.
■ **after dark** après la tombée de la nuit

darkness NOUN
l' obscurité *fem*
□ The room was in darkness. La chambre était dans l'obscurité.

darling NOUN
le chéri
la chérie
□ Thank you, darling! Merci, chéri!

dart NOUN
la fléchette
□ to play darts jouer aux fléchettes

to **dash** VERB
▷ *see also* **dash** NOUN
se précipiter
□ Everyone dashed to the window. Tout le monde s'est précipité vers la fenêtre.
■ **I must dash!** Il faut que je me sauve!

dash NOUN
▷ *see also* **dash** VERB
le tiret *(punctuation mark)*

data PL NOUN
les données *fem pl*

database NOUN
la base de données *(on computer)*

date NOUN
1 la date
□ my date of birth ma date de naissance
■ **What's the date today?** Quel jour sommes-nous?
■ **to have a date with somebody** sortir avec quelqu'un □ She's got a date with Ian tonight. Elle sort avec Ian ce soir.
■ **out of date 1** *(passport)* périmé **2** *(technology)* dépassé **3** *(clothes)* démodé
2 la datte *(fruit)*

daughter NOUN

la fille

daughter-in-law NOUN
la belle-fille (PL les belles-filles)

dawn NOUN
l' aube *fem*
□ at dawn à l'aube

day NOUN

> LANGUAGE TIP Use **jour** to refer to the whole 24-hour period. **journée** only refers to the time when you are awake.

1 le jour
□ We stayed in Nice for three days. Nous sommes restés trois jours à Nice.
■ **every day** tous les jours
2 la journée
□ during the day dans la journée □ I stayed at home all day. Je suis resté à la maison toute la journée.
■ **the day before** la veille □ the day before my birthday la veille de mon anniversaire
■ **the day after** le lendemain
■ **the day after tomorrow** après-demain
□ We're leaving the day after tomorrow. Nous partons après-demain.
■ **the day before yesterday** avant-hier
□ He arrived the day before yesterday. Il est arrivé avant-hier.

dead ADJECTIVE, ADVERB
1 mort (FEM morte)
□ He was already dead when the doctor came. Il était déjà mort quand le docteur est arrivé.
■ **He was shot dead.** Il a été abattu.
2 absolument *(totally)*
□ You're dead right! Tu as absolument raison!
■ **dead on time** à l'heure pile □ The train arrived dead on time. Le train est arrivé à l'heure pile.

dead end NOUN
l' impasse *fem*

deadline NOUN
la date limite
□ The deadline for entries is May 2nd. La date limite d'inscription est le deux mai.

deaf ADJECTIVE
sourd (FEM sourde)

deafening ADJECTIVE
assourdissant (FEM assourdissante)

deal NOUN
▷ *see also* **deal** VERB
le marché
■ **It's a deal!** Marché conclu!
■ **a great deal** beaucoup □ a great deal of money beaucoup d'argent

to **deal** VERB

▷ *see also* **deal** NOUN
donner *(cards)*
□ It's your turn to deal. C'est à toi de donner.
■ **to deal with something** s'occuper de quelque chose □ He promised to deal with it immediately. Il a promis de s'en occuper immédiatement.

dealer NOUN
1 le marchand
   la marchande
2 le dealer *(of drugs)*

dealt VERB ▷ *see* **deal**

dear ADJECTIVE
1 cher (FEM chère)
   □ Dear Mrs Duval Chère Madame Duval
   ■ **Dear Sir/Madam** *(in a circular)* Madame, Monsieur
2 coûteux (FEM coûteuse) *(expensive)*

death NOUN
   la mort
   □ after his death après sa mort
   ■ **I was bored to death.** Je me suis ennuyé à mourir.

debate NOUN
   ▷ *see also* **debate** VERB
   le débat

to **debate** VERB
   ▷ *see also* **debate** NOUN
   débattre

debt NOUN
   la dette
   □ He's got a lot of debts. Il a beaucoup de dettes.
   ■ **to be in debt** avoir des dettes

decade NOUN
   la décennie

decaffeinated ADJECTIVE
   décaféiné (FEM décaféinée)

to **decay** VERB
   se délabrer *(building)*
   □ a decaying mansion un manoir qui se délabre

to **deceive** VERB
   tromper

December NOUN
   décembre *masc*
   ■ **in December** en décembre

decent ADJECTIVE
   convenable (FEM convenable)
   □ a decent education une éducation convenable

to **decide** VERB
1 décider
   □ I decided to write to her. J'ai décidé de lui écrire. □ I decided not to go. J'ai décidé de ne pas y aller.

2 se décider
   □ I can't decide. Je n'arrive pas à me décider. □ Haven't you decided yet? Tu ne t'es pas encore décidé?
   ■ **to decide on something** se mettre d'accord sur quelque chose □ They haven't decided on a name yet. Ils ne se sont pas encore mis d'accord sur un nom.

decimal ADJECTIVE
   décimal (FEM décimale)
   □ the decimal system le système décimal

decision NOUN
   la décision
   ■ **to make a decision** prendre une décision

decisive ADJECTIVE
   décidé (FEM décidée) *(person)*

deck NOUN
1 le pont *(of ship)*
   ■ **on deck** sur le pont
2 le jeu (PL les jeux) *(of cards)*

deckchair NOUN
   la chaise longue

to **declare** VERB
   déclarer

to **decorate** VERB
1 décorer
   □ I decorated the cake with glacé cherries. J'ai décoré le gâteau avec des cerises confites.
2 peindre *(paint)*
3 tapisser *(wallpaper)*

decrease NOUN
   ▷ *see also* **decrease** VERB
   la diminution
   □ a decrease in the number of unemployed une diminution du nombre de chômeurs

to **decrease** VERB
   ▷ *see also* **decrease** NOUN
   diminuer

dedicated ADJECTIVE
   dévoué (FEM dévouée)
   □ a very dedicated teacher un professeur très dévoué
   ■ **dedicated to** 1 consacré à □ a museum dedicated to Napoleon un musée consacré à Napoléon 2 dédicacé à □ The book is dedicated to Emma. Le livre est dédicacé à Emma.

dedication NOUN
1 le dévouement *(commitment)*
2 la dédicace *(in book, on radio)*

to **deduct** VERB
   déduire

deep ADJECTIVE
1 profond (FEM profonde) *(water, hole, cut)*
   □ Is it deep? Est-ce que c'est profond?
   ■ **How deep is the lake?** Quelle est la

d

357

profondeur du lac?

■ **a hole 4 metres deep** un trou de quatre mètres de profondeur

2 épais (FEM épaisse) *(layer)*

□ a deep layer of snow une épaisse couche de neige □ The snow was really deep. Il y avait une épaisse couche de neige.

■ **He's got a deep voice.** Il a la voix grave.

■ **to take a deep breath** respirer à fond

deeply ADVERB
profondément *(depressed)*

deer NOUN
1 le cerf *(red deer)*
2 le daim *(fallow deer)*
3 le chevreuil *(roe deer)*

defeat NOUN
▷ *see also* **defeat** VERB
la défaite

to **defeat** VERB
▷ *see also* **defeat** NOUN
battre

defect NOUN
le défaut

defence NOUN
la défense

to **defend** VERB
défendre

defender NOUN
le défenseur

to **define** VERB
définir

definite ADJECTIVE
1 précis (FEM précise)
□ I haven't got any definite plans. Je n'ai pas de projets précis.
2 net (FEM nette)
□ It's a definite improvement. Cela constitue une nette amélioration.
3 sûr (FEM sûre)
□ We might go to Spain, but it's not definite. Nous irons peut-être en Espagne, mais ce n'est pas sûr.
■ **He was definite about it.** Il a été catégorique.

definitely ADVERB
vraiment
□ He's definitely the best player. C'est vraiment lui le meilleur joueur.
■ **He's the best player. — Definitely!** C'est le meilleur joueur. — C'est sûr!
■ **I definitely think he'll come.** Je suis sûr qu'il va venir.

definition NOUN
la définition

degree NOUN
1 le degré
□ a temperature of 30 degrees une

température de trente degrés
2 la licence
□ a degree in English une licence d'anglais

to **delay** VERB
▷ *see also* **delay** NOUN
1 retarder
□ We decided to delay our departure. Nous avons décidé de retarder notre départ.
2 tarder
□ Don't delay! Ne tarde pas!
■ **to be delayed** être retardé □ Our flight was delayed. Notre vol a été retardé.

delay NOUN
▷ *see also* **delay** VERB
le retard
□ There will be delays to trains on the London-Brighton line. Il y aura des retards sur la ligne Londres-Brighton.

LANGUAGE TIP Be careful not to translate **delay** by **délai**.

to **delete** VERB
effacer *(on computer, tape)*

deliberate ADJECTIVE
délibéré (FEM délibérée)

deliberately ADVERB
exprès
□ She did it deliberately. Elle l'a fait exprès.

delicate ADJECTIVE
délicat (FEM délicate)

delicatessen NOUN
l'épicerie fine *fem*

delicious ADJECTIVE
délicieux (FEM délicieuse)

delight NOUN
■ **to her delight** à sa plus grande joie

delighted ADJECTIVE
ravi (FEM ravie)
□ He'll be delighted to see you. Il sera ravi de vous voir.

delightful ADJECTIVE
délicieux (FEM délicieuse) *(meal, evening)*

to **deliver** VERB
1 livrer
□ I deliver newspapers. Je livre les journaux.
2 distribuer *(mail)*

delivery NOUN
la livraison

to **demand** VERB
▷ *see also* **demand** NOUN
exiger

LANGUAGE TIP Be careful not to translate **to demand** by **demander**.

demand NOUN
▷ *see also* **demand** VERB
la demande *(for product)*

demanding ADJECTIVE
astreignant (FEM astreignante)

□ It's a very demanding job. C'est un travail très astreignant.

demo NOUN
la manif *(protest)*

democracy NOUN
la démocratie

democratic ADJECTIVE
démocratique (FEM démocratique)

to **demolish** VERB
démolir

to **demonstrate** VERB
1 faire une démonstration de *(show)*
□ She demonstrated the technique. Elle a fait une démonstration de la technique.
2 manifester *(protest)*
□ to demonstrate against something manifester contre quelque chose

demonstration NOUN
1 la démonstration *(of method, technique)*
2 la manifestation *(protest)*

demonstrator NOUN *(protester)*
le manifestant
la manifestante

denim NOUN
le jean
□ a denim jacket une veste en jean

denims PL NOUN
le jean *sing (jeans)*

Denmark NOUN
le Danemark
■ **in Denmark** au Danemark
■ **to Denmark** au Danemark

dense ADJECTIVE
1 dense (FEM dense) *(crowd, fog)*
2 épais (FEM épaisse) *(smoke)*
■ **He's so dense!** Il est vraiment bouché!

dent NOUN
▷ *see also* **dent** VERB
la bosse

to **dent** VERB
▷ *see also* **dent** NOUN
cabosser

dental ADJECTIVE
dentaire (FEM dentaire)
■ **dental floss** le fil dentaire

dentist NOUN
le/la dentiste
□ Catherine is a dentist. Catherine est dentiste.

to **deny** VERB
nier
□ She denied everything. Elle a tout nié.

deodorant NOUN
le déodorant

to **depart** VERB
partir

department NOUN

1 le rayon *(in shop)*
□ the shoe department le rayon chaussures
2 le département *(in university, school)*
□ the English department le département d'anglais

department store NOUN
le grand magasin

departure NOUN
le départ

departure lounge NOUN
le hall des départs

to **depend** VERB
■ **to depend on** dépendre de □ The price depends on the quality. Le prix dépend de la qualité.
■ **depending on the weather** selon le temps
■ **It depends.** Ça dépend.

to **deport** VERB
expulser

deposit NOUN
1 les arrhes *fem pl (part payment)*
□ You have to pay a deposit when you book. Il faut verser des arrhes lors de la réservation.
2 la caution *(when hiring something)*
□ You get the deposit back when you return the bike. On vous remboursera la caution quand vous ramènerez le vélo.
3 la consigne *(on bottle)*

depressed ADJECTIVE
déprimé (FEM déprimée)
□ I'm feeling depressed. Je suis déprimé.

depressing ADJECTIVE
déprimant (FEM déprimante)

depth NOUN
la profondeur

deputy head NOUN
le directeur adjoint
la directrice adjointe

to **descend** VERB
descendre

to **describe** VERB
décrire

description NOUN
la description

desert NOUN
le désert

desert island NOUN
l' île déserte *fem*

to **deserve** VERB
mériter

design NOUN
▷ *see also* **design** VERB
1 la conception
□ It's a completely new design. C'est une conception entièrement nouvelle.

d

2 le motif

  □ a geometric design un motif géométrique

  ■ **fashion design** le stylisme

to **design** VERB

  ▷ *see also* **design** NOUN

  dessiner *(clothes, furniture)*

designer NOUN

  le/la styliste *(of clothes)*

  ■ **designer clothes** les vêtements griffés

desire NOUN

  ▷ *see also* **desire** VERB

  le désir

to **desire** VERB

  ▷ *see also* **desire** NOUN

  désirer

desk NOUN

1 le bureau (PL les bureaux) *(in office)*

2 le pupitre *(for pupil)*

3 la réception *(in hotel)*

4 le comptoir *(at airport)*

despair NOUN

  le désespoir

  ■ **I was in despair.** J'étais désespéré.

desperate ADJECTIVE

  désespéré (FEM désespérée)

  □ a desperate situation une situation désespérée

  ■ **to get desperate** désespérer □ I was getting desperate. Je commençais à désespérer.

desperately ADVERB

1 terriblement

  □ We're desperately worried. Nous sommes terriblement inquiets.

2 désespérément

  □ He was desperately trying to persuade her. Il essayait désespérément de la persuader.

to **despise** VERB

  mépriser

despite PREPOSITION

  malgré

dessert NOUN

  le dessert

  □ for dessert comme dessert

destination NOUN

  la destination

to **destroy** VERB

  détruire

destruction NOUN

  la destruction

detached house NOUN

  le pavillon

detail NOUN

  le détail

  □ in detail en détail

detailed ADJECTIVE

  détaillé (FEM détaillée)

detective NOUN

  l' inspecteur de police *masc*

  ■ **a private detective** un détective privé

  ■ **a detective story** un roman policier

detention NOUN

  ■ **to get a detention** être consigné

detergent NOUN

1 le détergent

2 la lessive (US)

determined ADJECTIVE

  déterminé (FEM déterminée)

  ■ **to be determined to do something** être déterminé à faire quelque chose □ She's determined to succeed. Elle est déterminée à réussir.

detour NOUN

  le détour

devaluation NOUN

  la dévaluation

devastated ADJECTIVE

  anéanti (FEM anéantie)

  □ I was devastated. J'étais anéanti.

devastating ADJECTIVE

1 accablant (FEM accablante) *(upsetting)*

2 dévastateur (FEM dévastatrice) *(flood, storm)*

to **develop** VERB

1 développer

  □ to get a film developed faire développer un film

2 se développer

  □ Girls develop faster than boys. Les filles se développent plus vite que les garçons.

  ■ **to develop into** se transformer en □ The argument developed into a fight. La dispute s'est transformée en bagarre.

  ■ **a developing country** un pays en voie de développement

development NOUN

  le développement

  □ the latest developments les derniers développements

device NOUN

  l' appareil *masc*

devil NOUN

  le diable

  □ Poor devil! Pauvre diable!

to **devise** VERB

  concevoir

devoted ADJECTIVE

  dévoué (FEM dévouée)

  □ He's completely devoted to her. Il lui est très dévoué.

diabetes NOUN

  le diabète

diabetic NOUN

  le/la diabétique

  □ I'm a diabetic. Je suis diabétique.

diagonal ADJECTIVE
diagonal (FEM diagonale, MASC PL diagonaux)

diagram NOUN
le diagramme

to **dial** VERB
composer (number)

dialling tone NOUN
la tonalité

dialogue NOUN
le dialogue

diamond NOUN
le diamant
□ a diamond ring une bague en diamant
■ **diamonds** (at cards) le carreau sing □ the
ace of diamonds l'as de carreau

diaper NOUN (US)
la couche

diarrhoea NOUN
la diarrhée
□ I've got diarrhoea. J'ai la diarrhée.

diary NOUN
1 l' agenda masc
□ I've got her phone number in my diary. J'ai
son numéro de téléphone dans mon
agenda.
2 le journal (PL les journaux)
□ I keep a diary. Je tiens un journal.

dice NOUN
le dé

dictation NOUN
la dictée

dictionary NOUN
le dictionnaire

did VERB ▷ see **do**

to **die** VERB
mourir
□ He died last year. Il est mort l'année
dernière.
■ **to be dying to do something** mourir
d'envie de faire quelque chose □ I'm dying
to see you. Je meurs d'envie de te voir.

diesel NOUN
1 le gazole (fuel)
□ 30 litres of diesel trente litres de gazole
2 la voiture diesel (car)
□ My car's a diesel. J'ai une voiture diesel.

diet NOUN
▷ see also **diet** VERB
1 l' alimentation fem
□ a healthy diet une alimentation saine
2 le régime (for slimming)
□ I'm on a diet. Je suis au régime.

to **diet** VERB
▷ see also **diet** NOUN
faire un régime
□ I've been dieting for two months. Je fais
un régime depuis deux mois.

difference NOUN
la différence
□ There's not much difference in age
between us. Il n'y a pas une grande
différence d'âge entre nous.
■ **It makes no difference.** Ça revient au
même.

different ADJECTIVE
différent (FEM différente)
□ We are very different. Nous sommes très
différents. □ Paris is different from London.
Paris est différent de Londres.

difficult ADJECTIVE
difficile (FEM difficile)
□ It's difficult to choose. C'est difficile de
choisir.

difficulty NOUN
la difficulté
□ without difficulty sans difficulté
■ **to have difficulty doing something**
avoir du mal à faire quelque chose

to **dig** VERB
1 creuser (hole)
2 bêcher (garden)
■ **to dig something up** déterrer quelque
chose

digestion NOUN
la digestion

digger NOUN
la pelleteuse (machine)

digital camera NOUN
l' appareil photo numérique masc

digital radio NOUN
la radio numérique

digital television NOUN
la télévision numérique

digital watch NOUN
la montre à affichage numérique

dim ADJECTIVE
1 faible (FEM faible) (light)
2 limité (FEM limitée) (stupid)

dimension NOUN
la dimension

to **diminish** VERB
diminuer

din NOUN
le vacarme

diner NOUN (US)
le snack

dinghy NOUN
■ **a rubber dinghy** un canot pneumatique
■ **a sailing dinghy** un dériveur

dining car NOUN
le wagon-restaurant (PL les wagons-
restaurants)

dining room NOUN
la salle à manger

d

d

dinner NOUN
1 le déjeuner (at midday)
2 le dîner (in the evening)
dinner jacket NOUN
le smoking
dinner lady NOUN
la dame de service
dinner party NOUN
le dîner
dinner time NOUN
1 l' heure du déjeuner fem (midday)
2 l' heure du dîner fem (in the evening)
dinosaur NOUN
le dinosaure
dip NOUN
▷ see also **dip** VERB
■ to go for a dip aller se baigner
to **dip** VERB
▷ see also **dip** NOUN
tremper
□ He dipped a biscuit into his tea. Il a trempé un biscuit dans son thé.
diploma NOUN
le diplôme
□ a diploma in social work un diplôme d'assistante sociale
diplomat NOUN
le/la diplomate
diplomatic ADJECTIVE
diplomatique (FEM diplomatique)
direct ADJECTIVE, ADVERB
▷ see also **direct** VERB
direct (FEM directe)
□ the most direct route le chemin le plus direct □ You can't fly to Nice direct from Cork. Il n'y a pas de vols directs de Cork à Nice.
to **direct** VERB
▷ see also **direct** ADJECTIVE
1 réaliser (film, programme)
2 mettre en scène (play, show)
direction NOUN
la direction
□ We're going in the wrong direction. Nous allons dans la mauvaise direction.
■ to ask somebody for directions demander son chemin à quelqu'un
director NOUN
1 le directeur
la directrice (of company)
2 le metteur en scène (of play)
3 le réalisateur
la réalisatrice (of film, programme)
directory NOUN
1 l' annuaire masc (phone book)
2 le répertoire (computing)
dirt NOUN

la saleté
dirty ADJECTIVE
sale (FEM sale)
■ to get dirty se salir
■ to get something dirty salir quelque chose
disabled ADJECTIVE
handicapé (FEM handicapée)
■ the disabled les handicapés
disadvantage NOUN
le désavantage
to **disagree** VERB
■ We always disagree. Nous ne sommes jamais d'accord.
■ I disagree! Je ne suis pas d'accord!
■ He disagrees with me. Il n'est pas d'accord avec moi.
disagreement NOUN
le désaccord
to **disappear** VERB
disparaître
disappearance NOUN
la disparition
disappointed ADJECTIVE
déçu (FEM déçue)
disappointing ADJECTIVE
décevant (FEM décevante)
disappointment NOUN
la déception
disaster NOUN
le désastre
disastrous ADJECTIVE
désastreux (FEM désastreuse)
disc NOUN
le disque
discipline NOUN
la discipline
disc jockey NOUN
le disc-jockey
disco NOUN
la soirée disco
□ There's a disco at the school tonight. Il y a une soirée disco à l'école ce soir.
to **disconnect** VERB
1 débrancher (electrical equipment)
2 couper (telephone, water supply)
discount NOUN
la réduction
□ a discount for students une réduction pour les étudiants
to **discourage** VERB
décourager
■ to get discouraged se décourager
□ Don't get discouraged! Ne te décourage pas!
to **discover** VERB
découvrir

discrimination NOUN
la discrimination
□ racial discrimination la discrimination raciale

to **discuss** VERB
1 discuter de
□ I'll discuss it with my parents. Je vais en discuter avec mes parents.
2 discuter sur *(topic)*
□ We discussed the problem of pollution. Nous avons discuté du problème de la pollution.

discussion NOUN
la discussion

disease NOUN
la maladie

disgraceful ADJECTIVE
scandaleux (FEM scandaleuse)

to **disguise** VERB
déguiser
□ He was disguised as a policeman. Il était déguisé en policier.

disgusted ADJECTIVE
dégoûté (FEM dégoûtée)
□ I was absolutely disgusted. J'étais complètement dégoûté.

disgusting ADJECTIVE
1 dégoûtant (FEM dégoûtante) *(food, smell)*
□ It looks disgusting. Ça a l'air dégoûtant.
2 honteux (FEM honteuse) *(disgraceful)*
□ That's disgusting! C'est honteux!

dish NOUN
le plat
□ a china dish un plat en porcelaine □ a vegetarian dish un plat végétarien
■ to do the dishes faire la vaisselle □ He never does the dishes. Il ne fait jamais la vaisselle.

dishonest ADJECTIVE
malhonnête (FEM malhonnête)

dish soap NOUN (US)
le produit à vaisselle

dish towel NOUN (US)
le torchon

dishwasher NOUN
le lave-vaisselle (PL les lave-vaisselle)

disinfectant NOUN
le désinfectant

disk NOUN
le disque
■ a floppy disk une disquette
■ the hard disk le disque dur

diskette NOUN
la disquette

to **dislike** VERB
▷ see also **dislike** NOUN
ne pas aimer

□ I really dislike cabbage. Je n'aime vraiment pas le chou.

dislike NOUN
▷ see also **dislike** VERB
■ my likes and dislikes ce que j'aime et ce que je n'aime pas

dismal ADJECTIVE
lugubre (FEM lugubre)

to **dismiss** VERB
renvoyer *(employee)*

disobedient ADJECTIVE
désobéissant (FEM désobéissante)

display NOUN
▷ see also **display** VERB
l' étalage *masc*
□ There was a lovely display of fruit in the window. Il y avait un superbe étalage de fruits en vitrine.
■ to be on display être exposé □ Her best paintings were on display. Ses meilleurs tableaux étaient exposés.
■ a firework display un feu d'artifice

to **display** VERB
▷ see also **display** NOUN
1 montrer
□ She proudly displayed her medal. Elle a montré sa médaille avec fierté.
2 exposer *(in shop window)*

disposable ADJECTIVE
jetable (FEM jetable)

to **disqualify** VERB
disqualifier
■ to be disqualified être disqualifié □ He was disqualified. Il a été disqualifié.

to **disrupt** VERB
perturber
□ Protesters disrupted the meeting. Des manifestants ont perturbé la réunion.
□ Train services are being disrupted by the strike. Les horaires de train sont perturbés par la grève.

dissatisfied ADJECTIVE
■ We were dissatisfied with the service. Nous n'étions pas satisfaits du service.

to **dissolve** VERB
dissoudre

distance NOUN
la distance
□ a distance of 40 kilometres une distance de quarante kilomètres
■ It's within walking distance. On peut y aller à pied.
■ in the distance au loin

distant ADJECTIVE
lointain (FEM lointaine)
□ in the distant future dans un avenir lointain

distillery NOUN
la distillerie
□ a whisky distillery une distillerie de whisky

distinction NOUN
1 la distinction
□ to make a distinction between ... faire la distinction entre ...
2 la mention très bien
□ I got a distinction in my piano exam. J'ai eu la mention très bien à mon examen de piano.

distinctive ADJECTIVE
distinctif (FEM distinctive)

to **distract** VERB
distraire

to **distribute** VERB
distribuer

district NOUN
1 le quartier (of town)
2 la région (of country)

to **disturb** VERB
déranger
□ I'm sorry to disturb you. Je suis désolé de vous déranger.

ditch NOUN
▷ see also **ditch** VERB
le fossé

to **ditch** VERB
▷ see also **ditch** NOUN
plaquer (informal)
□ She's just ditched her boyfriend. Elle vient de plaquer son copain.

dive NOUN
▷ see also **dive** VERB
le plongeon

to **dive** VERB
▷ see also **dive** NOUN
plonger

diver NOUN
le plongeur
la plongeuse

diversion NOUN
la déviation (for traffic)

to **divide** VERB
1 diviser
□ Divide the pastry in half. Divisez la pâte en deux. □ 12 divided by 3 is 4. Douze divisé par trois égalent quatre.
2 se diviser
□ We divided into two groups. Nous nous sommes divisés en deux groupes.

diving NOUN
la plongée
■ a diving board un plongeoir

division NOUN
la division

divorce NOUN
le divorce

divorced ADJECTIVE
divorcé (FEM divorcée)
□ My parents are divorced. Mes parents sont divorcés.

DIY NOUN
le bricolage
□ to do DIY faire du bricolage □ a DIY shop un magasin de bricolage

dizzy ADJECTIVE
■ to feel dizzy avoir la tête qui tourne □ I feel dizzy. J'ai la tête qui tourne.

DJ NOUN
le disc-jockey

to **do** VERB
1 faire
□ What are you doing this evening? Qu'est-ce que tu fais ce soir? □ I do a lot of cycling. Je fais beaucoup de vélo. □ I haven't done my homework. Je n'ai pas fait mes devoirs. □ She did it by herself. Elle l'a fait toute seule. □ I'll do my best. Je ferai de mon mieux.
■ to do well marcher bien □ The firm is doing well. L'entreprise marche bien.
□ She's doing well at school. Ses études marchent bien.
2 aller (be enough)
□ It's not very good, but it'll do. Ce n'est pas très bon, mais ça ira.
■ That'll do, thanks. Ça ira, merci.

LANGUAGE TIP In English 'do' is used to make questions. In French questions are made either with est-ce que or by reversing the order of verb and subject.

□ Do you like French food? Est-ce que vous aimez la cuisine française? □ Where does he live? Où est-ce qu'il habite? □ Do you speak English? Parlez-vous anglais? □ What do you do in your free time? Qu'est-ce que vous faites pendant vos loisirs? □ Where did you go for your holidays? Où es-tu allé pendant tes vacances?

LANGUAGE TIP Use ne ... pas in negative sentences for 'don't'.

□ I don't understand. Je ne comprends pas.
□ Why didn't you come? Pourquoi n'êtes-vous pas venus?

LANGUAGE TIP 'do' is not translated when it is used in place of another verb.

□ I hate maths. — So do I. Je déteste les maths. — Moi aussi. □ I didn't like the film. — Neither did I. Je n'ai pas aimé le film. — Moi non plus. □ Do you like horses? — No I

d

don't. Est-ce que tu aimes les chevaux? — Non.

☀ **LANGUAGE TIP** Use **n'est-ce pas** to check information.

□ You go swimming on Fridays, don't you? Tu fais de la natation le vendredi, n'est-ce pas? □ The bus stops at the youth hostel, doesn't it? Le bus s'arrête à l'auberge de jeunesse, n'est-ce pas?

■ **How do you do?** Enchanté!

to **do up** VERB

1 lacer *(shoes)*

□ Do up your shoes! Lace tes chaussures!

2 retaper *(renovate)*

□ They're doing up an old cottage. Ils retapent une vieille maison.

3 boutonner *(shirt, cardigan)*

■ **Do up your zip!** *(on trousers)* Ferme ta braguette!

to **do without** VERB

se passer de

□ I couldn't do without my computer. Je ne pourrais pas me passer de mon ordinateur.

dock NOUN

le dock *(for ships)*

doctor NOUN

le médecin

□ She's a doctor. Elle est médecin. □ I'd like to be a doctor. Je voudrais être médecin.

document NOUN

le document

documentary NOUN

le documentaire

to **dodge** VERB

échapper à *(attacker)*

dodgems PL NOUN

les autos tamponneuses *fem pl*

□ to go on the dodgems aller faire un tour d'autos tamponneuses

does VERB ▷ *see* **do**

doesn't = does not

dog NOUN

le chien

la chienne

□ Have you got a dog? Est-ce que tu as un chien?

do-it-yourself NOUN

le bricolage

dole NOUN

les allocations chômage *fem pl*

■ **to be on the dole** toucher le chômage

□ A lot of people are on the dole. Beaucoup de gens touchent le chômage.

■ **to go on the dole** s'inscrire au chômage

doll NOUN

la poupée

dollar NOUN

le dollar

dolphin NOUN

le dauphin

domestic ADJECTIVE

■ **a domestic flight** un vol intérieur

dominoes PL NOUN

■ **to have a game of dominoes** faire une partie de dominos

to **donate** VERB

donner

done VERB ▷ *see* **do**

donkey NOUN

l' âne *masc*

donor NOUN

1 le donateur

la donatrice *(to charity)*

2 le donneur

la donneuse *(of blood, organ for transplant)*

don't = do not

door NOUN

1 la porte

□ the first door on the right la première porte à droite

2 la portière *(of car, train)*

doorbell NOUN

la sonnette

■ **to ring the doorbell** sonner

■ **Suddenly the doorbell rang.** Soudain, on a sonné.

doorman NOUN

le portier

doorstep NOUN

le pas de la porte

dormitory NOUN

le dortoir

dose NOUN

la dose

dosh NOUN

le fric *(informal: money)*

dot NOUN

le point *(on letter 'i', in email address)*

■ **on the dot** à l'heure pile □ He arrived at 9 o'clock on the dot. Il est arrivé à neuf heures pile.

double ADJECTIVE, ADVERB

▷ *see also* **double** VERB

double (FEM double)

□ a double helping une double portion

■ **to cost double** coûter le double □ First-class tickets cost double. Les billets de première classe coûtent le double.

■ **a double bed** un grand lit

■ **a double room** une chambre pour deux personnes

■ **a double-decker bus** un autobus à impériale

to **double** VERB

▷ *see also* **double** ADJECTIVE
doubler
□ The number of attacks has doubled. Le nombre d'agressions a doublé.

double bass NOUN
la contrebasse
□ I play the double bass. Je joue de la contrebasse.

to **double-click** VERB
double-cliquer
□ to double-click on an icon double-cliquer sur une icône

double glazing NOUN
le double vitrage

doubles PL NOUN
le double *sing (in tennis)*
□ to play mixed doubles jouer en double mixte

doubt NOUN
▷ *see also* **doubt** VERB
le doute
□ I have my doubts. J'ai des doutes.

to **doubt** VERB
▷ *see also* **doubt** NOUN
douter de
■ I doubt it. J'en doute.
■ to doubt that douter que
  ⚬ **LANGUAGE TIP** **douter que** has to be followed by a verb in the subjunctive.
  □ I doubt he'll agree. Je doute qu'il soit d'accord.

doubtful ADJECTIVE
■ to be doubtful about doing something hésiter à faire quelque chose □ I'm doubtful about going by myself. J'hésite à y aller tout seul.
■ It's doubtful. Ce n'est pas sûr.
■ You sound doubtful. Tu n'as pas l'air sûr.

dough NOUN
la pâte

doughnut NOUN
le beignet
□ a jam doughnut un beignet à la confiture

Dover NOUN
Douvres
□ We went from Dover to Boulogne. Nous sommes allés de Douvres à Boulogne.
■ in Dover à Douvres

down ADVERB, ADJECTIVE, PREPOSITION
1 en bas *(below)*
□ His office is down on the first floor. Son bureau est en bas, au premier étage. □ It's down there. C'est là-bas.
2 à terre *(to the ground)*
□ He threw down his racket. Il a jeté sa raquette à terre.
■ They live just down the road. Ils

habitent tout à côté.
■ to come down descendre □ Come down here! Descends!
■ to go down descendre □ The rabbit went down the hole. Le lapin est descendu dans le terrier.
■ to sit down s'asseoir □ Sit down! Asseyez-vous!
■ to feel down avoir le cafard □ I'm feeling a bit down. J'ai un peu le cafard.
■ The computer's down. L'ordinateur est en panne.

to **download** VERB
▷ *see also* **download** NOUN
télécharger
□ to download a file télécharger un fichier

download NOUN
▷ *see also* **download** VERB
le téléchargement
□ a free download un téléchargement gratuit

downpour NOUN
la pluie torrentielle
□ a sudden downpour une pluie soudaine et torrentielle

downstairs ADVERB, ADJECTIVE
1 au rez-de-chaussée
□ The bathroom's downstairs. La salle de bain est au rez-de-chaussée.
2 du rez-de-chaussée
□ the downstairs bathroom la salle de bain du rez-de-chaussée
■ the people downstairs les voisins du dessous

downtown ADJECTIVE (US)
dans le centre

to **doze** VERB
sommeiller

to **doze off** VERB
s'assoupir

dozen NOUN
la douzaine
□ two dozen deux douzaines □ a dozen eggs une douzaine d'œufs
■ I've told you that dozens of times. Je t'ai dit ça des centaines de fois.

drab ADJECTIVE
terne (FEM terne) *(clothes)*

draft NOUN (US)
le courant d'air

to **drag** VERB
▷ *see also* **drag** NOUN
traîner *(thing, person)*
■ 'drag and drop' 'glisser déposer'

drag NOUN
▷ *see also* **drag** VERB
■ It's a real drag! *(informal)* C'est la barbe!

■ **in drag** travesti □ He was in drag. Il était travesti.

dragon NOUN
le dragon

drain NOUN
▷ *see also* **drain** VERB
l' égout *masc*
□ The drains are blocked. Les égouts sont bouchés.

to **drain** VERB
▷ *see also* **drain** NOUN
égoutter *(vegetables, pasta)*

draining board NOUN
l' égouttoir *masc*

drainpipe NOUN
le tuyau d'écoulement

drama NOUN
l' art dramatique *masc*
□ Drama is my favourite subject. L'art dramatique est ma matière préférée.
■ **drama school** l'école d'art dramatique □ I'd like to go to drama school. J'aimerais entrer dans une école d'art dramatique.
■ **Greek drama** le théâtre grec

dramatic ADJECTIVE
spectaculaire (FEM spectaculaire)
□ It was really dramatic! C'était vraiment spectaculaire! □ a dramatic improvement une amélioration spectaculaire
■ **dramatic news** une nouvelle extraordinaire

drank VERB ▷ *see* **drink**

drapes PL NOUN (US)
les rideaux *masc pl*

drastic ADJECTIVE
radical (FEM radicale, MASC PL radicaux) *(change)*
■ **to take drastic action** prendre des mesures énergiques

draught NOUN
le courant d'air

draughts NOUN
les dames *fem pl*
□ to play draughts jouer aux dames

to **draw** VERB
▷ *see also* **draw** NOUN
1 dessiner
□ He's good at drawing. Il dessine bien.
■ **to draw a picture** faire un dessin
■ **to draw a picture of somebody** faire le portrait de quelqu'un
■ **to draw a line** tirer un trait
2 faire match nul *(sport)*
□ We drew 2-2. Nous avons fait match nul deux à deux.
■ **to draw the curtains** tirer les rideaux
■ **to draw lots** tirer au sort

draw NOUN
▷ *see also* **draw** VERB
1 le match nul *(sport)*
□ The game ended in a draw. La partie s'est soldée par un match nul.
2 le tirage au sort *(in lottery)*
□ The draw takes place on Saturday. Le tirage au sort a lieu samedi.

drawback NOUN
l' inconvénient *masc*

drawer NOUN
le tiroir

drawing NOUN
le dessin

drawing pin NOUN
la punaise

drawn VERB ▷ *see* **draw**

dreadful ADJECTIVE
1 terrible (FEM terrible)
□ a dreadful mistake une terrible erreur
2 affreux (FEM affreuse)
□ The weather was dreadful. Il a fait un temps affreux.
■ **I feel dreadful.** Je ne me sens vraiment pas bien.
■ **You look dreadful.** *(ill)* Tu as une mine affreuse.

to **dream** VERB
▷ *see also* **dream** NOUN
rêver
□ I dreamed I was in Belgium. J'ai rêvé que j'étais en Belgique.

dream NOUN
▷ *see also* **dream** VERB
le rêve
□ It was just a dream. Ce n'était qu'un rêve.
■ **a bad dream** un cauchemar

to **drench** VERB
■ **to get drenched** se faire tremper □ We got drenched. Nous nous sommes fait tremper.

dress NOUN
▷ *see also* **dress** VERB
la robe

to **dress** VERB
▷ *see also* **dress** NOUN
s'habiller
□ I got up, dressed, and went downstairs. Je me suis levé, je me suis habillé et je suis descendu.
■ **to dress somebody** habiller quelqu'un
□ She dressed the children. Elle a habillé les enfants.
■ **to get dressed** s'habiller □ I got dressed quickly. Je me suis habillé rapidement.

to **dress up** VERB
se déguiser

□ I dressed up as a ghost. Je me suis déguisé en fantôme.

dressed ADJECTIVE
habillé (FEM habillée)
□ I'm not dressed yet. Je ne suis pas encore habillé. □ How was she dressed? Comment est-ce qu'elle était habillée?
■ **She was dressed in a green sweater and jeans.** Elle portait un pull vert et un jean.

dresser NOUN
le vaisselier (furniture)

dressing gown NOUN
la robe de chambre

dressing table NOUN
la coiffeuse

drew VERB ▷ see **draw**

dried VERB ▷ see **dry**

drier NOUN
le séchoir

drift NOUN
▷ see also **drift** VERB
■ **a snow drift** une congère

to **drift** VERB
▷ see also **drift** NOUN
1 aller à la dérive (boat)
2 s'amonceler (snow)

drill NOUN
▷ see also **drill** VERB
la perceuse

to **drill** VERB
▷ see also **drill** NOUN
percer

to **drink** VERB
▷ see also **drink** NOUN
boire
□ What would you like to drink? Qu'est-ce que vous voulez boire? □ She drank three cups of tea. Elle a bu trois tasses de thé. □ He'd been drinking. Il avait bu.
■ **I don't drink.** Je ne bois pas d'alcool.

drink NOUN
▷ see also **drink** VERB
1 la boisson
□ a cold drink une boisson fraîche □ a hot drink une boisson chaude
2 le verre (alcoholic)
□ They've gone out for a drink. Ils sont allés prendre un verre.
■ **to have a drink** prendre un verre

drinking water NOUN
l' eau potable fem

drive NOUN
▷ see also **drive** VERB
1 le tour en voiture
■ **to go for a drive** aller faire un tour en voiture □ We went for a drive in the country.

Nous sommes allés faire un tour à la campagne.
■ **We've got a long drive tomorrow.** Nous avons une longue route à faire demain.
2 l' allée fem (of house)
□ He parked his car in the drive. Il a garé sa voiture dans l'allée.

to **drive** VERB
▷ see also **drive** NOUN
1 conduire (a car)
□ She's learning to drive. Elle apprend à conduire. □ Can you drive? Tu sais conduire?
2 aller en voiture (go by car)
□ I'd rather drive than take the train. Je préfère conduire que de prendre le train.
3 emmener en voiture
□ My mother drives me to school. Ma mère m'emmène à l'école en voiture.
■ **to drive somebody home** raccompagner quelqu'un □ He offered to drive me home. Il m'a proposé de me raccompagner.
■ **to drive somebody mad** rendre quelqu'un fou □ He drives her mad. Il la rend folle.

driver NOUN
1 le conducteur
la conductrice
□ She's an excellent driver. C'est une excellente conductrice.
2 le chauffeur (of taxi, bus)
□ He's a bus driver. Il est chauffeur d'autobus.

driver's license NOUN (US)
le permis de conduire

driving instructor NOUN
le moniteur d'auto-école
□ He's a driving instructor. Il est moniteur d'auto-école.

driving lesson NOUN
la leçon de conduite

driving licence NOUN
le permis de conduire

driving test NOUN
■ **to take one's driving test** passer son permis de conduire □ He's taking his driving test tomorrow. Il passe son permis de conduire demain.
■ **She's just passed her driving test.** Elle vient d'avoir son permis.

drizzle NOUN
la bruine

drop NOUN
▷ see also **drop** VERB
la goutte
□ a drop of water une goutte d'eau

to **drop** VERB

▷ *see also* **drop** NOUN
1 laisser tomber
  □ I dropped the glass and it broke. J'ai laissé tomber le verre et il s'est cassé. □ I'm going to drop chemistry. Je vais laisser tomber la chimie.
2 déposer
  □ Could you drop me at the station? Pouvez-vous me déposer à la gare?

drought NOUN
la sécheresse

drove VERB ▷ *see* **drive**

to **drown** VERB
se noyer
  □ A boy drowned here yesterday. Un jeune garçon s'est noyé ici hier.

drug NOUN
1 le médicament *(medicine)*
  □ They need food and drugs. Ils ont besoin de nourriture et de médicaments.
2 la drogue *(illegal)*
  □ hard drugs les drogues dures □ soft drugs les drogues douces
  ■ **to take drugs** se droguer
  ■ **a drug addict** un drogué □ She's a drug addict. C'est une droguée.
  ■ **a drug pusher** un dealer
  ■ **a drug smuggler** un trafiquant de drogue
  ■ **the drugs squad** la brigade antidrogue
  ■ **the problem of drug abuse** le problème de la drogue

drugstore NOUN (US)
le drugstore

drum NOUN
le tambour
  □ an African drum un tambour africain
  ■ **a drum kit** une batterie
  ■ **drums** la batterie *sing* □ I play drums. Je joue de la batterie.

drummer NOUN
le batteur
la batteuse *(in rock group)*

drunk ADJECTIVE
▷ *see also* **drunk** NOUN
ivre (FEM ivre)
  □ He was drunk. Il était ivre.

drunk NOUN
▷ *see also* **drunk** ADJECTIVE
l' ivrogne *masc/fem*
  □ The streets were full of drunks. Les rues étaient pleines d'ivrognes.

dry ADJECTIVE
▷ *see also* **dry** VERB
1 sec (FEM sèche)
  □ The paint isn't dry yet. La peinture n'est pas encore sèche.
2 sans pluie *(weather)*

□ a long dry period une longue période sans pluie

to **dry** VERB
▷ *see also* **dry** ADJECTIVE
1 sécher
  □ The washing will dry quickly in the sun. Le linge va sécher vite au soleil. □ some dried flowers des fleurs séchées
  ■ **to dry one's hair** se sécher les cheveux
  □ I haven't dried my hair yet. Je ne me suis pas encore séché les cheveux.
2 faire sécher *(clothes)*
  □ There's nowhere to dry clothes here. Il n'y a pas d'endroit où faire sécher les vêtements ici.
  ■ **to dry the dishes** essuyer la vaisselle

dry-cleaner's NOUN
la teinturerie

dryer NOUN
le séchoir *(for clothes)*
  ■ **a tumble dryer** un séchoir à linge
  ■ **a hair dryer** un sèche-cheveux

DTP NOUN (= *desktop publishing*)
la PAO (= *publication assistée par ordinateur*)

dubbed ADJECTIVE
doublé (FEM doublée)
  □ The film was dubbed into French. Le film était doublé en français.

dubious ADJECTIVE
réticent (FEM réticente)
  □ My parents were a bit dubious about it. Mes parents étaient un peu réticents à ce sujet.

duck NOUN
le canard

due ADJECTIVE, ADVERB
  ■ **to be due to do something** devoir faire quelque chose □ He's due to arrive tomorrow. Il doit arriver demain.
  ■ **The plane's due in half an hour.** L'avion doit arriver dans une demi-heure.
  ■ **When's the baby due?** Le bébé est prévu pour quand?
  ■ **due to** à cause de □ The trip was cancelled due to bad weather. Le voyage a été annulé à cause du mauvais temps.

dug VERB ▷ *see* **dig**

dull ADJECTIVE
1 ennuyeux (FEM ennuyeuse)
  □ He's nice, but a bit dull. Il est sympathique, mais un peu ennuyeux.
2 maussade (FEM maussade) *(weather, day)*

dumb ADJECTIVE
1 muet (FEM muette)
  ■ **She's deaf and dumb.** Elle est sourde-muette.
2 bête (FEM bête) *(stupid)*

□ That was a really dumb thing I did! C'était vraiment bête de ma part!

dummy NOUN
la tétine *(for baby)*

dump NOUN
▷ *see also* **dump** VERB
■ **It's a real dump!** C'est un endroit minable!
■ **a rubbish dump** une décharge

to **dump** VERB
▷ *see also* **dump** NOUN
1 déposer *(waste)*
□ 'no dumping' 'défense de déposer des ordures'
2 plaquer *(informal)*
□ He's just dumped his girlfriend. Il vient de plaquer sa copine.

dungarees PL NOUN
la salopette *sing*

dungeon NOUN
le cachot

duration NOUN
la durée

during PREPOSITION
pendant
□ during the day pendant la journée

dusk NOUN
le crépuscule
□ at dusk au crépuscule

dust NOUN
▷ *see also* **dust** VERB
la poussière

to **dust** VERB
▷ *see also* **dust** NOUN
épousseter
□ I dusted the shelves. J'ai épousseté les étagères.
■ **I hate dusting!** Je déteste faire les poussières!

dustbin NOUN
la poubelle

dustman NOUN

l' éboueur *masc*
□ He's a dustman. Il est éboueur.

dusty ADJECTIVE
poussiéreux (FEM poussiéreuse)

Dutch NOUN
▷ *see also* **Dutch** ADJECTIVE
le hollandais *(language)*
■ **the Dutch** les Hollandais

Dutch ADJECTIVE
▷ *see also* **Dutch** NOUN
hollandais (FEM hollandaise)
□ She's Dutch. Elle est hollandaise.

Dutchman NOUN
le Hollandais

Dutchwoman NOUN
la Hollandaise

duty NOUN
le devoir
□ It was his duty to tell the police. C'était son devoir de prévenir la police.
■ **to be on duty 1** *(policeman)* être de service **2** *(doctor, nurse)* être de garde

duty-free ADJECTIVE
hors taxes
■ **the duty-free shop** la boutique hors taxes

duvet NOUN
la couette

DVD NOUN
le DVD (PL les DVD)
□ I've got that film on DVD. J'ai ce film en DVD.

DVD player NOUN
le lecteur de DVD

dwarf NOUN
le nain
la naine

dying VERB ▷ *see* **die**

dynamic ADJECTIVE
dynamique (FEM dynamique)

dyslexia NOUN
la dyslexie

Ee

each ADJECTIVE, PRONOUN
1 chaque (FEM chaque)
□ each day chaque jour □ Each house in our street has its own garden. Chaque maison dans notre rue a son propre jardin.
2 chacun (FEM chacune)
□ The girls each have their own bedroom. Les filles ont chacune leur chambre. □ They have 10 points each. Ils ont dix points chacun. □ The plates cost £5 each. Les assiettes coûtent cinq livres chacune. □ He gave each of us £10. Il nous a donné dix livres à chacun.

> LANGUAGE TIP Use a reflexive verb to translate 'each other'.

■ **They hate each other.** Ils se détestent.
■ **We wrote to each other.** Nous nous sommes écrit.
■ **They don't know each other.** Ils ne se connaissent pas.

eager ADJECTIVE
■ **to be eager to do something** être impatient de faire quelque chose

ear NOUN
l' oreille *fem*

earache NOUN
■ **to have earache** avoir mal aux oreilles

earlier ADVERB
1 tout à l'heure
□ I saw him earlier. Je l'ai vu tout à l'heure.
2 plus tôt *(in the morning)*
□ I ought to get up earlier. Je devrais me lever plus tôt.

early ADVERB, ADJECTIVE
1 tôt *(early in the day)*
□ I have to get up early. Je dois me lever tôt.
■ **to have an early night** se coucher tôt
2 en avance *(ahead of time)*
□ I came early to get a good seat. Je suis venu en avance pour avoir une bonne place.

to **earn** VERB
gagner
□ She earns £5 an hour. Elle gagne cinq livres de l'heure.

earnings PL NOUN
le salaire *sing*

earring NOUN
la boucle d'oreille

earth NOUN
la terre

earthquake NOUN
le tremblement de terre

easily ADVERB
facilement

east ADJECTIVE, ADVERB
> *see also* **east** NOUN
1 est (FEM+PL est)
□ the east coast la côte est
■ **an east wind** un vent d'est
■ **east of** à l'est de □ It's east of London. C'est à l'est de Londres.
2 vers l'est
□ We were travelling east. Nous allions vers l'est.

east NOUN
> *see also* **east** ADJECTIVE
l' est *masc*
□ in the east dans l'est

eastbound ADJECTIVE
■ **The car was eastbound on the M25.** Le voiture se trouvait sur la M25 en direction de l'est.
■ **Eastbound traffic is moving very slowly.** La circulation vers l'est avance très lentement.

Easter NOUN
Pâques *fem*
□ at Easter à Pâques □ We went to my grandparents' for Easter. Nous sommes allés chez mes grands-parents à Pâques.

Easter egg NOUN
l' œuf de Pâques *masc*

> DID YOU KNOW...?
> In France, Easter eggs are said to be brought by the Easter bells or **cloches de Pâques** which fly from Rome and drop them in people's gardens.

eastern ADJECTIVE
■ **the eastern part of the island** la partie est de l'île

■ **Eastern Europe** l'Europe de l'Est

easy ADJECTIVE
facile (FEM facile)

easy chair NOUN
le fauteuil

easy-going ADJECTIVE
facile à vivre (FEM facile à vivre)
□ She's very easy-going. Elle est très facile à vivre.

to **eat** VERB
manger
■ **Would you like something to eat?** Est-ce que tu veux manger quelque chose?

EC NOUN (= European Community)
la CE (= Communauté européenne)

eccentric ADJECTIVE
excentrique (FEM excentrique)

echo NOUN
l' écho masc

eco-friendly ADJECTIVE
respectueux de l'environnement (FEM respectueuse de l'environnement)

ecological ADJECTIVE
écologique (FEM écologique)

ecology NOUN
l' écologie fem

e-commerce NOUN
le commerce électronique

economic ADJECTIVE
rentable (FEM rentable) (profitable)

economical ADJECTIVE
1 économe (FEM économe) (person)
2 économique (FEM économique) (method, car)

economics NOUN
l' économie fem
□ He's studying economics. Il étudie les sciences économiques.

to **economize** VERB
faire des économies
□ to economize on something faire des économies sur quelque chose

economy NOUN
l' économie fem

ecstasy NOUN
l' ecstasy fem (drug)
■ **to be in ecstasy** s'extasier

eczema NOUN
l' eczéma masc

edge NOUN
le bord

edgy ADJECTIVE
tendu (FEM tendue)

Edinburgh NOUN
Édimbourg

editor NOUN
le rédacteur en chef
la rédactrice en chef (of newspaper)

educated ADJECTIVE
cultivé (FEM cultivée)

education NOUN
1 l' éducation fem
□ There should be more investment in education. On devrait investir plus dans l'éducation.
2 l' enseignement masc (teaching)
□ She works in education. Elle travaille dans l'enseignement.

educational ADJECTIVE
éducatif (FEM éducative) (experience, toy)
□ It was very educational. C'était très éducatif.

effect NOUN
l' effet masc
□ special effects les effets spéciaux

effective ADJECTIVE
efficace (FEM efficace)

effectively ADVERB
efficacement

LANGUAGE TIP Be careful not to translate **effectively** by effectivement.

efficient ADJECTIVE
efficace (FEM efficace)

effort NOUN
l' effort masc

e.g. ABBREVIATION
p. ex. (= par exemple)

egg NOUN
l' œuf masc
□ a hard-boiled egg un œuf dur □ a soft-boiled egg un œuf à la coque □ a fried egg un œuf sur le plat
■ **scrambled eggs** les œufs brouillés

egg cup NOUN
le coquetier

eggplant NOUN (US)
l' aubergine fem

Egypt NOUN
l' Égypte fem
■ **in Egypt** en Égypte

Eiffel Tower NOUN
la tour Eiffel

eight NUMBER
huit
□ She's eight. Elle a huit ans.

eighteen NUMBER
dix-huit
□ She's eighteen. Elle a dix-huit ans.

eighteenth ADJECTIVE
dix-huitième (FEM dix-huitième)
□ her eighteenth birthday son dix-huitième anniversaire □ the eighteenth floor le dix-huitième étage
■ **the eighteenth of August** le dix-huit

août

eighth ADJECTIVE
huitième (FEM huitième)
□ the eighth floor le huitième étage
■ **the eighth of August** le huit août

eighty NUMBER
quatre-vingts

Eire NOUN
la République d'Irlande
■ **in Eire** en République d'Irlande

either ADVERB, CONJUNCTION, PRONOUN
non plus
□ I don't like milk, and I don't like eggs either. Je n'aime pas le lait, et je n'aime pas les œufs non plus. □ I've never been to Spain. — I haven't either. Je ne suis jamais allé en Espagne. — Moi non plus.
■ **either … or …** soit … soit … □ You can have either ice cream or yoghurt. Tu peux prendre soit une glace soit un yaourt.
■ **either of them** l'un ou l'autre □ Take either of them. Prends l'un ou l'autre.
■ **I don't like either of them.** Je n'aime ni l'un ni l'autre.

elastic NOUN
l' élastique masc

elastic band NOUN
l' élastique masc

elbow NOUN
le coude

elder ADJECTIVE
aîné (FEM aînée)
□ my elder sister ma sœur aînée

elderly ADJECTIVE
âgé (FEM âgée)
■ **the elderly** les personnes âgées

eldest ADJECTIVE
aîné (FEM aînée)
□ my eldest sister ma sœur aînée □ He's the eldest. C'est l'aîné.

to **elect** VERB
élire

election NOUN
l' élection fem

electric ADJECTIVE
électrique (FEM électrique)
□ an electric fire un radiateur électrique
□ an electric guitar une guitare électrique
■ **an electric blanket** une couverture chauffante
■ **an electric shock** une décharge

electrical ADJECTIVE
électrique (FEM électrique)
■ **an electrical engineer** un ingénieur électricien

electrician NOUN
l' électricien masc

□ He's an electrician. Il est électricien.

electricity NOUN
l' électricité fem

electronic ADJECTIVE
électronique (FEM électronique)

electronics NOUN
l' électronique fem
□ My hobby is electronics. Ma passion, c'est l'électronique.

elegant ADJECTIVE
élégant (FEM élégante)

elementary school NOUN (US)
l' école primaire fem

elephant NOUN
l' éléphant masc

elevator NOUN (US)
l' ascenseur masc

eleven NUMBER
onze
□ She's eleven. Elle a onze ans.

eleventh ADJECTIVE
onzième (FEM onzième)
□ the eleventh floor le onzième étage □ the eleventh of August le onze août

else ADVERB
d'autre
□ somebody else quelqu'un d'autre
□ nobody else personne d'autre □ nothing else rien d'autre
■ **something else** autre chose
■ **anything else** autre chose □ Would you like anything else? Désirez-vous autre chose?
■ **I don't want anything else.** Je ne veux rien d'autre.
■ **somewhere else** ailleurs
■ **anywhere else** autre part

email NOUN
▷ see also **e-mail** VERB
le courrier électronique
■ **email address** l'adresse e-mail fem □ My email address is: … Mon adresse e-mail, c'est: …

to **email** VERB
▷ see also **email** NOUN
■ **to email somebody** envoyer un e-mail à quelqu'un

embankment NOUN
le talus

embarrassed ADJECTIVE
gêné (FEM gênée)
□ I was really embarrassed. J'étais vraiment gêné.

embarrassing ADJECTIVE
gênant (FEM gênante)
□ It was so embarrassing. C'était tellement gênant.

embassy NOUN
l' ambassade *fem*
□ the British Embassy l'ambassade de Grande-Bretagne □ the French Embassy l'ambassade de France

to **embroider** VERB
broder

embroidery NOUN
la broderie
□ I do embroidery. Je fais de la broderie.

emergency NOUN
l' urgence *fem*
□ This is an emergency! C'est une urgence!
■ **in an emergency** en cas d'urgence
■ **an emergency exit** une sortie de secours
■ **an emergency landing** un atterrissage forcé
■ **the emergency services** les services d'urgence *masc pl*

to **emigrate** VERB
émigrer

emotion NOUN
l' émotion *fem*

emotional ADJECTIVE
émotif (FEM émotive) *(person)*

emperor NOUN
l' empereur *masc*

to **emphasize** VERB
■ **to emphasize something** insister sur quelque chose
■ **to emphasize that ...** souligner que ...

empire NOUN
l' empire *masc*

to **employ** VERB
employer
□ The factory employs 600 people. L'usine emploie six cents personnes.

employee NOUN
l' employé *masc*
l' employée *fem*

employer NOUN
l' employeur *masc*

employment NOUN
l' emploi *masc*

empty ADJECTIVE
▷ *see also* **empty** VERB
vide (FEM vide)

to **empty** VERB
▷ *see also* **empty** ADJECTIVE
vider
■ **to empty something out** vider quelque chose

to **encourage** VERB
encourager
■ **to encourage somebody to do something** encourager quelqu'un à faire quelque chose

encouragement NOUN
l' encouragement *masc*

encyclopedia NOUN
l' encyclopédie *fem*

end NOUN
▷ *see also* **end** VERB
1 la fin
□ the end of the film la fin du film □ the end of the holidays la fin des vacances
■ **in the end** en fin de compte □ In the end I decided to stay at home. En fin de compte j'ai décidé de rester à la maison.
■ **It turned out all right in the end.** Ça s'est bien terminé.
2 le bout
□ at the end of the street au bout de la rue
□ at the other end of the table à l'autre bout de la table
■ **for hours on end** des heures entières

to **end** VERB
▷ *see also* **end** NOUN
finir
□ What time does the film end? À quelle heure est-ce que le film finit?
■ **to end up doing something** finir par faire quelque chose □ I ended up walking home. J'ai fini par rentrer chez moi à pied.

ending NOUN
la fin
□ It was an exciting film, especially the ending. C'était un film passionnant, surtout la fin.

endless ADJECTIVE
interminable (FEM interminable)
□ The journey seemed endless. Le voyage a paru interminable.

enemy NOUN
l' ennemi *masc*
l' ennemie *fem*

energetic ADJECTIVE
énergique (FEM énergique) *(person)*

energy NOUN
l' énergie *fem*

engaged ADJECTIVE
1 occupé (FEM occupée) *(busy, in use)*
□ I phoned, but it was engaged. J'ai téléphoné, mais c'était occupé.
2 fiancé (FEM fiancée) *(to be married)*
□ She's engaged to Brian. Elle est fiancée à Brian.
■ **to get engaged** se fiancer

engaged tone NOUN
la tonalité 'occupé'

engagement NOUN
les fiançailles *fem pl*
□ an engagement ring une bague de fiançailles

engine NOUN
le moteur

> LANGUAGE TIP Be careful not to translate **engine** by engin.

engineer NOUN
l' ingénieur *masc*
▫ He's an engineer. Il est ingénieur.

engineering NOUN
l' ingénierie *fem*

England NOUN
l' Angleterre *fem*
■ **in England** en Angleterre
■ **to England** en Angleterre
■ **I'm from England.** Je suis anglais.

English NOUN
▷ *see also* **English** ADJECTIVE
l' anglais *masc (language)*
▫ Do you speak English? Est-ce que vous parlez anglais?
■ **the English** les Anglais

English ADJECTIVE
▷ *see also* **English** NOUN
anglais (FEM anglaise)
▫ I'm English. Je suis anglais.
■ **English people** les Anglais

Englishman NOUN
l' Anglais *masc*

Englishwoman NOUN
l' Anglaise *fem*

to **enjoy** VERB
aimer
▫ Did you enjoy the film? Est-ce que vous avez aimé le film?
■ **to enjoy oneself** s'amuser ▫ I really enjoyed myself. Je me suis vraiment bien amusé. ▫ Did you enjoy yourselves at the party? Est-ce vous vous êtes bien amusés à la fête?

enjoyable ADJECTIVE
agréable (FEM agréable)

enlargement NOUN
l' agrandissement *masc (of photo)*

enormous ADJECTIVE
énorme (FEM énorme)

enough PRONOUN, ADJECTIVE
assez de
▫ enough time assez de temps ▫ I didn't have enough money. Je n'avais pas assez d'argent. ▫ Have you got enough? Tu en as assez? ▫ I've had enough! J'en ai assez!
■ **big enough** suffisamment grand
■ **warm enough** suffisamment chaud
■ **That's enough.** Ça suffit.

to **enquire** VERB
■ **to enquire about something** se renseigner sur quelque chose ▫ I am going to enquire about train times. Je vais me

renseigner sur les horaires de trains.

enquiry NOUN
■ **to make enquiries (about something)** se renseigner (sur quelque chose)
▫ 'enquiries' 'renseignements'

to **enter** VERB
entrer
■ **to enter a room** entrer dans une pièce
■ **to enter a competition** s'inscrire à une compétition

to **entertain** VERB
recevoir *(guests)*

entertainer NOUN
l' artiste de variétés *masc/fem*

entertaining ADJECTIVE
amusant (FEM amusante)

enthusiasm NOUN
l' enthousiasme *masc*

enthusiast NOUN
■ **a railway enthusiast** un passionné des trains
■ **She's a DIY enthusiast.** C'est une passionnée de bricolage.

enthusiastic ADJECTIVE
enthousiaste (FEM enthousiaste)

entire ADJECTIVE
entier (FEM entière)
▫ the entire world le monde entier

entirely ADVERB
entièrement

entrance NOUN
l' entrée *fem*
■ **an entrance exam** un concours d'entrée
■ **entrance fee** le prix d'entrée

entry NOUN
l' entrée *fem*
■ **'no entry' 1** *(on door)* 'défense d'entrer'
2 *(on road sign)* 'sens interdit'
■ **an entry form** une feuille d'inscription

entry phone NOUN
l' interphone *masc*

envelope NOUN
l' enveloppe *fem*

envious ADJECTIVE
envieux (FEM envieuse)

environment NOUN
l' environnement *masc*

environmental ADJECTIVE
écologique (FEM écologique)

environment-friendly ADJECTIVE
écologique (FEM écologique)

envy NOUN
▷ *see also* **envy** VERB
l' envie *fem*

to **envy** VERB
▷ *see also* **envy** NOUN
envier

e

□ I don't envy you! Je ne t'envie pas!

epileptic NOUN
l' épileptique *masc/fem*

episode NOUN
l' épisode *masc (of TV programme, story)*

equal ADJECTIVE
▷ *see also* **equal** VERB
égal (FEM égale, MASC PL égaux)

to **equal** VERB
▷ *see also* **equal** ADJECTIVE
égaler

equality NOUN
l' égalité *fem*

to **equalize** VERB
égaliser *(in sport)*

equator NOUN
l' équateur *masc*

equipment NOUN
l' équipement *masc*
□ fishing equipment l'équipement de pêche
□ skiing equipment l'équipement de ski

equipped ADJECTIVE
■ **equipped with** équipé de
■ **to be well equipped** être bien équipé

equivalent NOUN
l' équivalent *masc*
■ **equivalent to** équivalent à

error NOUN
l' erreur *fem*

escalator NOUN
l' escalier roulant *masc*

escape NOUN
▷ *see also* **escape** VERB
l' évasion *fem (from prison)*

to **escape** VERB
▷ *see also* **escape** NOUN
s'échapper
□ A lion has escaped. Un lion s'est échappé.
■ **to escape from prison** s'évader de prison

escort NOUN
l' escorte *fem*
□ a police escort une escorte de police

especially ADVERB
surtout
□ It's very hot there, especially in the summer. Il fait très chaud là-bas, surtout en été.

essay NOUN
la dissertation
□ a history essay une dissertation d'histoire

essential ADJECTIVE
essentiel (FEM essentielle)
□ It's essential to bring warm clothes. Il est essentiel d'apporter des vêtements chauds.

estate NOUN
la cité *(housing estate)*
□ I live on an estate. J'habite dans une cité.

estate agent NOUN
l' agent immobilier *masc*

estate car NOUN
le break

to **estimate** VERB
estimer
□ They estimated it would take three weeks. Ils ont estimé que cela prendrait trois semaines.

etc ABBREVIATION *(= et cetera)*
etc.

Ethiopia NOUN
l' Éthiopie *fem*
■ **in Ethiopia** en Éthiopie

ethnic ADJECTIVE
1 ethnique (FEM ethnique) *(racial)*
□ an ethnic minority une minorité ethnique
2 folklorique (FEM folklorique) *(clothes, music)*

e-ticket NOUN
le billet électronique

EU NOUN *(= European Union)*
l' Union européenne *fem*

euro NOUN
l' euro *masc*
□ 50 euros 50 euros

Europe NOUN
l' Europe *fem*
■ **in Europe** en Europe
■ **to Europe** en Europe

European NOUN
▷ *see also* **European** ADJECTIVE
l' Européen *masc*
l' Européenne *fem (person)*

European ADJECTIVE
▷ *see also* **European** NOUN
européen (FEM européenne)

to **evacuate** VERB
évacuer

eve NOUN
■ **Christmas Eve** la veille de Noël
■ **New Year's Eve** la Saint-Sylvestre

even ADVERB
▷ *see also* **even** ADJECTIVE
même
□ I like all animals, even snakes. J'aime tous les animaux, même les serpents.
■ **even if** même si □ I'd never do that, even if you asked me. Je ne ferais jamais ça, même si tu me le demandais.
■ **not even** même pas □ He never stops working, not even at the weekend. Il n'arrête jamais de travailler, même pas le week-end.
■ **even though** bien que
○ LANGUAGE TIP **bien que** has to be followed by a verb in the subjunctive.
□ He wants to go out, even though it's

raining. Il veut sortir bien qu'il pleuve.

■ **even more** encore plus □ I liked Boulogne even more than Paris. J'ai encore plus aimé Boulogne que Paris.

even ADJECTIVE

▷ *see also* **even** ADVERB

régulier (FEM régulière)

□ an even layer of snow une couche régulière de neige

■ **an even number** un nombre pair

■ **to get even with somebody** prendre sa revanche sur quelqu'un □ I le wanted to get even with her. Il voulait prendre sa revanche sur elle.

evening NOUN

le soir

□ in the evening le soir □ yesterday evening hier soir □ tomorrow evening demain soir

■ **all evening** toute la soirée

■ **Good evening!** Bonsoir!

evening class NOUN

le cours du soir (PL les cours du soir)

event NOUN

l' événement *masc*

■ **a sporting event** une épreuve sportive

eventful ADJECTIVE

mouvementé (FEM mouvementée)

eventual ADJECTIVE

final (FEM finale)

LANGUAGE TIP Be careful not to translate **eventual** by éventuel.

eventually ADVERB

finalement

LANGUAGE TIP Be careful not to translate **eventually** by éventuellement.

ever ADVERB

■ **Have you ever been to Germany?** Est-ce que tu es déjà allé en Allemagne?

■ **Have you ever seen her?** Vous l'avez déjà vue?

■ **I haven't ever done that.** Je ne l'ai jamais fait.

■ **the best I've ever seen** le meilleur que j'aie jamais vu

■ **for the first time ever** pour la première fois

■ **ever since** depuis que □ ever since I met him depuis que je l'ai rencontré

■ **ever since then** depuis ce moment-là

every ADJECTIVE

chaque (FEM chaque)

□ every pupil chaque élève

■ **every time** chaque fois □ Every time I see him he's depressed. Chaque fois que je le vois il est déprimé.

■ **every day** tous les jours

■ **every week** toutes les semaines

■ **every now and then** de temps en temps

everybody PRONOUN

tout le monde

□ Everybody had a good time. Tout le monde s'est bien amusé. □ Everybody makes mistakes. Tout le monde peut se tromper.

everyone PRONOUN

tout le monde

□ Everyone opened their presents. Tout le monde a ouvert ses cadeaux. □ Everyone should have a hobby. Tout le monde devrait avoir un passe-temps.

everything PRONOUN

tout

□ You've thought of everything! Tu as pensé à tout!

■ **Have you remembered everything?** Est-ce que tu n'as rien oublié?

■ **Money isn't everything.** L'argent ne fait pas le bonheur.

everywhere ADVERB

partout

□ I looked everywhere, but I couldn't find it. J'ai regardé partout, mais je n'ai pas pu le trouver. □ There were policemen everywhere. Il y avait des policiers partout.

evil ADJECTIVE

mauvais (FEM mauvaise)

ex- PREFIX

ex-

□ his ex-wife son ex-femme

exact ADJECTIVE

exact (FEM exacte)

exactly ADVERB

exactement

□ exactly the same exactement le même □ Not exactly. Pas exactement.

■ **it's exactly 10 o'clock.** Il est dix heures précises.

to **exaggerate** VERB

exagérer

exaggeration NOUN

l' exagération *fem*

exam NOUN

l' examen *masc*

□ a French exam un examen de français □ the exam results les résultats des examens *masc pl*

examination NOUN

l' examen *masc*

to **examine** VERB

examiner

□ He examined her passport. Il a examiné son passeport. □ The doctor examined him. Le docteur l'a examiné.

examiner NOUN
l' examinateur *masc*
l' examinatrice *fem*

example NOUN
l' exemple *masc*
■ **for example** par exemple

excellent ADJECTIVE
excellent (FEM excellente)
□ Her results were excellent. Elle a eu
d'excellents résultats.
■ **It was excellent fun.** C'était vraiment
super.

except PREPOSITION
sauf
□ everyone except me tout le monde sauf
moi
■ **except for** sauf
■ **except that** sauf que □ The holiday was
great, except that it rained. Les vacances
étaient super, sauf qu'il a plu.

exception NOUN
l' exception *fem*
■ **to make an exception** faire une
exception

exceptional ADJECTIVE
exceptionnel (FEM exceptionnelle)

excess baggage NOUN
l' excédent de bagages *masc*

to **exchange** VERB
échanger
□ I exchanged the book for a video. J'ai
échangé le livre contre une vidéo.

exchange rate NOUN
le taux de change

excited ADJECTIVE
excité (FEM excitée)

exciting ADJECTIVE
passionnant (FEM passionnante)

exclamation mark NOUN
le point d'exclamation

excuse NOUN
▷ *see also* **excuse** VERB
l' excuse *fem*

to **excuse** VERB
▷ *see also* **excuse** NOUN
■ **Excuse me!** Pardon!

ex-directory ADJECTIVE
■ **to be ex-directory** être sur liste rouge
■ **to go ex-directory** se mettre sur liste
rouge

to **execute** VERB
exécuter

execution NOUN
l' exécution *fem*

executive NOUN
le cadre *(in business)*
□ He's an executive. Il est cadre.

exercise NOUN
l' exercice *masc*
■ **an exercise bike** un vélo d'appartement
■ **an exercise book** un cahier

exhausted ADJECTIVE
épuisé (FEM épuisée)

exhaust fumes PL NOUN
les gaz d'échappement *masc pl*

exhaust pipe NOUN
le tuyau d'échappement

exhibition NOUN
l' exposition *fem*

ex-husband NOUN
l' ex-mari *masc*

to **exist** VERB
exister

exit NOUN
la sortie

exotic ADJECTIVE
exotique (FEM exotique)

to **expect** VERB
1 attendre
□ I'm expecting him for dinner. Je l'attends
pour dîner. □ She's expecting a baby. Elle
attend un enfant.
2 s'attendre à
□ I was expecting the worst. Je m'attendais
au pire.
3 supposer
□ I expect it's a mistake. Je suppose qu'il
s'agit d'une erreur.

expedition NOUN
l' expédition *fem*

to **expel** VERB
■ **to get expelled** *(from school)* se faire
renvoyer

expenses PL NOUN
les frais *masc pl*

expensive ADJECTIVE
cher (FEM chère)

experience NOUN
l' expérience *fem*

experienced ADJECTIVE
expérimenté (FEM expérimentée)

experiment NOUN
l' expérience *fem*

expert NOUN
le spécialiste
la spécialiste
□ He's a computer expert. C'est un
spécialiste en informatique.
■ **He's an expert cook.** Il cuisine très bien.

to **expire** VERB
expirer

to **explain** VERB
expliquer

explanation NOUN

l' explication *fem*

to **explode** VERB
exploser

to **exploit** VERB
exploiter

exploitation NOUN
l' exploitation *fem*

to **explore** VERB
explorer *(place)*

explorer NOUN
l' explorateur *masc*
l' exploratrice *fem*

explosion NOUN
l' explosion *fem*

explosive ADJECTIVE
▷ *see also* **explosive** NOUN
explosif (FEM explosive)

explosive NOUN
▷ *see also* **explosive** ADJECTIVE
l' explosif *masc*

to **express** VERB
exprimer
■ **to express oneself** s'exprimer □ It's hard
to express oneself in French. C'est dur de
s'exprimer en français.

expression NOUN
l' expression *fem*
□ It's an English expression. C'est une
expression anglaise.

expressway NOUN (US)
l' autoroute urbaine *fem*

extension NOUN
1 l' annexe *fem (of building)*
2 le poste *(telephone)*

> LANGUAGE TIP In France phone
> numbers are broken into groups of
> two digits where possible.

■ **Extension 3137, please.** Poste trente et
un trente-sept, s'il vous plaît.

extensive ADJECTIVE
1 vaste (FEM vaste) *(knowledge, range)*
□ The castle is set in extensive grounds. Le
château est situé au cœur d'un vaste
domaine.
2 considérable (FEM considérable) *(damage,
alterations)*
□ The earthquake caused extensive
damage. Le tremblement de terre a causé
des dommages considérables.

extensively ADVERB
■ **He has travelled extensively in Europe.**
Il a beaucoup voyagé en Europe.

■ **The building was extensively
renovated last year.** Le bâtiment a été
entièrement rénové l'année dernière.

extent NOUN
■ **to some extent** dans une certaine
mesure

exterior ADJECTIVE
extérieur (FEM extérieure)

extinct ADJECTIVE
■ **to become extinct** disparaître
■ **to be extinct** avoir disparu □ The species
is almost extinct. Cette espèce a presque
disparu.

extinguisher NOUN
l' extincteur *masc (fire extinguisher)*

extortionate ADJECTIVE
exorbitant (FEM exorbitante)

extra ADJECTIVE, ADVERB
supplémentaire (FEM supplémentaire)
□ an extra blanket une couverture
supplémentaire
■ **to pay extra** payer un supplément
■ **Breakfast is extra.** Il y a un supplément
pour le petit déjeuner.
■ **It costs extra.** Il y a un supplément.

extraordinary ADJECTIVE
extraordinaire (FEM extraordinaire)

extravagant ADJECTIVE
dépensier (FEM dépensière) *(person)*

extreme ADJECTIVE
extrême (FEM extrême)

extremely ADVERB
extrêmement

extremist NOUN
l' extrémiste *masc/fem*

eye NOUN
l' œil *masc* (PL les yeux)
□ I've got green eyes. J'ai les yeux verts.
■ **to keep an eye on something** surveiller
quelque chose

eyebrow NOUN
le sourcil

eyelash NOUN
le cil

eyelid NOUN
la paupière

eyeliner NOUN
l' eye-liner *masc*

eye shadow NOUN
l' ombre à paupières *fem*

eyesight NOUN
la vue

Ff

fabric NOUN
le tissu

fabulous ADJECTIVE
formidable (FEM formidable)
□ The show was fabulous. Le spectacle était formidable.

face NOUN
▷ see also **face** VERB
1 le visage (of person)
2 le cadran (of clock)
3 la paroi (of cliff)
■ **on the face of it** à première vue
■ **in the face of these difficulties** face à ces difficultés
■ **face to face** face à face

to **face** VERB
▷ see also **face** NOUN
faire face à (place, problem)
■ **to face up to something** faire face à quelque chose □ You must face up to your responsibilities. Vous devez faire face à vos responsabilités.

face cloth NOUN
le gant de toilette

> **DID YOU KNOW...?**
> The French traditionally wash with a towelling glove rather than a flannel.

facilities PL NOUN
l' équipement masc sing
□ This school has excellent facilities. Cette école dispose d'un excellent équipement.
■ **toilet facilities** les toilettes fem pl
■ **cooking facilities** la cuisine équipée sing

fact NOUN
le fait
■ **in fact** en fait

factory NOUN
l' usine fem

to **fade** VERB
1 passer (colour)
□ The colour has faded in the sun. La couleur a passé au soleil.
■ **My jeans have faded.** Mon jean est délavé.
2 baisser

□ The light was fading fast. La lumière baissait rapidement.
3 diminuer
□ The noise gradually faded. Le bruit a diminué peu à peu.

fag NOUN
la clope (cigarette)

to **fail** VERB
▷ see also **fail** NOUN
1 rater
□ I failed the history exam. J'ai raté l'examen d'histoire.
2 échouer
□ In our class, no one failed. Dans notre classe, personne n'a échoué.
3 lâcher
□ My brakes failed. Mes freins ont lâché.
■ **to fail to do something** ne pas faire quelque chose □ She failed to return her library books. Elle n'a pas rendu ses livres à la bibliothèque.

fail NOUN
▷ see also **fail** VERB
■ **without fail** sans faute

failure NOUN
1 l' échec masc
□ feelings of failure un sentiment d'échec sing
2 le raté
la ratée
□ He's a failure. C'est un raté.
3 la défaillance
□ a mechanical failure une défaillance mécanique

faint ADJECTIVE
▷ see also **faint** VERB
faible (FEM faible)
□ His voice was very faint. Sa voix était très faible.
■ **to feel faint** se trouver mal

to **faint** VERB
▷ see also **faint** ADJECTIVE
s'évanouir
□ All of a sudden she fainted. Tout à coup elle s'est évanouie.

fair ADJECTIVE
▷ *see also* **fair** NOUN
1 juste (FEM juste)
□ That's not fair. Ce n'est pas juste.
2 blond (FEM blonde) *(hair)*
□ He's got fair hair. Il a les cheveux blonds.
3 clair (FEM claire) *(skin)*
□ people with fair skin les gens qui ont la peau claire
4 beau (FEM belle) *(weather)*
□ The weather was fair. Il faisait beau.
5 assez bon (FEM assez bonne) *(good enough)*
□ I have a fair chance of winning. J'ai d'assez bonnes chances de gagner.
6 considérable (FEM considérable) *(sizeable)*
□ That's a fair distance. Ça représente une distance considérable.

fair NOUN
▷ *see also* **fair** ADJECTIVE
la foire
□ They went to the fair. Ils sont allés à la foire.
■ **a trade fair** une foire commerciale

fairground NOUN
le champ de foire

fair-haired ADJECTIVE
■ **My mother is fair-haired.** Ma mère a les cheveux blonds.

fairly ADVERB
1 équitablement
□ The cake was divided fairly. Le gâteau a été partagé équitablement.
2 assez *(quite)*
□ That's fairly good. C'est assez bien.

fairness NOUN
la justice

fairy NOUN
la fée

fairy tale NOUN
le conte de fées

faith NOUN
1 la foi
□ the Catholic faith la foi catholique
2 la confiance
□ People have lost faith in the government. Les gens ont perdu confiance dans le gouvernement.

faithful ADJECTIVE
fidèle (FEM fidèle)

faithfully ADVERB
■ **Yours faithfully ...** *(in letter)* Veuillez agréer mes salutations distinguées ...

fake NOUN
▷ *see also* **fake** ADJECTIVE
le faux
□ The painting was a fake. Le tableau était un faux.

fake ADJECTIVE
▷ *see also* **fake** NOUN
faux (FEM fausse)
□ She wore fake fur. Elle portait une fausse fourrure.

fall NOUN
▷ *see also* **fall** VERB
1 la chute
□ a fall of snow une chute de neige □ She had a nasty fall. Elle a fait une mauvaise chute.
■ **the Niagara Falls** les chutes du Niagara
2 l' automne *masc* (US: autumn)

to fall VERB
▷ *see also* **fall** NOUN
1 tomber
□ He tripped and fell. Il a trébuché et il est tombé.
2 baisser
□ Prices are falling. Les prix baissent.

to fall down VERB
1 tomber *(person)*
□ She's fallen down. Elle est tombée.
2 s'écrouler *(building)*
□ The house is slowly falling down. La maison est en train de s'écrouler.

to fall for VERB
1 se laisser prendre à
□ They fell for it. Ils s'y sont laissé prendre.
2 tomber amoureux de
□ She's falling for him. Elle est en train de tomber amoureuse de lui.

to fall off VERB
tomber de
□ The book fell off the shelf. Le livre est tombé de l'étagère.

to fall out VERB
■ **to fall out with somebody** se fâcher avec quelqu'un □ Sarah's fallen out with her boyfriend. Sarah s'est fâchée avec son copain.

to fall through VERB
tomber à l'eau
□ Our plans have fallen through. Nos projets sont tombés à l'eau.

fallen VERB ▷ *see* **fall**

false ADJECTIVE
faux (FEM fausse)
■ **a false alarm** une fausse alerte
■ **false teeth** les fausses dents

fame NOUN
la renommée

familiar ADJECTIVE
familier (FEM familière)
□ a familiar face un visage familier
■ **to be familiar with something** bien connaître quelque chose □ I'm familiar with

his work. Je connais bien ses œuvres.

family NOUN
la famille
■ **the Cooke family** la famille Cooke

famine NOUN
la famine

famous ADJECTIVE
célèbre (FEM célèbre)

fan NOUN
1 l' éventail *masc (hand-held)*
2 le ventilateur *(electric)*
3 le/la fan *(of person, band)*
□ I'm a fan of Coldplay. Je suis une fan de Coldplay.
4 le/la supporter *(of sport)*
□ football fans les supporters de football

fanatic NOUN
le/la fanatique

to **fancy** VERB
■ **to fancy something** avoir envie de quelque chose □ I fancy an ice cream. J'ai envie d'une glace.
■ **to fancy doing something** avoir envie de faire quelque chose
■ **He fancies her.** Elle lui plaît.

fancy dress NOUN
le déguisement
□ He was wearing fancy dress. Il portait un déguisement.
■ **a fancy-dress ball** un bal costumé

fantastic ADJECTIVE
fantastique (FEM fantastique)

far ADJECTIVE, ADVERB
loin
□ Is it far? Est-ce que c'est loin?
■ **far from** loin de □ It's not far from London. Ce n'est pas loin de Londres. □ It's far from easy. C'est loin d'être facile.
■ **How far is it?** C'est à quelle distance?
■ **How far is it to Geneva?** Combien y a-t-il jusqu'à Genève?
■ **How far have you got?** *(with a task)* Où en êtes-vous?
■ **at the far end** à l'autre bout □ at the far end of the room à l'autre bout de la pièce
■ **far better** beaucoup mieux
■ **as far as I know** pour autant que je sache

fare NOUN
1 le prix du billet *(on trains, buses)*
2 le prix de la course *(in taxi)*
■ **half fare** le demi-tarif
■ **full fare** le plein tarif

Far East NOUN
l' Extrême-Orient *masc*
■ **in the Far East** en Extrême-Orient

farm NOUN
la ferme

farmer NOUN
l' agriculteur *masc*
l' agricultrice *fem*
□ He's a farmer. Il est agriculteur.
■ **a farmers' market** un marché fermier

farmhouse NOUN
la ferme

farming NOUN
l' agriculture *fem*
■ **dairy farming** l'industrie laitière

fascinating ADJECTIVE
fascinant (FEM fascinante)

fashion NOUN
la mode
□ a fashion show un défilé de mode
■ **in fashion** à la mode

fashionable ADJECTIVE
à la mode
□ Jane wears very fashionable clothes. Jane porte des vêtements très à la mode. □ a fashionable restaurant un restaurant à la mode

fast ADJECTIVE, ADVERB
1 vite
□ He can run fast. Il sait courir vite.
2 rapide (FEM rapide)
□ a fast car une voiture rapide
■ **That clock's fast.** Cette pendule avance.
■ **He's fast asleep.** Il est profondément endormi.

fat ADJECTIVE
▷ *see also* **fat** NOUN
gros (FEM grosse)

WORD POWER
You can use a number of other words instead of **fat**:
chubby potelé
□ a chubby baby un bébé potelé
overweight trop gros
□ an overweight child un enfant trop gros
plump dodu
□ a plump woman une femme dodue

---

fat NOUN
▷ *see also* **fat** ADJECTIVE
1 le gras *(on meat, in food)*
□ It's very high in fat. C'est très gras.
2 la matière grasse *(for cooking)*

fatal ADJECTIVE
1 mortel (FEM mortelle) *(causing death)*
□ a fatal accident un accident mortel
2 fatal (FEM fatale) *(disastrous)*
□ He made a fatal mistake. Il a fait une erreur fatale.

father NOUN
le père

□ my father mon père
father-in-law NOUN
le beau-père (PL les beaux-pères)
faucet NOUN (US)
le robinet
fault NOUN
1 la faute *(mistake)*
□ It's my fault. C'est de ma faute.
2 le défaut *(defect)*
□ There's a fault in this material. Ce tissu a un défaut.
■ **a mechanical fault** une défaillance mécanique
faulty ADJECTIVE
défectueux (FEM défectueuse)
□ This machine is faulty. Cette machine est défectueuse.
favour (US **favor**) NOUN
le service
■ **to do somebody a favour** rendre service à quelqu'un □ Could you do me a favour? Tu peux me rendre service?
■ **to be in favour of something** être pour quelque chose □ I'm in favour of nuclear disarmament. Je suis pour le désarmement nucléaire.
favourite (US **favorite**) ADJECTIVE
▷ *see also* **favourite** NOUN
favori (FEM favorite)
□ Blue's my favourite colour. Le bleu est ma couleur favorite.
favourite (US **favorite**) NOUN
▷ *see also* **favourite** ADJECTIVE
1 le favori
2 la favorite
□ Liverpool are favourites to win the Cup.
L'équipe de Liverpool est favorite pour la coupe.
fax NOUN
▷ *see also* **fax** VERB
le fax
■ **to send somebody a fax** envoyer un fax à quelqu'un
to **fax** VERB
▷ *see also* **fax** NOUN
■ **to fax somebody** envoyer un fax à quelqu'un
fear NOUN
▷ *see also* **fear** VERB
la peur
to **fear** VERB
▷ *see also* **fear** NOUN
craindre
□ You have nothing to fear. Vous n'avez rien à craindre.
feather NOUN
la plume

feature NOUN
la caractéristique *(of person, object)*
□ an important feature une caractéristique essentielle
February NOUN
février *masc*
■ **in February** en février
fed VERB ▷ *see* **feed**
fed up ADJECTIVE
■ **to be fed up of something** en avoir marre de quelque chose □ I'm fed up of waiting for him. J'en ai marre de l'attendre.
to **feed** VERB
donner à manger à
□ Have you fed the cat? Est-ce que tu as donné à manger au chat?
■ **He worked hard to feed his family.** Il travaillait dur pour nourrir sa famille.
to **feel** VERB
1 se sentir
□ I don't feel well. Je ne me sens pas bien.
□ I feel a bit lonely. Je me sens un peu seul.
2 sentir
□ I didn't feel much pain. Je n'ai presque rien senti.
3 toucher
□ The doctor felt his forehead. Le docteur lui a touché le front.
■ **I was feeling hungry.** J'avais faim.
■ **I was feeling cold, so I went inside.**
J'avais froid, alors je suis rentré.
■ **I feel like ...** *(want)* J'ai envie de ... □ Do you feel like an ice cream? Tu as envie d'une glace?
feeling NOUN
1 la sensation *(physical)*
□ a burning feeling une sensation de brûlure
2 le sentiment *(emotional)*
□ a feeling of satisfaction un sentiment de satisfaction
feet PL NOUN ▷ *see* **foot**
fell VERB ▷ *see* **fall**
felt VERB ▷ *see* **feel**
felt-tip pen NOUN
le stylo-feutre
female ADJECTIVE
▷ *see also* **female** NOUN
1 femelle (FEM femelle)
□ a female animal un animal femelle
2 féminin (FEM féminine)
□ the female sex le sexe féminin
female NOUN
▷ *see also* **female** ADJECTIVE
la femelle *(animal)*
feminine ADJECTIVE
féminin (FEM féminine)

feminist NOUN
le/la féministe
fence NOUN
la barrière
fern NOUN
la fougère
ferret NOUN
le furet
ferry NOUN
le ferry
fertile ADJECTIVE
fertile (FEM fertile)
fertilizer NOUN
l' engrais *masc*
festival NOUN
le festival
□ a jazz festival un festival de jazz
to **fetch** VERB
1 aller chercher
□ Fetch the bucket. Va chercher le seau.
2 se vendre *(sell for)*
□ His painting fetched £5000. Son tableau s'est vendu cinq mille livres.
fever NOUN
la fièvre *(temperature)*
few ADJECTIVE, PRONOUN
peu de *(not many)*
□ few books peu de livres
■ **a few 1** quelques □ a few hours quelques heures **2** quelques-uns □ How many apples do you want? — A few. Tu veux combien de pommes? — Quelques-unes.
■ **quite a few people** pas mal de monde
fewer ADJECTIVE
moins de
□ There are fewer people than there were yesterday. Il y a moins de monde qu'hier. □ There are fewer pupils in this class. Il y a moins d'élèves dans cette classe.
fiancé NOUN
le fiancé
□ He's my fiancé. C'est mon fiancé.
fiancée NOUN
la fiancée
□ She's my fiancée. C'est ma fiancée.
fiction NOUN
les romans *masc pl (novels)*
field NOUN
1 le champ *(in countryside)*
□ a field of wheat un champ de blé
2 le terrain *(for sport)*
□ a football field un terrain de football
3 le domaine *(subject)*
□ He's an expert in his field. C'est un expert dans son domaine.
fierce ADJECTIVE
1 féroce (FEM féroce)

□ The dog looked very fierce. Le chien avait l'air très féroce.
2 violent (FEM violente)
□ The wind was very fierce. Le vent était très violent. □ a fierce attack une attaque violente
fifteen NUMBER
quinze
□ I'm fifteen. J'ai quinze ans.
fifteenth ADJECTIVE
quinzième (FEM quinzième)
□ the fifteenth floor le quinzième étage
■ **the fifteenth of August** le quinze août
fifth ADJECTIVE
cinquième (FEM cinquième)
□ the fifth floor le cinquième étage
■ **the fifth of August** le cinq août
fifty NUMBER
cinquante
□ He's fifty. Il a cinquante ans.
fifty-fifty ADJECTIVE, ADVERB
moitié-moitié
□ They split the prize money fifty-fifty. Ils ont partagé l'argent du prix moitié-moitié.
■ **a fifty-fifty chance** une chance sur deux
fight NOUN
▷ *see also* **fight** VERB
1 la bagarre
□ There was a fight in the pub. Il y a eu une bagarre au pub.
2 la lutte
□ the fight against cancer la lutte contre le cancer
to **fight** VERB
▷ *see also* **fight** NOUN
1 se battre
□ They were fighting. Ils se battaient.
2 lutter contre
□ The doctors tried to fight the disease. Les médecins ont essayé de lutter contre la maladie. □ He fought against the urge to smoke. Il a lutté contre son envie de fumer.
fighting NOUN
les bagarres *fem pl*
□ Fighting broke out outside the pub. Des bagarres ont éclaté devant le pub.
figure NOUN
1 le chiffre *(number)*
□ Can you give me the exact figures? Pouvez-vous me donner les chiffres exacts?
2 la silhouette *(outline of person)*
□ Hélène saw the figure of a man on the bridge. Hélène a vu la silhouette d'un homme sur le pont.
■ **She's got a good figure.** Elle est bien faite.
■ **I have to watch my figure.** Je dois faire

attention à ma ligne.

3 le personnage (*personality*)

□ She's an important political figure. C'est un personnage politique important.

to **figure out** VERB

1 calculer

□ I'll try to figure out how much it'll cost. Je vais essayer de calculer combien ça va coûter.

2 voir

□ I couldn't figure out what it meant. Je n'arrivais pas à voir ce que ça voulait dire.

3 cerner

□ I can't figure him out at all. Je n'arrive pas du tout à le cerner.

file NOUN

▷ *see also* **file** VERB

1 le dossier (*document*)

□ Have we got a file on the suspect? Est-ce que nous avons un dossier sur le suspect?

2 la chemise (*folder*)

□ She keeps all her letters in a cardboard file. Elle garde toutes ses lettres dans une chemise en carton.

3 le classeur (*ring binder*)

4 le fichier (*on computer*)

5 la lime (*for nails, metal*)

to **file** VERB

▷ *see also* **file** NOUN

1 classer (*papers*)

2 limer (*nails, metal*)

□ to file one's nails se limer les ongles

to **fill** VERB

remplir

□ She filled the glass with water. Elle a rempli le verre d'eau.

to **fill in** VERB

1 remplir

□ Can you fill this form in please? Est-ce que vous pouvez remplir ce formulaire s'il vous plaît?

2 boucher

□ He filled the hole in with soil. Il a bouché le trou avec de la terre.

to **fill up** VERB

remplir

□ He filled the cup up to the brim. Il a rempli la tasse à ras bords.

■ **Fill it up, please.** (*at petrol station*) Le plein, s'il vous plaît.

film NOUN

1 le film (*movie*)

2 la pellicule (*for camera*)

film star NOUN

la vedette de cinéma

□ He's a film star. C'est une vedette de cinéma.

filthy ADJECTIVE

dégoûtant (FEM dégoûtante)

final ADJECTIVE

▷ *see also* **final** NOUN

1 dernier (FEM dernière) (*last*)

□ our final farewells nos derniers adieux

2 définitif (FEM définitive) (*definite*)

□ a final decision une décision définitive

■ **I'm not going and that's final.** Je n'y vais pas, un point c'est tout.

final NOUN

▷ *see also* **final** ADJECTIVE

la finale

□ Andy Murray is in the final. Andy Murray va disputer la finale.

finally ADVERB

1 enfin (*lastly*)

□ Finally, I would like to say ... Enfin, je voudrais dire ...

2 finalement (*eventually*)

□ She finally chose the red shoes. Elle a finalement choisi les chaussures rouges.

to **find** VERB

1 trouver

□ I can't find the exit. Je ne trouve pas la sortie.

2 retrouver (*something lost*)

□ Did you find your pen? Est-ce que tu as retrouvé ton crayon?

to **find out** VERB

découvrir

□ I'm determined to find out the truth. Je suis décidé à découvrir la vérité.

■ **to find out about 1** (*make enquiries*) se renseigner sur □ Try to find out about the cost of a hotel. Essaye de te renseigner sur le prix d'un hôtel. **2** (*by chance*) apprendre □ I found out about their affair. J'ai appris leur liaison.

fine ADJECTIVE, ADVERB

▷ *see also* **fine** NOUN

1 excellent (FEM excellente) (*very good*)

□ He's a fine musician. C'est un excellent musicien.

■ **to be fine** aller bien □ How are you? — I'm fine. Comment ça va? — Ça va bien.

■ **I feel fine.** Je me sens bien.

■ **The weather is fine today.** Il fait beau aujourd'hui.

2 fin (FEM fine) (*not coarse*)

□ She's got very fine hair. Elle a les cheveux très fins.

fine NOUN

▷ *see also* **fine** ADJECTIVE

1 l' amende *fem*

□ She got a £50 fine. Elle a eu une amende de cinquante livres.

2 la contravention *(for traffic offence)*
□ I got a fine for speeding. J'ai eu une contravention pour excès de vitesse.

finger NOUN
le doigt

■ **my little finger** mon petit doigt

fingernail NOUN
l' ongle *masc*

finish NOUN
▷ *see also* **finish** VERB
l' arrivée *fem (of race)*
□ We saw the finish of the London Marathon. Nous avons vu l'arrivée du marathon de Londres.

to **finish** VERB
▷ *see also* **finish** NOUN

1 finir
□ I've finished! J'ai fini!

■ **to finish doing something** finir de faire quelque chose

2 terminer
□ I've finished the book. J'ai terminé ce livre.
□ The film has finished. Le film est terminé.

Finland NOUN
la Finlande

■ **in Finland** en Finlande
■ **to Finland** en Finlande

Finn NOUN
le Finlandais
la Finlandaise

Finnish NOUN
▷ *see also* **Finnish** ADJECTIVE
le finnois *(language)*

Finnish ADJECTIVE
▷ *see also* **Finnish** NOUN
finlandais (FEM finlandaise)

fire NOUN
▷ *see also* **fire** VERB

1 le feu (PL les feux)
□ He made a fire in the woods. Il a fait du feu dans les bois.

■ **to be on fire** être en feu

2 l' incendie *masc (accidental)*
□ The house was destroyed by fire. La maison a été détruite par un incendie.

3 le radiateur *(heater)*
□ Turn the fire on. Allume le radiateur.

■ **the fire brigade** les pompiers *masc pl*
■ **a fire alarm** un avertisseur d'incendie
■ **a fire engine** une voiture de pompiers
■ **a fire escape** un escalier de secours
■ **a fire extinguisher** un extincteur
■ **a fire station** une caserne de pompiers

to **fire** VERB
▷ *see also* **fire** NOUN
tirer *(shoot)*
□ She fired twice. Elle a tiré deux fois.

■ **to fire at somebody** tirer sur quelqu'un
□ The terrorist fired at the crowd. Le terroriste a tiré sur la foule.

■ **to fire a gun** tirer un coup de feu
■ **to fire somebody** mettre quelqu'un à la porte □ He was fired from his job. Il a été mis à la porte.

fireman NOUN
le pompier
□ He's a fireman. Il est pompier.

fireplace NOUN
la cheminée

fireworks PL NOUN
le feu d'artifice *sing*
□ Are you going to see the fireworks? Est-ce que tu vas voir le feu d'artifice?

firm ADJECTIVE
▷ *see also* **firm** NOUN
ferme (FEM ferme)
□ to be firm with somebody se montrer ferme avec quelqu'un

firm NOUN
▷ *see also* **firm** ADJECTIVE
l' entreprise *fem*
□ He works for a large firm in London. Il travaille pour une grande entreprise à Londres.

first ADJECTIVE, ADVERB
▷ *see also* **first** NOUN

1 premier (FEM première)
□ the first of September le premier septembre □ the first time la première fois

■ **to come first** *(in exam, race)* arriver premier □ Rachel came first. Rachel est arrivée première.

2 d'abord
□ I want to get a job, but first I have to graduate. Je veux trouver du travail, mais d'abord je dois finir mes études.

■ **first of all** tout d'abord

first NOUN
▷ *see also* **first** ADJECTIVE
le premier
la première
□ She was the first to arrive. Elle est arrivée la première.

■ **at first** au début

first aid NOUN
les premiers secours *masc pl*

■ **a first aid kit** une trousse de secours

first-class ADJECTIVE, ADVERB

1 de première classe
□ She has booked a first-class ticket. Elle a réservé un billet de première classe.

■ **to travel first class** voyager en première

2 excellent (FEM excellente)
□ a first-class meal un excellent repas

■ **a first-class stamp**

DID YOU KNOW...?

In France there is no first-class or second-class postage. However letters cost more to send than postcards, so you have to remember to say what you are sending when buying stamps.

firstly ADVERB

premièrement

□ Firstly, let's see what the book is about. Premièrement, voyons de quoi parle ce livre.

fir tree NOUN

le sapin

fish NOUN

▷ see also **fish** VERB

le poisson

□ I caught three fish. J'ai pêché trois poissons. □ I don't like fish. Je n'aime pas le poisson.

■ **a fish tank** un aquarium

to **fish** VERB

▷ see also **fish** NOUN

pêcher

■ **to go fishing** aller à la pêche □ We went fishing in the River Dee. Nous sommes allés à la pêche sur la Dee.

fisherman NOUN

le pêcheur

□ He's a fisherman. Il est pêcheur.

fish fingers PL NOUN

les bâtonnets de poisson masc pl

fishing NOUN

la pêche

□ My hobby is fishing. La pêche est mon passe-temps favori.

fishing boat NOUN

le bateau de pêche

fishing rod NOUN

la canne à pêche

fishing tackle NOUN

le matériel de pêche

fish sticks PL NOUN (US)

les bâtonnets de poisson masc pl

fist NOUN

le poing

fit ADJECTIVE

▷ see also **fit** VERB, NOUN

en forme (in condition)

□ He likes to stay fit. Il aime se maintenir en forme.

■ **to keep fit** se maintenir en forme □ She does aerobics to keep fit. Elle fait de l'aérobic pour se maintenir en forme.

fit NOUN

▷ see also **fit** ADJECTIVE, VERB

■ **to have a fit 1** (epileptic) avoir une crise

d'épilepsie **2** (be angry) piquer une crise de nerfs □ My Mum will have a fit when she sees the carpet! Ma mère va piquer une crise de nerfs quand elle va voir la moquette!

to **fit** VERB

▷ see also **fit** ADJECTIVE, NOUN

1 être la bonne taille (be the right size)

□ Does it fit? Est-ce que c'est la bonne taille?

LANGUAGE TIP In French you usually specify whether something is too big, small, tight etc.

■ **These trousers don't fit me. 1** (too big) Ce pantalon est trop grand pour moi. **2** (too small) Ce pantalon est trop petit pour moi.

2 installer (fix up)

□ He fitted an alarm in his car. Il a installé une alarme dans sa voiture.

3 adapter (attach)

□ She fitted a plug to the hair dryer. Elle a adapté une prise au sèche-cheveux.

to **fit in** VERB

1 correspondre (match up)

□ That story doesn't fit in with the facts. Cette histoire ne correspond pas aux faits.

2 s'adapter (person)

□ She fitted in well at her new school. Elle s'est bien adaptée à sa nouvelle école.

fitted carpet NOUN

la moquette

fitted kitchen NOUN

la cuisine aménagée

fitting room NOUN

la cabine d'essayage

five NUMBER

cinq

□ He's five. Il a cinq ans.

to **fix** VERB

1 réparer (mend)

□ Can you fix my bike? Est-ce que tu peux réparer mon vélo?

2 fixer (decide)

□ Let's fix a date for the party. Fixons une date pour la soirée. □ They fixed a price for the car. Ils ont fixé un prix pour la voiture.

3 préparer

□ Janice fixed some food for us. Janice nous a préparé à manger.

fixed ADJECTIVE

fixe (FEM fixe)

□ at a fixed time à une heure fixe □ at a fixed price à un prix fixe □ a fixed-price menu un menu à prix fixe

■ **My parents have very fixed ideas.** Mes parents ont des idées très arrêtées.

fizzy ADJECTIVE

gazeux (FEM gazeuse)

flabby – flood

□ I don't like fizzy drinks. Je n'aime pas les boissons gazeuses.

flabby ADJECTIVE
flasque (FEM flasque)

flag NOUN
le drapeau (PL les drapeaux)

flame NOUN
la flamme

flamingo NOUN
le flamant rose

flan NOUN
1 la tarte (sweet)
□ a raspberry flan une tarte aux framboises
2 la quiche (savoury)
□ a cheese and onion flan une quiche au fromage et aux oignons

flannel NOUN
le gant de toilette (for face)

> **DID YOU KNOW...?**
> The French traditionally wash with a towelling glove rather than a flannel.

to **flap** VERB
battre de
□ The bird flapped its wings. L'oiseau battait des ailes.

flash NOUN
▷ see also **flash** VERB
le flash (PL les flashes)
□ Has your camera got a flash? Est-ce que ton appareil photo a un flash?
■ a flash of lightning un éclair
■ in a flash en un clin d'œil

to **flash** VERB
▷ see also **flash** NOUN
1 clignoter
□ The police car's blue light was flashing. Le gyrophare de la voiture de police clignotait.
2 projeter
□ They flashed a torch in his face. Ils lui ont projeté la lumière d'une torche en plein visage.
■ She flashed her headlights. Elle a fait un appel de phares.

flask NOUN
le thermos (vacuum flask)

flat ADJECTIVE
▷ see also **flat** NOUN
1 plat (FEM plate)
□ a flat roof un toit plat □ flat shoes des chaussures plates
2 crevé (FEM crevée) (tyre)
□ I've got a flat tyre. J'ai un pneu crevé.

flat NOUN
▷ see also **flat** ADJECTIVE
l' appartement masc
□ She lives in a flat. Elle habite un appartement.

flatscreen ADJECTIVE
■ a flatscreen TV une télévision à écran plat

to **flatter** VERB
flatter

flattered ADJECTIVE
flatté (FEM flattée)

flavour (US **flavor**) NOUN
1 le goût (taste)
□ It has a very strong flavour. Ça a un goût très fort.
2 le parfum (variety)
□ Which flavour of ice cream would you like? Quel parfum de glace est-ce que tu veux?

flavouring (US **flavoring**) NOUN
le parfum

flew VERB ▷ see **fly**

flexible ADJECTIVE
flexible (FEM flexible)
□ flexible working hours les horaires flexibles

to **flick** VERB
appuyer sur
□ She flicked the switch to turn the light on. Elle a appuyé sur le bouton pour allumer la lumière.
■ to flick through a book feuilleter un livre

to **flicker** VERB
trembloter
□ The light flickered. La lumière a trembloté.

flight NOUN
le vol
□ What time is the flight to Paris? À quelle heure est le vol pour Paris?
■ a flight of stairs un escalier

flight attendant NOUN
1 l' hôtesse de l'air fem (woman)
2 le steward (man)

to **fling** VERB
jeter
□ He flung the book onto the floor. Il a jeté le livre par terre.

flippers NOUN
les palmes fem pl

to **float** VERB
flotter
□ A leaf was floating on the water. Une feuille flottait sur l'eau.

flock NOUN
■ a flock of sheep un troupeau de moutons
■ a flock of birds un vol d'oiseaux

flood NOUN
▷ see also **flood** VERB
1 l' inondation fem
□ We had a flood in the kitchen. On a eu

une inondation dans la cuisine.
2 le flot
□ He received a flood of letters. Il a reçu un flot de lettres.
to **flood** VERB
▷ *see also* **flood** NOUN
inonder
□ The river has flooded the village. La rivière a inondé le village.
flooding NOUN
les inondations *fem pl*
floor NOUN
1 le sol
□ a tiled floor un sol carrelé
■ **on the floor** par terre
2 l' étage *masc (storey)*
□ the first floor le premier étage
■ **the ground floor** le rez-de-chaussée
■ **on the third floor** au troisième étage
flop NOUN
le fiasco
□ The film was a flop. Le film a été un fiasco.
floppy disk NOUN
la disquette
florist NOUN
le/la fleuriste
flour NOUN
la farine
to **flow** VERB
1 couler *(river)*
2 s'écouler *(flow out)*
□ Water was flowing from the pipe. De l'eau s'écoulait du tuyau.
flower NOUN
▷ *see also* **flower** VERB
la fleur
to **flower** VERB
▷ *see also* **flower** NOUN
fleurir
flown VERB ▷ *see* **fly**
flu NOUN
la grippe
□ She's got flu. Elle a la grippe.
fluent ADJECTIVE
■ **He speaks fluent French.** Il parle couramment le français.
flung VERB ▷ *see* **fling**
flush NOUN
▷ *see also* **flush** VERB
la chasse d'eau *(of toilet)*
to **flush** VERB
▷ *see also* **flush** NOUN
■ **to flush the toilet** tirer la chasse
flute NOUN
la flûte
□ I play the flute. Je joue de la flûte.
fly NOUN

▷ *see also* **fly** VERB
la mouche *(insect)*
to **fly** VERB
▷ *see also* **fly** NOUN
1 voler
□ The plane flew through the night. L'avion a volé toute la nuit.
2 aller en avion *(passenger)*
□ He flew from Paris to New York. Il est allé de Paris à New York en avion.
to **fly away** VERB
s'envoler
□ The bird flew away. L'oiseau s'est envolé.
foal NOUN
le poulain
focus NOUN
▷ *see also* **focus** VERB
■ **to be out of focus** être flou □ The house is out of focus in this photo. La maison est floue sur cette photo.
to **focus** VERB
▷ *see also* **focus** NOUN
mettre au point
□ Try to focus the binoculars. Essaye de mettre au point les jumelles au point.
■ **to focus on something 1** *(with camera, telescope)* régler la mise au point sur quelque chose □ The cameraman focused on the bird. Le caméraman a réglé la mise au point sur l'oiseau. **2** *(concentrate)* se concentrer sur quelque chose □ Let's focus on the plot of the play. Concentrons-nous sur l'intrigue de la pièce.
fog NOUN
le brouillard
foggy ADJECTIVE
■ **It's foggy.** Il y a du brouillard.
■ **a foggy day** un jour de brouillard
foil NOUN
le papier d'aluminium *(kitchen foil)*
□ She wrapped the meat in foil. Elle a enveloppé la viande dans du papier d'aluminium.
fold NOUN
▷ *see also* **fold** VERB
le pli
to **fold** VERB
▷ *see also* **fold** NOUN
plier
□ He folded the newspaper in half. Il a plié le journal en deux.
■ **to fold something up** plier quelque chose
■ **to fold one's arms** croiser ses bras □ She folded her arms. Elle a croisé les bras.
folder NOUN
1 la chemise

folding – for

□ She kept all her letters in a folder. Elle gardait toutes ses lettres dans une chemise.
2 le classeur *(ring binder)*

folding ADJECTIVE
■ **a folding chair** une chaise pliante
■ **a folding bed** un lit pliant

to **follow** VERB
suivre
□ She followed him. Elle l'a suivi. □ You go first and I'll follow. Va devant, je te suis.

following ADJECTIVE
suivant (FEM suivante)
□ the following day le jour suivant

fond ADJECTIVE
■ **to be fond of somebody** aimer beaucoup quelqu'un □ I'm very fond of her. Je l'aime beaucoup.

food NOUN
la nourriture
■ **We need to buy some food.** Nous devons acheter à manger.
■ **cat food** la nourriture pour chat
■ **dog food** la nourriture pour chien

food processor NOUN
le robot

fool NOUN
l' idiot *masc*
l' idiote *fem*

foot NOUN
1 le pied *(of person)*
□ My feet are aching. J'ai mal aux pieds.
2 la patte *(of animal)*
□ The dog's foot was injured. Le chien était blessé à la patte.
■ **on foot** à pied
3 le pied *(12 inches)*

> **DID YOU KNOW...?**
> In France measurements are in metres and centimetres rather than feet and inches. A foot is about 30 centimetres.

■ **Dave is 6 foot tall.** Dave mesure un mètre quatre-vingt.
■ **That mountain is 5000 feet high.** Cette montagne fait mille six cents mètres de haut.

football NOUN
1 le football *(game)*
□ I like playing football. J'aime jouer au football.
2 le ballon *(ball)*
□ Paul threw the football over the fence. Paul a envoyé le ballon par dessus la clôture.

footballer NOUN
le footballeur
la footballeuse

football player NOUN

le joueur de football
la joueuse de football
□ He's a famous football player. C'est un joueur de football célèbre.

footie NOUN
le foot

footpath NOUN
le sentier
□ Jane followed the footpath through the forest. Jane a suivi le sentier à travers la forêt.

footprint NOUN
la trace de pas
□ He saw some footprints in the sand. Il a vu des traces de pas sur le sable.

footstep NOUN
le pas
□ I can hear footsteps on the stairs. J'entends des pas dans l'escalier.

for PREPOSITION

> **LANGUAGE TIP** There are several ways of translating 'for'. Scan the examples to find one that is similar to what you want to say.

1 pour
□ a present for me un cadeau pour moi □ the train for London le train pour Londres □ He works for the government. Il travaille pour le gouvernement. □ I'll do it for you. Je vais le faire pour toi. □ Can you do it for tomorrow? Est-ce que vous pouvez le faire pour demain? □ Are you for or against the idea? Êtes-vous pour ou contre cette idée? □ Oxford is famous for its university. Oxford est célèbre pour son université.

> **LANGUAGE TIP** When referring to periods of time, use **pendant** for the future and completed actions in the past, and **depuis** (with the French verb in the present tense) for something that started in the past and is still going on.

2 pendant
□ He worked in France for two years. Il a travaillé en France pendant deux ans. □ She will be away for a month. Elle sera absente pendant un mois. □ There are roadworks for three kilometres. Il y a des travaux pendant trois kilomètres.

3 depuis
□ He's been learning French for two years. Il apprend le français depuis deux ans. □ She's been away for a month. Elle est absente depuis un mois.

> **LANGUAGE TIP** When talking about amounts of money, you do not translate 'for'.

□ I sold it for £5. Je l'ai vendu cinq livres.
□ He paid fifty pence for his ticket. Il a payé son billet cinquante pence.
■ **What's the French for 'lion'?** Comment dit-on 'lion' en français?
■ **It's time for lunch.** C'est l'heure du déjeuner.
■ **What for?** Pour quoi faire? □ Give me some money! — What for? Donne-moi de l'argent! — Pour quoi faire?
■ **What's it for?** Ça sert à quoi?
■ **for sale** à vendre □ The factory's for sale. L'usine est en vente.

to **forbid** VERB
défendre
■ **to forbid somebody to do something** défendre à quelqu'un de faire quelque chose □ I forbid you to go out tonight! Je te défends de sortir ce soir.

forbidden ADJECTIVE
défendu (FEM défendue)
□ Smoking is strictly forbidden. Il est strictement défendu de fumer.

force NOUN
▷ see also **force** VERB
la force
□ the force of the explosion la force de l'explosion
■ **in force** en vigueur □ No-smoking rules are now in force. Un règlement qui interdit de fumer est maintenant en vigueur.

to **force** VERB
▷ see also **force** NOUN
forcer
□ They forced him to open the safe. Ils l'ont obligé à ouvrir le coffre-fort.

forecast NOUN
■ **the weather forecast** la météo

foreground NOUN
le premier plan
□ in the foreground au premier plan

forehead NOUN
le front

foreign ADJECTIVE
étranger (FEM étrangère)

foreigner NOUN
l' étranger masc
l' étrangère fem

to **foresee** VERB
prévoir
□ He had foreseen the problem. Il avait prévu ce problème.

forest NOUN
la forêt

forever ADVERB
1 pour toujours
□ He's gone forever. Il est parti pour

toujours.
2 toujours (always)
□ She's forever complaining. Elle est toujours en train de se plaindre.

forgave VERB ▷ see **forgive**
to **forge** VERB
contrefaire
□ She tried to forge his signature. Elle a essayé de contrefaire sa signature.

forged ADJECTIVE
faux (FEM fausse)
□ forged banknotes des faux billets

to **forget** VERB
oublier
□ I've forgotten his name. J'ai oublié son nom. □ I'm sorry, I completely forgot! Je suis désolé, j'ai complètement oublié!

to **forgive** VERB
■ **to forgive somebody** pardonner à quelqu'un □ I forgive you. Je te pardonne.
■ **to forgive somebody for doing something** pardonner à quelqu'un d'avoir fait quelque chose □ She forgave him for forgetting her birthday. Elle lui a pardonné d'avoir oublié son anniversaire.

forgot, forgotten VERB ▷ see **forget**
fork NOUN
1 la fourchette (for eating)
2 la fourche (for gardening)
3 la bifurcation (in road)

form NOUN
1 le formulaire (paper)
□ to fill in a form remplir un formulaire
2 la forme (type)
□ I'm against hunting in any form. Je suis contre la chasse sous toutes ses formes.
■ **in top form** en pleine forme
■ **She's in the fourth form.** Elle est en troisième.

formal ADJECTIVE
1 officiel (FEM officielle) (occasion)
□ a formal dinner un dîner officiel
2 guindé (FEM guindée) (person)
3 soutenu (FEM soutenue) (language)
□ In English, 'residence' is a formal term. En anglais, 'residence' est un terme soutenu.
■ **formal clothes** une tenue habillée
■ **He's got no formal education.** Il n'a pas fait beaucoup d'études.

former ADJECTIVE
ancien (FEM ancienne)
□ a former pupil un ancien élève □ the former Prime Minister l'ancien Premier ministre

formerly ADVERB
autrefois
fort NOUN

le fort

forth ADVERB
- **to go back and forth** aller et venir
- **and so forth** et ainsi de suite

fortnight NOUN
- **a fortnight** quinze jours □ I'm going on holiday for a fortnight. Je pars en vacances pendant quinze jours.

fortunate ADJECTIVE
- **to be fortunate** avoir de la chance □ He was extremely fortunate to survive. Il a eu énormément de chance de survivre.
- **It's fortunate that I remembered the map.** C'est une chance que j'aie pris la carte.

fortunately ADVERB
heureusement
□ Fortunately, it didn't rain. Heureusement, il n'a pas plu.

fortune NOUN
la fortune
□ Kate earns a fortune! Kate gagne une fortune!
- **to tell somebody's fortune** dire la bonne aventure à quelqu'un

forty NUMBER
quarante
□ He's forty. Il a quarante ans.

forward ADVERB
▷ see also **forward** VERB
- **to move forward** avancer

to **forward** VERB
▷ see also **forward** ADVERB
faire suivre
□ He forwarded all Janette's letters. Il a fait suivre toutes les lettres de Janette.

forward slash NOUN
la barre oblique

to **foster** VERB
- **She has fostered more than fifteen children.** Plus de quinze enfants ont été placés chez elle.

foster child NOUN
l' enfant adoptif *masc*
l' enfant adoptive *fem*

fought VERB ▷ see **fight**

foul ADJECTIVE
▷ see also **foul** NOUN
infect (FEM infecte)
□ The weather was foul. Le temps était infect. □ What a foul smell! Quelle odeur infecte!

foul NOUN
▷ see also **foul** ADJECTIVE
la faute
□ Ferguson committed a foul. Ferguson a fait une faute.

found VERB ▷ see **find**

to **found** VERB
fonder
□ Baden Powell founded the Scout Movement. Baden Powell a fondé le mouvement scout.

foundations PL NOUN
les fondations *fem pl*

fountain NOUN
la fontaine

fountain pen NOUN
le stylo à encre

four NUMBER
quatre
□ She's four. Elle a quatre ans.

fourteen NUMBER
quatorze
□ I'm fourteen. J'ai quatorze ans.

fourteenth ADJECTIVE
quatorzième (FEM quatorzième)
□ the fourteenth floor le quatorzième étage
- **the fourteenth of August** le quatorze août

fourth ADJECTIVE
quatrième (FEM quatrième)
□ the fourth floor le quatrième étage
- **the fourth of July** le quatre juillet

fox NOUN
le renard

fragile ADJECTIVE
fragile (FEM fragile)

frame NOUN
le cadre *(for picture)*

France NOUN
la France
- **in France** en France
- **to France** en France
- **He's from France.** Il est français.

frantic ADJECTIVE
- **I was going frantic.** J'étais dans tous mes états.
- **to be frantic with worry** être folle d'inquiétude

fraud NOUN
1 la fraude *(crime)*
□ He was jailed for fraud. On l'a mis en prison pour fraude.
2 l' imposteur *masc (person)*
□ He's not a real doctor, he's a fraud. Ce n'est pas un vrai médecin, c'est un imposteur.

freckles PL NOUN
les taches de rousseur *fem pl*

free ADJECTIVE
▷ see also **free** VERB
1 gratuit (FEM gratuite) *(free of charge)*
□ a free brochure une brochure gratuite

2 libre (FEM libre) (not busy, not taken)
  □ Is this seat free? Est-ce que cette place est libre? □ Are you free after school? Tu es libre après l'école?

to **free** VERB
  ▷ see also **free** ADJECTIVE
  libérer

freedom NOUN
  la liberté

freeway NOUN (US)
  l' autoroute fem

to **freeze** VERB
1 geler
  □ The water had frozen. L'eau avait gelé.
2 congeler (food)
  □ She froze the rest of the raspberries. Elle a congelé le reste des framboises.

freezer NOUN
  le congélateur

freezing ADJECTIVE
  ■ It's freezing! Il fait un froid de canard! (informal)
  ■ I'm freezing! Je suis gelé! (informal)
  ■ 3 degrees below freezing moins trois

freight NOUN
  la cargaison (goods)
  ■ a freight train un train de marchandises

French NOUN
  ▷ see also **French** ADJECTIVE
  le français (language)
  □ Do you speak French? Est-ce que tu parles français?
  ■ the French (people) les Français

French ADJECTIVE
  ▷ see also **French** NOUN
  français (FEM française)
  □ He's French. Il est français. □ She's French. Elle est française.

French beans PL NOUN
  les haricots verts masc pl

French fries PL NOUN
  les frites fem pl

French horn NOUN
  le cor (d'harmonie)
  □ I play the French horn. Je joue du cor.

French kiss NOUN
  le baiser profond

French loaf NOUN
  la baguette

Frenchman NOUN
  le Français

French windows PL NOUN
  la porte-fenêtre sing (PL les portes-fenêtres)

Frenchwoman NOUN
  la Française

frequent ADJECTIVE
  fréquent (FEM fréquente)

□ frequent showers des averses fréquentes
  ■ There are frequent buses to the town centre. Il y a beaucoup de bus pour le centre ville.

fresh ADJECTIVE
  frais (FEM fraîche)
  ■ I need some fresh air. J'ai besoin de prendre l'air.

to **freshen up** VERB
  faire un brin de toilette
  □ I'd like to go and freshen up. Je voudrais faire un brin de toilette.

to **fret** VERB
  se tracasser
  □ Philip was fretting about his exams. Philip se tracassait au sujet de ses examens.

Friday NOUN
  le vendredi
  □ on Friday vendredi □ on Fridays le vendredi □ every Friday tous les vendredis □ last Friday vendredi dernier □ next Friday vendredi prochain

fridge NOUN
  le frigo

fried ADJECTIVE
  frit (FEM frite)
  □ fried vegetables des légumes frits
  ■ a fried egg un œuf sur le plat

friend NOUN
  l' ami masc
  l' amie fem

friendly ADJECTIVE
1 gentil (FEM gentille)
  □ She's really friendly. Elle est vraiment gentille.
2 accueillant (FEM accueillante)
  □ Liverpool is a very friendly city. Liverpool est une ville très accueillante.

friendship NOUN
  l' amitié fem

fright NOUN
  la peur
  □ I got a terrible fright! Ça m'a fait une peur terrible!

to **frighten** VERB
  faire peur à
  □ Horror films frighten him. Les films d'horreur lui font peur.

frightened ADJECTIVE
  ■ to be frightened avoir peur □ I'm frightened! J'ai peur!
  ■ to be frightened of something avoir peur de quelque chose □ Anna's frightened of spiders. Anna a peur des araignées.

frightening ADJECTIVE
  effrayant (FEM effrayante)

fringe NOUN

la frange *(of hair)*
□ She's got a fringe. Elle a une frange.
Frisbee® NOUN
le Frisbee®
□ to play Frisbee jouer au Frisbee
fro ADVERB
■ **to go to and fro** aller et venir
frog NOUN
la grenouille
■ **frogs' legs** les cuisses de grenouille
from PREPOSITION
de
□ Where do you come from? D'où venez-vous? □ I come from Perth. Je viens de Perth. □ a letter from my sister une lettre de ma sœur □ The hotel is one kilometre from the beach. L'hôtel est à un kilomètre de la plage.
■ **from ... to ...** de ... à ... □ He flew from London to Paris. Il a pris l'avion de Londres à Paris. □ from 1 o'clock to 2 d'une heure à deux heures □ The price was reduced from £10 to £5. Ils ont réduit le prix de dix livres à cinq.
■ **from ... onwards** à partir de ... □ We'll be at home from 7 o'clock onwards. Nous serons chez nous à partir de sept heures.
front NOUN
▷ *see also* **front** ADJECTIVE
le devant
□ the front of the house le devant de la maison
■ **in front** devant □ a house with a car in front une maison avec une voiture devant □ the car in front la voiture de devant
■ **in front of** devant □ in front of the house devant la maison □ the car in front of us la voiture devant nous
■ **in the front** *(of car)* à l'avant □ I was sitting in the front. J'étais assis à l'avant.
■ **at the front of the train** à l'avant du train
front ADJECTIVE
▷ *see also* **front** NOUN
1 de devant
□ the front row la rangée de devant
2 avant
□ the front seats of the car les sièges avant de la voiture
■ **the front door** la porte d'entrée
frontier NOUN
la frontière
frost NOUN
le gel
frosting NOUN (US)
le glaçage *(on cake)*
frosty ADJECTIVE
■ **It's frosty today.** Il gèle aujourd'hui.

to **frown** VERB
froncer les sourcils
□ He frowned. Il a froncé les sourcils.
froze VERB ▷ *see* **freeze**
frozen ADJECTIVE
▷ *see also* **freeze**
surgelé (FEM surgelée) *(food)*
□ frozen chips des frites surgelées
fruit NOUN
le fruit
■ **fruit juice** le jus de fruits
■ **a fruit salad** une salade de fruits
fruit machine NOUN
la machine à sous
frustrated ADJECTIVE
frustré (FEM frustrée)
to **fry** VERB
faire frire
□ Fry the onions for 5 minutes. Faites frire les oignons pendant cinq minutes.
frying pan NOUN
la poêle
fuel NOUN
le carburant *(for car, aeroplane)*
□ to run out of fuel avoir une panne de carburant
to **fulfil** VERB
réaliser
□ Robert fulfilled his dream to visit China. Robert a réalisé son rêve de visiter la Chine.
full ADJECTIVE, ADVERB
1 plein (FEM pleine)
□ The tank's full. Le réservoir est plein.
2 complet (FEM complète)
□ He asked for full details about the job. Il a demandé des renseignements complets sur le poste.
■ **your full name** vos nom et prénoms
□ My full name is Ian John Marr. Je m'appelle Ian John Marr.
■ **I'm full.** *(after meal)* J'ai bien mangé.
■ **at full speed** à toute vitesse □ He drove at full speed. Il conduisait à toute vitesse.
■ **There was a full moon.** C'était la pleine lune.
full stop NOUN
le point
full-time ADJECTIVE, ADVERB
à plein temps
□ She's got a full-time job. Elle a un travail à plein temps. □ She works full-time. Elle travaille à plein temps.
fully ADVERB
complètement
□ He hasn't fully recovered from his illness. Il n'est pas complètement remis de sa maladie.

fumes PL NOUN
les fumées *fem pl*
▫ The factory emitted dangerous fumes.
L'usine rejetait des fumées dangereuses.
■ **exhaust fumes** les gaz d'échappement
masc pl

fun ADJECTIVE
▷ *see also* **fun** NOUN
marrant (FEM marrante)
▫ She's a fun person. Elle est marrante.

fun NOUN
▷ *see also* **fun** ADJECTIVE
■ **to have fun** s'amuser ▫ We had great fun
playing in the snow. Nous nous sommes
bien amusés à jouer dans la neige.
■ **for fun** pour rire ▫ He entered the
competition just for fun. Il a participé à la
compétition juste pour rire.
■ **to make fun of somebody** se moquer de
quelqu'un ▫ They made fun of him. Ils se
sont moqués de lui.
■ **It's fun!** C'est chouette!
■ **Have fun!** Amuse-toi bien!

funds PL NOUN
les fonds *masc pl*
▫ to raise funds collecter des fonds

funeral NOUN
l' enterrement *masc*

funfair NOUN
la fête foraine

funny ADJECTIVE
1 drôle (FEM drôle) *(amusing)*
▫ It was really funny. C'était vraiment drôle.
2 bizarre (FEM bizarre) *(strange)*
▫ There's something funny about him. Il est
un peu bizarre.

fur NOUN
1 la fourrure
▫ a fur coat un manteau de fourrure
2 le poil

▫ the dog's fur le poil du chien

furious ADJECTIVE
furieux (FEM furieuse)
▫ Dad was furious with me. Papa était
furieux contre moi.

furniture NOUN
les meubles *masc pl*
▫ a piece of furniture un meuble

further ADVERB, ADJECTIVE
plus loin
▫ London is further from Manchester than
Leeds is. Londres est plus loin de
Manchester que Leeds.
■ **How much further is it?** C'est encore
loin?

further education NOUN
l' enseignement postscolaire *masc*

fuse NOUN
le fusible
▫ The fuse has blown. Le fusible a sauté.

fuss NOUN
l' agitation *fem*
▫ What's all the fuss about? Qu'est-ce que
c'est que toute cette agitation?
■ **to make a fuss** faire des histoires ▫ He's
always making a fuss about nothing. Il fait
toujours des histoires pour rien.

fussy ADJECTIVE
difficile (FEM difficile)
▫ She is very fussy about her food. Elle est
très difficile sur la nourriture.

future NOUN
1 l' avenir *masc*
▫ What are your plans for the future? Quels
sont vos projets pour l'avenir?
■ **in future** à l'avenir ▫ Be more careful in
future. Sois plus prudent à l'avenir.
2 le futur *(in grammar)*
▫ Put this sentence into the future. Mettez
cette phrase au futur.

Gg

to **gain** VERB
- ■ **to gain weight** prendre du poids
- ■ **to gain speed** prendre de la vitesse

gallery NOUN
le musée
- □ an art gallery un musée d'art

to **gamble** VERB
jouer
- □ He gambled £100 at the casino. Il a joué cent livres au casino.

gambler NOUN
le joueur

gambling NOUN
le jeu
- □ He likes gambling. Il aime le jeu.

game NOUN
1 le jeu (PL les jeux)
- □ The children were playing a game. Les enfants jouaient à un jeu.
2 le match (sport)
- □ a game of football un match de football
- ■ **a game of cards** une partie de cartes

gang NOUN
la bande

gangster NOUN
le gangster

gap NOUN
1 le trou
- □ There's a gap in the hedge. Il y a un trou dans la haie.
2 l' intervalle masc
- □ a gap of four years un intervalle de quatre ans

gap year NOUN
l' année sabatique avant d'aller à l'université
- □ My sister's in Australia on her gap year. Ma sœur prend une année sabatique en Australie avant d'aller à l'université.

garage NOUN
le garage

garbage NOUN
les ordures fem pl

garden NOUN
le jardin

gardener NOUN
le jardinier
- □ He's a gardener. Il est jardinier.

gardening NOUN
le jardinage
- □ Margaret loves gardening. Margaret aime le jardinage.

gardens PL NOUN
le jardin public sing

garlic NOUN
l' ail masc

garment NOUN
le vêtement

gas NOUN
1 le gaz
- ■ **a gas cooker** une cuisinière à gaz
- ■ **a gas cylinder** une bouteille de gaz
- ■ **a gas fire** un radiateur à gaz
- ■ **a gas leak** une fuite de gaz
2 l' essence fem (us: petrol)

gasoline NOUN (US)
l' essence fem

gate NOUN
1 le portail (of garden)
2 la barrière (of field)
3 la porte (at airport)

gateau NOUN
le gâteau à la crème

to **gather** VERB
se rassembler (assemble)
- □ People gathered in front of Buckingham Palace. Les gens se sont rassemblés devant Buckingham Palace.
- ■ **to gather speed** prendre de la vitesse
- □ The train gathered speed. Le train a pris de la vitesse.

gave VERB ▷ see **give**

gay ADJECTIVE
homosexuel (FEM homosexuelle)

to **gaze** VERB
- ■ **to gaze at something** fixer quelque chose du regard □ He gazed at her. Il l'a fixée du regard.

GCSE NOUN
le brevet des collèges

gear NOUN
1 la vitesse *(in car)*
☐ in first gear en première vitesse ☐ to change gear changer de vitesse
2 le matériel
☐ camping gear le matériel de camping
■ **your sports gear** *(clothes)* tes affaires de sport

gear lever NOUN
le levier de vitesse

gearshift NOUN (US)
le levier de vitesse

geese PL NOUN ▷ *see* **goose**

gel NOUN
le gel
■ **hair gel** le gel pour les cheveux

gem NOUN
la pierre précieuse

Gemini NOUN
les Gémeaux *masc pl*
☐ I'm Gemini. Je suis Gémeaux.

gender NOUN
1 le sexe *(of person)*
2 le genre *(of noun)*

gene NOUN
le gène

general NOUN
▷ *see also* **general** ADJECTIVE
le général *(PL les généraux)*

general ADJECTIVE
▷ *see also* **general** NOUN
général *(FEM générale, MASC PL généraux)*
■ **in general** en général

general election NOUN
les élections législatives *fem pl*

general knowledge NOUN
les connaissances générales *fem pl*

generally ADVERB
généralement
☐ I generally go shopping on Saturday. Généralement, je fais mes courses le samedi.

generation NOUN
la génération
☐ the younger generation la nouvelle génération

generator NOUN
le générateur

generous ADJECTIVE
généreux *(FEM généreuse)*
☐ That's very generous of you. C'est très généreux de votre part.

genetic ADJECTIVE
génétique *(FEM génétique)*

genetically-modified ADJECTIVE
génétiquement modifié *(FEM génétiquement modifiée)*

genetics NOUN
la génétique

Geneva NOUN
Genève
■ **in Geneva** à Genève
■ **to Geneva** à Genève
■ **Lake Geneva** le lac Léman

genius NOUN
le génie
☐ She's a genius! C'est un génie!

gentle ADJECTIVE
doux *(FEM douce)*

gentleman NOUN
le monsieur *(PL les messieurs)*
☐ Good morning, gentlemen. Bonjour messieurs.

gently ADVERB
doucement

gents NOUN
les toilettes pour hommes *fem pl*
☐ Can you tell me where the gents is, please? Pouvez-vous me dire où sont les toilettes, s'il vous plaît?
■ **'gents'** *(on sign)* 'messieurs'

genuine ADJECTIVE
1 véritable *(FEM véritable) (real)*
☐ These are genuine diamonds. Ce sont de véritables diamants.
2 sincère *(FEM sincère) (sincere)*
☐ She's a very genuine person. C'est quelqu'un de très sincère.

geography NOUN
la géographie

gerbil NOUN
la gerbille

germ NOUN
le microbe

German NOUN
▷ *see also* **German** ADJECTIVE
1 l' Allemand *masc*
l' Allemande *fem (person)*
2 l' allemand *(language)*
☐ Do you speak German? Parlez-vous allemand?

German ADJECTIVE
▷ *see also* **German** NOUN
allemand *(FEM allemande)*

German measles NOUN
la rubéole

Germany NOUN
l' Allemagne *fem*

gesture NOUN
le geste

to **get** VERB

> LANGUAGE TIP There are several ways of translating 'get'. Scan the examples to find one that is similar to what you want to say.

1 avoir *(have, receive)*
□ I got lots of presents. J'ai eu beaucoup de cadeaux. □ He got first prize. Il a eu le premier prix. □ He got good exam results. Il a eu de bons résultats aux examens. □ How many have you got? Combien en avez-vous?

2 aller chercher *(fetch)*
□ Quick, get help! Allez vite chercher de l'aide!

3 attraper *(catch)*
□ They've got the thief. Ils ont attrapé le voleur.

4 prendre *(train, bus)*
□ I'm getting the bus into town. Je prends le bus pour aller en ville.

5 comprendre *(understand)*
□ I don't get it. Je ne comprends pas.

6 aller *(go)*
□ How do you get to the castle? Comment est-ce qu'on va au château?

7 arriver *(arrive)*
□ He should get here soon. Il devrait arriver bientôt.

8 devenir *(become)*
□ to get old devenir vieux

■ **to get something done** faire faire quelque chose □ to get one's hair cut se faire couper les cheveux

■ **to get something for somebody** trouver quelque chose pour quelqu'un □ The librarian got the book for me. Le bibliothécaire m'a trouvé le livre.

■ **to have got to do something** devoir faire quelque chose □ I've got to tell him. Je dois le lui dire.

to **get away** VEBR
s'échapper
□ One of the burglars got away. L'un des cambrioleurs s'est échappé.

to **get back** VERB
1 rentrer
□ What time did you get back? Tu es rentré à quelle heure?

2 récupérer
□ He got his money back. Il a récupéré son argent.

to **get in** VERB
rentrer

□ What time did you get in last night? Tu es rentré à quelle heure hier soir?

to **get into** VERB
monter dans
□ Sharon got into the car. Sharon est montée dans la voiture.

to **get off** VERB
descendre de *(vehicle, bike)*
□ Isobel got off the train. Isobel est descendue du train.

to **get on** VERB
1 monter dans *(vehicle)*
□ Phyllis got on the bus. Phyllis est montée dans le bus.

2 enfourcher *(bike)*
□ Carol got on her bike. Carol a enfourché son vélo.

■ **to get on with somebody** s'entendre avec quelqu'un □ He doesn't get on with his parents. Il ne s'entend pas avec ses parents. □ We got on really well. Nous nous sommes très bien entendus.

to **get out** VERB
sortir
□ Hélène got out of the car. Hélène est sortie de la voiture. □ Get out! Sortez!

■ **to get something out** sortir quelque chose □ She got the map out. Elle a sorti la carte.

to **get over** VERB
se remettre
□ She never got over his death. Elle ne s'est jamais remise de sa mort.

to **get together** VERB
se retrouver
□ Could we get together this evening? Pourrait-on se retrouver ce soir?

to **get up** VERB
se lever
□ What time do you get up? Tu te lèves à quelle heure?

ghetto blaster NOUN
le radiocassette portable

ghost NOUN
le fantôme

giant ADJECTIVE
▷ *see also* **giant** NOUN
énorme *(FEM* énorme*)*
□ They ate a giant meal. Ils ont mangé un énorme repas.

giant NOUN
▷ *see also* **giant** ADJECTIVE
le géant
la géante

gift NOUN
1 le cadeau *(PL* les cadeaux*) (present)*
2 le don *(talent)*

■ **to have a gift for something** être doué pour quelque chose □ Dave has a gift for painting. Dave est doué pour la peinture.

gifted ADJECTIVE
doué (FEM douée)
□ Janice is a gifted dancer. Janice est douée pour la danse.

gift shop NOUN
la boutique de cadeaux

gigantic ADJECTIVE
gigantesque (FEM gigantesque)

gin NOUN
le gin

ginger NOUN
▷ see also **ginger** ADJECTIVE
le gingembre
□ Add a teaspoon of ginger. Ajoutez une cuillère à café de gingembre.

ginger ADJECTIVE
▷ see also **ginger** NOUN
roux (FEM rousse)
□ Chris has ginger hair. Chris a les cheveux roux.

giraffe NOUN
la girafe

girl NOUN
1 la fille
□ They've got a girl and two boys. Ils ont une fille et deux garçons.
2 la petite fille (young)
□ a five-year-old girl une petite fille de cinq ans
3 la jeune fille (older)
□ a sixteen-year-old girl une jeune fille de seize ans □ an English girl une jeune Anglaise

girlfriend NOUN
1 la copine (lover)
□ Damon's girlfriend is called Justine. La copine de Damon s'appelle Justine.
2 l' amie fem (friend)
□ She often went out with her girlfriends. Elle sortait souvent avec ses amies.

to give VERB
donner
■ **to give something to somebody** donner quelque chose à quelqu'un □ He gave me £10. Il m'a donné dix livres.
■ **to give something back to somebody** rendre quelque chose à quelqu'un □ I gave the book back to him. Je lui ai rendu le livre.
■ **to give way** céder la priorité (in traffic)

to give in VERB
céder
□ His Mum gave in and let him go out. Sa mère a cédé et l'a laissé sortir.

to give out VERB

distribuer
□ He gave out the exam papers. Il a distribué les sujets d'examen.

to give up VERB
laisser tomber
□ I couldn't do it, so I gave up. Je n'arrivais pas à le faire, alors j'ai laissé tomber
■ **to give up doing something** arrêter de faire quelque chose □ He gave up smoking. Il a arrêté de fumer.
■ **to give oneself up** se rendre □ The thief gave himself up. Le voleur s'est rendu.

glad ADJECTIVE
content (FEM contente)
□ She's glad she's done it. Elle est contente de l'avoir fait.

glamorous ADJECTIVE
1 glamour (FEM+PL glamour) (person)
□ She's very glamourous. Elle est très glamour.
2 prestigieux (FEM prestigieuse) (job)
■ **to have a glamorous lifestyle** vivre comme une star

to glance VERB
▷ see also **glance** NOUN
■ **to glance at something** jeter un coup d'œil à quelque chose □ Peter glanced at his watch. Peter a jeté un coup d'œil à sa montre.

glance NOUN
▷ see also **glance** VERB
le coup d'œil
□ at first glance au premier coup d'œil

to glare VERB
■ **to glare at somebody** lancer un regard furieux à quelqu'un □ He glared at me. Il m'a lancé un regard furieux.

glaring ADJECTIVE
■ **a glaring mistake** une erreur qui saute aux yeux

glass NOUN
le verre
□ a glass of milk un verre de lait

glasses PL NOUN
les lunettes fem pl
□ Jean-Pierre wears glasses. Jean-Pierre porte des lunettes.

glider NOUN
le planeur

gliding NOUN
le vol à voile
□ My hobby is gliding. Je fais du vol à voile.

global ADJECTIVE
mondial (FEM mondiale, MASC PL mondiaux)
■ **on a global scale** à l'échelle mondiale

global warming NOUN
le réchauffement de la planète

globe NOUN
le globe

gloomy ADJECTIVE
1 morose (FEM morose)
□ She looked gloomy when she heard the news. Elle avait l'air morose quand elle a entendu les nouvelles.
2 lugubre (FEM lugubre)
□ He lives in a small gloomy flat. Il habite un petit appartement lugubre.

glorious ADJECTIVE
magnifique (FEM magnifique)

glove NOUN
le gant

glove compartment NOUN
la boîte à gants

glue NOUN
▷ see also **glue** VERB
la colle

to **glue** VERB
▷ see also **glue** NOUN
coller

GM ADJECTIVE (= genetically modified)
génétiquement modifié (FEM génétiquement modifiée)
□ GM foods les aliments génétiquement modifiés masc pl
■ **GM-free** sans OGM

GMO ABBREVIATION (= genetically-modified organism)
l' OGM masc (= l'organisme génétiquement modifié)

go NOUN
▷ see also **go** VERB
■ **to have a go at doing something** essayer de faire quelque chose □ He had a go at making a cake. Il a essayé de faire un gâteau.
■ **Whose go is it?** À qui le tour?

to **go** VERB
▷ see also **go** NOUN
1 aller
□ I'm going to the cinema tonight. Je vais au cinéma ce soir.
2 partir (leave)
□ Where's Pierre? — He's gone. Où est Pierre? — Il est parti.
3 s'en aller (go away)
□ I'm going now. Je m'en vais.
4 marcher (vehicle)
□ My car won't go. Ma voiture ne marche pas.
■ **to go home** rentrer à la maison □ I go home at about 4 o'clock. Je rentre à la maison vers quatre heures.
■ **to go for a walk** aller se promener
□ Shall we go for a walk? Si on allait se

promener?
■ **How did it go?** Comment est-ce que ça s'est passé?
■ **I'm going to do it tomorrow.** Je vais le faire demain.
■ **It's going to be difficult.** Ça va être difficile.

to **go after** VERB
suivre
□ Quick, go after them! Vite, suivez-les!

to **go ahead** VERB
■ **The meeting will go ahead as planned.** La réunion aura bien lieu comme prévu.
■ **We'll go ahead with your plan.** Nous allons mettre votre projet à exécution.
■ **Go ahead!** Vas-y!

to **go away** VERB
s'en aller
□ Go away! Allez-vous-en!

to **go back** VERB

> LANGUAGE TIP Use **retourner** in most cases, unless you are entering a building (usually your home) when you would use **rentrer**.

1 retourner
□ We went back to the same place. Nous sommes retournés au même endroit.
2 rentrer
□ After the film we went back home. Il est rentré chez lui après le film.

to **go by** VERB
passer
□ Two policemen went by. Deux policiers sont passés.

to **go down** VERB
1 descendre (person)
□ to go down the stairs descendre l'escalier
2 baisser (decrease)
□ The price of computers has gone down. Le prix des ordinateurs a baissé.
3 se dégonfler (deflate)
□ My airbed kept going down. Mon matelas pneumatique se dégonflait constamment.
■ **My brother's gone down with flu.** Mon frère a attrapé la grippe.

to **go for** VERB
attaquer (attack)
□ Suddenly the dog went for me. Soudain, le chien m'a attaqué.
■ **Go for it!** (go on!) Vas-y, fonce!

to **go in** VERB
entrer
□ He knocked on the door and went in. Il a frappé à la porte et il est entré.

to **go off** VERB
1 exploser (bomb)
□ The bomb went off. La bombe a explosé.

2 se déclencher *(alarm, gun)*
□ The fire alarm went off. L'avertisseur d'incendie s'est déclenché.

3 sonner *(alarm clock)*
□ My alarm clock goes off at seven every morning. Mon réveil sonne à sept heures tous les matins.

4 tourner *(food)*
□ The milk's gone off. Le lait a tourné.

5 partir *(go away)*
□ He went off in a huff. Il est parti de mauvaise humeur.

to **go on** VERB
1 se passer *(happen)*
□ What's going on? Qu'est-ce qui se passe?

2 continuer *(carry on)*
□ The concert went on until 11 o'clock at night. Le concert a continué jusqu'à onze heures du soir.

■ **to go on doing something** continuer à faire quelque chose □ He went on reading. Il a continué à lire.

■ **to go on at somebody** être sur le dos de quelqu'un □ My parents always go on at me. Mes parents sont toujours sur mon dos.

■ **Go on!** Allez! □ Go on, tell me what the problem is! Allez, dis-moi quel est le problème!

to **go out** VERB
1 sortir *(person)*
□ Are you going out tonight? Tu sors ce soir?

■ **to go out with somebody** sortir avec quelqu'un □ Are you going out with him? Est-ce que tu sors avec lui?

2 s'éteindre *(light, fire, candle)*
□ Suddenly the lights went out. Soudain, les lumières se sont éteintes.

to **go past** VERB
■ **to go past something** passer devant quelque chose □ He went past the shop. Il est passé devant la boutique.

to **go round** VERB
■ **to go round a corner** prendre un tournant

■ **to go round to somebody's house** aller chez quelqu'un

■ **to go round a museum** visiter un musée
■ **to go round the shops** faire les boutiques
■ **There's a bug going round.** Il y a un microbe qui circule.

to **go through** VERB
traverser
□ We went through Paris to get to Rennes. Nous avons traversé Paris pour aller à Rennes.

to **go up** VERB

1 monter *(person)*
□ to go up the stairs monter l'escalier
2 augmenter *(increase)*
□ The price has gone up. Le prix a augmenté.

■ **to go up in flames** s'embraser □ The whole factory went up in flames. L'usine toute entière s'est embrasée.

to **go with** VERB
aller avec
□ Does this blouse go with that skirt? Est-ce que ce chemisier va avec cette jupe?

goal NOUN
le but
□ to score a goal marquer un but □ His goal is to become the world champion. Son but est de devenir champion du monde.

goalkeeper NOUN
le gardien de but

goat NOUN
la chèvre
■ **goat's cheese** le fromage de chèvre

god NOUN
le dieu (PL les dieux)
□ I believe in God. Je crois en Dieu.

goddaughter NOUN
la filleule

godfather NOUN
le parrain

godmother NOUN
la marraine

godson NOUN
le filleul

goggles PL NOUN
1 les lunettes de protection *fem pl (of welder, mechanic etc)*
2 les lunettes de plongée *fem pl (of swimmer)*

gold NOUN
l' or *masc*
□ They found some gold. Ils ont trouvé de l'or. □ a gold necklace un collier en or

goldfish NOUN
le poisson rouge
□ I've got five goldfish. J'ai cinq poissons rouges.

gold-plated ADJECTIVE
plaqué or (FEM plaquée or)

golf NOUN
le golf
□ My dad plays golf. Mon père joue au golf.
■ **a golf club** un club de golf

golf course NOUN
le terrain de golf

gone VERB ▷ see go

good ADJECTIVE
1 bon (FEM bonne)
□ It's a very good film. C'est un très bon

401

film. □ Vegetables are good for you. Les
légumes sont bons pour la santé.

■ **to be good at something** être bon en
quelque chose □ Jane's very good at maths.
Jane est très bonne en maths.

> **WORD POWER**
>
> You can use a number of other words
> instead of **good** to mean 'great':
> **excellent** excellent
> □ an excellent book un livre excellent
> **fantastic** fantastique
> □ fantastic weather un temps fantastique
> **great** génial
> □ a great film un film génial
> **super** formidable
> □ a super idea une idée formidable

2 gentil (FEM gentille) *(kind)*
□ They were very good to me. Ils ont été très
gentils avec moi. □ That's very good of you.
C'est très gentil de votre part.

3 sage (FEM sage) *(not naughty)*
□ Be good! Sois sage!

■ **for good** pour de bon □ One day he left
for good. Un jour il est parti pour de bon.

■ **Good morning!** Bonjour!

■ **Good afternoon!** Bonjour!

■ **Good evening!** Bonsoir!

■ **Good night!** Bonne nuit!

■ **It's no good complaining.** Cela ne sert à
rien de se plaindre.

goodbye EXCLAMATION
au revoir!

Good Friday NOUN
le Vendredi saint

good-looking ADJECTIVE
beau (FEM belle, MASC PL beaux)
□ He's very good-looking. Il est très beau.

> **LANGUAGE TIP** beau changes to **bel**
> before a vowel and most words
> beginning with 'h'.

good-natured ADJECTIVE
facile à vivre (FEM facile à vivre) *(person)*

goods PL NOUN
les marchandises *fem pl (in shop)*

■ **a goods train** un train de marchandises

to **Google**® VERB
googler

goose NOUN
l' oie *fem*

gooseberry NOUN
la groseille à maquereau

gorgeous ADJECTIVE
1 superbe (FEM superbe)
□ She's gorgeous! Elle est superbe!

2 splendide (FEM splendide)

□ The weather was gorgeous. Il a fait un
temps splendide.

gorilla NOUN
le gorille

gospel NOUN
le gospel *(music)*

gossip NOUN
▷ *see also* **gossip** VERB
1 les cancans *masc pl (rumours)*
□ Tell me the gossip! Raconte-moi les
cancans!

2 la commère *(woman)*
□ She's such a gossip! C'est une vraie
commère!

3 le bavard *(man)*
□ What a gossip! Quel bavard!

to **gossip** VERB
▷ *see also* **gossip** NOUN
1 bavarder *(chat)*
□ They were always gossiping. Elles étaient
tout le temps en train de bavarder.

2 faire des commérages *(about somebody)*
□ They gossiped about her. Elles faisaient
des commérages à son sujet.

got VERB ▷ *see* **get**

gotten VERB (US) ▷ *see* **get**

government NOUN
le gouvernement

GP NOUN
le médecin généraliste

GPS NOUN
le GPS

to **grab** VERB
saisir

graceful ADJECTIVE
élégant (FEM élégante)

grade NOUN
la note *(at school)*
□ He got good grades in his exams. Il a eu
de bonnes notes à ses examens.

grade school NOUN (US)
l' école primaire *fem*

gradual ADJECTIVE
progressif (FEM progressive)

gradually ADVERB
peu à peu
□ We gradually got used to it. Nous nous y
sommes habitués peu à peu.

graduate NOUN
1 le diplômé
la diplômée *(from university)*

2 le bachelier
la bachelière *(from US high school)*

graffiti PL NOUN
les graffiti *masc pl*

grain NOUN
le grain

gram NOUN
le gramme

grammar NOUN
la grammaire

grammar school NOUN
1 le collège
2 le lycée

> **DID YOU KNOW...?**
> In France pupils go to a **collège** between the ages of 11 and 15, and then to a **lycée** until the age of 18. French schools are mostly non-selective.

grammatical ADJECTIVE
grammatical (FEM grammaticale, MASC PL grammaticaux)

gramme NOUN
le gramme
□ 500 grammes of cheese cinq cents grammes de fromage

grand ADJECTIVE
somptueux (FEM somptueuse)
□ Samantha lives in a very grand house. Samantha habite une maison somptueuse.

grandchild NOUN
le petit-fils
la petite-fille
■ my grandchildren mes petits-enfants *masc pl*

granddad NOUN
le papi
□ my granddad mon papi

granddaughter NOUN
la petite-fille (PL les petites-filles)

grandfather NOUN
le grand-père (PL les grands-pères)
□ my grandfather mon grand-père

grandma NOUN
la mamie
□ my grandma ma mamie

grandmother NOUN
la grand-mère (PL les grands-mères)
□ my grandmother ma grand-mère

grandpa NOUN
le papi
□ my grandpa mon papi

grandparents PL NOUN
les grands-parents *masc pl*
□ my grandparents mes grands-parents

grandson NOUN
le petit-fils (PL les petits-fils)

granny NOUN
la mamie
□ my granny ma mamie

grant NOUN
la bourse

grape NOUN
le raisin

grapefruit NOUN
le pamplemousse

graph NOUN
le graphique

graphics PL NOUN
les images de synthèse *fem pl*
□ I designed the graphics, she wrote the text. J'ai conçu les images de synthèse, elle a écrit le texte.
■ **He works in computer graphics.** Il fait de l'infographie.

to **grasp** VERB
saisir

grass NOUN
l' herbe *fem*
□ The grass is long. L'herbe est haute.
■ **to cut the grass** tondre le gazon

grasshopper NOUN
la sauterelle

to **grate** VERB
râper
□ to grate some cheese râper du fromage

grateful ADJECTIVE
reconnaissant (FEM reconnaissante)

grave NOUN
la tombe

gravel NOUN
le gravier

graveyard NOUN
le cimetière

gravy NOUN
la sauce au jus de viande

grease NOUN
le lubrifiant

greasy ADJECTIVE
gras (FEM grasse)
□ He has greasy hair. Il a les cheveux gras.
□ The food was very greasy. la nourriture était très grasse.

great ADJECTIVE
1 génial (FEM géniale, MASC PL géniaux)
□ That's great! C'est génial!

> **WORD POWER**
> You can use a number of other words instead of **great** to mean 'good':
> **amazing** extraordinaire
> □ an amazing view une vue extraordinaire
> **fabulous** formidable
> □ a fabulous idea une idée formidable
> **terrific** super
> □ a terrific party une super fête
> **wonderful** formidable
> □ a wonderful opportunity une occasion formidable

g

2 grand (FEM grande)
- □ a great mansion un grand manoir

Great Britain NOUN
la Grande-Bretagne
- ■ **in Great Britain** en Grande-Bretagne
- ■ **to Great Britain** en Grande-Bretagne
- ■ **I'm from Great Britain.** Je suis britannique.

great-grandfather NOUN
l' arrière-grand-père *masc* (PL les arrière-grands-pères)

great-grandmother NOUN
l' arrière-grand-mère *fem* (PL les arrière-grands-mères)

Greece NOUN
la Grèce
- ■ **in Greece** en Grèce
- ■ **to Greece** en Grèce

greedy ADJECTIVE
1 gourmand (FEM gourmande) *(for food)*
- □ I want some more cake. — Don't be so greedy! Je veux encore du gâteau. — Ne sois pas si gourmand!
2 avide (FEM avide) *(for money)*

Greek NOUN
▷ *see also* **Greek** ADJECTIVE
1 le Grec
la Grecque *(person)*
2 le grec *(language)*

Greek ADJECTIVE
▷ *see also* **Greek** NOUN
grec (FEM grecque)
- □ Dionysis is Greek. Dionysis est grec.
- □ She's Greek. Elle est grecque.

green ADJECTIVE
▷ *see also* **green** NOUN
1 vert (FEM verte)
- □ a green car une voiture verte □ a green light un feu vert □ a green salad une salade verte
2 écologiste (FEM écologiste) *(movement, candidate)*
- □ the Green Party le parti écologiste
- ■ **green beans** les haricots verts *masc pl*

green NOUN
▷ *see also* **green** ADJECTIVE
le vert
- □ a dark green un vert foncé
- ■ **greens** *(vegetables)* les légumes verts *masc pl*
- ■ **the Greens** *(party)* les Verts *masc pl*

greengrocer's NOUN
le marchand de fruits et légumes

greenhouse NOUN
la serre
- ■ **the greenhouse effect** l'effet de serre *masc*

Greenland NOUN
le Groenland

to greet VERB
accueillir
- □ He greeted me with a kiss. Il m'a accueillie en me donnant un baiser.

greeting NOUN
- ■ **Greetings from Bangor!** Bonjour de Bangor!
- ■ **'Season's greetings'** 'Meilleurs vœux pour les fêtes de fin d'année'

greetings card NOUN
la carte de vœux

grew VERB ▷ *see* **grow**

grey ADJECTIVE
gris (FEM grise)
- □ She's got grey hair. Elle a les cheveux gris.
- ■ **He's going grey.** Il grisonne.

grey-haired ADJECTIVE
grisonnant (FEM grisonnante)

grid NOUN
1 la grille *(in road)*
2 le réseau (PL les réseaux) *(of electricity)*

grief NOUN
le chagrin

grill NOUN
▷ *see also* **grill** VERB
le gril *(of cooker)*
- ■ **a mixed grill** un assortiment de grillades

to grill VERB
▷ *see also* **grill** NOUN
- ■ **to grill something** faire griller quelque chose

grim ADJECTIVE
sinistre (FEM sinistre)

to grin VERB
▷ *see also* **grin** NOUN
sourire
- □ Dave grinned at me. Dave m'a souri.

grin NOUN
▷ *see also* **grin** VERB
le large sourire

to grind VERB
moudre *(coffee, pepper)*

to grip VERB
saisir

gripping ADJECTIVE
palpitant (FEM palpitante) *(exciting)*

grit NOUN
le gravillon

to groan VERB
▷ *see also* **groan** NOUN
gémir
- □ He groaned with pain. Il a gémi sous l'effet de la douleur.

groan NOUN
▷ *see also* **groan** VERB

le gémissement *(of pain)*

grocer NOUN
l' épicier *masc*
□ He's a grocer. Il est épicier.

groceries PL NOUN
les provisions *fem pl*

grocer's NOUN
l' épicerie *fem*

grocer's shop NOUN
l' épicerie *fem*

grocery store NOUN (US)
l' épicerie *fem*

groom NOUN
le marié *(bridegroom)*
□ the groom and his best man le marié et son témoin

to **grope** VERB
■ **to grope for something** chercher quelque chose à tâtons □ He groped for the light switch. Il a cherché à tâtons l'interrupteur.

gross ADJECTIVE
dégoûtant *(FEM dégoûtante) (revolting)*
□ It was really gross! C'était vraiment dégoûtant!

grossly ADVERB
largement
□ We're grossly underpaid. Nous sommes largement sous-payés.

ground NOUN
▷ *see also* **ground** VERB
1 le sol *(earth)*
□ The ground's wet. Le sol est mouillé.
2 le terrain *(for sport)*
□ a football ground un terrain de football
3 la raison *(reason)*
□ We've got grounds for complaint. Nous avons des raisons de nous plaindre.
■ **on the ground** par terre □ We sat on the ground. Nous nous sommes assis par terre.

ground VERB ▷ *see* **grind**
▷ *see also* **ground** NOUN
■ **ground coffee** le café moulu

ground floor NOUN
le rez-de-chaussée
■ **on the ground floor** au rez-de-chaussée

group NOUN
le groupe

to **grow** VERB
1 pousser *(plant)*
□ Grass grows quickly. L'herbe pousse vite.
2 grandir *(person, animal)*
□ Haven't you grown! Comme tu as grandi!
3 augmenter *(increase)*
□ The number of unemployed people has grown. Le nombre de chômeurs a augmenté.

4 faire pousser *(cultivate)*
□ My Dad grows potatoes. Mon père fait pousser des pommes de terre.
■ **to grow a beard** se laisser pousser la barbe
■ **He's grown out of his jacket.** Sa veste est devenue trop petite pour lui.

to **grow up** VERB
grandir
□ Oh, grow up! Ne fais pas l'enfant!

to **growl** VERB
grogner

grown VERB ▷ *see* **grow**

growth NOUN
la croissance
□ economic growth la croissance économique

grub NOUN
la bouffe *(informal)*

grudge NOUN
la rancune
■ **to bear a grudge against somebody** garder rancune à quelqu'un

gruesome ADJECTIVE
horrible *(FEM horrible)*

guarantee NOUN
▷ *see also* **guarantee** VERB
la garantie
■ **a five-year guarantee** une garantie de cinq ans

to **guarantee** VERB
▷ *see also* **guarantee** NOUN
garantir
□ I can't guarantee he'll come. Je ne peux pas garantir qu'il viendra.

to **guard** VERB
▷ *see also* **guard** NOUN
garder
□ They guarded the palace. Ils gardaient le palais.
■ **to guard against something** protéger contre quelque chose

guard NOUN
▷ *see also* **guard** VERB
le chef de train *(of train)*
■ **a security guard** un vigile
■ **a guard dog** un chien de garde

to **guess** VERB
▷ *see also* **guess** NOUN
deviner
□ Guess what this is? Devine ce que c'est!
■ **to guess wrong** se tromper □ Janice guessed wrong. Janice s'est trompée.

guess NOUN
▷ *see also* **guess** VERB
la supposition
□ It's just a guess. C'est une simple

supposition.
- **Have a guess!** Devine!

guest NOUN
1 l' invité masc
l' invitée fem
□ We have guests staying with us. Nous
avons des invités.
2 le client
la cliente (of hotel)

guesthouse NOUN
le petit hôtel

guide NOUN
1 le guide (book, person)
□ We bought a guide to Paris. Nous avons
acheté un guide sur Paris. □ The guide
showed us round the castle. Le guide nous
a fait visiter le château.
2 l' éclaireuse fem (girl guide)
- **the Guides** les Éclaireuses

guidebook NOUN
le guide

guide dog NOUN
le chien d'aveugle

guilty ADJECTIVE
coupable (FEM coupable)
□ to feel guilty se sentir coupable □ She
was found guilty. Elle a été reconnue
coupable.

guinea pig NOUN
le cobaye

guitar NOUN
la guitare
□ I play the guitar. Je joue de la guitare.

gum NOUN
le chewing-gum (sweet)
- **gums** (in mouth) les gencives fem pl

gun NOUN
1 le revolver (small)
2 le fusil (rifle)

gunpoint NOUN
- **at gunpoint** sous la menace d'une
arme

gust NOUN
- **a gust of wind** une rafale de vent

guy NOUN
le type
□ Who's that guy? C'est qui ce type? □ He's
a nice guy. C'est un type sympa.

gym NOUN
la gym
□ I go to the gym every day. Je vais tous les
jours à la gym.
- **gym classes** les cours de gym masc pl

gymnast NOUN
le/la gymnaste
□ She's a gymnast. Elle est gymnaste.

gymnastics NOUN
la gymnastique
□ to do gymnastics faire de la gymnastique

gypsy NOUN
le Tzigane
la Tzigane

Hh

habit NOUN
l' habitude *fem*
□ a bad habit une mauvaise habitude
to **hack** VERB
■ **to hack into a system** s'introduire dans un système
hacker NOUN
le/la pirate informatique
had VERB ▷ *see* **have**
haddock NOUN
l' églefin *masc*
hadn't = had not
hail NOUN
▷ *see also* **hail** VERB
la grêle
to **hail** VERB
▷ *see also* **hail** NOUN
grêler
□ It's hailing. Il grêle.
hair NOUN
1 les cheveux *masc pl*
□ She's got long hair. Elle a les cheveux longs. □ He's got black hair. Il a les cheveux noirs. □ He's losing his hair. Il perd ses cheveux.
■ **to brush one's hair** se brosser les cheveux □ I'm brushing my hair. Je me brosse les cheveux.
■ **to wash one's hair** se laver les cheveux □ I need to wash my hair. Il faut que je me lave les cheveux.
■ **to have one's hair cut** se faire couper les cheveux □ I've just had my hair cut. Je viens de me faire couper les cheveux.
■ **a hair 1** *(from head)* un cheveu **2** *(from body)* un poil
2 le pelage *(fur of animal)*
hairbrush NOUN
la brosse à cheveux
haircut NOUN
la coupe
■ **to have a haircut** se faire couper les cheveux □ I've just had a haircut. Je viens de me faire couper les cheveux.
hairdresser NOUN

le coiffeur
la coiffeuse
□ He's a hairdresser. Il est coiffeur.
hairdresser's NOUN
le coiffeur
□ at the hairdresser's chez le coiffeur
hair dryer NOUN
le sèche-cheveux (PL les sèche-cheveux)
hair gel NOUN
le gel pour les cheveux
hairgrip NOUN
la pince à cheveux
hair spray NOUN
la laque
hairstyle NOUN
la coiffure
hairy ADJECTIVE
poilu (FEM poilue)
□ He's got hairy legs. Il a les jambes poilues.
half NOUN
▷ *see also* **half** ADJECTIVE
1 la moitié
□ half of the cake la moitié du gâteau
2 le billet demi-tarif *(ticket)*
□ A half to York, please. Un billet demi-tarif pour York, s'il vous plaît.
■ **two and a half** deux et demi
■ **half an hour** une demi-heure
■ **half past ten** dix heures et demie
■ **half a kilo** cinq cents grammes
■ **to cut something in half** couper quelque chose en deux
half ADJECTIVE, ADVERB
▷ *see also* **half** NOUN
1 demi (FEM demie)
□ a half chicken un demi-poulet
2 à moitié
□ He was half asleep. Il était à moitié endormi.
half-brother NOUN
le demi-frère (PL les demi-frères)
half-hour NOUN
la demi-heure
half-price ADJECTIVE, ADVERB
■ **at half-price** à moitié prix

h

half-sister – handy

half-sister NOUN
la demi-sœur (PL les demi-sœurs)

half-term NOUN
les petites vacances *fem pl*

> **DID YOU KNOW...?**
> There are two half-term holidays in France: **les vacances de la Toussaint** (in October/November) and **les vacances de février** (in February).

half-time NOUN
la mi-temps

halfway ADVERB
1 à mi-chemin
□ halfway between Oxford and London à mi-chemin entre Oxford et Londres
2 à la moitié
□ halfway through the chapter à la moitié du chapitre

hall NOUN
1 l' entrée *fem (in house)*
2 la salle
□ the village hall la salle des fêtes

Hallowe'en NOUN
la veille de la Toussaint

> **DID YOU KNOW...?**
> The French do not traditionally celebrate Hallowe'en (although it is starting to become more popular). The next day, All Saints' Day (November 1st), is a public holiday, and is the day when people often visit family graves.

hallway NOUN
le vestibule

halt NOUN
■ **to come to a halt** s'arrêter □ The train came to a halt at the station. Le train s'est arrêté dans la gare.

ham NOUN
le jambon
□ a ham sandwich un sandwich au jambon

hamburger NOUN
le hamburger

hammer NOUN
le marteau (PL les marteaux)

hamster NOUN
le hamster

hand NOUN
▷ *see also* **hand** VERB
1 la main *(of person)*
■ **to give somebody a hand** donner un coup de main à quelqu'un □ Can you give me a hand? Tu peux me donner un coup de main?
■ **on the one hand ..., on the other hand ...** d'une part ..., d'autre part ...
2 l' aiguille *fem (of clock)*

to **hand** VERB
▷ *see also* **hand** NOUN
passer
□ He handed me the book. Il m'a passé le livre.
■ **to hand something in** rendre quelque chose □ He handed his exam paper in. Il a rendu sa copie d'examen.
■ **to hand something out** distribuer quelque chose □ The teacher handed out the books. Le professeur a distribué les livres.
■ **to hand something over** remettre quelque chose □ She handed the keys over to me. Elle m'a remis les clés.

handbag NOUN
le sac à main

handball NOUN
le handball *(game)*
■ **to play handball** jouer au handball

handbook NOUN
le manuel

handcuffs PL NOUN
les menottes *fem pl*

handkerchief NOUN
le mouchoir

handle NOUN
▷ *see also* **handle** VERB
1 la poignée *(of door)*
2 l' anse *fem (of cup)*
3 le manche *(of knife)*
4 la queue *(of saucepan)*

to **handle** VERB
▷ *see also* **handle** NOUN
■ **He handled it well.** Il s'en est bien tiré.
■ **Kath handled the travel arrangements.** Kath s'est occupée de l'organisation du voyage.
■ **She's good at handling children.** Elle sait bien s'y prendre avec les enfants.

handlebars PL NOUN
le guidon *sing*

handmade ADJECTIVE
fait à la main (FEM faite à la main)

hands-free kit NOUN
le kit mains libres *(phone)*

handsome ADJECTIVE
beau (FEM belle, MASC PL beaux)
□ He's handsome. Il est beau.

> **LANGUAGE TIP** beau changes to **bel** after a vowel and most words beginning with 'h'.

handwriting NOUN
l' écriture *fem*

handy ADJECTIVE
1 pratique (FEM pratique)
□ This knife's very handy. Ce couteau est

très pratique.

2 sous la main

□ Have you got a pen handy? Est-ce que tu as un stylo sous la main?

to **hang** VERB

1 accrocher

□ Mike hung the painting on the wall. Mike a accroché le tableau au mur.

2 pendre

□ They hanged the criminal. Ils ont pendu le criminel.

to **hang around** VERB

traîner

□ On Saturdays we hang around in the park. Le samedi nous traînons dans le parc.

to **hang on** VERB

patienter

□ Hang on a minute please. Patientez une minute s'il vous plaît.

to **hang up** VERB

1 accrocher (clothes)

□ Hang your jacket up on the hook. Accrochez votre veste au portemanteau.

2 raccrocher (phone)

□ Don't hang up! Ne raccroche pas!

■ **to hang up on someone** raccrocher au nez de quelqu'un □ He always hangs up on me. Il me raccroche toujours au nez.

hanger NOUN

le cintre (coat hanger)

hang-gliding NOUN

le deltaplane

■ **to go hang-gliding** faire du deltaplane

hangover NOUN

la gueule de bois

□ I've got a terrible hangover. J'ai une gueule de bois terrible.

to **happen** VERB

se passer

□ What's happened? Qu'est-ce qui s'est passé?

■ **as it happens** justement □ As it happens, I don't want to go. Justement, je ne veux pas y aller.

happily ADVERB

1 joyeusement

□ 'Don't worry!' he said happily. 'Ne te fais pas de souci!' dit-il joyeusement.

2 heureusement (fortunately)

□ Happily, everything went well. Heureusement, tout s'est bien passé.

happiness NOUN

le bonheur

happy ADJECTIVE

heureux (FEM heureuse)

□ Janet looks happy. Janet a l'air heureuse.

■ **I'm very happy with your work.** Je suis

très satisfait de ton travail.

■ **Happy birthday!** Bon anniversaire!

WORD POWER

You can use a number of other words instead of **happy** to mean 'glad':

cheerful gai

□ a cheerful song une chanson gaie

delighted ravi

□ a delighted smile un sourire ravi

glad content

□ to be glad être content

satisfied satisfait

□ a satisfied customer un client satisfait

---

harassment NOUN

le harcèlement

□ police harassment le harcèlement policier

harbour (US **harbor**) NOUN

le port

hard ADJECTIVE, ADVERB

1 dur (FEM dure)

□ This cheese is very hard. Ce fromage est très dur. □ He's worked very hard. Il a travaillé très dur.

2 difficile (FEM difficile)

□ This question's too hard for me. Cette question est trop difficile pour moi.

hard disk NOUN

le disque dur (of computer)

hardly ADVERB

■ **I've hardly got any money.** Je n'ai presque pas d'argent.

■ **I hardly know you.** Je te connais à peine.

■ **hardly ever** presque jamais

hard up ADJECTIVE

fauché (FEM fauchée)

hardware NOUN

le hardware (computing)

hare NOUN

le lièvre

to **harm** VERB

■ **to harm somebody** faire du mal à quelqu'un □ I didn't mean to harm you. Je ne voulais pas te faire de mal.

■ **to harm something** nuire à quelque chose □ Chemicals harm the environment. Les produits chimiques nuisent à l'environnement.

harmful ADJECTIVE

nuisible (FEM nuisible)

□ harmful chemicals des produits chimiques nuisibles

harmless ADJECTIVE

inoffensif (FEM inoffensive)

□ Most spiders are harmless. La plupart des araignées sont inoffensives.

h

harsh ADJECTIVE
  dur (FEM dure)

has VERB ▷see **have**

hasn't = has not

hat NOUN
  le chapeau (PL les chapeaux)

to **hate** VERB
  détester
    □ I hate maths. Je déteste les maths.

hatred NOUN
  la haine

haunted ADJECTIVE
  hanté (FEM hantée)
    □ a haunted house une maison hantée

to **have** VERB
1 avoir
    □ Have you got a sister? Tu as une sœur?
    □ He's got blue eyes. Il a les yeux bleus.
    □ I've got a cold. J'ai un rhume. □ He's done
    it, hasn't he? Il l'a fait, non? □ Have you got
    any money? — No, I haven't! Est-ce que tu
    as de l'argent? — Non, je n'en ai pas!
2 être
    LANGUAGE TIP The perfect tense of
    some verbs is formed with **être**.
    □ They have arrived. Ils sont arrivés. □ Has
    he gone? Est-ce qu'il est parti?
3 prendre
    □ He had his breakfast. Il a pris son petit
    déjeuner. □ to have a shower prendre une
    douche
    ■ **to have got to do something** devoir faire
    quelque chose □ She's got to do it. Elle doit
    le faire.
    ■ **to have a party** faire une fête
    ■ **to have one's hair cut** se faire couper les
    cheveux

haven't = have not

hay NOUN
  le foin

hay fever NOUN
  le rhume des foins
    □ Do you get hay fever? Est-ce que vous
    êtes sujet au rhume des foins?

hazelnut NOUN
  la noisette

he PRONOUN
  il
    □ He loves dogs. Il aime les chiens.

head NOUN
  ▷ see also **head** VERB
1 la tête (of person)
    □ The wine went to my head. Le vin m'est
    monté à la tête.
2 le directeur
  la directrice (of private or primary school)
3 le proviseur (of state secondary school)

4 le chef (leader)
    □ a head of state un chef d'État
    ■ **to have a head for figures** être doué
    pour les chiffres
    ■ **Heads or tails? — Heads.** Pile ou face?
    — Face.

to **head** VERB
    ▷ see also **head** NOUN
    ■ **to head for something** se diriger vers
    quelque chose □ They headed for the
    church. Ils se sont dirigés vers l'église.

headache NOUN
    ■ **I've got a headache.** J'ai mal à la tête.

headlight NOUN
  le phare

headline NOUN
  le titre

headmaster NOUN
1 le directeur (of private or primary school)
2 le proviseur (of state secondary school)

headmistress NOUN
1 la directrice (of private or primary school)
2 le proviseur (of state secondary school)

headphones PL NOUN
  les écouteurs masc pl

headquarters PL NOUN
  le siège sing (of organization)

headteacher NOUN
1 le directeur
  la directrice (of private or primary school)
2 le proviseur (of state secondary school)
    □ She's a headteacher. Elle est proviseur.

to **heal** VERB
  cicatriser
    □ The wound soon healed. La blessure a vite
    cicatrisé.

health NOUN
  la santé

healthy ADJECTIVE
1 en bonne santé (person)
    □ Lesley's a healthy person. Lesley est en
    bonne santé.
2 sain (FEM saine) (climate, food)
    □ a healthy diet une alimentation saine

heap NOUN
  le tas
    □ a rubbish heap un tas d'ordures

to **hear** VERB
1 entendre
    □ He heard the dog bark. Il a entendu le
    chien aboyer. □ She can't hear very well.
    Elle entend mal. □ I heard that she was ill.
    J'ai entendu dire qu'elle était malade.
    ■ **to hear about something** entendre
    parler de quelque chose
2 apprendre (news)
    □ Did you hear the good news? Est-ce que

tu as appris la bonne nouvelle?

■ **to hear from somebody** avoir des nouvelles de quelqu'un □ I haven't heard from him recently. Je n'ai pas eu de ses nouvelles récemment.

heart NOUN
le cœur
□ My heart's beating very fast. J'ai le cœur qui bat très fort.

■ **to learn something by heart** apprendre quelque chose par cœur
■ **the ace of hearts** l'as de cœur

heart attack NOUN
la crise cardiaque

heartbroken ADJECTIVE
■ **to be heartbroken** avoir le cœur brisé

heat NOUN
▷ see also **heat** VERB
la chaleur

to **heat** VERB
▷ see also **heat** NOUN
faire chauffer
□ Heat gently for 5 minutes. Faire chauffer à feu doux pendant cinq minutes.

to **heat up** VERB
1 faire réchauffer (cooked food)
□ He heated the soup up. Il a fait réchauffer la soupe.
2 chauffer (water, oven)
□ The water is heating up. L'eau chauffe.

heater NOUN
le radiateur
□ an electric heater un radiateur électrique

heather NOUN
la bruyère

heating NOUN
le chauffage

heaven NOUN
le paradis

heavily ADVERB
lourdement
□ The car was heavily loaded. La voiture était lourdement chargée.
■ **He drinks heavily.** C'est un gros buveur.

heavy ADJECTIVE
1 lourd (FEM lourde)
□ This bag's very heavy. Ce sac est très lourd.
■ **heavy rain** une grosse averse
2 chargé (FEM chargée) (busy)
□ I've got a very heavy week ahead. Je vais avoir une semaine très chargée.
■ **to be a heavy drinker** être un gros buveur

he'd = he would, he had

hedge NOUN
la haie

hedgehog NOUN
le hérisson

heel NOUN
le talon

height NOUN
1 la taille (of person)
2 la hauteur (of object)
3 l' altitude fem (of mountain)

heir NOUN
l' héritier masc

heiress NOUN
l' héritière fem

held VERB ▷ see **hold**

helicopter NOUN
l' hélicoptère masc

hell NOUN
l' enfer masc

he'll = he will, he shall

hello EXCLAMATION
bonjour!

helmet NOUN
le casque

to **help** VERB
▷ see also **help** NOUN
aider
□ Can you help me? Est-ce que vous pouvez m'aider?
■ **Help!** Au secours!
■ **Help yourself!** Servez-vous!
■ **He can't help it.** Il n'y peut rien.

help NOUN
▷ see also **help** VERB
l' aide fem
□ Do you need any help? Vous avez besoin d'aide?

helpful ADJECTIVE
serviable (FEM serviable)
□ He was very helpful. Il a été très serviable.

hen NOUN
la poule

her ADJECTIVE
▷ see also **her** PRONOUN
son masc
□ her father son père
sa fem
□ her mother sa mère
ses pl
□ her parents ses parents

⟨ LANGUAGE TIP **sa** becomes **son** before a vowel sound.

■ **her friend 1** (male) son ami **2** (female) son amie

⟨ LANGUAGE TIP Do not use **son/sa/ses** with parts of the body.

□ She's going to wash her hair. Elle va se laver les cheveux. □ She's cleaning her teeth. Elle se brosse les dents. □ She's hurt

411

h

her foot. Elle s'est fait mal au pied.

her PRONOUN

▷ see also **her** ADJECTIVE

1 la

□ I can see her. Je la vois. □ Look at her!
Regarde-la!

> **LANGUAGE TIP** la becomes l' before a
> vowel sound.

l'

□ I saw her. Je l'ai vue.

> **LANGUAGE TIP** Use lui when 'her'
> means 'to her'.

2 lui

□ I gave her a book. Je lui ai donné un livre.
□ I told her the truth. Je lui ai dit la vérité.

3 elle

> **LANGUAGE TIP** Use elle after
> prepositions.

□ I'm going with her. Je vais avec elle. □ He
sat next to her. Il s'est assis à côté d'elle.

> **LANGUAGE TIP** elle is also used in
> comparisons.

□ I'm older than her. Je suis plus âgé qu'elle.

herb NOUN

l' herbe fem

■ **herbs** les fines herbes fem pl □ What
herbs do you use in this sauce? Quelles
fines herbes utilise-t-on pour cette sauce?

here ADVERB

ici

□ I live here. J'habite ici.

■ **here is …** voici … □ Here's Helen. Voici
Helen. □ Here he is! Le voici!

■ **here are …** voici … □ Here are the books.
Voici les livres.

heritage NOUN

le patrimoine

hero NOUN

le héros

□ He's a real hero! C'est un véritable héros!

heroin NOUN

l' héroïne fem

□ Heroin is a hard drug. L'héroïne est une
drogue dure.

■ **a heroin addict** un héroïnomane
□ She's a heroin addict. C'est une
héroïnomane.

heroine NOUN

l' héroïne fem

□ the heroine of the novel l'héroïne du
roman

hers PRONOUN

le sien + masc noun

□ Is this her coat? — No, hers is black. C'est
son manteau? — Non, le sien est noir.
la sienne + fem noun

□ Is this her car? — No, hers is white. C'est

sa voiture? — Non, la sienne est blanche.
les siens + masc pl noun

□ my parents and hers mes parents et les
siens
les siennes + fem pl noun

□ my reasons and hers mes raisons et les
siennes

■ **Is this hers?** C'est à elle? □ This book is
hers. Ce livre est à elle. □ Whose is this? —
It's hers. C'est à qui? — À elle.

herself PRONOUN

1 se

□ She's hurt herself. Elle s'est blessée.

2 elle (after preposition)

□ She talked mainly about herself. Elle a
surtout parlé d'elle.

3 elle-même

□ She did it herself. Elle l'a fait elle-même.

■ **by herself** toute seule □ She doesn't like
travelling by herself. Elle n'aime pas voyager
toute seule.

he's = he is, he has

to **hesitate** VERB

hésiter

heterosexual ADJECTIVE

hétérosexuel (FEM hétérosexuelle)

hi EXCLAMATION

salut!

hiccups PL NOUN

■ **to have hiccups** avoir le hoquet

to **hide** VERB

se cacher

□ He hid behind a bush. Il s'est caché
derrière un buisson.

■ **to hide something** cacher quelque chose
□ Paula hid the present. Paula a caché le
cadeau.

hide-and-seek NOUN

■ **to play hide-and-seek** jouer à cache-
cache

hideous ADJECTIVE

hideux (FEM hideuse)

hi-fi NOUN

la chaîne hi-fi (PL les chaînes hi-fi)

high ADJECTIVE, ADVERB

1 haut (FEM haute)

□ It's too high. C'est trop haut.

■ **How high is the wall?** Quelle est la
hauteur du mur?

■ **The wall's 2 metres high.** Le mur fait
deux mètres de haut.

2 élevé (FEM élevée)

□ a high price un prix élevé □ a high
temperature une température élevée

■ **at high speed** à grande vitesse

■ **It's very high in fat.** C'est très gras.

■ **She's got a very high voice.** Elle a la voix

h

très aiguë.

■ **to be high** *(on drugs)* être défoncé *(informal)*

■ **to get high** se défoncer *(informal)* □ to get high on crack se défoncer au crack

higher education NOUN
l' enseignement supérieur *masc*

high-heeled ADJECTIVE
à hauts talons

□ high-heeled shoes des chaussures à hauts talons

high jump NOUN
le saut en hauteur *(sport)*

highlight NOUN
▷ *see also* **highlight** VERB
le clou

□ the highlight of the evening le clou de la soirée

to **highlight** VERB
▷ *see also* **highlight** NOUN
1 souligner *(underline)*
2 surligner *(with highlighter pen)*

highlighter NOUN
le surligneur

high-rise NOUN
la tour

□ I live in a high-rise. J'habite dans une tour.

high school NOUN
1 le collège
2 le lycée

> **DID YOU KNOW...?**
> In France pupils go to a **collège** between the ages of 11 and 15, then to a **lycée** until the age of 18.

to **hijack** VERB
détourner

hijacker NOUN
le pirate de l'air

hike NOUN
la randonnée

hiking NOUN
■ **to go hiking** faire une randonnée

hilarious ADJECTIVE
hilarant *(FEM* hilarante*)*

□ It was hilarious! C'était hilarant!

hill NOUN
la colline

□ She walked up the hill. Elle a gravi la colline.

hill-walking NOUN
la randonnée de basse montagne

□ to go hill-walking faire de la randonnée de basse montagne

him PRONOUN
1 le

□ I can see him. Je le vois. □ Look at him! Regarde-le!

> **LANGUAGE TIP** le becomes l' before a vowel sound.

l'
□ I saw him. Je l'ai vu.
2 lui

> **LANGUAGE TIP** Use lui when 'him' means 'to him', and after prepositions.

□ I gave him a book. Je lui ai donné un livre. □ I told him the truth. Je lui ai dit la vérité. □ I'm going with him. Je vais avec lui. □ She sat next to him. Elle s'est assise à côté de lui.

> **LANGUAGE TIP** lui is also used in comparisons.

□ I'm older than him. Je suis plus âgé que lui.

himself PRONOUN
1 se
□ He's hurt himself. Il s'est blessé.
2 lui
□ He talked mainly about himself. Il a surtout parlé de lui.
3 lui-même
□ He did it himself. Il l'a fait lui-même.
■ **by himself** tout seul □ He was travelling by himself. Il voyageait tout seul.

Hindu ADJECTIVE
hindou *(FEM* hindoue*)*
□ a Hindu temple un temple hindou

hint NOUN
▷ *see also* **hint** VERB
l' allusion *fem*
■ **to drop a hint** faire une allusion

to **hint** VERB
▷ *see also* **hint** NOUN
laisser entendre
□ He hinted that something was going on. Il a laissé entendre qu'il se passait quelque chose.
■ **What are you hinting at?** Qu'est-ce que vous voulez dire par là ?

hip NOUN
la hanche

hippie NOUN
le hippie
la hippie

hippo NOUN
l' hippopotame *masc*

to **hire** VERB
▷ *see also* **hire** NOUN
1 louer
□ to hire a car louer une voiture
2 engager *(person)*
□ They hired a cleaner. Ils ont engagé une femme de ménage.

hire NOUN

▷ *see also* **hire** VERB
la location
■ **car hire** location de voitures
■ **for hire** à louer

hire car NOUN
la voiture de location

his ADJECTIVE
▷ *see also* **his** PRONOUN
son *masc*
□ his father son père
sa *fem*
□ his mother sa mère
ses *pl*
□ his parents ses parents

> **LANGUAGE TIP** **sa** becomes **son** before a vowel sound.

■ **his friend 1** *(male)* son ami **2** *(female)* son amie

> **LANGUAGE TIP** Do not use **son/sa/ses** with parts of the body.

□ He's going to wash his hair. Il va se laver les cheveux. □ He's cleaning his teeth. Il se brosse les dents. □ He's hurt his foot. Il s'est fait mal au pied.

his PRONOUN
▷ *see also* **his** ADJECTIVE
le sien + *masc noun*
□ Is this his coat? — No, his is black. C'est son manteau? — Non, le sien est noir.
la sienne + *fem noun*
□ Is this his car? — No, his is white. C'est sa voiture? — Non, la sienne est blanche.
les siens + *masc pl noun*
□ my parents and his mes parents et les siens
les siennes + *fem pl noun*
□ my reasons and his mes raisons et les siennes

■ **Is this his?** C'est à lui? □ This book is his. Ce livre est à lui. □ Whose is this? — It's his. C'est à qui? — À lui.

history NOUN
l' histoire *fem*

to **hit** VERB
▷ *see also* **hit** NOUN
1 frapper
□ Andrew hit him. Andrew l'a frappé.
2 renverser
□ He was hit by a car. Il a été renversé par une voiture.
3 toucher
□ The arrow hit the target. La flèche a touché la cible.

■ **to hit it off with somebody** bien s'entendre avec quelqu'un □ She hit it off with his parents. Elle s'est bien entendue avec ses parents.

hit NOUN
▷ *see also* **hit** VERB
1 le tube *(song)*
□ Madonna's latest hit le dernier tube de Madonna
2 le succès *(success)*
□ The film was a massive hit. Le film a eu un immense succès.

hitch NOUN
le contretemps
□ There's been a slight hitch. Il y a eu un léger contretemps.

to **hitchhike** VERB
faire de l'auto-stop

hitchhiker NOUN
l' auto-stoppeur *masc*
l' auto-stoppeuse *fem*

hitchhiking NOUN
l' auto-stop *masc*
□ Hitchhiking can be dangerous. Il peut être dangereux de faire de l'auto-stop.

hit man NOUN
le tueur à gages

HIV-negative ADJECTIVE
séronégatif (FEM séronégative)

HIV-positive ADJECTIVE
séropositif (FEM séropositive)

hobby NOUN
le passe-temps favori
□ What are your hobbies? Quels sont tes passe-temps favoris?

hockey NOUN
le hockey
□ I play hockey. Je joue au hockey.

to **hold** VERB
1 tenir *(hold on to)*
□ She held the baby. Elle tenait le bébé.
2 contenir *(contain)*
□ This bottle holds one litre. Cette bouteille contient un litre.

■ **to hold a meeting** avoir une réunion
■ **Hold the line!** *(on telephone)* Ne quittez pas!
■ **Hold it!** *(wait)* Attends!
■ **to get hold of something** *(obtain)* trouver quelque chose □ I couldn't get hold of it. Je n'ai pas réussi à en trouver.

to **hold on** VERB
1 tenir bon *(keep hold)*
□ Hold on! I'll help you get down. Tiens bon! Je vais t'aider à descendre.

■ **to hold on to something** se cramponner à quelque chose □ He held on to the chair. Il se cramponnait à la chaise.
2 attendre *(wait)*
□ Hold on, I'm coming! Attends, je viens!
■ **Hold on!** *(on telephone)* Ne quittez pas!

h

to **hold up** VERB
- **to hold up one's hand** lever la main
□ Pierre held up his hand. Pierre a levé la main.
- **to hold somebody up** (delay) retenir quelqu'un □ I was held up at the office. J'ai été retenu au bureau.
- **to hold up a bank** (rob) braquer une banque (informal)

hold-up NOUN
1 le hold-up (at bank)
2 le retard (delay)
3 le bouchon (traffic jam)

hole NOUN
le trou

holiday NOUN
1 les vacances fem pl
□ Did you have a good holiday? Tu as passé de bonnes vacances? □ our holidays in France nos vacances en France
- **on holiday** en vacances □ to go on holiday partir en vacances □ We are on holiday. Nous sommes en vacances.
- **the school holidays** les vacances scolaires
2 le jour férié (public holiday)
□ Next Wednesday is a holiday. Mercredi prochain est un jour férié.
3 le jour de congé (day off)
□ He took a day's holiday. Il a pris un jour de congé.
- **a holiday camp** un camp de vacances

holiday home NOUN
la maison de vacances

Holland NOUN
la Hollande
- **in Holland** en Hollande
- **to Holland** en Hollande

hollow ADJECTIVE
creux (FEM creuse)

holly NOUN
le houx
□ a sprig of holly un brin de houx

holy ADJECTIVE
saint (FEM sainte)

home NOUN
▷ see also **home** ADVERB
la maison
- **at home** à la maison
- **Make yourself at home.** Faites comme chez vous.
- **My aunt's at home from 5 p.m.** Ma tante est chez elle à partir de cinq heures.

home ADVERB
▷ see also **home** NOUN
à la maison
□ I'll be home at 5 o'clock. Je serai à la

maison à cinq heures.
- **to get home** rentrer □ What time did he get home? Il est rentré à quelle heure?

home address NOUN
l' adresse fem
□ What's your home address? Quelle est votre adresse?

homeland NOUN
la patrie

homeless ADJECTIVE
sans abri
- **the homeless** les sans-abri

home match NOUN
le match à domicile

homeopathy NOUN
l' homéopathie fem

home page NOUN
la page d'accueil

homesick ADJECTIVE
- **to be homesick** avoir le mal du pays

homework NOUN
les devoirs masc pl
□ Have you done your homework? Est-ce que tu as fait tes devoirs? □ my geography homework mes devoirs de géographie

homosexual ADJECTIVE
▷ see also **homosexual** NOUN
homosexuel (FEM homosexuelle)

homosexual NOUN
▷ see also **homosexual** ADJECTIVE
l' homosexuel masc
l' homosexuelle fem

honest ADJECTIVE
1 honnête (FEM honnête) (trustworthy)
□ She's a very honest person. Elle est très honnête.
2 franc (FEM franche) (sincere)
□ He was very honest with her. Il a été très franc avec elle.

honestly ADVERB
franchement
□ I honestly don't know. Franchement, je n'en sais rien.

honesty NOUN
l' honnêteté fem

honey NOUN
le miel

honeymoon NOUN
la lune de miel

honour (US honor) NOUN
l' honneur masc

hood NOUN
1 la capuche (on coat)
2 le capot (US: of car)

hook NOUN
le crochet
□ He hung the painting on the hook. Il a

suspendu le tableau au crochet.

■ **to take the phone off the hook** décrocher le téléphone

■ **a fish-hook** un hameçon

hooligan NOUN
le voyou (PL les voyoux)

hooray EXCLAMATION
hourra!

Hoover® NOUN
l' aspirateur *masc*

to **hoover** VERB
passer l'aspirateur
□ to hoover the lounge passer l'aspirateur dans le salon

to **hope** VERB
▷ *see also* **hope** NOUN
espérer
□ I hope he comes. J'espère qu'il va venir.
□ I'm hoping for good results. J'espère avoir de bons résultats.
■ **I hope so.** Je l'espère.
■ **I hope not.** J'espère que non.

hope NOUN
▷ *see also* **hope** VERB
l' espoir *masc*
■ **to give up hope** perdre espoir □ Don't give up hope! Ne perds pas espoir!

hopeful ADJECTIVE
1 plein d'espoir (FEM pleine d'espoir)
□ I'm hopeful. Je suis plein d'espoir.
■ **He's hopeful of winning.** Il a bon espoir de gagner.
2 prometteur (FEM prometteuse) *(situation)*
□ The prospects look hopeful. Les perspectives semblent prometteuses.

hopefully ADVERB
avec un peu de chance
□ Hopefully he'll make it in time. Avec un peu de chance, il arrivera à temps.

hopeless ADJECTIVE
nul (FEM nulle)
□ I'm hopeless at maths. Je suis nul en maths.

horizon NOUN
l' horizon *masc*

horizontal ADJECTIVE
horizontal (FEM horizontale, MASC PL horizontaux)

horn NOUN
1 le klaxon
□ He sounded his horn. Il a klaxonné.
2 le cor
□ I play the horn. Je joue du cor.

horoscope NOUN
l' horoscope *masc*

horrible ADJECTIVE
horrible (FEM horrible)

□ What a horrible dress! Quelle robe horrible!

horrifying ADJECTIVE
effrayant (FEM effrayante)

horror NOUN
l' horreur *fem*

horror film NOUN
le film d'horreur

horse NOUN
le cheval (PL les chevaux)

horse-racing NOUN
les courses de chevaux *fem pl*

horseshoe NOUN
le fer à cheval

hose NOUN
le tuyau (PL les tuyaux)
□ a garden hose un tuyau d'arrosage

hosepipe NOUN
le tuyau d'arrosage

hospital NOUN
l' hôpital *masc* (PL les hôpitaux)
□ Take me to the hospital! Emmenez-moi à l'hôpital! □ in hospital à l'hôpital

hospitality NOUN
l' hospitalité *fem*

host NOUN
l' hôte *masc*
l' hôtesse *fem*
□ Don't forget to write and thank your hosts. N'oublie pas d'écrire à tes hôtes pour les remercier.

hostage NOUN
l' otage *masc*
■ **to take somebody hostage** prendre quelqu'un en otage

hostel NOUN
le foyer *(for refugees, homeless people)*
■ **a youth hostel** une auberge de jeunesse

hostile ADJECTIVE
hostile (FEM hostile)

hot ADJECTIVE
1 chaud (FEM chaude) *(warm)*
□ a hot bath un bain chaud □ a hot country un pays chaud

> **LANGUAGE TIP** When you are talking about a person being hot, you use **avoir chaud.**

□ I'm hot. J'ai chaud. □ I'm too hot. J'ai trop chaud.

> **LANGUAGE TIP** When you mean that the weather is hot, you use **faire chaud.**

□ It's hot. Il fait chaud. □ It's very hot today. Il fait très chaud aujourd'hui.
2 épicé (FEM épicée) *(spicy)*
□ a very hot curry un curry très épicé

hot dog NOUN

le hot-dog
hotel NOUN
l' hôtel *masc*
□ We stayed in a hotel. Nous avons logé à l'hôtel.
hour NOUN
l' heure *fem*
□ She always takes hours to get ready. Elle passe toujours des heures à se préparer.
■ **a quarter of an hour** un quart d'heure
■ **half an hour** une demi-heure
■ **two and a half hours** deux heures et demie
hourly ADJECTIVE, ADVERB
toutes les heures
□ There are hourly buses. Il y a des bus toutes les heures.
■ **to be paid hourly** être payé à l'heure
house NOUN
la maison
□ Our house is at the end of the road. Notre maison est au bout de la rue.
■ **at his house** chez lui
■ **We stayed at their house.** Nous avons séjourné chez eux.
housewife NOUN
la femme au foyer
□ She's a housewife. Elle est femme au foyer.
housework NOUN
le ménage
■ **to do the housework** faire le ménage
hovercraft NOUN
l' aéroglisseur *masc*
how ADVERB
comment
□ How are you? Comment allez-vous?
■ **How many?** Combien?
■ **How many ...?** Combien de ...? □ How many pupils are there in the class? Combien d'élèves y a-t-il dans la classe?
■ **How much?** Combien?
■ **How much ...?** Combien de ...? □ How much sugar do you want? Combien de sucres voulez-vous?
■ **How old are you?** Quel âge as-tu?
■ **How far is it to Edinburgh?** Combien y a-t-il de kilomètres d'ici à Édimbourg?
■ **How long have you been here?** Depuis combien de temps êtes-vous là?
■ **How do you say 'apple' in French?** Comment dit-on 'apple' en français?
however CONJUNCTION
pourtant
□ This, however, isn't true. Pourtant, ce n'est pas vrai.
to **howl** VERB

hurler
HTML NOUN
le langage HTML
□ an HTML document un document en langage HTML
to **hug** VERB
▷ *see also* **hug** NOUN
serrer dans ses bras
□ He hugged her. Il l'a serrée dans ses bras.
hug NOUN
▷ *see also* **hug** VERB
■ **to give somebody a hug** serrer quelqu'un dans ses bras □ She gave them a hug. Elle les a serrés dans ses bras.
huge ADJECTIVE
immense (FEM immense)
to **hum** VERB
fredonner
human ADJECTIVE
humain (FEM humaine)
□ the human body le corps humain
human being NOUN
l' être humain *masc*
humble ADJECTIVE
humble (FEM humble)
humour (US **humor**) NOUN
l' humour *masc*
■ **to have a sense of humour** avoir le sens de l'humour
hundred NUMBER
■ **a hundred** cent □ a hundred euros cent euros
■ **five hundred** cinq cents
■ **five hundred and one** cinq cent un
■ **hundreds of people** des centaines de personnes
hung VERB ▷ *see* **hang**
Hungarian NOUN
▷ *see also* **Hungarian** ADJECTIVE
1 le Hongrois
la Hongroise *(person)*
2 le hongrois *(language)*
Hungarian ADJECTIVE
▷ *see also* **Hungarian** NOUN
hongrois (FEM hongroise)
□ She's Hungarian. Elle est hongroise.
Hungary NOUN
la Hongrie
■ **in Hungary** en Hongrie
■ **to Hungary** en Hongrie
hunger NOUN
la faim
hungry ADJECTIVE
■ **to be hungry** avoir faim □ I'm hungry. J'ai faim.
to **hunt** VERB

h

English-French

1 chasser *(animal)*
  □ People used to hunt wild boar. On chassait le sanglier autrefois.
  ■ **to go hunting** aller à la chasse
2 pourchasser *(criminal)*
  □ The police are hunting the killer. La police pourchasse le criminel.
  ■ **to hunt for something** *(search)* chercher quelque chose partout □ I hunted everywhere for that book. J'ai cherché ce livre partout.
hunting NOUN
  la chasse
  □ I'm against hunting. Je suis contre la chasse.
  ■ **fox-hunting** la chasse au renard
hurdle NOUN
  l' obstacle *masc*
hurricane NOUN
  l' ouragan *masc*
to **hurry** VERB
  ▷ *see also* **hurry** NOUN
  se dépêcher
  □ Sharon hurried back home. Sharon s'est dépêchée de rentrer chez elle.
  ■ **Hurry up!** Dépêche-toi!
hurry NOUN
  ▷ *see also* **hurry** VERB
  ■ **to be in a hurry** être pressé
  ■ **to do something in a hurry** faire quelque chose en vitesse
  ■ **There's no hurry.** Rien ne presse.
to **hurt** VERB

▷ *see also* **hurt** ADJECTIVE
  ■ **to hurt somebody 1** *(physically)* faire mal à quelqu'un □ You're hurting me! Tu me fais mal! **2** *(emotionally)* blesser quelqu'un □ His remarks really hurt me. Ses remarques m'ont vraiment blessé.
  ■ **to hurt oneself** se faire mal □ I fell over and hurt myself. Je me suis fait mal en tombant.
  ■ **That hurts.** Ça fait mal. □ It hurts to have a tooth out. Ça fait mal de se faire arracher une dent.
  ■ **My leg hurts.** J'ai mal à la jambe.
hurt ADJECTIVE
  ▷ *see also* **hurt** VERB
  blessé (FEM blessée)
  □ Is he badly hurt? Est-ce qu'il est grièvement blessé? □ He was hurt in the leg. Il a été blessé à la jambe. □ I was hurt by what he said. J'ai été blessé par ce qu'il a dit.
  ■ **Luckily, nobody got hurt.** Heureusement, il n'y a pas eu de blessés.
husband NOUN
  le mari
hut NOUN
  la hutte
hymn NOUN
  le cantique
hypermarket NOUN
  l' hypermarché *masc*
hyphen NOUN
  le trait d'union

I PRONOUN
1 je
   □ I speak French. Je parle français.

   > **LANGUAGE TIP** je changes to **j'** before a vowel and most words beginning with 'h'.

   j'
   □ I love cats. J'aime les chats.
2 moi
   □ Ann and I Ann et moi
ice NOUN
1 la glace
   □ There was ice on the lake. Il y avait de la glace sur le lac.
2 le verglas (on road)
iceberg NOUN
   l' iceberg masc
icebox NOUN (US)
   le frigo
ice cream NOUN
   la glace
   □ vanilla ice cream la glace à la vanille
ice cube NOUN
   le glaçon
ice hockey NOUN
   le hockey sur glace
Iceland NOUN
   l' Islande fem
   ■ **in Iceland** en Islande
   ■ **to Iceland** en Islande
ice lolly NOUN
   la glace à l'eau
ice rink NOUN
   la patinoire
ice-skating NOUN
   le patinage sur glace
   ■ **to go ice-skating** faire du patin à glace
icing NOUN
   le glaçage (on cake)
   ■ **icing sugar** le sucre glace
icon NOUN
   l' icône fem
ICT NOUN
   l' informatique fem
icy ADJECTIVE

glacial (FEM glaciale, MASC PL glaciaux)
   □ There was an icy wind. Il y avait un vent glacial.
   ■ **The roads are icy.** Il y a du verglas sur les routes.
I'd = I had, I would
idea NOUN
   l' idée fem
   □ Good idea! Bonne idée!
ideal ADJECTIVE
   idéal (FEM idéale, MASC PL idéaux)
identical ADJECTIVE
   identique (FEM identique)
identification NOUN
   l' identification fem
to **identify** VERB
   identifier
identity card NOUN
   la carte d'identité
idiot NOUN
   l' idiot masc
   l' idiote fem
idiotic ADJECTIVE
   stupide (FEM stupide)
idle ADJECTIVE
   fainéant (FEM fainéante) (lazy)
i.e. ABBREVIATION
   c.-à-d. (= c'est-à-dire)
if CONJUNCTION
   si
   □ You can have it if you like. Tu peux le prendre si tu veux.

   > **LANGUAGE TIP** si changes to **s'** before il and ils.

   s'
   □ Do you know if he's there? Savez-vous s'il est là?
   ■ **if only** si seulement □ If only I had more money! Si seulement j'avais plus d'argent!
   ■ **if not** sinon □ Are you coming? If not, I'll go with Mark. Est-ce que tu viens? Sinon, j'irai avec Mark.
ignorant ADJECTIVE
   ignorant (FEM ignorante)
to **ignore** VERB

■ **to ignore something** ne tenir aucun compte de quelque chose □ *She ignored my advice.* Elle n'a tenu aucun compte de mes conseils.

■ **to ignore somebody** ignorer quelqu'un □ *She saw me, but she ignored me.* Elle m'a vu, mais elle m'a ignoré.

■ **Just ignore him!** Ne fais pas attention à lui!

ill ADJECTIVE
malade (FEM malade) *(sick)*

■ **to be taken ill** tomber malade □ *She was taken ill while on holiday.* Elle est tombée malade pendant qu'elle était en vacances.

I'll = I will

illegal ADJECTIVE
illégal (FEM illégale, MASC PL illégaux)

illegible ADJECTIVE
illisible (FEM illisible)

illness NOUN
la maladie

to **ill-treat** VERB
maltraiter

illusion NOUN
l' illusion *fem*

illustration NOUN
l' illustration *fem*

image NOUN
l' image *fem*
□ *The company has changed its image.* La société a changé d'image.

imagination NOUN
l' imagination *fem*

to **imagine** VERB
imaginer
□ *You can imagine how I felt!* Tu peux imaginer ce que j'ai ressenti! □ *Is he angry?* — *I imagine so.* Est-ce qu'il est en colère? — J'imagine que oui.

to **imitate** VERB
imiter

imitation NOUN
l' imitation *fem*

immediate ADJECTIVE
immédiat (FEM immédiate)

immediately ADVERB
immédiatement
□ *I'll do it immediately.* Je vais le faire immédiatement.

immigrant NOUN
l' immigré *masc*
l' immigrée *fem*

immigration NOUN
l' immigration *fem*

immoral ADJECTIVE
immoral (FEM immorale, MASC PL immoraux)

impartial ADJECTIVE

impartial (FEM impartiale, MASC PL impartiaux)

impatience NOUN
l' impatience *fem*

impatient ADJECTIVE
impatient (FEM impatiente)

■ **to get impatient** s'impatienter □ *People are getting impatient.* Les gens commencent à s'impatienter.

impatiently ADVERB
avec impatience
□ *We waited impatiently.* Nous avons attendu avec impatience.

impersonal ADJECTIVE
impersonnel (FEM impersonnelle)

importance NOUN
l' importance *fem*

important ADJECTIVE
important (FEM importante)

impossible ADJECTIVE
impossible (FEM impossible)

to **impress** VERB
impressionner
□ *She's trying to impress you.* Elle essaie de t'impressionner.

impressed ADJECTIVE
impressionné (FEM impressionnée)
□ *I'm very impressed!* Je suis très impressionné!

impression NOUN
l' impression *fem*
□ *I was under the impression that ...* J'avais l'impression que ...

impressive ADJECTIVE
impressionnant (FEM impressionnante)

to **improve** VERB
1 améliorer *(make better)*
□ *They have improved the service.* Ils ont amélioré le service.
2 s'améliorer *(get better)*
□ *The weather is improving.* Le temps s'améliore. □ *My French has improved.* Mon français s'est amélioré.

improvement NOUN
1 l' amélioration *fem (of condition)*
□ *It's a great improvement.* C'est une nette amélioration.
2 le progrès *(of learner)*
□ *There's been an improvement in his French.* Il a fait des progrès en français.

in PREPOSITION, ADVERB

LANGUAGE TIP There are several ways of translating 'in'. Scan the examples to find one that is similar to what you want to say. For other expressions with 'in', see the verbs 'go', 'come', 'get', 'give' etc.

1 dans

□ in the house dans la maison □ in my bag dans mon sac □ in the sixties dans les années soixante □ I'll see you in three weeks. Je te verrai dans trois semaines.

2 à

□ in the country à la campagne □ in school à l'école □ in hospital à l'hôpital □ in London à Londres □ in spring au printemps □ in the sun au soleil □ in the shade à l'ombre □ in a loud voice à voix haute □ the boy in the blue shirt le garçon à la chemise bleue □ It was written in pencil. C'était écrit au crayon.

3 en

□ in French en français □ in summer en été □ in May en mai □ in 1996 en dix-neuf cent quatre-vingt seize □ I did it in 3 hours. Je l'ai fait en trois heures. □ in town en ville □ in prison en prison □ in tears en larmes □ in good condition en bon état

> **LANGUAGE TIP** When 'in' refers to a country which is feminine, use **en**; when the country is masculine, use **au**; when the country is plural, use **aux**.

□ in France en France □ in Portugal au Portugal □ in the United States aux États-Unis

4 de

□ the best pupil in the class le meilleur élève de la classe □ the best team in the world la meilleure équipe du monde □ the tallest person in the family le plus grand de la famille □ at 4 o'clock in the afternoon à quatre heures de l'après-midi □ at 6 in the morning à six heures du matin

■ **in the afternoon** l'après-midi

■ **You look good in that dress.** Tu es jolie avec cette robe.

■ **in time** à temps □ We arrived in time for dinner. Nous sommes arrivés à temps pour le dîner.

■ **in here** ici □ It's hot in here. Il fait chaud ici.

■ **in the rain** sous la pluie

■ **one person in ten** une personne sur dix

■ **to be in** (at home, work) être là □ He wasn't in. Il n'était pas là.

■ **to ask somebody in** inviter quelqu'un à entrer

inaccurate ADJECTIVE
inexact (FEM inexacte)

inadequate ADJECTIVE
inadéquat (FEM inadéquate) (measures, resources)

■ **I felt completely inadequate.** Je ne me sentais absolument pas à la hauteur.

inbox NOUN
la boîte de réception

incentive NOUN

■ **There is no incentive to work.** Il n'y a rien qui incite à travailler.

inch NOUN
le pouce

> **DID YOU KNOW...?**
> In France measurements are in metres and centimetres rather than feet and inches. An inch is about 2.5 centimetres.

■ **6 inches** quinze centimètres

incident NOUN
l' incident masc

inclined ADJECTIVE

■ **to be inclined to do something** avoir tendance à faire quelque chose □ He's inclined to arrive late. Il a tendance à arriver en retard.

to **include** VERB
comprendre
□ Service is not included. Le service n'est pas compris.

including PREPOSITION
compris
□ It will be 200 euros, including tax. Ça coûtera deux cents euros, toutes taxes comprises.

inclusive ADJECTIVE
compris (FEM comprise)
□ The inclusive price is 200 euros. Ça coûte deux cents euros tout compris.

■ **inclusive of tax** taxes comprises

income NOUN
le revenu

income tax NOUN
l' impôt sur le revenu masc

incompetent ADJECTIVE
incompétent (FEM incompétente)

incomplete ADJECTIVE
incomplet (FEM incomplète)

inconsistent ADJECTIVE
incohérent (FEM incohérente)

inconvenience NOUN

■ **I don't want to cause any inconvenience.** Je ne veux pas vous déranger.

inconvenient ADJECTIVE

■ **That's very inconvenient for me.** Ça ne m'arrange pas du tout.

incorrect ADJECTIVE
incorrect (FEM incorrecte)

increase NOUN
▷ see also **increase** VERB
l' augmentation fem
□ an increase in road accidents une

augmentation des accidents de la route

to **increase** VERB

▷ *see also* **increase** NOUN
augmenter

incredible ADJECTIVE
incroyable (FEM incroyable)

indecisive ADJECTIVE
indécis (FEM indécise) (*person*)

indeed ADVERB
vraiment

□ It's very hard indeed. C'est vraiment très difficile.

■ **Know what I mean? — Indeed I do.** Tu vois ce que je veux dire? — Oui, tout à fait.

■ **Thank you very much indeed!** Merci beaucoup!

independence NOUN
l' indépendance *fem*

independent ADJECTIVE
indépendant (FEM indépendante)

■ **an independent school** une école privée

index NOUN
l' index *masc* (*in book*)

index finger NOUN
l' index *masc*

India NOUN
l' Inde *fem*

■ **in India** en Inde

■ **to India** en Inde

Indian NOUN
▷ *see also* **Indian** ADJECTIVE
l' Indien *masc*
l' Indienne *fem* (*person*)

■ **an American Indian** un Indien d'Amérique

Indian ADJECTIVE
▷ *see also* **Indian** NOUN
indien (FEM indienne)

to **indicate** VERB
indiquer

indicator NOUN
le clignotant (*on car*)

□ Put your indicators on. Mets tes clignotants.

indigestion NOUN
l' indigestion *fem*

■ **I've got indigestion.** J'ai une indigestion.

individual ADJECTIVE
individuel (FEM individuelle)

indoor ADJECTIVE
■ **an indoor swimming pool** une piscine couverte

indoors ADVERB
à l'intérieur

□ They're indoors. Ils sont à l'intérieur.

■ **to go indoors** rentrer □ We'd better go indoors. Nous ferions mieux de rentrer.

industrial ADJECTIVE
industriel (FEM industrielle)

industrial estate NOUN
la zone industrielle

industry NOUN
l' industrie *fem*

□ the tourist industry l'industrie du tourisme □ the oil industry l'industrie pétrolière □ I'd like to work in industry. J'aimerais travailler dans l'industrie.

inefficient ADJECTIVE
inefficace (FEM inefficace)

inevitable ADJECTIVE
inévitable (FEM inévitable)

inexpensive ADJECTIVE
bon marché (FEM+PL bon marché)

□ an inexpensive hotel un hôtel bon marché □ inexpensive holidays des vacances bon marché

inexperienced ADJECTIVE
inexpérimenté (FEM inexpérimentée)

infant school NOUN
■ **He's just started at infant school.** Il vient d'entrer au cours préparatoire.

> **DID YOU KNOW...?**
> CP (cours préparatoire) is the equivalent of first-year infants, and CE1 (cours élémentaire première année) the equivalent of second-year infants.

infection NOUN
l' infection *fem*

□ an ear infection une infection de l'oreille

■ **a throat infection** une angine

infectious ADJECTIVE
contagieux (FEM contagieuse)

□ It's not infectious. Ce n'est pas contagieux.

infinitive NOUN
l' infinitif *masc*

infirmary NOUN
l' hôpital *masc* (PL les hôpitaux)

inflatable ADJECTIVE
gonflable (FEM gonflable) (*mattress, dinghy*)

inflation NOUN
l' inflation *fem*

influence NOUN
▷ *see also* **influence** VERB
l' influence *fem*

□ He's a bad influence on her. Il a mauvaise influence sur elle.

to **influence** VERB
▷ *see also* **influence** NOUN
influencer

influenza NOUN
la grippe

to **inform** VERB

informer
- **to inform somebody of something**
informer quelqu'un de quelque chose
□ Nobody informed me of the new plan.
Personne ne m'a informé de ce nouveau projet.

informal ADJECTIVE
1 décontracté (FEM décontractée) *(person, party)*
□ 'informal dress' 'tenue décontractée'
2 familier (FEM familière) *(colloquial)*
□ informal language le langage familier
- **an informal visit** une visite non officielle

information NOUN
les renseignements *masc pl*
□ important information les renseignements importants
- **a piece of information** un renseignement
- **Could you give me some information about trains to Paris?** Pourriez-vous me renseigner sur les trains pour Paris?

information office NOUN
le bureau des renseignements (PL les bureaux des renseignements)

infuriating ADJECTIVE
exaspérant (FEM exaspérante)

ingenious ADJECTIVE
ingénieux (FEM ingénieuse)

ingredient NOUN
l' ingrédient *masc*

inhabitant NOUN
l' habitant *masc*
l' habitante *fem*

inhaler NOUN
l' inhalateur
□ I mustn't forget my inhaler. Il ne faut pas que j'oublie mon inhalateur.

to inherit VERB
hériter de
□ She inherited her father's house. Elle a hérité de la maison de son père.

initials PL NOUN
les initiales *fem pl*
□ Her initials are CDT. Ses initiales sont CDT.

initiative NOUN
l' initiative *fem*

to inject VERB
injecter *(drug)*

injection NOUN
la piqûre

to injure VERB
blesser

injured ADJECTIVE
blessé (FEM blessée)

injury NOUN
la blessure

injury time NOUN
les arrêts de jeu *masc pl*

injustice NOUN
l' injustice *fem*

ink NOUN
l' encre *fem*

in-laws PL NOUN
les beaux-parents *masc pl*

inn NOUN
l' auberge *fem*

inner ADJECTIVE
intérieur (FEM intérieure)
- **the inner city** les quartiers déshérités du centre ville

inner tube NOUN
la chambre à air

innocent ADJECTIVE
innocent (FEM innocente)

inquest NOUN
l' enquête *fem*

to inquire VERB
- **to inquire about something** se renseigner sur quelque chose □ I'm going to inquire about train times. Je vais me renseigner sur les horaires des trains.

inquiries office NOUN
le bureau des renseignements (PL les bureaux des renseignements)

inquiry NOUN
- **to make inquiries about something** faire des demandes de renseignement
□ 'inquiries' 'renseignements'

inquisitive ADJECTIVE
curieux (FEM curieuse)

insane ADJECTIVE
fou (FEM folle)

> LANGUAGE TIP fou changes to fol before a vowel and most words beginning with 'h'.

inscription NOUN
l' inscription *fem*

insect NOUN
l' insecte *masc*

insect repellent NOUN
l' insectifuge *masc*

insensitive ADJECTIVE
indélicat (FEM indélicate)
□ That was a bit insensitive of you. C'était un peu indélicat de ta part.

inside NOUN
▷ *see also* **inside** ADVERB
l' intérieur *masc*

inside ADVERB, PREPOSITION
▷ *see also* **inside** NOUN
à l'intérieur
□ They're inside. Ils sont à l'intérieur.
□ inside the house à l'intérieur de la maison 423

insincere – interest

■ **to go inside** rentrer
■ **Come inside!** Rentrez!

insincere ADJECTIVE
peu sincère (FEM peu sincère)

to **insist** VERB
insister
□ I didn't want to, but he insisted. Je ne voulais pas, mais il a insisté.
■ **to insist on doing something** insister pour faire quelque chose □ She insisted on paying. Elle a insisté pour payer.
■ **He insisted he was innocent.** Il affirmait qu'il était innocent.

inspector NOUN
l' inspecteur masc (police)
□ Inspector Jill Brown l'inspecteur Jill Brown
■ **ticket inspector** (on buses) le contrôleur

instalment NOUN
1 le versement (payment)
□ to pay in instalments payer en plusieurs versements
2 l' épisode masc (episode)

instance NOUN
■ **for instance** par exemple

instant ADJECTIVE
immédiat (FEM immédiate)
□ It was an instant success. Ça a été un succès immédiat.
■ **instant coffee** le café instantané

instantly ADVERB
tout de suite

instead ADVERB
■ **instead of 1** (followed by noun) à la place de □ He went instead of Peter. Il y est allé à la place de Peter. **2** (followed by verb) au lieu de □ We played tennis instead of going swimming. Nous avons joué au tennis au lieu d'aller nager.
■ **The pool was closed, so we played tennis instead.** La piscine était fermée, alors nous avons joué au tennis.

instinct NOUN
l' instinct masc

institute NOUN
l' institut masc

institution NOUN
l' institution fem

to **instruct** VERB
■ **to instruct somebody to do something** donner l'ordre à quelqu'un de faire quelque chose □ She instructed us to wait outside. Elle nous a donné l'ordre d'attendre dehors.

instructions PL NOUN
1 les instructions fem pl
□ Follow the instructions carefully. Suivez soigneusement les instructions.
2 le mode d'emploi sing (booklet)
□ Where are the instructions? Où est le mode d'emploi?

instructor NOUN
le moniteur
la monitrice
□ a skiing instructor un moniteur de ski □ a driving instructor un moniteur d'auto-école

instrument NOUN
l' instrument masc
□ Do you play an instrument? Est-ce que tu joues d'un instrument?

insufficient ADJECTIVE
insuffisant (FEM insuffisante)

insulin NOUN
l' insuline fem

insult NOUN
▷ see also **insult** VERB
l' insulte fem

to **insult** VERB
▷ see also **insult** NOUN
insulter

insurance NOUN
l' assurance fem
□ his car insurance son assurance automobile
■ **an insurance policy** une police d'assurance

intelligent ADJECTIVE
intelligent (FEM intelligente)

to **intend** VERB
■ **to intend to do something** avoir l'intention de faire quelque chose □ I intend to do French at university. J'ai l'intention d'étudier le français à l'université.

intense ADJECTIVE
intense (FEM intense)

intensive ADJECTIVE
intensif (FEM intensive)

intention NOUN
l' intention fem

intercom NOUN
l' interphone masc

interest NOUN
▷ see also **interest** VERB
l' intérêt masc
□ to show an interest in something manifester de l'intérêt pour quelque chose
■ **What interests do you have?** Quels sont tes centres d'intérêt?
■ **My main interest is music.** Ce qui m'intéresse le plus c'est la musique.

to **interest** VERB
▷ see also **interest** NOUN
intéresser
□ It doesn't interest me. Ça ne m'intéresse pas.
■ **to be interested in something**

s'intéresser à quelque chose □ I'm not interested in politics. Je ne m'intéresse pas à la politique.

interesting ADJECTIVE
intéressant (FEM intéressante)

interior NOUN
l' intérieur *masc*

interior designer NOUN
l' architecte d'intérieur *masc/fem*

intermediate ADJECTIVE
moyen (FEM moyenne) *(course, level)*

internal ADJECTIVE
interne (FEM interne)

international ADJECTIVE
international (FEM internationale, MASC PL internationaux)

internet NOUN
l' Internet *masc*
□ on the internet sur Internet

internet café NOUN
le cybercafé

internet user NOUN
l' internaute *masc/fem*

to **interpret** VERB
faire d'interprète
□ Steve interpreted into English for his friend. Steve a fait l'interprète en anglais pour son ami.

interpreter NOUN
l' interprète *masc/fem*

to **interrupt** VERB
interrompre

interruption NOUN
l' interruption *fem*

interval NOUN
l' entracte *masc (in play, concert)*

interview NOUN
▷ see also **interview** VERB
1 l' interview *fem (on TV, radio)*
2 l' entretien *masc (for job)*

to **interview** VERB
▷ see also **interview** NOUN
interviewer *(on TV, radio)*
□ I was interviewed on the radio. J'ai été interviewé à la radio.

interviewer NOUN
l' interviewer *masc (on TV, radio)*

intimate ADJECTIVE
intime (FEM intime)

into PREPOSITION
1 dans
□ He got into the car. Il est monté dans la voiture.
2 en
□ I'm going into town. Je vais en ville.
□ Translate it into French. Traduisez ça en français. □ Divide into two groups.

Répartissez-vous en deux groupes.

to **introduce** VERB
présenter
□ I'd like to introduce Michelle Davies. Je vous présente Michelle Davies. □ He introduced me to his parents. Il m'a présenté à ses parents.

introduction NOUN
l' introduction *fem (in book)*

intruder NOUN
l' intrus *masc*
l' intruse *fem*

intuition NOUN
l' intuition *fem*

to **invade** VERB
envahir

invalid NOUN
le/la malade

to **invent** VERB
inventer

invention NOUN
l' invention *fem*

inventor NOUN
l' inventeur *masc*
l' inventrice *fem*

investigation NOUN
l' enquête *fem (police)*

investment NOUN
l' investissement *masc*
□ They bought the house as an investment. Ils ont acheté la maison comme investissement.

invigilator NOUN
le surveillant
la surveillante

invisible ADJECTIVE
invisible (FEM invisible)

invitation NOUN
l' invitation *fem*

to **invite** VERB
inviter
□ He's not invited. Il n'est pas invité.
■ **to invite somebody to a party** inviter quelqu'un à une fête

to **involve** VERB
nécessiter
□ His job involves a lot of travelling. Son travail nécessite de nombreux déplacements.
■ **to be involved in something** *(crime, drugs)* être impliqué dans quelque chose
■ **to be involved with somebody** *(in relationship)* avoir une relation avec quelqu'un

iPod® NOUN
l' iPod® *masc*

IQ NOUN *(= intelligence quotient)*

425

le Q.I. *(= quotient intellectuel)*

Iran NOUN
l' Iran *masc*
■ **in Iran** en Iran

Iranian NOUN
▷ *see also* **Iranian** ADJECTIVE
l' Iranien *masc*
l' Iranienne *fem*
■ **the Iranians** les Iraniens

Iranian ADJECTIVE
▷ *see also* **Iranian** NOUN
iranien (FEM iranienne)

Iraq NOUN
l' Iraq *masc*
■ **in Iraq** en Iraq

Iraqi NOUN
▷ *see also* **Iraqi** ADJECTIVE
l' Irakien *masc*
l' Irakienne *fem*
■ **the Iraqis** les Irakiens

Iraqi ADJECTIVE
▷ *see also* **Iraqi** NOUN
irakien (FEM irakienne)
□ the Iraqi government le gouvernement irakien

Ireland NOUN
l' Irlande *fem*
■ **in Ireland** en Irlande
■ **to Ireland** en Irlande
■ **I'm from Ireland.** Je suis irlandais.

Irish NOUN
▷ *see also* **Irish** ADJECTIVE
l' irlandais *masc (language)*
■ **the Irish** *(people)* les Irlandais

Irish ADJECTIVE
▷ *see also* **Irish** NOUN
irlandais (FEM irlandaise)
□ Irish music la musique irlandaise

Irishman NOUN
l' Irlandais *masc*

Irishwoman NOUN
l' Irlandaise *fem*

iron NOUN
▷ *see also* **iron** VERB
1 le fer *(metal)*
2 le fer à repasser *(for clothes)*

to **iron** VERB
▷ *see also* **iron** NOUN
repasser

ironic ADJECTIVE
ironique (FEM ironique)

ironing NOUN
le repassage
□ to do the ironing faire le repassage

ironing board NOUN
la planche à repasser

ironmonger's NOUN

la quincaillerie

ironmonger's shop NOUN
la quincaillerie

irrelevant ADJECTIVE
hors de propos
□ That's irrelevant. C'est hors de propos.

irresponsible ADJECTIVE *(person)*
irresponsable (FEM irresponsable)
□ That was irresponsible of him. C'était irresponsable de sa part.

irritating ADJECTIVE
irritant (FEM irritante)

is VERB ▷ *see* **be**

Islam NOUN
l' Islam *masc*

Islamic ADJECTIVE
islamique (FEM islamique)
□ Islamic law la loi islamique
■ **Islamic fundamentalists** les intégristes musulmans

island NOUN
l' île *fem*

isle NOUN
■ **the Isle of Man** l'île de Man *fem*
■ **the Isle of Wight** l'île de Wight *fem*

isolated ADJECTIVE
isolé (FEM isolée)

ISP NOUN *(= internet service provider)*
le fournisseur d'accès à Internet

Israel NOUN
Israël *masc*
■ **in Israel** en Israël

Israeli ADJECTIVE
▷ *see also* **Israeli** NOUN
israélien (FEM israélienne)

Israeli NOUN
▷ *see also* **Israeli** ADJECTIVE
l' Israélien *masc*
l' Israélienne *fem*

issue NOUN
▷ *see also* **issue** VERB
1 la question *(matter)*
□ a controversial issue une question controversée
2 le numéro *(of magazine)*

to **issue** VERB
▷ *see also* **issue** NOUN
distribuer *(equipment, supplies)*

it PRONOUN

LANGUAGE TIP Remember to check if 'it' stands for a masculine or feminine noun.

1 il
□ Where's my book? — It's on the table. Où est mon livre? — Il est sur la table.
elle
□ When does the pool close? — It closes at

8. La piscine ferme à quelle heure? — Elle ferme à vingt heures.

> LANGUAGE TIP Use **le** or **la** when 'it' is the object of the sentence. **le** and **la** change to **l'** before a vowel and most words beginning with 'h'.

2 le

□ There's a croissant left. Do you want it? Il reste un croissant. Tu le veux?
l'

□ It's a good film. Did you see it? C'est un bon film. L'as-tu vu?
la

□ I don't want this apple. Take it. Je ne veux pas de cette pomme. Prends-la.
l'

□ He's got a new car. — Yes, I saw it. Il a une nouvelle voiture. — Oui, je l'ai vue.

■ **It's raining.** Il pleut.

■ **It's 6 o'clock.** Il est six heures.

■ **It's Friday tomorrow.** Demain c'est vendredi.

■ **Who is it? — It's me.** Qui est-ce? — C'est moi.

■ **It's expensive.** C'est cher.

Italian NOUN

▷ see also **Italian** ADJECTIVE

1 l' Italien masc
l' Italienne fem (person)

2 l' italien masc (language)

Italian ADJECTIVE

▷ see also **Italian** NOUN

italien (FEM italienne)

Italy NOUN

l' Italie fem

■ **in Italy** en Italie

■ **to Italy** en Italie

to **itch** VERB

■ **It itches.** Ça me démange.

■ **My head's itching.** J'ai des démangeaisons à la tête.

itchy ADJECTIVE

■ **My arm is itchy.** J'ai des fourmis dans le bras.

it'd = it had, it would

item NOUN

l' article masc (object)

itinerary NOUN

l' itinéraire masc

it'll = it will

its ADJECTIVE

> LANGUAGE TIP Remember to check if 'its' refers to a masculine, feminine or plural noun.

son masc

□ What's its name? Quel est son nom?
sa fem

□ Every thing in its place. Chaque chose à sa place.
ses pl

□ The dog is losing its hair. Le chien perd ses poils.

it's = it is, it has

itself PRONOUN

se

> LANGUAGE TIP **se** changes to **s'** before a vowel and most words beginning with 'h'.

s'

□ The heating switches itself off. Le chauffage s'arrête automatiquement.

I've = I have

Jj

j

jab NOUN
la piqûre *(injection)*

jack NOUN
1 le cric *(for car)*
2 le valet *(playing card)*

jacket NOUN
la veste
■ **jacket potatoes** les pommes de terre en robe des champs

jackpot NOUN
le gros lot
□ to win the jackpot gagner le gros lot

jail NOUN
▷ *see also* **jail** VERB
la prison
■ **to go to jail** aller en prison

to **jail** VERB
▷ *see also* **jail** NOUN
emprisonner

jam NOUN
la confiture
□ strawberry jam la confiture de fraises
■ **a traffic jam** un embouteillage

jam jar NOUN
le pot à confiture

jammed ADJECTIVE
coincé (FEM coincée)
□ The window's jammed. La fenêtre est coincée.

jam-packed ADJECTIVE
bondé (FEM bondée)
□ The room was jam-packed. La salle était bondée.

janitor NOUN
le concierge
□ He's a janitor. Il est concierge.

January NOUN
janvier *masc*
■ **in January** en janvier

Japan NOUN
le Japon
■ **in Japan** au Japon
■ **from Japan** du Japon

Japanese NOUN
▷ *see also* **Japanese** ADJECTIVE

1 le Japonais
la Japonaise *(person)*
■ **the Japanese** les Japonais
2 le japonais *(language)*

Japanese ADJECTIVE
▷ *see also* **Japanese** NOUN
japonais (FEM japonaise)

jar NOUN
le bocal (PL les bocaux)
□ an empty jar un bocal vide
■ **a jar of honey** un pot de miel

jaundice NOUN
la jaunisse

javelin NOUN
le javelot

jaw NOUN
la mâchoire

jazz NOUN
le jazz

jealous ADJECTIVE
jaloux (FEM jalouse)

jeans PL NOUN
le jean *sing*

Jehovah's Witness NOUN
le témoin de Jéhovah
□ She's a Jehovah's Witness. Elle est témoin de Jéhovah.

Jello® NOUN (US)
la gelée

jelly NOUN
la gelée

jellyfish NOUN
la méduse

jersey NOUN
le pull-over *(pullover)*

Jesus NOUN
Jésus *masc*

jet NOUN
le jet *(plane)*

jetlag NOUN
■ **to be suffering from jetlag** être sous le coup du décalage horaire

jetty NOUN
la jetée

Jew NOUN

le Juif
la Juive

jewel NOUN
le bijou (PL les bijoux)

jeweller (US **jeweler**) NOUN
le bijoutier
la bijoutière
□ He's a jeweller. Il est bijoutier.

jeweller's shop (US **jeweler's shop**) NOUN
la bijouterie

jewellery (US **jewelry**) NOUN
les bijoux *masc pl*

Jewish ADJECTIVE
juif (FEM juive)

jigsaw NOUN
le puzzle

job NOUN
1 l' emploi *masc*
□ He's lost his job. Il a perdu son emploi.
■ **I've got a Saturday job.** Je travaille le samedi.
2 le travail (PL les travaux) *(chore, task)*
□ That was a difficult job. C'était un travail difficile.

job centre NOUN
l' agence pour l'emploi *fem*

jobless ADJECTIVE
sans emploi

jockey NOUN
le jockey

to **jog** VERB
faire du jogging

jogging NOUN
le jogging
■ **to go jogging** faire du jogging

john NOUN (US)
les toilettes *fem pl*

to **join** VERB
1 s'inscrire à *(become member of)*
□ I'm going to join the ski club. Je vais m'inscrire au club de ski.
2 se joindre à
□ Do you mind if I join you? Puis-je me joindre à vous?

joiner NOUN
le menuisier
□ He's a joiner. Il est menuisier.

joint NOUN
1 l' articulation *fem (in body)*
2 le rôti *(of meat)*
3 le joint *(drugs)*

joke NOUN
▷ *see also* **joke** VERB
la plaisanterie
□ to tell a joke raconter une plaisanterie

to **joke** VERB
▷ *see also* **joke** NOUN

plaisanter
□ I'm only joking. Je plaisante.

jolly ADJECTIVE
jovial (FEM joviale, MASC PL joviaux)

Jordan NOUN
la Jordanie *(country)*
■ **in Jordan** en Jordanie

to **jot down** VERB
noter

jotter NOUN
le bloc-notes (PL les blocs-notes) *(pad)*

journalism NOUN
le journalisme

journalist NOUN
le/la journaliste
□ She's a journalist. Elle est journaliste.

journey NOUN
1 le voyage
□ I don't like long journeys. Je n'aime pas les longs voyages.
■ **to go on a journey** faire un voyage
2 le trajet *(to school, work)*
□ The journey to school takes about half an hour. Il y a une demi-heure de trajet pour aller à l'école.
■ **a bus journey** un trajet en autobus

joy NOUN
la joie

joystick NOUN
le manette de jeu *(for computer game)*

judge NOUN
▷ *see also* **judge** VERB
le juge
□ She's a judge. Elle est juge.

to **judge** VERB
▷ *see also* **judge** NOUN
juger

judo NOUN
le judo
□ My hobby is judo. Je fais du judo.

jug NOUN
le pot

juggler NOUN
le jongleur
la jongleuse

juice NOUN
le jus
□ orange juice le jus d'orange

July NOUN
juillet *masc*
■ **in July** en juillet
DID YOU KNOW...?
The fourteenth of July (**la fête nationale**) is the French national holiday. There's a firework display and military parade in Paris.

jumble sale NOUN

la vente de charité

to **jump** verb
sauter
□ to jump over something sauter par-
dessus quelque chose □ to jump out of the
window sauter par la fenêtre □ to jump off
the roof sauter du toit

jumper noun
le pull-over (pullover)

junction noun
le carrefour (of roads)

June noun
juin masc
■ in June en juin

jungle noun
la jungle

junior noun
■ the juniors (in school) les élèves des
petites classes

junior school noun
l' école primaire fem

junk noun
le bric-à-brac (old things)
□ The attic's full of junk. Le grenier est

rempli de bric-à-brac.
■ to eat junk food manger n'importe
comment
■ a junk shop un magasin de brocante

jury noun
le jury

just adverb
juste
□ just after Christmas juste après Noël
□ We had just enough money. Nous avions
juste assez d'argent. □ just in time juste à
temps
■ just here ici
■ I'm rather busy just now. Je suis assez
occupé en ce moment.
■ I did it just now. Je viens de le faire.
■ He's just arrived. Il vient d'arriver.
■ I'm just coming! J'arrive!
■ It's just a suggestion. Ce n'est qu'une
suggestion.

justice noun
la justice

to **justify** verb
justifier

Kk

kangaroo NOUN
le kangourou

karaoke NOUN
le karaoké

karate NOUN
le karaté

kebab NOUN
1 la brochette *(shish kebab)*
2 le doner kebab *(doner kebab)*

keen ADJECTIVE
enthousiaste (FEM enthousiaste)
  □ He doesn't seem very keen. Il n'a pas l'air très enthousiaste.
  ■ **She's a keen student.** C'est une étudiante assidue.
  ■ **to be keen on something** aimer quelque chose □ I'm keen on maths. J'aime les maths. □ I'm not very keen on maths. Je n'aime pas trop les maths.
  ■ **to be keen on somebody** *(fancy them)* être très attiré par quelqu'un □ He's keen on her. Il est très attiré par elle.
  ■ **to be keen on doing something** avoir très envie de faire quelque chose □ I'm not very keen on going. Je n'ai pas très envie d'y aller.

to **keep** VERB
1 garder *(retain)*
  □ You can keep it. Tu peux le garder.
2 rester *(remain)*
  □ Keep still! Reste tranquille!
  ■ **Keep quiet!** Tais-toi!
  ■ **I keep forgetting my keys.** J'oublie tout le temps mes clés.

to **keep on** VERB
  ■ **to keep on doing something**
  1 *(continue)* continuer à faire quelque chose □ He kept on reading. Il a continué à lire.
  2 *(repeatedly)* ne pas arrêter de faire quelque chose □ The car keeps on breaking down. La voiture n'arrête pas de tomber en panne.

to **keep out** VERB
  ■ **'keep out'** 'défense d'entrer'

to **keep up** VERB
se maintenir à la hauteur de quelqu'un
  □ Matthew walks so fast I can't keep up. Matthew marche tellement vite que je n'arrive pas à me maintenir à sa hauteur.
  ■ **I can't keep up with the rest of the class.** Je n'arrive pas à suivre le reste de la classe.

keep-fit NOUN
la gymnastique d'entretien
  ■ **I go to keep-fit classes.** Je vais à des cours de gymnastique.

kennel NOUN
la niche

kept VERB ▷ see **keep**

kerosene NOUN (US)
le pétrole

kettle NOUN
la bouilloire

key NOUN
la clé

keyboard NOUN
le clavier
  □ ... with Mike Moran on keyboards ... avec Mike Moran aux claviers

keyring NOUN
le porte-clés (PL les porte-clés)

kick NOUN
  ▷ see also **kick** VERB
le coup de pied

to **kick** VERB
  ▷ see also **kick** NOUN
  ■ **to kick somebody** donner un coup de pied à quelqu'un □ He kicked me. Il m'a donné un coup de pied. □ He kicked the ball hard. Il a donné un bon coup de pied dans le ballon.

to **kick off** VERB
donner le coup d'envoi *(in football)*

kick-off NOUN
le coup d'envoi
  □ The kick-off is at 10 o'clock. Le coup d'envoi sera donné à dix heures.

kid NOUN
  ▷ see also **kid** VERB
le/la gosse *(child)*

to **kid** VERB
▷ *see also* **kid** NOUN
plaisanter
□ I'm just kidding. Je plaisante.
to **kidnap** VERB
kidnapper
kidney NOUN
1 le rein *(human)*
□ He's got kidney trouble. Il a des problèmes de reins.
2 le rognon *(to eat)*
□ I don't like kidneys. Je n'aime pas les rognons.
■ **kidney beans** les haricots rouges *masc pl*
to **kill** VERB
tuer
□ He was killed in a car accident. Il a été tué dans un accident de voiture.
■ **Luckily, nobody was killed.** Il n'y a heureusement pas eu de victimes.
■ **Six people were killed in the accident.** L'accident a fait six morts.
■ **to kill oneself** se suicider □ He killed himself. Il s'est suicidé.
killer NOUN
1 le meurtrier
la meurtrière *(murderer)*
□ The police are searching for the killer. La police recherche le meurtrier.
2 le tueur
la tueuse *(assassin)*
□ a hired killer un tueur à gages
■ **Meningitis can be a killer.** La méningite peut être mortelle.
kilo NOUN
le kilo
□ 10 euros a kilo dix euros le kilo
kilometre (US **kilometer**) NOUN
le kilomètre
kilt NOUN
le kilt
kind ADJECTIVE
▷ *see also* **kind** NOUN
gentil (FEM gentille)
■ **to be kind to somebody** être gentil avec quelqu'un
■ **Thank you for being so kind.** Merci pour votre gentillesse.
kind NOUN
▷ *see also* **kind** ADJECTIVE
la sorte
□ It's a kind of sausage. C'est une sorte de saucisse.
kindergarten NOUN
l' école maternelle *fem*
kindly ADVERB
gentiment

□ 'Don't worry,' she said kindly. 'Ne t'en fais pas', m'a-t-elle dit gentiment.
■ **Kindly refrain from smoking.** Veuillez vous abstenir de fumer.
kindness NOUN
la gentillesse
king NOUN
le roi
kingdom NOUN
le royaume
kiosk NOUN
la cabine téléphonique *(phone box)*
kipper NOUN
le hareng fumé
kiss NOUN
▷ *see also* **kiss** VERB
le baiser
□ a passionate kiss un baiser passionné

DID YOU KNOW…?
Between boys and girls, and between girls, the normal French way of saying hello and goodbye is with kisses, usually one on each cheek. Boys shake hands with each other instead.

to **kiss** VERB
▷ *see also* **kiss** NOUN
1 embrasser
□ He kissed her passionately. Il l'a embrassée passionnément.
2 s'embrasser
□ They kissed. Ils se sont embrassés.
kit NOUN
1 les affaires *fem pl (clothes for sport)*
□ I've forgotten my gym kit. J'ai oublié mes affaires de gym.
2 la trousse
□ a tool kit une trousse à outils □ a first aid kit une trousse de secours □ a puncture repair kit une trousse de réparations
■ **a drum kit** une batterie
■ **a sewing kit** un nécessaire à couture
kitchen NOUN
la cuisine
□ a fitted kitchen une cuisine aménagée
■ **the kitchen units** les éléments de cuisine
■ **a kitchen knife** un couteau de cuisine
kite NOUN
le cerf-volant (PL les cerfs-volants)
kitten NOUN
le chaton
knee NOUN
le genou (PL les genoux)
□ He was on his knees. Il était à genoux.
to **kneel** VERB
s'agenouiller
to **kneel down** VERB

s'agenouiller

knew VERB ▷ *see* **know**

knickers PL NOUN
la culotte *sing*

■ **a pair of knickers** une culotte

knife NOUN
le couteau (PL les couteaux)

■ **a kitchen knife** un couteau de cuisine
■ **a sheath knife** un couteau à gaine
■ **a penknife** un canif

to **knit** VERB
tricoter

knitting NOUN
le tricot

□ I like knitting. J'aime faire du tricot.

knives PL NOUN ▷ *see* **knife**

knob NOUN
le bouton *(on door, radio, TV, radiator)*

to **knock** VERB
▷ *see also* **knock** NOUN
frapper

□ Someone's knocking at the door.
Quelqu'un frappe à la porte.

knock NOUN
▷ *see also* **knock** VERB
le coup

to **knock down** VERB
renverser

□ She was knocked down by a car. Elle a été
renversée par une voiture.

to **knock out** VERB
1 éliminer *(defeat)*

□ They were knocked out early in the
tournament. Ils ont été éliminés au début
du tournoi.

2 assommer *(stun)*

□ They knocked out the security guard. Ils
ont assommé le vigile.

knot NOUN
le nœud

■ **to tie a knot in something** faire un
nœud à quelque chose

to **know** VERB

> LANGUAGE TIP Use **savoir** for knowing
> facts, **connaître** for knowing people
> and places.

1 savoir

□ It's a long way. — Yes, I know. C'est loin.
— Oui, je sais. □ I don't know. Je ne sais

pas. □ I don't know what to do. Je ne sais
pas quoi faire. □ I don't know how to do it.
Je ne sais pas comment faire.

2 connaître

□ I know her. Je la connais. □ I know Paris
well. Je connais bien Paris.

■ **I don't know any German.** Je ne parle
pas du tout allemand.

■ **to know that ...** savoir que ... □ I know
that you like chocolate. Je sais que tu aimes
le chocolat. □ I didn't know that your Dad
was a policeman. Je ne savais pas que ton
père était policier.

■ **to know about something** 1 *(be aware
of)* être au courant de quelque chose □ Do
you know about the meeting this
afternoon? Tu es au courant de la réunion
de cet après-midi? 2 *(be knowledgeable
about)* s'y connaître en quelque chose □ He
knows a lot about cars. Il s'y connaît en
voitures. □ I don't know much about
computers. Je ne m'y connais pas bien en
informatique.

■ **to get to know somebody** apprendre à
connaître quelqu'un

■ **How should I know?** *(I don't know!)*
Comment veux-tu que je le sache?

■ **You never know!** On ne sait jamais!

know-all NOUN
le/la je-sais-tout

□ He's such a know-all! C'est Monsieur
je-sais-tout!

know-how NOUN
le savoir-faire

knowledge NOUN
la connaissance

knowledgeable ADJECTIVE

■ **to be knowledgeable about something**
s'y connaître en quelque chose □ She's very
knowledgeable about computers. Elle s'y
connaît bien en informatique.

known VERB ▷ *see* **know**

Koran NOUN
le Coran

Korea NOUN
la Corée

■ **in Korea** en Corée

kosher ADJECTIVE
kascher (FEM+PL kascher)

k

433

lab NOUN (= *laboratory*)
le labo
- **a lab technician** un laborantin

label NOUN
l' étiquette *fem*

labor NOUN (US)
- **to be in labor** être en train d'accoucher
- **the labor market** le marché du travail
- **a labor union** un syndicat

laboratory NOUN
le laboratoire

Labour NOUN
les travaillistes *masc pl*
□ My parents vote Labour. Mes parents votent pour les travaillistes.
- **the Labour Party** le parti travailliste

labour NOUN
- **to be in labour** être en train d'accoucher
- **the labour market** le marché du travail

labourer NOUN
le manœuvre
- **a farm labourer** un ouvrier agricole

lace NOUN
1 le lacet *(of shoe)*
2 la dentelle
□ a lace collar un col en dentelle

lack NOUN
le manque
□ He got the job despite his lack of experience. Il a obtenu le poste en dépit de son manque d'expérience.
- **There was no lack of volunteers.** Les volontaires ne manquaient pas.

lacquer NOUN
la laque

lad NOUN
le gars

ladder NOUN
l' échelle *fem*

lady NOUN
la dame
- **a young lady** une jeune fille
- **Ladies and gentlemen ...** Mesdames, Messieurs ...
- **the ladies'** les toilettes pour dames

fem pl

ladybird NOUN
la coccinelle

to **lag behind** VERB
rester en arrière

lager NOUN
la bière blonde

laid VERB ▷ *see* **lay**

laid-back ADJECTIVE
relaxe (FEM relaxe)

lain VERB ▷ *see* **lie**

lake NOUN
le lac
- **Lake Geneva** le lac Léman

lamb NOUN
l' agneau *masc* (PL les agneaux)
- **a lamb chop** une côtelette d'agneau

lame ADJECTIVE
boiteux (FEM boiteuse)
□ My pony is lame. Mon poney boite.

lamp NOUN
la lampe

lamppost NOUN
le réverbère

lampshade NOUN
l' abat-jour *masc* (PL les abat-jour)

land NOUN
▷ *see also* **land** VERB
la terre
- **a piece of land** un terrain

to **land** VERB
▷ *see also* **land** NOUN
atterrir *(plane, passenger)*

landing NOUN
1 l' atterrissage *masc (of plane)*
2 le palier *(of staircase)*

landlady NOUN
la propriétaire

landlord NOUN
le propriétaire

landmark NOUN
le point de repère *(for finding your way)*
- **Big Ben is one of London's most famous landmarks.** Big Ben est l'un des sites les plus célèbres du paysage londonien.

landowner NOUN
le propriétaire terrien

landscape NOUN
le paysage

lane NOUN
1 le chemin (in country)
2 la voie (on motorway)

language NOUN
la langue
□ French isn't a difficult language. Le français n'est pas une langue difficile.
■ **to use bad language** dire des grossièretés

language laboratory NOUN
le laboratoire de langues

lanky ADJECTIVE
dégingandé (FEM dégingandée)
□ a lanky boy un garçon dégingandé

lap NOUN
le tour de piste (sport)
□ I ran ten laps. J'ai fait dix tours de piste en courant.
■ **on my lap** sur mes genoux

laptop NOUN (computer)
le portable

larder NOUN
le garde-manger (PL les garde-manger)

large ADJECTIVE
1 grand (FEM grande)
□ a large house une grande maison
2 gros (FEM grosse) (person, animal)
□ a large dog un gros chien

largely ADVERB
en grande partie
□ It's largely the fault of the government. C'est en grande partie la faute du gouvernement.

laser NOUN
le laser

lass NOUN
la jeune fille

last ADJECTIVE, ADVERB
▷ see also **last** VERB
1 dernier (FEM dernière)
□ last Friday vendredi dernier □ last week la semaine dernière □ last summer l'été dernier
2 en dernier
□ He arrived last. Il est arrivé en dernier.
3 pour la dernière fois
□ I've lost my bag. — When did you see it last? J'ai perdu mon sac. — Quand est-ce que tu l'as vu pour la dernière fois? □ When I last saw him, he was wearing a blue shirt. La dernière fois que je l'ai vu, il portait une chemise bleue.
■ **the last time** la dernière fois □ the last

time I saw her la dernière fois que je l'ai vue
□ That's the last time I take your advice! C'est la dernière fois que je suis tes conseils!
■ **last night 1** (evening) hier soir □ I got home at midnight last night. Je suis rentré à minuit hier soir. **2** (sleeping hours) la nuit dernière □ I couldn't sleep last night. J'ai eu du mal à dormir la nuit dernière.
■ **at last** enfin

to **last** VERB
▷ see also **last** ADJECTIVE
durer
□ The concert lasts two hours. Le concert dure deux heures.

lastly ADVERB
finalement
□ Lastly, what time do you arrive? Finalement, à quelle heure arrives-tu?

late ADJECTIVE, ADVERB
1 en retard
□ Hurry up or you'll be late! Dépêche-toi, sinon tu vas être en retard! □ I'm often late for school. J'arrive souvent en retard à l'école.
■ **to arrive late** arriver en retard □ She arrived late. Elle est arrivée en retard.
2 tard
□ I went to bed late. Je me suis couché tard.
■ **in the late afternoon** en fin d'après-midi
■ **in late May** fin mai

lately ADVERB
ces derniers temps
□ I haven't seen him lately. Je ne l'ai pas vu ces derniers temps.

later ADVERB
plus tard
□ I'll do it later. Je ferai ça plus tard.
■ **See you later!** À tout à l'heure!

latest ADJECTIVE
dernier (FEM dernière)
□ their latest album leur dernier album
■ **at the latest** au plus tard □ by 10 o'clock at the latest à dix heures au plus tard

Latin NOUN
le latin
□ I do Latin. Je fais du latin.

Latin America NOUN
l' Amérique latine fem
■ **in Latin America** en Amérique latine

Latin American ADJECTIVE
latino-américain (FEM latino-américaine)

latter NOUN
le second
la seconde
■ **the former ..., the latter ...** le premier ..., le second ... □ The former lives in the US, the latter in Australia. Le premier habite aux

États-Unis, le second en Australie.
■ **The latter is the more expensive of the two systems.** Ce dernier système est le plus coûteux des deux.

laugh NOUN
▷ see also **laugh** VERB
le rire
■ **It was a good laugh.** (it was fun) On s'est bien amusés.

to **laugh** VERB
▷ see also **laugh** NOUN
rire
■ **to laugh at something** se moquer de quelque chose □ They laughed at her. Ils se sont moqués d'elle.

to **launch** VERB
lancer (product, rocket, boat)
□ They're going to launch a new model. Ils vont lancer un nouveau modèle.

Launderette® NOUN
la laverie

Laundromat® NOUN (US)
la laverie

laundry NOUN
le linge (clothes)

lavatory NOUN
les toilettes fem pl

lavender NOUN
la lavande

law NOUN
1 la loi
□ The laws are very strict. Les lois sont très sévères.
■ **It's against the law.** C'est illégal.
2 le droit (subject)
□ My sister's studying law. Ma sœur fait des études de droit.

lawn NOUN
la pelouse

lawnmower NOUN
la tondeuse à gazon

law school NOUN (US)
la faculté de droit

lawyer NOUN
l' avocat masc
l' avocate fem
□ My mother's a lawyer. Ma mère est avocate.

to **lay** VERB
LANGUAGE TIP 'lay' is also a form of 'lie' VERB.
mettre
□ She laid the baby in her cot. Elle a mis le bébé dans son lit.
■ **to lay the table** mettre la table
■ **to lay something on 1** (provide) organiser quelque chose □ They laid on

extra buses. Ils ont organisé un service de bus supplémentaire. **2** (prepare) préparer quelque chose □ They laid on a special meal. Ils ont préparé un repas soigné.

to **lay off** VERB
licencier
□ My father's been laid off. Mon père a été licencié.

lay-by NOUN
l' aire de stationnement fem

layer NOUN
la couche
□ the ozone layer la couche d'ozone

layout NOUN
1 la mise en page (of newspaper article)
2 la disposition (of house, buildings)
□ No one likes the new office layout. Personne n'aime la nouvelle disposition des bureaux.

lazy ADJECTIVE
paresseux (FEM paresseuse)

lead NOUN
LANGUAGE TIP This word has two pronunciations. Make sure you choose the right translation.
▷ see also **lead** VERB
1 le fil (cable)
2 la laisse (for dog)
■ **to be in the lead** être en tête □ Our team is in the lead. Notre équipe est en tête.
3 le plomb (metal)

to **lead** VERB
▷ see also **lead** NOUN
mener
□ the street that leads to the station la rue qui mène à la gare
■ **to lead the way** montrer le chemin
■ **to lead somebody away** emmener quelqu'un □ The police led the man away. La police a emmené l'homme.

leaded NOUN
■ **leaded petrol** l' essence au plomb fem

leader NOUN
1 le chef (of expedition, gang)
2 le dirigeant
la dirigeante (of political party)

lead-free ADJECTIVE
■ **lead-free petrol** de l'essence sans plomb

lead singer NOUN
le chanteur principal
la chanteuse principale

leaf NOUN
la feuille

leaflet NOUN
la brochure

league NOUN
le championnat

□ They are at the top of the league. Ils sont en tête du championnat.

■ **the Premier League** la première division

leak NOUN
▷ *see also* **leak** VERB
la fuite

□ a gas leak une fuite de gaz

to **leak** VERB
▷ *see also* **leak** NOUN
fuir *(pipe, water, gas)*

to **lean** VERB
se pencher

■ **to be leaning against something** être appuyé contre quelque chose □ The ladder was leaning against the wall. L'échelle était appuyée contre le mur.

■ **to lean something against a wall** appuyer quelque chose contre un mur □ He leant his bike against the wall. Il a appuyé son vélo contre le mur.

to **lean forward** VERB
se pencher en avant

to **lean on** VERB
■ **to lean on something** s'appuyer contre quelque chose □ He leant on the wall. Il s'est appuyé contre le mur.

to **lean out** VERB
se pencher au dehors

■ **She leant out of the window.** Elle s'est penchée par la fenêtre.

to **lean over** VERB
se pencher

□ Don't lean over too far. Ne te penche pas trop loin.

to **leap** VERB
sauter

□ They leapt over the stream. Ils ont sauté pour traverser la rivière.

■ **He leapt out of his chair when his team scored.** Il s'est levé d'un bond lorsque son équipe a marqué.

leap year NOUN
l'année bissextile *fem*

to **learn** VERB
apprendre

□ I'm learning to ski. J'apprends à skier.

learner NOUN
■ **She's a quick learner.** Elle apprend vite.
■ **French learners** *(people learning French)* ceux qui apprennent le français

learner driver NOUN
le conducteur débutant
la conductrice débutante

learnt VERB ▷ *see* **learn**

least ADVERB, ADJECTIVE, PRONOUN
■ **the least 1** *(followed by noun)* le moins de □ It takes the least time. C'est ce qui

prend le moins de temps. **2** *(after a verb)* le moins □ Maths is the subject I like the least. Les maths sont la matière que j'aime le moins.

LANGUAGE TIP When 'least' is followed by an adjective, the translation depends on whether the noun referred to is masculine, feminine or plural.

■ **the least ... 1** le moins ... □ the least expensive hotel l'hôtel le moins cher **2** la moins ... □ the least expensive seat la place la moins chère **3** les moins ... □ the least expensive hotels les hôtels les moins chers □ the least expensive seats les places les moins chères

■ **It's the least I can do.** C'est le moins que je puisse faire.

■ **at least 1** au moins □ It'll cost at least £200. Ça va coûter au moins deux cents livres. **2** du moins □ ... but at least nobody was hurt. ... mais du moins personne n'a été blessé. □ It's totally unfair – at least, that's my opinion. C'est vraiment injuste – du moins c'est ce que je pense.

leather NOUN
le cuir

□ a black leather jacket un blouson en cuir noir

leave NOUN
▷ *see also* **leave** VERB
1 le congé *(from job)*
2 la permission *(from army)*

□ My brother is on leave for a week. Mon frère est en permission pendant une semaine.

to **leave** VERB
▷ *see also* **leave** NOUN
1 laisser *(deliberately)*

□ Don't leave your camera in the car. Ne laisse pas ton appareil-photo dans la voiture.

2 oublier *(by mistake)*

□ I've left my book at home. J'ai oublié mon livre à la maison. □ Make sure you haven't left anything behind. Vérifiez bien que vous n'avez rien oublié.

3 partir *(go)*

□ The bus leaves at 8. Le car part à huit heures. □ She's just left. Elle vient de partir.

4 quitter *(go away from)*

□ We leave London at six o'clock. Nous quittons Londres à six heures. □ My sister left home last year. Ma sœur a quitté la maison l'an dernier.

■ **to leave somebody alone** laisser quelqu'un tranquille □ Leave me alone!

437

leave out – less

Laisse-moi tranquille!

to leave out VERB
mettre à l'écart
□ As the new girl, I felt really left out. En tant que nouvelle, je me suis vraiment sentie à l'écart.

leaves PL NOUN ▷ see **leaf**

Lebanon NOUN
le Liban
■ **in Lebanon** au Liban

lecture NOUN
▷ see also **lecture** VERB
1 la conférence (public)
2 le cours magistral (PL les cours magistraux) (at university)

> LANGUAGE TIP Be careful not to translate **lecture** by the French word **lecture**.

to lecture VERB
▷ see also **lecture** NOUN
1 enseigner
□ She lectures at the technical college. Elle enseigne au collège technique.
2 faire la morale
□ He's always lecturing us. Il n'arrête pas de nous faire la morale.

lecturer NOUN
le professeur d'université
□ She's a lecturer. Elle est professeur d'université.

led VERB ▷ see **lead**

leek NOUN
le poireau (PL les poireaux)

left VERB ▷ see **leave**

left ADJECTIVE, ADVERB
▷ see also **left** NOUN
1 gauche (FEM gauche) (not right)
□ my left hand ma main gauche □ on the left side of the road sur le côté gauche de la route
2 à gauche
□ Turn left at the traffic lights. Tournez à gauche aux prochains feux.
■ **I haven't got any money left.** Il ne me reste plus d'argent.

left NOUN
▷ see also **left** ADJECTIVE
la gauche
■ **on the left** à gauche □ Remember to drive on the left. N'oubliez pas de conduire à gauche.

left-hand ADJECTIVE
■ **the left-hand side** la gauche □ It's on the left-hand side. C'est à gauche.

left-handed ADJECTIVE
gaucher (FEM gauchère)

left-luggage office NOUN

la consigne

left-luggage locker NOUN
la consigne automatique

leg NOUN
la jambe
□ She's broken her leg. Elle s'est cassé la jambe.
■ **a chicken leg** une cuisse de poulet
■ **a leg of lamb** un gigot d'agneau

legal ADJECTIVE
légal (FEM légale, MASC PL légaux)

leggings NOUN
le caleçon sing

leisure NOUN
les loisirs masc pl
□ What do you do in your leisure time? Qu'est-ce que tu fais pendant tes loisirs?

leisure centre NOUN
le centre de loisirs

lemon NOUN
le citron

lemonade NOUN
la limonade

to lend VERB
prêter
□ I can lend you some money. Je peux te prêter de l'argent.

length NOUN
la longueur
■ **It's about a metre in length.** Ça fait environ un mètre de long.

lens NOUN
1 la lentille (contact lens)
2 le verre (of spectacles)
3 l' objectif masc (of camera)

Lent NOUN
le carême

lent VERB ▷ see **lend**

lentil NOUN
la lentille

Leo NOUN
le Lion
□ I'm Leo. Je suis Lion.

leotard NOUN
le justaucorps

lesbian NOUN
la lesbienne

less PRONOUN, ADVERB, ADJECTIVE
1 moins
□ He's less intelligent than her. Il est moins intelligent qu'elle. □ A bit less, please. Un peu moins, s'il vous plaît.
2 moins de
□ I've got less time for hobbies now. J'ai moins de temps pour les loisirs maintenant.
■ **less than 1** (with amounts) moins de
□ It's less than a kilometre from here. C'est

à moins d'un kilomètre d'ici. □ It costs less than 100 euros. Ça coûte moins de cent euros. □ less than half moins de la moitié **2** (in comparisons) moins que □ He spent less than me. Il a dépensé moins que moi. □ I've got less than you. J'en ai moins que toi. □ It cost less than we thought. Ça a coûté moins cher que nous ne le pensions.

lesson NOUN
1 la leçon

□ a French lesson une leçon de français □ 'Lesson Sixteen' (in textbook) 'Leçon seize'
2 le cours (class)

□ The lessons last forty minutes each. Chaque cours dure quarante minutes.

to **let** VERB
1 laisser (allow)

■ **to let somebody do something** laisser quelqu'un faire quelque chose □ Let me have a look. Laisse-moi voir. □ My parents won't let me stay out that late. Mes parents ne me laissent pas sortir aussi tard.

■ **to let somebody know** faire savoir à quelqu'un □ I'll let you know as soon as possible. Je vous le ferai savoir dès que possible.

■ **to let somebody go** lâcher quelqu'un □ Let me go! Lâche-moi!

⸰⸰ **LANGUAGE TIP** To make suggestions using 'let's', you can ask questions beginning with **si on**.

□ Let's go to the cinema! Si on allait au cinéma?

■ **Let's go!** Allons-y!
2 louer (hire out)

■ **'to let'** 'à louer'

to **let down** VERB
décevoir

□ I won't let you down. Je ne vous décevrai pas.

to **let in** VERB
laisser entrer

□ They wouldn't let me in because I was under 18. Ils ne m'ont pas laissé entrer parce que j'avais moins de dix-huit ans.

letter NOUN
la lettre

letterbox NOUN
la boîte à lettres

lettuce NOUN
la salade

leukaemia NOUN
la leucémie

level ADJECTIVE
▷ see also **level** NOUN
plan (FEM plane)

□ A snooker table must be perfectly level.

Un billard doit être parfaitement plan.

level NOUN
▷ see also **level** ADJECTIVE
le niveau (PL les niveaux)

□ The level of the river is rising. Le niveau de la rivière monte.

■ **A levels** le baccalauréat

⸰⸰ **DID YOU KNOW…?**
The French **baccalauréat** (or **bac** for short) is taken at the age of 17 or 18. Students have to sit one of a variety of set subject combinations, rather than being able to choose any combination of subjects they want. If you pass you have the right to a place at university.

level crossing NOUN
le passage à niveau

lever NOUN
le levier

liable ADJECTIVE
■ **He's liable to lose his temper.** Il se met facilement en colère.

liar NOUN
le menteur
la menteuse

liberal ADJECTIVE
libéral (FEM libérale, MASC PL libéraux) (opinions)

■ **the Liberal Democrats** le parti libéral-démocrate

liberation NOUN
la libération

Libra NOUN
la Balance

□ I'm Libra. Je suis Balance.

librarian NOUN
le/la bibliothécaire

□ She's a librarian. Elle est bibliothécaire.

library NOUN
la bibliothèque

⸰⸰ **LANGUAGE TIP** Be careful not to translate **library** by librairie.

Libya NOUN
la Libye

■ **in Libya** en Libye

licence (US **license**) NOUN
le permis

■ **a driving licence** un permis de conduire

to **lick** VERB
lécher

lid NOUN
le couvercle

to **lie** VERB
▷ see also **lie** NOUN
mentir (not tell the truth)

□ I know she's lying. Je sais qu'elle ment.

- **to lie down** s'allonger
- **to be lying down** être allongé □ He was lying down on the sofa. Il était allongé sur le canapé.
- **to lie on the beach** être allongé sur la plage

lie NOUN
▷ *see also* **lie** VERB
le mensonge
- **to tell a lie** mentir
- **That's a lie!** Ce n'est pas vrai!

lie-in NOUN
- **to have a lie-in** faire la grasse matinée
□ I have a lie-in on Sundays. Je fais la grasse matinée le dimanche.

lieutenant NOUN
le lieutenant

life NOUN
la vie

lifebelt NOUN
la bouée de sauvetage

lifeboat NOUN
le canot de sauvetage

lifeguard NOUN
le maître nageur

life jacket NOUN
le gilet de sauvetage

life-saving NOUN
le sauvetage
□ I've done a course in life-saving. J'ai pris des cours de sauvetage.

lifestyle NOUN
le style de vie

to lift VERB
▷ *see also* **lift** NOUN
soulever
□ It's too heavy, I can't lift it. C'est trop lourd, je ne peux pas le soulever.

lift NOUN
▷ *see also* **lift** VERB
l'ascenseur *masc*
□ The lift isn't working. L'ascenseur est en panne.
- **He gave me a lift to the cinema.** Il m'a emmené au cinéma en voiture.
- **Would you like a lift?** Est-ce que je peux vous déposer quelque part?

light ADJECTIVE
▷ *see also* **light** NOUN, VERB
1 léger (FEM légère) *(not heavy)*
□ a light jacket une veste légère □ a light meal un repas léger
2 clair (FEM claire) *(colour)*
□ a light blue sweater un pull bleu clair

light NOUN
▷ *see also* **light** ADJECTIVE, VERB
1 la lumière

□ to switch on the light allumer la lumière
□ to switch off the light éteindre la lumière
2 la lampe
□ There's a light by my bed. Il y a une lampe près de mon lit.
- **the traffic lights** les feux *masc pl*
- **Have you got a light?** *(for cigarette)* Avez-vous du feu?

to light VERB
▷ *see also* **light** ADJECTIVE, NOUN
allumer *(candle, cigarette, fire)*

light bulb NOUN
l'ampoule *fem*

lighter NOUN
le briquet *(for cigarettes)*

lighthouse NOUN
le phare

lightning NOUN
les éclairs *masc pl*
- **a flash of lightning** un éclair

to like VERB
▷ *see also* **like** PREPOSITION
1 aimer
□ I don't like mustard. Je n'aime pas la moutarde. □ I like riding. J'aime monter à cheval.

> **LANGUAGE TIP** Note that aimer also means to love, so make sure you use aimer bien for just liking somebody.

2 aimer bien
□ I like Paul, but I don't want to go out with him. J'aime bien Paul, mais je ne veux pas sortir avec lui.
- **I'd like ...** Je voudrais ... □ I'd like an orange juice, please. Je voudrais un jus d'orange, s'il vous plaît. □ Would you like some coffee? Voulez-vous du café?
- **I'd like to ...** J'aimerais ... □ I'd like to go to Russia one day. J'aimerais aller en Russie un jour. □ I'd like to wash my hands. J'aimerais me laver les mains.
- **Would you like to go for a walk?** Tu veux aller faire une promenade?
- **... if you like** ... si tu veux

like PREPOSITION
▷ *see also* **like** VERB
comme
□ It's fine like that. C'est bien comme ça. □ Do it like this. Fais-le comme ça. □ a city like Paris une ville comme Paris □ It's a bit like salmon. C'est un peu comme du saumon.
- **What's the weather like?** Quel temps fait-il?
- **to look like somebody** ressembler à quelqu'un □ You look like my brother. Tu ressembles à mon frère.

likely ADJECTIVE
probable (FEM probable)
□ That's not very likely. C'est peu probable.
■ **She's likely to come.** Elle viendra
probablement.
■ **She's not likely to come.** Elle ne viendra
probablement pas.

Lilo® NOUN
le matelas pneumatique

lily of the valley NOUN
le muguet

> **DID YOU KNOW...?**
> On May 1st French people celebrate
> May Day by giving each other small
> bunches of lily of the valley.

lime NOUN
le citron vert (fruit)

limit NOUN
la limite
□ The speed limit is 70 mph. La vitesse est
limitée à cent dix kilomètres à l'heure.

limousine NOUN
la limousine

to **limp** VERB
boiter

line NOUN
1 la ligne
□ a straight line une ligne droite
2 le trait (to divide, cancel)
□ Draw a line under each answer. Tirez un
trait après chaque réponse.
3 la voie (railway track)
■ **Hold the line, please.** Ne quittez pas.
■ **It's a very bad line.** La ligne est très
mauvaise.

linen NOUN
le lin
□ a linen jacket une veste en lin

liner NOUN
le paquebot (ship)

linguist NOUN
■ **to be a good linguist** être doué pour les
langues □ She's a good linguist. Elle est
douée pour les langues.

lining NOUN
la doublure (of jacket, skirt etc)

link NOUN
▷ see also **link** VERB
1 le rapport
□ the link between smoking and cancer le
rapport entre le tabagisme et le cancer
2 le lien (computing)

to **link** VERB
▷ see also **link** NOUN
relier

lino NOUN
le linoléum

lion NOUN
le lion

lioness NOUN
la lionne

lip NOUN
la lèvre

to **lip-read** VERB
lire sur les lèvres

lip salve NOUN
la pommade pour les lèvres

lipstick NOUN
le rouge à lèvres

> **LANGUAGE TIP** Word for word, this
> means 'red for lips'.

liqueur NOUN
la liqueur

liquid NOUN
le liquide

liquidizer NOUN
le mixer

list NOUN
▷ see also **list** VERB
la liste

to **list** VERB
▷ see also **list** NOUN
faire une liste de
□ List your hobbies! Fais une liste de tes
hobbies!

to **listen** VERB
écouter
□ Listen to this! Écoutez ceci! □ Listen to
me! Écoutez-moi!

listener NOUN
l' auditeur masc
l' auditrice fem

lit VERB ▷ see **light**

liter NOUN (US)
le litre

literally ADVERB
vraiment (completely)
□ It was literally impossible to find a seat. Il
était vraiment impossible de trouver une
place.
■ **to translate literally** faire une traduction
littérale

literature NOUN
la littérature
□ I'm studying English Literature. J'étudie la
littérature anglaise.

litre NOUN
le litre

litter NOUN
les ordures fem pl

litter bin NOUN
la poubelle

little ADJECTIVE
petit (FEM petite)

I

□ a little girl une petite fille

WORD POWER
You can use a number of other words instead of **little** to mean 'small':
miniature miniature
□ a miniature version une version miniature
minute minuscule
□ a minute plant une plante minuscule
tiny minuscule
□ a tiny garden un jardin minuscule

■ **a little** un peu □ How much would you like? — Just a little. Combien en voulez-vous? — Juste un peu.
■ **very little** très peu □ We've got very little time. Nous avons très peu de temps.
■ **little by little** petit à petit

live ADJECTIVE
▷ see also **live** VERB
1 vivant (FEM vivante) (animal)
2 en direct (broadcast)
■ **There's live music on Fridays.** Il y a des musiciens qui jouent le vendredi.

to **live** VERB
▷ see also **live** ADJECTIVE
1 vivre
□ I live with my grandmother. Je vis avec ma grand-mère.
2 habiter (reside)
□ Where do you live? Où est-ce que tu habites? □ I live in Edinburgh. J'habite à Édimbourg.

to **live on** VERB
■ **to live on something** vivre de quelque chose □ He lives on benefit. Il vit de ses indemnités.

to **live together** VERB
1 partager un appartement (as flatmates)
□ She's living with two Greek students. Elle partage un appartement avec deux étudiants grecs.
2 vivre ensemble
□ My parents aren't living together any more. Mes parents ne vivent plus ensemble.
■ **They're not married, they're living together.** Ils ne sont pas mariés, ils vivent en concubinage.

lively ADJECTIVE
■ **She's got a lively personality.** Elle est pleine de vitalité.
animé (FEM animée)
□ It was a lively party. C'était une soirée animée.

liver NOUN
le foie

lives PL NOUN ▷ see **life**

living NOUN
■ **to make a living** gagner sa vie
■ **What does she do for a living?** Qu'est-ce qu'elle fait dans la vie?

living room NOUN
la salle de séjour

lizard NOUN
le lézard

load NOUN
▷ see also **load** VERB
■ **loads of** un tas de □ loads of people un tas de gens □ loads of money un tas d'argent
■ **You're talking a load of rubbish!** Tu ne dis que des bêtises!

to **load** VERB
▷ see also **load** NOUN
charger
□ a trolley loaded with luggage un chariot chargé de bagages

loaf NOUN
le pain
■ **a loaf of bread** un pain

loan NOUN
▷ see also **loan** VERB
le prêt

to **loan** VERB
▷ see also **loan** NOUN
prêter

to **loathe** VERB
détester
□ I loathe her. Je la déteste.

loaves PL NOUN ▷ see **loaf**

lobster NOUN
le homard

local ADJECTIVE
local (FEM locale, MASC PL locaux)
□ the local paper le journal local
■ **a local call** une communication urbaine

location NOUN
l' endroit masc
■ **a hotel set in a beautiful location** un hôtel situé dans un endroit magnifique
LANGUAGE TIP Be careful not to translate **location** by the French word **location**.

loch NOUN
le loch

lock NOUN
▷ see also **lock** VERB
la serrure
□ The lock is broken. La serrure est cassée.

to **lock** VERB
▷ see also **lock** NOUN
fermer à clé
□ Make sure you lock your door. N'oubliez

pas de fermer votre porte à clé.

to **lock out** VERB
- ■ **The door slammed and I was locked out.** La porte a claqué et je me suis retrouvé à la porte.

locker NOUN
le casier
- ■ **the locker room** le vestiaire
- ■ **the left-luggage lockers** la consigne automatique *sing*

locket NOUN
le médaillon

lodger NOUN
le/la locataire

loft NOUN
le grenier

log NOUN
la bûche *(of wood)*

to **log in** VERB
se connecter

to **log off** VERB
se déconnecter

to **log on** VERB
se connecter

to **log out** VERB
se déconnecter

logical ADJECTIVE
logique (FEM logique)

lollipop NOUN
la sucette

lolly NOUN
la glace à l'eau *(ice lolly)*

London NOUN
Londres
- ■ **in London** à Londres
- ■ **to London** à Londres
- ■ **I'm from London.** Je suis de Londres.

Londoner NOUN
le Londonien
la Londonienne

loneliness NOUN
la solitude

lonely ADJECTIVE
seul (FEM seule)
- ■ **to feel lonely** se sentir seul □ She feels a bit lonely. Elle se sent un peu seule.

lonesome ADJECTIVE
- ■ **to feel lonesome** se sentir seul

long ADJECTIVE, ADVERB
▷ *see also* **long** VERB
long (FEM longue)
- □ She's got long hair. Elle a les cheveux longs.
- ■ **The room is 6 metres long.** La pièce fait six mètres de long.
- ■ **how long?** *(time)* combien de temps? □ How long did you stay there? Combien de temps êtes-vous resté là-bas? □ How long have you been here? Depuis combien de temps êtes-vous ici? □ How long is the flight? Combien de temps dure le vol?
- ■ **I've been waiting a long time.** J'attends depuis longtemps.
- ■ **It takes a long time.** Ça prend du temps.
- ■ **as long as** si □ I'll come as long as it's not too expensive. Je viendrai si ce n'est pas trop cher.

to **long** VERB
▷ *see also* **long** ADJECTIVE
- ■ **to long to do something** attendre avec impatience de faire quelque chose □ I'm longing to see my boyfriend again. J'attends avec impatience de revoir mon copain.

long-distance ADJECTIVE
- ■ **a long-distance call** une communication interurbaine

longer ADVERB
▷ *see also* **long** ADJECTIVE
- ■ **They're no longer going out together.** Ils ne sortent plus ensemble.
- ■ **I can't stand it any longer.** Je ne peux plus le supporter.

long jump NOUN
le saut en longueur

loo NOUN
les toilettes *fem pl*
- □ Where's the loo? Où sont les toilettes?

look NOUN
▷ *see also* **look** VERB
- ■ **to have a look** regarder □ Have a look at this! Regardez ceci!
- ■ **I don't like the look of it.** Ça ne me dit rien.

to **look** VERB
▷ *see also* **look** NOUN
1 regarder
- □ Look! Regardez!
- ■ **to look at something** regarder quelque chose □ Look at the picture. Regardez cette image.
2 avoir l'air *(seem)*
- □ She looks surprised. Elle a l'air surprise.
- □ That cake looks nice. Ce gâteau a l'air bon.
- □ It looks fine. Ça a l'air bien.
- ■ **to look like somebody** ressembler à quelqu'un □ He looks like his brother. Il ressemble à son frère.
- ■ **What does she look like?** Comment est-elle physiquement?
- ■ **to look forward to something** attendre quelque chose avec impatience □ I'm looking forward to the holidays. J'attends les vacances avec impatience.
- ■ **Looking forward to hearing from you ...** 443

J'espère avoir bientôt de tes nouvelles ...
■ **Look out!** Attention!

to **look after** VERB
s'occuper de
□ I look after my little sister. Je m'occupe de ma petite sœur.

to **look for** VERB
chercher
□ I'm looking for my passport. Je cherche mon passeport.

to **look round** VERB
1 se retourner *(look behind)*
□ I shouted and he looked round. J'ai crié et il s'est retourné.
2 jeter un coup d'œil *(have a look)*
□ I'm just looking round. Je jette simplement un coup d'œil.
■ **to look round a museum** visiter un musée
■ **I like looking round the shops.** J'aime faire les boutiques.

to **look up** VERB
chercher *(word, name)*
□ Look the word up in the dictionary. Cherchez le mot ans le dictionnaire.

loose ADJECTIVE
ample *(FEM ample) (clothes)*
■ **loose change** la petite monnaie

lord NOUN
le seigneur *(feudal)*
■ **the House of Lords** la Chambre des lords
■ **good Lord!** mon Dieu!

lorry NOUN
le camion

lorry driver NOUN
le routier
□ He's a lorry driver. Il est routier.

to **lose** VERB
perdre
□ I've lost my purse. J'ai perdu mon porte-monnaie.
■ **to get lost** se perdre □ I was afraid of getting lost. J'avais peur de me perdre.

loser NOUN
1 le perdant
la perdante
■ **to be a bad loser** être mauvais perdant
2 le loser *(pathetic person)*
□ He's such a loser! C'est un vrai loser!

loss NOUN
la perte

lost VERB ▷ see **lose**

lost ADJECTIVE
perdu *(FEM perdue)*

lost-and-found NOUN (US)
les objets trouvés *masc pl (word, name)*

lost property office NOUN

les objets trouvés *masc pl*
○ **LANGUAGE TIP** Word for word, this means 'things that have been found'.

lot NOUN
■ **a lot** beaucoup
■ **a lot of** beaucoup de □ We saw a lot of interesting things. Nous avons vu beaucoup de choses intéressantes.
■ **lots of** un tas de □ She's got lots of money. Elle a un tas d'argent. □ He's got lots of friends. Il a un tas d'amis.
■ **What did you do at the weekend? — Not a lot.** Qu'as-tu fait ce week-end? — Pas grand-chose.
■ **Do you like football? — Not a lot.** Tu aimes le football? — Pas tellement.
■ **That's the lot.** C'est tout.

lottery NOUN
la loterie
□ to win the lottery gagner à la loterie

loud ADJECTIVE
fort *(FEM forte)*
□ The television is too loud. La télévision est trop forte.

loudly ADVERB
fort

loudspeaker NOUN
le haut-parleur

lounge NOUN
le salon

lousy ADJECTIVE
infect *(FEM infecte)*
□ The food in the canteen is lousy. La nourriture de la cantine est infecte.
■ **I feel lousy.** Je suis mal fichu. *(informal)*

love NOUN
▷ see also **love** VERB
l' amour *masc*
■ **to be in love** être amoureux □ She's in love with Paul. Elle est amoureuse de Paul.
■ **to make love** faire l'amour
■ **Give Delphine my love.** Embrasse Delphine pour moi.
■ **Love, Rosemary.** Amitiés, Rosemary.

to **love** VERB
▷ see also **love** NOUN
1 aimer *(be in love with)*
□ I love you. Je t'aime.
2 aimer beaucoup *(like a lot)*
□ Everybody loves her. Tout le monde l'aime beaucoup. □ I'd love to come. J'aimerais beaucoup venir.
3 adorer *(things)*
□ I love chocolate. J'adore le chocolat. □ I love skiing. J'adore le ski.

lovely ADJECTIVE
charmant *(FEM charmante)*

□ What a lovely surprise! Quelle charmante surprise! □ She's a lovely person. Elle est charmante.
■ **It's a lovely day.** Il fait très beau aujourd'hui.
■ **Is your meal OK? — Yes, it's lovely.** Est-ce que c'est bon? — Oui, c'est délicieux.
■ **They've got a lovely house.** Ils ont une très belle maison.
■ **Have a lovely time!** Amusez-vous bien!

lover NOUN
1 l' amant *masc*
la maîtresse *(in relationship)*
2 l' amateur *masc (of hobby, wine)*
□ an art lover un amateur d'art □ She is a lover of good food. Elle est amateur de bonne cuisine.

low ADJECTIVE, ADVERB
bas (FEM basse) *(price, level)*
□ That plane is flying very low. Cet avion vole très bas.
■ **the low season** la basse saison □ in the low season en basse saison

lower ADJECTIVE
▷ *see also* **lower** VERB
inférieur (FEM inférieure)
□ on the lower floor a l'étage inférieur

to **lower** VERB
▷ *see also* **lower** ADJECTIVE
baisser

lower sixth NOUN
la première
□ He's in the lower sixth. Il est en première.

DID YOU KNOW...?
In French secondary schools the years are counted from the **sixième** (lowest) to **première** and **terminale** (oldest).

low-fat ADJECTIVE
allégé (FEM allégée)
□ a low-fat yoghurt un yaourt allégé

loyalty NOUN
la fidélité

loyalty card NOUN
la carte de fidélité

L-plates PL NOUN
les plaques de conducteur débutant *fem pl*

luck NOUN
la chance
□ She hasn't had much luck. Elle n'a pas eu beaucoup de chance.
■ **Good luck!** Bonne chance!
■ **Bad luck!** Pas de chance!

luckily ADVERB
heureusement

lucky ADJECTIVE
■ **to be lucky 1** *(be fortunate)* avoir de la chance □ Lucky you! Tu as de la chance!
□ He's lucky, he's got a job. Il a de la chance, il a un emploi. □ He wasn't hurt. — That was lucky! Il n'a pas été blessé. — C'est une chance! **2** *(bring luck)* porter bonheur
□ Black cats are lucky in Britain. Les chats noirs portent bonheur en Grande-Bretagne.
■ **a lucky horseshoe** un fer à cheval porte-bonheur

luggage NOUN
les bagages *masc pl*

lukewarm ADJECTIVE
tiède (FEM tiède) *(water, food)*
■ **The response was lukewarm.** Sa réaction a été peu enthousiaste.

lump NOUN
1 le morceau (PL les morceaux)
□ a lump of butter un morceau de beurre
2 la bosse *(swelling)*
□ He's got a lump on his forehead. Il a une bosse sur le front.

lunatic NOUN
le fou
la folle
□ He drives like a lunatic. Il conduit comme un fou.

lunch NOUN
le déjeuner
■ **to have lunch** déjeuner □ We have lunch at 12.30. Nous déjeunons à midi et demie.

luncheon voucher NOUN
le ticket-restaurant

lung NOUN
le poumon
□ lung cancer le cancer du poumon

luscious ADJECTIVE
délicieux (FEM délicieuse)

lush ADJECTIVE
luxuriant (FEM luxuriante)

lust NOUN
le désir

Luxembourg NOUN
1 le Luxembourg *(country)*
■ **in Luxembourg** au Luxembourg
■ **to Luxembourg** au Luxembourg
2 Luxembourg *(city)*
■ **in Luxembourg** à Luxembourg

luxurious ADJECTIVE
luxueux (FEM luxueuse)

luxury NOUN
le luxe
□ It was luxury! C'était un vrai luxe!
■ **a luxury hotel** un hôtel de luxe

lying VERB ▷ *see* **lie**

lyrics PL NOUN
les paroles *fem pl (of song)*

445

Mm

mac NOUN
l' imper *masc*

macaroni NOUN
les macaronis *masc pl*

machine NOUN
la machine

machine gun NOUN
la mitrailleuse

machinery NOUN
les machines *fem pl*

mackerel NOUN
le maquereau (PL les maquereaux)

mad ADJECTIVE
1 fou (FEM folle) *(insane)*
  □ You're mad! Tu es fou!

> **LANGUAGE TIP** fou changes to fol before a vowel and most words beginning with 'h'.

2 furieux (FEM furieuse) *(angry)*
  □ She'll be mad when she finds out. Elle sera furieuse quand elle va s'en apercevoir.
  ■ **to be mad about 1** *(sport, activity)* être enragé de □ He's mad about football. Il est enragé de foot. **2** *(person, animal)* adorer □ She's mad about horses. Elle adore les chevaux.

madam NOUN
madame *fem*
  □ Would you like to order, Madam? Désirez-vous commander, Madame?

made VERB ▷ see **make**

madly ADVERB
  ■ **They're madly in love.** Ils sont éperdument amoureux.

madman NOUN
le fou

madness NOUN
la folie
  □ It's absolute madness. C'est de la pure folie.

magazine NOUN
le magazine

maggot NOUN
l' asticot *masc*

magic ADJECTIVE

▷ *see also* **magic** NOUN
1 magique (FEM magique) *(magical)*
  □ a magic wand une baguette magique
2 super (FEM+PL super) *(brilliant)*
  □ It was magic! C'était super!

magic NOUN
▷ *see also* **magic** ADJECTIVE
la magie
  ■ **a magic trick** un tour de magie
  ■ **My hobby is magic.** Je fais des tours de magie.

magician NOUN
le prestidigitateur *(conjurer)*

magnet NOUN
l' aimant *masc*

magnificent ADJECTIVE
1 magnifique (FEM magnifique) *(beautiful)*
  □ a magnificent view une vue magnifique
2 superbe (FEM superbe) *(outstanding)*
  □ It was a magnificent effort. Ils ont fait un superbe effort.

magnifying glass NOUN
la loupe

maid NOUN
la domestique *(servant)*
  ■ **an old maid** *(spinster)* une vieille fille

maiden name NOUN
le nom de jeune fille

mail NOUN
▷ *see also* **mail** VERB
1 le courrier
  □ Here's your mail. Voici ton courrier.
2 le courrier électronique *(email)*
  □ Can I check my mail on your PC? Je peux consulter mon courrier électronique sur ton PC?
  ■ **by mail** par la poste

to **mail** VERB
▷ *see also* **mail** NOUN
  ■ **to mail something** *(email)* envoyer quelque chose par courrier électronique
  □ I'll mail you my address. Je t'enverrai mon adresse par courrier électronique.

mailbox NOUN (US)
la boîte à lettres

mailing list NOUN
la liste d'adresses

mailman NOUN (US)
le facteur

main ADJECTIVE
principal (FEM principale, MASC PL principaux)
□ the main problem le principal problème
■ the main thing is to ... l'essentiel est
de ...

mainly ADVERB
principalement

main road NOUN
la grande route
□ I don't like cycling on main roads. Je
n'aime pas faire du vélo sur les grandes
routes.

to **maintain** VERB
entretenir (machine, building)

maintenance NOUN
l' entretien masc (of machine, building)

maize NOUN
le maïs

majesty NOUN
la majesté
■ Your Majesty Votre Majesté

major ADJECTIVE
majeur (FEM majeure)
□ a major problem un problème majeur
■ in C major en do majeur

Majorca NOUN
Majorque fem
□ We went to Majorca in August. Nous
sommes allés à Majorque en août.

majority NOUN
la majorité

make NOUN
▷ see also **make** VERB
la marque
□ What make is that car? De quelle marque
est cette voiture?

to **make** VERB
▷ see also **make** NOUN
1 faire
□ I'm going to make a cake. Je vais faire un
gâteau. □ He made it himself. Il l'a fait lui-
même. □ I make my bed every morning. Je
fais mon lit tous les matins. □ 2 and 2 make
4. Deux et deux font quatre.
2 fabriquer (manufacture)
□ made in France fabriqué en France
3 gagner (earn)
□ He makes a lot of money. Il gagne
beaucoup d'argent.
■ to make somebody do something
obliger quelqu'un à faire quelque chose
□ My mother makes me do my homework.
Ma mère m'oblige à faire mes devoirs.

■ to make lunch préparer le repas □ She's
making lunch. Elle prépare le repas.
■ to make a phone call donner un coup
de téléphone □ I'd like to make a phone
call. J'aimerais donner un coup de
téléphone.
■ to make fun of somebody se moquer de
quelqu'un □ They made fun of him. Ils se
sont moqués de lui.
■ What time do you make it? Quelle
heure avez-vous?

to **make out** VERB
1 déchiffrer (read)
□ I can't make out the address on the label.
Je n'arrive pas à déchiffrer l'adresse sur
l'étiquette.
2 comprendre (understand)
□ I can't make her out at all. Je n'arrive pas
du tout à la comprendre.
3 prétendre (claim, pretend)
□ They're making out it was my fault. Ils
prétendent que c'était ma faute.
■ to make a cheque out to somebody
libeller un chèque à l'ordre de quelqu'un

to **make up** VERB
1 inventer (invent)
□ He made up the whole story. Il a inventé
cette histoire de toutes pièces.
2 se réconcilier (after argument)
□ They had a quarrel, but soon made up. Ils
se sont disputés, mais se sont vite
réconciliés.
■ to make oneself up se maquiller □ She
spends hours making herself up. Elle passe
des heures à se maquiller.

makeover NOUN
le relookage
■ She had a complete makeover. Elle est
relooké des pieds à la tête.

maker NOUN
le fabricant
□ Europe's biggest car maker le plus grand
fabriquant de voitures d'Europe
■ a film maker un cinéaste

make-up NOUN
le maquillage

Malaysia NOUN
la Malaisie
■ in Malaysia en Malaisie

male ADJECTIVE
1 mâle (FEM mâle) (animals, plants)
□ a male kitten un chaton mâle
2 masculin (FEM masculine) (person, on official
forms)
□ Sex: male. Sexe : masculin.
■ Most football players are male. La
plupart des joueurs de football sont des

447

hommes.

■ **a male chauvinist** un macho
■ **a male nurse** un infirmier

malicious ADJECTIVE
malveillant (FEM malveillante)
□ a malicious rumour une rumeur
malveillante

> LANGUAGE TIP Be careful not to
> translate **malicious** by **malicieux**.

mall NOUN
le centre commercial

Malta NOUN
Malte

■ **in Malta** à Malte
■ **to Malta** à Malte

mammoth NOUN
▷ see also **mammoth** ADJECTIVE
le mammouth

mammoth ADJECTIVE
▷ see also **mammoth** NOUN
monstre (FEM monstre)
□ a mammoth task un travail monstre

man NOUN
l' homme masc
□ an old man un vieil homme

to **manage** VERB
1 diriger (be in charge of)
□ She manages a big store. Elle dirige un
grand magasin. □ He manages our football
team. Il dirige notre équipe de foot.
2 se débrouiller (get by)
□ We haven't got much money, but we
manage. Nous n'avons pas beaucoup
d'argent, mais nous nous débrouillons.
□ It's okay, I can manage. Ça va, je me
débrouille.
■ **Can you manage okay?** Tu y arrives?
■ **to manage to do something** réussir à
faire quelque chose □ Luckily I managed to
pass the exam. J'ai heureusement réussi à
avoir mon examen.
■ **I can't manage all that.** (food) C'est trop
pour moi.

manageable ADJECTIVE
faisable (FEM faisable) (task)

management NOUN
1 la gestion (organization)
□ He's responsible for the management of
the company. Il est responsable de la
gestion de la société.
2 la direction (people in charge)
■ **'under new management'** 'changement
de direction'

manager NOUN
1 le directeur
la directrice (of company)
2 le gérant

la gérante (of shop, restaurant)
3 le manager (of team, performer)

manageress NOUN
la gérante

mandarin NOUN
la mandarine (fruit)

mango NOUN
la mangue

mania NOUN
la manie

maniac NOUN
le fou
la folle
□ He drives like a maniac. Il conduit comme
un fou.
■ **a religious maniac** un fanatique religieux

to **manipulate** VERB
manipuler

mankind NOUN
l' humanité fem

man-made ADJECTIVE
synthétique (FEM synthétique) (fibre)

manner NOUN
la façon
□ She behaves in an odd manner. Elle se
comporte de façon étrange.
■ **He has a confident manner.** Il a de
l'assurance.

manners PL NOUN
les manières fem pl
□ good manners les bonnes manières
□ Her manners are appalling. Elle a de très
mauvaises manières.
■ **It's bad manners to speak with your
mouth full.** Ce n'est pas poli de parler la
bouche pleine.

manpower NOUN
la main-d'œuvre

mansion NOUN
le manoir

mantelpiece NOUN
la cheminée

manual NOUN
le manuel

to **manufacture** VERB
fabriquer

manufacturer NOUN
le fabricant

manure NOUN
le fumier

manuscript NOUN
le manuscrit

many ADJECTIVE, PRONOUN
beaucoup de
□ The film has many special effects. Le film
a beaucoup d'effets spéciaux. □ He hasn't
got many friends. Il n'a pas beaucoup

d'amis. ▫ Were there many people at the concert? Est-ce qu'il y avait beaucoup de gens au concert?

■ **very many** beaucoup de ▫ I haven't got very many CDs. Je n'ai pas beaucoup de CD.

■ **Not many.** Pas beaucoup.

■ **How many?** Combien? ▫ How many do you want? Combien en veux-tu?

■ **how many ...?** combien de ...? ▫ How many euros do you get for £1? Combien d'euros a-t-on pour une livre?

■ **too many** trop ▫ That's too many. C'est trop.

■ **too many ...** trop de ... ▫ She makes too many mistakes. Elle fait trop d'erreurs.

■ **so many** autant ▫ I didn't know there would be so many. Je ne pensais pas qu'il y en aurait autant.

■ **so many ...** autant de ... ▫ I've never seen so many policemen. Je n'ai jamais vu autant de policiers.

map NOUN
1 la carte *(of country, area)*
2 le plan *(of town)*

marathon NOUN
le marathon

▫ the London marathon le marathon de Londres

marble NOUN
le marbre

▫ a marble statue une statue en marbre

■ **to play marbles** jouer aux billes

March NOUN
mars *masc*

■ **in March** en mars

march NOUN
▷ *see also* **march** VERB
la manifestation *(demonstration)*

to **march** VERB
▷ *see also* **march** NOUN
1 marcher au pas *(soldiers)*
2 défiler *(protesters)*

mare NOUN
la jument

margarine NOUN
la margarine

margin NOUN
la marge

▫ Write notes in the margin. Écrivez vos notes dans la marge.

marijuana NOUN
la marijuana

marina NOUN
la marina

marital status NOUN
la situation de famille

mark NOUN

▷ *see also* **mark** VERB
1 la note *(in school)*

▫ I get good marks for French. J'ai de bonnes notes en français.
2 la tache *(stain)*

▫ You've got a mark on your skirt. Tu as une tache sur ta jupe.
3 le mark *(former German currency)*

to **mark** VERB
▷ *see also* **mark** NOUN
corriger

▫ The teacher hasn't marked my homework yet. Le professeur n'a pas encore corrigé mon devoir.

market NOUN
le marché

marketing NOUN
le marketing

marketplace NOUN
la place du marché

marmalade NOUN
la confiture d'oranges

maroon ADJECTIVE
bordeaux (FEM+PL bordeaux) *(colour)*

marriage NOUN
le mariage

married ADJECTIVE
marié (FEM mariée)

▫ They are not married. Ils ne sont pas mariés. ▫ They have been married for 15 years. Ils sont mariés depuis quinze ans. ▫ a married couple un couple marié

marrow NOUN
la courge *(vegetable)*

■ **bone marrow** la moelle

to **marry** VERB
épouser

▫ He wants to marry her. Il veut l'épouser.

■ **to get married** se marier ▫ My sister's getting married in June. Ma sœur se marie en juin.

marvellous (US **marvelous**) ADJECTIVE
1 excellent (FEM excellente)

▫ She's a marvellous cook. C'est une excellente cuisinière.
2 superbe (FEM superbe)

▫ The weather was marvellous. Il a fait un temps superbe.

marzipan NOUN
la pâte d'amandes

mascara NOUN
le mascara

masculine ADJECTIVE
masculin (FEM masculine)

mashed potatoes PL NOUN
la purée *sing*

▫ sausages and mashed potatoes des

saucisses avec de la purée

mask NOUN
le masque

masked ADJECTIVE
masqué (FEM masquée)

mass NOUN
1 la multitude
□ a mass of books and papers une multitude de livres et de papiers
2 la messe (in church)
□ We go to mass on Sunday. Nous allons à la messe le dimanche.
■ **the mass media** les médias

massage NOUN
le massage

massive ADJECTIVE
énorme (FEM énorme)

to **master** VERB
maîtriser

masterpiece NOUN
le chef-d'œuvre (PL les chefs-d'œuvre)

mat NOUN
le paillasson (doormat)
■ **a table mat** un set de table
■ **a beach mat** un tapis de plage

match NOUN
▷ see also **match** VERB
1 l' allumette fem
□ a box of matches une boîte d'allumettes
2 le match (sport)
□ a football match un match de foot

to **match** VERB
▷ see also **match** NOUN
être assorti à
□ The jacket matches the trousers. La veste est assortie au pantalon.
■ **These colours don't match.** Ces couleurs ne vont pas ensemble.

matching ADJECTIVE
assorti (FEM assortie)
□ My bedroom has matching wallpaper and curtains. Ma chambre a du papier peint et des rideaux assortis.

mate NOUN
le pote (informal)
□ On Friday night I go out with my mates. Vendredi soir, je sors avec mes potes.

material NOUN
1 le tissu (cloth)
2 la documentation (information, data)
□ I'm collecting material for my project. Je rassemble une documentation pour mon dossier.
■ **raw materials** les matières premières fem pl

mathematics NOUN
les mathématiques fem pl

maths NOUN
les maths fem pl

matron NOUN
l' infirmière-chef fem (PL les infirmières-chefs) (in hospital)

matter NOUN
▷ see also **matter** VERB
la question
□ It's a matter of life and death. C'est une question de vie ou de mort.
■ **What's the matter?** Qu'est-ce qui ne va pas?
■ **as a matter of fact** en fait

to **matter** VERB
▷ see also **matter** NOUN
■ **it doesn't matter 1** (I don't mind) ça ne fait rien □ I can't give you the money today. — It doesn't matter. Je ne peux pas te donner l'argent aujourd'hui. — Ça ne fait rien. **2** (it makes no difference) ça n'a pas d'importance □ It doesn't matter if you're late. Ça n'a pas d'importance si tu es en retard.
■ **It matters a lot to me.** C'est très important pour moi.

mattress NOUN
le matelas

mature ADJECTIVE
mûr (FEM mûre)
□ She's quite mature for her age. Elle est très mûre pour son âge.

maximum NOUN
▷ see also **maximum** ADJECTIVE
le maximum

maximum ADJECTIVE
▷ see also **maximum** NOUN
maximum (FEM+PL maximum)
□ The maximum speed is 100 km/h. La vitesse maximum autorisée est de cent kilomètres à l'heure.
■ **the maximum amount** le maximum

May NOUN
mai masc
■ **in May** en mai
■ **May Day** le Premier Mai

may VERB
■ **He may come.** Il va peut-être venir. □ It may rain. Il va peut-être pleuvoir.
■ **May I smoke?** Est-ce que je peux fumer?

maybe ADVERB
peut-être
□ maybe not peut-être pas □ a bit boring, maybe peut-être un peu ennuyeux
□ Maybe she's at home. Elle est peut-être chez elle. □ Maybe he'll change his mind. Il va peut-être changer d'avis.

mayonnaise NOUN

la mayonnaise

mayor NOUN
le maire

maze NOUN
le labyrinthe

me PRONOUN
1 me
  □ Could you lend me your pen? Est-ce que
  tu peux me prêter ton stylo?

  LANGUAGE TIP me becomes m' before
  a vowel sound.

  m'
  □ Can you tell me the way to the station?
  Est-ce que vous pouvez m'indiquer le
  chemin de la gare? □ Can you help me? Est-
  ce que tu peux m'aider? □ He heard me. Il
  m'a entendu.

2 moi
  LANGUAGE TIP moi is used in
  exclamations.

  □ Me too! Moi aussi! □ Excuse me!
  Excusez-moi! □ Look at me! Regarde-moi!
  □ Wait for me! Attends-moi! □ Come with
  me! Suivez-moi!

  LANGUAGE TIP moi is also used after
  prepositions and in comparisons.

  □ You're after me. Tu es après moi. □ Is it
  for me? C'est pour moi? □ She's older than
  me. Elle est plus âgée que moi.

meal NOUN
le repas

mealtime NOUN
  ■ at mealtimes aux heures des repas

to **mean** VERB
  ▷ see also **mean** ADJECTIVE, **means** NOUN
  vouloir dire

  □ What does 'complet' mean? Qu'est-ce
  que 'complet' veut dire? □ I don't know
  what it means. Je ne sais pas ce que ça veut
  dire. □ What do you mean? Qu'est que vous
  voulez dire? □ That's not what I meant. Ce
  n'est pas ce que je voulais dire.
  ■ Which one do you mean? Duquel veux-
  tu parler?
  ■ Do you really mean it? Tu es sérieux?
  ■ to mean to do something avoir
  l'intention de faire quelque chose □ I didn't
  mean to offend you. Je n'avais pas
  l'intention de vous blesser.

mean ADJECTIVE
  ▷ see also **mean** VERB, **means** NOUN
1 radin (FEM radine) (with money)
  □ He's too mean to buy Christmas presents.
  Il est trop radin pour acheter des cadeaux de
  Noël.
2 méchant (FEM méchante) (unkind)
  □ You're being mean to me. Tu es méchant

avec moi.
  ■ That's a really mean thing to say! Ce
  n'est vraiment pas gentil de dire ça!

meaning NOUN
le sens

means NOUN
  ▷ see also **mean** VERB, ADJECTIVE
  le moyen
  □ He'll do it by any possible means. Il le fera
  par tous les moyens. □ a means of transport
  un moyen de transport
  ■ by means of au moyen de □ He got in by
  means of a stolen key. Il est entré au moyen
  d'une clé volée.
  ■ by all means bien sûr □ Can I come? —
  By all means! Est-ce que je peux venir? —
  Bien sûr!

meant VERB ▷ see **mean**

meanwhile ADVERB
pendant ce temps

measles NOUN
la rougeole

to **measure** VERB
1 mesurer
  □ I measured the page. J'ai mesuré la page.
2 faire
  □ The room measures 3 metres by 4. La
  pièce fait trois mètres sur quatre.

measurements PL NOUN
1 les dimensions fem pl (of object)
  □ What are the measurements of the room?
  Quelles sont les dimensions de la pièce?
2 les mensurations fem pl (of body)
  □ What are your measurements? Quelles
  sont tes mensurations?
  ■ my waist measurement mon tour de
  taille
  ■ What's your neck measurement? Quel
  est votre tour de cou?

meat NOUN
la viande
  □ I don't eat meat. Je ne mange pas de
  viande.

Mecca NOUN
La Mecque

mechanic NOUN
le mécanicien
  □ He's a mechanic. Il est mécanicien.

mechanical ADJECTIVE
mécanique (FEM mécanique)

medal NOUN
la médaille
  ■ the gold medal la médaille d'or

medallion NOUN
le médaillon

media PL NOUN
les médias masc pl

451

median strip NOUN (US)
le terre-plein central

medical ADJECTIVE
▷ *see also* **medical** NOUN
médical (FEM médicale, MASC PL médicaux)
□ medical treatment les soins médicaux
■ **medical insurance** l'assurance maladie
■ **to have medical problems** avoir des problèmes de santé
■ **She's a medical student.** Elle est étudiante en médecine.

medical NOUN
▷ *see also* **medical** ADJECTIVE
■ **to have a medical** passer une visite médicale

medicine NOUN
1 la médecine (*subject*)
□ I want to study medicine. Je veux faire médecine.
■ **alternative medicine** la médecine douce
2 le médicament (*medication*)
□ I need some medicine. J'ai besoin d'un médicament.

Mediterranean ADJECTIVE
méditerranéen (FEM méditerranéenne)
■ **the Mediterranean** la Méditerranée

medium ADJECTIVE
moyen (FEM moyenne)
□ a man of medium height un homme de taille moyenne

medium-sized ADJECTIVE
de taille moyenne
□ a medium-sized town une ville de taille moyenne

to **meet** VERB
1 rencontrer (*by chance*)
□ I met Paul in the street. J'ai rencontré Paul dans la rue. □ Have you met him before? Tu l'as déjà rencontré?
2 se rencontrer
□ We met by chance in the shopping centre. Nous nous sommes rencontrés par hasard dans le centre commercial.
3 retrouver (*by arrangement*)
□ I'm going to meet my friends. Je vais retrouver mes amis.
4 se retrouver
□ Let's meet in front of the tourist office. Retrouvons-nous devant l'office de tourisme.
■ **I like meeting new people.** J'aime faire de nouvelles connaissances.
5 aller chercher (*pick up*)
□ I'll meet you at the station. J'irai te chercher à la gare.

to **meet up** VERB
se retrouver

□ What time shall we meet up? On se retrouve à quelle heure?

meeting NOUN
1 la réunion (*for work*)
□ a business meeting une réunion d'affaires
2 la rencontre (*socially*)
□ their first meeting leur première rencontre

mega ADJECTIVE
■ **He's mega rich.** Il est hyper-riche. (*informal*)

melody NOUN
la mélodie

melon NOUN
le melon

to **melt** VERB
fondre
□ The snow is melting. La neige est en train de fondre.

member NOUN
le membre
■ **a Member of Parliament** un député

membership NOUN
l' adhésion *fem* (*of party, union*)
□ to apply for membership faire une demande d'adhésion

membership card NOUN
la carte de membre

memento NOUN
le souvenir

memorial NOUN
le monument
□ a war memorial un monument aux morts

to **memorize** VERB
apprendre par cœur

memory NOUN
1 la mémoire (*also for computer*)
□ I haven't got a good memory. Je n'ai pas une bonne mémoire.
2 le souvenir (*recollection*)
□ to bring back memories rappeler des souvenirs

men PL NOUN ▷ *see* **man**

to **mend** VERB
réparer

meningitis NOUN
la méningite

mental ADJECTIVE
1 mental (FEM mentale, MASC PL mentaux)
□ a mental illness une maladie mentale
2 fou (FEM folle) (*mad*)
□ You're mental! Tu es fou!

LANGUAGE TIP fou changes to fol before a vowel and most words beginning with 'h'.

■ **a mental hospital** un hôpital psychiatrique

mentality NOUN
la mentalité

to **mention** VERB
mentionner
■ Thank you! — Don't mention it! Merci!
— Il n'y a pas de quoi!

menu NOUN
le menu
▢ Could I have the menu please? Est-ce que
je pourrais avoir le menu s'il vous plaît?

merchant NOUN
le marchand
▢ a wine merchant un marchand de vin

mercy NOUN
la pitié

mere ADJECTIVE
■ a mere five percent à peine cinq pour
cent
■ It's a mere formality. C'est une simple
formalité.
■ the merest hint of criticism la moindre
petite critique

meringue NOUN
la meringue

merry ADJECTIVE
■ Merry Christmas! Joyeux Noël!

merry-go-round NOUN
le manège

mess NOUN
le fouillis
▢ My bedroom's usually in a mess. Il y a
généralement du fouillis dans ma chambre.

to **mess about** VERB
■ to mess about with something (interfere
with) tripoter quelque chose ▢ Stop
messing about with my computer! Arrête
de tripoter mon ordinateur!
■ Don't mess about with my things! Ne
touche pas à mes affaires!

to **mess up** VERB
■ to mess something up mettre la pagaille
dans quelque chose ▢ My little brother has
messed up my DVDs. Mon petit frère a mis
la pagaille dans mes DVDs.

message NOUN
le message

messenger NOUN
le messager

messy ADJECTIVE
1 salissant (FEM salissante) (dirty)
▢ a messy job un travail salissant
2 en désordre (untidy)
▢ Your desk is really messy. Ton bureau est
vraiment en désordre.
3 désordonné (FEM désordonnée) (person)
▢ She's so messy! Elle est tellement
désordonnée!

■ My writing is terribly messy. J'ai une
écriture de cochon.

met VERB ▷ see **meet**

metal NOUN
le métal (PL les métaux)

meter NOUN
1 le compteur (for gas, electricity, taxi)
2 le parcmètre (parking meter)
3 le mètre (US: unit of measurement)

method NOUN
la méthode

Methodist NOUN
le/la méthodiste
▢ I'm a Methodist. Je suis méthodiste.

metre NOUN
le mètre

metric ADJECTIVE
métrique (FEM métrique)

Mexico NOUN
le Mexique
■ in Mexico au Mexique
■ to Mexico au Mexique

to **miaow** VERB
miauler

mice PL NOUN ▷ see **mouse**

microchip NOUN
la puce

microphone NOUN
le microphone

microscope NOUN
le microscope

microwave oven NOUN
le four à micro-ondes

mid ADJECTIVE
■ in mid May à la mi-mai

midday NOUN
le midi
■ at midday à midi

middle NOUN
le milieu
▢ in the middle of the road au milieu de la
route ▢ in the middle of the night au milieu
de la nuit ▢ the middle seat la place du
milieu

middle-aged ADJECTIVE
d'un certain âge
▢ a middle-aged man un homme d'un
certain âge
■ to be middle-aged avoir la cinquantaine
■ She's middle-aged. Elle a la
cinquantaine.

Middle Ages PL NOUN
■ the Middle Ages le Moyen Âge sing

middle-class ADJECTIVE
de la classe moyenne
▢ a middle-class family une famille de la
classe moyenne

Middle East NOUN
le Moyen-Orient
- **in the Middle East** au Moyen-Orient

middle name NOUN
le deuxième nom

midge NOUN
le moucheron

midnight NOUN
minuit *masc*
- **at midnight** à minuit

midwife NOUN
la sage-femme (PL les sages-femmes)
□ She's a midwife. Elle est sage-femme.

might VERB
□ He might come later. Il va peut-être venir plus tard. □ We might go to Spain next year. Nous irons peut-être en Espagne l'an prochain. □ She might not have understood. Elle n'a peut-être pas compris.

migraine NOUN
la migraine
□ I've got a migraine. J'ai la migraine.

mike NOUN
le micro

mild ADJECTIVE
doux (FEM douce)
□ The winters are quite mild. Les hivers sont assez doux.

mile NOUN
le mille
□ It's 5 miles from here. C'est à huit kilomètres d'ici.

> **DID YOU KNOW...?**
> In France distances are expressed in kilometres. A mile is about 1.6 kilometres.

- **We walked miles!** Nous avons fait des kilomètres à pied!

military ADJECTIVE
militaire (FEM militaire)

milk NOUN
▷ *see also* **milk** VERB
le lait
□ tea with milk du thé au lait

to **milk** VERB
▷ *see also* **milk** NOUN
traire

milk chocolate NOUN
le chocolat au lait

milkman NOUN
- **He's a milkman.** Il livre le lait à domicile.

> **DID YOU KNOW...?**
> In France milk is not delivered to people's homes.

milk shake NOUN
le milk-shake

mill NOUN

le moulin *(for grain)*

millennium NOUN
le millénaire
□ the third millennium le troisième millénaire
- **the millennium** le millénium

millimetre (US **millimeter**) NOUN
le millimètre

million NOUN
le million

millionaire NOUN
le millionnaire

to **mimic** VERB
imiter

mince NOUN
la viande hachée

mince pie NOUN
la tartelette de Noël

to **mind** VERB
▷ *see also* **mind** NOUN
1 garder
□ Could you mind the baby this afternoon? Est-ce que tu pourrais garder le bébé cet après-midi?
2 surveiller *(keep an eye on)*
□ Could you mind my bags for a few minutes? Est-ce que vous pourriez surveiller mes bagages pendant quelques minutes?
- **Do you mind if I open the window?** Est-ce que je pourrais ouvrir la fenêtre?
- **I don't mind.** Ça ne me dérange pas. □ I don't mind the noise. Le bruit ne me dérange pas.
- **Never mind!** Ça ne fait rien!
- **Mind that bike!** Attention au vélo!
- **Mind the step!** Attention à la marche!

mind NOUN
▷ *see also* **mind** VERB
- **to make up one's mind** se décider □ I haven't made up my mind yet. Je ne me suis pas encore décidé.
- **to change one's mind** changer d'avis
□ He's changed his mind. Il a changé d'avis.
- **Are you out of your mind?** Tu as perdu la tête?

mine PRONOUN
▷ *see also* **mine** NOUN
le mien + *masc noun*
□ Is this your coat? — No, mine's black. C'est ton manteau? — Non, le mien est noir.
la mienne + *fem noun*
□ Is this your car? — No, mine's green. C'est ta voiture? — Non, la mienne est verte.
les miens + *masc pl noun*
□ her parents and mine ses parents et les miens

les miennes + *fem pl noun*

□ Your hands are dirty, mine are clean. Tes mains sont sales, les miennes sont propres.
■ **It's mine.** C'est à moi. □ This book is mine. Ce livre est à moi. □ Whose is this? — It's mine. C'est à qui? — À moi.

mine NOUN
▷ *see also* **mine** PRONOUN
la mine

□ a coal mine une mine de charbon □ a land mine une mine terrestre

miner NOUN
le mineur

mineral water NOUN
l' eau minérale *fem*

miniature ADJECTIVE
▷ *see also* **miniature** NOUN
miniature (FEM miniature)

□ a miniature version une version miniature

miniature NOUN
▷ *see also* **miniature** ADJECTIVE
la miniature

minibus NOUN
le minibus

minicab NOUN
le taxi

> **DID YOU KNOW...?**
> In France the distinction between black taxis and minicabs does not exist.

Minidisc® NOUN
le minidisque

minimum NOUN
▷ *see also* **minimum** ADJECTIVE
le minimum

minimum ADJECTIVE
▷ *see also* **minimum** NOUN
minimum (FEM+PL minimum)

□ The minimum age for driving is 17. L'âge minimum pour conduire est dix-sept ans.
■ **the minimum amount** le minimum

miniskirt NOUN
la mini-jupe

minister NOUN
1 le ministre (*in government*)
2 le pasteur (*of church*)

ministry NOUN
le ministère (*in government*)

□ The Ministry of Culture Le Ministère de la Culture

mink NOUN
le vison

□ a mink coat un manteau en vison

minor ADJECTIVE
mineur (FEM mineure)

□ a minor problem un problème mineur
■ **in D minor** en ré mineur

■ **a minor operation** une opération bénigne

minority NOUN
la minorité

mint NOUN
1 la menthe (*plant*)

□ mint sauce la sauce à la menthe
2 le bonbon à la menthe (*sweet*)

minus PREPOSITION
moins

□ 16 minus 3 is 13. Seize moins trois égale treize. □ It's minus two degrees outside. Il fait moins deux dehors. □ I got a B minus. J'ai eu un B moins.

minute NOUN
▷ *see also* **minute** ADJECTIVE
la minute

□ Wait a minute! Attends une minute!

minute ADJECTIVE
▷ *see also* **minute** NOUN
minuscule (FEM minuscule)

□ Her flat is minute. Son appartement est minuscule.

miracle NOUN
le miracle

mirror NOUN
1 la glace (*on wall*)
2 le rétroviseur (*in car*)

to **misbehave** VERB
se conduire mal

miscellaneous ADJECTIVE
divers (FEM diverse)

mischief NOUN
les bêtises *fem pl*

□ My little sister's always up to mischief. Ma petite sœur fait constamment des bêtises.

mischievous ADJECTIVE
coquin (FEM coquine)

miser NOUN
l' avare *masc/fem*

miserable ADJECTIVE
1 malheureux (FEM malheureuse) (*person*)

□ You're looking miserable. Tu as l'air malheureux.
2 épouvantable (FEM épouvantable) (*weather*)

□ The weather was miserable. Il faisait un temps épouvantable.
■ **to feel miserable** ne pas avoir le moral
□ I'm feeling miserable. Je n'ai pas le moral.

misery NOUN
1 la tristesse (*unhappiness*)

□ All that money brought nothing but misery. Tout cet argent n'a apporté que de la tristesse.
2 le pleurnicheur
la pleurnicheuse (*unhappy person*)

□ She's a real misery. C'est une vraie

pleurnicheuse.

misfortune NOUN
le malheur

mishap NOUN
la mésaventure

to **misjudge** VERB
mal juger *(person)*
▢ I've misjudged her. Je l'ai mal jugée.
■ He misjudged the bend. Il a mal pris le virage.

to **mislay** VERB
égarer
▢ I've mislaid my passport. J'ai égaré mon passeport.

misleading ADJECTIVE
trompeur (FEM trompeuse)

Miss NOUN
1 Mademoiselle (PL Mesdemoiselles)
2 Mlle (PL Mlles) *(in address)*

to **miss** VERB
1 rater
▢ Hurry or you'll miss the bus. Dépêche-toi ou tu vas rater le bus. ▢ He missed the target. Il a raté la cible.
2 manquer
▢ to miss an opportunity manquer une occasion
■ I miss you. Tu me manques. ▢ I'm missing my family. Ma famille me manque. ▢ I miss him. Il me manque. ▢ I miss them. Ils me manquent.

missing ADJECTIVE
manquant (FEM manquante)
▢ the missing part la pièce manquante
■ to be missing avoir disparu ▢ My rucksack is missing. Mon sac à dos a disparu. ▢ Two members of the group are missing. Deux membres du groupe ont disparu.

missionary NOUN
le/la missionnaire

mist NOUN
la brume

mistake NOUN
▷ *see also* **mistake** VERB
1 la faute *(slip)*
▢ a spelling mistake une faute d'orthographe
■ to make a mistake 1 *(in writing, speaking)* faire une faute 2 *(get mixed up)* se tromper ▢ I'm sorry, I made a mistake. Je suis désolé, je me suis trompé.
2 l' erreur *fem (misjudgement)*
▢ It was a mistake to come. J'ai fait une erreur en venant.
■ by mistake par erreur ▢ I took his bag by mistake. J'ai pris son sac par erreur.

to **mistake** VERB
▷ *see also* **mistake** NOUN
■ He mistook me for my sister. Il m'a prise pour ma sœur.

mistaken ADJECTIVE
■ to be mistaken se tromper ▢ If you think I'm coming with you, you're mistaken. Si tu penses que je vais venir avec toi, tu te trompes.

mistakenly ADVERB
à tort

mistletoe NOUN
le gui

mistook VERB ▷ *see* **mistake**

mistress NOUN
1 le professeur *(teacher)*
▢ our French mistress notre professeur de français
2 la maîtresse *(lover)*
▢ He's got a mistress. Il a une maîtresse.

misty ADJECTIVE
brumeux (FEM brumeuse)
▢ a misty morning un matin brumeux

to **misunderstand** VERB
mal comprendre
▢ Sorry, I misunderstood you. Je suis désolé, je t'avais mal compris.

misunderstanding NOUN
le malentendu

misunderstood VERB ▷ *see* **misunderstand**

mix NOUN
▷ *see also* **mix** VERB
le mélange
▢ It's a mix of science fiction and comedy. C'est un mélange de science-fiction et de comédie.
■ a cake mix une préparation pour gâteau

to **mix** VERB
▷ *see also* **mix** NOUN
1 mélanger
▢ Mix the flour with the sugar. Mélangez la farine au sucre.
2 combiner
▢ He's mixing business with pleasure. Il combine les affaires et le plaisir.
■ to mix with somebody *(associate)* fréquenter quelqu'un
■ He doesn't mix much. Il se tient à l'écart.

to **mix up** VERB *(people)*
confondre
▢ He always mixes me up with my sister. Il me confond toujours avec ma sœur.
■ The travel agent mixed up the bookings. L'agence de voyage s'est embrouillée dans les réservations.
■ I'm getting mixed up. Je ne m'y retrouve

plus.

mixed ADJECTIVE
- ■ **a mixed salad** une salade composée
- ■ **a mixed school** une école mixte
- ■ **a mixed grill** un assortiment de grillades

mixer NOUN
- ■ **She's a good mixer.** Elle est très sociable.

mixture NOUN
le mélange
- □ **a mixture of spices** un mélange d'épices
- ■ **cough mixture** le sirop pour la toux

mix-up NOUN
la confusion

MMS NOUN
le MMS

to **moan** VERB
râler
- □ **She's always moaning.** Elle est toujours en train de râler.

mobile NOUN
le portable (phone)

mobile home NOUN
le mobile home

mobile phone NOUN
le portable

to **mock** VERB
▷ see also **mock** ADJECTIVE
ridiculiser

mock ADJECTIVE
▷ see also **mock** VERB
- ■ **a mock exam** un examen blanc

mod cons PL NOUN
- ■ **'all mod cons'** 'tout confort'

model NOUN
▷ see also **model** ADJECTIVE
1 le modèle (type)
- □ **His car is the latest model.** Sa voiture est le tout dernier modèle.
2 la maquette (mock-up)
- □ **a model of the castle** une maquette du château
3 le mannequin (fashion)
- □ **She's a famous model.** C'est un mannequin célèbre.

model ADJECTIVE
▷ see also **model** NOUN
- ■ **a model plane** un modèle réduit d'avion
- ■ **a model railway** un modèle réduit de voie ferrée
- ■ **He's a model pupil.** C'est un élève modèle.

to **model** VERB
▷ see also **model** NOUN
- ■ **She was modelling a Lorna Bailey outfit.** Elle présentait une tenue de la collection Lorna Bailey.

modem NOUN
le modem

moderate ADJECTIVE
modéré (FEM modérée)
- □ **His views are quite moderate.** Ses opinions sont assez modérées.
- ■ **a moderate amount of** un peu de
- ■ **a moderate price** un prix raisonnable

modern ADJECTIVE
moderne (FEM moderne)

to **modernize** VERB
moderniser

modest ADJECTIVE
modeste (FEM modeste)

to **modify** VERB
modifier

moist ADJECTIVE
humide (FEM humide) (skin, soil)
- □ **Make sure the soil is moist.** Assurez-vous que la terre est humide.

moisture NOUN
l' humidité fem

moisturizer NOUN
1 la crème hydratante (cream)
2 le lait hydratant (lotion)

moldy ADJECTIVE (US)
moisi (FEM moisie)

mole NOUN
1 la taupe (animal)
2 le grain de beauté (on skin)

moment NOUN
l' instant masc
- □ **Could you wait a moment?** Pouvez-vous attendre un instant? □ **in a moment** dans un instant □ **Just a moment!** Un instant!
- ■ **at the moment** en ce moment
- ■ **any moment now** d'un moment à l'autre
- □ **They'll be arriving any moment now.** Ils vont arriver d'un moment à l'autre.

momentous ADJECTIVE
capital (FEM capitale) (event)

Monaco NOUN
Monaco
- ■ **in Monaco** à Monaco

monarch NOUN
le monarque

monarchy NOUN
la monarchie

monastery NOUN
le monastère

Monday NOUN
le lundi
- □ **on Monday** lundi □ **on Mondays** le lundi □ **every Monday** tous les lundis □ **last Monday** lundi dernier □ **next Monday** lundi prochain

money NOUN
l' argent masc

m

□ I need to change some money. J'ai besoin de changer de l'argent.

■ **to make money** gagner de l'argent

mongrel NOUN
le bâtard

□ My dog's a mongrel. Mon chien est un bâtard.

monitor NOUN
le moniteur *(of computer)*

monk NOUN
le moine

monkey NOUN
le singe

monotonous ADJECTIVE
monotone (FEM monotone)

monster NOUN
le monstre

month NOUN
le mois

□ this month ce mois-ci □ next month le mois prochain □ last month le mois dernier □ every month tous les mois □ at the end of the month à la fin du mois

monthly ADJECTIVE
mensuel (FEM mensuelle)

monument NOUN
le monument

mood NOUN
l' humeur *fem*

■ **to be in a bad mood** être de mauvaise humeur

■ **to be in a good mood** être de bonne humeur

moody ADJECTIVE
1 lunatique (FEM lunatique) *(temperamental)*
2 maussade (FEM maussade) *(in a bad mood)*

moon NOUN
la lune

□ There's a full moon tonight. Il y a pleine lune ce soir.

■ **to be over the moon** *(happy)* être aux anges

moor NOUN
▷ *see also* **moor** VERB
la lande

to **moor** VERB
▷ *see also* **moor** NOUN
amarrer *(boat)*

mop NOUN
le balai laveur *(for floor)*

moped NOUN
le cyclomoteur

moral ADJECTIVE
▷ *see also* **moral** NOUN
moral (FEM morale, MASC PL moraux)

moral NOUN
▷ *see also* **moral** ADJECTIVE

la morale

□ the moral of the story la morale de l'histoire

■ **morals** la moralité

morale NOUN
le moral

□ Their morale is very low. Leur moral est très bas.

more ADJECTIVE, PRONOUN, ADVERB

LANGUAGE TIP When comparing one amount with another, you usually use **plus**.

1 plus

□ Beer is more expensive in Britain. La bière est plus chère en Grande-Bretagne. □ Could you speak more slowly? Est-ce que vous pourriez parler plus lentement? □ a bit more un peu plus □ There isn't any more. Il n'y en a plus.

■ **more ... than** plus ... que □ He's more intelligent than me. Il est plus intelligent que moi. □ She practises more than I do. Elle s'entraîne plus que moi. □ More girls than boys do French. Il y a plus de filles que de garçons qui font du français.

2 plus de *(followed by noun)*

□ There are more girls in the class. Il y a plus de filles dans la classe. □ I get more homework than you do. J'ai plus de devoirs que toi. □ I spent more than 500 euros. J'ai dépensé plus de cinq cents euros.

LANGUAGE TIP When referring to an additional amount, more than there is already, you usually use **encore**.

3 encore

□ Is there any more? Est-ce qu'il y en a encore? □ Would you like some more? Vous en voulez encore? □ It'll take a few more days. Ça prendra encore quelques jours.

4 encore de *(followed by noun)*

□ Could I have some more chips? Est-ce que je pourrais avoir encore des frites? □ Do you want some more tea? Voulez-vous encore du thé?

■ **more or less** plus ou moins

■ **more than ever** plus que jamais

moreover ADVERB
en outre

morning NOUN
le matin

□ this morning ce matin □ tomorrow morning demain matin □ every morning tous les matins

■ **in the morning** le matin □ at 7 o'clock in the morning à sept heures du matin

■ **a morning paper** un journal du matin

Morocco NOUN

le Maroc

■ **in Morocco** au Maroc

Moscow NOUN
Moscou

■ **in Moscow** à Moscou

Moslem NOUN
le musulman
la musulmane

□ He's a Moslem. Il est musulman.

mosque NOUN
la mosquée

mosquito NOUN
le moustique

■ **a mosquito bite** une piqûre de moustique

most ADVERB, ADJECTIVE, PRONOUN

> **LANGUAGE TIP** Use **la plupart de** when 'most (of)' is followed by a plural noun and **la majeure partie (de)** when 'most (of)' is followed by a singular noun.

1 la plupart de

□ most of my friends la plupart de mes amis □ most people la plupart des gens □ Most cats are affectionate. La plupart des chats sont affectueux.

■ **most of them** la plupart d'entre eux
■ **most of the time** la plupart du temps

2 la majeure partie de

□ most of the work la majeure partie du travail □ most of the class la majeure partie de la classe □ most of the night la majeure partie de la nuit

■ **the most** le plus □ He's the one who talks the most. C'est lui qui parle le plus.

> **LANGUAGE TIP** When 'most' is followed by adjective, the translation depends on whether the noun referred to is masculine, feminine or plural.

■ **the most ... 1** le plus ... □ the most expensive restaurant le restaurant le plus cher **2** la plus ... □ the most expensive seat la place la plus chère **3** les plus ... □ the most expensive restaurants les restaurants les plus chers □ the most expensive seats les places les plus chères

■ **to make the most of something** profiter au maximum de quelque chose

■ **at the most** au maximum □ Two hours at the most. Deux heures au maximum.

mostly ADVERB

■ **The teachers are mostly quite nice.** La plupart des professeurs sont assez gentils.

MOT NOUN
le contrôle technique

□ Her car failed its MOT. Sa voiture n'a pas

obtenu le certificat du contrôle technique.

motel NOUN
le motel

moth NOUN
le papillon de nuit

> **LANGUAGE TIP** Word for word, this means 'butterfly of the night'

mother NOUN
la mère

□ my mother ma mère

■ **mother tongue** la langue maternelle

mother-in-law NOUN
la belle-mère (PL les belles-mères)

Mother's Day NOUN
la fête des Mères

> **DID YOU KNOW...?** Mother's Day is usually on the last Sunday of May in France.

motionless ADJECTIVE
immobile (FEM immobile)

motivated ADJECTIVE
motivé (FEM motivée)

□ He is highly motivated. Il est très motivé.

motivation NOUN
la motivation

motive NOUN
le mobile

□ the motive for the killing le mobile du crime

motor NOUN
le moteur

□ The boat has a motor. Le bateau a un moteur.

motorbike NOUN
la moto

motorboat NOUN
le bateau à moteur (PL les bateaux à moteur)

motorcycle NOUN
le vélomoteur

motorcyclist NOUN
le motard

motorist NOUN
l' automobiliste *masc/fem*

motor mechanic NOUN
le mécanicien garagiste

motor racing NOUN
la course automobile

motorway NOUN
l' autoroute *fem*

□ on the motorway sur l'autoroute

mouldy ADJECTIVE
moisi (FEM moisie)

to **mount** VERB

1 monter

□ They're mounting a publicity campaign. Ils montent une campagne publicitaire.

2 augmenter

□ Tension is mounting. La tension augmente.

to **mount up** VERB
1 s'accumuler
□ The bills are mounting up. Les factures s'accumulent.
2 augmenter
□ My savings are mounting up gradually. Mes économies augmentent progressivement.

mountain NOUN
la montagne
■ **a mountain bike** un VTT (= *vélo tout-terrain*)

mountaineer NOUN
l' alpiniste *masc/fem*

mountaineering NOUN
l' alpinisme *masc*
□ I go mountaineering. Je fais de l'alpinisme.

mountainous ADJECTIVE
montagneux (FEM montagneuse)

mouse NOUN
la souris *(also for computer)*
□ white mice des souris blanches

mouse mat NOUN
le tapis de souris

mousse NOUN
1 la mousse *(food)*
□ chocolate mousse la mousse au chocolat
2 la mousse coiffante *(for hair)*

moustache NOUN
la moustache
□ He's got a moustache. Il a une moustache.
■ **a man with a moustache** un moustachu

mouth NOUN
la bouche

mouthful NOUN
la bouchée

mouth organ NOUN
l' harmonica *masc*
□ I play the mouth organ. Je joue de l'harmonica.

mouthwash NOUN
le bain de bouche

move NOUN
▷ *see also* **move** VERB
1 le tour
□ It's your move. C'est ton tour.
2 le déménagement
□ Our move from Oxford to Luton ... Notre déménagement d'Oxford à Luton ...
■ **to get a move on** se remuer □ Get a move on! Remue-toi!

460 to **move** VERB

▷ *see also* **move** NOUN
1 bouger
□ Don't move! Ne bouge pas! □ Could you move your stuff please? Est-ce que tu peux bouger tes affaires s'il te plaît?
2 avancer
□ The car was moving very slowly. La voiture avançait très lentement.
3 émouvoir
□ I was very moved by the film. J'ai été très émue par ce film.
■ **to move house** déménager □ We're moving in July. Nous allons déménager en juillet.

to **move forward** VERB
avancer

to **move in** VEBR
emménager
□ They're moving in next week. Ils emménagent la semaine prochaine.

to **move over** VERB
se pousser
□ Could you move over a bit? Est-ce que vous pouvez vous pousser un peu?

movement NOUN
le mouvement

movie NOUN
le film
■ **the movies** le cinéma □ Let's go to the movies! Si on allait au cinéma?

moving ADJECTIVE
1 en marche *(not stationary)*
□ a moving bus un bus en marche
2 touchant (FEM touchante) *(touching)*
□ a moving story une histoire touchante

to **mow** VERB
tondre
□ to mow the lawn tondre le gazon

mower NOUN
la tondeuse à gazon

mown VERB ▷ *see* **mow**

MP NOUN
le député
□ She's an MP. Elle est député.

MP3 player NOUN
le baladeur numérique
□ I need a new MP3 player. Il me faut un nouveau baladeur numérique.

mph ABBREVIATION (= *miles per hour*)
km/h (= *kilomètres-heure*)
□ to drive at 50 mph rouler à 80 km/h

DID YOU KNOW...?
In France, speed is expressed in kilometres per hour. 50 mph is about 80 km/h.

Mr NOUN
1 Monsieur (PL Messieurs)

2 M. (PL MM.) *(in address)*

Mrs NOUN
1 Madame (PL Mesdames)
2 Mme (PL Mmes) *(in address)*

MS NOUN (= *multiple sclerosis*)
la sclérose en plaques
□ She's got MS. Elle a la sclérose en plaques.

Ms NOUN
1 Madame (PL Mesdames)
2 Mme (PL Mmes) *(in address)*

> **DID YOU KNOW...?**
> There isn't a direct equivalent of 'Ms' in French. If you are writing to somebody and don't know whether she is married, use **Madame**.

much ADJECTIVE, ADVERB, PRONOUN
1 beaucoup *(with verb)*
□ Do you go out much? Tu sors beaucoup? □ I don't like sport much. Je n'aime pas beaucoup le sport. □ I feel much better now. Je me sens beaucoup mieux maintenant.
2 beaucoup de *(with noun)*
□ I haven't got much money. Je n'ai pas beaucoup d'argent. □ I don't want much rice. Je ne veux pas beaucoup de riz.

■ **very much 1** *(with verb)* beaucoup □ I enjoyed the film very much. J'ai beaucoup apprécié le film. □ Thank you very much. Merci beaucoup. **2** *(followed by noun)* beaucoup de □ I haven't got very much money. Je n'ai pas beaucoup d'argent.

■ **not much 1** pas beaucoup □ Have you got a lot of luggage? — No, not much. As-tu beaucoup de bagages? — Non, pas beaucoup. **2** pas grand-chose □ What's on TV? — Not much. Qu'est-ce qu'il y a à la télé? — Pas grand-chose. □ What did you think of it? — Not much. Qu'est-ce que tu en as pensé? — Pas grand-chose.

■ **How much?** Combien? □ How much do you want? Tu en veux combien? □ How much time have you got? Tu as combien de temps? □ How much is it? *(cost)* Combien est-ce que ça coûte?

■ **too much** trop □ That's too much! C'est trop! □ It costs too much. Ça coûte trop cher. □ They give us too much homework. Ils nous donnent trop de devoirs.

■ **so much** autant □ I didn't think it would cost so much. Je ne pensais pas que ça coûterait autant. □ I've never seen so much traffic. Je n'ai jamais vu autant de circulation.

mud NOUN
la boue

muddle NOUN
le désordre
□ The photos are in a muddle. Les photos sont en désordre.

to **muddle up** VERB
confondre *(people)*
□ He muddles me up with my sister. Il me confond avec ma sœur.
■ **to get muddled up** s'embrouiller □ I'm getting muddled up. Je m'embrouille.

muddy ADJECTIVE
boueux (FEM boueuse)

muesli NOUN
le muesli

muffler NOUN (US)
le silencieux

mug NOUN
▷ *see also* **mug** VERB
la grande tasse
□ Do you want a cup or a mug? Est-ce que vous voulez une tasse normale ou une grande tasse?

to **mug** VERB
▷ *see also* **mug** NOUN
agresser
□ He was mugged in the city centre. Il s'est fait agresser au centre ville.

mugger NOUN
l' agresseur *masc*

mugging NOUN
l' agression *fem*

muggy ADJECTIVE
lourd (FEM lourde)
□ It's muggy today. Il fait lourd aujourd'hui.

multiple choice test NOUN
le QCM (= *le questionnaire à choix multiples*)

multiple sclerosis NOUN
la sclérose en plaques
□ She's got multiple sclerosis. Elle a la sclérose en plaques.

multiplication NOUN
la multiplication

to **multiply** VERB
multiplier
□ to multiply 6 by 3 multiplier six par trois

multi-storey car park NOUN
le parking à plusieurs étages

mum NOUN
> **LANGUAGE TIP** You use **mère** in most cases, except when you are talking to your mother or using it as her name, then you would use **maman**.
1 la mère
□ my mum ma mère □ her mum sa mère
2 la maman
□ Mum! Maman! □ I'll ask Mum. Je vais demander à maman.

mummy NOUN
1 la maman *(mum)*
□ Mummy says I can go. Maman dit que je peux y aller.
2 la momie *(Egyptian)*

mumps NOUN
les oreillons *masc pl*

murder NOUN
▷ *see also* **murder** VERB
le meurtre

to **murder** VERB
▷ *see also* **murder** NOUN
assassiner
□ He was murdered. Il a été assassiné.

murderer NOUN
l' assassin *masc*

muscle NOUN
le muscle

muscular ADJECTIVE
musclé (FEM musclée)

museum NOUN
le musée

mushroom NOUN
le champignon
□ mushroom omelette l'omelette aux champignons

music NOUN
la musique

musical ADJECTIVE
▷ *see also* **musical** NOUN
doué pour la musique (FEM douée pour la musique)
□ I'm not musical. Je ne suis pas doué pour la musique.
■ a musical instrument un instrument de musique

musical NOUN
▷ *see also* **musical** ADJECTIVE
la comédie musicale

music centre NOUN
la chaîne stéréo (PL les chaînes stéréo)

musician NOUN
le musicien
la musicienne

Muslim NOUN
le musulman
la musulmane
□ He's a Muslim. Il est musulman.

mussel NOUN
la moule

must VERB
⋮ **LANGUAGE TIP** When 'must' means that you assume or suppose something, use **devoir**; when it means it's necessary to do something, eg 'I must buy some presents', use **il faut que** ..., which

comes from the verb **falloir** and is followed by a verb in the subjunctive.
1 devoir *(I suppose)*
□ You must be tired. Tu dois être fatigué.
□ They must have plenty of money. Ils doivent avoir beaucoup d'argent. □ There must be some problem. Il doit y avoir un problème.
2 il faut que
□ I must buy some presents. Il faut que j'achète des cadeaux. □ I really must go now. Il faut que j'y aille.
■ You mustn't forget to send her a card. N'oublie surtout pas de lui envoyer une carte.
■ You must come and see us. *(invitation)* Venez donc nous voir.

mustard NOUN
la moutarde

mustn't VERB = must not

to **mutter** VERB
marmonner

mutton NOUN
le mouton

my ADJECTIVE
mon *masc*
□ my father mon père
ma *fem*
□ my aunt ma tante
mes *pl*
□ my parents mes parents
⋮ **LANGUAGE TIP** ma becomes mon before a vowel sound.
■ my friend 1 *(male)* mon ami 2 *(female)* mon amie
⋮ **LANGUAGE TIP** Do not use mon/ma/mes with parts of the body.
□ I want to wash my hair. Je voudrais me laver les cheveux. □ I'm going to clean my teeth. Je vais me brosser les dents.
□ I've hurt my foot. Je me suis fait mal au pied.

myself PRONOUN
1 me
□ I've hurt myself. Je me suis fait mal. □ I really enjoyed myself. Je me suis vraiment bien amusé. □ ... when I look at myself in the mirror. ... quand je me regarde dans la glace.
2 moi
□ I don't like talking about myself. Je n'aime pas parler de moi.
3 moi-même
□ I made it myself. Je l'ai fait moi-même.
■ by myself tout seul □ I don't like travelling by myself. Je n'aime pas voyager

tout seul.

mysterious ADJECTIVE
mystérieux (FEM mystérieuse)

mystery NOUN
le mystère
■ **a murder mystery** *(novel)* un roman policier

myth NOUN
1 le mythe *(legend)*
   □ a Greek myth un mythe grec
2 l' idée reçue *fem (untrue idea)*
   □ That's a myth. C'est une idée reçue.

mythology NOUN
la mythologie

m

Nn

naff ADJECTIVE
nul (FEM nulle)

to **nag** VERB
harceler (scold)
□ She's always nagging me. Elle me harcèle constamment.

nail NOUN
1 l' ongle masc (on finger, toe)
□ Don't bite your nails! Ne te ronge pas les ongles!
2 le clou (made of metal)

nailbrush NOUN
la brosse à ongles

nailfile NOUN
la lime à ongles

nail scissors PL NOUN
les ciseaux à ongles masc pl

nail varnish NOUN
le vernis à ongles
■ nail varnish remover le dissolvant

naked ADJECTIVE
nu (FEM nue)

name NOUN
le nom
■ What's your name? Comment vous appelez-vous?

nanny NOUN
la garde d'enfants
□ She's a nanny. C'est une garde d'enfants.

nap NOUN
le petit somme
■ to have a nap faire un petit somme

napkin NOUN
la serviette

nappy NOUN
la couche

narrow ADJECTIVE
étroit (FEM étroite)

narrow-minded ADJECTIVE
borné (FEM bornée)

nasty ADJECTIVE
1 mauvais (FEM mauvaise) (bad)
□ a nasty cold un mauvais rhume □ a nasty smell une mauvaise odeur
2 méchant (FEM méchante) (unfriendly)

□ He gave me a nasty look. Il m'a regardé d'un air méchant.

nation NOUN
la nation

national ADJECTIVE
national (FEM nationale, MASC PL nationaux)
□ He's the national champion. C'est le champion national.
■ the national elections les élections législatives

national anthem NOUN
l' hymne national masc

National Health Service NOUN
la Sécurité sociale

> **DID YOU KNOW...?**
> In France you have to pay for medical treatment when you receive it, and then claim it back from the **Sécurité sociale**.

nationalism NOUN
le nationalisme
□ Scottish nationalism le nationalisme écossais

nationalist NOUN
le/la nationaliste

nationality NOUN
la nationalité

National Lottery NOUN
la Loterie nationale

national park NOUN
le parc national (PL les parcs nationaux)

native ADJECTIVE
natal (FEM natale)
□ my native country mon pays natal
■ native language la langue maternelle
□ English is not their native language. L'anglais n'est pas leur langue maternelle.

natural ADJECTIVE
naturel (FEM naturelle)

naturalist NOUN
le naturaliste

naturally ADVERB
naturellement
□ Naturally, we were very disappointed. Nous avons naturellement été très déçus.

nature NOUN
la nature

naughty ADJECTIVE
vilain (FEM vilaine)
□ Naughty girl! Vilaine! □ Don't be naughty!
Ne fais pas le vilain!

navy NOUN
la marine
□ He's in the navy. Il est dans la marine.

navy-blue ADJECTIVE
bleu marine (FEM+PL bleu marine)
□ a navy-blue skirt une jupe bleu marine

Nazi NOUN
le Nazi
la Nazie
□ the Nazis les Nazis

near ADJECTIVE
▷ see also **near** PREPOSITION
proche (FEM proche)
□ It's fairly near. C'est assez proche.
■ **It's near enough to walk.** On peut
facilement y aller à pied.
■ **the nearest** le plus proche □ Where's
the nearest service station? Où est la
station-service la plus proche? □ The
nearest shops were three kilometres away.
Les magasins les plus proches étaient à trois
kilomètres.

near PREPOSITION, ADVERB
▷ see also **near** ADJECTIVE
près de
□ I live near Liverpool. J'habite près de
Liverpool. □ near my house près de chez
moi
■ **near here** près d'ici □ Is there a bank
near here? Est-ce qu'il y a une banque près
d'ici?
■ **near to** près de □ It's very near to the
school. C'est tout près de l'école.

nearby ADVERB
▷ see also **nearby** ADJECTIVE
à proximité
□ There's a supermarket nearby. Il y a un
supermarché à proximité.

nearby ADJECTIVE
▷ see also **nearby** ADVERB
1 proche (FEM proche) (close)
□ a nearby garage un garage proche
2 voisin (FEM voisine) (neighbouring)
□ We went to the nearby village of Torrance.
Nous sommes allés à Torrance, le village
voisin.

nearly ADVERB
presque
□ Dinner's nearly ready. Le dîner est
presque prêt. □ I'm nearly 15. J'ai presque
quinze ans.
■ **I nearly missed the train.** J'ai failli rater
le train.

neat ADJECTIVE
soigné (FEM soignée)
□ She has very neat writing. Elle a une
écriture très soignée.
■ **a neat whisky** un whisky sec

neatly ADVERB
soigneusement
□ neatly folded soigneusement plié
■ **neatly dressed** impeccable

necessarily ADVERB
■ **not necessarily** pas forcément

necessary ADJECTIVE
nécessaire (FEM nécessaire)

necessity NOUN
la chose nécessaire
□ A car is a necessity, not a luxury. Une
voiture est une chose nécessaire et non pas
un luxe.

neck NOUN
1 le cou (of body)
■ **a stiff neck** un torticolis
2 l' encolure fem (of garment)
□ a V-neck sweater un pull avec une
encolure en V

necklace NOUN
le collier

to **need** VERB
▷ see also **need** NOUN
avoir besoin de
□ I need a bigger size. J'ai besoin d'une plus
grande taille.
■ **to need to do something** avoir besoin de
faire quelque chose □ I need to change
some money. J'ai besoin de changer de
l'argent.

need NOUN
▷ see also **need** VERB
■ **There's no need to book.** Il n'est pas
nécessaire de réserver.

needle NOUN
l' aiguille fem

negative NOUN
▷ see also **negative** ADJECTIVE
le négatif (photo)

negative ADJECTIVE
▷ see also **negative** NOUN
négatif (FEM négative)
□ He's got a very negative attitude. Il a une
attitude très négative.

neglected ADJECTIVE
mal tenu (FEM mal tenue) (untidy)
□ The garden is neglected. Le jardin est mal
tenu.

negligee NOUN
le déshabillé

to **negotiate** VERB
négocier

negotiations PL NOUN
les négociations *fem pl*

neighbour (US **neighbor**) NOUN
le voisin
la voisine
□ the neighbours' garden le jardin des voisins

neighbourhood (US **neighborhood**) NOUN
le quartier

neither PRONOUN, CONJUNCTION, ADVERB
aucun des deux
aucune des deux
□ Carrots or peas? — Neither, thanks. Des carottes ou des petits pois? — Aucun des deux merci. □ Neither of them is coming. Aucun des deux ne vient.
■ **neither … nor …** ni … ni … □ Neither Sarah nor Tamsin is coming to the party. Ni Sarah ni Tamsin ne viennent à la soirée.
■ **Neither do I.** Moi non plus. □ I don't like him. — Neither do I! Je ne l'aime pas. — Moi non plus!
■ **Neither have I.** Moi non plus. □ I've never been to Spain. — Neither have I. Je ne suis jamais allé en Espagne. — Moi non plus.

neon NOUN
le néon
□ a neon light une lampe au néon

nephew NOUN
le neveu (PL les neveux)
□ my nephew mon neveu

nerve NOUN
1 le nerf
□ She sometimes gets on my nerves. Elle me tape quelquefois sur les nerfs.
2 le toupet (*cheek*)
□ He's got a nerve! Il a du toupet!

nerve-racking ADJECTIVE
angoissant (FEM angoissante)

nervous ADJECTIVE
tendu (FEM tendue) (*tense*)
□ I bite my nails when I'm nervous. Je me ronge les ongles quand je suis tendu.
■ **to be nervous about something** appréhender de faire quelque chose □ I'm a bit nervous about flying to Paris by myself. J'appréhende un peu d'aller toute seule en avion à Paris.

nest NOUN
le nid

Net NOUN
le Net
□ to surf the Net surfer sur le Net

le filet
□ a fishing net un filet de pêche

netball NOUN
■ **Netball is a bit like basketball.** Le netball ressemble un peu au basket.

DID YOU KNOW…?
Netball is not played in France. Both sexes play basketball or volleyball instead.

Netherlands PL NOUN
les Pays-Bas *masc*
■ **in the Netherlands** aux Pays-Bas

network NOUN
1 le réseau (PL les réseaux)
2 l' opérateur *masc* (*for mobile phone*)
□ Which network are you on? Tu es avec quel opérateur?

neurotic ADJECTIVE
névrosé (FEM névrosée)

never ADVERB
1 jamais
□ Have you ever been to Germany? — No, never. Est-ce que tu es déjà allé en Allemagne? — Non, jamais. □ When are you going to phone him? — Never! Quand est-ce que tu vas l'appeler? — Jamais!
2 ne … jamais

LANGUAGE TIP Add **ne** if the sentence contains a verb.

□ I never write letters. Je n'écris jamais. □ I have never been camping. Je n'ai jamais fait de camping. □ Never leave valuables in your car. Ne laissez jamais d'objets de valeur dans votre voiture.
■ **Never again!** Plus jamais!
■ **Never mind.** Ça ne fait rien.

new ADJECTIVE
1 nouveau (FEM nouvelle, MASC PL nouveaux)
□ her new boyfriend son nouveau copain □ I need a new dress. J'ai besoin d'une nouvelle robe.

LANGUAGE TIP nouveau changes to **nouvel** before a vowel and most words beginning with 'h'.

2 neuf (FEM neuve) (*brand new*)
□ They've got a new car. Ils ont une voiture neuve.

newborn ADJECTIVE
■ **a newborn baby** un nouveau-né

newcomer NOUN
le nouveau venu (MASC PL les nouveaux venus)
la nouvelle venue

news NOUN
1 les nouvelles *fem pl*
□ good news de bonnes nouvelles □ I've had some bad news. J'ai reçu de mauvaises

n

nouvelles. □ It was nice to have your news. J'ai été content d'avoir de tes nouvelles.

2 la nouvelle *(single piece of news)*
□ That's wonderful news! Quelle bonne nouvelle!

3 le journal télévisé *(on TV)*
□ I watch the news every evening Je regarde le journal télévisé tous les soirs.

4 les informations *fem pl (on radio)*
□ I listen to the news every morning. J'écoute les informations tous les matins.

newsagent NOUN
le marchand de journaux

newsdealer NOUN (US)
le marchand de journaux

newspaper NOUN
le journal (PL les journaux)
□ I deliver newspapers. Je distribue des journaux.

newsreader NOUN
le présentateur
la présentatrice

New Year NOUN
le Nouvel An
□ to celebrate New Year fêter le Nouvel An
■ **Happy New Year!** Bonne Année!
■ **New Year's Day** le premier de l'An
■ **New Year's Eve** la Saint-Sylvestre

New Zealand NOUN
la Nouvelle-Zélande
■ **in New Zealand** en Nouvelle-Zélande

New Zealander NOUN
le Néo-Zélandais
la Néo-Zélandaise

next ADJECTIVE, ADVERB, PREPOSITION
1 prochain (FEM prochaine) *(in time)*
□ next Saturday samedi prochain □ next year l'année prochaine □ next summer l'été prochain

2 suivant (FEM suivante) *(in sequence)*
□ the next train le train suivant □ Next please! Au suivant!

3 ensuite *(afterwards)*
□ What shall I do next? Qu'est-ce que je fais ensuite? □ What happened next? Qu'est-ce qui s'est passé ensuite?
■ **next to** à côté de □ next to the bank à côté de la banque
■ **the next day** le lendemain □ The next day we visited Versailles. Le lendemain nous avons visité Versailles.
■ **the next time** la prochaine fois □ the next time you see her la prochaine fois que tu la verras
■ **next door** à côté □ They live next door. Ils habitent à côté. □ the people next door les gens d'à côté

■ **the next room** la pièce d'à côté

NHS NOUN
la Sécurité sociale

> **DID YOU KNOW...?**
> In France you have to pay for medical treatment when you receive it, and then claim it back from the Sécurité sociale.

nice ADJECTIVE
1 gentil (FEM gentille) *(kind)*
□ Your parents are very nice. Tes parents sont très gentils. □ It was nice of you to remember my birthday. C'était gentil de ta part de te souvenir de mon anniversaire.
■ **to be nice to somebody** être gentil avec quelqu'un

2 joli (FEM jolie) *(pretty)*
□ That's a nice dress! Qu'est-ce qu'elle est jolie, cette robe! □ Aix is a nice town. Aix est une jolie ville.

> **WORD POWER**
> You can use a number of other words instead of **nice** to mean 'pretty':
> **attractive** séduisant
> □ an attractive girl une fille séduisante
> **beautiful** beau
> □ a beautiful painting un beau tableau
> **lovely** charmant
> □ a lovely surprise une charmante surprise
> **pretty** joli
> □ a pretty dress une jolie robe

3 bon (FEM bonne) *(food)*
□ It's very nice. C'est très bon. □ a nice cup of coffee une bonne tasse de café
■ **Have a nice time!** Amuse-toi bien!
■ **nice weather** le beau temps
■ **It's a nice day.** Il fait beau.

nickname NOUN
le surnom

niece NOUN
la nièce
□ my niece ma nièce

Nigeria NOUN
le Nigéria
■ **in Nigeria** au Nigéria

night NOUN
1 la nuit
□ I want a single room for two nights. Je veux une chambre à un lit pour deux nuits.
■ **My mother works nights.** Ma mère travaille de nuit.
■ **at night** la nuit
■ **Goodnight!** Bonne nuit!

2 le soir *(evening)*
□ last night hier soir

night club NOUN
la boîte de nuit

nightdress NOUN
la chemise de nuit

nightie NOUN
la chemise de nuit

nightlife NOUN
■ **There's plenty of nightlife.** Il y a plein de choses à faire le soir.

nightmare NOUN
le cauchemar
□ It was a real nightmare! Ça a été un vrai cauchemar!
■ **to have a nightmare** faire un cauchemar

nightshirt NOUN
la chemise de nuit

nil NOUN
le zéro
□ We won one-nil. Nous avons gagné un à zéro.

nine NUMBER
neuf
□ She's nine. Elle a neuf ans.

nineteen NUMBER
dix-neuf
□ She's nineteen. Elle a dix-neuf ans.

nineteenth ADJECTIVE
dix-neuvième (FEM dix-neuvième)
□ her nineteenth birthday son dix-neuvième anniversaire □ the nineteenth floor le dix-neuvième étage
■ **the nineteenth of August** le dix-neuf août

ninety NUMBER
quatre-vingt-dix

ninth ADJECTIVE
neuvième (FEM neuvième)
□ the ninth floor le neuvième étage
■ **the ninth of August** le neuf août

no ADVERB, ADJECTIVE
1 non
□ Are you coming? — No. Est-ce que vous venez? — Non. □ Would you like some more? — No thank you. Vous en voulez encore? — Non merci.
2 pas de (not any)
□ There's no hot water. Il n'y a pas d'eau chaude. □ There are no trains on Sundays. Il n'y a pas de trains le dimanche. □ No problem. Pas de problème.
■ **I've got no idea.** Je n'en ai aucune idée.
■ **No way!** Pas question!
■ **'no smoking'** 'défense de fumer'

nobody PRONOUN
1 personne
□ Who's going with you? — Nobody. Qui t'accompagne? — Personne.

2 ne ... personne
⊙ **LANGUAGE TIP** Add **ne** if the sentence contains a verb.
□ There was nobody in the office. Il n'y avait personne au bureau.
■ **Nobody likes him.** Personne ne l'aime.

to nod VERB
acquiescer d'un signe de tête (in agreement)
■ **to nod at somebody** (as greeting) saluer quelqu'un d'un signe de tête

noise NOUN
le bruit
□ Please make less noise. Faites moins de bruit s'il vous plaît.

noisy ADJECTIVE
bruyant (FEM bruyante)

to nominate VERB
1 nommer (appoint)
□ She was nominated as director. Elle a été nommée directrice.
2 proposer (propose)
□ I nominate Ian Alexander as president of the society. Je propose Ian Alexander comme président de la société.
■ **He was nominated for an Oscar.** Il a été nominé pour un Oscar.

none PRONOUN
1 aucun
aucune
□ How many sisters have you got? — None. Tu as combien de sœurs? — Aucune.
□ What sports do you do? — None. Qu'est-ce que tu fais comme sport? — Je n'en fais aucun.
2 aucun ... ne
⊙ **LANGUAGE TIP** Add **ne** if the sentence contains a verb.
□ None of my friends wanted to come. Aucun de mes amis n'a voulu venir.
■ **There's none left.** Il n'y en a plus.
■ **There are none left.** Il n'y en a plus.

nonsense NOUN
les bêtises fem pl
□ She talks a lot of nonsense. Elle dit beaucoup de bêtises. □ Nonsense! Ne dis pas de bêtises!

non-smoker NOUN
le non-fumeur
□ He's a non-smoker. Il est non-fumeur.

non-smoking ADJECTIVE
non-fumeurs
□ a non-smoking carriage une voiture non-fumeurs

non-stop ADJECTIVE, ADVERB
1 direct (FEM directe)
□ a non-stop flight un vol direct □ We flew non-stop. Nous avons pris un vol direct.

2 sans arrêt
- ☐ He talks non-stop. Il parle sans arrêt.

noodles PL NOUN
les nouilles *fem pl*

noon NOUN
midi *masc*
- ☐ at noon à midi ☐ before noon avant midi

no one PRONOUN
1 personne
- ☐ Who's going with you? — No one. Qui t'accompagne? — Personne.
2 ne ... personne
- ⚬ **LANGUAGE TIP** Add ne if the sentence contains a verb.
- ☐ There was no one in the office. Il n'y avait personne au bureau.
- ■ No one likes Christopher. Personne n'aime Christopher.

nor CONJUNCTION
- ■ **neither ... nor** ni ... ni ☐ neither the cinema nor the swimming pool ni le cinéma, ni la piscine
- ■ **Nor do I.** Moi non plus. ☐ I didn't like the film. — Nor did I. Je n'ai pas aimé le film. — Moi non plus.
- ■ **Nor have I.** Moi non plus. ☐ I haven't seen him. — Nor have I. Je ne l'ai pas vu. — Moi non plus.

normal ADJECTIVE
1 habituel (FEM habituelle) *(usual)*
- ☐ at the normal time à l'heure habituelle
2 normal (FEM normale, MASC PL normaux) *(standard)*
- ☐ a normal car une voiture normale

normally ADVERB
1 généralement *(usually)*
- ☐ I normally arrive at nine o'clock. J'arrive généralement à neuf heures.
2 normalement *(as normal)*
- ☐ In spite of the strike, the airports are working normally. Malgré la grève, les aéroports fonctionnent normalement.

Normandy NOUN
la Normandie
- ■ **in Normandy** en Normandie
- ■ **to Normandy** en Normandie

north ADJECTIVE, ADVERB
▷ *see also* **north** NOUN
1 nord (FEM+PL nord)
- ☐ the north coast la côte nord
- ■ **a north wind** un vent du nord
2 vers le nord
- ☐ We were travelling north. Nous allions vers le nord.
- ■ **north of** au nord de ☐ It's north of London. C'est au nord de Londres.

north NOUN
▷ *see also* **north** ADJECTIVE
le nord
- ☐ in the north dans le nord

North America NOUN
l' Amérique du Nord *fem*

northbound ADJECTIVE
- ■ **The truck was northbound on the M5.** Le camion se trouvait sur la M5 en direction du nord.
- ■ **Northbound traffic is moving very slowly.** La circulation vers le nord avance très lentement.

northeast NOUN
le nord-est
- ☐ in the northeast au nord-est

northern ADJECTIVE
- ■ **the northern part of the island** la partie nord de l'île
- ■ **Northern Europe** l'Europe du Nord

Northern Ireland NOUN
l' Irlande du Nord *fem*
- ■ **in Northern Ireland** en Irlande du Nord
- ■ **to Northern Ireland** en Irlande du Nord
- ■ **I'm from Northern Ireland.** Je viens d'Irlande du Nord.

North Pole NOUN
le pôle Nord

North Sea NOUN
la mer du Nord

northwest NOUN
le nord-ouest
- ☐ in the northwest au nord-ouest

Norway NOUN
la Norvège
- ■ **in Norway** en Norvège

Norwegian NOUN
▷ *see also* **Norwegian** ADJECTIVE
1 le Norvégien
la Norvégienne *(person)*
2 le norvégien *(language)*

Norwegian ADJECTIVE
▷ *see also* **Norwegian** NOUN
norvégien (FEM norvégienne)

nose NOUN
le nez (PL les nez)

nosebleed NOUN
- ■ **to have a nosebleed** saigner du nez ☐ I often get nosebleeds. Je saigne souvent du nez.

nosy ADJECTIVE
fouineur (FEM fouineuse)

not ADVERB
1 pas
- ☐ Are you coming or not? Est-ce que tu viens ou pas?
- ■ **not really** pas vraiment
- ■ **not at all** pas du tout

- **not yet** pas encore □ Have you finished? — Not yet. As-tu fini? — Pas encore.

2 ne ... pas

> **LANGUAGE TIP** Add **ne** if the sentence contains a verb.

□ I'm not sure. Je ne suis pas sûr. □ It's not raining. Il ne pleut pas. □ You shouldn't do that. Tu ne devrais pas faire ça. □ They haven't arrived yet. Ils ne sont pas encore arrivés.

3 non

□ I hope not. J'espère que non. □ Can you lend me £10? — I'm afraid not. Est-ce que tu peux me prêter dix livres? — Non, désolé.

note NOUN

1 la note

□ to take notes prendre des notes

2 le mot (letter)

□ I'll write her a note. Je vais lui écrire un mot.

3 le billet (banknote)

□ a £5 note un billet de cinq livres

to **note down** VERB

noter

notebook NOUN

le carnet

notepad NOUN

le bloc-notes (PL les blocs-notes)

notepaper NOUN

le papier à lettres

nothing NOUN

1 rien

□ What's wrong? — Nothing. Qu'est-ce qui ne va pas? — Rien. □ nothing special rien de particulier

2 ne ... rien

> **LANGUAGE TIP** Add **ne** if the sentence contains a verb.

□ He does nothing. Il ne fait rien. □ He ate nothing for breakfast. Il n'a rien mangé au petit-déjeuner.

- **Nothing is open on Sundays.** Rien n'est ouvert le dimanche.

notice NOUN

> see also **notice** VERB

le panneau (PL les panneaux) (sign)

- **to put up a notice** mettre un panneau
- **a warning notice** un avertissement
- **Don't take any notice of him!** Ne fais pas attention à lui!

to **notice** VERB

> see also **notice** NOUN

remarquer

notice board NOUN

le panneau d'affichage (PL les panneaux d'affichage)

nought NOUN

le zéro

noun NOUN

le nom

novel NOUN

le roman

novelist NOUN

le romancier
la romancière

November NOUN

novembre masc

- **in November** en novembre

now ADVERB, CONJUNCTION

maintenant

□ What are you doing now? Qu'est-ce que tu fais maintenant?

- **just now** en ce moment □ I'm rather busy just now. Je suis très occupé en ce moment.
- **I did it just now.** Je viens de le faire.
- **He should be there by now.** Il doit être arrivé à l'heure qu'il est.
- **It should be ready by now.** Ça devrait être déjà prêt.
- **now and then** de temps en temps

nowhere ADVERB

nulle part

□ nowhere else nulle part ailleurs

nuclear ADJECTIVE

nucléaire (FEM nucléaire)

□ nuclear power l'énergie nucléaire □ a nuclear power station une centrale nucléaire

nude ADJECTIVE

> see also **nude** NOUN

nu (FEM nue)

- **to sunbathe nude** faire du bronzage intégral

nude NOUN

> see also **nude** ADJECTIVE

- **in the nude** nu

nudist NOUN

le/la nudiste

nuisance NOUN

- **It's a nuisance.** C'est très embêtant.
- **Sorry to be a nuisance.** Désolé de vous déranger.

numb ADJECTIVE

engourdi (FEM engourdie)

□ My leg's gone numb. J'ai les jambes engourdies.

- **numb with cold** engourdi par le froid

number NOUN

1 le nombre (total amount)

□ a large number of people un grand nombre de gens

2 le numéro (of house, telephone, bank account)

□ They live at number 5. Ils habitent au

numéro cinq. □ What's your phone number? Quel est votre numéro de téléphone? □ You've got the wrong number. Vous vous êtes trompé de numéro.

3 le chiffre *(figure, digit)*

□ I can't read the second number. Je n'arrive pas à lire le deuxième chiffre.

number plate NOUN
la plaque d'immatriculation

nun NOUN
la religieuse

□ She's a nun. Elle est religieuse.

nurse NOUN
l' infirmier *masc*
l' infirmière *fem*

□ She's a nurse. Elle est infirmière.

nursery NOUN
1 la crèche *(for children)*
2 la pépinière *(for plants)*

nursery school NOUN
l' école maternelle *fem*

⊙ **DID YOU KNOW...?**
The **école maternelle** is a state school for 2-6 year-olds.

nursery slope NOUN
la piste pour débutants

nut NOUN
1 la cacahuète *(peanut)*
2 la noisette *(hazelnut)*
3 la noix (PL les noix) *(walnut)*
4 l' écrou *masc (made of metal)*

nutmeg NOUN
la noix de muscade

nutritious ADJECTIVE
nourrissant (FEM nourrissante)

nuts ADJECTIVE
■ He's nuts. Il est dingue.

nutter NOUN
■ He's a nutter. Il est complètement cinglé. *(informal)*

nylon NOUN
le nylon

Oo

oak NOUN
le chêne
□ an oak table une table en chêne

oar NOUN
l' aviron *masc*

oats NOUN
l' avoine *fem*

obedient ADJECTIVE
obéissant (FEM obéissante)

to **obey** VERB
■ **to obey the rules** respecter le règlement

object NOUN
l' objet *masc*
□ a familiar object un objet familier

objection NOUN
l' objection *fem*

objective NOUN
l' objectif *masc*

oblong ADJECTIVE
rectangulaire (FEM rectangulaire)

oboe NOUN
le hautbois
□ I play the oboe. Je joue du hautbois.

obscene ADJECTIVE
obscène (FEM obscène)

observant ADJECTIVE
observateur (FEM observatrice)

to **observe** VERB
observer

obsessed ADJECTIVE
obsédé (FEM obsédée)
□ He's obsessed with trains. Il est obsédé par les trains.

obsession NOUN
l' obsession *fem*
□ It's getting to be an obsession with you. Ça devient une obsession chez toi.
■ **Football's an obsession of mine.** Le football est une de mes passions.

obsolete ADJECTIVE
dépassé (FEM dépassée)

obstacle NOUN
l' obstacle *masc*

obstinate ADJECTIVE
obstiné (FEM obstinée)

to **obstruct** VERB
bloquer
□ A lorry was obstructing the traffic. Un camion bloquait la circulation.

to **obtain** VERB
obtenir

obvious ADJECTIVE
évident (FEM évidente)

obviously ADVERB
1 évidemment *(of course)*
□ Do you want to pass the exam? — Obviously! Tu veux être reçu à l'examen? — Évidemment!
■ **Obviously not!** Bien sûr que non!
2 manifestement *(visibly)*
□ She was obviously exhausted. Elle était manifestement épuisée.

occasion NOUN
l' occasion *fem*
□ a special occasion une occasion spéciale
■ **on several occasions** à plusieurs reprises

occasionally ADVERB
de temps en temps

occupation NOUN
la profession

to **occupy** VERB
occuper
□ That seat is occupied. Cette place est occupée.

to **occur** VERB
avoir lieu *(happen)*
□ The accident occurred yesterday. L'accident a eu lieu hier.
■ **It suddenly occurred to me that ...** Il m'est soudain venu à l'esprit que ...

ocean NOUN
l' océan *masc*

o'clock ADVERB
■ **at four o'clock** à quatre heures
■ **It's five o'clock.** Il est cinq heures.

October NOUN
octobre *masc*
■ **in October** en octobre

octopus NOUN
la pieuvre

odd ADJECTIVE
1 bizarre (FEM bizarre)
□ That's odd! C'est bizarre!
2 impair (FEM impaire)
□ an odd number un chiffre impair

of PREPOSITION
1 de
□ some photos of my holiday des photos de
mes vacances □ a boy of ten un garçon de
dix ans

⟨ LANGUAGE TIP de changes to d' before
a vowel and most words beginning
with 'h'. ⟩

d'
□ a kilo of oranges un kilo d'oranges

⟨ LANGUAGE TIP de + le changes to du,
and de + les changes to des. ⟩

du
□ the end of the film la fin du film
des
□ the end of the holidays la fin des vacances
2 en (with quantity, amount)
□ He's got four sisters. I've met two of them.
Il a quatre sœurs. J'en ai rencontré deux.
□ Can I have half of that? Je peux en avoir la
moitié?
■ **three of us** trois d'entre nous
■ **a friend of mine** un de mes amis
■ **the 14th of September** le quatorze
septembre
■ **That's very kind of you.** C'est très gentil
de votre part.
■ **It's made of wood.** C'est en bois.

off ADVERB, PREPOSITION, ADJECTIVE

⟨ LANGUAGE TIP For other expressions
with 'off', see the verbs 'get', 'take',
'turn' etc. ⟩

1 éteint (FEM éteinte) (heater, light, TV)
□ All the lights are off. Toutes les lumières
sont éteintes.
2 fermé (FEM fermée) (tap, gas)
□ Are you sure the tap is off? Tu es sûr que
le robinet est fermé?
3 annulé (FEM annulée) (cancelled)
□ The match is off. Le match est annulé.
■ **to be off sick** être malade
■ **a day off** un jour de congé □ to take a day
off work prendre un jour de congé
■ **She's off school today.** Elle n'est pas à
l'école aujourd'hui.
■ **I must be off now.** Je dois m'en aller
maintenant.
■ **I'm off.** Je m'en vais.

offence (US **offense**) NOUN
le délit (crime)

offensive ADJECTIVE
choquant (FEM choquante)

offer NOUN
▷ see also **offer** VERB
la proposition
□ a good offer une proposition intéressante
■ **'on special offer'** 'en promotion'

to **offer** VERB
▷ see also **offer** NOUN
proposer
□ He offered to help me. Il m'a proposé de
m'aider. □ I offered to go with them. Je leur
ai proposé de les accompagner.

office NOUN
le bureau (PL les bureaux)
□ She works in an office. Elle travaille dans
un bureau.

officer NOUN
l' officier masc

official ADJECTIVE
officiel (FEM officielle)

off-licence NOUN
le marchand de vins et spiritueux

off-peak ADVERB
hors saison (off-season)
□ It's cheaper to go on holiday off-peak.
C'est moins cher de partir en vacances hors
saison.
■ **to phone off-peak** appeler pendant les
heures creuses

offside ADJECTIVE
hors jeu (in football)

often ADVERB
souvent
□ It often rains. Il pleut souvent. □ How
often do you go to the gym? Tu vas souvent
à la gym? □ I'd like to go skiing more often.
J'aimerais aller skier plus souvent.

oil NOUN
▷ see also **oil** VERB
1 l' huile fem (for lubrication, cooking)
■ **an oil painting** une peinture à l'huile
2 le pétrole (crude oil)
□ North Sea oil le pétrole de la mer du Nord

to **oil** VERB
▷ see also **oil** NOUN
graisser

oil rig NOUN
la plateforme pétrolière
□ He works on an oil rig. Il travaille sur une
plateforme pétrolière.

oil slick NOUN
la marée noire

oil well NOUN
le puits de pétrole (PL les puits de pétrole)

ointment NOUN
la pommade

okay EXCLAMATION, ADJECTIVE
d'accord (agreed)

o

□ Could you call back later? — Okay! Tu peux rappeler plus tard? — D'accord! □ I'll meet you at six o'clock, okay? Je te retrouve à six heures, d'accord? □ Is that okay? C'est d'accord?

■ **I'll do it tomorrow, if that's okay with you.** Je le ferai demain, si tu es d'accord.

■ **Are you okay?** Ça va?

■ **How was your holiday? — It was okay.** C'était comment tes vacances? — Pas mal.

■ **What's your teacher like? — He's okay.** Il est comment ton prof? — Il est sympa. (*informal*)

old ADJECTIVE

1 vieux (FEM vieille, MASC PL vieux)

□ an old dog un vieux chien □ an old house une vieille maison

> LANGUAGE TIP **vieux** changes to **vieil** before a vowel and most words beginning with 'h'.

vieil

□ an old man un vieil homme

> LANGUAGE TIP When talking about people it is more polite to use **âgé** instead of **vieux**.

âgé

□ old people les personnes âgées

2 ancien (FEM ancienne) (*former*)

□ my old English teacher mon ancien professeur d'anglais

■ **How old are you?** Quel âge as-tu?

■ **He's ten years old.** Il a dix ans.

■ **my older brother** mon frère aîné □ my older sister ma sœur aînée

■ **She's two years older than me.** Elle a deux ans de plus que moi.

■ **I'm the oldest in the family.** Je suis l'aîné de la famille.

old age pensioner NOUN

le retraité
la retraitée

□ She's an old age pensioner. Elle est retraitée.

old-fashioned ADJECTIVE

1 démodé (FEM démodée)

□ She wears old-fashioned clothes. Elle porte des vêtements démodés.

2 vieux jeu (FEM+PL vieux jeu) (*person*)

□ My parents are rather old-fashioned. Mes parents sont plutôt vieux jeu.

olive NOUN

l' olive *fem*

olive oil NOUN

l' huile d'olive *fem*

olive tree NOUN

l' olivier *masc*

Olympic ADJECTIVE

olympique (FEM olympique)

■ **the Olympics** les Jeux olympiques *masc pl*

omelette NOUN

l' omelette *fem*

on PREPOSITION, ADVERB

▷ *see also* **on** ADJECTIVE

> LANGUAGE TIP There are several ways of translating 'on'. Scan the examples to find one that is similar to what you want to say. For other expressions with 'on', see the verbs 'go', 'put', 'turn' etc.

1 sur

□ on the table sur la table □ on an island sur une île

2 à

□ on the left à gauche □ on the 2nd floor au deuxième étage □ I go to school on my bike. Je vais à l'école à vélo.

■ **on TV** à la télé □ What's on TV? Qu'est-ce qu'il y a à la télé?

■ **on the radio** à la radio □ I heard it on the radio. Je l'ai entendu à la radio.

■ **on the bus 1** (*by bus*) en bus □ I go into town on the bus. Je vais en ville en bus.

2 (*inside bus*) dans le bus □ There were no empty seats on the bus. Il n'y avait pas de places libres dans le bus.

■ **on holiday** en vacances □ They're on holiday. Ils sont en vacances.

■ **on strike** en grève

> LANGUAGE TIP With days and dates 'on' is not translated.

□ on Friday vendredi □ on Fridays le vendredi □ on Christmas Day le jour de Noël □ on June 20th le vingt juin □ on my birthday le jour de mon anniversaire

on ADJECTIVE

▷ *see also* **on** PREPOSITION

1 allumé (FEM allumée) (*heater, light, TV*)

□ I think I left the light on. Je crois que j'ai laissé la lumière allumée.

2 ouvert (FEM ouverte) (*tap, gas*)

□ Leave the tap on. Laisse le robinet ouvert.

3 en marche (*machine*)

□ Is the dishwasher on? Est-ce que le lave-vaisselle est en marche?

■ **What's on at the cinema?** Qu'est-ce qui passe au cinéma?

once ADVERB

une fois

□ once a week une fois par semaine □ once more encore une fois □ I've been to France once before. J'ai déjà été une fois en France.

■ **Once upon a time ...** Il était une fois ...

■ **at once** tout de suite

■ **once in a while** de temps en temps

one NUMBER, PRONOUN

> LANGUAGE TIP Use **un** for masculine nouns and **une** for feminine nouns.

1 un

□ one day un jour □ Do you need a stamp? — No thanks, I've got one. Est-ce que tu as besoin d'un timbre? — Non merci, j'en ai un.

une

□ one minute une minute □ I've got one brother and one sister. J'ai un frère et une sœur.

2 on *(impersonal)*

□ One never knows. On ne sait jamais.

■ **this one 1** celui-ci *masc* □ Which foot is hurting? — This one. Quel pied te fait mal? — Celui-ci. **2** celle-ci *fem* □ Which is the best photo? — This one. Quelle est la meilleure photo? — Celle-ci.

■ **that one 1** celui-là *masc* □ Which bag is yours? — That one. Lequel est ton sac? — Celui-là. **2** celle-là *fem* □ Which seat do you want? — That one. Quelle place voulez-vous? — Celle-là.

oneself PRONOUN

1 se

□ to hurt oneself se faire mal

2 soi-même

□ It's quicker to do it oneself. C'est plus rapide de le faire soi-même.

one-way ADJECTIVE

■ **a one-way street** une impasse

onion NOUN

l' oignon *masc*

□ onion soup la soupe à l'oignon

online ADJECTIVE, ADVERB

en ligne

□ They like to chat online. Ils aiment chatter en ligne.

only ADVERB, ADJECTIVE, CONJUNCTION

1 seul (FEM seule)

□ Monday is the only day I'm free. Le lundi est le seul jour où je suis libre. □ French is the only subject I like. Le français est la seule matière que j'aime.

2 seulement

□ How much was it? — Only 10 euros. Combien c'était? — Seulement dix euros.

3 ne ... que

□ We only want to stay for one night. Nous ne voulons rester qu'une nuit. □ These books are only 3 euros. Ces livres ne coûtent que trois euros.

4 mais

□ I'd like the same sweater, only in black. Je voudrais le même pull, mais en noir.

■ **an only child** un enfant unique

onwards ADVERB

à partir de

□ from July onwards à partir de juillet

open ADJECTIVE

▷ *see also* **open** VERB

ouvert (FEM ouverte)

□ The baker's is open on Sunday morning. La boulangerie est ouverte le dimanche matin.

■ **in the open air** en plein air

to **open** VERB

▷ *see also* **open** ADJECTIVE

1 ouvrir

□ Can I open the window? Est-ce que je peux ouvrir la fenêtre? □ What time do the shops open? Les magasins ouvrent à quelle heure?

2 s'ouvrir

□ The door opens automatically. La porte s'ouvre automatiquement. □ The door opened and in came the teacher. La porte s'est ouverte et le professeur est entré.

opening hours PL NOUN

les heures d'ouverture *fem pl*

opera NOUN

l' opéra *masc*

to **operate** VERB

1 fonctionner

□ The lights operate on a timer. Les lumières fonctionnent avec une minuterie.

2 faire fonctionner

□ How do you operate the camcorder? Comment fait-on fonctionner le caméscope?

3 opérer *(perform surgery)*

■ **to operate on someone** opérer quelqu'un

operation NOUN

l' opération *fem*

□ a major operation une grave opération

■ **to have an operation** se faire opérer

□ I have never had an operation. Je ne me suis jamais fait opérer.

operator NOUN

le/la standardiste *(on telephone)*

opinion NOUN

l' avis *masc*

□ in my opinion à mon avis □ He asked me my opinion. Il m'a demandé mon avis.

■ **What's your opinion?** Qu'est-ce que vous en pensez?

opinion poll NOUN

le sondage

opponent NOUN

l' adversaire *masc/fem*

opportunity NOUN

opposed – origin

l' occasion *fem*

■ **to have the opportunity to do something** avoir l'occasion de faire quelque chose □ I've never had the opportunity to go to France. Je n'ai jamais eu l'occasion d'aller en France.

opposed ADJECTIVE

■ **I've always been opposed to violence.** J'ai toujours été contre la violence.

■ **as opposed to** par opposition à

opposing ADJECTIVE
opposé (FEM opposée) *(team)*

opposite ADJECTIVE, ADVERB, PREPOSITION

1 opposé (FEM opposée)
□ It's in the opposite direction. C'est dans la direction opposée.

2 en face
□ They live opposite. Ils habitent en face.

3 en face de
□ the girl sitting opposite me la fille assise en face de moi

■ **the opposite sex** l'autre sexe

opposition NOUN
l' opposition *fem*

optician NOUN
l' opticien *masc*
l' opticienne *fem*
□ She's an optician. Elle est opticienne.

optimist NOUN
l' optimiste *masc/fem*

optimistic ADJECTIVE
optimiste (FEM optimiste)

option NOUN

1 le choix *(choice)*
□ I've got no option. Je n'ai pas le choix.

2 la matière à option *(optional subject)*
□ I'm doing geology as my option. La géologie est ma matière à option.

optional ADJECTIVE
facultatif (FEM facultative)

or CONJUNCTION

1 ou
□ Would you like tea or coffee? Est-ce que tu veux du thé ou du café?

☀ **LANGUAGE TIP** Use ni ... ni in negative sentences.

□ I don't eat meat or fish. Je ne mange ni viande, ni poisson.

2 sinon *(otherwise)*
□ Hurry up or you'll miss the bus. Dépêche-toi, sinon tu vas rater le bus.

■ **Give me the money, or else!** Donne-moi l'argent, sinon tu vas le regretter!

oral ADJECTIVE
▷ *see also* **oral** NOUN
oral (FEM orale, MASC PL oraux)

■ **an oral exam** un oral

oral NOUN
▷ *see also* **oral** ADJECTIVE
l' oral *masc* (PL les oraux)
□ I've got my French oral soon. Je vais bientôt passer mon oral de français.

orange NOUN
▷ *see also* **orange** ADJECTIVE
l' orange *fem*

■ **an orange juice** un jus d'orange

orange ADJECTIVE
▷ *see also* **orange** NOUN
orange (FEM+PL orange)

orchard NOUN
le verger

orchestra NOUN
l' orchestre *masc*
□ I play in the school orchestra. Je joue dans l'orchestre de l'école.

order NOUN
▷ *see also* **order** VERB

1 l' ordre *masc (sequence)*
□ in alphabetical order dans l'ordre alphabétique

2 la commande *(instruction)*
□ The waiter took our order. Le garçon a pris notre commande.

■ **in order to** pour □ He does it in order to earn money. Il le fait pour gagner de l'argent.

■ **'out of order'** 'en panne'

to **order** VERB
▷ *see also* **order** NOUN
commander
□ We ordered steak and chips. Nous avons commandé un steak frites. □ Are you ready to order? Vous êtes prêt à commander?

■ **to order somebody about** donner des ordres à quelqu'un □ She liked to order him about. Elle aimait lui donner des ordres.

ordinary ADJECTIVE

1 ordinaire (FEM ordinaire)
□ an ordinary day une journée ordinaire

2 comme les autres *(people)*
□ an ordinary family une famille comme les autres □ He's just an ordinary guy. C'est un type comme les autres.

organ NOUN
l' orgue *masc (instrument)*
□ I play the organ. Je joue de l'orgue.

organic ADJECTIVE
biologique (FEM biologique) *(vegetables, fruit)*

organization NOUN
l' organisation *fem*

to **organize** VERB
organiser

origin NOUN
l' origine *fem*

o

original ADJECTIVE
original (FEM originale, MASC PL originaux)
□ It's a very original idea. C'est une idée très originale.
■ Our original plan was to go camping. A l'origine nous avions l'intention de faire du camping.

originally ADVERB
à l'origine

Orkneys PL NOUN
les Orcades fem pl
■ in the Orkneys dans les Orcades

ornament NOUN
le bibelot

orphan NOUN
l' orphelin masc
l' orpheline fem

ostrich NOUN
l' autruche fem

other ADJECTIVE, PRONOUN
autre (FEM autre)
□ Have you got these jeans in other colours? Est-ce que vous avez ce jean dans d'autres couleurs? □ on the other side of the street de l'autre côté de la rue □ the other day l'autre jour
■ the other one l'autre □ This one? — No, the other one. Celui-ci? — Non, l'autre.
■ the others les autres □ The others are going but I'm not. Les autres y vont mais pas moi.

otherwise ADVERB, CONJUNCTION
1 sinon (if not)
□ Note down the number, otherwise you'll forget it. Note le numéro, sinon tu vas l'oublier. □ Put some sunscreen on, you'll get burned otherwise. Mets une crème solaire, sinon tu vas attraper des coups de soleil.
2 à part ça (in other ways)
□ I'm tired, but otherwise I'm fine. Je suis fatigué, mais à part ça, ça va.

ought VERB

> LANGUAGE TIP To translate 'ought to' use the conditional tense of **devoir**.

□ I ought to phone my parents. Je devrais appeler mes parents. □ You ought not to do that. Tu ne devrais pas faire ça. □ He ought to win. Il devrait gagner.

ounce NOUN
l' once fem

> DID YOU KNOW...?
> In France measurements are in grammes and kilogrammes. One ounce is about 30 grammes.

□ 8 ounces of cheese 250 grammes de fromage

our ADJECTIVE
notre (FEM notre, PL nos)
□ Our house is quite big. Notre maison est plutôt grande. □ Our neighbours are very nice. Nos voisins sont très gentils.

ours PRONOUN
le nôtre + masc noun
□ Your garden is very big, ours is much smaller. Votre jardin est très grand, le nôtre est beaucoup plus petit.
la nôtre + fem noun
□ Your school is very different from ours. Votre école est très différente de la nôtre.
les nôtres + pl noun
□ Our teachers are strict. — Ours are too. Nos professeurs sont sévères. — Les nôtres aussi.
■ Is this ours? C'est à nous? □ This car is ours. Cette voiture est à nous. □ Whose is this? — It's ours. C'est à qui? — À nous.

ourselves PRONOUN
1 nous
□ We really enjoyed ourselves. Nous nous sommes vraiment bien amusés.
2 nous-mêmes
□ We built our garage ourselves. Nous avons construit notre garage nous-mêmes.

out ADVERB, ADJECTIVE

> LANGUAGE TIP There are several ways of translating 'out'. Scan the examples to find one that is similar to what you want to say. For other expressions with 'out', see the verbs 'go', 'put', 'turn' etc.

1 dehors (outside)
□ It's cold out. Il fait froid dehors.
2 éteint (FEM éteinte) (light, fire)
□ All the lights are out. Toutes les lumières sont éteintes.
■ She's out. Elle est sortie.
■ She's out shopping. Elle est sortie faire des courses.
■ She's out for the afternoon. Elle ne sera pas là de tout l'après-midi.
■ out there dehors □ It's cold out there. Il fait froid dehors.
■ to go out sortir □ I'm going out tonight. Je sors ce soir.
■ to go out with somebody sortir avec quelqu'un □ I've been going out with him for two months. Je sors avec lui depuis deux mois.
■ out of 1 dans □ to drink out of a glass boire dans un verre 2 sur □ in 9 cases out of 10 dans neuf cas sur dix 3 en dehors de □ He lives out of town. Il habite en dehors de la ville.

■ **3 km out of town** à trois kilomètres de la ville
■ **out of curiosity** par curiosité
■ **out of work** sans emploi
■ **That is out of the question.** C'est hors de question.
■ **You're out!** *(in game)* Tu es éliminé!
■ **'way out'** 'sortie'

outbreak NOUN
1 l' épidémie *fem (of disease)*
  □ a salmonella outbreak une épidémie de salmonelle
2 le début
  □ the outbreak of war le début de la guerre

outcome NOUN
l' issue *fem*
  □ What was the outcome of the negotiations? Quelle a été l'issue des négociations?

outdoor ADJECTIVE
en plein air
  □ an outdoor swimming pool une piscine en plein air
  ■ **outdoor activities** les activités de plein air

outdoors ADVERB
au grand air

outfit NOUN
la tenue
  □ She bought a new outfit for the wedding. Elle a acheté une nouvelle tenue pour le mariage.
  ■ **a cowboy outfit** une panoplie de cowboy

outgoing ADJECTIVE
extraverti (FEM extravertie)
  □ She's very outgoing. Elle est très extravertie.

outing NOUN
la sortie
  □ to go on an outing faire une sortie

outline NOUN
1 les grandes lignes *fem pl (summary)*
  □ This is an outline of the plan. Voici les grandes lignes du projet.
2 les contours *masc pl (shape)*
  □ We could see the outline of the mountain in the mist. Nous distinguions les contours de la montagne dans la brume.

outlook NOUN
1 l' attitude *fem (attitude)*
  □ my outlook on life mon attitude face à la vie
2 les perspectives *fem pl (prospects)*
  □ the economic outlook les perspectives économiques
  ■ **The outlook is poor.** Les choses s'annoncent mal.

outrageous ADJECTIVE
1 scandaleux (FEM scandaleuse) *(behaviour)*
2 exorbitant (FEM exorbitante) *(price)*

outset NOUN
le début
  □ at the outset dès le début

outside NOUN
  ▷ *see also* **outside** ADJECTIVE
l' extérieur *masc*

outside ADJECTIVE, ADVERB, PREPOSITION
  ▷ *see also* **outside** NOUN
1 extérieur (FEM extérieure)
  □ the outside walls les murs extérieurs
2 dehors
  □ It's very cold outside. Il fait très froid dehors.
3 en dehors de
  □ outside the school en dehors de l'école
  □ outside school hours en dehors des heures de cours

outsize ADJECTIVE
énorme (FEM énorme)

outskirts PL NOUN
la banlieue
  □ on the outskirts of the town dans les banlieues de la ville

outstanding ADJECTIVE
remarquable (FEM remarquable)

oval ADJECTIVE
ovale (FEM ovale)

oven NOUN
le four

over PREPOSITION, ADVERB, ADJECTIVE
  LANGUAGE TIP When there is movement over something, use **par-dessus**; when something is located above something, use **au-dessus de**.
1 par-dessus
  □ The ball went over the wall. Le ballon est passé par-dessus le mur.
2 au-dessus de
  □ There's a mirror over the washbasin. Il y a une glace au-dessus du lavabo.
3 plus de *(more than)*
  □ It's over twenty kilos. Ça pèse plus de vingt kilos. □ The temperature was over thirty degrees. Il faisait une température de plus de trente degrés.
4 pendant *(during)*
  □ over the holidays pendant les vacances
  □ over Christmas pendant les fêtes de Noël
5 terminé (FEM terminée) *(finished)*
  □ I'll be happy when the exams are over. Je serai content quand les examens seront terminés.
  ■ **over here** ici
  ■ **over there** là-bas

O

■ **all over Scotland** dans toute l'Écosse
■ **The baker's is over the road.** La boulangerie est de l'autre côté de la rue.
■ **I spilled coffee over my shirt.** J'ai renversé du café sur ma chemise.

overall ADVERB
dans l'ensemble *(generally)*
□ My results were quite good overall. Mes résultats étaient assez bons dans l'ensemble.

overalls PL NOUN
les bleus de travail *masc pl*

overcast ADJECTIVE
couvert (FEM couverte)
□ The sky was overcast. Le ciel était couvert.

to **overcharge** VERB
■ **He overcharged me.** Il m'a fait payer trop cher.
■ **They overcharged us for the meal.** Ils nous ont fait payer de trop pour le repas.

overcoat NOUN
le pardessus

overdone ADJECTIVE
trop cuit (FEM trop cuite) *(food)*

overdose NOUN
l' overdose *fem (of drugs)*
□ to take an overdose prendre une overdose

overdraft NOUN
le découvert
■ **to have an overdraft** être à découvert

to **overestimate** VERB
surestimer

overhead projector NOUN
le rétroprojecteur

to **overlook** VERB
1 donner sur *(have view of)*
□ The hotel overlooked the beach. L'hôtel donnait sur la plage.
2 négliger *(forget about)*
□ He had overlooked one important problem. Il avait négligé un problème important.

overseas ADVERB
à l'étranger
□ I'd like to work overseas. J'aimerais travailler à l'étranger.

oversight NOUN
l' oubli *masc*

to **oversleep** VERB
se réveiller en retard
□ I overslept this morning. Je me suis réveillé en retard ce matin.

to **overtake** VERB
dépasser

overtime NOUN
les heures supplémentaires *fem pl*
□ to work overtime faire des heures supplémentaires

overtook VERB ▷ *see* overtake

overweight ADJECTIVE
trop gros (FEM trop grosse)

to **owe** VERB
devoir
■ **to owe somebody something** devoir quelque chose à quelqu'un □ I owe you 50 euros. Je te dois cinquante euros.

owing to PREPOSITION
en raison de
□ owing to bad weather en raison du mauvais temps

owl NOUN
le hibou (PL les hiboux)

own ADJECTIVE
▷ *see also* **own** VERB
propre (FEM propre)
□ I've got my own bathroom. J'ai ma propre salle de bain.
■ **I'd like a room of my own.** J'aimerais avoir une chambre à moi.
■ **on his own** tout seul □ on her own toute seule □ on our own tout seuls

to **own** VERB
▷ *see also* **own** ADJECTIVE
posséder

to **own up** VERB
avouer
■ **to own up to something** admettre quelque chose

owner NOUN
le/la propriétaire

oxygen NOUN
l' oxygène *masc*

oyster NOUN
l' huître *fem*

ozone NOUN
l' ozone *fem*

ozone layer NOUN
la couche d'ozone

o

Pp

PA NOUN
la secrétaire de direction *(personal assistant)*
  □ She's a PA. Elle est secrétaire de direction.
  ■ **the PA system** *(public address)* les haut-parleurs

pace NOUN
l' allure *fem (speed)*
  □ He was walking at a brisk pace. Il marchait à vive allure.

Pacific NOUN
le Pacifique

pacifier NOUN (US)
la tétine

to **pack** VERB
  ▷ *see also* **pack** NOUN
  faire ses bagages
  □ I'll help you pack. Je vais t'aider à faire tes bagages.
  ■ **I've already packed my case.** J'ai déjà fait ma valise.
  ■ **Pack it in!** *(stop it)* Laisse tomber!

pack NOUN
  ▷ *see also* **pack** VERB
1 le paquet *(packet)*
  □ a pack of cigarettes un paquet de cigarettes
2 le pack *(of yoghurts, cans)*
  □ a six-pack un pack de six
  ■ **a pack of cards** un jeu de cartes

package NOUN
le paquet
  ■ **a package holiday** un voyage organisé

packed ADJECTIVE
bondé (FEM bondée)
  □ The cinema was packed. Le cinéma était bondé.

packed lunch NOUN
le repas froid
  □ I take a packed lunch to school. J'apporte un repas froid à l'école.

> **DID YOU KNOW...?**
> French schoolchildren do not take packed lunches to school. They either eat at the canteen or go home.

packet NOUN
le paquet
  □ a packet of cigarettes un paquet de cigarettes

pad NOUN
le bloc-notes (PL les blocs-notes) *(notepad)*

to **paddle** VERB
  ▷ *see also* **paddle** NOUN
1 pagayer *(canoe)*
2 faire trempette *(in water)*

paddle NOUN
  ▷ *see also* **paddle** VERB
la pagaie *(for canoe)*
  ■ **to go for a paddle** faire trempette

padlock NOUN
le cadenas

paedophile NOUN
le pédophile

page NOUN
  ▷ *see also* **page** VERB
la page *(of book)*

to **page** VERB
  ▷ *see also* **page** NOUN
  ■ **to page somebody** faire appeler quelqu'un

pager NOUN
le récepteur d'appel

paid VERB ▷ *see* **pay**

paid ADJECTIVE
1 rémunéré (FEM rémunérée) *(work)*
2 payé (FEM payée)
  □ 3 weeks' paid holiday trois semaines de congés payés

pail NOUN
le seau (PL les seaux)

pain NOUN
la douleur
  □ a terrible pain une douleur insupportable
  ■ **I've got a pain in my stomach.** J'ai mal à l'estomac.
  ■ **to be in pain** souffrir □ She's in a lot of pain. Elle souffre beaucoup.
  ■ **He's a real pain.** Il est vraiment pénible.

painful ADJECTIVE
douloureux (FEM douloureuse)
  □ to suffer from painful periods souffrir de

règles douloureuses
- **Is it painful?** Ça te fait mal?

painkiller NOUN
l' analgésique *masc*

paint NOUN
▷ *see also* **paint** VERB
la peinture

to **paint** VERB
▷ *see also* **paint** NOUN
peindre
□ to paint something green peindre quelque chose en vert

paintbrush NOUN
le pinceau (PL les pinceaux)

painter NOUN
le peintre

painting NOUN
1 la peinture
□ My hobby is painting. Je fais de la peinture.
2 le tableau (PL les tableaux) *(picture)*
□ a painting by Picasso un tableau de Picasso

pair NOUN
la paire
□ a pair of shoes une paire de chaussures
□ a pair of scissors une paire de ciseaux
- **a pair of trousers** un pantalon
- **a pair of jeans** un jean
- **a pair of pants 1** *(briefs)* un slip **2** *(boxer shorts)* un caleçon **3** *(trousers)* (US) un pantalon
- **in pairs** deux par deux □ We work in pairs. On travaille deux par deux.

pajamas PL NOUN
le pyjama *sing*
□ my pajamas mon pyjama □ a pair of pajamas un pyjama
- **a pajama top** une veste de pyjama

Pakistan NOUN
le Pakistan
- **in Pakistan** au Pakistan
- **to Pakistan** au Pakistan
- **He's from Pakistan.** Il est pakistanais.

Pakistani NOUN
▷ *see also* **Pakistani** ADJECTIVE
le Pakistanais
la Pakistanaise

Pakistani ADJECTIVE
▷ *see also* **Pakistani** NOUN
pakistanais (FEM pakistanaise)

pal NOUN
le copain
la copine

palace NOUN
le palais

pale ADJECTIVE

pâle (FEM pâle)
□ a pale blue shirt une chemise bleu pâle

Palestine NOUN
la Palestine
- **in Palestine** en Palestine

Palestinian NOUN
▷ *see also* **Palestinian** ADJECTIVE
le Palestinien
la Palestinienne

Palestinian ADJECTIVE
▷ *see also* **Palestinian** NOUN
palestinien (FEM palestinienne)

palm NOUN
la paume *(of hand)*
- **a palm tree** un palmier

pamphlet NOUN
la brochure

pan NOUN
1 la casserole *(saucepan)*
2 la poêle *(frying pan)*

pancake NOUN
la crêpe
- **Pancake Day** mardi gras

DID YOU KNOW...?
Pancake Day is celebrated in France as well. Children dress up and eat crêpes.

panic NOUN
▷ *see also* **panic** VERB
la panique

to **panic** VERB
▷ *see also* **panic** NOUN
s'affoler
□ Don't panic! Pas de panique!

panther NOUN
la panthère

panties PL NOUN
le slip *sing*

pantomime NOUN
le spectacle de Noël pour enfants

DID YOU KNOW...?
Pantomimes don't exist in France.

pants PL NOUN
1 le slip *sing (briefs)*
□ a pair of pants un slip
2 le caleçon *sing (boxer shorts)*
□ a pair of pants un caleçon
3 le pantalon *sing (us: trousers)*
□ a pair of pants un pantalon

pantyhose PL NOUN (US)
le collant *sing*

paper NOUN
1 le papier
□ a piece of paper un morceau de papier
- **a paper towel** une serviette en papier
- **an exam paper** une épreuve écrite
2 le journal (PL les journaux) *(newspaper)*

□ I saw an advert in the paper. J'ai vu une annonce dans le journal.

paperback NOUN
le livre de poche

paper boy NOUN
le livreur de journaux

paper clip NOUN
le trombone

paper girl NOUN
la livreuse de journaux

paper round NOUN
la tournée de distribution de journaux

paperweight NOUN
le presse-papiers

paperwork NOUN
la paperasse
□ He had a lot of paperwork to do. Il avait beaucoup de paperasse à faire.

parachute NOUN
le parachute

parade NOUN
le défilé

paradise NOUN
le paradis

paraffin NOUN
le pétrole
□ a paraffin lamp une lampe à pétrole

paragraph NOUN
le paragraphe

parallel ADJECTIVE
parallèle (FEM parallèle)

paralysed ADJECTIVE
paralysé (FEM paralysée)

paramedic NOUN
l' auxiliaire médical *masc*
l' auxiliaire médicale *fem*

parcel NOUN
le colis

pardon NOUN
■ **Pardon?** Pardon?

parent NOUN
1 le père *(father)*
2 la mère *(mother)*
■ **my parents** mes parents *masc pl*

Paris NOUN
Paris *fem*
■ **in Paris** à Paris
■ **to Paris** à Paris
■ **She's from Paris.** Elle est parisienne.

Parisian NOUN
▷ *see also* **Parisian** ADJECTIVE
le Parisien
la Parisienne

Parisian ADJECTIVE
▷ *see also* **Parisian** NOUN
parisien (FEM parisienne)

park NOUN

▷ *see also* **park** VERB
le parc
■ **a national park** un parc national
■ **a theme park** un parc à thème
■ **a car park** un parking

to **park** VERB
▷ *see also* **park** NOUN
1 garer
□ Where can I park my car? Où est-ce que je peux garer ma voiture?
2 se garer
□ We couldn't find anywhere to park. Nous avons eu du mal à nous garer.

parking NOUN
le stationnement
□ 'no parking' 'stationnement interdit'
LANGUAGE TIP Be careful not to translate **parking** by the French word **parking**.

parking lot NOUN (US)
le parking

parking meter NOUN
le parcmètre

parking ticket NOUN
le p.-v. *(informal)*

parliament NOUN
le parlement

parole NOUN
■ **on parole** en liberté conditionnelle

parrot NOUN
le perroquet

parsley NOUN
le persil

part NOUN
1 la partie *(section)*
□ The first part of the film was boring. La première partie du film était ennuyeuse.
2 la pièce *(component)*
□ spare parts les pièces de rechange
3 le rôle *(in play, film)*
■ **to take part in something** participer à quelque chose □ A lot of people took part in the demonstration. Beaucoup de gens ont participé à la manifestation.

particular ADJECTIVE
particulier (FEM particulière)
□ Are you looking for anything particular? Est-ce que vous voulez quelque chose de particulier?
■ **nothing in particular** rien de particulier

particularly ADVERB
particulièrement

parting NOUN
la raie *(in hair)*

partly ADVERB
en partie

partner NOUN

1 le/la partenaire *(in game)*
2 l' associé *masc*
l' associée *fem (in business)*
3 le cavalier
la cavalière *(in dance)*
4 le compagnon
la compagne *(in relationship)*

part-time ADJECTIVE, ADVERB
à temps partiel
□ a part-time job un travail à temps partiel
□ She works part-time. Elle travaille à temps partiel.

to **part with** VERB
■ **to part with something** se défaire de quelque chose

party NOUN
1 la fête
□ a birthday party une fête d'anniversaire
□ a Christmas party une fête de Noël □ a New Year party une fête du Nouvel An
2 la soirée *(more formal)*
□ I'm going to a party on Saturday. Je vais à une soirée samedi.
3 le parti *(political)*
□ the Conservative Party le Parti conservateur
4 le groupe *(group)*
□ a party of tourists un groupe de touristes

pass NOUN
▷ *see also* **pass** VERB
1 le col *(in mountains)*
□ The pass was blocked with snow. Le col était enneigé.
2 la passe *(in football)*
■ **to get a pass** *(in exam)* être reçu □ She got a pass in her piano exam. Elle a été reçue à son examen de piano. □ I got six passes. J'ai été reçu dans six matières.
■ **a bus pass** une carte de bus

to **pass** VERB
▷ *see also* **pass** NOUN
1 être reçu *(exam)*
□ Did you pass? Tu as été reçu?
■ **to pass an exam** être reçu à un examen
□ I hope I'll pass the exam. J'espère que je serai reçu à l'examen.

> **LANGUAGE TIP** Be careful not to translate **to pass an exam** by passer un examen.

2 passer
□ Could you pass me the salt, please? Est-ce que vous pourriez me passer le sel, s'il vous plaît? □ The time has passed quickly. Le temps a passé rapidement.
3 passer devant
□ I pass his house on my way to school. Je passe devant chez lui en allant à l'école.

to **pass out** VERB
s'évanouir *(faint)*

passage NOUN
1 le passage *(piece of writing)*
□ Read the passage carefully. Lisez attentivement le passage.
2 le couloir *(corridor)*

passenger NOUN
le passager
la passagère

passion NOUN
la passion

passive ADJECTIVE
passif (FEM passive)
■ **passive smoking** le tabagisme passif

Passover NOUN
la Pâque juive
□ at Passover à la Pâque juive

passport NOUN
le passeport
□ passport control le contrôle des passeports

password NOUN
le mot de passe

past ADVERB, PREPOSITION
▷ *see also* **past** NOUN
après *(beyond)*
□ It's on the right, just past the station. C'est sur la droite, juste après la gare.
■ **to go past 1** passer □ The bus went past without stopping. Le bus est passé sans s'arrêter. **2** passer devant □ The bus goes past our house. Le bus passe devant notre maison.
■ **It's half past ten.** Il est dix heures et demie.
■ **It's quarter past nine.** Il est neuf heures et quart.
■ **It's ten past eight.** Il est huit heures dix.
■ **It's past midnight.** Il est minuit passé.

past NOUN
▷ *see also* **past** ADVERB
le passé
□ She lives in the past. Elle vit dans le passé.
■ **in the past** *(previously)* autrefois □ This was common in the past. C'était courant autrefois.

pasta NOUN
les pâtes *fem pl*
□ Pasta is easy to cook. Les pâtes sont faciles à préparer.

paste NOUN
la colle *(glue)*

pasteurized ADJECTIVE
pasteurisé (FEM pasteurisée)

pastime NOUN
le passe-temps (PL les passe-temps)

□ Her favourite pastime is knitting. Son passe-temps favori est le tricot.

pastry NOUN
la pâte

■ **pastries** les pâtisseries *fem pl*

patch NOUN
1 la pièce
□ a patch of material une pièce de tissu
2 la rustine *(for flat tyre)*

■ **He's got a bald patch.** Il a le crâne dégarni.

patched ADJECTIVE
rapiécé (FEM rapiécée)
□ a pair of patched jeans un jean rapiécé

pâté NOUN
le pâté

path NOUN
1 le chemin *(footpath)*
2 l' allée *fem (in garden, park)*

pathetic ADJECTIVE
lamentable (FEM lamentable)
□ Our team was pathetic. Notre équipe a été lamentable.

patience NOUN
1 la patience
□ He hasn't got much patience. Il n'a pas beaucoup de patience.
2 la réussite *(card game)*
□ to play patience faire une réussite

patient NOUN
▷ *see also* **patient** ADJECTIVE
le patient
la patiente

patient ADJECTIVE
▷ *see also* **patient** NOUN
patient (FEM patiente)

patio NOUN
le patio

patriotic ADJECTIVE
patriote (FEM patriote)

patrol NOUN
la patrouille

patrol car NOUN
la voiture de police

pattern NOUN
le motif
□ a geometric pattern un motif géométrique

■ **a sewing pattern** un patron

pause NOUN
la pause

pavement NOUN
le trottoir

pavilion NOUN
le pavillon

paw NOUN
la patte

pay NOUN
▷ *see also* **pay** VERB
le salaire

to **pay** VERB
▷ *see also* **pay** NOUN
1 payer
□ They pay me more on Sundays. Je suis payé davantage le dimanche.
2 régler
□ to pay by cheque régler par chèque □ to pay by credit card régler par carte de crédit

■ **to pay for something** payer quelque chose □ I paid for my ticket. J'ai payé mon billet. □ I paid 50 euros for it. Je l'ai payé cinquante euros.

■ **to pay extra for something** payer un supplément pour quelque chose □ You have to pay extra for breakfast. Il faut payer un supplément pour le petit déjeuner.

■ **to pay attention** faire attention □ Don't pay any attention to him! Ne fais pas attention à lui!

■ **to pay somebody a visit** rendre visite à quelqu'un □ Paul paid us a visit last night. Paul nous a rendu visite hier soir.

■ **to pay somebody back** rembourser quelqu'un □ I'll pay you back tomorrow. Je te rembourserai demain.

payable ADJECTIVE
■ **Make the cheque payable to 'ABC Ltd'.** Libellez le chèque à l'ordre de 'ABC Ltd'.

payment NOUN
le paiement

payphone NOUN
le téléphone public

PC NOUN (= *personal computer*)
le PC
□ She typed the report on her PC. Elle a tapé le rapport sur son PC.

■ **a PC game** un jeu d'ordinateur

PE NOUN
l' EPS *fem*
□ We do PE twice a week. Nous avons EPS deux fois par semaine.

pea NOUN
le petit pois

peace NOUN
1 la paix *(after war)*
2 le calme *(quietness)*

peaceful ADJECTIVE
1 paisible (FEM paisible) *(calm)*
□ a peaceful afternoon un après-midi paisible
2 pacifique (FEM pacifique) *(not violent)*
□ a peaceful protest une manifestation pacifique

peach NOUN

la pêche

peacock NOUN
le paon

peak NOUN
la cime (of mountain)
■ **the peak rate** le plein tarif □ You pay the peak rate for calls at this time of day. On paie le plein tarif quand on appelle à cette heure-ci.
■ **in peak season** en haute saison

peanut NOUN
la cacahuète
□ a packet of peanuts un paquet de cacahuètes

peanut butter NOUN
le beurre de cacahuètes
□ a peanut-butter sandwich un sandwich au beurre de cacahuètes

pear NOUN
la poire

pearl NOUN
la perle

pebble NOUN
le galet
□ a pebble beach une plage de galets

peckish ADJECTIVE
■ **to feel a bit peckish** avoir un petit creux

peculiar ADJECTIVE
bizarre (FEM bizarre)
□ He's a peculiar person. Il est bizarre. □ It tastes peculiar. Ça a un goût bizarre.

pedal NOUN
la pédale

pedestrian NOUN
le piéton

pedestrian crossing NOUN
le passage pour piétons

pedestrianized ADJECTIVE
■ **a pedestrianized street** une rue piétonne

pedestrian precinct NOUN
la zone piétonnière

pedigree ADJECTIVE
de race (animal)
□ a pedigree dog un chien de race □ a pedigree labrador un labrador de pure race

pee NOUN
■ **to have a pee** faire pipi

peek NOUN
■ **to have a peek at something** jeter un coup d'œil à quelque chose
■ **No peeking!** On ne regarde pas!

peel NOUN
▷ see also **peel** VERB
l' écorce fem (of orange)

to **peel** VERB
▷ see also **peel** NOUN

1 éplucher
□ Shall I peel the potatoes? J'épluche les pommes de terre?
2 peler
□ My nose is peeling. Mon nez pèle.

peg NOUN
1 le portemanteau (PL les portemanteaux) (for coats)
2 la pince à linge (clothes peg)
3 le piquet (tent peg)

Pekinese NOUN
le pékinois

pelican crossing NOUN
le passage pour piétons

pellet NOUN
le plomb (for gun)

pelvis NOUN
le bassin

pen NOUN
le stylo

to **penalize** VERB
pénaliser

penalty NOUN
1 la peine (punishment)
■ **the death penalty** la peine de mort
2 le penalty (in football)
3 la pénalité (in rugby)
■ **a penalty shoot-out** les tirs au but

pence PL NOUN
les pence masc pl

pencil NOUN
le crayon
■ **in pencil** au crayon

pencil case NOUN
la trousse

pencil sharpener NOUN
le taille-crayon (PL les taille-crayons)

pendant NOUN
le pendentif

penfriend NOUN
le correspondant
la correspondante

penguin NOUN
le pingouin

penicillin NOUN
la pénicilline

penis NOUN
le pénis

penitentiary NOUN (US)
la prison

penknife NOUN
le canif

penny NOUN
le penny (PL les pence)

pension NOUN
la retraite

pensioner NOUN

le retraité
la retraitée

pentathlon NOUN
le pentathlon

people PL NOUN
1 les gens *masc pl*
□ The people were nice. Les gens étaient sympathiques. □ a lot of people beaucoup de gens
2 les personnes *fem pl (individuals)*
□ six people six personnes □ several people plusieurs personnes
■ **How many people are there in your family?** Vous êtes combien dans votre famille?
■ **French people** les Français
■ **black people** les Noirs
■ **People say that …** On dit que …

pepper NOUN
1 le poivre *(spice)*
□ Pass the pepper, please. Passez-moi le poivre, s'il vous plaît.
2 le poivron *(vegetable)*
□ a green pepper un poivron vert

peppermill NOUN
le moulin à poivre

peppermint NOUN
la pastille de menthe *(sweet)*
■ **peppermint chewing gum** le chewing-gum à la menthe

per PREPOSITION
par
□ per day par jour □ per week par semaine
■ **30 miles per hour** trente miles à l'heure

per cent ADVERB
pour cent
□ fifty per cent cinquante pour cent

percentage NOUN
le pourcentage

percolator NOUN
la cafetière électrique

percussion NOUN
la percussion
□ I play percussion. Je joue des percussions.

perfect ADJECTIVE
parfait (FEM parfaite)
□ Chantal speaks perfect English. Chantal parle un anglais parfait.

perfectly ADVERB
parfaitement

to **perform** VERB
jouer *(act, play)*

performance NOUN
1 le spectacle *(show)*
□ The performance lasts two hours. Le spectacle dure deux heures.
2 l' interprétation *fem (acting)*

□ his performance as Hamlet son interprétation d'Hamlet
3 la performance *(results)*
□ the team's poor performance la médiocre performance de l'équipe

perfume NOUN
le parfum

perhaps ADVERB
peut-être
□ a bit boring, perhaps peut-être un peu ennuyeux □ Perhaps he's ill. Il est peut-être malade.
■ **perhaps not** peut-être pas

period NOUN
1 la période
□ for a limited period pour une période limitée
2 l' époque *fem (in history)*
□ the Victorian period l'époque victorienne
3 les règles *fem pl (menstruation)*
□ I'm having my period. J'ai mes règles.
4 le cours *(lesson time)*
□ Each period lasts forty minutes. Chaque cours dure quarante minutes.

perm NOUN
la permanente
□ She's got a perm. Elle a une permanente.
■ **to have a perm** se faire faire une permanente

permanent ADJECTIVE
permanent (FEM permanente)

permission NOUN
la permission
□ Could I have permission to leave early? Pourrais-je avoir la permission de partir plus tôt?

permit NOUN
le permis
□ a fishing permit un permis de pêche

to **persecute** VERB
persécuter

Persian ADJECTIVE
■ **a Persian cat** un chat persan

persistent ADJECTIVE
tenace (FEM tenace) *(person)*

person NOUN
la personne
□ She's a very nice person. C'est une personne très sympathique.
■ **in person** en personne

personal ADJECTIVE
personnel (FEM personnelle)
■ **personal column** les annonces personnelles *fem pl*

personality NOUN
la personnalité

personally ADVERB

personnellement

□ I don't know him personally. Je ne le connais pas personnellement. □ Personally I don't agree. Personnellement, je ne suis pas d'accord.

personal stereo NOUN
le walkman®

personnel NOUN
le personnel

perspiration NOUN
la transpiration

to **persuade** VERB
persuader

■ **to persuade somebody to do something** persuader quelqu'un de faire quelque chose □ She persuaded me to go with her. Elle m'a persuadé de l'accompagner.

pessimist NOUN
le/la pessimiste

□ I'm a pessimist. Je suis pessimiste.

pessimistic ADJECTIVE
pessimiste (FEM pessimiste)

pest NOUN
le/la casse-pieds (person)

□ He's a real pest! C'est un vrai casse-pieds!

to **pester** VERB
importuner

pet NOUN
l' animal familier masc

□ Have you got a pet? Est-ce que tu as un animal familier?

■ **She's the teacher's pet.** C'est la chouchoute de la maîtresse.

petition NOUN
la pétition

petrified ADJECTIVE
pétrifié (FEM pétrifiée)

petrol NOUN
l' essence fem

■ **unleaded petrol** l'essence sans plomb

⋮ **LANGUAGE TIP** Be careful not to
⋮ translate **petrol** by **pétrole**.

petrol station NOUN
la station-service (PL les stations-service)

petrol tank NOUN
le réservoir d'essence

phantom NOUN
le fantôme

pharmacy NOUN
la pharmacie

⋮ **DID YOU KNOW...?**
⋮ Pharmacies in France are identified
⋮ by a special green cross outside the
⋮ shop.

pheasant NOUN
le faisan

philosophy NOUN

la philosophie

phobia NOUN
la phobie

phone NOUN
▷ see also **phone** VERB
le téléphone

□ Where's the phone? Où est le téléphone? □ Is there a phone here? Est-ce qu'il y a un téléphone ici?

■ **by phone** par téléphone

■ **to be on the phone** être au téléphone □ She's on the phone at the moment. Elle est au téléphone en ce moment.

■ **Can I use the phone, please?** Est-ce que je peux téléphoner, s'il vous plaît?

to **phone** VERB
▷ see also **phone** NOUN
appeler

□ I'll phone the station. Je vais appeler la gare.

phone bill NOUN
la facture de téléphone

phone book NOUN
l' annuaire masc

phone box NOUN
la cabine téléphonique

phone call NOUN
l' appel masc

□ There's a phone call for you. Il y a un appel pour vous.

■ **to make a phone call** téléphoner □ Can I make a phone call? Est-ce que peux téléphoner?

phonecard NOUN
la carte de téléphone

phone number NOUN
le numéro de téléphone

photo NOUN
la photo

■ **to take a photo** prendre une photo

■ **to take a photo of somebody** prendre quelqu'un en photo

photocopier NOUN
la photocopieuse

photocopy NOUN
▷ see also **photocopy** VERB
la photocopie

to **photocopy** VERB
▷ see also **photocopy** NOUN
photocopier

photograph NOUN
▷ see also **photograph** VERB
la photo

■ **to take a photograph** prendre une photo

■ **to take a photograph of somebody** prendre quelqu'un en photo

to **photograph** VERB

photographer - pierce

▷ see also **photograph** NOUN
photographier

photographer NOUN
le/la photographe
□ She's a photographer. Elle est
photographe.

photography NOUN
la photo
□ My hobby is photography. Je fais de la
photo.

phrase NOUN
l' expression *fem*

phrase book NOUN
le guide de conversation

physical ADJECTIVE
▷ see also **physical** NOUN
physique (FEM physique)

physical NOUN (US)
▷ see also **physical** ADJECTIVE
l' examen médical *masc*

physicist NOUN
le physicien
la physicienne
□ He's a physicist. Il est physicien.

physics NOUN
la physique
□ She teaches physics. Elle enseigne la
physique.

physiotherapist NOUN
le/la kinésithérapeute

physiotherapy NOUN
la kinésithérapie

pianist NOUN
le/la pianiste

piano NOUN
le piano
□ I play the piano. Je joue du piano. □ I have
piano lessons. Je prends des leçons de
piano.

pick NOUN
▷ see also **pick** VERB
■ **Take your pick!** Faites votre choix!

to **pick** VERB
▷ see also **pick** NOUN
1 choisir *(choose)*
□ I picked the biggest piece. J'ai choisi le
plus gros morceau.
2 sélectionner *(for team)*
□ I've been picked for the team. J'ai été
sélectionné pour faire partie de l'équipe.
3 cueillir *(fruit, flowers)*

to **pick on** VERB
harceler
□ She's always picking on me. Elle me
harcèle constamment.

to **pick out** VERB
choisir

□ I like them all — it's difficult to pick one
out. Ils me plaisent tous — c'est difficile
d'en choisir un.

to **pick up** VERB
1 venir chercher *(collect)*
□ We'll come to the airport to pick you up.
Nous irons vous chercher à l'aéroport.
2 ramasser *(from floor)*
□ Could you help me pick up the toys? Tu
peux m'aider à ramasser les jouets?
3 apprendre *(learn)*
□ I picked up some Spanish during my
holiday. J'ai appris quelques mots d'espagnol
pendant mes vacances.

pickpocket NOUN
le pickpocket

picnic NOUN
le pique-nique
■ **to have a picnic** pique-niquer □ We had
a picnic on the beach. Nous avons pique-
niqué sur la plage.

picture NOUN
1 l' illustration *fem*
□ Children's books have lots of pictures. Il y
a beaucoup d'illustrations dans les livres
pour enfants.
2 la photo
□ My picture was in the paper. Ma photo
était dans le journal.
3 le tableau (PL les tableaux) *(painting)*
□ a famous picture un tableau célèbre
■ **to paint a picture of something** peindre
quelque chose
4 le dessin *(drawing)*
■ **to draw a picture of something** dessiner
quelque chose
■ **the pictures** *(cinema)* le cinéma □ Shall
we go to the pictures? On va au cinéma?

picture messaging NOUN
l' envoi de photos par MMS *masc*

picturesque ADJECTIVE
pittoresque (FEM pittoresque)

pie NOUN
la tourte
□ an apple pie une tourte aux pommes

piece NOUN
le morceau (PL les morceaux)
□ A small piece, please. Un petit morceau,
s'il vous plaît.
■ **a piece of furniture** un meuble
■ **a piece of advice** un conseil

pier NOUN
la jetée

to **pierce** VERB
percer
□ She's going to have her ears pierced. Elle
va se faire percer les oreilles.

pierced ADJECTIVE
percé (FEM percée)
□ I've got pierced ears. J'ai les oreilles percées.

piercing NOUN
le piercing
□ She has several piercings. Elle a plusieurs piercings.

pig NOUN
le cochon

pigeon NOUN
le pigeon

piggyback NOUN
■ to give somebody a piggyback porter quelqu'un sur son dos □ I can't give you a piggyback, you're too heavy. Je ne peux pas te porter sur mon dos, tu es trop lourd.

piggy bank NOUN
la tirelire

pigtail NOUN
la natte

pile NOUN
1 le tas (untidy heap)
2 la pile (tidy stack)

piles PL NOUN
les hémorroïdes fem pl
□ to suffer from piles avoir des hémorroïdes

pile-up NOUN
le carambolage

pill NOUN
la pilule
■ to be on the pill prendre la pilule

pillar NOUN
le pilier

pillar box NOUN
la boîte aux lettres

pillow NOUN
l' oreiller masc

pilot NOUN
le pilote
□ He's a pilot. Il est pilote.

pimple NOUN
le bouton

pin NOUN
l' épingle fem
■ I've got pins and needles. J'ai des fourmis dans les jambes.

PIN NOUN (= personal identification number)
le code confidentiel
■ chip and PIN la CB

pinafore NOUN
le tablier

pinball NOUN
le flipper
□ to play pinball jouer au flipper
■ a pinball machine un flipper

to **pinch** VERB

1 pincer
□ He pinched me! Il m'a pincé!
2 piquer (informal: steal)
□ Who's pinched my pen? Qui est-ce qui m'a piqué mon stylo?

pine NOUN
le pin
□ a pine table une table en pin

pineapple NOUN
l' ananas masc

pink ADJECTIVE
rose (FEM rose)

pint NOUN
la pinte

> DID YOU KNOW...?
> In France measurements are in litres and centilitres. A pint is about 0.6 litres.

■ to have a pint boire une bière □ He's gone out for a pint. Il est parti boire une bière.
■ a pint of milk un demi-litre de lait

pipe NOUN
1 la conduite (for water, gas)
□ The pipes froze. Les conduites d'eau ont gelé.
2 la pipe (for smoking)
□ He smokes a pipe. Il fume la pipe.
■ the pipes (bagpipes) la cornemuse □ He plays the pipes. Il joue de la cornemuse.

pirate NOUN
le pirate

pirated ADJECTIVE
pirate (FEM pirate)
□ a pirated DVD un DVD pirate

Pisces NOUN
les Poissons masc
□ I'm Pisces. Je suis Poissons.

pissed ADJECTIVE
bourré (FEM bourrée) (informal)

pistol NOUN
le pistolet

pitch NOUN
▷ see also pitch VERB
le terrain
□ a football pitch un terrain de football

to **pitch** VERB
▷ see also pitch NOUN
dresser (tent)
□ We pitched our tent near the beach. Nous avons dressé notre tente près de la plage.

pity NOUN
▷ see also pity VERB
la pitié
■ What a pity! Quel dommage!

to **pity** VERB
▷ see also pity NOUN

plaindre

pizza NOUN
la pizza

place NOUN
▷ see also **place** VERB
1 l' endroit *masc (location)*
□ It's a quiet place. C'est un endroit tranquille. □ There are a lot of interesting places to visit. Il y a beaucoup d'endroits intéressants à visiter.
2 la place *(space)*
□ a parking place une place de parking □ a university place une place à l'université
■ **to change places** changer de place
□ Tamsin, change places with Delphine! Tamsin, change de place avec Delphine!
■ **to take place** avoir lieu
■ **at your place** chez toi □ Shall we meet at your place? On se retrouve chez toi?
■ **to my place** chez moi □ Do you want to come round to my place? Tu veux venir chez moi?

to **place** VERB
▷ see also **place** NOUN
1 poser
□ He placed his hand on hers. Il a posé la main sur la sienne.
2 classer *(in competition, contest)*

placement NOUN
le stage
■ **to do a work placement** faire un stage en entreprise

plaid ADJECTIVE
écossais (FEM écossaise)
□ a plaid shirt une chemise écossaise

plain NOUN
▷ see also **plain** ADJECTIVE
la plaine

plain ADJECTIVE, ADVERB
▷ see also **plain** NOUN
1 uni (FEM unie) *(not patterned)*
□ a plain carpet un tapis uni
2 simple (FEM simple) *(not fancy)*
□ a plain white blouse un chemisier blanc simple

plain chocolate NOUN
le chocolat à croquer

plait NOUN
la natte
□ She wears her hair in a plait. Elle a une natte.

plan NOUN
▷ see also **plan** VERB
1 le projet
□ What are your plans for the holidays? Quels sont tes projets pour les vacances?
□ to make plans faire des projets

■ **Everything went according to plan.** Tout s'est passé comme prévu.
2 le plan *(map)*
□ a plan of the campsite un plan du terrain de camping
■ **my essay plan** le plan de ma dissertation

to **plan** VERB
▷ see also **plan** NOUN
1 préparer *(make plans for)*
□ We're planning a trip to France. Nous préparons un voyage en France.
2 planifier *(make schedule for)*
□ Plan your revision carefully. Planifiez vos révisions avec soin.
■ **to plan to do something** avoir l'intention de faire quelque chose □ I'm planning to get a job in the holidays. J'ai l'intention de trouver un job pour les vacances.

plane NOUN
l' avion *masc*
□ by plane en avion

planet NOUN
la planète

planning NOUN
la préparation
□ The trip needs careful planning. Le voyage nécessite une préparation méticuleuse.
■ **family planning** le planning familial

plant NOUN
▷ see also **plant** VERB
1 la plante
□ to water the plants arroser les plantes
2 l' usine *fem (factory)*

to **plant** VERB
▷ see also **plant** NOUN
planter

plant pot NOUN
le pot de fleurs

plaque NOUN
la plaque *(on wall)*

plaster NOUN
1 le pansement adhésif *(sticking plaster)*
□ Have you got a plaster, by any chance? Vous n'auriez pas un pansement adhésif, par hasard?
2 le plâtre *(for fracture)*
□ Her leg's in plaster. Elle a la jambe dans le plâtre.

plastic NOUN
▷ see also **plastic** ADJECTIVE
le plastique
□ It's made of plastic. C'est en plastique.

plastic ADJECTIVE
▷ see also **plastic** NOUN
en plastique
□ a plastic bag un sac en plastique □ a plastic mac un imperméable en plastique

plate NOUN
l' assiette *fem (for food)*

platform NOUN
1 le quai *(at station)*
□ on platform 7 sur le quai numéro sept
2 l' estrade *fem (for performers)*

play NOUN
▷ *see also* **play** VERB
la pièce
□ a play by Shakespeare une pièce de
Shakespeare
■ **to put on a play** monter une pièce

to **play** VERB
▷ *see also* **play** NOUN
1 jouer
□ He's playing with his friends. Il joue avec
ses amis. □ What sort of music do they
play? Quel genre de musique jouent-ils?
2 jouer contre *(against person, team)*
□ France will play Scotland next month. La
France jouera contre l'Écosse le mois
prochain.
3 jouer à *(sport, game)*
□ I play hockey. Je joue au hockey. □ Can
you play pool? Tu sais jouer au billard
américain?
4 jouer de *(instrument)*
□ I play the guitar. Je joue de la guitare.
5 écouter *(CD, music)*
□ She's always playing that song. Elle
écoute tout le temps cette chanson.

to **play down** VERB
dédramatiser
□ He tried to play down his illness. Il a
essayé de dédramatiser sa maladie.

player NOUN
1 le joueur
la joueuse *(of sport)*
□ a football player un joueur de football
2 le musicien
la musicienne *(of instrument)*
■ **a piano player** un pianiste
■ **a saxophone player** un saxophoniste

playful ADJECTIVE
espiègle *(FEM espiègle)*

playground NOUN
1 la cour de récréation *(at school)*
2 l' aire de jeux *fem (in park)*

playgroup NOUN
la garderie

playing card NOUN
la carte à jouer

playing field NOUN
le terrain de sport

playtime NOUN
la récréation

playwright NOUN
le dramaturge

pleasant ADJECTIVE
agréable *(FEM agréable)*

please EXCLAMATION
1 s'il vous plaît *(polite form)*
□ Two coffees, please. Deux cafés, s'il vous
plaît.
2 s'il te plaît *(familiar form)*
□ Please write back soon. Réponds vite, s'il
te plaît.

pleased ADJECTIVE
content *(FEM contente)*
□ My mother's not going to be very pleased.
Ma mère ne va pas être contente du tout.
□ It's beautiful: she'll be pleased with it.
C'est beau: elle va être contente.
■ **Pleased to meet you!** Enchanté!

pleasure NOUN
le plaisir
□ I read for pleasure. Je lis pour le plaisir.

plenty NOUN
largement assez
□ I've got plenty. J'en ai largement assez.
□ That's plenty, thanks. Ça suffit largement,
merci.
■ **plenty of 1** *(a lot)* beaucoup de □ I've
got plenty of things to do. J'ai beaucoup de
choses à faire. **2** *(enough)* largement assez
de □ I've got plenty of money. J'ai
largement assez d'argent. □ We've got
plenty of time. Nous avons largement le
temps.

pliers PL NOUN
la pince *sing*
■ **a pair of pliers** une pince

plot NOUN
▷ *see also* **plot** VERB
1 l' intrigue *fem (of story, play)*
2 la conspiration *(against somebody)*
□ a plot against the president une
conspiration contre le président
3 le carré *(of land)*
□ a vegetable plot un carré de légumes

to **plot** VERB
▷ *see also* **plot** NOUN
comploter
□ They were plotting to kill him. Ils
complotaient de le tuer.

plough NOUN
▷ *see also* **plough** VERB
la charrue

to **plough** VERB
▷ *see also* **plough** NOUN
labourer

plug NOUN
1 la prise de courant *(electrical)*
□ The plug is faulty. La prise est

P

491

défectueuse.

2 le bouchon (for sink)

to **plug in** VERB
brancher
□ Is it plugged in? Est-ce que c'est branché?

plum NOUN
la prune
□ plum jam la confiture de prunes

plumber NOUN
le plombier
□ He's a plumber. Il est plombier.

plump ADJECTIVE
dodu (FEM dodue)

to **plunge** VERB
plonger

plural NOUN
le pluriel

plus PREPOSITION, ADJECTIVE
plus
□ 4 plus 3 equals 7. Quatre plus trois
égalent sept. □ three children plus a dog
trois enfants plus un chien
■ I got a B plus. J'ai eu un Bien.

p.m. ABBREVIATION
■ at 8 p.m. à huit heures du soir
■ at 2 p.m. à quatorze heures

> DID YOU KNOW...?
> In France times are often given using
> the 24-hour clock.

pneumonia NOUN
la pneumonie

poached ADJECTIVE
■ a poached egg un œuf poché

pocket NOUN
la poche
■ pocket money l'argent de poche masc
□ £8 a week pocket money huit livres
d'argent de poche par semaine

pocket calculator NOUN
la calculette

poem NOUN
le poème

poet NOUN
le poète

poetry NOUN
la poésie

point NOUN
▷ see also **point** VERB
1 le point (spot, score)
□ a point on the horizon un point à l'horizon
□ They scored 5 points. Ils ont marqué cinq
points.
2 la remarque (comment)
□ He made some interesting points. Il a fait
quelque remarques intéressantes.
3 la pointe (tip)
□ a pencil with a sharp point un crayon à la

pointe aiguisée
4 le moment (in time)
□ At that point, we decided to leave. À ce
moment-là, nous avons décidé de partir.
■ a point of view un point de vue
■ to get the point comprendre □ Sorry, I
don't get the point. Désolé, je ne
comprends pas.
■ That's a good point! C'est vrai!
■ There's no point. Cela ne sert à rien.
□ There's no point in waiting. Cela ne sert à
rien d'attendre.
■ What's the point? À quoi bon? □ What's
the point of leaving so early? À quoi bon
partir si tôt?
■ Punctuality isn't my strong point. La
ponctualité n'est pas mon fort.
■ two point five (2.5) deux virgule cinq
(2,5)

> DID YOU KNOW...?
> In decimal numbers, the French use a
> comma instead of a point.

to **point** VERB
▷ see also **point** NOUN
montrer du doigt
□ Don't point! Ne montre pas du doigt!
■ to point at somebody montrer
quelqu'un du doigt □ She pointed at Anne.
Elle a montré Anne du doigt.
■ to point a gun at somebody braquer un
revolver sur quelqu'un

to **point out** VERB
1 montrer (show)
□ The guide pointed out Notre-Dame to us.
Le guide nous a montré Notre-Dame.
2 signaler (mention)
□ I should point out that ... Je dois vous
signaler que ...

pointless ADJECTIVE
inutile (FEM inutile)
□ It's pointless to argue. Il est inutile de
discuter.

poison NOUN
▷ see also **poison** VERB
le poison

to **poison** VERB
▷ see also **poison** NOUN
empoisonner

poisonous ADJECTIVE
1 venimeux (FEM venimeuse) (snake)
2 vénéneux (FEM vénéneuse) (plant,
mushroom)
3 toxique (FEM toxique) (gas)

to **poke** VERB
■ He poked the ground with his stick. Il
tapotait le sol avec sa canne.
■ She poked me in the ribs. Elle m'a

P

enfoncé le doigt dans les côtes.

poker NOUN
le poker
□ I play poker. Je joue au poker.

Poland NOUN
la Pologne
■ **in Poland** en Pologne
■ **to Poland** en Pologne

polar bear NOUN
l' ours blanc *masc*

Pole NOUN
le Polonais
la Polonaise

pole NOUN
le poteau (PL les poteaux)
□ a telegraph pole un poteau télégraphique
■ **a tent pole** un montant de tente
■ **a ski pole** un bâton de ski
■ **the North Pole** le pôle Nord
■ **the South Pole** le pôle Sud

pole vault NOUN
le saut à la perche

police PL NOUN
la police
□ We called the police. Nous avons appelé la police.
■ **a police car** une voiture de police
■ **a police station** un commissariat de police

> DID YOU KNOW...?
> There are several different types of police force in France. The **police nationale** are in charge of national security and public order in general, while the **police municipale** mainly deal with traffic and minor crimes. The **gendarmerie municipale** look after rural policing and border patrols.

policeman NOUN
le policier
□ He's a policeman. Il est policier.

policewoman NOUN
la femme policier
□ She's a policewoman. Elle est femme policier.

polio NOUN
la polio

Polish NOUN
▷ *see also* **Polish** ADJECTIVE
le polonais *(language)*

Polish ADJECTIVE
▷ *see also* **Polish** NOUN
polonais (FEM polonaise)

polish NOUN
▷ *see also* **polish** VERB
1 le cirage *(for shoes)*
2 la cire *(for furniture)*

to **polish** VERB
▷ *see also* **polish** NOUN
1 cirer *(shoes, furniture)*
2 faire briller *(glass)*

polite ADJECTIVE
poli (FEM polie)

politely ADVERB
poliment

politeness NOUN
la politesse

political ADJECTIVE
politique (FEM politique)

politician NOUN
le politicien
la politicienne

politics PL NOUN
la politique *sing*
□ I'm not interested in politics. La politique ne m'intéresse pas.

poll NOUN
le sondage
□ A recent poll revealed that ... Un sondage récent a révélé que ...

pollen NOUN
le pollen

to **pollute** VERB
polluer

polluted ADJECTIVE
pollué (FEM polluée)

pollution NOUN
la pollution

polo-necked sweater NOUN
le pull à col roulé

polo shirt NOUN
le polo

polythene bag NOUN
le sac en plastique

pond NOUN
1 l' étang *masc (big)*
2 la mare *(smaller)*
3 le bassin *(in garden)*
□ We've got a pond in our garden. Nous avons un bassin dans notre jardin.

pony NOUN
le poney

ponytail NOUN
la queue de cheval
□ He's got a ponytail. Il a une queue de cheval.

pony trekking NOUN
■ **to go pony trekking** faire une randonnée à dos de poney

poodle NOUN
le caniche

pool NOUN
1 la flaque *(puddle)*
2 l' étang *masc (pond)*

P

3 la piscine *(for swimming)*
4 le billard américain *(game)*
□ Shall we have a game of pool? Si on jouait au billard américain?
■ **the pools** *(football)* le loto sportif □ to do the pools jouer au loto sportif
poor ADJECTIVE
1 pauvre (FEM pauvre)
□ a poor family une famille pauvre □ Poor David, he's very unlucky! Le pauvre David, il n'a vraiment pas de chance!
■ **the poor** les pauvres *masc*
2 médiocre (FEM médiocre) *(bad)*
□ a poor mark une note médiocre
poorly ADJECTIVE
souffrant (FEM souffrante)
□ She's poorly. Elle est souffrante.
pop ADJECTIVE
pop (FEM + PL pop)
□ pop music la musique pop □ a pop star une pop star □ a pop group un groupe pop □ a pop song une chanson pop
to **pop in** VERB
passer
□ I just popped in to say hello. Je suis juste passé dire bonjour. □ I need to pop in to the supermarket for some milk. Je dois passer au supermarché pour chercher du lait.
to **pop out** VERB
sortir
□ He's just popped out to the supermarket. Il vient de sortir pour aller au supermarché.
to **pop round** VERB
passer
□ I'm just popping round to John's. Je vais juste passer chez John.
popcorn NOUN
le pop-corn
pope NOUN
le pape
poppy NOUN
le coquelicot
Popsicle® NOUN (US)
la glace à l'eau
popular ADJECTIVE
populaire (FEM populaire)
□ She's a very popular girl. C'est une fille très populaire. □ This is a very popular style. C'est un style très populaire.
population NOUN
la population
porch NOUN
le porche
pork NOUN
le porc
□ a pork chop une côtelette de porc □ I don't eat pork. Je ne mange pas de porc.

porn NOUN
▷ *see also* **porn** ADJECTIVE
le porno
porn ADJECTIVE
▷ *see also* **porn** NOUN
porno (FEM+PL porno)
□ a porn film un film porno □ a porn mag un magazine porno
pornographic ADJECTIVE
pornographique (FEM pornographique)
□ a pornographic magazine un magazine pornographique
pornography NOUN
la pornographie
porridge NOUN
le porridge
port NOUN
1 le port *(harbour)*
2 le porto *(wine)*
□ a glass of port un verre de porto
portable ADJECTIVE
portable (FEM portable)
□ a portable TV un téléviseur portable
porter NOUN
1 le portier *(in hotel)*
2 le porteur *(at station)*
portion NOUN
la portion
□ a large portion of chips une grosse portion de frites
portrait NOUN
le portrait
Portugal NOUN
le Portugal
■ **in Portugal** au Portugal
■ **We went to Portugal.** Nous sommes allés au Portugal.
Portuguese NOUN
▷ *see also* **Portuguese** ADJECTIVE
1 le Portugais
la Portugaise *(person)*
2 le portugais *(language)*
Portuguese ADJECTIVE
▷ *see also* **Portuguese** NOUN
portugais (FEM portugaise)
posh ADJECTIVE
chic (FEM+PL chic)
□ a posh hotel un hôtel chic
position NOUN
la position
□ an uncomfortable position une position inconfortable
positive ADJECTIVE
1 positif (FEM positive) *(good)*
□ a positive attitude une attitude positive
2 certain (FEM certaine) *(sure)*
□ I'm positive. J'en suis certain.

to **possess** VERB
posséder

possession NOUN
■ **Have you got all your possessions?** Est-ce tu as toutes tes affaires?

possibility NOUN
■ **It's a possibility.** C'est possible.

possible ADJECTIVE
possible (FEM possible)
□ as soon as possible aussitôt que possible

possibly ADVERB
peut-être (perhaps)
□ Are you coming to the party? — Possibly. Est-ce que tu viens à la soirée? — Peut-être.
■ **... if you possibly can.** ... si cela vous est possible.
■ **I can't possibly come.** Je ne peux vraiment pas venir.

post NOUN
▷ see also post VERB
1 le courrier (letters)
□ Is there any post for me? Est-ce qu'il y a du courrier pour moi?
2 le poteau (PL les poteaux) (pole)
□ The ball hit the post. Le ballon a heurté le poteau.

to **post** VERB
▷ see also post NOUN
poster
□ I've got some cards to post. J'ai quelques cartes à poster.

postage NOUN
l' affranchissement masc

postbox NOUN
la boîte aux lettres
DID YOU KNOW...?
French postboxes are yellow.

postcard NOUN
la carte postale

postcode NOUN
le code postal

poster NOUN
1 le poster
□ I've got posters on my bedroom walls. J'ai des posters sur les murs de ma chambre.
2 l' affiche fem (advertising)
□ There are posters all over town. Il y a des affiches dans toute la ville.

postman NOUN
le facteur
□ He's a postman. Il est facteur.

postmark NOUN
le cachet de la poste

post office NOUN
la poste
□ Where's the post office, please? Où est la poste, s'il vous plaît? □ She works for the post office. Elle travaille à la poste.

to **postpone** VERB
remettre à plus tard
□ The match has been postponed. Le match a été remis à plus tard.

postwoman NOUN
la factrice
□ She's a postwoman. Elle est factrice.

pot NOUN
1 le pot
□ a pot of jam un pot de confiture
■ **the pots and pans** les casseroles
2 la théière (teapot)
3 la cafetière (coffeepot)
4 l' herbe fem (marijuana)
□ to smoke pot fumer de l'herbe

potato NOUN
la pomme de terre
□ potato salad la salade de pommes de terre
■ **mashed potatoes** la purée
■ **boiled potatoes** les pommes vapeur
■ **a baked potato** une pomme de terre en robe des champs

potential NOUN
▷ see also potential ADJECTIVE
■ **He has great potential.** Il a de l'avenir.

potential ADJECTIVE
▷ see also potential NOUN
possible (FEM possible)
□ a potential problem un problème possible

pothole NOUN
le nid de poule (in road)

pot plant NOUN
la plante en pot

pottery NOUN
la poterie

pound NOUN
▷ see also pound VERB
la livre (weight, money)
□ How many euros do you get for a pound? Combien d'euros a-t-on pour une livre? □ a pound coin une pièce d'une livre
DID YOU KNOW...?
In France measurements are in grammes and kilogrammes. One pound is about 450 grammes.
□ a pound of carrots un demi-kilo de carottes

to **pound** VERB
▷ see also pound NOUN
battre
□ My heart was pounding. J'avais le cœur qui battait.

to **pour** VERB
1 verser (liquid)
□ She poured some water into the pan. Elle

a versé de l'eau dans la casserole.
- **She poured him a drink.** Elle lui a servi à boire.
- **Shall I pour you a cup of tea?** Je vous sers une tasse de thé?

2 pleuvoir à verse *(rain)*
  □ It's pouring. Il pleut à verse.
- **in the pouring rain** sous une pluie torrentielle

poverty NOUN
la pauvreté

powder NOUN
la poudre

power NOUN
1 le courant *(electricity)*
  □ The power's off. Le courant est coupé.
- **a power cut** une coupure de courant
- **a power point** une prise de courant
- **a power station** une centrale électrique
2 l' énergie *fem (energy)*
  □ nuclear power l'énergie nucléaire □ solar power l'énergie solaire
3 le pouvoir *(authority)*
  □ to be in power être au pouvoir

powerful ADJECTIVE
puissant *(FEM puissante)*

practical ADJECTIVE
pratique *(FEM pratique)*
  □ a practical suggestion un conseil pratique
- **She's very practical.** Elle a l'esprit pratique.

practically ADVERB
pratiquement
  □ It's practically impossible. C'est pratiquement impossible.

practice NOUN
l' entraînement *masc (for sport)*
  □ football practice l'entraînement de foot
- **I've got to do my piano practice.** Je dois travailler mon piano.
- **It's normal practice in our school.** C'est ce qui se fait dans notre école.
- **in practice** en pratique
- **a medical practice** un cabinet médical

to **practise** (US **practice**) VERB
1 s'exercer *(music, hobby)*
  □ I ought to practise more. Je devrais m'exercer davantage.
2 travailler *(instrument)*
  □ I practise the flute every evening. Je travaille ma flûte tous les soirs.
3 pratiquer *(language)*
  □ I practised my French when we were on holiday. J'ai pratiqué mon français pendant les vacances.
4 s'entraîner *(sport)*
  □ The team practises on Thursdays.

L'équipe s'entraîne le jeudi. □ I don't practise enough. Je ne m'entraîne pas assez.

practising ADJECTIVE
pratiquant *(FEM pratiquante)*
  □ She's a practising Catholic. Elle est catholique pratiquante.

to **praise** VERB
faire l'éloge de
  □ Everyone praises her cooking. Tout le monde fait l'éloge de sa cuisine. □ The teachers praised our work. Les professeurs ont fait l'éloge de notre travail.

pram NOUN
le landau

prawn NOUN
la crevette

prawn cocktail NOUN
le cocktail de crevettes

to **pray** VERB
prier
  □ to pray for something prier pour quelque chose

prayer NOUN
la prière

precaution NOUN
la précaution
- **to take precautions** prendre ses précautions

preceding ADJECTIVE
précédent *(FEM précédente)*

precinct NOUN
- **a shopping precinct** un centre commercial
- **a pedestrian precinct** une zone piétonnière

precious ADJECTIVE
précieux *(FEM précieuse)*

precise ADJECTIVE
précis *(FEM précise)*
  □ at that precise moment à cet instant précis

precisely ADVERB
précisément
  □ Precisely! Précisément!
- **at 10 a.m. precisely** à dix heures précises

to **predict** VERB
prédire

predictable ADJECTIVE
prévisible *(FEM prévisible)*

prefect NOUN

> **DID YOU KNOW...?**
> French schools do not have prefects. You could explain what a prefect is using the example given.

- **My sister's a prefect.** Ma sœur est en dernière année et est chargée de maintenir

la discipline.

to **prefer** VERB
préférer
□ Which would you prefer? Lequel préfères-tu? □ I prefer French to chemistry. Je préfère le français à la chimie.

preference NOUN
la préférence

pregnant ADJECTIVE
enceinte
□ She's six months pregnant. Elle est enceinte de six mois.

prehistoric ADJECTIVE
préhistorique (FEM préhistorique)

prejudice NOUN
1 le préjugé
□ That's just a prejudice. C'est un préjugé.
2 les préjugés masc pl
□ There's a lot of racial prejudice. Il y a beaucoup de préjugés raciaux.

prejudiced ADJECTIVE
■ **to be prejudiced against somebody** avoir des préjugés contre quelqu'un

premature ADJECTIVE
prématuré (FEM prématurée)
■ **a premature baby** un prématuré

Premier League NOUN
la première division
□ in the Premier League en première division

premises PL NOUN
les locaux masc pl
□ They're moving to new premises. Ils vont occuper de nouveaux locaux.

premonition NOUN
la prémonition

preoccupied ADJECTIVE
préoccupé (FEM préoccupée)

prep NOUN
les devoirs masc pl (homework)
□ history prep les devoirs d'histoire

preparation NOUN
la préparation

to **prepare** VERB
préparer
□ She has to prepare lessons in the evening. Elle doit préparer ses cours le soir.
■ **to prepare for something** se préparer pour quelque chose □ We're preparing for our skiing holiday. Nous nous préparons pour nos vacances à la neige.

prepared ADJECTIVE
■ **to be prepared to do something** être prêt à faire quelque chose □ I'm prepared to help you. Je suis prêt à t'aider.

prep school NOUN
l' école primaire privée fem

Presbyterian NOUN
▷ see also **Presbyterian** ADJECTIVE
le presbytérien
la presbytérienne

Presbyterian ADJECTIVE
▷ see also **Presbyterian** NOUN
presbytérien (FEM presbytérienne)

to **prescribe** VERB
prescrire

prescription NOUN
l' ordonnance fem
□ You can't get it without a prescription. On ne peut pas se le procurer sans ordonnance.

presence NOUN
la présence
■ **presence of mind** présence d'esprit

present ADJECTIVE
▷ see also **present** NOUN, VERB
1 présent (FEM présente) (in attendance)
□ He wasn't present at the meeting. Il n'était pas présent à la réunion.
2 actuel (FEM actuelle) (current)
□ the present situation la situation actuelle
■ **the present tense** le présent

present NOUN
▷ see also **present** ADJECTIVE, VERB
1 le cadeau (PL les cadeaux) (gift)
□ I'm going to buy presents. Je vais acheter des cadeaux.
■ **to give somebody a present** offrir un cadeau à quelqu'un
2 le présent (time)
□ up to the present jusqu'à présent
■ **for the present** pour l'instant
■ **at present** en ce moment

to **present** VERB
▷ see also **present** ADJECTIVE, NOUN
■ **to present somebody with something** (prize, medal) remettre quelque chose à quelqu'un

presenter NOUN
le présentateur
la présentatrice (on TV)

presently ADVERB
1 bientôt (soon)
□ You'll feel better presently. Tu vas bientôt te sentir mieux.
2 actuellement (at present)
□ They're presently on tour. Ils sont actuellement en tournée.

president NOUN
le président
la présidente

press NOUN
▷ see also **press** VERB
la presse
■ **a press conference** une conférence de

P

497

presse

to **press** VERB

▷ *see also* **press** NOUN

1 appuyer

□ Don't press too hard! N'appuie pas trop fort!

2 appuyer sur

□ He pressed the accelerator. Il a appuyé sur l'accélérateur.

pressed ADJECTIVE

■ **We are pressed for time.** Le temps nous manque.

press-up NOUN

■ **to do press-ups** faire des pompes □ I do twenty press-ups every morning. Je fais vingt pompes tous les matins.

pressure NOUN

▷ *see also* **pressure** VERB

la pression

□ He's under a lot of pressure at work. Il est sous pression au travail.

■ **a pressure group** un groupe de pression

to **pressure** VERB

▷ *see also* **pressure** NOUN

faire pression sur

□ My parents are pressuring me. Mes parents font pression sur moi.

to **pressurize** VERB

■ **to pressurize somebody to do something** faire pression sur quelqu'un pour qu'il fasse quelque chose □ My parents are pressurizing me to stay on at school. Mes parents font pression sur moi pour que je reste à l'école.

prestige NOUN

le prestige

prestigious ADJECTIVE

prestigieux (FEM prestigieuse)

presumably ADVERB

vraisemblablement

to **presume** VERB

supposer

□ I presume so. Je suppose que oui.

to **pretend** VERB

■ **to pretend to do something** faire semblant de faire quelque chose □ He pretended to be asleep. Il faisait semblant de dormir.

> LANGUAGE TIP Be careful not to translate **to pretend** by **prétendre**.

pretty ADJECTIVE, ADVERB

1 joli (FEM jolie)

□ She's very pretty. Elle est très jolie.

2 plutôt *(rather)*

□ That film was pretty bad. Ce film était plutôt mauvais.

■ **The weather was pretty awful.** Il faisait

un temps minable.

■ **It's pretty much the same.** C'est pratiquement la même chose.

to **prevent** VERB

empêcher

■ **to prevent somebody from doing something** empêcher quelqu'un de faire quelque chose □ They try to prevent us from smoking. Ils essaient de nous empêcher de fumer.

previous ADJECTIVE

précédent (FEM précédente)

previously ADVERB

auparavant

prey NOUN

la proie

□ a bird of prey un oiseau de proie

price NOUN

le prix

price list NOUN

la liste des prix

to **prick** VERB

piquer

□ I've pricked my finger. Je me suis piqué le doigt.

pride NOUN

la fierté

priest NOUN

le prêtre

□ He's a priest. Il est prêtre.

primarily ADVERB

principalement

primary ADJECTIVE

principal (FEM principale, MASC PL principaux)

primary school NOUN

l' école primaire *fem*

□ She's still at primary school. Elle est encore à l'école primaire.

> DID YOU KNOW...?
> In France, children start primary school at the age of six. The first year is **CP**, followed by **CE1** and **CE2**. The last two years are **CM1** and **CM2**.

prime minister NOUN

le Premier ministre

primitive ADJECTIVE

primitif (FEM primitive)

prince NOUN

le prince

□ the Prince of Wales le prince de Galles

princess NOUN

la princesse

□ Princess Anne la princesse Anne

principal ADJECTIVE

▷ *see also* **principal** NOUN

principal (FEM principale, MASC PL principaux)

principal NOUN

▷ *see also* **principal** ADJECTIVE
le principal *(of college)*

principle NOUN
le principe (PL les principaux)
■ **on principle** par principe

print NOUN
1 le tirage *(photo)*
  □ colour prints des tirages en couleur
2 les caractères *masc pl (letters)*
  □ in small print en petits caractères
3 l' empreinte digitale *fem (fingerprint)*
4 la gravure *(picture)*
  □ a framed print une gravure encadrée

printer NOUN
l' imprimante *fem (machine)*

printout NOUN
le tirage

priority NOUN
la priorité

prison NOUN
la prison
■ **in prison** en prison

prisoner NOUN
le prisonnier
la prisonnière

prison officer NOUN
le gardien de prison
la gardienne de prison

privacy NOUN
l' intimité *fem*

private ADJECTIVE
privé (FEM privée)
  □ a private school une école privée
■ **'private property'** 'propriété privée'
■ **'private'** *(on envelope)* 'personnel'
■ **a private bathroom** une salle de bain individuelle
■ **I have private lessons.** Je prends des cours particuliers.

to **privatize** VERB
privatiser

privilege NOUN
le privilège

prize NOUN
le prix
  □ to win a prize gagner un prix

prize-giving NOUN
la distribution des prix

prizewinner NOUN
le gagnant
la gagnante

pro NOUN
■ **the pros and cons** le pour et le contre
  □ We weighed up the pros and cons. Nous avons pesé le pour et le contre.

probability NOUN
la probabilité

probable ADJECTIVE
probable (FEM probable)

probably ADVERB
probablement
  □ probably not probablement pas

problem NOUN
le problème
  □ No problem! Pas de problème!

proceeds PL NOUN
la recette *sing*

process NOUN
le processus
  □ the peace process le processus de paix
■ **to be in the process of doing something** être en train de faire quelque chose □ We're in the process of painting the kitchen. Nous sommes en train de peindre la cuisine.

procession NOUN
la procession *(religious)*

to **produce** VERB
1 produire *(manufacture)*
2 monter *(play, show)*

producer NOUN
le metteur en scène *(of play, show)*

product NOUN
le produit

production NOUN
1 la production
  □ They're increasing production of luxury models. Ils augmentent la production des modèles de luxe.
2 la mise en scène *(play, show)*
  □ a production of 'Hamlet' une mise en scène de 'Hamlet'

profession NOUN
la profession

professional NOUN
▷ *see also* **professional** ADJECTIVE
le professionnel
la professionnelle

professional ADJECTIVE
▷ *see also* **professional** NOUN
professionnel (FEM professionnelle) *(player)*
  □ a professional musician un musicien professionnel
■ **a very professional piece of work** un vrai travail de professionnel

professionally ADVERB
■ **She sings professionally.** C'est une chanteuse professionnelle.

professor NOUN
le professeur d'université
■ **He's the French professor.** Il est titulaire de la chaire de français.

profit NOUN
le bénéfice

profitable ADJECTIVE

rentable (FEM rentable)

program NOUN
▷ *see also* **program** VERB
le programme
□ a computer program un programme informatique
■ **a TV program** (US) une émission de télévision

to **program** VERB
▷ *see also* **program** NOUN
programmer *(computer)*

programme NOUN
1 l' émission *fem (on TV, radio)*
2 le programme *(of events)*

programmer NOUN
le programmeur
la programmeuse
□ She's a programmer. Elle est programmeuse.

programming NOUN
la programmation

progress NOUN
le progrès
□ You're making progress! Vous faites des progrès!

to **prohibit** VERB
interdire
□ Smoking is prohibited. Il est interdit de fumer.

project NOUN
1 le projet *(plan)*
□ a development project un projet de développement
2 le dossier *(research)*
□ I'm doing a project on education in France. Je prépare un dossier sur l'éducation en France.

projector NOUN
le projecteur

promenade NOUN
le front de mer

promise NOUN
▷ *see also* **promise** VERB
la promesse
□ He made me a promise. Il m'a fait une promesse.
■ **That's a promise!** C'est promis!

to **promise** VERB
▷ *see also* **promise** NOUN
promettre
□ She promised to write. Elle a promis d'écrire. □ I'll write, I promise! J'écrirai, c'est promis!

promising ADJECTIVE
■ **a promising player** un joueur qui a de l'avenir

to **promote** VERB

■ **to be promoted** être promu □ She was promoted after six months. Elle a été promue au bout de six mois.

promotion NOUN
la promotion

prompt ADJECTIVE, ADVERB
rapide (FEM rapide)
□ a prompt reply une réponse rapide
■ **at eight o'clock prompt** à huit heures précises

promptly ADVERB
■ **We left promptly at seven.** Nous sommes partis à sept heures précises.

pronoun NOUN
le pronom

to **pronounce** VERB
prononcer
□ How do you pronounce that word? Comment est-ce qu'on prononce ce mot?

pronunciation NOUN
la prononciation

proof NOUN
la preuve

proper ADJECTIVE
1 vrai (FEM vraie) *(genuine)*
□ proper French bread du vrai pain français
□ We didn't have a proper lunch, just sandwiches. Nous n'avons pas pris de vrai repas, juste des sandwichs.
■ **It's difficult to get a proper job.** Il est difficile de trouver un travail correct.
2 adéquat (FEM adéquate)
□ You have to have the proper equipment. Il faut avoir l'équipement adéquat. □ We need proper training. Il nous faut une formation adéquate.
■ **If you had come at the proper time ...** Si tu étais venu à l'heure dite ...

properly ADVERB
1 comme il faut *(correctly)*
□ You're not doing it properly. Tu ne t'y prends pas comme il faut.
2 convenablement *(appropriately)*
□ Dress properly for your interview. Habille-toi convenablement pour ton entretien.

property NOUN
la propriété
■ **'private property'** 'propriété privée'
■ **stolen property** les objets volés

proportional ADJECTIVE
proportionnel (FEM proportionnelle)
□ proportional representation la représentation proportionnelle

proposal NOUN
la proposition *(suggestion)*

to **propose** VERB
proposer

◻ I propose a new plan. Je propose un changement de programme.

■ **to propose to do something** avoir l'intention de faire quelque chose ◻ What do you propose to do? Qu'est-ce que tu as l'intention de faire?

■ **to propose to somebody** (*for marriage*) demander quelqu'un en mariage ◻ He proposed to her at the restaurant. Il l'a demandée en mariage au restaurant.

to **prosecute** VERB
poursuivre en justice

◻ They were prosecuted for murder. Ils ont été poursuivis en justice pour meurtre.

■ **'Trespassers will be prosecuted'** 'Défense d'entrer sous peine de poursuites'

prospect NOUN
la perspective

◻ It'll improve my career prospects. Ça va améliorer mes perspectives d'avenir.

prospectus NOUN
le prospectus

prostitute NOUN
la prostituée

■ **a male prostitute** un prostitué

to **protect** VERB
protéger

protection NOUN
la protection

protein NOUN
la protéine

protest NOUN
▷ *see also* **protest** VERB
la protestation

◻ He ignored their protests. Il a ignoré leurs protestations.

■ **a protest march** une manifestation

to **protest** VERB
▷ *see also* **protest** NOUN
protester

Protestant NOUN
▷ *see also* **Protestant** ADJECTIVE
le protestant
la protestante

◻ I'm a Protestant. Je suis protestant.

Protestant ADJECTIVE
▷ *see also* **Protestant** NOUN
protestant (FEM protestante)

◻ a Protestant church une église protestante

protester NOUN
le manifestant
la manifestante

proud ADJECTIVE
fier (FEM fière)

◻ Her parents are proud of her. Ses parents sont fiers d'elle.

to **prove** VERB
prouver

◻ The police couldn't prove it. La police n'a pas pu le prouver.

proverb NOUN
le proverbe

to **provide** VERB
fournir

■ **to provide somebody with something** fournir quelque chose à quelqu'un ◻ They provided us with maps. Ils nous ont fourni des cartes.

to **provide for** VERB
subvenir aux besoins de

◻ He can't provide for his family any more. Il ne peut plus subvenir aux besoins de sa famille.

provided CONJUNCTION
à condition que

○ **LANGUAGE TIP** à condition que has to be followed by the subjunctive.

◻ He'll play in the next match provided he's fit. Il jouera dans le prochain match, à condition qu'il soit en forme.

provisional ADJECTIVE
provisoire (FEM provisoire)

prowler NOUN
le rôdeur
la rôdeuse

prune NOUN
le pruneau (PL les pruneaux)

to **pry** VERB
■ **He's always prying into other people's affairs.** Il met toujours son nez dans les affaires des autres.

pseudonym NOUN
le pseudonyme

psychiatrist NOUN
le/la psychiatre

◻ She's a psychiatrist. Elle est psychiatre.

psychoanalyst NOUN
le/la psychanalyste

psychological ADJECTIVE
psychologique (FEM psychologique)

psychologist NOUN
le/la psychologue

◻ He's a psychologist. Il est psychologue.

psychology NOUN
la psychologie

PTO ABBREVIATION (= *please turn over*)
T.S.V.P. (= *tournez, s'il vous plaît*)

pub NOUN
le pub

public NOUN
▷ *see also* **public** ADJECTIVE
le public

◻ open to the public ouvert au public

P

- **in public** en public

public ADJECTIVE
▷ see also **public** NOUN
public (FEM publique)
- **a public holiday** un jour férié
- **public opinion** l'opinion publique fem
- **the public address system** les haut-parleurs

publican NOUN
le patron de pub
la patronne de pub
- **My uncle's a publican.** Mon oncle tient un pub.

publicity NOUN
la publicité

public school NOUN
l' école privée fem

public transport NOUN
les transports en commun masc pl

to **publish** VERB
publier

publisher NOUN
l' éditeur masc

pudding NOUN
le dessert
□ What's for pudding? Qu'est-ce qu'il y a comme dessert?
- **rice pudding** le riz au lait
- **black pudding** le boudin noir

puddle NOUN
la flaque

puff pastry NOUN
la pâte feuilletée

to **pull** VERB
tirer
□ Pull! Tirez!
- **He pulled the trigger.** Il a appuyé sur la gâchette.
- **to pull a muscle** se froisser un muscle
□ I pulled a muscle when I was training. Je me suis froissé un muscle à l'entraînement.
- **You're pulling my leg!** Tu me fais marcher!

to **pull down** VERB
démolir

to **pull out** VERB
1 arracher (tooth, weed)
2 déboîter (car)
□ The car pulled out to overtake. La voiture a déboîté pour doubler.
3 se retirer (withdraw)
□ She pulled out of the tournament. Elle s'est retirée du tournoi.

to **pull through** VERB
s'en sortir
□ They think he'll pull through. Ils pensent qu'il va s'en sortir.

P

to **pull up** VERB
s'arrêter (car)
□ A black car pulled up beside me. Une voiture noire s'est arrêtée à côté de moi.

pullover NOUN
le pull-over

pulse NOUN
le pouls
□ The nurse felt his pulse. L'infirmière a pris son pouls.

pulses PL NOUN
les légumes secs masc pl

pump NOUN
▷ see also **pump** VERB
1 la pompe
□ a bicycle pump une pompe à vélo □ a petrol pump une pompe à essence
2 le chausson de gym (shoe)

to **pump** VERB
▷ see also **pump** NOUN
pomper

to **pump up** VERB
gonfler (tyre)

pumpkin NOUN
le potiron

punch NOUN
▷ see also **punch** VERB
1 le coup de poing (blow)
□ He gave me a punch. Il m'a donné un coup de poing.
2 le punch (drink)

to **punch** VERB
▷ see also **punch** NOUN
1 donner un coup de poing à (hit)
□ He punched me! Il m'a donné un coup de poing!
2 composter (in ticket machine)
□ Punch your ticket before you get on the train. Compostez votre billet avant de monter dans le train.
3 poinçonner (by hand)
□ He forgot to punch my ticket. Il a oublié de poinçonner mon billet.

> **DID YOU KNOW...?**
> In France, you have to punch your ticket before you get on the train. If you don't, you could be fined.

punch-up NOUN
la bagarre (informal)

punctual ADJECTIVE
ponctuel (FEM ponctuelle)

punctuation NOUN
la ponctuation

puncture NOUN
la crevaison
□ I had to mend a puncture. J'ai dû réparer une crevaison.

■ **to have a puncture** crever □ I had a
puncture on the motorway. J'ai crevé sur
l'autoroute.

to **punish** VERB
punir
■ **to punish somebody for something**
punir quelqu'un de quelque chose
■ **to punish somebody for doing
something** punir quelqu'un d'avoir fait
quelque chose

punishment NOUN
la punition

punk NOUN
le/la punk (person)
■ **a punk rock band** un groupe de punk
rock

pupil NOUN
l' élève masc/fem

puppet NOUN
la marionnette

puppy NOUN
le chiot

to **purchase** VERB
acheter

pure ADJECTIVE
pur (FEM pure)
□ pure orange juice du pur jus d'orange
□ He's doing pure maths. Il fait des maths
pures.

purple ADJECTIVE
violet (FEM violette)

purpose NOUN
le but
□ What is the purpose of these changes?
Quel est le but de ces changements? □ his
purpose in life son but dans la vie
■ **on purpose** exprès □ He did it on
purpose. Il l'a fait exprès.

to **purr** VERB
ronronner

purse NOUN
1 le porte-monnaie (PL les porte-monnaie)
2 le sac à main (us: handbag)

to **pursue** VERB
poursuivre

pursuit NOUN
l' activité fem
□ outdoor pursuits les activités de plein air

push NOUN
▷ see also **push** VERB
■ **to give somebody a push** pousser
quelqu'un □ He gave me a push. Il m'a
poussé.

to **push** VERB
▷ see also **push** NOUN
1 pousser
□ Don't push! Arrêtez de pousser!

2 appuyer sur (button)
■ **to push somebody to do something**
pousser quelqu'un à faire quelque chose
□ My parents are pushing me to go to
university. Mes parents me poussent à
entrer à l'université.
■ **to push drugs** revendre de la drogue
■ **Push off!** Dégage!

to **push around** VERB
bousculer
□ He likes pushing people around. Il aime
bien bousculer les gens.

to **push through** VERB
se frayer un passage
□ The ambulancemen pushed through the
crowd. Les ambulanciers se sont frayé un
passage dans la foule.
■ **I pushed my way through.** Je me suis
frayé un passage.

pushchair NOUN
la poussette

pusher NOUN
le revendeur
la revendeuse (of drugs)

push-up NOUN
■ **to do push-ups** faire des pompes

to **put** VERB
1 mettre (place)
□ Where shall I put my things? Où est-ce
que je peux mettre mes affaires? □ She's
putting the baby to bed. Elle met le bébé au
lit.
2 écrire (write)
□ Don't forget to put your name on the
paper. N'oubliez pas d'écrire votre nom sur
la feuille.

to **put aside** VERB
mettre de côté
□ Can you put this aside for me till
tomorrow? Est-ce que vous pouvez mettre
ça de côté pour moi jusqu'à demain?

to **put away** VERB
ranger
□ Can you put away the dishes, please? Tu
peux ranger la vaisselle, s'il te plaît?

to **put back** VERB
remettre en place (replace)
□ Put it back when you've finished with it.
Remets-le en place une fois que tu auras
fini.

to **put down** VERB
1 poser
□ I'll put these bags down for a minute. Je
vais poser ces sacs une minute.
2 noter (in writing)
□ I've put down a few ideas. J'ai noté
quelques idées.

P

■ **to have an animal put down** faire piquer un animal □ We had to have our old dog put down. Nous avons dû faire piquer notre vieux chien.

to **put forward** VERB
1 avancer *(clock)*
□ Don't forget to put the clocks forward. N'oubliez pas d'avancer les pendules d'une heure.
2 proposer *(idea, argument)*
□ to put forward a suggestion proposer une suggestion

to **put in** VERB
installer *(install)*
□ We're going to get central heating put in. Nous allons faire installer le chauffage central.
■ **He has put in a lot of work on this project.** Il a fourni beaucoup de travail pour ce projet.

to **put off** VERB
1 éteindre *(switch off)*
□ Shall I put the light off? Est-ce que j'éteins la lumière?
2 remettre à plus tard *(postpone)*
□ I keep putting it off. Je n'arrête pas de remettre ça à plus tard.
3 déranger *(distract)*
□ Stop putting me off! Arrête de me déranger!
4 décourager *(discourage)*
□ He's not easily put off. Il ne se laisse pas facilement décourager.

to **put on** VERB
1 mettre *(clothes, lipstick, CD)*
□ I'll put my coat on. Je vais mettre mon manteau.
2 allumer *(light, heater, TV)*
□ Shall I put the heater on? J'allume le chauffage?
3 monter *(play, show)*
□ We're putting on 'Bugsy Malone'. Nous sommes en train de monter 'Bugsy Malone'.
4 mettre à cuire
□ I'll put the potatoes on. Je vais mettre les pommes de terre à cuire.
■ **to put on weight** grossir □ He's put on a lot of weight. Il a beaucoup grossi.

to **put out** VERB

éteindre *(light, cigarette, fire)*
□ It took them five hours to put out the fire. Ils ont mis cinq heures à éteindre l'incendie.

to **put through** VERB
passer
□ Can you put me through to the manager? Est-ce que vous pouvez me passer le directeur?
■ **I'm putting you through.** Je vous passe la communication.

to **put up** VERB
1 mettre *(pin up)*
□ I'll put the poster up on my wall. Je vais mettre le poster sur mon mur.
2 monter *(tent)*
□ We put up our tent in a field. Nous avons monté la tente dans un champ.
3 augmenter *(price)*
□ They've put up the price. Ils ont augmenté le prix.
4 héberger *(accommodate)*
□ My friend will put me up for the night. Mon ami va m'héberger pour la nuit.
■ **to put one's hand up** lever la main □ If you have any questions, put up your hand. Si vous avez une question, levez la main.
■ **to put up with something** supporter quelque chose □ I'm not going to put up with it any longer. Je ne vais pas supporter ça plus longtemps.

puzzle NOUN
le puzzle *(jigsaw)*

puzzled ADJECTIVE
perplexe (FEM perplexe)
□ You look puzzled! Tu as l'air perplexe!

puzzling ADJECTIVE
déconcertant (FEM déconcertante)

pyjamas PL NOUN
le pyjama *sing*
□ my pyjamas mon pyjama □ a pair of pyjamas un pyjama
■ **a pyjama top** un haut de pyjama

pyramid NOUN
la pyramide

Pyrenees PL NOUN
les Pyrénées *fem pl*
■ **in the Pyrenees** dans les Pyrénées
■ **We went to the Pyrenees.** Nous sommes allés dans les Pyrénées.

Qq

quaint ADJECTIVE
  pittoresque (FEM pittoresque) (house, village)
qualification NOUN
  le diplôme
  □ to leave school without any qualifications
  quitter l'école sans aucun diplôme
  ■ **vocational qualifications** des
  qualifications professionnelles
qualified ADJECTIVE
1 qualifié (FEM qualifiée) (trained)
  □ a qualified driving instructor un moniteur
  d'auto-école qualifié
2 diplômé (FEM diplômée) (nurse, teacher)
  □ a qualified nurse une infirmière diplômée
to **qualify** VERB
1 obtenir son diplôme (for job)
  □ She qualified as a teacher last year. Elle a
  obtenu son diplôme de professeur l'année
  dernière.
2 se qualifier (in competition)
  □ Our team didn't qualify. Notre équipe ne
  s'est pas qualifiée.
quality NOUN
  la qualité
  □ a good quality of life une bonne qualité de
  vie □ good-quality ingredients des
  ingrédients de bonne qualité □ She's got
  lots of good qualities. Elle a beaucoup de
  qualités.
quantity NOUN
  la quantité
quarantine NOUN
  la quarantaine
  □ in quarantine en quarantaine
quarrel NOUN
  ▷ see also **quarrel** VERB
  la dispute
to **quarrel** VERB
  ▷ see also **quarrel** NOUN
  se disputer
quarry NOUN
  la carrière (for stone)
quarter NOUN
  le quart
  ■ **three quarters** trois quarts

  ■ **a quarter of an hour** un quart d'heure
  □ three quarters of an hour trois quarts
  d'heure
  ■ **a quarter past ten** dix heures et quart
  ■ **a quarter to eleven** onze heures moins
  le quart
quarter final NOUN
  le quart de finale
quartet NOUN
  le quatuor
  □ a string quartet un quatuor à cordes
quay NOUN
  le quai
queasy ADJECTIVE
  ■ **to feel queasy** avoir mal au cœur □ I'm
  feeling queasy. J'ai mal au cœur.
queen NOUN
1 la reine
  □ Queen Elizabeth la reine Élisabeth
2 la dame (playing card)
  □ the queen of hearts la dame de cœur
  ■ **the Queen Mother** la reine mère
query NOUN
  ▷ see also **query** VERB
  la question
to **query** VERB
  ▷ see also **query** NOUN
  mettre en question
  □ No one queried my decision. Personne
  n'a mis en question ma décision.
question NOUN
  ▷ see also **question** VERB
  la question
  □ Can I ask a question? Est-ce que je peux
  poser une question? □ That's a difficult
  question. C'est une question difficile.
  ■ **It's out of the question.** C'est hors de
  question.
to **question** VERB
  ▷ see also **question** NOUN
  interroger
  □ He was questioned by the police. Il a été
  interrogé par la police.
question mark NOUN
  le point d'interrogation

q

questionnaire NOUN
le questionnaire

queue NOUN
▷ *see also* **queue** VERB
la queue

to **queue** VERB
▷ *see also* **queue** NOUN
faire la queue
■ **to queue for something** faire la queue
pour avoir quelque chose ▫ We had to
queue for tickets. Nous avons dû faire la
queue pour avoir les billets.

quick ADJECTIVE, ADVERB
rapide (FEM rapide)
▫ a quick lunch un déjeuner rapide ▫ It's
quicker by train. C'est plus rapide en train.
■ **Be quick!** Dépêche-toi!
■ **She's a quick learner.** Elle apprend vite.
■ **Quick, phone the police!** Téléphonez
vite à la police!

quickly ADVERB
vite
▫ It was all over very quickly. Ça s'est passé
très vite.

quiet ADJECTIVE
1 silencieux (FEM silencieuse) *(not talkative or
noisy)*
▫ You're very quiet today. Tu es bien
silencieux aujourd'hui. ▫ The engine's very
quiet. Le moteur est très silencieux.
2 tranquille (FEM tranquille) *(peaceful)*
▫ a quiet little town une petite ville
tranquille ▫ a quiet weekend un week-end
tranquille
■ **Be quiet!** Tais-toi!
■ **Quiet!** Silence!

quietly ADVERB
1 doucement *(speak)*
▫ 'She's dead,' he said quietly. 'Elle est
morte' dit-il doucement.
2 silencieusement *(move)*
■ **He quietly opened the door.** Il a ouvert
la porte sans faire de bruit.

quilt NOUN
la couette *(duvet)*

to **quit** VERB
quitter *(place, premises, job)*
▫ She's decided to quit her job. Elle a décidé
de quitter son emploi.
■ **I quit!** J'abandonne!

quite ADVERB
1 assez *(rather)*
▫ It's quite warm today. Il fait assez bon
aujourd'hui. ▫ I quite liked the film, but...
J'ai trouvé le film assez bon, mais...
2 tout à fait *(entirely)*
▫ I'm not quite sure. Je n'en suis pas tout à
fait sûr. ▫ It's not quite the same. Ce n'est
pas tout à fait la même chose.
■ **quite good** pas mal
■ **I've been there quite a lot.** J'y suis allé
pas mal de fois.
■ **quite a lot of money** pas mal d'argent
■ **It costs quite a lot to go abroad.** Ça
coûte assez cher d'aller à l'étranger.
■ **It's quite a long way.** C'est assez loin.
■ **It was quite a shock.** Ça a été un sacré
choc.
■ **There were quite a few people there.** Il
y avait pas mal de gens.

quiz NOUN
le jeu-concours

quota NOUN
le quota

quotation NOUN
la citation
▫ a quotation from Shakespeare une
citation de Shakespeare

quote NOUN
▷ *see also* **quote** VERB
la citation
▫ a Shakespeare quote une citation de
Shakespeare
■ **quotes** *(quotation marks)* les guillemets
masc pl ▫ in quotes entre guillemets

to **quote** VERB
▷ *see also* **quote** NOUN
citer
▫ He's always quoting Shakespeare. Il
n'arrête pas de citer Shakespeare.

q

Rr

rabbi NOUN
le rabbin

rabbit NOUN
le lapin

■ **a rabbit hutch** un clapier

rabies NOUN
la rage

■ **a dog with rabies** un chien enragé

race NOUN
▷ see also **race** VERB
1 la course *(sport)*
□ a cycle race une course cycliste
2 la race *(species)*
□ the human race la race humaine
■ **race relations** les relations interraciales *fem pl*

to **race** VERB
▷ see also **race** NOUN
1 courir
□ We raced to catch the bus. Nous avons couru pour attraper le bus.
2 faire la course *(have a race)*
■ **I'll race you!** On fait la course!

racecourse NOUN
le champ de courses

racehorse NOUN
le cheval de course (PL les chevaux de course)

racer NOUN
le vélo de course *(bike)*

racetrack NOUN
la piste

racial ADJECTIVE
racial (FEM raciale, MASC PL raciaux)
□ racial discrimination la discrimination raciale

racing car NOUN
la voiture de course

racing driver NOUN
le pilote de course

racism NOUN
le racisme

racist ADJECTIVE
▷ see also **racist** NOUN
raciste (FEM raciste)

racist NOUN
▷ see also **racist** ADJECTIVE
le/la raciste

rack NOUN *(for luggage)*
le porte-bagages (PL les porte-bagages)

racket NOUN
1 la raquette *(for sport)*
□ my tennis racket ma raquette de tennis
2 le boucan *(noise)*
□ They're making a terrible racket. Ils font un boucan de tous les diables. *(informal)*

racquet NOUN
la raquette

radar NOUN
le radar

radiation NOUN
la radiation

radiator NOUN
le radiateur

radio NOUN
la radio
■ **on the radio** à la radio
■ **a radio station** une station de radio

radioactive ADJECTIVE
radioactif (FEM radioactive)

radio-controlled ADJECTIVE
téléguidé (FEM téléguidée) *(model plane, car)*

radish NOUN
le radis

RAF NOUN (= Royal Air Force)
la R.A.F.
□ He's in the RAF. Il est dans la R.A.F.

raffle NOUN
la tombola
□ a raffle ticket un billet de tombola

raft NOUN
le radeau (PL les radeaux)

rag NOUN
le chiffon
□ a piece of rag un chiffon
■ **dressed in rags** en haillons

rage NOUN
la rage
□ mad with rage fou de rage
■ **to be in a rage** être furieux □ She was in

a rage. Elle était furieuse.
■ **It's all the rage.** Ça fait fureur.

raid NOUN
▷ *see also* **raid** VERB
1 le hold-up (PL les hold-up) *(burglary)*
□ There was a bank raid near my house. Il y a eu un hold-up dans une banque près de chez moi.
2 la descente
□ a police raid une descente de police

to **raid** VERB
▷ *see also* **raid** NOUN
faire une descente dans *(police)*
□ The police raided the club. La police a fait une descente dans le club.

rail NOUN
1 la rampe *(on stairs)*
2 la balustrade *(on bridge, balcony)*
□ Don't lean over the rail! Ne vous penchez pas sur la balustrade!
3 le rail *(on railway line)*
■ **by rail** en train

railcard NOUN
la carte de chemin de fer
□ a young person's railcard une carte de chemin de fer tarif jeune

railroad NOUN (US)
le chemin de fer
■ **a railroad line** une ligne de chemin de fer
■ **a railroad station** une gare

railway NOUN
le chemin de fer
□ the privatization of the railways la privatisation des chemins de fer
■ **a railway line** une ligne de chemin de fer
■ **a railway station** une gare

rain NOUN
▷ *see also* **rain** VERB
la pluie
□ in the rain sous la pluie

to **rain** VERB
▷ *see also* **rain** NOUN
pleuvoir
□ It rains a lot here. Il pleut beaucoup par ici.
■ **It's raining.** Il pleut.

rainbow NOUN
l' arc-en-ciel *masc* (PL les arcs-en-ciel)

raincoat NOUN
l' imperméable *masc*

rainforest NOUN
la forêt tropicale humide

rainy ADJECTIVE
pluvieux (FEM pluvieuse)

to **raise** VERB
1 lever *(lift)*
□ He raised his hand. Il a levé la main.

2 améliorer *(improve)*
□ They want to raise standards in schools. Ils veulent améliorer le niveau dans les écoles.
■ **to raise money** collecter des fonds □ The school is raising money for a new gym. L'école collecte des fonds pour un nouveau gymnase.

raisin NOUN
le raisin sec

rake NOUN
le râteau (PL les râteaux)

rally NOUN
1 le rassemblement *(of people)*
2 le rallye *(sport)*
□ a rally driver un pilote de rallye
3 l' échange *masc (in tennis)*

ram NOUN
▷ *see also* **ram** VERB
le bélier *(sheep)*

to **ram** VERB
▷ *see also* **ram** NOUN
emboutir *(vehicle)*
□ The thieves rammed a police car. Les voleurs ont embouti une voiture de police.

Ramadan NOUN
le ramadan

ramble NOUN
la randonnée
□ to go for a ramble faire une randonnée

rambler NOUN
le randonneur
la randonneuse

ramp NOUN
la rampe d'accès *(for wheelchairs)*

ran VERB ▷ *see* **run**

ranch NOUN
le ranch

random ADJECTIVE
■ **a random selection** une sélection effectuée au hasard
■ **at random** au hasard □ We picked the number at random. Nous avons choisi le numéro au hasard.

rang VERB ▷ *see* **ring**

range NOUN
▷ *see also* **range** VERB
le choix
□ a wide range of colours un grand choix de coloris
■ **a range of subjects** diverses matières
□ We study a range of subjects. Nous étudions diverses matières.
■ **a mountain range** une chaîne de montagnes

to **range** VERB
▷ *see also* **range** NOUN

■ **to range from ... to** se situer entre ... et
□ Temperatures in summer range from 20 to 35 degrees. Les températures estivales se situent entre vingt et trente-cinq degrés.

■ **Tickets range from £2 to £20.** Les billets coûtent entre deux et vingt livres.

rank NOUN
▷ *see also* **rank** VERB
■ **a taxi rank** une station de taxis

to **rank** VERB
▷ *see also* **rank** NOUN
■ **He's ranked third in the United States.** Il est classé troisième aux Etats-Unis.

ransom NOUN
la rançon

rap NOUN
le rap *(music)*

rape NOUN
▷ *see also* **rape** VERB
le viol

to **rape** VERB
▷ *see also* **rape** NOUN
violer

rapids PL NOUN
les rapides *masc pl*

rapist NOUN
le violeur

rare ADJECTIVE
1 rare (FEM rare) *(unusual)*
□ a rare plant une plante rare
2 saignant (FEM saignante) *(steak)*

rash NOUN
l' éruption de boutons *fem*
□ I've got a rash on my chest. J'ai une éruption de boutons sur la poitrine.

rasher NOUN
la tranche
□ an egg and two rashers of bacon un œuf et deux tranches de bacon

raspberry NOUN
la framboise
□ raspberry jam la confiture de framboises

rat NOUN
le rat

rate NOUN
▷ *see also* **rate** VERB
1 le tarif *(price)*
□ There are reduced rates for students. Il y a des tarifs réduits pour les étudiants.
2 le taux *(level)*
□ the divorce rate le taux de divorce □ a high rate of interest un taux d'intérêt élevé

to **rate** VERB
▷ *see also* **rate** NOUN
considérer comme
■ **He is rated the best.** Il est considéré comme le meilleur.

■ **How do you rate him?** Qu'est-ce que vous pensez de lui?

rather ADVERB
plutôt
□ I was rather disappointed. J'étais plutôt déçu. □ £20! That's rather a lot! Vingt livres! C'est plutôt cher!

■ **rather a lot of** pas mal de □ I've got rather a lot of homework to do. J'ai pas mal de devoirs à faire.

■ **rather than** plutôt que □ We decided to camp, rather than stay at a hotel. Nous avons décidé de camper plutôt que d'aller à l'hôtel.

■ **I'd rather ...** J'aimerais mieux ... □ I'd rather stay in tonight. J'aimerais mieux rester à la maison ce soir. □ I'd rather have an apple than a banana. J'aimerais mieux une pomme qu'une banane.

rattle NOUN
le hochet *(for baby)*

rattlesnake NOUN
le serpent à sonnette

to **rave** VERB
▷ *see also* **rave** NOUN
s'extasier
□ They raved about the film. Ils se sont extasiés sur le film.

rave NOUN
▷ *see also* **rave** VERB
la rave *(party)*
■ **rave music** le rave

raven NOUN
le corbeau (PL les corbeaux)

ravenous ADJECTIVE
■ **to be ravenous** avoir une faim de loup
□ I'm ravenous! J'ai une faim de loup!

‿‿ **LANGUAGE TIP** Word for word, this means 'I'm as hungry as a wolf'.

raving ADJECTIVE
■ **raving mad** fou à lier □ She's raving mad! Elle est folle à lier.

raw ADJECTIVE
cru (FEM crue) *(food)*
■ **raw materials** les matières premières *fem pl*

razor NOUN
le rasoir
□ some disposable razors des rasoirs jetables
■ **a razor blade** une lame de rasoir

RE NOUN
l' éducation religieuse *fem*

reach NOUN
▷ *see also* **reach** VERB
■ **out of reach** hors de portée □ The light switch was out of reach. L'interrupteur était

hors de portée.

- **within easy reach of** à proximité de
□ The hotel is within easy reach of the town centre. L'hôtel se trouve à proximité du centre-ville.

to **reach** VERB
▷ *see also* **reach** NOUN
1 arriver à
□ We reached the hotel at 7 p.m. Nous sommes arrivés à l'hôtel à sept heures du soir.
- **We hope to reach the final.** Nous espérons aller en finale.
2 parvenir à *(decision)*
□ Eventually they reached a decision. Ils sont finalement parvenus à une décision.
- **He reached for his gun.** Il a tendu la main pour prendre son revolver.

to **react** VERB
réagir

reaction NOUN
la réaction

reactor NOUN
le réacteur
□ a nuclear reactor un réacteur nucléaire

to **read** VERB
lire
□ I don't read much. Je ne lis pas beaucoup.
□ Have you read 'Animal Farm'? Est-ce que tu as lu 'La ferme des animaux'? □ Read the text out loud. Lis le texte à haute voix.

to **read out** VERB
lire
□ He read out the article to me. Il m'a lu l'article.
- **to read out the results** annoncer les résultats

reader NOUN
le lecteur
la lectrice *(person)*

readily ADVERB
volontiers
□ She readily agreed. Elle a accepté volontiers.

reading NOUN
la lecture
□ Reading is one of my hobbies. La lecture est l'une de mes activités favorites.

ready ADJECTIVE
prêt (FEM prête)
□ She's nearly ready. Elle est presque prête.
□ He's always ready to help. Il est toujours prêt à rendre service.
- **a ready meal** un plat cuisiné
- **to get ready** se préparer □ She's getting ready to go out. Elle est en train de se préparer pour sortir.

- **to get something ready** préparer quelque chose □ He's getting the dinner ready. Il est en train de préparer le dîner.

real ADJECTIVE
1 vrai (FEM vraie)
□ He wasn't a real policeman. Ce n'était pas un vrai policier. □ Her real name is Cordelia. Son vrai nom est Cordelia.
2 véritable (FEM véritable)
□ It's real leather. C'est du cuir véritable.
□ It was a real nightmare. C'était un véritable cauchemar.
- **in real life** dans la réalité

realistic ADJECTIVE
réaliste (FEM réaliste)

reality NOUN
la réalité

reality TV NOUN
la téléréalité
□ a reality TV show une émission de téléréalité

to **realize** VERB
- **to realize that ...** se rendre compte que ... □ We realized that something was wrong. Nous nous sommes rendu compte que quelque chose n'allait pas.

really ADVERB
vraiment
□ She's really nice. Elle est vraiment sympathique. □ Do you want to go? — Not really. Tu veux y aller? — Pas vraiment.
- **I'm learning German. — Really?** J'apprends l'allemand. — Ah bon?
- **Do you really think so?** Tu es sûr?

realtor NOUN (US)
l' agent immobilier *masc*

rear ADJECTIVE
▷ *see also* **rear** NOUN
arrière (FEM+PL arrière)
□ a rear wheel une roue arrière

rear NOUN
▷ *see also* **rear** ADJECTIVE
l' arrière *masc*
□ at the rear of the train à l'arrière du train

reason NOUN
la raison
□ There's no reason to think that ... Il n'y a aucune raison de penser que ... □ for security reasons pour des raisons de sécurité
- **That was the main reason I went.** C'est surtout pour ça que j'y suis allé.

reasonable ADJECTIVE
1 raisonnable (FEM raisonnable) *(sensible)*
□ Be reasonable! Sois raisonnable!
2 correct (FEM correcte) *(not bad)*
□ He wrote a reasonable essay. Sa

dissertation était correcte.

reasonably ADVERB
raisonnablement
▢ The team played reasonably well. L'équipe
a joué raisonnablement bien.
■ **reasonably priced accommodation** un
logement à un prix raisonnable

to **reassure** VERB
rassurer

reassuring ADJECTIVE
rassurant (FEM rassurante)

rebellious ADJECTIVE
rebelle (FEM rebelle)

receipt NOUN
le reçu

to **receive** VERB
recevoir

receiver NOUN
le combiné (of phone)
■ **to pick up the receiver** décrocher

recent ADJECTIVE
récent (FEM récente)

recently ADVERB
ces derniers temps
▢ I've been doing a lot of training recently.
Je me suis beaucoup entraîné ces derniers
temps.

reception NOUN
la réception
▢ Please leave your key at reception. Merci
de laisser votre clé à la réception. ▢ The
reception will be at a big hotel. La réception
aura lieu dans un grand hôtel.

receptionist NOUN
le/la réceptionniste

recession NOUN
la récession

recipe NOUN
la recette

to **reckon** VERB
penser
▢ What do you reckon? Qu'est-ce que tu en
penses?

reclining ADJECTIVE
■ **a reclining seat** un siège inclinable

recognizable ADJECTIVE
reconnaissable (FEM reconnaissable)

to **recognize** VERB
reconnaître
▢ You'll recognize me by my red hair. Vous
me reconnaîtrez à mes cheveux roux.

to **recommend** VERB
conseiller
▢ What do you recommend? Qu'est-ce que
vous me conseillez?

to **reconsider** VERB
reconsidérer

record NOUN
▷ see also **record** VERB
1 le record (sport)
▢ the world record le record du monde
■ **in record time** en un temps record ▢ She
finished the job in record time. Elle a
terminé le travail en un temps record
2 le disque (recording)
▢ my favourite record mon disque préféré
■ **a criminal record** un casier judiciaire
▢ He's got a criminal record. Il a un casier
judiciaire.
■ **records** (of police, hospital) les archives
fem pl ▢ I'll check in the records. Je vais
vérifier dans les archives.
■ **There is no record of your booking.** Il
n'y a aucune trace de votre réservation.

to **record** VERB
▷ see also **record** NOUN
enregistrer (on film)
▢ They've just recorded their new album. Ils
viennent d'enregistrer leur nouveau disque.

recorded delivery NOUN
■ **to send something recorded delivery**
envoyer quelque chose en recommandé

recorder NOUN
la flûte à bec (instrument)
▢ She plays the recorder. Elle joue de la flûte
à bec.
■ **a video recorder** un magnétoscope

recording NOUN
l' enregistrement masc

record player NOUN
le tourne-disque

to **recover** VERB
se remettre
▢ He's recovering from a knee injury. Il se
remet d'une blessure au genou.

recovery NOUN
le rétablissement
■ **Best wishes for a speedy recovery!**
Meilleurs vœux de prompt rétablissement!

rectangle NOUN
le rectangle

rectangular ADJECTIVE
rectangulaire (FEM rectangulaire)

to **recycle** VERB
recycler

recycling NOUN
le recyclage

red ADJECTIVE
1 rouge (FEM rouge)
▢ a red rose une rose rouge ▢ red meat la
viande rouge
■ **a red light** (traffic light) un feu rouge ▢ to
go through a red light brûler un feu rouge
2 roux (FEM rousse) (hair)

r

□ Sam's got red hair. Sam a les cheveux roux.

Red Cross NOUN
la Croix-Rouge

redcurrant NOUN
la groseille

to **redecorate** VERB
1 retapisser *(with wallpaper)*
2 refaire les peintures *(with paint)*

red-haired ADJECTIVE
roux (FEM rousse)

red-handed ADJECTIVE
■ **to catch somebody red-handed** prendre quelqu'un la main dans le sac □ He was caught red-handed. Il a été pris la main dans le sac.

LANGUAGE TIP Word for word, this means 'He was caught with his hand in the bag'.

redhead NOUN
le roux
la rousse

to **redo** VERB
refaire

to **reduce** VERB
réduire
□ at a reduced price à prix réduit
■ **'reduce speed now'** 'ralentir'

reduction NOUN
la réduction
□ a 5% reduction une réduction de cinq pour cent
■ **'huge reductions!'** 'prix sacrifiés!'

redundancy NOUN
le licenciement
□ There were fifty redundancies. Il y a eu cinquante licenciements.
■ **his redundancy payment** ses indemnités de licenciement

redundant ADJECTIVE
■ **to be made redundant** être licencié □ He was made redundant yesterday. Il a été licencié hier.

red wine NOUN
le vin rouge

reed NOUN
le roseau (PL les roseaux) *(plant)*

reel NOUN
la bobine *(of thread)*

to **refer** VERB
■ **to refer to** faire allusion à □ What are you referring to? À quoi faites-vous allusion?

referee NOUN
l' arbitre *masc*

reference NOUN
1 l' allusion *fem*

□ He made no reference to the murder. Il n'a fait aucune allusion au meurtre.
2 les références *fem pl (for job application)*
□ Would you please give me a reference? Pouvez-vous me fournir des références?
■ **a reference book** un ouvrage de référence

to **refill** VERB
remplir à nouveau
□ He refilled my glass. Il a rempli mon verre à nouveau.

refinery NOUN
la raffinerie

to **reflect** VERB
refléter *(light, image)*

reflection NOUN
le reflet *(in mirror)*

reflex NOUN
le réflexe

reflexive ADJECTIVE
réfléchi (FEM réfléchie)
□ a reflexive verb un verbe réfléchi

refresher course NOUN
le cours de recyclage

refreshing ADJECTIVE
rafraîchissant (FEM rafraîchissante)

refreshments PL NOUN
les rafraîchissements *masc pl*

refrigerator NOUN
le réfrigérateur

to **refuel** VERB
se ravitailler en carburant
□ The plane stops in Boston to refuel. L'avion s'arrête à Boston pour se ravitailler en carburant.

refuge NOUN
le refuge

refugee NOUN
le réfugié
la réfugiée

refund NOUN
▷ *see also* **refund** VERB
le remboursement

to **refund** VERB
▷ *see also* **refund** NOUN
rembourser

refusal NOUN
le refus

to **refuse** VERB
▷ *see also* **refuse** NOUN
refuser

refuse NOUN
▷ *see also* **refuse** VERB
les ordures *fem pl*
■ **refuse collection** le ramassage des ordures

to **regain** VERB

■ **to regain consciousness** reprendre connaissance

regard NOUN
▷ *see also* **regard** VERB
■ **Give my regards to Alice.** Transmettez mon bon souvenir à Alice.
■ **Louis sends his regards.** Vous avez le bonjour de Louis.
■ **'with kind regards'** 'bien cordialement'

to **regard** VERB
▷ *see also* **regard** NOUN
■ **to regard something as** considérer quelque chose comme
■ **as regards ...** concernant ...

regarding PREPOSITION
relatif à (FEM relative à)
□ the laws regarding the export of animals les lois relatives à l'exportation des animaux
■ **Regarding John, ...** Quant à John, ...

regardless ADVERB
■ **regardless of the weather** peu importe le temps
■ **regardless of the consequences** peu importent les conséquences

regiment NOUN
le régiment

region NOUN
la région

regional ADJECTIVE
régional (FEM régionale, MASC PL régionaux)

register NOUN
▷ *see also* **register** VERB
le registre d'absences *(in school)*

to **register** VERB
▷ *see also* **register** NOUN
s'inscrire *(at school, college)*

registered ADJECTIVE
■ **a registered letter** une lettre recommandée

registration NOUN
1 l'appel *masc (roll call)*
2 le numéro d'immatriculation *(of car)*

regret NOUN
▷ *see also* **regret** VERB
le regret
■ **I've got no regrets.** Je ne regrette rien.

to **regret** VERB
▷ *see also* **regret** NOUN
regretter
□ Give me the money or you'll regret it! Donne-moi l'argent, sinon tu vas le regretter!
■ **to regret doing something** regretter d'avoir fait quelque chose □ I regret saying that. Je regrette d'avoir dit ça.

regular ADJECTIVE
1 régulier (FEM régulière)
□ at regular intervals à intervalles réguliers
□ a regular verb un verbe régulier
■ **to take regular exercise** faire régulièrement de l'exercice
2 normal (FEM normale, MASC PL normaux) *(average)*
□ a regular portion of fries une portion de frites normale

regularly ADVERB
régulièrement

regulation NOUN
le règlement

rehearsal NOUN
la répétition

to **rehearse** VERB
répéter

rein NOUN
la rêne
□ the reins les rênes

reindeer NOUN
le renne

to **reject** VERB
rejeter *(idea, suggestion)*
□ We rejected that idea straight away. Nous avons immédiatement rejeté cette idée.
■ **I applied but they rejected me.** J'ai posé ma candidature mais ils l'ont rejetée.

relapse NOUN
la rechute
□ to have a relapse faire une rechute

related ADJECTIVE
apparenté (FEM apparentée) *(people)*
□ We're related. Nous sommes apparentés.
■ **The two events were not related.** Il n'y avait aucun rapport entre les deux événements.

relation NOUN
1 le parent
la parente *(person)*
□ He's a distant relation. C'est un parent éloigné. □ my close relations mes parents proches
■ **my relations** ma famille
■ **I've got relations in London.** J'ai de la famille à Londres.
2 le rapport *(connection)*
□ It has no relation to reality. Cela n'a aucun rapport avec la réalité.
■ **in relation to** par rapport à

relationship NOUN
les relations *fem pl*
□ We have a good relationship. Nous avons de bonnes relations.
■ **I'm not in a relationship at the moment.** Je ne sors avec personne en ce moment.

relative NOUN

le parent
la parente
□ my close relatives mes proches parents
■ **all her relatives** toute sa famille
relatively ADVERB
relativement
to **relax** VERB
se détendre
□ I relax listening to music. Je me détends
en écoutant de la musique.
■ **Relax! Everything's fine.** Ne t'en fais
pas! Tout va bien.
relaxation NOUN
la détente
□ I don't have much time for relaxation. Je
n'ai pas beaucoup de moments de détente.
relaxed ADJECTIVE
détendu (FEM détendue)
relaxing ADJECTIVE
reposant (FEM reposante)
■ **I find cooking relaxing.** Cela me détend
de faire la cuisine.
relay NOUN
■ **a relay race** une course de relais
to **release** VERB
▷ see also **release** NOUN
1 libérer (prisoner)
2 divulguer (report, news)
3 sortir (CD, DVD)
release NOUN
▷ see also **release** VERB
la libération (from prison)
□ the release of the prisoners la libération
des prisoniers
■ **the band's latest release** le dernier
disque du groupe
relegated ADJECTIVE
déclassé (FEM déclassée) (sport)
relevant ADJECTIVE
approprié (FEM appropriée) (documents)
■ **That's not relevant.** Ça n'a aucun
rapport.
■ **to be relevant to something** être en
rapport avec quelque chose □ Education
should be relevant to real life.
L'enseignement devrait être en rapport avec
la réalité.
reliable ADJECTIVE
fiable (FEM fiable)
□ a reliable car une voiture fiable □ He's not
very reliable. Il n'est pas très fiable.
relief NOUN
le soulagement
□ That's a relief! Quel soulagement!
to **relieve** VERB
soulager
□ This injection will relieve the pain. Cette

piqûre va soulager la douleur.
relieved ADJECTIVE
soulagé (FEM soulagée)
□ I was relieved to hear ... J'ai été soulagé
d'apprendre ...
religion NOUN
la religion
□ What religion are you? Quelle est votre
religion?
religious ADJECTIVE
1 religieux (FEM religieuse)
□ my religious beliefs mes croyances
religieuses
2 croyant (FEM croyante)
□ I'm not religious. Je ne suis pas croyant.
reluctant ADJECTIVE
■ **to be reluctant to do something** être
peu disposé à faire quelque chose □ They
were reluctant to help us. Ils étaient peu
disposés à nous aider.
reluctantly ADVERB
à contrecœur
□ She reluctantly accepted. Elle a accepté à
contrecœur.
to **rely on** VERB
compter sur
□ I'm relying on you. Je compte sur toi.
to **remain** VERB
rester
■ **to remain silent** garder le silence
remaining ADJECTIVE
le reste de
□ the remaining ingredients le reste des
ingrédients
remains PL NOUN
les restes masc pl
□ the remains of the picnic les restes du
pique-nique □ human remains des restes
humains
■ **Roman remains** les vestiges romains
remake NOUN
le remake (of film)
remark NOUN
la remarque
remarkable ADJECTIVE
remarquable (FEM remarquable)
remarkably ADVERB
remarquablement
to **remarry** VERB
se remarier
□ She remarried three years ago. Elle s'est
remariée il y a trois ans.
remedy NOUN
le remède
□ a good remedy for a sore throat un bon
remède contre le mal de gorge
to **remember** VERB

se souvenir de
□ I can't remember his name. Je ne me souviens pas de son nom. □ I don't remember. Je ne m'en souviens pas.

○ **LANGUAGE TIP** In French you often say 'don't forget' instead of 'remember'. □ Remember your passport! N'oublie pas ton passeport! □ Remember to write your name on the form. N'oubliez pas d'écrire votre nom sur le formulaire.

Remembrance Day NOUN
le jour de l'Armistice *masc*
□ on Remembrance Day le jour de l'Armistice

to **remind** VERB
rappeler
□ It reminds me of Scotland. Cela me rappelle l'Écosse. □ I'll remind you tomorrow. Je te le rappellerai demain. □ Remind me to speak to Daniel. Rappelle-moi de parler à Daniel.

remorse NOUN
le remords
□ He showed no remorse. Il a manifesté aucun remords.

remote ADJECTIVE
isolé (FEM isolée)
□ a remote village un village isolé

remote control NOUN
la télécommande

remotely ADVERB
■ I'm not remotely interested. Je ne suis absolument pas intéressé.
■ Do you think it would be remotely possible? Pensez-vous que cela serait éventuellement possible?

removable ADJECTIVE
amovible (FEM amovible)

removal NOUN
le déménagement *(from house)*
■ a removal van un camion de déménagement

to **remove** VERB
1 enlever
□ Please remove your bag from my seat. Est-ce que vous pouvez enlever votre sac de mon siège?
2 faire partir *(stain)*
□ Did you remove the stain? Est-ce que tu as fait partir la tache?

rendezvous NOUN
le rendez-vous (PL les rendez-vous)

to **renew** VERB
renouveler *(passport, licence)*

renewable ADJECTIVE
renouvelable (FEM renouvelable) *(energy, resource)*

to **renovate** VERB
rénover
□ The building's been renovated. Le bâtiment a été rénové.

renowned ADJECTIVE
renommé (FEM renommée)

rent NOUN
▷ see also **rent** VERB
le loyer

to **rent** VERB
▷ see also **rent** NOUN
louer
□ We rented a car. Nous avons loué une voiture.

rental NOUN
la location
□ Car rental is included in the price. Le prix comprend la location d'une voiture.

rental car NOUN
la voiture de location

to **reorganize** VERB
réorganiser

rep NOUN *(= representative)*
le représentant
la représentante

repaid VERB ▷ see **repay**

to **repair** VERB
▷ see also **repair** NOUN
réparer
■ to get something repaired faire réparer quelque chose □ I got the washing machine repaired. J'ai fait réparer la machine à laver.

repair NOUN
▷ see also **repair** VERB
la réparation

to **repay** VERB
rembourser *(money)*

repayment NOUN
le remboursement

to **repeat** VERB
▷ see also **repeat** NOUN
répéter

repeat NOUN
▷ see also **repeat** VERB
la reprise
□ There are too many repeats on TV. Il y a trop de reprises à la télé.

repeatedly ADVERB
à plusieurs reprises

repellent NOUN
■ insect repellent l'insectifuge *masc*

repetitive ADJECTIVE
répétitif (FEM répétitive) *(movement, work)*

to **replace** VERB
remplacer

replay NOUN
▷ see also **replay** VERB

r

■ **There will be a replay on Friday.** Le match sera rejoué vendredi.

to **replay** VERB
▷ *see also* **replay** NOUN
rejouer *(match)*

replica NOUN
la réplique

reply NOUN
▷ *see also* **reply** VERB
la réponse

to **reply** VERB
▷ *see also* **reply** NOUN
répondre

report NOUN
▷ *see also* **report** VERB
1 le compte rendu (PL les comptes rendus) *(of event)*
2 le reportage *(news report)*
  □ a report in the paper un reportage dans le journal
3 le bulletin scolaire *(at school)*
  □ I got a good report this term. J'ai un bon bulletin scolaire ce trimestre.

to **report** VERB
▷ *see also* **report** NOUN
1 signaler
  □ I reported the theft to the police. J'ai signalé le vol au commissariat.
2 se présenter
  □ Report to reception when you arrive. Présentez-vous à la réception à votre arrivée.

reporter NOUN
le reporter
  □ I'd like to be a reporter. J'aimerais être reporter.

to **represent** VERB
représenter

representative ADJECTIVE
représentatif (FEM représentative)

reproduction NOUN
la reproduction

reptile NOUN
le reptile

republic NOUN
la république

repulsive ADJECTIVE
repoussant (FEM repoussante)

reputable ADJECTIVE
de bonne réputation

reputation NOUN
la réputation

request NOUN
▷ *see also* **request** VERB
la demande

to **request** VERB
▷ *see also* **request** NOUN

demander

to **require** VERB
exiger
  □ The job requires good computational skills. Cet emploi exige une bonne connaissance de l'informatique.
■ **What qualifications are required?** Quelles sont les diplômes requis?

requirement NOUN
la condition requise
  □ What are the requirements for the job? Quelles sont les conditions requises pour le poste?
■ **entry requirements** *(for university)* les critères d'entrée

to **rescue** VERB
▷ *see also* **rescue** NOUN
sauver

rescue NOUN
▷ *see also* **rescue** VERB
1 le sauvetage
  □ a rescue operation une opération de sauvetage
■ **a mountain rescue team** une équipe de sauvetage en montagne
2 le secours
  □ the rescue services les services de secours
■ **to come to somebody's rescue** venir au secours de quelqu'un □ He came to my rescue. Il est venu à mon secours.

research NOUN
1 la recherche *(experimental)*
  □ He's doing research. Il fait de la recherche.
2 les recherches *fem pl (theoretical)*
  □ She's doing some research in the library. Elle fait des recherches à la bibliothèque.

resemblance NOUN
la ressemblance

to **resent** VERB
être contrarié par
  □ I really resented your criticism. J'ai été vraiment contrarié par tes critiques.

resentful ADJECTIVE
plein de ressentiment (FEM pleine de ressentiment)
■ **to feel resentful towards somebody** en vouloir à quelqu'un

reservation NOUN
la réservation *(booking)*
  □ I've got a reservation for two nights. J'ai une réservation pour deux nuits. □ I'd like to make a reservation for this evening. J'aimerais faire une réservation pour ce soir.

reserve NOUN
▷ *see also* **reserve** VERB
1 la réserve *(place)*

□ a nature reserve une réserve naturelle

2 le remplaçant
la remplaçante *(person)*

□ I was reserve in the game last Saturday. J'étais remplaçant dans le match de samedi dernier.

to **reserve** VERB
 ▷ *see also* **reserve** NOUN
réserver

□ I'd like to reserve a table for tomorrow evening. J'aimerais réserver une table pour demain soir.

reserved ADJECTIVE
réservé (FEM réservée)

□ a reserved seat une place réservée □ He's quite reserved. Il est assez réservé.

reservoir NOUN
le réservoir

resident NOUN
le résident
la résidente

residential ADJECTIVE
résidentiel (FEM résidentielle)

□ a residential area un quartier résidentiel

to **resign** VERB
donner sa démission

resistance NOUN

■ He was in the resistance. Il faisait de la résistance.

■ the French Resistance la Résistance

to **resit** VERB
repasser

□ I'm resitting the exam in December. Je vais repasser l'examen en décembre.

resolution NOUN
la résolution

■ Have you made any New Year's resolutions? Tu as pris de bonnes résolutions pour l'année nouvelle?

resort NOUN
la station balnéaire *(at seaside)*

□ It's a resort on the Costa del Sol. C'est une station balnéaire sur la Costa del Sol.

■ a ski resort une station de ski

■ as a last resort en dernier recours

resource NOUN
la ressource

respect NOUN
 ▷ *see also* **respect** VERB
le respect

to **respect** VERB
 ▷ *see also* **respect** NOUN
respecter

respectable ADJECTIVE

1 respectable (FEM respectable)

2 correct (FEM correcte) *(standard, marks)*

respectively ADVERB
respectivement

responsibility NOUN
la responsabilité

responsible ADJECTIVE

1 responsable (FEM responsable) *(in charge)*

■ to be responsible for something être responsable de quelque chose □ He's responsible for booking the tickets. Il est responsable de la réservation des billets.

■ It's a responsible job. C'est un poste à responsabilités.

2 sérieux (FEM sérieuse) *(mature)*

□ You should be more responsible. Tu devrais être un peu plus sérieux.

rest NOUN
 ▷ *see also* **rest** VERB

1 le repos *(relaxation)*

□ five minutes' rest cinq minutes de repos

■ to have a rest se reposer □ We stopped to have a rest. Nous nous sommes arrêtés pour nous reposer.

2 le reste *(remainder)*

□ I'll do the rest. Je ferai le reste. □ the rest of the money le reste de l'argent

■ the rest of them les autres □ The rest of them went swimming. Les autres sont allés nager.

to **rest** VERB
 ▷ *see also* **rest** NOUN

1 se reposer *(relax)*

□ She's resting in her room. Elle se repose dans sa chambre.

2 ménager *(not overstrain)*

□ He has to rest his knee. Il doit ménager son genou.

3 appuyer *(lean)*

□ I rested my bike against the window. J'ai appuyé mon vélo contre la fenêtre.

restaurant NOUN
le restaurant

□ We don't often go to restaurants. Nous n'allons pas souvent au restaurant.

■ a restaurant car un wagon-restaurant

restful ADJECTIVE
reposant (FEM reposante)

restless ADJECTIVE
agité (FEM agitée)

restoration NOUN
la restauration

to **restore** VERB
restaurer *(building, picture)*

to **restrict** VERB
limiter

rest room NOUN (US)
les toilettes *fem pl*

result NOUN
 ▷ *see also* **result** VERB

le résultat
□ my exam results mes résultats d'examen
□ What was the result? — One-nil. Quel a été le résultat? — Un à zéro.

to **result** VERB
▷ see also **result** NOUN
■ **to result in** occasioner □ Many road accidents result in head injuries. De nombreux accidents de la route occasionnent des blessures à la tête.

to **resume** VERB
reprendre
□ They've resumed work. Ils ont repris le travail.

> LANGUAGE TIP Be careful not to translate **to resume** by résumer.

résumé NOUN (US)
le curriculum vitae

to **retire** VERB
prendre sa retraite
□ He retired last year. Il a pris sa retraite l'an dernier.

retired ADJECTIVE
retraité (FEM retraitée)
□ She's retired. Elle est retraitée.
■ **a retired teacher** un professeur à la retraite

retirement NOUN
la retraite

to **retrace** VERB
■ **to retrace one's steps** revenir sur ses pas □ I retraced my steps. Je suis revenu sur mes pas.

return NOUN
▷ see also **return** VERB
1 le retour
□ after our return à notre retour
■ **the return journey** le voyage de retour
■ **a return match** un match retour
2 l' aller retour masc (ticket)
□ A return to Avignon, please. Un aller retour pour Avignon, s'il vous plaît.
■ **in return** en échange □ ... and I help her in return ... et je l'aide en échange
■ **in return for** en échange de
■ **Many happy returns!** Bon anniversaire!

to **return** VERB
▷ see also **return** NOUN
1 revenir (come back)
□ I've just returned from holiday. Je viens de revenir de vacances.
■ **to return home** rentrer à la maison
2 retourner (go back)
□ He returned to France the following year. Il est retourné en France l'année suivante.
3 rendre (give back)
□ She borrows my things and doesn't return

them. Elle m'emprunte mes affaires et ne me les rend pas.

reunion NOUN
la réunion

to **reuse** VERB
réutiliser

to **reveal** VERB
révéler

revenge NOUN
la vengeance
□ in revenge par vengeance
■ **to take revenge** se venger □ They planned to take revenge on him. Ils voulaient se venger de lui.

to **reverse** VERB
▷ see also **reverse** ADJECTIVE
faire marche arrière (car)
□ He reversed without looking. Il a fait marche arrière sans regarder.
■ **to reverse the charges** (telephone) appeler en PCV □ I'd like reverse the charges to Britain. Je voudrais appeler la Grande-Bretagne en PCV.

reverse ADJECTIVE
▷ see also **reverse** VERB
inverse (FEM inverse)
□ in reverse order dans l'ordre inverse
■ **in reverse gear** en marche arrière

review NOUN
la critique (of book, film, programme)
□ The book had good reviews. Ce livre a eu de bonnes critiques.

to **revise** VERB
réviser
□ I haven't started revising yet. Je n'ai pas encore commencé à réviser.
■ **I've revised my opinion.** J'ai changé d'opinion.

revision NOUN
les révisions fem pl
□ Have you done a lot of revision? Est-ce que tu as fait beaucoup de révisions?

to **revive** VERB
ranimer
□ The nurses tried to revive him. Les infirmières ont essayé de le ranimer.

revolting ADJECTIVE
dégoûtant (FEM dégoûtante)

revolution NOUN
la révolution
■ **the French Revolution** la Révolution française

revolutionary ADJECTIVE
révolutionnaire (FEM révolutionnaire)

revolver NOUN
le revolver

reward NOUN

la récompense

rewarding ADJECTIVE
gratifiant (FEM gratifiante)
□ a rewarding job un travail gratifiant

to **rewind** VERB
rembobiner
□ to rewind a cassette rembobiner une cassette

rheumatism NOUN
le rhumatisme

Rhine NOUN
le Rhin

rhinoceros NOUN
le rhinocéros

Rhone NOUN
le Rhône

rhubarb NOUN
la rhubarbe
□ a rhubarb tart une tarte à la rhubarbe

rhythm NOUN
le rythme

rib NOUN
la côte

ribbon NOUN
le ruban

rice NOUN
le riz
■ **rice pudding** le riz au lait

rich ADJECTIVE
riche (FEM riche)
■ **the rich** les riches *masc pl*

to **rid** VERB
■ **to get rid of** se débarrasser de □ I want to get rid of some old clothes. Je veux me débarrasser de vieux vêtements.

ridden VERB ▷ *see* **ride**

ride NOUN
▷ *see also* **ride** VERB
■ **to go for a ride 1** *(on horse)* monter à cheval **2** *(on bike)* faire un tour en vélo
□ We went for a bike ride. Nous sommes allés faire un tour en vélo.
■ **It's a short bus ride to the town centre.** Ce n'est pas loin du centre-ville en bus.

to **ride** VERB
▷ *see also* **ride** NOUN
monter à cheval *(on horse)*
□ I'm learning to ride. J'apprends à monter à cheval.
■ **to ride a bike** faire du vélo □ Can you ride a bike? Tu sais faire du vélo?

rider NOUN
1 le cavalier
la cavalière *(on horse)*
□ She's a good rider. C'est une bonne cavalière.
2 le/la cycliste *(on bike)*

ridiculous ADJECTIVE
ridicule (FEM ridicule)
□ Don't be ridiculous! Ne sois pas ridicule!

riding NOUN
l' équitation *fem*
■ **to go riding** faire de l'équitation
■ **a riding school** une école d'équitation

rifle NOUN
le fusil
□ a hunting rifle un fusil de chasse

rig NOUN
■ **an oil rig** une plate-forme pétrolière

right ADJECTIVE, ADVERB
▷ *see also* **right** NOUN

> **LANGUAGE TIP** There are several ways of translating 'right'. Scan the examples to find one that is similar to what you want to say.

1 bon (FEM bonne) *(factually correct, suitable)*
□ the right answer la bonne réponse □ It isn't the right size. Ce n'est pas la bonne taille. □ We're on the right train. Nous sommes dans le bon train.
■ **Is this the right road for Arles?** Est-ce que c'est bien la route pour aller à Arles?
2 correctement *(correctly)*
□ Am I pronouncing it right? Est-ce que je prononce ça correctement?
■ **to be right 1** *(person)* avoir raison □ You were right! Tu avais raison! **2** *(statement, opinion)* être vrai □ That's right! C'est vrai!
3 juste (FEM juste) *(accurate)*
□ Do you have the right time? Est-ce que vous avez l'heure juste?
4 bien *(morally correct)*
□ It's not right to behave like that. Ce n'est pas bien d'agir comme ça.
■ **I think you did the right thing.** Je pense que tu as bien fait.
5 droit (FEM droite) *(not left)*
□ my right hand ma main droite
6 à droite *(turn, look)*
□ Turn right at the traffic lights. Tournez à droite aux prochains feux.
■ **Right! Let's get started.** Bon! On commence.
■ **right away** tout de suite □ I'll do it right away. Je vais le faire tout de suite.

right NOUN
▷ *see also* **right** ADJECTIVE
1 le droit
■ **You've got no right to do that.** Vous n'avez pas le droit de faire ça.
2 la droite *(not left)*
■ **on the right** à droite □ Remember to drive on the right. N'oubliez pas de conduire à droite.

r

■ **right of way** la priorité ▫ It was our right of way. Nous avions la priorité.
right-hand ADJECTIVE
■ **the right-hand side** la droite ▫ It's on the right-hand side. C'est à droite.
right-handed ADJECTIVE
droitier (FEM droitière)
rightly ADVERB
avec raison
▫ She rightly decided not to go. Elle a décidé, avec raison, de ne pas y aller.
■ **if I remember rightly** si je me souviens bien
rim NOUN
la monture
▫ glasses with wire rims des lunettes avec une monture métallique
ring NOUN
▷ see also **ring** VERB
1 l' anneau masc (PL les anneaux)
▫ a gold ring un anneau en or
2 la bague (with stones)
▫ a diamond ring une bague de diamants
■ **a wedding ring** une alliance
3 le cercle (circle)
▫ to stand in a ring se mettre en cercle
4 le coup de sonnette (of bell)
▫ I was woken by a ring at the door. J'ai été réveillé par un coup de sonnette.
■ **to give somebody a ring** appeler quelqu'un ▫ I'll give you a ring this evening. Je t'appellerai ce soir.
to ring VERB
▷ see also **ring** NOUN
1 téléphoner
▫ Your mother rang this morning. Ta mère a téléphoné ce matin.
■ **to ring somebody** appeler quelqu'un
▫ I'll ring you tomorrow morning. Je t'appellerai demain matin.
2 sonner
▫ The phone's ringing. Le téléphone sonne.
■ **to ring the bell** (doorbell) sonner à la porte ▫ I rang the bell three times. J'ai sonné trois fois à la porte.
to ring back VERB
rappeler
▫ I'll ring back later. Je rappellerai plus tard.
to ring up VERB
■ **to ring somebody up** donner un coup de fil à quelqu'un
ring binder NOUN
le classeur
ring road NOUN
1 la rocade (ordinary road)
2 le périphérique (motorway)
ringtone NOUN

la sonnerie
rink NOUN
1 la patinoire (for ice-skating)
2 la piste (for roller-skating)
to rinse VERB
rincer
riot NOUN
▷ see also **riot** VERB
l' émeute fem
to riot VERB
▷ see also **riot** NOUN
faire une émeute
to rip VERB
1 déchirer
▫ I've ripped my jeans. J'ai déchiré mon jean.
2 se déchirer
▫ My skirt's ripped. Ma jupe s'est déchirée.
to rip off VERB
arnaquer
▫ The hotel ripped us off. L'hôtel nous a arnaqués.
to rip up VERB
déchirer
▫ He read the note and then ripped it up. Il a lu le mot, puis l'a déchiré.
ripe ADJECTIVE
mûr (FEM mûre)
rip-off NOUN
■ **It's a rip-off!** C'est de l'arnaque! (informal)
rise NOUN
▷ see also **rise** VERB
1 la hausse (in prices, temperature)
▫ a sudden rise in temperature une hausse subite de température
2 l' augmentation fem (pay rise)
to rise VERB
▷ see also **rise** NOUN
1 augmenter (increase)
▫ Prices are rising. Les prix augmentent.
2 se lever
▫ The sun rises early in June. Le soleil se lève tôt en juin.
riser NOUN
■ **to be an early riser** être matinal
risk NOUN
▷ see also **risk** VERB
le risque
■ **to take risks** prendre des risques
■ **It's at your own risk.** C'est à vos risques et périls.
to risk VERB
▷ see also **risk** NOUN
risquer
▫ You risk getting a fine. Vous risquez de recevoir une amende.

■ **I wouldn't risk it if I were you.** À votre place, je ne prendrais pas ce risque.

risky ADJECTIVE
risqué (FEM risquée)

rival NOUN
▷ *see also* **rival** ADJECTIVE
le rival (PL les rivaux)
la rivale

rival ADJECTIVE
▷ *see also* **rival** NOUN
1 rival (FEM rivale)
□ a rival gang une bande rivale
2 concurrent (FEM concurrente)
□ a rival company une société concurrente

rivalry NOUN
la rivalité *(between towns, schools)*

river NOUN
1 la rivière
□ The river runs alongside the canal. La rivière longe le canal.
2 le fleuve *(major)*
□ the rivers of France les fleuves de France
■ **the river Seine** la Seine

Riviera NOUN
■ **the French Riviera** la Côte d'Azur
■ **the Italian Riviera** la Riviera italienne

road NOUN
1 la route
□ There's a lot of traffic on the roads. Il y a beaucoup de circulation sur les routes.
2 la rue *(street)*
□ They live across the road. Ils habitent de l'autre côté de la rue.

road map NOUN
la carte routière

road rage NOUN
l' agressivité au volant *fem*

road sign NOUN
le panneau de signalisation (PL les panneaux de signalisation)

roadworks PL NOUN
les travaux *masc pl*

roast ADJECTIVE
rôti (FEM rôtie)
□ roast chicken le poulet rôti □ roast potatoes les pommes de terre rôties
■ **roast pork** le rôti de porc
■ **roast beef** le rôti de bœuf

to **rob** VERB
■ **to rob somebody** voler quelqu'un □ I've been robbed. On m'a volé.
■ **to rob somebody of something** voler quelque chose à quelqu'un □ He was robbed of his wallet. On lui a volé son portefeuille.
■ **to rob a bank** dévaliser une banque

robber NOUN

le voleur
■ **a bank-robber** un cambrioleur de banques

robbery NOUN
le vol
■ **a bank robbery** un hold-up
■ **armed robbery** le vol à main armée

robin NOUN
le rouge-gorge

robot NOUN
le robot

rock NOUN
▷ *see also* **rock** VERB
1 la roche *(substance)*
□ They tunnelled through the rock. Ils ont creusé un tunnel dans la roche.
2 le rocher *(boulder)*
□ I sat on a rock. Je me suis assis sur un rocher.
3 la pierre *(stone)*
□ The crowd started to throw rocks. La foule s'est mise à lancer des pierres.
4 le rock *(music)*
□ a rock concert un concert de rock □ He's a rock star. C'est une rock star.
5 le sucre d'orge *(sweet)*
□ a stick of rock un bâton de sucre d'orge
■ **rock and roll** le rock'n'roll

to **rock** VERB
▷ *see also* **rock** NOUN
ébranler
□ The explosion rocked the building. L'explosion a ébranlé le bâtiment.

rockery NOUN
la rocaille

rocket NOUN
la fusée *(firework, spacecraft)*

rocking chair NOUN
le rocking-chair

rocking horse NOUN
le cheval à bascule (PL les chevaux à bascule)

rod NOUN
la canne à pêche *(for fishing)*

rode VERB ▷ *see* **ride**

role NOUN
le rôle

role play NOUN
le jeu de rôle (PL les jeux de rôles)
□ to do a role play faire un jeu de rôle

roll NOUN
▷ *see also* **roll** VERB
1 le rouleau (PL les rouleaux)
□ a roll of tape un rouleau de ruban adhésif
□ a toilet roll un rouleau de papier hygiénique
2 le petit pain *(bread)*

to **roll** VERB

▷ *see also* **roll** NOUN
rouler
■ **to roll out the pastry** abaisser la pâte
roll call NOUN
l' appel *masc*
roller NOUN
le rouleau (PL les rouleaux)
Rollerblade® NOUN
le roller
□ a pair of Rollerblades une paire de rollers
rollercoaster NOUN
les montagnes russes *fem pl*
roller skates PL NOUN
les patins à roulettes *masc pl*
roller-skating NOUN
le patin à roulettes
■ **to go roller-skating** faire du patin à
roulettes
rolling pin NOUN
le rouleau à pâtisserie
Roman ADJECTIVE, NOUN
romain (FEM romaine) *(ancient)*
□ a Roman villa une villa romaine □ the
Roman empire l'empire romain
■ **the Romans** les Romains
Roman Catholic NOUN
le/la catholique
□ He's a Roman Catholic. Il est catholique.
romance NOUN
1 les romans d'amour *masc pl (novels)*
□ I read a lot of romance. Je lis beaucoup de
romans d'amour.
2 le charme *(glamour)*
□ the romance of Paris le charme de Paris
■ **a holiday romance** une idylle de
vacances
Romania NOUN
la Roumanie
■ **in Romania** en Roumanie
Romanian ADJECTIVE
roumain (FEM roumaine)
romantic ADJECTIVE
romantique (FEM romantique)
roof NOUN
le toit
roof rack NOUN
la galerie
room NOUN
1 la pièce
□ the biggest room in the house la plus
grande pièce de la maison
2 la chambre *(bedroom)*
□ She's in her room. Elle est dans sa
chambre.
■ **a single room** une chambre pour une
personne
■ **a double room** une chambre pour deux

personnes
3 la salle *(in school)*
□ the music room la salle de musique
4 la place *(space)*
□ There's no room for that box. Il n'y a pas
de place pour cette boîte.
roommate NOUN
le/la camarade de chambre
root NOUN
la racine
to root around VERB
fouiller
□ She started rooting around in her
handbag. Elle a commencé à fouiller dans
son sac à main.
to root out VERB
traquer
□ They are determined to root out
corruption. Ils sont déterminés à traquer la
corruption.
rope NOUN
la corde
to rope in VERB
enrôler
□ I was roped in to help with the
refreshments. J'ai été enrôlé pour servir les
rafraîchissements.
rose VERB ▷ *see* **rise**
rose NOUN
la rose *(flower)*
to rot VERB
pourrir
rotten ADJECTIVE
pourri (FEM pourrie) *(decayed)*
□ a rotten apple une pomme pourrie
■ **rotten weather** un temps pourri
■ **That's a rotten thing to do.** Ce n'est
vraiment pas gentil.
■ **to feel rotten** être mal fichu *(informal)*
rough ADJECTIVE
1 rêche (FEM rêche) *(surface)*
□ My hands are rough. J'ai les mains rêches.
2 violent (FEM violente) *(game)*
□ Rugby's a rough sport. Le rugby est un
sport violent.
3 difficile (FEM difficile) *(place)*
□ It's a rough area. C'est un quartier
difficile.
4 houleux (FEM houleuse) *(water)*
□ The sea was rough. La mer était houleuse.
5 approximatif (FEM approximative)
□ I've got a rough idea. J'en ai une idée
approximative.
■ **to feel rough** ne pas être dans son
assiette □ I feel rough. Je ne suis pas dans
mon assiette.
roughly ADVERB

à peu près

□ It weighs roughly 20 kilos. Ça pèse à peu près vingt kilos.

round ADJECTIVE, ADVERB, PREPOSITION

▷ *see also* **round** NOUN

1 rond (FEM ronde)

□ a round table une table ronde

2 autour de *(around)*

□ We were sitting round the table. Nous étions assis autour de la table. □ She wore a scarf round her neck. Elle portait une écharpe autour du cou.

■ **It's just round the corner.** *(very near)* C'est tout près.

■ **to go round to somebody's house** aller chez quelqu'un □ I went round to my friend's house. Je suis allé chez mon ami.

■ **to have a look round** faire un tour □ We're going to have a look round. Nous allons faire un tour.

■ **to go round a museum** visiter un musée

■ **round here** près d'ici □ Is there a chemist's round here? Est-ce qu'il y a une pharmacie près d'ici?

■ **He lives round here.** Il habite dans les parages.

■ **all round** partout □ There were vineyards all round. Il y avait des vignobles partout.

■ **all year round** toute l'année

■ **round about** *(roughly)* environ □ It costs round about £100. Cela coûte environ cent livres. □ round about 8 o'clock à huit heures environ

round NOUN

▷ *see also* **round** ADJECTIVE

1 la manche *(of tournament)*

2 le round *(of boxing match)*

■ **a round of golf** une partie de golf

■ **a round of drinks** une tournée □ He bought a round of drinks. Il a offert une tournée.

to round off VERB

terminer

□ They rounded off the meal with liqueurs. Ils ont terminé le repas par des liqueurs.

to round up VERB

1 rassembler *(sheep, cattle, suspects)*

2 arrondir *(figure)*

roundabout NOUN

1 le rond-point (PL les ronds-points) *(at junction)*

2 le manège *(at funfair)*

rounders NOUN

■ **Rounders is a bit like baseball.** Le 'rounders' ressemble un peu au base-balll.

☼ **DID YOU KNOW...?**

Rounders is not played in France.

round trip NOUN (US)

l' aller et retour *masc*

■ **a round-trip ticket** un billet de aller-retour

route NOUN

1 l' itinéraire *masc*

□ We're planning our route. Nous établissons notre itinéraire.

2 le parcours *(of bus)*

routine NOUN

■ **my daily routine** mes occupations quotidiennes

row NOUN

▷ *see also* **row** VERB

1 la rangée

□ a row of houses une rangée de maisons

2 le rang *(of seats)*

□ Our seats are in the front row. Nos places se trouvent au premier rang.

■ **five times in a row** cinq fois d'affilée

3 le vacarme *(noise)*

□ What's that terrible row? Qu'est-ce que c'est que ce vacarme?

4 la dispute *(quarrel)*

■ **to have a row** se disputer □ They've had a row. Ils se sont disputés.

to row VERB

▷ *see also* **row** NOUN

1 ramer

□ We took turns to row. Nous avons ramé à tour de rôle.

2 faire de l'aviron *(as sport)*

rowboat NOUN (US)

le bateau à rames

rowing NOUN

l' aviron *masc (sport)*

□ My hobby is rowing. Je fais de l'aviron.

■ **a rowing boat** un bateau à rames

royal ADJECTIVE

royal (FEM royale, MASC PL royaux)

■ **the royal family** la famille royale

to rub VERB

1 frotter *(stain)*

2 se frotter *(part of body)*

□ Don't rub your eyes! Ne te frotte pas les yeux!

■ **to rub something out** effacer quelque chose

rubber NOUN

1 le caoutchouc

□ rubber soles des semelles en caoutchouc

2 la gomme *(eraser)*

□ Can I borrow your rubber? Je peux emprunter ta gomme?

■ **a rubber band** un élastique

rubbish NOUN

▷ *see also* **rubbish** ADJECTIVE

1 les ordures *fem pl (refuse)*
  □ When do they collect the rubbish? Quand est-ce qu'ils ramassent les ordures?
2 la camelote *(junk)*
  □ They sell a lot of rubbish at the market. Ils vendent beaucoup de camelote au marché.
3 les bêtises *fem pl (nonsense)*
  □ Don't talk rubbish! Ne dis pas de bêtises!
  ■ **That's a load of rubbish!** C'est vraiment n'importe quoi! *(informal)*
  ■ **a rubbish bin** une poubelle
  ■ **a rubbish dump** une décharge
rubbish ADJECTIVE
  ▷ *see also* **rubbish** NOUN
  nul (FEM nulle)
  □ They're a rubbish team! Cette équipe est nulle!
rucksack NOUN
  le sac à dos
rude ADJECTIVE
1 impoli (FEM impolie) *(impolite)*
  □ It's rude to interrupt. C'est impoli de couper la parole aux gens.
2 grossier (FEM grossière) *(offensive)*
  □ a rude joke une plaisanterie grossière
  □ He was very rude to me. Il a été très grossier avec moi.
  ■ **a rude word** un gros mot
rug NOUN
1 le tapis
  □ a Persian rug un tapis persan
2 la couverture *(blanket)*
  □ a tartan rug une couverture écossaise
rugby NOUN
  le rugby
  □ I play rugby. Je joue au rugby.
ruin NOUN
  ▷ *see also* **ruin** VERB
  la ruine
  □ the ruins of the castle les ruines du château
  ■ **in ruins** en ruine
to **ruin** VERB
  ▷ *see also* **ruin** NOUN
1 abîmer
  □ You'll ruin your shoes. Tu vas abîmer tes chaussures.
2 gâcher
  □ It ruined our holiday. Ça a gâché nos vacances.
3 ruiner *(financially)*
  □ That one mistake ruined the business. Cette une erreur a ruiné l'entreprise.
rule NOUN
1 la règle
  □ the rules of grammar les règles de grammaire

  ■ **as a rule** en règle générale
2 le règlement *(regulation)*
  □ It's against the rules. C'est contre le règlement.
to **rule out** VERB
  écarter *(possibility)*
  □ I'm not ruling anything out. Je n'écarte aucune possibilité.
ruler NOUN
  la règle
  □ Can I borrow your ruler? Je peux emprunter ta règle?
rum NOUN
  le rhum
rumour (US **rumor**) NOUN
  la rumeur
  □ It's just a rumour. Ce n'est qu'une rumeur.
rump steak NOUN
  le romsteak
run NOUN
  ▷ *see also* **run** VERB
  le point *(in cricket)*
  □ to score a run marquer un point
  ■ **to go for a run** courir □ I go for a run every morning. Je cours tous les matins.
  ■ **I did a ten-kilometre run.** J'ai couru dix kilomètres.
  ■ **on the run** en fuite □ The criminals are still on the run. Les criminels sont toujours en fuite.
  ■ **in the long run** à long terme
to **run** VERB
  ▷ *see also* **run** NOUN
1 courir
  □ I ran five kilometres. J'ai couru cinq kilomètres.
  ■ **to run a marathon** participer à un marathon
2 diriger *(manage)*
  □ He runs a large company. Il dirige une grosse société.
3 organiser *(organize)*
  □ They run music courses in the holidays. Ils organisent des cours de musique pendant les vacances.
4 couler *(water)*
  □ Don't leave the tap running. Ne laisse pas couler le robinet.
  ■ **to run a bath** faire couler un bain
5 conduire *(by car)*
  □ I can run you to the station. Je peux te conduire à la gare.
to **run away** VERB
  s'enfuir
  □ They ran away before the police came. Ils se sont enfuis avant l'arrivée de la police.

to **run out** VERB
- **Time is running out.** Il ne reste plus beaucoup de temps.
- **to run out of something** se trouver à court de quelque chose □ We ran out of money. Nous nous sommes trouvés à court d'argent.

to **run over** VERB
- **to run somebody over** écraser quelqu'un
- **to get run over** se faire écraser □ Be careful, or you'll get run over! Fais attention, sinon tu vas te faire écraser!

rung VERB ▷ see **ring**

runner NOUN
le coureur
la coureuse

runner beans PL NOUN
les haricots verts *masc pl*

runner-up NOUN
le second
la seconde

running NOUN
la course
□ Running is my favourite sport. La course est mon sport préféré.

run-up NOUN
- **in the run-up to Christmas** pendant la période de préparation de Noël

runway NOUN
la piste

rural ADJECTIVE
rural (FEM rurale, MASC PL ruraux)

rush NOUN
▷ see also **rush** VERB
la hâte

- **in a rush** à la hâte

to **rush** VERB
▷ see also **rush** NOUN
1 se précipiter *(run)*
□ Everyone rushed outside. Tout le monde s'est précipité dehors.
2 se dépêcher *(hurry)*
□ There's no need to rush. Ce n'est pas la peine de se dépêcher.

rush hour NOUN
les heures de pointe *fem pl*
□ in the rush hour aux heures de pointe

rusk NOUN
la biscotte

Russia NOUN
la Russie

- **in Russia** en Russie
- **to Russia** en Russie

Russian NOUN
▷ see also **Russian** ADJECTIVE
1 le/la Russe *(person)*
2 le russe *(language)*

Russian ADJECTIVE
▷ see also **Russian** NOUN
russe (FEM russe)

rust NOUN
la rouille

rusty ADJECTIVE
rouillé (FEM rouillée)
□ a rusty bike un vélo rouillé □ My French is very rusty. Mon français est très rouillé.

ruthless ADJECTIVE
sans pitié

rye NOUN
le seigle

- **rye bread** le pain de seigle

r

Ss

Sabbath NOUN
1 le dimanche (*Christian*)
2 le sabbat (*Jewish*)

sack NOUN
▷ *see also* **sack** VERB
le sac
■ **to get the sack** être mis à la porte

to **sack** VERB
▷ *see also* **sack** NOUN
■ **to sack somebody** mettre quelqu'un à la porte □ He was sacked. On l'a mis à la porte.

sacred ADJECTIVE
sacré (FEM sacrée)

sacrifice NOUN
le sacrifice

sad ADJECTIVE
triste (FEM triste)

saddle NOUN
la selle

saddlebag NOUN
la sacoche

sadly ADVERB
1 tristement
□ 'She's gone,' he said sadly. 'Elle est partie,' a-t-il dit tristement.
2 malheureusement (*unfortunately*)
□ Sadly, it was too late. Malheureusement, il était trop tard.

safe NOUN
▷ *see also* **safe** ADJECTIVE
le coffre-fort (PL les coffres-forts)
□ She put the money in the safe. Elle a mis l'argent dans le coffre-fort.

safe ADJECTIVE
▷ *see also* **safe** NOUN
1 sans danger
□ Don't worry, it's perfectly safe. Ne vous inquiétez pas, c'est absolument sans danger.
■ **Is it safe?** Ça n'est pas dangereux?
2 sûr (FEM sûre) (*machine, ladder*)
□ This car isn't safe. Cette voiture n'est pas sûre.
3 hors de danger (*out of danger*)

□ You're safe now. Vous êtes hors de danger maintenant.
■ **to feel safe** se sentir en sécurité
■ **safe sex** le sexe sans risques

safety NOUN
la sécurité
■ **a safety belt** une ceinture de sécurité
■ **a safety pin** une épingle de nourrice

Sagittarius NOUN
le/la Sagittaire
□ I'm Sagittarius. Je suis Sagittaire.

Sahara NOUN
■ **the Sahara Desert** le Sahara

said VERB ▷ *see* **say**

sail NOUN
▷ *see also* **sail** VERB
la voile

to **sail** VERB
▷ *see also* **sail** NOUN
1 naviguer (*travel*)
2 prendre la mer (*set off*)
□ The boat sails at eight o'clock. Le bateau prend la mer à huit heures.

sailing NOUN
la voile
□ His hobby is sailing. Son passe-temps, c'est la voile.
■ **to go sailing** faire de la voile
■ **a sailing boat** un voilier
■ **a sailing ship** un grand voilier

sailor NOUN
le marin
□ He's a sailor. Il est marin.

saint NOUN
le saint
la sainte

sake NOUN
■ **for the sake of** dans l'intérêt de

salad NOUN
la salade
■ **salad cream** la mayonnaise
■ **salad dressing** la vinaigrette

salami NOUN
le salami

salary NOUN

le salaire

sale NOUN
les soldes *masc pl (reductions)*
□ There's a sale on at Harrods. Ce sont les soldes chez Harrods.
■ **on sale** en vente
■ **The factory's for sale.** L'usine est en vente.
■ **'for sale'** 'à vendre'

sales assistant NOUN
le vendeur
la vendeuse
□ She's a sales assistant. Elle est vendeuse.

salesman NOUN
1 le représentant *(sales rep)*
□ He's a salesman. Il est représentant.
■ **a double-glazing salesman** un représentant en doubles vitrages
2 le vendeur *(sales assistant)*

sales rep NOUN
le représentant
la représentante

saleswoman NOUN
1 la représentante *(sales rep)*
□ She's a saleswoman. Elle est représentante.
2 la vendeuse *(sales assistant)*

salmon NOUN
le saumon

salon NOUN
le salon
□ a hair salon un salon de coiffure □ a beauty salon un salon de beauté

saloon car NOUN
la berline

salt NOUN
le sel

salty ADJECTIVE
salé *(FEM salée)*

to **salute** VERB
saluer

Salvation Army NOUN
l' armée du Salut *fem*

same ADJECTIVE
même *(FEM même)*
□ the same model le même modèle □ at the same time en même temps
■ **They're exactly the same.** Ils sont exactement pareils.
■ **It's not the same.** Ça n'est pas pareil.

sample NOUN
l' échantillon *masc*

sand NOUN
le sable

sandal NOUN
la sandale
□ a pair of sandals une paire de sandales

sand castle NOUN
le château de sable *(PL les châteaux de sable)*

sandwich NOUN
le sandwich
□ a cheese sandwich un sandwich au fromage

sandwich course NOUN
le cours avec stage pratique

sang VERB ▷ see sing

sanitary towel NOUN
la serviette hygiénique

sank VERB ▷ see sink

Santa Claus NOUN
le père Noël

sarcastic ADJECTIVE
sarcastique *(FEM sarcastique)*

sardine NOUN
la sardine

sat VERB ▷ see sit

satchel NOUN
le cartable

satellite NOUN
le satellite
□ satellite television la télévision par satellite
■ **a satellite dish** une antenne parabolique

satisfactory ADJECTIVE
satisfaisant *(FEM satisfaisante)*

satisfied ADJECTIVE
satisfait *(FEM satisfaite)*

sat nav NOUN
le GPS

Saturday NOUN
le samedi
□ on Saturday samedi □ on Saturdays le samedi □ every Saturday tous les samedis □ last Saturday samedi dernier □ next Saturday samedi prochain
■ **I've got a Saturday job.** Je travaille le samedi.

sauce NOUN
la sauce

saucepan NOUN
la casserole

saucer NOUN
la soucoupe

Saudi Arabia NOUN
l' Arabie Saoudite *fem*
■ **in Saudi Arabia** en Arabie Saoudite

sauna NOUN
le sauna

sausage NOUN
1 la saucisse
2 le saucisson *(salami)*
■ **a sausage roll** un friand à la saucisse

to **save** VERB

1 mettre de côté *(save up money)*
□ I've saved £50 already. J'ai déjà mis cinquante livres de côté.

2 économiser *(spend less)*
□ I saved £20 by waiting for the sales. J'ai économisé vingt livres en attendant les soldes.

■ **to save time** gagner du temps □ We took a taxi to save time. Nous avons pris un taxi pour gagner du temps. □ It saved us time. Ça nous a fait gagner du temps.

3 sauver *(rescue)*
□ Luckily, all the passengers were saved. Heureusement, tous les passagers ont été sauvés.

4 sauvegarder *(on computer)*
□ Don't forget to save your work regularly. N'oublie pas de sauvegarder ton travail régulièrement.

to **save up** VERB
mettre de l'argent de côté
□ I'm saving up for a new bike. Je mets de l'argent de côté pour un nouveau vélo.

savings PL NOUN
les économies *fem pl*
□ She spent all her savings on a computer. Elle a dépensé toutes ses économies en achetant un ordinateur.

savoury ADJECTIVE
salé (FEM salée)
□ Is it sweet or savoury? C'est sucré ou salé?

saw VERB ▷ see **see**

saw NOUN
la scie

sax NOUN
le saxo *(informal)*
□ I play the sax. Je joue du saxo.

saxophone NOUN
le saxophone
□ I play the saxophone. Je joue du saxophone.

to **say** VERB
dire
□ What did he say? Qu'est-ce qu'il a dit?
□ Did you hear what she said? Tu as entendu ce qu'elle a dit?

■ **Could you say that again?** Pourriez-vous répéter s'il vous plaît?

■ **That goes without saying.** Cela va sans dire.

saying NOUN
le dicton
□ It's just a saying. C'est juste un dicton.

scale NOUN
1 l' échelle *fem (of map)*
□ a large-scale map une carte à grande échelle

2 l' ampleur *fem (size, extent)*
□ a disaster on a massive scale un désastre d'une ampleur incroyable

3 la gamme *(in music)*

scales PL NOUN
la balance *sing (in kitchen, shop)*
■ **bathroom scales** le pèse-personne *sing*

scampi PL NOUN
les scampi *masc pl*

scandal NOUN
1 le scandale *(outrage)*
□ It caused a scandal. Ça a fait scandale.

2 les ragots *masc pl (gossip)*
□ It's just scandal. Ce ne sont que des ragots.

Scandinavia NOUN
la Scandinavie
■ **in Scandinavia** en Scandinavie

Scandinavian ADJECTIVE
scandinave (FEM scandinave)

scar NOUN
la cicatrice

scarce ADJECTIVE
limité (FEM limitée)
□ scarce resources des ressources limitées
■ **Jobs are scarce these days.** Il y a peu de travail ces temps-ci.

scarcely ADVERB
à peine
□ I scarcely knew him. Je le connaissais à peine.

scare NOUN
▷ see also **scare** VERB
la panique
■ **a bomb scare** une alerte à la bombe

to **scare** VERB
▷ see also **scare** NOUN
■ **to scare somebody** faire peur à quelqu'un □ He scares me. Il me fait peur.

scarecrow NOUN
l' épouvantail *masc*

scared ADJECTIVE
■ **to be scared** avoir peur □ I was scared stiff. J'avais terriblement peur.
■ **to be scared of** avoir peur de □ Are you scared of him? Est-ce que tu as peur de lui?

scarf NOUN
1 l' écharpe *fem (long)*
2 le foulard *(square)*

scary ADJECTIVE
effrayant (FEM effrayante)
□ It was really scary. C'était vraiment effrayant.

scene NOUN
1 les lieux *masc pl (place)*
□ The police were soon on the scene. La police est vite arrivée sur les lieux. □ the

scene of the crime les lieux du crime

2 le spectacle *(event, sight)*

□ It was an amazing scene. C'était un spectacle étonnant.

■ **to make a scene** faire une scène

scenery NOUN
le paysage *(landscape)*

scent NOUN
le parfum *(perfume)*

schedule NOUN
le programme

□ a busy schedule un programme chargé

■ **on schedule** comme prévu

■ **to be behind schedule** avoir du retard

scheduled flight NOUN
le vol régulier

scheme NOUN

1 le truc *(idea)*

□ a crazy scheme he dreamed up un truc farfelu qu'il a inventé

2 le projet *(project)*

□ a council road-widening scheme un projet municipal d'élargissement des routes

scholarship NOUN
la bourse

school NOUN
l' école *fem*

■ **to go to school** aller à l'école

schoolbag NOUN
le cartable

schoolbook NOUN
le livre scolaire

schoolboy NOUN
l' écolier *masc*

schoolchildren NOUN
les écoliers *masc pl*

schoolgirl NOUN
l' écolière *fem*

school uniform NOUN
l' uniforme scolaire *masc*

science NOUN
la science

science fiction NOUN
la science-fiction

scientific ADJECTIVE
scientifique (FEM scientifique)

scientist NOUN
le chercheur
la chercheuse

■ **He trained as a scientist.** Il a une formation scientifique.

scissors PL NOUN
les ciseaux *masc pl*

□ a pair of scissors une paire de ciseaux

to **scoff** VERB
bouffer *(eat)*

□ My brother scoffed all the sandwiches.

Mon frere a boutté tous les sandwichs.

scone NOUN
le scone

scooter NOUN

1 le scooter

2 la trottinette *(child's toy)*

score NOUN

▷ *see also* **score** VERB

le score

□ The score was three nil. Le score était trois à zéro.

to **score** VERB

▷ *see also* **score** NOUN

1 marquer *(goal, point)*

□ to score a goal marquer un but

■ **to score 6 out of 10** obtenir un score de six sur dix

2 compter les points *(keep score)*

□ Who's going to score? Qui va compter les points?

Scorpio NOUN
le Scorpion

□ I'm Scorpio. Je suis Scorpion.

Scot NOUN
l' Écossais *masc*
l' Écossaise *fem*

Scotch tape® NOUN (US)
le scotch®

Scotland NOUN
l' Écosse *fem*

■ **in Scotland** en Écosse

■ **to Scotland** en Écosse

■ **I'm from Scotland.** Je suis écossais.

Scots ADJECTIVE
écossais (FEM écossaise)

□ a Scots accent un accent écossais

Scotsman NOUN
l' Écossais *masc*

Scotswoman NOUN
l' Écossaise *fem*

Scottish ADJECTIVE
écossais (FEM écossaise)

□ a Scottish accent un accent écossais

scout NOUN
le scout

□ I'm in the Scouts. Je suis scout.

scrambled eggs PL NOUN
les œufs brouillés *masc pl*

scrap NOUN

▷ *see also* **scrap** VERB

1 le bout

□ a scrap of paper un bout de papier

2 la bagarre *(fight)*

■ **scrap iron** la ferraille

to **scrap** VERB

▷ *see also* **scrap** NOUN

abandonner *(plan)*

□ The idea was scrapped. L'idée a été abandonnée.

scrapbook NOUN
l' album *masc*

to **scratch** VERB
▷ *see also* **scratch** NOUN
se gratter

□ Stop scratching! Arrête de te gratter!

scratch NOUN
▷ *see also* **scratch** VERB
l' égratignure *fem (on skin)*

■ to start from scratch partir de zéro

scream NOUN
▷ *see also* **scream** VERB
le hurlement

to **scream** VERB
▷ *see also* **scream** NOUN
hurler

screen NOUN
l' écran *masc*

screen-saver NOUN
l' économiseur d'écran *masc*

screw NOUN
la vis

screwdriver NOUN
le tournevis

to **scribble** VERB
griffonner

to **scrub** VERB
récurer

□ to scrub a pan récurer une casserole

sculpture NOUN
la sculpture

sea NOUN
la mer

seafood NOUN
les fruits de mer *masc pl*

□ I don't like seafood. Je n'aime pas les fruits de mer.

seagull NOUN
la mouette

seal NOUN
▷ *see also* **seal** VERB
1 le phoque *(animal)*
2 le cachet *(on letter)*

to **seal** VERB
▷ *see also* **seal** NOUN
1 sceller *(document)*
2 coller *(letter)*

seaman NOUN
le marin

to **search** VERB
▷ *see also* **search** NOUN
fouiller

□ They searched the woods for her. Ils ont fouillé les bois pour la trouver.

■ to search for something chercher

quelque chose □ He searched for evidence. Il cherchait des preuves.

search NOUN
▷ *see also* **search** VERB
la fouille

search engine NOUN
le moteur de recherche

search party NOUN
l' expédition de secours *fem*

seashore NOUN
le bord de la mer

□ on the seashore au bord de la mer

seasick ADJECTIVE
■ to be seasick avoir le mal de mer

seaside NOUN
le bord de la mer

□ at the seaside au bord de la mer

season NOUN
la saison

□ What's your favourite season? Quelle est ta saison préférée?

■ out of season hors saison □ It's cheaper to go there out of season. C'est moins cher d'y aller hors saison.

■ during the holiday season en période de vacances

■ a season ticket une carte d'abonnement

seat NOUN
le siège

seat belt NOUN
la ceinture de sécurité

sea water NOUN
l' eau de mer *fem*

seaweed NOUN
les algues *fem pl*

second ADJECTIVE
▷ *see also* **second** NOUN
deuxième (FEM deuxième)

□ on the second page à la deuxième page

■ to come second *(in race)* arriver deuxième

■ the second of March le deux mars

second NOUN
▷ *see also* **second** ADJECTIVE
la seconde

□ It'll only take a second. Ça va prendre juste une seconde.

secondary school NOUN
1 le collège
2 le lycée

> **DID YOU KNOW...?**
> In France pupils go to a **collège** between the ages of 11 and 15, and then to a **lycée** until the age of 18.

second-class ADJECTIVE, ADVERB
1 de seconde classe *(ticket, compartment)*
■ to travel second class voyager en

seconde

2 à tarif réduit *(stamp, letter)*

□ to send something second class envoyer quelque chose à tarif réduit

secondhand ADJECTIVE

d'occasion

□ a secondhand car une voiture d'occasion

secondly ADVERB

deuxièmement

■ **firstly ... secondly ...** d'abord ... ensuite ... □ Firstly, it's too expensive. Secondly, it wouldn't work anyway. D'abord, c'est trop cher. Ensuite, ça ne marcherait pas de toute façon.

secret ADJECTIVE

▷ *see also* **secret** NOUN

secret (FEM secrète)

□ a secret mission une mission secrète

secret NOUN

▷ *see also* **secret** ADJECTIVE

le secret

□ It's a secret. C'est un secret. □ Can you keep a secret? Tu sais garder un secret?

■ **in secret** en secret

secretary NOUN

le/la secrétaire

□ She's a secretary. Elle est secrétaire.

secretly NOUN

secrètement

section NOUN

la section

security NOUN

la sécurité

□ a feeling of security un sentiment de sécurité □ a campaign to improve airport security une campagne visant à améliorer la sécurité dans les aéroports

■ **job security** la sécurité de l'emploi

security guard NOUN

1 le garde chargé de la sécurité *(on guard)*

2 un convoyeur de fonds *(transporting money)*

sedan NOUN (US)

la berline

to **see** VERB

voir

□ I can't see. Je n'y vois rien. □ I saw him yesterday. Je l'ai vu hier. □ Have you seen him? Est-ce que tu l'as vu?

■ **See you!** Salut!

■ **See you soon!** À bientôt!

■ **to see to something** s'occuper de quelque chose □ Can you see to the kids, please? Tu peux t'occuper des enfants, s'il te plaît?

seed NOUN

la graine

□ sunflower seeds des graines de tournesol

to **seek** VERB

chercher

■ **to seek help** chercher de l'aide

to **seem** VERB

avoir l'air

□ She seems tired. Elle a l'air fatiguée. □ The shop seemed to be closed. Le magasin avait l'air d'être fermé.

■ **That seems like a good idea.** Ce n'est pas une mauvaise idée.

■ **It seems that ...** Il paraît que ... □ It seems she's getting married. Il paraît qu'elle va se marier.

■ **There seems to be a problem.** Il semble y avoir un problème.

seen VERB ▷ *see* **see**

seesaw NOUN

le tapecul

see-through ADJECTIVE

transparent (FEM transparente)

seldom ADVERB

rarement

to **select** VERB

sélectionner

selection NOUN

la sélection

self-assured ADJECTIVE

sûr de soi (FEM sûre de soi)

□ He's very self-assured. Il est très sûr de lui.

self-catering ADJECTIVE

■ **a self-catering apartment** un appartement de vacances

self-centred (US **self-centered**) ADJECTIVE

égocentrique (FEM égocentrique)

self-confidence NOUN

la confiance en soi

□ He hasn't got much self-confidence. Il n'a pas très confiance en lui.

self-conscious ADJECTIVE

■ **to be self-conscious 1** *(embarrassed)* être mal à l'aise □ She was really self-conscious at first. Elle était vraiment mal à l'aise au début. **2** *(shy)* manquer d'assurance □ He's always been rather self-conscious. Il a toujours manqué un peu d'assurance.

self-contained ADJECTIVE

■ **a self-contained flat** un appartement indépendant

self-control NOUN

le sang-froid

self-defence (US **self-defense**) NOUN

l' autodéfense *fem*

□ self-defence classes les cours d'autodéfense

■ **She killed him in self-defence.** Elle l'a

S

English-French

tué en légitime défense.

self-discipline NOUN
l' autodiscipline *fem*

self-employed ADJECTIVE
■ **to be self-employed** travailler à son compte □ He's self-employed. Il travaille à son compte.
■ **the self-employed** les travailleurs indépendants

selfish ADJECTIVE
égoïste (FEM égoïste)
□ Don't be so selfish. Ne sois pas si égoïste.

self-respect NOUN
l' amour-propre *masc*

self-service ADJECTIVE
■ It's self-service. *(café, shop)* C'est un self-service.
■ **a self-service restaurant** un restaurant self-service

to **sell** VERB
vendre
□ He sold it to me. Il me l'a vendu.

to **sell off** VERB
liquider

to **sell out** VERB
se vendre
□ The tickets sold out in three hours. Les billets se sont tous vendus en trois heures.
□ The show didn't quite sell out. Ce spectacle ne s'est pas très bien vendu.
■ **The tickets are all sold out.** Il ne reste plus de billets.

sell-by date NOUN
la date limite de vente

selling price NOUN
le prix de vente

Sellotape® NOUN
le scotch®

semi NOUN
la maison jumelée
□ We live in a semi. Nous habitons dans une maison jumelée.

semicircle NOUN
le demi-cercle

semicolon NOUN
le point-virgule

semi-detached house NOUN
la maison jumelée
□ We live in a semi-detached house. Nous habitons dans une maison jumelée.

semi-final NOUN
la demi-finale

semi-skimmed milk NOUN
le lait demi-écrémé

to **send** VERB
envoyer
□ She sent me a birthday card. Elle m'a

envoyé une carte d'anniversaire.

to **send back** VERB
renvoyer

to **send off** VERB
1 envoyer *(goods, letter)*
2 renvoyer du terrain *(in sports match)*
□ He was sent off. On l'a renvoyé du terrain.
■ **to send off for something 1** *(free)* se faire envoyer quelque chose □ I've sent off for a brochure. Je me suis fait envoyer une brochure. **2** *(paid for)* commander quelque chose par correspondance □ She sent off for a book. Elle a commandé un livre par correspondance.

to **send out** VERB
envoyer
■ **to send out for** commander par téléphone □ Shall we send out for a pizza? Et si on commandait une pizza par téléphone?

sender NOUN
l' expéditeur *masc*
l' expéditrice *fem*

senior ADJECTIVE
haut placé (FEM haut placée)
■ **senior management** les cadres supérieurs
■ **senior school** le lycée
■ **senior pupils** les grandes classes

senior citizen NOUN
la personne du troisième âge

sensational ADJECTIVE
sensationnel (FEM sensationnelle)

sense NOUN
1 le bon sens *(wisdom)*
□ Use your common sense! Un peu de bon sens, voyons!
■ **It makes sense.** C'est logique.
■ **It doesn't make sense.** Ça n'a pas de sens.
2 le sens *(faculty)*
□ the five senses les cinq sens
■ **the sense of touch** le toucher
■ **the sense of smell** l'odorat *masc*
■ **the sixth sense** le sixième sens
■ **sense of humour** le sens de l'humour
□ He's got no sense of humour. Il n'a aucun sens de l'humour.

senseless ADJECTIVE
insensé (FEM insensée)

sensible ADJECTIVE
raisonnable (FEM raisonnable)
□ Be sensible! Sois raisonnable!

LANGUAGE TIP Be careful not to translate **sensible** by the French word **sensible**.

sensitive ADJECTIVE

S

sensible (FEM sensible)

□ She's very sensitive. Elle est très sensible.

sensuous ADJECTIVE
sensuel (FEM sensuelle)

sent VERB ▷ *see* **send**

sentence NOUN
▷ *see also* **sentence** VERB

1 la phrase

□ What does this sentence mean? Que veut dire cette phrase?

2 la condamnation (judgment)

3 la peine (punishment)

□ the death sentence la peine de mort

■ **He got a life sentence.** Il a été condamné à la réclusion à perpétuité.

to **sentence** VERB
▷ *see also* **sentence** NOUN
condamner

■ **to sentence somebody to life imprisonment** condamner quelqu'un à la réclusion à perpétuité

■ **to sentence somebody to death** condamner quelqu'un à mort

sentimental ADJECTIVE
sentimental (FEM sentimentale, MASC PL sentimentaux)

separate ADJECTIVE
▷ *see also* **separate** VERB
séparé (FEM séparée)

□ I wrote it on a separate sheet. Je l'ai écrit sur une feuille séparée.

■ **The children have separate rooms.** Les enfants ont chacun leur chambre.

■ **on separate occasions** à différentes reprises

to **separate** VERB
▷ *see also* **separate** ADJECTIVE

1 séparer

2 se séparer (married couple)

□ My parents are separated. Mes parents sont séparés.

separately ADVERB
séparément

separation NOUN
la séparation

September NOUN
septembre masc

■ **in September** en septembre

sequel NOUN
la suite (book, film)

sequence NOUN

1 l' ordre masc

■ **in sequence** par ordre

■ **a sequence of events** une succession d'événements

2 la séquence (in film)

sergeant NOUN

1 le sergent (army)

2 le brigadier (police)

serial NOUN
le feuilleton

series NOUN

1 la série

□ a TV series une série télévisée

2 la suite (of numbers)

serious ADJECTIVE

1 sérieux (FEM sérieuse)

□ You look very serious. Tu as l'air sérieux.

■ **Are you serious?** Sérieusement?

2 grave (FEM grave) (illness, mistake)

seriously ADVERB
sérieusement

□ No, but seriously ... Non, mais sérieusement ...

■ **to take somebody seriously** prendre quelqu'un au sérieux

■ **seriously injured** gravement blessé

■ **Seriously?** Vraiment?

sermon NOUN
le sermon

servant NOUN
le/la domestique

to **serve** VERB
▷ *see also* **serve** NOUN

1 servir

□ Dinner is served. Le dîner est servi. □ It's Murray's turn to serve. C'est à Murray de servir.

2 purger (prison sentence)

■ **to serve time** être en prison

■ **It serves you right.** C'est bien fait pour toi.

serve NOUN
▷ *see also* **serve** VERB
le service (tennis)

■ **It's your serve.** C'est à toi de servir.

server NOUN
le serveur (computing)

to **service** VERB
▷ *see also* **service** NOUN
réviser (car, washing machine)

service NOUN
▷ *see also* **service** VERB

1 le service

□ Service is included. Le service est compris.

2 la révision (of car)

3 l' office masc (church service)

■ **the Fire Service** les sapeurs-pompiers

■ **the armed services** les forces armées

service area NOUN
l' aire de service fem

service charge NOUN
le service

□ There's no service charge. Le service est

compris.

serviceman NOUN
le militaire
□ He's a serviceman. Il est militaire.

service station NOUN
la station-service (PL les stations-service)

servicewoman NOUN
la femme soldat
□ She's a servicewoman. Elle est femme soldat.

serviette NOUN
la serviette

session NOUN
la séance

set NOUN
▷ see also **set** VERB
1 le jeu (PL les jeux)
□ a set of keys un jeu de clés □ a chess set un jeu d'échecs
■ a train set un train électrique
2 le set (in tennis)

to **set** VERB
▷ see also **set** NOUN
1 mettre à sonner (alarm clock)
□ I set the alarm for 7 o'clock. J'ai mis le réveil à sonner pour sept heures.
2 établir (record)
□ The world record was set last year. Le record du monde a été établi l'année dernière.
3 se coucher (sun)
□ The sun was setting. Le soleil se couchait.
■ The film is set in Morocco. L'action du film se déroule au Maroc.
■ to set sail prendre la mer
■ to set the table mettre le couvert

to **set off** VERB
partir
□ We set off for London at 9 o'clock. Nous sommes partis pour Londres à neuf heures.

to **set out** VERB
partir
□ We set out for London at 9 o'clock. Nous sommes partis pour Londres à neuf heures.

settee NOUN
le canapé

to **settle** VERB
1 résoudre (problem)
2 régler (argument, account)
■ to settle on something opter pour quelque chose

to **settle down** VERB (calm down)
se calmer
■ Settle down! Du calme!

to **settle in** VERB
s'installer

seven NUMBER

sept
□ She's seven. Elle a sept ans.

seventeen NUMBER
dix-sept
□ He's seventeen. Il a dix-sept ans.

seventeenth ADJECTIVE
dix-septième (FEM dix-septième)
□ her seventeenth birthday son dix-septième anniversaire □ the seventeenth floor le dix-septième étage
■ the seventeenth of August le dix-sept août

seventh ADJECTIVE
septième (FEM septième)
□ the seventh floor le septième étage
■ the seventh of August le sept août

seventy NUMBER
soixante-dix

several ADJECTIVE, PRONOUN
plusieurs
□ several schools plusieurs écoles
■ several of them plusieurs □ I've seen several of them. J'en ai vu plusieurs.

to **sew** VERB
coudre

to **sew up** VERB
recoudre (tear)

sewing NOUN
la couture
□ I like sewing. J'aime faire de la couture.
■ a sewing machine une machine à coudre

sewn VERB ▷ see **sew**

sex NOUN
le sexe
■ to have sex with somebody coucher avec quelqu'un
■ sex education l'éducation sexuelle fem

sexism NOUN
le sexisme

sexist ADJECTIVE
sexiste (FEM sexiste)

sexual ADJECTIVE
sexuel (FEM sexuelle)
□ sexual discrimination la discrimination sexuelle □ sexual harassment le harcèlement sexuel

sexuality NOUN
la sexualité

sexy ADJECTIVE
sexy (FEM+PL sexy)

shabby ADJECTIVE
miteux (FEM miteuse)

shade NOUN
1 l' ombre fem
■ in the shade à l'ombre □ It was 35 degrees in the shade. Il faisait trente-cinq à

l'ombre.

2 la nuance *(colour)*
□ a shade of blue une nuance de bleu

shadow NOUN
l' ombre *fem*

to shake VERB
1 secouer
□ She shook the rug. Elle a secoué le tapis.
2 trembler *(tremble)*
□ He was shaking with cold. Il tremblait de froid.

■ **to shake one's head** *(in refusal)* faire non de la tête

■ **to shake hands with somebody** serrer la main à quelqu'un □ They shook hands. Ils se sont serré la main.

> **DID YOU KNOW...?**
> Boys shake hands with their friends when they arrive at school in the morning.

shaken ADJECTIVE
secoué *(FEM secouée)*
□ I was feeling a bit shaken. J'étais un peu secoué.

shaky ADJECTIVE
tremblant *(FEM tremblante) (hand, voice)*

shall VERB
■ **Shall I shut the window?** Vous voulez que je ferme la fenêtre?

■ **Shall we ask him to come with us?** Si on lui demandait de venir avec nous?

shallow ADJECTIVE
peu profond *(FEM peu profonde) (water, pool)*

shambles NOUN
la pagaille
□ It's a complete shambles. C'est la pagaille complète.

shame NOUN
la honte
□ The shame of it! Quelle honte!

■ **What a shame!** Quel dommage!

■ **It's a shame that ...** C'est dommage que ... □ It's a shame he isn't here. C'est dommage qu'il ne soit pas ici.

> **LANGUAGE TIP c'est dommage que** has to be followed by a verb in the subjunctive.

shampoo NOUN
le shampooing
□ a bottle of shampoo une bouteille de shampooing

shandy NOUN
le panaché

shan't = shall not

shape NOUN
la forme

share NOUN

▷ *see also* **share** VERB

1 l' action *fem (in company)*
□ They've got shares in the company. Ils ont des actions dans la société.

2 la part
□ Everybody pays their share. Tout le monde paie sa part.

to share VERB

▷ *see also* **share** NOUN

partager
□ to share a room with somebody partager une chambre avec quelqu'un

to share out VERB
distribuer
□ They shared the sweets out among the children. Ils ont distribué les bonbons aux enfants.

shark NOUN
le requin

sharp ADJECTIVE
1 tranchant *(FEM tranchante) (razor, knife)*
2 pointu *(FEM pointue) (spike, point)*
3 intelligent *(FEM intelligente) (clever)*
□ She's very sharp. Elle est très intelligente.

■ **at two o'clock sharp** à deux heures pile

to shave VERB
se raser *(have a shave)*

■ **to shave one's legs** se raser les jambes

shaver NOUN
■ **an electric shaver** un rasoir électrique

shaving cream NOUN
la crème à raser

shaving foam NOUN
la mousse à raser

she PRONOUN
elle
□ She's very nice. Elle est très gentille.

shed NOUN
la remise

she'd = she had, she would

sheep NOUN
le mouton

sheepdog NOUN
le chien de berger

sheer ADJECTIVE
pur *(FEM pure)*
□ It's sheer greed. C'est de l'avidité pure.

sheet NOUN
le drap *(on bed)*

■ **a sheet of paper** une feuille de papier

shelf NOUN
1 l' étagère *fem (in house)*
2 le rayon *(in shop)*

shell NOUN
1 le coquillage *(on beach)*
2 la coquille *(of egg, nut)*
3 l' obus *masc (explosive)*

she'll = she will

shellfish NOUN
les fruits de mer *masc pl*

shell suit NOUN
le survêtement

shelter NOUN
■ **to take shelter** se mettre à l'abri
■ **a bus shelter** un arrêt d'autobus

shelves PL NOUN ▷ *see* **shelf**

shepherd NOUN
le berger

sheriff NOUN
le shérif

sherry NOUN
le xérès

she's = she is, she has

Shetland Islands PL NOUN
les îles Shetland *fem pl*

shield NOUN
le bouclier

shift NOUN
▷ *see also* **shift** VERB
le service
□ His shift starts at 8 o'clock. Il prend son service à huit heures. □ the night shift le service de nuit
■ **to do shift work** faire les trois-huit

to shift VERB
▷ *see also* **shift** NOUN
déplacer *(move)*
□ I couldn't shift the wardrobe on my own. Je n'ai pas pu déplacer l'armoire tout seul.
■ **Shift yourself!** Pousse-toi de là! *(informal)*

shifty ADJECTIVE
1 louche (FEM louche) *(person)*
□ He looked shifty. Il avait l'air louche.
2 fuyant (FEM fuyante) *(eyes)*

shin NOUN
le tibia

to shine VERB
briller
□ The sun was shining. Le soleil brillait.

shiny ADJECTIVE
brillant (FEM brillante)

ship NOUN
1 le bateau (PL les bateaux)
2 le navire *(warship)*

shipbuilding NOUN
la construction navale

shipwreck NOUN
le naufrage

shipwrecked ADJECTIVE
■ **to be shipwrecked** faire naufrage

shipyard NOUN
le chantier naval

shirt NOUN

1 la chemise *(man's)*
2 le chemisier *(woman's)*

to shiver VERB
frissonner

shock NOUN
▷ *see also* **shock** VERB
le choc
■ **to get a shock 1** *(surprise)* avoir un choc
2 *(electric)* recevoir une décharge
■ **an electric shock** une décharge

to shock VERB
▷ *see also* **shock** NOUN
1 bouleverser *(upset)*
□ They were shocked by the tragedy. Ils ont été bouleversés par la tragédie.
2 choquer *(scandalize)*
□ I was rather shocked by her attitude. J'ai été assez choqué par son attitude. □ He'll be shocked if you say that. Tu vas le choquer si tu dis ça.

shocking ADJECTIVE
choquant (FEM choquante)
□ It's shocking! C'est choquant!
■ **a shocking waste** un gaspillage épouvantable

shoe NOUN
la chaussure

shoelace NOUN
le lacet

shoe polish NOUN
le cirage

shoe shop NOUN
le magasin de chaussures

shone VERB ▷ *see* **shine**

shook VERB ▷ *see* **shake**

to shoot VERB
1 abattre *(kill)*
□ He was shot by a sniper. Il a été abattu par un franc-tireur.
2 fusiller *(execute)*
□ He was shot at dawn. Il a été fusillé à l'aube.
3 tirer *(gun)*
□ Don't shoot! Ne tirez pas!
■ **to shoot at somebody** tirer sur quelqu'un
■ **He shot himself with a revolver.** *(dead)* Il s'est suicidé d'un coup de revolver.
■ **He was shot in the leg.** *(wounded)* Il a reçu une balle dans la jambe.
■ **to shoot an arrow** envoyer une flèche
4 tourner *(film)*
□ The film was shot in Prague. Le film a été tourné à Prague.
5 shooter *(in football)*

shooting NOUN
1 les coups de feu *masc pl*

□ They heard shooting. Ils ont entendu des coups de feu.

■ **a shooting** une fusillade □ a drive-by shooting une fusillade au volant d'une voiture

2 la chasse *(hunting)*

□ to go shooting aller à la chasse

shop NOUN
le magasin

□ a sports shop un magasin de sports

shop assistant NOUN
le vendeur
la vendeuse

□ She's a shop assistant. Elle est vendeuse.

shopkeeper NOUN
le commerçant
la commerçante

□ He's a shopkeeper. Il est commerçant.

shoplifting NOUN
le vol à l'étalage

shopping NOUN
les courses *fem pl (purchases)*

□ Can you get the shopping from the car? Tu peux aller chercher les courses dans la voiture?

■ **I love shopping.** J'adore faire du shopping.

■ **to go shopping 1** *(for food)* faire des courses **2** *(for pleasure)* faire du shopping

■ **a shopping bag** un sac à provisions

■ **a shopping centre** un centre commercial

shop window NOUN
la vitrine

shore NOUN
le rivage

■ **on shore** à terre

short ADJECTIVE
1 court *(FEM courte)*

□ a short skirt une jupe courte □ short hair les cheveux courts

■ **too short** trop court □ It was a great holiday, but too short. C'étaient des vacances super, mais trop courtes.

2 petit *(FEM petite) (person, period of time)*

□ She's quite short. Elle est assez petite.
□ a short break une petite pause □ a short walk une petite promenade

■ **to be short of something** être à court de quelque chose □ I'm short of money. Je suis à court d'argent.

■ **at short notice** au dernier moment

■ **In short, the answer's no.** Bref, la réponse est non.

shortage NOUN
la pénurie

□ a water shortage une pénurie d'eau

short cut NOUN

le raccourci

□ I took a short cut. J'ai pris un raccourci.

shorthand NOUN
la sténo

shortly ADVERB
bientôt

shorts PL NOUN
le short *sing*

■ **a pair of shorts** un short

short-sighted ADJECTIVE
myope *(FEM myope)*

short story NOUN
la nouvelle

shot VERB ▷ see **shoot**

shot NOUN
1 le coup de feu *(gunshot)*
2 la photo *(photo)*

□ a shot of Edinburgh Castle une photo du château d'Édimbourg

3 le vaccin *(vaccination)*

shotgun NOUN
le fusil de chasse

should VERB

LANGUAGE TIP When 'should' means 'ought to', use **devoir**.

devoir

□ You should take more exercise. Vous devriez faire plus d'exercice. □ He should be there by now. Il devrait être arrivé maintenant. □ That shouldn't be too hard. Ça ne devrait pas être trop difficile.

■ **should have** avoir dû □ I should have told you before. J'aurais dû te le dire avant.

LANGUAGE TIP When 'should' means 'would', use the conditional tense.

■ I should go if I were you. Si j'étais vous, j'irais.

■ I should be so lucky! Ça serait trop beau!

shoulder NOUN
l' épaule *fem*

■ **a shoulder bag** un sac à bandoulière

shouldn't = should not

to **shout** VERB
▷ see also **shout** NOUN
crier

□ Don't shout! Ne criez pas! □ 'Go away!' he shouted. 'Allez-vous-en!' a-t-il crié.

shout NOUN
▷ see also **shout** VERB
le cri

shovel NOUN
la pelle

show NOUN
▷ see also **show** VERB
1 le spectacle *(performance)*
2 l' émission *fem (programme)*
3 le salon *(exhibition)*

to show VERB
▷ *see also* **show** NOUN
1 montrer
■ **to show somebody something** montrer quelque chose à quelqu'un □ Have I shown you my new trainers? Je t'ai montré mes nouvelles baskets?
2 faire preuve de
□ She showed great courage. Elle a fait preuve de beaucoup de courage.
■ **It shows.** Ça se voit. □ I've never been riding before. — It shows. Je n'ai jamais fait de cheval. — Ça se voit.

to show off VERB
frimer *(informal)*

to show up VERB
se pointer *(turn up)*
□ He showed up late as usual. Il s'est pointé en retard comme d'habitude.

shower NOUN
1 la douche
■ **to have a shower** prendre une douche
2 l' averse *fem (of rain)*

showerproof ADJECTIVE
imperméabilisé (FEM imperméabilisée)

showing NOUN
la projection *(of film)*

shown VERB ▷ *see* **show**

show-off NOUN
le frimeur
la frimeuse

shrank VERB ▷ *see* **shrink**

to shriek VERB
hurler

shrimps PL NOUN
les crevettes *fem pl*

to shrink VERB
rétrécir *(clothes, fabric)*

Shrove Tuesday NOUN
le mardi gras

to shrug VERB
■ **to shrug one's shoulders** hausser les épaules

shrunk VERB ▷ *see* **shrink**

to shudder VERB
frissonner

to shuffle VERB
■ **to shuffle the cards** battre les cartes

to shut VERB
fermer
□ What time do you shut? À quelle heure est-ce que vous fermez? □ What time do the shops shut? À quelle heure est-ce que les magasins ferment?

to shut down VERB
fermer
□ The cinema shut down last year. Le cinéma a fermé l'année dernière.

to shut up VERB
1 fermer *(close)*
2 se taire *(be quiet)*
□ Shut up! Tais-toi!

shutters NOUN
les volets *masc pl*

shuttle NOUN
la navette

shuttlecock NOUN
le volant *(badminton)*

shy ADJECTIVE
timide (FEM timide)

Sicily NOUN
la Sicile
■ **in Sicily** en Sicile
■ **to Sicily** en Sicile

sick ADJECTIVE
1 malade (FEM malade) *(ill)*
□ He was sick for four days. Il a été malade pendant quatre jours.
2 de mauvais goût *(joke, humour)*
□ That's really sick! C'est vraiment de mauvais goût!
■ **to be sick** *(vomit)* vomir
■ **I feel sick.** J'ai envie de vomir.
■ **to be sick of something** en avoir assez de quelque chose □ I'm sick of your jokes. J'en ai assez de tes plaisanteries.

sickening ADJECTIVE
écœurant (FEM écœurante)

sick leave NOUN
le congé de maladie

sickness NOUN
la maladie

sick note NOUN
1 le mot d'absence *(from parents)*
2 le certificat médical *(from doctor)*

sick pay NOUN
l' indemnité de maladie *fem*

side NOUN
1 le côté *(of object, building, car)*
□ He was driving on the wrong side of the road. Il roulait du mauvais côté de la route.
2 le bord *(of pool, river, road)*
□ by the side of the lake au bord du lac
3 le flanc *(of hill)*
4 l' équipe *fem (team)*
■ **He's on my side.** **1** *(on my team)* Il est dans mon équipe. **2** *(supporting me)* Il est de mon côté.
■ **side by side** côte à côte
■ **the side entrance** l'entrée latérale
■ **to take sides** prendre parti □ She always takes his side. Elle prend toujours son parti.

sideboard NOUN
le buffet

side-effect NOUN
l'effet secondaire *masc*

side street NOUN
la petite rue transversale

sidewalk NOUN (US)
le trottoir

sideways ADVERB
1 de côté (*look, be facing*)
2 de travers (*move*)
  ■ **sideways on** de profil

sieve NOUN
la passoire

sigh NOUN
▷ *see also* **sigh** VERB
le soupir

to **sigh** VERB
▷ *see also* **sigh** NOUN
soupirer

sight NOUN
1 la vue
  □ **to have poor sight** avoir une mauvaise vue
  ■ **to know somebody by sight** connaître quelqu'un de vue
2 le spectacle
  □ **It was an amazing sight.** C'était un spectacle étonnant.
  ■ **in sight** visible
  ■ **out of sight** hors de vue
  ■ **the sights** (*tourist spots*) les attractions touristiques
  ■ **to see the sights of London** visiter Londres

sightseeing NOUN
le tourisme
  ■ **to go sightseeing** faire du tourisme

sign NOUN
▷ *see also* **sign** VERB
1 le panneau (PL les panneaux) (*notice*)
  □ **There was a big sign saying 'private'.** Il y avait un grand panneau indiquant 'privé'.
  ■ **a road sign** un panneau
2 le signe (*gesture, indication*)
  □ **There's no sign of improvement.** Il n'y a aucun signe d'amélioration.
  ■ **What sign are you?** (*star sign*) Tu es de quel signe?

to **sign** VERB
▷ *see also* **sign** NOUN
signer

to **sign on** VERB
1 s'inscrire au chômage (*as unemployed*)
2 s'inscrire (*for course*)

signal NOUN
▷ *see also* **signal** VERB
le signal (PL les signaux)

to **signal** VERB
▷ *see also* **signal** NOUN

  ■ **to signal to somebody** faire un signe à quelqu'un

signalman NOUN
l'aiguilleur *masc*

signature NOUN
la signature

significance NOUN
l'importance *fem*

significant ADJECTIVE
important (FEM importante)

sign language NOUN
le langage des signes

signpost NOUN
le poteau indicateur

silence NOUN
le silence

silencer NOUN
le silencieux

silent ADJECTIVE
silencieux (FEM silencieuse)

silicon chip NOUN
la puce électronique

silk NOUN
▷ *see also* **silk** ADJECTIVE
la soie

silk ADJECTIVE
▷ *see also* **silk** NOUN
en soie
  □ **a silk scarf** un foulard en soie

silky ADJECTIVE
soyeux (FEM soyeuse)

silly ADJECTIVE
bête (FEM bête)

silver NOUN
l'argent *masc*
  □ **a silver medal** une médaille d'argent

similar ADJECTIVE
semblable (FEM semblable)
  ■ **similar to** semblable à

simple ADJECTIVE
1 simple (FEM simple)
  □ **It's very simple.** C'est très simple.
2 simplet (FEM simplette) (*simple-minded*)
  □ **He's a bit simple.** Il est un peu simplet.

simply ADVERB
simplement
  □ **It's simply not possible.** Ça n'est tout simplement pas possible.

simultaneous ADJECTIVE
simultané (FEM simultanée)

sin NOUN
▷ *see also* **sin** VERB
le péché

to **sin** VERB
▷ *see also* **sin** NOUN
pécher

since PREPOSITION, ADVERB, CONJUNCTION

S

English-French

1 depuis
   □ since Christmas depuis Noël □ since then depuis ce moment-là □ I haven't seen him since. Je ne l'ai pas vu depuis.
   ■ **ever since** depuis ce moment-là
2 depuis que
   □ I haven't seen her since she left. Je ne l'ai pas vue depuis qu'elle est partie.
3 puisque *(because)*
   □ Since you're tired, let's stay at home. Puisque tu es fatigué, restons à la maison.

sincere ADJECTIVE
   sincère (FEM sincère)

sincerely ADVERB
   ■ **Yours sincerely ... 1** *(in business letter)* Veuillez agréer l'expression de mes sentiments les meilleurs ... **2** *(in personal letter)* Cordialement ...

to **sing** VERB
   chanter
   □ He sang out of tune. Il chantait faux.
   □ Have you ever sung this tune before? Vous avez déjà chanté cet air-là?

singer NOUN
   le chanteur
   la chanteuse

singing NOUN
   le chant

single ADJECTIVE
   ▷ *see also* **single** NOUN
   célibataire (FEM célibataire) *(unmarried)*
   ■ **a single room** une chambre pour une personne
   ■ **not a single thing** rien du tout

single NOUN
   ▷ *see also* **single** ADJECTIVE
   l' aller simple *masc (ticket)*
   □ A single to Toulouse, please. Un aller simple pour Toulouse, s'il vous plaît.
   ■ **a CD single** un CD single

single parent NOUN
   ■ **She's a single parent.** Elle élève ses enfants toute seule.
   ■ **a single parent family** une famille monoparentale

singles PL NOUN
   le simple sing *(in tennis)*
   □ the women's singles le simple dames

singular NOUN
   le singulier
   □ in the singular au singulier

sinister ADJECTIVE
   sinistre (FEM sinistre)

sink NOUN
   ▷ *see also* **sink** VERB
   l' évier *masc*
to **sink** VERB

   ▷ *see also* **sink** NOUN
   couler

sir NOUN
   monsieur *masc*
   ■ **Yes sir.** Oui, Monsieur.

siren NOUN
   la sirène

sister NOUN
1 la sœur
   □ my little sister ma petite sœur
2 l' infirmière en chef *fem (nurse)*

sister-in-law NOUN
   la belle-sœur (PL les belles-sœurs)

to **sit** VERB
   s'asseoir
   ■ **to sit on something** s'asseoir sur quelque chose □ She sat on the chair. Elle s'est assise sur la chaise.
   ■ **to be sitting** être assis
   ■ **to sit an exam** passer un examen

to **sit down** VERB
   s'asseoir

sitcom NOUN
   la comédie de situation

site NOUN
1 le site
   □ an archaeological site un site archéologique
   ■ **the site of the accident** le lieu de l'accident
2 le camping *(campsite)*
   ■ **a building site** un chantier

sitting room NOUN
   le salon

situated ADJECTIVE
   ■ **to be situated** être situé □ The village is situated on a hill. Le village est situé sur une colline.

situation NOUN
   la situation

six NUMBER
   six
   □ He's six. Il a six ans.

sixteen NUMBER
   seize
   □ He's sixteen. Il a seize ans.

sixteenth ADJECTIVE
   seizième (FEM seizième)
   □ the sixteenth floor le seizième étage
   ■ **the sixteenth of August** le seize août

sixth ADJECTIVE
   sixième (FEM sixième)
   □ the sixth floor le sixième étage
   ■ **the sixth of August** le six août

sixth form NOUN
   le lycée

sixty NUMBER

S

soixante

size NOUN

> **DID YOU KNOW...?**
> France uses the European system to show clothing and shoe sizes.

1 la taille *(of object, clothing)*
□ What size do you take? Quelle taille est-ce que vous faites?
■ **I'm a size ten.** Je fais du trente-huit.

2 la pointure *(of shoes)*
■ **I take size six.** Je fais du trente-neuf.

to **skate** VERB

1 faire du patin à glace *(ice-skate)*

2 faire du patin à roulettes *(roller-skate)*

skateboard NOUN
le skateboard

skateboarding NOUN
le skateboard
□ to go skateboarding faire du skateboard

skates NOUN
les patins *masc pl*

skating NOUN
le patin à glace
□ to go skating faire du patin à glace
■ **a skating rink** une patinoire

skeleton NOUN
le squelette

sketch NOUN
▷ *see also* **sketch** VERB
le croquis *(drawing)*

to **sketch** VERB
▷ *see also* **sketch** NOUN
■ **to sketch something** faire un croquis de quelque chose

ski NOUN
▷ *see also* **ski** VERB
le ski
■ **ski boots** les chaussures de ski *fem pl*
■ **a ski lift** un remonte-pente
■ **ski pants** le fuseau *sing*
■ **a ski pole** un bâton de ski
■ **a ski slope** une piste de ski
■ **a ski suit** une combinaison de ski

to **ski** VERB
▷ *see also* **ski** NOUN
skier
□ Can you ski? Tu sais skier?

to **skid** VERB
déraper

skier NOUN
le skieur
la skieuse

skiing NOUN
le ski
■ **to go skiing** faire du ski
■ **to go on a skiing holiday** aller aux sports d'hiver

skilful ADJECTIVE
adroit (FEM adroite)

skill NOUN
le talent
□ He played with great skill. Il a joué avec beaucoup de talent.

skilled ADJECTIVE
■ **a skilled worker** un ouvrier spécialisé

skimmed milk NOUN
le lait écrémé

skimpy ADJECTIVE

1 minuscule (FEM minuscule) *(clothes)*

2 maigre (FEM maigre) *(meal)*

skin NOUN
la peau (PL les peaux)
■ **skin cancer** le cancer de la peau

skinhead NOUN
le/la skinhead

skinny ADJECTIVE
maigre (FEM maigre)

skin-tight ADJECTIVE
collant (FEM collante)

skip NOUN
▷ *see also* **skip** VERB
la benne *(container)*

to **skip** VERB
▷ *see also* **skip** NOUN
sauter
□ to skip a meal sauter un repas
■ **to skip a lesson** sécher un cours

skirt NOUN
la jupe

skittles NOUN
les quilles *fem pl*
□ to play skittles jouer aux quilles

to **skive** VERB
tirer au flanc *(be lazy)*

to **skive off** VERB
sécher *(informal)*
□ to skive off school sécher les cours

skull NOUN
le crâne

sky NOUN
le ciel

skyscraper NOUN
le gratte-ciel (PL les gratte-ciel)

slack ADJECTIVE

1 lâche (FEM lâche) *(rope)*

2 négligent (FEM négligente) *(person)*

to **slag off** VERB
■ **to slag somebody off** dire du mal de quelqu'un

to **slam** VERB
claquer
□ The door slammed. La porte a claqué.
□ She slammed the door. Elle a claqué la porte.

slang NOUN
l' argot *masc*

slap NOUN
▷ *see also* **slap** VERB
la claque

to **slap** VERB
▷ *see also* **slap** NOUN
■ **to slap somebody** donner une claque à quelqu'un

slate NOUN
l' ardoise *fem*

sledge NOUN
la luge

sledging NOUN
■ **to go sledging** faire de la luge

sleep NOUN
▷ *see also* **sleep** VERB
le sommeil
■ **I need some sleep.** J'ai besoin de dormir.
■ **to go to sleep** s'endormir

to **sleep** VERB
▷ *see also* **sleep** NOUN
dormir
□ I couldn't sleep last night. J'ai mal dormi la nuit dernière.
■ **to sleep with somebody** coucher avec quelqu'un

to **sleep around** VERB
coucher à droite et à gauche

to **sleep in** VERB
1 ne pas se réveiller (*accidentally*)
□ I'm sorry I'm late, I slept in. Désolé d'être en retard: je ne me suis pas réveillé.
2 faire la grasse matinée (*on purpose*)

to **sleep together** VERB
coucher ensemble

sleeping bag NOUN
le sac de couchage

sleeping car NOUN
le wagon-lit (PL les wagons-lits)

sleeping pill NOUN
le somnifère

sleepy ADJECTIVE
■ **to feel sleepy** avoir sommeil □ I was feeling sleepy. J'avais sommeil.
■ **a sleepy little village** un petit village tranquille

sleet NOUN
▷ *see also* **sleet** VERB
la neige fondue

to **sleet** VERB
▷ *see also* **sleet** NOUN
■ **It's sleeting.** Il tombe de la neige fondue.

sleeve NOUN
la manche
□ long sleeves les manches longues □ short sleeves les manches courtes

sleigh NOUN
le traîneau (PL les traîneaux)

slept VERB ▷ *see* **sleep**

slice NOUN
▷ *see also* **slice** VERB
la tranche

to **slice** VERB
▷ *see also* **slice** NOUN
couper en tranches

slick NOUN
■ **an oil slick** une marée noire

slide NOUN
▷ *see also* **slide** VERB
1 le toboggan (*in playground*)
2 la diapositive (*photo*)
3 la barrette (*hair slide*)

to **slide** VERB
▷ *see also* **slide** NOUN
glisser

slight ADJECTIVE
léger (FEM légère)
□ a slight problem un léger problème □ a slight improvement une légère amélioration

slightly ADVERB
légèrement

slim ADJECTIVE
▷ *see also* **slim** VERB
mince (FEM mince)

to **slim** VERB
▷ *see also* **slim** ADJECTIVE
faire un régime (*be on a diet*)
□ I'm slimming. Je fais un régime.

sling NOUN
l' écharpe *fem*
□ She had her arm in a sling. Elle avait le bras en écharpe.

slip NOUN
▷ *see also* **slip** VERB
1 l' erreur *fem* (*mistake*)
2 le jupon (*underskirt*)
3 la combinaison (*full-length underskirt*)
■ **a slip of paper** un bout de papier
■ **a slip of the tongue** un lapsus

to **slip** VERB
▷ *see also* **slip** NOUN
glisser
□ He slipped on the ice. Il a glissé sur le verglas.

to **slip up** VERB
faire une erreur (*make a mistake*)

slipper NOUN
le chausson
■ **a pair of slippers** des chaussons

slippery ADJECTIVE
glissant (FEM glissante)

slip-up NOUN

l' erreur *fem*

slope NOUN
la pente

sloppy ADJECTIVE
1 bâclé (FEM bâclée) *(work)*
2 négligé (FEM négligée) *(person, appearance)*

slot NOUN
la fente

slot machine NOUN
1 la machine à sous *(for gambling)*
2 le distributeur automatique *(vending machine)*

slow ADJECTIVE, ADVERB
1 lent (FEM lente)
　□ We are behind a very slow lorry. On est derrière un camion très lent.
2 lentement
　□ to go slow *(person, car)* aller lentement
　□ Drive slower! Conduisez plus lentement!
　■ My watch is slow. Ma montre retarde.

to slow down VERB
ralentir

slowly ADVERB
lentement

slug NOUN
la limace

slum NOUN
1 le quartier insalubre *(area)*
2 le taudis *(house)*

slush NOUN
la neige fondue

sly ADJECTIVE
rusé (FEM rusée) *(person)*
　■ a sly smile un sourire sournois

smack NOUN
　▷ *see also* **smack** VERB
la tape

to smack VERB
　▷ *see also* **smack** NOUN
　■ to smack somebody donner une tape à quelqu'un

small ADJECTIVE
petit (FEM petite)
　■ small change la petite monnaie

WORD POWER
You can use a number of other words instead of **small** to mean 'little':
miniature miniature
　□ a miniature version une version miniature
minute minuscule
　□ a minute plant une plante minuscule
tiny minuscule
　□ a tiny garden un jardin minuscule

---

smart ADJECTIVE

1 chic (FEM+PL chic) *(elegant)*
2 intelligent (FEM intelligente) *(clever)*
　■ a smart idea une idée astucieuse

smart phone NOUN
le smartphone

smash NOUN
　▷ *see also* **smash** VERB
l' accident *masc*

to smash VERB
　▷ *see also* **smash** NOUN
1 casser *(break)*
　□ I've smashed my watch. J'ai cassé ma montre.
2 se briser *(get broken)*
　□ The glass smashed into tiny pieces. Le verre s'est brisé en mille morceaux.

smashing ADJECTIVE
formidable (FEM formidable)
　□ I think he's smashing. Je le trouve formidable.

smell NOUN
　▷ *see also* **smell** VERB
l' odeur *fem*
　■ the sense of smell l'odorat *masc*

to smell VERB
　▷ *see also* **smell** NOUN
1 sentir mauvais
　□ That old dog really smells! Qu'est-ce qu'il sent mauvais, ce vieux chien!
　■ to smell of something sentir quelque chose □ It smells of petrol. Ça sent l'essence.
2 sentir *(detect)*
　□ I can't smell anything. Je ne sens rien.

smelly ADJECTIVE
qui sent mauvais
　□ He's got smelly feet. Il a les pieds qui sentent mauvais.

smelt VERB ▷ *see* **smell**

smile NOUN
　▷ *see also* **smile** VERB
le sourire

to smile VERB
　▷ *see also* **smile** NOUN
sourire

smiley NOUN
l' émoticon *masc*

smoke NOUN
　▷ *see also* **smoke** VERB
la fumée

to smoke VERB
　▷ *see also* **smoke** NOUN
fumer
　□ I don't smoke. Je ne fume pas. □ He smokes cigars. Il fume le cigare.

smoker NOUN
le fumeur

la fumeuse
smoking NOUN
- ■ **to give up smoking** arrêter de fumer
- ■ **Smoking is bad for you.** Le tabac est mauvais pour la santé.
- ■ **'no smoking'** 'défense de fumer'

smooth ADJECTIVE
1 lisse (FEM lisse) (surface)
2 mielleux (FEM mielleuse) (person)

SMS NOUN
le SMS
□ I'll send you an SMS. Je t'enverrai un SMS.

smudge NOUN
la bavure

smug ADJECTIVE
suffisant (FEM suffisante)

to **smuggle** VERB
passer en fraude (goods)
□ to smuggle cigarettes into a country faire passer des cigarettes en fraude dans un pays
- ■ **They managed to smuggle him out of prison.** Ils ont réussi à le faire sortir de prison clandestinement.

smuggler NOUN
le contrebandier
la contrebandière

smuggling NOUN
la contrebande

smutty ADJECTIVE
cochon (FEM cochonne)
□ a smutty story une histoire cochonne

snack NOUN
l' en-cas masc (PL les en-cas)
- ■ **to have a snack** prendre un en-cas

snack bar NOUN
le snack-bar

snail NOUN
l' escargot masc

snake NOUN
le serpent

to **snap** VERB
casser net (break)
□ The branch snapped. La branche a cassé net.
- ■ **to snap one's fingers** faire claquer ses doigts

snap fastener NOUN
le bouton-pression (PL les boutons-pression)

snapshot NOUN
la photo

to **snarl** VERB
gronder (animal)

to **snatch** VERB
- ■ **to snatch something from somebody** arracher quelque chose à quelqu'un □ He snatched the keys from my hand. Il m'a

arraché les clés des mains.
- ■ **My bag was snatched.** On m'a arraché mon sac.

to **sneak** VERB
- ■ **to sneak in** entrer furtivement
- ■ **to sneak out** sortir furtivement
- ■ **to sneak up on somebody** s'approcher de quelqu'un sans faire de bruit

to **sneeze** VERB
éternuer

to **sniff** VERB
1 renifler
□ Stop sniffing! Arrête de renifler!
2 flairer
□ The dog sniffed my hand. Le chien m'a flairé la main.
- ■ **to sniff glue** sniffer de la colle

snob NOUN
le/la snob

snooker NOUN
le billard
□ to play snooker jouer au billard

snooze NOUN
le petit somme
□ to have a snooze faire un petit somme

to **snore** VERB
ronfler

snow NOUN
▷ see also **snow** VERB
la neige

to **snow** VERB
▷ see also **snow** NOUN
neiger
□ It's snowing. Il neige.

snowball NOUN
la boule de neige

snowflake NOUN
le flocon de neige

snowman NOUN
le bonhomme de neige
□ to build a snowman faire un bonhomme de neige

so CONJUNCTION, ADVERB
1 alors
□ The shop was closed, so I went home. Le magasin était fermé, alors je suis rentré chez moi. □ So, have you always lived in London? Alors, vous avez toujours vécu à Londres?
- ■ **So what?** Et alors?
2 donc (so that)
□ It rained, so I got wet. Il pleuvait, donc j'ai été mouillé.
3 tellement (very)
□ It was so heavy! C'était tellement lourd!
□ He was talking so fast I couldn't understand. Il parlait tellement vite que je

ne comprenais pas.

■ **It's not so heavy!** Ça n'est pas si lourd que ça!

■ **How's your father? — Not so good.** Comment va ton père? — Pas très bien.

■ **so much** *(a lot)* tellement □ I love you so much. Je t'aime tellement

■ **so much ...** tellement de ... □ I've got so much work. J'ai tellement de travail.

■ **so many...** tellement de ... □ I've got so many things to do today. J'ai tellement de choses à faire aujourd'hui.

4   aussi *(in comparisons)*

□ He's like his sister but not so clever. Il est comme sa sœur mais pas aussi intelligent.

■ **so do I** moi aussi □ I love horses. — So do I. J'aime les chevaux. — Moi aussi.

■ **so have we** nous aussi □ I've been to France twice. — So have we. Je suis allé en France deux fois. — Nous aussi.

■ **I think so.** Je crois.

■ **I hope so.** J'espère bien.

■ **That's not so.** Ça n'est pas le cas.

■ **so far** jusqu'à présent □ It's been easy so far. Ça a été facile jusqu'à présent.

■ **so far so good** jusqu'ici ça va

■ **ten or so people** environ dix personnes

■ **at five o'clock or so** à environ cinq heures

to **soak** VERB
tremper

soaked ADJECTIVE
trempé (FEM trempée)

□ By the time we got back we were soaked. Nous sommes rentrés trempés.

soaking ADJECTIVE
trempé (FEM trempée)

□ By the time we got back we were soaking. Nous sommes rentrés trempés.

■ **soaking wet** trempé □ Your shoes are soaking wet. Tes chaussures sont trempées.

soap NOUN
le savon

soap opera NOUN
le feuilleton à l'eau de rose

soap powder NOUN
la lessive

to **sob** VERB
sangloter

□ She was sobbing. Elle sanglotait.

sober ADJECTIVE
sobre (FEM sobre)

to **sober up** VERB
dessoûler

soccer NOUN
le football

□ to play soccer jouer au football

■ **a soccer player** un joueur de football

social ADJECTIVE
social (FEM sociale, MASC PL sociaux)

□ a social class une classe sociale

■ **I have a good social life.** Je vois beaucoup de monde.

socialism NOUN
le socialisme

socialist ADJECTIVE
▷ *see also* **socialist** NOUN
socialiste (FEM socialiste)

socialist NOUN
▷ *see also* **socialist** ADJECTIVE
le/la socialiste

social security NOUN
1   l' aide sociale *fem (money)*

■ **to be on social security** recevoir de l'aide sociale

2   la sécurité sociale *(organization)*

social worker NOUN
1   l' assistante sociale *fem (woman)*

□ She's a social worker. Elle est assistante sociale.

2   le travailleur social (PL les travailleurs sociaux) *(man)*

□ He's a social worker. Il est travailleur social.

society NOUN
1   la société

□ We live in a multi-cultural society. Nous vivons dans une société multiculturelle.

2   le club

□ a drama society un club de théâtre

sociology NOUN
la sociologie

sock NOUN
la chaussette

socket NOUN
la prise de courant

soda NOUN
le soda *(soda water)*

soda pop NOUN (US)
le soda

sofa NOUN
le canapé

soft ADJECTIVE
1   doux (FEM douce) *(fabric, texture)*
2   mou (FEM molle) *(pillow, bed)*

⸝ **LANGUAGE TIP** mou changes to mol before a vowel and most words beginning with 'h'.

■ **soft cheeses** les fromages à pâte molle
3   fin (FEM fine) *(hair)*

■ **to be soft on somebody** *(be kind to)* être indulgent avec quelqu'un

■ **a soft drink** une boisson non alcoolisée

■ **soft drugs** les drogues douces *fem*

545

■ **a soft option** une solution de facilité
software NOUN
le logiciel
soggy ADJECTIVE
1 trempé (FEM trempée) (soaked)
□ a soggy tissue un mouchoir trempé
2 mou (FEM molle) (not crisp)
□ soggy chips des frites molles

> LANGUAGE TIP **mou** changes to **mol** before a vowel and most words beginning with 'h'.

soil NOUN
la terre
solar ADJECTIVE
solaire (FEM solaire)
■ **a solar panel** un panneau solaire
solar power NOUN
l' énergie solaire fem
sold VERB ▷ see **sell**
soldier NOUN
le soldat
□ He's a soldier. Il est soldat.
solicitor NOUN
1 l' avocat masc
l' avocate fem (for lawsuits)
□ He's a solicitor. Il est avocat.
2 le notaire (for wills, property)
□ She's a solicitor. Elle est notaire.
solid ADJECTIVE
1 massif (FEM massive) (not hollow)
□ solid gold l'or massif
2 solide (FEM solide)
□ a solid wall un mur solide
■ **for three hours solid** pendant trois heures entières
solo NOUN
le solo
□ a guitar solo un solo de guitare
solution NOUN
la solution
to **solve** VERB
résoudre
some ADJECTIVE, PRONOUN

> LANGUAGE TIP When 'some' means 'a certain amount of', use **du**, **de la** or **des** according to the gender of the French noun that follows it. **du** and **de la** become **de l'** when they are followed by a noun starting with a vowel.

1 du
□ Would you like some bread? Voulez-vous du pain?
de la
□ Would you like some beer? Voulez-vous de la bière?
de l'

□ Have you got some mineral water? Avez-vous de l'eau minérale?
des
□ I've got some Madonna albums. J'ai des albums de Madonna.
■ **Some people say that ...** Il y a des gens qui disent que ...
■ **some day** un de ces jours
■ **some day next week** un jour la semaine prochaine
2 certains (FEM certaines) (some but not all)
□ Are these mushrooms poisonous? — Only some. Est-ce que ces champignons sont vénéneux? — Certains le sont.
■ **some of them** quelques-uns □ I only sold some of them. J'en ai seulement vendu quelques-uns.
■ **I only took some of it.** J'en ai seulement pris un peu.
■ **I'm going to buy some stamps. Do you want some too?** Je vais acheter des timbres. Tu en veux aussi?
■ **Would you like some coffee? — No thanks, I've got some.** Tu veux du café? — Non merci, j'en ai déjà.
somebody PRONOUN
quelqu'un
□ Somebody stole my bag. Quelqu'un a volé mon sac.
somehow ADVERB
■ **I'll do it somehow.** Je trouverai le moyen de le faire.
■ **Somehow I don't think he believed me.** Quelque chose me dit qu'il ne m'a pas cru.
someone PRONOUN
quelqu'un
□ Someone stole my bag. Quelqu'un a volé mon sac.
someplace ADVERB (US)
quelque part
something PRONOUN
quelque chose
□ something special quelque chose de spécial □ Wear something warm. Mets quelque chose de chaud. □ That's really something! C'est vraiment quelque chose! □ It cost £100, or something like that. Ça a coûté cent livres, ou quelque chose comme ça. □ His name is Pierre or something. Il s'appelle Pierre, ou quelque chose comme ça.
sometime ADVERB
un de ces jours
□ You must come and see us sometime. Passez donc nous voir un de ces jours.
■ **sometime last month** dans le courant du mois dernier

S

sometimes ADVERB
quelquefois

□ Sometimes I think she hates me.
Quelquefois j'ai l'impression qu'elle me
déteste.

somewhere ADVERB
quelque part

□ I left my keys somewhere. J'ai laissé mes
clés quelque part. □ I'd like to go on holiday,
somewhere sunny. J'aimerais aller en
vacances, quelque part où il fait du soleil.

son NOUN
le fils

song NOUN
la chanson

son-in-law NOUN
le gendre

soon ADVERB
bientôt

□ very soon très bientôt
■ **soon afterwards** peu après
■ **as soon as possible** aussitôt que possible

sooner ADVERB
plus tôt

□ Can't you come a bit sooner? Tu ne peux
pas venir un peu plus tôt?
■ **sooner or later** tôt ou tard

soot NOUN
la suie

soppy ADJECTIVE
sentimental (FEM sentimentale, MASC PL
sentimentaux)

soprano NOUN (singer)
le/la soprano

sorcerer NOUN
le sorcier

sore ADJECTIVE
▷ see also **sore** NOUN
■ **My feet are sore.** J'ai mal aux pieds.
■ **It's sore.** Ça fait mal.
■ **That's a sore point.** C'est un point
sensible.

sore NOUN
▷ see also **sore** ADJECTIVE
la plaie

sorry ADJECTIVE
désolé (FEM désolée)

□ I'm really sorry. Je suis vraiment désolé.
□ I'm sorry, I haven't got any change. Je suis
désolé, je n'ai pas de monnaie. □ I'm sorry
I'm late. Je suis désolé d'être en retard.
■ **sorry!** pardon!
■ **sorry?** pardon?
■ **I'm sorry about the noise.** Je m'excuse
pour le bruit.
■ **You'll be sorry!** Tu le regretteras!
■ **to feel sorry for somebody** plaindre

quelqu'un

sort NOUN
la sorte

□ What sort of bike have you got? Quelle
sorte de vélo as-tu?

to sort out VERB
1 ranger (objects)
2 résoudre (problems)

so-so ADVERB
comme ci comme ça

□ How are you feeling? — So-so. Comment
est-ce que tu te sens? — Comme ci comme
ça.

sought VERB ▷ see **to seek**

soul NOUN
1 l' âme fem (spirit)
2 la soul (music)

sound NOUN
▷ see also **sound** VERB, ADJECTIVE
1 le bruit (noise)

□ Don't make a sound! Pas un bruit! □ the
sound of footsteps des bruits de pas
2 le son

□ Can I turn the sound down? Je peux
baisser le son?

to sound VERB
▷ see also **sound** NOUN, ADJECTIVE
■ **That sounds interesting.** Ça a l'air
intéressant.
■ **It sounds as if she's doing well at
school.** Elle a l'air de bien travailler à l'école.
■ **That sounds like a good idea.** C'est une
bonne idée.

sound ADJECTIVE, ADVERB
▷ see also **sound** NOUN, VERB
bon (FEM bonne)

□ That's sound advice. C'est un bon conseil.
■ **sound asleep** profondément endormi

soundtrack NOUN
la bande sonore

soup NOUN
la soupe

□ vegetable soup la soupe aux légumes

sour ADJECTIVE
aigre (FEM aigre)

south ADJECTIVE, ADVERB
▷ see also **south** NOUN
1 sud (FEM ı PL sud)

□ the south coast la côte sud
2 vers le sud

□ We were travelling south. Nous allions
vers le sud.
■ **south of** au sud de □ It's south of
London. C'est au sud de Londres.

south NOUN
▷ see also **south** ADJECTIVE
le sud

S

547

□ in the south dans le sud □ the South of France le sud de la France

South Africa NOUN
l' Afrique du Sud *fem*
■ **in South Africa** en Afrique du Sud
■ **to South Africa** en Afrique du Sud

South America NOUN
l' Amérique du Sud *fem*
■ **in South America** en Amérique du Sud
■ **to South America** en Amérique du Sud

South American NOUN
▷ *see also* **South American** ADJECTIVE
le Sud-Américain
la Sud-Américaine

South American ADJECTIVE
▷ *see also* **South American** NOUN
sud-américain (FEM sud-américaine)

southbound ADJECTIVE
■ **The southbound carriageway is blocked.** La route est bloquée en direction du sud.
■ **We were going southbound on the M1.** Nous étions sur la M1 en direction du sud.

southeast NOUN
le sud-est
□ southeast England le sud-est de l'Angleterre

southern ADJECTIVE
■ **the southern part of the island** la partie sud de l'île
■ **Southern England** le sud de l'Angleterre

South Pole NOUN
le pôle Sud

South Wales NOUN
le sud du Pays de Galles

southwest NOUN
le sud-ouest
□ southwest France le sud-ouest de la France

souvenir NOUN
le souvenir
■ **a souvenir shop** une boutique de souvenirs

Soviet ADJECTIVE
■ **the former Soviet Union** l'ex-Union Soviétique *fem*

soya NOUN
le soja

soy sauce NOUN
la sauce de soja

space NOUN
1 la place
□ There isn't enough space. Il n'y a pas suffisamment de place.
■ **a parking space** une place de parking
2 l' espace *masc (universe, gap)*
□ to go into space aller dans l'espace
□ Leave a space after your answer. Laissez

un espace après votre réponse.
■ **a space shuttle** une navette spatiale

spacecraft NOUN
l' engin spatial *masc*

spade NOUN
la pelle
■ **spades** *(in cards)* le pique *sing* □ the ace of spades l'as de pique

Spain NOUN
l' Espagne *fem*
■ **in Spain** en Espagne
■ **to Spain** en Espagne

Spaniard NOUN
l' Espagnol *masc*
l' Espagnole *fem*

spaniel NOUN
l' épagneul *masc*

Spanish NOUN
▷ *see also* **Spanish** ADJECTIVE
l' espagnol *masc (language)*
■ **the Spanish** les Espagnols

Spanish ADJECTIVE
▷ *see also* **Spanish** NOUN
espagnol (FEM espagnole)
□ She's Spanish. Elle est espagnole.

to **spank** VERB
■ **to spank somebody** donner une fessée à quelqu'un

spanner NOUN
la clé anglaise

spare ADJECTIVE
▷ *see also* **spare** VERB, NOUN
de rechange
□ spare batteries des piles de rechange □ a spare part une pièce de rechange
■ **a spare room** une chambre d'amis
■ **spare time** le temps libre □ What do you do in your spare time? Qu'est-ce que tu fais pendant ton temps libre?
■ **spare wheel** une roue de secours

to **spare** VERB
▷ *see also* **spare** ADJECTIVE, NOUN
■ **Can you spare a moment?** Vous pouvez m'accorder un instant?
■ **I can't spare the time.** Je n'ai pas le temps.
■ **There's no room to spare.** Il n'y a plus de place.
■ **We arrived with time to spare.** Nous sommes arrivés en avance.

spare NOUN
▷ *see also* **spare** ADJECTIVE, VERB
■ **a spare** un autre □ I've lost my key. — Have you got a spare? J'ai perdu ma clé. — Tu en as une autre?

sparkling ADJECTIVE
pétillant (FEM pétillante) *(water)*

■ **sparkling wine** le mousseux

sparrow NOUN
le moineau (PL les moineaux)

spat VERB ▷see **spit**

to **speak** VERB
parler
□ Do you speak English? Est-ce que vous parlez anglais?
■ **to speak to somebody** parler à quelqu'un □ Have you spoken to him? Tu lui as parlé? □ She spoke to him about it. Elle lui en a parlé.

to **speak up** VERB
parler plus fort
□ Speak up, we can't hear you. Parle plus fort, nous ne t'entendons pas.

speaker NOUN
1 l' enceinte fem (loudspeaker)
2 l' intervenant masc
l' intervenante fem (in debate)

special ADJECTIVE
spécial (FEM spéciale, MASC PL spéciaux)

specialist NOUN
le/la spécialiste

speciality NOUN
la spécialité

to **specialize** VERB
se spécialiser
□ We specialize in skiing equipment. Nous nous spécialisons dans les articles de ski.

specially ADVERB
1 spécialement
□ It's specially designed for teenagers. C'est spécialement conçu pour les adolescents.
■ **not specially** pas spécialement □ Do you like opera? — Not specially. Tu aimes l'opéra? — Pas spécialement.
2 surtout
□ It can be very cold here, specially in winter. Il peut faire très froid ici, surtout en hiver.

species NOUN
l' espèce fem

specific ADJECTIVE
1 particulier (FEM particulière) (particular)
□ certain specific issues certains problèmes particuliers
2 précis (FEM précise) (precise)
□ Could you be more specific? Est-ce que vous pourriez être plus précis?

specifically ADVERB
1 spécialement
□ It's specifically designed for teenagers. C'est spécialement conçu pour les adolescents.
2 particulièrement
□ in Britain, or more specifically in England en Grande-Bretagne, ou plus

particulièrement en Angleterre
■ **I specifically said that ...** J'ai clairement dit que ...

specs, spectacles PL NOUN
les lunettes fem pl

spectacular ADJECTIVE
spectaculaire (FEM spectaculaire)

spectator NOUN
le spectateur
la spectatrice

speech NOUN
le discours
□ to make a speech faire un discours

speechless ADJECTIVE
muet (FEM muette)
□ speechless with admiration muet d'admiration
■ **I was speechless.** Je suis resté sans voix.

speed NOUN
la vitesse
□ a three-speed bike un vélo à trois vitesses
□ at top speed à toute vitesse

to **speed up** VERB
accélérer

speedboat NOUN
la vedette

speeding NOUN
l' excès de vitesse masc
□ He was fined for speeding. Il a reçu une contravention pour excès de vitesse.

speed limit NOUN
la limitation de vitesse
■ **to break the speed limit** faire un excès de vitesse

speedometer NOUN
le compteur

to **spell** VERB
▷see also **spell** NOUN
1 écrire (in writing)
□ How do you spell that? Comment est-ce que ça s'écrit?
2 épeler (out loud)
□ Can you spell that please? Est-ce que vous pouvez épeler, s'il vous plaît?
■ **I can't spell.** Je fais des fautes d'orthographe.

spell NOUN
▷see also **spell** VERB
■ **to cast a spell on somebody** jeter un sort à quelqu'un
■ **to be under somebody's spell** être sous le charme de quelqu'un

spelling NOUN
l' orthographe fem
□ My spelling is terrible. Je fais beaucoup de fautes d'orthographe.
■ **a spelling mistake** une faute

S

d'orthographe

spelt VERB ▷ see **spell**

to spend VERB
1 dépenser (money)
2 passer (time)
□ He spent a month in France. Il a passé un mois en France.

spice NOUN
l'épice fem

spicy ADJECTIVE
épicé (FEM épicée)

spider NOUN
l'araignée fem

to spill VERB
1 renverser (tip over)
□ He spilled his coffee over his trousers. Il a renversé son café sur son pantalon.
2 se répandre (get spilt)
□ The soup spilled all over the table. La soupe s'est répandue sur la table.

spinach NOUN
les épinards masc pl

spin drier NOUN
l'essoreuse fem

spine NOUN
la colonne vertébrale

spinster NOUN
la célibataire

spire NOUN
la flèche

spirit NOUN
1 le courage (courage)
■ to be in good spirits être de bonne humeur
2 l'énergie fem (energy)

spirits PL NOUN
les alcools forts masc pl
□ I don't drink spirits. Je ne bois pas d'alcools forts.

spiritual ADJECTIVE
religieux (FEM religieuse)
□ the spiritual leader of Tibet le chef religieux du Tibet

spit NOUN
▷ see also **spit** VERB
la salive

to spit VERB
▷ see also **spit** NOUN
cracher
■ to spit something out cracher quelque chose

spite NOUN
▷ see also **spite** VERB
■ in spite of malgré
■ out of spite par méchanceté

to spite VERB
▷ see also **spite** NOUN

contrarier
□ He just did it to spite me. Il a fait ça juste pour me contrarier.

spiteful ADJECTIVE
1 méchant (FEM méchante) (action)
2 rancunier (FEM rancunière) (person)

to splash VERB
▷ see also **splash** NOUN
éclabousser
□ Careful! Don't splash me! Attention! Ne m'éclabousse pas!

splash NOUN
▷ see also **splash** VERB
le plouf
□ I heard a splash. J'ai entendu un plouf.
■ a splash of colour une touche de couleur

splendid ADJECTIVE
splendide (FEM splendide)

splint NOUN
l'attelle fem

splinter NOUN
l'écharde fem

to split VERB
1 fendre (break apart)
□ He split the wood with an axe. Il a fendu le bois avec une hache.
2 se fendre
□ The ship hit a rock and split in two. Le bateau a percuté un rocher et s'est fendu en deux.
3 partager (divide up)
□ They decided to split the profits. Ils ont décidé de partager les bénéfices.

to split up VERB
1 rompre (couple)
□ My parents have split up. Mes parents ont rompu.
2 se disperser (group)

to spoil VERB
1 abîmer (object)
2 gâcher (occasion)
3 gâter (child)

spoiled ADJECTIVE
gâté (FEM gâtée)
□ a spoiled child un enfant gâté

spoilsport NOUN
le/la trouble-fête

spoilt ADJECTIVE
gâté (FEM gâtée)
□ a spoilt child un enfant gâté

spoilt VERB ▷ see **spoil**

spoke VERB ▷ see **speak**

spoke NOUN
le rayon (of wheel)

spoken VERB ▷ see **speak**
■ spoken French le français parlé

spokesman NOUN

le porte-parole (PL les porte-parole)

spokeswoman NOUN
le porte-parole (PL les porte-parole)

sponge NOUN
l' éponge *fem*
■ **a sponge bag** une trousse de toilette
■ **a sponge cake** un biscuit de Savoie

sponsor NOUN
▷ *see also* **sponsor** VERB
le donateur
la donatrice

to **sponsor** VERB
▷ *see also* **sponsor** NOUN
parrainer
□ The festival was sponsored by ... Le festival a été parrainé par ...

spontaneous ADJECTIVE
spontané (FEM spontanée)

spooky ADJECTIVE
1 sinistre (FEM sinistre) *(eerie)*
■ **a spooky story** une histoire qui fait froid dans le dos
2 étrange (FEM étrange) *(strange)*
□ a spooky coincidence une étrange coïncidence

spoon NOUN
la cuiller

spoonful NOUN
la cuillerée
□ two spoonfuls of sugar deux cuillerées de sucre

sport NOUN
le sport
□ What's your favourite sport? Quel est ton sport préféré?
■ **a sports bag** un sac de sport
■ **a sports car** une voiture de sport
■ **a sports jacket** une veste sport
■ **Go on, be a sport!** Allez, sois sympa!

sportsman NOUN
le sportif

sportswear NOUN
les vêtements de sport *masc pl*

sportswoman NOUN
la sportive

sporty ADJECTIVE
sportif (FEM sportive)
□ I'm not very sporty. Je ne suis pas très sportif.

spot NOUN
▷ *see also* **spot** VERB
1 la tache *(mark)*
□ There's a spot on your shirt. Il y a une tache sur ta chemise.
2 le pois *(in pattern)*
□ a red dress with white spots une robe rouge à pois blancs

3 le bouton *(pimple)*
□ He's covered in spots. Il est couvert de boutons.
4 le coin *(place)*
□ It's a lovely spot for a picnic. C'est un coin agréable pour un pique-nique.
■ **on the spot 1** *(immediately)* sur-le-champ □ They gave her the job on the spot. Ils lui ont offert le poste sur-le-champ. **2** *(at the same place)* sur place □ Luckily they were able to mend the car on the spot. Heureusement ils ont pu réparer la voiture sur place.

to **spot** VERB
▷ *see also* **spot** NOUN
repérer
□ I spotted a mistake. J'ai repéré une faute.

spotless ADJECTIVE
immaculé (FEM immaculée)

spotlight NOUN
le projecteur
□ The universities have been in the spotlight recently. Les universités ont été sous le feu des projecteurs ces derniers temps.

spotty ADJECTIVE
boutonneux (FEM boutonneuse) *(pimply)*

spouse NOUN
l' époux *masc*
l' épouse *fem*

to **sprain** VERB
▷ *see also* **sprain** NOUN
■ **to sprain one's ankle** se faire une entorse à la cheville

sprain NOUN
▷ *see also* **sprain** VERB
l' entorse *fem*
□ It's just a sprain. C'est juste une entorse.

spray NOUN
▷ *see also* **spray** VERB
la bombe *(spray can)*

to **spray** VERB
▷ *see also* **spray** NOUN
1 vaporiser
□ to spray perfume on one's hand se vaporiser du parfum sur la main
2 traiter *(crops)*
3 peindre avec une bombe *(graffiti)*
□ Somebody had sprayed graffiti on the wall. Quelqu'un avait peint des graffiti avec une bombe sur le mur.

spread NOUN
▷ *see also* **spread** VERB
■ **cheese spread** le fromage à tartiner
■ **chocolate spread** le chocolat à tartiner

to **spread** VERB
▷ *see also* **spread** NOUN
1 étaler

□ to spread butter on a slice of bread étaler du beurre sur une tranche de pain

2 se propager *(disease, news)*

□ The news spread rapidly. La nouvelle s'est propagée rapidement.

to **spread out** VERB
se disperser *(people)*

□ The soldiers spread out across the field. Les soldats se sont dispersés dans le champ.

spreadsheet NOUN
le tableur *(computer program)*

spring NOUN

1 le printemps *(season)*

■ **in spring** au printemps

2 le ressort *(metal coil)*

3 la source *(water hole)*

spring-cleaning NOUN
le grand nettoyage de printemps

springtime NOUN
le printemps

■ **in springtime** au printemps

sprinkler NOUN
l' arroseur *masc (for lawn)*

sprint NOUN
▷ *see also* **sprint** VERB
le sprint

to **sprint** VERB
▷ *see also* **sprint** NOUN
courir à toute vitesse

□ She sprinted for the bus. Elle a couru à toute vitesse pour attraper le bus.

sprinter NOUN
le sprinteur
la sprinteuse

sprouts PL NOUN

■ **Brussels sprouts** les choux de Bruxelles *masc pl*

spy NOUN
▷ *see also* **spy** VERB
l' espion *masc*
l' espionne *fem*

to **spy** VERB
▷ *see also* **spy** NOUN

■ **to spy on somebody** espionner quelqu'un

spying NOUN
l' espionnage *masc*

to **squabble** VERB
se chamailler

□ Stop squabbling! Arrêtez de vous chamailler!

square NOUN
▷ *see also* **square** ADJECTIVE

1 le carré

□ a square and a triangle un carré et un triangle

2 la place

□ the town square la place de l'hôtel de ville

square ADJECTIVE
▷ *see also* **square** NOUN
carré (FEM carrée)

□ two square metres deux mètres carrés

■ **It's 2 metres square.** Ça fait deux mètres sur deux.

squash NOUN
▷ *see also* **squash** VERB
le squash *(sport)*

□ I play squash. Je joue au squash.

■ **a squash court** un court de squash

■ **a squash racket** une raquette de squash

■ **orange squash** l' orangeade *fem*

■ **lemon squash** la citronnade

to **squash** VERB
▷ *see also* **squash** NOUN
écraser

□ You're squashing me. Tu m'écrases.

to **squeak** VERB

1 pousser un petit cri *(mouse, child)*

2 grincer *(creak)*

to **squeeze** VERB

1 presser *(fruit, toothpaste)*

2 serrer *(hand, arm)*

to **squeeze in** VERB

1 trouver une petite place

□ It was a tiny car, but we managed to squeeze in. La voiture était toute petite, mais nous avons réussi à trouver une petite place.

2 caser *(for appointment)*

□ I can squeeze you in at two o'clock. Je peux vous caser demain à deux heures.

to **squint** VERB
▷ *see also* **squint** NOUN
loucher

squint NOUN
▷ *see also* **squint** VERB

■ **He has a squint.** Il louche.

squirrel NOUN
l' écureuil *masc*

to **stab** VERB
poignarder

stable NOUN
▷ *see also* **stable** ADJECTIVE
l' écurie *fem*

stable ADJECTIVE
▷ *see also* **stable** NOUN
stable (FEM stable)

□ a stable relationship une relation stable

stack NOUN
la pile

□ a stack of books une pile de livres

stadium NOUN
le stade

staff NOUN

1 le personnel *(in company)*
2 les professeurs *masc pl (in school)*
staffroom NOUN
  la salle des professeurs
stage NOUN
1 la scène *(in plays)*
2 l' estrade *fem (for speeches, lectures)*
  ■ **at this stage 1** à ce stade □ at this stage in the negotiations à ce stade des négociations **2** pour l'instant □ At this stage, it's too early to comment. Pour l'instant, il est trop tôt pour se prononcer.
  ■ **to do something in stages** faire quelque chose étape par étape
  ⸨ **LANGUAGE TIP** Be careful not to translate **stage** by the French word **stage**.
to **stagger** VERB
  chanceler
stain NOUN
  ▷ *see also* **stain** VERB
  la tache
to **stain** VERB
  ▷ *see also* **stain** NOUN
  tacher
stainless steel NOUN
  l' inox *masc*
stain remover NOUN
  le détachant
stair NOUN
  la marche *(step)*
staircase NOUN
  l' escalier *masc*
stairs PL NOUN
  l' escalier *masc sing*
stale ADJECTIVE
  rassis *(FEM rassie) (bread)*
stalemate NOUN
  le pat *(in chess)*
stall NOUN
  le stand *masc*
  □ He's got a market stall. Il a un stand au marché.
  ■ **the stalls** *(in cinema, theatre)* l'orchestre *masc sing*
stamina NOUN
  l' endurance *fem*
stammer NOUN
  le bégaiement
  ■ **He's got a stammer.** Il bégaie.
to **stamp** VERB
  ▷ *see also* **stamp** NOUN
  affranchir *(letter)*
  ■ **to stamp one's foot** taper du pied
stamp NOUN
  ▷ *see also* **stamp** VERB
1 le timbre

□ My hobby is stamp collecting. Je collectionne les timbres.
  ■ **a stamp album** un album de timbres
  ■ **a stamp collection** une collection de timbres
2 le tampon *(rubber stamp)*
stamped ADJECTIVE
  affranchi *(FEM affranchie)*
  □ The letter wasn't stamped. La lettre n'était pas affranchie.
  ■ **Enclose a stamped addressed envelope.** Joindre une enveloppe affranchie à vos nom et adresse.
to **stand** VERB
1 être debout *(be standing)*
  □ He was standing by the door. Il était debout à la porte.
2 se lever *(stand up)*
3 supporter *(tolerate, withstand)*
  □ I can't stand all this noise. Je ne supporte pas tout ce bruit.
to **stand for** VERB
1 être l'abréviation de *(be short for)*
  □ 'BT' stands for 'British Telecom'. 'BT' est l'abréviation de 'British Telecom'.
2 supporter *(tolerate)*
  □ I won't stand for it! Je ne supporterai pas ça!
  ■ **to stand in for somebody** remplacer quelqu'un
to **stand out** VERB
  se distinguer
  □ None of the candidates really stood out. Aucun des candidats ne s'est distingué.
  ■ **She really stands out in that orange coat.** Tout le monde la remarque avec ce manteau orange.
to **stand up** VERB
  se lever *(get up)*
  ■ **to stand up for** défendre □ Stand up for your rights! Défendez vos droits!
standard ADJECTIVE
  ▷ *see also* **standard** NOUN
1 courant *(FEM courante)*
  □ standard French le français courant
2 ordinaire *(FEM ordinaire) (equipment)*
  ■ **the standard procedure** la procédure normale
standard NOUN
  ▷ *see also* **standard** ADJECTIVE
  le niveau *(PL les niveaux)*
  □ The standard is very high. Le niveau est très haut.
  ■ **the standard of living** le niveau de vie
  ■ **She's got high standards.** Elle est très exigeante.
stand-by ticket NOUN

S

le billet stand-by

standpoint NOUN
le point de vue

stands PL NOUN
la tribune *sing (at sports ground)*

stank VERB ▷ *see* **stink**

staple NOUN
▷ *see also* **staple** VERB
l' agrafe *fem*

to **staple** VERB
▷ *see also* **staple** NOUN
agrafer

stapler NOUN
l' agrafeuse *fem*

star NOUN
▷ *see also* **star** VERB
1 l' étoile *fem (in sky)*
2 la vedette *(celebrity)*
□ He's a TV star. C'est une vedette de la télé.
■ **the stars** *(horoscope)* l' horoscope *masc*

to **star** VERB
▷ *see also* **star** NOUN
être la vedette
□ to star in a film être la vedette d'un film
■ **The film stars Glenda Jackson.** Le film a pour vedette Glenda Jackson.
■ **... starring Johnny Depp** ... avec Johnny Depp

to **stare** VERB
■ **to stare at something** fixer quelque chose

stark ADVERB
■ **stark naked** complètement nu

start NOUN
▷ *see also* **start** VERB
1 le début
□ It's not much, but it's a start. Ce n'est pas grand chose, mais c'est un début.
■ **Shall we make a start on the washing-up?** On commence à faire la vaisselle?
2 le départ *(of race)*

to **start** VERB
▷ *see also* **start** NOUN
1 commencer
□ What time does it start? À quelle heure est-ce que ça commence?
■ **to start doing something** commencer à faire quelque chose □ I started learning French three years ago. J'ai commencé à apprendre le français il y a trois ans.
2 créer *(organization)*
□ He wants to start his own business. Il veut créer sa propre entreprise.
3 organiser *(campaign)*
□ She started a campaign against drugs. Elle a organisé une campagne contre la drogue.

4 démarrer *(car)*
□ He couldn't start the car. Il n'a pas réussi à démarrer la voiture. □ The car wouldn't start. La voiture ne voulait pas démarrer.

to **start off** VERB
partir *(leave)*
□ We started off first thing in the morning. Nous sommes partis en début de matinée.

starter NOUN
l' entrée *fem (first course)*

to **starve** VERB
mourir de faim
□ People were literally starving. Les gens mouraient littéralement de faim.
■ **I'm starving!** Je meurs de faim!

state NOUN
▷ *see also* **state** VERB
l' état *masc*
■ **He was in a real state.** Il était dans tous ses états.
■ **the state** *(government)* l'État
■ **the States** *(USA)* les États-Unis *masc pl*

to **state** VERB
▷ *see also* **state** NOUN
1 déclarer *(say)*
□ He stated his intention to resign. Il a déclaré son intention de démissionner.
2 donner *(give)*
□ Please state your name and address. Veuillez donner vos nom et adresse.

stately home NOUN
le château *(PL les châteaux)*

statement NOUN
la déclaration

station NOUN
la gare *(railway)*
■ **the bus station** la gare routière
■ **a police station** un poste de police
■ **a radio station** une station de radio

stationer's NOUN
la papeterie

station wagon NOUN *(US)*
le break

statue NOUN
la statue

stay NOUN
▷ *see also* **stay** VERB
le séjour
□ my stay in France mon séjour en France

to **stay** VERB
▷ *see also* **stay** NOUN
1 rester *(remain)*
□ Stay here! Reste ici!
2 loger *(spend the night)*
□ to stay with friends loger chez des amis
□ Where are you staying? Où est-ce que vous logez?

■ **to stay the night** passer la nuit

■ **We stayed in Belgium for a few days.** Nous avons passé quelques jours en Belgique.

to **stay in** VERB
rester à la maison *(not go out)*

to **stay up** VERB
rester debout

□ We stayed up till midnight. Nous sommes restés debout jusqu'à minuit.

steady ADJECTIVE
1 régulier (FEM régulière)

□ steady progress des progrès réguliers
2 stable (FEM stable)

□ a steady job un emploi stable
3 ferme (FEM ferme) *(voice, hand)*
4 calme (FEM calme) *(person)*

■ **a steady boyfriend** un copain

■ **a steady girlfriend** une copine

steak NOUN
le steak *(beef)*

□ steak and chips un steak frites

to **steal** VERB
voler

steam NOUN
la vapeur

□ a steam engine une locomotive à vapeur

steel NOUN
l' acier *masc*

□ a steel door une porte en acier

steep ADJECTIVE
raide (FEM raide) *(slope)*

steeple NOUN
le clocher

steering wheel NOUN
le volant

step NOUN
▷ *see also* **step** VERB
1 le pas *(pace)*

□ He took a step forward. Il a fait un pas en avant.
2 la marche *(stair)*

□ She tripped over the step. Elle a trébuché sur la marche.

to **step** VERB
▷ *see also* **step** NOUN

■ **to step aside** faire un pas de côté

■ **to step back** faire un pas en arrière

stepbrother NOUN
le demi-frère

stepdaughter NOUN
la belle-fille (PL les belles-filles)

stepfather NOUN
le beau-père (PL les beaux-pères)

stepladder NOUN
l' escabeau *masc* (PL les escabeaux)

stepmother NOUN

la belle-mère (PL les belles-mères)

stepsister NOUN
la demi-sœur

stepson NOUN
le beau-fils (PL les beaux-fils)

stereo NOUN
la chaîne stéréo (PL les chaînes stéréo)

sterling ADJECTIVE

■ **£5 sterling** cinq livres sterling

stew NOUN
le ragoût

steward NOUN
le steward

stewardess NOUN
l' hôtesse de l'air *fem*

stick NOUN
▷ *see also* **stick** VERB
1 le bâton
2 la canne *(walking stick)*

to **stick** VERB
▷ *see also* **stick** NOUN
coller *(with adhesive)*

□ Stick the stamps on the envelope. Collez les timbres sur l'enveloppe.

to **stick out** VERB
sortir *(project)*

□ A pen was sticking out of his pocket. Un stylo sortait de sa poche.

■ **Stick your tongue out and say 'ah'.** Tirez la langue et dites 'ah'.

stick insect NOUN
le phasme

sticker NOUN
l' autocollant *masc*

sticky ADJECTIVE
1 poisseux (FEM poisseuse)

□ to have sticky hands avoir les mains poisseuses
2 adhésif (FEM adhésive)

□ a sticky label une étiquette adhésive

stiff ADJECTIVE, ADVERB
rigide (FEM rigide) *(rigid)*

■ **to have a stiff neck** avoir un torticolis

■ **to feel stiff** avoir des courbatures

■ **to be bored stiff** s'ennuyer à mourir

■ **to be frozen stiff** être mort de froid

■ **to be scared stiff** être mort de peur

still ADVERB
▷ *see also* **still** ADJECTIVE
1 encore

□ I still haven't finished. Je n'ai pas encore fini. □ Are you still in bed? Tu es encore au lit?

■ **better still** encore mieux
2 quand même *(even so)*

□ She knows I don't like it, but she still does it. Elle sait que je n'aime pas ça, mais elle le

S

fait quand même.
3 enfin *(after all)*
  □ Still, it's the thought that counts. Enfin,
  c'est l'intention qui compte.
still ADJECTIVE
  ▷ *see also* **still** ADVERB
  ■ **Keep still!** Ne bouge pas!
  ■ **Sit still!** Reste tranquille!
sting NOUN
  ▷ *see also* **sting** VERB
  la piqûre
  □ a bee sting une piqûre d'abeille
to **sting** VERB
  ▷ *see also* **sting** NOUN
  piquer
  □ I've been stung. J'ai été piqué.
stingy ADJECTIVE
  pingre (FEM pingre)
to **stink** VERB
  ▷ *see also* **stink** NOUN
  puer
  □ It stinks! Ça pue!
stink NOUN
  ▷ *see also* **stink** VERB
  la puanteur
to **stir** VERB
  remuer
to **stitch** VERB
  ▷ *see also* **stitch** NOUN
  coudre *(cloth)*
stitch NOUN
  ▷ *see also* **stitch** VERB
1 le point *(in sewing)*
2 le point de suture *(in wound)*
  □ I had five stitches. J'ai eu cinq points de
  suture.
stock NOUN
  ▷ *see also* **stock** VERB
1 la réserve *(supply)*
2 le stock *(in shop)*
  □ in stock en stock
  ■ **out of stock** épuisé
3 le bouillon
  □ chicken stock du bouillon de volaille
to **stock** VERB
  ▷ *see also* **stock** NOUN
  avoir *(have in stock)*
  □ Do you stock camping stoves? Vous avez
  des camping-gaz?
to **stock up** VERB
  s'approvisionner
  □ to stock up with something
  s'approvisionner en quelque chose
stock cube NOUN
  le cube de bouillon
stocking NOUN
  le bas

stole, stolen VERB ▷ *see* **steal**
stomach NOUN
  l' estomac *masc*
  □ to have an upset stomach avoir l'estomac
  barbouillé
stomachache NOUN
  ■ **to have stomachache** avoir mal au
  ventre
stone NOUN
1 la pierre *(rock)*
  □ a stone wall un mur en pierre
2 le noyau (PL les noyaux) *(in fruit)*
  □ a peach stone un noyau de pêche

> **DID YOU KNOW…?**
> In France, weight is expressed in kilos.
> A stone is about 6.3 kg.

  ■ **I weigh eight stone.** Je pèse cinquante
  kilos.
stood VERB ▷ *see* **stand**
stool NOUN
  le tabouret
to **stop** VERB
  ▷ *see also* **stop** NOUN
1 arrêter
  □ a campaign to stop whaling une
  campagne pour arrêter la chasse à la baleine
2 s'arrêter
  □ The bus doesn't stop there. Le bus ne
  s'arrête pas là. □ I think the rain's going to
  stop. Je pense qu'il va s'arrêter de pleuvoir.
  ■ **to stop doing something** arrêter de faire
  quelque chose □ to stop smoking arrêter de
  fumer
  ■ **to stop somebody doing something**
  empêcher quelqu'un de faire quelque chose
  ■ **Stop!** Stop!
stop NOUN
  ▷ *see also* **stop** VERB
  l' arrêt *masc*
  □ a bus stop un arrêt de bus
  ■ **This is my stop.** Je descends ici.
stopwatch NOUN
  le chronomètre
store NOUN
  ▷ *see also* **store** VERB
1 le magasin *(shop)*
  □ a furniture store un magasin de meubles
2 la réserve *(stock, storeroom)*
to **store** VERB
  ▷ *see also* **store** NOUN
1 garder
  □ They store potatoes in the cellar. Ils
  gardent des pommes de terre dans la cave.
2 enregistrer *(information)*
storey NOUN
  l' étage *masc*
  □ a three-storey building un immeuble à

trois étages

storm NOUN
1 la tempête *(gale)*
2 l' orage *masc (thunderstorm)*

stormy ADJECTIVE
orageux *(FEM orageuse)*

story NOUN
l' histoire *fem*

stove NOUN
1 la cuisinière *(in kitchen)*
2 le réchaud *(camping stove)*

straight ADJECTIVE
1 droit *(FEM droite)*
□ a straight line une ligne droite
2 raide *(FEM raide)*
□ straight hair les cheveux raides
3 hétéro *(FEM hétéro) (heterosexual)*
■ **straight away** tout de suite
■ **straight on** tout droit

straighteners PL NOUN
le fer à lisser *sing*
■ **a pair of straighteners** un fer à lisser

straightforward ADJECTIVE
simple *(FEM simple)*

strain NOUN
▷ *see also* **strain** VERB
le stress
■ **It was a strain.** C'était éprouvant.

to **strain** VERB
▷ *see also* **strain** NOUN
se faire mal à
□ I strained my back. Je me suis fait mal au dos.
■ **to strain a muscle** se froisser un muscle

strained ADJECTIVE
froissé *(FEM froissée) (muscle)*

stranded ADJECTIVE
■ **We were stranded.** Nous étions coincés.

strange ADJECTIVE
bizarre *(FEM bizarre)*
□ That's strange! C'est bizarre!

stranger NOUN
l' inconnu *masc*
l' inconnue *fem*
□ Don't talk to strangers. Ne parle pas aux inconnus.
■ **I'm a stranger here.** Je ne suis pas d'ici.

to **strangle** VERB
étrangler

strap NOUN
1 la courroie *(of bag, camera, suitcase)*
2 la bretelle *(of bra, dress)*
3 la lanière *(on shoe)*
4 le bracelet *(of watch)*

straw NOUN
la paille
■ **That's the last straw!** Ça, c'est le comble!

strawberry NOUN
la fraise
□ strawberry jam la confiture de fraises □ a strawberry ice cream une glace à la fraise

stray NOUN
■ **a stray cat** un chat perdu

stream NOUN
le ruisseau *(PL les ruisseaux)*

street NOUN
la rue
□ in the street dans la rue

streetcar NOUN *(US)*
le tramway

streetlamp NOUN
le réverbère

street plan NOUN
le plan de la ville

streetwise ADJECTIVE
dégourdi *(FEM dégourdie)*

strength NOUN
la force

to **stress** VERB
▷ *see also* **stress** NOUN
souligner
□ I would like to stress that ... J'aimerais souligner que ...

stress NOUN
▷ *see also* **stress** VERB
le stress

to **stretch** VERB
1 s'étirer *(person, animal)*
□ The dog woke up and stretched. Le chien s'est réveillé et s'est étiré.
2 se détendre *(get bigger)*
□ My sweater stretched when I washed it. Mon pull s'est détendu au lavage.
3 tendre *(stretch out)*
□ They stretched a rope between two trees. Ils ont tendu une corde entre deux arbres.
■ **to stretch out one's arms** tendre les bras

stretcher NOUN
le brancard

stretchy ADJECTIVE
élastique *(FEM élastique)*

strict ADJECTIVE
strict *(FEM stricte)*

strike NOUN
▷ *see also* **strike** VERB
la grève
■ **to be on strike** être en grève
■ **to go on strike** faire grève

to **strike** VERB
▷ *see also* **strike** NOUN
1 sonner *(clock)*
□ The clock struck three. L'horloge a sonné trois heures.

S

English-French

2 faire grève *(go on strike)*
3 frapper *(hit)*
■ **to strike a match** frotter une allumette
striker NOUN
1 le/la gréviste *(person on strike)*
2 le buteur *(footballer)*
striking ADJECTIVE
1 en grève *(on strike)*
  □ striking miners les mineurs en grève
2 frappant (FEM frappante) *(noticeable)*
  □ a striking difference une différence frappante
string NOUN
1 la ficelle
  □ a piece of string un bout de ficelle
2 la corde *(of violin, guitar)*
to **strip** VERB
  ▷ *see also* **strip** NOUN
  se déshabiller *(get undressed)*
strip NOUN
  ▷ *see also* **strip** VERB
  la bande
  ■ **a strip cartoon** une bande dessinée
stripe NOUN
  la rayure
striped ADJECTIVE
  à rayures
  □ a striped skirt une jupe à rayures
stripper NOUN
  le strip-teaseur
  la strip-teaseuse
stripy ADJECTIVE
  rayé (FEM rayée)
  □ a stripy shirt une chemise rayée
to **stroke** VERB
  ▷ *see also* **stroke** NOUN
  caresser
stroke NOUN
  ▷ *see also* **stroke** VERB
  l' attaque *fem*
  □ to have a stroke avoir une attaque
stroll NOUN
  ■ **to go for a stroll** aller faire une petite promenade
stroller NOUN (US)
  le landau
strong ADJECTIVE
1 fort (FEM forte)
  □ She's very strong. Elle est très forte.
2 résistant (FEM résistante) *(material)*
strongly ADVERB
  fortement
  □ We recommend strongly that … Nous recommandons fortement que …
  ■ **He smelt strongly of tobacco.** Il sentait fort le tabac.
■ **strongly built** solidement bâti

■ **I don't feel strongly about it.** Ça m'est égal.
struck VERB ▷ *see* **strike**
to **struggle** VERB
  ▷ *see also* **struggle** NOUN
  se débattre *(physically)*
  □ He struggled, but he couldn't escape. Il s'est débattu, mais il n'a pas pu s'échapper.
  ■ **to struggle to do something 1** *(fight)* se battre pour faire quelque chose □ He struggled to get custody of his daughter. Il s'est battu pour obtenir la garde de sa fille.
  2 *(have difficulty)* avoir du mal à faire quelque chose □ She struggled to get the door open. Elle a eu du mal à ouvrir la porte.
struggle NOUN
  ▷ *see also* **struggle** VERB
  la lutte *(for independence, equality)*
  ■ **It was a struggle.** Ça a été laborieux.
stub NOUN
  le mégot *(of cigarette)*
to **stub out** VERB
  écraser *(cigarette)*
stubborn ADJECTIVE
  têtu (FEM têtue)
stuck VERB ▷ *see* **stick**
stuck ADJECTIVE
  coincé (FEM coincée) *(jammed)*
  □ It's stuck. C'est coincé.
  ■ **to get stuck** rester coincé □ We got stuck in a traffic jam. Nous sommes restés coincés dans un embouteillage.
stuck-up ADJECTIVE
  coincé (FEM coincée) *(informal)*
stud NOUN
1 la boucle d'oreille *(earring)*
2 le clou *(on football boots)*
student NOUN
  l' étudiant *masc*
  l' étudiante *fem*
studio NOUN
  le studio
  □ a TV studio un studio de télévision
  ■ **a studio flat** un studio
to **study** VERB
1 faire des études *(at university)*
  □ I plan to study biology. J'ai l'intention de faire des études de biologie.
2 travailler *(do homework)*
  □ I've got to study tonight. Je dois travailler ce soir.
stuff NOUN
1 le truc *(substance)*
  □ I need some stuff for hay fever. J'ai besoin d'un truc contre le rhume des foins.
2 les trucs *masc pl (things)*
  □ There's some stuff on the table for you. Il

S

y à des trucs sur la table pour toi.

3 les affaires *fem pl (possessions)*

□ Have you got all your stuff? Est-ce que tu as toutes tes affaires?

stuffy ADJECTIVE
mal aéré (FEM mal aérée) *(room)*

■ **It's really stuffy in here.** On étouffe ici.

to **stumble** VERB
trébucher

stung VERB ▷ see **sting**

stunk VERB ▷ see **stink**

stunned ADJECTIVE
sidéré (FEM sidérée) *(amazed)*

□ I was stunned. J'étais sidéré.

stunning ADJECTIVE
superbe (FEM superbe)

stunt NOUN
la cascade *(in film)*

stuntman NOUN
le cascadeur

stupid ADJECTIVE
stupide (FEM stupide)

□ a stupid joke une plaisanterie stupide

■ **Me, go jogging? Don't be stupid!** Moi, faire du footing? Ne dis pas de bêtises!

to **stutter** VERB
▷ see also **stutter** NOUN
bégayer

stutter NOUN
▷ see also **stutter** VERB

■ **He's got a stutter.** Il bégaie.

style NOUN
le style

□ That's not his style. Ça n'est pas son style.

subject NOUN
1 le sujet

□ The subject of my project was the internet. Le sujet de mon projet était l'Internet.

2 la matière *(at school)*

□ What's your favourite subject? Quelle est ta matière préférée?

subjunctive NOUN
le subjonctif

□ in the subjunctive au subjonctif

submarine NOUN
le sous-marin

subscription NOUN
l' abonnement *masc (to paper, magazine)*

■ **to take out a subscription to something** s'abonner à quelque chose

subsequently ADVERB
en conséquence

to **subsidize** VERB
subventionner

subsidy NOUN
la subvention

substance NOUN
la substance

substitute NOUN
▷ see also **substitute** VERB
le remplaçant
la remplaçante *(person)*

to **substitute** VERB
▷ see also **substitute** NOUN
substituer

□ to substitute A for B substituer A à B

subtitled ADJECTIVE
sous-titré (FEM sous-titrée)

subtitles PL NOUN
les sous-titres *masc pl*

□ a French film with English subtitles un film français avec des sous-titres en anglais

subtle ADJECTIVE
subtil (FEM subtile)

to **subtract** VERB
retrancher

□ to subtract 3 from 5 retrancher trois de cinq

suburb NOUN
la banlieue

□ a suburb of Paris une banlieue de Paris

■ **the suburbs** la banlieue □ They live in the suburbs. Ils habitent en banlieue.

suburban ADJECTIVE
de banlieue

□ a suburban train un train de banlieue

subway NOUN
le passage souterrain *(underpass)*

to **succeed** VERB
réussir

□ to succeed in doing something réussir à faire quelque chose

success NOUN
le succès

□ The play was a great success. La pièce a eu beaucoup de succès.

successful ADJECTIVE
réussi (FEM réussie)

□ a successful attempt une tentative réussie

■ **to be successful in doing something** réussir à faire quelque chose

■ **He's a successful businessman.** Ses affaires marchent bien.

successfully ADVERB
avec succès

successive ADJECTIVE

■ **on four successive occasions** quatre fois de suite

such ADJECTIVE, ADVERB
si

□ such nice people des gens si gentils
□ such a long journey un voyage si long

■ **such a lot of** tellement de ☐ such a lot of work tellement de travail

■ **such as** *(like)* comme ☐ hot countries, such as India les pays chauds, comme l'Inde

■ **not as such** pas exactement ☐ He's not an expert as such, but ... Ce n'est pas exactement un expert, mais ...

■ **There's no such thing.** Ça n'existe pas. ☐ There's no such thing as the yeti. Le yéti n'existe pas.

such-and-such ADJECTIVE
tel ou tel (FEM telle ou telle)
☐ such-and-such a place tel ou tel endroit

to **suck** VERB
sucer
☐ to suck one's thumb sucer son pouce

sudden ADJECTIVE
soudain (FEM soudaine)
☐ a sudden change un changement soudain

■ **all of a sudden** tout à coup

suddenly ADVERB
1 brusquement *(stop, leave, change)*
2 subitement *(die)*
3 soudain *(at beginning of sentence)*
☐ Suddenly, the door opened. Soudain, la porte s'est ouverte.

suede NOUN
le daim
☐ a suede jacket une veste en daim

to **suffer** VERB
souffrir
☐ She was really suffering. Elle souffrait beaucoup.

■ **to suffer from a disease** avoir une maladie ☐ I suffer from hay fever. J'ai le rhume des foins.

to **suffocate** VERB
suffoquer

sugar NOUN
le sucre
☐ Do you take sugar? Est-ce que vous prenez du sucre?

to **suggest** VERB
suggérer
☐ I suggested they set off early. Je leur ai suggéré de partir de bonne heure.

suggestion NOUN
la suggestion
☐ to make a suggestion faire une suggestion

suicide NOUN
le suicide

■ **to commit suicide** se suicider

suicide bomber NOUN
le/la kamikaze

suit NOUN
▷ *see also* **suit** VERB
1 le costume *(man's)*
2 le tailleur *(woman's)*

to **suit** VERB
▷ *see also* **suit** NOUN
1 convenir à *(be convenient for)*
☐ What time would suit you? Quelle heure vous conviendrait?

■ **That suits me fine.** Ça m'arrange.
■ **Suit yourself!** Comme tu veux!

2 aller bien à *(look good on)*
☐ That dress really suits you. Cette robe te va vraiment bien.

suitable ADJECTIVE
1 convenable (FEM convenable)
☐ a suitable time une heure convenable
2 approprié (FEM appropriée) *(clothes)*
☐ suitable clothing des vêtements appropriés

suitcase NOUN
la valise

suite NOUN
la suite *(of rooms)*
■ **a bedroom suite** une chambre à coucher

to **sulk** VERB
bouder

sulky ADJECTIVE
boudeur (FEM boudeuse)

sultana NOUN
le raisin sec (PL les raisins secs)

sum NOUN
1 le calcul *(calculation)*
☐ She's good at sums. Elle est bonne en calcul.
2 la somme *(amount)*
☐ a sum of money une somme d'argent

to **sum up** VERB
résumer

to **summarize** VERB
résumer

summary NOUN
le résumé

summer NOUN
l'été masc

■ **in summer** en été
■ **summer clothes** les vêtements d'été
■ **the summer holidays** les vacances d'été
■ **a summer camp** (US) une colonie de vacances

summertime NOUN
l'été masc

■ **in summertime** en été

summit NOUN
le sommet

sun NOUN
le soleil

□ in the sun au soleil

to **sunbathe** VERB
se bronzer

sunblock NOUN
l' écran total *masc*

sunburn NOUN
le coup de soleil

sunburnt ADJECTIVE
■ **I got sunburnt.** J'ai attrapé un coup de soleil.

Sunday NOUN
le dimanche
□ on Sunday dimanche □ on Sundays le dimanche □ every Sunday tous les dimanches □ last Sunday dimanche dernier □ next Sunday dimanche prochain

Sunday school NOUN
le catéchisme
□ to go to Sunday school aller au catéchisme

> **DID YOU KNOW...?**
> **le catéchisme**, the French equivalent of 'Sunday school', takes place during the week after school rather than on a Sunday.

sunflower NOUN
le tournesol
□ sunflower seeds des grains de tournesol

sung VERB ▷ see **sing**

sunglasses PL NOUN
les lunettes de soleil *fem pl*

sunk VERB ▷ see **sink**

sunlight NOUN
le soleil

sunny ADJECTIVE
ensoleillé (FEM ensoleillée)
□ a sunny morning une matinée ensoleillée
■ **It's sunny.** Il fait du soleil.
■ **a sunny day** une belle journée

sunrise NOUN
le lever du soleil

sunroof NOUN
le toit ouvrant

sunscreen NOUN
la crème solaire

sunset NOUN
le coucher du soleil

sunshine NOUN
le soleil

sunstroke NOUN
l' insolation *fem*
□ to get sunstroke attraper une insolation

suntan NOUN
le bronzage
■ **suntan lotion** le lait solaire
■ **suntan oil** l'huile solaire *fem*

super ADJECTIVE

formidable (FEM formidable)

superb ADJECTIVE
superbe (FEM superbe)

supermarket NOUN
le supermarché

supernatural ADJECTIVE
surnaturel (FEM surnaturelle)

superstitious ADJECTIVE
superstitieux (FEM superstitieuse)

to **supervise** VERB
surveiller

supervisor NOUN
1 le surveillant
la surveillante (in factory)
2 le chef de rayon (in department store)

supper NOUN
le dîner

supplement NOUN
le supplément

supplies PL NOUN
les vivres *masc pl* (food)

to **supply** VERB
▷ see also **supply** NOUN
fournir (provide)
■ **to supply somebody with something** fournir quelque chose à quelqu'un □ The centre supplied us with all the equipment. Le centre nous a fourni tout l'équipement.

supply NOUN
▷ see also **supply** VERB
la provision
□ a supply of paper une provision de papier
■ **the water supply** (to town)
l'approvisionnement en eau *masc*

supply teacher NOUN
le suppléant
la suppléante

to **support** VERB
▷ see also **support** NOUN
1 soutenir
□ My mum has always supported me. Ma mère m'a toujours soutenu.
2 être supporter de
□ What team do you support? Tu es supporter de quelle équipe?
3 subvenir aux besoins de (financially)
□ She had to support five children on her own. Elle a dû subvenir toute seule aux besoins de cinq enfants.

> **LANGUAGE TIP** Be careful not to translate **to support** by **supporter**.

support NOUN
▷ see also **support** VERB
le soutien (backing)

supporter NOUN
1 le supporter
□ a Liverpool supporter un supporter de

561

Liverpool

2 le sympathisant
la sympathisante

□ a supporter of the Labour Party un sympathisant du parti travailliste

to **suppose** VERB
imaginer

□ I suppose he's late. J'imagine qu'il est en retard. □ Suppose you won the lottery. Imaginez que vous gagniez à la loterie.

■ **I suppose so.** J'imagine.

■ **to be supposed to do something** être censé faire quelque chose □ You're supposed to show your passport. On est censé montrer son passeport.

supposing CONJUNCTION
si

□ Supposing you won the lottery ... Si tu gagnais à la loterie ...

surcharge NOUN
la surcharge

sure ADJECTIVE
sûr (FEM sûre)

□ Are you sure? Tu es sûr?

■ **Sure!** Bien sûr!

■ **to make sure that ...** vérifier que ... □ I'm going to make sure the door's locked. Je vais vérifier que la porte est fermée à clé.

surely ADVERB

■ **Surely you've been to London?** J'imagine que tu es allé à Londres, non?

■ **The shops are closed on Sundays, surely?** J'imagine que les magasins sont fermés le dimanche, non?

surf NOUN
▷ see also **surf** VERB
le ressac

to **surf** VERB
▷ see also **surf** NOUN
surfer

■ **to go surfing** faire du surf

■ **to surf the Net** surfer sur le Net

surface NOUN
la surface

surfboard NOUN
la planche de surf

surfing NOUN
le surf

□ to go surfing faire du surf

surgeon NOUN
le chirurgien

□ She's a surgeon. Elle est chirurgien.

surgery NOUN
le cabinet médical (doctor's surgery)

■ **surgery hours** les heures de consultation fem pl

surname NOUN

le nom de famille

surprise NOUN
la surprise

surprised ADJECTIVE
surpris (FEM surprise)

□ I was surprised to see him. J'ai été surpris de le voir.

surprising ADJECTIVE
surprenant (FEM surprenante)

to **surrender** VERB
capituler

surrogate mother NOUN
la mère porteuse

to **surround** VERB
encercler

□ The police surrounded the house. La police a encerclé la maison. □ You're surrounded! Vous êtes encerclé!

■ **surrounded by** entouré de □ The house is surrounded by trees. La maison est entourée d'arbres.

surroundings PL NOUN
le cadre sing

□ a hotel in beautiful surroundings un hôtel situé dans un beau cadre

survey NOUN
l' enquête fem (research)

surveyor NOUN
1 l' expert en bâtiment masc (of buildings)
2 le/la géomètre (of land)

survivor NOUN
le survivant
la survivante

□ There were no survivors. Il n'y a pas eu de survivants.

to **suspect** VERB
▷ see also **suspect** NOUN
soupçonner

suspect NOUN
▷ see also **suspect** VERB
le suspect
la suspecte

to **suspend** VERB
1 exclure (from school, team)

□ He's been suspended. Il s'est fait exclure.

2 suspendre (from job)

suspenders PL NOUN (US)
les bretelles fem pl (braces)

suspense NOUN
1 l' attente fem (waiting)

□ The suspense was terrible. L'attente a été terrible.

2 le suspense (in story)

□ a film with lots of suspense un film avec beaucoup de suspense

suspension NOUN
1 l' exclusion fem (from school, team)

2 la suspension *(from job)*
suspicious ADJECTIVE
1 méfiant (FEM méfiante)
  □ He was suspicious at first. Il était méfiant au début.
2 louche (FEM louche) *(suspicious-looking)*
  □ a suspicious person un individu louche
to **swallow** VERB
  avaler
swam VERB ▷ *see* **swim**
swan NOUN
  le cygne
to **swap** VERB
  échanger
  □ Do you want to swap? Tu veux échanger?
  □ to swap A for B échanger A contre B
to **swat** VERB
  écraser
to **sway** VERB
  osciller
to **swear** VERB
  jurer *(make an oath, curse)*
swearword NOUN
  le gros mot
sweat NOUN
  ▷ *see also* **sweat** VERB
  la transpiration
to **sweat** VERB
  ▷ *see also* **sweat** NOUN
  transpirer
sweater NOUN
  le pull
sweatshirt NOUN
  le sweat
sweaty ADJECTIVE
1 en sueur *(person, face)*
  □ I'm all sweaty. Je suis en sueur.
2 moite (FEM moite) *(hands)*
Swede NOUN
  le Suédois
  la Suédoise *(person)*
swede NOUN
  le rutabaga *(vegetable)*
Sweden NOUN
  la Suède
  ■ in Sweden en Suède
  ■ to Sweden en Suède
Swedish NOUN
  ▷ *see also* **Swedish** ADJECTIVE
  le suédois *(language)*
Swedish ADJECTIVE
  ▷ *see also* **Swedish** NOUN
  suédois (FEM suédoise)
  □ She's Swedish. Elle est suédoise.
to **sweep** VERB
  balayer
  ■ to sweep the floor balayer

sweet NOUN
  ▷ *see also* **sweet** ADJECTIVE
1 le bonbon *(candy)*
  □ a bag of sweets un paquet de bonbons
2 le dessert *(pudding)*
  □ What sweet did you have? Qu'est-ce que vous avez mangé comme dessert?
sweet ADJECTIVE
  ▷ *see also* **sweet** NOUN
1 sucré (FEM sucrée) *(not savoury)*
2 gentil (FEM gentille) *(kind)*
  □ That was really sweet of you. C'était vraiment gentil de ta part.
3 mignon (FEM mignonne) *(cute)*
  □ Isn't she sweet? Comme elle est mignonne!
  ■ sweet and sour pork le porc à la sauce aigre-douce
sweetcorn NOUN
  le maïs doux
sweltering ADJECTIVE
  ■ It was sweltering. Il faisait une chaleur étouffante.
swept VERB ▷ *see* **sweep**
to **swerve** VERB
  faire une embardée
  □ He swerved to avoid the cyclist. Il a fait une embardée pour éviter le cycliste.
swim NOUN
  ▷ *see also* **swim** VERB
  ■ to go for a swim aller se baigner
to **swim** VERB
  ▷ *see also* **swim** NOUN
  nager
  □ Can you swim? Tu sais nager?
  ■ She swam across the river. Elle a traversé la rivière à la nage.
swimmer NOUN
  le nageur
  la nageuse
  □ She's a good swimmer. C'est une bonne nageuse.
swimming NOUN
  la natation
  □ Do you like swimming? Tu aimes la natation?
  ■ to go swimming *(in a pool)* aller à la piscine
  ■ a swimming cap un bonnet de bain
  ■ a swimming costume un maillot de bain
  ■ a swimming pool une piscine
  ■ swimming trunks le maillot de bain
swimsuit NOUN
  le maillot de bain
swing NOUN
  ▷ *see also* **swing** VERB
  la balançoire *(in playground, garden)*

to **swing** VERB
▷ *see also* **swing** NOUN
1 se balancer
□ A bunch of keys swung from his belt. Un trousseau de clés se balançait à sa ceinture.
■ **Sam was swinging an umbrella as he walked.** Sam balançait son parapluie en marchant.
2 virer
□ The canoe swung round sharply. Le canoë a viré brusquement.

Swiss NOUN
▷ *see also* **Swiss** ADJECTIVE
le/la Suisse *(person)*
■ **the Swiss** les Suisses

Swiss ADJECTIVE
▷ *see also* **Swiss** NOUN
suisse (FEM suisse)
□ Sabine's Swiss. Sabine est suisse.

switch NOUN
▷ *see also* **switch** VERB
le bouton *(for light, radio etc)*

to **switch** VERB
▷ *see also* **switch** NOUN
changer de
□ We switched partners. Nous avons changé de partenaire.

to **switch off** VERB
1 éteindre *(electrical appliance)*
2 arrêter *(engine, machine)*

to **switch on** VERB
1 allumer *(electrical appliance)*
2 mettre en marche *(engine, machine)*

Switzerland NOUN
la Suisse
■ **in Switzerland** en Suisse

swollen ADJECTIVE
enflé (FEM enflée) *(arm, leg)*

to **swop** VERB

échanger
□ Do you want to swop? Tu veux échanger?
□ to swop A for B échanger A contre B

sword NOUN
l' épée *fem*

swore, sworn VERB ▷ *see* **swear**

swot NOUN
▷ *see also* **swot** VERB
le bûcheur
la bûcheuse

to **swot** VERB
▷ *see also* **swot** NOUN
bosser dur
□ I'll have to swot for my maths exam. Je vais devoir bosser dur pour mon examen de maths.

swum VERB ▷ *see* **swim**

swung VERB ▷ *see* **swing**

syllabus NOUN
le programme
□ on the syllabus au programme

symbol NOUN
le symbole

sympathetic ADJECTIVE
compréhensif (FEM compréhensive)

> **LANGUAGE TIP** Be careful not to translate **sympathetic** by sympathique.

to **sympathize** VERB
■ **to sympathize with somebody** comprendre quelqu'un

sympathy NOUN
la compassion

symptom NOUN
le symptôme

syringe NOUN
la seringue

system NOUN
le système

S

Tt

table NOUN
la table
  □ to lay the table mettre la table
tablecloth NOUN
la nappe
tablespoon NOUN
la grande cuillère
  ■ **two tablespoons of sugar** deux cuillerées à soupe de sucre
tablet NOUN
le comprimé
table tennis NOUN
le ping-pong
  □ to play table tennis jouer au ping-pong
tabloid NOUN
le quotidien populaire
tackle NOUN
  ▷ see also **tackle** VERB
1 le tacle (in football)
2 le plaquage (in rugby)
  ■ **fishing tackle** le matériel de pêche
to **tackle** VERB
  ▷ see also **tackle** NOUN
1 tacler (in football)
2 plaquer (in rugby)
  ■ **to tackle a problem** s'attaquer à un problème
tact NOUN
le tact
tactful ADJECTIVE
plein de tact (FEM pleine de tact)
tactics PL NOUN
la tactique sing
tactless ADJECTIVE
  ■ **to be tactless** manquer de tact □ a tactless remark une remarque qui manque de tact
tadpole NOUN
le têtard
tag NOUN
l' étiquette fem (label)
tail NOUN
la queue
  ■ **Heads or tails?** Pile ou face?
tailor NOUN

le tailleur
to **take** VERB
1 prendre
  □ Are you taking your new camera? Tu prends ton nouvel appareil photo? □ He took a plate from the cupboard. Il a pris une assiette dans le placard. □ It takes about an hour. Ça prend environ une heure.
2 emmener (person)
  □ When will you take me to London? Quand est-ce que tu vas m'emmener à Londres?
  ■ **to take something somewhere** emporter quelque chose quelque part □ Do you take your exercise books home? Vous emportez vos cahiers chez vous? □ Don't take anything valuable with you. N'emportez pas d'objets de valeur.
  ■ **I'm going to take my coat to the cleaner's.** Je vais donner mon manteau à nettoyer.
3 demander (effort, skill)
  □ That takes a lot of courage. Cela demande beaucoup de courage.
  ■ **It takes a lot of money to do that.** Il faut beaucoup d'argent pour faire ça.
4 supporter (tolerate)
  □ He can't take being criticized. Il ne supporte pas d'être critiqué.
5 passer (exam, test)
  □ Have you taken your driving test yet? Est-ce que tu as déjà passé ton permis de conduire?
6 faire (subject)
  □ I decided to take French instead of German. J'ai décidé de faire du français au lieu de l'allemand.
to **take after** VERB
ressembler à
  □ She takes after her mother. Elle ressemble à sa mère.
to **take apart** VERB
  ■ **to take something apart** démonter quelque chose
to **take away** VERB
1 emporter (object)

t

2 emmener *(person)*
- **to take something away** *(confiscate)* confisquer quelque chose
- **hot meals to take away** des plats chauds à emporter

to **take back** VERB
rapporter
□ I took it back to the shop. Je l'ai rapporté au magasin.
- **I take it all back!** Je n'ai rien dit!

to **take down** VERB
1 enlever *(poster, sign)*
2 décrocher *(painting, curtains)*
3 démonter *(tent, scaffolding)*
4 prendre en note *(make a note of)*
□ He took down the details in his notebook. Il a pris tous les détails en note dans son carnet.

to **take in** VERB
comprendre *(understand)*
□ I didn't really take it in. Je n'ai pas bien compris.

to **take off** VERB
1 décoller *(plane)*
□ The plane took off twenty minutes late. L'avion a décollé avec vingt minutes de retard.
2 enlever *(clothes)*
□ Take your coat off. Enlevez votre manteau.

to **take out** VERB
sortir *(from container, pocket)*
- **He took her out to the theatre.** Il l'a emmenée au théâtre.

to **take over** VERB
prendre la relève
□ I'll take over now. Je vais prendre la relève.
- **to take over from somebody** remplacer quelqu'un

takeaway NOUN
le plat à emporter *(meal)*
- **a Chinese takeaway** un restaurant chinois qui vend des plats à emporter

taken VERB ▷ *see* **take**

takeoff NOUN
le décollage *(of plane)*

talcum powder NOUN
le talc

tale NOUN
le conte *fem (story)*

talent NOUN
le talent
□ She's got lots of talent. Elle a beaucoup de talent.
- **to have a talent for something** être doué pour quelque chose □ He's got a real

talent for languages. Il est vraiment doué pour les langues.

talented ADJECTIVE
- **She's a talented pianist.** C'est une pianiste de talent.

talk NOUN
▷ *see also* **talk** VERB
1 l' exposé *masc (speech)*
□ She gave a talk on rock climbing. Elle a fait un exposé sur la varappe.
2 la conversation *(conversation)*
□ I had a talk with my Mum about it. J'ai eu une petite conversation avec ma mère à ce sujet.
3 les racontars *masc pl (gossip)*
□ It's just talk. Ce sont des racontars.

to **talk** VERB
▷ *see also* **talk** NOUN
parler
□ to talk about something parler de quelque chose
- **to talk something over with somebody** discuter de quelque chose avec quelqu'un

talkative ADJECTIVE
bavard (FEM bavarde)

tall ADJECTIVE
1 grand (FEM grande) *(person, tree)*
- **to be 2 metres tall** mesurer deux mètres
2 haut (FEM haute) *(building)*

tame ADJECTIVE
apprivoisé (FEM apprivoisée) *(animal)*
□ They've got a tame hedgehog. Ils ont un hérisson apprivoisé.

tampon NOUN
le tampon

tan NOUN
le bronzage
□ She's got an amazing tan. Elle a un bronzage superbe.

tangerine NOUN
la mandarine

tangle NOUN
1 l' enchevêtrement *masc (ropes, cables)*
2 le nœud *(hair)*
- **to be in a tangle 1** *(ropes, cables)* être enchevêtré **2** *(hair)* être emmêlé

tank NOUN
1 le réservoir *(for water, petrol)*
2 le char d'assaut *(military)*
- **a fish tank** un aquarium

tanker NOUN
1 le pétrolier *(ship)*
- **an oil tanker** un pétrolier
2 le camion-citerne *(truck)*
- **a petrol tanker** un camion-citerne

tap NOUN
1 le robinet *(water tap)*

2 la petite tape *(gentle blow)*

tap-dancing NOUN
les claquettes *fem pl*
□ I do tap-dancing. Je fais des claquettes.

to **tape** VERB
▷ *see also* **tape** NOUN
enregistrer *(record)*
□ Did you tape that film last night? As-tu enregistré le film hier soir?

tape NOUN
▷ *see also* **tape** VERB
1 la cassette
2 le scotch® *(sticky tape)*

tape measure NOUN
le mètre à ruban

tape recorder NOUN
le magnétophone

target NOUN
la cible

tarmac NOUN
le macadam *(on road)*

tart NOUN
la tarte
□ an apple tart une tarte aux pommes

tartan ADJECTIVE
écossais (FEM écossaise)
□ a tartan scarf une écharpe écossaise

task NOUN
la tâche

taste NOUN
▷ *see also* **taste** VERB
le goût
□ It's got a really strange taste. Ça a un goût vraiment bizarre. □ a joke in bad taste une plaisanterie de mauvais goût
■ **Would you like a taste?** Tu veux goûter?

to **taste** VERB
▷ *see also* **taste** NOUN
goûter
□ Would you like to taste it? Vous voulez y goûter?
■ **to taste of something** avoir un goût de quelque chose □ It tastes of fish. Ça a un goût de poisson.
■ **You can taste the garlic in it.** Ça a bien le goût d'ail.

tasteful ADJECTIVE
de bon goût

tasteless ADJECTIVE
1 fade (FEM fade) *(food)*
2 de mauvais goût *(in bad taste)*
□ a tasteless remark une remarque de mauvais goût

tasty ADJECTIVE
savoureux (FEM savoureuse)

tattoo NOUN
le tatouage

taught VERB ▷ *see* **teach**

Taurus NOUN
le Taureau
□ I'm Taurus. Je suis Taureau.

tax NOUN
1 les impôts *masc pl (on income)*
2 la taxe *(on goods, alcohol)*

taxi NOUN
le taxi
■ **a taxi driver** un chauffeur de taxi

taxi rank NOUN
la station de taxis

TB NOUN
la tuberculose

tea NOUN
1 le thé
□ a cup of tea une tasse de thé
■ **a tea bag** un sachet de thé
2 le dîner *(evening meal)*
■ **We were having tea.** Nous étions en train de dîner.

> **DID YOU KNOW...?**
> In France, it is more common to have lemon with your tea.

to **teach** VERB
1 apprendre
□ My sister taught me to swim. Ma sœur m'a appris à nager. □ That'll teach you! Ça t'apprendra!
2 enseigner *(in school)*
□ She teaches physics. Elle enseigne la physique.

teacher NOUN
1 le professeur *(in secondary school)*
□ a maths teacher un professeur de maths
□ She's a teacher. Elle est professeur.
2 l' instituteur *masc*
l' institutrice *fem (in primary school)*
□ He's a primary school teacher. Il est instituteur.

teacher's pet NOUN
le chouchou
la chouchoute

tea cloth NOUN
le torchon

team NOUN
l' équipe *fem*
□ a football team une équipe de football
□ She was in my team. Elle était dans mon équipe.

teapot NOUN
la théière

tear NOUN
▷ *see also* **tear** VERB
la larme
□ She was in tears. Elle était en larmes.

to **tear** VERB

▷ *see also* **tear** NOUN
1 déchirer
□ Be careful or you'll tear the page. Fais attention, tu vas déchirer la page.
2 se déchirer
□ It won't tear, it's very strong. Ça ne se déchire pas, c'est très solide.

to **tear up** VERB
déchirer
□ He tore up the letter. Il a déchiré la lettre.

tear gas NOUN
le gaz lacrymogène

to **tease** VERB
1 tourmenter *(unkindly)*
□ Stop teasing that poor animal! Arrête de tourmenter cette pauvre bête!
2 taquiner *(jokingly)*
□ He's teasing you. Il te taquine.
■ I was only teasing. Je plaisantais.

teaspoon NOUN
la petite cuillère
■ two teaspoons of sugar deux cuillerées à café de sucre

teatime NOUN
l' heure du dîner *fem (in evening)*
□ It was nearly teatime. C'était presque l'heure du dîner.
■ Teatime! À table!

tea towel NOUN
le torchon

technical ADJECTIVE
technique (FEM technique)
■ a technical college un lycée technique

technician NOUN
le technicien
la technicienne

technique NOUN
la technique

techno NOUN
la techno *(music)*

technological ADJECTIVE
technologique (FEM technologique)

technology NOUN
la technologie

teddy bear NOUN
le nounours

teenage ADJECTIVE
1 pour les jeunes
□ a teenage magazine un magazine pour les jeunes
2 adolescent (FEM adolescente) *(boys, girls)*
□ She has two teenage daughters. Elle a deux filles adolescentes.

teenager NOUN
l' adolescent *masc*
l' adolescente *fem*

teens PL NOUN

■ She's in her teens. C'est une adolescente.

tee-shirt NOUN
le tee-shirt

teeth PL NOUN
les dents *fem pl*

to **teethe** VERB
faire ses dents

teetotal ADJECTIVE
■ I'm teetotal. Je ne bois jamais d'alcool.

telecommunications PL NOUN
les télécommunications *fem pl*

telephone NOUN
le téléphone
□ on the telephone au téléphone
■ a telephone box une cabine téléphonique
■ a telephone call un coup de téléphone
■ the telephone directory l'annuaire *masc*
■ a telephone number un numéro de téléphone

telesales PL NOUN
la vente par téléphone *sing*
□ She works in telesales. Elle travaille dans la vente par téléphone.

telescope NOUN
le télescope

television NOUN
la télévision
■ on television à la télévision
■ a television licence une redevance de télévision
■ a television programme une émission de télévision

to **tell** VERB
dire
■ to tell somebody something dire quelque chose à quelqu'un □ Did you tell your mother? Tu l'as dit à ta mère? □ I told him that I was going on holiday. Je lui ai dit que je partais en vacances.
■ to tell somebody to do something dire à quelqu'un de faire quelque chose □ He told me to wait a moment. Il m'a dit d'attendre un moment.
■ to tell lies dire des mensonges
■ to tell a story raconter une histoire
■ I can't tell the difference between them. Je n'arrive pas à les distinguer.

to **tell off** VERB
gronder

telly NOUN
la télé
□ to watch telly regarder la télé
■ on telly à la télé

temper NOUN
le caractère

□ He's got a terrible temper. Il a un sale caractère.

■ **to be in a temper** être en colère

■ **to lose one's temper** se mettre en colère

□ I lost my temper. Je me suis mis en colère.

temperature NOUN
la température (of oven, water, person)

■ **The temperature was 30 degrees.** Il faisait trente degrés.

■ **to have a temperature** avoir de la fièvre

temple NOUN
le temple

temporary ADJECTIVE
temporaire (FEM temporaire)

to **tempt** VERB
tenter

□ I'm very tempted! Je suis très tenté!

■ **to tempt somebody to do something** persuader quelqu'un de faire quelque chose

temptation NOUN
la tentation

tempting ADJECTIVE
tentant (FEM tentante)

ten NUMBER
dix

□ She's ten. Elle a dix ans.

tenant NOUN
le locataire
la locataire

to **tend** VERB

■ **to tend to do something** avoir tendance à faire quelque chose □ He tends to arrive late. Il a tendance à arriver en retard.

tender ADJECTIVE
1 tendre (FEM tendre) (food)
2 sensible (FEM sensible) (part of body)

□ My feet are really tender. J'ai les pieds très sensibles.

tennis NOUN
le tennis

□ Do you play tennis? Vous jouez au tennis?

■ **a tennis ball** une balle de tennis

■ **a tennis court** un court de tennis

■ **a tennis racket** une raquette de tennis

tennis player NOUN
le joueur de tennis
la joueuse de tennis

□ He's a tennis player. Il est joueur de tennis.

tenor NOUN
le ténor

tenpin bowling NOUN
le bowling

□ to go tenpin bowling jouer au bowling

tense ADJECTIVE
▷ see also **tense** NOUN

tendu (FEM tendue)

tense NOUN
▷ see also **tense** ADJECTIVE

■ **the present tense** le présent

■ **the future tense** le futur

tension NOUN
la tension

tent NOUN
la tente

■ **a tent peg** un piquet de tente

■ **a tent pole** un montant de tente

tenth ADJECTIVE
dixième (FEM dixième)

□ the tenth floor le dixième étage

■ **the tenth of August** le dix août

term NOUN
1 le trimestre (at school)
2 le terme

□ a short-term solution une solution à court terme

■ **to come to terms with something** accepter quelque chose

terminal ADJECTIVE
▷ see also **terminal** NOUN

incurable (FEM incurable) (illness, patient)

terminal NOUN
▷ see also **terminal** ADJECTIVE

un terminal (of computer)

■ **an oil terminal** un terminal pétrolier

■ **an air terminal** une aérogare

terminally ADVERB

■ **to be terminally ill** être condamné

terrace NOUN
1 la terrasse (patio)
2 la rangée de maisons (row of houses)

■ **the terraces** (at stadium) les gradins masc pl

terraced ADJECTIVE

■ **a terraced house** une maison mitoyenne

terrible ADJECTIVE
épouvantable (FEM épouvantable)

□ My French is terrible. Mon français est épouvantable.

terribly ADVERB
1 terriblement

□ He suffered terribly. Il souffre terriblement.

2 vraiment

□ I'm terribly sorry. Je suis vraiment désolé.

terrier NOUN
le terrier

terrific ADJECTIVE
super (FEM + PL super) (wonderful)

□ That's terrific! C'est super!

■ **You look terrific!** Tu es superbe!

terrified ADJECTIVE

terrifié (FEM terrifiée)
- □ I was terrified! J'étais terrifié!

terrorism NOUN
le terrorisme

terrorist NOUN
le/la terroriste
- ■ a terrorist attack un attentat terroriste

test NOUN
▷ see also **test** VERB
1 l' interrogation *fem (at school)*
- □ I've got a test tomorrow. J'ai une interrogation demain.
2 l' essai *masc (trial, check)*
- □ nuclear tests les essais nucléaires
3 l' analyse *fem (medical)*
- □ a blood test une analyse de sang
- □ They're going to do some more tests. Ils vont faire d'autres analyses.
- ■ driving test l'examen du permis de conduire □ He's got his driving test tomorrow. Il passe son permis de conduire demain.

to **test** VERB
▷ see also **test** NOUN
1 essayer
- □ to test something out essayer quelque chose
2 interroger *(class)*
- □ He tested us on the vocabulary. Il nous a interrogés sur le vocabulaire.
- ■ She was tested for drugs. On lui a fait subir un contrôle antidopage.

test match NOUN
le match international

test tube NOUN
l' éprouvette *fem*

tetanus NOUN
le tétanos
- □ a tetanus injection un vaccin contre le tétanos

text NOUN
▷ see also **text** VERB
1 le texte
2 le SMS *(on mobile phone)*

to **text** VERB
▷ see also **text** NOUN
- ■ to text someone envoyer un SMS à quelqu'un

textbook NOUN
le manuel
- □ a French textbook un manuel de français

text message NOUN
le SMS

Thames NOUN
la Tamise

than CONJUNCTION

que
- □ She's taller than me. Elle est plus grande que moi. □ I've got more books than him. J'ai plus de livres que lui.
- ■ more than ten years plus de dix ans
- ■ more than once plus d'une fois

to **thank** VERB
remercier
- □ Don't forget to write and thank them. N'oublie pas de leur écrire pour les remercier.
- ■ thank you merci
- ■ thank you very much merci beaucoup

thanks EXCLAMATION
merci!
- ■ thanks to grâce à □ Thanks to him, everything went OK. Grâce à lui, tout s'est bien passé.

that ADJECTIVE, PRONOUN, CONJUNCTION

> **LANGUAGE TIP** Use **ce** when 'that' is followed by a masculine noun, and **cette** when 'that' is followed by a feminine noun. **ce** changes to **cet** before a vowel and before most words beginning with 'h'.

1 ce
- □ that book ce livre
cet
- □ that man cet homme
cette
- □ that woman cette femme □ that road cette route
- ■ *that* road cette route-là
- ■ *that* one 1 celui-là *masc* □ This man? — No, that one. Cet homme-ci? — Non, celui-là. 2 celle-là *fem* □ Do you like this photo? — No, I prefer that one. Tu aimes cette photo? — Non, je préfère celle-là.
2 ça
- □ You see that? Tu vois ça?
- ■ What's that? Qu'est-ce que c'est?
- ■ Who's that? Qui est-ce?
- ■ Is that you? C'est toi?
- ■ That's ... C'est ... □ That's my teacher. C'est mon prof. □ That's what he said. C'est ce qu'il a dit.

> **LANGUAGE TIP** In relative phrases use **qui** when 'that' refers to the subject of the sentence, and **que** when it refers to the object.

3 qui
- □ the man that saw us l'homme qui nous a vus □ the man that spoke to us l'homme qui nous a parlé
4 que
- □ the man that we saw l'homme que nous avons vu □ the man that we spoke to

l'homme à qui nous avons parlé

> **LANGUAGE TIP** **que** changes to **qu'** before a vowel and before most words beginning with 'h'.

▢ the dog that she bought le chien qu'elle a acheté ▢ He thought that Henri was ill. Il pensait qu'Henri était malade. ▢ I know that she likes chocolate. Je sais qu'elle aime le chocolat.

■ **It was that big.** Il était grand comme ça.
■ **It's about that high.** C'est à peu près haut comme ça.
■ **It's not that difficult.** Ça n'est pas si difficile que ça.

thatched ADJECTIVE
■ **a thatched cottage** une chaumière

the ARTICLE

> **LANGUAGE TIP** Use **le** with a masculine noun, and **la** with a feminine noun. Use **l'** before a vowel and most words beginning with 'h'. For plural nouns always use **les**.

le
▢ the boy le garçon
l'
▢ the man l'homme *masc* ▢ the air l'air *masc* ▢ the habit l'habitude *fem*
la
▢ the girl la fille
les
▢ the children les enfants

theatre (US **theater**) NOUN
le théâtre

theft NOUN
le vol

their ADJECTIVE
leur (PL leurs)
▢ their house leur maison ▢ their parents leurs parents

theirs PRONOUN
le leur + *masc noun*
▢ It's not our garage, it's theirs. Ce n'est pas notre garage, c'est le leur.
la leur + *fem noun*
▢ It's not our car, it's theirs. Ce n'est pas notre voiture, c'est la leur.
les leurs + *pl noun*
▢ They're not our ideas, they're theirs. Ce ne sont pas nos idées, ce sont les leurs.
■ **Is this theirs?** **1** *(masculine owners)* C'est à eux? **2** *(feminine owners)* C'est à elles?
▢ This car is theirs. Cette voiture est à eux.
▢ Whose is this? — It's theirs. C'est à qui? — À eux.

them PRONOUN
1 les
▢ I didn't see them. Je ne les ai pas vus.

> **LANGUAGE TIP** Use **leur** when 'them' means 'to them'.

2 leur
▢ I gave them some brochures. Je leur ai donné des brochures. ▢ I told them the truth. Je leur ai dit la vérité.

> **LANGUAGE TIP** Use **eux** or **elles** after a preposition.

3 eux *masc*
▢ It's for them. C'est pour eux.
elles *fem*
▢ Ann and Sophie came — Graham was with them. Ann et Sophie sont venues — Graham était avec elles.

theme NOUN
le thème

theme park NOUN
le parc d'attractions

themselves PRONOUN
1 se
▢ Did they hurt themselves? Est-ce qu'ils se sont fait mal?
2 eux-mêmes *masc*
elles-mêmes *fem*
▢ They did it themselves. Ils l'ont fait eux-mêmes.

then ADVERB, CONJUNCTION
1 ensuite *(next)*
▢ I get dressed. Then I have breakfast. Je m'habille. Ensuite je prends mon petit déjeuner.
2 alors *(in that case)*
▢ My pen's run out. — Use a pencil then! Il n'y a plus d'encre dans mon stylo. — Alors utilise un crayon!
3 à l'époque *(at that time)*
▢ There was no electricity then. Il n'y avait pas l'électricité à l'époque.
■ **now and then** de temps en temps ▢ Do you play chess? — Now and then. Vous jouez aux échecs? — De temps en temps.
■ **By then it was too late.** Il était déjà trop tard.

therapy NOUN
la thérapie

there ADVERB
1 là
▢ Put it there, on the table. Mets-le là, sur la table.
■ **over there** là-bas
■ **in there** là
■ **on there** là
■ **up there** là-haut
■ **down there** là-bas
■ **There he is!** Le voilà!
2 y
▢ He went there on Friday. Il y est allé

vendredi. □ Paris? I've never been there.
Paris? Je n'y suis jamais allé.

■ **There is ...** Il y a ... □ There's a factory
near my house. Il y a une usine près de chez
moi.

■ **There are ...** Il y a ... □ There are five
people in my family. Il y a cinq personnes
dans ma famille.

■ **There has been an accident.** Il y a eu un
accident.

■ **Will there be a buffet?** Est-ce qu'il y
aura un buffet?

therefore ADVERB
donc

there's = there is, there has

thermometer NOUN
le thermomètre

Thermos® NOUN
le thermos®

these ADJECTIVE, PRONOUN
1 ces
□ these shoes ces chaussures
■ *these* shoes ces chaussures-là
2 ceux-ci *masc*
□ I want these! Je veux ceux-ci!
celles-ci *fem*
□ I'm looking for some sandals. Can I try
these? Je cherche des sandales. Je peux
essayer celles-ci?

they PRONOUN

LANGUAGE TIP Check if 'they' stands
for a masculine or feminine noun.

ils
□ Are there any tickets left? — No, they're all
sold. Est-ce qu'il reste des billets? — Non,
ils sont tous vendus.
elles
□ Do you like those shoes? — No, they're
horrible. Tu aimes ces chaussures? — Non,
elles sont affreuses.
■ **They say that ...** On dit que ...

they'd = they had, they would
they'll = they will
they're = they are
they've = they have

thick ADJECTIVE
1 épais (FEM épaisse) *(not thin)*
■ **The walls are one metre thick.** Les
murs font un mètre d'épaisseur.
2 bête (FEM bête) *(stupid)*

thief NOUN
le voleur
la voleuse
■ **Stop thief!** Au voleur!

thigh NOUN
la cuisse

thin ADJECTIVE

1 mince (FEM mince) *(person, slice)*
2 maigre (FEM maigre) *(skinny)*

WORD POWER
You can use a number of other words
instead of **thin** to mean 'skinny':
lanky dégingandé
□ a lanky boy un garçon dégingandé
skinny maigre
□ a skinny dog un chien maigre
slim mince
□ a slim girl une fille mince

---

thing NOUN
1 la chose
□ beautiful things de belles choses
2 le truc *(thingy)*
□ What's that thing called? Comment
s'appelle ce truc?
■ **my things** *(belongings)* mes affaires *fem pl*
■ **You poor thing!** Mon pauvre!

to **think** VERB
1 penser *(believe)*
□ I think you're wrong. Je pense que vous
avez tort. □ What do you think about the
war? Que pensez-vous de la guerre?
2 réfléchir *(spend time thinking)*
□ Think carefully before you reply. Réfléchis
bien avant de répondre. □ I'll think about it.
Je vais y réfléchir.
■ **What are you thinking about?** À quoi tu
penses?
3 imaginer *(imagine)*
□ Think what life would be like without cars.
Imaginez la vie sans voitures.
■ **I think so.** Oui, je crois.
■ **I don't think so.** Je ne crois pas.
■ **I'll think it over.** Je vais y réfléchir.

third ADJECTIVE
▷ *see also* **third** NOUN
troisième (FEM troisième)
□ the third day le troisième jour □ the third
time la troisième fois □ I came third. Je suis
arrivé troisième.
■ **the third of March** le trois mars

third NOUN
▷ *see also* **third** ADJECTIVE
le tiers
□ a third of the population un tiers de la
population

thirdly ADVERB
troisièmement

Third World NOUN
le tiers monde

thirst NOUN
la soif

thirsty ADJECTIVE

■ **to be thirsty** avoir soif

thirteen NUMBER
treize
▫ I'm thirteen. J'ai treize ans.

thirteenth ADJECTIVE
treizième (FEM treizième)
▫ her thirteenth birthday son treizième
anniversaire ▫ the thirteenth floor le
treizième étage
■ **the eighteenth of August** le treize août

thirty NUMBER
trente

this ADJECTIVE, PRONOUN

> **LANGUAGE TIP** Use **ce** when 'this' is
> followed by a masculine noun, and
> **cette** when 'this' is followed by a
> feminine noun. **ce** changes to **cet**
> before a vowel and before most words
> beginning with 'h'.

1 ce
▫ this book ce livre
cet
▫ this man cet homme
cette
▫ this woman cette femme ▫ this road
cette route
■ **this** road cette route-ci
■ **this one 1** celui-ci *masc* ▫ Pass me that
pen. — This one? Passe-moi ce stylo. —
Celui-ci? **2** celle-ci *fem* ▫ Of the two
photos, I prefer this one. Des deux photos,
c'est celle-ci que je préfère.
2 ça
▫ You see this? Tu vois ça?
■ **What's this?** Qu'est-ce que c'est?
■ **This is my mother.** *(introduction)* Je te
présente ma mère.
■ **This is Gavin speaking.** *(on the phone)*
C'est Gavin à l'appareil.

thistle NOUN
le chardon

thorough ADJECTIVE
minutieux (FEM minutieuse)
▫ She's very thorough. Elle est très
minutieuse.

thoroughly ADVERB
à fond *(examine)*

those ADJECTIVE, PRONOUN
1 ces
▫ those shoes ces chaussures
■ **those** shoes ces chaussures-là
2 ceux-là *masc*
▫ I want those! Je veux ceux-là!
celles-là *fem*
▫ I'm looking for some sandals. Can I try
those? Je cherche des sandales. Je peux
essayer celles-là?

though CONJUNCTION, ADVERB
bien que
▫ Though it's raining ... Bien qu'il pleuve ...

> **LANGUAGE TIP** **bien que** has to be
> followed by a verb in the subjunctive.

■ **He's a nice person, though he's not
very clever.** Il est sympa, mais pas très
malin.

thought VERB ▷ see **think**

thought NOUN
l' idée *fem (idea)*
▫ I've just had a thought. Je viens d'avoir
une idée.
■ **It was a nice thought, thank you.** C'est
gentil de ta part, merci.

thoughtful ADJECTIVE
1 pensif (FEM pensive) *(deep in thought)*
▫ You look thoughtful. Tu as l'air pensif.
2 prévenant (FEM prévenante) *(considerate)*
▫ She's very thoughtful. Elle est très
prévenante.

thoughtless ADJECTIVE
■ **He's completely thoughtless.** Il ne
pense absolument pas aux autres.

thousand NUMBER
■ **a thousand** mille ▫ a thousand euros
mille euros
■ **£2000** deux mille livres
■ **thousands of people** des milliers de
personnes

thousandth ADJECTIVE, NOUN
le millième

thread NOUN
le fil

threat NOUN
la menace

to **threaten** VERB
menacer
▫ to threaten to do something menacer de
faire quelque chose

three NUMBER
trois
▫ She's three. Elle a trois ans.

three-dimensional ADJECTIVE
à trois dimensions

threw VERB ▷ see **throw**

thrifty ADJECTIVE
économe (FEM économe)

thrill NOUN
l' émotion *fem (excitement)*

thrilled ADJECTIVE
■ **I was thrilled.** *(pleased)* J'étais
absolument ravi.

thriller NOUN
le thriller

thrilling ADJECTIVE
palpitant (FEM palpitante)

t

throat NOUN
la gorge
□ to have a sore throat avoir mal à la gorge
to **throb** VERB
■ **a throbbing pain** un élancement
■ **My arm's throbbing.** J'ai des élancements dans le bras.
throne NOUN
le trône
through PREPOSITION, ADJECTIVE, ADVERB
1 par
□ through the window par la fenêtre □ I know her through my sister. Je la connais par ma sœur. □ to go through Birmingham passer par Birmingham
■ **to go through a tunnel** traverser un tunnel
2 à travers
□ through the mist à travers la brume □ through the crowd à travers la foule □ The window was dirty and I couldn't see through. La fenêtre était sale et je n'arrivais pas à voir à travers.
■ **a through train** un train direct
■ **'no through road'** 'impasse'
throughout PREPOSITION
■ **throughout Britain** dans toute la Grande-Bretagne
■ **throughout the year** pendant toute l'année
to **throw** VERB
lancer
□ He threw the ball to me. Il m'a lancé le ballon.
■ **to throw a party** organiser une soirée
■ **That really threw him.** Ça l'a décontenancé.
to **throw away** VERB
1 jeter (rubbish)
2 perdre (chance)
to **throw out** VERB
1 jeter (throw away)
2 mettre à la porte (person)
□ I threw him out. Je l'ai mis à la porte.
to **throw up** VERB
vomir
thug NOUN
le voyou
thumb NOUN
le pouce
thumb tack NOUN (US)
la punaise
to **thump** VERB
■ **to thump somebody** donner un coup de poing à quelqu'un
thunder NOUN
le tonnerre

thunderstorm NOUN
l' orage masc
thundery ADJECTIVE
orageux (FEM orageuse)
Thursday NOUN
le jeudi
□ on Thursday jeudi □ on Thursdays le jeudi □ every Thursday tous les jeudis □ last Thursday jeudi dernier □ next Thursday jeudi prochain
thyme NOUN
le thym
tick NOUN
▷ see also **tick** VERB
1 la coche (mark)
2 le tic-tac (of clock)
■ **I'll be back in a tick.** J'en ai pour une seconde.
to **tick** VERB
▷ see also **tick** NOUN
1 cocher
□ Tick the appropriate box. Cochez la case correspondante.
2 faire tic-tac (clock)
to **tick off** VERB
1 cocher (check)
□ He ticked off our names on the list. Il a coché nos noms sur la liste.
2 passer un savon à (tell off)
□ She ticked me off for being late. Elle m'a passé un savon à cause de mon retard.
ticket NOUN

LANGUAGE TIP Be careful to choose correctly between **le ticket** and **le billet**.

1 le ticket (for bus, tube, cinema, museum)
□ an underground ticket un ticket de métro
2 le billet (for plane, train, theatre, concert)
■ **a parking ticket** un p.-v. (informal)
ticket inspector NOUN
le contrôleur
la contrôleuse
ticket office NOUN
le guichet
to **tickle** VERB
chatouiller
ticklish ADJECTIVE
chatouilleux (FEM chatouilleuse)
□ Are you ticklish? Tu es chatouilleux?
tide NOUN
la marée
■ **high tide** la marée haute
■ **low tide** la marée basse
tidy ADJECTIVE
▷ see also **tidy** VERB
1 bien rangé (FEM bien rangée) (room)
□ Your room's very tidy. Ta chambre est

bien rangée.

2 ordonné (FEM ordonnée) *(person)*
□ She's very tidy. Elle est très ordonnée.

to **tidy** VERB
▷ *see also* **tidy** ADJECTIVE
ranger
□ Go and tidy your room. Va ranger ta chambre.

to **tidy up** VERB
ranger
□ Don't forget to tidy up afterwards. N'oubliez pas de ranger après.

tie NOUN
▷ *see also* **tie** VERB
la cravate *(necktie)*
■ **It was a tie.** *(in sport)* Ils ont fait match nul.

to **tie** VERB
▷ *see also* **tie** NOUN
1 nouer *(ribbon, shoelaces)*
■ **to tie a knot in something** faire un nœud à quelque chose
2 faire match nul *(in sport)*
□ They tied three all. Ils ont fait match nul, trois à trois.

to **tie up** VERB
1 ficeler *(parcel)*
2 attacher *(dog, boat)*
3 ligoter *(prisoner)*

tiger NOUN
le tigre

tight ADJECTIVE
1 moulant (FEM moulante) *(tight-fitting)*
□ tight clothes les vêtements moulants
2 juste (FEM juste) *(too tight)*
□ This dress is a bit tight. Cette robe est un peu juste.

to **tighten** VERB
1 tendre *(rope)*
2 resserrer *(screw)*

tightly ADVERB
fort *(hold)*

tights PL NOUN
le collant *sing*

tile NOUN
1 la tuile *(on roof)*
2 le carreau (PL les carreaux) *(on wall, floor)*

tiled ADJECTIVE
1 en tuiles *(roof)*
2 carrelé (FEM carrelée) *(wall, floor, room)*

till NOUN
▷ *see also* **till** PREPOSITION
la caisse

till PREPOSITION, CONJUNCTION
▷ *see also* **till** NOUN
1 jusqu'à
□ I waited till ten o'clock. J'ai attendu

jusqu'à dix heures.
■ **till now** jusqu'à présent
■ **till then** jusque-là
2 avant

LANGUAGE TIP Use **avant** if the sentence you want to translate contains a negative such as 'not' or 'never'.

□ It won't be ready till next week. Ça ne sera pas prêt avant la semaine prochaine. □ Till last year I'd never been to France. Avant l'année dernière, je n'étais jamais allé en France.

time NOUN
1 l' heure *fem (on clock)*
□ What time is it? Quelle heure est-il?
□ What time do you get up? À quelle heure tu te lèves? □ It was two o'clock, French time. Il était deux heures, heure française.
■ **on time** à l'heure □ He never arrives on time. Il n'arrive jamais à l'heure.
2 le temps *(amount of time)*
□ I'm sorry, I haven't got time. Je suis désolé, je n'ai pas le temps.
■ **from time to time** de temps en temps
■ **in time** à temps □ We arrived in time for lunch. Nous sommes arrivés à temps pour le déjeuner.
■ **just in time** juste à temps
■ **in no time** en un rien de temps □ It was ready in no time. Ça a été prêt en un rien de temps.
■ **It's time to go.** Il est temps de partir.
■ **a long time** longtemps □ Have you lived here for a long time? Vous habitez ici depuis longtemps?
3 le moment *(moment)*
□ This isn't a good time to ask him. Ce n'est pas le bon moment pour lui demander.
■ **for the time being** pour le moment
4 la fois *(occasion)*
□ this time cette fois-ci □ next time la prochaine fois □ two at a time deux à la fois
■ **How many times?** Combien de fois?
■ **at times** parfois
■ **in a week's time** dans une semaine □ I'll come back in a month's time. Je reviendrai dans un mois.
■ **Come and see us any time.** Venez nous voir quand vous voulez.
■ **to have a good time** bien s'amuser
□ Did you have a good time? Vous vous êtes bien amusés?
■ **2 times 2 is 4** deux fois deux égalent quatre

time bomb NOUN
la bombe à retardement

time off NOUN
le temps libre

timer NOUN
le minuteur

time-share NOUN
l' appartement en multipropriété *masc*

timetable NOUN
1 l' horaire *masc (for train, bus)*
2 l' emploi du temps *masc (at school)*

time zone NOUN
le fuseau horaire

tin NOUN
1 la boîte
□ a tin of soup une boîte de soupe □ a biscuit tin une boîte à biscuits
2 la boîte de conserve
□ The bin was full of tins. La poubelle était pleine de boîtes de conserve.
3 l' étain *masc (type of metal)*

tinned ADJECTIVE
en boîte *(food)*
□ tinned peaches des pêches en boîte

tin opener NOUN
l' ouvre-boîte *masc*

tinsel NOUN
les guirlandes de Noël *fem pl*

tinted ADJECTIVE
teinté (FEM teintée) *(spectacles, glass)*

tiny ADJECTIVE
minuscule (FEM minuscule)

tip NOUN
▷ see also **tip** VERB
1 le pourboire *(money)*
□ Shall I give him a tip? Je lui donne un pourboire?
2 le tuyau (PL les tuyaux) *(advice)*
□ a useful tip un bon tuyau *(informal)*
3 le bout *(end)*
□ It's on the tip of my tongue. Je l'ai sur le bout de la langue.
■ a rubbish tip une décharge
■ This place is a complete tip! Quel fouillis!

to **tip** VERB
▷ see also **tip** NOUN
donner un pourboire à
□ Don't forget to tip the taxi driver. N'oubliez pas de donner un pourboire au chauffeur de taxi.

tipsy ADJECTIVE
pompette (FEM pompette)

tiptoe NOUN
■ on tiptoe sur la pointe des pieds

tired ADJECTIVE
fatigué (FEM fatiguée)
□ I'm tired. Je suis fatigué.
■ to be tired of something en avoir assez

de quelque chose

tiring ADJECTIVE
fatigant (FEM fatigante)

tissue NOUN
le kleenex®
□ Have you got a tissue? Tu as un kleenex®?

title NOUN
le titre

title role NOUN
le rôle principal

to PREPOSITION

LANGUAGE TIP à + **le** changes to **au**. à + **les** changes to **aux**.

1 à
□ to go to Paris aller à Paris □ to go to school aller à l'école □ a letter to his mother une lettre à sa mère □ the answer to the question la réponse à la question
au
□ to go to the theatre aller au théâtre
aux
□ We said goodbye to the neighbours. Nous avons dit au revoir aux voisins.
■ ready to go prêt à partir
■ ready to eat prêt à manger
■ It's easy to do. C'est facile à faire.
■ something to drink quelque chose à boire
■ I've got things to do. J'ai des choses à faire.
■ from ... to ... de ... à ... □ from nine o'clock to half past three de neuf heures à trois heures et demie

2 de
□ the train to London le train de Londres □ the road to Edinburgh la route d'Édimbourg □ the key to the front door la clé de la porte d'entrée
■ It's difficult to say. C'est difficile à dire.
■ It's easy to criticize. C'est facile de critiquer.

3 chez

LANGUAGE TIP When referring to someone's house, shop or office, use **chez**.

□ to go to the doctor's aller chez le docteur □ to go to the butcher's aller chez le boucher □ Let's go to Anne's house. Si on allait chez Anne?

LANGUAGE TIP When 'to' refers to a country which is feminine, use **en**; when the country is masculine, use **au**.

4 en
□ to go to France aller en France
au

□ to go to Portugal aller au Portugal
5 jusqu'à *(up to)*

□ to count to ten compter jusqu'à dix
6 pour *(in order to)*

□ I did it to help you. Je l'ai fait pour vous aider. □ She's too young to go to school. Elle est trop jeune pour aller à l'école.

toad NOUN
le crapaud

toadstool NOUN
le champignon vénéneux

toast NOUN
1 le pain grillé

□ a piece of toast une tranche de pain grillé
2 le toast *(speech)*

□ to drink a toast to somebody porter un toast à quelqu'un

toaster NOUN
le grille-pain (PL les grille-pain)

toastie NOUN
le sandwich chaud

■ a cheese and ham toastie un croque-monsieur

tobacco NOUN
le tabac

tobacconist's NOUN
le bureau de tabac (PL les bureaux de tabac)

toboggan NOUN
la luge

tobogganing NOUN
■ to go tobogganing faire de la luge

today ADVERB
aujourd'hui

□ What did you do today? Qu'est-ce tu as fait aujourd'hui?

toddler NOUN
le bambin

toe NOUN
le doigt de pied

toffee NOUN
le caramel

together ADVERB
1 ensemble

□ Are they still together? Ils sont toujours ensemble?
2 en même temps *(at the same time)*

□ Don't all speak together! Ne parlez pas tous en même temps!

■ together with *(with person)* avec

toilet NOUN
les toilettes *fem pl*

toilet paper NOUN
le papier hygiénique

toiletries PL NOUN
les articles de toilette *masc pl*

toilet roll NOUN
le rouleau de papier hygiénique (PL les

rouleaux de papier hygiénique)

token NOUN
■ a gift token un bon-cadeau

told VERB ▷ *see* **tell**

tolerant ADJECTIVE
tolérant (FEM tolérante)

toll NOUN
le péage *(on bridge, motorway)*

tomato NOUN
la tomate

□ tomato sauce la sauce tomate □ tomato soup la soupe à la tomate

tomboy NOUN
le garçon manqué

□ She's a real tomboy. C'est un vrai garçon manqué.

tomorrow ADVERB
demain

□ tomorrow morning demain matin
□ tomorrow night demain soir

■ the day after tomorrow après-demain

ton NOUN
la tonne

□ That old bike weighs a ton. Ce vieux vélo pèse une tonne.

> **DID YOU KNOW...?**
> In France measurements are in metric tonnes rather than tons. A ton is slightly more than a **tonne**.

tongue NOUN
la langue

■ to say something tongue in cheek dire quelque chose en plaisantant

tonic NOUN
le Schweppes® *(tonic water)*

■ a gin and tonic un gin tonic

tonight ADVERB
1 ce soir *(this evening)*

□ Are you going out tonight? Tu sors ce soir?
2 cette nuit *(during the night)*

□ I'll sleep well tonight. Je dormirai bien cette nuit.

tonsillitis NOUN
l' angine *fem*

tonsils PL NOUN
les amygdales *fem pl*

too ADVERB, ADJECTIVE
1 aussi *(as well)*

□ My sister came too. Ma sœur est venue aussi.
2 trop (FEM trope) *(excessively)*

□ The water's too hot. L'eau est trop chaude. □ We arrived too late. Nous sommes arrivés trop tard.

■ too much 1 *(with noun)* trop de □ too much noise trop de bruit 2 *(with verb)* trop
□ At Christmas we always eat too much. À

Noël nous mangeons toujours trop. **3** *(too expensive)* trop cher □ Fifty euros? That's too much. Cinquante euros? C'est trop cher.
■ **too many** trop de □ **too many hamburgers** trop de hamburgers
■ **Too bad!** Tant pis!

took VERB ▷ see **take**

tool NOUN
l' outil *masc*
■ **a tool box** une boîte à outils

tooth NOUN
la dent

toothache NOUN
le mal de dents
□ to have toothache avoir mal aux dents

toothbrush NOUN
la brosse à dents

toothpaste NOUN
le dentifrice

top NOUN
▷ see also **top** ADJECTIVE
1 le haut *(of page, ladder, garment)*
□ at the top of the page en haut de la page
■ **a bikini top** un haut de bikini
2 le sommet *(of mountain)*
3 le dessus *(of table)*
■ **on top of** *(on)* sur □ on top of the fridge sur le frigo
■ **There's a surcharge on top of that.** Il a un supplément en plus.
■ **from top to bottom** de fond en comble
□ I searched the house from top to bottom. J'ai fouillé la maison de fond en comble.
4 le couvercle *(of box, jar)*
5 le bouchon *(of bottle)*

top ADJECTIVE
▷ see also **top** NOUN
grand (FEM grande) *(first-class)*
□ a top surgeon un grand chirurgien
■ **a top model** un top model
■ **He always gets top marks in French.** Il a toujours d'excellentes notes en français.
■ **the top floor** le dernier étage □ on the top floor au dernier étage

topic NOUN
le sujet
□ The essay can be on any topic. Cette dissertation peut être sur n'importe quel sujet.

topical ADJECTIVE
d'actualité
□ a topical issue un sujet d'actualité

topless ADJECTIVE
aux seins nus *(model)*
■ **to go topless** enlever le haut

top-secret ADJECTIVE
top secret (FEM top secrète)

□ top-secret documents des documents top secrets

torch NOUN
la lampe de poche

tore, torn VERB ▷ see **tear**

tortoise NOUN
la tortue

torture NOUN
▷ see also **torture** VERB
la torture
□ It was pure torture. C'était une vraie torture.

to **torture** VERB
▷ see also **torture** NOUN
torturer
□ Stop torturing that poor animal! Arrête de torturer cette pauvre bête!

Tory ADJECTIVE
▷ see also **Tory** NOUN
conservateur (FEM conservatrice)
□ the Tory government le gouvernement conservateur

Tory NOUN
▷ see also **Tory** ADJECTIVE
le conservateur
la conservatrice
■ **the Tories** les conservateurs

to **toss** VERB
■ **to toss pancakes** faire sauter les crêpes
■ **Shall we toss for it?** On joue à pile ou face?

total ADJECTIVE
▷ see also **total** NOUN
total (FEM totale, MASC PL totaux)
■ **the total amount** le total

total NOUN
▷ see also **total** ADJECTIVE
le total (PL les totaux)
■ **the grand total** le total

totally ADVERB
complètement
□ He's totally useless. Il est complètement nul.

touch NOUN
▷ see also **touch** VERB
■ **to get in touch with somebody** prendre contact avec quelqu'un
■ **to keep in touch with somebody** ne pas perdre contact avec quelqu'un
■ **Keep in touch!** Donne-moi de tes nouvelles!
■ **to lose touch** se perdre de vue
■ **to lose touch with somebody** perdre quelqu'un de vue

to **touch** VERB
▷ see also **touch** NOUN
toucher

■ **Don't touch that!** N'y touche pas!

touchdown NOUN
l' atterrissage *masc*

touched ADJECTIVE
touché (FEM touchée)

□ **I was really touched.** Ça m'a beaucoup touché.

touching ADJECTIVE
touchant (FEM touchante)

touchline NOUN
la ligne de touche

touchpad NOUN
le pavé tactile

touchy ADJECTIVE
susceptible (FEM susceptible)

□ **She's a bit touchy.** Elle est susceptible.

tough ADJECTIVE
1 dur (FEM dure)

□ **It was tough, but I managed OK.** C'était dur, mais je m'en suis tiré. □ **It's a tough job.** C'est dur.

■ **The meat's tough.** La viande est coriace.
2 solide (FEM solide) *(strong)*

□ **tough leather gloves** de solides gants en cuir □ **She's tough. She can take it.** Elle est solide. Elle tiendra le coup.
3 dangereux (FEM dangereuse) *(rough, violent)*

■ **He thinks he's a tough guy.** Il se prend pour un gros dur.

■ **Tough luck!** C'est comme ça!

toupee NOUN
le postiche

tour NOUN
▷ *see also* **tour** VERB
1 la visite *(of town, museum)*

□ **We went on a tour of the city.** Nous avons visité la ville.

■ **a package tour** un voyage organisé
2 la tournée *(by singer, group)*

□ **on tour** en tournée

■ **to go on tour** faire une tournée

to **tour** VERB
▷ *see also* **tour** NOUN

■ **Robbie Williams is touring Europe.** Robbie Williams est en tournée en Europe.

tour guide NOUN
le/la guide

tourism NOUN
le tourisme

tourist NOUN
le/la touriste

■ **tourist information office** l'office du tourisme *masc*

tournament NOUN
le tournoi

tour operator NOUN
le tour-opérateur

towards PREPOSITION
1 vers *(in the direction of)*

□ **He came towards me.** Il est venu vers moi.
2 envers *(of attitude)*

□ **my feelings towards him** mes sentiments envers lui

towel NOUN
la serviette

tower NOUN
la tour

■ **a tower block** une tour

town NOUN
la ville

□ **a town plan** un plan de ville

■ **the town centre** le centre-ville

■ **the town hall** la mairie

tow truck NOUN (US)
la dépanneuse

toy NOUN
le jouet

□ **a toy shop** un magasin de jouets

■ **a toy car** une petite voiture

trace NOUN
▷ *see also* **trace** VERB
la trace

□ **There was no trace of the robbers.** Il n'y avait pas de trace des voleurs.

to **trace** VERB
▷ *see also* **trace** NOUN
décalquer *(draw)*

tracing paper NOUN
le papier calque

track NOUN
1 le chemin *(dirt road)*
2 la voie ferrée *(railway line)*
3 la piste *(in sport)*

□ **two laps of the track** deux tours de piste
4 la chanson *(song)*

□ **This is my favourite track.** C'est ma chanson préférée.
5 les traces *fem pl (trail)*

□ **They followed the tracks for miles.** Ils ont suivi les traces pendant des kilomètres.

to **track down** VERB

■ **to track somebody down** retrouver quelqu'un □ **The police never tracked down the killer.** La police n'a jamais retrouvé l'assassin.

tracksuit NOUN
le jogging

tractor NOUN
le tracteur

trade NOUN
le métier *(skill, job)*

□ **to learn a trade** apprendre un métier

trade union NOUN

le syndicat

trade unionist NOUN
le/la syndicaliste

tradition NOUN
la tradition

traditional ADJECTIVE
traditionnel (FEM traditionnelle)

traffic NOUN
la circulation
□ The traffic was terrible. Il y avait une circulation épouvantable.

traffic circle NOUN (US)
le rond-point (PL les ronds-points)

traffic jam NOUN
l' embouteillage masc

traffic lights PL NOUN
les feux masc pl

traffic warden NOUN
le contractuel
la contractuelle

tragedy NOUN
la tragédie

tragic ADJECTIVE
tragique (FEM tragique)

trailer NOUN
1 la remorque (vehicle)
2 la bande-annonce (film advert)

train NOUN
▷ see also **train** VERB
1 le train
■ a train set un train électrique
2 la rame (on underground)

to **train** VERB
▷ see also **train** NOUN
s'entraîner (sport)
□ to train for a race s'entraîner pour une course
■ to train as a teacher suivre une formation d'enseignant
■ to train an animal to do something dresser un animal à faire quelque chose

trained ADJECTIVE
■ She's a trained nurse. Elle est infirmière diplômée.

trainee NOUN
1 le/la stagiaire (in profession)
□ She's a trainee. Elle est stagiaire.
2 l' apprenti masc
l' apprentie fem (apprentice)
□ a trainee plumber un apprenti plombier

trainer NOUN
1 l' entraîneur masc (sports coach)
2 le dompteur
la dompteuse (of animals)

trainers PL NOUN
les baskets fem pl
□ a pair of trainers une paire de baskets

training NOUN
1 la formation
□ a training course un stage de formation
2 l' entraînement masc (sport)

tram NOUN
le tramway

tramp NOUN
le clochard
la clocharde

trampoline NOUN
le trampoline

tranquillizer NOUN
le tranquillisant
□ She's on tranquillizers. Elle prend des tranquillisants.

transfer NOUN
la décalcomanie (sticker)

transfusion NOUN
la transfusion

transistor NOUN
le transistor

transit NOUN
le transit
□ in transit en transit

transit lounge NOUN
la salle de transit

to **translate** VERB
traduire
□ to translate something into English traduire quelque chose en anglais

translation NOUN
la traduction

translator NOUN
le traducteur
la traductrice
□ Anita's a translator. Anita est traductrice.

transparent ADJECTIVE
transparent (FEM transparente)

transplant NOUN
la greffe
□ a heart transplant une greffe du cardiaque

transport NOUN
▷ see also **transport** VERB
le transport
□ public transport les transports en commun

to **transport** VERB
▷ see also **transport** NOUN
transporter

trap NOUN
le piège

trash NOUN (US)
les ordures fem pl
■ the trash can la poubelle

trashy ADJECTIVE
nul (FEM nulle)
□ a really trashy film un film vraiment nul

t

traumatic ADJECTIVE
traumatisant (FEM traumatisante)
□ It was a traumatic experience. Ça a été une expérience traumatisante.

travel NOUN
▷ see also **travel** VERB
les voyages masc pl

to **travel** VERB
▷ see also **travel** NOUN
voyager
□ I prefer to travel by train. Je préfère voyager en train.
■ I'd like to travel round the world. J'aimerais faire le tour du monde.
■ We travelled over 800 kilometres. Nous avons fait plus de huit cents kilomètres.
■ News travels fast! Les nouvelles circulent vite!

travel agency NOUN
l' agence de voyages fem

travel agent NOUN
■ She's a travel agent. Elle travaille dans une agence de voyages.

traveller (US **traveler**) NOUN
1 le voyageur
la voyageuse (on bus, train, plane)
2 le/la nomade (gypsy)

traveller's cheque (US **traveler's check**) NOUN
le chèque de voyage

travelling (US **traveling**) NOUN
■ I love travelling. J'adore les voyages.

travel sickness NOUN
le mal des transports

tray NOUN
le plateau (PL les plateaux)

to **tread** VERB
marcher
□ to tread on something marcher sur quelque chose

treasure NOUN
le trésor

treat NOUN
▷ see also **treat** VERB
1 le petit cadeau (PL les petits cadeaux) (present)
2 la gâterie (food)
■ to give somebody a treat faire plaisir à quelqu'un

to **treat** VERB
▷ see also **treat** NOUN
traiter (well, badly)
■ to treat somebody to something offrir quelque chose à quelqu'un □ He treated us to an ice cream. Il nous a offert une glace.

treatment NOUN
le traitement

to **treble** VERB
tripler
□ The cost of living there has trebled. Le coût de la vie là-bas a triplé.

tree NOUN
l' arbre masc

to **tremble** VERB
trembler

tremendous ADJECTIVE
énorme (FEM énorme)
□ a tremendous success un succès énorme

trend NOUN
la mode (fashion)

trendy ADJECTIVE
branché (FEM branchée)

trial NOUN
le procès (in court)

triangle NOUN
le triangle

tribe NOUN
la tribu

trick NOUN
▷ see also **trick** VERB
1 le tour
□ to play a trick on somebody jouer un tour à quelqu'un
2 le truc (knack)
□ It's not easy: there's a trick to it. Ce n'est pas facile: il y a un truc.

to **trick** VERB
▷ see also **trick** NOUN
■ to trick somebody rouler quelqu'un

tricky ADJECTIVE
délicat (FEM délicate)

tricycle NOUN
le tricycle

trifle NOUN
le diplomate (dessert)

to **trim** VERB
▷ see also **trim** NOUN
1 égaliser (hair)
2 tondre (grass)

trim NOUN
▷ see also **trim** VERB
la coupe d'entretien (haircut)
□ to have a trim se faire faire une coupe d'entretien

trip NOUN
▷ see also **trip** VERB
le voyage
□ to go on a trip faire un voyage □ Have a good trip! Bon voyage!
■ a day trip une excursion d'une journée

to **trip** VERB
▷ see also **trip** NOUN
trébucher (stumble)

triple ADJECTIVE
triple (FEM triple)

triplets PL NOUN
les triplés *masc pl*
les triplées *fem pl*

trivial ADJECTIVE
insignifiant (FEM insignifiante)

trod, trodden VERB ▷ *see* **tread**

trolley NOUN
le chariot

trombone NOUN
le trombone
□ I play the trombone. Je joue du trombone.

troops PL NOUN
les troupes *masc pl*
□ British troops les troupes britanniques

trophy NOUN
le trophée
□ to win a trophy gagner un trophée

tropical ADJECTIVE
tropical (FEM tropicale)
□ The weather was tropical. Il faisait une chaleur tropicale.

to **trot** VERB
trotter

trouble NOUN
le problème
□ The trouble is, it's too expensive. Le problème, c'est que c'est trop cher.
■ to be in trouble avoir des ennuis
■ What's the trouble? Qu'est-ce qui ne va pas?
■ stomach trouble troubles gastriques
■ to take a lot of trouble over something se donner beaucoup de mal pour quelque chose
■ Don't worry, it's no trouble. Mais non, ça ne me dérange pas du tout.

troublemaker NOUN
l' élément perturbateur *masc*

trousers PL NOUN
le pantalon *sing*
□ a pair of trousers un pantalon

trout NOUN
la truite

truant NOUN
■ to play truant faire l'école buissonnière

truck NOUN
le camion
■ a truck driver un camionneur □ He's a truck driver. Il est camionneur.

trucker NOUN (US)
le camionneur

true ADJECTIVE
vrai (FEM vraie)
■ That's true. C'est vrai.
■ to come true se réaliser □ I hope my

dream will come true. J'espère que mon rêve se réalisera.
■ true love le grand amour

truly ADVERB
vraiment
□ It was a truly remarkable victory. C'était vraiment une victoire remarquable.
■ Yours truly. Je vous prie d'agréer mes salutations distinguées.

trumpet NOUN
la trompette
□ She plays the trumpet. Elle joue de la trompette.

trunk NOUN
1 le tronc *(of tree)*
2 la trompe *(of elephant)*
3 la malle *(luggage)*
4 le coffre *(us: of car)*

trunks PL NOUN
■ swimming trunks le maillot de bain
■ a pair of trunks un maillot de bain

trust NOUN
▷ *see also* **trust** VERB
la confiance
□ to have trust in somebody avoir confiance en quelqu'un

to **trust** VERB
▷ *see also* **trust** NOUN
■ to trust somebody faire confiance à quelqu'un □ Don't you trust me? Tu ne me fais pas confiance? □ Trust me! Fais-moi confiance!

trusting ADJECTIVE
confiant (FEM confiante)

truth NOUN
la vérité

truthful ADJECTIVE
■ She's a very truthful person. Elle dit toujours la vérité.

try NOUN
▷ *see also* **try** VERB
l' essai *masc*
□ his third try son troisième essai
■ to have a try essayer
■ It's worth a try. Ça vaut la peine d'essayer.
■ to give something a try essayer quelque chose

to **try** VERB
▷ *see also* **try** NOUN
1 essayer *(attempt)*
□ to try to do something essayer de faire quelque chose
■ to try again refaire un essai
2 goûter *(taste)*
□ Would you like to try some? Voulez-vous goûter?

to **try on** VERB
essayer (clothes)

to **try out** VERB
essayer

T-shirt NOUN
le tee-shirt

tube NOUN
le tube

■ **the Tube** (underground) le métro

tuberculosis NOUN
la tuberculose

Tuesday NOUN
le mardi

▫ on Tuesday mardi ▫ on Tuesdays le mardi ▫ every Tuesday tous les mardis ▫ last Tuesday mardi dernier ▫ next Tuesday mardi prochain

■ **Shrove Tuesday, Pancake Tuesday** le mardi gras

tug-of-war NOUN
la lutte à la corde

tuition NOUN
les cours masc pl

■ **private tuition** les cours particuliers

tulip NOUN
la tulipe

tumble dryer NOUN
le sèche-linge (PL les sèche-linge)

tummy NOUN
le ventre

tuna NOUN
le thon

tune NOUN
l' air masc (melody)

■ **to play in tune** jouer juste
■ **to sing out of tune** chanter faux

Tunisia NOUN
la Tunisie

■ **in Tunisia** en Tunisie

tunnel NOUN
le tunnel

■ **the Channel Tunnel** le tunnel sous la Manche

Turk NOUN
le Turc
la Turque

Turkey NOUN
la Turquie

■ **in Turkey** en Turquie
■ **to Turkey** en Turquie

turkey NOUN
1 la dinde (meat)
2 le dindon (live bird)

Turkish NOUN
▷ see also **Turkish** ADJECTIVE
le turc (language)

Turkish ADJECTIVE

▷ see also **Turkish** NOUN
turc (FEM turque)

turn NOUN
▷ see also **turn** VERB
1 le tournant (bend in road)

■ **'no left turn'** 'défense de tourner à gauche'
2 le tour (go)

▫ It's my turn! C'est mon tour!

to **turn** VERB
▷ see also **turn** NOUN
1 tourner

▫ Turn right at the lights. Tournez à droite aux feux.
2 devenir (become)

▫ to turn red devenir rouge

■ **to turn into something** se transformer en quelque chose ▫ The frog turned into a prince. La grenouille s'est transformée en prince.

to **turn back** VERB
faire demi-tour

▫ We turned back. Nous avons fait demi-tour.

to **turn down** VERB
1 refuser (offer)
2 baisser (radio, TV, heating)

▫ Shall I turn the heating down? Je baisse le chauffage?

to **turn off** VERB
1 éteindre (light, radio)
2 fermer (tap)
3 arrêter (engine)

to **turn on** VERB
1 allumer (light, radio)
2 ouvrir (tap)
3 mettre en marche (engine)

to **turn out** VERB

■ **It turned out to be a mistake.** Il s'est avéré que c'était une erreur.
■ **It turned out that she was right.** Il s'est avéré qu'elle avait raison.

to **turn round** VERB
1 faire demi-tour (car)
2 se retourner (person)

to **turn up** VERB
1 arriver (arrive)
2 monter (heater)

■ **Could you turn up the radio?** Tu peux monter le son de la radio?

turning NOUN

■ **It's the third turning on the left.** C'est la troisième à gauche.
■ **We took the wrong turning.** Nous n'avons pas tourné au bon endroit.

turnip NOUN
le navet

583

t

turquoise ADJECTIVE
turquoise (FEM+PL turquoise) (colour)

turtle NOUN
la tortue

tutor NOUN
le professeur particulier (private teacher)

tuxedo NOUN (US)
le smoking

TV NOUN
la télé

tweezers PL NOUN
la pince à épiler sing

twelfth ADJECTIVE
douzième (FEM douzième)
□ the twelfth floor le douzième étage
■ **the twelfth of August** le douze août

twelve NUMBER
douze
□ She's twelve. Elle a douze ans.
■ **twelve o'clock 1** (midday) midi
2 (midnight) minuit

twentieth ADJECTIVE
vingtième (FEM vingtième)
□ the twentieth time la vingtième fois
■ **the twentieth of May** le vingt mai

twenty NUMBER
vingt
□ He's twenty. Il a vingt ans.

twice ADVERB
deux fois
■ **twice as much** deux fois plus □ He gets
twice as much pocket money as me. Il a
deux fois plus d'argent de poche que moi.

twin NOUN
le jumeau (MASC PL les jumeaux)
la jumelle
■ **my twin brother** mon frère jumeau

■ **her twin sister** sa sœur jumelle
■ **identical twins** les vrais jumeaux
■ **a twin room** une chambre à deux lits

twinned ADJECTIVE
jumelé (FEM jumelée)
□ Stroud is twinned with Châteaubriant.
Stroud est jumelée avec Châteaubriant.

to **twist** VERB
1 tordre (bend)
2 déformer (distort)
□ You're twisting my words. Tu déformes ce
que j'ai dit.

twit NOUN
le crétin
la crétine

two NUMBER
deux
□ She's two. Elle a deux ans.

type NOUN
▷ see also **type** VERB
le type
□ What type of camera have you got? Quel
type d'appareil photo as-tu?

to **type** VERB
▷ see also **type** NOUN
taper à la machine
□ Can you type? Tu sais taper à la
machine?
■ **to type a letter** taper une lettre

typewriter NOUN
la machine à écrire

typical ADJECTIVE
typique (FEM typique)
□ That's just typical! C'est typique!

tyre NOUN
le pneu
■ **the tyre pressure** la pression des pneus

Uu

UFO NOUN
l' OVNI *masc (= objet volant non identifié)*

ugh EXCLAMATION
pouah!

ugly ADJECTIVE
laid (FEM laide)

UK NOUN (= *United Kingdom*)
le Royaume-Uni

■ **from the UK** du Royaume-Uni
■ **in the UK** au Royaume-Uni
■ **to the UK** au Royaume-Uni

ulcer NOUN
l' ulcère *masc*

■ **a mouth ulcer** un aphte

Ulster NOUN
l' Irlande du Nord *fem*

■ **in Ulster** en Irlande du Nord

ultimate ADJECTIVE
suprême (FEM suprême)
□ the ultimate challenge le défi suprême
■ **It was the ultimate adventure.** C'était
la grande aventure.

ultimately ADVERB
au bout du compte
□ Ultimately, it's your decision. Au bout du
compte, c'est votre décision.

umbrella NOUN
1 le parapluie
2 le parasol *(for sun)*

umpire NOUN
1 l' arbitre *masc (in cricket)*
2 le juge de chaise *(in tennis)*

UN NOUN
l' ONU *fem (= Organisation des Nations
unies)*

unable ADJECTIVE
■ **to be unable to do something** ne pas
pouvoir faire quelque chose □ I was unable
to come. Je n'ai pas pu venir.

unacceptable ADJECTIVE
inacceptable (FEM inacceptable)

unanimous ADJECTIVE
unanime (FEM unanime)
□ a unanimous decision une décision
unanime

unattended ADJECTIVE
■ **to leave something unattended** laisser
quelque chose sans surveillance □ Never
leave pets unattended in your car. Ne
laisser jamais d'animaux domestiques sans
surveillance dans votre voiture.

unavoidable ADJECTIVE
inévitable (FEM inévitable)

unaware ADJECTIVE
■ **to be unaware 1** *(not know about)*
ignorer □ I was unaware of the regulations.
J'ignorais le règlement. **2** *(not notice)* ne
pas se rendre compte □ She was unaware
that she was being filmed. Elle ne s'était pas
rendu compte qu'on la filmait.

unbearable ADJECTIVE
insupportable (FEM insupportable)

unbeatable ADJECTIVE
imbattable (FEM imbattable)

unbelievable ADJECTIVE
incroyable (FEM incroyable)

unborn ADJECTIVE
■ **the unborn child** le fœtus

unbreakable ADJECTIVE
incassable (FEM incassable)

uncanny ADJECTIVE
étrange (FEM étrange)
□ That's uncanny! C'est étrange!
■ **an uncanny resemblance** une
ressemblance troublante

uncertain ADJECTIVE
incertain (FEM incertaine)
□ The future is uncertain. L'avenir est
incertain.
■ **to be uncertain about something** ne
pas être sûr de quelque chose

uncivilized ADJECTIVE
barbare (FEM barbare)

uncle NOUN
l' oncle *masc*
□ my uncle mon oncle

uncomfortable ADJECTIVE
pas confortable (FEM pas confortable)
□ The seats are rather uncomfortable. Les
sièges ne sont pas très confortables.

u

unconscious ADJECTIVE
sans connaissance

uncontrollable ADJECTIVE
incontrôlable (FEM incontrôlable)

unconventional ADJECTIVE
peu conventionnel (FEM peu
conventionnelle)

under PREPOSITION
1 sous
  □ The cat's under the table. Le chat est sous
  la table. □ The tunnel goes under the
  Channel. Le tunnel passe sous la Manche.
  ■ **under there** là-dessous □ What's under
  there? Qu'est-ce qu'il y a là-dessous?
2 moins de (less than)
  □ under 20 people moins de vingt
  personnes □ children under 10 les enfants
  de moins de dix ans

underage ADJECTIVE
  ■ **He's underage.** Il n'a pas l'âge
  réglementaire.

undercover ADJECTIVE, ADVERB
secret (FEM secrète)
  □ an undercover agent un agent secret
  ■ **She was working undercover.** Elle
  travaillait sous une fausse identité.

to **underestimate** VERB
sous-estimer
  □ I underestimated her. Je l'ai sous-
  estimée.

to **undergo** VERB
subir (operation, examination, change)
  ■ **to be undergoing repairs** être en
  réparation

underground ADJECTIVE, ADVERB
  ▷ see also **underground** NOUN
1 souterrain (FEM souterraine)
  □ an underground car park un parking
  souterrain
2 sous terre
  □ Moles live underground. Les taupes vivent
  sous terre.

underground NOUN
  ▷ see also **underground** ADJECTIVE
le métro
  □ Is there an underground in Lille? Est-ce
  qu'il y a un métro à Lille?

to **underline** VERB
souligner

underneath PREPOSITION, ADVERB
1 sous
  □ underneath the carpet sous la moquette
2 dessous
  □ I got out of the car and looked
  underneath. Je suis descendu de la voiture
  et j'ai regardé dessous.

586 **underpaid** ADJECTIVE

sous-payé (FEM sous-payée)
  □ I'm underpaid. Je suis sous-payé.

underpants PL NOUN
le slip sing

underpass NOUN
1 le passage souterrain (for people)
2 le passage inférieur (for cars)

undershirt NOUN (US)
le maillot de corps

underskirt NOUN
le jupon

to **understand** VERB
comprendre
  □ Do you understand? Vous comprenez? □ I
  don't understand this word. Je ne
  comprends pas ce mot. □ Is that
  understood? C'est compris?

understanding ADJECTIVE
compréhensif (FEM compréhensive)
  □ She's very understanding. Elle est très
  compréhensive.

understood VERB ▷ see **understand**

undertaker NOUN
l' entrepreneur des pompes funèbres masc

underwater ADJECTIVE, ADVERB
sous l'eau
  □ This sequence was filmed underwater.
  Cette séquence a été filmée sous l'eau.
  ■ **an underwater camera** un appareil
  photographique de plongée
  ■ **underwater photography** la
  photographie subaquatique

underwear NOUN
les sous-vêtements masc pl

underwent VERB ▷ see **undergo**

to **undo** VERB
1 défaire (buttons, knot)
2 déballer (parcel)

to **undress** VERB
se déshabiller (get undressed)
  □ The doctor told me to undress. Le
  médecin m'a dit de me déshabiller.

uneconomic ADJECTIVE
pas rentable (FEM pas rentable)

unemployed ADJECTIVE
au chômage
  □ He's unemployed. Il est au chômage.
  □ He's been unemployed for a year. Ça fait
  un an qu'il est au chômage.
  ■ **the unemployed** les chômeurs masc pl

unemployment NOUN
le chômage

unexpected ADJECTIVE
inattendu (FEM inattendue)
  □ an unexpected visitor un visiteur
  inattendu

unexpectedly ADVERB

à l'improviste

□ They arrived unexpectedly. Ils sont arrivés à l'improviste.

unfair ADJECTIVE
injuste (FEM injuste)

□ It's unfair to girls. C'est injuste pour les filles.

unfamiliar ADJECTIVE

■ I heard an unfamiliar voice. J'ai entendu une voix que je ne connaissais pas.

unfashionable ADJECTIVE
démodé (FEM démodée)

unfit ADJECTIVE

■ I'm rather unfit. Je ne suis pas en très bonne condition physique.

to **unfold** VERB
déplier

□ She unfolded the map. Elle a déplié la carte.

unforgettable ADJECTIVE
inoubliable (FEM inoubliable)

unfortunately ADVERB
malheureusement

□ Unfortunately, I arrived late. Malheureusement, je suis arrivé en retard.

unfriendly ADJECTIVE
pas aimable (FEM pas aimable)

□ The waiters are a bit unfriendly. Les serveurs ne sont pas très aimables.

ungrateful ADJECTIVE
ingrat (FEM ingrate)

unhappy ADJECTIVE
malheureux (FEM malheureuse)

□ He was very unhappy as a child. Il était très malheureux quand il était petit.

■ to look unhappy avoir l'air triste

unhealthy ADJECTIVE
1 maladif (FEM maladive) (person)
2 malsain (FEM malsaine) (place, habit)
3 pas sain (FEM pas saine) (food)

uni NOUN
la fac (university)

□ to go to uni aller à la fac

uniform NOUN
l' uniforme masc

□ school uniform l'uniforme scolaire

> **DID YOU KNOW...?**
> French children don't wear school uniform.

uninhabited ADJECTIVE
inhabité (FEM inhabitée)

union NOUN
le syndicat (trade union)

Union Jack NOUN
le drapeau du Royaume-Uni

unique ADJECTIVE
unique (FEM unique)

unit NOUN
1 l' unité fem

□ a unit of measurement une unité de mesure

2 l' élément masc (piece of furniture)

□ a kitchen unit un élément de cuisine

United Kingdom NOUN
le Royaume-Uni

United Nations NOUN
l' O.N.U. fem (= Organisation des Nations Unies)

United States NOUN
les États-Unis masc pl

■ in the United States aux États-Unis

■ to the United States aux États-Unis

universe NOUN
l' univers masc

university NOUN
l' université fem

□ She's at university. Elle va à l'université.

□ Do you want to go to university? Tu veux aller à l'université? □ Lancaster University l'université de Lancaster

unleaded petrol NOUN
l' essence sans plomb fem

unless CONJUNCTION

■ unless he leaves à moins qu'il ne parte

□ I won't come unless you phone me. Je ne viendrai pas à moins que tu ne me téléphones.

unlike PREPOSITION
contrairement à

□ Unlike him, I really enjoy flying. Contrairement à lui, j'adore prendre l'avion.

unlikely ADJECTIVE
peu probable (FEM peu probable)

□ It's possible, but unlikely. C'est possible, mais peu probable.

unlisted ADJECTIVE (US)

■ an unlisted number un numéro qui est sur la liste rouge

to **unload** VERB
décharger

□ We unloaded the car. Nous avons déchargé la voiture. □ The lorries go there to unload. Les camions y vont pour être déchargés.

to **unlock** VERB
ouvrir

□ He unlocked the door of the car. Il a ouvert la portière de la voiture.

unlucky ADJECTIVE

■ to be unlucky 1 (number, object) porter malheur □ They say thirteen is an unlucky number. On dit que le nombre treize porte malheur. 2 (person) ne pas avoir de chance □ Did you win? — No, I was unlucky. Vous

avez gagné? — Non, je n'ai pas eu de chance.

unmarried ADJECTIVE
célibataire (FEM célibataire) *(person)*
□ an unmarried mother une mère célibataire
■ **an unmarried couple** un couple non marié

unnatural ADJECTIVE
pas naturel (FEM pas naturelle)

unnecessary ADJECTIVE
inutile (FEM inutile)

unofficial ADJECTIVE
1 non officiel (FEM non officielle) *(meeting, leader)*
2 sauvage (FEM sauvage) *(strike)*

to **unpack** VERB
1 défaire
□ I unpacked my suitcase. J'ai défait ma valise.
2 déballer ses affaires
□ I went to my room to unpack. Je suis allé dans ma chambre pour déballer mes affaires. □ I haven't unpacked my clothes yet. Je n'ai pas encore déballé mes affaires.

unpleasant ADJECTIVE
désagréable (FEM désagréable)

to **unplug** VERB
débrancher

unpopular ADJECTIVE
impopulaire (FEM impopulaire)

unpredictable ADJECTIVE
imprévisible (FEM imprévisible)

unreal ADJECTIVE
incroyable (FEM incroyable) *(incredible)*
□ It was unreal! C'était incroyable!

unrealistic ADJECTIVE
peu réaliste (FEM peu réaliste)

unreasonable ADJECTIVE
pas raisonnable (FEM pas raisonnable)
□ Her attitude was completely unreasonable. Son attitude n'était pas du tout raisonnable.

unreliable ADJECTIVE
pas fiable (FEM pas fiable) *(car, machine)*
□ It's a nice car, but a bit unreliable. C'est une belle voiture, mais elle n'est pas très fiable.
■ **He's completely unreliable.** On ne peut pas du tout compter sur lui.

to **unroll** VERB
dérouler

unsatisfactory ADJECTIVE
insatisfaisant (FEM insatisfaisante)

to **unscrew** VERB
dévisser
□ She unscrewed the top of the bottle. Elle a

dévissé le bouchon de la bouteille.

unshaven ADJECTIVE
mal rasé

unskilled ADJECTIVE
■ **unskilled worker** le manœuvre

unstable ADJECTIVE
instable (FEM instable)

unsteady ADJECTIVE
mal assuré (FEM mal assurée) *(walk, voice)*
■ **He was unsteady on his feet.** Il marchait d'un pas mal assuré.

unsuccessful ADJECTIVE
vain (FEM vaine) *(attempt)*
■ **to be unsuccessful in doing something** ne pas réussir à faire quelque chose □ an unsuccessful artist un artiste qui n'a pas réussi

unsuitable ADJECTIVE
inapproprié (FEM inappropriée) *(clothes, equipment)*

untidy ADJECTIVE
1 en désordre
□ My bedroom's always untidy. Ma chambre est toujours en désordre.
2 débraillé (FEM débraillée) *(appearance, person)*
□ He's always untidy. Il est toujours débraillé.
3 désordonné (FEM désordonnée) *(in character)*
□ He's a very untidy person. Il est très désordonné.

to **untie** VERB
1 défaire *(knot, parcel)*
2 détacher *(animal)*

until PREPOSITION, CONJUNCTION
1 jusqu'à
□ I waited until ten o'clock. J'ai attendu jusqu'à dix heures.
■ **until now** jusqu'à présent □ It's never been a problem until now. Ça n'a jamais été un problème jusqu'à présent.
■ **until then** jusque-là □ Until then I'd never been to France. Jusque-là je n'étais jamais allé en France.
2 avant

> **LANGUAGE TIP** Use **avant** if the sentence you want to translate contains a negative, such as 'not' or 'never'

□ It won't be ready until next week. Ça ne sera pas prêt avant la semaine prochaine. □ Until last year I'd never been to France. Avant l'année dernière, je n'étais jamais allé en France.

unusual ADJECTIVE
1 insolite (FEM insolite)
□ an unusual shape une forme insolite

2 rare (FEM rare)
☐ It's unusual to get snow at this time of year. Il est rare qu'il neige à cette époque de l'année.

unwilling ADJECTIVE
■ **to be unwilling to do something** ne pas être disposé à faire quelque chose ☐ He was unwilling to help me. Il n'était pas disposé à m'aider.

to **unwind** VERB
se détendre (relax)

unwise ADJECTIVE
imprudent (FEM imprudente) (person)
☐ That was rather unwise of you. C'était plutôt imprudent de votre part.

unwound VERB ▷see **unwind**

to **unwrap** VERB
déballer
☐ After the meal we unwrapped the presents. Après le repas nous avons déballé les cadeaux.

up PREPOSITION, ADVERB

> **LANGUAGE TIP** For other expressions with 'up', see the verbs 'go', 'come', 'put', 'turn' etc.

en haut
☐ up on the hill en haut de la colline
■ **up here** ici
■ **up there** là-haut
■ **up north** dans le nord
■ **to be up** (out of bed) être levé ☐ We were up at 6. Nous étions levés à six heures.
☐ He's not up yet. Il n'est pas encore levé.
■ **What's up?** Qu'est-ce qu'il y a? ☐ What's up with her? Qu'est-ce qu'elle a?
■ **to get up** (in the morning) se lever ☐ What time do you get up? À quelle heure est-ce que tu te lèves?
■ **to go up** monter ☐ The bus went up the hill. Le bus a monté la colline.
■ **to go up to somebody** s'approcher de quelqu'un ☐ She came up to me. Elle s'est approchée de moi.
■ **up to** (as far as) jusqu'à ☐ to count up to fifty compter jusqu'à cinquante ☐ up to three hours jusqu'à trois heures ☐ up to now jusqu'à présent
■ **It's up to you.** C'est à vous de décider.

upbringing NOUN
l' éducation fem

uphill ADVERB
■ **to go uphill** monter

upper ADJECTIVE
supérieur (FEM supérieure)
☐ on the upper floor à l'étage supérieur

upper sixth NOUN
■ **the upper sixth** la terminale ☐ She's in the upper sixth. Elle est en terminale.

> **DID YOU KNOW...?**
> In French secondary schools the years are counted from the **sixième** (youngest) to the **première** and **terminale** (oldest).

upright ADJECTIVE
■ **to stand upright** se tenir droit

upset NOUN
▷see also **upset** ADJECTIVE, VERB
■ **a stomach upset** une indigestion

upset ADJECTIVE
▷see also **upset** NOUN, VERB
contrarié (FEM contrariée)
☐ She's still a bit upset. Elle est encore un peu contrariée.
■ **I had an upset stomach.** J'avais l'estomac dérangé.

to **upset** VERB
▷see also **upset** NOUN, ADJECTIVE
■ **to upset somebody** contrarier quelqu'un

upside down ADVERB
à l'envers
☐ That painting is upside down. Ce tableau est à l'envers.

upstairs ADVERB
en haut
☐ Where's your coat? — It's upstairs. Où est ton manteau? — Il est en haut.
■ **to go upstairs** monter

uptight ADJECTIVE
tendu (FEM tendue)
☐ She's really uptight. Elle est très tendue.

up-to-date ADJECTIVE
1 moderne (FEM moderne) (car, stereo)
2 à jour (information)
☐ an up-to-date timetable un horaire à jour
■ **to bring something up to date** moderniser quelque chose

upwards ADVERB
vers le haut
☐ to look upwards regarder vers le haut

urgent ADJECTIVE
urgent (FEM urgente)
☐ Is it urgent? C'est urgent?

urine NOUN
l' urine fem

US NOUN
les USA masc pl

us PRONOUN
nous
☐ They helped us. Ils nous ont aidés. ☐ They gave us a map. Ils nous ont donné une carte.

USA NOUN
les USA masc pl

use NOUN

▷ *see also* **use** VERB

■ **It's no use.** Ça ne sert à rien. □ It's no use shouting, she's deaf. Ça ne sert à rien de crier, elle est sourde.

■ **It's no use, I can't do it.** Il n'y a rien à faire, je n'y arrive pas.

■ **to make use of something** utiliser quelque chose

to **use** VERB

▷ *see also* **use** NOUN

utiliser

□ Can we use a dictionary in the exam? Est-ce qu'on peut utiliser un dictionnaire à l'examen?

■ **Can I use your phone?** Je peux téléphoner?

■ **to use the toilet** aller aux W.C.

■ **I used to live in London.** J'habitais à Londres autrefois.

■ **I used not to like maths, but now …** Avant, je n'aimais pas les maths, mais maintenant …

■ **to be used to something** avoir l'habitude de quelque chose □ He wasn't used to driving on the right. Il n'avait pas l'habitude de conduire à droite. □ Don't worry, I'm used to it. Ne t'inquiète pas, j'ai l'habitude.

■ **a used car** une voiture d'occasion

to **use up** VERB

1 finir

□ We've used up all the paint. Nous avons fini la peinture.

2 dépenser *(money)*

useful ADJECTIVE

utile (FEM utile)

useless ADJECTIVE

nul (FEM nulle)

□ This map is just useless. Cette carte est vraiment nulle. □ You're useless! Tu es nul!

■ **It's useless!** Ça ne sert à rien!

user NOUN

l' utilisateur *masc*

l' utilisatrice *fem*

user-friendly ADJECTIVE

facile à utiliser (FEM facile à utiliser)

usual ADJECTIVE

habituel (FEM habituelle)

■ **as usual** comme d'habitude

usually ADVERB

1 en général *(generally)*

□ I usually get to school at about half past eight. En général, j'arrive à l'école vers huit heures et demie.

2 d'habitude *(when making a contrast)*

□ Usually I don't wear make-up, but today is a special occasion. D'habitude je ne me maquille pas, mais aujourd'hui c'est spécial.

utility room NOUN

la buanderie

U-turn NOUN

le demi-tour

□ to do a U-turn faire demi-tour

Vv

vacancy NOUN
1 le poste vacant (job)
2 la chambre disponible (room in hotel)
   ■ 'no vacancies' (on sign) 'complet'

vacant ADJECTIVE
   libre (FEM libre)

vacation NOUN (US)
   les vacances fem pl
   □ to be on vacation être en vacances □ to
   take a vacation prendre des vacances

to **vaccinate** VERB
   vacciner

to **vacuum** VERB
   passer l'aspirateur
   □ to vacuum the hall passer l'aspirateur
   dans le couloir

vacuum cleaner NOUN
   l' aspirateur masc

vagina NOUN
   le vagin

vague ADJECTIVE
   vague (FEM vague)

vain ADJECTIVE
   vaniteux (FEM vaniteuse)
   □ He's so vain! Qu'est-ce qu'il est vaniteux!
   ■ in vain en vain

Valentine card NOUN
   la carte de la Saint-Valentin

Valentine's Day NOUN
   la Saint-Valentin

valid ADJECTIVE
   valable (FEM valable)
   □ This ticket is valid for three months. Ce
   billet est valable trois mois.

valley NOUN
   la vallée

valuable ADJECTIVE
1 de valeur
   □ a valuable picture un tableau de valeur
2 précieux (FEM précieuse)
   □ valuable help une aide précieuse

valuables PL NOUN
   les objets de valeur masc pl
   □ Don't take any valuables with you.
   N'emportez pas d'objets de valeur.

value NOUN
   la valeur

van NOUN
   la camionnette

vandal NOUN
   le/la vandale

vandalism NOUN
   le vandalisme

to **vandalize** VERB
   saccager

vanilla NOUN
   la vanille
   □ vanilla ice cream la glace à la vanille

to **vanish** VERB
   disparaître

variable ADJECTIVE
   variable (FEM variable)

varied ADJECTIVE
   varié (FEM variée)

variety NOUN
   la variété

various ADJECTIVE
   plusieurs
   □ We visited various villages in the area.
   Nous avons visité plusieurs villages de la
   région.

to **vary** VERB
   varier

vase NOUN
   le vase

VAT NOUN (= value added tax)
   la TVA (= taxe sur la valeur ajoutée)

VCR NOUN (= video cassette recorder)
   le magnétoscope

VDU NOUN (= visual display unit)
   la console

veal NOUN
   le veau

vegan NOUN
   le végétalien
   la végétalienne
   □ I'm a vegan. Je suis végétalien.

vegetable NOUN
   le légume
   □ vegetable soup la soupe aux légumes

v

vegetarian ADJECTIVE
▷ see also **vegetarian** NOUN
végétarien (FEM végétarienne)
□ I'm vegetarian. Je suis végétarien.
□ vegetarian lasagne les lasagnes
végétariennes *fem pl*

vegetarian NOUN
▷ see also **vegetarian** ADJECTIVE
le végétarien
la végétarienne
□ I'm a vegetarian. Je suis végétarien.

vehicle NOUN
le véhicule

vein NOUN
la veine

velvet NOUN
le velours

vending machine NOUN
le distributeur automatique

Venetian blind NOUN
le store vénitien

verb NOUN
le verbe

verdict NOUN
le verdict

vertical ADJECTIVE
vertical (FEM verticale, MASC PL verticaux)

vertigo NOUN
le vertige
□ I get vertigo. J'ai le vertige.

very ADVERB
très
□ very tall très grand □ not very interesting
pas très intéressant
■ **very much** beaucoup

vest NOUN
1 le maillot de corps *(underclothing)*
2 le gilet (US: *waistcoat*)

vet NOUN
le/la vétérinaire
□ She's a vet. Elle est vétérinaire.

via PREPOSITION
en passant par
□ We went to Paris via Boulogne. Nous
sommes allés à Paris en passant par
Boulogne.

vicar NOUN
le pasteur
□ He's a vicar. Il est pasteur.

vice NOUN
l' étau *masc (for holding things)*

vice versa ADVERB
vice versa

vicious ADJECTIVE
1 brutal (FEM brutale, MASC PL brutaux)
□ a vicious attack une agression brutale
2 méchant (FEM méchante) *(dog, person)*

■ **a vicious circle** un cercle vicieux

victim NOUN
la victime
□ He was the victim of a mugging. Il a été
victime d'une agression.

victory NOUN
la victoire

to **video** VERB
▷ see also **video** NOUN
1 enregistrer *(from TV)*
2 filmer *(with video camera)*

video NOUN
▷ see also **video** VERB
1 la vidéo *(film)*
□ to watch a video regarder une vidéo □ a
video of my family on holiday une vidéo de
ma famille en vacances
2 la cassette vidéo *(video cassette)*
□ She lent me a video. Elle m'a prêté une
cassette vidéo.
3 le magnétoscope *(video recorder)*
□ Have you got a video? Tu as un
magnétoscope?
■ **a video camera** une caméra vidéo
■ **a video cassette** une cassette vidéo
■ **a video game** un jeu vidéo □ He likes
playing video games. Il aime les jeux vidéo.
■ **a video recorder** un magnétoscope
■ **a video shop** un vidéoclub

videophone NOUN
le téléphone mobile vidéo

Vietnam NOUN
le Viêt-Nam
■ **in Vietnam** au Viêt-Nam

Vietnamese ADJECTIVE
vietnamien (FEM vietnamienne)

view NOUN
1 la vue
□ There's an amazing view. Il y a une vue
extraordinaire.
2 l' avis *masc (opinion)*
□ in my view à mon avis

viewer NOUN
le téléspectateur
la téléspectatrice

viewpoint NOUN
le point de vue

vile ADJECTIVE
dégoûtant (FEM dégoûtante) *(smell, food)*

villa NOUN
la villa

village NOUN
le village

villain NOUN
1 le malfrat *(criminal)*
2 le méchant *(in film)*

vine NOUN

v

la vigne

vinegar NOUN
le vinaigre

vineyard NOUN
le vignoble

viola NOUN
l' alto *masc*
◻ I play the viola. Je joue de l'alto.

violence NOUN
la violence

violent ADJECTIVE
violent (FEM violente)

violin NOUN
le violon
◻ I play the violin. Je joue du violon.

violinist NOUN
le/la violoniste

virgin NOUN
la vierge
◻ to be a virgin être vierge

Virgo NOUN
la Vierge
◻ I'm Virgo. Je suis Vierge.

virtual reality NOUN
la réalité virtuelle

virus NOUN
le virus *(also computing)*

visa NOUN
le visa

visible ADJECTIVE
visible (FEM visible)

visit NOUN
▷ *see also* **visit** VERB
1 la visite *(to museum)*
2 le séjour *(to country)*
◻ Did you enjoy your visit to France? Ton séjour en France s'est bien passé?
■ **my last visit to my grandmother** la dernière fois que je suis allé voir ma grand-mère

to **visit** VERB
▷ *see also* **visit** NOUN
1 rendre visite à *(person)*
◻ to visit somebody rendre visite à quelqu'un
2 visiter *(place)*
◻ We'd like to visit the castle. Nous voudrions visiter le château.

visitor NOUN
1 le visiteur
la visiteuse *(tourist)*
2 l' invité *masc*
l' invitée *fem (guest)*
■ **to have a visitor** avoir de la visite

visual ADJECTIVE

visuel (FEM visuelle)

to **visualize** VERB
imaginer

vital ADJECTIVE
vital (FEM vitale, MASC PL vitaux)

vitamin NOUN
la vitamine

vivid ADJECTIVE
vif (FEM vive) *(colour)*
■ **to have a vivid imagination** avoir une imagination débordante

vocabulary NOUN
le vocabulaire

vocational ADJECTIVE
professionnel (FEM professionnelle)
■ **a vocational course** un stage de formation professionnelle

vodka NOUN
la vodka

voice NOUN
la voix (PL les voix)

voice mail NOUN
la boîte vocale

volcano NOUN
le volcan

volleyball NOUN
le volley-ball
◻ to play volleyball jouer au volley-ball

volt NOUN
le volt

voltage NOUN
le voltage

voluntary ADJECTIVE
volontaire (FEM volontaire) *(contribution, statement)*
■ **to do voluntary work** travailler bénévolement

volunteer NOUN
▷ *see also* **volunteer** VERB
le/la volontaire

to **volunteer** VERB
▷ *see also* **volunteer** NOUN
■ **to volunteer to do something** se proposer pour faire quelque chose

to **vomit** VERB
vomir

to **vote** VERB
voter

voucher NOUN
le bon
◻ a gift voucher un bon d'achat

vowel NOUN
la voyelle

vulgar ADJECTIVE
vulgaire (FEM vulgaire)

V

Ww

wafer NOUN
la gaufrette

wage NOUN
le salaire
□ He collected his wages. Il a retiré son salaire.

waist NOUN
la taille

waistcoat NOUN
le gilet

to **wait** VERB
attendre
■ **to wait for something** attendre quelque chose
■ **to wait for somebody** attendre quelqu'un □ I'll wait for you. Je t'attendrai.
■ **Wait for me!** Attends-moi!
■ **Wait a minute!** Attends!
■ **to keep somebody waiting** faire attendre quelqu'un □ They kept us waiting for hours. Ils nous ont fait attendre pendant des heures.
■ **I can't wait for the holidays.** J'ai hâte d'être en vacances.
■ **I can't wait to see him again.** J'ai hâte de le revoir.

to **wait up** VERB
attendre pour se coucher
□ My mum always waits up till I get in. Ma mère attend toujours que je rentre pour se coucher.

waiter NOUN
le serveur
■ **Waiter!** Excusez-moi!

waiting list NOUN
la liste d'attente

waiting room NOUN
la salle d'attente

waitress NOUN
la serveuse

to **wake up** VERB
se réveiller
□ I woke up at six o'clock. Je me suis réveillé à six heures.
■ **to wake somebody up** réveiller

quelqu'un □ Please would you wake me up at seven o'clock? Pourriez-vous me réveiller à sept heures?

Wales NOUN
le pays de Galles
■ **in Wales** au pays de Galles
■ **to Wales** au pays de Galles
■ **I'm from Wales.** Je suis gallois.
■ **the Prince of Wales** le prince de Galles

to **walk** VERB
▷ see also **walk** NOUN
1 marcher
□ He walks fast. Il marche vite.
2 aller à pied (go on foot)
□ Are you walking or going by bus? Tu y vas à pied ou en bus? □ We walked 10 kilometres. Nous avons fait dix kilomètres à pied.
■ **to walk the dog** promener le chien

walk NOUN
▷ see also **walk** VERB
la promenade
□ to go for a walk faire une promenade
■ **It's 10 minutes' walk from here.** C'est à dix minutes d'ici à pied.

walkie-talkie NOUN
le talkie-walkie

walking NOUN
la randonnée
□ I did some walking in the Alps last summer. J'ai fait de la randonnée dans les Alpes l'été dernier.

walking stick NOUN
la canne

Walkman® NOUN
le baladeur

wall NOUN
le mur

wallet NOUN
le portefeuille

wallpaper NOUN
1 le papier peint
2 le fond d'écran (for phone, PC)

walnut NOUN
la noix (PL les noix)

to **wander** VERB
- **to wander around** flâner ▢ I just wandered around for a while. J'ai flâné un peu.

to **want** VERB
vouloir
▢ Do you want some cake? Tu veux du gâteau?
- **to want to do something** vouloir faire quelque chose ▢ I want to go to the cinema. Je veux aller au cinéma. ▢ What do you want to do tomorrow? Qu'est-ce que tu veux faire demain?

war NOUN
la guerre

ward NOUN
la salle (room in hospital)

warden NOUN
le directeur
la directrice (of youth hostel)

wardrobe NOUN
l' armoire fem (piece of furniture)

warehouse NOUN
l' entrepôt masc

warm ADJECTIVE
1 chaud (FEM chaude)
▢ warm water l'eau chaude
- **It's warm in here.** Il fait chaud ici.
- **to be warm** (person) avoir chaud ▢ I'm too warm. J'ai trop chaud.
2 chaleureux (FEM chaleureuse)
▢ a warm welcome un accueil chaleureux

to **warm up** VERB
1 s'échauffer (for sport)
2 réchauffer (food)
▢ I'll warm up some lasagne for you. Je vais te réchauffer des lasagnes.

to **warn** VERB
prévenir
▢ Well, I warned you! Je t'avais prévenu!
- **to warn somebody to do something** conseiller à quelqu'un de faire quelque chose

warning NOUN
l' avertissement masc

Warsaw NOUN
Varsovie

wart NOUN
la verrue

was VERB ▷ see **be**

wash NOUN
▷ see also **wash** VERB
- **to have a wash** se laver ▢ I had a wash. Je me suis lavé.
- **to give something a wash** laver quelque chose ▢ He gave the car a wash. Il a lavé la voiture.

to **wash** VERB
▷ see also **wash** NOUN
1 laver
▢ to wash something laver quelque chose
2 se laver (have a wash)
▢ Every morning I get up, wash and get dressed. Tous les matins je me lève, je me lave et je m'habille.
- **to wash one's hands** se laver les mains
- **to wash one's hair** se laver les cheveux

to **wash up** VERB
faire la vaisselle

washbasin NOUN
le lavabo

washcloth NOUN (US)
le gant de toilette

> **DID YOU KNOW...?**
> The French traditionally wash with a towelling glove rather than a flannel.

washing NOUN
le linge
▢ dirty washing du linge sale
- **Have you got any washing?** Tu as du linge à laver?
- **to do the washing** faire la lessive

washing machine NOUN
la machine à laver

washing powder NOUN
la lessive

washing-up NOUN
- **to do the washing-up** faire la vaisselle

washing-up liquid NOUN
le produit à vaisselle

wasn't = was not

wasp NOUN
la guêpe

waste NOUN
▷ see also **waste** VERB
1 le gaspillage
▢ It's such a waste! C'est vraiment du gaspillage!
- **It's a waste of time.** C'est une perte de temps.
2 les déchets masc pl (rubbish)
▢ nuclear waste les déchets nucléaires

to **waste** VERB
▷ see also **waste** NOUN
gaspiller
▢ I don't like wasting money. Je n'aime pas gaspiller de l'argent.
- **to waste time** perdre du temps
▢ There's no time to waste. Il n'y a pas de temps à perdre.

wastepaper basket NOUN
la corbeille à papier

watch NOUN
▷ see also **watch** VERB

la montre

to **watch** VERB
▷ *see also* **watch** NOUN
1 regarder
□ to watch television regarder la télévision
□ Watch me! Regarde-moi!
2 surveiller *(keep a watch on)*
□ The police were watching the house. La police surveillait la maison.

to **watch out** VERB
faire attention
■ Watch out! Attention!

water NOUN
▷ *see also* **water** VERB
l' eau *fem*

to **water** VERB
▷ *see also* **water** NOUN
arroser
□ He was watering his tulips. Il arrosait ses tulipes.

waterfall NOUN
la cascade

watering can NOUN
l' arrosoir *masc*

watermelon NOUN
la pastèque

waterproof ADJECTIVE
imperméable (FEM imperméable)
□ Is this jacket waterproof? Ce blouson est-il imperméable?
■ a waterproof watch une montre étanche

water-skiing NOUN
le ski nautique
□ to go water-skiing faire du ski nautique

wave NOUN
▷ *see also* **wave** VERB
1 la vague *(in water)*
2 le signe *(of hand)*
□ We gave him a wave. Nous lui avons fait signe.

to **wave** VERB
▷ *see also* **wave** NOUN
faire un signe de la main
□ to wave at somebody faire un signe de la main à quelqu'un
■ to wave goodbye faire au revoir de la main □ I waved her goodbye. Je lui ai fait au revoir de la main.

wavy ADJECTIVE
ondulé (FEM ondulée)
□ wavy hair les cheveux ondulés

wax NOUN
la cire

way NOUN
1 la façon *(manner)*
□ She looked at me in a strange way. Elle

m'a regardé d'une façon étrange.
■ This book tells you the right way to do it. Ce livre explique comment il faut faire.
■ You're doing it the wrong way. Ce n'est pas comme ça qu'il faut faire.
■ in a way ... dans un sens ...
■ a way of life un mode de vie
2 le chemin *(route)*
□ I don't know the way. Je ne connais pas le chemin.
■ on the way en chemin □ We stopped on the way. Nous nous sommes arrêtés en chemin.
■ It's a long way. C'est loin. □ Paris is a long way from London. Paris est loin de Londres.
■ Which way is it? C'est par où?
■ The supermarket is this way. Le supermarché est par ici.
■ Do you know the way to the station? Vous savez comment aller à la gare?
■ He's on his way. Il arrive.
■ 'way in' 'entrée'
■ 'way out' 'sortie'
■ by the way ... au fait ...

we PRONOUN
nous
□ We're staying here for a week. Nous restons une semaine ici.

weak ADJECTIVE
faible (FEM faible)

wealthy ADJECTIVE
riche (FEM riche)

weapon NOUN
l' arme *fem*

to **wear** VERB
porter *(clothes)*
□ She was wearing a hat. Elle portait un chapeau.
■ She was wearing black. Elle était en noir.

weather NOUN
le temps
□ What was the weather like? Quel temps a-t-il fait? □ The weather was lovely. Il a fait un temps magnifique.

weather forecast NOUN
la météo

web NOUN
le web

web address NOUN
l' adresse web *fem*

web browser NOUN
le navigateur

webcam NOUN
la webcam

webmaster NOUN
le/la gestionnaire de site

website NOUN
le site web

webzine NOUN
le webzine

we'd = we had, we would

wedding NOUN
le mariage

■ **wedding anniversary** l'anniversaire de
mariage *masc*

■ **wedding dress** la robe de mariée

Wednesday NOUN
le mercredi

□ on Wednesday mercredi □ on
Wednesdays le mercredi □ every
Wednesday tous les mercredis □ last
Wednesday mercredi dernier □ next
Wednesday mercredi prochain

weed NOUN
la mauvaise herbe

□ The garden's full of weeds. Le jardin est
plein de mauvaises herbes.

week NOUN
la semaine

□ last week la semaine dernière □ every
week toutes les semaines □ next week la
semaine prochaine □ in a week's time dans
une semaine

■ **a week on Friday** vendredi en huit

weekday NOUN
■ **on weekdays** en semaine

weekend NOUN
le week-end

□ at weekends le week-end □ last weekend
le week-end dernier □ next weekend le
week-end prochain

to weep VERB
pleurer

to weigh VERB
peser

□ How much do you weigh? Combien
est-ce que tu pèses? □ First, weigh the
flour. Tout d'abord, pesez la farine.

■ **to weigh oneself** se peser

weight NOUN
le poids

■ **to lose weight** maigrir

■ **to put on weight** grossir

weightlifter NOUN
l' haltérophile *masc*

weightlifting NOUN
l' haltérophilie *fem*

weird ADJECTIVE
bizarre (FEM bizarre)

welcome NOUN
▷ *see also* **welcome** VERB
l' accueil *masc*

□ They gave her a warm welcome. Ils lui ont
fait un accueil chaleureux.

■ **Welcome!** Bienvenue! □ Welcome to
France! Bienvenue en France!

to welcome VERB
▷ *see also* **welcome** NOUN

■ **to welcome somebody** accueillir
quelqu'un

■ **Thank you! — You're welcome!** Merci!
— De rien!

well ADJECTIVE, ADVERB
▷ *see also* **well** NOUN

1 bien

□ You did that really well. Tu as très bien fait
ça.

■ **to do well** réussir bien □ She's doing
really well at school. Elle réussit vraiment
bien à l'école.

■ **to be well** *(in good health)* aller bien □ I'm
not very well at the moment. Je ne vais pas
très bien en ce moment.

■ **get well soon!** remets-toi vite!

■ **well done!** bravo!

2 enfin

□ It's enormous! Well, quite big anyway.
C'est énorme! Enfin, c'est assez grand.

■ **as well** aussi □ I decided to have dessert
as well. J'ai décidé de prendre aussi un
dessert. □ We went to Chartres as well as
Paris. Nous sommes allés à Paris et à
Chartres aussi.

well NOUN
▷ *see also* **well** ADJECTIVE
le puits (PL les puits)

we'll = we will

well-behaved ADJECTIVE
sage (FEM sage)

well-dressed ADJECTIVE
bien habillé (FEM bien habillée)

wellingtons PL NOUN
les bottes en caoutchouc *fem pl*

well-known ADJECTIVE
célèbre (FEM célèbre)

□ a well-known film star une vedette de
cinéma célèbre

well-off ADJECTIVE
aisé (FEM aisée)

Welsh NOUN
▷ *see also* **Welsh** ADJECTIVE
le gallois *(language)*

Welsh ADJECTIVE
▷ *see also* **Welsh** NOUN
gallois (FEM galloise)

□ She's Welsh. Elle est galloise.

■ **Welsh people** les Gallois *masc pl*

Welshman NOUN
le Gallois

Welshwoman NOUN

la Galloise

went VERB ▷ *see* **go**

wept VERB ▷ *see* **weep**

were VERB ▷ *see* **be**

we're = we are

weren't = were not

west NOUN

▷ *see also* **west** ADJECTIVE
l' ouest *masc*

□ in the west dans l'ouest

west ADJECTIVE, ADVERB

▷ *see also* **west** NOUN

1 ouest (FEM + PL ouest)

□ the west coast la côte ouest

■ **west of** à l'ouest de □ Stroud is west of Oxford. Stroud est à l'ouest d'Oxford.

2 vers l'ouest

□ We were travelling west. Nous allions vers l'ouest.

■ **the West Country** le sud-ouest de l'Angleterre

westbound ADJECTIVE

■ **The truck was westbound on the M5.** Le camion roulait sur la M5 en direction de l'ouest.

■ **Westbound traffic is moving very slowly.** La circulation en direction de l'ouest est très ralentie.

western NOUN

▷ *see also* **western** ADJECTIVE
le western *(film)*

western ADJECTIVE

▷ *see also* **western** NOUN

■ **the western part of the island** la partie ouest de l'île

■ **Western Europe** l'Europe de l'Ouest

West Indian NOUN

▷ *see also* **West Indian** ADJECTIVE
l' Antillais *masc*
l' Antillaise *fem (person)*

West Indian ADJECTIVE

▷ *see also* **West Indian** NOUN
antillais (FEM antillaise)

□ She's West Indian. Elle est antillaise.

West Indies PL NOUN
les Antilles *fem pl*

■ **in the West Indies** aux Antilles

wet ADJECTIVE
mouillé (FEM mouillée)

□ wet clothes les vêtements mouillés

■ **to get wet** se faire mouiller

■ **dripping wet** trempé

■ **wet weather** le temps pluvieux

■ **It was wet all week.** Il a plu toute la semaine.

wetsuit NOUN
la combinaison de plongée

we've = we have

whale NOUN
la baleine

what ADJECTIVE, PRONOUN

1 quel (FEM quelle) *(which)*

□ What subjects are you studying? Quelles matières est-ce que tu fais? □ What colour is it? C'est de quelle couleur? □ What's the capital of Finland? Quelle est la capitale de la Finlande? □ What a mess! Quel fouillis!

2 qu'est-ce que

□ What are you doing? Qu'est-ce que vous faites? □ What did you say? Qu'est-ce que vous avez dit? □ What is it? Qu'est-ce que c'est? □ What's the matter? Qu'est-ce qu'il y a?

3 qu'est-ce qui

□ What happened? Qu'est-ce qui s'est passé? □ What's bothering you? Qu'est-ce qui te préoccupe?

LANGUAGE TIP In relative phrases use **ce qui** or **ce que** depending on whether 'what' refers to the subject or the object of the sentence.

4 ce qui *(subject)*

□ I saw what happened. J'ai vu ce qui est arrivé. □ I know what's bothering you. Je sais ce qui te préoccupe.

ce que *(object)*

□ Tell me what you did. Dites-moi ce que vous avez fait. □ I heard what he said. J'ai entendu ce qu'il a dit.

■ **What?** *(what did you say)* Comment?

■ **What!** *(shocked)* Quoi!

wheat NOUN
le blé

wheel NOUN
la roue

■ **the steering wheel** le volant

wheelchair NOUN
le fauteuil roulant

when ADVERB, CONJUNCTION
quand

□ When did he go? Quand est-ce qu'il est parti? □ She was reading when I came in. Elle lisait quand je suis entré.

where ADVERB, CONJUNCTION
où

□ Where's Emma today? Où est Emma aujourd'hui? □ Where do you live? Où habites-tu? □ Where are you going? Où vas-tu? □ a shop where you can buy croissants un magasin où l'on peut acheter des croissants

whether CONJUNCTION
si

□ I don't know whether to go or not. Je ne

sais pas si y aller ou non.

which ADJECTIVE, PRONOUN

1 quel (FEM quelle)

□ Which flavour do you want? Quel parfum est-ce que tu veux?

> **LANGUAGE TIP** When asking 'which one' use **lequel or laquelle**, depending on whether the noun is masculine or feminine.

■ **I know his brother. — Which one?** Je connais son frère. — Lequel?

■ **I know his sister. — Which one?** Je connais sa sœur. — Laquelle?

■ **Which would you like?** Lequel est-ce que vous voulez?

■ **Which of these are yours?** Lesquels sont à vous?

> **LANGUAGE TIP** In relative phrases use **qui** or **que** depending on whether 'which' refers to the subject or the object of the sentence.

2 qui (subject)

□ the CD which is playing now le CD qui passe maintenant

que (object)

□ the CD which I bought today le CD que j'ai acheté hier

while CONJUNCTION

▷ see also **while** NOUN

1 pendant que

□ You hold the torch while I look inside. Tiens la lampe électrique pendant que je regarde à l'intérieur.

2 alors que

□ Isobel is very dynamic, while Kay is more laid-back. Isobel est très dynamique, alors que Kay est plus relax.

while NOUN

▷ see also **while** CONJUNCTION

le moment

□ after a while au bout d'un moment

■ **a while ago** il y a un moment □ He was here a while ago. Il était là il y a un moment.

■ **for a while** pendant quelque temps □ I lived in London for a while. J'ai vécu à Londres pendant quelque temps.

■ **quite a while** longtemps □ quite a while ago il y a longtemps □ I haven't seen him for quite a while. Ça fait longtemps que je ne l'ai pas vu.

whip NOUN

▷ see also **whip** VERB

le fouet

to **whip** VERB

▷ see also **whip** NOUN

1 fouetter (person, animal)

2 battre (eggs)

whipped cream NOUN

la crème fouettée

whisk NOUN

le fouet

whiskers PL NOUN

les moustaches fem pl

whisky NOUN

le whisky (PL les whiskies)

to **whisper** VERB

chuchoter

whistle NOUN

▷ see also **whistle** VERB

le sifflet

■ **The referee blew his whistle.** L'arbitre a sifflé.

to **whistle** VERB

▷ see also **whistle** NOUN

siffler

white ADJECTIVE

blanc (FEM blanche)

□ He's got white hair. Il a les cheveux blancs.

■ **white wine** le vin blanc

■ **white bread** le pain blanc

■ **white coffee** le café au lait

■ **a white man** un Blanc

■ **a white woman** une Blanche

■ **white people** les Blancs

Whitsun NOUN

la Pentecôte

who PRONOUN

1 qui

□ Who said that? Qui a dit ça? □ Who is Jacques Chirac? Qui est Jacques Chirac?

> **LANGUAGE TIP** In relative phrases use **qui** or **que** depending on whether 'who' refers to the subject or the object of the verb.

2 qui (subject)

□ the man who saw us l'homme qui nous a vus □ the man who spoke to us l'homme qui nous a parlé

que (object)

□ the man who we saw l'homme que nous avons vu □ the man who she married l'homme qu'elle a épousé

whole ADJECTIVE

▷ see also **whole** NOUN

tout (FEM toute)

□ the whole class toute la classe □ the whole afternoon tout l'après-midi

■ **a whole box of chocolates** toute une boîte de chocolats

■ **the whole world** le monde entier

whole NOUN

▷ see also **whole** ADJECTIVE

■ **The whole of Wales was affected.** Le

pays de Galles tout entier a été touché.

■ **on the whole** dans l'ensemble

wholemeal ADJECTIVE
complet (FEM complète)

■ **wholemeal bread** le pain complet

wholewheat ADJECTIVE (US)
complet (FEM complète)

whom PRONOUN
qui

□ Whom did you see? Qui avez-vous vu? □ the man to whom I spoke l'homme à qui j'ai parlé

whose PRONOUN, ADJECTIVE

1 à qui

□ Whose is this? À qui est-ce? □ I know whose it is. Je sais à qui c'est. □ Whose book is this? À qui est ce livre?

2 dont (after noun)

□ the girl whose picture was in the paper la jeune fille dont la photo était dans le journal

why ADVERB
pourquoi

□ Why did you do that? Pourquoi avez-vous fait ça? □ That's why he did it. Voilà pourquoi il a fait ça. □ Tell me why. Dis-moi pourquoi.

■ **I've never been to France. — Why not?** Je ne suis jamais allé en France. — Pourquoi?

■ **All right, why not?** D'accord, pourquoi pas?

wicked ADJECTIVE

1 méchant (FEM méchante) (evil)

2 génial (FEM géniale, MASC PL géniaux) (really great)

wicket NOUN
le guichet (stumps)

wide ADJECTIVE, ADVERB
large (FEM large)

□ a wide road une route large

■ **wide open** grand ouvert □ The door was wide open. La porte était grande ouverte. □ The windows were wide open. Les fenêtres étaient grandes ouvertes.

■ **wide awake** complètement réveillé

widow NOUN
la veuve

□ She's a widow. Elle est veuve.

widower NOUN
le veuf

□ He's a widower. Il est veuf.

width NOUN
la largeur

wife NOUN
la femme

□ She's his wife. C'est sa femme.

wig NOUN

la perruque

wild ADJECTIVE

1 sauvage (FEM sauvage) (not tame)

□ a wild animal un animal sauvage

2 fou (FEM folle) (crazy)

□ She's a bit wild. Elle est un peu folle.

> **LANGUAGE TIP** fou changes to **fol** before a vowel and most words beginning with 'h'.

wildlife NOUN
la nature

□ I'm interested in wildlife. Je m'intéresse à la nature.

will NOUN

▷ see also **will** VERB

le testament

□ He left me some money in his will. Il m'a laissé de l'argent dans son testament.

will VERB

▷ see also **will** NOUN

■ **I'll show you your room.** Je vais te montrer ta chambre.

■ **I'll give you a hand.** Je vais t'aider.

> **LANGUAGE TIP** Use the French future tense when referring to the more distant future.

■ **I will finish it tomorrow.** Je le finirai demain.

■ **It won't take long.** Ça ne prendra pas longtemps.

■ **Will you wash up? — No, I won't.** Est-ce que tu peux faire la vaisselle? — Non.

■ **Will you help me?** Est-ce que tu peux m'aider?

■ **Will you be quiet!** Voulez-vous bien vous taire!

■ **That will be the postman.** Ça doit être le facteur.

willing ADJECTIVE

■ **to be willing to do something** être prêt à faire quelque chose

to **win** VERB

▷ see also **win** NOUN

gagner

□ Did you win? Est-ce que tu as gagné?

■ **to win a prize** remporter un prix

win NOUN

▷ see also **win** VERB

la victoire

to **wind** VERB

▷ see also **wind** NOUN

1 enrouler (rope, wool, wire)

2 serpenter (river, path)

□ The road winds through the valley. La route serpente à travers la vallée.

wind NOUN

▷ see also **wind** VERB

le vent
□ There was a strong wind. Il y avait
beaucoup de vent.
■ **a wind instrument** un instrument à vent
■ **wind power** l'énergie éolienne *fem*
windmill NOUN
le moulin à vent
window NOUN
1 la fenêtre *(of building)*
2 la vitre *(in car, train)*
■ **a shop window** une vitrine
3 le carreau (PL les carreaux) *(window pane)*
□ to break a window casser un carreau □ a
broken window un carreau cassé
windscreen NOUN
le pare-brise (PL les pare-brise)
windscreen wiper NOUN
l' essuie-glace *masc* (PL les essuie-glace)
windshield NOUN (US)
le pare-brise (PL les pare-brise)
windshield wiper NOUN (US)
l' essuie-glace *masc* (PL les essuie-glace)
windy ADJECTIVE
venteux (FEM venteuse) *(place)*
■ **It's windy.** Il y a du vent.
wine NOUN
le vin
□ a bottle of wine une bouteille de vin □ a
glass of wine un verre de vin
■ **white wine** le vin blanc
■ **red wine** le vin rouge
■ **a wine bar** un bar à vin
■ **a wine glass** un verre à vin
■ **the wine list** la carte des vins
wing NOUN
l' aile *fem*
to **wink** VERB
■ **to wink at somebody** faire un clin d'œil à
quelqu'un □ He winked at me. Il m'a fait un
clin d'œil.
winner NOUN
le gagnant
la gagnante
winning ADJECTIVE
■ **the winning team** l'équipe gagnante
■ **the winning goal** le but décisif
winter NOUN
l' hiver *masc*
■ **in winter** en hiver
winter sports PL NOUN
les sports d'hiver *masc pl*
to **wipe** VERB
essuyer
■ **to wipe one's feet** s'essuyer les pieds
□ Wipe your feet! Essuie-toi les pieds!
to **wipe up** VERB
essuyer

wire NOUN
le fil de fer
wisdom tooth NOUN
la dent de sagesse
wise ADJECTIVE
sage (FEM sage)
to **wish** VERB
▷ *see also* **wish** NOUN
■ **to wish for something** souhaiter
quelque chose □ What more could you wish
for? Que pourrais-tu souhaiter de plus?
■ **to wish to do something** désirer faire
quelque chose □ I wish to make a
complaint. Je désire porter plainte.
■ **I wish you were here!** Si seulement tu
étais ici!
■ **I wish you'd told me!** Si seulement tu
m'en avais parlé!
wish NOUN
▷ *see also* **wish** VERB
le vœu (PL les vœux)
□ to make a wish faire un vœu
■ **'best wishes'** *(on greetings card)*
'meilleurs vœux'
■ **'with best wishes, Kathy'** 'bien
amicalement, Kathy'
wit NOUN
l' esprit *masc (humour)*
with PREPOSITION
1 avec
□ Come with me. Venez avec moi. □ He
walks with a stick. Il marche avec une
canne.
■ **a woman with blue eyes** une femme
aux yeux bleus
2 chez *(at the home of)*
□ We stayed with friends. Nous avons logé
chez des amis.
3 de
□ green with envy vert de jalousie □ to
shake with fear trembler de peur □ Fill the
jug with water. Remplis la carafe d'eau.
within PREPOSITION
■ **The shops are within easy reach.** Les
magasins sont à proximité.
■ **within the week** avant la fin de la
semaine
without PREPOSITION
sans
□ without a coat sans manteau □ without
speaking sans parler
witness NOUN
le témoin
□ There were no witnesses. Il n'a pas eu de
témoins.
witty ADJECTIVE
spirituel (FEM spirituelle)

601

wives PL NOUN ▷ see **wife**
woke up, woken up VERB ▷ see **wake up**
wolf NOUN
le loup
woman NOUN
la femme
▫ a woman doctor une femme médecin
won VERB ▷ see **win**
to **wonder** VERB
se demander
▫ I wonder why she said that. Je me demande pourquoi elle a dit ça. ▫ I wonder what that means. Je me demande ce que ça veut dire. ▫ I wonder where Caroline is. Je me demande où est Caroline.
wonderful ADJECTIVE
formidable (FEM formidable)
won't = will not
wood NOUN
le bois (timber, forest)
▫ It's made of wood. C'est en bois. ▫ We went for a walk in the wood. Nous sommes allés nous promener dans le bois.
wooden ADJECTIVE
en bois
▫ a wooden chair une chaise en bois
woodwork NOUN
la menuiserie
▫ My hobby is woodwork. Je fais de la menuiserie.
wool NOUN
la laine
▫ It's made of wool. C'est en laine.
word NOUN
le mot
▫ a difficult word un mot difficile
■ **What's the word for 'shop' in French?** Comment dit-on 'shop' en français?
■ **in other words** en d'autres termes
■ **to have a word with somebody** parler avec quelqu'un
■ **the words** (lyrics) les paroles fem pl ▫ I really like the words of this song. J'adore les paroles de cette chanson.
word processing NOUN
le traitement de texte
word processor NOUN
la machine de traitement de texte
wore VERB ▷ see **wear**
work NOUN
▷ see also **work** VERB
le travail (PL les travaux)
▫ She's looking for work. Elle cherche du travail. ▫ He's at work at the moment. Il est au travail en ce moment.
■ **It's hard work.** C'est dur.
■ **to be off work** (sick) être malade ▫ He's

been off work for a week. Il est malade depuis une semaine.
■ **He's out of work.** Il est sans emploi.
to **work** VERB
▷ see also **work** NOUN
1 travailler (person)
▫ She works in a shop. Elle travaille dans un magasin. ▫ to work hard travailler dur
2 marcher (machine, plan)
▫ The heating isn't working. Le chauffage ne marche pas. ▫ My plan worked perfectly. Mon plan a marché impeccablement.
to **work out** VERB
1 faire de l'exercice (exercise)
▫ I work out twice a week. Je fais de l'exercice deux fois par semaine.
2 marcher (turn out)
▫ In the end it worked out really well. Au bout du compte, ça a très bien marché.
3 arriver à comprendre (figure out)
▫ I just couldn't work it out. Je n'arrivais pas du tout à comprendre.
■ **It works out at £10 each.** Ça fait dix livres chacun.
worker NOUN
l' ouvrier masc
l' ouvrière fem (in factory)
■ **He's a factory worker.** Il est ouvrier.
■ **She's a good worker.** Elle travaille bien.
work experience NOUN
le stage
▫ I'm going to do work experience in a factory. Je vais faire un stage dans une usine.
working-class ADJECTIVE
ouvrier (FEM ouvrière)
▫ a working-class family une famille ouvrière
workman NOUN
l' ouvrier masc
works NOUN
l' usine fem (factory)
worksheet NOUN
la feuille d'exercices
workshop NOUN
l' atelier masc
▫ a drama workshop un atelier de théâtre
workspace NOUN
l' espace de travail masc (computing)
workstation NOUN
le poste de travail
world NOUN
le monde
■ **He's the world champion.** Il est champion du monde.
worm NOUN
le ver

worn VERB ▷ *see* **wear**

worn ADJECTIVE

usé (FEM usée)

□ The carpet is a bit worn. La moquette est un peu usée.

■ **worn out** *(tired)* épuisé (FEM épuisée)

worried ADJECTIVE

inquiet (FEM inquiète)

□ She's very worried. Elle est très inquiète.

■ **to be worried about something** s'inquiéter pour quelque chose □ I'm worried about the exams. Je m'inquiète pour les examens.

■ **to look worried** avoir l'air inquiet □ She looks a bit worried. Elle a l'air un peu inquiète.

to **worry** VERB

s'inquiéter

■ **Don't worry!** Ne t'inquiète pas!

worse ADJECTIVE, ADVERB

1 pire (FEM pire)

□ It was even worse than that. C'était encore pire que ça. □ My results were bad, but his were even worse. Mes notes étaient mauvaises, mais les siennes étaient encore pires.

2 plus mal

□ I'm feeling worse. Je me sens plus mal.

to **worship** VERB

vénérer *(God)*

■ **He really worships her.** Il est en adoration devant elle.

worst ADJECTIVE

▷ *see also* **worst** NOUN

■ **the worst** le plus mauvais □ the worst student in the class le plus mauvais élève de la classe □ He got the worst mark in the whole class. Il a eu la plus mauvaise note de toute la classe.

■ **my worst enemy** mon pire ennemi

■ **Maths is my worst subject.** Je suis vraiment nul en maths.

worst NOUN

▷ *see also* **worst** ADJECTIVE

le pire

□ The worst of it is that ... Le pire c'est que ...

■ **at worst** au pire

■ **if the worst comes to the worst** au pire

worth ADJECTIVE

■ **to be worth** valoir □ It's worth a lot of money. Ça vaut très cher. □ How much is it worth? Ça vaut combien?

■ **It's worth it.** Ça vaut la peine. □ Is it worth it? Est-ce que ça vaut la peine? □ It's not worth it. Ça ne vaut pas la peine.

would VERB

■ **Would you like a biscuit?** Vous voulez un biscuit?

■ **Would you like to go and see a film?** Est-ce que tu veux aller voir un film?

■ **Would you close the door please?** Vous pouvez fermer la porte, s'il vous plaît?

■ **I'd like ...** J'aimerais ... □ I'd like to go to America. J'aimerais aller en Amérique.

□ Shall we go and see a film? — Yes, I'd like that. Si on allait voir un film? — Oui, j'aimerais bien.

■ **I said I would do it.** J'ai dit que je le ferais.

■ **If you asked him he'd do it.** Si vous le lui demandiez, il le ferait.

■ **If you had asked him he would have done it.** Si vous le lui aviez demandé, il l'aurait fait.

wouldn't = would not

wound NOUN

▷ *see also* **wound** VERB

la blessure

to **wound** VERB

▷ *see also* **wound** NOUN

blesser

□ He was wounded in the leg. Il a été blessé à la jambe.

to **wrap** VERB

emballer

□ She's wrapping her Christmas presents. Elle est en train d'emballer ses cadeaux de Noël.

■ **Can you wrap it for me please?** *(in shop)* Vous pouvez me faire un papier cadeau, s'il vous plaît?

to **wrap up** VERB

emballer

wrapping paper NOUN

le papier cadeau

wreck NOUN

▷ *see also* **wreck** VERB

1 le tas de ferraille *(vehicle, machine)*

□ That car is a wreck! Cette voiture est un tas de ferraille!

2 la loque *(person)*

□ After the exams I was a complete wreck. Après les examens j'étais une véritable loque.

to **wreck** VERB

▷ *see also* **wreck** NOUN

1 démolir *(building, vehicle)*

□ The explosion wrecked the whole house. L'explosion a démoli toute la maison.

2 ruiner *(plan, holiday)*

□ The trip was wrecked by bad weather. Le voyage a été ruiné par le mauvais temps.

wreckage NOUN

1 les débris *masc pl (of vehicle)*

2 les décombres *masc pl (of building)*

wrestler NOUN
le lutteur
la lutteuse

wrestling NOUN
la lutte

wrinkled ADJECTIVE
ridé (FEM ridée)

wrist NOUN
le poignet

to **write** VERB
écrire
  □ to write a letter écrire une lettre
  ■ **to write to somebody** écrire à quelqu'un
  □ I'm going to write to her in French. Je vais lui écrire en français.

to **write down** VERB
noter
  □ I wrote down the address. J'ai noté l'adresse.
  ■ **Can you write it down for me, please?** Vous pouvez me l'écrire, s'il vous plaît?

writer NOUN
l'écrivain *masc*
  □ She's a writer. Elle est écrivain.

writing NOUN
l'écriture *fem*
  □ I can't read your writing. Je n'arrive pas à lire ton écriture.
  ■ **in writing** par écrit

written VERB ▷ *see* **write**

wrong ADJECTIVE, ADVERB
1 faux (FEM fausse) *(incorrect)*
  □ The information they gave us was wrong. Les renseignements qu'ils nous ont donnés étaient faux.
  ■ **the wrong answer** la mauvaise réponse
  ■ **You've got the wrong number.** Vous vous êtes trompé de numéro.
2 mal *(morally bad)*
  □ I think hunting is wrong. Je trouve que c'est mal de chasser.
  ■ **to be wrong** *(mistaken)* se tromper
  □ You're wrong about that. Tu te trompes.
  ■ **to do something wrong** se tromper
  □ You've done it wrong. Tu t'es trompé.
  ■ **to go wrong** *(plan)* mal tourner □ The robbery went wrong and they got caught. Le cambriolage a mal tourné et ils ont été pris.
  ■ **What's wrong?** Qu'est-ce qu'il y a?
  ■ **What's wrong with her?** Qu'est-ce qu'elle a?

wrote VERB ▷ *see* **write**

WWW NOUN *(= World Wide Web)*
le Web

Xerox® NOUN
▷ *see also* **xerox** VERB
la photocopie

to **xerox** VERB
▷ *see also* **Xerox** NOUN
photocopier

Xmas NOUN *(= Christmas)*
Noël

to **X-ray** VERB

▷ *see also* **X-ray** NOUN
■ **to X-ray something** faire une radio de quelque chose □ They X-rayed my arm. Ils ont fait une radio de mon bras.

X-ray NOUN
▷ *see also* **X-ray** VERB
la radio

□ to have an X-ray passer une radio

yacht NOUN
1 le voilier *(sailing boat)*
2 le yacht *(luxury motorboat)*

yard NOUN
1 la cour *(of building)*
  □ in the yard dans la cour
2 le mètre

> **DID YOU KNOW...?**
> In France measurements are in metres rather than yards. A yard is slightly less than a metre.

to **yawn** VERB
bâiller

year NOUN
l'an *masc*
  □ last year l'an dernier □ next year l'an prochain
  ■ **to be 15 years old** avoir quinze ans
  ■ **an eight-year-old child** un enfant de huit ans

> **DID YOU KNOW...?**
> In French secondary schools, years are counted from the **sixième** (youngest) to **première** and **terminale** (oldest).

  □ year 7 la sixième □ year 8 la cinquième
  □ year 9 la quatrième □ year 10 la troisième
  □ year 11 la seconde
  ■ **She's in year 11.** Elle est en seconde.
  ■ **He's a first-year.** Il est en sixième.

to **yell** VERB
hurler

yellow ADJECTIVE
jaune *(FEM jaune)*

yes ADVERB
1 oui
  □ Do you like it? — Yes. Tu aimes ça? — Oui.
  ■ **Would you like a cup of tea? — Yes please.** Voulez-vous une tasse de thé? — Je veux bien.
2 si

> **LANGUAGE TIP** Use **si** when answering negative questions.

  □ Don't you like it? — Yes! Tu n'aimes pas ça? — Si! □ You're not Swiss, are you? — Yes

I am! Tu n'es pas suisse, si? — Si!

yesterday ADVERB
hier
  □ yesterday morning hier matin
  □ yesterday afternoon hier après-midi
  □ yesterday evening hier soir □ all day yesterday toute la journée d'hier

yet ADVERB
encore
  ■ **not yet** pas encore □ It's not finished yet. Ce n'est pas encore fini.
  ■ **not as yet** pas encore □ There's no news as yet. Nous n'avons pas encore de nouvelles.
  ■ **Have you finished yet?** Vous avez fini?

to **yield** VERB (US)
céder le passage *(on road sign)*

yob NOUN
le loubard

yoghurt NOUN
le yaourt

yolk NOUN
le jaune d'œuf

you PRONOUN

> **LANGUAGE TIP** Only use **tu** when speaking to one person of your own age or younger. If in doubt use **vous**.

1 vous *(polite form or plural)*
  □ Do you like football? Est-ce que vous aimez le football? □ Can I help you? Est-ce que je peux vous aider? □ It's for you. C'est pour vous.
2 tu *(familiar singular)*
  □ Do you like football? Tu aimes le football?

> **LANGUAGE TIP** **vous** never changes, but **tu** has different forms. When 'you' is the object of the sentence use **te** not **tu**. **te** becomes **t'** before a vowel sound.

3 te
  □ I know you. Je te connais. □ I gave it you. Je te l'ai donné.
  t'
  □ I saw you. Je t'ai vu. □ I'll help you. Je vais t'aider.
4 toi

LANGUAGE TIP **toi** is used instead of **tu** after a preposition and in comparisons. □ It's for you. C'est pour toi. □ I'll come with you. Je viens avec toi. □ She's younger than you. Elle est plus jeune que toi.

young ADJECTIVE
jeune (FEM jeune)

■ **young people** les jeunes

younger ADJECTIVE
plus jeune (FEM plus jeune)
□ He's younger than me. Il est plus jeune que moi.

■ **my younger brother** mon frère cadet
■ **my younger sister** ma sœur cadette

youngest ADJECTIVE
plus jeune (FEM plus jeune)
□ my youngest brother mon plus jeune frère □ She's the youngest. C'est la plus jeune.

your ADJECTIVE

LANGUAGE TIP Only use **ton/ta/tes** when speaking to one person of your own age or younger. If in doubt use **votre/vos**.

1 votre (FEM votre)
□ your house
vos pl (polite form or plural)
□ your seats vos places

2 ton masc
□ your brother ton frère (familiar singular)
ta fem
□ your sister ta sœur
tes pl
□ your parents tes parents

LANGUAGE TIP **ta** becomes **ton** before a vowel sound

■ **your friend 1** (male) ton ami **2** (female) ton amie

LANGUAGE TIP Do not use **votre/vos** or **ton/ta/tes** with parts of the body.
□ Would you like to wash your hands? Est-ce que vous voulez vous laver les mains?
□ Do you want to wash your hair? Tu veux te laver les cheveux?

yours PRONOUN

LANGUAGE TIP Only use **le tien/la tienne/les tiens/les tiennes** when talking to one person of your own age or younger. If in doubt use **le vôtre/la vôtre/les vôtres**. The same applies to **à toi** and **à vous**.

1 le vôtre + masc noun
□ I've lost my pen. Can I use yours? J'ai perdu mon stylo. Je peux utiliser le vôtre?
la vôtre + fem noun
□ I like that car. Is it yours? J'aime cette voiture-là. C'est la vôtre?

les vôtres + pl noun
□ my parents and yours mes parents et les vôtres

■ **Is this yours?** C'est à vous? □ This book is yours. Ce livre est à vous.

■ **Yours sincerely ...** Veuillez agréer l'expression de mes sentiments les meilleurs ...

2 le tien + masc noun
□ I've lost my pen. Can I use yours? J'ai perdu mon stylo. Je peux utiliser le tien?
la tienne + fem noun
□ I like that car. Is it yours? J'aime cette voiture-là. C'est la tienne?
les tiens + masc pl noun
□ my parents and yours mes parents et les tiens
les tiennes + fem pl noun
□ My hands are dirty, yours are clean. Mes mains sont sales, les tiennes sont propres.

■ **Is this yours?** C'est à toi? □ This book is yours. Ce livre est à toi.

yourself PRONOUN

LANGUAGE TIP Only use **te** when talking to one person of your own age or younger; use **vous** to everyone else. If in doubt use **vous**.

1 vous (polite form)
□ Have you hurt yourself? Est-ce que vous vous êtes fait mal? □ Tell me about yourself! Parlez-moi de vous!

2 te (familiar form)
□ Have you hurt yourself? Est-ce que tu t'es fait mal?

3 toi (familiar form)

LANGUAGE TIP After a preposition, use **toi** instead of **te**.
□ Tell me about yourself! Parle-moi de toi!

4 toi-même
□ Do it yourself! Fais-le toi-même!

5 vous-même
□ Do it yourself! Faites-le vous-même!

yourselves PRONOUN

1 vous
□ Did you enjoy yourselves? Vous vous êtes bien amusés?

2 vous-mêmes
□ Did you make it yourselves? Vous l'avez fait vous-mêmes?

youth club NOUN
le centre de jeunes

youth hostel NOUN
l' auberge de jeunesse fem

Yugoslavia NOUN
la Yougoslavie

■ **in the former Yugoslavia** en ex-Yougoslavie

Zz

zany ADJECTIVE
　loufoque (FEM loufoque)

zebra NOUN
　le zèbre

zebra crossing NOUN
　le passage clouté

zero NOUN
　le zéro

Zimbabwe NOUN
　le Zimbabwe
　■ **in Zimbabwe** au Zimbabwe

Zimmer frame® NOUN
　le déambulateur

zip NOUN
　la fermeture éclair® (PL les fermetures
　éclair)

zip code NOUN (US)
　le code postal

zipper NOUN (US)
　la fermeture éclair® (PL les fermetures
　éclair)

zit NOUN
　le bouton

zodiac NOUN
　le zodiaque
　□ the signs of the zodiac les signes du
　zodiaque

zone NOUN
　la zone

zoo NOUN
　le zoo

zoom lens NOUN
　le zoom

zucchini NOUN (US)
　la courgette